D1271060

A MODERN STUDY IN

THE BOOK OF PROVERBS

A MODERN STUDY IN

THE BOOK OF PROVERBS

Charles Bridges' Classic Revised
for Today's Reader
by

George F. Santa

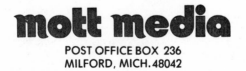

mott media
POST OFFICE BOX 236
MILFORD, MICH. 48042

Scripture quotations are from the New American Standard Bible, © The Lockman Foundation 1960, 1962, 1963, 1968, 1971, 1972, 1973, 1975, and are used by permission.

Copyright © 1978 by Mott Media

All rights reserved. No portion of this book may be reproduced by any process such as mimeograph, photocopying, recording, storage in a retrieval system or transmitted by any means without written permission of the publisher. Brief quotations embodied in critical reviews are permitted. For information write Mott Media, Box 236, Milford, MI 48042.

Printed in the United States of America

Library of Congress Cataloging in Publication Data

Bridges, Charles, 1794-1869.
A modern study in the Book of Proverbs.
Previous ed. published under title: An exposition of the Book of Proverbs.
1. Bible: O.T. Proverbs—Commentaries.
I. Santa, George Frederick, 1914- II. Title.
BS1465.3.B74 1978 223'.7'077 78-7667
ISBN 0-915134-27-6

CONTENTS

PREFACE

Why a new edition of Charles Bridges' magnificent exposition of Proverbs?

For more than a century, its greatness has been consistently recognized, and its usefulness and impact have continued to the present day of this twentieth century, even in the outdated English of the author's own day.

Why then should an exposition already so successful and of such stature and proven usefulness require adaptation, revision, rewrite, or even editing?

The answer is obvious. To increase its usefulness to today's reader, the language in which it was originally written needs updating.

Therefore, the publishers of this new, contemporary edition have responded to a valid concern. Though the book has served other generations well, just as it came from the pen of the author in the early nineteenth century, it still could be lost to present and future generations, simply because, to them, the language is neither readily nor fully understandable.

NOT IN THE VERNACULAR

The goal of the publishers of this new edition, however, has not been to reduce the original writing to the vernacular of our day. It is designed primarily for you who desire to read and study comfortably and at ease in the language of our time.

Only obviously archaic terminology and passages obscured by expressions not totally familiar in our day have been revised. However, neither Bridges' meaning nor intent have been tampered with.

THE AUTHOR'S CONCERN—OURS TOO!

One of the primary desires of the author was that his exposition of Proverbs be read *profitably*. All too many earnest Christians and readers of this superb portion of God's Word confess honestly but regretfully: "I don't get 'spiritual' food from it, as I do from other parts of the Bible, and therefore am less interested. I am impressed with its great wisdom. I know it is God's inspired Word, equally with the rest of the Bible, and therefore, was not written in vain. But the question still baffles me: How can I read this portion of God's Word profitably and with the blessing God intended?"

To address himself to this very problem, Bridges devoted years of intensive study to all parts of Scripture that shed light upon this very practical portion of God's Word.

CROSS REFERENCES PRESERVED

The illuminating cross references Bridges brought to bear upon the truths of Proverbs, thereby making God His own interpreter, have been carefully retained. In addition, they have been set apart, conspicuously, in a separate column for the reader's ready application.

WHY THE NASB TRANSLATION?

The publishers were aware of the need, not only for the *commentary* but also the biblical text, to appear in *contemporary* language. Therefore, the highly respected and accurate *New American Standard Bible,* its aims coinciding with those of the publishers of this updated edition of Bridges' exposition, was chosen, and for these specific reasons:

- the language of the NASB is grammatically correct, contemporary English
- it is faithful to the original languages
- it was designed to be understood by the masses
- it gives the Lord Jesus Christ the same vital place in this portion of God's Word as He occupies in all other parts of Scripture

VALUABLE TOPICAL INDEX

The essentials of Bridges' own topical index have also been retained. They lead not only to the Scripture text but to Bridges' illuminating comments, as well.

The author fervently desired that the very practical, life-changing truths of Proverbs should be presented so meaningfully as to become practical in the lives and walk of his readers. To the accomplishment of this hoped-for achievement, also earnestly desired by the publishers, this updated edition is dedicated.

It has been prepared and released with you, today's reader, in mind, that you may read with utmost understanding and personal and practical application.

"While other parts of Scripture," to quote the commentator himself, "shew us the glory of our high calling; this [Book] may instruct in all minuteness of detail how to 'walk worthy of it.' Elsewhere we learn our completeness in Christ (Col. 2:10): and most justly we glory in our high exaltation as 'joint-heirs' with Christ, made to sit together in heavenly places in Christ Jesus (Rom. 8:17; Eph. 2:6). We look into this Book, and, as by the aid of the microscope, we see the minuteness of our Christian obligations; that there is not a temper, a look, a word, a movement, the most important action of the day, the smallest relative duty, in which we do not either deface or adorn the image of our Lord, and the profession of his name."

Proverbs, then, is a guidebook and directory for godly conduct. All ranks and classes are given divine instruction on virtually all activities and responsibilities of life, with special caution and counsel given to the rich and poor, to national rulers and leaders, to family members in their relationships one to another, to young and old, to employers and employees.

It condemns laziness, praises diligence, warns against the base temptations of life, and gives wise rules for self-control of the tongue, the eye, the heart.

Even the minute courtesies of life, such as self-denying consideration for, and liberality toward, others, are given detailed attention.

All this diversified instruction is based upon *the principles of true godliness.* That is not sound faith that does not issue in practical godliness, nor is there any true morality apart from the principles of Christ.

Proverbs may surely be taken as a valuable Rule of Conduct, even as the New Testament is a Rule of Faith.

Great profit will most certainly come to those who will take the time to read even a few of these godly principles and apply them to their lives daily. "If the world were governed by the wisdom of this single Book," said one who knew it and loved it, "it would be 'a new earth wherein dwelleth righteousness.' "

Though this Book of Proverbs has a message for all, it has a special one for the young. Solomon's father, David, in the Psalms, asked the question: "How can a young man keep his way pure?" He answered, "By keeping *it* according to Thy word" (Psalm 119:9). Solomon, in Proverbs, fully expounds his father's answer. Proverbs, Bridges says, concerning its teachings for youth, "takes them as it were by the hand, sets up way-marks to warn against coming danger and imminent temptations, and allures them into the bright ways of God by the most engaging motives."

If the Psalms, as someone has expressed it, bring a glow to the heart, then Proverbs makes the face shine.

STOREHOUSE OF PRACTICAL INSTRUCTION

It was recorded of one Mary Jane Graham, Bridges recalls, that she was delighted in the course of her study of the Book of Proverbs to have Christ so much and so frequently before her mind—a recollection of great moment for the spiritual discernment of the divine wisdom treasured up in this storehouse of practical instruction.

PERSONALIZED—FOR YOU!

The author, in the introduction to the original volume (from which we have drawn sparingly for the preface to this new edition) strongly desired that the truths of Proverbs become engraved on the reader's heart and find true expression in his life. So it is the sincere hope of all involved in the production of this updated version that the efforts put forth for your better understanding and application will make these truths real and applicable for this generation and many more to come.

Above all it is our earnest prayer that this life-changing Book of Proverbs, and this enduring commentary upon it, will cause you to see Jesus only. May it bring a fresh glow to your heart, a new and holy purpose to your life, and a heavenly shine upon your face, to the eternal glory of our wonderful Lord.

George F. Santa

CHAPTER ONE

1 *The proverbs of Solomon the son of David, king of Israel:*
2 *To know wisdom and instruction,*
To discern the sayings of understanding,
3 *To receive instruction in wise behavior,*
Righteousness, justice and equity;
4 *To give prudence to the naive,*
To the youth knowledge and discretion,

THE WRITER: HIS CREDENTIALS

Proverbs naturally opens with a short account of its author. Solomon is recorded as the wisest of men. He was a man of wisdom, because he was a man of prayer.[a] His extraordinary wisdom was the admiration of the world.[b] Had Solomon been, for example, the son of Jeroboam, even then he would have commanded great respect; but how much more as *the son of David*, shaped by David's godly prayers[c] and teaching.[d] And if a king's sayings, even without special merit, are preserved, how much more should the wise teaching of this great king of Israel, and wisest of all men[e] demand our special interest.

But though Solomon's sayings were extremely valuable because of his own great wisdom (exceeding the wise men of his own or any other time),[f] they claim our reverence upon much, much higher ground. "Behold, something greater than Solomon is here."[g] Very often Solomon speaks in the person of God[h] and always under the inspiration[i] of the wisdom of God; so that his sayings are truly *divine* sentences "in the lips of the King."[j]

[a] 1 Kings 3:12. Comp. Prov 2:1–9
[b] 1 Kings 3:28; 4:34
[c] Ps 72:1
[d] Prov 4:1–4; 1 Kings 2:1–4; 1 Chron 28:9
[e] Eccl 1:1; 12:9, 10
[f] 1 Kings 4:29–31
[g] Matt 12:42
[h] Verse 20; Prov 8:9; 23:26
[i] 2 Tim 3:16
[j] Prov 16:10

PURPOSES OF THIS BOOK

The great purpose of this most valuable book is to teach, that to know God is more important than every-

[k]Prov 6:1–11; 27:23–27, with 11:14; 13:28, 34; 20:18
[l]2 Tim 3:15
[m]Verse 7
[n]2 Tim 3:15–17; Titus 2:11, 12
[o]Prov 3:13–18
[p]Prov 4:5–9, 13
[q]Comp. Prov 2:9
[r]Prov 14:15; 21:11; Ezek 14:20
[s]Phil 1:10; 1 Thess 5:21
[t]Ps 17:4; 1 John 4:1. Comp. Acts 17:11
[u]Titus 1:9; 2:8. Comp. Matt 22:15–46

thing else[k] in life.[l] It gives us "wisdom that leads to salvation."[m]

It perfects and equips the man of God for every good work.[n] Its glowing privileges are set forth[o] with intense earnestness, and we see it, not only as more important than all else, but as our very *life.*[p] Then we are shown how to make it ours, that we obtain it through *instruction.* And we accept that instruction as a complete rule of wisdom: *behavior, righteousness, justice, and equity,*[q] sound principles, and their practical application. Here also *the naive*, so easily misled,[r] learn to distinguish between truth and error;[s] to guard themselves from false teachers;[t] and to refute those who contradict God's Word.[u] Especially is the young man directed to Proverbs.[1] His undisciplined enthusiasm goes to waste, and he is easily swayed by the winds of opinion in the world around him. He greatly needs some settled master-principles to fix his goals, choices, and conduct. In this book he will find *knowledge and discretion;* not a religion of imagination, impulse, or sentiment; but sound practical, scriptural truth.

5 *A wise man will hear and increase in learning,*
And a man of understanding will acquire wise counsel,
6 *To understand a proverb and a figure,*
The words of the wise and their riddles.

[v]Phil 3:12. Comp. 1 Cor 3:18; 8:2
[w]Ps 119:98–100, with 18, 33, 34

Not only the *naive* and the *youth*, but even the *wise,* can learn from Proverbs. For a truly *wise man* is not one who has attained, but who knows that he has *not* attained and is still pressing onward to perfection.[v] David was conscious of great attainments, but he was ever reaching out for higher light.[w] And he was wise.

Unless we constantly add to our knowledge, the reserves we already have will soon waste away.

LISTEN AND LEARN!

[x]Exod 18:17–26; Matt 13:11–16; John 16:12
[y]Acts 11:2–18

Hearing is a great medium of knowledge. Moses was instructed by Jethro; the disciples, by our Lord;[x] and the apostles, by Peter.[y] Apollos was instructed by Priscilla

[1] *Ps 119:9. Over the gates of Plato's school, it was written: Let no one who is not a geometrician enter. But very different is the inscription over these doors of Solomon—Let the ignorant, simple, foolish, young enter. CARTWRIGHT.–LAVATER c. 4:20–22.*

and Aquila in "the way of God more accurately."[z] In fact, we all must be hearers, before we can be teachers. Bishop Hall has said that we gather knowledge when we listen, we spend it when we teach, but if we spend before we gather, we'll soon be bankrupt. The longer we learn, the more we feel that we are learners; and the more willing we are to listen, the more we believe we can learn.[a]

Living in a world full of crises, in the church and out of it, how anxious we should be to gain knowledge through every available means! This is how we become *men of understanding* and learn what we ought to do![b] The wise man himself taught to the delight and instruction of his royal scholar the queen of Sheba;[c] so to a teachable hearer "even the depths of God" will be made plain.[d] And there is the value of the minister of God! He is "a mediator for him, one out of a thousand"[e] divinely appointed to bring others to the perfection of knowledge.[f] The church might have been spared many disorders and heresies, if man had honored God's appointed messenger, and in humble simplicity had sought the Word through him,[g] coming to learn, not to teach; not to have his curiosity fed, but his conscience satisfied. This reverence for God's Word "is good for the heart to be strengthened by grace."[h]

[z] Acts 18:24–26
[a] Prov 9:9; 18:15
[b] 1 Chron 12:32
[c] 1 Kings 10:1–5
[d] 1 Cor 2:9, 10
[e] Job 33:23. Comp. Acts 8:27–35
[f] Eph 4:11–15; 1 Thess 3:10
[g] Mal 2:7. Comp. Heb 13:17, with 1 Cor 4:8; 3:2–4
[h] Heb 13:9

7 *The fear of the* L*ORD is the beginning*[i] *of knowledge;*
Fools despise wisdom and instruction.[j]

The preface has stated the object of this Book of Wisdom. Now, the book, itself, opens with a noble sentence. "There is not," Bishop Patrick observed, "such a wise instruction to be found in all their books [speaking of heathen ethics], as the very first of all in Solomon's, which he lays as the ground of all wisdom."[2] *The fear of the Lord, that is wisdom.* Job said it before.[k] So did the wise man's father, David.[l] Such is the impact of this saying that Solomon repeats it.[m] No—after having gone 'round the whole circuit; after having carefully considered all the sources of knowledge; his conclusion of the whole matter is this, that *the fear of God* in its practical exercise "applies to every person"[n]—all his duty; all his happiness; his first lesson and his last. So . . . when about

[i] principal part
[j] Verses 1–6
[k] Job 28:28
[l] Ps 111:10
[m] Prov 9:10
[n] Eccl 12:13. Comp. Job 28:12–14, with 28

[2] *Preface to his Paraphrase.*

to instruct us from the mouth of God, he begins at the beginning.

THE MAIN THING ABOUT IT ALL

All heathen wisdom is foolishness. Of everything we can learn in the world, the first and most important is to know God. There is no true knowledge without godliness.[o]

But what is the fear of the Lord? It is that affectionate reverence, by which the child of God submits himself humbly and carefully to his Father's law. God's wrath is so bitter, and his love so sweet; that there naturally arises an earnest desire to please Him. And also—in view of the danger of falling short because of his own weakness and temptations—a holy watchfulness and fear, so "that I may not sin against Thee."[p] This enters into every thought and every activity of life.[q] The most mature pupil in God's school wants to be more completely molded by His teaching. The godly parent trains up his family under the Word's influence.[r] The Christian scholar honors it as the beginning, the most important part of all his knowledge. He sees that it gives meaning and purpose to learning, and saves him from all the treacherous temptations that accompany knowledge.

[o]Comp. Deut 4:6, 7
[p]Ps 119:11; Heb 12:28, 29
[q]Prov 23:17
[r]Gen 18:19; Eph 6:4

WHY DOESN'T EVERYBODY WANT WISDOM?

Why then do multitudes around us despise wisdom and instruction? Because the beginning of wisdom—the "fear of God"—is not before their eyes.[s] They don't know its value. They laugh at its holy demands. They may be wise in their own sight. But God knows them far better than they know themselves. And He calls them by their right name—fools! For that's what they must be, to *despise* such a blessing;[t] to rush into wilful ruin.[u] Blessed Lord! May my childlike *fear* be my *wisdom*, my security, my happiness!

[s]Ps 36:1
[t]Jer 8:9
[u]Verses 22, 24–32. Comp. 1 Sam 2:25; 1 Kings 12:13; Jer 26:22–32. Prov 5:12, 13; 29:1

8 *Hear, my son, your father's instruction,*
And do not forsake your mother's teaching;
9 *Indeed, they are a graceful wreath to your head,*
And ornaments about your neck.

YOU AND YOUR PARENTS

Let the young see how *the fear of the Lord* is connected with reverence to parents. Thus the first part of this book puts honor upon the first commandment with promise. "Honor your father and mother (which is the first commandment with a promise)."[v] God here speaks with the mouth of a parent or teacher[3] blending fatherly tenderness with divine authority—*My son.* The command assumes the godly character of parents and recognizes the responsibility of *both* father and mother.[4] Children are rational creatures. *Instruction,* not blind submission, must be taught. Still they are wayward. Instruction must therefore be enforced with the authority of law. God puts his own stamp upon parental discipline. Listen to it—do not forsake it. Reverence for his mother's law was the honorable mark of Timothy's godly life.[w] And this reverence must not be limited to just the first years of a child's life—the years of restraint. The student of the Bible will admit he is a child in obligations to his parents, long after he has ceased to be a child in years.[x] Neither age nor rank frees him from such responsibilities. Joseph in manhood, the head of a family, and the first Lord in Egypt—bowed before his father's feet.[y] Solomon, even as king, didn't forget the respect justly due to his mother.[5] The crown upon his head, and the chain of gold about Joseph's neck[z] were not so graceful an ornament as the respect he paid his parents.[a] This commands the praise of the world. Sometimes, though, it might be a deceptive, self-righteous dependence. But wherever it is grounded upon right principle, it is the putting "on of the Lord Jesus Christ" in His lovely example.[b] Though angels were subject to Him, yet "He continued in subjection to them [His parents]."[c] And consider how He honored His mother in His last dying command to His disciple—"Behold your mother!"[d]

[v] Eph 6:2. Comp. 1 Tim 5:4
[w] 2 Tim 1:5; 3:14, 15
[x] Jer 35:8–10, 18
[y] Gen 46:29; 48:12
[z] Comp. Prov 4:9, with Gen 41:39, 42
[a] 1 Peter 5:5
[b] Rom 13:14
[c] Luke 2:51, with Heb 1:6
[d] John 19:27

A mutual obligation binds the spiritual father and his children. Authority softened by tenderness—instruction

[3] *Thus the prophets were called fathers—2 Kings 2:12; 13:14. Our blessed Lord used the same endearing address—John 21:5. Comp. Matt 9:2; 22. Thus the apostles also acknowledged both their individual converts and collective churches—1 Tim 1:2; 2 Tim 1:2; Titus 1:4; 1 Cor 4:15; with 1 John 2:1; 5:21.*

[4] *See Judg 13:12. No ancient system, so fully as the Bible, recognizes the mother's just and equal claims. Comp. 6:20; 15:20; 20:20; 23:22; 30:17; Lev 19:3; Deut 21:18–21. Cartwright observes, that the names of mothers of good and bad kings are mentioned in Kings and Chronicles, as partakers in their credit or reproach.*

[5] *1 Kings 2:19, 20. See also Queen Esther's respect for Mordecai, her reputed father—2:20.*

moulded in parental love—will always command its measure of reverential and affectionate response. Such was Paul's ministry to the churches of Philippi and Thessalonica. Humility, tenderness, mutual communion, and cheerful subjection formed the harmony of Christian love and happiness.[e]

[e]Phil 4:9–19; 1 Thess 2:7–13

10 *My son, if sinners entice you,*
Do not consent.
11 *If they say, "Come with us,*
Let us lie in wait for blood,
Let us ambush the innocent without cause;
12 *Let us swallow them alive like Sheol,*
Even whole, as those who go down to the pit;
13 *We shall find all* kinds *of precious wealth,*
We shall fill our houses with spoil;
14 *Throw in your lot with us,*
We shall all have one purse,"
15 *My son, do not walk in the way with them.*
Keep your feet from their path,
16 *For their feet run to evil,*
And they hasten to shed blood.

Let the young pay attention to the instruction and law of the godly parent and minister. What youth worker doesn't mourn over the bad influence of evil companions among his youth? If only the Lord's servants were as energetic in His work, as sinners are in serving Satan! Almost as soon as Satan rebelled and turned from the Lord, he became a tempter. And he is most successful in training his servants in his ways![f]

[f]Prov 16:29; Gen 11:4; Num 31:16; Isa 56:12

HOW TO HANDLE TEMPTATION

If sinners tempt you—this isn't just some far-fetched possibility! It is an almost certain one. Yet we have one rule against all temptations—and they are many[g]—don't give in! Agreeing to do evil is sin! Eve consented, before she plucked the fruit;[h] David consented, before he committed his act of sin.[i] Joseph resisted and was saved.[j] Job was sorely tried; "yet through all this Job did not sin."[k] If you are overcome by temptation, don't blame God—or the devil. The worst the devil can do is tempt us to sin. He can't force us to give in. When he turns his greatest

[g]Prov 7:5–23. Comp. Deut 13:6–8; 1 Chron 21:1; 1 Kings 13:15–19
[h]Gen 3:6
[i]2 Sam 11:2–4. Comp. Josh 7:21
[j]Gen 39:8, 9
[k]Job 1:22; 2:10

power and cleverest tricks against us, whether we give in, or not, is up to us. We, ourselves, make the final decision.[l] Constantly resisting with our will clears us of responsibility.[m] But if we consent—even though we don't actually carry out the act, we are still responsible.

The temptation here was to rob and shed blood; greedy desire was to lead to murder. The plot was terribly wicked. The innocent was to be murdered without cause,[n] *swallow them* alive, like Korah and his company, going down into the pit in their full strength.[o] At first, the temptation seems harmless enough—just come with us. Then they demand more—join us. The reply comes, "But we shall be discovered." "No," they reply, "we'll do it so cleverly, there won't be any more blood around to be seen than there would be if the earth swallowed them up; or they died a natural death and were decently buried."[p] You can't imagine how great the reward will be, when our victim is destroyed.[q] Great reward! Precious substance! Why! That is as great a promise as the Son of God gives us.[r] But how can reality be found in a world of shadows?[s] And more than that! How can the fruit of robbery be precious with the curse of God upon it?[t]

Not that the plot *starts out* to be as horrible as that. It doesn't. But step by step, unless the Lord graciously holds us back, it may *end up* like that. When the veneer is removed, we see what sin is really like and how terrible its end is! What young man wouldn't tremble and run away from such wickedness, if he could just imagine the results? But how many a deceived sinner is led away by his companions into sins he never even dreamed of. Other temptations are prepared for the easygoing and naive young person just entering into life. They are less fearful and obvious, and therefore more dangerous. That's why Satan can take advantage of us—just because we're so ignorant of his devices.[u]

Is it safe then, to trust in our good resolutions or principles? Not for a minute! Don't walk in the way with them. Their invitation is—*Come with us.* God's warning is—*do not enter the path of the wicked.*[v] Stay away from them![w] Don't even discuss things with them. No one becomes extravagantly sinful all at once. But "bad company corrupts good morals."[x]

[l] James 1:13–15
[m] Comp. Rom 7:14–17, 19, 20, 23
[n] Gen 4:8; Ps 10:8
[o] Num 16:33
[p] Gen 4:10; 2 Kings 9:26
[q] Comp. Matt 21:38
[r] Prov 8:21
[s] Ps 39:6
[t] Prov 21:6; Ps 62:9, 10
[u] 2 Cor 2:11
[v] Prov 4:14, 15
[w] Comp. Ps 1:1
[x] 1 Cor 15:33

TOBOGGAN SLIDE TO HELL

Your tender conscience becomes less sensitive every time you give in. Who can stop himself on the downhill road? One sin demands another. We live and have to lie again to cover the first lie. We sin once and then have to commit worse sin to conceal the first. David committed murder to hid his adultery.[y]

[y]2 Sam 11:4, 17, 25

PATH OF BLOOD—SATAN'S GROUND

Again then—we repeat with all earnestness—hold back! Don't give in. The *path* may be strewn with flowers; but it is a path of *evil,* maybe even of *blood.*[6] Every step on Satan's ground deprives us of the security of the promises of God. Ruin is often followed by not refusing to take the first step into sin. Your only hope is to get away from the temptation as fast as you can,[z] like Joseph did.[a] Just come right out and tell your tempter to "get lost" and leave you alone. Then run away and hide.[b]

[z]Comp. Mark 14:54, 71
[a]Gen 39:10, 12
[b]Ps 119:114, 115. Comp. Matt 4:10

Here's an awful thought! There is no sin, that the best Christian if trusting in himself, might not commit. "You stand only by your faith. Do not be conceited, but fear."[c]

[c]Rom 11:20

17 *Indeed, it is useless to spread the net*
In the eyes of any bird;
18 *But they lie in wait for their own blood;*
They ambush their own lives.
19 *So are the ways of everyone who gains by violence;*
It takes away the life of its possessors.

DON'T DIG YOUR OWN GRAVE!

The sight of danger leads, when possible, to the avoiding of it. The bird is directed by instinct; man by reason. Yet, sin can so warp a man's sound judgment, that even with his boasted wisdom, he won't do what the bird does by instinct (*avoids* the net she sees but man *rushes* into it.) These men thirsted for their neighbor's *blood.* But in the end *they lie in wait for their own.* They hid secretly, waiting to pounce on the innocent without cause. But it proved to be *ambush for their own lives.*[d] Ahab and his guilty partner, in plotting to destroy their *innocent* victim, brought about their own ruin.[e] Little did Haman, when determined to murder Mordecai;[f] or Judas, when

[d]Verse 11, with 18. Comp. Job 18:8; Heb 2:10
[e]1 Kings 21:4–24
[f]Esther 7:9

[6] *Verse 16. Isa 59:7. An apt illustration of the total depravity of man in the perverted use of the members of his body—Rom 3:15.*

looking for a chance to betray his Master,[g] see, that they were digging their own grave.[h] Yet the sinner, if he would just look around a little, might see hell at the end of his path.[i] But sin is misleading and self-destroying. So are the ways—and such is the goal—of greedy, murderous, gain.[7] *My son*—once more, *hear* your Father's instruction, "Flee from these things."[j]

[g]Matt 26:14–16; 27:3–5
[h]Ps 7:15, 16; 9:15, 16
[i]Matt 7:13
[j]Verse 8, with 1 Tim 6:9–11

20 *Wisdom shouts in the street,*
She lifts her voice in the square;
21 *At the head of the noisy* streets *she cries out;*
At the entrance of the gates in the city, she utters her sayings:
22 *"How long, O naive ones, will you love simplicity?*
And scoffers delight themselves in scoffing,
And fools hate knowledge?
23 *"Turn to my reproof,*
Behold, I will pour out my spirit on you;
I will make my words known to you.

A father's instruction has warned us against the temptations of Satan. *Wisdom*—the Son of God Himself, now invites us,—in all His divine authority and grace. Full of yearning love to sinners, he *shouts,* not only in the temple, but out in the streets with the crowds.[k]—*How long? Naive* is another word for folly. It's the frame of mind of those who do not fear God. They don't weigh what they say or do. They live as though there is no God and no eternity. Their understanding is blinded by their love of sin. Other men don't delight in their ignorance. They want to get rid of it. But these *naive ones* are ignorant of the value of their soul and the dangers it is exposed to, and they don't want to be disturbed. They consider all efforts to help them, as breaking in upon their repose, and raising needless alarm. For while they live wildly and lazily, or disregarding the rules, they don't consider that God is aware of all their wickedness, and "that God will bring you to judgment for all these things."[l] They are encouraged by a few scoffers—more violent than they, themselves, who have neither fear nor shame; neither regret nor decency of manner—people who just take

[k]Comp. Prov 8:1–5; Matt 13:2; John 7:37–39; 18:20, 21; Ps 40:9, 10
[l]Hos 7:2; Eccl 11:9

[7] *Comp. Job 31:39, 40; Jer 22:17–19; Mic 3:10–12. "How great a cheat is wickedness! It ensnareth the ensnarers, and murders the murderers; holds a dark lantern in one hand, while with the other it discharges silently a pistol into our bosom"—JERMIN (Dr. M.),* Comment on Proverbs, *folio, 1638.*

great delight in shooting off their mouths, who shoot their poisoned arrows against godliness.[m] Christianity to them is a weakness beneath the dignity of educated people. The very terms of the Bible are revolting to them. A saint in Scripture means one sanctified by the Spirit of God, but to these high and mighty scoffers, it means either a fool or a hypocrite. They are so exalted in their own opinion that they can't stoop to the vulgar thoughts and habits of the Christian. So . . . that's how they prove themselves (both the lazy crowd of *naive ones*, and their scoffing leaders) to be fools, that hate true *knowledge.*[n] Trying to keep out fear, they also shut out everything that would make them wise and happy. If they don't want to think about their lost condition, they also rule out of their thinking everything that's able to give them "wisdom that leads to salvation."[o] Oh, they have plenty of other knowledge, but often, all it does is to keep out better things. It gives them an evil eye and fills their soul with darkness, making them hate the light and "not come to the light, lest" their deeds should be exposed.[p]

[m] Ps 64:3, 4
[n] Verses 7, 29, 30; Job 21:14; 24:13
[o] 2 Tim 3:15
[p] John 3:19, 20

Our Lord deals with people like that by melting down the hardness of their hearts with compassionate pleading—*How long?*[q] He brushes away all suggestions of unbelief and all their empty excuses. He says, "Turn to My reproof." And they say, "I can't turn myself." And He responds, "I will pour out My spirit on you." And—as the result of this blessing—*I will make My words known to you.* The Bible, once a dark and sealed book, will be made clear to you. Bishop Hall interprets, "I offer to you both My Word outwardly to your ears, and My Spirit in your heart, to make it understandable to you."

[q] Comp. Matt 23:37; Luke 19:41, 42

But many tell us, the only illumination we can expect today is the written Word, and we will have to interpret it like we would any other book, by our own reason. They argue that there is no such thing as the Spirit's teaching—that it is all just enthusiastic delusion. This may get by with the *naive and the scoffers*—who know nothing of the blindness of their hearts and of the power of natural prejudice, which only God's grace can conquer. But the man that knows his own darkness and that nothing less than the power of God can teach him, he will "cry for discernment, lift your voice for understanding;"[r] not be-

[r] Prov 2:3

cause the word is dark (for it is light itself), but because he is dark and therefore utterly unable to receive its instructions.[s] We don't need a new revelation, all we need is a divine teacher. We need *the pouring out of the Spirit to make known the Word.* The Word is the same divine Word as it always was. But it was not understood, not recognized, and therefore, it wasn't practically effectual. Now there is joy, a power and sweetness, we had no idea of before. It humbled us in the sense of our ignorance and makes us long for more of its heavenly light and influence.

[s]1 Cor 2:9–14

But the proud faultfinder complains against God, as if he blames Him for a blindness and inability he cannot help, inborn without his consent. "Who are you, O man, who answers back to God?"[t] He at once answers this Satanic plea by offering you present, suitable, and sufficient relief. He meets you on your way to condemnation with the promise of free and full forgiveness.[u] Your plea would be forceful, only if you go to Him and find Him unable to help—and that will never happen! The power indeed is of Him. But He has said, "Ask, and it shall be given to you."[v]

[t]Rom 9:20

[u]Isa 1:18; 43:23, 26

[v]Matt 7:7

BRING YOUR HELPLESSNESS TO HIM

If your helplessness is a real grievance, bring it to Him with an honest desire to get rid of it. If you have never prayed, now is the time for prayer. If you cannot pray, at least make the effort. Stretch out the withered hand in the obedience of faith.[w] If your heart is hard, your convictions weak, your resolves unsteady; all is provided in the promise—*I will pour out my Spirit on you.*

[w]Mark 3:5

Take the first step—now. Act in dependence upon God—the almighty mover and agent.[x] Christian experience explains a mystery too deep for human reason. It harmonizes man's energy and God's grace. There is no limiting, no being shut out, with God. His promises assure a welcome to the willing heart. If it cannot move, His Spirit can compel, point, draw it to the Savior. In fact, doesn't the very desire you have to turn, show that the Savior has already touched it, and drawn it to Himself?

[x]Comp. Phil 2:12, 13

But remember—the call—*How long?* is to an instant conversion; not to be considered or resolved tomorrow, but to be decided today. When we delay, we mock God. "Do not quench the Spirit" now striving, but which "shall not strive with man forever."[y] Don't add even more to the guilt that is about to sink you into perdition.

[y] 1 Thess 5:19; Gen 6:3

24 *Because I called, and you refused;*
I stretched out my hand, and no one paid attention;
25 *And you neglected all my counsel,*
And did not want my reproof;
26 *I will even laugh at your calamity;*
I will mock when your dread comes,
27 *When your dread comes like a storm,*
And your calamity comes on like a whirlwind,
When distress and *anguish come on you.*
28 *"Then they will call on me, but I will not answer;*
They will seek me diligently, but they shall not find me,
29 *Because they hated knowledge,*
And did not choose the fear of the LORD.
30 *"They would not accept my counsel,*
They spurned all my reproof.
31 *"So they shall eat of the fruit of their own way,*
And be satiated with their own devices.

The Savior *calls* by His Word, His providence, His ministers, and conscience. But *you refused.* Yet, not until His *calls* have been *refused,* does He thunder forth His warnings. But who can measure the guilt of rejection of grace, so rich and free? All creatures apart from man are His servants.[z] Only man resists His control. *"I have spread out my hands"*[a] to offer help; to give blessing; to ask acceptance; yes, even to command attention to His call.[b] But no *one paid attention.* The wisest *counsel,* the most solemn reproof, comes to nothing. So he endures "with much patience vessels of wrath prepared for destruction."[c] But, O sinner! the day will come, when He, who once yearned, and wept, and prayed, and died for you, will have no pity;[d] when He shall be, as though He *laughs and mocks at your calamity.*[e] He shall delight in the exercise of His almighty justice over you.[f]

[z] Ps 119:91
[a] Isa 65:2
[b] Acts 21:40
[c] Rom 9:22
[d] Ezek 5:11; 8:18 with 33:11
[e] Comp. Judg 10:14; Isa 1:24
[f] Comp. Deut 28:63; Ezek 5:13

IS YOURS THE LONELY GRIEF?

All will then be the lonely grief of fear fulfilled;[g] sud-

[g] Prov 10:24

den as *a whirlwind;*[8] the *distress and anguish* of utter despair.[h]

[h]Job 15:24; Dan 5:5, 6, 30

This is His solemn condemnation. And then, as if He can't bear the scorn and rejection a moment longer, He pictures the scene itself in strongest colors. They would not hear when I called. *Then they will call on me, but I will not answer.* They would not listen to my warnings; I will not listen to their cries. *They will call on me*—yea, *they will seek me diligently, but they shall not find me.*[9] Prayer, once all-powerful, will then be powerless. "The last judgment before the very last of all is come; the very outward court or portal of hell" (*Bishop Reynolds' Works*, p. 971); the misery of deserted souls. To be forsaken of God at any time brings unspeakable sorrow.[i] But how much more in the time of trouble![j] Yet, to have His face not only turned from us, but turned against us, and to see His eternal frown instead of His smile—this will be hell instead of heaven.

[i]Hos 9:12
[j]1 Sam 28:15

Does this terrible wrath seem inconsistent with a God of love? "The Lord your God is a consuming fire."[k] Look at it this way, His wisdom was hated instead of loved. He wasn't revered as God; His fear was not chosen; none of His gracious *counsel* was regarded; all His *reproof* was spurned. Isn't it right, then, that the sinner, determined to choose his *own way*, should, not only gather the fruit of it, but eat it, too?[l] And it should enter into him, and become a part of his being; that he should be filled with it, even to having more than enough;[m] and that—not only on the road of life,[n] but at the end of it, and throughout eternity as well?[o] Sin, itself, apart from the material fire, constitutes a hell. The fruit of sin in time, when ripe, is just the fruit of sin through eternity. It is merely the sinner reaping what he has sown. There is no violent or random step from sin in time, to hell in eternity. The one emerges from the other, as does the fruit from the flower.

[k]Deut 4:24
[l]Prov 13:2
[m]Prov 24:14. Comp. 25:16
[n]Num 11:4, 20; Ps 56:13–15
[o]Isa 3:11; Gal 6:7

[8] *Chap. 10:25; Ps 58:9; Isa 17:13; 40:24. Eastern travelers furnish abundant illustration of this striking figure. Paxton's* Illustrations of Scripture Geography, *pp. 412–416—(Oliphant).*

[9] *Matt 25:6–12; Luke 13:24–26. Dr. Owen, admirably remarks upon this remonstrance as a proof of the personality of Wisdom—"If these things express not a person, and* that *a divine person, the Scripture gives us no due apprehension of anything whatever. Who is it that pours out the Holy Spirit? Who is it that men sin against, in refusing to be obedient? Who is it, that in their distress they call upon, and seek early in their trouble? The whole Scripture declare to whom, and to whom alone, these things belong, and may be ascribed."* —Expos. of Hebrews. *Prelim. Exercit. 27:8–12. We might add—Who besides could threaten rebels with ruin and promise peace and security to the obedient?*

It is simply, that the sinner is filled with his own ways, and eats the fruit of his own evil doings.[p]

[p] Rom 6:21

This picture might seem to be the prediction of despair. Yet, we've seen such miracles of God's grace—in fact, such are we ourselves—that we don't despair concerning anyone. But, even so, we must not soften down God's words by a misplaced presumptuous tenderness. Haven't we seen His words fulfilled in the agonies of the dying sinner, who has neglected and scoffed at the gospel, and never sent up one cry for mercy on his soul? Isn't this a warning of the danger of prolonging repentence; of the worthlessness of confessions extorted by terror; "wail on their beds," not weeping at the cross?[q] And doesn't it solemnly tell us, that the day of grace has its limits;[r] that there is a knock, which will be the last knock; that a sinner may be lost on this side of hell; begged, pleaded with, wept over—yet lost, lost even in the day of salvation? To have "insulted the Spirit *of grace*" (mark the endearing name)—the Spirit of all kindness, of alluring love; who pleads so tenderly with us—to wound Him, as it were, to His very soul[s]—this is a provocation beyond words, beyond thought. There remains only that, which might strike into the very center of the man, the "terrifying expectation of judgment and the fury of a fire, which will consume the adversaries . . . it is a terrifying thing to fall into the hands of the living God."[t]

[q] Hos 7:14, with Luke 18:13
[r] Gen 6:3; Heb 4:7
[s] Heb 10:29, Gr.
[t] Heb 10:26, 27, 31

WAYWARDNESS OF THE NAIVE

32 *For the waywardness* [AV—*turning away*] *of the naive shall kill them,*
And the complacency of fools shall destroy them.
33 *"But he who listens to me shall live securely,*
And shall be at ease from the dread of evil."

Once more, the sinner's ruin is laid at his own door. His *waywardness* turns him away from Wisdom's pleading voice. He despises the only remedy. He dies a suicide. It doesn't matter a bit what we turn to. If we turn away from God, we turn from our true and eternal interests. And, oh! remember—every inattention, every wilful neglect, is a step toward this fearful falling away. The word gradually becomes a burden, then a scorn. The *fool* may seem to be spared from judgment. But *complacency* is his destruction.[10] To desire ease, therefore, is to embrace a deadly enemy. Anyone that knows his own heart will feel it a matter, not of commendation, but of deep and anxious prayer— "In all our times of prosperity. Blessed Lord, deliver us" (Litany).

But to close with the sunshine of promise—are you, like God's own child, listening to Him? If so, you are under His cover, out of reach of evil; *living* not only *securely,* but certain of safety; even *at ease* from dread of evil.[u] You are in conscious security, like Noah was in the ark, while the world was perishing around him.[v] You are as fearless as David was, when in imminent danger, because you know your refuge is in God.[w] Yes—even the coming *day of calamity and dread* brings with it no fear of evil.[x] "The day is coming, like a burning furnace."[y] You will see the world on fire and feel you have lost, but, really, you can't lose anything. To you, the day of darkness and gloominess will be a day of unclouded sunshine, the entrance into everlasting joy.[z]

[u] Prov 3:31–26; Job 5:21; Ps 91:5; 112:6, 7; Isa 32:17–19
[v] Gen 7:11–16
[w] Ps 3. Comp. 1 Sam 30:6
[x] Contrasting verses 26, 27. Luke 21:26. Rev 6:16–17
[y] Mal 4:1, 2
[z] Luke 21:28. 2 Peter 3:10–13

[10] *Job 21:11–13; Ps 55:19; 73:3–20; Jer 12:1–3; Luke 6:24, 25; 12:16–20; 16:19–24; James 5:1–5. Examples of Israel—Deut 32:15–25; Jer 22:20–22; Hos 13:6–9; Amos 6:1–6. Babylon—Isa 47:7–9. Moab—Jer 48:11–15. Sodom—Ezek 16:49. Tyre—Ezek 27:2, 25–27.*

CHAPTER TWO

1 *My son, if you will receive my sayings,*
And treasure my commandments within you,
2 *Make your ear attentive to wisdom,*
Incline your heart to understanding;
3 *For if you cry for discernment,*
Lift your voice for understanding;
4 *If you seek her as silver,*
And search for her as for hidden treasures;
5 *Then you will discern the fear of the* LORD.
And discover the knowledge of God.
6 *For the* LORD *gives wisdom;*
From His mouth come *knowledge and understanding.*

WHERE CAN WE FIND WISDOM?

Wisdom, having solemnly warned rebellious scorners, now instructs her faithful children. The dark question asked long before—"Where can wisdom be found?"[a]—is now answered. It is here set before us, as *the fear and knowledge of God;*[b] a principle of practical godliness;[c] a preservation from besetting temptations;[d] and a guide into the right and safe path.[e] So follow the security of its scholars[f] and the certain ruin of its ungodly despisers.[g]

[a]Job 28:12, 20, 21
[b]Verse 5
[c]Verses 7–9
[d]Verses 10–19
[e]Verse 20
[f]Verse 21
[g]Verse 22

HOW TO UNDERSTAND THE WHOLE WORD OF GOD

The rules for getting *wisdom* are such that the simplest comprehension can apply. Carefully considered and diligently improved, they will furnish a key for the understanding of the whole Word of God. Let us examine them more closely.

Receive my sayings—Let them be the seed cast into the ground of "an honest and good heart"[h]—a heart pre-

[h]Luke 8:15

pared by God.[i] Read the Book of God as one who sat at the feet of Jesus, and heard His Word.[j] Like the Bereans, "received the word with great eagerness";[k] like the Thessalonians, with reverential faith, acknowledging its supreme authority.[l] *Treasure my commandments within you.* Carry them about with you as the choicest treasure for greater security,[m] as your furniture always at hand for present use.[n] Let the heart be the hiding place for the treasure.[o] Satan can never snatch it there.

[i]Prov 16:1
[j]Luke 10:39
[k]Acts 17:11
[l]1 Thess 2:13
[m]Col 3:16, with Matt 13:44
[n]Prov 4:20, 21; 7:3. Job 22:22
[o]Luke 2:19, 51; Ps 119:11

But there must be an active, practical habit of *attention.*[1] Yet to *make your ear attentive, and incline your heart*—"who is adequate for these things?"[p] Oh! my Lord! Let it be your own work in me! You alone can do it.[q] Jerome said, "Thou giving me the ear, I have heard, as thou wouldest Thy Word to be heard" (*Hab* 3:2). Let it be with me, as with your Beloved Son—"He awakens *me* morning by morning. He awakens my ear to listen as a disciple."[r] So let me, under your grace, listen as You say, "incline your ear and come to Me. Listen, that you may live."[s]

[p]2 Cor 2:16
[q]Prov 20:12
[r]Isa 50:4
[s]Isa 55:3

HOW YOU CAN GET HEAVENLY WISDOM

Without this spirit of prayer—there may be attention and earnestness; yet not one spiritual impression upon the conscience; not one ray of divine light in the soul. Earthly wisdom is gained by study; heavenly wisdom by prayer. Study may make a Biblical scholar; but prayer puts the heart under heavenly teaching and forms the wise and spiritual Christian. The Word first comes into the ears; then it enters into the heart; there it is safely hid; and from there rises the *cry—the lifting up of the voice.* Thus, "the unfolding of Thy Words gives light; It gives understanding to the simple."[t] God keeps the key of the treasure-house in His own hand. "This also I will let the house of Israel ask Me to do for them,"[u] and he will open it to you. We look for no other inspiration than divine grace to make His Word clear and impressive. Every verse read and meditated on furnishes material for prayer. Every text prayed over opens a mine of "un-

[t]Ps 119:130
[u]Ezek 36:37

[1] *Prov 22:17; 23:12. The Emperor Constantine stood hours to hear the Word; replying, when asked to sit, "that he thought it wicked to give negligent ears, when the truth handled was spoken of God"*—Euseb. de Vita Constant. *lib. 4. Foxe records of Edward VI: "That never was he present at any sermon commonly, but would excerpt them, or note them with his own hand"—Vol. 5, p. 700. And yet, Bishop Hooper thought, that his royal master's love for the preached Word needed to be increased*—Sermon 7th on Jonas.

[v]Eph 3:8
[w]Ps 119:18 and Ps 50
[x]1 Kings 3:9–12
[y]Eph 1:17, 18

fathomable riches,"[v] with a light from above, more clear and full than the most intelligent instruction. David[w] and his wise son[x] searched for this learning upon their knees; and the most matured Christian will continue to the end to lift up his voice for a greater *knowledge of Him.*[y]

HERE'S BURIED TREASURE FOR YOU!

[z]Job 28:1
[a]Eph 3:18, 19

But prayer must not replace hard work. Instead, let prayer energize it![2] The miner's tireless efforts; his invincible resolution; his untiring perseverance; seeking, yes, searching for *hidden treasures,*—such must be our *searching* into the sacred storehouse. To read, instead of *searching* the Scriptures, is only to skim the surface, and gather up a few superficial notions.[3] The rule of success is dig up and down the field; and if the search is discouraging, dig again. The patient, systematic effort required by reading and rereading will uncover the buried treasure. "Surely there is a mine for silver."[z] Yes, what miner would be content with the first ore? Would he not search deeper and deeper, until he has found it all; not satisfied with taking away much, but determined to leave nothing? So let us daily explore "the breadth, and length, and height and depth" of our boundless stores, until we be "filled up to all the fullness of God."[a]

This habit of living in the very atmosphere of Scripture is priceless! To be filled from this divine treasury; to have large portions of the Word daily passing through the mind; gives us a firmer grasp, and a more suitable and varied application of it. Yet this profit can only be fully reaped in solitude. We may *read* the Scriptures, one with another. But to *search* them, we must be alone with God.

[2] *Comp. Matt 11:12. "We are all," says the heavenly Leighton, "too little in the humble seeking and begging this divine knowledge; and that is the cause why we are so shallow and small proficients. 'If thou cry, and lift up thy voice for understanding, search for it as for hid treasures;' sit down upon thy knees, and dig for it. That is the best posture, to fall right upon the golden vein, and go deepest to know the mind of God, in searching the Scriptures, to be directed and regulated in His ways; to be made skilful in ways of honoring Him, and doing Him service. This, neither man nor angels can teach Him, but God alone"*—Sermon on Ps 107:43.

[3] *Comp. John 5:39. Gr.—a similar allusion to the miner's toil. "I can speak it by experience," said a wise man "that there is little good to be gotten by reading the Bible cursorily and carelessly. But do it daily and diligently, with attention and affection; and you shall find such efficacy, as is to be found in no other book that can be named."—ERASMUS'S* Preface to Luke. *Peter Martyr gives the same testimony*—Epist. Dedic. to Comment. on Rom. *The following relic of Queen Elizabeth I will interest and profit. It was written on a blank leaf of a black-letter edition of St. Paul's Epistles, which she used during her lonely imprisonment at Woodstock. The volume itself, curiously embroidered by her own hand, is preserved in the Bodleian Library:—"August. I walk many times into the pleasant fields of the Holy Scriptures, where I pluck the goodlisome herbs of sentences by pruning, eat them by reading, chew them by musing, and lay them up, at length, in the high seat of memorie, by gathering them together, that so, having tasted their sweetness, I may the less perceive the bitterness of this miserable life"—MISS STRICKLAND'S* Queen of England, *Ch. 6, p. 113.*

Here we learn to apply ourselves wholly to the Word, and the Word wholly to us. This enriching study gives a purer vein of sound judgment. The one who merely reads often hardly knows where to begin, and he reads routinely without purpose. The knowledge gained will therefore be very limited and ineffective. Nor is the neglect of this habit less hurtful to the church. All fundamental errors and heresies in the church may be traced to this source—"You are mistaken, not understanding the Scriptures."[b] They are mostly based on partial or disjointed statements of truth. Truth separated from truth becomes error.

[b] Matt 22:29

TWO PRINCIPLES OF GODLINESS

But the mind prayerfully occupied in the *search* for divine truth—*crying and lifting up the voice*—will never fail to discern the two great principles of godliness—*the fear and knowledge of God.* There is no chance and no disappointment in this search. *Then you will discern. The Lord gives wisdom; it comes out of His mouth.* None shall search in vain.[c] Never has apostasy from the faith been connected with a prayerful and earnest study of the Word of God.

[c] Job 32:8; Isa 48:17; 54:13; James 1:5, 17. Comp. Gen 41:38, 39; Exod 4:12; Dan 1:17

7 *He stores up sound wisdom for the upright;*
He is *a shield to those who walk in integrity,*
8 *Guarding the paths of justice,*
And He preserves the way of His godly ones.
9 *Then you will discern righteousness and justice*
And equity and *every good course.*

Vanity[d] and foolishness[e] are the stamp on the wisdom of this world. Here is *sound wisdom.*

[d] Eccl 1:18
[e] 1 Cor 3:19

NEW TREASURES DAILY

It looks at things not in their notions but in their substance. It is *sound*, because it is practical. It is indeed a hid *treasure*;[f] so protected, that no thief can reach it; yet so free, that every sinner may have access to it. Yes; in the Son of God Himself "are hidden all the treasures of wisdom and knowledge." All these treasures in Him are laid up for the righteous—made over to them.[g] Oh, let us draw upon this infinite treasure daily, hourly, for light to direct an *upright* walk. "To those that are true and *upright* in heart, He will in His own good time reveal true

[f] Verse 4
[g] Col 2:3; 1 Cor 1:30

and saving knowledge, and that *sound* spiritual *wisdom*, which shall make them eternally happy," stated Bishop Hall. Our faithful God is a *shield* to them that *walk uprightly.*[h] His wisdom covers us from that clever reasoning, which would rob us of our treasure.[i] The way of the saints is indeed full of danger; surrounded with temptation: yet it is safe[j]—kept and preserved by almighty power, even on the very edge of the enemy's ground.[k]

And so complete is this godly privilege, that, not only does it enlarge our *knowledge of God,*[l] but it brings us to a full *understanding* of every practical obligation. Indeed, only that which guides our feet into every good *path* is *sound wisdom;* that "the man of God may be adequate, equipped for every good work."[m] The gracious wisdom that saves the soul, sanctifies the heart and life.[n]

[h]Prov 30:5; Ps 84:11
[i]Prov 22:12
[j]Prov 4:11; 8:20; Deut 33:26–29; 1 Sam 2:9; Ps 37:23, 24; 106:9
[k]1 Sam 25:39; 27:1, with Prov 29; 2 Cor 12:7–9
[l]Verse 5
[m]2 Tim 3:15–17
[n]Titus 2:11, 12

10 *For wisdom will enter your heart,*
And knowledge will be pleasant to your soul;
11 *Discretion will guard you,*
Understanding will watch over you,

THE HEART'S TRUE RESTING PLACE

We have seen the good that wisdom brings to us.[o] Now see what evil it *guards* us from. But note its place—*in the heart.* Here only has it any light, life, or power.[p] Clear knowledge floating in the head is deep ignorance. If it only glitters in the understanding, it is dry, speculative, and barren. When it enters into *your heart,* light beams out, all the affections are engaged; and how pleasant it is *to your soul*![q] Christianity now is no lifeless notion. It is handled, tasted, enjoyed. It gives a *discreet and understanding* direction to the whole life. It becomes not only an external rule, but a *guarding, watching* principle;[r] like royalty's bodyguard.[s] Before, it was the object of our search. Now, having found it, it is our *pleasure*. Until it is so, it can have no practical influence. It is the man, whose "*delight is in the law of the Lord,*" who is preserved from walking "in the counsel of the wicked."[t] Education, conviction, and high moral principle are at best only partially operative. The reclaimed drunkard may be true to his Alcoholics Anonymous pledge, but if the "root of bitterness"[u] is untouched, he may revel in some other equally ruinous course. External wickedness may be exchanged

[o]Verse 5
[p]Prov 4:23
[q]Prov 24:13, 14; Job 23:12; Ps 119:103; Jer 15:16
[r]Prov 4:6; 6:22–24; Ps 17:4; 119:9–11, 104
[s]1 Sam 26:16; 2 Kings 11:11
[t]Ps 1:1, 2. Comp. Prov 7:4, 5
[u]Heb 12:15

for decent formality. Wandering affections may be turned from some object of desire without being fixed upon God. The mind may be disciplined from utter unprofitableness, only to idolize talent, or to become fascinated with literature. The folly of the pride of life may be resisted; yet in other forms it may be tenderly cherished. In all these cases, the principle is unconquered. The forsaken sin only makes way for some more plausible, but no less deadly passion. The heart, cast into the mold of the gospel, is the only cover from those snares within and without,[v] which so unnoticeably, yet so fatally, estrange us from God. Never, till the vital principle is implanted, is their mischief really seen. Never, till then, does the heart find its proper object, its true resting place.

[v]Rom 6:17, 18; 2 Cor 3:18

12 *To deliver you from the way of evil,*
From the man who speaks perverse things;
13 *From those who leave the paths of uprightness,*
To walk in the ways of darkness;
14 *Who delight in doing evil,*
And rejoice in the perversity of evil;
15 *Whose paths are crooked,*
And who are devious in their ways;

SATAN'S SECRET AGENTS

The various snares for the young, about to be described, furnish a fearful picture of the temptations to which young people are exposed. Will it not awaken our earnest cries for their deep and solid conversion to God; that *wisdom may indeed enter into their hearts,* and its *pleasures* be really enjoyed; that they may have a spiritual hunger, as well as a religious education; that they may know the gospel, not only in the conviction of their conscience, or the excitement of their feelings, but in the entire renewal of their hearts before God? This, and nothing less, will preserve them from the snare of their cruel foe. Every town and village swarms with his secret agents; first, they initiate themselves into the mysteries of his art; then, they go forth, as hard-working and skilled teachers, well prepared for his murderous work. We have been warned against one of these temptations before.[w]

[w]Prov 1:10–13

POISONED WATERS

And now, here's something else to beware of: the tempter, himself! You can tell him by his speech. He's *the man who speaks perverse things* against God and His law. He is like a polluted fountain sending out poisoned waters. How quickly the contamination spreads! It isn't that he sins in ignorance. He and his companions[4] have probably been trained in *the paths of justice.* But having come in contact with the poisonous breath of the ungodly, they have caught the contagion and eagerly spread it. They are quick to *leave the paths,* which they never really loved, choosing, instead, *to walk the ways of darkness,* which their hearts *do* love.[x] Having left the good paths they hated, they become therefore leaders in iniquity. Poisoned themselves, they delight in poisoning everything around them. Like Satan himself, they love *doing evil;*[5] to draw their fellow-sinners into the net; and they *rejoice* in those, who are most strongly established in their *evil.*[6]

[x]Prov 4:16, 17; Job 24:13–16; John 3:19, 20

THE DECEITFULNESS OF SIN— AND ITS CERTAIN END

Therefore, they plunge deeper and deeper into sin, till they leave the straight way altogether, and all their *paths become crooked,* leading them to certain and eternal ruin. Isn't this the true-life story of many a Sunday school pupil or child of godly parents, who has been the object of deep and tender care, and yet, becomes "hardened by the deceitfulness of sin,"[y] the neglect of faithful warnings, the stifling of solemn conviction? If God deserted them, it would serve them right, since they first left Him with such fearful aggravation! Most of all, young people, don't make friends with those, who are sinning against better knowledge and instruction. They are totally dedicated to their master's work. Oh! if misguided sinners could only see sin as it really is—in all its horrid ugliness and its awful end, wouldn't they give serious thought to its terrors? But they don't! *The crookedness of their ways* hides the end from view. Satan dangles the bait before them, makes the sin seem far less serious than it really is, blinds the sinner's eyes and keeps the person from see-

[y]Heb 3:13

[4] *The change to the plural number* (the man . . . who leave) *implies confederacy.*
[5] *Comp. Isa 3:9; Jer 11:15. God's heavy judgment, 2 Thess 2:12.*
[6] *The sin of the heathen, Rom 1:32.*

ing the certain end of it all—Hell.[z] Those who are stubbornly confirmed in their ways cannot—will not—turn back.

[z]Ps 125:5; Rom 6:21, with 2 Cor 4:3, 4

16 *To deliver you from the strange woman,*
From the adulteress [AV—"*stranger*"] *who flatters with her words;*
17 *That leaves the companion of her youth,*
And forgets the covenant of her God;
18 *For her house sinks down to death,*
And her tracks lead *to the dead;*
19 *None who go to her return again,*
Nor do they reach the paths of life.

WATCH OUT FOR FLATTERING LIPS!

Another snare of the hunter is here graphically portrayed.[7] *Wisdom hidden in the heart* is, as before, the most effectual deliverance; restraining even the eye from the harmful object.[8] Shouldn't the unknown woman, even if she is born and baptized in a Christian land, be counted as a stranger among us? One who had *forsaken the companion of her youth,*[9] and forgotten the solemn bond of *the covenant of her God*[10]—what else could she be to the incautious and reckless, but a vile *flatterer with her words*?[a] Being the slave of unlawful desire; and no pleasure but sensual gratification; she quickly becomes her own and her victim's murderer. Her house is the land of death.[b] Eternal death is her doom.[c] She prefers the dead. Her paths lead toward them, despite the awful examples of God's vengeance in old times.[d] There are some instances of deliverance; but they are not so much typical, as they are special miracles of grace. Their purpose is to show how far the arm of the Lord can reach.[e] Solomon's own case is an example. However, cases are rare. Actually, there are scarcely, in comparison, very few cases—*none*[f] *who go to her,* who ever return. And what madness it is to rush into the snare upon so faint and

[a]Prov 5:3; 7:5, 21

[b]Prov 5:5
[c]Gal 5:19–21; Eph 5:5; Rev 21:8; 22:15
[d]Comp. Prov 9:18

[e]Comp. Luke 7:37–50; 1 Cor 6:9–11

[f]Comp. Isa 59:4; 64:7

[7] *Prov 5:3–20; 6:24; 7:5–23; 22:14; 23:27. Some commentators interpret these pictures allegorically, as descriptive of idolatry or false doctrine. "But surely," as Holden well observes, "if they be any dependence to be placed upon the language of the sacred writer, any propriety in his expressions, it is to be understood in its literal sense, as a warning against the seduction of harlots. The spirit of allegorical interpretation may make the Scriptures speak whatever is prompted by the wildest fancy, or the deepest fanaticism"—HOLDEN. Comp. SCOTT.*

[8] *Comp. Job 31:1, and our Lord's rule—Matt 5:28.*

[9] *Though a harlot, she might be (Prov 7:5, 10, 19) or might have been (John 4:17, 18) a married woman.*

[10] *Mal 2:14–16. Does not this sacred view of marriage ordinance rebuke the legal authorization which has now degraded it to a mere civil contract?*

glimmering hope of escape![g] The spell of lust makes powerless the grasp by which its victim might have taken hold of the paths of life for deliverance. He that is "saved, yet so as through fire"[h] the wonder of heaven and earth. "Is this not a brand plucked out of the fire?"[i]

[g]Eccl 7:26
[h]1 Cor 3:15
[i]Zech 3:2

20 *So you will walk in the way of good men,*
And keep to the paths of the righteous.
21 *For the upright will live in the land,*
And the blameless will remain in it;
22 *But the wicked will be cut off from the land,*
And the treacherous will be uprooted from it.

PATHS OF REST

Here is the ultimate blessing of *implanted wisdom.* Not only does it deliver from evil men; but it guides us *into the way of good men.* Protected with this divine armor, you will have courage, like Joseph, to turn your face from the enchantment of sin,[j] *and keep to the paths of the righteous.* Rugged though they are, still they are the only paths of rest and security.[k] So shall you *live and remain in the land,* as its original inheritor;[l] having the best portion on earth, and an infinitely better portion in heaven; while *the wicked and treacherous,* though they may "enjoy the passing pleasures of sin"[m] shall be ultimately *cut off, uprooted,* and driven away into everlasting ruin.[n]

[j]Gen 39:9, 10
[k]Song of Sol 1:7, 8; Jer 6:16
[l]Ps 37:9, 11, 22, 29, 34; Matt 5:5
[m]Heb 11:25
[n]Prov 10:30; 14:32; 15:25; Ps 52:5–7; 92:7; Matt 3:10

RULE OF LIFE—GUIDE TO HEAVEN

And now, what serious reader of this chapter can fail to see the unspeakable blessing of enlisting under the banner of the cross early in life; of desiring and being taught in the ways, and disciplined in the school, of the Bible while young; and being led, in earliest childhood, to hide that blessed Book in the heart, as the rule of life, the principle of holiness, the guide to heaven!

Parents, sponsors, teachers of youth; consider your deep responsibility with unceasing prayer for special grace and wisdom. Beware of glossing over sin or making it seem less serious than it is. Let young people be always led to look upon sinful habits with horror, as appallingly evil; to restrain their passion and all badly controlled excitement. Steer them away from pornographic books and magazines designed to stir up evil thoughts. To encourage glowing passion may stimulate wickedness to the most dangerous results. Oh! what wisdom is needed to guide, to repress, to bring forth, develop safely, and to improve fully, the mind, energies, and sensibilities of youth!

CORDS OF SIN

Young man, beware! Don't flatter yourself for a moment that God will ever wink at your sinful passions; that He will allow for them, as mistakes and weaknesses of youth. They are the cords "of your own sins, which, if the power of God's grace doesn't break them in time, will "hold" you for eternity.[o] Avoid sin as you would the infection of a plague. Keep your distance from it, as from the pit of destruction. Store your mind with those things which will preserve heavenly wisdom. Cultivate the taste for purer pleasures. Listen to the fatherly, pleading protest, inviting you to your rest—"Have you not just now called to Me, from this time cry, 'My Father, Thou art the friend of my youth?' "[p]

[o] Prov 5:22

[p] Jer 3:4

CHAPTER THREE

1 *My son, do not forget my teaching,*
But let your heart keep my commandments;
2 *For length of days and years of life,*
And peace they will add to you.

THE HEART'S FORGETFULNESS

This is not the stern language of command. It is our Father's voice in all the endearing persuasiveness of promise—*My son.* He had before instructed us to *seek and search* after wisdom, and He described its invaluable blessings. Now He calls us to put into practice what He told us—*do not forget my teaching.* The wilful forgetfulness of the heart,[a] not the failing of the memory (for which a special, though we fear too much neglected, help, is provided)[b] is here implied. *Let your heart,* like the Ark of the covenant, *be the keeping-place of my commandments.*[c] And isn't this the child's desire—"Oh that my ways were directed to keep thy statutes?"[d], while his conscious helplessness takes hold of God's promise—"I will put My law within them, and on their hearts I will write it."[e]

Indeed, no laws, but God's bind the heart. All acceptable obedience begins here. The heart is the first thing that wanders from God, and the first that returns. Here is the vital principle.[f] Religion without it is merely a name; and no matter how much the believer tries to put life into it, all his efforts will fail, "Their root will become like rot and their blossom blow away as dust."[g] Even if every moment were filled with good deeds, or outward piety; yet, unless *the heart* were quickened to *keep the commandments,* the voice of rebuke would be heard—"Who requires of you this trampling of My courts?"[h] The inner man's delight in the law of God[i] is what determines the

[a] Prov 2:17; Ps 9:17; 10:4. Comp. Prov 4:5; Deut 4:23; Ps 119:93, 176
[b] John 14:26
[c] Prov 4:4; Deut 11:18; Isa 51:7, with Ezek 11:20; Heb 9:4
[d] Ps 119:6. Comp. verses 69, 129
[e] Jer 31:33
[f] Prov 4:23; Rom 6:17
[g] Isa 5:24
[h] Isa 1:11, 12
[i] Rom 7:22

reality and true value of service. And this pleasure and perseverance in duty are the result of a changed heart.[j]

[j]See Ezek 11:19; 36:26, 27

REWARD OF OBEDIENCE

Herein also lies our interest, not less than our obligation. The reward of this hearty obedience (need we add—a reward of grace?) is a long and happy life—the highest earthly good.[k] The wicked indeed live long, and the godly often live out only half their days. The wicked die in outward comfort; the righteous in outward trouble.[l] But *length of days* is the promise to the righteous; whether for earth or for heaven, as their Father sees best for them. In itself the promise, as it pertains to this life, has no charm. To the ungodly it is a curse;[m] to the people of God a trial of faith and patience;[n] to everybody a weariness.[o] But *peace* added provides sunshine for the toilsome way:[p] "peace with God through our Lord Jesus Christ";[q] eternal peace in his home and in his heart;[r] where all the fightings of a rebellious human nature, all the counter strivings of a contrary and unrestrained will, shall have ceased forever. "*Blessed are those who wash their robes,* that they may have the right to the *tree* of life, and may enter by the gates into the city."[s]

[k]Ps 34:12. Comp. verse 16; 4:10; 9:11; 10:27; Job 10:12
[l]Eccl 9:2
[m]Gen 4:11–15; Isa 65:20
[n]Gen 27:46; 47:9; 1 Kings 19:4; Job 7:16; Phil 1:23, 24; Rev 22:20
[o]Prov 15:15; Ps 90:10; Eccl 12:1
[p]Ps 119:165; Isa 32:17; 48:17, 18
[q]Rom 5:1; Eph 2:13, 14; Col 1:20
[r]Ps 37:37; Isa 57:2
[s]Rev 22:14

3 *Do not let kindness and truth leave you;*
Bind them around your neck,
Write them on the tablet of your heart.
4 *So you will find favor and good repute*
In the sight of God and man.

Kindness and truth are the glorious perfections of God; always together[t] for His people's good. While we rest upon them for salvation, let us imitate them in our lives. Are not His children newly created in His image? Let then our Father's image be seen in us, "as beloved children."[u] Let these graces be, as with God, in combination—always together. "The want of one buries the commendation of the other. Such a one is a *merciful* man to the poor; but there is no *truth* in him. Such a one is very just in his dealings, but as hard as flint."[1] "Put on a heart of compassion, kindness, humility, gentleness and patience ... Do not lie to one another ... Speak truth, each one of you, with his neighbor."[v] Indeed, Bishop

[t]Gen 32:10; Ps 25:10; 85:10; 89:14; 100:5; 117:2; Mic 7:18–20
[u]Eph 4:24; 5:1, 2, 8
[v]Col 3:12, 9, with Eph 4:25

[1] F. TAYLOR'S Comment on Chap. 1—9, p. 4 and 1655—1657.

Sanderson said, "As a rich sparkling diamond adds both value and lustre to a golden ring; so do these virtues of justice and mercy, well-attuned to one another, bring a rich addition of glory to the crowns of the greatest monarchs" (*Sermon on Chap. 24:10–12*).

But these virtues must not be in temporary or occasional use. *Do not forget them. Bind them* as jewels around your neck.[w] "Write them on the tablet of your heart... written not with ink, but with the Spirit of the living God."[x] God indeed is not your debtor; yet none shall serve Him without reward. The man who shows *kindness* to his neighbor shall find kindness with him.[y] "Those who deal faithfully are His delight."[z] So you will *find favor and good repute*[a]—(success)[b]—*both in the sight of God and man.* Witness Joseph in Egypt;[c] David in the family of Saul[d] the servants of God in the eastern courts;[2] the early Christians with the people around them.[e] What is more beautiful than to live down reproach in this way by consistent godliness? What is more acceptable to God or more edifying to the church?[f] The Scripture connects the favor of God with the favor of men, as if the one were often the fruit of the other.[g] Such was the record of the holy child.[h] The highest crown of a youthful testimony is conformity to this divine pattern.[i]

[w] Prov 6:21; 7:3; Deut 6:8
[x] Prov 7:3; 2 Cor 3:3
[y] Ps 18:25; Matt 5:7
[z] Prov 12:22
[a] Ps 111:10
[b] Josh 1:7, 8
[c] Gen 39:2–4, 21–23; 41:37–43; 45:16
[d] 1 Sam 18:5, 14–16
[e] Acts 2:44–47
[f] Rom 14:16–19
[g] Comp. Prov 16:7
[h] Luke 2:52
[i] Comp. 1 Sam 2:26

5 *Trust in the LORD with all your heart,*
And do not lean on your own understanding.
6 *In all your ways acknowledge Him,*
And He will make your paths straight.

This is the polar star of a child of God—faith in his Father's care, promises, and grace. The meaningless expression of *trust* on the lips of the ignorant and ungodly is a fearful delusion. What ground of confidence can there be when there is everything to fear? Can the sinner's God—a just, avenging God—be an object of *trust?* How much we owe to that precious atonement, which has opened up our way to a reconciled God,[j] and assured our confidence in Him as our friend and counselor! Nor is this the cold assent of enlightened judgment. It is the *trust of the heart, of all the heart.* It is a childlike, unwavering[k] confidence in our Father's well-proved Wis-

[j] Rom 5:11
[k] Ps 78; 2 Chron 14:11. Contrast Jer 1:6–8

[2] *Dan 1:8, 9; 4:8, 9; 5:11; 6:1–3, 27, 28—His three companions, 3:30; Ezra 7:9–12; Neh 2:1–6. Mordecai, Esther 10:3.*

dom, faithfulness, and love. Any limit to this confidence is a hateful provocation.[l] He is truth itself. Therefore He would have us take Him at His Word and prove His Word to the utmost extent of His power.

[l]Ps 78:18–21

NO OTHER CONFIDENCE

But our *trust* must not only be entire: it must be exclusive. No other confidence, no confidence in the flesh, can exist in harmony with it.[m] Man with all his pride feels that he wants something to *lean on.* As a fallen being, he naturally leans to himself, to his own foolish notions and false fancies. Human power is his idol. His *understanding* is his God. Many would rather be convicted of lack of principle than lack of talent. Many bring God's truth to their own judgment and find fault with it, as an excuse for rejecting it. In these and other ways, man "who trusts in mankind" his heart "turns away from the Lord."[n] This is the history of the fall; the history of man from the fall; the dominant sin of every unhumbled heart; the lamented and resisted sin of every child of God. Need we refer to it as the sin of youth? How rare is the sight of the younger men being subject to the elder![o] If advice is asked, is it not with the hope that it will confirm a decision already made? In case the counselor doesn't agree and offers contrary judgment, then the young man's *own understanding* usually determines his course.

[m]Comp. Phil 3:3

[n]Jer 17:5

[o]1 Peter 5:5

BEWARE OF FALSE GUIDES!

This is why there's such need for the warning—*do not lean on your own understanding.* At one time, man's understanding was reliable and gave forth a clear, unclouded light. That was man's high and rightful power, when he was created "in the image of God."[p] But now, degraded as it is by the fall,[q] and darkened by the corruption of the heart,[r] man's own reason is certain to be a false guide. Even in a prophet of God it proved a mistaken counselor.[s] Yet, though we refuse to lean to it, to follow it may be implicit *trust in the Lord;* because it is a trust in His divine power, enlightening our reason and making it His lamp for our guidance. The Christian on his knees, as if he cast his understanding away, confesses himself utterly unable to guide his path. But see him in his active life. He carefully improves his mind. He conscientiously

[p]Gen 1:27; Col 3:10

[q]Ps 99:20

[r]Eph 4:18

[s]2 Sam 7:2–5

follows what it tells him to do. So then, practical faith strengthens, not destroys, its power; fills with energy, but does not take the place of exercise and effort.[t]

[t]Comp. Gen 32:9–20; Neh 2:4–20; 4:9

It is therefore our plain duty not to neglect *our understanding* but to cultivate it diligently in all its faculties. In a world of such available knowledge, ignorance is the fruit of laziness, wasteful use of time and energy, or misguided and false opinion. But *do not lean to your own understanding. Lean—upon the Lord, instead.* Self-dependence is folly,[u] rebellion,[v] ruin.[w] "The great folly of man in trials," Dr. Owen justly remarks, "*is leaning to or upon his own understanding* and counsels. What's the outcome? Whenever in our trials we consult our own understandings—that is, listen to our self-reasonings, though they seem to be good, and helping to preserve us—yet the principle of living by faith is stifled, and we shall in the issue be cast down by our own counsels." (*Treatise on temptation,* chap. 8)[x]

[u]Prov 28:26
[v]Jer 2:13; 9:23
[w]Gen 3:5, 6; Isa 47:10, 11
[x]Comp. Job 18:7; Hos 10:8

WHAT TO DO WITH YOUR DIFFICULTIES

Next, let our confidence be uniform—in all your ways acknowledge Him. Take one step at a time, every step under divine order and direction.[y] Always plan for yourself in simple dependence on God.[3] It is nothing less than undue self-exaltation to think that we can carry on even the ordinary matters of the day without His counsel. He loves to be consulted. Therefore take all your difficulties to Him to be resolved. Be in the habit of going to Him *in the first place*—before self-will, self-pleasing,[4] self-wisdom, human friends, convenience, self-interest. Before any of these have been consulted, go to God. Consider no circumstances so clear you do not need His direction.[5] *In all your ways,* small as well as great; in all your concerns, personal or relative, temporal or eternal, let Him be supreme. Who of us has not found the unspeakable "peace" of bringing to God matters too insignificant or personal, to be entrusted to the most confidential ear? We must remember "in everything."[z] That's the way Abraham *acknowledged God.* Wherever he pitched

[y]Comp. Ezek 8:21–23; Neh 1:11
[z]Phil 4:6, 7

[3] *James 4:15.* If the Lord will—*as Fuller remarks, in his own quaint way—"a parenthesis, and yet the most important part of the sentence."*
[4] *See the awful hypocrisy and judgment of asking counsel of God under this deadly influence. Jer 42:1–3, 19–22. Ezek 14:1–6.*
[5] *See the evil result of this inconsiderate neglect, Josh 9:14.*

a tent for himself, he also always established an altar for God.[a] In choosing a wife for his son there was a total absence of worldliness. No mention was made of riches, fame, beauty; only of what concerned the name and honor of his God.[b] So did the wise man's father *in all his ways acknowledge God*, asking counsel of Him in all his difficulties. He was never disappointed.[6]

[a]Gen 12:7; 13:18

[b]Gen 24:1–8. Comp. also his servant, verse 12–27

DOES GOD'S INFALLIBLE GUIDANCE MAKE US INFALLIBLE?

Now, if we wean ourselves from being our own counselors; if in true poverty of spirit we go every morning to our Lord, admitting we don't know how to guide ourselves for this day, with our eye constantly looking upward for *direction*,[c] the light will come down.[7] *He will make your paths straight*. We don't want any new revelations or visible tokens.[d] Study the Word with prayer. Note the divine Spirit shedding light upon it. Compare it with the observation of God's provisions of the day.[e] Don't judge by personal prejudice (a most undependable interpreter), but ponder with sober, practical, reverent faith. Let your will be kept in a quiet, subdued, cheerful readiness, to move, stay, retreat, turn to the right hand or to the left, at the Lord's command, always remembering that, whatever is least our own doing is best, and that a pliable spirit always gets the needful guidance.[f] We may be led, so that our faith may be exercised, "in paths they do not know"[g]—maybe a way of disappointment, or even of mistake. Yet no step well prayed over will bring ultimate regret. Though God's promise for guidance doesn't make us infallible; our very errors will be overruled to produce greater humility and wisdom; so that, even this mysterious direction will at least be gratefully acknowledged. "He led them also by a straight way."[h]

[c]Ps 5:3; 143:8–10; 25:4, 5

[d]Such as Exod 13:21, 22

[e]Ps 117:43

[f]Comp. Ps 32:8, 9; Isa 48:17, 18, with 30:21

[g]Isa 47:16; 1:10

[h]Ps 107:7

7 *Do not be wise in your own eyes;*
Fear the LORD *and turn away from evil.*
8 *It will be healing to your body,*
And refreshment to your bones.

[6] *1 Sam 23:9–11; 30:6–8; 2 Sam 2:1; 5:19. Comp. the smarting rod from the neglect of this godly habit. 1 Sam 27:1, with 29.*

[7] *Matt 6:22. Comp. Ps 32:8; 34:5; Neh 1:4–11; 2:4–8. Sir M. Hale testified that, when nearly eighty years old, it was his experience, that whenever he had committed his way to the Lord, simply and without reservation, God had always* directed his path.

WHO IS REALLY SELF-CONFIDENT?

This warning against self-confidence is closely connected with the preceding verse. The *wise* in his own eyes, is he, who *leans on* his own understanding.[8] Such wisdom is foolishness and self-delusion.[9] Put it away, and let it be your wisdom to *fear the Lord and turn away from evil.* How striking is this connection between the *fear of God* and the fear of sin.[i] Where God is honored, sin is hated, loathed, and resisted.[j] It lives indeed; but it is condemned to die.[k] It clings to the child of God; but his heart *turns away from it.* Often, it is the cause of the sickness of the body,[10] and always of the soul.[l] *Turning away from it,* in exercising self-denial and godly discipline, is health to the body.[m] The soul, bending under the harmful influence of spiritual disease, revives in fruitfulness.[n] The man that *fears the Lord,* under the sun of righteousness will rise with healing"[o] as from his sick chamber, full of life and Christian energy. "The joy of the Lord is your strength."[p]

[i] Prov 14:27; 16:6; Prov 39:9, 10; Neh 5:15; Job 28:28
[j] Rom 7:18–24
[k] Rom 6:6
[l] Hos 7:9
[m] Verses 1, 2
[n] Hos 14:5–7
[o] Mal 4:2
[p] Neh 8:10

9 *Honor the* LORD *from your wealth,*
And from the first of all your produce;
10 *So your barns will be filled with plenty,*
And your vats will overflow with new wine.

TRUE ROAD TO RICHES

This rule of sacrifice is costly to the man of the world and the person excessively attached to external observances. But to the servant of God, it is a privilege to lay aside a part of our money with this sacred stamp—"This is for God."[q] *The first-fruits of the increase* were the acknowledgment of redemption from Egypt.[r] And shall we, redeemed from sin, Satan, death, and hell, deny the claim?[s] "Well, may we think *our substance due,* where we owe ourselves," Bishop Hall commented. Nay, could we be happy in spending that *substance* on ourselves which He has given us wherewith *to honor* Him?[t] What value, what dignity, does it give to the talent, that He

[q] 1 Cor 16:2
[r] Exod 13:12, 13 Deut 26:1–10
[s] 1 Cor 6:19, 20
[t] Luke 19:13. Contrast Luke 12:16–22

[8] *Verse 5. Comp. 23:4; Rom 7:3–16. See the mind of God expressed in that solemn woe (Isa 5:21).*

[9] *Even a heathen could remark, "I suppose that many might have attained to wisdom, had they not thought they had already attained it."* SENECA, de Ira, *Lib. 3. c. 36. Comp. 1 Cor 8:2; Gal 6:3. "Our knowledge should hold the light before us, and help us for the better discovery of our ignorance, and so dispose us to humility, not pride"—Bishop SANDERSON'S* Sermon on Rom 14:3.

[10] *In sensual indulgence—Prov 5:8–11. Intemperance—23:29, 30. As a judicial infliction—Ps 32:3, 4; 38:1–8; 1 Cor 11:30.*

should condescend to use it for his own grand, eternal purposes! This sacred dedication is the true road to riches.[u] God challenges us to "test Me now in this," if the abundant harvest, and the overflowing vintage, shall not put unbelief and covetousness to shame.[v] A selfish spirit is, therefore, narrow policy; shrinking the harvest, by sparing the seed corn.[w] It's not out of order to enthusiastically look for the literal fulfillment of the promise. If we doubt the material promises, shouldn't we question our assumed confidence in the spiritual? For if the Lord's Word isn't enough security for physical and material matters, much more must it be for the tremendously more important safekeeping of our soul!

[u]Prov 11:24

[v]Mal 3:10; 2 Chron 31:5–10

[w]2 Cor 9:6; Hag 1:4–6

The rule and responsibility are therefore clear. The law dealt with us as children, and prescribed the exact amount. The gospel treats us as men and leaves it to circumstance, principle, and conscience. This consecration of our material wealth, as the seed corn for the harvest, is as strange to the world, as casting the seed into the earth would be to an ignorant savage. Now, is the result guaranteed in both cases? Yes, but with one difference. The disposition or mood of the earthly sower has no influence on the harvest; but the fruitfulness of the spiritual harvest depends mainly upon our attitude toward our work. It is most important that we beware of selfish principles; that we *honor the Lord,* not ourselves. There must be a denying of self;[x] complete and unquestioning faith;[y] compelling love;[z] special concern for His own people. Don't ever doubt that He will affix His own seal—"Those who honor Me I will honor."[a]

[x]1 Chron 29:14–16; Matt 6:1–4; 25:37–39

[y]1 Kings 17:12–16

[z]Rom 12:1; 2 Cor 5:14, 15; Matt 10:42

[a]1 Sam 2:30. Comp. Prov 11:25; 22:9; Heb 6:10

11 *My son, do not reject the discipline of the* LORD,
Or loathe His reproof,
12 *For whom the* LORD *loves He reproves,*
Even as a father, the son in whom he delights.

GOD'S MOST ENDEARING ROLE

Prosperity and adversity are wisely and proportionately mixed in our present condition. Each is equally fruitful in opportunity for honoring the Lord; in prosperity—by the full consecration of *our material goods;*[b] in our poverty and trouble—by a humble and cheerful yielding to His will and direction. Bishop Patrick said,

[b]Verse 9, 10

"In prosperity it is well to expect the rod; and suppose it to be His pleasure." But don't let it make you doubt His kind care. And don't be impatient and try any unlawful way to get out of it! His "exhortation"—the apostle Paul reminds us—"is addressed to you as sons."[11] And indeed, in no role does He come so near to us, and endear Himself so much to us, as in the role of Father. Most precious at all times, especially under *discipline,* is the privilege of adoption—*My son.*

Nowhere, indeed, are our corruptions so plainly evident, or our graces so shining, as under the rod. We need it as much as our daily bread. Children of God are still children of Adam; with Adam's will, pride, independence, and waywardness. And nothing more distinctly requires divine teaching and grace, than how to preserve, in our behavior, the right balance between hardness and despondency; neither *rejecting the discipline of the Lord,* nor getting tired of His correction.[12]

DON'T DESPISE HIS DISCIPLINE

Often, while we guard against an error on the right hand, we forget one no less hurtful on the left; like the man, who, in guarding against the precipice on the one side, rushes into some fearful hazard on the other. The middle path is the right path. Doubtless the Lord intends for His chastening to be felt.[c] A great iron-heartedness[d] is the stubbornness of the flesh, not the triumph of the Spirit; an attitude most offensive to God, and most inappropriate for the reception of His gracious discipline. To be as though no pain were felt or cared for; sullenly to "kick against the pricks"[e] and to dare God to do His worst—this is, indeed, to reject His discipline.[13] But pride will lift up its head and keep it stiff and unbending. It will take many a stroke to bring it down.

And sadly enough, this is not the sin of just the ungodly. Often we see even the child of God in a rebellious spirit,[f] caring little whether His Father smiles or frowns. The *discipline* is passed over lightly. He considers only second causes or immediate instruments.[g] He is irritated

[c] 2 Sam 15:26; Ps 39:10, 11
[d] Job 41:24–29; Jer 5:3
[e] Av—Acts 9:5. Comp. Prov 19:3
[f] Job 5:17; Heb 12:6
[g] Amos 3:6

[11] *Heb 12:5. We must not overlook the apostle's testimony to the divine inspiration of the Bible; showing the instruction throughout to be the teaching of our heavenly Father to His beloved sons or children.*

[12] *It is inhuman not to feel your afflictions and unmanly not to bear them—SENECA,* Consol. ad Polyb. *c. 36.*

[13] *Comp. Pharaoh—Exod 7:23; Jehoram—2 Kings 6:31. Ahaz—2 Chron 28:22; Israel—Isa 1:5; Zeph 3:2. Comp. Job 15:25, 26.*

by looking at the rod,[h] rather than at the hand that inflicts it.[i] He shrinks from looking for the cause. He disregards his Father's loving voice and purpose. And so, there is no softening humiliation;[j] no "amends for their iniquity;"[k] no childlike submission; no exercise of faith in looking for support. Isn't this *rejecting the discipline of the Lord?*

[h]Prov 10:13
[i]2 Chron 16:10–12
[j]Ps 32:3, 4
[k]Lev 26:41, 43

But ... though some *reject* the hand of God as light, others "faint" under it as heavy.[l] They are tired of His correction. Beware of yielding to unfeeling despondency, or peevish impatience.[m] Resist harsh and disgraceful thoughts of God.[n] Just by letting them into our minds, we spread destruction. We're very apt to misunderstand our Father's dealings;[o] to neglect present duty; to enjoy morbid brooding over our sorrows;[p] to forget our title and privilege of adoption;[q] or in stubborn grief to "refuse to be comforted" with the "hope of the end."[r] And isn't this *loathing His reproof?*

[l]Heb 12:5; Ps 38:2, 3; 39:10
[m]Ps 73:14; 77:7–10
[n]Gen 42:36; Judg 6:13; Jonah 4:9
[o]Prov 24:10; Isa 40:27–31. Comp. 1 Sam 27:1; 1 Kings 19:4; Job 3:1–3; Jer 20:14–18
[p]Job 6:1–16
[q]Heb 12:5
[r]Ps 77:2. Comp. Jer 29:11; 31:15–17

REVERENCE GOD'S DISCIPLINE

But these rules have much more than just negative meaning. Instead of *rejecting* the *discipline of the Lord,* reverence it. Solemnly remember that you are under your Father's *reproof* or correction.[s] Receive it then in good spirit. Instead of *loathing* it, hang upon His chastening hand and pour your heart out to God.[t] Kiss the rod.[u] Acknowledge its humbling, but enriching, benefit.[v] Expect a richer blessing from God's sustaining grace than from the removal of the painful affliction.[w]

[s]Lam 3:28, 29; Mic 7:9
[t]1 Sam 1:10–15
[u]Prov 10:13; Job 34:31, 32; 1 Peter 5:6
[v]Ps 119:67–71
[w]2 Cor 12:7–10

After all we must add, that chastening is a trial to the flesh;[x] yet it is overruled by wonder-working wisdom and faithfulness to an end above and contrary to its nature. This very rod was sent in love to the soul. Perhaps we were living at ease or in heartless backsliding. The awakening voice called us to our Bible and to prayer. So ... seeing God in it, we recognize it to be love, not anger; receiving, not casting out. Perhaps we might have wished it a little different; that the weight had been shifted, and the cross smoothed out a little, where it pressed upon the shoulder. But now that we see more clearly, we find enough blessing to soothe the most painful smart. In it all, we see God's plan to preserve us from near-at-hand danger[y] and for the trial of our faith. We

[x]Heb 12:11
[y]Comp. Prov 1:22; Ps 55:19

[z]Ps 51:4; 119:75
[a]1 Peter 1:6, 7
[b]Deut 8:2, 15, 16
[c]Ps 89:30–32
[d]James 5:11

come to a prompt verdict in favor of the absolute perfection of God's plan.[z] Faith understands the reasons for the discipline;[a] recognizes it as a part of God's gracious guidance,[b] and the provision of His everlasting covenant;[c] waits to see the final outcome the Lord had planned;[d] and meanwhile draws its main support from the seal of adoption.

FAMILY DISCIPLINE

[e]Heb 12:7, 8; Rev 3:19
[f]Eph 1:6
[g]Heb 12:10
[h]Jer 32:41
[i]Prov 13:24; Deut 8:5
[j]Isa 30:18; 1 Peter 5:6
[k]Isa 27:7, 8; Jer 30:11; Lam 3:31–33
[l]Ezra 9:13; Ps 103:10; Lam 3:39

After all, that's the final, certain test of our legitimacy,[e] He *reproves whom He loves, the son in whom He delighteth.* His discipline is that of the family; not of the school; much less of the prison. He corrects His children, not as criminals but as those whom He sees without spot, "bestowed on us in the Beloved."[f] Nor is there ever any impulsive change of mind or action, in His discipline, as is so often true of the earthly father.[g] He acts with wisdom in the spirit of love. "I will rejoice over them [children] to do them good";[h] yet as a wise and affectionate Father, He would not suffer him to be ruined for want of *reproof.*[i] It is correction. It is for your humbling. It is only correction—that is your consolation. The intolerable sting of legal punishment is removed. Here then the child has rest indeed.[14] The rod is now meekly, yes, thankfully borne, because it is in the hand of Him supreme in wisdom and love, who knows our need, and how to apply the discipline. He chooses the best time,[j] the surest yet gentlest means, the most considerate measure,[k] the most effective instruments. And ... when we compare our sufferings with our sin, the marvel is that it's so light![l] Haven't we more than deserved it all? "I love the rod of my heavenly Father," exclaimed the saintly Fletcher. "How gentle are the stripes I feel! How heavy those I deserve!" (*Life of Rev. H. Venn,* pp. 238, 584.) "O God, I have made an ill use of Thy mercies," said Bishop Hall, "if I have not learned to be content with Thy correction."

[14] *1 Sam 3:18; 2 Sam 15:25; 16:10, 11; Ps 39:9; Job 1:21; Isa 39:8. Comp. John 18:11. The heathen philosopher has accurately drawn the line—"Chastisement is on the sufferer's account. Vengeance is for the satisfaction of him that inflicts it"—ARIST.* de Rhetor *b. i. 10.*

WHAT TO DO WITH YOUR MISERY

Should he then at any dark season ask—"If that's true, then how is it that I'm so miserable? You're miserable, because this is your Father's training discipline for heaven.[m] He loves you so much, that He will lay all necessary pain upon you. He will melt you in His furnace, so that He may stamp His image upon you.[n] He would make you "share His holiness,"[o] that you might share His happiness. But unless you understand His purposes, you will, so far as you can, defeat His purpose, and lose the benefit—a loss too great to describe.[p] So try to understand God's purposes with you.[q] Every rod is your Father's messenger; and He will not permit His messenger to be *rejected.* Be anxious to "hear the rod, and who hath appointed it;";[r] knowing well that "I have not done in vain whatever I did."[s] Be more concerned to have it blessed by God to your good, than to plead against its removal, until it has fully accomplished its appointed work.[t] We can only admire God's loving management of affairs on our behalf, which uses these light afflictions as a means to deliver us from deadly evil. Should flesh and blood rebel; should the earthly tabernacle shake with "the opposition of Thy hand."[u]

[m] Job 33:14–29; 36:8–10; Heb 12:7, 8
[n] Isa 27:9; 48:10; Zech 13:9
[o] Mal 3:3
[p] Comp. Jer 6:8
[q] Job 10:2; Ps 139:23, 24; Eccl 7:14; Lam 3:40
[r] AV—Mic 6:9
[s] Ezek 14:23
[t] Isa 4:4
[u] Ps 39:10

HIDDEN STEPS

Still you will praise and thank Him throughout eternity that even by this crushing discipline He should accomplish His most merciful purpose. Meanwhile, give Him unlimited confidence; and if some steps of the way are hid, wait and see "the outcome."[v] Watch for the first signs of His will, the first glimpse of His care, the guidance of His eye.[w] You'll be spared a lot of discipline, and that will put your mind at ease. It's a golden opportunity, requiring that, which should be improved upon, through much study, prayer, and seclusion. No communion is so close, so endearing, so fruitful, as with a *disciplining* God. Never is Christ more precious to us; His love never more sweet, than in the midst of *disciplining.* Never do we have such a full revelation of God's character[x] and perfections. What we have learned before in theory, we now learn experimentally; and what we have understood

[v] Job 23:8–10; James 5:11
[w] Ps 32:8, 9
[x] Ps 119:75

imperfectly before is more fully revealed.[15] When you consider the total picture, and consider the trial as a whole, and also all the small, individual circumstances, which were successively so bitter and piercing—we may ask—"Which of them could be spared?" It is quite clear, when you consider the whole time, the whole weight, the whole number and variety of circumstances, that all of them together and each, individually, was every bit as important as each of the others. Where could we have stopped, without making that stop fatal to the final and total purpose? What does it all mean, if not that the Lord is holding to His determination to save us; all the thoughts of His heart, every exercise of His power, centering in this purpose of His sovereign mercy?

13 *How blessed is the man who finds wisdom,*
And the man who gains understanding.
14 *For its profit is better than the profit of silver,*
And its gain than fine gold.
15 *She is more precious than jewels;*
And nothing you desire compares with her.

THE BLESSED MAN'S TREASURE

Who does not admire this glowing picture of blessed happiness?[y] The wisdom of this world affords no such happiness.[z] Yet cold and barren is admiration, without an interest in the blessing. The *blessed man has found* a treasure, where possibly he least expected it, under *the discipline of the* Lord. David[a] and Manasseh[b] found (as who hath not found?) "God's house of correction to be a school of instruction," said Trapp. Under all circumstances, however, prayerful diligence in the search of *wisdom* ensures success.[c] The naturally wise man is a fool in heavenly *wisdom*. The man of prayer *gains understanding*, draws it out to the light, as out of the hid treasure.[d] We don't wonder at the merchant's concentrated interest, at his untiring toil. Here the wise man, himself

[y] Ps 1:1; 32:1
[z] Eccl 1:18
[a] Ps 119:67, 71; Ps 94:12
[b] 2 Chron 33:12, 13
[c] Prov 2:1–6
[d] Comp. Prov 8:35; Prov 2:4; Matt 13:44

[15] *Job 42:5. Comp. the apostle Paul's most instructive and encouraging exposition, Heb 12. There is some slight variation between Heb 12:6 and verse 12. The one describes the mode and subject of* the disciplining. *The other shows the Father's delight in His chastened child. Some by inverting the first clause, verse 12, grossly pervert the meaning and conclude themselves to be the Lord's children,* because they are afflicted. *But this isn't the case, It's true that every child is corrected, but not every one that is corrected is a child. The same hand—but not the same character—gives the stroke, to both godly and ungodly. The punishment of the Judge is widely different from the rod of the Father. Comp. 1 Sam 28:15–20, with 2 Sam 12:13, 14; Prov 1:26; Isa 1:24, with Jer 31:18–20; Hos 11:7, 8; also Isa 17:7–9. Nor is it* disciplining, *but the* endurance of disciplining, *according to the rules prescribed, that seals our adoption, Heb 12:7.*

enriched with the *profit of fine gold*[e] points out to us a *better profit.* It's the search for the pearl of great price, more precious than rubies. Yes, more than all other things that could be desired![16] That's the value the apostle placed upon it. And that's how valuable he found it when he put it to the test. All the world's show, all his former valuable gain, he counted as less than nothing, when Paul compared it with "the true wisdom"—"the surpassing value of knowing Christ Jesus my Lord."[f] We can never know true and abiding happiness without this singleness of judgment and purpose. This greatest of all blessings must have the throne. But the half-decided and half-seeking fail to find it. Only determined perseverance wins the prize.[g]

[e] 1 Kings 9:26–28
[f] Phil 3:4–8
[g] Phil 3:12–14

16 *Long life is in her right hand;*
In her left hand are riches and honor.
17 *Her ways are pleasant ways,*
And all her paths are peace.
18 *She is a tree of life to those who take hold of her,*
And happy are all who hold her fast.

HAPPINESS IN TWO WORLDS

Behold this heavenly queen dispensing her blessings! *Her right hand* presents the promise of both worlds[h]—the rich enjoyment of the world's lawful comforts,[i] and the yet higher joy of serving the Lord and His church. The apostle Paul regarded it as such a privilege, he was even willing, in order to have it, to be detained from heaven for awhile.[j] Add long life for eternity to the balance; and the total value just can't be computed. *Her left hand* offers *riches and honor,*[17] so far as may be for her children's good; yet in their highest splendor, they are only a faint shadow of her more "durable *riches,*" and of the *honor* of a heavenly crown.

[h] Verse 2. Ps 91:16; 1 Tim 6:8
[i] 1 Tim 6:17
[j] Phil 1:23, 24

NO MORE GOOD TIMES—ONLY GLOOM?

But what about *her ways?* Is she a sullen matron, who entertains her followers only on sighs and tears? In order to obtain the joys of the next life, must we say good-bye to all of this life? No more fun, no more good times, no more

[16] *Matt 13:45, 46, with Prov 23:23. Comp. Prov 8:11, 19; Job 38:15–18. Most truly does the great moralist define wisdom to be "the knowledge of the most honourable things"—ARIST. Ethic. b. vi. chap. vii.*
[17] *See the treasures of* right and left hand *promised to the wise man himself, 1 Kings 3:12–14.*

sunshine, only gloom? That's what the world tells us. It's a slander of the great forger of lies, to turn us from *wisdom's ways.* Actually, they are *ways of great pleasantness,* because the Lord saith it. And if we feel they aren't, we just don't know them.

The man of pleasure utterly mistakes both his object and his pursuit of it. The only happiness worth seeking is found here—that which will live in all circumstances and endure through ceaseless changes of life. *The ways* may be dark and lonely; yet how brightly the sunshine or reconciliation beams upon their entrance! Every step is lighted from above and accompanied by promises; a step in happiness, a step to heaven. Wisdom's work is its own reward[k]—strictness without bondage.[l] God rules children, not slaves. They don't work because they're compelled to nor because they are hired. They work out of gratitude to their benefactor; family delight in their Father. *Pleasant* therefore must be the labor—yes, the sacrifices—of love; short the path; cheerful the way, when the heart goes freely in it.

[k]Ps 19:11; Isa 32:17
[l]Matt 11:29, 30

SUNSHINE IN GLOOM

It is saying far too little, that the trials of *these* ways are not inconsistent with their *pleasantness.* They are the very principles of the most elevated pleasure. "The verdict of Christ," says Dr. South in *Sermons,* "makes the discipline of self-denial and the cross—those terrible blows to flesh and blood—the indispensable requisite to being His disciples."[m] And yet, contrary as it may appear, in this deep gloom is the sunshine of joy. For if our natural will be "hostile toward God,"[n] it must be the enemy to our own happiness. Our pleasure, therefore, must be to deny it, not to indulge it; to kill sinful appetites, that only "bear fruit for death."[o] Even what may be called the harsh and painful aspects of godliness are more joyous than the pleasures of sin. Far better to cross the will than to wound the conscience. The very chains of Christ are glorious.[p] Moses endured not "his reproach" as a trial. He "considered it as a treasure—"greater riches than the treasures of Egypt."[q] Our principles are never more consoling than when we are making a sacrifice for them. Hannah yielded up her dearest earthly joy. But did she sink under the trial? Did she

[m]Matt 26:24
[n]Rom 8:7
[o]Rom 7:5
[p]Acts 5:41, 42; 16:24, 25
[q]Heb 11:26

grudge the sacrifice? "Hannah prayed and said—*my heart exults in the Lord;*"[r] while—to show that none ever serve Him for nothing—for one child that was given to the Lord, five were added.[s]

[r] 1 Sam 2:1; 26

[s] 1 Sam 2:20, 21

SINGING WAYS

In fact, the world has no idea of the real character of *wisdom's ways.* Christianity, to them, is associated with cold, heartless forms and irksome restraints—much to do, but nothing to enjoy. But they only see half the picture. They see what Christianity takes away. But they don't see what it gives. They can't discern, that, while it denies sinful activities it abounds in spiritual pleasures. We work hard in the ways of sin. But we "will sing of the ways of the Lord."[t] Here is the only thing in this life worth the name of joy—solid—abiding—overflowing—satisfying[u] —God's own joy.[v] It is not a mere impulse of dull, lifeless emotionalism, but a principle of Christian energy, strengthening for duty, supporting for trial.[w] Here, then, we have less toil, and we reap more fruit. Won't any reasonable man, just by hearing the names of these things only, quickly admit that love, joy, peace, and patience, which are fruits of the Spirit,[x] are far more beautiful, easier, fuller of sweetness and calmness, less annoying, than hatreds, ambitious rivalries, murders, and those other works of the flesh?

[t] Isa 57:10, with Ps 138:5

[u] Hab 3:18

[v] John 15:11; 17:13

[w] Neh 8:10

[x] Gal 5:22, 23

But *pleasant ways* are not always safe. Yet *all wisdom's paths are peace.* The deadly breach is healed. The cloud vanishes. Heaven smiles. And *peace,* the Savior's last bequest, is realized even in the heat of this world's "tribulation."[y] "Shod your feet" for the rugged path "with the preparation of the gospel of peace."[z] The conquering of the will, the sorrow of repentance, the weariness of the cross—all end in peace.[a]

[y] John 16:33

[z] Eph 6:15, with Deut 33:25

[a] Ps 37:37; Isa 57:2, with 20, 21

Yet nothing can make *wisdom's ways* agreeable to a carnal mind. "For those who are according to the flesh set their minds on the things of the flesh"; so that, as they "cannot please God," *God's ways* cannot please them.[b] Nor again—though *wisdom's ways are ways of pleasantness,* are wisdom's children always happy? Sometimes a naturally sullen disposition gives a gloomy tinge to religion. Professing believers forget that it's not a matter of choice, whether they should be happy or not; that it is

[b] Rom 8:5, 8

their *obligation* no less than their *privilege* to be so; that the commands of God on this duty[c] carry weight and demand obedience. The prophets, in their excitement and enthusiasm, search heaven and earth, bring forth the most beautiful objects of nature. In fact, they call the lifeless, inanimate creation into glowing sympathy with the joys of the gospel.[d] A happy spirit characterizes the servants of God[e] especially in suffering.[f] So then ... is your happiness clouded? If so, is it because there has been some straying from *wisdom's paths*? Your God calls you to search, to humble yourself, to return.[g]

[c]Ps 32:11; 37:4; Phil 4:4; 1 Thess 5:16. Comp. Deut 28:47, 48
[d]Ps 96:11–13; 198; Isa 44:23; 55:12, 13
[e]Phil 3:3; Acts 2:46, 47
[f]2 Cor 6:10; 8:2; 1 Peter 1:6–8
[g]Jer 2:17–19; Hos 5:15; 6:1

A BETTER PARADISE

And one last thought—the paradise of God alone can furnish the full counterpart to the glory, beauty, and fruitfulness of wisdom.[h] *The tree of life* was the means God chose for preserving lasting life, and continual vigor and health, before man sinned. So true wisdom maintains man in the spiritual life of God's grace and the communion of His Spirit. Once our way was barred, and no one could touch her.[i] Now our way is opened to her in a better paradise.[j] We sit down under the shade with great delight. Her branches bend down upon this world of sin and misery. Her clusters hang within the reach of the youngest child, and the "fruit was sweet to my taste";[k] sweeter than ever man tasted, since he became an exile from Eden. For what is so refreshing, as near communion with God; access to Him; boldness in His presence; admission to His most holy delights? And if the earthly shadow and fruit be so rich, what will be "on either side of the river?" Her monthly fruits, her healing leaves![l] And yet, only the weeping, wrestling soul can *take hold of* the beloved object,[m] and embrace it, in spite of all the enemy's struggles to loosen the grasp.[n] And even, when almighty power has enabled us to *take hold,* the same continual miracle of grace, the same continually renewed effort of faith, is needed to *hold fast.*[o] We must "continue in the faith firmly established and steadfast";[p] "firmly rooted"[q] "keeps My deeds"; holding the beginning of our confidence steadfast "until the end."[r] *Happy are all who hold her fast.* The promises are to those that have perseverance and have endured."[s] God honors perseverance in the weakest saint.

[h]Rev 2:7
[i]Gen 3:22–24
[j]Heb 10:19–22
[k]Song of Sol 2:3
[l]Rev 22:2
[m]Gen 32:26–28; Hos 12:3, 4
[n]Matt 11:12
[o]1 Tim 6:12
[p]John 8:31
[q]Col 1:23; 2:7
[r]Rev 2:26; Heb 3:6, 14
[s]Rev 2:3

This lovely description of wisdom's blessing is no fancy picture but divine reality. Don't rest at all, until your heart is filled with its substance. Take it to the Lord in prayer and, before long, you shall have your share.

19 *The* L*ORD by wisdom founded the earth;*
By understanding He established the heavens.
20 *By His knowledge the deeps were broken up,*
And the skies drip with dew.

We have seen *wisdom,* as it is in man, with all its enriching blessings. Here we behold its majesty, as it is in the bosom of God, and gloriously displayed in His works. Hereby He showeth, that this wisdom, that He speaks about, was everlasting, because it was before all creatures; and that all things, even the whole world, were made by it. Behold it founded the earth "on nothing"; and yet "so established, it will not be moved."[t] See how this great architect *has established the heavens,* fixing all their bright luminaries in their own special orbits[u]—such a glorious covering, set with such sparkling diamonds! Each of these divisions declares His *knowledge*—in the earth, by *deeps broken up,* and gathering them up into rivers and streams for the refreshment of man,[v] and—*in the heavens,* by collecting the moisture into a gentle rain, and dropping down fatness upon the dry and thirsty ground;[18] each of these countless drops falling from this fountain of life.[w] In this way, every particle of the universe glitters with infinite skill.[x] The earth is its pavement, and the *heavens*—its ceiling; both miracles of wisdom, to "tell of the glory of God."[y] How beautiful is the uniformity of the two great systems of God! Both are the work of the same architect. Both display the wisdom and knowledge of God.[z] The universe is a parable, a mirror of the gospel. The showing of these divine perfections in the field of creation opens a rich provision for our happiness. But, in addition, let their more glorious exhibition in the great work of redemption fill us

[t] Job 26:7; Ps 93:1

[u] Gen 1:14–16; Ps 136:5; Jer 10:12; 51:15

[v] Prov 7:24–29; Gen 1:9, 10; Job 38:8–12; Ps 104:8–13

[w] Job 38:28

[x] Ps 104:24

[y] Ps 19:1

[z] John 1:1–14; Eph 1:8; 3:10; Col 1:13–17

[18] *Gen 27:28, 29. There is a philosophical difficulty in supposing* "the clouds *to drop down the dew," which is the moisture rising from the lower region, sometimes a very few feet from the earth. In the east, however, the dew is said to fall from a considerable height. Gesenius states, that the Hebrew word represents a "gentle rain."*

with adoring praise—"O the depth of the riches, both of the *wisdom and knowledge of God!"*[19]

21 *My son, let them not depart from your sight;*
Keep sound wisdom and discretion,
22 *So they will be life to your soul,*
And adornment to your neck.

Again we listen to wisdom's voice. Her repetitions are not vain repetitions; but well fitted to impress upon youth[a] the importance of her teachings.[b] As your much loved treasure, as your daily guide—*let them not depart from* your eyes.[c] They are worse than valueless, if they are received as notions; but they are of inestimable price, if *kept* as principles. God's teaching is *sound wisdom;*[d] full of light and matter; transforming divine truth with heavenly glory. Therefore *keep* it close to your heart. Exercise it in that practical *wisdom,* which disciplines all our dispositions and duties. Man's wisdom is utterly without energy. The soul, "excluded from the life of God,"[e] is in a state of death, until "the unfolding" of God's Word gives light and gives understanding[f]—"the light of life."[g] "The advantage of knowledge is that wisdom preserves the lives of its possessors." Yes, it gives *life* to them that have it.[h] Every truth influenced by it, springs up into the new creature with a heavenly glow, and with all *the grace* of "the beauty of the Lord";[20] outshining, even in the most despised dress, the richest glory of an earthly crown.

[a]Isa 28:9, 10
[b]Phil 3:1; 2 Peter 1:12
[c]Prov 7:1–3
[d]Deut 4:9; 6:8; Josh 1:7, 8
[e]Eph 4:18
[f]Ps 119:130
[g]John 8:12
[h]Eccl 7:12. Comp. Prov 4:22; 6:23

23 *Then you will walk in your way securely,*
And your foot will not stumble.
24 *When you lie down, you will not be afraid;*
When you lie down, your sleep will be sweet.
25 *Do not be afraid of sudden fear,*
Nor of the onslaught of the wicked, when it comes;
26 *For the* Lord *will be your confidence,*
And will keep your foot from being caught.

[19] *Rom 11:33. Full of deep thought are the words of our admirable Mr. Hooker—"That which moveth God to work is Goodness; that which ordereth His work is Wisdom; that which perfecteth His work is Power. All things, which God in these times and seasons hath brought forth, were eternally and before all time in God; as a work unbegun is in the artificer, which afterwards bringeth it into effect. Therefore whatsoever we do behold now in this present world, it was enwrapped within the bowels of Divine Mercy, written in the book of Eternal Wisdom, and held in the hands of Omnipotent Power, the first foundations of the earth being as yet unlaid. So that all things which God hath made are in that respect the Offspring of God. They are in Him, as effects in their highest cause. He likewise is actually in them; the assistance and influence of his Deity is their life"—Book 5:56.5.*

[20] *Ps 90:17; 149:4. Comp. Prov 1:9. "Grace to thy jaws"—is the Douay Version, with the Marg. Explanation—"Merit for the words of thy mouth."*

WALK SECURELY, SLEEP SOUNDLY

Habitually examining the Word keeps the feet in a slippery path.[i] When David neglected wisdom's words, his feet came "close to stumbling."[j] Peter from the same neglect fearfully stumbled.[k] But our sleeping hours, no less than our waking steps, are divinely guarded. "He gives to His beloved even in his sleep."[l] "Underneath are the everlasting arms."[m] They enjoy a childlike repose, sleeping in His bosom without fear. In the same way, David slept in God and in a state of salvation, amid the noisy warfare with his dutiful son.[21] Peter in prison, in chains, between two soldiers, on the eve of his probable execution, when there seemed but a step between him and death. Yet, in such a place, in such company, at such a moment, he lay down so fearlessly, and slept so soundly, that even the shining light failed to disturb him, and an angel's stroke was needed to wake him.[22] What wouldn't many of us, in turbulent times, waking at every sound, give for one night of such *sweet sleep!* And yet, how many such nights have we actually enjoyed, waking, as Jacob did, on his stony—but, to him, feathery, soft pillow, fully aware of our Father's keeping! But what has happened to our renewed dedication to God?[n]

Sudden fear may come. Yet *do not be afraid.*[o] It is the wicked, who have no refuge—they are the ones who must fear.[p] Child of God! Run to your refuge, and be safe.[q] Surely *He will keep your foot from being caught.*[r] Noah found this security in the flood of the ungodly; Lot in the destruction of Sodom;[s] the Christians in Pella, in the desolation of the wicked city. Echoing a psalm Luther sung his song of *confidence*—"God is our refuge and strength."[t] In the final onslaught of the wicked when it comes—what will be the *sudden fear*—the undismayed *confidence?* "All the tribes of the earth will mourn" at the sight of their despised Savior—then their Judge.[u] But, "when these things begin to take place, straighten up and lift up your heads, because your redemption is drawing near."[v]

[i] Prov 4:11, 12; Ps 17:4; 37:23; 119:9, 11, 133
[j] Ps 73:2–17
[k] Matt 26:33–35, 69–75
[l] Ps 127:2. Comp. 121:3, 4
[m] Deut 33:27. Comp. Lev 26:6
[n] Gen 38:11, 18–22
[o] Job 5:21–24. Comp. 2 Kings 6:16, 17; Jer 39:15–18
[p] Isa 57:20, 21
[q] Prov 14:26; 18:10; Isa 26:1, 20
[r] Ps 91:1–3
[s] 2 Peter 2:5–9
[t] Ps 46
[u] Prov 1:27; Luke 21:26; Rev 1:7; 6:15–17
[v] Luke 21:28. Comp. 2 Thess 1:7–10.

[21] *Ps 3; 4:8. Compare the beautiful picture, Ezek 34:25–28, in contrast with Prov 4:16; Deut 28:66.*

[22] *Acts 12:6, 7. Our Martyrologist records of John Rogers, the proto-martyr in the Marian persecution: "on the morning of his execution, being found fast asleep,* scarce with much shogging could he be *awakened"—FOXE, vi. 699.*

27 *Do not withhold good from those to whom it is due,*
When it is in your power to do it.

28 *Do not say to your neighbor, "Go, and come back,*
And tomorrow I will give it,"
When you have it with you.

The wise man now comes to practical points. He shows the fruit of selfishness—*withholding dues*. Many are the forms of this dishonesty—borrowing without payment;[w] evading the taxes;[23] keeping back "the pay of the laborers."[x] But the rule probes deeper than the surface. If we have no legal debt to any, we have a gospel debt to all.[y] Even the poor is bound by this universal law to his poorer neighbor.[z] Every one has a claim upon our love.[a] Every opportunity of doing good is our call to do it. Our neighbors are the real *owners of our good.* The Lord of all has transferred His right to them, with a special reference to His own "brothers."[b] Kindness, therefore, is not a matter of option, but of obligation. It is an act of justice, as well as mercy. It isn't that it may be demanded by our fellow-men. But the obligation lies upon our conscience; and to *withhold* what we owe will be our eternal condemnation.[c]

Christian love will also do good in the kindest way. Delay offends the law of love. Too often the cold rejection—*Go, and come back*—is a cover for selfishness. There is a secret hope that the matter will be forgotten, dropped, or taken up by someone else. Often an application is put off from mere thoughtlessness. *We mean to do something about it.*[24] But it doesn't suit our convenience just now. This is a serious injury to the applicant. A little, in time of need, is more than much, when the time is gone. We should develop a keen understanding of the wants and sufferings of others; putting ourselves as much as possible in their place; not only doing a "good deed, but be generous and *ready* to share."[d] If we are to do justly—which sometimes (as in the punishment of criminals) may grieve us; we are like our gracious God,[e] to *love* mercy;[f] seizing the present, perhaps the only,[g] opportunity. We should anticipate the need rather than wantonly or thoughtlessly delaying to relieve it.[h]

[w] Ps 37:21
[x] James 5:4; Jer 22:13–17. Comp. Gen 31:7; Deut 24:14, 15
[y] Rom 13:8
[z] Eph 4:28. Comp. 2 Cor 8:1–3
[a] Comp. Luke 10:29–37
[b] Gal 6:10; Mark 9:41; Matt 25:31–40
[c] Matt 25:41–45. Comp. Deut 23:3, 4
[d] Titus 3:1; 1 Tim 6:18
[e] Mic 7:18
[f] Mic 6:8. Comp. Rom 12:8; 2 Cor 9:7
[g] Prov 27:1; Gal 6:10
[h] 2 Cor 8:10

[23] *The example and admonition of Christ are evidently directed against this sin. Matt 17:24–27; 22:15–21.*
[24] *See how Job rebutted his friend's accusation, 22:9, with 31:16. Comp. James 2:15, 16.*

The gospel regards every neighbor as a brother or sister needing our help, and to be loved and cared for "as yourself."[i] Why don't we more quickly acknowledge this standard? The Lord deliver us out of our selfishness and mold us to His own image of mercy and love![25]

[i] Lev 19:18

29 *Do not devise harm against your neighbor,*
While he lives in security beside you.
30 *Do not contend with a man without cause,*
If he has done you no harm.

BITTER HERBS IN THE CUP

The command—*do not withhold good*—is naturally followed by the command against doing *harm*. The deceipt here rebuked was a disgrace even to a heathen. It is generally hated by the world and should be doubly hated by a godly man. With him everything should be out in the open. *A harmful scheme against a neighbor,* whatever the cause, is a cursed sin.[j] But to take unfair advantage of another's trust, betrays "this wisdom is not that which comes down from above ... demonic."[k] Such was the underhandedness of Jacob's sons against the unsuspecting Shechemites;[l] Saul's hatred of David, when under his protection;[m] Joab's murder of Abner and Amasa;[n] Ishmael's of Gedaliah.[o] No testing hurts so much.[p] This was one of the bitter herbs in the Savior's cup of suffering.[q] And many a wounded spirit has been cheered by His sympathy with this painful sorrow.[r]

[j] Prov 6:14–18; Deut 27:24; Ps 35:20; 55:20; Jer 18:18–20
[k] James 3:15
[l] Gen 34:13–29; 49:5–7
[m] 1 Sam 18:22–26
[n] 2 Sam 3:27; 20:9, 10
[o] Jer 41:1, 2
[p] Ps 55:12–14
[q] John 13:21, with Ps 41:9; Matt 26:46–50
[r] Heb 4:15

Yet, we must guard, not only against secret hatred, but against *causeless struggles*. A tendency to involve ourselves in quarrels[s] causes strife, instead of peace.[t] This spirit greatly hinders holiness,[u] and is inconsistent with a true servant of God.[v] Irritable people strongly insist upon their rights—how they think they deserve to be treated by others. "Is there not," they say, "a cause?" But impartial onlookers frequently regard it as *quarreling for no reason at all;* that no harm has been done; none at least to

[s] Prov 17:14; 18:6; 25:8, 9
[t] Rom 12:18
[u] Heb 12:14; Col 3:12–15
[v] 2 Tim 2:24

[25] *Dr. South's caustic application may be wholesome probing—"Was ever the hungry fed, or the naked clothed, with good looks or fair speeches? These are but thin garments to keep out the cold, and but a slender repast to conjure down the rage of a craving appetite. My enemy, perhaps, is ready to starve; and I tell him I am heartily glad to see him, and should be very ready to serve him. But still my hand is closed, and my purse shut. I neither bring him to my table, nor lodge him under my roof. He asks for bread, and I give him a compliment—a thing indeed not so hard as a stone, but altogether as dry. I treat him with art and outside, and lastly, at parting, with all the ceremonial of dearness, I shake him by the hand, but put nothing into it. I play with his distress, and dally with that which was not to be dallied with—want, and misery, and a clamorous necessity"*—Sermon on Matt. 5:44.

justify the breach of love; that more love on one side, and more forbearance on the other, would have prevented the break; that there is "already a defeat ... Why not rather be wronged?"[w] How valuable is a close application of the self-denying law of Christ![x] How earnestly should we seek from the Lord His own meek and loving spirit![y] "O Lord, pour into our hearts that most excellent gift of love, the very bond of peace, and of all virtues; without which, whosoever liveth is counted dead before thee,"[z] reads the collection prayer for Quinguagesima Sunday.

[w]1 Cor 6:1–7
[x]Such as Matt 5:39–41
[y]1 Peter 2:21–23
[z]1 Cor 13:4–7

31 *Do not envy a man of violence,*
And do not choose any of his ways.
32 *For the crooked* man *is an abomination to the* LORD;
But He is intimate with the upright.

THE FROWN OF HEAVEN

What is there—we might ask—to *envy in the man of violence?* The love of power is a ruling passion; and the slave of his own will enjoys a brutish pleasure in tyranny. Yet we have little reason to envy him, much less *to choose his ways.*[a] Can he be happy, going stubbornly in his own way, obstinately disobedient to the will of the Lord, with the frown of heaven? For God who hateth nothing that He has made, hates those who have, in that way, disfigured themselves. They are disgusting, in His sight.[b] Really to be *envied,* to be eagerly desired, is the portion of the righteous in life, made rich by *being intimate with the Lord*—"His covenant and fatherly affection, which is hid and *secret* from the world" *(Reformer's Notes).*

[a]Prov 24:1; Eccl 4:1
[b]Prov 6:14–18; 11:20; 15:9; Mic 2:1, 2. Comp. Exod 9:16; 14:28. Isa 37:21–38. Acts 12:1, 2, 23

Sinners are repulsive. But Christians are God's delight. They are God's friends, He gives to whom He familiarly imparts, as men used to do to their friends, His thoughts and advice, or His *intimate* favor and comforts, to which other men are strangers. Communion with Him;[c] peace;[d] joy;[e] assurance;[f] teaching;[g] confidence;[h] an enlightening understanding of God's care;[i] yes, all the blessings of His covenant.[j] This is *intimate* between God and the soul, a closed-in part, hidden from the world, sealed to His beloved people. Here then the child of God "dwells in the shelter of the Most High."[k]

[c]John 14:21–23
[d]Phil 4:6, 7
[e]Prov 14:10
[f]Rev 2:17
[g]Matt 11:25; 13:11–17; 16:17; John 7:17; 1 Cor 2:12, 15
[h]John 15:15
[i]Gen 18:17, 18; Ps 107:43
[j]Ps 25:14
[k]Ps 91:1

If He has given you knowledge of Himself, and your interest in Him; and to the *stubbornly disobedient man of violence,* only worldly advantage; is it not the seal of His love to you, and rejection of Him? Is it not infinitely more to dwell on high with your God, than in the vain show of an ungodly world?[l]

[l]Ps 84:10

33 *The curse of the LORD is on the house of the wicked.*
But He blesses the dwelling of the righteous.

AN IDLE DREAM

The contrast between the sinner and the saint, affects us not only personally, but relatively.

The curse or blessing of the Lord follows us to our homes. Shall we then envy *the wicked,* with his cup of earthly joy filled to the brim? *The curse of the Lord is in his house*[m]—"a curse without cause does not alight."[n] Let him think—"It is my Maker's curse—how awful, that my being and my curse should come from the same sacred source!"

[m]Mal 2:2
[n]Prov 26:2

It is not the impotent wishing of ill. If we could trace its deadly work, we should see the man wasting, withering, and being consumed under it. Look at the scroll in the house of the thief, and in the house of the swearer—"twenty cubits" long—a long catalog of woes; "flying"—to mark its swiftness; "it will spend the night within the house and consume it with its timber and stones."[o]

[o]Zech 5:1–4

Is this an idle dream? Surely—except for the blindness of his heart, *the wicked sinner* would see the naked sword hanging by a hair over his head, or the awful handwriting upon the wall, solemnly proclaiming—"There is no peace," says my God, *"for the wicked."*[p]

[p]Dan 5:5, 6; Isa 57:21

Vainly the proud worm resists. Ahab multiplied his *house* beyond all human average, as if to set at defiance *the curse* pronounced against it. Yet at one stroke all was swept away.[q] Similar instances[26] conclusively prove whose words shall stand—man's or God's.[r] "Who has defied Him without harm? . . . For who resists His will?"[s]

[q]1 Kings 21:20–22; 2 Kings 10:1–11
[r]Jer 44:28
[s]Job 9:4; Rom 9:19

[26] *JEROBOAM: 1 Kings 14:9–11; Amos 7:9. BAASHA—1 Kings 16:1–4, 12, 13. JEHU—2 Kings 15:8–12; Hos 1:4. HAZAEL—Amos 1:4. JEHOIAKIM—Jer 22:13–19. CONIAH—Jer 24–30. ESAU—Obad 18. Comp. Prov 14:11; 15:25.*

PROMISES—CLOUDS OF BLESSING

But bright is the sunshine of *the righteous*. Not only *is the secret of the Lord with their souls*, but *His blessings is on their home*. And when He blesses, who can reverse it?[t] Many a homely cottage, occupied by a child of Abraham, shines more splendidly than the princely palace of the ungodly.[u] An heir of glory dwells here. A family altar of prayer and praise consecrates it as the temple of Jehovah.[v]

[t]Num 23:20; Job 34:29
[u]Job 29:4; Isa 4:5
[v]Gen 12:8

Promises, like clouds of blessings, rest over it. God has been honored, and God will honor.[w] "Those who live in his shadow will again raise grain."[x] Is then my *house* under *the curse or blessing of the Lord?* Let my God be honored in His own gifts: that I and mine may be plainly sealed with the full tokens of His love.

[w]2 Sam 6:11; Jer 35:18, 19; 2 Tim 1:18
[x]Hos 14:7

34 *Though He scoffs at the scoffers,*
Yet He gives grace to the afflicted.

Two apostles have combined with the wise man, to set out this rule of the divine government.[27] On no point is the mind of God more fully declared than against pride—the spirit of scoffing. It displaces man, and would, if possible, displace God Himself. Jealous therefore of His own glory, God sets Himself in battle array, as against the thief of His rightful power, the rebel against His dominion. Witness the Babel-builders;[y] Pharaoh;[z] Sennacherib;[a] the proud opposers of His gospel[b]—all the objects of *His scoffing*. But most hateful to Him is the sinner, that will not submit to His righteousness, that scorns the cornerstone of salvation. How fearfully does it then become a stone of offense, of eternal ruin![c] Surely without doubt, without way of escape from His frown, *He scoffs the scoffers*.

[y]Gen 11:1–9
[z]Exod 14:13
[a]Isa 37:33–38
[b]Ps 2:1–4
[c]Rom 10:3, with 9:32, 33; Matt 21:41–44

A MOST ADORNING GRACE

A *lowly* spirit—a deep conviction of utter nothingness and guilt—is a most adorning grace. Not just an occasional or temporary feeling, the result of some unexpected hateful revelation, but a costume, "clothing" the man[d] from the sole of the foot to the head. It combines

[d]1 Peter 5:5

[27]*James 4:6. 1 Peter 5:5. AV is "scorners." "The Apostle's quotation of this passage, though somewhat different in the words, is the same in the sense as the original. For scorners in Scripture are* proud, insolent, wicked men. *And to resist such persons, by making their schemes abortive, and by humbling them, is emphatically called* a scorning of them"—*MACKNIGHT on James 4:6.*

the highest level of joy with the deepest humbling of spirit. And those who sink the lowest, stand nearest to the highest advancement. For *"God is opposed to the proud, but gives grace to the humble"*—"greater grace,"[e] till his work is perfected in them. "He pours it out plentifully upon humble hearts. His sweet dews and showers of grace slide off the mountains of pride, and fall on the low valleys of humble hearts, and make them pleasant and fertile, said Leighton on 1 Peter 5:5.[f] The centurion;[g] the Canaanite;[h] the penitent;[i] the publican;[j] such as these are the objects of His favor.[k] Their hearts are His dwelling place.[l] Their inheritance is His kingdom.[m] The soul, swelling with its proud fancies, has no room for His humbling grace. Blessed exchange of the little idol of self-esteem *for Him*; who alone has the right when even His own graces are only desired, as instruments to set out His glory.

[e]James 4:6
[f]Comp. Prov 3:8
[g]Matt 8:5–10
[h]Matt 15:21–28
[i]Luke 7:44–50
[j]Luke 18:13, 14
[k]Isa 66:2
[l]Isa 67:15
[m]Matt 5:3

35 *The wise will inherit honor,*
But fools display dishonor.

WHAT HIGHER GLORY?

This is the last contrast drawn to hold back our envy at the prosperity of the wicked.[n] It carries us forward to the coming day when everyone shall see in the full light of eternity.[o] *The wise—the heirs of honor*—are identified with *the lowly*[p]—the heirs of grace. Self-knowledge—the principle of lowliness—is the very substance of *wisdom*. Their inheritance also is one—*grace and glory.*[q] For what higher *glory* can there be than the grace, which "purchased for God" a repulsive worm of the earth, "and Thou hast made them to be a kingdom and priests to our God?"[r] Oh! let the redeemed cherish honorable thoughts of their present *honor*. Be careful to clear it from the filth and pollution of the world's dust and enjoy it in adorning praise to Him, who has chosen you to this totally undeserved grace.[s]

But who can tell *the honor* of the after-*inheritance*—not like this world's glory—the shadow of a name; but real, and solid; "an infinite gain, in the exchange of dross for down-weight [full-weight] of pure gold," said Leighton.[t] All occasion of sin and temptation is shut out forever. "The tree of knowledge shall not be fenced in.

[n]Verse 31
[o]Mal 3:18
[p]Verse 34; 11:2
[q]Ps 84:11
[r]Rev 5:9, 10
[s]Rev 1:5, 6
[t]1 Peter 5:1

There shall be neither lust, nor forbidden fruit; no withholding of desirable knowledge, nor pretense of undesirable. The glorified spirits touch nothing that can defile, and defile nothing they touch, said Mr. Howe in *Blessedness of Righteous,* chap. 5, p. 11. But after all, the glory of this glory will be communion and likeness with our Lord—"be with Me—where I am—behold My glory."[u] We don't need to look too closely. Much is clear. The value of our inheritance is beyond all price; its happiness unspeakable; its security unchangeable; its duration eternal. *The wise shall inherit glory.* "Those who have insight will shine like the brightness of the expanse of heaven . . . forever and ever."[v]

[u] John 17:24; 1 John 3:2

[v] Dan 12:3; Matt 13:43

Oh! Won't the fools then discover the worthlessness of this world's glory too late to make a wise choice? *Shame* is their present fruit.[w] Honor doesn't seem right upon them.[x] But what fruit will eternity bring concerning those things, of which they will then be "ashamed?"[y] Certainly *shame will be their promotion.* Their fame will be notorious, their disgrace plainly visible, lifting them up, like Haman upon his elevated gallows[z]—a laughingstock to the world. How solemn and final will be the great separation for eternity! "Many of those who sleep in the dust of the ground will awake, these to everlasting life, but the others to disgrace and everlasting contempt."[a]

[w] Prov 13:18; 10:9

[x] Prov 26:1

[y] Rom 6:21

[z] Esther 7:9

[a] Dan 12:2

CHAPTER FOUR

1 *Hear,* O *sons, the instruction of a father,*
And give attention that you may gain understanding,
2 *For I give you sound teaching;*
Do not abandon my instruction.

Surely these frequent repetitions are as the angel's visit to the prophet—waking him, "as a man who is awakened from his sleep."[a] "God gave Solomon wisdom," and Solomon had the "breadth of mind, like the sand that is on the seashore,"[b] might readily have made every sentence a fresh discovery of his knowledge. But more suitable to our sluggish and forgetful heart is "the Word of the Lord . . . order on order."[c] Children are often deprived of a parental instructor. Here these orphans are taken up, and called to *hear the instruction of a father.* For truly we see the wise man, like the apostle in after days, "exhorting, encouraging . . . as a father would his own children."[d]

[a] Zech 4:1
[b] 1 Kings 4:29
[c] Isa 28:13
[d] 1 Thess 2:11

FROM THE MOUTH OF GOD

Solomon evidently speaks from the mouth of God, declaring His *teaching*—His *instruction.* Therefore he claims attention to know understanding, for he gives good teachings.[e] To many, exciting,[f] curious and thoughtful,[g] compromising,[h] self-righteous, self-exalting teaching,[i] is more attractive. But, young people, remember—that which humbles the soul before God; that which exhibits the free grace of the gospel; which melts down the will, consecrates the heart, fills with the spirit of the cross—however disagreeable to the flesh—is alone *sound teaching* for the soul. Therefore, do not *abandon it.* Don't be carried away with the senseless cry, "Everybody thinks opposite." Of what worth is the judgment of all mankind on the great subject of religion? "This is the

[e] Eccl 12:9–11
[f] Ezek 33:31, 32
[g] 2 Tim 4:3, 4
[h] Isa 30:10; Jer 5:31
[i] Gal 1:6, 7

way of those who are foolish." This is God's stamp upon man's "words," however applauded and "approved" by successive generations.[j] Shall this world's judgment be preferred to the Word of God? "The morning" of the resurrection will reflect the glory of eternity upon the choice of the narrow path.[k]

[j]Ps 49:13

[k]Ps 49:14

3 *When I was a son to my father,*
Tender and the only son in the sight of my mother,
4 *Then he taught me and said to me,*
"Let your heart hold fast my words;
Keep my commandments, and live;
5 *Acquire wisdom! Acquire understanding!*
Do not forget, nor turn away from the words of my mouth.
6 *"Do not forsake her, and she will guard you;*
Love her, and she will watch over you.
7 *"The beginning of wisdom* is: *Acquire wisdom;*
And with all your acquiring, get understanding.
8 *"Prize her, and she will exalt you;*
She will honor you if you embrace her.
9 *"She will place on your head a garland of grace;*
She will present you with a crown of beauty."

GARLAND OF GRACE, CROWN OF BEAUTY

Solomon here claims our attention as teacher of youth, because of his own godly education by such a *father*. He was a *tender* child,[l] well-beloved, as an *only* son.[1] The more dearly he was loved, the more carefully was he *taught*. Thus we are brought into the family of "the man after God's heart," to hear him commanding His child in the fear and service of the Lord.[m] What a blessing to us, if we can tell of an Abraham or a David—of a Lois or Eunice, who have *taught*, and bound us to the ways of God![n] Parents! Remember, a child untaught will be a living shame.[o] Training discipline, not foolish leniency, is the truest evidence of affection to our young beloved ones.[p]

[l]1 Chron 22:5; 29:1

[m]Comp. also 1 Kings 2:2–4; 1 Chron 22:6–16; 18:9, 19, 20. Comp. Gen 18:19; Deut 6:7

[n]2 Tim 1:5; 3:14, 15

[o]Prov 29:15

[p]Prov 13:24, with 1 Kings 1:6

[1] *Not really the only son. 2 Sam 5:14; 1 Chron 3:5. Thus Isaac was called the only son (i.e., most beloved), when Ishmael was another son: Gen 22:2, 12, 16, with 17:19. So the church is called the only one*—the choice—*implying others, out of which the choice was made. Song of Sol 6:9.*

TREASURE FOR YOUR HAPPINESS

But let us examine this beautiful example of parental instruction.[2] Observe the anxiety for his son's heart-relationship with God. *Let your heart hold fast my words.* Often (and this is a comfort to a weak memory) *words* may be lost to the memory, yet practically *held in the heart.* This *heartkeeping* is the path of life,[q] without which all is dead. Note again the extreme earnestness of the plea. Many a parent, like Augustine's father,[3] insists, "Get wealth, worldly honor, or wisdom." This godly parent teaches "line upon line"—Get heavenly wisdom; get it with all your getting—at any cost,[r] as the principal thing; and when you have got it—*do not forget it*—don't turn from it—don't forsake it[4]—*love—embrace —prize—her.* Such a caretaker she is for your soul.[s] Such an *exalting honor* even in this life! Such a *garland of grace* in the church! Such a *crown of beauty* in heaven.

[q] Verse 13; 6:23; 8:34, 35; Isa 55:3; Zech 3:7

[r] Prov 23:23. Comp. 1 Kings 10:1; Matt 12:42

[s] Prov 2:10–18

This is not the way of a cold pleader, seriously enforcing some unimportant truth. It is the father, feeling that his child's soul is perishing, unless it be taught and led in wisdom's ways.

Parents! Do we know this stirring concern, anxiously looking out for the first dawn of light upon our child's soul? Do we eagerly point out to him wisdom as the principal thing, to be gotten *first*?[t] Is it our own first choice, infinitely above this world's shining brightness,[u] not only important, but all-important? It can have no place, if it doesn't have first place. If it is anything, then it must be everything. Earthly wisdom may be a goodly pearl. But this wisdom from above is the pearl "of great value"; worth getting indeed; but only to be obtained, by selling all that we have, to buy it.[v]

[t] Matt 6:33

[u] 1 Kings 3:5–12; Phil 3:7, 8

[v] Matt 13:45, 46

[2] *Where David's instruction begins, is obvious. Where it ends, is not so clear—whether it be verse 6, 10, 12, or 13; or as F. Taylor asserts, at the close of chap. 9. But as Geier observes, "Let the reader form his own judgment; provided that we pay due obedience to the instruction, it matters little, whether we have it in the words of David or Solomon."*

[3] *Of whom he records, "This father of mine never troubled himself with any thought of—How I might improve myself towards Thee, so that I proved eloquent, though I were withal left undrest by thy tillage"*—Confess. 2:3.

[4] *See the great importance of this continuance, John 8:30, 31; Col 1:22, 23; Heb 3:6, 14, contrasted with Matt 13:20, 21.*

[5] *Thus Jerome wrote to a friend—"Beg now for me, who am grey-headed, of the Lord, that I may have Wisdom for my companion, of which it is written—'Love her, and she shall keep thee.'"*

10 *Hear, my son, and accept my sayings,*
And the years of your life will be many.
11 *I have directed you in the way of wisdom;*
I have led you in upright paths.
12 *When you walk, your steps will not be impeded;*
And if you run, you will not stumble.
13 *Take hold of instruction; do not let go.*
Guard her, for she is your life.

RUN AND NOT STUMBLE

It is educational to see a king (whether David or Solomon) not forgetting in the midst of his royal cares his domestic responsibilities. We are told, "Youth will have its fling." "So," adds Taylor solemnly, "it may—to Hell." For where else can a wayward will lead? Let us see the need of guidance of every step, both to take and to avoid. *The ways of wisdom* assure a happy life in the favor of God.[w] And what comfort to the dying parent's conscience will be the memory of children, brought up not for the world, but taught in these ways! Yet this can't be, if the rod of punishment, when needed, has been spared; if the will has been indulged; and the love of the world cherished. This will be—if godly discipline has been exercised; if the Bible has been laid down as the rule of life; if habits of prayer, love to the service of God, fellowship with His people, have been encouraged. The path, though rough and lonely sometimes, is *an upright path,* and a path of liberty.[x] The single eye will preserve a steady walk.[y] You will run, and not stumble.[z]

And yet, the lively exhortation *to take a firm hold,* shows what kind of struggle is needed to retain our principles. Feeble, indeed, is our *hold,* when connected merely with the excitement of novelty,[a] temporary convictions,[b] the restraint of education,[c] unestablished knowledge,[d] or the indulgence of sin.[e] Truths received only in the understand, not becoming the daily nourishment of the soul, never lay hold of the heart. *The hold* exercised by instruction is by a personal living faith; including an intense interest, and persevering pursuit; continuing "in the things you have learned and become convinced of"; clinging with purpose of heart unto the Lord.[f] As Jacob detained the angel;[g] as the wife took hold of her Beloved;[h] as the disciples "urging the Savior to stay with

[w] 1 Tim 4:8, with Prov 3:1, 2; Ps 34:12–14; 1 Peter 3:10–12
[x] Ps 119:32, 45
[y] Prov 10:9; Isa 48:17, 18; Matt 6:22
[z] Prov 3:21–26; Hos 14:9
[a] Matt 13:20, 21
[b] Ps 78:34–36; 106:12, 13
[c] 2 Chron 12:1; 24:2, 15–18
[d] Gal 3:1–4
[e] Mark 6:18–26
[f] 2 Tim 3:14; Acts 11:23; 2:42
[g] Gen 32:26–29
[h] Song of Sol 3:4

them"[i]—so, young Christians, *let her not go, keep her*, as the man from "joy" guarded his precious treasure.[j] So let your heavenly treasure stand above every earthly blessing. Then will it be your life.[k] And while others "turn back, and walk no more" in the way, your heart will turn to its only spring of happiness—"Lord, to whom shall we go? You have words of eternal life."[l]

[i]Luke 24:28, 29
[j]Matt 13:44
[k]Prov 3:18; Eccl 7:12
[l]John 6:67–69

14 *Do not enter the path of the wicked,*
And do not proceed in the way of evil men.
15 *Avoid it, do not pass by it;*
Turn away from it and pass on.
16 *For they cannot sleep unless they do evil;*
And they are robbed of sleep unless they make
someone *stumble.*
17 *For they eat the bread of wickedness,*
And drink the wine of violence.

How often does fellowship with *the wicked* loosen even the strong grip of instruction! Their *path* is so contrary to the way *of instruction* that just entering into it is forsaking the way of God. Their character is here drawn in their father's image—first sinners, then tempters. They live to sin.[m] "To do evil is more proper and natural than to sleep, eat or drink," reads *Reformers' Notes*. They pursue their wicked activities around the clock.[n] They show little concern for their extremes of violence, just so they can do mischief, or cause others to stumble and fall.[o] Judas with his midnight torches;[p] the early morning gathering of the Jewish rulers;[q] the frenzied vow of the enemies of Paul;[r] and many a plot through centuries against the church—all vividly portray this untiring wickedness.

[m]Job 15:16; Ps 14:4
[n]Job 24:15, 16; Ps 36:4; Mic 2:1
[o]Prov 2:10–14, 16; 2:14; 24:2; Ps 10:8; 2 Peter 2:14
[p]John 18:3
[q]Luke 22:66
[r]Acts 23:12

THE MURDERER'S STAB

Yet, if we are preserved from these open and destructive tendencies, what are all the attractions for every class and circumstance of life, but the deceptive poison of the murderer? A light-minded young person pours into his companion's ear—simple and inexperienced in the ways of sin—filthy talk; or shows him pornography. What but established habits of purity can save the unsuspecting victim? Or again—the wicked unbeliever, anxious to rob[s] others of their most precious treasure, repeats the

[s]Col 2:8

[t]Gen 3:4

first lie.[t] No principle seems to be given up, no basic teaching set aside; yet the foundation of an unwavering confidence is shaken to pieces. Isn't this as bad as being the murderer's stab?

[u]Eph 5:11

Surely then it is mercy that forbids needless communication with *the evil men.*[u] With a disposition prone to evil, when the alternative is, whether we shall shun or dare the danger, can we doubt our path? The whole Word of God is on the side of caution, to hazard nothing, except on a plain call of God. Just because we're free, doesn't mean we can run wild. Half the time we're good only because we aren't tempted. Notice how the wise man piles up word upon word: *do not enter the path*—don't even set your foot on it.

KEEP OUT OF THE QUARANTINE WARD

[v]Prov 5:8

Even if you are thrown into it by accident, don't continue on it. Avoid it at any cost. Don't even go near it, so you don't accidentally fall into it.[v] Not only avoid it when you come close to it, but don't let yourself go near it. It's like being near someone with a contagious and fatal disease. The fact that the warning is earnestly repeated, again and again, shows how close at hand the danger is and how certain injury is. The world around us is the action of mind upon mind.

[w]1 Cor 15:33; Ps 106:35; Prov 22:24, 25
[x]Prov 9:10, 15; Gen 31:9, 10

Through continual communication, we are molded by other minds, and other minds are molded by our own. Communication with the ungodly must, therefore, be filled with fatal contamination.[w] The occasions, the company, the borders of temptation—all must be avoided.[x] Stay away from the quarantine.

[y]Gen 13:10–13; 14:12
[z]Gen 34:1, 2
[a]1 Kings 11:1–5
[b]Matt 26:58, 69–74

Young people are apt to plead with those who have their interest at heart, "What harm is there in this or that path?" Apart from other evils—this much is plain. It's a contagious atmosphere. You are drinking in poison. It is far easier to steer clear of the *occasion* of sin, than the sin, itself, when the occasion presents it; to resist the beginnings, than the progress, of sin. There must, therefore, be no tampering with it; no testing our strength, to see how well our resolutions are able to keep us from sin. Let the examples of Lot;[y] Dinah;[z] Solomon;[a] Peter;[b] warn us, how far, just *entrance into the path of the wicked* might carry us; lengths that we could never have dreamed of, looking ahead without horror.

DON'T CONTRADICT YOUR PRAYERS!

It may appear harmless at the start.

But how about farther on? The beginning is fatally connected with the next step forward. The frightful probability of falling might make the boldest tremble. Those at least, that know their own corruption and weakness, will shrink back, where you tread lightly. Here and there, indeed, there may be some special miracle of preservation. But no one comes out *of the path* without hurt;[c] and the general outcome is an open door to ruin. To pretend to dread sin without fearing temptation is self-delusion. Satan has bound them too closely together for us to separate them. First, the evil company is loved, then the evil of the company.[6] To pray not to be led into temptation; yet not to watch, that we enter not into it—is really to contradict our prayers; to mock our God, by asking for what we really don't want. Walk then with God and with His people, separate from an ungodly world.[d] Yet, don't take safety for granted, even though separated from the ungodly. The whole tempting world may be presented to your imagination. The unsearchable deceitfulness of the heart may bear fearfully upon you. The tempter may, in solitude, as he did with our Lord, put forth his special power.[e] Walk closely with God in secret, and He will spread His almighty covering over you for your security. Avoid fellowship with those, who hinder your fellowship with God.[f]

[c]2 Chron 18:1–3; 19:2; 20:35–37

[d]Prov 9:6; 2 Cor 6:17

[e]Matt 4:1

[f]Ps 119:63, 114, 115, also 17:4; 26:4, 5

18 *But the path of the righteous is like the light of dawn,*
That shines brighter and brighter until the full day.

YOUR CHOICE: CANDLE, METEOR, OR SUN?

This is an excellent contrast of the Christian's *path* of light with the dark and dangerous *path of the wicked.* It is not the feeble wasting light of a candle, nor the momentary flash of the meteor; but the majestic sun of heaven, "coming out of his chamber" and rejoicing "as a strong man to run his course,"[g] from earliest dawn to his noonday glory. And a beautiful sight it is, to see the

[g]Ps 19:5

[6] *Eusebius mentions a young man, whom John committed to the special charge of the Bishop of Ephesus; but who by evil company was drawn away to be a captain of robbers, until John went after him and brought him back. B. 3. c. 20. Augustine's recollections of his youthful theft was—"by myself alone I would not have done it. It was the company that I loved, with whom I did it." When they said, "Come, let us go and do it, I was ashamed not to be as shameless as they"—Confess. Lib. 2:8, 9.*

Christian rising like that out of darkness; not with uniform brightness, it's true, but deepening from the first faint beginning of his course; rising higher and higher; widening his circle; advancing onward with increasing brightness *unto the perfect day*. Knowledge, faith, love, holiness light up every step.

WALK IN THE CLEARER LIGHT

It is at first but a faint, flickering ray, the first dawn of day. He does not come at once into the marvelous light. There is much—often long-continued—struggle with his own wisdom and self-righteousness. And even when brought to a simple dependence on the great work of Christ, it is still long before he sees how all its parts fit together, providing for the honor of every perfection of God, as well as the supply of every want of man. And it takes a long time, too, before he can see the balance between promise and command; the sure connection between justification and sanctification; the accurate arrangement, by which, though we are not saved by works, we cannot be saved without them; and while we work of ourselves, our strength and trust is in another. Nor is it at the beginning that we see how happiness identifies with conformity to Christ and find heaven in communion with God and consecration to His service. So also, in the indistinct beginning of the course, sin lies within a narrow sphere. It includes little besides glaring wickedness. Many things are thought harmless, which the spiritual law condemns. But as the line becomes more marked, old habits and associations, until now unsuspected, become convicted by a clearer light, and are finally given up. It is in this path that, as Christians "press on," the eye is more unveiled,[h] the heart more enlightened, the truth more vividly impressed upon the conscience, the "understanding" more alive to "the fear of the Lord," the taste better able to recognize the difference between good and evil. Faith now becomes more strong in the Savior's love, more simple in the promises of God.

[h]Hos 6:3. Comp. Mark 8:22–25

EXPANDING LIGHT—INCREASING LOVE

Obviously also, love will increase as light expands. In proportion to the knowledge of our sinfulness and ruin must be our gratitude for the remedy. The view of heaven—in proportion to the clearness of our understanding of it—must enlarge our love to Him, who has obtained our title to it. Thus our knowledge converts itself into a motive, expanding our love more widely to all the legitimate objects of it. We can't always compare its warmth at different periods. But knowledge and love, like light and heat, must go together under the beams of knowledge; subjection to the Redeemer's rule is more gladly accepted; love rises to new heights, into a closer union with Him, to a more intimate rest in Him. Experience may be confused. But light will clear away the mists. Practice in some points may be inconsistent. *But the advances, however weak, will be sure.* "Beholding as in a mirror the glory of the Lord, being transformed into the same image from glory to glory, just as from the Lord, the Spirit."[i] Such is the *path of the just.* The devout Nathanael was cheered with the promise of a brighter day.[j] The clouds on the minds of the apostles gradually melted away before a brighter sun.[k] The eunuch and Cornelius, sincerely seeking, rejoiced in the full sunshine of gospel light.[l] The Thessalonian church *shone more and more* with Christian graces.[m]

[i] 2 Cor 3:18; Job 17:9; Ps 84:7

[j] John 1:46–51

[k] Mark 6:52; 10:35; 16:14, with John 16:13; Acts 2

[l] Acts 7:27–39; 10

[m] 1 Thess 1:3; 2 Thess 1:3

NO SETTING SUN!

But is this *shining light* the picture of my *path*? There is no command given—"O sun, stand still."[n] Therefore, it rebukes a static profession. It is a rising and advancing, not a setting, sun. Therefore, it rebukes a backsliding state. It is not necessary that everything should be perfect at once. There may be an occasional cloud, or even (as in the cases of David and Peter) a temporary eclipse. But when did the sun fail to carry its early dawn *until the full day?* Despise not, then, "the day of small things."[o] But don't be satisfied with it. Aim high, and you will reach nearer the mark. A fitful, fluctuating course, instead of illustrating this beautiful figure, throws around the profession a saddening uncertainty. Christian living must be a *shining* and progressive *light.* We must not mistake the beginning for the end of the course. We must not sit down on the entry and say to our soul, "Soul—take thine ease." There is no point, where we may repose at ease, as if there were no loftier heights, which it was our duty to climb. *Christian perfection is the continual aim-*

[n] Josh 10:12

[o] Zech 4:10

[p]See Phil 3:12–15

ing at perfection.[p] Let us hasten on to *the full day,* when the *path of the righteous* shall be eternally realized; when "they shall come to full perfection, which is—when they shall be joined to their Head in the heavens," says *Reformers' Notes.* "Then the righteous will shine forth as the sun in the kingdom of their father."[q] And yet even here will not *the path* of eternity, no less than of time, *be shining brighter and brighter?* Shall we not be exploring that unsearchable "breadth and length and height and depth ... which surpasses knowledge," until we "be filled up to all the fullness of God"?[r] Will not light therefore be more glorious, and love more full of praise and adoration? Yes, surely, the world of eternity will be one *full day* of ever-increasing light and joy. "Their sun shall no more go down—for the Lord shall be their everlasting light. The city had no need of the sun, neither of the moon, to shine in it, for the glory of the Lord did lighten it, and the Lamb is the light thereof."[7]

[q]Matt 13:43

[r]Eph 3:18, 19

19 *The way of the wicked is like darkness;*
They do not know over what they stumble.

THE DARK MOUNTAINS

The contrast is more clearly repeated.[8] Each has his own way. *The path of the just* is glowing light and joy. *The way of the wicked is darkness;* without direction, comfort, safety, or peace, till "your feet stumble on the dusky mountains;" till he falls into "the black darkness ... reserved forever."[s] His *way* is not only dark, but *as darkness,* a compound of ignorance, error, sin, and misery. The love of sin rebels "against the light."[t] The *darkness* is wilful and therefore accountable. There is *no stumbling in the path of the just.* So far as he is upright, the Lord keeps him.[u] The wicked go on, "groping like those who have no eyes";[v] hurrying on blindly into misery, that they can neither forsee nor avoid.[w] *They don't know what they're stumbling over.* Oh, if they did, wouldn't they be startled, and shrink back? For *they stumble* on the very foundation of the gospel; making the

[s]Jer 13:16; Jude 13. Comp. Job 18:5, 6, 18

[t]Job 24:13; John 3:19. Comp. Isa 5:20

[u]Verse 12; 3:23; Ps 91:11, 12

[v]Isa 59:10

[w]Job 5:14; 12:25; Jer 23:12; Zeph 1:17

[7] *Isa 60:20; Rev 21:23. The Septuagint version is very beautiful: "The way of the righteous shine like the light; they go on shining, until the day be perfected." Dr. Watts' Hymn on the Summer Evening, written for the infant mind, but glowing to the finest taste, furnishes a most exquisite exposition of this verse: "How fine has the day been; how bright was the sun ...."*

[8] *See the same contrast drawn by our Lord, Matt 6:22, 23—Schultens considers the original to express* increasing darkness, *answering to the* increasing light *of the opposite path. Job 15:23.*

rock of salvation a rock of offense.[x] If they would just listen to the merciful warning of their Lord—"For a little while longer the light is among you. Walk while you have the light, that darkness may not overtake you; *for he who walks in the darkness does not know where he goes.*[y]

[x]Rom 9:32, 33; 1 Peter 2:3

[y]John 12:35, 36

20 *My son, give attention to my words;*
Incline your ear to my sayings.
21 *Do not let them depart from your sight;*
Keep them in the midst of your heart.
22 *For they are life to those who find them,*
And health to all their whole body.

IN THE HEART'S CHAMBERS

These repeated commands[z] are a splendid pattern to the Christian parent or minister. The desire of wisdom, the first step in the path, is encouraged. The means of obtaining, and the privilege when obtained, are pointed out. Look, then, at the treasure of wisdom regularly. A neglected Bible is the sad proof of a heart "excluded from the life of God."[a] For how can we have a spark of love for Him, if that Book, which so fully reveals His glory, is despised? And yet a superficial acquaintance with it is of no value. Even if our ears were glued to the doors of the sanctuary; *if the words were always before our eyes;* yet unless they were *kept in* our heart, our Christianity would be only a notion, not a reality; theoretical, not practical; belief, not love. Even here, they do not possess more than the beginning. Let the Word be *kept in the midst of the heart.* Only there can it be effective,[b] for out of the heart "flow the springs of life."[c] Here it becomes a real and substantial truth. And here we should make a home for it,[d] a holy temple in the most honored *chambers of the heart.* This indwelling of the Word is a binding promise—the test of our interest in the Lord.[e]

[z]Prov 3:1; 5:1; 6:20, 21; 22:17

[a]Eph 4:18

[b]Prov 23:26; Ps 40:8; 119:11

[c]Verse 23

[d]Col 3:16

[e]Jer 31:33

THE VITAL GLOW

This keeping of the Word will be *life to those who find it.*[f] "Some medicines are good for one part of the body; some for another. This is good for all the body, and all the soul," said Cartwright.[g] In feeding upon this heavenly manna, we'll be vigorous and healthy. We shall not then bear our Christianity as our cross—as a heavy, unwieldy weight. We won't drag Christian duties around like a

[f]Verses 4, 10, 13; 3:18

[g]Prov 3:8

chain. Godliness will be a joy. Its actions will be free and alive. The spirit will be a vital glow. The mind will be enriched with divine wisdom. The heart will be established with gospel grace.

23 *Watch over your heart with all diligence,*
For from it flow *the springs of life.*
24 *Put away from you a deceitful mouth,*
And put devious lips far from you.
25 *Let your eyes look directly ahead,*
And let your gaze be fixed straight in front of you.
26 *Watch the path of your feet,*
And all your ways will be established.
27 *Do not turn to the right nor to the left;*
Turn your foot from evil.

KEEP YOUR HEART

These rules are invaluable as our safeguard. Because we are assaulted at every point, every inlet of sin must be strongly guarded: *the heart, the mouth, the eye, the feet.*

First, *the heart,* "the citadel of man," said Schultens—the seat of his dearest treasure. It's frightening to think of its many watchful and sly attackers. Be sure it is closely guarded. Don't ever let the guard sleep at his post. "Give heed to yourself and *keep your soul diligently.*"[h]

[h]Deut 4:9

But we must know our hearts, if we are going to be able to keep them from evil. Nothing is more difficult, and yet nothing is more necessary. If we don't know our hearts, we know nothing to any purpose. Whatever else we know, if we neglect this knowledge, we'll be a fool at best. If we don't know our weak points, Satan does. He knows them well—"the sin which so easily entangles us."[i]

[i]Heb 12:1

Then when I know my heart, and feel it to be so dangerous, and in such dangers, the question is—"Can *I keep my heart?*" Certainly not. But, even if it is God's work, we are His agency. Our efforts are His instrumentality. He implants an active principle and sustains the exercise of it unceasingly.[j] Conscious faith entrusts "their souls to a faithful Creator."[k] This done—in His strength and guidance faithfully improves all the ways of preservation. Watch with prayer. Place high value on a dependent, humble spirit. Live in the atmosphere of the

[j]Phil 2:12, 13; Jude 24 with 21
[k]1 Peter 4:19; Ps 25:20

Word of God. Don't let the evil world enter, even in its best forms.[l] Here's where the conflict lies. In *Saint Indeed,* Flavel says, "The greatest difficulty in conversion is to win the heart to God, and after conversion to keep it with Him." "What is there," asks Mede, in his sermon on Proverbs 4 "that will not entice and allure so fickle a thing as the heart from God?" *More than all watching—* advises the wise man—*watch your heart.* Here Satan keeps special watch and so should we. If the fortress is taken, the whole town must surrender. If the heart is captured, the whole man—the affections, desires, motives, pursuits—all will be given up. The most important part of the body is the heart. A wound here is sure death. So—spiritually, as well as naturally—*out of the heart are the issues of life.* It is the great vital spring of the soul, the fountain of actions, the center and the seat of principle, both of sin and of holiness.[m] The natural heart is a fountain of poison. The purified heart is "water springing up to eternal life."[n] The way the fountain is, that's the way streams will be.

[l] Judg 8:22, 23; 2 Kings 5:5, 16

[m] Matt 12:34, 35; 15:19

[n] John 4:14. Comp. Prov 14:14

GUARD THE FOUNTAIN!

The way the heart is—that's the way *the mouth, the eyes,* and *the feet* will be. But *above all watching, watch your heart.* Guard the fountain, so the waters won't be poisoned.[o] The bitter moments, from the neglect of this guard, have been many. And, if the *heart isn't watched,* all watching is in vain.

[o] Comp. Gen 26:18–21

WATCH YOUR MOUTH

But with this watching, let us not forget to guard the outlets of sin![p] What a world of evil the heart pours out from the *deceitful mouth!* Therefore, commit both heart and mouth to God's discipline.[q] Then let prayer and faith be the practical principles of Christian watchfulness. Not only *avoid*, but *put away*—yes, *far away from you*—the *devious lips.* Their evil—remember—extends beyond us. Even though the "blood" that speaks peace to us, will bring the painful sense of injury to our fellow creatures, perhaps without remedy.

[p] Prov 13:3

[q] Ps 19:13; 141:3, 4

GUARD YOUR EYES

Next to the heart and mouth—watch your eyes—"the lamp of the body;"[r] the directing power of the soul. Yet

[r] Matt 6:22

too often they are a most dangerous gateway to sin.[s] Therefore, like Job, "I have made a covenant with my eyes."[t] Place them under heavenly restraint.[u] Let your eyes look directly ahead, "like one plowing, who must not look back," comments Cartwright.[v] Look straight before us. If Eve had done that, she would have listened to God's command, instead of looking at the forbidden tree.[w] If Lot's wife had looked *directly ahead,* instead of, "behind" her, she would, like her husband, have been a monument of mercy.[x] Achan was ruined by neglecting this rule of wisdom.[y] David's example calls the holiest of us to godly jealousy.[z] In asking the way to Zion, be sure that your *faces are turned in that direction.*[a] The pleasure of sin, and the temptations of the world, don't lie in the road. They wouldn't be likely to be seen there by the eye that looks straight ahead. They belong to the by-paths on the right hand and on the left, or to some backward track. It's only when the Christian lingers, turns aside, or turns back, that they come in sight. Take the racer's motto—"one thing I do." Fix your eyes on the mark and move toward it.[b] Onward—upward—heavenward.

WATCH YOUR FEET

Lastly, *watch your feet.* Oh! has not experience, no less than Scripture, shown your need of a cautious walk?[c] Traps are set along every path, even for every step in your path; for your meat, your drink, your calling—perhaps more than all—for the service of God. What careful thought should be given to a path so filled with danger! Every step should be carefully considered.[d] Joseph *pondered*, and thereby *established* his way.[e] Peter, neglecting to *watch*, was fearfully sifted.[f] David, also, looking at the trial of the path, instead of thinking about its direction, brought shame upon himself;[g] like the trouble, which Christian in *The Pilgrim's Progress* made for himself in exchanging By-Path Meadow for the rough and straight road. "The habit of calm and serious thinking makes the real difference between one man and another," said Dr. Abercrombie.

NO STEP FORWARD WITHOUT GOD

Here, then, is the voice of wisdom. *Don't mistake presumption for faith, temptations for God's appointments.*

[s] Gen 3:6; 6:2; 39:7; Matt 5:28; 2 Peter 2:14
[t] Job 31:1
[u] Ps 119:37
[v] Comp. Luke 9:62
[w] Gen 3:3–6
[x] Gen 19:17; 26
[y] Josh 7:21
[z] 2 Sam 11:2
[a] Jer 1:5
[b] Phil 3:12–14
[c] Eph 5:15
[d] Gen 24:5; Ps 39:1; Dan 1:8; 6:3, 4
[e] Gen 39:9, 10. Comp. verses 14, 15
[f] Matt 26:58, 69–75
[g] 1 Sam 27–29

Never forsake a plain for a doubtful command.[h] Estimate every step by its conformity to the known will of God. Don't move one step forward without God.[i] *In His path* you may "tread upon the lion and cobra" without hurt.[j] But who shall venture into a path of his own choosing, without a wound? See that your feet are straight, like those of the cherubim.[k] The pleasures of sin lie *on the right and on the left*. The eyes therefore, *fixed straight in front of you* escape the sight. *The pondering foot is established* in steady perseverance. And by noting small turnings aside[l] and never turning out of the straight path to avoid a cross, it *is turned from evil.*

[h]1 Kings 12:18–22
[i]Josh 9:14
[j]Ps 91:11–13
[k]Ezek 1:7–9. Comp. Heb 12:13
[l]Eccl 19:1

PUT ASIDE THE CHURCH?—SOMETIMES

May we all have grace and wisdom to ponder these sound practical rules! The man of God must have only one standard.[m] He must "recognize no man according to the flesh."[n] He must often put aside the church, no less than the world, that he may listen more closely to God's command—*Walk before Me.*[o] He must recognize and remove the first signs of decay; guarding every avenue of sin: the senses, the memory, the imagination, the touch, the taste. He must walk by the straight rule of the gospel; otherwise, he will not only bring discomfort upon himself, but stumbling to the church.[p] A single eye—steadily fixed upon the one object, God—will throw light on the path.[q] *Straightforward* progress will guarantee prosperity.[r] Keep in the middle path, and daily lift up your voice for restraint and guidance.[s]

[m]Isa 8:20
[n]2 Cor 5:16
[o]Gen 17:1
[p]Gal 2:11–14
[q]Matt 6:22
[r]Deut 17:20; Josh 1:7, 8
[s]Ps 119:37; 143:8–10

"And your ears will hear a word behind you, 'This is the way, walk in it,' whenever you turn to the right or to the left.[9]

[9] *Isa 30:21. Comp. Deut 2:27; 5:32. The Septuagint adds, "For God knows the ways on the right hand. But those on the left are crooked. But He shall make straight your paths, and advance your goings in peace." Geier remarks, "We have no ear for these words, as not belonging to the holy fountain." A paraphrase of Cartwright's exposition of this middle path is valuable. It is as though the royal way was hemmed in by the sea, and a fall over either side could result in drowning. Some are too greedy; others too self-denying. Some are too bold; others too shy. Some neglect the Mediator; others seek* new *Mediators. Some flee the cross; others make one.*

CHAPTER FIVE

1 *My son, give attention to my wisdom,*
Incline your ear to my understanding;
2 *That you may observe discretion,*
And your lips may reserve knowledge.
3 *For the lips of an adulteress drip honey,*
And smoother than oil is her speech;
4 *But in the end she is bitter as wormwood,*
Sharp as a two-edged sword.
5 *Her feet go down to death,*
Her steps lay hold of Sheol.
6 *She does not ponder the path of life;*
Her ways are unstable, she does not know it.
7 *Now then,* my *sons, listen to me,*
And do not depart from the words of my mouth.
8 *Keep your way far from her,*
And do not go near the door of her house,
9 *Lest you give your vigor to others,*
And your years to the cruel one;
10 *Lest strangers be filled with your strength,*
And your hard-earned goods go *to the house of an alien;*
11 *And you groan at your latter end,*
When your flesh and your body are consumed;
12 *And you say, "How I have hated instruction!*
And my heart spurned reproof!
13 *"And I have not listened to the voice of my teachers,*
Nor inclined my ear to my instructors!
14 *"I was almost in utter ruin*
In the midst of the assembly and congregation."

Think about this chapter—you, who don't know the poison and corruption of fleshly lusts. Perhaps painful experience[a] had given the wise man *wisdom and under-*

[a] 1 Kings 11:1–8; Eccl 7:26

standing. Therefore, *give attention* to it with fear and trembling. Your own strength, education or self-discipline are as powerless to keep you from sin as green twigs are to bind the giant.[b] Firmly established wisdom is the only effective safeguard. This heavenly influence teaches us to observe discretion for the warning of our fellow-sinners.[c]

PATH OF DEATH

The extreme possibility of the temptation calls our *attention*. The deceived victim only tastes, or expects to taste, *the honey:* only hears the *slick smoothness* of the charmer's voice.[d] But the beginning is never so sweet as the end is *bitter*. God shows *the wormwood—the two-edged sword*[e]—her path of death—every step *lay hold of all Hell*, as if invading it with a high hand; grasping it as her home. One feature of the tempter's wiliness is most remarkable, noted Schultens.[f] She winds herself in a thousand *unstable ways*, to meet the different frames of mind and circumstances;[g] she works upon every weakness; seizes every unguarded moment—all with one deeply hidden object—to keep you from *seriously considering the path of life*. The restraints of conscience must be put aside. No time should be allowed for reflections. The intrusion of one serious thought might break the spell, and open the way of escape.[h]

Are we surprised at parental concern that makes them force back children playing on the brink of a precipice? *Listen*, young people, we're not trying to put any stern restraint upon youthful pleasures. All we ask is that you avoid the tempter's touch, her word, even her look. *Keep as far away from her as possible*. Not only should you not go to her; but—so bad is the disease—that *you shouldn't even go near the door*.[i] *To throw ourselves into the way of temptation is to throw ourselves out of God's protection*. The snare as it approaches becomes more enticing. The voice of wisdom therefore is—*"Flee from youthful lusts."*[j]

The loss of honor,[k] taking the crown from the victim's head;[l] *years given to the cruel* mockers of his misery;[m] the waste of the family wealth;[n] servitude *in a stranger's house;*[o] *being consumed*, slowly bringing *the body* to the grave[p]—that's the bitter fruit of the neglected warning.

[b] Judg 16:9
[c] Prov 2:10, 11, 16; 6:20, 24; 7:1–5; Ps 17:4; 119:9, 11
[d] Prov 2:16; 6:24; 7:21
[e] Comp. Ps 55:21
[f] Prov 2:18; 7:17; 9:18; 1 Cor 6:9, 10; Rev 21:8
[g] Prov 7:21
[h] See Ps 119:59; Ezek 18:28; Luke 15:17
[i] Comp. Prov 4:14, 15; 6:27, 28
[j] 2 Tim 2:22
[k] Prov 6:32, 33; Gen 38:23–26
[l] 2 Sam 12:11; 15:30; Neh 13:26
[m] Prov 6:26; 31:3; Judg 16:18–21
[n] Prov 6:26, 35; 29:3; Job 31:12; Hos 7:9; Luke 15:13, 30
[o] Luke 15:15, 16
[p] 1 Cor 6:18

Add to this the voice of conscience *at the latter end*, telling of neglected privileges, putting down convictions, misusing knowledge. And won't this be the pain of thousands taught in our schools, or the children of godly parents, now *spurning the reproof* of God, and the voice of their teachers; announcing their shame openly; perhaps making Christian *assemblies* the scenes *of almost utter ruin?*[q]

[q] Num 25:6, 7; Ezek 8:5–16

THE ACCUSING CONSCIENCE

That's the picture of sin. It's "passing pleasures of sin" result in wages of eternal death.[r] Every sin we don't repent of here will bring its never ending torment in eternity. *Being impenitent doesn't put away our sorrow.* It just delays it. Someday, when mercy shall have fled forever,[s] then nothing will remain, except the piercing cry of the accusing conscience, "Son! remember."[t] There are no unbelievers in eternity and only a very few on deathbeds. Sinner! *The path of life* is now open to you. Consider it anxiously, prayerfully. The light of the Word, and the teaching of the Spirit, guide you to it.

[r] Heb 11:25; Rom 6:23

[s] Prov 1:24–31

[t] Luke 16:25

15 *Drink water from your own cistern,*
And fresh water from your own well.
16 *Should your springs be dispersed abroad,*
Streams of water in the streets?
17 *Let them be yours alone,*
And not for strangers with you.
18 *Let your fountain be blessed,*
And rejoice in the wife of your youth.
19 *As loving hind and a graceful doe,*
Let her breasts satisfy you at all times;
Be exhilarated always with her love.

GOD'S SPECIAL GIFT

A desire for forbidding joys springs from dissatisfaction with blessings we already have. When we don't find contentment at home—*drinking out of our own cistern*[1]—out we go—vainly searching for happiness elsewhere. Conjugal love is first among earthly blessings that God in mercy gives us, His fallen and rebellious creatures. Enjoy then with thankfulness what's yours, and don't de-

[1] *The beauty of the figure is illustrated from the circumstance, that the houses of the East appear to have had their own cistern. 2 Kings 18:31.*

sire your neighbor's *well.*[u] If a happy issue is given;[v] let it be as *springs*[w] sent forth to enrich with godly influence the way through which their course may be directed.[x] *Rejoice in the wife of your youth.*[y] Regard her as God's special gift.[z] Treat her with gentleness and purity,[a] *as the loving hind and graceful doe.*[2] Remember, whatever upsets your marriage relationship, opens the door to temptation waiting nearby. Tender, well-ordered domestic affection is the best defense against wandering desires of unlawful passion. Yes—it's set apart by the Word of God, itself, to the high purpose of symbolizing the great mystery—loving and cherishing our own flesh, even as the Lord the church.[b]

[u]Exod 20:17; 2 Sam 11:2, 3
[v]Ps 127:3–5; 128
[w]Comp. Num 24:7; Deut 33:28; Ps 68:26; Isa 48:1
[x]Comp. Zech 8:5
[y]Deut 24:5; Eccl 9:9
[z]Prov 19:14
[a]Gen 24:67
[b]Eph 5:25, 29

20 *For why should you, my son, be exhilarated with an adulteress,*
And embrace the bosom of a foreigner?
21 *For the ways of a man are before the eyes of the* LORD,
And He watches all his paths.
22 *His own iniquities will capture the wicked,*
And he will be held with the cords of his sin.
23 *He will die for lack of instruction,*
And in the greatness of his folly he will go astray.

THE FORBIDDEN SPRING

With a view like we've had on the deadly enticement of sin on the one hand,[c] and the calm happiness provided on the other by the command of God,[d] surely no one with sound judgment would leave the wholesome well for the poisoned spring. If he were not stupefied, would he treat the honorable state of marriage disrespectfully,[e] to *embrace the bosom of a foreigner,* loveless, joyless, unendeared? Would not the thought that, *the ways of man are before the eyes of the Lord,* arrest him in his course?[f] But no. Practical atheism is the root of human depravity.[g] The eye of man, even of a child, is a check upon him;[h] but the thought of an all-seeing god, even if it enters his mind,[i] inspires no alarm, conviction, or restraint. Oh! if men would but read—would but *believe*—their Bibles, how

[c]Verses 9–11
[d]Verses 15–19
[e]Heb 13:4
[f]Job 34:21, 22; Ps 94:6–9; Jer 13:25–27; 16:17; 29:23; Hos 7:2
[g]Ps 14:1–3
[h]Job 24:15; Isa 29:15
[i]Ps 10:4

[2] *Comp. 2 Sam 12:3. The* hind and the doe *were objects of special delight (Song of Sol 2:17; 3:5) and endearment—a picture of the lively delight, which the wife naturally engages; relaxing in her society from severer duties, and taking the liveliest pleasure in her company. As Bishop Davenant beautifully observes, "Abroad the man may consider himself as tossing in the waves; but at home with his wife, in repose, as in a desired haven"—On Col 3:19.*

[j]Job 31:4; Ps 139:1–4
[k]Prov 16:2; 1 Sam 2:3; Dan 5:27
[l]Heb 4:13
[m]Eccl 12:14
[n]Mal 3:2; Eph 5:5

would this solemn truth—*he watches all his paths*—flash upon their consciences! Not only does He see and mark them, as the Omniscient God;[j] but he *watches them* as the just Judge.[k] Not one is hidden from His piercing eye.[l] "God will bring every act to judgment."[m] He will be a swift witness against the adulterers. No unclean person shall enter into "the kingdom of Christ and God."[n]

[o]Prov 6:3, 5, 6; 29:6; 1 Sam 28:5–10
[p]Verse 12. Prov 1:29; 10:21; Job 4:21; 36:12; Hos 4:14, 17
[q]2 Peter 2:14, 15

But if no regard to reason, or to the all-seeing eye of God, will restrain the sinner, let him think of the trouble that he is bringing upon himself. God needs no chains or prison to bring him under His hand. Wherever he goes, *his iniquities* go with him, as *cords to hold him* for judgment.[o] Does he think that he can give them up when he pleases? Repetition forms the habit. The habit becomes a ruling principle. "Every lust deals with him, as Delilah with Samson—not only robs him of his strength, but leaves him fast bound."[3] Shutting his eyes against the light, *he dies for lack of instruction.*[p]—*the greatness of his folly leads him astray*—to perdition.[q]

[r]Zech 13:1; 1 Cor 6:11
[s]Isa 61:1

But isn't there a remedy for this deadly curse? Thanks be to God, cleansing is provided for the impure;[r] "deliverance is proclaimed to the captive."[s] Blessed Savior! cleanse the leper in Your precious springs. Perform Your mighty commission. Set the captive free.

[3] *Archbishop Tillotson quoted in NICHOLL'S* Commentary. *Judg 16:19–21. "Thus I," said Augustine, adverting to this hateful sin, "delighted with the disease of the flesh, and with the deadly sweetness of it, drew my shackles along with me, much afraid to have them knocked off; and as if my wound had been too hard rubbed by it, I put back my friend's good persuasions, as it were the hand of one that would unchain me"*—Confess. *b. vi. c.12. Comp. Prov 23:29–35.*

CHAPTER SIX

1 *My son, if you have become surety for your neighbor,*
Have given a pledge for a stranger,
2 If *you have been snared with the words of your mouth,*
Have been caught with the words of your mouth,
3 *Do this then, my son, and deliver yourself;*
Since you have come into the hand of your neighbor,
Go, humble yourself, and importune your neighbor.
4 *Do not give sleep to your eyes,*
Nor slumber to your eyelids;
5 *Deliver yourself like a gazelle from* the hunter's *hand,*
And like a bird from the hand of the fowler.

AVOID RASH AGREEMENTS

The *son has* just been warned against the deadly wound of a stranger. He is now cautioned against a hurt from a false friend. Our God has so graciously made His Book, not only our guide to heaven, but also to our everyday living. But often we need to take its wise rules with some restriction. We are here earnestly warned against making oneself liable for someone else—his debts, damages, or default. In some cases it is plainly allowed and approved.[1] And the giving of our word, in a binding agreement, may be an act of concerned friendship and of strong and lasting advantage. The caution is evidently directed against rash agreements,[a] to which the young and inexperienced are especially exposed; *shaking hands* (the usual way of making a pledge),[b] in an unguarded moment. Often you may be *snared with the words of your mouth,* by entering into virtual promises, without knowing how far they were pledged, or what the

[a]Comp. also Prov 11:15; 17:18; 20:16; 22:26, 27
[b]Prov 17:18; 22:26; Job 17:3

[1] *Reuben and Judah for Benjamin—Gen 42:37; 43:9; 44:32, 33. Paul for Onesimus—Phil 18, 19.*

outcome might be. Christian caution will keep us free of such agreements, which bring distress upon our families, dishonor upon our name, and reproach upon our Christian testimony. While the "good man showeth favor, and lendeth, he must guide his affairs with good judgment";[2] however annoying it may be to bring on the suspicion of unkindness. If, however, by any inconsiderate pledge, you have *come into the hand of your neighbor;* your first duty is, *to humble yourself for your poor judgment and make sure your friendship.* If you can, persuade him to answer for himself; and give yourself no rest, until, *like as the gazelle and the bird,* you are released from the snare.

Our God, though He warns us against making ourselves liable for someone else's debts, has taken our debts upon Himself. Praise His name! He has given His word, His bond, yes—His blood—for sinners—a guarantee, that no powers of Hell can shake.

6 *Go to the ant, O sluggard,*
Observe her ways and be wise,
7 *Which, having no chief,*
Officer or ruler,
8 *Prepares her food in the summer,*
And *gathers her provision in the harvest.*
9 *How long will you lie down, O sluggard?*
When will you arise from your sleep?
10 *"A little sleep, a little slumber,*
A little folding of the hands to rest"—
11 *And your poverty will come in like a vagabond,*
And your need like an armed man.

"It's a shame," said the heathen philosopher, "not to learn morals from the small animals." Yet what a proof it is of the degradation of the fall, that man, created in the image of God, and made wiser than the creation,[c] should be sent, as here to this insignificant school for instruction! *The ant, having no chief* to direct her work, no *officer* to inspect her, or *ruler* to call her to account;[d] yet *prepares* with careful foresight the *summer and harvest*

[c]Gen 1:26; Job 35:11

[d]Comp. Prov 30:27, and contrast Exod 5:13, 14; 1 Kings 5:16

[2] *Ps 92:5. P. Henry always advised that those binding themselves to be responsible for someone else's debts should not be bound for more than they were able to pay nor for more than they would be* willing *to pay, if the principal failed—*Life. *chap.* 5.

store for her winter need.[3] *Let the sluggard observe her ways and be wise.* He sleeps over his work, and if for a moment half-startled by some rousing call, still pleads for a *little more sleep, and folds his hands to sleep.* Present ease is all he counts on, all he provides for. The future he carefully keeps out of sight, to be provided for, like the present, when it comes. So life will be wasted. *Poverty comes* step by step *like a vagabond, and, like an armed man,* with irresistible violence.[e]

Perhaps he perverts his Master's word to excuse his laziness. But, if we are told "do not be *anxious* for tomorrow,"[f] aren't we to take any thought at all? Care is a duty, a parental obligation,[g] and, therefore, a part of godliness.[4] Carefulness is a sin,[h] a needless burden to ourselves, an unworthy distrust of God.[i] The careful use of God's provisions honors God.[j]

[e]Prov 10:4; 13:4; 19:15, 24; 20:4; 21:25; 24:33, 34

[f]Matt 6:34. Comp. Phil 4:6

[g]2 Cor 12:14. Comp. Gen 30:30; 41:33

[h]Luke 10:41; 1 Cor 7:32

[i]Matt 6:25–33

[j]Prov 10:5; 24:27

THE SLUMBER OF DEATH

But much more loudly would we speak to the spiritual *sluggard.* You who are sleeping away the opportunities of grace; not striving "to enter by the narrow door";[k] taking your salvation for granted; hoping that you will "reap where [you] did not sow, and gather where [you] scattered no seed[l]—*go to the ant, O sluggard; observe her ways, and be wise.* Follow this pattern and improve, the *summer and harvest* season—the time of youth, the present, perhaps the only, moment. *The ant has no chief.* Think how many chiefs you have—conscience—the Bible—ministers![m] *She has no officer.* You are living before Him, whose eyes are "like a flame of fire."[n] *She has no ruler* calling her to account. "Each one of us shall give account of himself to God."[o] *How long will you lie down, O sluggard?*—is the solemn protest of your God.[p] Your sleep is not like that of the body, refreshing at the dawn of day; but it is that of the poisoned drink, heavier and heavier; the slumber of death. "Awake, sleeper . . . and Christ will shine on you."[q] Don't ignore the call of the present moment. The spell grows stronger, as resistance

[k]Luke 13:24

[l]Matt 25:26

[m]Job 32:8; Ps 119:105; Mal 2:7

[n]Prov 15:3; Rev 1:14; 2:18

[o]Rom 14:12

[p]Comp. Prov 1:22; 1 Kings 18:21

[q]Eph 5:14

[3] *Prov 10:5; 30:25. Horace's miser quotes this example as an excuse for hoarding. But—as the poet replies—it was to use the hoard in the winter—wise and thrifty care, not coveteousness. See also Virgil's exquisite picture. The hoarding spirit of the ants, though confirmed by many writers and naturalists, does not characterize those known to us; though the habits of the species in a warmer climate would probably widely differ from our own. Some, however, have thought, that Solomon only refers to their wisdom and care in preparing suitable food in summer and harvest, when it is most plentiful.*

[4] *1 Tim 5:8. Our Lord had a bag for the provision of his family. John 13:29.*

is delayed. Every day's slumber makes it more improbable that you will ever awaken at all. The intended struggle of tomorrow is a delusion. A thousand such tomorrows there may be; and yet you may finally be found perishing in your *poverty,* and the King of terror will *come* as an *armed man* to call you to judgment.

But how strongly one feels that no voice but God's can rouse him from this deep slumber. Enter the *sluggard's* chamber; pull his curtain aside; lean over his bed; sound a solemn cry in his ears—*How long?* Try even to open his eyes to the light of day; and yet the spell is too strong for man. He turns over, cries, "*a little more sleep*" and slumbers again. Christians! you feel the helplessness of your work. Then call in the power of God in your brother's behalf—"Enlighten his eyes, lest [he] sleep the *sleep* of death."[r]

[r]Ps 13:3

THE SIN OF LAZINESS

And then, as for yourself, grown in intense energy in your high calling. Remember, faith without diligence is sleeping delusion. Faith is the practical energy of a *living* faith. Always, therefore, look at laziness, not as an infirmity, but as a sin, affecting the whole man; growing upon us with unseen power. Therefore, don't allow it any rest—no time to root itself. Resist it in all its forms—bodily, mentally, spiritually. Don't allow it any indulgence of sleep and appetites—self-pleasing in all its subtle and plausible workings. Live by rule. Have your time strictly arranged. Employ yourself in early work for God. Store your mind with useful knowledge; always reserving the first place for earnest and prayerful study of the Word of God. Mortify deadly lust through God's Spirit[s] drawing all your motives from the death,[t] the life,[u] and the teachings of Christ.[v] Victory will soon be yours; and how rewarding the spoil.

[s]Rom 8:13
[t]Rom 6:6
[u]Mark 1:32–35
[v]Luke 9:23; Rom 8:11–14

12 *A worthless person, a wicked man,*
Is the one who walks with a false mouth,
13 *Who winks with his eyes, who signals with his feet,*
Who points with his fingers;
14 *Who* with *perversity in his heart devises evil continually,*
Who spreads strife.

15 *Therefore his calamity will come suddenly;*
Instantly he will be broken, and there will be no healing.

What a contrast between the inactivity of the sluggard and the unwearied perseverance of the stubbornly wilful person! This devilish man of Belial—as if his *false mouth* itself "a world of iniquity"[w]—does not have enough room for his hatred, now he makes every member—*eyes, feet, and fingers*—vocal and significant,[x] active "instruments of unrighteousness."[y] These, however, are only the external evidences. Deep within lies the laboratory of evil—"the room of carved images," teeming with greater and yet "greater abominations."[z] *Perversity is in the heart.*[a] Here is the restless *devising of evil,*[b] *spreading strife,* instead of piety and love.[c] Such a pest to society brings on himself his own ruin, *suddenly and with no healing.*

[w] James 3:6
[x] Isa 3:16
[y] Prov 10:10; Rom 6:13–19
[z] Ezek 8:8–15; Matt 15:19
[a] Gen 6:5; Acts 13:10
[b] Ps 10:7–9; 36:2–4. Comp. Hos 7:6; Prov 16:28; Ps 52:2
[c] Prov 10:12

The sight of this all-pervading power of sin is truly affecting. How utterly powerless is any remedy, except that involved in the solemn declaration—"You must be born again!"[d]

[d] John 3:7; Titus 3:3–5

16 *There are six things which the* LORD *hates,*
Yes, seven which are an abomination to Him:
17 *Haughty eyes, a lying tongue,*
And hands that shed innocent blood,
18 *A heart that devises wicked plans,*
Feet that run rapidly to evil,
19 *A false witness* who *utters lies,*
And one who spreads strife among brothers.

Man conceives of God in his heart as "such a one as himself,"[e] looking with indifference at sin. Here therefore Solomon names *six—yes—seven*[f] *abominations* (most of them mentioned in the preceding list) *which the Lord hates*—haughty eyes,[5] a lying tongue,[6] a blood-stained hand.[7] And, lest we should think, that he "looks at the outward appearance";[g] *the heart,* active in *devising wicked plans,*[h] is brought out; and its willing organ, *the feet swift in running to evil.*[i] How hateful also is the *false* witness,[j] surely reserved by him for judgment![k] Let the

[e] Ps 50:21
[f] Comp. Prov 30:15–18
[g] 1 Sam 16:7
[h] 2 Sam 16:20–23; 17:23; Mic 2:1; 2 Peter 2:14
[i] Prov 1:16; Isa 59:7; Rom 3:15
[j] Zech 8:17
[k] Prov 9:5. Zech 5:4; Mal 3:5

[5] *Prov 8:13; 30:13; Ps 18:27; Isa 2:12; Jer 1:31—the examples of Pharaoh—Exod 9:16; Haman—Esther 7:10; Nebuchadnezzar—Dan 4:28–33; Herod—Acts 12:21–23.*
[6] *Prov 12:22; Ps 5:6; Rev 21:8; Gehazi—2 Kings 5:25–27; Ananias and Sapphira—Acts 5:1–10.*
[7] *Gen 9:6; Cain—4:8–12; Manasseh—2 Kings 21:15–16. Specially the murderers of His dear Son—Matt 23:31–38.*

self-willed dissenter remember the marks against anyone[l] *who spreads strife among brothers.* If the heavenly dew descends on the brothers who "dwell together in unity,"[m] a withering blast will fall on those, who, mistaking prejudice for principle, selfishly "cause dissensions."[n] Terrible is the Lord's mark upon them, who are "worldly-minded, devoid of the Spirit."[8] If we can't agree—can't be "complete in the same mind," and in the same judgment,[9] at least let's try to promote unity of spirit—"Let us keep living by that same *standard* to which we have attained."[o]

[l] Verses 14, 19
[m] Ps 133
[n] Rom 16:17, 18
[o] Phil 3:16

20 *My son, observe the commandment of your father,*
And do not forsake the teaching of your mother;
21 *Bind them continually on your heart;*
Tie them around your neck.
22 *When you walk about, they will guide you;*
When you sleep, they will watch over you;
And when you awake, they will talk to you.
23 *For the commandment is a lamp, and the teaching is light;*
And reproofs for discipline are the way of life,
24 *To keep you from the evil woman,*[10]
From the smooth tongue of the adulteress.

The authority of parental instruction is commanded over and over.[p] God never intended young people to be independent of their parents. The right kind of instruction from anyone is valuable. But from *parents*—always supposing them to be godly parents—it is as though it is from God, Himself. They will give you God's word, not their own. Therefore *bind it continually on your heart,*[q] as your rule; *around your neck*[r] as an ornament. Let God's Word be your friend for all times and circumstances—a guide by day;[s] a comfort by night,[t]

[p] Prov 1:8, 9; 4:1
[q] Prov 3:3; 4:21; 7:3
[r] Prov 3:3. Comp. Job 31:36
[s] Prov 3:22, 23; 4:12
[t] Prov 3:24; Ps 63:5

[8] *Jude 19. 1 Cor 3:3, 4. In this paraphrase of his statement let the wisdom of experience given by Baxter who knows himself and the church, be seriously considered—I am much more sensitive to the evil of divisiveness and of the separating disposition and of gathering parties, and making several sects in the church, than I have ever been before. For the effects have shown us more of the harm. I am much more aware of how many young professing believers are given to spiritual pride and self-conceit, and unruliness, and division. They prove a disappointment to their teachers, and stir up people in the church to cause strife. I am much more aware than ever of the breadth, and length, and depth of the radical, universal, hateful sin of selfishness, and the superiority and necessity of self-denial, and of a public mind, and of loving our neighbor as ourselves*—Narrative of his Life and Times.

[9] *1 Cor 1:10—"A text," says the godly Flavel, "to be commented upon rather by tears than by words"*—Sermon on Text.

[10] *Heb—woman of wickedness, the woman full of wickedness, wholly given to it. Comp. Zech 5:7, 8.*

yes—a friend for *your waking* moments.[u] Be careful, so that nothing keeps you from having early communion with this faithful counselor before the world comes in. It's the best means of keeping the world out. "Happy is the mind to which the Word is an undivided companion," said Bernard ("Sermon 32" in *Cant*). A *lamp* so full of *light,* in this dark world[v] is a gift beyond measure. Its *reproofs* of instruction, the *discipline* of our wayward will, are as *the way of life* to us.[w]

[u]Ps 139:17, 18
[v]Ps 119:105
[w]Ps 19:11; 2 Tim 3:16, 17. Comp. Matt 7:13, 14

Specially valuable are this *lamp and light* in sensual temptation.[x] Those who choose their own light fall into a flattering snare.[y] The neglect of parental warning will finally prove a bitter matter for futile repentance.[z] Oh! let the Father's instruction be heard before it's too late—"How can a young man keep his way pure? By keeping *it* according to Thy Word."[a]

[x]Prov 2:10, 11, 16–19; 5:1–8; 7:1–5
[y]Prov 2:16; 7:21
[z]Prov 5:11–13
[a]Ps 119:9. Comp. 5:11; 17:4

25 *Do not desire her beauty in your heart,*
Nor let her catch you with her eyelids.
26 *For on account of a harlot* one is reduced *to a loaf of bread,*
And an adulteress hunts for the precious life.
27 *Can a man take fire in his bosom,*
And his clothes not be burned?
28 *Or can a man walk on hot coals,*
And his feet not be scorched?
29 *So is the one who goes in to his neighbor's wife;*
Whoever touches her will not go unpunished.

ON THE BORDERS OF SIN

Solomon here gives our Lord's own rule.[b] Resist *the desire* when it first rises in your heart. By vain *beauty,*[c] and lustful *eyes,*[11] many a deceived victim has been *reduced to a loaf of bread.*[12] Like the greedy huntsman, who never loses sight of his prey, till he has pursued it to death; never does the seducer cease to solicit, till she has *hunted for the precious life.*[d] Yet neither the present miseries, nor the certain end, of this wretched course, can draw away the foot, that has dared to walk in a forbidden path. Self-confidence sees and fears no danger. A young person says, "I can look to myself; I need not go

[b]Matt 5:28. Comp. James 1:14, 15; Job 31:1; Ps 109:37
[c]Prov 31:30; Gen 6:21; 39:6; 2 Sam 11:2
[d]Gen 39:14; Judg 16:18–21. Comp. Ezek 8:18, 20, 21

[11] *Gen 39:7; 2 Kings 9:30; Isa 3:16; 2 Peter 2:14. Comp.* Paradise Lost, *Book 11, l 620.*
[12] *Prov 5:10; 29:3; 1 Sam 2:26, 36; Job 31:9, 12; Luke 15:13, 30. Comp. the difference between Solomon's indecent and unholy age. 1 Kings 10:21, 27 with 12:4.*

too far, and I shall get no harm." But the temptation acts upon a congenial nature like fuel, not water, on the fire. We might just as well expect to *take fire into our inmost being, and our clothes not be burned, or to walk on hot coals, and not be burned;* as to go wilfully into sin, and to escape the punishment.[13] Sin and punishment are linked together by an unbreakable chain. "The fire of lust kindles the fire of Hell," said Henry.[e] He cannot afterward plead the strength of the temptation. Why didn't he avoid it? Who is he that knows the amount of dry tinder he carries with him that would wilfully light up the sparks? Carelessly rushing into temptation, is to provoke the evil, that is too ready to stir itself. The influence of temptation, though not always sensible, is immediate. A man has to move along in a hurry, if he would successfully resist it. Look out for suspicious familiarities on the borders of sin.[f] The temptation to crime in this atmosphere is terrible. *Whoever touches shall not be innocent.*[g]

[e]Comp. Job 31:12; James 1:14, 15

[f]Gen 39:10; Rom 13:13; 1 Thess 5:22; 2 Sam 11:2–4

[g]Gen 20:6; 39:9; 1 Cor 7:1

30 *Men do not despise a thief if he steals*
To satisfy himself when he is hungry;
31 *But when he is found, he must repay sevenfold;*
He must give all the substance of his house.
32 *The one who commits adultery with a woman is lacking sense;*
He who would destroy himself does it.
33 *Wounds and disgrace he will find,*
And his reproach will not be blotted out.
34 *For jealousy enrages a man,*
And he will not spare in the day of vengeance.
35 *He will not accept any ransom,*
Nor will he be content though you give many gifts.

There's no excuse or exemption here for *the thief.* The full *repayment* that he is forced to make[14]—perhaps sweeping away *all the money of his house*—proves that not even extreme need can excuse the breaking of the law.[h] Let him earn his bread by honest, hard work. If the fruits of hard work fail, let him, trusting in God, seek the

[h]Comp. 1 Cor 6:10, with 1 John 3:4

[13] *Exod 20:14, 17; Lev 20:10; 2 Sam 12:9; Mal 3:5. Even as a sin of ignorance it was liable to be investigated. Gen 12:15–18; 20:1–6; 26:10. So strictly has the holy Lord fenced His own command! See MEDE'S* Sermon on Chap. 4:23.

[14] *Exod 22:1–4.* Sevenfold—*not literally. Four or fivefold was the extent of God's requirement. Comp. Luke 19:8. It means full (v. 3) and satisfactory—an indefinite number. Comp. Gen 4:15, 24; Ps 79:12. Comp. Job 20:18.*

help of his fellowmen. If he has faith to trust, he will never be forced to steal.[i] Yet his extreme temptation makes him an object, more of pity than of scorn—men do not despise him.

[i]Matt 6:25–33

But the sin of the adulterer has no right to sympathy. His plea is not the cry of hunger, but of desire; not want, but wantonness; not the *lack* of bread, but of *sense.*[j] He deliberately and intentionally gives himself up to sin. *He destroys his own self.*[k] *He gets a wound*—not like the soldier or the martyr for Christ—full of honor; but irritates his conscience,[l] and brings *disgrace* and indelible *reproach* upon his name.[m] The tremendous passions of *jealousy and rage* shut out all forgiveness.[15] *The face* of no one who offered a *ransom* would be *accepted.* No compensation,[n] no matter how great, will bring contentment.

[j]Comp. Eccl 7:25, 26; Jer 5:8, 21

[k]Lev 20:10; Prov 2:18, 19; 5:22, 23; 7:22, 23; Eph 5:5

[l]Ps 32:3, 4

[m]Prov 5:9; Gen 38:23; 49:4; 2 Sam 3:13; 13:13; 1 Kings 15:5; Matt 1:6; Neb 13:26. Comp. Deut 23:2

[n]Gen 39:19, 20; Judg 19:29, 30

Such are the many sins,[o] the awfully destructive miseries, flowing from the breaking of God's holy law. Oh! how great iniquity," exclaimed the godly Augustine, "is this adultery! How great a perverseness! The soul, redeemed by the precious blood of Christ, is thus for the pleasures of an hour given to the devil; a thing much to be lamented and bewailed; when that which delighteth is soon gone, that which tormenteth remaineth without end."

[o]2 Sam 11:6–24

And won't this fearful picture of sin and its consequences (which Solomon, sadly enough was too well fitted to draw) teach us to avoid everything that *may be* temptation; to be sensitive to the first hints of its becoming so; to close every avenue of sense to the entrance of this seductive poison; to turn away from all communications that spoil the taste, that familiarize the mind with impurity, that arouses keen interest in associations that a pure imagination recoils from with disgust? Let us learn to seek God's divine strength to "keep watching and praying"[p] continually; and let him who thinks he stands, "take heed lest he fall."[q]

[p]Mark 14:38

[q]1 Cor 10:12

[15] *Gen 34:7; 49:5–7; Num 5:14; Esther 7:7–10; Ezek 16:38. Schultens remarks that no version fully expresses the strength of the original.*

CHAPTER SEVEN

1 *My son, keep my words,*
And treasure my commandments within you.
2 *Keep my commandments and live,*
And my teaching as the apple of your eye.
3 *Bind them on your fingers;*
Write them on the tablet of your heart.
4 *Say to wisdom, "You are my sister,"*
And call understanding your *intimate friend;*
5 *That they may keep you from an adulteress,*
From the foreigner who flatters with her words.

The study of wisdom in the Word of God is here commended to us with loving earnestness and with a beautiful variety of imagery. Let us ponder these valuable rules for practical application.

LAND OF PROMISE

Let your whole mind and heart be occupied with it. *Keep my words* as the daily means of life.[a] Sir Matthew Hale told his children, "If I omit reading a portion of Scripture in the morning, it never goes well with me through the day." *Treasure* it up[b] carefully, not on our shelves, but in our hearts. Let the whole Word of God be our precious treasure. Receive the promises from His grace with simple trust and *the commandments* from His holiness with ready obedience. Stand with your eye in the land of promise; but with your feet "on level ground."[c]

[a]Prov 3:21, 22; 4:4, 13; Isa 55:2, 3; Jer 22:15

[b]Prov 10:14; Deut 11:18; Luke 2:19, 51

[c]Ps 143:10

Maintain a jealous regard for His teaching. What care is necessary to keep *the apple of your eye*—that the most tender part of the most tender member![d] With the same care preserve the integrity of God's teaching in your life. Let every part of it have its full weight. To explain it away, or to lower its requirements, breaks down the bar-

[d]Deut 32:10; Ps 17:8; Zech 2:8

rier, and gives an easy entrance to temptation. The sensual sinner is often a disguised infidel.

Let it be at hand for constant use. *Bind them upon your fingers.*[e] Always in sight, they may be always ready for the present moment. And for their practical influence, *write them on the tablets of your heart.* Oh, Lord, this is Your almighty Work.[f] But You have promised to do it for Your people.[g] I take hold of Your "covenant." Lord! Seal Your promised favor.

[e] Prov 3:3; Deut 6:8; 11:18

[f] Isa 26:12; 2 Cor 3:3

[g] Jer 31:33

Let it be the object of tender affection—*as our sister*—your intimate friend. It is her embrace that throws the harlot's beauty into the shade. Man must have his object of delight. If wisdom is not loved, lust will be indulged. The Bible therefore—not merely read, but the cherished object of familiar conversation—proves a sacred exorcist to expel the power of evil.[h]

[h] Prov 2:10, 16; 6:23, 24; 23:26, 27

6 *For at the window of my house*
I looked out through my lattice,
7 *And I saw among the naive,*
I discerned among the youths,
A young man lacking sense,
8 *Passing through the street near her corner;*
And he takes the way to her house,
9 *In the twilight, in the evening,*
In the middle of the night and in *the darkness.*
10 *And behold, a woman* comes *to meet him,*
Dressed as a harlot and cunning of heart.
11 *She is boisterous and rebellious;*
Her feet do not remain at home;
12 She *is now in the streets, now in the squares,*
And lurks by every corner.
13 *So she seizes him and kisses him,*
And with a brazen face she says to him:
14 *"I was due to offer peace offerings;*
Today I have paid my vows.
15 *"Therefore I have come out to meet you,*
To seek your presence earnestly, and I have found you.
16 *"I have spread my couch with coverings,*
With colored linens of Egypt.
17 *"I have sprinkled my bed*
With myrrh, aloes and cinnamon.

18 *"Come, let us drink our fill of love until morning;*
Let us delight ourselves with caresses.
19 *"For the man is not at home,*
He has gone on a long journey;
20 *He has taken a bag of money with him,*
At full moon he will come home."
21 *With her many persuasions she entices him;*
With her flattering lips she seduces him.
22 *Suddenly he follows her,*
As an ox goes to the slaughter,
Or as one in *fetters to the discipline of a fool,*
23 *Until an arrow pierces through his liver;*
As a bird hastens to the snare,
So he does not know that it will cost him *his life.*

[i]Prov 1:4, 22; 13:66

[j]Gen 38:14, 15
[k]Prov 23:27; Eccl 7:26; Judg 16:4–20
[l]Prov 9:13
[m]Comp. 1 Tim 5:13; Titus 2:5
[n]See Gen 39:7, 12; Jer 3:3

Solomon paints the deadly snare of the adulteress with a master's hand, and with exquisitely true coloring. A *young man lacking sense,*[i] in company with *youths* as *naive* as he, *goes to the harlot's house in the dark of the evening.* She *meets* him. Her *clothing;*[j] her *cunning;*[k] *her boisterous and rebellious voice;*[l] *her feet* at this late hour *do not remain* at home;[m] *lurking at every corner of the street;*[1] her *brazen face* and conduct—all are the harlot's.[n] She lures her victim with the garb of sanctity. She had just been taking part in special religious duties. Now she *had come out to earnestly seek* her lover, that they might feast together upon her *peace offerings,*[2] and *delight themselves with love,* with every indulgence. *The man* (her husband which might have awakened her conscience) *is gone on a long journey till the full moon.* Meanwhile, therefore, we can *drink our fill of love* without fear of interruption. Unarmed with principle, the weakness of resolution yields to the seduction of lust; and her unsuspecting prey rushes on to ruin.

[o]2 Sam 11:2
[p]Job 24:15; Rom 13:12, 13
[q]Prov 13:20; 1 Cor 15:33

Trace this sad ending back to its beginning. Wasn't this mischief caused by idleness?[o] The loitering evening walk; the untimely hour;[p] the vacant mind—all bringing the youth into contact with evil company[q]—wasn't this courting sin, tempting the tempter? The house was

[1] *Prov 9:14, 15; 23:28. Dr. Richardson mentions seeing "these wretched women in a large commercial town in Egypt, in the harlot's attire, sitting at the doors of their houses, and calling on the passengers as they went by, in the same manner as we read in the Book of Proverbs*—Travels, *vol. 1. p. 270.*

[2] *See HOLDEN. Comp. Lev 7:16; 19:6; Deut 12:6. Scott takes the same view—adding—"that it is no wonder, that these sacred ordinances should have given occasion to carnal indulgence, when our Christian festivals (Christmas especially) are abused for similar profanations."*

empty, and therefore ready for his reception, and soon it was altogether in his possession.[r] How valuable are self-discipline, self-control, constant employment, active energy of pursuit, as preservatives under the divine blessing from fearful danger!

[r]Matt 12:44, 45

See also the base varnish of religion. It is often a cover for sin![s] "She dared not play the harlot with the man till she had played the hypocrite with God, and stopped the mouth of her conscience with *her peace offerings*."[3] No—she seems to have made herself bolder in her wickedness, as if her meeting was a happy providence, the reward of her religious services.[t] Beware of any voice, though most respected, that plainly encourages forbidden indulgence.

[s]1 Sam 2:22; 2 Sam 15:8–11; John 18:28

[t]Verses 14, 15; 1 Sam 23:7; Zech 11:5

Observe also the infatuation of the snare. South says, "Man cannot be ruined till he has been made confident *to the contrary*. A man must get into his victim's heart with fair speeches and promises, before he can come at it with a dagger" (*Sermons*, 3.130). Thus the harlot's *flattering lips* chained the youth, blindfolded for destruction. As *the ox goes to the slaughter*, unconscious of his fate, perhaps dreaming of rich pasture: *or as a fool is locked in fetters*,[u] careless and unfeeling; so does this poor deluded victim rush on with pitiable mirth or indifference, *until an arrow pierces through his liver*.[v]

[u]Eccl 7:26; Judg 16:16–19

[v]Hos 4:11, 14

He hastens as a bird to the snare[w] thinking only of the bait, *not knowing it will cost his life*.[x] What will recollection bring, but the fragrance of exciting perfume,[y] changed into the bitterness of wormwood and gall; the short night of pleasure succeeded by the eternal night of internal torment—for a cup of pleasure drinking an ocean of wrath![z]

[w]Eccl 9:12

[x]Prov 9:18

[y]Verses 16, 17

[z]Verse 27; 9:18

Lastly—mark the danger of venturing into temptation. Could we expect any other results, when we saw the youth going the way to the harlot's house?[a] He intended merely to gratify his own idle pleasure; and when he yielded, it was probably not without some struggle. But it's a deserved judgment, that those who don't fear temptation should fall. Those who would avoid danger must avoid temptation to sin. And those who would avoid sin must avoid temptation to sin. He couldn't blame it on

[a]Prov 4:15; 5:8; Judg 16:1

[3] *GURNAL. It is a well-known fact, that the favorite mistress of Louis XIV was so rigid in her religious duties, that her bread was weighed during Lent, lest she should transgress the austerity of fasting.*

the force to which his own foolishness subjected him. When the first bounds of modesty are broken through, the door of the fancy is opened to the tempter for the kindling of desire. To rush into the very jaws of ruin is to "enter into temptation" by our own will, not to be led into it, or to fall into it, under the providential discipline and dispensation of God.[b] Self-confidence has ruined many a promising testimony. Tenderness of conscience, sensibility of weakness, dependence on divine strength and promise—in this frame "No one who is born of God sins; but He who was born of God keeps him and the evil one does not touch him."[c]

[b] Matt 26:41, with 4:1; James 1:2

[c] 1 John 5:18

24 *Now therefore* my *sons, listen to me,*
And pay attention to the words of my mouth.
25 *Do not let your heart turn aside to her ways,*
Do not stray into her paths.
26 *For many are the victims she has cast down,*
And numerous are all her slain.
27 *Her house is the way to Sheol—*
Descending to the chambers of death.

THE WAY TO HELL AND THE CHAMBERS OF DEATH

In the hand of a morally unrestrained poet or painter, this picture might defile the unholy imagination. But on the page of inspiration, it is God's solemn warning *to youth,* whether in years, understanding, or experience. *Now* that you have seen the end of sin,[d] *listen to me.* So that you *do not stray into her paths, do not let your heart turn aside.*[e] An impure thought, a polluted fancy, an idle book, filthy conversation, foolish company, theaters or places of empty pleasure—these are *her ways.* Dread the first step, and don't imagine that you can stop yourself in her course, just any time you please. Familiarity with sin weakens your hatred of it. Soon you will begin to love the thing you now hate. And what if you should find too late, that you have chosen her house for your home, which is *the way to Sheol, and to the chambers of death?*[4] Many victims not of the weaker kind, but

[d] Verses 22, 23

[e] Prov 4:23; 5:8

[4] *Prov 2:18; 9:18 The plural number (the ways, Heb) seems to imply "many other ways of guilt branching out, many other paths of ruin coinciding"—HERVEY'S* Theron and Aspassio. *Letter v. Schultens insists, that the present most wretched state, full of all horror and loathing, is included; so that the man who has entered the seducer's house, may be said to have entered alive into Hell, and gone down to the chamber of death—Prov 5:5.*

strong men has *she cast down wounded and slain.* And it's a miracle of almighty power and grace, that plucks the child of God from the brink of destruction.

So even the most established Christian shouldn't dismiss this subject as of no personal concern. It's true—"you have been raised up with Christ"; you have "set your mind on the things above";[f] "your life is hidden with Christ in God"; you are looking for the glorious hope of being with "Him in glory." It's to you, in whom "fleshly lusts, which wage war against the soul,"[g] that the exhortation is given—your earthly body is dead, therefore, your members that are upon the earth—even the worst members of the old man—*adultery, uncleanness, evil sensuality.*[5] And who, with the picture of the wounded and slain before him will revolt?—"Is your servant, who is but a dog, that he should do this great thing?"[h]—that he should need this warning? Look at the footsteps of the men who have gone in.[6] Whom do we see come out whole? "Behold, the two kings did not stand before him; how can we stand.?"[i]

[f]Col 3:1–4
[g]1 Peter 2:11
[h]2 Kings 8:13
[i]2 Kings 10:4

And don't let your present steadfastness or separation from temptation, blind your eyes to the possibility of yielding to the vilest sin. The eye of God sees a far deeper corruption that appears in the outer man—such total depravity, that even the affections planned for our greatest delight, lead to the most awful departures from purity and peace.

The gospel presents the only remedy. The love of Christ is the counteracting principle to the love of lust. If impure love solicits, remember the holy love of your Savior to you, proved by His most shameful death. Think of Him, as looking into your heart boiling over with corruption, showing you His wounds, and exciting you to an answering love of Himself.[j] The crucifixion of the flesh by a living union with Him will "keep us from our iniquity."[k] "How shall we who died to sin still live in it?"[l] "The flesh sets its desire against the Spirit."[m] But the man, who walks with God in gospel liberty, and Christian discipline and watchfulness, is safe.[n]

[j]Comp. 1 Cor 6:18, 20; 2 Cor 5:14
[k]Gal 5:24, with Ps 18:23
[l]Rom 6:2, 3
[m]Gal 5:17
[n]Rom 6:14, with 1 Cor 9:27

[5] *Col 3:1–5. Compare the exhortation to the flourishing Thessalonian church, 1 Thess 4:3–5; and to a Christian Bishop, 2 Tim 2:22.*
[6] *Samson—David—Solomon. Neh 13:26.*

But if sin isn't destroyed by these principles, sooner or later it will break out; if not, as here, to open disgrace; yet it will defile the conscience, "quench the Spirit,"[o] and by a sure, though perhaps unseen, course, bring soul and body to Hell—to the chambers of eternal death.[p]

[o] 2 Thess 5:19

[p] Rom 6:21; James 1:14, 15

CHAPTER EIGHT

1 *Does not wisdom call,*
And understanding lift up her voice?
2 *On top of the heights beside the way,*
Where the paths meet, she takes her stand;
3 *Beside the gates, at the opening to the city,*
At the entrance of the doors, she cries out:
4 *"To you, O men, I call,*
And my voice is to the sons of men.

Now we listen to the calls of heavenly Wisdom—to the voice of the Son of God.[1] Careless soul! Should God's call be slighted, when the charms of sin and vanity have had the power to catch your ear?[2] Can you plead ignorance? *Doesn't wisdom call?* and that—not in the hour of darkness, and in the secret corners, but in the high places—*the paths of the city*—the doors of your house? Hasn't she followed you to your places of business—or diversion—of sin? Hasn't she *lifted up her voice* in the Bible, in the family, in sermons? The loudness—the perseverance of the *call* shows earnestness in your friend and danger in your condition. For would she have cried so loud, or continued so long, if she had not loved your

[1] *We assume the speaker to be personal—Wisdom in its Being. Consider the following personal attributes: 1)* Personal existence—*"brought forth" (v. 24). 2)* Personal properties—*"everlasting" (v. 23); "master workman" (vv. 27–30); having "wisdom" and "power" (v. 14); having authority (vv. 15, 16, 32–36). 3)* Personal affections—*hatred (v. 13); love (v. 17); joy (vv. 30, 31).*
Whether or not Solomon fully understood the significance of his words may be a question, but receiving the words as from God (1 Peter 1:10, 11), and comparing them with other Scriptures, we do not doubt that they describe, not an attribute, but the Eternal and Omniscient Creator, Mediator, Savior.

[2] *Prov 7: "Imagination cannot form to itself a more exquisite and affecting piece of scenery, than that exhibited by Solomon in the Book of Proverbs. In his seventh chapter he introduces the world, by its meretricious blandishments, alluring the unwary to the chambers of destruction. In the succeeding chapter, by way of perfect contrast, appears in the beauty and majesty of holiness, the Son of the Father, the true and eternal Wisdom of God, with all the tender love and affectionate concern of a parent, inviting men to the substantial joys and enduring pleasures of immortality, in the house of salvation"—Bishop HORNE'S* Sermon on *the Tree of Knowledge.*

soul; if she had not known the wrath that was hanging over you?

The call is let loose; not to devils, but *to men;* not to the righteous, but *to the sons of men.* Therefore, every child, of guilty Adam has his name in the warrant. It's the proclamation of the gospel "to all creation."[a] Wherever the Word reaches, the offer is made. Wherever a lost sinner is found on this side of the grave, the free welcome of the gospel meets him. If he isn't saved, he is more lost than ever. His ruin lies at his own door.[b]

[a]Mark 16:15

[b]Matt 23:37

5 *"O naive ones, discern prudence;*
And, O fools, discern wisdom.
6 *"Listen, for I shall speak noble things;*
And the opening of my lips will produce *right things.*
7 *"For my mouth will utter truth;*
And wickedness is an abomination to my lips.
8 *"All the utterances of my mouth are in righteousness;*
There is nothing crooked or perverted in them.
9 *"They are all straightforward to him who understands,*
And right to those who find knowledge.
10 *"Take my instruction, and not*[3] *silver,*
And knowledge rather than choicest gold.
11 *"For wisdom is better than jewels;*
And all desirable things can not compare with her.

The great teacher (God) calls *the naive and fools to hear.*[c] And where else can they hear such *noble things?* They are worthy of the attention of princes—His glorious person; His everlasting covenant; His rich and sovereign love to sinners.[d] Often the truth of God, by the tradition of men,[4] or the subtility of the father of lies,[e] becomes virtually a principle of error.[f] But here *all* is unchangeable *righteousness.* There is no stubbornly wilful deviation from the normal. Every such wickedness is an abomination.[g]

[c]Prov 1:23; 9:4, 5

[d]Verses 12–31

[e]Comp. Matt 4:6, 7, with Ps 91:11

[f]Gal 1:7–9

[g]Prov 30:5; Ps 19:9; 33:4; 119:152, 160

[3] *Rather than silver. See next clause, and Comp. Hos 6:6.*

[4] *It was a keen reply of one of the martyrs, when asking of Bonner's chaplain—"Is not God's book sufficient for my salvation?" The answer was—"Yes, it is sufficient for our salvation; but not for our instruction." God send me the salvation, and you the instruction"—Exam. of Thomas Hawkes. FOXE, vii. 100.*

THE VOICE OUT OF THE WHIRLWIND

But are they within the reach of the multitude? They who "lean on your own understanding,"[h] who care more to be educated than to be holy; who value the tree of knowledge more than the tree of life; who desire "food according to their desire,"[i] rather than manna for their souls. Such, indeed, make difficulties for themselves. The voice "out of the whirlwind" rebukes them, as darkening "counsel by words without knowledge."[j] Scripture difficulties belong not to the Book itself, but to man's blind and corrupt heart. The carnal man can't understand it, any more than the blind can see the noonday light of the sun. But "it is easy to all that a desire to it, and which are not blinded by the prince of this world."[5] "The babes" are taught of God.[k] He not only unfolds the truth but opens their hearts to receive it. There will be, indeed, great depths. But they will grasp important, saving truths. Here "the wisest Solomon may fetch jewels for ornament, and the poorest Lazarus bread for life," said Bishop Reynolds on Hos 14:9. Come then—sinner—"be seated," with one of old, "at His feet"—your divine teacher.[l] *Take His instruction,* more precious *than silver or choicest gold.*[m] Enrich yourself with His satisfying and enduring treasures, compared with which all the things that may be desired are lighter than vanity.[n] And will not the children of God daily draw more abundantly from these treasures? Oh! let them not be like the pomp of this world, the object of gaze, but of active desire and increasing enjoyment.

[h] Prov 3:5; 1 Cor 1:20; 3:18
[i] Ps 78:18
[j] Job 38:1, 2
[k] Matt 11:25; 18:4
[l] Luke 10:39
[m] Verse 19; 16:16; Job 28:15–19; Ps 19:10; 119:127
[n] Prov 3:15

12 *"I, wisdom, dwell with prudence,*
And I find knowledge and *discretion.*

How adorable is the Being before us! His glorious perfections, each dwelling with the other in such harmonious combination! All the witty inventions of science are ultimately traceable to this heavenly source.[o] But His great mind was soaring far beyond. The vast discovery of man's salvation was now before His eyes;[p] found out, not by laborious investigation, but by the intuition of the infinite Godhead. Here is His most splendid display of *wisdom*[q] *dwelling with prudence—wisdom* contriving for

[o] Exod 31:3–6; 35:30–35; 1 Chron 28:19; Isa 28:24–29
[p] Verses 22–31
[q] Eph 3:10

[5] Reformer's Notes. *Comp. Prov 14:6; 17:24. "What wonder, if the unlettered and despised Christian knows more of the mysteries of Heaven than the naturalists, though both wise and learned? Christ admits the believer into His bosom, and* He *is in the bosom of the Father"—LEIGHTON'S* Sermon on Heavenly Wisdom.

the highest end: *prudence* directing the most effective means. The same perfect combination controls all His arrangements, both as the "head of the body, the church,"[r] and the "head over all things to the church,"[s] for her present good, and His eternal glory. And what do we owe individually, to "the riches of His grace, "by the removal of impossible difficulties, and the communication of suitable grace, "He lavished upon us. In all wisdom and insight!"[t]

[r]Col 1:18
[s]Eph 1:22
[t]Eph 1:7, 8

Prudence is commonly thought to be only a moral quality. Here we see it to be an attribute of deity. The humanity of our beloved Lord was filled with this perfection.[u] With what divine penetration of *wisdom* did He find out the knowledge of the inventions of His enemies, and put them to shame![v] And how this combination of caution restrained him from hasty confidence,[w] removed Him from premature danger;[x] and preserved Him from giving needless offense![y] Praised be our God for such "treasures of wisdom," hid in our glorious head, ready for distribution for every emergency of His people's need![z]

[u]Isa 11:2
[v]Matt 9:4–8; 22:15–46
[w]John 2:23, 24
[x]Matt 12:14–16; John 6:15
[y]Matt 17:27
[z]Col 1:19; 2:3

13 *"The fear of the LORD is to hate evil;*
Pride and arrogance and the evil way,
And the perverted mouth, I hate.

Such is the holiness of divine *wisdom!* She dwells with discretion. But she cannot dwell with evil. Therefore, the *fear of the Lord,* which is her very nature, is *to hate evil.*[a] So ... in speaking of *pride* in all its branches—*haughtiness* of spirit, *the evil way and the perverted mouth*—the Wisdom of God declares without reserve—*I hate them.*[b] How clearly He marked His *hatred* in the days of His flesh by the full exhibition of the opposite grace! "The Son of Man did not come to be served, but to serve."[c] A proud disciple of a lowly Savior! How offensive is this contradiction to our Master! What a cause of stumbling to the world!

[a]Prov 3:7; 16:6
[b]Prov 6:16–19; 16:5; Ps 45:7; Zech 8:17
[c]Matt 20:28; Luke 22:27

14 *"Counsel is mine and sound wisdom;*
I am understanding, power is mine.

This *counsel,* as we have just hinted,[d] is not, as with man, the fruit of deliberation, but divine intuition. It is not that it flows from Him; but that He is Himself the essence—the fountainhead.[e] It is not that He has under-

[d]See verse 12
[e]Isa 40:13, 14; Rom 11:34

standing to order and govern the world. He *is understanding*. All is in Him. All begins with Him.[f] "Great is our Lord, and abundant in strength; His understanding is infinite."[g] Therefore we adore Him—we rest in Him—as the great "counselor";[h] one with His Father in the everlasting plan of salvation;[i] one with His church, undertaking her cause,[j] guiding her in all her difficulties and perplexities.[k] His self-existent power is always ready to execute the purpose of His *counsel.*[l] Behold Him then, surrounded with the majesty of His mighty perfections—"Christ the power of God and the Wisdom of God."[m] In all your doubts and anxieties—counsel is mine, and sound wisdom.[n] In all your conflicts and weariness—I have strength.[o] See Him as man filled with these divine perfections.[p] Remember—His fullness is your portion.[q]

[f] John 1:9
[g] Ps 147:5; Isa 40:28; 26:4
[h] Isa 9:6
[i] Zech 6:12, 13
[j] Zech 3:1
[k] Isa 63:9–14
[l] Isa 63:1–6; Ps 89:19; Job 9:4; 12:13, 16; Dan 2:20
[m] 1 Cor 1:24
[n] Isa 48:17
[o] Isa 40:28, 29
[p] Isa 11:2
[q] 1 Cor 1:30; Col 2:10

15 *"By me kings reign,*
And rulers decree justice.
16 *"By me princes rule, and nobles,*
All who judge rightly.

NO POWER BUT OF GOD

Another glorious look at this divine person! He proclaims Himself to be the source of power and authority, no less than of *counsel and wisdom.* "KING OF KINGS" was the mysterious name written upon His garments.[r] Yet His crown does not take the place of the regal diadem from the brow of earthly princes; nor take their authority from them. These symbols of power are to be held, but in subordination to His own. *By me kings reign;* not only by my permission, but by my appointment. They bear my name. They are stamped with my authority.[s] Proud anarchy disputes God's authority, and traces it to the people; just so they can cast off the yoke of God, and "every man did what was right in his own eyes."[t] Scripture lays down the offensive truth—"There is no authority except from God, and those which exist are established by God." They are ministers of God, not servants of the people.[u] Government in all its administrations—kings, princes, nobles, judges—is a divinely-consecrated system.[6]

[r] Rev 19:16; 1:5; 17:14
[s] Exod 22:28; Ps 82:6; John 10:35
[t] Judg 17:6; 19:1; Hos 8:4; 2 Peter 2:10; Jude 8
[u] Rom 13:1–6

[6] *Ps 75:7; Jer 27:5–7; Dan 2:37, 38; 4:25; 5:18. Comp. John 19:11. It is interesting to trace this acknowledgment even in the darkness of heathenism. Kings inherited their scepter from Jove; magistracy was consecrated by augurs, the assessors and counselors of Jove.*

OUR REST—OUR ANCHOR

Every kingdom is a province of the universal empire of the "King of Kings." Men may mix their own pride, folly, and self-will with this appointment. But God's providential counterworking preserves the substantial blessing. Yet, if the power is *exclusively* of God, then is Wisdom, by whom kings reign, the very essence and person of God. And here is our rest, our anchor in this world's agitating storm. "The government will rest on His shoulders" of the head of the church.[v] All things—all power in heaven and in earth—is delivered unto Him of His Father.[7] "The Lord reigns; let the earth rejoice."[w]

[v]Isa 9:6
[w]Ps 97:1

17 *"I love those who love me;*
And those who diligently seek me will find me.

Now behold the grace of this divine person to his *loving* children. None by nature is interested in it.[x] But His free grace first implants *love* in their hearts, and then cheers them with the assurance of His own love.[y] The first kindling of the flame is of Him. We *love,* because we are drawn.[z] We *seek,* not by the impulse from within, but by the grace from above;[a] and who *seeks, finds.*[b] But it must be early seeking—the first desire and choice of the heart.[c] It must be early in the day;[d] the first-fruits of ou time. Consecrate everything to Him.

[x]Rom 8:7
[y]John 4:19; 14:21
[z]Jer 31:3
[a]Prov 16:1; Ps 119:32
[b]Isa 45:19; Jer 29:13; Matt 7:7, 8
[c]Prov 23:26; Ps 63:1; Hos 5:15; Matt 6:33
[d]Ps 5:3; 119:147; Isa 26:9; Mark 1:35

SEEK HIM FIRST

Make sure that God is the first person we speak to in the morning; that we see His face first before any other; otherwise our lamp will be untrimmed, our soul estranged from His presence, our heart unready for His service. Let it be the early breaking in of the day of grace;[e] the improvement of the first, who knows that they won't be the only, opportunities of salvation?[f] Every present opportunity for the soul is worth worlds. Mercy is in it—grace and glory are in it—heaven and eternity are in it. But remember, the door of grace, that is opened today, may be shut tomorrow—forever.

[e]Job 8:5–7; Isa 55:6; 2 Cor 6:2
[f]Prov 27:1; Heb 4:7

Again—this early seeking. Oh! let it be the early spring and morning of life[g]—when the eye is full of life and the heart of gladness. Let it be "the devotion of your youth,"[h]

[g]1 Kings 18:12; 2 Chron 34:3
[h]Jer 2:2

[7] *Matt 11:27; 28:18. Scott remarks the future tense in the original, as seeming to agree with the prediction of righteous kings and rulers in the latter times of the church. Comp. Ps 72:1–3; Isa 49:23; 60:16, 17. See the national blessing of godly rulers—2 Chron 9:8, Isa 1:26.*

the first love before it has been devoted to the world; before the hardening habits of sin have been formed and fixed. Is He not the greatest—the most desirable—the most satisfying good? Therefore, let Him be to us, as He deserves to be, the first of the first—the best of the best.

Children! Here is a special encouragement for you, added to the general one. It can never be too early for you. Even now it is too late. God has claimed you from the moment that you passed from unconscious infancy to the dignity of a responsible being. The time spent estranged from God has been all too long. Early devotedness saves from much foolishness and many mistakes, retracing of steps, and the after-misery of being made "to inherit the iniquities of my youth."[i]

[i]Job 13:26

EARLY SEEKERS FIND

Early satisfaction, the pure fruit of early seeking (for *who seeks, finds*) will be the joy of your whole life,[j]—the dawn of your blessed eternity. Remember—the bud and bloom of life is especially acceptable to God;[k] specially honored by Him.[l] But is it reasonable? No, it is a most humbling thought—to offer the flower of youth to Satan; and, when you have well-worn yourself out in his service, to reserve only the dregs and sweepings of life for your Savior?[m] Every day you lose a world of happiness; you bind a chain of sin; you take a step to Hell. Come, then, and answer the call that is drawing you to Him, who is worthy of all.[n] Never will you regret that you have come too soon. But many have been the sorrowing cries, "Lord, I have loved thee too late!"[o] Come, then, by His help, and in dependence on His grace make Him your first, your present choice. Lay claim by faith to this promise to early seekers, and you shall find.

[j]Ps 90:14, with verses 34, 35

[k]Hos 11:1–4

[l]1 Sam 2:18; 3:19; Ps 92:12–15

[m]Mal 1:8

[n]1 Sam 3:9; Ps 32:8; Jer 3:4

[o]Matt 25:6–12; Luke 13:24, 25

18 *"Riches and honor are with me,*
Enduring wealth and righteousness.
19 *"My fruit is better than gold, even pure gold,*
And my yield than choicest silver.
20 *"I walk in the way of righteousness,*
In the midst of the paths of justice,
21 *To endow those who love me with wealth,*
That I may fill their treasuries.

What a treasure early seekers find! This fading world is too poor a portion.[p] Theirs are durable riches of eternity[q] the *honor* of reigning as kings "in life";[r] a *righteousness*, in which they are accepted with God, and conformed to His image.[s] Is not this *fruit and yield better than choicest silver?*[t] And then when our way is shut up, how valuable is wisdom's counsel[u] so carefully *walking in the midst of the paths;* "at a distance from the extreme," said Scott,[8] on either side of the narrow way. The sober-minded Christian is equally remote from formal service and enthusiastic delusion. His grasp of truth is, alike, distinguished from the dryness of system, and from loose, unconnected principles.

[p]Ps 17:14, 15
[q]Matt 6:19, 20; Luke 10:42; Rev 3:18
[r]Rom 5:17; 8:17, Rev 1:6
[s]Rom 3:22; 13:14; Eph 4:24
[t]Verses 10, 11; 3:14, 15; Eccl 7:12
[u]Prov 3:6; 4:11, 12; 6:22; Isa 48:17; 49:10

THINGS THAT HAVE A MEANING

The intelligent and spiritually-minded churchman is, alike, separate from exclusiveness or idolatry on the one side, and from indiscriminate Christianity on the other. He values highly his scriptural ordinances; yet he neither mistakes them for the substance of the gospel, nor substitutes self-willed effervescence in their place. This is the Via Media—Christian unity, consistency, and fruitfulness. Here also is *wealth*—things that have a being, in contrast with things that have not;[v] solid realities;[w] "faith is the assurance of *things* hoped for."[x] Sin pardoned: the Father smiling acceptance; the comforter witnessing our peace; a new molding of our mind and spirit. Here is no yawning vacuum, but a grand object to give interest to life, to fill up every vacancy in the heart—"perfect happiness," said Cartwright. All that we could add from the world would only make us poorer, by diminishing that enjoyment of God, for the loss of which there is no compensation. There is one point, only one, in the universe, where we can look up, and cry with the saintly martyr, "With Thee, there is no disappointment" (*Journals*, vol. 2:130).

[v]Prov 23:5; Ps 39:6; 1 Cor 7:31
[w]Isa 29:8, contrasted with Isa 55:2
[x]Heb 11:1

Now contrast the portion in this life—of the men of this world. Mark how the Word of God pictures it—a fashion[y]—a dream[z]—a shadow with no substance[a]—a lie.[b] So, men are spread over the world, feeding "on ashes; a deceived heart has turned him aside."[c] The inlet

[y]1 Cor 7:31
[z]Ps 73:20
[a]Prov 23:5; Amos 6:13
[b]Jon 2:8
[c]Isa 44:20

[8] *Prov 4:25–27. See Bunyan's fine description of the middle path.*

of their misery is, that they walk in a vain shadow, and therefore "they make an uproar for nothing." The child of God finds wealth in returning to his true rest. Now, Lord, what do I wait for—"my hope is in Thee."[d] [d]Ps 39:6, 7

OUT OF HIS ROYAL BOUNTIES

But how does he get his portion? Is there any way in which he deserves it? Far from it. Free grace, not free will, is the obtaining cause. It is an endowment or "inheritance," now indeed "obtained," while the pledge is in hand;[e] but to be fully enjoyed at the great final day. Then, indeed, what God promises here, He will fully make good. His joyous welcome "to those on His right" will indeed be causing them that love Him to have better possessions[f]—eternal, unfading, and abiding.[g] Even now, from His royal bounty He fills their *treasuries*. But what a burst of joy at that day—what unbounded delight throughout eternity, when, endowing them with such a royal yes—divine bounty, the glorious giver shall proclaim—*I* will fill their treasuries![h] And the countless throng of the redeemed shall unite in the testimony—*one Christ hath abundantly filled us all!*

[e]Eph 1:11
[f]Heb 10:34
[g]Matt 25:34
[h]1 Peter 1:4, 5

22 *"The LORD possessed me at the beginning of His way,*
Before His works of old.
23 *"From everlasting I was established,*
From the beginning, from the earliest times of the earth.
24 *"When there were no depths I was brought forth,*
When there were no springs abounding with water.
25 *"Before the mountains were settled,*
Before the hills I was brought forth;
26 *While He had not yet made the earth and the fields,*
Nor the first dust of the world.
27 *"When He established the heavens, I was there,*
When He inscribed a circle on the face of the deep,
28 *When He made firm the skies above,*
When the springs of the deep became fixed,
29 *When He set for the sea its boundary,*
So that the water should not transgress His command,
When He marked out the foundations of the earth;

30 *Then I was beside Him,* as *a master workman;*
And I was daily His *delight,*
Rejoicing always before Him,
31 *Rejoicing in the world, His earth,*
And having *my delight in the sons of men.*

UNSEARCHABLE MYSTERIES

It must be a twisted imagination that dares to pry into mysteries, such as these. So glorious are the rays of eternal supreme deity, distinct personality, and basic unity, that the mysterious, ever-blessed Being—"In the beginning was the Word [Jesus Christ], and the Word was with God, and the Word was God. He was in the beginning with God"[i]—now undoubtedly stands before us. Curiously to pry into the nature of His previous existence would be intruding into things which "No man has seen or can see."[j] To receive His own revelation of Himself is our reverential privilege.

[i]John 1:1, 2

[j]Col 2:18; 1 Tim 6:16

How clear is His original and basic unity with the Father! The Lord possessed me—present with Him in the innermost being of deity. Every movement of the divine mind was known to the last detail—every purpose of divine counsel eternally present—fully developed, I was by Him[9]—in the same basic substance and blessedness.[k] Such was "the glory which I ever had with Thee [the Father] before the world was."[l] Neither man nor angel could declare it. No created intelligence could set one foot in the course, that realizes any general notion of the mystery. The mode of His existence in the Godhead (and this is all that is revealed of this mysterious subject) is: *I was brought forth*—the "only begotten Son"[m] [10]—a term which it is much safer to adore than to expound; expressing, as it does, what is unsearchable. "Take care,"—to paraphrase Michael Cope in *Exposition of Proverbs,* "that in this beginning of all things we invent nothing worldly, carnal, or human. But rather let us worship this beginning, seeing it by faith; and let us be careful about prying further into what Scripture teaches us

[k]John 10:30

[l]John 17:5

[m]John 3:16

[9]*John 1 and 2. Geier remarks, that out of above sixty instances, where this preposition occurs, not one can be produced, where vicinity is not supposed between two distinct persons or substances.*

[10]*John 1:18; 3:16; Col 1:15—"begotten before every creature"*—Bishop MIDDLETON.

here. Otherwise we should deserve to be blinded and punished for our great curiosity.

No less clear is His external existence—in the beginning[11] of the way of God—existing at the same time with His eternal counsels—before His works of old[12]—set up or anointed[13] from everlasting for His covenant offices;[n] "destined and advanced to be the Wisdom and Power of the Father, Light and Life, and All in All, both in the creation and the redemption of the world," said Henry.[o]

Connected with His eternity was His activity in the works of the Creation. Before those works were even begun, He was brought forth. But when they were in operation *I was there*—and that, not, like "the sons of God," an interested spectator,[p] but an efficient cause.[14] The whole detail of the creative work is brought out—the highest part or summits of the dust of the world, with its deep and unsearchable foundations. This is Wisdom (uncreated) on display in plain glory—"the divinity and eternity of Wisdom, that is, the eternal Son of God, Jesus Christ, our Savior," says *Reformers' Notes*.

[n] 1 Peter 1:20

[o] Comp. Eph 3:9

[p] Job 38:6, 7

UNSPEAKABLE COMMUNION

Next, he describes his unspeakable blessedness in communion with His Father. I was by Him, as one brought up *with* Him—sheltered in Him as the object of daily delight;[15] rejoicing before Him as the fountain and center of infinite joy. All this mutual intimate satisfaction and delight related to the beginning of the way of God—His eternal purpose, and the "counsel of peace, will be between the two offices."[q] There the Father once

[q] Zech 6:13

[11] *Holden strongly advocates the translation—supported by many ancient versions, and some of the best critics (see POOLE'S Synopsis)—"the beginning of the way"—and expounds it—"That Jehovah possessed by an eternal generation Wisdom or the Son, who is the origin, or efficient cause, of all the works of God"—Comp. Col 1:18; Rev 3:14, also 1:8; 22:13. Geier and other accredited authorities prefer the received version upon critical grounds. Holden's remark, however, holds good on either hypothesis:—"It is scarcely possible in the whole compass of the Hebrew language to select terms more expressive of the eternity of Wisdom than those which Solomon employs from this verse to the thirtieth."*

[12] *Contrast Job 38:4, 5. Comp. Prov 23–25, with Ps 90:2—the sublime adoration of the eternity of God. Comp. also Exod 3:14; with John 8:58; Mic 5:2; Rev 1:11.*

[13] *Heb. Anointing was the inaugurating ceremony in the consecration of prophets, priests, and kings—a figure of the eternal consecration of the Messiah to those high offices. Comp. 1 Kings 19:16; with Isa 41:1; 62:1; Exod 29:7; with Ps 110:4; 1 Sam 10:1; 16:13. 2 Kings 9:6 with Ps 2:6.*

[14] *John 1:3, Col 1:16. Even in the creation of man he was a co-worker, Gen 2:7, with 1:26.*

[15] *Comp. John 1:18*—the only-begotten Son, who is in the bosom of the Father—*"exhibiting at once," as Dr. Jamieson admirably observes—"the idea conveyed by both the terms—*brought forth, and brought up"—Vindication of Doctrine of Deity of Christ, *1. 224. Holden with some others prefers the rendering "Fabricator" for* brought up. *But the scope appears to be—not the power of the Messiah, but the mutual delight and communion between Himself and His Father, as it were, never absent from each other.*

and again proclaimed Him to be His delight; His elect, in "whom I upheld; my chosen one *in whom* My soul delights; . . . My beloved Son, in whom I am well-pleased";[r] "willing that by the Son we should approach to him; in the Son we should honour and adore him; and honour the Son as himself," said Scott.

[r] Isa 42:1; Matt 3:17; 17:5. Comp. Col 1:13

WHY WAS MAN'S FALL PERMITTED?

Yet how deeply interesting it is to see Him rejoicing, not only before His Father, but in the habitable part of the earth! And what was it that here attracted His interest? Man had been created in the image of God—free to stand or fall. This freedom was the perfection of his nature. His fall was permitted as the mysterious means of his higher elevation. His ruin was overruled for his greater security. This earth was to be the grand theater of the work, that should fill the whole creation with wonder and joy.[s] Here the serpent's head was to be visibly bruised,[t] the kingdom of Satan to be destroyed; "He will divide the bounty with the strong."[u] Here was the church to be framed, as the manifestation of His glory, the mirror of all His divine perfections.[v]

[s] Ps 98; Isa 44:23
[t] Gen 3:15; Heb 2:14, 15; 1 John 3:8
[u] Isa 53:12; Luke 11:21, 22
[v] Eph 3:10, 21

Considering the infinite cost at which He was to accomplish this work—it's a wonder, that He should have endured it—a greater wonder that, even before a single atom of the creation was formed—before the first blossom had been put forth in Paradise, He should have rejoiced in it.

THE WONDER OF ALL WONDERS

But the wonder of wonders yet remains—that He, who was His Father's infinite delight, and infinitely delighting in Him, should find *His delights* from all eternity *in the sons of men;* that He should, actually, long to be with us; that He should comfort His heart with the prospect; that He should look forward to the moment with joyous readiness;[w] that He should pass by the far nobler nature of angels and "gives help to the seed of Abraham"[x] to embrace man as one with His all-perfect self! Even though He foresaw how they would despise, reject, and put Him to shame; yet they were the objects of His everlasting love,[y] the purchase and satisfaction "of the anguish of His soul,"[z] the eternal monuments to His

[w] Ps 40:6–8; Heb 10:7
[x] Heb 2:16
[y] Jer 31:3
[z] Isa 53:10, 11

praise.[a] Yet for their sakes He made humanity a temple of God, for them He exchanged the throne of glory for the accursed cross[b]—the worship of the seraphim for the scorn and buffeting of men[c]—inexpressible joy for unknown sorrow.[d] Yes—adorable Redeemer, nothing but the strength of Your own love could have brought You out from the bosom of inexpressible delight to suffer such things for such sinners! But this was "the joy set before Him" for which—unfathomable love!—He was content to "endure the cross, despising the shame."[e] For this love You inherit Your Father's justly proportioned reward.[f] On this foundation is Your people's confidence—rest—security.

[a]Isa 55:13
[b]Phil 2:6–8
[c]Isa 6:1, 2, with Matt 27:22–31
[d]John 17:5, with Matt 26:38; 27:46
[e]Heb 12:2
[f]Phil 2:8–11

32 *"Now therefore, O sons, listen to me,*
For blessed are they who keep my ways.
33 *"Heed instruction and be wise,*
And do not neglect it.

HE IS WORTHY TO BE HEARD

Now therefore listen. It is no lowly, undeserving person that calls. It is none other than the Wisdom of God; the source of all light and knowledge;[g] the King of Kings;[h] the loving rewarder of His children, especially of His young children;[i] the rich portion and unfailing guide of His people.[j] Look at Him once again in his divine glory, as "the only-begotten Son of God";[k] the mediator in the everlasting councils of redemption;[l] the almighty Creator of the world;[m] the adorable friend of sinners.[n] How should His divine majesty and condescending love endear His *instruction* to us![16]

[g]Verses 12–14
[h]Verses 15, 16
[i]Verse 17. Comp. Heb 11:6
[j]Verses 18, 19
[k]Verses 22, 24
[l]Verse 23
[m]Verses 27–30
[n]Verse 31

PROMISED BLESSING FOR THOSE WHO OBEY

Yet His promised blessing belongs only to practical hearing—*to those who keep His ways*[o] with godly fear, constancy, and perseverance; keeping their eye *on* them, their hearts *toward* them, their feet *in* them. Such *are* truly *blessed.* They choose rightly; they walk surely; they live happily; they progress honorably; they end gloriously. Is it not therefore our *wisdom to hear instruction* with the obedience of faith—not doing what He commands—(in which we may sometimes do—not His

[o]Isa 55:2, 3; Luke 11:28; John 14:21–23; James 1:25

[16] *See how the Father manifested the glory of His divine Son to give constraining force to His instruction. Matt 17: 1–5.*

will, but our own) but doing *because* He commands—doing His will in it—obeying as well when it rubs us the wrong way, as when it is more congenial? But for this cheerful, childlike obedience, sovereign grace must open the heart, and give the ear.[p] The guilt of *neglecting* is inexcusable—a resolved will against the most gracious call.[q]

[p]Prov 20:12, with Acts 16:14

[q]Acts 3:22, 23; Heb 2:1–3

Now therefore, listen, O sons. Oh! happy moment, when the soul is made willing in the day of His power;[r] when the "bonds of love" are drawing[s] unto Him! The cold, dead indifference is gone. The enmity is slain. And who will not now joyfully swear loyalty; yes, count it His unspeakable delight to take such a yoke; to be bound to such a service, where there is nothing but for our good?[t] Oh, my Prince, my Savior! you have based your dominion on your blood. You have purchased your right by your cross.[u] You rule, only that you might save. Take to yourself the glory of your victory. I am thine—not my own—forever.

[r]Ps 90:3

[s]Hos 11:4

[t]Deut 10:12, 13

[u]1 Cor 6:19, 20; Rom 14:9

34 *"Blessed is the man who listens to me,*
Watching daily at my gates,
Waiting at my doorposts.
35 *"For he who finds me finds life,*
And obtains favor from the LORD.
36 *"But he who sins against me injures himself;*
All those who hate me love death."

WHEN THE HEART HEARS

This is the hearing of faith—the voice of Christ to the inmost ear—the impression of His Word upon the heart.[v] The effect is untiring effort and patient expectation; like the *priest* waiting *at the doorway* of the tabernacle for the assured blessing;[w] or the people *watching at the temple gates* for his return from his holy service.[x] This free and habitual attention to sacred practices indicates a healthy appetite for divine nourishment. The superficial professor excuses himself from this "how tiresome it is"[y] by the fear of legality, or the danger of overvaluing the means. But is there not at least as much danger of undervaluing the means, to which our gracious Lord has pledged His blessing?[z] In gazing on the heavenly Jerusalem, the apostle "saw no temple in it."[a]

[v]John 5:25; Rev 3:20

[w]Exod 29:42

[x]Luke 1:10, 21

[y]Mal 1:13

[z]Exod 20:24; Isa 56:7; Matt 18:20

[a]Rev 21:22

STAY CLOSE TO THE "FOOTPRINTS OF THE FLOCK"

But what right-hearted Christian will doubt that the lifeblood of his soul while on earth consists in *watching*, like the servants of the temple, *daily in God's courts*,[b] without neglecting imperative obligations. Wisdom's child will ever be familiar with *wisdom's courts*. The *weekday* as well as Sunday assemblies will be his delight. He will be most thankful for the services which invigorate him in the midst of the duties of his work-a-day world. He will frequently find himself near the way of the footsteps of the flock, "by the *tents of the Shepherd*."[c] And he would never hurt the feelings of his shepherd by willfully avoiding the well, when he comes to water his flock. He will find spiritual help in prayer, meditation, Scripture reading, and Christian fellowship. When that is no longer the case; when you find yourself satisfied with the usual routine; when the time between Sundays passes, week after week, and you don't have any appetite for spiritual things; when you don't even make any effort to strengthen yourself spiritually—Christian, doesn't that show that your spiritual life's pulse is beating feebly? Think now! Haven't you missed many a precious message from the Lord[d]—the fruit of your minister's special study, a word that applied to some particular need or weakness in your life, and which might have guided and comforted you to the end of your life? Oh, listen to your Lord's rebuke, "Be watchful and strengthen the things that remain that are ready to die?"[17]

[b]Ps 84:1, 4, 10
[c]Song of Sol 1:7, 8
[d]John 20:19, 24

See the *blessing* that comes down upon the Lord's waiting ones. They *find life*.[e] For He on whom they wait is the author,[f] the dispenser,[g] and the keeper of life.[h] "He therefore that hath him, hath life,[i] with all its present privileges of favor from the Lord.[j] "The smiles of God make heaven; and they that *obtain favor of the Lord*, have a heaven upon earth." said George Lawson in *Ex-*

[e]Isa 55:3; John 5:24
[f]John 1:4; 11:25; 14:6
[g]John 10:10
[h]Col 3:3; 1 John 5:11; Jude 1
[i]1 John 5:12
[j]Isa 64:5

[17] *Rev 3:2. "The places where the gospel is faithfully preached, are 'the gates, and the posts of the doors of Wisdom,' at which Christ would have His disciples to 'wait daily.' And may not Christians, consistently with other duties, redeem time for this waiting, as well as the children of this world find time for their vain amusements, who yet do not neglect* their *one thing needful? Is not the time spared from attending on a weekday, often spent in unprofitable visits or vain discourse? Ought ministers to be 'instant in-season, and out-of-season,' in preaching the Word; and ought not the people be glad for the opportunity to hear it?"—SCOTT.*

position of Proverbs. So, keep this expectation before your eyes in waiting on your God. "I am seeking *life* for my soul; I will *wait at the post of his doors,* missing no opportunity that will help me grow in grace; I shall not wait in vain," says the faithful Christian.

BEWARE OF SOUL-SUICIDE

If only the *sinner*—the thoughtless sinner—not the daring and ungodly only—would just stop to think how his heartless neglect of wisdom has wronged his own soul.[k] How cruel he is to himself, while he is despising his Savior. Every bait of sin is the temptation to suicide—to soul-murder. When men snatch at it, it's as though they are in love with damnation. *Those who hate me love death.* They love that which will be their death and put away from them that which would be their life. Sinners die, because they *choose* to die; and that leaves them inexcusable. It makes their condemnation more intolerable and will forever justify God when He judges. "*It is* your destruction, O Israel."[l]

[k] Prov 1:17–19, 31; 9:12; Jer 7:19; Acts 13:46; Num 16:38

[l] Hos 13:9

CHAPTER NINE

1 *Wisdom*[1] *has built her house,*
She has hewn out her seven pillars;
2 *She has prepared her food, she has mixed her wine;*
She has also set her table;
3 *She has sent out her maidens, she calls*
From the tops of the heights of the city:
4 *"Whoever is naive, let him turn in here!"*
To him who lacks understanding she says,
5 *"Come eat of my food,*
And drink of the wine I have mixed.
6 *"Forsake* your *folly and live,*
And proceed in the way of understanding."

We have delighted in looking upon the divine Savior in His glorious majesty, and especially in His wondrous love to *the sons of men.*[a] Here His love is poured out before us. The parable of the marriage-feast clearly identifies the speaker. Then the king made the feast and sent his servants to invite the guest.[b] Here *Wisdom* is a queen, according to Eastern custom, attended by her *maidens,*[c] and *she sends them out* to invite others to the feast. *She has built her house*—"the church of the living God"—firm upon the *pillars* of eternal truth.[d] The great sacrifice supplies her feast.[e] She *has prepared her food, and mixed her wine* with the choicest spices, and *set her table.*

[a] Prov 8:22–31
[b] Matt 22:1–4, also Luke 14:16, 17
[c] Exod 2:5; Esther 4:4
[d] 1 Tim 3:15; Eph 2:20–22; Heb 3:3, 4; Matt 16:18
[e] 1 Cor 5:7; Ps 36:8; Isa 25:6

INVITATION TO THE GOSPEL FEAST

And now she *cries to the naive,* ignorant of his danger,[f] and easily deceived[g]—*to him that lacks understanding*[h]—who is unaware of his need and has no desire for the blessing—*let him turn in here.* Here is a feast, not to see, but to enjoy. Come, eat of the food of life;

[f] Prov 22:3
[g] Prov 14:15
[h] Hos 7:11

[1] *Wisdoms. Heb. Comp. note on Prov 1:20.*

drink of the wine of gospel grace and joy.[i] Is there not besides a special invitation for her children—*a table* richly *furnished* for their refreshment; where they *eat of the food, and drink of the wine,* that the world does not know?[j]

[i]Matt 22:4; Isa 55:1
[j]Matt 26:26–28

But isn't everyone who comes, welcome to the gospel feast? The Master's heart goes out with every offer of His grace. His servants are ministers of reconciliation.[k] Their message is to tell of the wealth and plenty of the Messiah's house and to bid sinners welcome to Him. Here, sinner, is your authorization—not your worthiness, but your need, and the invitation of your Lord. All the blessings of His gospel are set before you—love without beginning, end, or change. Honor the freeness of His mercy. Let Him have the full glory of His own grace, who invites you to a feast, when He might have sent you to Hell.[2] Let His heavenly hope be enthroned in your soul, taking the place of every subordinate object from its hold on your affections, eclipsing the glories of this present world, absorbing your whole mind, consecrating your whole heart.

[k]2 Cor 5:18–20

THE WAYS OF PEACE

Here only are the ways of peace. The very severities of the gospel prepare the way for its consolations. But these blessings can never be valued, until you forsake the path of folly. You must *forsake* either them or Christ.[l] To abide with them, is to "rest in the assembly of the dead."[m] *To forsake them,* is the way of *life and understanding.*[n] Are they more to you than salvation? To be the friend of the world is to be the enemy of God. "Come out from their midst and be separate ... do not touch what is unclean; and I will welcome you ... says the Lord Almighty."[o]

[l]James 4:4
[m]Prov 21:16
[n]Prov 13:20; Ps 26:3–6; 34:12–14; 119:115; Amos 5:15
[o]2 Cor 6:17, 18

7 *He who corrects a scoffer gets dishonor for himself,*
And he who reproves a wicked man gets *insults for himself.*

8 *Do not reprove a scoffer, lest he hate you,*
Reprove a wise man, and he will love you.

9 *Give* instruction *to a wise man, and he will be still wiser,*
Teach a righteous man, and he will increase his *learning.*

[2] *Calvin speaks of the pleading invitations of Christ, as "His sweet and more than motherly allurements," and beautifully adds—that "the Word of God is never opened to us, but that He with a motherly sweetness opens his bosom to us." On Matt 23:37.*

THE RULE OF CHRISTIAN WISDOM

Wisdom's messengers must discriminate in the proclamation of their message. If *the naive* welcome it, the *scoffer and wicked* will rebel. Yet we must distinguish between the *ignorant* and the *wilful* scoffer. Paul "acted ignorantly in unbelief."[p] His countrymen deliberately refused the blessing and shut themselves out from the free offers of salvation.[q]

[p]1 Tim 1:13

[q]Acts 13:45, 46, 50; 18:6; Matt 10:14, 15

One cannot think of the scoffer without compassion. He cannot bear to commune with himself. Under an assumed gaiety, he would envy—as did Colonel Gardiner—the dog, his existence. "I hate life," said Voltaire, "yet I am afraid to die." Such is the bitterness of a soul linked with rebellion against God! Wretched indeed must he be, when the thought of God is an abomination, and when it is necessary to his peace to completely banish Him from his thinking.[r]

[r]Ps 14:1

Yet, in dealing with him, Solomon here gives us the rule of Christian wisdom. The gospel is a thing too holy to be exposed to scoffing fools.[s] Why should we *correct*, where more harm than good may be occasioned? Avoid irritations. Await the favorable opportunity. Sometimes a sad, serious, intelligible silence is the most effective reproof.[t] Whereas open *reproves* might stir up a torrent of *hatred*[u] and abuse;[v] and under provocation of spirit, the reprover might be insulted.[w]

[s]Matt 7:6

[t]Amos 5:13; 6:10
[u]Prov 15:12; 23:9; 1 Kings 22:8; 2 Chron 25:16
[v]Gen 19:9; Amos 7:10; Matt 7:6
[w]Isa 29:21

SPEAK THE WORD IN DUE SEASON

Yet this wisdom must not degenerate into cowardice and compromise the primary obligation to boldly rebuke sin;[x] and confess our Master.[y] Every sinner is not a *scoffer.* And "how delightful is a timely word," how good it is![z] That false show of distaste, therefore, which draws back from an unyielding profession, is treachery to our Lord, and deep—perhaps eternal—injury to our fellow-sinners. Hasn't each of us a tongue to speak? To permit any, therefore, to rush into perdition without opening our mouths to save them, is a sin of omission, which will cause a bitter pang to the awakened conscience.

[x]Eph 5:11; 1 Thess 5:14; 1 Tim 5:20; Matt 14:3
[y]Matt 10:32, 33; Acts 4:19, 20
[z]Prov 15:23

The wise and righteous man gladly encourages well-timed reproof.[a] Conscious of his own failings, he loves his reprover as a friend to his best interest;[b] and he would

[a]Prov 28:23
[b]Lev 19:17; Ps 41:5; 1 Sam 25:33; 2 Sam 12:7–14

receive *instruction* from the lowest, as a means of becoming *yet wiser, and increasing in learning.*[c]

[c]Prov 1:5; Exod 18:17–24; Acts 18:26

After all—it takes a lot of prayer to wisely give and humbly receive reproof. But where the mind of Christ is mutually exhibited, it cements a bond of the warmest affection.[d] "Faithful are the wounds of a friend."[e] Happy is that church which receives the loving admonitions of the Christian pastor with humility and thankfulness.[3]

[d]1 Sam 25:32–42
[e]Prov 27:6

10 *The fear of the LORD is the beginning of wisdom,*
And the knowledge of the Holy One is understanding.
11 *For by me your days will be multiplied,*
And years of life will be added to you.

THE CHILD OF GOD'S ONE DREAD, ONE DESIRE

The repetition of this significant sentence[f] deepens our estimate of its importance. *The fear of the Lord* was a lovely grace in the perfect humanity of Jesus.[g] Let it be the test of our predestination "*to become* conformed to the image of His Son."[h] It is the genuine spirit of adoption. The child of God has only one dread—to offend his Father; only one desire—to please and delight in Him. Thus is *the fear of the Lord* connected with His love. "The heart that is touched with the loadstone of divine love, trembles still with godly fear," Leighton said on 1 Peter 2:17. If this temper is *the beginning,* it is also (as the word signifies) the head—of wisdom—not only its first principle, but its matured exercise. It is obviously combined with *the knowledge of the Holy One.*[4] For if men only knew *His holiness*—"who will not fear, O Lord, and glorify Thy name?"[i] *Years added to life* was the reward in Old Testament times.[j] And truly the value of life is only realized in the *knowledge* and service of

[f]Prov 1:7; Job 28:28; Ps 111:10
[g]Isa 11:2, 3
[h]Rom 8:29
[i]Rev 15:4
[j]Prov 3:2, 16; 4:10; 10:27

[3] *2 Cor 2:1–9. Mr. Martyn—his biographer observes—"felt reproof to be 'a duty of unlimited extent and almost insuperable difficulty.' But, said he, 'the way to know when to address men, and when to abstain, is to love.' And, as love is most genuine, where the heart is most abased, he resolved not to reprove others, when he could conscientiously be silent, except he experienced at the same time a peculiar contrition of spirit"—Life, chap. 2.*

[4] *The parallelism with the former clause seems to demand this meaning. The application of the plural number to the sacred name is elsewhere used by Solomon (verse 1:1–20; Eccl 12:1) as well as by others of the inspired writers. Gen 1:26; Job 35:10; Isa 14:5. Compare the Hebrew of Hos 12:1; Josh 24:19. Bishop Horseley remarks—"God is the only Being, to whom the same name in the singular and in the plural may be indiscriminately applied. And this change from the one number to the other, without anything in the principles of language to account for it, is frequent in speaking of God in the Hebrew tongue, but unexampled in the case of any other Being." Sermon 29 on the Watchers. The reason of this peculiar usage, we may add, is obvious to any one, who receives with implicit and reverential faith the scriptural revelation of the divine essence.*

God. Inconceivably joyous to us is the prospect of *years of life* increased into a boundless eternity—infinite desires; fully satisfied, yet aroused unceasingly to more full and heavenly enjoyment.

12 *If you are wise, you are wise for yourself,*
And if you scoff, you alone will bear it.

The consequences of our conduct, good or bad, chiefly reflect on ourselves most of all.[k] God cannot be profited by us;[l] and He is far above any possible injury by us.[m] *The wise* man's light is a blessing to the church and to the world.[n] But he *is wise for himself*—for his own advantage.[o] *The scoffer* grieves his minister and is a stumbling block to his church. But he hurts no one so much as himself. *He alone will bear it.*[p] Jesus is there to stand liable for him, but his scoffing rejects Him. He sinks therefore into Hell under a millstone of guilt without remedy.[q] This then is the law of God. "For each one shall bear his own load . . . whatever a man sows, this he will also reap;" life or death—a double harvest—for time and for eternity.[r]

[k] Prov 16:26
[l] Job 22:2, 3; Ps 16:2; Luke 17:10
[m] Job 35:6, 7
[n] Matt 5:14, 16
[o] Prov 3:13–18; 24:3; Eccl 8:1
[p] Prov 8:36; Ezek 18:20; Luke 7:30
[q] Prov 39:1; Heb 10:28, 29; Lev 24:15
[r] Gal 6:5, 7, 8

13 *The woman of folly is boisterous,*
She is *naive, and knows nothing.*
14 *And she sits at the doorway of her house,*
On a seat by the high places of the city,
15 *Calling to those who pass by,*
Who are making their paths straight:
16 *"Whoever is naive, let him turn in here,"*
And to him who lacks understanding she says,
17 *"Stolen water is sweet;*
And bread eaten *in secret is pleasant."*
18 *But he does not know that the dead are there,*
That *her guests are in the depths of Sheol.*

Wisdom's free and gracious invitation has been before us. And we might almost ask—who could resist it? Now we have an allurement from the opposite quarter. For sin is no less anxious to destroy, than wisdom is to save. The distinct character of folly referred to, may be gathered from the pictures formerly given.[s]

[s] Prov 2, 5, 7

DON'T BE FOOLED BY THE SPARKLING CUP

Fleshly lusts are in open opposition to divine wisdom. "The delight of the soul fixed on anything but God and

His grace, is but spiritual adultery," said Diodati. *The woman of foolishness is loudly demanding,*[t] and, though "cunning of heart"[u] in the devices of Satan, she is *naive* in her utter ignorance of right. So fearfully do sensual pleasures darken the understanding, that the tempter, from the very habit of deceiving, becomes the victim of her own delusion![v] With a shameless front she dares to present herself *in the high places of the city,*[w] tempting, not only those who are going "the way to her house,"[x] but the inexperienced who are *going straight on their paths.* Thus, even the highway of God, though a path of safety,[y] is beset with temptation. Satan is angry with none so much as with those, *who are making their paths straight.* When Israel was in the straight path, quickly did He turn them aside by the golden calf.[z] And now enticements or assaults wait on every step. The temptation to open sin would be revolting. But must you give up all your pleasures? May not some *stolen waters,*[a] some *secret* indulgences,[b] be allowed? Ah! sinner, there is no such thing as *secret* sin. All is naked and open as day before the eye of God.[c] All will soon be proclaimed before the assembled world.[d] But the strength of this temptation is, that they are forbidden pleasures.[e] Restraint arouses the sleeping power of sin,[5] as children will do that which is forbidden, *because* it is forbidden. But what will be the end? Satan shows only the sparkling cup, and the glaring light. Ask to look into the inner chamber. The blinded fool hath wilfully closed his eyes;[f] otherwise he might *know that the dead are there; and that her guests*—the willful despisers of wisdom, are *in the very depths of Shoel.*[g] Reader, *the Wisdom of God* and the great deceiver of man stand before you. Both are wooing your heart; the one for life—the other for death. Both are intensely anxious for success. *Wisdom crieth. The woman of folly is boisterous.*[h] Both take their position in the high places of the city.[i] Both spread out their feast *for the naive* and ignorant,[j] smiling and happy on the brink of ruin. But how opposite their end? The one makes *the naive* wise unto eternal life. The other bears away her

[t] Prov 7:11
[u] Verse 10
[v] Hos 4:11; 2 Tim 3:13
[w] Gen 38:14, 21; Jer 3:2, 3; Ezek 16:24, 25, 31
[x] Prov 7:8
[y] Prov 10:9
[z] Exod 24:7, with 32
[a] Prov 5:15–17; 2 Sam 11:2
[b] Prov 20:17; Job 20:12–14
[c] Job 24:15; 34:21, 22
[d] Luke 12:1, 2
[e] Gen 3:1–6
[f] Prov 7:22; Isa 1:3; 2 Peter 3:5
[g] Prov 2:18; 7:27
[h] Verse 3 with 13
[i] Verse 3 with 15
[j] Verse 4 and 16

[5] *Rom 7:8; 1 Cor 15:56. See Augustine's description of his robbing the pear tree—not for the gain of the fruit (the greater part of which he threw away), but for the mere pleasure of sin* as sin—as breaking God's law. *Truly affecting also is it to see him, like the Psalmist (Ps 51:5) tracing the sin to its root—"Behold my heart, O lord, behold my heart, which thou hadst pity upon in the very bottom of the bottomless pit!"—Confess.* 3:4, 6.

willing captive into unutterable misery. Which voice arrests your ear and allures your heart? Which feast excites your appetite? Whose *guest* are you? Will you not open your eyes to the infatuation and pollution of this house of horror and death? Oh! remember that every listening to the enticement rivets your chain, rejoices your strong enemy, cheats you out of your present, no less than your eternal, happiness, and will banish you forever from the paradise reopened as your home. You may sink into the grave and perish. But it will be with the Savior's voice crying in your ears, "How long, *O naive* ones, will you love simplicity?"[k] The voice of mercy now warns you against estranging yourself from your God. But mercy is limited to time. Then justice, without mercy, will hold the scales with relentless severity, and the sentence of condemnation will bind you in the lost and damned kingdom of eternal death. What then is our heart's desire and prayer, but that the free grace and love of the gospel may draw and fix your heart; and that the Lord may preserve you from the tempter's snare, by keeping you closely walking with Himself.

[k]Prov 1:22

CHAPTER TEN

1 *The proverbs of Solomon.*
A wise son makes a father glad,
But a foolish son is a grief to his mother.

PROVERBS—WHAT THEY ARE

The former chapters have beautifully set forth in continuous discourse the nature and value of heavenly wisdom, contrasted with the fascinations of sinful folly. We now come to what are more properly (not excluding the foregoing)[a]—*The Proverbs of Solomon.* They are for the most part unconnected sentences, remarkable for profound thought, and acute observation expressed usually in two opposite phrases or illustrative form; the whole comprising a divine system of morals of universal application; a treasury of wisdom in all its diversified details, personal, domestic, social, civil. The previous chapters form a striking introduction to the book. The glorious description of God as the great counselor[b] commends to us His gracious instruction as the principles of true happiness and practical godliness.

Perhaps this first sentence may have been placed in the front, to point to the value of a godly education in its personal, social, national influence, connected both with time and eternity. We naturally look for rest in our children—the choicest gift of God.[c] Faith, indeed, may be tried, perhaps severely.[d] But the child, watched, prayed over, instructed, and disciplined, shall, in the Lord's best time, choose *wisdom's* paths,[e] and be the *gladness of his father's heart.*[f]

Many a *mother,* sadly enough, is chastened with the *grief* of a *foolish son.*[g] In such cases, has not indulgence, instead of wholesome restraint; pleasure, instead of godliness; the world, instead of the Bible—educated the

[a]Prov 1:2
[b]Prov 1:8
[c]Gen 5:28, 29; 33:5; Ps 127:3
[d]Eccl 11:1
[e]Prov 22:6
[f]Prov 15:20; 23:15, 16, 24, 25; 27:11; 29:3; Gen 45:28; 46:30
[g]Gen 26:34, 35; 27:26

child? Want of early discipline; passing over trifles; yielding when we ought to command—how little do we think to what they may grow![h] God has laid down plain rules, plain duties, and plain consequences flowing from their observance[i] or neglect.[j] To forget a daily reference to them; to choose our own wisdom before God's[k]—can we wonder that the result should be grief?[1]

[h] 1 Sam 2:24; 3:13; 1 Kings 1:5, 6; 2:25
[i] Prov 22:6; 23:13, 14
[j] Prov 29:15
[k] 1 Sam 2:29

2 *Ill-gotten gains do not profit,*
But righteousness delivers from death.

WHAT PROFIT IN EARTHLY GAINS?

The most substantial earthly *gains do not profit*[l] and neither do *gains of wickedness.*[m] Bishop Sanderson said, "A man may seem to *profit* by them, and to come up wonderfully for a time" (Sermon on 1 Sam 12:3). But what was the *profit* of Naboth's vineyard to Ahab, when in his "ivory house" he was withering under the curse of God?[n] What was the *profit* of the thirty pieces of silver to Judas? Instead of *delivering from death,* their intolerable sting plunged him into death eternal.[o] What else will be the fruit of covetousness, but shame,[p] disappointment,[q] and ruin?[r] "Flee from these things, you man of God; and pursue *righteousness.*"[s] This is "the breastplate,"[t] that covers the vitals in the fearful conflict. This is the pathway to eternal life.[u] This is the *deliverance* from the sting, the terror, the taste of death.[v] We must not flinch from this Scriptural statement from fear of legality. Lay the foundation of acceptance deep and clear upon the righteousness of Christ. But upon this foundation fear not to raise the superstructure of inherent *righteousness.* Take up the prayer and confidence of the man of God—"Let integrity and uprightness preserve me. For I wait for Thee."[w]

[l] Prov 23:5; Matt 6:19
[m] Jer 22:13; Ezra 7:19; Amos 3:10, 11; Hab 2:6–9
[n] 1 Kings 21:4–24, with 22:39
[o] Matt 27:5
[p] 2 Kings 5:23–27; Rom 6:21
[q] Jer 17:11
[r] Prov 21:6, 7; Josh 7:20–26; Dan 5:1–6
[s] 1 Tim 6:11
[t] Eph 6:14; 1 Thess 5:8
[u] Prov 12:28; Ps 15:24: 3–5; Isa 35:8; Matt 5:8
[v] Prov 11:4; John 8:51
[w] Ps 25:21

3 *The LORD will not allow the righteous to hunger,*
But He will thrust aside *the craving of the wicked.*

To spiritualize the temporal promises would be to lose great enlargement of faith. They are not restricted to Old

[1] *Bishop Lowth supposes an antithesis between the relative terms* (Prelim. Dissert. Isaiah), *which Bishop Jebb illustrates by the distinctive character of* the father's gladness, *whose affections are more disciplined, and* the mother's grief, *whose tenderness might blind her to the faults of her children, or lead her weakly to excuse them*—Sacred Literature, *Sect. ii. But, probably, this refinement of criticism is beside the meaning of the inspired writer, who interchangeably ascribes these exercises of feeling to both parents. Prov 17:24, 25; 19:13; 23:24, 25. Comp. Gen 26:35; 2 Sam 13:37–39. Comp.* Glass Phil. Sacr. *Lib. 4 Trace 2 Obs. 13. SCHULTENS.*

Testament times. If David was preserved from hunger, and that too by those most unlikely to help him,[2] Paul could also in similar trial set to his seal—"I have received everything in full, and have an abundance; I am amply supplied."[x] How does our gracious God double and redouble His engagements![3] He sends us to the fowls of the air for the confirmation of our little faith, "Are you not worth much more than they?"[y] "Yet the promises require faith, whereby we believe that God helps us," said Cope. He may for the exercise of faith allow us to hunger;[z] yet not to famish.[a]

[x]Phil 4:18
[y]Matt 6:25, 26
[z]1 Cor 4:11; 2 Cor 11:27, with Deut 8:3; Matt 4:2–4
[a]Ps 37:3; Isa 33:16; Matt 6:32

SAFE IN THE SHEPHERD'S FOLD

And doesn't His unfailing care for temporal provision convey the assurance, that *He will not allow the righteous to hunger?* "I am the good shepherd; and I know My own."[b] He seeks them out in the "cloudy and gloomy day," and brings them into His fold, where they "go in and out, and find pasture."[c] Awful indeed is the contrast of *the wicked—their substance cast out;*[d] themselves buried in the ruins of their own family.[e]

[b]John 10:14
[c]John 10:9; Ezek 34:12
[d]Job 20:15
[e]Ps 49:6; Luke 12:19, 20; 16:23

4 *Poor is he who works with a negligent hand,*
But the hand of the diligent makes rich.

Every day's observation confirms the fact, that *a negligent hand* leads to poverty;[f] and *the hand of the diligent enriches*[g] the harvest's lord. Actually the negligent person is deceitful; because he pretends to serve his master, when in truth he has been doing nothing.[h] He *becomes poor* by wasting his trust.[i] His life, which might have been a continual feast, is instead, a continual vexation. Wholesome, earnest work was the law of Paradise;[j] and though now it bears the stamp of the Fall,[k] it is overruled as a blessing; and in the ordinary course of God's care *makes rich.*[l]

[f]Prov 19:15; 20:4; 23:21; 24:30–34; Eccl 10:18
[g]Prov 13:4; 21:5
[h]Matt 25:26; Jer 48:10
[i]Prov 18:9. Comp. Matt 25:28, 29
[j]Gen 2:15
[k]Gen 3:19
[l]Prov 12:24, 27; 22:29

OUR IDLE TIME—THE DEVIL'S BUSY TIME

The Lord's visits of favor were never given to loiterers. Moses and the shepherds of Bethlehem were keeping their flocks.[m] Gideon was at the threshing floor.[n] "*Our idle* days," Bishop Hall observes, "are Satan's busy days." Active employment gives us a ready answer to his

[m]Exod 3:1, 2; Luke 2:8, 9
[n]Judg 6:11

[2] *By Shobi the brother of his bitter enemy. 2 Sam 17:27, with 10:4. Machir also of the house of Saul. 2 Sam 9:4. Comp. Ps 37:25.*
[3] *Heb 13:5; five negatives in the original.*

present temptation—"I am doing a great work and I cannot come down."[o]

[o]Neh 6:3

Are the Christian's reserve supplies getting low? Hasn't there been a *negligent hand* in using the sacred treasury? Hasn't he looked upon the heavenly treasures, but has none for himself?[p] Hasn't he *become poor* by slighting his rich comforts? The Lord gives His blessing, as He gives the fruits of the earth, not to those that wish[q] but to those that "work";[r] not to sentimental idolence, but to Christian energy and perseverance. The trade of the world is uncertain. The trade of godliness is sure. There are no bankrupts here. The diligent servant is honored with an increase of his grace,[s] and the enlargement of his confidence.[t]

[p]Prov 19:24
[q]Prov 13:4; 20:4
[r]Verse 3 with 4; John 6:27
[s]Matt 25:29
[t]2 Peter 1:5–11; 1 Cor 7:24

5 *He who gathers in summer is a son who acts wisely,*
But *he who sleeps in harvest is a son who acts*
shamefully.

IMPROVE YOUR PRESENT OPPORTUNITIES

Laziness has just been contrasted with diligence. Forethought is here opposed to lack of foresight.[u] The importance of opportunity is practically admitted in temporal matters.[v] Joseph *wisely gathered in summer and harvest* for the coming need.[w] The woman of Canaan[x] and the blind men[y] improved their present opportunities. *So also will the wise son* gather his blessing at the right time. The freshness of youth is a summer harvest. It is as much the will of God, that the young should gather knowledge, as that the farmer should gather his harvest. The *wise gathering in this summer* gives substance, vigor, high-tone, and power of usefulness in afterlife! How often may we trace poverty of mind, weakness of character, unprofitable habits, to *sleeping* in this fruitful *harvest!* "He who idles away the time of his youth will bear the shame of it when he is old," said Henry.[4] Specially looking at this, as the season of Christian instruction, anxious promise, our Father's pleading time with the wayward heart;[z] before it becomes hardened in

[u]Prov 6:6–8
[v]Ecc 3:1; 8:5
[w]Gen 41:46–56
[x]Matt 15:22–28
[y]Matt 20:30
[z]Jer 3:40

[4] *See Bishop HORNE'S* Sermon on the Redemption of Time. *Sir Walter Scott's testimony in his Autobiography is most instructive—"If it should ever fall to the lot of youth to peruse these pages, let such a reader remember, that it is with the deepest regret that I recollect in my manhood the opportunities of learning which I neglected in my youth; that through every part of my literary career I have felt pinched and hampered by my own ignorance; and that I would at this moment give half the reputation I have had the good fortune to acquire, if, by doing so, I could rest the remaining part upon a sound foundation of learning and science."*

habits of sin—is not the *sleeper in such a harvest, a son* that causes shame? Look also at the large harvest of opportunity in laboring for God—the great and diversified machinery of Christian organizations, needing guidance and help; the throngs of fellow-sinners around us, claiming our sympathy and helpfulness—"While we have opportunity, let us do good."[a]

[a]Gal 6:10

ANY BANKRUPTS HERE?

How high is the privilege of laboring with Christ in such a harvest![b] How great the *shame* of doing nothing, where there is so much to be done! What a harvest also is the present "acceptable time"![c] Mark the abundance of the means of grace, the living freshness of the gospel. The Bible opens the way. The Savior invites. The Holy Spirit strives with the conscience. The Lord's Day is a golden gathering time for the week. It draws us aside from the world; it is filled with the peace, joy, and hope of heaven. Now, am I diligently improving this harvest? Or am I *sleeping*—perhaps in the very house of God—instead of listening to the voice from heaven—*a shame* to my minister, to my church, to my Lord?

The Lord preserve me from the ruin of *sleeping*[d] away the invaluable hours of "the day of salvation"![e] Can I bear the thought of that desponding cry of eternal remorse—"*Harvest* is past, *summer* is ended, and we are not saved"?[f]

[b]Matt 12:30
[c]2 Cor 6:2
[d]Matt 25:5. Comp. Isa 55:6; Luke 13:28, 29; Prov 1:24–28
[e]2 Cor 6:2
[f]Jer 8:20. Comp. Prov 5:11–13

6 *Blessings are on the head of the righteous,*
But the mouth of the wicked conceals violence.
7 *The memory of the righteous is blessed,*
But the name of the wicked will rot.

AFFLICTIONS, YES!—
BUT ALL KINDS OF BLESSINGS, TOO!

Is not affliction the lot of the righteous?[g] Yet how abundantly is it compensated by the *blessings that are upon his head*[h]—blessings temporal[i] and spiritual;[j] from man[k] and from God.[l] His very *memory is a blessing* to his family and to the church.[m] Fragrant is faith "for by it the men of old gained approval" and were immortalized in the Apostolic Book of Martyrs.[n] Truly blessed is the memory of a godly parent;[o] of a faithful minister;[p] of a

[g]John 16:33; Acts 14:22; 2 Tim 3:12
[h]Prov 28:20; Gen 49:26
[i]Deut 28:1–6; 1 Tim 4:8
[j]Isa 32:17
[k]Prov 16:7; Job 29:11–13
[l]Ps 3:8; 5:12; Isa 64:4, 5; Matt 5:3–12
[m]Ps 112:6
[n]Heb 11:2
[o]Prov 31:28
[p]Heb 13:7

righteous king;[q] of a public benefactor;[r] of a self-denying Christian.[5]

[q]2 Chron 35:24, 25
[r]2 Chron 24:6

No such honor belongs to *the wicked*. Violence is concealed by their mouth[s] and marks them for condemnation,[t] as they will all be so marked at the day of retribution.[u] And even now *their memory rots* in corruption. Contrast the memory of the man after God's heart, with that of "Jeroboam the son of Nebat";[v] or in later times, Ridley and Latimer with the *name of their wicked* persecutors. Such is *the blessing* and curse of God, long after the men had passed into eternity. "Thou mayest choose," said godly Bishop Pilkington, "whether thou wilt be remembered to thy praise or thy shame" *(Works,* Parker Society, p. 366).

[s]Ps 107:42
[t]Esther 7:8; Job 9:24; Rom 3:19
[u]Job 18:17; Ps 49:11, 12; 109:13; Eccl 8:10; Isa 65:15; Jer 22:18, 19; 29:22, 23
[v]1 Kings 11:26; 14:14–16; 2 Kings 14:3

8 *The wise of heart will receive commands,*
But a babbling fool will be thrown down.

COMMANDMENTS FROM HEAVEN

The *heart* is the seat of true *wisdom,* and a teachable spirit is the best proof of its influence. For which of us, who knows himself, would not be thankful for further light? No sooner, therefore, *do the commands* come down from Heaven, than the well-instructed Christian eagerly reaches out to receive them, like his father, with unquestioning simplicity;[w] welcomes the voice of his heavenly teacher;[x] and, when he knows that "it is the Lord . . . put his outer garment on" with all the ardor of the disciple to be found at His feet.[y]

[w]Heb 11:8; Gen 22:1–3
[x]1 Sam 3:10; Acts 10:33; Ps 27:8; 86:11; 143:10
[y]John 21:7

But look at the pretender, who merely professes to have religion, and is totally without this heart-felt wisdom. We find him a man of creeds and doctrines, not of prayers, asking strange questions, rather than listening to plain truths;[z] wanting to know events rather than duties; occupied with other men's business, while neglecting his own.[a] In this wandering spirit, with all his thoughts outward bound, he wanders from church to church, and from house to house, *a babbling fool* upon religion; bold in his own conceit,[b] while his life and temper fearfully contradict his fluent tongue. Too blind to respect him-

[z]John 21:21, 22
[a]Luke 13:23, 24; 1 Tim 5:13
[b]3 John 10

[5] *Mark 14:9. "No spices can so embalm a man; no monument can so preserve his name and memory, as a pious conversation, whereby God has been honoured, and man benefited. The fame of such a person is, in the best judgments, far more precious and truly glorious, than is the fame of those, who have excelled in any other deeds or qualities"—BARROW's Sermons.*

[c]Prov 18:2
[d]Verse 17; 15:32

[e]Prov 18:6, 7; Eccl 10:12; 2 Kings 14:8–14

self,[c] too proud to listen to counsel,[d] he will surely *be thrown down* into disgrace, beaten with the rod of his own foolishness.[e] Let me look at this picture as a beacon against the foolishness of my own heart. Young Christian! beware of a deceitful and empty religion, without humility, consistency, and love, because it is separated from a close walk with God.

9 *He who walks in integrity walks securely,*
But he who perverts his ways will be found out.

[f]Job 1:8
[g]Gen 17:1

[h]Prov 2:7; Ps 84:11;
[i]Prov 1:33; Eccl 8:5; Isa 33:15, 16
[j]Ps 24:3–6
[k]1 John 3:18–22
[l]Ps 37:37; Isa 57:1, 2

[m]Dan 3:21–29

A *walk in integrity* is Christian, not sinless, perfection;[f] "walk before Me [God]," not before man.[g] Impurity indeed defiles the holiest activity. But if the will is rightly bent, the integrity will be maintained. "Show me an easier path," nature cries. "Show me," cries the child of God, "a *secure* path." Such is *the walk in integrity* under the shield of the Lord's protection,[h] and provision and care;[i] under the shadow of His promises;[j] in the assurance of His present favor,[k] and in its peaceful end.[l] There will be difficulties. But a deliverance will be worked out through them; as the Babylonian captives were delivered through the fire from the infinite greater danger of apostasy.[m]

HERE'S HOW FOR SELF-ASSURANCE

[n]Gal 2:14

[o]Acts 5:31

[p]1 Cor 10:31; Col 3:17

From the lack of *this walk in integrity*, Peter denied the foundation of the gospel.[n] Learn then the value of this principle for an enlightened and full reception of the truth; that we may welcome "a Prince and a Savior;"[o] combine His sceptre with His sacrifice, His holy rules with His precious promises; and prove the influence of a vital faith in godly practice. In this way, we carry out the rule of the gospel into everything, making God the master of every thought, word, temper, motive, no less in our secular calling than in our spiritual devotedness.[p] Such a *walk in integrity* will bring a happy self-assurance. A paraphrase of Barrow is "The man, conscious to himself of an honest meaning, and a due course of prosecuting it, feels no check or struggling of mind, no regret or sting of heart. He therefore briskly moves forward with courage, with nothing within him to cause him to stop, to distract or disturb him."

HOW TO LOSE YOUR SELF-CONFIDENCE

But to bend our rule to suit our own fancy; to pervert our *ways* to escape trouble, or for some other self-centered end, will shake our confidence far more than the heaviest cross. The eye of God *knows* the straying already[q] and will bring it to shame.[r] So Jacob was chastened to the end of his days.[s] Peter was openly rebuked.[t] Judas[u] and Ananias[v] are known in the records of the church as a beacon to the end of time. "May my heart be blameless in Thy statutes, That I may not be ashamed. . . . I shall walk in my integrity; Redeem me, and be gracious to me."[w]

[q]John 6:70, 71
[r]Luke 12:1, 2; 1 Tim 5:24
[s]Gen 27, with 42:36–38
[t]Gal 2:11–14
[u]Matt 27:3–5
[v]Acts 5:1–10
[w]Ps 119:80; 26:11

10 *He who winks the eye causes trouble,*
And a babbling fool will be thrown down.

The contrast meant here seems to be between the man who brings trouble on his fellow-creatures and one who brings it upon himself. Mischievous sport indeed is it to *cause trouble* for selfish gratification;[x] to make the eye an instrument of wilful sin.[y] Scarcely less moving is it to see the tongue a world of *foolishness.* But not a trace is visible of the likeness in which man was first created. Every member is turned from its proper use and glorious end. Man is a plague to his neighbor, because he is an enemy to his God. And because "*fools* despise wisdom,"[z] they *will be thrown down* and the victim of their own foolishness.

[x]Verse 23; 26:18, 19
[y]Prov 6:13; Ps 35:19
[z]Prov 1:7

11 *The mouth of the righteous is a fountain of life,*
But the mouth of the wicked conceals violence.

INCREASE YOUR SPIRITUAL RESERVES

The indwelling Spirit—"a well of water springing up to eternal life"—is the glorious privilege of *the righteous.*[a] So, *his mouth,* replenished from the heavenly source, is *a fountain of life,* sending forth refreshing waters.[b] The precious talent of speech is in this way consecrated to His service, who made man's mouth. Wit, originality, imagination may furnish the feast of reason, and the flow of soul. But how poor is this pleasure compared with the godly instruction—perhaps with little intellectual attraction—that pours forth from a *fountain of*

[a]John 4:14; 7:38
[b]Prov 16:23

[c]Verse 21; 15:7; Eph 4:29

life! Servant of God! Honor your high privilege of ministering such a blessing to the church.[c] Enlarge its exercise by increasing your spiritual store and walking in closer fellowship with your God. What do you owe to His grace, who hath made *your mouth a fountain of life;* while *the violence of the wicked* falls back upon themselves, and covers their mouth with confusion?

12 *Hatred stirs up strife,*
But love covers all transgressions.

BEWARE OF THE UNDERGROUND FIRE!

[d]Titus 3:3

[e]Isa 29:21

[f]Prov 15:18, 16:27, 28:25; 29:22

[g]Prov 17:9; Gen 45:5–8

[h]Gen 9:23

[i]Matt 18:21

[j]Matt 18:22–35

A simple but forcible contrast! *Hatred,* however varnished by smooth pretense, is the selfish principle of man.[d] Like an underground fire, it continually *stirs up* mischief, creates or keeps alive resentful coldness, disgusts, dislikes, envyings and evil surmisings; finds fault with the infirmities of others; aggravates the least slip;[e] or resents the most trifling, or even imaginary, provocation. These *strifes* are kindled[f] to the great dishonor of God and the marring of the beauty and consistency of the gospel. Is there not here abundant matter for prayer, watchfulness, and resistance? Study 1 Cor 13 in all its detail. Let it be the looking glass for our hearts and the standard of our profession. *Love covers,* overlooks, speedily forgives and forgets.[g] Full of candor and inventiveness, it puts the best construction on doubtful matters, searches out ways to make excuses for another's unpleasant actions, does not rigidly eye or arrogantly expose a brother's faults;[h] nor will it uncover them at all, except insofar as it may be needful for his ultimate good. To refrain from vile slander, when there's plenty of opportunity for needless and unkind gossip, is not *covering transgressions.* Nor is the seven-times forgiveness the true standard of love,[i] which, like its divine author, *covers all transgressions.* And who does not need the full extent of this *covering?* What is our brother's worst against us, compared with the way we've treated God? And how can we, who look *for the covering* of the debt of thousands of dollars, hesitate to forgive a few pennies someone owes us?[j] Oh! let us "put on the Lord Jesus" in

His spirit of long-suffering, impartial, sacrificing love—"Just as the Lord forgave you, so also should you."[6]

13 *On the lips of the discerning, wisdom is found,*
But a rod is for the back of him who lacks understanding.

Solomon and his son admirably illustrate this contrast. *Such wisdom was found on his lips*—the fruit of an *understanding*[k] heart—that "his fame was *known* in all the surrounding nations."[l] And those, who stood before him, and heard his "*wisdom,*" were justly said to be very happy.[m] Rehoboam was as lacking in understanding, as his father was full of it. His foolishness prepared *a rod for his back.*[7]

[k]1 Kings 3:12
[l]1 Kings 4:31; 10:1
[m]1 Kings 10:8

WHERE TO LOOK FOR WISDOM

Learn then to seek for *wisdom* at the lips of the wise.[n] The lack of this wisdom, or rather the want of *a* heart to seek it, will surely bring us under *the rod.* Often, in discipline, we'll feel its pain—for our laxity in raising our children;[o] for the neglect of family discipline;[p] for fleshly indulgence.[q] And how different is this *rod* from our Father's loving chastisement! That—the seal of our adoption[r]—this the mark of disgrace.[s] Will not the children of God cry—"Turn away my reproach which I dread, For Thine ordinances are good."[t]

[n]Prov 10:11, 21; 13:20; 15:7
[o]Prov 29:15
[p]Prov 29:21
[q]2 Sam 12:9–11
[r]Prov 3:11, 12; Heb 12:6, 7
[s]1 Peter 2:20
[t]Ps 119:39

14 *Wise men store up knowledge,*
But with the mouth of the foolish, ruin is at hand.

STORE UP KNOWLEDGE

Did Solomon prove his title as *a wise man* by his diligence *in storing up knowledge?*[u] No wonder that *wisdom is found in the lips,* where "the mouth speaks out of that which fills the heart."[8] It is "a householder" storing his mind not for selfish gratification, but for liberal and useful distribution.[v] If the storing up of wisdom is learned

[u]Eccl 12:9, 10
[v]Matt 13:52

[6] *Col 3:13. Comp. 1 Peter 4:8. The first clause of the verse, compared with the apostle's application of the second, clearly proves that the subject is* the covering *of our brother's* sin *before men. Este—one of the most evangelical of the Roman interpreters—thus limits the application. The gloss, therefore, of man's covering sins before God is utterly groundless. Comp. Prov 17:9. Calvin and Geier conceive James 5:20, to be only an allusion to the Prov. The latter adds—"It is one thing to cover sin before men; another thing to cover it before God. The first is the act of love. 1 Cor 13:4; Gal 6:2. The last requires an infinite price, equal to the turning away of the eternal wrath of God." Rom 3:25; 1 John 1:7; Ps 32:1.*

[7] *1 Kings 12:13–24. Comp. Prov 19:29; 26:3. The rod was the usual corporal punishment under the Mosaic law. Deut 22:18; 25:2, 3.*

[8] *Matt 12:34. Jerome mentions of his friend Nepotian, that, "by daily reading and meditating in the sacred volume, he had made his soul a library of Christ"*—Letter to Nepotian.

and practiced in youth,[w] what a store of valuable treasure he would have laid up! Yet even all that will be little enough to meet the coming trial. We need to add something every day to our storehouse of wisdom. The supply from which to draw is so inexhaustible, that no doubt, difficulty, temptation, or duty needs to be unprovided for!

Wise men store up knowledge, for their own use. *Fools* lacking true wisdom, only open their mouths to their own harm, in blasphemous rebellion;[x] selfishness;[y] ungodly worldliness;[z] or hateful pride[a]—*near to destruction.*[b] How *near*—who can say? But if they are not taken away with a stroke without remedy;[c] they only stand out as monuments of the much long-suffering of God who "endured with much patience vessels of wrath prepared for destruction."[d]

15 *The rich man's wealth is his fortress,*
The ruin of the poor is their poverty.

CITY WITHOUT WALLS

This is as it appears on the surface. The *rich man's wealth* fences him from many invading evils,[e] obtains for him influence and respect,[f] and defends him against many sorrows.[g] Thus, "in his own imagination" it is *his fortress.*[h] So prone are we to rest on the creature as the stay and comfort of life.[i] All notions of God are blotted out, and man becomes a god to himself. *The poor,* having no such defense, dwell as in a city without walls, exposed to every assault.[j] "Poverty will come in like a vagabond . . . your need like an armed man"[k] and sinks the spirit in dismay.

How secure—how happy then—we are ready to say—are the rich! How wretched the condition of the poor! But the glass of God's Word discovers a more equal balance. "Did not God choose *the poor* of this world to be rich in faith and heirs of the kingdom?"[l] Think of Jesus sanctifying the state of poverty by His own blessed example.[m] Think of the riches of His grace, raising the poor out of the dunghill, that He may set Him with the princes of His people.[n]

Both states, however, have their besetting temptations, needing special grace.[o] The safety of both is, when the

[w] Prov 6:6; 18:1, 15
[x] Exod 5:2; Ps 12:3–5; 52:1–5
[y] 1 Sam 25:10, 11, 38
[z] Luke 12:18–20
[a] Acts 12:21–23
[b] Prov 12:13; 13:3; 18:7; Eccl 10:12, 13
[c] Job 36:12
[d] Rom 9:22
[e] Eccl 7:12
[f] Prov 19:4, 6; Gen 23:6
[g] Eccl 10:19
[h] Prov 18:11
[i] Ps 49:6; 62:10; Jer 9:23; 1 Tim 6:17
[j] Prov 14:20; 19:7; 22:7; John 7:48, 49
[k] Prov 6:11
[l] James 2:5; Zeph 3:12
[m] Luke 2:7–12; 4:22; 8:3; Matt 8:20
[n] Ps 113:7, 8; 1 Sam 2:8
[o] Prov 30:8, 9

rich are poor in spirit[p] and large in heart; and *the poor* rich in faith, and contented with the gain of godliness.[q] "Let the brother of humble circumstances glory in his high position; and let *the rich* man *glory* in his humiliation."[r]

[p] 1 Chron 19:14
[q] Job 1:21; 1 Tim 6:6–8
[r] James 1:9, 10

16 *The wages (AV—labor) of the righteous is life,*
The income of the wicked, punishment.

GLOWING CONFIDENCE

Labor, not idleness, is the mark of a servant of God: and so, the Christian is cheered by the glowing confidence, that it moves toward life.[s] "Do business *with this* until I come *back* . . . do all to the glory of God."[t] This is the standard. So, even the duties of our daily calling are *life*.[u] God works in us, by us, with us, through us.[v] We work in and through Him. Our labor therefore is His work—wrought in dependence on Him; not for life, but *to life*.[w] And this is life indeed; the only exercise deserving the name; the only object worth living for.[x] Lord! quicken us to *life* more abundantly.[y] And sowing "to the Spirit shall from the Spirit reap eternal life."[z] With *the wicked*, self is both the object and the end. *His income* therefore *is punishment*.[a] His master, so long as he serves him faithfully cares little how or in what sphere. He that "sows to his own flesh shall from the flesh reap corruption."[b] Each has its own end. "Whatever a man sows, this he will also reap."[c]

[s] John 6:27
[t] Luke 19:13; 1 Cor 10:31
[u] Prov 11:19; Jer 22:15, 16
[v] Isa 26:12
[w] Rom 8:13; 1 Cor 15:10; Phil 2:12, 13
[x] Phil 1:21
[y] John 10:10
[z] Gal 6:8
[a] Prov 21:4; Titus 1:15; Matt 12:33; 15:19
[b] Gal 6:8
[c] Gal 6:7

17 *He is* on *the path of life who heeds instruction,*
But he who forsakes reproof goes astray.

It is unspeakable mercy, that *the path of life* is opened! *Instruction* sets the way before us, and he who keeps instruction, cannot fail to find and enjoy it.[d]

[d] Prov 8:34, 35

THAT MOST NEEDFUL PART

The more we value that most needful part of instruction—discipline,[e] the more we shall regard every practical lesson in the heavenly school. *To forsake the reproof;* to be deaf to the voice that would save us from ruin—is a most fearful error—the proof of a foolish and unhumbled heart;[f] the certain forerunner, if not corrected, of irremediable destruction.[g] Child of God, is it not a matter of shame and sorrow, that you should be so

[e] Prov 6:23; 22:17
[f] Prov 12:1; 2 Chron 16:7–10; 25:15, 16
[g] Prov 1:25, 25, 30; 5:12; 15:10; 29:1; Jer 6:10; Zeph 3:2

slow to *heed* such inestimable *instruction;* so prone to stray *from the path of life;* and, though having the full promise of divine guidance, still so often acting as the slave of your own will?

18 *He who conceals hatred* has *lying lips,*
And he who spreads slander is a fool.

HOW THE FOOLISH HIDE THEIR HATRED

Scripture history, from the first chapter of fallen man, abundantly illustrates this proverb. Cain talking with his brother;[h] Saul plotting against David;[i] Joab's treachery to Abner and Amasa;[j] the enemies of the people of God on the return from Babylon[k]—*all concealed hatred and had lying lips.* Such was also the smooth tongue of the Herodians,[l] and more than all—the deadly kiss of Judas.[m] So perfectly, yet with the most exquisite sensibility of pain, did our blessed Lord identify Himself with the trials of His people! Closely allied with the hypocrite is *the slanderer*[n]—both stamped by God with the mark of *fools.* For what good is this mask when God's eye looks right through, and His hand tears off the flimsy cover?[o] And if their *hatred* is turned against the godly, isn't the day at hand, when "He will remove the reproach of His people from all the earth?"[p]

[h] Gen 4:8
[i] 1 Sam 18:21, 22, 29
[j] 2 Sam 3:27; 20:9, 10. Comp. 13:23, 29; Ps 5:9; 55:21
[k] Ezra 4:1–16; Neh 6:2
[l] Luke 20:20, 21
[m] Luke 22:47, 48, with Ps 55:12–14; 41:9
[n] Ps 50:16–20
[o] Prov 26:23–28. Comp. Ps 50:21; Luke 12:1, 2
[p] Isa 25:8
[q] Heb 12:15

But is this "root of bitterness"[q] thoroughly mortified in the Christian's heart? Is there no insincerity in our contact with those we hate or strongly dislike? In the language of polite courtesy, there is much that is hollow, if not false. Do we really mean what we say? Or, is our profession of regard often just the reverse of our real feelings? Don't we ever bring them under ridicule, talk about them in an unfavorable light, speak against them on mere suspicion,[9] or attempt to raise our own name upon the ruin of their reputation? How disappointing it is when we run out of gossip, and how compelled we feel to continue in the same vein, whether what we say is true or

[9] *"Occasions of evil report can never be wanting to them who seek, or are ready to embrace them. No innocence, no wisdom, can in anywise prevent them; and if they be admitted as grounds of defamation, no man's good name can be secure. It is not every possibility, every seeming, every faint show, or glimmering appearance, which sufficeth to ground bad opinion, or reproachful discourse concerning our fellow-creature. The matter should be clear, notorious, and palpable, before we admit a disadvantageous conceit into our head, a distasteful resentment into our heart, a harsh word into our mouth about him.... Justice requireth full proff. 'Charity thinketh no evil, and believeth all things' for the best. Wisdom is not forward to pronounce before full evidence"—BARROW'S* Sermons.

not! The very opposite ought to be true! We ought to be glad when the gossip stops. In the eyes of God, this is surely *slander;* an offense against the "new commandment . . . love"—which is the badge of all the disciples of Jesus.[r] These poisonous indulgences are the ruin of true godliness. They must not only be restrained, but "putting aside," if we would ever "like newborn babes, long for the pure milk of the Word, that by it [we] may grow."[s] Lord, purge our hearts from these hateful hidden corruptions; even though it be by "the spirit of judgment and the spirit of burning."[t]

[r]John 13:34, 35

[s]1 Peter 2:1, 2; James 1:21

[t]Isa 4:4

19 *When there are many words, transgression is unavoidable,*
But he who restrains his lips is wise.

BEWARE OF THE CORRUPTING FOUNTAIN

Hypocrisy and *slander* are not the only sins of the tongue. Indeed, considering the corrupt fountain from which they flow,[u] we cannot conceive of words, much less *many words,* without *transgression.* There is the sin of egotism. "Let another praise you, and not your own mouth."[v] We love to hear ourselves talk; and present our own judgment intrusively. There is also the sin of vain babbling, a canker to true godliness.[w] The fool talks forever about nothing; not because he is full, but because he is empty; not for instruction, but for the pure love of talking. Such is a sin of the flesh, trifling with this most responsible talent, conversation. When "conversation is," as Bishop Butler truly remarks, "merely the exercise of the tongue; no other human faculty has any place in it."[10] The control of the tongue is therefore a searching test of the reality of our experience with the Lord.[x] Considering, therefore, the *sin* connected with *many words,* it is surely *wisdom to strain our lips,*[y] not indeed in silence, but in caution; to weigh our words before uttering them; never speaking, except when we have something to say; speaking only just enough; considering the time, circumstances, and person;[z] what is solid, suitable, and profitable.[a] Indeed a talent for conversation is valueless

[u]Gen 6:5; Matt 12:34

[v]Prov 27:2

[w]2 Tim 2:16, 17; Eccl 10:13, 14; 1 Tim 5:13

[x]James 1:26; 3:2

[y]Prov 17:27, 28; Job 13:5; Eccl 5:3; James 1:19

[z]Job 32:4–7

[a]Prov 15:23; Eph 4:29; Col 4:6

[10] Sermon on the Government of the Tongue. *"One meets with people in the world, who never seem to have made the wise man's observation, that 'there is a time to keep silence.' These times, one would think, should be easily distinguished by everybody; namely, when a man has nothing to say, or nothing but what is better unsaid."*

both to the possessor and to the listeners, unless it's connected with a talent for silence. The sphere of social communication, that stimulates the conversational powers, at the same time teaches the wholesome discipline of the tongue—beautiful silence; which however, alike with its opposite grace, derives its chief loveliness, as the fruit of Christian humility and kindness. The *wisdom* is especially valuable under pressure.[b] And even in the unbending of innocent recreation, the discipline of godly sobriety is most important. The sins of this "small part"[c] are not trifles. They need the full application of the gospel. What but "the sprinkled blood,"[d] could enable us to "render account" for every careless word in the day of judgment? "Light words weigh heavy in God's balance," said Nicholls.[e] Woe to us, if the great substitute did not bear the sins of our vain words, no less than of our greater wickedness! Never let us think of these sins as anything less than the nails that pierced His hands and His feet. And won't this awareness of sin quicken our prayer for an increase of *restraining wisdom*? "Set a guard, O Lord, over my mouth; Keep watch over the door of my lips."[f]

[b] 1 Sam 10:27; 2 Kings 18:36
[c] James 3:5
[d] Heb 12:24
[e] Matt 12:36
[f] Ps 141:3

20 *The tongue of the righteous is* as *choice silver,*
The heart of the wicked is worth *little.*
21 *The lips of the righteous feed many,*
But the fools die for lack of understanding.

The wisdom of restraining our lips must always be connected with earnest effort in improving our talent. If our tongue is our shame in the overflowing of sin:[g] is it not also our glory?[h] When addressing "my verses to the King,"[i] or sketching the features of His transcendant loveliness;[j] is it not then *as choice silver,* refined from this world's rubbish, and shining with heavenly brightness? Who would not eagerly gather up the *silver* scattered in the streets? And shall we not enrich our store from *the choice silver of the just man's tongue,* pouring out its precious instruction before us? If, as regards this world's wealth, the Lord's poor must say—"I do not possess silver and gold";[k] at least they may scatter *choice silver* with a widely extended blessing—"As poor yet making many rich."[l]

[g] Verses 18, 19
[h] Ps 57:8; 108:1
[i] Ps 45:1
[j] Ps 2; Song of Sol 5:10–16
[k] Acts 3:6
[l] 2 Cor 6:10

THE TONGUE'S USEFULNESS

Note also the usefulness of this member. If we are living with God, it will spread out a salt with a heavenly savor, and multiply holiness in our various circles. *The lips of the righteous feed many* from the stores that richly dwell within";[m] giving "grace to those who hear," the soul's true and proper nourishment![n] "Their breath is food to others, as well as life to them," said Flavel in *On Soul of Man.* When the "priest's *lips* keep knowledge, and they seek the law at his mouth," he feeds the people of God.[11] And as our great Master broke the bread and gave it to His disciples for their distribution,[o] so does He now give to His servants heavenly provision, suitable, and abundantly sufficient for their needs. And every Lord's Day is the wondrous miracle displayed before our eyes. The imperishable bread multiplies in the breaking. The hungry, the mourners, the weary, and fainting: yes, all that feel their need, are refreshed and invigorated.

[m]Col 3:16
[n]Eph 4:29; Job 4:3, 4; 29:22, 23
[o]John 6:11

FAMINE IN RICH PASTURES

The wicked—his coffers may be full. But *his heart,* being empty of the *choice silver, is worth little.*[p] So far from feeding others, *the fool dies himself for lack of understanding;* or rather *for lack of heart* to seek it. He despises *the lips that would feed him,* and "dies of famine in the midst of the rich pastures of the Gospel," said Schultens.[q] Oh! How often we are reminded that sin is self-destruction![r]

[p]Jer 22:28
[q]Acts 13:41, 45, 46
[r]Hos 13:9

22 *It is the blessing of the* L*ORD that makes rich,*
And He adds no sorrow to it.

We have been told,[s] that *the hand of the diligent*—and here, *the blessing of the Lord—make rich.* This is no contradiction. Both are true. The one marks the primary cause; the other, the instrumental and subordinate. Neither will be effective without the other. The lazy man looks for prosperity without working for it, the practical atheist from hard effort alone. But the sound-hearted Christian expects it from the *blessing of the Lord* through his own diligent effort. This wise combination keeps him

[s]Verse 4

[11] *Mal 2:7 with Jer 3:15; John 21:15; Acts 20:28; 1 Peter 5:2. Of Bishop Ridley, our Martyrologist records in his own beautiful style, that "to his Sermon the people resorted, swarming about him like bees, and coveting the sweet flowers and wholesome juice of his fruitful doctrine"—FOXE, vii. 407.*

[t]John 6:27
[u]Ps 127:1; Eccl 9:11
[v]Eccl 2:24–26; 3:13; 5:18–20
[w]Gen 24:35; 26:12; 1 Chron 29:14; Deut 8:17, 18
[x]Luke 19:13
[y]1 Tim 6:17, 18
[z]1 Tim 6:6
[a]Rom 8:38, 39

dependent on God.[t] For "unless the Lord builds the house, They labor in vain who build it . . . the race is not to the swift, and the battle is not to the warriors."[u] The rich then may receive their portion[v] as the blessing of the Lord;[w] carefully using it as a talent for His service,[x] and for the good of their fellow creatures.[y] The poor may enjoy the same *enriching blessing* in the gain of godly "contentment."[z] Their cottage is a palace, as the habitation of the King of Kings; and neither life nor death, neither time nor eternity, can separate them from their God.[a]

[b]Prov 20:21; 28:22; 1 Tim 6:9, 10
[c]Gen 13:10, 11; 14:12; 19:15; 2 Peter 2:8
[d]1 Kings 21:4
[e]2 Kings 5:27
[f]Esther 5:13
[g]Luke 18:23
[h]Ps 127:2; Eccl 2:26; 5:12
[i]Phil 4:12
[j]1 Cor 3:21
[k]Ps 3:8

The blessing of the Lord moreover has this right. *He adds no sorrow to it;* at least no sorrow, except what will turn to a blessing. Adding riches may mean adding sorrows.[b] Lot's covetous choice was filled with bitterness.[c] Ahab wore a crown, and "lay down on his bed" in discontent.[d] Gehazi had his riches; but the plague of leprosy was on him.[e] Haman's mortification was the canker in his boasted glory.[f] The rich youth's rejection of Christ was the source of present—must we not fear?—everlasting *sorrow.*[g] The worldling's recompense for his daily toil is eating "the bread of painful labors." Mark the striking contrast—"He gives to His beloved even in his sleep."[h] Happy portion of the children of God! They "know how to get along with humble means, . . . how to live in prosperity."[i] "All things belong to you."[j] "Thy blessing *be* upon Thy people!"[k]

23 *Doing wickedness is like sport to a fool;*
And so is *wisdom to a man of understanding.*

CRUEL SPORT

[l]Prov 26:18, 19; 2 Sam 2:14–16
[m]Prov 1:11–14
[n]Prov 14:9

The cruel *sport* of putting others to pain shows the contrariness of *a fool* both in judgment and heart.[l] Sometimes this cruel amusement may draw a man into the tempter's work.[m] For *fools, who make sport of wickedness,* may heedlessly go on to "mock at sin."[n] But even without going so far, shouldn't we guard against mischievous jokes, tending to wound a neighbor's character, or to give him uneasiness? Are we sufficiently careful against indulging our wit or humor at his expense? All this is not less unmanly, than it is inconsistent with the sobriety and gravity of a Christian profession. It is the pure inborn selfishness of the human heart. Shouldn't children's play be sometimes under restraint? Young people cannot be too strongly disciplined to thoughtfulness and consideration of others. Never let their hilarity of spirits lead to make fun of what ought to call forth sympathy and tenderness. *A man of understanding is too wise* to find a reckless delight in his neighbor's injury. The spirit of our divine Master was according to His own law[o]—eminently considerate and sympathizing.[p] Let us who bear His name, cultivate His self-denying, loving mind.[q]

[o]Gal 6:2
[p]Luke 7:13
[q]Phil 2:4, 5

24 *What the wicked fears will come upon him,*
And the desire of the righteous will be granted.

THE FEARS OF THE WICKED

The sport of the wicked: how soon it is gone![r] But *his fear*—the evil which he *feared—comes upon him.* The Babel builders were punished with the evil, which they had labored to prevent.[s] Ahab's device could not shelter him from the judgment he feared.[t] The rebellious Jews rushed into the ruin from which they fled.[u] Belshazzar's trembling was realized in his speedy destruction.[v] So "*the* wicked are like a tossing sea."[w] Do not their "hearts" in solitude "meditate on terror?"[x] Don't their consciences turn pale at the question—"What will become of the godless man and the sinner?"[y] And won't it be the constrained confession at the great day—according to your fear, so is your punishment![z] Unwilling are they now to be reckoned among *the righteous.* Even more likely will they then be found in their sins—*fear* their portion—hate their doom—without hope—without end.

[r]Eccl 7:6
[s]Gen 11:4, 8
[t]1 Kings 22:28–37
[u]Jer 42:43
[v]Dan 5:6, 30
[w]Isa 57:20, 21
[x]Isa 33:18. Comp. Deut 28:67; Job 3:25; 15:21
[y]1 Peter 4:18
[z]Ps 90:11; Mal 4:1

But if *the fear of the wicked* will be fully realized, so will the desire *of righteous.* One cannot fear anything as bad as what is really in store for him. The other cannot *desire* anything as good as what awaits him. *Desires* bounded by the will[a] and centered in the enjoyment of God[b] *will be granted* to the utmost.[c] God did not raise them to torment us, but for our rest.

[a]1 John 5:14
[b]Ps 4:6; 37:4
[c]Ps 81:10; Jer 33:3; John 16:23, 24

HOW RIGHTEOUS ARE THE DESIRES OF THE RIGHTEOUS?

Granted they are upon the principle, that they "are

[d]Prov 11:23
[e]Mark 10:37
[f]Ps 106:15; James 4:3
[g]Exod 33:18, 20
[h]Exod 33:19

only good."[d] Yet too often *the desires of the righteous* are not righteous. The defilement of a worldly spirit,[e] or the hastiness of an impatient spirit[12]—it's far better that they should be denied than granted.[f] So generally indeed are they mixed with infirmity, that their unreserved gratification might be our destruction.[g] But He is no less wise than kind; He separates the evil, and fulfills the good;[h] answering, not according to our wishes, but our wants; not as in our ignorance we may have asked, but as an enlightened regard to our best interests would have led us to ask.

[i]Isa 41:17
[j]Prov 13:12

But "I have *desired* a thousand times on my knees, and yet it has not been *granted*," the Christian says. Yet is it not worth being upon our knees for it a thousand times more? May not the blessing be withheld a while, till our sensibility of need is speeded up;[i] or to prepare us ultimately for a richer enjoyment?[j]

HOW WE GROW IN GRACE

[k]Gen 48:11; 1 Kings 3:13; Eph 3:20
[l]Ps 17:15; 16:11

But if our desires be granted, and even exceeded;[k] faith and patience will be tried in the very *granting*. Growth in grace is given by deep and humbling views of our corruption. Longings for holiness are fulfilled by painful suffering. Prayers are answered by crosses. Our Father's orderings of events are not what they seem to be, but what He is pleased to make them. Yet in the darkest cloud the ground of our confidence is firm. All things needful will be given, and at the grand conclusion every *desire* will be eternally fulfilled—"As for me, I shall behold Thy face in righteousness; I will be satisfied with Thy likeness when I awake."[l]

25 *When the whirlwind passes, the wicked is no more,*
But the righteous has *an everlasting foundation.*

GONE WITH THE WHIRLWIND

[m]Comp. Jer 23:19; Hos 13:3; Job 20:8, 9; 21:13, 19–21; Ps 73:19, 20
[n]Luke 17:26–29
[o]2 Kings 19:35
[p]Luke 17:30; 1 Thess 5:2, 3

Suddenly, as the whirlwind,[m] the fear of the wicked often comes upon him. All his hopes, pleasures, and supports; all his opportunities of grace, and offers of mercy, are swept away in a moment *forever.* The destruction of the old world, of the cities of the plain[n] was a whirlwind like that of Sennacherib's army.[o] But an infinitely more terrible *whirlwind* will be the coming of the Lord.[p] "But

[12] *Elijah—1 Kings 19:4; Jonah 4:1–4. The disciples—Luke 9:54–56.*

the one who does the will of God abides forever,"[q] as an *everlasting foundation.* Faith has fastened him to the rock of ages; has built his house upon this rock; and no storm can root him up.[r] This is the confidence of *the righteous.* But remember, sin allowed and indulged will shake the confidence far more than all the outward assaults of earth and Hell. Hold fast then your rejoicing in a jealous godly fear. Your portion is secure. Your hopes, joys, and prospects are unchangeable. You can look at trouble—yes, even death itself—without dismay, and say, "I am safe." But while you stand by faith, "Do not be conceited, but fear."[s]

[q]1 John 2:17

[r]Matt 7:25; Ps 112:7

[s]Rom 11:20

26 *Like vinegar to the teeth and smoke to the eyes,*
So is the lazy one to those who send him.

YES, SMOKE CAN GET IN YOUR EYES!

That's what the lazy employee is to his employers![t] Suppose there's a fire to be put out, medical assistance needed, an urgent message to be delivered—he's no help at all! Common sense tells the employer to hire active and hard-working employees. And workers with these qualities, guided by godly principles, are doubly valuable.[u]

There's a lesson for the Christian here. The lazy worker is such a "headache" to his earthly boss, we need to make certain we'll not be that kind of disappointment to our heavenly Master. He has no use for hypocrites who claim to know Him and love Him, and yet are not dependable and zealous in His service.[v] There's no one more pitiable than someone with all kinds of time to spare, with no all-absorbing interest or consuming passion and is going on to the very end of life, as though it has been all child's play, and he hasn't done one useful thing. Oh, it's true that he might have set aside some part of his day for prayer—what he regarded as "religious duty"—but he might just as well have been asleep as on his knees, there was so little heart in it, so little effort put forth! Why standeth he idle in the marketplace? It cannot be—"Because no one hired" him. His Master's call sounds in his ears—"You too go into the vineyard."[w] At his peril he disobeys.[x]

[t]Contrast Prov 26:6, with 13:17; 25:13

[u]Prov 22:29; Gen 24:1–14; 1 Tim 5:17

[v]Rev 3:16

[w]Matt 20:7

[x]Matt 25:30

27 *The fear of the* LORD *prolongs life,*
But the years of the wicked will be shortened.

HOW TO LENGTHEN YOUR LIFE

The fear of the Lord is not a single grace. It includes the substance of all godly emotions. For all are radically one principle, from one source. It essentially differs from *the fear of the wicked.* They fear those whom they hate. The child of God—whom he loves. Whether his earthly life is *shortened* or *prolonged,* he lives long in a little time. He gains infinitely by the contraction of life; *when his days are prolonged* and swallowed up in the one unclouded day, on which "no longer will you have the sun for light by day."[y] *The fear of the Lord* is rightly contrasted with *the wicked;* because the absence of this grace is their distinguishing mark,[z] the principle of all their ungodliness.[a] And often do we see the letter of this curse realized in *the shortening of their years.* Excessive worldliness wears out the spring of life[b] and often brings it to an untimely end.[13] Sometimes the God of vengeance breaks out, and He takes away the daring offender.[c] Yet, if he "die the death of all men,"[d] awful is the course of a long life, wasted in folly and sin; living little in a long time—"The sinner *being* a hundred years old shall be accursed."[e]

[y]Prov 9:11; Ps 91:16; Isa 60:19
[z]Ps 36:11
[a]Rom 3:10–18
[b]Eccl 5:10–12
[c]1 Sam 2:32; 4:11; Acts 5:1–10
[d]Num 16:29
[e]AV—Isa 65:20

28 *The hope of the righteous is gladness,*
But the expectation of the wicked perishes.

THE CHRISTIAN'S HOPE

The fear of the Lord is far from being opposed to the *hope of the righteous.* Often, it is connected with it.[f] And well may this *hope be gladness;* for it is "accompanied with sweet patience, joyful hope, and crowned with a happy outcome," said Diodati. It has its origin in eternity.[g] Its substance is Christ and Heaven.[h] The foundation is the Work of Christ.[i] The security, the unchangeable commitments of God.[j] Who then can help but see it as the hope that "does not disappoint?"[k] The fear of the Lord, doesn't put an end to happiness, as is often supposed. Instead, it brings in the only sunshine of the soul. Beaming from the precious cross, how it dries up the penitent's

[f]Ps 33:18; 147:11
[g]Titus 1:2
[h]Rom 5:2; 1 Peter 1:3, 4; Col 1:27
[i]1 Peter 1:3, 21
[j]Heb 6:17, 18
[k]Rom 5:5; Heb 6:19; 2 Thess 2:16

[13] *Impurity, Prov 5:9–11; Drunkenness, 23:29–32; Malice, Ps 55:23; 1 Kings 2:31–44. Wickedness, Ps 37:9, 20. Eccl 7:17; Jer 17:11. Comp. Job 15:32, 33; 22:15, 16.*

tears![l] Or, if the *gladness* is withheld for a time, yet it has been sown; and the sheaves of joy shall doubtless follow the "weeping."[m] And then—as it were—carrying Heaven in and about us[n]—how refreshing is *this hope* in its clear insight into eternity, as Bunyan, in one of his beautiful touches in *The Pilgrim's Progress,* describes his feeling on witnessing Christian and Hopeful's welcome into the heavenly city—"which when I had seen, I wished myself among them." Oh! there must be a reality in that *hope*, which bears us away from earth, and makes its lowest citizen richer and happier, than if he were the sole possessor of this world's glory. Let me hurry on toward it, longing, yet not impatient. For how can I but desire to change my traveler's lot for my home; my labors for rest; my sorrow for joy; my body of sin for likeness to my Lord; "the tents of Kedar" for "the myriads of angels ... and the church of the first-born"?[o] Do I grasp this *hope?* Then—as a godly man exclaimed, "Let who will, be miserable; I will not—I cannot!"

[l]Isa 12:2
[m]Ps 97:11; 126:6; Isa 35:10
[n]Heb 10:34
[o]Ps 120:5, with Heb 12:22, 23

THE HOPELESSNESS OF THE WICKED

But *the wicked*—they too have *their expectation.* For none have a stronger hope than those, who have no grounds for hope.[p] And this delusion often reaches to the moment of eternity[q]—more than that, even to the "day" of the Lord;[r] expecting the door to be opened to them, after it has been shut forever;[s] dreaming of Heaven, and waking in Hell! *The expectation of the wicked perishes.*

[p]Deut 29:19
[q]Matt 25:10
[r]Matt 7:22, 23
[s]Matt 25:11

Christian! make sure what the ground *of your hope* really is.[t] Then show forth its *gladness*, in a way befitting an heir of glory. Don't let a drooping spirit tell the world how weak *your hope* really is. Show them, instead, that you can live upon its *gladness,* until you enter into its perfect and everlasting fruition.[u] Doubt brings believers and infidels nearly to the same level. A clear understanding of its infinite joy stimulates our diligence "to make certain about His calling and choosing you."[v]

[t]2 Peter 1:10
[u]Ps 16:11
[v]2 Peter 1:10

29 *The way of the* LORD *is a stronghold to the upright,*
But ruin to the workers of iniquity.

[14] *See the hope of the worldling, Ps 49:6–14; Luke 12:19, 20. Of the wicked, Job 11:20; 18:14. Of the hypocrite, Job 8:13, 14; 27:8.*

FLEX THOSE (SPIRITUAL) MUSCLES!

[w]Neh 8:10
[x]Judg 6:14
[y]Isa 40:29

Note that *the gladness of the righteous* is "your *strength.*"[w] In the roughness of *the way*—"Go in this your strength"—is the cheering voice—"Have I not sent you?"[x] "He gives strength to the weary, And to him who lacks might He increases power."[y] This promise, however, implies help for our work, not rest from our labor. We shall have strength for the conflict. But there is no discharge from the war. There is supply for real, not for imaginary, wants; for present, not for future, need. The healthful energy of the man of God is also supposed. He is alive in the way. His heart is set in it. This makes it practicable. What before was drudgery is now meat and drink. Indeed, the more godly we are, the more godly we shall be. The habit of grace increases by exercise. One step helps on the next.

[z]Job 17:9
[a]John 3:2; 7:50, 51; 19:39
[b]2 Chron 15:2
[c]Gen 39:10
[d]1 Kings 18:3
[e]Dan 6:10
[f]Job 17:9; Ps 84:5–7; Zech 10:12
[g]Phil 4:13

Thus was *the way of the Lord a stronghold to the upright* Nicodemus. His first step was feebleness and fear. Walking onward, he grew stronger;[z] standing up in the ungodly council, and ultimately the bold confessor of his Savior, when his self-confident disciples slunk back.[a] We don't have inborn sufficiency. The strongest in their own strength shall faint and be weary. The weakest in the Lord's strength shall "march on, and not faint," is Bishop Lowth's version of Isa 40:31. Thus, in the hour of temptation, *the upright* will find their *way* to be strength.[b] Joseph in Potiphar's house;[c] Obadiah in Ahab's house;[d] Daniel in the Persian court,[e] held on a fiery trial, sustained from on high. Thus—*thus alone*—"the righteous shall hold to his way ... blessed is the man whose strength is in Thee ... And in His name they will walk."[f] When we look at our resources, we might "as well despair of moving sin from our hearts, as of casting down the mountains with our fingers," said Bishop Reynolds. Yet none of us needs to shrink from the confession—"I can do all things through Him who strengthens me."[g]

[h]Isa 59:7; Rom 3:16; Isa 1:11
[i]Luke 13:27; Prov 21:15; Job 31:3; Ps 36:12

No such resources support the *workers of iniquity.* Captives instead of soldiers, they know no conflicts; they realize no need of *strength.* Even now devastation and "destruction are in their paths';[h] and the voice of the Judge will fearfully seal their doom. "Depart from me, all you evildoers."[i]

30 *The righteous will never be shaken,*
But the wicked will not dwell in the land.

THE BEST OF TWO WORLDS

The frailty of our present condition, common to all,[j] was not in the wise man's eye; but the state of the two classes was in the purpose and mind of God. *His way is a stronghold to the upright. The righteous,* walking steadily in the way, *shall never be shaken.*[k] "They enjoy in this life, by faith and hope, their everlasting life," says *Reformers' Notes.* "No weapon that is formed against you shall prosper."[l] "The mountains may be removed and the hills may shake, But My loving kindness will not be removed from you, and My covenant of *peace will not be shaken;* says the Lord who has compassion on you."[m] Is not this a confidence, that neither earth nor Hell can ever shake?[n]

The wicked—have they any such confidence? So far from being *never removed, they shall never dwell.* They have no title, like *the righteous,*[o] as sons and heirs, to the blessings of *earth;* no hope or interest in the land, of which *the earth* is the type.[p] How often are they cut off from dwelling in the one.[q] And yet, they never will be allowed to dwell in the other.[r] As our character is, so is our hope and prospect. We gain or lose both worlds.

[j] Eccl 9:2, 11
[k] Ps 15; 37:22; 112:6; 125:1; 2 Peter 1:5–11
[l] Isa 54:17
[m] Isa 54:10
[n] Rom 8:38, 39
[o] Matt 5:5; 1 Cor 3:22
[p] Ps 37:29
[q] Verse 27; 2:22; Ps 37:23; Ezek 33:24–26
[r] 1 Cor 6:9; Rev 21:27

31 *The mouth of the righteous flows with wisdom,*
But the perverted tongue will be cut out.
32 *The lips of the righteous bring forth what is acceptable,*
But the mouth of the wicked, what is perverted.

THE GRACIOUS TONGUE

Another image[s] of the fruitfulness of a gracious tongue! It *bringeth forth wisdom,*[t] and that too in the practical exercise of *knowing what is acceptable.* This gift needs to be deeply pondered, and carefully cultivated,[u] to give it a free scope, while we jealously confine it to its own sphere of influence. There is evidently many kinds of application. The same statement of truth does not satisfy everyone. And how—what—when—to whom—to speak—is a matter of great wisdom.[v] Yet this consideration of *acceptableness* must involve no compromise of principle. Let it be a thoughtful adjustment of manner to

[s] Comp. 10:11, 20, 21
[t] Ps 37:30
[u] Prov 15:23; 25:11; Job 6:25
[v] Eccl 8:5

the many kinds of tastes; a patience with lesser prejudices and inborn infirmities; avoiding—not all offense (which faithfulness to our Lord forbids), but all *needless* offense; all uncalled-for occasions of scheming and impatience. "The gentleness of wisdom"[w] should be clearly visible in Christian faithfulness. Thus Gideon melted the rebellion of the men of Ephraim.[x] Abigail held back David's hands from blood.[y] Daniel stood fearless before the mighty monarch of Babylon.[z] *Their lips knew what was acceptable,* and their God honored them.

[w]James 3:13
[x]Judg 8:2, 3
[y]1 Sam 25:23–33
[z]Dan 4:27

THE SWEETNESS OF PERSUASION

But most of all—let the minister of God study to clothe his most unwelcome message in *acceptable* dress. Let him mold it in all the sweetness of persuasion,[a] compassion,[b] and sympathy.[c] With what parental earnestness does the "Preacher" of Jerusalem, in his introductory chapters, allure us to wisdom's voice and instruction! Yet were his "delightful words . . . words of truth."[d] And thus must "the lips of a priest . . . preserve knowledge," if he would have his people "seek instruction from his mouth: for he is the messenger of the Lord of hosts."[e] He must weigh carefully his statements, without diluting them. The truth is to "be proclaimed upon the housetops"[f] to the multitude. But it is to be kept back from ungodly scorners.[g] He must always gain his people's ears, that he may win their hearts.

The perverted tongue, pouring forth its own wickedness provokes its own ruin. It shall be cut out.[h] O my God, what I owe Thee for the bridle of discipline, that holds me back from self-destruction!

[a]2 Cor 5:11, 20
[b]Rom 9:1–3; 2 Cor 2:4
[c]Titus 3:2, 3; 2 Cor 11:29
[d]Eccl 12:10
[e]Mal 2:7
[f]Luke 12:3
[g]Matt 10:27, with 7:6
[h]Prov 8:13; 18:7; Ps 12:3; 52:1–5; 120:3, 4; Num 16:1–33

CHAPTER ELEVEN

1 *A false balance is an abomination to the* *LORD*,
But a just weight is His delight.

TESTIMONY ABOVE PRAISE

How valuable is God's Word in its minute detail of principles for everyday living! Business is a providential appointment for our social communication and mutual helpfulness. With men, it is grounded upon human faith; with God, upon divine faith. *Balances, weights,* money, are its necessary materials. Cheating; double-dealings; the hard bargain struck with self-complacent shrewdness[a]—this is the *false balance* forbidden by both the law[b] and the gospel.[c] Men may "praise" its wisdom;[d] God not only forbids, but He hates it.[e] The honest *weight* often passes unnoticed. But such a just weight or "perfect stone," said Jermin, is a perfect jewel, and a precious stone in the sight of God. It is *His delight*[f]—a testimony infinitely above all human praise!

We must not put away this proverb as a mere moral saying. It was given as a warning to a flourishing Christian church;[g] and the sin denounced here has been a leprous spot upon many a highly gifted professing believer.[h] Is it not a solemn thought that the eye of God sees all our everyday dealings of life, either as hateful or as a delight? Haven't we ever found, when upon our knees, the frown of God upon some breach in our daily walk?[i] Look and see, whether you "maintain always a blameless conscience *both* before God and before men."[j] "The Lord is righteous; He loves righteousness; the upright will behold His face."[k] They—they only—"may abide in Thy tent."[l]

[a] Prov 20:14
[b] Lev 19:36
[c] Matt 7:12; Phil 4:8
[d] Luke 16:8
[e] Prov 20:10; Deut 25:13–16; Amos 8:5
[f] Prov 16:11; 12:22
[g] 1 Thess 4:6
[h] 1 Cor 6:8
[i] Ps 66:18
[j] Acts 24:16
[k] Ps 11:7
[l] Ps 15:1, 2; 24:3–5; 149:13

2 *When pride comes, then comes dishonor.*
But with the humble is wisdom.

THE FOOLISHNESS OF PRIDE

[m]Gen 3:5
[n]Mark 7:22
[o]Gen 3:7, with 2:25
[p]Gen 11:4
[q]Num 12:2, 10
[r]2 Chron 26:16–21
[s]Esther 5:11; 7:10
[t]Dan 4:29–32
[u]Acts 12:22, 23
[v]Luke 14:11
[w]Luke 18:14; Isa 2:17

Pride was the principle of the fall,[m] and therefore the native principle of fallen man.[n] When pride had stripped us of our honor, then—not till then—did dishonor come.[o] This is the wise discipline of our God to punish one by the other. The Babel-builders;[p] Miriam;[q] Uzziah;[r] Haman;[s] Nebuchadnezzar;[t] Herod;[u] all are instances of *dishonor,* treading upon the heels of *pride.* Even in common life, a man will never attempt to raise himself above his own level—but then comes dishonor[v]—the most revolting repayment. And so our God puts to shame the man who doesn't know his limits and who refuses to stand on the low ground on which God has placed him. "Every one who exalts himself shall be humbled."[w]

[x]Luke 2:47
[y]Luke 10:21
[z]Col 2:18

Such is the foolishness of *pride. With the humble is wisdom.* What a splendor of *wisdom* shone in the *humble* child, sitting at the doctors' feet, amazing them "at His understanding and His answers!"[x] And won't this spirit be the path of *wisdom* to us? For the divine Teacher "didst hide these things from *the* wise and intelligent and didst reveal them to babes."[y] There is no greater proof of proud folly, than believing only what we understand. So faith is grounded on knowledge, not on testimony; as if the Word of God could not be fully received, unless it is strengthened and supported by other witnesses. Happy are the *humble* of spirit, that come to God's revelation, as it were, without any will or mind of their own; humbly receiving what He is pleased to give; but willing—yes—thankful to be ignorant, when He forbids them to intrude![z]

3 *The integrity of the upright will guide them,*
But the falseness of the treacherous will destroy them.
4 *Riches do not profit in the day of wrath,*
But righteousness delivers from death.
5 *The righteousness of the blameless will smooth his way,*
But the wicked will fall by his own wickedness.
6 *The righteousness of the upright will deliver them,*
But the treacherous will be caught by their own *greed.*

7 *When a wicked man dies,* his *expectation will perish,*
And the hope of strong men perishes.

TO KNOW GOD'S WILL—AND DO IT!

Integrity or righteousness is a most valuable *guide* in all perplexities.[a] The single desire to know the will of God, only that we may do it,[b] will always bring light upon our path. It is also a hiding place from many dreaded evils. God is a defense to them that walk uprightly. "And who is there to harm you if you prove zealous for what is good?"[c] Let the Christian "stand firm therefore, having girded your loins with truth, and having put on the breastplate of *righteousness* . . . and the evil one does not touch him."[d] Often indeed does it deliver from temporal, always from eternal, *death.* "In the way of righteousness is life, And in *its* pathway there is no death . . . If anyone keeps My Word, he shall never taste of death."[e]

[a] Matt 6:22
[b] Ps 143:10
[c] 1 Peter 3:13
[d] Eph 6:14; 1 John 5:18
[e] Prov 12:28; John 8:52; Gen 7:1; 2 Kings 20:3–6

The obstinate disobedience, that neglects this godly principle, is the sinner's own snare and destruction.[f] And when the day of wrath comes—as come it will—a great ransom will not deliver.[g] Riches will profit nothing;[h] not even will they obtain a drop of water to "cool off" the tormented tongue.[i] In vain will the rich men of the earth seek a shelter from "the wrath of the Lamb."[j] They and their hopes will perish together.[1] They were not living, but lying, dying hopes.[k] What a contrast to that "hope we have as an anchor of the soul, a *hope* both sure and steadfast and one which enters within the veil"![2]

[f] Prov 28:18; John 8:51; Ezra 18:27
[g] Deut 1:43, 44; Num 22:32; Isa 1:28; Ezra 9:9, 10; Hos 14:9
[h] Job 36:18, 19
[i] Luke 16:19–24
[j] Rev 6:15–17
[k] 1 Peter 1:3

8 *The righteous is delivered from trouble,*
But the wicked takes his place.

So these two classes change places in the management of God. The same providence often marks divine faithfulness and earned punishment. The Israelites were *delivered from the trouble* of the Red Sea; the Egyptians took their *place.*[l] Mordecai was *delivered* from the gallows; Haman was hanged upon it.[m] The noble confessors in Babylon were saved from the fire; their executioners were slain by it.[n] Daniel was preserved from the lions;

[l] Exod 14:21–28
[m] Esther 5:14; 7:10
[n] Dan 3:22–26

[1] *Chap. 10:28; Job 8:13, 14; 11:20; 18:14–18; Ps 49:17, 18; 146:4.* In The Pilgrim's Progress *one of Bunyan's graphic and accurate sketches represents Ignorance ferried over the river by one Vain Hope, ascending the hill alone, without encouragement, and ultimately bound and carried away. "Then I saw," adds he with fearful solemnity, "that there was a way to Hell, even from the gates of Heaven!"*

[2] *Heb 6:19. Doesn't this verse prove the knowledge of a future state; since, as respects this life, the* expectation of the righteous—*alike with that of* the wicked—*perishes? Comp. 1 Cor 15:19.*

his accusers were devoured by them.[o] Peter was snatched from death; his jailors and persecutors were condemned.[p] So "precious in the sight of the Lord is" the life, no less than "the death of His godly ones."[q] In order to deliver one precious soul out of trouble, He will bring a nation into distress.[r] Yes—for the ransom of His own chosen people, He gave not only "Egypt" of old, but in later times "Cush and Seba . . . other men in your place and other peoples in exchange for your life."[3] To what source but His own free and sovereign love can we trace this special regard? "*Since you are precious in My sight, since you are honored and I love you.*"[s] We don't always see the same outward evidence. But the love is unchangeably the same. And how should it at the same time lay us in the dust and build our confidence upon an unshaking foundation!

[o] Dan 6:22–24
[p] Acts 12:6, 19, 23
[q] Ps 116:15
[r] 1 Sam 23:25–28
[s] Isa 43:4

9 *With* his *mouth the godless man destroys his neighbor,*
But through knowledge the righteous will be delivered.

THE MOUTH OF THE HYPOCRITE

Haman under the pretense of loyalty would have *destroyed* a whole nation.[t] Ziba under the same false cover would have *destroyed his neighbor.*[u] The lying prophet from mere willfulness ruined his brother. Such is *the godless man's mouth*—"a small part"; but a world of iniquity "set on fire by Hell."[v]

Then look at him in the church—a ravening wolf "in sheep's clothing," devouring the flock;[w] exploiting you "with false words";[x] an apostle of Satan, so diligent is he in his master's work of *destruction!*[y] "For false Christs," we are warned, "mislead, if possible, even the elect."[z] But they—*the righteous are delivered through knowledge*—Diodati said, "by the light and direction of the Holy Spirit, and by the lively *knowledge* of God's word, which gives unto the faithful man all the wisdom he needs for his preservation."[a] Learn the value of solid *knowledge.* Feeling, excitement, imagination expose us to an unsteady testimony.[b] *Knowledge* supplies principle

[t] Esther 3:8–13
[u] 2 Sam 16:1–4
[v] James 3:5, 6
[w] Matt 7:15
[x] 2 Peter 2:1–3
[y] 2 Cor 11:3, 13
[z] Matt 24:24
[a] Comp. Heb 5:14; 1 John 2:20, 27; 2 Peter 3:17, 18
[b] Eph 4:14

[3] *Isa 43:3, 4, with 2 Chron 14:9–11; 2 Kings 19:9. Comp. Prov 21:18. How different their estimation in the eyes of man, when an Eastern autocrat was willing to cut them off at a single blow as a worthless thing! Esther 3:8–15. Comp. 1 Cor 4:13.*

and steadfastness. Add to your faith knowledge.[c] Guard against plausible error, usually built upon some single truth, separated from its connection, and given more than its due proportion. Don't the many delusions of our day give force to the earnest exhortation—"Take hold of instruction; do not let go, Guard her, for she is your life"?[d]

[c]2 Peter 1:5

[d]Prov 4:13

10 *When it goes well with the righteous, the city rejoices,*
And when the wicked perish, there is glad shouting.
11 *By the blessing of the upright a city is exalted,*
But by the mouth of the wicked it is torn down.

The world, contempt of the unborn enmity of the heart, bears its testimony to consistent godliness,[e] and *rejoices* in the prosperity of the *righteous.* Their elevation to authority is a matter of general joy.[f] A godly king,[4] a premier, using his authority for the glory of God;[g] a man of God of high influence in the church[h]—these are justly regarded as national rejoicing. Their prayers,[i] wisdom,[j] disinterestedness, and example[k] are a public blessing.

The wicked are only a curse to the community. How often has *it been torn down,* or endangered *by their mouth.*[l] So that their *perishing* is a matter of present joy.[m] Such was the joy of Rome on the death of Nero, and the public rejoicings in Germany at the death of Hitler. The people of God unite *in the glad shouting;* not from any selfish feeling of revenge; much less from unfeeling hardness toward their fellow-sinners. But when a hindrance to the good cause is removed;[n] when the justice of God against sin,[o] and His faithful preservation of His people,[p] are displayed, shouldn't every feeling be taken with a supreme interest in His glory? Shouldn't they shout?[q] The "Alleluia" of Heaven is a joyful testimony to the righteous judgments of the Lord our God, hastening forward His glorious kingdom.[r]

[e]Prov 16:7; Mark 6:20
[f]Prov 19:2; Esther 8:15
[g]2 Chron 24:16
[h]2 Kings 2:12
[i]Exod 33:12; Isa 37:14–36; James 5:16–18
[j]Gen 41:38–42
[k]Job 22:30
[l]Num 16:3, 41; 2 Sam 15:1–14; 20:1
[m]Job 27:23
[n]Prov 28:28; Eccl 9:18
[o]2 Sam 18:14–28
[p]Exod 15:21; Judg 5:31
[q]Ps 52:6, 7; 58:10; Rev 18:20
[r]Rev 19:1, 2

12 *He who despises his neighbor lacks sense,*
But a man of understanding keeps silent.

DON'T DESPISE YOUR NEIGHBOR—
HE MIGHT BE RELATED!

Pride and lack of love show a man to *lack sense;* ignor-

[4] *2 Chron 30:25, 26. "All things prosper in every respect, so long as thou rulest well"—was the speech of the Senate to the Emperor Severus. Comp. Isa 32:1, 2; 1 Tim 2:1, 2.*

ant alike of himself, his neighbor, and his God. For if you delight in magnifying "the speck in your brother's eye," then you ought to have enough *wisdom* to "notice the log that is in your own eye?"[s] Could he *despise his neighbor*, if he really knew him to be his own flesh;[t] perhaps even a member "of His body" and of the flesh, and of the bones of his Lord?[u] Could He look down upon him in the fullness of pride, if he realized the consciousness, that, if he differs, it is God—not himself, who has made him to differ?[v] Surely this blindness is to be void *of understanding*, and destitute of heart. "It shows the need for a right state of mind, judgment, and affections. Such a man is *without heart* toward what is wise and good," said Scott.[w]

[s] Matt 7:3–5
[t] Isa 58:7; Mal 2:10; Acts 17:26
[u] Eph 5:30
[v] 1 Cor 4:7
[w] Comp. Prov 14:21; John 7:47–49

A man of understanding may see much in *his neighbor* to excite his pity and stir up his prayers, but nothing to *despise*. He may be called openly to condemn him. But his general course will be loving forbearance; *keeping silent;* keeping himself from speaking or doing anything in scorn of another, "looking to yourselves lest you too be tempted."[x] Self-knowledge shows the *man of understanding* and forms the man of love.

[x] Gal 6:1

13 *He who goes about as a talebearer reveals secrets,*
But he who is trustworthy conceals a matter.

BREACH OF LOVE

Another breach of love is here rebuked.[y] The gospel does not shut us up to our own private interests, as if we had no sympathy with our neighbor. The gospel is a universal brotherhood of love. Yet it rebukes the *talebearer*, who, having no business of his own, trifles with his neighbor's name and honor and sells his wares of scandal, as it may be, whether for gain or spite.[z] It is most unsafe to be within the breath of this cruel trifler with the happiness of his fellow-creatures.[a] For just as readily as he *reveals our* neighbor's secrets to us, will he reveal ours to him. All the bonds of confidence and friendship are shattered. Keep your lips closed against him. If there is no one around to listen, your words will fall to the ground and die away. Children, servants, and visitors in the family should guard most carefully against *revealing secrets*, that have been talked about in the home. *The*

[y] Lev 19:16, 17
[z] Neh 6:17–19
[a] Prov 16:28; 26:22

talebearer, having lots of time on his hands, worms out family secrets. He is always delighted to make a discovery. The most idle rumor is a treasure. A quarrel already made up before he has time to *reveal* it is a disappointment. This busy idleness has always been a problem in the church.[b] It is a religion always abroad, occupied offensively with foreign interference; while at home it is "the field of the slothful, grown over with thorns."[c] If we would have our friend share his anxieties with us,[d] we shouldn't allow his confidence in us to be shaken by learning that, after all, we didn't keep the secret he asked us to keep. It is vital to our peace, that our close friends should be so trustworthy, that we don't always have to be swearing them to secrecy; it is to our interest, as well as theirs. We should rather refuse, than betray, a trust, needing concealment, except when the honor of God and the interests of society plainly forbid.[e] A friend like that is invaluable, but, in this deceitful world, he is very rare, indeed.[f] Yet, if we would be consistent Christians, we should have a faithful spirit. Its habitual absence could make others wonder whether we're really saved or not.

[b] 2 Thess 3:10–12; 1 Tim 5:13; 1 Peter 4:15
[c] Prov 24:30, 31
[d] Prov 17:17
[e] 1 Sam 3:17, 18; Jer 38:24–27. Contrast Judg 16:16–20
[f] Prov 20:6

14 *Where there is no guidance, the people fall,*
But in abundance of counselors there is victory.

WISE COUNSELORS CAN HELP!

Even in private matters the value of wise counselors is generally recognized. The agreement of *the abundance of counselors* makes us more sure of our decision. And even their differences, by giving both sides of the question, enable us to consider our path more wisely. The nation, therefore, without *counselors* is like a ship in the midst of the rocks without a pilot—in imminent peril. God has given to some the gift of government—"wisdom has the advantage of giving success."[g] *Where there is no guidance, the people fall.* In the dark time of the Judges, the desire for a king led to anarchy, and the *people fell* into the enemies' hands.[h] Ten parts of the people fell when Rehoboam listened to evil *counsel.*[i] The people fell again, when the counsel of godly Jehoiada was taken away.[j] The good Lord deliver us from the deserved national judgment of weak and blinded counselors![k]

[g] Eccl 10:10
[h] Judg 2:8–23; 21:25
[i] 1 Kings 12:16–19
[j] 2 Chron 24:17–21
[k] Eccl 10:16; Isa 3:1–4; 19:11–14

David and Solomon, though themselves specially gifted with wisdom, governed their kingdoms prosperously with the help of wise counselors.[l] The larger the multitude of *such counselors*,[m] the greater the safety. To a counselor, like that, a heathen monarch's kingdom was saved from a devastating famine.[n]

[l]Ps 119:98–100, with 2 Sam 15:12; 17:14, also 1 Kings 12:6
[m]Contrast Isa 47:13
[n]Gen 41:38–57

The church has often been preserved by this belssing.[o] Shouldn't we now plead for the church's survival, in this day of her distress, that *her people* may not *fall*, for want of *counsel;*[p] that her ordained *counselors* may be filled with the spirit of "power and love and discipline,"[q] in order that her people may be established more firmly in the pure faith of the gospel?[r]

[o]Acts 15:6–31. Comp. Prov 15:22; 24:6
[p]Ezra 34:4–6; Matt 15:14
[q]2 Tim 1:7
[r]Acts 16:4, 5

15 *He who is surety for a stranger will surely suffer for it,*
But he who hates going surety is safe.

This repeated warning against *suretyship*[s] is intended to instill consideration for others; not to excuse selfishness, or to dry up the sources of helpful sympathy. It must not be *for a stranger,*[t] whose character and responsibilities are unknown to us. For such incautious kindness, too often causing our family to suffer, we shall pay a price. To *hate* such engagements is therefore our wise security.

[s]Prov 6:1–5
[t]Prov 27:13

UNDER THE STROKE OF THE FATHER'S HAND

But one exception we can never forget. The blessed Jesus, from His free grace—unsought, unasked[u]—became *surety*—not for a friend (in which case we should have had no interest), but *for a stranger.* He became one with us in nature, that He might be one with us in law. He took our place under the curse of the broken law.[v] He put His soul to the fullest extent in our soul's place; and then He made our nature pay the debt, which all the angels of Heaven could never have paid. Oh! this was suffering, indeed. How He suffered under the stroke of His Father's hand.[5] The upholder of the universe was prostrate in the dust;[w] His own creature strengthening His sinking frame.[x] Had He *hated suretyship, He would have been sure;* (for what could have disturbed His self-existent happiness?) but we should have perished. Glory

[u]John 10:15, 17, 18; Phil 2:6–8
[v]Gal 3:13
[w]Mark 14:35, with Heb 1:3
[x]Luke 22:43

[5]*Isa 53:5, 10*—bruised—sore broken.

to His name! Though from all eternity He knew the bitterness of the pain, instead of *hating.* He rejoiced and delighted in His Work.[y] His was no rash engagement. It was the arrangement of the everlasting covenant.[z] It was lawful in every way. There was an infinite treasure to discharge the liabilities. The claims of justice were fully satisfied.[a] Sin was as thoroughly punished, as it was thoroughly pardoned. The family of God suffered no injury, but received direct benefit instead.[b] What is there left for us to do, but to fall down before this grace, and to spend our days, as we shall spend our eternity, in adoring this wondrous display of divine glory![c]

[y] Prov 8:31; Heb 10:7; Ps 40:6–8
[z] Isa 53:10–12; 1 Peter 1:20
[a] Isa 1:27; 42:21; Rom 3:26
[b] Eph 1:10; Col 1:20
[c] Rev 1:5, 6; 5:12

16 *A gracious woman attains honor,*
And violent men attain riches.

THE GRACIOUS WOMAN

Everywhere the excellency of godliness meets our eyes. What loveliness, dignity, and influence it imparts to womanly character![d] A gracious woman is known, not by her outward beauty but by "beautiful inner ornaments";[e] which retain their full beauty when external beauties have faded away.[f] And though "a weaker vessel,"[g] she retains *honor,* as firmly as *violent men attain riches.* She preserves her character unblemished.[h] She wins her children[i]—perhaps her ungodly husband[j]—into the ways of holiness. Thus Deborah *attained honor* as "a mother in Israel," the counselor and the stay of a sinking people.[k] Esther *attained* her influence over her heathen husband for the good of her nation.[l] And still the *gracious woman attains honor* long after she has mingled with the dust. Sarah the obedient wife;[m] Hannah the consecrating mother;[n] Lois, Eunice, and "the chosen lady"[o] in the family sphere; Phoebe and her companions in the annals of the church;[p] the rich contributor to the temple;[q] the self-denying lover of her Lord;[r] Mary in contemplative withdrawal;[s] Dorcas in active usefulness[t]—are not these good names still honorably remembered?[u]

[d] Prov 31:10
[e] 1 Tim 2:9, 10; 1 Peter 3:3, 4
[f] Prov 31:25
[g] 1 Peter 3:7
[h] Ruth 3:11
[i] Prov 31:28
[j] Prov 31:12, 28; 1 Peter 3:1, 2
[k] Judg 4:4; 5:7
[l] Esther 9:12, 13, 25
[m] 1 Peter 3:5, 6
[n] 1 Sam 1:28
[o] 2 Tim 1:5; 3:15; 2 John 1–4
[p] Rom 16:2–6; Phil 4:3
[q] Mark 12:42–44
[r] Mark 14:3–9
[s] Luke 10:39
[t] Acts 9:36
[u] Ps 112:6

17 *The merciful man does himself good,*
But the cruel man does himself harm.

OUR NEIGHBOR'S TROUBLE IN OUR HEARTS

Mercifulness is not natural benevolence, without God or godliness. It is the "fruit of the Spirit";[v] the image of our Father;[w] the constraint of the love of Christ;[x] the adorning of the "chosen of God."[y] It is not pity in words and looks. It is when our neighbor's trouble descends into the depths of our hearts and draws out kindness and practical sympathy.[z] The *merciful man* will always find a merciful God.[a] The widow of Sarepta and the woman of Shunam, each for their kindness to the Lord's prophets, received a prophet's reward.[b] The alms of Cornelius brought *good* to his own soul.[c] In watering others with our mercy, our own souls "will be like a watered garden."[d] Even now "God is not unjust so as to forget your work and the love which you have shown toward His name."[e] At the great day He will honor it before the assembled universe.[f]

But no less certainly will *cruelty* bring its own penalty.[g] With our unsubdued passion, we carry around with us the very element of Hell, lacking nothing but immortality to complete the misery. Cain found his brother's murder an intolerable *harm* to his flesh.[h] Joseph's brethren all suffered for their unfeeling *cruelty.*[i] Adoni-bezek had to admit the justice of his punishment.[j] The doom of Ahab and Jezebel was the curse of their own *cruelty.*[k] The treasures of selfishness will eat as does a canker *harm.*[l] O my God, save me from the tyranny of my own lust, and may your perfect image of mercy be my standard and my pattern!

[v]Gal 5:22
[w]Luke 6:36
[x]2 Cor 8:9
[y]Col 3:12
[z]Luke 10:33
[a]Ps 41:1; Matt 5:7
[b]2 Kings 4:16; 8:1–6
[c]Acts 10:2–4
[d]Isa 58:11; Isa 32:8; Ps 112:4
[e]Heb 6:10; Matt 10:42
[f]Matt 25:34
[g]James 2:13; Matt 18:34, 35
[h]Gen 4:13, 14
[i]Gen 42:21
[j]Judg 1:6, 7
[k]1 Kings 22:38; 2 Kings 9:36, 37
[l]James 5:1–3

18 *The wicked earns deceptive wages,*
But he who sows righteousness gets *a true reward.*
19 *He who is steadfast in righteousness* will attain *to life,*
And he who pursues evil will bring about *his own death.*

TWO MASTERS

Both the masters that claim the heart put forth their promise of *reward.* If Satan fulfilled all his promises, truly his servants would be abundantly enriched.[m] But *the wicked* one works a deceitful work, ending in disappointment.[n] Pharaoh's exterminating project against Is-

[m]Gen 3:4, 5; Matt 4:8, 9
[n]Heb 2:13; Rom 6:21

rael *deceived* him in its results, issuing in their increase, and the ruin of himself and his people.[o] Abimelech doubtless expected peace as the result of his murderous work.[p] But *he pursued evil to his own death.*

[o]Acts 7:19; Exod 1:20

[p]Judg 9:22–51

THE PIERCINGS OF THE SWORD

Ahab hoped to find rest by getting rid of Naboth. But the words of his troublesome reprover were to him as the "thrusts of a sword."[q] How little did Gehazi expect to suffer leprosy, as the result of his well-contrived plan![r] Were the temptation presented in a naked form—"For this pleasure sell your soul, your God, your heaven"—who wouldn't run from it in horror? But the tempter *works deceitfully,* making the present pleasure, seem so wonderful, and hiding the certain reality of ruin.[s]

[q]Prov 12:18; 1 Kings 21:19

[r]2 Kings 5:27

[s]Prov 1:15–18

How moving it is to see Satan's poor victim eagerly *pursuing evil*[t]—yet *to his own death.* Not only his open acts, but his thoughts, motions, pursuits, ends—all *tend to death.*[u] God has no place in his heart, and what else can be the end of a life without God? Yes, the religious pretender *deceives* others, perhaps himself. But his *deceitful work* will be the delusion of a moment, an eternity of confusion.

[t]Prov 4:16, 17

[u]Prov 5:1–5; 9:18

THE SURE REWARD

The *true reward of righteousness* stands out in bright contrast. The "seed" is precious; and "his sheaves" shall doubtless follow.[v] No sinner since the fall of man has ever known the *full reward* of righteousness even in this life. It may be given to cause pain or misery—grace to support in trouble, and to triumph in its results. It will probably be given as the harvest to the sower—after difficult and anxious waiting.[w] But whenever granted, or however delayed, it is a *true reward. Righteousness* is the seed. Happiness is the harvest. *The reward* indeed is not from cause, but by consequence; not of debt, but of grace; depending upon a free promise; mercifully, yet surely, linked with Christian perseverance.[x] It must however be true righteousness—not according to man's profession, but according to God's standard. A routine of duties may skirt the borders of religion, at the utmost distance from the Spirit of God, and equally far from the vital principle of the heart. But *righteousness* not only

[v]Ps 126:6

[w]James 5:7, 8

[x]Eccl 11:6; Hos 10:12; 1 Cor 15:58; Gal 6:7, 8

[y]Verse 4
[z]Gen 19:16; Jer 45:5
[a]Prov 10:16; Isa 3:10; Rom 2:7; Gal 6:8
[b]Ps 19:11; 37:3–6; Isa 32:17
[c]Rev 22:12

"delivers from death"[y] (a special mercy even with the loss of all);[z] but it tends to life;[a] full of living enjoyment, of infinite, eternal pleasure. What importance is attached to every godly principle! All refer to eternity. If *righteousness* is our main end, God will make it our best friend; and He won't, as the world has done, reward us with ciphers instead of gold. Who will not love and serve the Lord when in keeping His commandments "there is *great reward?*"[b] At the last, the conviction of *the wicked* will be irresistible. "Had I but *sown righteousness* in the service of God, it would have been infinitely happy for me to eternity!" mumbles the dying sinner. But how joyous will be the great final outcome to the righteous—"Behold, I am coming quickly, and *My reward* is with Me, to render every man according to what he has done."[c]

20 *The perverse in heart are an abomination to the* LORD,
But the blameless in their *walk are His delight.*
21 *Assuredly, the evil man will not go unpunished,*
But the descendants of the righteous will be delivered.

[d]Verse 3; Prov 3:32; Ps 11:5–7
[e]Prov 8:13
[f]Exod 5:2; 9:17; Jer 44:16, 28
[g]Ps 119:67, 71
[h]Prov 16:5
[i]Isa 65:2–5; Luke 16:15

The *perverse and the blameless* are often contrasted, as God looks at them.[d] *Perverseness is abomination to the Lord.*[e] All the contests between God and man are—whose will shall prevail?[f] We ought to be most thankful for the school of discipline that makes us feel the privilege of subjection to the obedience of Christ.[g] *Perverseness in* the heart is specially hateful;[h] most of all under the guise of external religion.[i]

ARM OF VENGEANCE

[j]Prov 1:11–14; Isa 41:7
[k]Isa 8:9; Gen 11:8; Num 16:1–33; Josh 9:1, 2
[l]1 Sam 14:6
[m]Job 34:29
[n]Prov 16:5

Sinners encourage one another in sin,[j]—hand joining in hand. But all such partnerships shall be "broken . . . shattered."[k] For "The Lord is not restrained to save by many or by few";[l] so when He lifts his arm of vengeance, it is the same whether it be against a nation or a man only.[m] The flood; the judgment on Egypt; the chastenings of rebellious Israel in the wilderness; the destruction of Sennacherib's army—plainly prove, that *the evil man will not go unpunished,* and it is vain to resist the hand of God.[n]

The *blameless* are those, whom God makes blameless. They are His own workmanship. The *blameless in the way* are contrasted with the *perverse in heart:* because as the heart is, so is the way. Yet He is not said to delight in their way. (Though this is a known fact.) They themselves are *His delight.*[o] He singles them out from the ungodly world.[p] He even points to one of them as a challenge to Satan to do his worst.[q] Such is the condescension of His sovereign love—accepting His own Word; stamping with open honor the graces of His people, stained though they may be with such base defilement! "The Lord knows the days of the blameless"—the first day of going to their Bibles, the first day of prayer; all their cloudy and dark days. Nor does He put them off with a portion in this life. "Their inheritance will be forever."[r] It is but a moment, and they that love Him shall be with Him forever.

[o]Prov 12:22; Ps 84:11
[p]Gen 7:1; Num 14:24
[q]Job 1:8
[r]Ps 37:18

And their blessing isn't confined to themselves. The descendents of the righteous shall be delivered.[s]

[s]Prov 20:7; Ps 37:26; 1 Kings 15:4

THE BEST WAY TO HELP YOUR CHILDREN

"The best way for any man to do his children good, is to be godly himself."[6t] Isn't this an encouragement—not indeed to laziness and forwardness—but to parental faith, in leaving our children in this wicked world unprotected and alone?[u] "The children of Thy servants will continue, And their descendants will be established before Thee."[v]

[t]Gen 17:7; Acts 2:39
[u]Ps 103:17
[v]Ps 102:28

22 As *a ring of gold in a swine's snout,*
So is *a beautiful woman who lacks (departeth from)*[w] *discretion.*

[w]Prov 7:10; 9:13

THE FADING VANITY

A most distasteful, and yet an apt comparison! Let us see things as the Bible shows them to us. If a *beautiful,* light-minded young *woman* should see her own face in this mirror, she might well be startled with horror. Beauty indeed is to be honored, as the gift of God.[7] Yet in itself it is a fading vanity;[x] and, *without discretion,* it's as out-of-place and unbecoming, *as a ring of gold in a*

[x]Prov 31:30

[6] Exposition of Proverbs, *by JOHN DODD and ROBERT CLEAVER, 4 to 1614.*
[7] *See Moses, Acts 7:20; Joseph, Gen 39:6; David, 1 Sam 16:12; Esther 2:7; Job's daughters, 42:15.*

swine's snout.[y] Would the ornament beautify the filthy animal? Instead, wouldn't the unnatural combination make it more than ever an object of disgust? All the charms of beauty are lost upon a foolish woman. Instead of attaining "honor,"[z] she only brings disgrace upon herself. For just as *the ring* is soon employed and besmeared in raking the mire; so too often does the beauty of the *indiscreet woman* become servant to the vilest passions.[a] No ornament can give comeliness to a fool;[b] but "wisdom maketh the face to shine."[c]

[y]Isa 3:21
[z]Verse 16
[a]2 Sam 11:2
[b]Prov 26:8
[c]Eccl 8:1

"Lightness and fantastic elegance in apparel is the very bush or sign hanging out, that tells a vain mind lodges within. The soul fallen from God hath lost its true worth and beauty; and therefore it basely descends to these mean things, to serve and dress the body, and take share with it of its unworthy borrowed ornaments, while it hath lost and forgotten God, and seeks not after Him, knows not that He alone is the beauty and ornament of the soul, and His spirit, and the grace of it, His rich attire," said Leighton.[d]

[d]1 Peter 3:3, 4

INNER BEAUTY

Learn then to value, far beyond beauty of face, the inner ornaments of grace, which are "precious in the sight of God."[e] Many a lovely form enshrines a revolting mind. All external, even all intellectual, accomplishments *without discretion* result in barrenness. So fully do we depend upon God's grace for a fruitful improvement of His own gifts!

[e]1 Peter 3:4, 5

23 *The desire of the righteous is only good,*
But *the expectation of the wicked is wrath.*

THE SOUL HAS WINGS

Desire is the wing of the soul, by which it flies to what it loves, as the eagle to the carcass, in the Scripture Proverbs,[f] to feed itself upon it, and to be satisfied with it. *The desire of the righteous* must be good, because it is God's own work.[g] It must be *only good,* because it centers in Himself.[h] God in Christ is his portion: and what earthly portion can compare with it?[i]—his object; and what other object is worth living for—worth half a serious thought?[j] Only let me yield my desires to His will;[k]

[f]Job 39:30; Matt 24:28
[g]Ps 10:17; Rom 8:26, 27
[h]Ps 73:25; Isa 26:8, 9
[i]Ps 4:6, 7
[j]Rom 14:8, 9; 1 Cor 6:19, 20; Phil 1:21
[k]1 John 5:14

and I shall be happy, whether they be granted or withheld.[l] As a physician, "He Himself knows our frame";[m] what is, and what is not, good for me. "As a father", He has compassion on my weakness.[n] As a God, He fully supplies my *real* need.[o] The desire, therefore, inwrought by Him, fixed on Him, submitted to His will, must be *good.* But wouldn't an angel weep to see the corrupt mixture of worldliness;[p] selfishness;[q] pride?[r] Yet is this against our better will.[s] The main strength of *the desire* is toward God; even though the tossing tempest of sin and Satan may combine to drive it out of its course.[t] In spite of this mighty assault—"Lord, all my desire is before Thee . . . Lord, You know all things; You know that I love You."[u] "Thou didst put into my mind good desires; and Thou wilt bring the same to good effect!" reads the Collection for Easter Day.

[l]1 Kings 8:17, 18
[m]Ps 103:14
[n]Ps 103:13
[o]Phil 4:19
[p]Mark 10:35–37
[q]2 Sam 23:15; Jonah 4:8, 9
[r]1 Chron 21:1, 2
[s]Rom 7:15
[t]Rom 7:22
[u]Ps 38:9; John 21:17

But the *expectation of the wicked* is discontent and opposition to God. It is often indulged, but with the fearful accompaniment of *wrath.*[v]

[v]Num 11:18; Ps 78:29–31; 106:15

THE DELUDING DREAM

And how quickly will the deluding dream end in inexpressible, eternal *wrath!*[w] Oh! let me daily test my desires by the true standard, and discipline them, that they may be fixed upon the true object; so that, delighting myself "in the Lord," I may find them "*granted* . . . exceeding abundantly beyond" my greatest expectations.[x]

[w]Verse 7: Luke 16:23; Rom 2:8, 9; Heb 10:27
[x]Prov 10:24; Ps 37:4; Eph 3:20

24 *There is one who scatters, yet increases all the more,*
And there is one who withholds what is justly due,
but it results *only in want.*
25 *The generous man will be prosperous,*
And he who waters will himself be watered.

THE WAY TO PROSPERITY

God has put a mark of distinguishing favor upon the exercises of that mercy, which is His own attribute. He *scatters* His blessings richly around us;[y] and those that partake of His Spirit do the same. Men may *scatter* with lack of foresight and in sin, *and the result is want.*[z] But *there are those who scatter, and still increase.* The farmer, *scattering* his seed plentifully over his field, expects a proportionate increase. And shouldn't the man of

[y]Ps 33:5; 36:5–7
[z]Prov 21:17

God give "freely" the seed of godliness; consecrating his possessions and influence to the Lord; "while we have opportunity, let us do good to all men"[a]—shall not he receive a plentiful increase?[b] The men of the world risk everything they have in uncertain, and often, ruinous, speculations. But in this *scattering* there is no uncertainty, no speculation. Bounty is the way to plenty. Have faith in God; and laying out for Him will be laying up for ourselves.[c] This will be abundantly revealed, either in an evident enlargement of earthly blessing,[d] or in a satisfying enjoyment of a more limited portion.[e] The reward of grace will be given in the gracious acceptance of our God,[f] and in a blissful reception into "eternal dwellings."[g]

[a]Ps 112:9; Gal 6:10
[b]2 Cor 9:6, 11
[c]Prov 3:9, 10; 19:17
[d]Luke 6:38
[e]Deut 15:10
[f]Heb 13:16
[g]Luke 16:9; 1 Tim 6:18, 19

But is the covetous worldling happier? Is he richer—in withholding more than is right?[h] "Seldom does he prosper much even in the world. For God meters to men in their own measure; and bad crops, bad debts, expensive sickness, and a variety of similar deductions, soon amount to far more than *liberal* alms [giving] would have done," said Scott.

[h]Hag 1:4–10

Still more clearly does the Lord mark His blessing and His blight in the spiritual life. *The generous man will be prosperous* in the healthful vigor of practical godliness;[i] and while he is the soul of blessing to others; *he is watered himself* with the falling showers.[8] The minister is refreshed by his own message of salvation to his people. The Sunday school teacher learns many valuable lessons in his teaching. The soul of the church visitor or the Christian friend glows in sharing the precious name of Jesus with another person. Every holy mood, every spiritual gift, every active grace is increased by exercise; while its efficiency withers by neglect.[j]

[i]Verse 17; Isa 32:8
[j]Matt 25:29

26 *He who withholds grain, the people will curse him,*
But blessing will be on the head of him who sells it.

STEWARDS OF GOD'S GIFTS

This is a piece of sacred "political economy." It reminds us, that we are the stewards of the gifts of God.[k] To

[k]2 Cor 9:11

[8] *Isa 58:10, 11. "How often, when my heart has been cold and dead, have I been quickened by the loving-kindness of the Lord, upon doing something kind and loving for a fellow-creature, and more especially for a fellow-Christian!"—VENN'S Life, pp. 501, 502.*

use them therefore for our own interest, without due regard to our neighbor is unfaithfulness to our trust.[l] It is a flagrant sin, therefore, to withhold the very "staff of life";[m] holding back the hand of God stretched out in bounty over our land. This may indeed be a wise restraint in the time of scarcity.[n] Private interest may also claim a measure of consideration. But a grinding spirit; a spirit of selfish monopoly; raising the price for gain, with obvious suffering to the poor—will bring a piercing curse.[9] And here *the curse of the people* may be the curse of God. For if the cry of oppressed individuals[o]—much more that of an oppressed people—will enter into the ears of the Lord of Sabaoth.[p] His withering blight upon food withheld has often scourged this merciless greed.

[l] Matt 25:26, 27
[m] Isa 3:17
[n] Gen 41:46–49
[o] Exod 22:22–24; James 5:4
[p] Amos 8:4–8

The point of the opposite apparently fails, only to give stronger security to the blessing. *The curse* comes directly from *the people; the blessing* from above. To him who subordinates his own interest to the public good—blessings shall be upon his head,[q] descending immediately from the fountain of all grace.

[q] Prov 10:6

Would that the cry for Jesus, the "bread of life," were as earnest and universal as for the bread that perishes! But if he who withholds the one is justly cursed; how much more he, who unfaithfully and cruelly *withholds* the other! And if *blessings be upon the head of him, who sells the grain* of this life; what is his privilege, who doesn't sell the bread of life, but freely distributes it to people lost in sin! "The blessing of the one ready to perish came upon me."[r] The supply is abundant. Let the invitation be welcomed.[s]

[r] Job 29:13
[s] Isa 55:1

[9] *The original implies the piercing of a sword, or dagger, as if the selfish spoiler was, as it were, pierced through and stabbed to death by the* curses of the people—*CARTWRIGHT. The system of speculating in corn, in cruel disregard of the poor, was rebuked by a popular preacher in the latter days of Queen Elizabeth I, in the true spirit of Latimer—The poor man must needs sell presently to maintain his family, to pay his rents. And that which he sells, the rich glutton, who has hoarded up enough money, buys, that he may sell it at a much higher price. These buyers usually live in market towns, and wait to get into their hands all the corn (if it were possible) in the country. They don't only wait at home; they travel into the country to those men, whom they know have a great plenty of corn to sell. They bargain with them for as much as they can spare and so corner the market. And when they have it in their granaries, they set the price as they please. Surely this is a wolf of the soul. Some others will sell at home to their poor neighbors; but they will make them pay well above the market, or else get nothing. They know the poor man must have it. He can't buy it at the market, because he has no way to get it home; and, knowing how much he needs what they have, they will make him pay above all reason. And that also which makes their sin more heinous; if they send any corn to market, they will dress it very clean, and it has to be their best corn. But if they sell at home, then those who buy it will have to take the worst they have to offer. (A paraphrase of a godly and fruitful sermon, preached at Grantham A.D. 1592, by Francis Trigge.)*

27 *He who diligently seeks good seeks favor,*
But he who searches after evil, it will come to him.

BORN FOR ACTION

[t]Job 5:7
[u]Acts 10:38
[v]Ps 15:5
[w]James 1:27; Matt 25:35, 36
[x]Eccl 11:4
[y]Prov 16:7
[z]Prov 12:2; Neh 5:19
[a]Rev 3:8
[b]2 Cor 8:12

There is no negative existence. Man is born for action, "as sparks fly upward,"[t] or the stone tends downward. All of us are living with a stupendous measure of vital activity for *good* or for *evil*. Man was never intended—least of all the Christian—to be idle. Our divine Master "went about doing good";[u] always in motion; active in beneficence. And he is a counterfeit who does not live after this pattern. Usefulness is everything. We must not rest in life received. We should feel ashamed of our depravity, that we could ever spend a day without the great object—*seeking good.* Nor must we wait to have it brought to us. We must *seek it* diligently, rise up early, and hurry happily to work. Let's wake up to the fact that we have in our hands the means of blessing our fellow-sinners. And let's take our responsibility seriously. Every talent finds its suitable sphere, and may be put out "at interest"[v] with big returns. There is the practical exercise of "pure and undefiled religion";[w] the teaching of the ignorant; the instruction of the young—the rising hope of our church—a work of deepening interest and anxiety. Let each of us try to do what we can do; and, whether it's little or much, do it prayerfully, faithfully, heartily, not discouraged by trifling hindrances[x] and not making our inability to do much, an excuse for doing *nothing.* In living for others, we live for our true happiness. In *seeking diligently their good, we get favor;* often from man;[y] always from God.[z] He honors a little strength,[a] the single talent,[b] laid out for Him. And "filling up every hour with some profitable labor, either of heart, head, or hands" (as Brainerd justly observed) "is an excellent means of spiritual peace and boldness before God."[10]

[c]Ps 36:4
[d]Esther 7:10; Ps 57:6
[e]Gen 3:1–6, 14, 15
[f]2 Thess 2:10, 11

The ceaseless energy of Satan's servants in *searching after evil*[c] puts to shame our indifference. Yet *their own evil often comes to them.*[d] Satan himself found the *evil* that he brought upon man come unto him.[e] His servants often become the victims of their own delusions,[f] with

[10] Life of Brainerd—*Edwards' Works, vol. 3:148. "Religious people are heavy and moping, and cast down, principally because they are idle and selfish—Living and working for God and to save souls, is the only way to knowing more and more of his truth and his salvation"—VENN'S Life, pp. 321, 354.*

the fearful aggravation of having dragged multitudes with them into the pit of ruin. What then will be the fruit of my diligence? Will it be a blessing or a curse to my fellow-sinners? O my God! may it be from Thee, and for Thee!

28 *He who trusts in his riches will fall,*
But the righteous will flourish like the green *leaf.*

RICHES—STAFF OR PIERCING SPEAR?

Here is the cause and misery of the fall. Man seeks his rest in God's blessings, in opposition to himself.[g] *Riches* are one of his grounds of trust.[h] Man depends on them, as the saint upon his God.[i] And isn't this the denial of the "God above"?[j] An offensive truth indeed! Such as only the heart crucified to the world by the cross of Christ can receive. It's not that the possession of riches is a sin,[11] it's *trusting* in them, that is.[k] It certainly isn't always wrong to seize an opportunity for increasing riches. But no one that cares for his own soul, and believes the testimony of God,[l] will seek the opportunity; or even take advantage of it without a plain call, and a clear sign it's to the glory of God.[m] Let God be our satisfying portion. Let Him be supremely loved and honored, and He will determine for us, whether the worldly advantage be in God's care or in temptation.

[g] Jer 9:23, 24
[h] Prov 10:15; Luke 12:19
[i] Prov 18:10, 11
[j] Job 31:24, 25, 28
[k] Mark 10:24
[l] Mark 10:25–27; 1 Tim 6:9, 10
[m] 1 Tim 6:18, 19

Disappointment will be the certain end of this *trust.*[n] When we need a staff, we shall find a piercing spear.[o] Or we shall *fall,* like the withered leaf or blossom before the wind's blast.[p] And how many a lovely blossom has *fallen* in just that way![q] So it is that "the rich man in the midst of his pursuits will fade away"![r]

[n] Ps 49:6–12; Eccl 5:10, 11
[o] 1 Tim 6:10
[p] Deut 8:17–19
[q] Mark 10:21, 22
[r] James 1:10, 11

But *the righteous is the green leaf;* not like the blossom easily shaken and withered;[12] but abiding in the true vine; full of life and fruit.[s] There may be, as in nature's winter, times of apparent barrenness. But the spring returns, and with it *the leaf flourishes;* never ceasing from yielding fruit; yes—filled with the fruit of righteousness:[t] the branch of the Lord's "planting; The work of My hands, That I may be glorified"; to be transplanted in His own best time to the other side of the river, where "the

[s] John 15:5
[t] Jer 17:8

[11] *See the gift of God to Abraham, Gen 24:35; to David, 1 Chron 29:12; to Solomon, 2 Chron 1:11, 12; to Job, 42:11, 12.*
[12] *See the same contrast, Ps 3:7, 8.*

[u]Isa 60:21; Ezek 47:12

leaves will not wither and their fruit will not fail."[u] Shall not this prospect fill us with lively joy and praise?

29 *He who troubles his own house will inherit wind,*
And the foolish will be servant to the wisehearted.

INHERIT THE WIND

[v]Ps 133
[w]Matt 12:25
[x]1 Sam 25:17
[y]Hos 8:7
[z]Num 16:32, 33
[a]Josh 7:24, 25
[b]1 Sam 2:32, 33
[c]1 Kings 14:9–11; 21:20–22
[d]1 Kings 16:34
[e]Isa 5:24
[f]Comp. Prov 17:2
[g]Luke 15:13–15

A house at unity with itself, flourishes under the special favor of God.[v] But a house troubled with division, "is laid waste."[w] Often also the unspiritual, or ungoverned passion of the father in the home, blights the comfort of the family.[x] Indeed a parent cannot neglect his own soul without injury to his family. The father deprives the family of the blessing of holy prayers and godly example; while he *troubles* them with the positive mischief of his ungodliness, and himself *inherits the wind* in utter disappointment.[y] It was that way with the rebellion of Korah;[z] the sin of Achan;[a] the neglect of Eli;[b] the wickedness of Jeroboam and Ahab;[c] the stubborn contrariness of the rebuilder of Jericho[d]—they *troubled their house* to its ruin. Prayerless, careless parents ponder the responsibility of bringing a curse, instead of a blessing, upon your families. What if their "root will become like rot and their blossom blow away as dust"?[e] What if a man, instead of building up his house, should be "so foolish as to misspend himself, and come to be *a servant* at the last to him that is wise to get and keep his own?" said Bishop Hall.[f] Such retributions have been known[g] for the abuse of the gifts of God and the neglect of Christian responsibility.

30 *The fruit of the righteous is a tree of life,*
And he who is wise wins souls.

TREE OF LIFE-FLOURISHING BRANCH

[h]Verse 28
[i]Rev 22:2, with Prov 10:11, 31, 32
[j]Rev 2:7, with Prov 10:21
[k]Prov 12:18; 15:4

Here is *the fruit* of the flourishing branch.[h] The whole course of the *righteous*—his influence, his prayers, his instruction, his example—*is a tree of life.* What the tree of life was in Paradise: what it will be in Heaven, that he is in this wilderness, fruitful,[i] nourishing,[j] healing.[k] "And surely he, who by these means wins souls to righteousness and salvation, *is wise* indeed," said Bishop Horne in *Sermon on the Tree of Life.* He only, who purchased them by His blood, can *win* them to Himself; (and who ever knows the work, but will give Him all the praise!) yet has He set apart men for the work of "drawing souls to God, and to the love of Him; sweetly gaining, and making a holy conquest of them to God," said Diodati. This was the *wisdom* of our blessed Lord. He taught "the word to them as they were able to hear it";[l] accommodating himself to their convenience,[m] and their prejudices,[n] in order that He might *win their souls*. And these opportunities were truly His meat and drink. For when "wearied from His journey, was sitting thus by the well," thirsting for water; far more intensely did He thirst *for* the soul of the poor sinner before Him; and, having *won* her to Himself, He forgot His own want in the joy of her salvation.[o] In close walking after this pattern of *wisdom*, did the great apostle "become all things to all men, that I may by all means save some."[p] God grant that no minister of Christ may spend a day, without laboring to *win* at least *one soul* for heaven!

[l]Mark 4:33
[m]Mark 6:31–34
[n]Matt 11:16–19
[o]John 4:6, 32–34
[p]1 Cor 9:20–22; 10:33

But—blessed be God!—this fruit—this wisdom—is not confined to the ministry. Do we love our Lord? If so, let us follow in this happy work of soul-winning, and He will honor us. *The righteous wife wins her husband's soul* by the *wisdom* of meekness and sobriety.[q] The godly neighbor *wins* his fellow-sinner by patient faith and love.[r] "Not one of us" in the true church of God "lives for himself."[s] The Christian who neglects his brother's salvation, if he does not exhibit that love and kindness of God, which hath appeared unto men—he has gone back to his inborn selfishness. We should be diamonds of shining, magnets with strong drawing power to attract souls to Christ. How poor are the marks of office—headdress or crown; how debasing the wisdom of the philosopher, the scholar, or the statesman, compared with this wisdom! For we must be very wise, indeed, *to win souls*—they are so hard to win! If only one soul is won, the honor is beyond human comprehension. "A soul is a kingdom. As many as we can bring back to God are so many kingdoms reconquered," said Quesnel.[t] No ambition so great, no results so glorious as winning souls. Those who have insight will shine brightly like the brightness of the expanse of Heaven, and those who lead the many to righteousness, like the stars forever and ever."[u] Every soul

[q]1 Peter 3:1, 2
[r]James 5:19, 20
[s]Rom 14:7
[t]Luke 15:6
[u]Dan 12:3

won by this wisdom, will be a fresh jewel in the Savior's crown; a polished stone in that temple, in which He will be honored throughout eternity.

31 *If the righteous will be rewarded in the earth,*
How much more the wicked and the sinner!

The inspired application of this proverb always, without fail, makes plain the mind of God. It is introduced to us with special emphasis. Let *the righteous* expect from their relation to God—not exemption, but strict *reward.*[v] They are under the discipline, though not under the curse, of the rod. We think so highly of the world, conform so much to its ways and spirit, and are so forgetful of our inheritance and home; that, if it weren't for the rod, we should soon backslide to our stubborn waywardness. The *righteous* therefore are *rewarded in the earth.*[13] Every perfection of God is glorified in this dispensation. As a wise Father, He will not excuse their sin. As a holy God, He must show His hatred of it. As a faithful God, He will make the punishment of His rod the means of their restoration.[w] But—blessed be God—all the penal curse is eliminated. We *are rewarded on earth;* not as we deserve to be, in Hell. Really—"we are disciplined by the Lord in order that we may not be condemned along with the world";[x] punished here, that we might be spared forever; *rewarded on earth,* to be made fit for heaven.[y]

Much more then will the wicked and the sinner get what he deserves. If the children are punished, how much more those who turn from God. If the fatherly corrections are so terrible, even when the child is accepted; what must God's righteous unrestrained worth against the willful sinner be like? "If it is with difficulty that the righteous are saved; what will become of the godless man and the sinner?"[z] "If they do these things in the green tree, what will happen in the dry?"[a] "Behold, the day is coming, burning like a furnace; and all the arrogant and every evildoer will be chaff."[b] Let the *wicked* tremble. Let the child of God be humbled in the dust—"My flesh trembles for fear of Thee, And I am afraid of Thy judgments."[c]

[v] Amos 3:2; 1 Peter 4:17
[w] Ps 89:30–32
[x] 1 Cor 11:32
[y] Heb 12:10
[z] 1 Peter 4:18
[a] Luke 23:31
[b] Mal 4:1
[c] Ps 119:120

[13] Jacob—*Gen 27 with 33. Moses and Aaron—Num 20:12, with Deut 3:23–26; 33:48–52; Ps 99:6–8; Eli, 1 Sam 2:27–36; David—2 Sam 12:9–12; Ps 32:3, 4; 38:1–5; Solomon—1 Kings 11:9–13. The disobedient prophet—1 Kings 13:21–24; Hezekiah—Isa 39:1–7.*

CHAPTER TWELVE

1 *Whoever loves discipline loves knowledge,*
But he who hates reproof is stupid.

THE ONLY ROAD TO SPIRITUAL ATTAINMENT

Discipline, as the contrast teaches, mainly implies instruction[a]—that most needful means of acquiring *knowledge.*[b] You see, it's so contrary to our proud hearts, that the yielding of our will is our only road to Christian attainment.[c] Yet the value of this attainment more than covers the cost.[d] A faithful ministry, therefore, is a most valuable blessing; and all instructive *discipline* may well be *loved* as the way of life.[e]

But that irritable pride, that *hates reproof,* as if it were an insult to be told of our faults, shows not only a lack of grace;[f] but also understanding—*stupid* foolishness;[g] like the horse, which bites and kicks at the man, who performs a painful operation upon him, which is absolutely necessary for removing a dangerous disorder. He is surely not a rational creature. Anyone who swallows poison and would rather let it kill him than take the necessary medicine to save his life, is certainly out of his mind—especially, if it's because he doesn't want to admit his need for it, since he then would have to acknowledge his sin. Oh for a teachable spirit to sit at the feet of our divine Master, and learn of Him!

[a] Judg 8:16; Jer 6:8
[b] Ps 119:67, 71
[c] Matt 18:3, 4
[d] Phil 3:8
[e] Prov 9:8; Ps 141:5, with Prov 6:23. Comp. Ps 16:7; 94:12; Jer 31:18
[f] Prov 10:17; 15:10
[g] Isa 1:3; Jer 8:7

2 *A good man will obtain favor from the* LORD,
But He will condemn a man who devises evil.

PLEASURE FOREVERMORE!

Goodness is "the fruit of the Spirit."[h] *The good man* therefore is a man filled with the Spirit. He reflects the loving goodness of God.[i] He is not only the object of

[h] Gal 5:22
[i] Matt 5:44, 45

grace, but the giver of it, as well; not only "enriched" with all blessings for himself, but "for all liberality"[j] for the service of other people. As a benefactor to mankind, he commands our devoted gratitude. But as a far richer reward (or grace indeed, not of debt)[k] he obtains favor of the Lord.[l] What are all this world's treasures compared with it?[m] Is it not the joy of our salvation; our soothing mercy;[n] our covering shield;[o] in the near prospect of eternity, our absorbing interest?[p] And if here, in a world of sin, it is life, yes even better than life;[q] what will that unclouded sunshine be like: "the path of life"; the "fullness of joy; In Thy right hand there are pleasures forever"![r]

[j]2 Cor 9:11
[k]Luke 17:10
[l]Isa 58:8–11; Neh 13:14; 1 Peter 3:12
[m]Ps 4:6, 7
[n]Ps 119:76
[o]Ps 5:12
[p]2 Cor 5:9, 10
[q]Ps 58:3
[r]Ps 16:11

The contrast to *the good man* is—not the man (which alas! may be a child of God)[s] in whom, *evil devices* are found, but *the man of these devices.* He lives in them as his element; his mind is set upon them. He invites them. He follows them as his course and delight.[t] Instead of having favor, he is condemned already.[u] His sting of conscience and the curse of God are present *condemnation.*[v] And in the great day, the all-seeing Judge "will be a swift witness against" him![w]

[s]2 Sam 11:12–15
[t]Prov 1:10–12; 6:18; Isa 32:6, 7
[u]John 3:19, 20
[v]Zech 5:3, 4; 1 Kings 12:25–30; 14:10
[w]Mal 3:5; Ps 1:16–21

3 *A man will not be established by wickedness,*
But the root of the righteous will not be moved.

The man of evil schemes may prosper for a time, but *he will not be established by wickedness,* except as God may permit it, in the sovereignty of His purposes, and the fair punishment of His wrath. But how soon was the successful treason of Abimelech,[x] and the Israelitish kings,[y] brought to an end! Ahab strove to *establish* himself in spite of the threatened curse of God. He increased his family and had them trained with care under the teaching of his choice nobles. And surely, at least one out of seventy might remain to inherit his throne. But this was the vain striving of the worm with his Maker. One hour swept them all away; and not a word of the threatening fell to the ground.[1] *The wicked scheming* of Caiaphas also *to establish his* nation by wickedness was the means of its overthrow.[z] Such is the infatuation of sin!

[x]Judg 9:54–57
[y]1 Kings 16:9, 10; 2 Kings 15:10–14; 2 Chron 21:4, 13–15
[z]John 11:49, 50, with Matt 21:43, 44

[1] *1 Kings 21, with 2 Kings 10:1–7. Comp. the striking figures in the book of Job 15:29; 20:5–9; 27:13–17.*

IN THE FURY OF THE TEMPEST

Firm and unshaken is the condition of *the righteous.* Their leaves may wither in the blast; their branches may tremble in the fury of the tempest; but *their root*—the true principle of life—*will not be moved.* They are saved with "difficulty,"[a] not without many tossings. But they are surely saved. The powers of Hell cannot destroy them. Doesn't your faith, Christian, sometimes faint in the wearisome assaults of your relentless enemy? Rejoice in the assurance, that it cannot *fail.*[b] You are "rooted and grounded" in a sure foundation.[c] Let the Lord, God who "is my strength . . . and song. . . . He only is my rock and my salvation . . . I shall not be greatly shaken"; I shall *not be moved at all.*[d]

And how bright is this prospect for the church! *It cannot be moved.*[e] Triumphant is her confidence in the day of conflict. "The gates of Hades shall not overpower it. . . . No weapon that is formed against you shall prosper."[f]

[a] 1 Peter 4:18
[b] Luke 22:31, 32
[c] Eph 3:17; Col 2:7
[d] Isa 12:2; Ps 62:2, 6; Mic 7:8; Rom 8:31–39
[e] Ps 125:1, 2; Isa 26:1
[f] Matt 16:18; Isa 54:17

4 *An excellent wife is the crown of her husband,*
But she who shames him *is as rottenness in his bones.*

THE VIRTUOUS WOMAN

Faithful,[g] chaste,[h] reverentially obedient,[i] immovable in affection,[j] delighting to see her husband honored, respected, and loved; covering, as far as may be, his failings; prudent in the management of her family,[k] conscientious in the discharge of her domestic duties;[l] kind and considerate to all around her;[m] and as the root of all—"fears the Lord"[n]—such is *the excellent wife;* "a weaker vessel"[o] indeed, but a woman of strength,[2] with all her graces in godly energy. She isn't the ring on her husband's finger, or the chain of gold around his neck. Those are far too low. She is his crown; his brightest ornament;[3] drawing the eyes of all upon him, as eminently honored and blessed.[p]

[g] Prov 31:11, 12
[h] Titus 2:5; 1 Peter 3:2
[i] Eph 5:22, 23; 1 Peter 3:1, 4–6
[j] Titus 2:4
[k] Prov 14:1
[l] Prov 31:27, 28
[m] Prov 31:20, 26
[n] Prov 31:30
[o] 1 Peter 3:7
[p] Prov 31:23

THE CONTENTIOUS WIFE

Truly affecting is the contrast of a contentious,[q] domineering, extravagant, perhaps unfaithful wife; in the

[q] Prov 19:13; 21:9, 19

[2] *1 Peter 3:7, with Prov 31:10; Ruth 3:11. Here is given the meaning of manly courage. In the first ages of barbarism this was the primary virtue, and therefore it naturally became the generic term of virtue.*

[3] *Perhaps there may be some allusion to* the crown *on the wedding day. Comp. 1 Cor 11:7.*

flippancy of her conduct forgetting her proper place and subjection; seeking the admiration of others, instead of being satisfied with her husband's regard. This is indeed a living disease—*rottenness in his bones*[4] marring his usefulness; undermining his happiness; perhaps driving him into temptation, and a "snare of the devil." Let a young woman, in contemplating this holy union, ponder well and in deep prayer its weighty responsibility. Will she be *a crown to her husband,* or one *that shames* him? Will she be what God made the woman—"a helper";[r] or—what Satan made her—a tempter—to *her husband?*[s] If she is not a *crown* to him, she will be a shame to herself. If she is *rottenness to his bones,* she will be a plague to her own. For what is the woman's happiness, but to be the helper of her husband's joy? Oh! let their mutual comfort be looked for, the only place it can be solidly found, in living together "as a fellow-heir of the grace of life."[t] Better never to have seen each other, than to live together forgetful of this great end of improving their union as a loving gift of God, and an important talent for His service, and their own eternal happiness.

[r]Gen 2:18
[s]Gen 3:6; 1 Kings 21:25; Job 2:9
[t]1 Peter 3:7

5 *The thoughts of the righteous are just,*
But *the counsels of the wicked are deceitful.*
6 *The words of the wicked lie in wait for blood,*
But the mouth of the upright will deliver them.
7 *The wicked are overthrown and are no more,*
But the house of the righteous will stand.

OUT OF THE CORRUPT FOUNTAIN . . . BITTER WATERS

The workings of good and evil are here traced to the fountainhead.[u] *The thoughts of the righteous,* "renewed in the spirit of your mind,"[v] *are just.*[w] He learns to measure everything by the unerring rule and to lean upon his God in the careful distrust of himself. Many indeed are his errors, but there is an overcoming law within, that, in spite of all oppositions, fixes *his thoughts* with delight on God and His law[x] and gives to them a single love for His service. But the thoughts of *the wicked* are far different! They ripen into *counsels* full of *deceit.* The *counsels* of Joseph's brethren were intended to deceive their father;

[u]Gen 6:5
[v]Eph 4:23
[w]Prov 11:23
[x]Ps 139:17, 18; Rom 7:15–23

[4]*Jerome aptly compares it to the worm eating into the heart of the tree and destroying it.*

of Jeroboam, under pretended consideration of the people; of Daniel's enemies, under pretense of honoring the king; of Sanballat, under the guise of friendship; of Haman, under the cover of patriotism; of Herod, under the profession of worshiping the infant Savior.[y] Indeed from such "a polluted well" as man's heart, what else can be expected but bitter waters?[z]

[y]Gen 37:18–20; 1 Kings 12:26–28; Dan 6:4–7; Neh 6:2; Esther 3:8–10; Matt 2:7, 8

[z]Prov 25:26; Exod 15:23; Jer 17:9; Matt 15:19

Then look at *words*—the natural organ of *the thoughts*. How murderous were *the words* of Ahithophel; the trap laid for our beloved Lord; the conspiracy against the great apostle[a]—all lying *in wait for blood!*[b] The fiercer outbursts of humanity may indeed be softened down and restrained.[5] But the principles remain the same. The fiery elements only lie in slumbering cover, and often break out, wasting the very face of society. Yet even in this bursting storm *the mouth of the upright will deliver them.*[c] The wisdom of our precious Lord was an unfailing *deliverance.*[d] The same mouth was a cover to his *upright* disciples, with little of man's help, and much of man's opposition; "None . . . will be able to resist or refute."[e]

[a]2 Sam 17:1–4; Luke 20:19–21; Acts 23:14, 15

[b]Prov 29:10; Ps 37:12, 14

[c]Prov 11:9

[d]Matt 22:34, 35, 46

[e]Luke 21:14, 15; Acts 4:13, 14

THEY SHALL BE MINE—MY JEWELS

We can only wonder at the long-suffering, that allows *the wicked* to load the earth with such a mass of guilt and misery. Yet their triumphing is but for a moment.[f] Look at Haman—*his deceitful advice,* his bloody words. *He is* overthrown, and destroyed.[g] "Now shall not God bring about justice for His elect?"[h] *Their house,* feeble as it often is, and brought low,[i] *will stand.* They will have "an everlasting name which will not be cut off" immovable here,[j] and in eternity.[k] Yes—those, whose thoughts and words are upright, shall stand, when all else is falling—" 'They will be Mine,' says the LORD of hosts, 'on the day that I prepare My own possession.' "[l]

[f]Job 20:5; Ps 37:35, 36

[g]Esther 7:10

[h]Luke 18:7

[i]Prov 12:3; 1 Kings 15:4

[j]Isa 56:4, 5

[k]Rev 3:12

[l]Mal 3:17

8 *A man will be praised according to his insight*
[AV—wisdom],
But one of perverse mind will be despised.

The usual way of this world is to "substitute darkness for light,"[m] to commend foolishness rather than *insight.* And yet, even hated *wisdom* often convicts both conscience and judgment; and *a man is praised according to*

[m]Isa 5:20

[5] *See Rom 3:15, as proof of universal and total depravity, verses 9, 10.*

it. Hence the promotions of Joseph and Daniel to high office; the honor paid to David in private life; and the universal respect shown to his wise son.[n] Our Lord's *wisdom* was also *praised,* not only by popular voice,[o] but even by the testimony of His enemies.[p] The wisdom of Stephen, making "his face like the face of an angel," overpowered his beholders with solemn awe.[q] How thrilling will be *the praise of wisdom* before the assembled universe![r] Who will not then acknowledge the *wise* choice of an earthly cross with a heavenly crown?[s] Wisdom[t] then—not dignity, riches, or talent—brings honor. This is the Lord's *praise.* It must be right.[u] It will stand for eternity.

[n]Gen 41:39; Dan 1:19, 20; 2:46; 1 Sam 16:18; 18:30; 1 Kings 3:28; 4:29–34
[o]Matt 7:28, 29
[p]John 7:46
[q]Acts 6:10, 15
[r]Luke 12:42–44
[s]Matt 5:11, 12
[t]2 Sam 20:18–22
[u]2 Cor 5:18

What then makes a man *despised?* Not his poverty, obscure circumstances, or misfortune; but stubbornness of spirit,[v] too proud to be taught; following a mad course to ruin. *Perverse* Nabal was *despised* by his own family;[w] the prodigal by his former companions.[x] And of all such, shame will be their present promotion,[y] their eternal doom.[z]

[v]1 Kings 12:16; Mal 2:8, 9
[w]1 Sam 25:17, 25
[x]Luke 15:15, 16
[y]Prov 3:35; 11:2; 18:3
[z]Dan 12:2

9 *Better is he who is lightly esteemed and has a servant,*
Than he who honors himself and lacks bread.

EARTHLY CROSS—HEAVENLY CROWN

A man who is successful enough *to have a servant,*[a] but not enough to make an outward show, may be *lightly esteemed* by his richer neighbors.[b] But still, he's better off than those who make a big show of things but are unable to back it up; or those humbled outwardly but not in their heart.[c] Nothing is so detestable as to be proud, where there is nothing to be proud of. Sometimes by foolishly trying to "keep up with the Joneses" a man deprives himself of the common comforts of life. He makes a name for himself but goes without food to do it. That's the kind of slaves men are to public opinion! Principle is sacrificed for pride; and men rebel against God, who makes no mistake in His dealings with men, often disciplining those in high places by bringing them low.[d] Yet it is hard, even for the Christian, as Bunyan reminds us in *The Pilgrim's Progress,* to go down into the Valley of Humiliation, without a fall somewhere along the way.

[a]Prov 30:8, 9
[b]1 Sam 18:23
[c]Prov 13:7; Luke 14:11
[d]James 1:10, 11; Dan 4:32–37

We need our Lord's unworldly, elevated spirit[e] to make a safe descent. Remember—"the boastful pride of life, is not from the Father, but is from the world."[f] "Let your forbearing *spirit* be known to all men," remembering—"The Lord is near."[g] We need to constantly remember how the dazzling glare of man's esteem will someday fade away before the glory of His appearing!

[e]John 6:15

[f]1 John 2:16

[g]Phil 4:5; Mark 13:1, 2

10 *A righteous man has regard for the life of his beast,*
But the compassion of the wicked is cruel.

The attention of the Bible to minute detail is one of its most valuable qualities. It shows the mind of God on many seemingly trivial points.

THE CHRISTIAN'S ATTITUDE TOWARD GOD'S ANIMAL CREATION

Here it tests our profession by our treatment of God's creatures. He gave them to man, as the Lord of the Creation, for his use, comfort, and food;[h] not for wantonness. A *righteous man is concerned about his pets and animals,* tending to their comfort,[i] and never pushing them beyond their strength.[j] The brutal habits, therefore, the coarse words, inhuman blows,[k] and hard tyranny to horses at the public riding academies and at jumping events are disgraceful to our nature. The delight of children in putting animals to pain for amusement, if not early restrained, will mature them in cruelty, demoralize their whole character, and harden them against all the sympathies of social life. For, as Mr. Locke wisely observed in *Thoughts Concerning Education,* "they who delight in the sufferings and destruction of inferior creatures, will not be apt to be very compassionate and benign to those of their own kind." Thus *the compassion* of the wicked are cruel, having no right feeling;[l] only a milder exercise of barbarity;[m] and usually given out for some selfish end.[6]

[h]Gen 1:28; 9:3

[i]Gen 24:32

[j]Gen 23:13, 14

[k]Num 22:27

[l]Gen 27:26–28

[m]1 Sam 11:1, 2; Luke 23:13–16

But why does this humane attitude mark *a righteous man?* Because it is the image of our heavenly Father,

[6] *Acts 24:26, 27. To paraphrase Holden—We have been used to hearing much about the kindliness of infidels, and the desire of believers in God to help mankind. But it's all a pretense. Self is the idol, and self-indulgence the object, and it doesn't matter much how they reach their goals. Where self is the idol, the heart is cruel. While they talk of universal love, they overlook the cruelty of robbing millions of the comfort of religion. While they clamor about reform, they would with unfeeling barbarity exult in the demolition of revered establishments. While they speak of harmless gaiety and pleasure, they would treacherously corrupt piety, and pollute unsuspecting innocence.*

[n]Ps 33:5; 145:9, 16; 147:9
[o]Ps 36:6, 7
[p]Exod 12:30; Deut 5:14; 25:4
[q]Jon 4:11
[r]Num 22:28–30
[s]Matt 5:44, 45

who spreads His covering wings over His whole creation.[n] As though the field of man was too small for His goodness, He regards the life of the beast.[o] Note the approvals of His law,[p] and the giving out of His judgments.[q] Yet, God even miraculously enabled the stupid donkey to plead the cause of the animal creation.[r] Then shouldn't His children reflect His whole image of love?[s] And isn't the lack of any part of this image a mark of doubtful relationship to Him?

11 *He who tills his land will have plenty of bread,*
But he who pursues vain things *lacks sense.*

[t]Gen 2:15
[u]Gen 4:2
[v]Isa 28:23–26
[w]Gen 26:12
[x]Prov 27:23–27

Special honor is given to the work of cultivating the land. God assigned it to Adam in Paradise.[t] That was the work of his oldest son.[u] Its origin seems to have been under God's direct teaching.[v] In early times it was the business or relaxation of kings.[7]. A blessing is ensured to diligence; sometimes abundant;[w] always what we should be satisfied with.[x]

SATAN'S THRONE—AND PILLOW

[y]Prov 31:13–22
[z]Rom 12:11; 1 Thess 4:11
[a]2 Thess 3:10–12
[b]Prov 13:20; Acts 5:36, 37

The principle applies alike to every lawful calling. Hard work is an ornamental grace,[y] and a Christian obligation.[z] Its reward in God's work is all it should be and more! How great are the rewards for the diligent student of the Scriptures! Truly he shall *have plenty of bread.* But idleness is a blot upon our royal name.[a] An old writer said, "The proud person is Satan's *throne,* and the *idle* man his pillow. He sits in the one and sleeps quietly on the other." The man therefore who takes idle people as his example, instead of working hard, is unwise, and he will certainly reap the fruits of his foolishness[b]—perhaps for all eternity.

12 *The wicked desires the booty* [AV—*net*] *of evil men,*
But the root of the righteous yields fruit.

ROOTS OF RIGHTEOUSNESS

Man is always anxious to press onward to something not yet enjoyed. The Christian reaches out to higher

[7] *2 Chron 26:10. Such was the judgment of the Roman moralist: "Of all the arts of civilized man, agriculture is transcendently the most essential and valuable. Other arts may contribute to the comfort, the convenience, and the embellishment of life. But the cultivation of the soil stands in immediate connection with our very existence. The life itself, to whose comfort, and convenience, and embellishment, other arts contribute, is by this sustained; so that others without it can avail nothing"—WARDLAW on Eccl 5:9.*

privileges and greater holiness.[c] *The wicked* try to outdo each other in wickedness; and if they see *evil men* more successful than themselves, *they want their booty;*[d] to discover their plans in order to imitate them. They aren't satisfied with the honest gain of godliness, they *desire a net,* in which they can grasp rich treasures of this world's goods.[e] The history of the church strongly illustrates the power of sin; one *net* following another with a more cunning scheme. Such is the root of evil, loaded with destruction. *But the root of the righteous yields fruit*—true, solid abundant fruit; not always visible, but always acceptable.[f] Dependence on Christ is the source of this blessing; necessary in order *to yield fruit,*[8] and never failing to produce it.[g] The spiritual branches "are nourished and increased by the living root of God's grace and blessing," said Diodati.

[c]Phil 3:12–14
[d]Ps 10:8–10; Jer 5:26–28
[e]1 Tim 6:10
[f]Heb 13:15, 16
[g]John 15:5

13 *An evil man is ensnared by the transgression of his lips,*
But the righteous will escape from trouble.

We have seen the intense *desire* of *the wicked* to catch others in the *net*. Here he is *ensnared* himself; the *sins* of his lips become the *snare* of his life.[h] Many have felt the whip upon their backs because they have failed to bridle their tongues. That's what happened to the Amalekite who brought tidings of Saul's death. He expected a reward but, instead, he found death.[i] The same was true of Adonijah and his deceitful request;[j] the hypocritical loyalty of Daniel's enemies;[k] the fearful curse of the devoted nation.[l] *The lips of the evil man* miss their mark and become the instruments of his ruin.[m]

On the other hand, the godly exercise of the lips often delivers *from trouble,* into which the wicked rush headlong.[n] The noble confession of Caleb and Joshua brought them safe out of the *trouble*, which was threatening their rebellious brethren.[o] And even when *the righteous* are overtaken with a sin of the *lips*, still their faithful God makes a difference. He will not indeed overlook sin in His own children.[p] But while He promises punishment

[h]Prov 18:7; Ps 64:8
[i]2 Sam 4:9–12
[j]1 Kings 2:22, 23
[k]Dan 6:7, 8, 24
[l]Matt 27:25
[m]Ps 35:8
[n]Jer 26:12–16
[o]Num 14:6–10, 24
[p]Amos 3:2

[8]*John 15:4; Rom 7:4. It was the remark of a venerable relative of the writer's, who was never suspected of enthusiasm—"As surely as the vine-branch can have no powers, independent of the root; so surely cannot the Christian* think, act, or live, as such, *but only so far as he derives his abilities from the stock, on which he is engrafted"—The Rev. WILLIAM JONES' (Nayland)* Enquiry Upon the Spring, *p. 36.*

for *their transgressions,* He assures deliverance in the end.[q] Thus arrogant confidence is restrained; and a humbling, self-abasing, tender confidence is established.

[q] Ps 89:32, 33

14 *A man will be satisfied with good by the fruit of his words,*
And the deeds of man's hands will return to him.

ALL OF OUR BODY—GOD'S BY PURCHASE

We have seen the snare of the tongue. Here is it blessing, not to others[r] only, but to ourselves. Have we the mark of "the saints of God, to speak of the glory of His kingdom?"[s] What dignity this grand subject will give to our conversation! What a preservative from that frivolous "talk of the lips, which tendeth only to poverty!"[t] What a lift to our whole character![u] *How satisfied we shall be with good by the fruit of our words!*[v] When our God, not only visits us, but actually lives within us, then the *fruit* of our mouth doesn't have to be forced out, it just pours out of our hearts without effort.

Then, when the lips are devoted, so are *the hands,* and they willingly serve. Every member of the body is God's by purchase,[w] and when we serve Him, we are always rewarded. For whoever served God for nothing?[x] "God is not unjust so as to forget your work and the love which you have shown toward His name. A cup of cold water given in His name shall not lose its reward.[y] The smallest show of love will be abundantly and eternally rewarded.

[r] Prov 10:20, 21
[s] Ps 145:10, 11
[t] Prov 14:23
[u] Mal 3:16, 17
[v] Prov 13:2; 15:23
[w] 1 Cor 6:19, 20
[x] Job 1:9, 10
[y] Heb 6:10; Matt 10:42

15 *The way of a fool is right in his own eyes,*
But a wise man is he who listens to counsel.

THE PATH TO RUIN

The *fool's* conceit hinders his wisdom.[z] A discouraging case![a] He thinks whatever *he does is right.*[b] He doesn't need any guidance. He doesn't ask for any advice. He just goes on in his own stubborn way, just because it's his own,[c] and follows it to his own ruin. His chief danger is his self-security.[d] He may not be guilty of any great sin, or be any worse than his respectable neighbor. He has no doubt of Heaven. He doesn't think of the way as being so narrow that few find it;[e] he thinks of it as so easy to find that few can miss it. So . . . Christianity to him is really

[z] Job 11:12
[a] Prov 26:12
[b] Prov 16:2
[c] Judg 2:19
[d] Deut 29:19
[e] Matt 7:14

just self-delusion.[f] O Lord, save me from myself—from my own self-deceitfulness. [f]Prov 14:12

What a proof of wisdom is a teachable spirit! What an excellent means of increasing it![g] Wasn't Moses wiser for having listened to Jethro's *counsel;*[h] and David for listening to the restraining advice of Abigail?[i] How precious then to the child of God is the office of the divine counselor![j] How wise the reverential faith, that *listens to His counsel!* Whom does God ever disappoint? Whom does He scold or reprove?[k]

[g]Prov 1:5
[h]Exod 18:14–24
[i]1 Sam 25:23–32
[j]Isa 9:6
[k]James 1:5

16 *A fool's vexation* [AV—*wrath*] *is known at once,*
But a prudent man conceals dishonor.

BEWARE THAT TEMPORARY MADNESS!

Let the tongue always be under discipline. An unbridled tongue is the proof of an unrenewed heart.[l] Most of all, don't ever let your tongue be loose in a moment of *vexation.* How readily is *the fool known by his wrath!* He has no command of himself. On the first rising, he bursts out with an uncontrollable impulse.[m] Truly is *wrath* called *dishonor.* For is it not a dishonor, that unruly passions should trample reason under foot, change a man's whole appearance, and conquer the whole man by a temporary madness?[n] What else were Saul's unbecoming attacks against David and Jonathan;[o] Jezebel's boiling rage against Elijah;[p] Nebuchadnezzar's unreasonable decree to kill his wise men, because they could not interpret his vision?[q]

[l]James 1:26; 3:2
[m]Prov 14:17, 29; 25:28
[n]Dan 3:19
[o]1 Sam 18:10, 11; 19:9–11; 20:30–34
[p]1 Kings 19:1, 2
[q]Dan 2:12, 13

Yet far more painful is the sight of the fool's vexation in the children of God; in Moses, the meekest of men;[r] in David, the man after God's own heart;[s] in Asa, whose heart was "completely" with God all his days.[t] Nothing more excites the scoff of the ungodly, than the sight of these sinful outbursts, which divine grace ought to restrain. But "man at his best is a mere breath," left to himself! Animated with the spirit of a wild beast; in that day he becomes an object of *dishonor.*[u]

[r]Num 20:10, 11
[s]1 Sam 25:21, 22
[t]2 Chron 16:10
[u]Ps 39:5; Prov 17:12

LET HIM QUIET THE STORM

Self-control, that *conceals the dishonor,* and represses the rising agitation, is true Christian prudence.[v] Even as a matter of policy, it is most commendable.[w] But as a

[v]Prov 29;11; Judg 8:2, 3
[w]1 Sam 10:27

gracious principle, it is indeed a victory more honorable than the martial triumph;[x] not only subduing our own spirit, but melting the hardness of our adversary.[y]

[x] Prov 16:32; 19:11; 20:3
[y] Rom 12:18–21

Do we feel our temper at any time ready to rise? Cry instantly to Him who quiets the storm.[z] Keep before our eyes His blessed example, who "being reviled, He did not revile in return,"[a] and be what we behold.[b]

[z] Matt 8:26; Ps 65:7
[a] 1 Peter 2:23
[b] 2 Cor 3:18

17 *He who speaks truth tells what is right,*
But a false witness, deceit.

LET'S LOVE WHAT WE PREACH

This proverb may appear almost too obvious to need any comment. But the Scripture not only sets out what is deep and searching, but stamps the everyday truths with the seal of God for our more reverential obedience. Yet there is more here than lies on the surface. Maybe it seems like enough for a Christian to *speak the truth*. But it takes more than that. He must live righteously: what he preaches, what is just and what is true. The best-intentioned purpose must not lead us to cover up what is needed to bring the cause to a righteous issue; we must "not rejoice in unrighteousness, but rejoice with the truth."[c]

[c] 1 Cor 13:6

A false witness does not always deal with open lying, but with *deceit*—truth misrepresented, concealed, turned into falsehood. Doeg as a *false witness* like that—against the priests. He stated the fact, but by suppression of circumstances gave a false impression.[d] The false *witness* condemned our Lord by a similar perverse misuse of his words.[e] Oh, always keep a deep hatred of *deceit* in all its forms and beginnings.[f] Christian obligation and privilege alike forbid it.[g] *Truth and deceit* are not just moral qualities; they are the distinctive mark of the two classes of the world. Make sure that the broad stamp of *truth and righteousness* brings out the testimony—"Behold, an Israelite indeed, in whom is no guile!"[h]

[d] 1 Sam 21:1–7; 22:9, 10
[e] Matt 21:60, 61; John 2:19–21
[f] Prov 13:5; Ps 119:163
[g] Eph 4:22, 25
[h] John 1:47

18 *There is one who speaks rashly like the thrusts of a sword,*
But the tongue of the wise brings healing.

Who has not felt the piercings of false, unkind, inconsiderate gossip? How keenly have the servants of God suffered from this sword![9]

ABLE TO HURT, ABLE TO HEAL

Many will *speak* daggers without compunction, but they would be afraid to use them. Surely it was not without reason that our Lord charges an angry word or tongue with the guilt of murder.[i] The source of this mischief demonstrably shows its hateful character. "The tongue is a fire, the very world of iniquity ... and is set on fire by Hell."[j] How great and almost incredible a calamity it is, that man, who was created for humanity, should be so corrupted, that he is more ferocious and dangerous than any animal in the world.[k]

[i]Matt 5:21, 22

[j]James 3:6

[k]Col 3:8

Yet this little member is as able to heal as to hurt. It gives instant healing to *the thrusts of a sword,*[l] even to the very wound, which it may have inflicted.[10] But it is *the tongue of the wise, that brings healing.* Its unrestrained and unregulated expression might be hurtful. *Wisdom* is the guiding principle; not loose talk, but a delicate discriminating tact, directing us to whom to speak, when and what to say, and how to say it. Sometimes we should hold back, and other times let go. "Lord, God has given Me the tongue of disciples, That I may know how to sustain the weary one with a word."[m] This is no negative responsibility. It is not enough, that there is no poison in the tongue, that it is purified from any "unwholesome word." It must also "give *grace* to those who hear."[n] What need we have of the "word of Christ richly dwelling within you, with all wisdom," that in "teaching and admonishing one another," our speech may be always with grace, wholesome and edifying, to the glory of our blessed Lord![o]

[l]Judg 7:1–3; 1 Sam 19:1–7; 25:32, 33

[m]Isa 50:4

[n]Eph 4:29

[o]Col 3:16; 4:6

19 *Truthful lips will be established forever,*
But a lying tongue is only for a moment.

How important it is for us to keep eternity in mind whenever we speak! *Truth* would then be seen in its permanent value and results. The profession could bring us into present trouble.[p] But *it's lips shall be established forever.*

[p]Matt 10:32–39

[9] *Job 13:4; 16, 19; David—Ps 42:10; 52:2; Jeremiah—18:18–23; Lam 3:14; Paul–2 Cor 10:1, 2, 10; 13:2, 3.*

[10] *Ps 141:5. Comp. the healing counsel, 2 Cor 2:6–11, with 1 Cor 5.*

LIGHT A CANDLE NEVER TO BE PUT OUT

Who will argue against the martyr's testimony—"Be of good comfort, Master Ridley; play the man? We shall this day light such a candle by God's grace in England, as, I trust, *shall never be put out,"* said Foxe (7.550). *The lips* also of the faithful minister of God is *established forever.* For "whatever you shall bind . . . and loose on earth shall have been loosed in Heaven."[q]

[q] Matt 18:18; John 20:23

Truth is eternal. *Lying,* even if it suits our purpose as an easy escape from difficulty (a miserable—short-lived policy!) *is only for a moment.*[r] No,—if it should escape detection for a whole lifetime; yet, compared with eternity before us, what a short moment that is! And, anyway, what relief it will provide under the tremendous wrath of God?[s]

[r] Ps 52:4, 5

[s] Rev 21:8; 22:15

THE COST OF A LIE

God's own people have always found this momentary escape from trouble to be followed by shame and confusion.[11] The lie of the Gibeonites ended in their confusion.[t] The fruit of Gehazi's lie was the pleasure *for a moment.* The shame endured unto the end.[u] Under the same withering curse, *the lying tongue* of false teachers passes away;[v] while truth remains constant. "None are so visibly damned, as those who make no conscience of a life," said Matthew Henry (*Life,* ch. 13). Children, consider it well—eternity is, at the same time, the gain of truth and the cost of a lie![w] But oh, the infinite difference between Heaven and Hell!

[t] Josh 9

[u] 2 Kings 5:25–27

[v] 2 Tim 3:6–9

[w] Ps 15:1, 2; Rev 21:8

20 *Deceit is in the heart of those who devise evil,*
But counselors of peace have joy.
21 *No harm befalls the righteous,*
But the wicked are filled with trouble.
22 *Lying lips are an abomination to the* L*ORD,*
But those who deal faithfully are His delight.

The principle of *deceit* is here traced to its fountain—the *heart.* The first lispings of infancy, all too plainly prove how early it is found there! A lie is ready upon the child's lips when the temptation is presented to it; though nothing is to be gained by it, but the hateful pleasure of sin.

[11] *Abraham—Gen 20:1–16; Isaac—26:7–10; Peter—Matt 26:69–75.*

FRUIT OF THE HEART

Yet, though *deceit* is the native fruit of *the heart,* all are not equally ready to imagine evil—not all are, equally devisers "of evil."[x] The principle is not equally active, or equally developed at all. But when it does operate, *the wicked are filled with trouble,* and reap the full harvest in disappointment and ruin.[y]

[x]Prov 14:22; Mic 2:1

[y]Esther 7:10; Job 5:12, 13

How frightful also it is to make the outward expression of *deceit* in *lying lips!* Many and varied are its forms—falsehood, exaggeration, coloring, wilful perversion, wrong impressions produced or encouraged.[12] No part of Christian education is more important than the training of children in the deepest reverence for the simplicity of truth. Dr. Johnson has well observed, that the prevalence of falsehood arises more from carelessness about truth, than from intentional lying. If a child is relating what he has seen in the street, Dr. Johnson advises, don't allow "him to say, that he had seen it out of one window, if he has seen it out of another." Let him know that every willful departure from strict accuracy bears the stamp of *lying lips,* which is (and let the sentence be pondered, not only by children, but by all) *an abomination to the Lord.*[z] It was this sin that hurried Ananias and Sapphira into eternity.[a] The willful liar proves his parentage[b] and will be classed in eternity with all that is hateful. And fearfully will a righteous God, even in forgiving His own child, "yet [be] an avenger of their evil deeds."[13]

[z]Prov 6:16, 17; Ps 5:6

[a]Acts 5:1–10

[b]John 8:44

HOW TO STAND OUT FROM THE CROWD

Here however is *peace*—the contrast to evil inventions; and, intead of that sorrow which is connected with *deceit,*[c] to them that seek and pursue it, there is *joy.* Thus doubtless did Jonathan and Abigail *rejoice* in the success of their good *counsels.*[d] And most responsible is the obligation of Christians to be *counselors of peace,* breathing their Master's spirit of peace and love.[e] It's a blessed

[c]Judg 9; 2 Sam 15:6; 18:15

[d]1 Sam 19:4–7; 25:23–32

[e]Col 3:14, 15

[12] *"As one common but most responsible instance of this," (observes Mr. Goode in his valuable Sermon on this text), "is instructing servants to say—'Not at home.' Great is their guilt, who thus tempt a fellow-creature to utter a palpable untruth for the paltry convenience of a master. No Christian servant will consent to defile his conscience by acquiescing in any such iniquity. 'It is a matter of common consent, and everyone understands it.' Be it so—it is untruth still, and* lying lips are abomination to the Lord. *Moreover, if it be so generally understood, and admitted without offence; then how much more honorable and Christian to say at once—'We are engaged. We wish to be alone!' Who that accepts one excuse will not readily accept the other?"*

[13] *Ps 99:8. Comp. the example of Jacob, Gen 27 with 37:31–35. David's lie punished with such dreadful results, 1 Sam 21:2; 22:18, 19.*

office—to pour in the balm of peaceful counsel upon irritated feeling. They will mediate, explain, tactfully and considerately cover all the little causes of irritation. They will bring out the strong and unchangeable obligations of Christian love. They will seize the happy moment of softening to rekindle confidence. Happy are they, in *the joy* of their own conscience, in their dignity as "sons of God,"[f] in the rich harvest of their Christian efforts.[g] Instead of being *filled with mischief, no harm will happen to them. Evil* against them, whenever permitted, will become their good.[h] They will be supported in it,[i] delivered out of it,[j] sanctified by it.[k] Its sharpness will pierce their corruptions. Its bitterness will wean them from the creature. Its furnace will mold them into the image of their Lord, so that, what to the ungodly would be a mass of sorrow, *to the righteous* becomes a world of blessing.

[f]Matt 5:9
[g]James 3:17, 18
[h]Rom 8:28
[i]1 Cor 10:13; 2 Cor 12:7–10
[j]Verse 13. Ps 34:19
[k]Ps 119:67, 71

Freedom from *deceit* makes them stand out from the crowd. They not only speak truthfully, but they deal honestly, too, uniform in light and life.[l] They bear the image of a God of truth, and He delights in them.[m] " 'Surely, they are My people, Sons who will not deal falsely.' So He became their Savior."[n]

[l]John 3:21
[m]Prov 11:1
[n]Isa 63:8; 33:15, 16

23 *A prudent man conceals knowledge,*
But the heart of fools proclaims folly.

Knowledge is a talent to be wisely, not indiscriminately communicated.[o] In scriptural *knowledge* indeed there must be no *concealment* of fundamental truths;[p] or in declaring on suitable occasions, or to suitable persons, the gracious dealings of God to our own souls. Much harm would be done by forcing upon the ungodly those inner matters of Christian experience, which we are invited to tell to those "who fear God."[q] Every truth is not therefore fitting for every person or for every time.[r] Our blessed Lord charged upon His disciples *the wise concealment of knowledge,* after His example till a more favorable time.[s] The apostle *concealed his knowledge* for fourteen years, and even then mentioned it reluctantly to vindicate his own rightful claims of apostleship.[t] Elihu, though "full of words," and longing to give expression, yet *wisely concealed* it, till his elders had opened his way.[u]

[o]Prov 9:9; Matt 7:6
[p]Ps 40:9, 10; 1 Cor 15:3
[q]Ps 66:16
[r]Eccl 3:7; Amos 5:13
[s]Matt 16:20; 17:9; John 16:12
[t]2 Cor 12:1–6
[u]Job 32:6, 18, 19

Circumstances also may sometimes discreetly dictate *concealment.* Abraham spared the feelings of his family and cleared his own path by hiding the dreadful message of his God.[14] Joseph *concealed* his kindred for the discipline of his brethren;[v] Esther from a wise regard for consequences to herself.[w]

[v] Gen 42:7
[w] Esther 2:10

MUST WE ALWAYS TELL THE WHOLE TRUTH?

Nothing can justify speaking contrary to the truth. But we are not always obligated to tell the whole truth. Jeremiah answered all that he was obligated to speak; not all that he might have spoken.[x] In all these cases "a wise heart knows the proper time and procedure;"[y] cherishing at once a sound judgment and an ardent love for truth.

[x] Jer 38:24–27
[y] Eccl 8:5; Prov 15:2

The fool however everywhere *proclaims his folly.*[z] He unwisely opens his heart.[a] He is dogmatic in dispute when wiser men are cautious. He is teaching when he ought to take the learner's place; his self-confidence *proclaiming* his emptiness.[b] Self-distrust and humility are most important to enable us to improve the gifts of God for His glory.

[z] Eccl 10:3, 12–14
[a] Judg 16:17
[b] 1 Tim 6:3, 4

24 *The hand of the diligent will rule,*
But the slack hand *will be put to forced labor.*

ROYAL ROAD TO ADVANCEMENT

Hard work is the ordinary path to advancement. Pharaoh required men of activity to take charge of his cattle;[c] Solomon for the administration of his kingdom.[d] This was Joseph's road to rulership.[e] But if hard work does not raise one in a world-wide sphere, it will still command influence in its own sphere. The faithful steward is made *ruler* over his Lord's household.[f] The active trader *bears rule* over many cities.[g] Hard work, then, is not a moral virtue apart from religion. It is rather a component part of it.[h]

[c] Gen 47:6
[d] 1 Kings 11:28
[e] Prov 22:29
[f] Matt 24:45–47
[g] Matt 25:21
[h] Rom 12:11

The lazy spirit brings a man under bondage. "He is perpetually needing cousel of others, and hanging upon it."[15] He is the slave of his own lust; in the worst service, under the most degrading tyranny; "wicked" because "lazy," and "cast out" and condemned as an unprofitable

[14] *Gen 22:1–7. Comp. Moses' conduct, Exod 4:18.*
[15] *"The slothful shall become subservient to others"—FRENCH AND SKINNER'S* Translation of Proverbs, *with notes, 1831. Comp. Prov 10:4; 11:29.*

servant.[i] You, who profess to be a Christian, tremble at this responsibility of doing nothing, of living for your own indulgence; neglecting the great object of life—the only object that counts for eternity.

[i]Matt 25:26–30

25 *Anxiety in the heart of a man weighs it down,*
But a good word makes it glad.

WANT TO BE USEFUL—HERE'S HOW!

Anxiety in heart is a palsy that *weighs it down,* as if under an unbearable burden.[j] And gladdening indeed is a good word of sympathy and comfort![k] "This maxim therefore points out an easy and cheerful way of being useful," said Scott. Here we realize the precious effectiveness of the gospel. How full it is of these *good words!* Is it distress for sin? "Come to Me, all who are weary and heavy laden, and I will give you rest."[l] Is it the pressure of affliction? How *good is the word,* "the exhortation which is addressed to you as sons;" warning us not to "faint when you are reproved by Him."[m] Is it despondency? Often the good word—"Do not fear"—is repeated.[n] Don't we recognize the voice, "It is I; do not be afraid?"[o] Human sympathy may give temporary relief. But Leighton said, "that was the grace, softer than oil, sweether than roses, which flows from the Savior's lips into the sinner's wounds; and being poured into the contrite heart, not only heals, but blesses it, yea, and marks it out for eternal blessedness. Oh! how sweet is the voice of pardon to a soul groaning under the burden of sin!" *(Meditations on Ps 130:4).* David, but for these *good words,* said, "I would have perished in my affliction."[p] What else made the jailor's burdened heart glad.[q] Precious indeed is the privilege to strengthen the weak hands with "take courage, fear not";[r] to sit at the mourner's side, and "comfort those ... with the comfort with which we ourselves are comforted by God."[s] Precious is the ministry of the gospel commissioned with *the gladdening word to the heavy* of heart.[t] Yet more precious is the office of the beloved Savior, "anointed ... to bring good news," and filled with the unction of the Spirit, for the express purpose to "comfort all who mourn."[u] From His last sermon, you can tell just how Christ performed his office.[v] See then the provision for

[j]Gen 37:33, 35; 42:38
[k]Neh 1:4, with 2:1–8
[l]Matt 11:28
[m]Heb 12:5
[n]Isa 41:10, 14; 43:1
[o]Matt 14:27
[p]Ps 119:92
[q]Acts 16:28–34
[r]Isa 35:3, 4
[s]2 Cor 1:4
[t]Job 33:23–26; Isa 40:1, 2
[u]Isa 1:4; 61:1, 2
[v]John 14 to 16

joy, so rich, so free, so ready. Beware lest Satan somehow overwhelm you by "excessive sorrow."[w] Think on your obligation and your privilege to "rejoice in the Lord."[x]

[w]2 Cor 2:7
[x]Phil 3:1; 4:4

26 *The righteous is a guide to his neighbor,*
But the way of the wicked leads them astray.

TAKE A CLOSER LOOK AT YOURSELF—AND REJOICE!

God and the world don't agree in their estimate of His own people. *The righteous* are low indeed in man's eyes. But place him beside the wicked[y]—even upon the same level,[z] and his superiority is acknowledged. More excellent is he in character, more abundant in privilege, than his *neighbor,* no matter how great his outward advantages and gifts. Look at his birth, a child of God;[a] his dignity, a king,[b] his connections, a member of the family of Heaven;[c] his inheritance, a title to both worlds;[d] his food, the bread of everlasting life;[e] his clothing, the righteousness of the Savior;[f] his prospects, infinite and everlasting joy.[g] Note the honor which his God places upon him. He is the fullness of Christ;[h] "a temple of the Holy Spirit,"[i] throwing the splendor of Solomon's temple into the shade.[j] Angels, "behold the face of My Father who is in Heaven," and count it an honor to worship Him.[k] How can *his neighbor's* most exalted privileges compare with his? Contrast his high walk with God in "the holy place";[l] his heavenly profession before men;[m] his Christian victory over himself,[n] with his groveling *neighbor.* For "what an unprofitable drudgery is the service of the greatest prince in the world, in comparison with the work of a poor Christian, living in communion with God!"[16] And then—passing to the last contemplation—see him in the full enjoyment of his present prospects, "carried away by the angels to Abraham's bosom;"[o] "enter into the joy of your Master";[p] welcome before the assembled world;[q] then fixed on the throne of his Lord,[r] to be with Him,[s] near Him,[t] like Him,[u] forever—what are *his neighbor's* prospects, but as Hell compared with Heaven?[v] Can we doubt this testimony—the righteous is more excellent than his neighbor?

[y]Mark 6:20
[z]2 Kings 3:14
[a]John 1:12, 13
[b]Rev 1:6
[c]Heb 12:22, 23
[d]Matt 5:5; 1 Cor 3:22, 23
[e]John 6:35–58
[f]Isa 61:10
[g]Isa 35:10
[h]Eph 1:23
[i]1 Cor 6:19
[j]Isa 66:1, 2
[k]Matt 18:10; Heb 1:4–6
[l]Heb 10:19, 20
[m]Phil 2:15
[n]Prov 16:32; Matt 16:24
[o]Luke 16:22
[p]Matt 25:21
[q]Matt 5:34
[r]Rev 3:21
[s]John 14:3
[t]Rev 7:15
[u]1 John 3:2
[v]Prov 14:32; Matt 25:41

[16] *MANTON* on Ps. 119:45. *"God knows how much rather I would be the obscure tenant of a lath-and-plaster cottage, with a lively sense of my interest in a Redeemer, than the most admired object of public notice without it"—COWPER'S* Private Correspondence.

But we must not determine the Christian's character according to the standard of this world. It includes all that is meant in that important but despised word—conversion. What is commonly meant by amendment comes very far short of it. That is only an external work. Conversion is an inward change. The external is only partial. This is total. That concerns only the outward conduct and leaves the heart untouched. But whatever good may be in it of moral restraint, the principles are to be found with a far higher standard and tone in the inward change, which reaches the heart, infuses there a new and heavenly principle, and turns it to God by Christ, as its center of rest, peace, and holiness. Here alone is the real excellence, bearing the stamp of God, and commanding often the reluctant admiration of the world.

But though *wicked* Balaam acknowledged the higher excellence of the righteous, his own way tempted him and dragged him to his own ruin.[w] Saul's testimony to David, and Joash's reverence for Elisha, still left them tempted by the power of their own corruptions.[x] This way is always more pleasant to the flesh, and therefore more generally desired. That's why *the wicked* is easily deceived and tempted by the appearance of the right way and blinded to his own ruin.[y] Let me consider my path most carefully—with whom am I walking? In what way?

[w] Num 31:8

[x] Isa 44:20

[y] 1 Sam 24:17; 2 Kings 13:14, with 11

27 *A slothful man does not roast his prey,*
But the precious possession of a man is *diligence.*

DON'T GET TOO COMFORTABLE RESTING ON YOUR ATTAINMENTS

How miserable and ruinous is the habit of laziness. It is a dead palsy. Under God, it can only be checked by early discipline and constant resistance. Sometimes, however, the man makes a vigorous and successful effort. He rouses himself even to the hard work of hunting. But his fit of exertion is soon over. He can't go to the trouble to *roast his prey* for his meals.[z] He gives it to others, perhaps even to his dogs; and quickly falls back into his lazy habits again.

[z] Contrast Gen 27:30, 31

Isn't this a graphic picture of the slothful, professing Christian? He becomes "religious" in a fit of excitement.

He begins a new course and perhaps makes some advances in it. But he "has no *firm* root in himself," and his good resolutions wither away.[a] The continued exertion required;[b] the violence that must be done to his deep-rooted habits; the difficulties in his new path; the invitations to present ease and comfort; the delusive hope of better success at a future day—all these hang as a weight upon his efforts. So that, not knowing the only secret of resistance to his powerful enemy—earnest and persevering prayer; he grows slack, and with just life enough to feel himself dying, he sits down upon his little attainments; thus virtually throwing them away; content to lose heaven itself, if it is to be gained at such a cost.[c] What's the point, pretender, in making an effort, if you do not seek the grace of perseverance? No present blessing can be enjoyed without grasping something beyond.[d] Godliness without energy loses its full reward.[e] The weakening influence of doubts and fears often arises, not from a deep feeling of corruption, but from a lazy habit, and for want of a realized conviction of the infinite stake of the soul, calling for instant and persevering labor.

[a]Matt 13:20, 21
[b]Matt 11:12
[c]Prov 13:4; 21:25; 26:15
[d]Phil 3:12–14
[e]2 John 8

SPEND AND BE SPENT

Real substance[f] is the reward of the *diligent man; precious,* as the results of his toil; and increasing by his unwearied exercise.[g] Live then—Christian—more in your work—spend and be spent in it. Your privileges will be enlarged. Your substance will be enriched; Your God will be honored.[h] Your crown will be secured.[i]

[f]Prov 8:21; 15:6
[g]Matt 25:16, 28, 29
[h]John 15:8; Phil 1:11
[i]2 Peter 1:11

28 *In the way of righteousness is life,*
And in its *pathway there is no death.*

SUNBEAMS OF GLORY

Righteousness is here crowned with "*life* and immortality."[17] The wise man saw clearly beyond this dying world; and caught the sunbeams of glory that "brought life and immortality to light through the gospel"![j] *The way of righteousness* is the way of God's salvation,[k] in which his children come to Him; the way of His commandments, in which they love to walk with Him.[l] *In this way* is present life,[m] a passage "out of death into *life*"

[j]2 Tim 1:10
[k]John 14:6
[l]Isa 35:8
[m]Prov 8:35; 10:16

[17] *"In the path of righteousness is life; yea—the highway is immortality"—MSS.* Translation of Proverbs, *by Dr. GOOD.*

[n]John 5:24

eternal.[n] Enjoying the sense of God's love; confiding in His unspeakable, satisfying friendship; consecrating ourselves in spiritual devotedness to His service; eagerly looking to the fullness of His eternal joy—this is life indeed for eternity.[18] For where the life of grace is possessed, the life of glory is secured. It is "hidden with Christ in God;"[o] so that—"Because I live, you shall live also."[p]

[o]Col 3:3
[p]John 14:19

NO DEATH ON THIS ROAD

[q]John 8:51; 11:25
[r]Rom 5:21
[s]Rev 2:11; 20:6
[t]Rom 8:10; 5:12
[u]Acts 7:60; 1 Thess 4:14
[v]1 Cor 15:55

In this pathway there is no death.[q] The curse of the first death has passed away.[r] The power of "the second death" cannot hurt.[s] "The body is dead because of sin."[t] Yet it is "asleep," rather than dead, under the care of Jesus.[u] Surely the bitterness of death is passed. Now, "O death! Where is your sting?"[v] It is sheathed in the body of Jesus.

[w]Rom 8:6; Eph 2:1; 1 Tim 5:6
[x]Matt 7:13; Rom 6:21
[y]Prov 8:36
[z]Jude 23

And is not this cheering privilege, this glorious hope, an infinite recompense for all the crosses of *the way?* Contrast the ways of sin, full of death,[w] ending in death eternal.[x] Then wonder at the multitudes who "love death."[y] Pity, pray for them, "snatching them out of the fire."[z] Adore the riches of that sovereign grace, which has brought you to *righteousness to life,* to salvation.

[18] *"Those who seek after* righteousness *preserve, and increase in themselves the spiritual life of God's grace and the presence of his Spirit, and so attain to life everlasting"—DIODATI.*

CHAPTER THIRTEEN

1 *A wise son* accepts his *father's discipline,*
But a scoffer does not listen to rebuke.

Such *a wise son,* in son-like reverence, was Solomon himself.[a] The connection however of *discipline with rebuke* mainly points us to that instruction, which is obtained by discipline.[b] See how He condescended to this painful school and "learned obedience!"[c]

[a]Prov 4:3, 4
[b]Prov 12:1; Isa 1:5
[c]Heb 5:8

KEEP YOUR EYES ON HIM

How good is it in our daily practical walk to keep our eyes steadily fixed on Him, following Him closely in this childlike habit!

But the proud spirit of the scoffing son doesn't bend easily. He has never *accepted his father's discipline* with respect. Soon therefore he takes "the seat of scoffers."[d] When *rebuke* becomes necessary, he doesn't listen.[e] He just turns back again to his own unwise course at the extreme point from wisdom,[f] on the brink of ruin;[g] carrying about him a fearful mark of disapproval![h] Let me remember—if I am reluctant to listen to the rebuke of men, I will also resist the rebuke of God. And how long will it be before my revolt will bring His long-suffering to an end;[i] and my soul to destruction![j] "From hardness of heart, and contempt of Thy word and commandment, Good Lord, deliver me" (Litany).

[d]Ps 1:1
[e]Prov 15:12
[f]Prov 12:1; 15:5
[g]Prov 15:10; 29:1
[h]1 Sam 2:25
[i]2 Chron 36:16
[j]Jer 5:3; Zeph 3:2

2 *From the fruit of a man's mouth he enjoys good,*
But the desire of the treacherous is violence.

IF WE'RE WALKING WITH CHRIST OUR TALK WILL SHOW IT

The first clause has been before us a great deal lately.[k] But let's keep this in mind forever—that, if the Christian

[k]Prov 12:14

is walking with God, his speech will be godly. Whether, or not, it does anybody else any good, it will at least warm, refresh, and edify his own soul. The *fruit of a man's mouth he enjoys good.* We will never carry on our lips that beloved name to our fellow-sinners in simplicity, but to our own souls, it will be as "oils have a pleasant fragrance."[l] In distributing the heavenly manna to others, we shall feed our own souls.

[l]Song of Sol 1:3

The treacherous also eats the fruit of his mouth—but it won't be good. His soul sets his tongue aflame. He loves *violence* and therefore eats it to his own ruin.[m] "Death and life are in the power of the tongue."[n] Let's take a look. Under the influence of divine grace, restrained from evil, disciplined for usefulness, the tongue is a fruitful instrument of our own happiness.

[m]Ps 64:8
[n]Prov 18:21

3 *The one who guards his mouth preserves his life;*
The one who opens wide his lips comes to ruin.

YES, YOU CAN TAME YOUR TONGUE—HERE'S HOW!

The last Proverb contrasted a fruitful and evil—a cautious and ungoverned—tongue. "Keep over your heart."[o] This guards the citadel. *Guard your mouth.* This sets a watch at the gates. If the gates are well guarded, the city is safe. But leave them unprotected, and, like Babylon, it will be taken. He who carefully guards his tongue protects his life, which is often endangered by a lot of wild talking, noted Bishop Hall.[p] Think before we speak; ponder our words, and what they mean. Note the time, place, and audience. The tongue, that unruly member needs a strong bridle and a strong hand to hold it.[q] Of course, it's necessary to open our lips; but to *open them wide;* to let everything come out, is extremely risky.[r] For if, in the multitude of words, transgression is there,[s] it will bring us into the very jaws of *ruin.*

[o]Prov 4:23
[p]Prov 21:23; Ps 34:12, 13
[q]James 3:2, 3
[r]Prov 10:14; 12:13
[s]Prov 10:19

"Set a guard; O Lord, over my mouth. Keep watch over the door of my lips"[t]—was the prayer of one who knew the danger of an uncontrolled tongue and the only way to tame it. Shouldn't we call on God for help, in the recollection, remembering how often our unguarded tongue has given "the devil an opportunity,"[u] and grieved "the Holy Spirit"?[v] How much more do we have to repent of

[t]Ps 141:3
[u]Eph 4:27
[v]Eph 4:30

by our speaking than by our silence! Let the practical power of faith make us more watchful and prayerful, may it lead to self-abasement and self-discipline and godly fear, and may it help us keep our tongue under control. Two things are clear. Except for the blood of Christ, the mass of guilt from the sins of the tongue would have condemned us forever; and in proportion as that little member is bridled, the peace of God rules in the heart.

4 *The soul of the sluggard craves* [AV—*desires*] *and* gets *nothing,*
But the soul of the diligent is made fat.

Another vivid contrast of the *suggard with the diligent!*[w] *The sluggard craves* the gain of diligence but without doing the work required to get it. He would be wise without study and rich without labor. His religious profession is of the same easygoing character. *He craves* to overcome his bad habits, to enjoy the happiness of God's people. So far, well. Desires are a part of religion. There can be no attainment without them. But many don't even have the desire. They ridicule it as enthusiasm. The sluggard has nothing, except craving without effort. "He ever desireth; but he taketh no pains to get anything," reads *Reformer's Notes*. Why, he'd be glad to go to heaven if a morning dream would carry him there. He longs to die as a Christian (he knows nothing of prayer).[x] He would gladly be a Christian, if it didn't cost him anything. His duties, he feels are forced upon him; and when they are over, he feels as if he has been relieved of a heavy weight. This is no rare case. We often hear the cry—year after year—"I desire to be a child of God," and yet, I'm disappointed. I don't see God's children around me making any progress. Instead, they just settle down, ever more firmly, in a lifeless profession. "Hell," says an old writer, "is paved with such desires."

[w] Prov 10:4; 12:24

[x] Num 23:10

WANT TO BE SUCCESSFUL? THEN READ CAREFULLY HERE

Oh! If you're going to be in earnest about *anything*, let it be about spiritual things. Remember eternity is at stake. First, you lose only hours and days, but then, years. Just for the lack of energy, all can be lost. Empty wishing won't give life. Walking with uncertainty and hesitation won't bring us to God. A few minutes' cold prayer won't win the prize. To expect the blessing without hard work is just false hope. Earnestness and hard work bring their own reward in the world.[y] This is even more true in the Christian realm. It won't settle for just simply desiring, without the *reality of possession.* "Godliness is profitable" and leads to health and profit.[z] Good habits are formed; dormant energy is excited. The conflict of faith and the power of prayer ensure success.[a] God honors the use of our talents when the gifts He has given are used to His glory.[b] He gives, not only the wisdom, but "the manifestation," as well—and not for selfish gain, but for the blessing of others.[c] The talent must not be "put away in a handkerchief"[d] or the light "under the peck-measure."[e] False humility—a cover-up for laziness—must not hinder the faithful discharge of our trust.

[y] Prov 22:29
[z] 1 Tim 4:8
[a] Matt 11:12
[b] Matt 25:14–29
[c] 1 Cor 12:7
[d] Luke 19:20
[e] Matt 5:15

Child of God! shake off the dust of sloth. Be careful that a life of ease doesn't kill your appetite and keep you from seeking food for your soul; or from actively serving the Lord. Let your good will be vigorous and radiant. Let your profession be always progressing, deepening, expanding. If you're *in* Christ, seek to be "firmly rooted and now being built up in Him."[f] Let there be "life . . . abundantly."[g] "Be strong in the grace that is in Christ Jesus."[h] Let "the joy of the Lord [be] your strength."[i] Then *your soul shall be made fat,* healthful, and vigorous in all fruit and grace.[j]

[f] Col 2:7
[g] John 10:10
[h] 2 Tim 2:1
[i] Neh 8:10
[j] Ps 92:12–14

5 *A righteous man hates falsehood,*
But a wicked man acts disgustingly and shamefully.

DO CHRISTIANS EVER LIE?

Note the accuracy of Scripture. It is not that *a righteous man never lies.* David lied.[k] Peter lied.[l] Yet David could say, "I hate and despise falsehood."[m] He prayed to "remove the false way from me."[n] He said "deceit shall not dwell within my house."[o] Peter painfully remembered his sin, but he showed great happiness at delivery from it.[p] The child of God, though always a sinner, maintains holy hatred against sin—"I am doing the very thing I hate."[q]

[k] 1 Sam 21:2; 27:9, 10
[l] Matt 26:70–74
[m] Ps 119:163
[n] Ps 119:29
[o] Ps 101:7; 26:4
[p] 1 Peter 3:10; 2:1
[q] Rom 7:15, 19

But just because a man doesn't lie, doesn't prove that he is righteous. Selfish motives, regard for character, without any hatred of the sin as sin, may dictate restraint. But Christianity gives a man new tastes and conformity to the mind of God. "Lying lips"—however common, profitable, convenient, or pardonable, they may be thought to be—"are an abomination to the Lord." Therefore, the *righteous man hates them.*[r] He would rather suffer by telling the truth, than sin by lying.[s]

[r]Prov 12:22; Rom 12:9
[s]Dan 3:16–18

And yet how often, even in the church, this aspect of godliness is ignored! Isn't strict truth often sacrificed to courtesy? Don't we lie by our actions sometimes, or insinuations, or indirect meaning? What we would be ashamed to speak? Isn't the simple truth often colored with exaggeration? "Abstain from every form of evil"[t]—is the rule for the man of God. Commit your tongue to the only safe use, the restraint and guidance of the God of truth.[u]

[t]1 Thess 5:22
[u]Ps 19:14; 141:3

A *wicked man* indeed takes pleasure in deceit. Scripture gives him his right name. His base means often bring him *to shame* on this side of the grave.[v] But no matter what, shame will be his "everlasting contempt."[w]

[v]2 Kings 5:27; Acts 12:21–23
[w]Dan 12:2; Rev 21:8

6 *Righteousness guards the one whose way is blameless,*
But wickedness subverts the sinner.

If only this repetition of the truth,[x] might deepen its impression! It most certainly is a straight way to heaven. "O Lord, lead me in Thy righteousness,"[y] and keep me there. The many deviations even of the children of God prove our need of divine keeping. The fear of man;[z] the flinching of the flesh from positive duty,[a] the grasp of some desired object;[b] the subtle allurements of sin[c]—all these have turned him out of the path. In many things he obeys his Father's will; in others, he prefers his own. *Righteousness*—steady conformity to the mind of God—keeps the soul blameless, and so *keeps it in the way.*[d] We do not regard it as any meritorious virtue, or put it in the place of simply "fixing our eyes on Jesus"[e] for life and salvation. The Christian "shall walk in my integrity,"[f] he must never lose his sense of sin, or forget his need of mercy. Yet his "*righteousness*" is a breastplate[g] *keeping* him from many assaults of sin,[h] and covering him from threatening wrath.[i] But this is *righteousness*, not perfection, mixed with clinging infirmity.

[x]Prov 11:3, 5, 6
[y]Ps 5:8
[z]Gen 12:11–13; 20:2
[a]Jon 1:1–3
[b]Gen 27:19–24
[c]2 Sam 11:2; 1 Kings 11:1–4
[d]Ps 25:21
[e]Heb 12:2
[f]Ps 26:11
[g]Eph 6:14
[h]Gen 39:9
[i]Gen 7:1; 2 Peter 2:7–9

[j]2 Chron 15:17

Yet—blessed be God—the uprightness is accepted, and the fault is covered.[j]

THE SURE ROAD TO DESTRUCTION

[k]2 Chron 28:23

But while saints are secured *from* ruin, sinners are secured *for* ruin. *The sinner's own wickedness subverts him.*[k] He is determined to have his own way, which is the sure road to destruction. Peter Muffet said, "Let him not blame the Lord, or any mortal man beside himself, inasmuch as he is the author of ruin to himself" (Commentary on Proverbs).

7 *There is one that pretends to be rich, but has nothing;*
Another *pretends to be poor, but has great wealth.*

[l]Prov 12:9

[m]1 Tim 6:18

How fleeting the world's riches are! Yet some will put on a front, in order to gain the respect usually connected with them;[l] *pretending themselves rich, yet they have nothing.* Others *pretend themselves poor,* "and live as if they were rich," said Scott. In any case, riches are judged more accurately by their use than by their possession. But in both cases, those involved are practicing deceit against God—one by *pretending to have received,* the other by *virtually denying, His gracious gifts.* Both dishonor His wisdom and goodness; the one by being discontented with what God gives; the other by neglecting what He gives.[m]

THE PROUD BEGGAR

[n]Luke 18:11, 12
[o]1 Cor 4:8, 10
[p]Rev 3:17, 18

[q]Rev 2:9

The church presents the counterpart of both of these classes. The boasting Pharisee,[n] the gifted Corinthian;[o] the proud beggarly Laodicean[p]—all admire what they lack, as if it were *great wealth.* Others again *make themselves poor* in voluntary humility. Describing their whole course as unmixed sin, they deny the almighty work of grace. They excuse their lying on the basis of their own dominating corruptions, instead of devoting greater energy into a successful conflict. In this way, they promote the very evil of which they disapprove and sink the soul into a hopeless despondency, a hindrance to their happiness and usefulness. It's true that sometimes the Christian, from the deep sense of corruption still lingering with him, may be blind to what is evident to everyone else and known to his God.[q]

DON'T PUT YOURSELF DOWN!

But if it is the ruin of the self-deceiver to think himself better than he is, it's the hindrance of the upright to think himself worse, than he is.

The true path of simplicity is to turn away from all dependence on the flesh and to gladly welcome the gospel of grace, instead.[r] Such disciples, rich in their holy poverty, are honored of the Lord.[s] "O blessed Lord, who resistest the proud, and givest grace to the humble, give me more humility, that I may receive more grace from Thee. And Thou, whose gracious rain shelves down from the steep mountains, and sweetly drenches the humble valleys, depress thou my heart more and more with true lowliness of spirit; that the showers of your heavenly grace may sink into it, and make it more fruitful in all good affection and all holy obedience," said Bishop Hall (*Devotional Works*, vol. viii, 276).

[r] Phil 3:3–9
[s] Isa 66:2; Luke 18:13

8 *The ransom of a man's life is his riches,*
But the poor hears no rebuke.

WILL THE TRUE RICH MAN STAND UP?

The last Proverb rebukes discontent with our lot, whether of riches or poverty. The wise man strikes a sane balance between these two conditions. *A man's riches may be the ransom of his life.* Extortion of money may prompt false accusation, and *riches* may be a *ransom* cheerfully paid.[1] Or they may be the wealthy man's price of deliverance from his enemies. They may save him from the punishment of the law[t] or from imminent danger of his life.[u] Medical bills are easily paid. Yet if "money is protection,"[v] so also is the lack of it. If "the rich man's wealth is his fortress,"[w] *the poor man's poverty is often his safeguard.* He is usually out of sight and doesn't hear many rebukes; and thereby, he escapes many a danger, which is destruction to his richer neighbor.[x] If Isaac had had fewer flocks,[y] or Jacob had been less prosperous,[z] they would not *have heard so much rebuke* from their selfish enemies. *The poor* with his empty pocket travels with security, and his humble cottage offers little temptation to burglars. "Not *even*" therefore—his true happi-

[t] Exod 21:29, 30
[u] Jer 41:8
[v] Eccl 7:12
[w] Prov 10:15
[x] 2 Kings 24:14; 25:12
[y] Gen 26:13, 14
[z] Gen 31:1

[1] *See Job 2:4. The apostle refused to avail himself of this ransom. Acts 24:26. "The primitive Christians quoted this proverb in defense of their occasional habit of giving money to restrain the fury of their persecutors"—Geier.*

ness—"when one has an abundance does his life consist of his possessions."[a]

[a]Luke 12:15

His riches may save his life. But "what will a man give in exchange for his soul?"[b] which is too precious to be "redeemed with perishable things like silver or gold."[c] So far as he is concerned, "cease trying forever."[d] Praise the Lord! When all the treasures of earth would have been as nothing in the *ransom*, the riches of heaven were freely poured out.[e] The blood of the Son of God was the acceptable price. The voice was heard from heaven—"Deliver him from going down to the pit, I have found *a ransom.*"[f]

[b]Matt 16:26
[c]1 Peter 1:18
[d]Ps 49:8
[e]1 Peter 1:19; Heb 10:5–8
[f]Job 33:24

9 *The light of the righteous rejoices* [*AV—shines brightly*],
But the lamp of the wicked goes out.

LET YOUR LIGHT SO SHINE

Who can estimate the worth of a Christian's bright shining *light?*[g] Happy in his own soul, like his counterpart in the heavens, he sheds a joyous light around him. But how glowing, then, is the light of the church in the combined shining of all her members! Many of them have no remarkable individual splendor; yet, like the lesser stars forming the milky way, they present a bright path of holiness in the spiritual firmament. This happy heavenly *light* "an everlasting light," and that day will never set.[h] Sometimes it may be grey and gloomy, but only that it may break out more gloriously;[i] and soon will it be a day without a cloud.[j]

[g]Matt 5:14–16; Phil 2:15; Prov 4:18
[h]Isa 60:19, 20
[i]Mic 7:8
[j]Rev 21:23, 24

But it is *the light of the righteous that rejoices.* Sin therefore will bring the cloud. Do we hope to shine in the heavenly firmament? Then we must shine with present glory in the firmament of the church. So delicate is the divine principle, that every breath of this world dims its luster.

The wicked have their *lamp,* a cold profession of the name of religion. But being without oil, it will soon *go out.*[k] Even while it lasts, it doesn't rejoice. It sheds no light upon the soul. It guides no fellow-pilgrim with its light. Fearful will be the end. He leaves the light of this world, only to enter into eternal darkness, without even a flickering way to cheer—"They shall never see the light."[l]

[k]Job 18:5, 6; Matt 25:8
[l]Ps 49:19; Matt 22:13

10 *Through presumption comes nothing but strife [AV—contention],*
But with those who receive counsel is wisdom.

WHERE DO QUARRELS COME FROM?

Most accurately is *strife* here traced to its proper source.[m] All the crudities of the day, all the novelties of doctrine producing *strife,*[n] originate in the proud swelling of "the fleshly mind."[o] Men scorn the beaten track. They must strike out a new path. Individuality and excess are primary charms. They are ready to quarrel with every one, who does not value their notions as highly as they do. The desire of preeminence;[p] revolt from authority[q] or sound doctrine;[r] party spirit, with the pride of knowledge and gifts[s]—all produce the same results. Is it too much to say that empty pride has lighted up all the sinful *strife* that has ever kindled in the church? We must indeed contend for "the truth of the gospel,"[t] even though it's without our own compromising brethren.[u] But even here, however unnoticeably, presumption may introduce itself under the cover of glorifying God! Truly "it is the inmost coat, which we put on first, and put off last," said Bishop Hall.

[m] Prov 28:25
[n] 1 Tim 1:4; 2 Tim 2:23
[o] Col 2:18; 1 Tim 6:3, 4
[p] Matt 20:21; 3 John 9
[q] Num 12:2
[r] 2 Tim 4:3, 4
[s] 1 Cor 3:3, 4, with 4:8
[t] Gal 2:5; 1 Thess 2:2; Jude 3
[u] Gal 2:11

This mischievous principle spreads in families or among friends. "Some point of honor must be maintained; some insult must be resented; some rival must be crushed or eclipsed; some renowned character emulated; or some superior equalled and surpassed," stated Scott. Even in trifling disputes between relatives or neighbors—perhaps between Christians—each party contends vehemently for his rights, instead of satisfying himself with the testimony of his conscience, and submitting rather to be misunderstood and misjudged, than to break the bond of the divine brotherhood.[v] In the wide field of the world we may well ask—"What is the source of quarrels and conflicts among you? Is not the source your pleasure?"[w] Often wounded pride has[x] even without any proved injury,[y] brought destructive *strife* upon a land.

[v] 1 Cor 6:7
[w] James 4:1
[x] Judg 12:1
[y] 2 Kings 14:10

IMPROVE YOUR GIFTS

The proud man conceives himself wise enough. He asks no counsel, and thereby proves his lack of wisdom.

But with the modest and those *who receive counsel, there is* the *wisdom* that is from above, which is "first pure, then peaceable."[z] How many a rising contention it has quelled.[a] "Do nothing from selfishness or empty conceit, but with humility of mind let each of you regard one another as more important than himself."[b] Christian *wisdom* will keep us within our own line; knowing our own measure and bounds;[c] and—whatever our place or gifts may be—we will remain humble, active, loving, constant, and thankful in improving them.

[z] James 3:17, with 14–16
[a] Gen 13:8; Judg 8:1–3; Acts 6:1–6
[b] Phil 2:3
[c] 2 Cor 10:13–16

11 *Wealth* obtained *by fraud dwindles,*
But the one who gathers by labor increases it.

DON'T GIVE YOUR RICHES WINGS!

This Proverb does not imply the means by which *wealth has been gotten;* but the impoverishing use to which it is applied. However large, *by fraud* it will soon *dwindle.* Frivolous and expensive pursuits, empty amusements, and the vain pomp and show of dress, will soon prove that "wealth certainly makes itself wings";[d] that the treasure is "put into a purse with holes";[e] and that nothing remains but the awful account of unfaithfulness to a solemn trust.

[d] Prov 23:5
[e] Hag 1:6

GOD'S PROPERTY FOR GOD'S GLORY

On the other hand—God's blessing is upon Christian industry; and, so far as is good, *he that gathers by labor increases.* Just let him remember, that the security for his *increasing wealth* is the dedication of himself and his substance to the Lord; the ready acknowledgment, that "you are not your own," but God's property for God's glory.[f] "All that man can have, we have it on this condition; to use it, to have it, to lay it out, to lay it down unto the honor of our Master, from whose bounty we received it," said Swinnock *(True Christian,* p. 169). The Lord deliver us from the guilt of wasting what is rightfully His!

[f] 1 Cor 6:19, 20

12 *Hope deferred* makes *the heart sick,*
But desire fulfilled is a tree of life.

TRIED IN FAITH, NEVER DISAPPOINTED IN HOPE

The first springing of *hope* is a pleasurable sensation, but it is mixed with pain. It is the hunger that makes our food acceptable. But *hope deferred,* like hunger prolonged, brings torture. *It makes the heart sick.*[g] Yet when the *desire*—the fulfillment of the *hope*—does come, what a *tree of life it is*—so invigorating![h]

[g] Ps 119:82, 123; 143:7

[h] Verse 19

But we must limit this application to the spiritual world. Anywhere else, the fulfillment of the desire is not a *tree of life* but vanity.[i] Here, however, the child of God is often tried in his faith but never disappointed in his hope. We may have to wait a long time. But we never have cause to despair. "The steadfastness of hope" issues in "the full assurance of hope." What was it to Abraham, when, after hope had been long delayed, the desire finally came, and he called the child of promise—Laughter![j] What was it "when the Lord brought back the captive ones of Zion, We were like those who dream"![k] What was it to old Simeon and the waiting remnant, when "*the desire* of all nations" came![l] What to the disciples, when at the sight of their risen Lord, their despairing hearts "still could not believe *it* and were marveling"![m] What to the little flock met together in the faintness of *deferred hope* to plead for Peter's deliverance, when *the desire came*—the answer to prayer, so marvelously granted![n]

[i] Eccl 2:11

[j] 1 Thess 1:3; Heb 6:11; Gen 15:3; 21:3–6

[k] Ps 137, with 126

[l] Luke 2:25–30, with AV—Hag 2:7. Comp. Matt 13:16, 17

[m] Luke 24:41

[n] Acts 12:12–16

WHEN TIME SEEMS LONG

Now, to bring it all into personal experience, such was the trial of faith appointed for our beloved Lord. Such was the joyful issue.[o] Many a waiting, *sickened heart* has been gloriously refreshed from *a tree of life.* But just think what the joy of the grand consummation of hope will be![p] "The anxious longing of the creation waits eagerly for the revealing of the sons of God."[q] Time seems long, trials heavy, hearts failing. But "yet in a little while, He who is coming will come, will not delay."[r] The first moment of His glorious appearing will blot out all remembrance of labors, weariness, and trial. Yes—*the desire comes*—come it will in God's best time—"quickly." One moment sick; the next—living in that land, where there is no more sickness.[s] One moment, in the rags of the flesh; then, "in the twinkling of an eye," clothed in the glory of the Savior's image.[t] "Come, Lord Jesus"! Come quickly.[u]

[o] Ps 22:1–3, with 22–25; 69:1–3, with 30–35

[p] Rom 8:23–25; 2 Cor 5:1–4

[q] Rom 8:19

[r] Heb 10:37, 28; Hab 2:3; Rev 22:7, 12, 20

[s] Rev 22:20; Isa 33:24; Rev 21:4

[t] 1 Cor 15:51–54

[u] Rev 22:20

13 *The one who despises the word will be in debt to it,*
But the one who fears the commandment will be rewarded.

WATCH YOUR ATTITUDE TOWARD GOD'S WORD

God as a God of holiness will not be trifled with. But as a God of grace, no one ever serves Him for nothing. The arrogant *despiser* of His Word cannot escape. The word before the flood was the object of his long-suffering. "A preacher of righteousness" warned them of their danger. But the *despisers* brought about their own ruin.[v] Pharaoh was often reproved. Sometimes he half-resolved, yet finally *despised the word* and was destroyed.[w] Jehoiakim's daring rebellion brought its just reward.[x] The warnings of Sinai are like a voice of thunder—"For if the word spoken through angels proved unalterable, and every transgression and disobedience received a just recompense, how shall we escape if we neglect so great a salvation? . . . For if those did not escape when they refused him who warned *them* on earth, much less *shall* we *escape* who turn away from Him who warns from heaven . . . See to it that you do not refuse Him who is speaking."[y]

[v] 1 Peter 3:20; 2 Peter 2:5

[w] Exod 5:2; 10:16, 17; 14:28

[x] Jer 36:23–32

[y] Heb 2:2, 3; Heb 12:25

Let God and His word be our *fear*, not our terror. Faith is the principle of *fear*, of respectful childlike obedience.[z] Certainly the heart can never be right, till *it fears the commandment* above every earthly consideration. The slave *fears* the penalty; the child *the commandment*. And *this* he fears more, than if an angel from heaven were standing in his way with a flaming sword. He fears the Father, not the Judge. Here is no bondage, no legality. It brings its own reward. The "heart stands in awe of Thy words," rejoices in it, "as one who finds great spoil."[a] Here too is sunshine in the special favor of God—"To this one I will look, To him who is humble and contrite of spirit, and who *trembles at My Word.*"[b]

[z] Heb 11:7

[a] Ps 119:161, 162

[b] Isa 66:2. Comp. Ezra 10:3

14 *The teaching* [AV—*law*] *of the wise is a fountain of life,*
To turn aside from the snares of death.

THE ONLY SAFE WALK

Reverence to God's commandment has just been enforced. The blessing of *the law* or instruction[c] *of the wise* is here shown. It is *a fountain of life*[d] to a teachable and thirsting heart. It is a grand preserving principle in a world full of *snares*, not of danger only, but *of death*. There is no safe walking but in the ways of God. The Word of God gives the necessary warning.[e] *The teaching of the wise*—his instruction with all the authority of *a law*—applies it. This was David's timely instruction to Solomon[f] and Solomon's to us.[g] Hear this warning *law of the wise* from an apostle's mouth. The love of money was fearfully destroying souls. "Flee from these things, you man of God."[h] This is the grand purpose of the ministry of the gospel; to "come to their senses *and escape* from the snare of the devil, having been held captive by him to do his will."[i] Let the young watch their walk where every step is *a snare of death*. Let the instruction of your God and His ministers be *the teaching of the wise* to keep your path in safety. Even without direct orders, the spirit of *the teaching* will supply practical rules for keeping the heart and life—e.g. to do nothing, of which the lawfulness is questionable—to consider everything as unlawful, which interferes with prayer and interrupts communion with God—never to go into any company, business, or situation, in which the presence and blessing of God cannot be conscientiously asked and expected.[2] Such rules are in the spirit of the teaching and well worthy of adoption. "Watch the path of your feet, And all your ways will be established."[j]

[c] Prov 3:1; 4:2
[d] Prov 10:11
[e] Ps 17:4; 119:9, 11
[f] Prov 4:4
[g] Prov 5:1–13; 7:24–27
[h] 1 Tim 6:9–11
[i] 2 Tim 2:24–26
[j] Prov 4:26

15 *Good understanding produces favor,*
But the way of the treacherous is hard.

CHRISTIAN HABITS NEED DISCIPLINE

It's good for the young to have to "bear the yoke in his youth."[k] Under God's control, it strengthens the character, producing and firmly preserving manly virtues and practical godliness. This *is a good understanding*[l]—not cold and dry but glowing with heavenly light and love in all the discipline of Christian habits. Natural conviction

[k] Lam 3:27
[l] Ps 111:10

[2] *"By the help of these three rules, I soon settle all my doubts, and find that many things I have hitherto indulged in, are, if not utterly unlawful, at least inexpedient, and I can renounce them without many sighs"*—Life, *Rev. Dr.* PAYSON, *chap. iii.*

often reverences it as the image of God stamped upon His servants. Joseph applied many of those valuable rules and gained much *favor*. They were of great service to him in his many and important responsibilities.[m] It was good for him, for his people, and for the whole church of God through the centuries, that he had been trained in this school of *understanding*. And the histories of Samuel,[n] and David,[o] prove the same thing. *Good understanding*—the effect of early discipline—gave Daniel *favor*, even when he was past his ninetieth year and the premier of the largest empire of the world.[3] Our blessed Lord, as "Jesus kept increasing in wisdom and stature, and in *favor* with God and men."[p] So . . . the way of wisdom, with all its crosses, is brightened up with sunshine. Wisdom exalts her children.

[m]Gen 39–41
[n]1 Sam 2:6
[o]1 Sam 18:14–16
[p]Luke 2:52

LOOK OUT FOR THE FLOWERY PATH

Can we say this *of the way of the treacherous?* They dream of a flowery path; but they make their way very difficult—pleasing at first, in order to trap them and hold them to the end. "Wicked men live under a hard task-master," said Caryl.[q] "I was held before conversion," said Augustine, "not with an iron chain, but with the obstinacy of my own will." The philosophical infidel bears the same testimony, "I begin to fancy myself in a most deplorable condition, surrounded by deepest darkness on every side" (*Essays,* i. 458). Voltaire, judging of course from his own heart, concludes, "In man is more wretchedness than in all other animals put together. Man loves life, yet knows he must die." Voltaire despaired, "I wish I had never been born." Other worldly infidels agree. Colonel Gardiner declared that during his wicked life he had often envied the existence of a dog. How miserable a man must be who can't get along himself and whose peace depends on getting rid of every thought of God and his own soul!

[q]Job 15:20

In every shape and form, the service of this merciless tyrant is *a hard way.*[r] Men fight their way to hell, as they do to heaven[s]—"through many tribulations." The inborn contrariness of the will;[t] the continual battle with conscience;[u] the absence of peace;[v] the sting of sin;[w] the

[r]Isa 5:18; 47:13; 57:10; Jer 9:5
[s]Acts 14:22
[t]Num 22:32
[u]Acts 9:5
[v]Isa 57:20, 21; 59:8
[w]Prov 23:29–32; Jer 2:17–19

[3] *Dan 1:9, 19, 20; 6:1–3, 28. See also Abraham—Gen 23:10, 11. Paul—Acts 27:43; 28:2. Comp. Rom 14:18.*

certainty of destruction[x]—all prove a way of thorns.

Which then is the way of my choice? Lord, please choose for me. Help me under your guidance to choose the safe and pleasant path of wisdom,[y] the rich portion of godliness for both worlds.[z] *The way of the treacherous is hard.* The end of that way is death.[a] The taskmaster will have his full quota of work. The paymaster will pay the sinner's well-earned wages to the last penny—Death eternal.[b]

[x] Isa 59:7
[y] Prov 3:7
[z] 1 Tim 4:8
[a] Rom 6:21
[b] Rom 6:23

16 *Every prudent man acts with knowledge,*
But a fool displays folly.

SEE WHAT KNOWLEDGE CAN DO!

How often is even valuable *knowledge* wasted for lack of wise application! We need to be careful to use knowledge to full advantage.[c] Just think of all that knowledge can do! In daily life it provides against foreseen dangers[d] and makes a way to escape in trying difficulties.[e] And it's no less useful in family matters: in the training of children;[f] in the guidance of affairs;[g] in caring for household responsibilities.[h] Shouldn't we also make use of it in the church; in a wise adjustment to circumstances;[i] in the conviction of those who contradict;[j] in forbearing with the prejudices of the weak;[k] in the exercise of Christian advice?[l] The lack of it is the main course of an unstable profession. In understanding we are children, not men.[m] Most precious therefore is the word of knowledge, as "the manifestation of the Spirit for the common good."[n] How greatly we need this gift in our communication with the world; to avoid times of stumbling;[o] to mark seasonable periods of reproof;[p] to refrain from needless offence.[4] Yes—even in the political world what need we have for understanding "the times, with knowledge of what Israel should do"![q] Therefore, to deal with *knowledge* in these many applications, is the responsibility of a wise man of God.[r]

Lacking such wisdom, *the fool displays* his stupidity, and pours out his wrath.[s] He exhibits his vanity.[t] He reveals his thoughtlessness.[u] He exercises no judgment,[v] and fills his sphere of influence with evil.

[c] Prov 15:2
[d] Prov 22:3
[e] Acts 16:37, 38; 22:25; 23:7
[f] Judg 13:8–12
[g] Prov 14:1
[h] Prov 31:27
[i] Gal 2:2
[j] Titus 1:9
[k] Acts 15:22–29
[l] Rom 15:14
[m] 1 Cor 14:20
[n] 1 Cor 12:7
[o] Ezra 8:22; Neh 6:11
[p] Prov 9:7, 8; 15:23; 1 Sam 25:36; Amos 5:13; Matt 7:6
[q] 1 Chron 12:32
[r] Prov 14:8, 15
[s] Prov 12:16; Num 22:29, 30
[t] 1 Sam 17:44
[u] Matt 14:7
[v] Prov 18:13

[4] *Neh 2:5. Speaking of his land before a heathen King, in reference not to the God of Israel, but to the sepulchers of his fathers.*

Let us study the minute details of our Lord's well-filled life. He shall deal wisely.[w] This was His distinctive character. The Spirit of *wisdom* was basis for His work.[x] How gloriously it shone forth in the confounding of His enemies[y] and in tender sympathy with His afflicted people![z] How good it is to have our *knowledge* disciplined by His teaching and consecrated to His service!

[w] Isa 52:13
[x] Isa 11:2, 3
[y] Matt 21:24; 22:42–46
[z] Isa 1:4

17 *A wicked messenger falls into adversity,*
But a faithful envoy brings *healing.*

THE SERVANT'S GLORY

A messenger proves his character by either his neglect or his discharge of his trust. *A wicked messenger* betrays his trust,[a] damages his master,[b] and, as a just recompence, *falls into adversity. Faithfulness* is the servant's glory and his master's gain. He brings and receives a blessing. Gehazi's unfaithfulness brought him into evil.[c] Eliezer, "showing all good faith," was blessed himself, and was healing to his master.[d]

But now, let us speak of the messenger and ambassador of the Lord.[e] What words can tell the awful evil of *the wicked messenger,* ignorant of the worth of his commission, and utterly careless in the discharge of it! Yet his evil returns upon his own head; weighed down, as he is, with the guilt of the blood of souls, eternally damned through his neglect.[f]

Faithfulness marks the true *ambassador.*[g] He "did not shrink from declaring to you the whole purpose of God"[h] not forcing offensive truths into unnatural prominence; but also, not withholding them in their just scriptural proportion. He condescends to the capacities of his people: but he will not humor their prejudices or antipathies. He does not walk "in craftiness or adulterating the Word of God, but by the manifestation of truth commending [himself] to every man's conscience in the sight of God."[i] The tongue "of such an ambassador" brings healing,[j] both to himself and to his people.[k] "The wilderness and the desert will be glad" under his enriching blessing; and the burst of joy and peace is heard on every side—"How beautiful are the feet of those who bring glad tidings of good things!"[l]

[a] Luke 16:1
[b] Prov 10:26; Matt 25:26
[c] 2 Kings 5:26, 27
[d] Titus 2:10; Gen 24:33–56
[e] Mal 2:7; 2 Cor 5:20
[f] Ezek 3:17, 18; 1 Cor 9:16
[g] 1 Cor 4:1, 2; 1 Thess 2:3–6
[h] Acts 20:27
[i] 2 Cor 4:2; 2:17
[j] Prov 12:18
[k] Job 33:23–26
[l] Isa 35:1; Rom 10:15

18 *Poverty and shame* will come *to him who neglects*
discipline [AV—*instruction*],
But he who regards reproof will be honored.

DON'T LOSE THE BLESSINGS OF GOD'S DISCIPLINE

The instruction of discipline is God's law. Little do those who *neglect* it know what blessings they lose![m] *Poverty and shame* are often the Lord's rod for His wayward children;[n] two dreaded evils—*poverty,* bringing them into great need; and *shame,* causing them to hang their heads; both disappoint "the lust of the flesh and the lust of the eyes and the boastful pride of life."[o] Young people, learn to dread the freedom that leaves you to your own choice. Dread the first step in the downward course—*neglecting instruction.* Remember your birth, as "the foal of a wild donkey."[p] Know your besetting temptation—to resist control, "as the horse or as the mule."[q]

If you refuse godly restraint, you may end up in *poverty and shame,* embittered with the painful sting of deathbed remorse.[r]

But here *honor* is contrasted with *shame.* To reverently accept *reproof* will surely bring *honor* from man.[s] *Honor* from God will be plentiful. "It is for discipline that you endure; God deals with you as with sons."[t] If we are humbled under His reproof, we shall be raised to His throne.[u] His words are truly pleasant to his well-trained child. To have our ears open to receive discipline is to walk in the path of life and happiness;[v] and to have *the honor* of conformity to our divine Savior.[w] Our pride makes us think that reproof is degrading. But by God's standards "Who hates reproof is stupid."[x] Which judgment is true and right?

[m] Heb 12:10, 11
[n] Luke 15:12–16
[o] 1 John 2:16
[p] Job 11:12
[q] Ps 32:9
[r] Prov 5:11
[s] Prov 25:12
[t] Heb 12:7
[u] 1 Peter 5:6
[v] Prov 6:23; Job 36:10–12
[w] Heb 5:8
[x] Prov 12:1

19 *Desire realized is sweet to the soul,*
But it is an abomination to fools to depart from evil.

HOW TO GET YOUR DESIRES

This must be limited to the desire of the righteous as in verse 12. When that desire is "only good," it will be granted";[y] and the *desire realized is sweet to the soul.* Infinitely *sweeter* will be the full, the eternal,

[y] Prov 13:4; 11:23; 10:24

accomplishment—"I will be satisfied with Thy likeness when I awake."[z] Can't everyone enjoy this blessing? Everyone *can*, but everyone *won't*. Why not? Because it's so opposite to the desires of the carnal mind. Now, if you've been trained in the ways of God since early youth, you're in no position to know just how bitter this enmity really is. But what can make it more plain than to realize that what is hateful to God to see is something for the fool to stay away from![a] A striking figure of heaven and hell, in full contrast; with the great gulf that is fixed between them! Holiness makes heaven; sin makes hell. Take a look then and see which place the ungodly are preparing for. Hatred of holiness belongs to hell. Oh! what a mighty change it must take to make a man right about-face and love the *evil* that he now hates.

[z]Ps 17:15
[a]Prov 15:21

20 *He who walks with wise men will be wise,*
But the companion of fools will suffer harm.

IT'S WISE TO WALK WITH THE WISE

Everyone likes to try to make his friends like himself. So, naturally, we are all molded by the company we keep. It's not up to us to determine whether or not we *will* be influenced, but only *how* we *will* be influenced. *Walking with the wise*—under their instruction, encouragement, and example—*we will be wise*. Our principles and habits will be established, our interest aroused, and the decision made: "Let us go with you, for we have heard that God is with you."[b] Here you can see the blessing of living in a godly family, listening day by day to "the wise,"[c] or in a church where the members edify and help one another.[d]

[b]Zech 8:23
[c]Prov 16:23; 1 Kings 10:8
[d]Eph 4:15, 16

CHOOSE YOUR FRIENDS CAREFULLY

Young people, let us think about your responsibility in the choice of friends. How much depends on your decision to be "a companion of all those who fear Thee, And of those who keep Thy precepts"?[e] And, though the world may allure, the ungodly may mock, the evil heart may consent to their voice, you should seek your strength from God and resolve *to walk with wise men*—"as the Lord lives, and as you yourself live, I will not leave you."[f] Walk with those, whose acquaintance will be a special talent, to give account of to God.

[e]Ps 119:63
[f]2 Kings 2:4

Joash, while he *walked with his wise* guardian, *was wise*. But after his guardian's death, he became a *companion of fools*, and was destroyed.[g] And how often the punishment of criminals warns us that "bad company corrupts good morals"![h] Many a professing (but not true) "believer" has been brought step by step to destruction. The horror of sin, the instinctive drawing back from it, gradually disappears. The fear of God—that cover from sin[i]—is weakened. The hold on the great hopes of the gospel is relaxed. More and more, other objects take first place, and soon the ruin is complete. And when—we might ask—have the godly been able to keep company with fools, without his testimony suffering?[j] If we can live in a worldly element, without feeling out of place; if we can breathe a tainted atmosphere without being sensitive to possible infection; if we find ourselves getting used to the absence of spiritual things in the ordinary course of life, shouldn't we be concerned that worldliness might be regaining control in our lives?

[g]2 Chron 24
[h]1 Cor 15:33; Ps 1:18–21; 106:28, 35
[i]Gen 39:9; Neh 5:15
[j]2 Chron 18:3; 19:2

The first warning to sinners just plucked out of the fire, was—"Be saved from this perverse generation!"[k] And the rule will be to the end—"Do not participate in the unfruitful deeds of darkness, but instead even expose them."[l] Of course, we must have frequent contact with them.[m] But let us find our happiness in being with the saints of God.[n] God may soon decide for a professing believer who halts too long between two opinions. His patience may be exhausted. His justice may take its course; and those, who are now his companions in crime, will be his tormentors in hopeless misery.

[k]Acts 2:40
[l]Eph 5:11; 2 Cor 6:14–16
[m]1 Cor 5:10
[n]Ps 16:3

21 *Adversity* [AV—*evil*] *pursues sinners,*
But the righteous will be rewarded with prosperity.

Sinners are sure to find *evil* at last; the righteous, good. The histories of sin from the beginning—Cain,[o] Achan,[p] Abimelech,[q] Ahab,[r] and his wicked wife,[s] with many others—are solemn demonstrations, that *adversity pursues sinners*, even when they seem to have found a refuge.[t] The delay even of centuries does not lessen the certainty.[u] As sure as the shadow follows the substance, the avenger of blood pursued "the murderer,"[v] "evil may hunt the violent man speedily."[w] Yet often the sinner goes on in his blind infatuation. No one has been witness

[o]Gen 4:10–13
[p]Josh 7:20–26
[q]Judg 9:24, 56, 57
[r]1 Kings 21:19; 22:38; 2 Kings 9:26
[s]1 Kings 21:23; 2 Kings 9:30–36
[t]1 Kings 2:28–31
[u]Exod 17:14; 1 Sam 15:3–7
[v]Num 35:19
[w]Ps 140:11

to his sin. Or no one will make account of it. Or his accusers, being as guilty as he, will hold their peace; or, should he be discovered, prudence or pleading will save him from punishment. And then, though "the iniquity of my foes surrounds me,"[x] he thinks only of present gratification, never looks back, and therefore doesn't see the *evil pursuing him.* And his blindness makes his ruin more certain.[y] And how dearly are his momentary pleasures purchased at the cost of eternity![z]

[x] Ps 49:5
[y] Deut 29:19, 20; Job 11:20; 1 Thess 5:3
[z] Eccl 11:9

Not less sure is the *prosperity,* which shall be *rewarded to the righteous.*[a] The *evil* follows in just retribution. The other is the reward of grace. Not the smallest good—even "a cup of cold water" to a disciple,[b] or honor shown to his servants[c]—shall lose his reward.[d] And if a single act is thus remembered, much more "the good fight," held out to the end.[e] How plainly is this the constitution of grace; that when perfect obedience can claim no recompence,[f] such unworthy, such defiled, work should be so honored with an infinite, overwhelming acceptance!

[a] Isa 3:10, 11; Rom 2:6–10
[b] Matt 10:42
[c] Matt 10:41, 42; 1 Kings 17:16–23
[d] Heb 6:10
[e] 2 Tim 4:7, 8
[f] Luke 17:10

22 *A good man leaves an inheritance to his children's children,*
And the wealth of the sinner is stored up for the righteous.

WHAT KIND OF INHERITANCE WILL YOU LEAVE?

Here we have a particular instance of the good to be repaid to the *righteous*. It cannot, however, be taken as a blanket statement. Many *good* men have no inheritance to leave; or they have no *children;* or none that survive them; or no *children's children;* or this generation may be in poverty. *The wealth of the sinner* also, instead of being *stored up for the righteous,* is given to his posterity for successive generations.[g] Yet Scripture gives many examples of this dispensation of God's care; showing the blessing of personal godliness to unborn posterity. Abraham left his covenanted *inheritance to his children's children.*[h] Caleb's children inherited their father's possession.[i] Although David's house was not so with God, as he might have desired; yet his lamp continued to burn for some seventeen generations.[j] Also, the divine blessing

[g] Ps 17:14
[h] Gen 17:7, 8; Ps 112:2
[i] Josh 14:14
[j] 2 Sam 23:5; 2 Chron 21:7

has often come upon the discreet guidance of his affairs,[k] and the special promise to Christian liberality,[l] preserved *the good man's inheritance*. And if there is no earthly substance to leave; yet a church in the house; a family altar; the record of holy example and instruction; and above all, a store of believing prayer laid up for accomplishment, when we shall be silent in the grave—will be *an inheritance* to our children of inestimable value. For though no trust can be placed in inherited Christianity;[m] yet the recollection of the path in which their fathers walked, and in which they themselves were trained, may, under God's grace, continue a godly inheritance in our families, so that "fathers . . . shall teach them to their children."[n]

[k]Ps 112:5
[l]Prov 3:9, 10
[m]John 1:13
[n]Ps 78:5, 6; 45:16

But *the good man's inheritance* is also increased from *the wealth of the sinner*. Laban's *wealth was laid up for* Jacob,[o] the spoils of Egypt and Canaan[p] for Israel; Haman's wealth for Esther and Mordecai.[q] Indeed this appears to have been a prominent feature of the Old Dispensation,[r] and it will be openly renewed in the latter-day glory of the church.[s] Therefore, the fulfillment is probably far more frequent than meets the eye. Often also *the wealth of the sinner, stored up* for the glory of his own name in his offspring becomes the portion of the just in their own holy seed; consecrated to the service of their Lord and His church.[t]

[o]Gen 31:1, 9, 16
[p]Exod 12:35, 36; Josh 11:14; Ps 105:44
[q]Esther 8:1, 2
[r]Prov 38:8; Job 27:16, 17
[s]Isa 61:6
[t]Eccl 2:26

23 *Abundant food* is in *the fallow ground of the poor,*
But it is swept away by injustice [AV—*want of judgment*].

The produce of the soil is the fruit of hard work.[u] Much food comes from the farming of the poor; because, being wholly dependent on their own efforts, they spare no pains or labor. So that by careful husbandry they can get their living from a small plot of ground; while a large and fertile estate of a rich man may be destroyed for lack of good judgment.[v] The rich may then through injustice take from the poor. Indeed, for lack of wise management, the richest farming may be wasted. Egypt with her abundant crops would have been *swept away*, but for Joseph's wisdom in preserving a large portion of the crops.[w] Solomon's wise administration of his household did away with waste and extravagance.[x] Even our divine Master,

[u]Prov 12:11; Gen 3:19
[v]Prov 24:30–34
[w]Gen 41:33–36
[x]1 Kings 4:27, 28

in the distribution of food, directed his disciples to "Gather up the leftover fragments that nothing may be lost,"[y] or destroyed for want of care and judgment.

[y]John 6:12

A PRACTICAL APPLICATION

But what is the practical and extended application of all this? If talents lie inactive, or if their activity is not wisely directed, a rich harvest is lost for lack of good judgment. The same ruin flows from the neglect of spiritual advantages. The harvest of grace withers into a famine. Lazy pretender! Wake up and get busy cultivating the ground. Otherwise you'll starve for lack of food. Then let your roused energy be directed by a sound judgment. Without it, the fruits of hard work, temporal, intellectual, and spiritual, will go to waste.

24 *He who spares his rod hates his son,*
But he who loves him disciplines him diligently.

SPARING THE ROD OF DISCIPLINE—TRUE LOVE?

Among the many modern theories of education, how often God's system is overlooked, when actually, it should be our pattern and standard! *The rod* of discipline is its main mark—not harsh severity, but a wise, considerate, faithful exercise; always aimed at the conquering of the will and the humbling and purifying of the heart. Here, however, God and man are in conflict. Man often *spares his rod,* because he loves the child. At least, he calls it love. But isn't our Father's love to His children, inconceivably more intense than that of an earthly parent? Yet, He doesn't spare his rod—"What son is there whom his father does not discipline?"[z] Is *His rod* proof of his *hatred?* Not for a minute. "Whom the Lord *loves* He disciplines."[a] No! He teaches us, in His divine judgment that—*He who spares the rod hates* the child. Doesn't he at least act as if he hated him—by bypassing a duty so necessary for his welfare; overlooking his vicious habits and wayward will, which must surely issue in bitter sorrow.[b] Isn't this delivering him up to his worst enemy? Better that the child had been trained in the house of strangers, than that he should be the unhappy victim of the cruelty of parental love.

[z]Heb 12:7

[a]Heb 12:6; Deut 8:5; Rev 3:19

[b]Prov 29:15; 1 Sam 3:13; 1 Kings 1:6; 2:25. Comp. 2 Sam 13:39; 18:33

WHERE DOES DISCIPLINE OF OUR CHILDREN BEGIN?

The discipline of our children must therefore begin with self-discipline. Nature teaches us to love them much. But we need a controlling principle to teach us to love them wisely. The indulgence of our children has its root in self-indulgence. We don't like putting ourselves to pain. The difficulties indeed can only be learned by experience. And even in this school, no one parent can measure the trials of another. But all our children are children of Adam. "Foolishness is bound up in the heart."[c] All choose from the first dawn of reason, the broad road of destruction.[d] And can we bear the thought that they should walk in that road? We pray for their conversion. But prayer without teaching is mockery, and Scripture teaching implies the exercise of discipline.[e] Therefore, discipline *just must be*. Everyone of us needs the rod, some again and again. Yet, it must be the father's rod, yearning over his chastened child,[f] even yet "discipline your son while there is hope."[g] The rod without affection is revolting tyranny.

But often do we hear mourning over failure. And isn't this the main reason? We don't discipline early enough.[h] Satan begins with the infant in arms![i] The cry of passion is his first stir of inborn corruption. Do we begin that early? Every sin begins in the nursery. The great secret is, to establish authority in the dawn of life; to bend the tender twig, before the knotty oak is beyond our power. A child, trained early by parental discipline, will probably preserve that wholesome influence to the end of life.

But great is the difficulty, when the child has been the *early* master—to begin disciplining when the habit of disobedience has already been formed and hardened; to have the first work to do when the child is growing out of childhood and when unrestrained confidence needs to be established. The parent, who starts to discipline late in his child's life, rarely succeeds. "*It is* good for a man that he should bear the yoke in his youth."[j]

25 *The righteous has enough to satisfy his appetite,*
But the stomach of the wicked is in want.

This is one of the many proofs, that "the righteous is a guide to his neighbor."[k] Temporal blessings are assured,

[c] Prov 22:15; Gen 8:21
[d] Isa 53:6
[e] Prov 13:18; Eph 6:4; Heb 12:6. Comp. Ps 94:12; 119:67, 71
[f] Ps 103:13
[g] Prov 19:18
[h] Prov 19:18
[i] Ps 58:3; Isa 48:8
[j] Lam 3:27
[k] Prov 12:26

[l]Prov 10:3; Ps 34:10; 37:3, 18

[m]Gen 47:11–13

[n]1 Kings 17:1–11; 18:5

[o]Dan 1:12–16

[p]Ps 132:16. Comp. Ps 36:8; John 6:35, 55

[q]1 Kings 21:1–4; Job 20:20, 22

[r]Ps 17:14; Isa 65:13, 14; Hos 4:10; Mic 6:14

[s]Luke 16:24

so far as they are really good for him; whether little or much; enough to satisfy his wants, not to fulfill "craving"[l] of the wicked. Indeed he will never want very much, "because his desires are moderate, and he makes a temperate use of God's blessings," said Bishop Patrick. He therefore shall eat to his *satisfaction*, though the Egyptians are destitute.[m] Elijah was fed, first by ravens, afterward by a widow, when the wicked nation was in extremity.[n] The food of *the righteous* may be coarse, and that of *the wicked* sumptuous. But didn't Daniel and his friends eat their pulse (vegetables) with more *satisfaction*, than their fellow-captives did their richer dainties?[o] And—as to higher food and heavenly *satisfaction*, Christ is a substitute for everything; nothing for Him. "If then," as Luther declares, "we live here by begging our bread, is not this well recompensed, that we are nourished with the food of angels, with eternal life, and Christ himself?"[p]

So chaotic in its desires is the soul of *the wicked* that no abundance will ever satisfy *his want*. Ahab's crown could give him no rest without Naboth's vineyard.[q] That's how much the ungodly heart craves![r] But how intolerable this conscious want will be throughout eternity when a drop of water to cool the tormented tongue shall be denied![s]

CHAPTER FOURTEEN

1 *The wise woman builds her house,*
But the foolish tears it down with her own hands.

HOW IMPORTANT THE MARRIAGE CHOICE

A wife is either a blessing or a curse to her husband.[a] Her *wisdom* may make up for many of his defects; while all the results of his care and good stewardship may be wasted by her *foolishness*. The godly wife is the very soul of the *house*. She instructs her children by her example, no less than by her teaching. She educates them for God and for eternity; not for worldly glory, but for God. Her household management combines economy with liberality;[b] strict integrity in the fear of God.[c] So . . . as godly servants bring a blessing to the house,[d] so *does the wise woman build her house*[e] under the blessing of God, "establishing it in a firm and durable state," said Diodati.[f] Who can estimate the worth of a Christian mother—a Hannah[g]—or Eunice?[h]

But consider *the foolish woman*—her idleness, waste, love of pleasure, want of forethought and care, her children allowed their own way, their happiness ruined! We see her *house torn down* in confusion. A sad issue, if an enemy had done this! But it is the doing, or rather the undoing, of *her own hands*. In proportion to her power and influence is her capability to cause family trouble. Such was Jezebel, the destroyer of her house.[i]

What responsibility then belongs to the marriage choice, linked with the highest interests of unborn generations! If ever there was a matter for special prayer and consideration, this is it. One mistake here, may be an undoing of ourselves and of our house. Of how little ac-

[a] Prov 12:4
[b] Prov 31:13, 18–27
[c] Prov 31:30
[d] Gen 30:27; 39:5
[e] Prov 24:3
[f] Prov 31:28–31
[g] 1 Sam 1:27, 28
[h] 2 Tim 1:5; 3:15
[i] 1 Kings 16:31–33; 21:24, 25. Comp. 2 Kings 11:1

count are birth, fortune, external accomplishments, compared with godly wisdom![1]

2 *He who walks in his uprightness fears the* L*ORD*,
But he who is crooked in his ways despises Him.

YOU CAN'T LIVE THE CHRISTIAN LIFE BY HALVES

There can be no stream without the fountain. Grace in the heart is the spring of the upright walk.[j] The proof that we believe the reality of Christianity is that we walk in the power of it. The proof of the influence of "the *fear of the Lord*" is that we are in it always,[k] not saints in our prayers and worldlings in our conduct; not substituting active zeal for personal devotedness; not teaching our families half of the Christian life—to read and pray; but "whatever is true . . . honorable . . . right . . . pure . . . lovely . . . of good repute . . . let your mind dwell on these things."[l] Man may boast of his moral *uprightness* that he would not stoop to a mean action. But the heart-searching Savior lays open the root of worldly selfishness and shows *his way to be crooked* before him.[m] Does he remember, or does he know, while he slumbers in the delusion of external decency, that the allowed supremacy of any earthly object,[n] or the indulgence of a secret lust,[o] brings him under the fearful guilt of *despising God?*

[j] Prov 4:23; Matt 12:33–35
[k] Prov 23:17
[l] Phil 4:8
[m] Luke 16:14, 15
[n] 1 Sam 2:29, 30
[o] 2 Sam 12:9, 10

3 *In the mouth of the foolish is a rod* [AV—*of pride*] *for* his *back*,
But the lips of the wise will preserve them.

How many symbols the wise man Solomon uses to show the destructive evils of the mouth! Here it is a rod,[p] *a rod of pride. The rod in the mouth* is often sharper than the rod in the hand.[q] Sometimes it strikes against God;[r] sometimes it is "the rod of My anger"[s] against his people; permitted,[t] yet restrained.[u] And in the end, it's always *the rod* for the *fool* himself.[v] Yet when the heart is humbled and filled with wisdom, it's the tongue that preserves from imminent danger,[w] even from the threatened scourge of the *rod of pride.*[x]

[p] Ezek 7:10, 11
[q] Jer 18:18
[r] Exod 5:2; Ps 12:3, 4; 2 Kings 19:10
[s] Isa 10:5
[t] Rev 13:5
[u] Ps 125:3
[v] Ps 64:8
[w] Prov 12:6
[x] Job 5:21; Ps 31:20

[1] *Mr. Scott here aptly quotes the proverb—that "a fortune in a wife is better than a fortune with a wife." "For the* building of a house *three things are principally necessary; first, a holy marriage; secondly, a special fitness in the head of the family; and lastly, a holy living together. As many order the matter, they so provoke God by the first entering upon a family, that the family travels ever after under the burden of God's anger"—BYFIELD* on Col 3:18.

Just think what would happen if the tongues were to rule the earth! How could people ever stand to live together?[y] But how wonderful the grace that transforms our mouths—this unruly, boasting instrument of unrighteousness into "instruments of righteousness to God!"[z]

[y]Ps 57:4; 120:5
[z]Rom 6:13

4 *Where no oxen are, the manger is clean,*
But much increase comes by the strength of the ox.

Oxen are used in farming.[a] Therefore, where there are *no oxen* to till the ground, there is no food in the stall.[b] Why? Because, where there is no labor, no food can be supplied. God works by *means,* not by *miracles.* We must take good care of the farm, if we want an abundant harvest. Let our cattle be put to work, and the harvest will be greatly increased.[c] Spiritual fields, too, where there are no laborers, remain empty. But see the *much increase*—the harvest of precious souls—the fruit of their *strength* and effectiveness.[2] "In all labor," both in natural and spiritual farming, "there is profit."[d] But God will never acknowledge a lazy servant.

[a]Deut 25:4; 1 Kings 19:19
[b]Amos 4:6
[c]Ps 144:14
[d]Verse 23

5 *A faithful witness will not lie,*
But a false witness speaks lies.

On the surface, this seems perfectly obvious. But a closer look shows it to be a valuable statement of practical wisdom. *A faithful witness* is not moved to swerve from truth, by pleas or bribes, not by promise or threats. He is the man to trust. *He will not lie. But a false witness* has lost all principle of truth. *He will tell lies* without any inducement but his own interest or pleasure. Flee from his very breath.[e]

[e]Prov 25:19

THE FAITHFUL WITNESS

The faithful witness answers God's requirements.[f] He is therefore God's delight.[g] He is the citizen of the heavenly Zion,[h] and the ornament of godliness.[i] In the sacred office *he will not lie.* His spirit is firm and independent. His message is full and transparent truth.[j] But the *false witness* is a true child of "the father of lies."[k] Awful indeed is his utterance in common life;[l] more awful in the profession of the gospel;[m] awful beyond

[f]Ps 51:6
[g]John 1:47
[h]Ps 15:2; Isa 33:15
[i]Phil 4:8
[j]1 Thess 2:3, 4
[k]John 8:44; 1 Kings 21:13
[l]Prov 25:18
[m]Acts 5:1–4

[2] *1 Cor 3:9; 9:9, 10; 1 Tim 5:18, and the image of the minister, Rev 4:7, seem to warrant this application of the proverb.*

conception in the sanctuary.[n] A minister of God in his commission! A minister of Satan in his work[o] delivering a lying message; "to distort the gospel of Christ,"[p] to the destruction of his people, to the double destruction of his own soul.

[n] Jer 5:31
[o] 2 Cor 11:13–15
[p] Gal 1:7

Thus the "good tree" and "the rotten tree," each brings forth its own fruit.[q] Let us remember that our principles, good and evil, are exemplified in the most trivial transactions, and gather strength from the slightest, as well as from the most important, exercise.[r]

[q] Matt 7:17, 18
[r] Luke 16:10

6 *A scoffer seeks wisdom, and* finds *none,*
But knowledge is easy to him who has
understanding.

What then? Is the promise—"He who seeks finds"? —made untrue?[s] No! The failure lies at *the scoffer's* own door. He seeks indeed but without seriousness,[t] without honesty of purpose;[u] without delight;[v] solely for his own interest.[w] He "finds therefore matter enough for his humor, but none for his instruction!" said Lord Bacon. He blames the darkness on the Scripture, not where it really belongs, on his own heart. He feels himself able to comprehend the subject and therefore free to reject what is beyond his conception or contrary to his prejudices. He scorns the humbling submission of faith, so that the glory even of the wisdom of God is foolishness with him.[x] No wonder that, while he makes an effort to *seek,* he doesn't find what he is seeking.[y] He seeks his object, but neglects the means and perishes in the scornfulness of his own unbelief.[z]

[s] Matt 7:7, 8; Isa 45:19
[t] John 18:38
[u] Jer 42:1–3; 43:1–4; Ezra 14:1–4; 20:1–3; Matt 22:15, 16
[v] Prov 17:16; 18:2
[w] Acts 8:18–23
[x] Rom 9:31, 32; 10:3
[y] Prov 24:7; 2 Tim 3:7
[z] 1 Cor 3:19

THE PATH OF UNDERSTANDING

To another class of seekers, *knowledge is easy.*[a] The Ethiopian eunuch gathered his knowledge from simplicity.[b] God gave him a ready will, a right taste; and in doing his will he knew "the teaching."[c] Obedience is the path of *understanding.* "Whoever then humbles himself as this child, he is the greatest in the kingdom of heaven."[d]

[a] Prov 8:9
[b] Acts 8:31
[c] John 7:17
[d] Matt 18:4

Shouldn't we unite with our divine Master in adoring the gracious sovereignty of this dispensation?—"Thou didst hide these things from *the* wise and intelligent and didst reveal them to babes."[e] Shouldn't we seek for deeper humility as the pathway to higher instruction?

[e] Matt 11:25

While we are in our Father's "hand" as the object of His love, think of the privilege of sitting down at his feet where "*everyone* receives of Thy words."[f]

[f]Deut 33:3

7 *Leave the presence of a fool,*
Or you will not discern words of knowledge.

DON'T HAVE FELLOWSHIP WITH THE UNGODLY

Fellowship with the ungodly is absolutely forbidden, and it is never safe to contradict a plain command.[g] Let us labor to win their souls to Christ. But the rule of prudence directs, "Do not throw your pearls before swine." "Avoid," says Leighton (vol. 3), "the mixture of an irreverent commonness of speaking of holy things indifferently in all companies."[h] Therefore *when we perceive not in the foolish man the words of knowledge, leave him.* Some may be called to argue with him. But be careful that the call is clear. The safest way to go is to transact your business with him quickly and leave.

[g]Prov 9:6; 2 Cor 6:17

[h]Matt 7:6

DON'T TRY TO SEE HOW MUCH POISON YOUR SYSTEM CAN TAKE!

Thrilling, indeed, is the glow of the Savior's name upon the young Christian's lips. Its warmth may put elder Christians to shame. But we need to warn him, he may be harmed in an unwise effort to do good. Testify for your Savior wherever He may open your door and your mouth. But it's better to retreat from fault finders.[i] You may be fooled by plausible reasonings. Beware of tampering with your simplicity by the hazardous experiment of trying to see how much poison your constitution can take.[j] If our Lord exposed Himself to moral danger; just think of the impenetrable cover of His sanctity, His perfect self-government. His rules of godly wisdom. Do we feel secure in the strength of our Christian habits? None of us is so secure that we are able to relax our watchfulness and recklessly rush into danger. We are in perpetual warfare with the old principles of corruption. We just can't place dependence on habits that do not produce right conduct and correct understanding of present duty. It's far easier to avoid the path of sin than to leave it, once we begin to follow it; far easier to keep out of the course of the stream than to stem the torrent. Walk closely with God; and under His cover and shield, bear a protest

[i]Prov 26:4; 1 Tim 6:4, 5

[j]1 Cor 15:33

against the ungodly.[k] Spend much time in fellowship with His people. The very sight of a man of God is refreshing.[l]

[k]Ps 119:114–115
[l]Prov 27:9

8 *The wisdom of the prudent is to understand his way,*
But the folly of fools is deceit.

This is not *the wisdom* of the educated, but *of the prudent;* not academic and abstract, but sound and practical. It is self-knowledge and self-control, looking to God for His guidance. And how much we need this *wisdom* to *understand* our way! The restless professing Christian eagerly follows his own impulse. His inborn bias interprets providences and makes openings for himself. Everything is out of place. He is so "fervent in spirit," that he begins "lagging behind in diligence."[m] He conceives himself to be doing good; the more so, because it is different from his brethren. He pleads the constraint of zeal as an excuse for indiscretion; as if Christianity were meant to destroy rather than correct his judgment.

[m]Rom 12:11

AS GOD HAS DISTRIBUTED TO US, LET US WALK

But "He has made everything appropriate in its time. Christianity is orderly, as wise as it is warm. Whatever excitement a disorderly course may offer, more good is done in steady consistency. To break the ranks in disorder; by "acting like busybodies";[n] to be eager to *understand* our neighbor's way,[o] obscures the light upon our own. The true *wisdom is to understand* what belongs to us personally and relatively.[p] "As God has called each, in this manner let him walk."[q] Let the eye do the work of the eye and the hand of the hand. If Moses prayed on the mount and Joshua fought in the valley,[r] it was not because the one lacked courage or the other didn't pray; but just because each had his appointed work and *understood his own way*. Many steps of *our way* are different from our neighbor's and may often be difficult to determine; involved in the principles, rather than the detail expressed in Scripture. But the spiritually wise will understand what the will of the Lord is."[s] "Your eye is clear" and a sound heart will make our way plain.[t]

[n]Eccl 3:11; 1 Peter 4:15; 2 Thess 3:11, 12
[o]John 21:21, 22
[p]1 Kings 3:6–9 Eccl 8:5
[q]1 Cor 7:17
[r]Exod 17:10, 11
[s]Eph 5:17; Col 1:9, 10
[t]Matt 6:22

[3] *FRENCH and SKINNER'S* Translation of Proverbs.

But while the attention of a truly wise man is occupied in *understanding his way;* "the arts of *deceit* control the polluted minds of the wicked."[3] Their wisdom of *deceit* is really foolishness. Gehazi's overreaching wisdom proved foolish in the end. Daniel's accusers were taken "in their craftiness."[u] Ananias and Sapphira vainly tried to hide their covetousness under the cover of liberality.[v] Who can deceive a heart-searching God? The attempt to do so is fearful provocation, certain confusion.

[u] Dan 6:24; 1 Cor 3:19

[v] Acts 5:1–10

9 *Fools mock at sin,*
But among the upright there is good will.

What! Are there those who regard sin as a sport? They have never seen the sight, never felt the weight. Look into eternity. Heaven sees it as a very serious matter. And hell regards it in the same way. So . . . why should it be made a *mockery* on earth? "It brought death into the world, and all our woe," said Milton. Is this a joking matter? If you think so, just see how God feels about it.[w] Go to Gethsemane. Go to Calvary. Learn there what sin is. Shall we mock that which was such a crushing burden to the Son of God?[x] Ask converted souls, awakened consciences, dying sinners—do they speak lightly of sin? In eternity, *the mocker* will feel far differently about it all—he'll call himself, then, what God calls him now—*a fool!* The *mocking* can't go beyond the grave; unless it becomes the sport of the cruel enemy as he sees the hopeless, unchangeable torments of his deluded victim. The damnation of souls is sport in hell. Shouldn't the mocker, rushing into this hell, be the object of our pity and prayer? We warn, we weep, we would yearn over him.

[w] Isa 43:24; Jer 44:4; Ezek 6:9; Amos 2:13

[x] Matt 26:37, 38; 27:46

The upright cannot *mock,* like this hardened *fool.* While "he makes himself merry with his sin, and scoffs at the reproof and judgment which pertains thereunto," stated Bishop Hall. "They have the mark of those that sigh and cry over the abominations of the land"—the sure seal of the Lord's *favor.*[4] Soon the sport of the fool comes to an end. Here is *good will* from God abundant and unchangeable. Our God looks over, pities, bears

[4] *Ezek 9:4–6; 2 Kings 22:19, 20; Dan 9:4–21. See the contrast set out by God Himself. Isa 66:2–5.*

with, guides, loves, saves, eternally. What are crowns and kingdoms compared with such a portion!

10 *The heart knows its own bitterness,*
And a stranger does not share its joy.

EVERY MAN IS AN ISLAND

What a graphic illustration of man's proper individuality! "Who among men knows the *thoughts* of a man except the spirit of the man, which is in him?"[y] Everyone knows himself as no one else does. Inwardly, he is the only true judge of his own joys and sorrows.[z] Our most painful sufferings are often caused by things we can't reveal to even our dearest friend.[5] No two of us are made alike; and these differences of mind and character prevent perfect understanding, even in the warmest glow of human sympathy. Each only knows where his own heart pains. Therefore, each must, in a measure, tread a solitary path, and be often misunderstood. Hannah, *knowing her own bitterness,* was rashly rebuked by him, who ought to have been her comfort.[a] Gehazi harshly rejected the Shunamite, and pushed her away, through ignorance of her bitter sorrow.[b] Job's friends misunderstood his problems and proved to be "worthless physicians ... sorry comforters."[c]

[y]1 Cor 2:11
[z]1 Kings 8:38, 39
[a]1 Sam 1:10–13
[b]2 Kings 4:27
[c]Job 13:4; 16:2

ONE HEART ALONE INTO WHICH WE CAN POUR OUR SORROWS

But think of Him, who made Himself "a man of sorrows," that He might be "tempted in all things as *we* are."[d] This is not the common love to the whole family of God, but an individual interest of fellowship with each loved alone. The heart's *bitterness* is experimentally *known* and effectually relieved.[e] Very man that He is, even on the throne of God—Jesus Christ is alive to all our sorrows.[f] None of the members of His body—the church—are too low for His highest and most endearing thoughts. Into His heart, we may pour our tale of woe, which no other ear may receive. We may not be able to comprehend it. But He will make us feel that His sympathy with sorrow is a precious reality. My Savior! Has *my heart a bitterness,* that you do not know, that you do

[d]Isa 53:3; Heb 4:15
[e]Isa 50:4, 5
[f]Isa 63:9

[5] *Thus the Savior separated Himself even from His chosen disciples. Mark 14:32–35.*

not feel with me, and for which you do not have a present cure?

No less individual is the *heart's joy.* It lies deep within itself. *A stranger does not share it.* Michal could understand David's bravery, not *his joy.* She knew him as a man of war, not as a man of God.[g] Indeed, joy is a plant in "a garden locked," a stream from "a spring sealed up."[h] It is "the secret of the Lord . . . He is intimate with the upright."[i] it is the indwelling "Helper . . . whom the world cannot receive."[j] Yes, truly—that's the highest joy, that the man hides in his own heart, hidden from view. There is no noise or froth on the surface. They are deep waters of a divine spring. Christ takes the believer aside from the crowd, feeds him on hidden manna,[k] and makes him partaker of His own joy. Whatever cause there may be for mourning, He "will turn their mourning into joy,"[l] in the *midst* of it,[m] and as the everlasting fruit of it.[n]

[g]1 Sam 18:20; 2 Sam 6:16
[h]Song of Sol 4:12
[i]Prov 3:32; Ps 25:14
[j]John 14:16, 17
[k]Rev 2:17
[l]Jer 31:13
[m]Rom 5:3
[n]Isa 60:20

11 *The house of the wicked will be destroyed,*
But the tent of the upright will flourish.

PILGRIMS AND STRANGERS HERE

The feeblest state of *the upright* is more stable than the prosperity of *the wicked.* The wicked build *a house.* The earth is their home, where they would settle, and take their rest. *The upright*—knowing the uncertainty of earth, and seeking a better house—only pitch a tent[o]—weak and trembling. Yet *the house is destroyed,* and the *tent flourishes.*[p] The strongest support of man totters.[q] The support of God to the weakest is Omnipotence.[r] But the natural eye seems to see the contrary—the flourishing of *the wicked* and the overthrow of *the upright.* And how confusing it is to the servant of God![s] But "we walk by faith, not by sight."[t] "The sanctuary"—the Word of God—will explain.[u] Wait awhile. The great day will set all in order before us and show that "shall not the Judge of all the earth deal justly?"[v] Meanwhile let Him do His own work and fulfill His own Word in His own time.

[o]Heb 11:9
[p]Prov 3:33; 12:7
[q]Job 8:15; Ps 49:12
[r]Isa 40:29; 41:10
[s]Jer 12:1
[t]2 Cor 5:7
[u]Ps 73:16, 17; Job 18:14–21
[v]Gen 18:25; Ps 58:11

12 *There is a way* which seems *right to a man,*
But its end is the way of death.

SEARCH CAREFULLY BOTH YOUR BIBLE AND YOUR HEART

[w]1 Cor 6:9; 1 Tim 5:24

[x]Prov 14:14; Ps 36:2, 3

[y]Deut 29:19; Isa 44:20; Rev 3:17, 18

No one can doubt the outcome of open ungodliness.[w] But other paths in the broad road, seemingly right, are just as certainly in the *end, the way of death.* Vice passes under the guise of virtue. Covetousness is disguised under the name of foresight. Indeed it is the fearful character of sin to hide its own traits and tendencies. Our lack of understanding of it increases in proportion to our familiarity with it. The self-deceiver has often been a "backslider in heart."[x] He lost his humility, relaxed his watchfulness, neglected the diligent keeping of the heart. Sin soon found acceptance and entrance. When it could not be wholly covered, it was excused. Appearances were kept up; misgivings gradually vanished, and the fool mistook death for life.[y] But oh! How soon will the disguise drop off, and the discovery be made, that, all along, sin was cherished in self-delusion.

[z]1 Peter 3:21

[a]2 Cor 13:5

[b]1 Sam 12:23; Mal 2:7

[c]Gal 6:4; Ps 139:23, 24

[d]Matt 25:1–12

"Take care then," Leighton warns us, "of sleeping unto death in carnal ease."[z] Look well to the foundation and soundness of your faith.[a] Search carefully both your Bible and your heart. Go to the Lord in prayer, and to His ministers, to show you the true way.[b] Let each one "examine his own work."[c] If you're not in open rebellion against God, have you freely yielded your heart to Him? If you're free from open wickedness, are you not equally free from true godliness? The most moral, but unsaved, pretender is the slave of sin. It will be terrible, indeed, to be carrying a beautiful but unlit lamp when you meet the heavenly bridegroom and plunge then from high expectations of heaven into the depths of hell![d] May the Lord keep our eye steadily on the *end of our way* and make that end sure for heaven!

13 *Even in laughter the heart may be in pain,*
And the end of joy may be grief.

A SMILING FACE DOESN'T ALWAYS MEAN A HAPPY HEART

[e]Esther 5:9–13

Many a sigh is heaved amid the loud *laughter* of folly.[e] It would be as easy to find true joy in hell as in the worldly heart. We could just as easily gather grapes "from thorn bushes, nor figs from thistles," as this fruit of the Spirit[f] from nature's barren soil. As soon might the tempest-tossed ocean be at rest as the sinner's conscience.[g] He may feast in his prison or dance in his chains. He may drink away his trouble. But it is a vain show of happiness. Ask him what is in his heart. You'll find that his smile is a counterfeit to hide a reality of woe? The voice of conscience and experience will make itself heard—"It is madness—what does it accomplish?"[h] If he has found a diversion from present trouble, has he found a cover from everlasting misery? It is far easier to drown conviction, than to escape damnation. And to be merry for a day and in torment for eternity—who wants that? And who wouldn't run from it?

[f]Matt 7:16
[g]Isa 57:20, 21
[h]Eccl 2:2

And we're not talking just about the crude *joy* of the vulgar. Take the fullest cup of earth's best joys. Can it satisfy our desires, ease our troubles, prepare us for eternity? Even the present *end of this* short-lived *joy is grief,*[i] sometimes so intolerable, that suicide is turned to as the cure of anguish; and to avoid the fear of hell, the wretched sinner leaps into it.[j] At best, eternity will change the face of our pretended joy, when that, which remains, will be *what* we most desired to get rid of—the sting of conscience, as enduring as the pleasures of sin were momentary.[k]

[i]Amos 6:3–7
[j]Matt 27:3–5
[k]Luke 6:24; 16:21–24; Rom 6:21

But the end of those pleasures implies other pleasure with a different end. Contrast the prodigal's joy in the far country, with his return to his father's house, when *"they began to be merry."*[l] The fruit of carnal pleasure ends in sorrow. But penitential sorrow begets happiness that ends in everlasting joy.[m] Lord! Choose my inheritance for me among your weeping people.

[l]Luke 15:13–24
[m]Ps 126:5, 6; Isa 35:10

14 *The backslider in heart will have his fill of his own ways,*
But a good man will be satisfied *with his.*

LOOK OUT FOR THE CANKER OF UNWATCHFULNESS!

Every spot is not leprosy. Every mark of sin does not prove a Christian to be a *backslider.* A man may be "caught in any trespass;"[n] or it may be the sin of ignorance;[o] or sin abhorred, resisted, yet still cleaving.[p] *Backsliding* implies a willful step; not always in the

[n]Gal 6:1
[o]Lev 4:2; Heb 5:2
[p]Rom 7:15–24

open, but the more dangerous, because hidden. Here was no open apostasy, perhaps no tangible inconsistency. No—the man may be looked up to as an eminent saint. But he is a *backslider in heart.* A secret canker of unwatchfulness; worldly conformity,[q] neglect, or indulgence, has insensibly devoured "his strength."[r] He was once pressing onward. A languor has now stolen upon him. His heart beats unsteadily. He has become formal and hurried in his prayers; lukewarm in the means of grace: reading his Bible to soothe his conscience, rather than to feed his soul. The first steps, instead of alarming, and bringing him to secret sorrow,[s] hurried him onward from one liberty to another, till he lost all power of resistance. His unsoundness was known to God long before it was openly manifested. Before David's great sin, indolence and security had probably unhinged him and laid him open to the tempter.[t] Perhaps this example may teach the child of God his need of watchfulness and dependence.[u] *The backslider's* folly and wretchedness is graphically portrayed as a merciful warning to the church. He needs no other rod than *his own ways. To be filled with them;* thus to become the fountain of his own misery; is the most fearful of all divine judgments.[v]

[q]Hos 7:8
[r]Hos 7:9; Judg 16:20
[s]Matt 26:75
[t]2 Sam 11:1, 2
[u]2 Chron 32:31; Phil 2:12
[v]Ps 32:3, 4; Jer 2:19; 4:8. Comp. 1 Sam 28:15; Matt 27:3–5

DRINK DEEPLY FROM A HIGHER FOUNTAIN

The good man is also filled from himself;[6] yet not as the *backslider,* with misery, but with solid *satisfaction.* God has given him a fountain fed from a higher fountain; a living spring within himself;[w] the witness of the Spirit;[x] the life and joy of the heavenly Comforter;[y] the rejoicing testimony of his conscience;[z] the assured hope of glory.[a] This is not independent of God, the one source of self-sufficiency. But it is Himself dwelling in the heart and filling it with His fullness. Let the sinner compare the satisfaction of sin and godliness—the curse and the blessing; and lift up his heart for the direction of a right choice. Let *the backslider* return to the gospel to awaken his contrition and to reanimate his faith.[b] Let *the good man* invigorate his soul daily from his well of consolation.

[w]John 4:14
[x]Rom 8:16
[y]John 14:16, 17
[z]2 Cor 1:12
[a]Col 1:27
[b]Hos 14

[6] *Phil 4:11, self-sufficiency. Comp. 2 Cor 9:8.*

15 *The naive believes everything,*
But the prudent man considers his steps.

DON'T DRINK FROM EVERY CUP PRESENTED TO YOU

To *believe everything* of God is faith. To *believe everything* of man is folly. Faith is a principle of infinite importance. Eternal life and death hang upon it.[c] But it must be grounded upon evidence, and it can only be exercised according to the character and measure of the evidence. An indiscriminate faith is therefore very harmful. The world was ruined by this weakness.[d] And often since, it has been the occasion of sin,[e] and even of downfall.[f]

[c]Mark 16:16; John 3:36
[d]Gen 3:1–6
[e]2 Sam 16:1–4; Esther 3:8–11
[f]1 Kings 13:11–19

Look at the fruit of this folly in the church, when "faith should not rest on the wisdom of men, but on the power of God."[g] Men become loose in fundamental principles. They are "carried away by varied and strange teachings," and never know that it is "good for the heart to be strengthened by grace."[h] The novelties of fancy, accredited by some favorite name, readily pass for revelation of God. We do not sit down to our food blindfolded, not knowing whether we take food or poison. But here men are ready to drink of any cup that is presented to them, like children, who think everything that is sweet is good. In that way, "your minds should be led astray, from the simplicity and purity of devotion to Christ."[i] Errors, never solitary, are built upon some partial, insulated, or perverted truth. Feeling and excitement come in the place of solid practical principle.

[g]1 Cor 2:5
[h]Heb 13:9; Eph 4:14
[i]2 Cor 11:3

But the prudent considers his steps. Cautious consideration should mark our general conduct; trying before we trust; never trusting an uncertain profession.[j] Especially in the church should we carefully consider whom we follow. Weigh the most plausible pretensions.[k] Never set a person with a great name against God's Word.[l] Admit only the one standard; like the noble Bereans, who would not believe even an apostle's word, except it was confirmed by God's Word.[m] Ask wisdom of God. Carefully regulate the energy of religion by God's rule. Enlist feeling on the side and under the direction of sound judgment. This wise carefulness will exhibit a well-ordered Christian profession.

[j]Neh 6:2–4; John 2:24
[k]1 Thess 5:21; 1 John 4:1
[l]Isa 8:20
[m]Acts 17:11

16 *A wise man is cautious* [AV—*feareth*] *and turns away from evil,*
But a fool is arrogant and careless.

FEAR EVIL WORSE THAN DEATH!

Fear is sometimes thought to be an unmanly principle. But look at the terrible extent of *the evil* dreaded. Without—it is vanity and disappointment.[n] Within—it is the sting of guilt.[o] Upward—we see the form of God.[p] Downward—everlasting burnings.[q] Surely then to *turn away from this evil,*[r] yes—to fear it worse than death,[s] is true *wisdom.*

[n]Rom 6:21
[o]Prov 13:15; 1 Cor 15:56
[p]John 3:36
[q]Ps 9:17; Mark 9:44
[r]Gen 39:9, 10
[s]Dan 3:16–18; 6:10; Luke 12:5

The fool however, stout and stubborn in his mind, never *fears* till he falls. The voice of God is unheard amid the uproar of passion's raving tempest. Bravely independent, he sits amid the threatenings of God as unalarmed, as Solomon amid his brass lions; "carried by his rash will, and blind passion, without apprehending the end and issue of things," said Diodati.[t] His character is here shown to be true-to-life. *He is arrogant and careless.* Such *a fool* was Rehoboam, when his self-willed confidence rejected the counsel of wisdom and experience.[u] Such *a fool* was the raging Assyrian, blindly *arrogant* in his own might, until the God he despised turned him back to his destruction.[v] And will not the child of God bless his Father's painful discipline, so needful to curb his *raging* will and bring down his high *confidence*—"Thou hast chastised me, and I was chastised, Like an untrained calf; Bring me back that I may be restored, For Thou art the Lord my God"?[w]

[t]2 Chron 25:15–20
[u]1 Kings 12:13–15
[v]2 Kings 19:28–37
[w]Jer 31:18

17 *A quick-tempered man acts foolishly,*
And a man of evil devices is hated.

Different graduations of sin are here opposed to each other—the sudden passion and the deliberate purpose; the gust and the continuance of the storm. A hasty temper convicts of *foolishness* before our fellowmen.[x] What frightful evil may be the consequence of an *angry* word![y] How fearfully did the man after God's own heart allow the fire to burst out![z] Who then with this example before us, will dare to relax his watch? But are these sins of temper matters of sorrow and humiliation? Does the remembrance of their cost to our crucified Lord exercise

[x]2 Kings 5:11–13
[y]James 3:5
[z]1 Sam 25:21

our constant watchfulness and prayerful resistance? Is not our loving Father's rod sometimes needed to bring conviction of their guilty *foolishness*?[a] Oh, for a strong protection of that charity, that "is not provoked"![b] "Let us give our hearts no rest, until we have purged their gall, and tempered them with the sweetness and gentleness of our Lord and Savior," said Daille.[c]

[a]Num 20:10–12
[b]1 Cor 13:5
[c]Col 3:8. Comp. Col 3:13

But sin grows from weakness to wilfulness. "The first makes a man contemptible; the second, abominable," stated Diodati. *Evil devices;*[d] cherished malice;[e] one act preparing for another; almost aiming at the uttermost[f]—all this shows the true picture of man, *"hateful,* and hating one another."[g] Such a man is hated of God, as "an abomination."[h] Man holds him up to his righteous scorn.[i] Absalom's pillar, the monument to his name, is to this day the object of universal contempt.[7] The *hatred* of Haman's *evil devices* is perpetuated from generation to generation.[j] Why these warnings if we regard them not? Our dignity is our likeness to God! What shame and degradation must there be in being so contrary to Him!

[d]Ps 36:2–4; 64:2–9; Jer 5:26
[e]Gen 4:8; 27:41
[f]2 Sam 15:2–12
[g]Titus 3:3
[h]Prov 6:16–18
[i]Ps 52:2–7
[j]Esther 9:23–28

18 *The naive inherit folly,*
But the prudent are crowned with knowledge.

WISDOM IS FOR THE ASKING

The naive and prudent are again contrasted. The child of Adam is born to *folly.*[k] That is his *inheritance.* He "inherited from your forefathers"[l]: yes, from his first father.[m] So long as he remains *naive,* he confirms his title. Unlike an earthly inheritance, it cannot be relinquished. He holds it in life; and, when he naked "shall return" to the earth, from whence he came,[n] he still holds it firm in death and reaps its bitter fruits throughout eternity. Here is no injustice, no just cause of complaint. Sinner! Is not wisdom freely offered to you for the asking?[o] Don't you, therefore, remain ignorant only by your own wilful neglect? If knowledge is at hand, to be satisfied with ignorance, is to throw away a talent of inestimable price. "I confess," says Doctor South, "God has no need of any man's *learning;* much less need of his *ignorance"* (*Sermon* on 1 Kings 13:33, 34. Vol. 1). *The prudent,* instructed

[k]Job 11:12
[l]1 Peter 1:18
[m]Gen 5:3; Ps 51:5
[n]Job 1:21; 1 Tim 6:7
[o]James 1:5

[7] *Calmet mentions the habit of passing travelers throwing stones at Absalom's pillar to show their hatred of a son's rebellion against his father; and that now the accumulation of stones hides the lower part of the monument. This tradition is confirmed by recent travelers.*

in heavenly *knowledge* are enabled to see divine objects in a divine light. Is not this *knowledge* therefore their *crown*, not of laurel, not of perishing gold; but beautifying the man with all the light, holiness, joy, and glory of life eternal? This is not that religion of strange features, which obscures the glory of the divine image. Steady consistency is stamped upon it, such as enthrones its possessor in the conviction and regard even of those, who are unfriendly to his principles.[p] Thus "the wise" in this life "inherit honor."[q] What shall be their glory in eternity, sitting on the throne of God, crowned with the hand of God Himself!

[p] 1 Peter 2:12
[q] Prov 3:35

19 *The evil will bow down before the good,*
And the wicked at the gates of the righteous.

THE WICKED WILL NOT PROSPER FOREVER!

This is not the general rule of the present dispensation. *Righteous* Lazarus *bowed at the wicked man's gate*.[r] So faith is tried[s] and the foundations of our heavenly hopes more deeply grounded.[t] And yet often has the very letter of the proverb been verified. The Egyptians and Joseph's brethren *bowed before Joseph;*[u] the proud Pharaoh and his people before Moses;[v] Saul to David;[w] Jehoram ane Naaman before Elisha;[x] Haman before Esther;[y] the magistrates before the apostles.[z] More often still is the spirit of this proverb illustrated in the forced testimony of *the wicked* to the preeminence of the righteous.[a] The millennial era will exhibit a more glorious fulfillment.[b] The grand fulfillment will set all things right and shed a divine splendor over this profound statement: "The upright shall rule over them in the morning."[c] "The saints will judge the world."[d] They shall there appear in their suitable rank, exalted with their glorious Head over the whole creation.[e] Oh! let the sunshine of this glory light up every clouded morn. If this isn't enough to counterbalance the scorn of the ungodly, where is our faith? Had we a clear apprehension of this glory, should we have an eye for anything else.

[r] Luke 16:20
[s] Ps 73:12
[t] 2 Cor 4:17, 18
[u] Gen 41:43; 42:6
[v] Exod 8:8; 9:27, 28; 11:8
[w] 1 Sam 24:16–21; 26:21
[x] 2 Kings 3:12; 5:9
[y] Esther 7:7
[z] Acts 16:39
[a] Rev 3:9
[b] Isa 49:23; 60:14; Rev 20:4
[c] Ps 49:14; Mal 4:1–3
[d] 1 Cor 6:2
[e] Rev 2:26

20 *The poor is hated even by his neighbor,*
But those who love the rich are many.

HERE THEY ARE AGAIN— FAIR-WEATHER FRIENDS

A humbling, but common illustration of inborn selfishness. Sometimes however we hear of cheering exceptions. "Ruth clung to" Naomi in her poverty;[f] Jonathan to David, when stripped of royal favor.[g] But too generally *the poor,* instead of being pitied and comforted,[h] is *hated* or neglected *by his own neighbor.*[i] Yet *the rich* is no better off. He has *many friends* indeed (to his money and favor), but few to himself. Many would be the deserters, should a change of circumstance cut off supplies for their appetites, pleasures, or covetousness.[j] But how endearing is the love of Jesus! He was emphatically the poor man's Friend.[k] He sought *his many friends* among the wretched and forlorn;[l] and still His powerful compassion pleads for those *hated* ones among their fellow-sinners.[m] Shouldn't we, like Job, the tested saint of old, learn to look off from earthly destitution in a cleaving confidence on Him, as the Rock of our salvation?[n] The practical exercise of this confidence will be an overcoming of our selfish tendencies, cultivating that tenderness, which, instead of shrinking from the sight of misery, hastens, though at the expense of personal sacrifice, to its sympathizing relief.[o]

[f] Ruth 1:14, 21, 22
[g] 1 Sam 19:1–7; 23:16
[h] Job 6:14; Isa 58:7
[i] Prov 10:15; 19:4, 7; Luke 16:21
[j] Prov 19:4, 6
[k] Ps 72:12, 14
[l] Matt 4:18–22
[m] Ps 119:31
[n] Job 19:13–27
[o] Luke 10:33–35

21 *He who despises his neighbor sins,*
But happy is he who is gracious to the poor.

FROM DUNG HILL TO A PRINCELY THRONE

The last proverb showed the general standard of selfishness. Here we see its positive sinfulness. Some men are so high that they cannot see their lower brother. Yet this *despised* one may be infinitely precious and honored in the Savior's eyes, as one purchased by His own blood. But how small is the distance between him and his most elevated fellow-creature, compared with the infinite space between him and his God! Yet He that dwells on high, instead of *despising,* writes His name upon Him, "raises the poor from the dust, And lifts the needy from the ash heap, to make *them* sit . . . with the princes of His people."[p] The plain command is—"Honor all men,"[q] not all with equal measure, but in all honor our own nature,

[p] Ps 113:7, 8
[q] 1 Peter 2:17

the remains, however defaced, of the image of God. To look therefore upon the meanest, as if he were made to be *despised*, shows a lack of wisdom and heart.[r] "Because we think we are above him; therefore we think we may overlook him," said Bishop Sanderson, and neglect to *have mercy* on him[s]—this is reflecting on God's own care;[t] forgetting His example;[u] setting up our own judgment against his *sinning* against His law of love.[v] And most fearfully will he visit this sin at the day of recompense.[w]

[r] Prov 11:12
[s] Rom 14:3; Prov 21:13; James 2:16
[t] Verse 31
[u] 2 Cor 8:9
[v] James 2:1–9
[w] Job 31:13–15; Matt 25:42–45

HOW TO INCREASE YOUR HAPPINESS

But oh! the happiness of him *who is gracious to the poor;*[x] "expecting nothing in return";[y] constrained by love to Christ and his fellow-sinners! He shall be happy beyond expression. *Doesn't every exercise of love enlarge our own* happiness?[z] Don't we, ourselves, richly feed on the bread, with which we feed the hungry?[a] And will not the great day declare and honor every act of love for our divine Master?[b]

[x] Comp. Ps 41:3; 112:9; Jer 22:16; Dan 4:27; Matt 5:7
[y] Luke 6:35
[z] Prov 11:17
[a] Isa 58:8
[b] Matt 25:35–40

22 *Will they not go astray who devise evil?*
But kindness and truth will be to *those who devise good.*

YOUR INTENTIONS ARE MOST IMPORTANT

Scripture traces actions to principles. Wicked as it is to *do evil,* it is far more hateful to *devise it.*[c] *Devising* is the first stage working of the principle. *Devising evil* therefore, even if it doesn't come to the act, shows the purpose.[d] People who do this may be men of complete wisdom in other matters; but here, at least, don't they err? They miss either their object, or their anticipated happiness from it. Witness the shame of the Babel-builders;[e] the confusion of Haman's device;[f] the overruling of the wicked plot against our beloved Lord.[g] How the *devisers* thwart their own purpose to their own fearful cost! How little did Judas estimate the result of his *devising of evil*—A little matter kindling an unquenchable fire![h]

Children of God! Do you exhibit the same diligence and determination in *devising good?* Even if it doesn't materialize, your work will be accepted.[i] *Kindness and truth* are often set out as a reward of grace, the cheering encouragement to practical godliness. What can be more

[c] Verse 17
[d] Prov 24:8
[e] Gen 11:9
[f] Esther 7:10
[g] Ps 2:1–4; Matt 21:41–44
[h] Matt 26:14–16; 27:3–5
[i] 1 Kings 8:18

joyous than the glorious perfections of Jehovah, pouring into the soul the quickening energy of divine blessing; *kindness* the fountainhead, *truth* the pledge and fulfillment of unchangeable mercy![8]

23 *In all labor there is profit,*
But more talk leads *only to poverty.*

THE LAZY MAN TALKS HIMSELF POOR

This is not universally true. What *profit is there in the labor* of sin,[j] or of ill-timed work? Fruitful also *is the talk* of teaching.[k] But the contrast is intended between what is solid on the one hand and what is shadowy on the other, between lawful, well-directed *labor,* and empty *talk.* Bread eaten in "the sweat of your face" is the *profit* of bodily labor.[l] But the idler is condemned to *poverty* by *talk.*[m] Enlargement of mind is also the profit of mental labor.[n] But the "babbling fool"[o] cuts himself off from all advantage, except that of being entertained by his own talk. His reason for joining in the company of others is not "at all to be informed, to hear, to listen, but to display himself, and to talk without any design at all," said Bishop Butler in *Sermon on the Government of the Tongue.* Clearly therefore *talk tends only to poverty.* Rich beyond conception is *the profit of spiritual labor.*[p] The Son of Man gives to *the laborer* "food which endures to eternal life." But "God is not unjust so as to forget your work and the love which you have shown toward His name."[q] *But talk* gives husks, not bread. Where there are only shallow conceptions of the gospel and no experimental enjoyment of Christian establishment, it is "all running out in noise," said Henry.[9] There is no instruction, because there is no "good treasure" within.[r] "What are these words that you are exchanging with one another . . . ?"[s]—is a searching question. Ministers, doctrines, the externals, circumstantials, debates on religion—all may be the mere borders of the great subject, utterly remote from the heart and other vital organs. And indeed, the discussion of the substance of Christianity without reverence, without a sense of the divine pres-

[j] Rom 6:21
[k] Prov 10:21; 15:7
[l] Gen 3:19
[m] Prov 20:4; 21:25
[n] Eccl 12:9, 10
[o] Prov 10:8
[p] Prov 10:16
[q] John 6:27; Heb 6:10
[r] Matt 12:35
[s] Luke 24:17

[8] *Gen 24:27; 2 Sam 15:20; Ps 25:10; 61:7; 117:2; Mic 7:20. "Note," says an old expositor, "that Solomon here is no lawgiver, but an evangelist, leading us unto Jesus Christ. For we can obtain no mercy but in Him only. For 'the promises of God are yea and amen in him' "—Cope.*

[9] *1 Tim 5:13. See Bunyan's graphical portrait of Talkative in* The Pilgrim's Progress.

ence and a single eye to edification, only profanes holy things, and at best must alienate the precious truths from their true purpose. Nothing comes from a broken heart. It is only the deluding indulgence of a refined lust, a religious tongue without a godly heart—*all leading only to poverty.* Make sure that religious conversation deserves the name. Let the stamp of the profession of the saints of God be visible.[t] Let the burning theme of the Savior's love flow from the heart.[u] Let that name "far above every name that is named," be upon our lips, as "oils with a pleasing fragrance"; so that "the house"—all that are living with us—may be "filled with the fragrance of the ointment."[v]

[t]Ps 145:10–12
[u]Luke 24:14–32
[v]Eph 1:21; Song of Sol 1:3; John 12:3

24 *The crown of the wise is their riches,*
But *the folly of fools is foolishness.*

IS MONEY ALWAYS EVIL?

The godly first are made *wise* by being "crowned with knowledge."[w] Then *the crown of the wise is their riches.* For though, as a fearful temptation,[x] no *wise* man would desire them; yet as the gift of God[y] (the gift indeed of his left hand)[z] they may become his *crown.* They enhance his reputation and enlarge his usefulness as a consecrated talent for God. What *a crown* were they to David and his wise son, as the materials for building the temple;[a] and to Job, as employed for the good of his fellow-creatures![b] So that, though wisdom under all circumstances is a blessing, it is specially pronounced to be good with *"an inheritance."*[c] It is necessary to distinguish between the thing itself, and the abuse of it. Wealth is in fact a blessing when honestly acquired and conscientiously used. And when otherwise, the man not his treasure is to be blamed.

But if riches *are the crown of the wise,* they cannot disguise fools. They only seem to make their *folly* more open. Riches spent on selfish gratification become, not their *crown,* but their *foolishness.*[d] The *foolish* son of this wise father, with all his riches, only exposed his *folly* very badly, and lost ten precious jewels from his royal crown.[e] Whatever our talents may be, let us use them for eternity, and they will be our everlasting crown.[f]

[w]Verse 18
[x]Matt 13:22; 19:23
[y]1 Kings 3:13; Ps 112:3
[z]Prov 3:16
[a]1 Chron 29:1–5; 2 Chron 5:1
[b]Job 29:6–17. Comp. Ps 112:9
[c]Eccl 7:11, 12
[d]1 Sam 25:36–38; Ps 49:10–13; Luke 12:19, 20
[e]1 Kings 12:16
[f]Luke 19:13; 16:9; 1 Tim 6:19

25 *A truthful witness saves lives,*
But he who speaks lies is treacherous.

BY OUR WORDS—JUSTIFIED OR CONDEMNED

How great is the responsibility of testimony![g] Every Christian has in him a principle of conscientious faithfulness. As *a truthful witness he would save* the innocent from oppression or ruin. But an ungodly man would prove *treacherous,* the agent of Satan,[h] *speaking lies* for his neighbor's destruction.[i] How important it is that we walk "with integrity" before God in our speech, ready to hazard everything for the interests of truth;[j] considering our obligations to one another;[k] mindful of that true and faithful witness, which every man carries in his heart, which no gift or power can silence; and realizing our solemn appearing before the God of truth, when "by your words you shall be justified . . . " or "condemned"![l] If the responsibility is so great to the *witness* in court, how much more to the *witness* in the pulpit, observed Lavater and Scott. Oh! Is the minister of God a *truthful witness?* Is he convinced that by his message alone—not by any other truth, and not by the watering-down of this truth—will souls be saved?[m] Or is *he speaking lies,* holding back or denying truth, to the ruin of the soul, whom he was charged to deliver?[n] As those who preach Jesus Christ are the most profitable witnesses; even so, the most dangerous deceivers are they, who, under the guise of Christianity, set forth men's traditions.

[g] Prov 24:12
[h] 1 Kings 21:13
[i] Matt 26:60; Acts 6:13. Comp. Prov 12:6, 17
[j] Ps 15:2; 24:3–5
[k] Eph 4:25
[l] Matt 12:37
[m] 1 Tim 4:16
[n] Jer 5:31; Exod 3:17. Comp. verse 5.

26 *In the fear of the* LORD *there is strong confidence,*
And his children will have refuge.

HOW TO FEAR AND NOT BE AFRAID

"Fear involves punishment."[o] It is the trembling of the slave;[p] the dread of wrath, not of sin. There is no *confidence* here. It is pure selfishness. It ends in self. There is no homage to God. But the true *fear of God* is a holy, happy[q] reverential principle; not that which "love casts out,"[r] but which love brings in. It is reverence tempered with love. We fear, because we love. We fear "His goodness"[s] no less than His justice; not because we doubt His love, but because we are assured of it.[t] We fear, yet we are not afraid.[u] The holiest and humblest is the most

[o] 1 John 4:18; Acts 24:25
[p] Rom 8:15
[q] Ps 112:1; 33:18; 147:11
[r] 1 John 4:18
[s] Hos 3:5; Ps 130:4
[t] Heb 12:28; 1 Peter 1:17, 18
[u] Ps 112:1, 7

fixed and trusting heart. The fear of man produces faintness.[v] *The fear of the Lord*—such is the Christian paradox—emboldens. Its childlike spirit shuts out all terrors of conscience, all forebodings of eternity. *Confidence—strong confidence*—issues out of it. Abraham sacrificed his son in *the fear of God;* yet fully *confident,* "that God is able to raise men even from the dead."[w]

[v]Prov 29:25; Jon 1:3; Gal 2:12

[w]Gen 22:12, with Heb 11:17–19

WHERE REVERENTIAL FEAR MAY LEAD

The fear of God led the Babylonish captives with unshaken *confidence* into the fiery furnace.[x] And thus does the child of God, while walking in godly *fear,* rejoice in *confidence,* even in the most frowning dispensation.[y] God's promise covers him;[z] "and the evil one does not touch him."[a]

[x]Dan 3:16–18

[y]Job 1:1, with 13:15; Mic 7:7–9; Heb 3:16–19

[z]Jer 32:40

[a]1 John 5:18. Comp. 3:21–26; 19:23

And how happy is the change wrought on our testimony! Before, as criminals we fled *from God*—now, as *His* children, we *flee* to Him to hide us.[b] The atonement, which has made an end of sin; the righteousness, which brought in the sunshine of favor; the intercession which maintains our standing of acceptance—this is our ground of confidence, strong as death, stronger than hell.[c] Yes—if heaven and earth shake, God has ordained and secured, that *His children will have a place of refuge,* such as they need, and when they need it:[d] when the enemy is most strongly assaulting[e] at the last extremity, when every other refuge shall have been swept away.[f] How every act of faith strengthens our *confidence* and helps us realize more sensibly the peaceful security of our *refuge?*[g] But remember—nothing short of a full application of the atonement can establish our *confidence* and deliver us from slavish *fear* and uncertainty.

[b]Gen 3:8, with Ps 143:9

[c]Rom 8:31–39

[d]Ps 46:1; 48:3; Isa 32:2

[e]Ps 56:1–4; Isa 25:4

[f]Isa 28:16, 17

[g]Prov 1:33; 18:10; Isa 32:18, 19

27 *The fear of the* LORD *is a fountain of life,*
That one may avoid the snares of death.

HOW TO AVOID THE SNARES OF DEATH

How glowing is this divine principle, refreshing like the springs of Anaan;[h] full of life,[i] temporal,[j] spiritual,[k] eternal.[l] It is the influence of the heavenly Comforter, as a *fountain* "springing up to eternal life."[m] Its preserving tendency is invaluable. It is always connected with the fear of sin,[n] as grieving our most beloved friend, and

[h]Deut 8:7; Josh 15:19

[i]Prov 22:4

[j]Prov 10:27

[k]Prov 19:23; Mal 4:2

[l]Ps 103:17

[m]John 4:14

[n]Prov 3:7; 16:6

separating us from our only happiness; while it keeps us *from the snares of death,*[o] the end "and wages of sin."[p] How complete then is its application! Not only is it *a refuge* from danger, but *a fountain of life.* Not only does Christian *confidence* open a cover from the guilt, but its holy influence roots out the power of sin. For among the countless throngs of the redeemed, not one finds a cover from condemnation, who is not renovated unto spiritual life. Thus, this invaluable grace flows with the full streams of gospel blessing. How much of that worldliness that soils our profession, and of the restraint that contracts our spiritual joy, may be traced to the sparing or defective application of this Christian principle!

[o]Eccl 7:26
[p]Rom 6:23

28 *In a multitude of people is a king's glory,*
But in the dearth of people is a prince's ruin.

The Bible is a book for all. Even the king is interested in it and was commanded to treasure it.[q] It describes him as a curse or a blessing to his people, as he is led by his own whims,[r] or directed by divine wisdom.[s] "He is not appointed for luxury or for pleasure; but that as a Head he may preside over his members [people]; as a Shepherd, he may care for his flock; as a tree, he may nourish those who dwell under his shadow," stated Geier. *In the multitude of people is his glory.* They are the support and strength of his kingdom.[10] The shortage *of people* in his kingdom *is his ruin.* His revenue fails. His strength is impaired. His enemies take advantage of his weakness.[t] His interests and his *people's* are one. In promoting their happiness, *the prince* secures his own *glory.*[u] If he is the father of his numerous family, he will always have a quiver "full of them."[v] How great then is *the glory* of our heavenly *King in the countless multitude of His people!* How overwhelmingly glorious will it appear when the completed number shall stand before His throne;[w] each the medium of reflecting His glory;[x] each with a crown to cast at His feet,[y] and a song of everlasting joy to tune to His praise![z]

[q]Deut 17:18
[r]1 Kings 12:13
[s]2 Chron 9:8
[t]2 Kings 13:4–7
[u]Ps 72
[v]Ps 127
[w]Rev 7:9, 10
[x]2 Thess 1:10
[y]Rev 4:10, 11
[z]Rev 5:9

29 *He who is slow to anger has great understanding,*
But he who is quick-tempered exalts folly.

[10] *1 Kings 4:20; 2 Chron 17:14–19. Yet this* honor *had just about proved* the destruction of the prince *in the chastisement of his pride. 2 Sam 24.*

People aren't bothered much by a *quick-temper*—until it touches them. It is a fit of passion, soon over and forgotten. But is that the way God judges it? See how His word stamps the basic principle. It is "giving the devil an opportunity";[a] grieving the Holy Spirit;[b] contrary to the mind and example of Christ;[c] inconsistent with the profession of the gospel;[d] degrading human nature;[e] a work of the flesh, that shuts out from heaven,[f] and condemns to hell.[g] Surely then to be *slow to anger*—such a fruitful source of sin and misery—is a proof of *great understanding.*[h] It is as if we felt our rightful dignity and high obligations. But too often, instead of being *slow to anger,* the *quick-tempered* finds a short path to anger. It is as tinder to every spark of provocation, and at one step hurries into the midst of *anger.* There is often a sourness of spirit, that sits upon men, that causes them to become angry, and they don't know why; exploding into flame at the most trifling matters, things that, in cooler moments, we would be ashamed at having quarrelled over such silliness. Terrible flames have arisen from these trifling sparks as we see in verse 17. This is indeed exalting folly on a height visible to all.[i] Yet too often passion takes the place of law and reason, and this *folly* is thought to be high-mindedness and proper spirit. Oh! It is a mercy to be delivered from the standard of this world, and to live, act, and judge by the standard of God and His Word.

[a]Eph 4:26, 27
[b]Eph 4:30
[c]Matt 11:29; Phil 2:3–5; 1 Peter 2:23
[d]Col 3:8, 12, 13
[e]Prov 17:12; 25:8; 29:20
[f]Gal 5:19–21
[g]Matt 5:22
[h]Prov 19:11; 20:3; James 3:17
[i]Prov 3:35

But let the children of God remember, that *a quick-temper* condemned the meekest of men.[j] Never was a lack of good sense *more exalted* than by the fretful selfishness of a prophet of the Lord.[k] The gentlest spirit needs to be cast into a deep mold of lowliness and love for communion with God.[l] Who can plead inability to resist? Hasn't God given understanding to expose temper; reason to govern it; His Word and Spirit to crucify it? Realize our obligations to governing grace as the effective discipline for this harmful learning.[m]

[j]Ps 106:32, 33
[k]Jon 4
[l]Isa 57:15; 1 John 4:16
[m]James 1:18, 19

30 *A tranquil heart is life to the body,*
But passion is rottenness to the bones.

Many will admit Christianity is good for the soul. But they consider its fancied gloom to be harmful to the body. The wise man, however, teaches, that it is *life to the body.*[n] And surely *a tranquil heart,* freed from gnawing passions, and filled with Christian habits, though it will not bring immortality, must conspicuously contribute to good health. The contrast, however, distinguishes a *tranquil heart* by the absence of selfishness, and rejoicing in another's happiness or honor.[o] *Passion,* on the other hand, is wounded by our neighbor's prosperity.[p] His ruin, at least, injury, would give pleasure. But it turns sick when hearing of his praises, and even complains about his virtues. Something is always wrong in his conduct, something at least, which, if not deserving to be blamed, greatly detracts from his unbearable praise. This evil is indeed the deadliest fruit of selfishness. Nothing flourishes under its shade.[q] Often it's a fretting sickness[r] or a painful despair,[s] like the destruction of the bodily system by the *rottenness to the bones.* "Truly," as Bishop Hall observes in his *Sermon on Rom 12:2,* "this vice is executioner enough to itself!" (*Works* 5:21). Such hell does the man carry in his own heart, it's a pity, that this plant should be the growth of our own fleshly soil. That is so contrary to the mind of Christ,[t] and to the spirit of His gospel.[u] So certainly will it exclude from heaven![v]

[n] Prov 3:7, 8
[o] Num 11:29
[p] Gen 26:14; 1 Sam 18:9
[q] James 3:16
[r] Esther 6:6, 12
[s] Ps 112:10
[t] Mark 7:22; James 4:5; Rom 13:13
[u] 1 Cor 13:4
[v] Gal 5:21

31 *He who oppresses the poor reproaches his Maker,*
But he who is gracious to the needy honors Him.

Aren't *the poor* just as much as the rich made "in the image of God"?[w] Both "the rich and the poor have a common bond" before their Maker without respect of persons.[x] Both carry the same undying principle in their bosom. Both sink to the same humiliating level of death. Both rise to the same position of immortality. Besides—don't the poor have a special interest in the gospel?[y] Wasn't the gospel first spread by the poor?[z] Hasn't the voluntary poverty of the Son of God for us put high honor upon a lowly condition?[a] Then, what ground is there to *oppress the poor,* as if they don't amount to nearly as much as we? This involves the guilt of *reproaching our Maker.*[b] It is slighting His own work; despising His own laws,[c] and charging Him with injustice, as if He had formed *the poor* to be the footstool of *their oppressors.*[d] Do you want to honor God? Then, don't just hold back from oppressing the poor; have mercy on them, as well!

[w] Gen 9:6
[x] Prov 22:2; Job 31:15
[y] Matt 11:5; James 2:5; Ps 68:10
[z] Matt 28:19, 20; Acts 4:13
[a] Luke 2:7; Phil 2:7; 2 Cor 8:9; Matt 8:20
[b] Prov 17:5
[c] Deut 15:11
[d] 1 Sam 2:7

His reward is certain and, in the case of the Lord's poor, it will be a good one.[e] High is the privilege and everlasting the compensation for *honoring* the Savior in *His* own person.[f]

[e] Prov 19:17; Ps 41:1
[f] Matt 25:40

32 *The wicked is thrust down by his wrong-doing,*
But the righteous has a refuge [AV—*hope*] *when he dies.*

We can't judge men by their outward condition, for *the righteous and the wicked* have one event in common.[g] Such a judgment would often tip the scales on the wrong side.[h] The standard of the world is just as erroneous. While men rarely speak very highly of their neighbors, in talking with others, yet (they say) as far as God is concerned (they think), everybody's good enough for heaven. A hope is entertained by the most criminal that they will receive mercy at the last. And so the distinctive terms—*righteous and wicked*—are so confounded, and brought so near each other, that there is little meaning in either.

[g] Eccl 9:2
[h] Ps 73:12

But now, look at this striking picture before us, sweeping away all human standards. Here we stand, looking out into eternity, seeing—the wicked and the righteous—each "to go to his own place."[i] Let's think about what we've seen—O my soul, make your calling sure! *The wicked* includes many kinds of character—the amiable, useful, and in a variety of ways exemplary. Others are absorbed in vanity; or they wear themselves away by the lamp of study; or they are given up to selfish indulgence. But whatever external shape or feature, the stamp is broad—those "who forget God"—and the condemnation sealed—return to Sheol."[j]

[i] Acts 1:25
[j] Ps 9:17

WHERE DOES HELL BEGIN?

Truly *the wicked* is pictured as *thrust down* in his wickedness. He is dragged out of life, like a criminal to execution; torn away from whatever "heaven" he has on earth, with no joyous heaven beyond.[k] To be forced out of the body, to die a violent death—these are dreadful beyond imagination. With all his heart he wants to stay. But he can't. He can't live. And he doesn't dare to die. Sometimes he leaves this life with a horror no words can paint. Hell really begins this side of eternity[l]—*thrust* out of a world, which has cheated and damned his soul

[k] Job 18:18; 27:21
[l] 1 Sam 28:15

forever. And even where he has "no pains in their death,"[m] where do we hear of "a desire to depart?"[n] Though he may fall asleep as softly as a lamb, he will wake to live forever with "the devil and his angels."[o] His few moments of peace are only a moment's relief from hopeless, never-ending torments. His wickedness was his element in life. It will cleave to him still, the sting of the undying worm, the fuel of unquenchable fire.

[m] Ps 73:4
[n] Phil 1:23
[o] Matt 25:41

IN CHRIST—COURAGE TO FACE THE KING OF TERRORS

But is *the righteous really thrust away,* driven out of this life? No, he dies by his own consent. It's a glad surrender, not a forced separation.[p] The tabernacle is not rent or torn away but laid "aside."[q] He can take death by his cold hand and bid him welcome. "I can smile on death," said a dying saint, "because my Savior smiles on me." There is courage to face the king of terrors, and delight in looking homeward to God.[r] There is such loveliness and sunshine in his death, that it flashes conviction upon the most hardened conscience.[s] *The righteous has a refuge when he dies.* His death is full of hope. Job pierced his dark cloud of sorrow with this joyous hope.[t] David rested his way-worn spirit upon the Rock of Salvation.[u] Stephen anchored within the vail, undisturbed by the volley of stones without.[v] Paul triumphed in the crown, as if it were already on his head.[w] And don't we hear daily the "voice from heaven," assuring us that "blessed are the dead who die in the Lord"?[x] Praise to our Immanuel! When you overcame the pain of death, You opened the kingdom of heaven to all believers. By You, as the way to the kingdom, we go freely, gladly, out of life. We go to what we love, to our native home, to our Savior's bosom, to our rest, our crown, our everlasting joy. "Now, Lord, what wait I for? I have waited for thy salvation, O Lord."[11]

[p] Ps 31:5
[q] 2 Peter 1:14
[r] 2 Cor 5:8. Comp. Matt 3:17
[s] Num 23:10
[t] Job 19:25–27
[u] 2 Sam 23:5
[v] Acts 7:55–60
[w] 2 Tim 4:6–8; 2 Cor 5:1
[x] Rev 14:13

[11] *Ps 39:7; Gen 49:18. Doesn't this text clearly prove that, while life and immortality were brought* to light *through the gospel (2 Tim 1:10), the dawn of the day beamed upon the Old Testament saints? What could* this hope of the righteous be, *but the finalizing prospect of the gospel? Bishop Warburton teaches "that they shall be delivered from the most iminent danger." That keen mind could never have confused two things so totally different, as hope* in *death, and hope of* escape from *death, had it not been necessary to support a favorite theory. Just as satisfactory and beautiful is a paraphrase of the note of a learned German critic—A splendid testimony of the knowledge of the Old Testament believer in a future life. The wicked in this disaster is terrified. He doesn't know where to turn. But the godly in this last evil has no fear. He knows to whom to flee, and where he is going—DATHE* in loco. *Again—"He (the righteous) dieth in God's grace, and in an assured confidence of the salvation of his soul, and of the glorious resurrection of his body"—DIODATI.*

33 *Wisdom rests in the heart of one who has understanding,*
But in the bosom of fools it is made known.

TRUE WISDOM'S THRONE IS IN THE HEART

Often the wise man shows the blessing of *wisdom* on the lips.[y] Here we trace it to its home. It flows from the head and *rests in the heart.* That's *where it rested* without measure in the humanity of Jesus;[z] and most glorious was its manifestation.[a] When it rests in our hearts, its value is beyond all measure. And it's there as a fixed principle. It preserves us from being tossed about by all kinds of strange doctrines, and "it is good for the heart to be strengthened by grace."[b] We see now the vital difference between *thinking about something* and *experiencing it;* between the convictions of the judgment and the movement of the will.

It's not just worldly debate. This—as Bishop Taylor preached before the University of Dublin—"*covers* no vices, but *kindles* a great many. Though men esteem its learning, it is the most useless learning in the world" (*Via* Intelligentiae). True *wisdom,* while it secures its *rest,* sets up its throne, *in the heart.* All is therefore Christian order and holiness.

But there is another fountain always bubbling up.[c] The *fool's* many words,[d] selfish giving in to one's own desires,[e] and uncontrolled passions,[f] all these plainly show what's in the midst of him.[g] Let him stand out as a warning beacon against display, self-conceit, self-ignorance. Never let our prayers cease, until He who is the Wisdom of God[h] takes His *rest in our hearts.* Have we received the precious gift? Then let us seek the increase by a close union with Him and an entire dependence upon him.[i]

[y] Prov 10:11, 20, 21; 15:2, 7
[z] John 3:34
[a] Luke 2:47, 52; 4:22; Matt 22:46; John 7:46
[b] Heb 13:9
[c] Prov 15:2, 28; 29:11
[d] Eccl 5:3; 10:14
[e] 1 Sam 25:10
[f] 1 Sam 20:30–34; 1 Kings 19:1, 2. Comp. v. 16; 12:16
[g] Prov 10:9; 12:23; 13:16; 18:2; Eccl 10:3
[h] 1 Cor 1:24
[i] 1 Cor 1:30

34 *Righteousness exalts a nation,*
But sin is a disgrace to any *people.*

WHAT REALLY MAKES A NATION GREAT?

If it isn't beneath statesmen to take lessons from the Bible, let them deeply ponder this sound political maxim, which commends itself to every instinct of the simple mind. Actually, it would be a strange paradox in the divine government, if the connection between godliness and prosperity, ungodliness and misery, established in individual cases, should not be fulfilled by the multiplication of individuals into nations. The Scripture records, however—confirmed by the result of impartial and extended observation—clearly prove this to be the rule of national, no less than personal, management. The history of the chosen people, as they were a *righteous or sinful nation*, is marked by corresponding *exaltation or disgrace.*[12] Not the wisdom of policy, extent of empire, splendid conquests, flourishing trade, abundant resources—but *righteousness exalts a nation.* It is both the prop to make it continue to remain alive, "firm in itself, and a crown to render it glorious in the eyes of others."[13] Greece in her proud science, Rome at the peak of her glory—both were sunk in the lowest depths of moral degradation.[14] Their true greatness existed only in the visions of poetry or the dreams of philosophy. Contrast the influence of *righteousness*, bringing out of the most debased barbarism a community, of the highest principles, that form a nation's well-being. The missionary records of New Zealand and the South Seas furnish ample proof of this statement. Thus, to Christianize, is to regenerate, the community; to elevate it to a more dignified position; to *exalt the nation,*[j] and that, not with a sudden flash of shadowy splendor, but with solid glory, filled with every practical blessing. *But sin is a disgrace to any people.* No nation is so low, as not to sink low under it; while to the mightiest people, it is a stain on their honor, that no worldly glory can blot out. What an enemy ungodly man is to his country! Loudly as he may talk of his patriotism, and even though God should make him an instrument of advancing her temporal interest; yet he contributes, as much as possible, to her deepest *disgrace.*

[j] Deut 26:16–19

[12] Exaltation. *Deut 28:13; Josh 10:42; 1 Kings 4:20–24; 2 Chron 17:2–5, 11, 12, 32:22, 23.* Disgrace, *Deut 28:43, 44; Judg 2:7–15; 2 Kings 10:31, 32; 18:11, 12; 2 Chron 15:2–6; 36:11–17; Jer 7:29. See the name of* disgrace *given by God Himself. Isa 1:10; 57:3; Hos 1:6–9; Zeph 2:1.*

[13] *Bishop SANDERSON'S* Sermon on Exod *23:1–3. Even a heathen wise man spoke of moral righteousness—the pillar and support of the city.—PLATO* de Legibus, *book 6. "Those princes and commonwealths, who would keep their governments entire and uncorrupt, are, above all things, to have a care of religion and its ceremonies, and preserve them in due veneration. For in the whole world there is not a greater sign of threatening ruin, than when God and his worship are despised." Such was the testimony of the infidel and profligate politician—Machiaveli—*Discourses on Livy.

[14] *Rom 1:22–32 was a picture of the heathen world in the best ages of refinement.*

35 *The king's favor is toward a servant who acts wisely,*
But his anger is toward him who acts shamefully.

THE DAY OF RECKONING—WHAT WILL IT BRING?

The wise servant's management is often the working cause of *national exaltation.*[k] *The king's favor toward him*[l] is therefore the rule of sound policy. But *his anger is no less against him that acts shamefully*[m] "to the office which he bears and to the Prince's choice," said Diodati.

So it is with the great King. All of us are His *servants,* bound to Him by the highest obligations,[n] animated by the most glowing encouragements.[o] All of us have our responsibilities, our talents, our work, our account. Toward the faithful and *wise servant,* who has traded with his talents, who has been diligent in his work, and who is ready for his account—*his favor* will be infinitely condescending and honorable.[p] *But against him that acts shamefully*—to reflect upon his Master, who is neglectful of his work, and unprepared for his account—*His anger* will be tremendous and eternal.[q] What will the solemn day of reckoning bring to me? May I—may we all—be found *wise servants* to the best of *kings,* looking with confidence for his welcome!

[k] 2 Chron 24:1–16
[l] Gen 41:38–40; Dan 6:3. Comp. Prov 16:13; 22:29
[m] Esther 7:6–10
[n] Ps 116:16; 1 Cor 6:19, 20; 7:23
[o] Matt 25:21, 23; 24:44–46
[p] John 12:26
[q] Matt 25:24–30

CHAPTER FIFTEEN

1 *A gentle answer turns away wrath,*
But a harsh word stirs up anger.

TO FEED OR QUENCH THE ANGRY FLAME?

What a mine of practical wisdom is this Book of God! Let's think about this valuable rule for self-discipline, family peace, and church unity. Scripture often illustrates the different effects of the tongue. *The gentle answer* is the water to quench.[1] *Harsh words* are the oil to *stir up* the fire.[2] And this is, alas! man's natural tendency, to feed rather than to quench, the *angry* flame. We yield to irritation; reply in kind to our neighbor; have recourse to self-justification; insist upon the last word; say all that we could say; and think we "have good reason to be angry."[a] Neither party gives up the smallest part of the will. Pride and passion on both sides strike together like two flints; and "behold, how great a forest is set aflame by such a small fire!"[b] So then, there is the self-pleasing sarcasm; as if we would rather lose a friend, than pass up a clever remark. All this the world excuses as a sensitive and lively temper. But the gospel sets before us our Savior's example;[c] imbues with His spirit;[d] and imparts that blessed charity, that "is not provoked";[e] and therefore is careful not to provoke a chafed or wounded spirit. If others begin, may we refrain from continuing the strife.[3] "Patience is the true peacemaker," said Bishop Sanderson in *Sermon on Rom 15:5. Gentle* and healing words[f] gain a double victory—over ourselves[g] and our brother.[h]

[a] Jon 4:9
[b] James 3:5
[c] 1 Peter 2:23
[d] 2 Cor 3:18; Phil 2:3–5
[e] 1 Cor 13:5
[f] Prov 25:15. Comp. Eccl 7:8; James 3:17, 18
[g] Prov 16:32
[h] Rom 12:19–21

[1] *See Jacob with Esau—Gen 32:33; Aaron with Moses—Lev 10:16–20; the Reubenites with their brethren—Josh 22:15–34; Gideon with the men of Ephraim—Judg 8:1–3; David with Saul—1 Sam 24:9–21; 26:21; Abigail with David—25:23–32.*

[2] *See the instances of Jephthah—Judg 12:1–6; Saul—1 Sam 20:30–34; Nabal—25:10–12; Rehoboam—1 Kings 12:12–15; the Apostles, Acts 15:39. Comp. Prov 30:33.*

[3] *Prov 17:14. Even a Heathen could give this excellent advice—"Let dissension begin from others, but reconciliation from Thee"—SENECA.*

2 *The tongue of the wise makes knowledge acceptable,*
But the mouth of fools spouts folly.

THE TONGUE OF WISDOM

Earlier we had the tongue of love. Here is the *tongue of wisdom.* The tongue reveals the man. *The wise* commands *his tongue.* But the fool's tongue commands him. He may possess great *knowledge* but without knowing how to use it, it goes to waste. Wisdom is proved, not by the amount of *knowledge* we possess, but by its right application. Observe "the spirit of *wisdom* and understanding" rests upon our divine Lord.[i] In condescending to the ignorance of the people;[j] in commanding their respect;[k] in silencing His opponents;[l] in alluring sinners to Himself[m]—how *wisely His tongue used His knowledge.* His great apostle (Paul) gave to all the same *knowledge,* but wisely—not, in the same form or to the same degree.[n] Instead of antagonizing his heathen congregation by condemning their deficiency, he told them how their acknowledged lack (worshiping an unknown god) could be overcome—by bringing before them the true God they were ignorantly worshiping.[o] He pointed an arrow to Agrippa's conscience by the kindly admission of his openness and intelligence.[p] This right use of *knowledge* distinguishes the workman approved of God, "who does not need to be ashamed."[q] The workman, lacking it, often gives out truth so loosely and unsuitably, that it opens, rather than shuts, the mouth of opponents; discredits the truth, rather than convicts the adversary. *The tongue of the wise* will especially direct a right application of *knowledge* to the newly-saved. Don't we sometimes, in our present spiritual stature, forget our former feeble infancy? If now we "take root like the *cedars of* Lebanon," was it not once with us only "smaller than all *other* seeds"?[r] Let our thoughtful directions pluck the thorn out of their tender feet, "*the limb* which is lame may not be put out of joint, but rather be healed."[s]

But to judge the waters flowing from a *fool's* fountain; listen to Baal's worshippers;[t] Rabshakeh's proud boasting;[u] the fretting murmurings of the people of God[v] all *spouting out folly.* Oh! for a large filling of sound *knowledge* in the treasure house within, that the tongue may be disciplined and consecrated at once.

[i] Isa 11:2
[j] Mark 4:33
[k] Matt 7:29; John 7:46
[l] Matt 22:15–46
[m] Matt 11:28–30; John 4:1–26
[n] 1 Cor 3:2
[o] Acts 17:23
[p] Acts 26:27–29
[q] 2 Tim 2:15
[r] Hos 14:5; Matt 13:32
[s] Heb 12:13
[t] 1 Kings 18:26
[u] 2 Kings 18:26–29
[v] Num 14:2–10; 16:13

3 *The eyes of the* LORD *are in every place,*
Watching the evil and the good.

GOD'S ALL-SEEING EYE

May He be adored—this all-seeing God![w] His inspection of the universe so minute, exact, unwearied![x] The first mark of the apostasy was a dread of His presence.[y] The ungodly try to forget it[z] and often succeed in banishing Him out of their thoughts.[a] Yet, despite all their efforts to hide, still He sees them. *His eyes are in every place.* Heaven, hell, the secret places of the earth are all open before Him.[b] He is *watching the evil;* whether the king on his throne;[c] or in his palace;[d] or the servant indulging his secret sin.[e] Yes—he may shut out the sun from his retreat, but he cannot shut out the eye of God, no darkness or deep shadow "can hide man."[f] Reckless indeed is he to do or think that he would hide from God; and then—such is the secret root of atheism[g]—thinking he can do so.[h]

But *His eyes also watch the good.* He sees them in outward destitution,[i] in secret retirement,[j] in deep affliction.[k] He pierces the prison walls.[l] He covers their heads "in the day of battle."[m] He is with them in the furnace[n] and in the tempest.[o] His eye guides them as their journeying God and will guide them safely home;[p] full of blessing,[q] protection,[r] and support.[s] "He fills Hell with His severity, heaven with His glory, His people with His grace," commented Charnock.

But how shall I meet these *eyes?* As a rebel or a child? Do they inspire me with terror or with love? Do I walk carefully under their lively impressions?[t] Conscious corruption leads me to shrink from the eyes of man. But oh! my God! I would lay myself naked and open to Thee. Search me; try me; show me to myself. Bring out my hidden iniquities and slay them before Thee.[u] How is the overwhelming thought of this piercing *eye* more than counterbalanced by the view of the great High Priest, who covers and cleanses all infirmities and defilements, and pleads and maintains my acceptance, despite all discouragement![v]

[w] Ps 139:1–6
[x] Jer 23:24; Ps 11:4
[y] Gen 3:8
[z] Ps 10:11; Ezra 8:12
[a] Ps 10:4
[b] Verse 11; Ps 139:8
[c] Acts 12:23
[d] Dan 5:5
[e] 2 Kings 5:20
[f] Job 34:21, 22; Jer 16:17
[g] Ps 14:1
[h] Isa 29:15
[i] Gen 16:7, 13
[j] John 1:48
[k] Exod 3:7; Ps 91:15
[l] Gen 39:21; 2 Chron 33:12, 13
[m] Ps 140:7
[n] Dan 3:25
[o] Acts 27:23
[p] Ps 23:4; 48:14; Isa 42:16
[q] Gen 26:3
[r] 2 Chron 16:9; 1 Peter 3:12
[s] Isa 41:10
[t] Gen 17:1
[u] Ps 139:24
[v] Heb 4:13, 14

4 *A soothing tongue is a tree of life,*
But perversion in it crushes the spirit.

THE HEALING TONGUE

[w]Prov 3:18
[x]Prov 11:30
[y]2 Kings 2:21
[z]Prov 12:18
[a]Col 4:6

Wisdom is finely portrayed as a tree of life.[w] So is also the friendly influence of the righteous[x]—here the fruitfulness of the tongue. A high image of what it ought to be; not negative, not harmless, but *soothing*. As the salt, cast into the spring, cleansed the bitter waters;[y] so *when there is grace in the heart, there will be healing in the tongue.*[z] "Let your speech always be with grace, seasoned, as it were, with salt."[a] Large indeed is the sphere and abundant the blessing. When employed in soothing the afflicted, calming the troubled waters with words of peace, it creates a surrounding paradise. It is not like "the thorny bush, pricking and hurting those that are about us, but a fruitful tree—a *tree of life*," stated Leighton in *Exposition of the Ninth Commandment*, vol. 4.

THE WOUNDING TONGUE

[b]Num 16:8–15
[c]Job 13:1–5
[d]Ps 69:19, 20

But if the gracious tongue is healing, *the perverse tongue* is wounding. The meekest of men felt ill-temper and a *breach* in the spirit.[b] The tongue of Job's friends broke the bruised reed, which needed to be bound up.[c] Even our Beloved Lord, who never shrunk from external evil, keenly felt the piercing edge of this sword to his inmost soul.[d]

THE WHOLESOME TONGUE

[e]Ps 45:2

May "grace be poured upon" my lips, as upon my divine Master's,[e] so that it may be a *soothing tongue*, full of blessing and of good fruits! "Everlasting benediction be upon that tongue, which spake, as no other ever did, or could speak, pardon, peace, and comfort to lost mankind! This was *the tree of life*, whose leaves were for the healing of the nations," said Bishop Horne in *Sermon on The Tree of Life*.

5 *A fool rejects his father's discipline,*
But he who regards reproof is prudent.

THE AUTHORITY OF PARENTS

[f]Job 11:12

We cannot wonder at this folly. Remember the birth of the fool, as "the foal of a wild donkey,"[f] *rejecting discipline* and restraint. Yet subjection to parents is the law of nature, recognized by the most uncivilized nations.

Much more is it the law of God.[g] *The authority of parents is the authority of God.* The wayward resistance of the ungodly will be fearfully scourged.[h] And even the Christian penitent has felt the smart of the rod to the end of life.[4] If example would put this folly to shame, do we not read of one child (Christ), able to teach, yea to command, His parents, who yet set the example of filial subjection?[5] But pride must be broken down, and the clothing of "humility" worn[i] before the child will see that his parents know better than he, and that to count their word law—to "bear the yoke in his youth"[j] and to regard reproof, is the path of prudence[k] no less than of honor.[l] Solomon's wisdom, though the special gift of God, was doubtless connected with his filial *regard* to his *father's discipline.*[m] Will those, who despise their earthly *father's discipline,* listen to their Heavenly Father? How surely therefore will this unyielding spirit exclude from the Kingdom of God![n]

[g]Exod 20:12; Eph 6:1, 2. Comp. Deut 21:18–21
[h]1 Sam 2:22–25
[i]1 Peter 5:5
[j]Lam 3:27
[k]Verses 31, 32; 19:20
[l]Prov 13:18
[m]1 Chron 22:11–13; 28:9, 20
[n]Matt 18:3, 4

6 *Much wealth is* in *the house of the righteous,*
But trouble is in the income of the wicked.

UNSEEN TREASURES

The comparison between *the righteous and the wicked* always turns in favor of *the righteous.* Even in wealth[o] the world's idol, he exceeds. For though *his house* may be without money, there still is *much wealth;* often unseen,[p] yet such, that *the income of the wicked,* compared with it, sinks into nothing. Divine teaching alone cannot convey any right understanding of it.[q] Even eternity cannot fully grasp it; as throughout eternity it will be progressively increasing. "Drop millions of gold, boundless *revenues,* ample territories, crowns and scepters; and a poor contemptible worm lays his One God against all of them," said Bishop Hopkins in *Treaties on Vanity of the World.* The *wealth* of the wicked is too much for their good, and too little for their lust. They cannot satisfy their senses, much less their souls.[r] *Wealth* may *make* itself "wings"[s] at any moment; and, while they continue, unlike the *wealth* of the righteous,[t] they are burdened with *trouble.*[u] But is it not the crown of the Christian's crown, and the glory of his glory, that his portion is so full, that

[o]Verses 16, 17; 3:33
[p]2 Cor 6:10
[q]1 Cor 2:9
[r]Eccl 5:10
[s]Prov 23:5
[t]Prov 10:22
[u]Eccl 4:6

[4] *See* Memoirs of Mrs. Hawkes, *p. 524—A most instructive biography.*
[5] *Luke 2:49–51. "Who was subject? And to whom? God to men"—BERNARD, Homily i.*

he cannot desire more? All the excellence of the creation are only dark shadows of its more substantial excellency. What a mercy to be delivered from the idolatrous bait, so ruinous to both our present peace and eternal welfare![v] But a greater mercy still, to be enriched with that *wealth*, beyond the reach of harm, that raises to heaven; a portion in God, His favor, His image, His everlasting joy.

[v] 1 Tim 6:9, 10

7 *The lips of the wise spread knowledge,*
But the hearts of fools are not so.

THE RIGHT USE OF KNOWLEDGE

The right use of knowledge is, first to "store" it up in a storehouse;[w] then go out of the storehouse and *spread it*. The sower scatters the seed in the furrow and counts on an adequate harvest.[x] Thus the *lips of the wise spread* the precious seed, "divide your portion to seven, or even to eight"; not discouraged by trifling difficulties, but "sow your seed in the morning, and ... evening," and commit the result to God.[y] Our Lord thus gave out the heavenly *knowledge* of His gospel.[z] He commanded His apostles to scatter the seed through the vast field of the world.[a] The persecution of the church was overruled for this great end.[b] The reformers widely spread their treasures, both by preaching and writing, and rich indeed was the fruit. Do we remember, that our gifts and talents are the riches of the church;[c] that, like our father Abraham, *we are blessed, not for our own sakes, but to be a blessing?*[d] And doesn't conscience remind us of many wasted opportunities to talk with our fellow-sinners or fellow-Christians about Christ, when we didn't even open our mouths? We don't argue for any peculiar irregularity, no going beyond proper bounds, no intrusion into supreme obligations. But be careful, that, in quenching unnatural fire, we don't accidentally quench some genuine spark of holy flame. Be mindful of small opportunities. The careful cultivation of the smallest field assumes an abundant harvest. The acceptance is not according to the *number* of talents but according to the *improvement* of the talents; not only where much has been given; but where we "were faithful with a few things."[e]

[w] Prov 10:14
[x] 2 Cor 9:6
[y] Eccl 11:2, 4, 6
[z] Matt 4:23; 9:35
[a] Matt 28:19, 20
[b] Acts 8:4
[c] 1 Cor 12:7; 1 Peter 4:10
[d] Gen 12:2
[e] Matt 25:21

The sin of *the wicked* is not always, that their mouth "spouts folly";[f] but that they don't give out blessing. They neglect to *spread.* If they do not abuse their talent, they fail to improve it. If they aren't *blots* in the church, they are *blanks.* If they do no harm, *they don't do any good, or* they do nothing.[g] How can they *spread* anything from their empty storehouse? They have only trash to trade with the world, not the commerce of substantial *knowledge.* The end of both is according to their works—"For to everyone who has [actively improves] shall *more* be given, and he shall have an abundance; but from the one who does not have [uses not], even what he does have shall be taken away."[h]

[f]Verse 2

[g]Matt 25:25–28

[h]Matt 25:29

8 *The sacrifice of the wicked is an abomination to the*
LORD,
But the prayer of the upright is His delight.
9 *The way of the wicked is an abomination to the*
LORD,
But He loves him who pursues righteousness.

WHEN THE HEART IS ABSENT

Let the reader think about this difficult question—"What am I—what is my service—when I'm on my knees before God? Am I *an abomination or a delight?*" Man judges by acts; God by principles. The *sacrifice of the wicked,* though it is part of God's own service, yet "it will be found in His register in the catalog of sins to be accounted for."[6] At best, little is said or done, where nothing would be lost. But it is "the sacrifice of fools"[i]—heedless and unreflecting, performed without interest, with the heart asleep. But even more—where the heart is deliberately and habitually absent[j]—it is the acting of a lie. And whether it be smoothly fashioned to impose on man, or whether it be forced by the sting of an awakened conscience—instead of possessing the virtue of *a sacrifice,* it is an insulting provocation; not only vain,[k] but abominable—yea *abomination* itself.[l] That is wanting without which it is impossible to please God; the lack of which stamped *the sacrifice* of Cain as an *abomination.*[m] It is a work that does not flow from a lively faith and therefore has in it the nature of sin.

[i]Eccl 5:1

[j]Isa 29:13

[k]Matt 15:7–9

[l]Prov 21:27

[m]Gen 4:3–5, with Heb 11:4

[6] *Bishop HOPKINS'* Works, *ii. 481. Comp. Isa 66:3; Hag 2:12–14.*

Not that prayer itself is a sin. "It is," as Archbishop Usher expounds in *Eighteen Sermons on Eph 2:1,* "a good duty, but spoiled in the carriage." And far indeed would we be from discouraging *the wicked* from prayer.[n] We would only press the awakening conviction that it must be done in God's order and way or it can never find His acceptance.

[n]Acts 8:22

THE WAY OF THE WICKED

But not only *the sacrifice* but *the way, of the wicked;* not only his religion, but his normal living, natural as well as moral, is *abomination.*[o] It is all the way of a rebel against God. All his doings are a corrupt stream from a corrupt fountain. Awful, indeed, is the thought of every step of life as being hateful to God!

[o]Prov 21:4; Titus 1:15

Is he then finally rejected? Far from it. His desire to seek the Lord would be the beginning of *the prayer* that ensures acceptance. *The prayer of the upright* from its first, feeblest utterance is not only acceptable to the Lord but *His delight.*[p] It is not the perfection but the simplicity of uprightness that brings the acceptance. The man feelingly knows his own defilement. If he has not fathomed the depths of his corruptions, he has made the discovery that to him at least they are unfathomable.[q] This consciousness of hidden sins only makes him more concerned to tear them from their hiding place. His sacrifice therefore is that of truth, as contrasted with that of falsehood. That was the service of the outer—this of the inner—man. That seems what it is not and covers what it is. This "comes to the light," and the deed is made manifest, with all its infirmities, that it is "wrought in God."[r] *This prayer of the upright is the Lord's delight.* It is suited to His own spiritual nature. The Father seeks such people "to be His worshipers."[s] The golden censer above,[t] and the gracious intercession within,[u] combine with fragrant odor before our God. Never should we faint in prayer if we realize more habitually this pure ground of acceptance. Not less pleasing to Him is the course of the upright. He has given him a measure of *righteousness* and an effort for more. And though he fulfills it not, he *pursues after it,* cheered with the smile of his Father's gracious *love.*[v]

[p]Song of Sol 2:14; 4:11; Dan 9:23; 10:12

[q]Jer 17:9

[r]John 3:21

[s]John 4:23, 24

[t]Heb 10:19–22

[u]Rom 8:26, 27

[v]Prov 21:21; Phil 3:12

10 *Stern discipline is* [AV—*grievous*] *for him who forsakes the way;*
He who hates reproof will die.

THE SUREST WAY TO RUIN

But isn't it also "sorrowful" for the moment to the child of God? He knows his need of it, bows his will, and reaps a fruitful blessing.[w] But grievous indeed *is it to him that forsakes the way.* He is humbled by force, not in spirit. He kicks at it, and, like an unmanageable child under the rod, only increases the severity of his punishment. There is no surer step to ruin than this *hatred of reproof.*[7] How do the sins of God's children[x] here warn us—"stop regarding man"![y]

[w]Heb 12:11
[x]Deut 32:5; 2 Chron 16:10
[y]Isa 2:22

But when correction turns him back, who had *forsaken the way,* then it is no longer grievous. Had not Manasseh more cause to bless God for his chains than for his crown, for his dungeon than for his palace?[8] The real man was born there. We would always look hopefully at a sinner under *reproof.* For surely so long as the doctor is giving the medicine, there is no cause for despair.

Child of God! Isn't it true that you still need correction to perfect you for more difficult and refined obedience? It demands a price, but it pays wonderful dividends. May the Lord teach you when the thorn is in the flesh to pray for grace in the heart![z] Seek your Father's favor more than your own ease. Desire the sanctifying of his rod rather than its removal. Don't mock Him by the empty ceremonial of repentance. But in true penitence look up to your smiter to be your healer;[a] yet not till His *discipline* has fully accomplished His gracious work. Lord! Let me know the smart of your rod, rather than the eclipse of your love. Show me your love; then do with me what you will.

[z]2 Cor 12:7
[a]Hos 6:1

11 *Sheol and Abaddon* [*hell and destruction*] lie open *before the* LORD*,*
How much more the hearts of men!

Once more we see an Omniscient—Omnipresent God.[b] *Hell and destruction;* every recess of the vast Hades; the state of the dead, and the place of the damned—*are be-*

[b]Verse 3

[7] *Prov 1:30; 5:11, 12, 23; 29:1; Pharaoh—Ex 10:24–29; Ahab—1 Kings 18:17; 21:20; 22:8, 37; Amaziah—2 Chron 25:15, 16, 27; Ahaz—28:22, 23; the Jews—36:15–17; Jer 6:16–19.*
[8] *2 Chron 33:11–13. Comp. David—Ps 119:67, 71; Ephraim—Jer 31:18–20; the Prodigal—Luke 15:12–20.*

fore the Lord,[9] before His eye; completely known to Him. How *much more, then, the hearts* of the children of men,[c] no matter how unsearchable they are![d] There's no depth in them that He cannot fathom; no deceit so complicated, that he can't track them. Words aren't needed in order for Him to lay open the heart. He perceived Aaron's rebellious feelings as easily as Moses' angry words.[e] The inward hypocrisy of His people was as open before Him, as if it had been stamped upon their foreheads.[f]

[c] 1 John 3:20
[d] Jer 17:9, 10
[e] Num 20:12, 24
[f] Deut 5:28, 29; Zeph 1:12

GOD'S SEARCHING EYE

Yet, what a mass of practical unbelief there is in this plainly conclusive truth! For would men dare to tolerate their vain thoughts, light notions, trifles, impurities, if they really believed that the Lord searches their hearts? Would they attempt to conceal anything from His eye;[g] as though outward service or lip worship would meet every requirement, while the heart would be cherishing its unrepented sin? Wouldn't they be afraid to *even think* in front of Him what they would shrink *from doing* before men? Oh! Isn't it an awesome moment when a man has to stand the test of this searching eye? How awful just the thought of it is to the idolatrous sinner, or the lover of pleasure, fame, or low ambition! Make no mistake about it, your heart is open before your God. And He will never stoop to occupy second place there. No covering of deceit can ever stand His searching eye. And all refuges of lies are pierced and laid bare.

[g] Isa 29:15

While the conscious sinner tries to hide from this appalling view, the believer walks boldly in the sight of this consuming fire.[h] His godly fear is the exercise of filial confidence.[i] The sins, that are opened to His Father's knowledge, are covered from His justice.[j] When he finds "the principle, that evil is present in me, the one who wishes to do good"; he can look up—"All my desire is before Thee."[k] Thus does the gospel clothe God's attributes with light and love.

[h] Deut 32:22
[i] Heb 12:28, 29
[j] Heb 4:13; Ps 32:1
[k] Rom 7:21; Ps 38:9

Don't we see that there is a testimony here to the divine glory of Immanuel? For *are not hell and destruction before Him*[l] as His vast empire? And didn't He often

[l] Rev 1:18

[9] *Job 26:6; Ps 139:7, 8.* Destruction, *Heb. Abaddon. Comp. Rev 9:11.*

prove His right of searching *the hearts of men;* charging sin in the inner world, beyond the knowledge of any, but the one all-seeing eye? And this, indeed, is the confidence His people have in Him. Each of them appeals to this all-seeing eye despite all the enemy's accusations—'Lord, You know all things; You know that I love You"![m]

[m]John 21:17; Rev 2:23

12 *A scoffer does not love one who reproves him,*
He will not go to the wise.

How different from David's spirit, thankful that the "righteous smite me in kindness";[n] and from the lovely humility of an apostle, who showed his honor before the church and *love to his reprover!*[o] Yet he had need to be wise with the wisdom that is from above to give reproof aright. So closely does the mixture of our own spirit cleave to every Christian exercise! And it takes no less grace and wisdom, instead of turning from our reprover, to go to *Him,* and ask Him to continue his faithful work in us. That most sensitive, delicate, and unvarying of all feelings, self-love—has been wounded, and the wound is not easily healed. *The scoffer* has been his own flatterer so long, that he cannot bear to be brought down to his proper level. And the truth-telling friend, therefore, he regards as his enemy.[p] He *loves not*—in fact, he hates *anyone who reproves him,*[q] though he is someone he formerly revered.[r] "The Pharisee" scoffed at our Lord with external scorn, when He struck at their right eye and reproved their hypocrisy.[10] "Everyone who does evil hates the light, and does not come to the light, lest his deeds should be exposed."[s]

[n]Ps 141:5
[o]Gal 2:11–14, with 2 Peter 3:15
[p]Gal 4:15, 16
[q]Prov 9:8; 1 Kings 21:20; 22:8; Amos 5:10; 7:10–13
[r]Mark 6:17–20; Luke 16:14
[s]John 3:20

13 *A joyful heart makes a cheerful face,*
But when the heart is sad, the spirit is broken.

How close is the sympathy between the body and soul, though made of such opposite elements! A man's face reveals his mood. When a man is happy, "the *heart* sits smiling in the face, and looks *merrily* out of the windows of the eyes," said Trapp.[11] Yet too often a high spirit, a face lighted up is really a matter of sadness, rather than

[10] *Luke 16:13, 14. Literally from the Greek, nostril—contempt shown by the nostrils—to blow the nose—"They blowed their nose at him." See LEIGH'S Critica Sacra, and PARKHURST.*
[11] *This merriment, however, widely differs from the noisy mirth of the ungodly (Prov 14:13). The word is of frequent use among our old writers. It is Foxe's favorite description of the holy joys of the martyrs. Comp. Eccl 9:7.*

pleasure, because it's connected with the wrong kind of happiness—that which estranges the heart from God. Who has a true right to a merry heart, but he that is walking in the joy of God's approval?[t] This spring of joy lighted up Hannah's sorrowful countenance into godly cheerfulness.[u] Stephen stood before his judge with his heavenly prospects beaming in his face as "of an angel."[v] Everywhere the hearty reception of the gospel gives beauty "instead of ashes" and sunshine for gloom.[w]

[t]Ps 32:1, 2, 11
[u]1 Sam 1:18
[v]Acts 6:15; 7:55
[w]Isa 61:3

A sad contrast is *a heart broken* by worldly *sadness.*[x] Too often an evil gloom worms itself into the vitals of the child of God.[y] The melancholy victim drags on a weary, heavy-laden existence, clouding a distinct feature of his character,[z] and one of the most attractive ornaments of his Christian profession.[a] His hands slacken; all of his energies are paralyzed for the work of God; and he sinks into despondent apathy and indolence, as if he has left life and the sun no longer shines upon him.[b]

[x]1 Sam 28:16; 2 Cor 7:10
[y]Prov 18:14
[z]Phil 3:3
[a]Ps 33:1; Phil 4:4
[b]Prov 17:22

Every effort should be made to get rid of this black hovering cloud. Keep sense and feeling within their bounds, and you will hear the Savior's voice, encouraging confidence.[c] Even our very "sigh and groan over all the abominations"[d] must not issue in heartless complaints, but rather stimulate us to the diligently improved present opportunities. If we realized, as we should, our present privilege, and grasp our eternal prospects; *no sorrow of the heart would break our spirit.* "I wonder many times," says Rutherford, "that ever a child of God should have a sad heart, considering what his Lord is preparing for him." The gleam of the present sunshine is the earnest of what it will be, when—as he again beautifully observes—"we shall be on the sunny side of the Brae," said Rutherford in *Letters.* Meanwhile the first step in our Christian walk, is, not only beginning to be serious, but to be happy. In order for us to maintain our Christian balance, even godly "sorrow" must be disciplined; lest it *break the heart that it was intended only to humble;* lest it give advantage to the enemy and bring hindrance to the church.[e]

[c]Isa 1:10
[d]Ezek 9:4
[e]2 Cor 2:7

14 *The mind of the intelligent seeks knowledge,*
But the mouth of fools feeds on folly.

Look at the man with natural *knowledge.* Every new thing *learned quickens his thirst for more knowledge.* He is ready to learn from any source, even from a child. He is all eye, ear, heart, for the object of his interest. And this is even more true of spiritual *understanding.*[f] Hold down the desire to be wise above "what is written," but make strong and energetic effort to be wise to the full extent of God's Word. David, with his high attainments, was ever crying for divine teaching.[g] His wise son *sought knowledge* upon his knees,[h] and just as hard in study.[i] The Queen of Sheba, coming a long distance;[j] Nicodemus and Mary, sitting at the feet of Jesus;[k] the Eunuch, journeying to Jerusalem;[l] Cornelius and his company, taking in the precious message of salvation;[m] the Bereans, carefully "examining the Scriptures daily"[n]—all these show *the intelligent person's heart, seeks* a larger interest in the blessing.

[f]Prov 1:5; 9:9
[g]1 Cor 4:6; Ps 119:98–100, with 33, 34
[h]1 Kings 3:5–10
[i]Eccl 12:9, 10
[j]1 Kings 10:1; Matt 12:42
[k]John 3:1, 2; Luke 10:39
[l]Acts 8:28
[m]Acts 10:33
[n]Acts 17:11

Invaluable, indeed, is the gift. Warm affections need the discipline of *knowledge* to form Christian consistency and completeness:[o] seeking for wholesome food, not intoxicating drinks; not deeming novelty the most desirable thing; but, rather, with the wise Sir M. Hale, desiring "to be impressed and affected, and to have old and known truths reduced to experience and practice."

[o]Phil 1:9; Ps 119:66

But while the *mind of the intelligent* is never satisfied with *knowledge,* the fool is fully satisfied with folly. His brutish taste feeds on folly, as his meat and his drink. His spirit is of "the earth, earthy." Young people, guard against this folly at every turn. Avoid trifling amusements, frivolous reading, profane merriment. In your Christian walk beware of preferring empty speculations and disputings on matters having no part of the rich pasture of the children of God.[p] Let us all seriously think of the responsibility of pressing on to "maturity," that, being of full age, we may have our senses trained to discern good and evil."[q]

[p]1 Cor 15:45; Prov 15:21; Acts 17:21
[q]Heb 6:1; 5:14

15 *All the days of the afflicted are bad,*
But a cheerful heart has *a continual feast.*

Affliction, as the fruit and chastening of sin, is *bad.* Therefore, all the days of the afflicted are bad.[r] Yet solid inward satisfaction will bring real comfort in most dif-

[r]Gen 47:9; Ps 90:7–9

ficult circumstances. Therefore, though the abounding consolation of Christian affliction does not blot out his penal character; yet the child of God is not so miserable as he seems to be.[s] The darkest of these evil days can never make "the consolations of God too small for you."[t] He can sing in the prison as in a palace.[u] He can accept "joyfully the seizure of . . . property."[v] He can praise his God when He hath stripped him naked.[w] He can rejoice in Him as his portion in poverty.[x] "Who is it," said the heavenly martyn in a moment of faintness, "that maketh my comforts to be a source of enjoyment? Cannot the same hand make cold, and hunger, and nakedness, and peril, to be a train of ministering angels conducting me to glory?" (*Life,* chap. 2).

[s] 2 Cor 6:10
[t] Job 15:11
[u] Acts 16:25
[v] Heb 10:34
[w] Job 1:21
[x] Hab 3:17, 18

What *bad* then can affliction bring? Or rather, what does it bring but many feast days?[y] A few days' feasting would soon weary even great food lovers. But here *the cheerful heart has a continual feast.* His temporal mercies are filled with cheerfulness. And "all his trouble is but the rattling hail upon the tiles of his house," not disturbing his enjoyment, said Leighton.[z] Having this heavenly portion, shall I not thank my God, that he has drawn me away from present satisfactions? "Do not let me eat of their delicacies . . . Thou hast put gladness in my heart, More than when their grain and new wine abound."[a]

[y] Eccl 9:7
[z] 1 Peter 1:2; 3; 3:17
[a] Ps 141:4; 4:6, 7

16 *Better is a little with the fear of the* L*ORD,*
Than great treasure and turmoil with it.
17 *Better is a dish of vegetables where love is,*
Than a fattened ox and hatred with it.

Here are the sources of the merry heart—*the fear of the Lord,* and *love* to man. And here also is the continual feast, so satisfying, that the saint's *little* is better than the worldling's all.[b] It is his Father's gift;[c] the fruit of his Savior's love;[d] enjoyed by special promise,[e] and sweetened with the great gain "of godly" contentment.[f] If it be only *little*, it is not from lack of his Father's care and love; but because His wisdom knows what he really needs[g] and that all beyond would be a temptation and snare. Truly a man's life does not consist in the "abundance" of

[b] Prov 16:8; Ps 37:16
[c] Matt 6:11
[d] 2 Peter 1:3
[e] Ps 34:10; 37:3, 19; Isa 33:15, 16
[f] 1 Tim 6:6; Phil 4:11, 12
[g] Matt 6:32

the things which he possesses.[h] "Riches and proverty are more in the heart than in the hand. He is wealthy, that is contented. He is poor, that wanteth more, said Bishop Hall. The universe will not fill a worldly heart,[i] but it takes only a little to fill a heavenly heart.[j] The children of light content themselves willingly with the small pittances, which their Father allows them during the time of their minority; knowing that their main portion is reserved for them in safekeeping "in heaven,"[k] They are well satisfied on their way home to live rather more scantily by the way; like Joseph's brethren, who were provided with food for their journey; but their full sacks were unopened, till they reached their home.[l] Here their God compensates for everything. But what could compensate for Him?

On the other hand, there must be *turmoil even with great treasure,* without *the fear of the Lord.*[m] And far more destitute is that possessor of great treasure, in his unsubstantial happiness, than the man of God, who "by the sweat of your face . . . shall eat bread."[n] "Jacob's ladder, which conveys to heaven, may have its foot in the smoking cottage," said Bishop Reynolds (*Sermon on 1 Tim 6:17–19*). And as to this world's comforts—the *dish of vegetables,* the homely meal *of love,* is better than *the fattened ox* prepared for a sumptuous feast without love.[o] *Love* sweetens the poorest food. *Hatred* embitters the richest feast.[p] How did the presence and fellowship of the Lord of angels dignify the humble fare![q] How much more refreshing were the social meals of the Pentecostal Christians, than the well-furnished tables of their enemies![r] When the Lord's ordinance of marriage is marred by man's selfishness; when wealth, rank, or accidental accomplishments determine the choice of a life's companion, rather than *the fear of the Lord;* what wonder if *the fattened ox, and hatred with it* be the order of the house? Mutual disappointment is too often the source of criminal indulgence abroad; always the ruin of peace and unity at home.

How sad that so few believe this divine testimony. Parents! do you seek solid happiness for your children? Then lead them to expect little from the world, everything from God.

[h]Luke 12:15
[i]Eccl 1:8
[j]Gen 28:29
[k]1 Peter 1:4
[l]Gen 42:25
[m]Eccl 4:6; 5:12
[n]Gen 3:19
[o]Prov 17:1; 21:19; 23:6
[p]1 Sam 20:24–34; 2 Sam 13:23–29
[q]John 21:9–12
[r]Acts 2:46. Comp. Ps 133

18 *A hot-tempered man*[12] *stirs up strife,*
But the slow to anger pacifies contention.

This proverb requires no explanation. But observe the principles of hatred and love contrasted in active exercise. Some persons make it their occupation to sit by the fire, to feed and fan the flame, lest it be extinguished. If it were a fire to get warm by, it would be a useful and friendly occupation. But when it's an injurious, consuming, and destructive element, it would seem difficult to determine the motive of these incendiaries,[s] do we not read that "out of the heart of men, proceed evil thoughts and fornications, thefts, murders, adulteries . . . pride and foolishness."[t]

[s]Prov 10:12; 16:27, 28; 26:21

[t]Mark 7:21, 22

What then is the Christian's exercise? Not to *stir up* strife but to *pacify* it; to bring water, not fuel, to the fire; by "a gentle answer" to turn away wrath;[13] by a yielding spirit to melt, subdue, and bring peace.[u] Let me remember, that I owe my very salvation to this attribute, *slow to anger.*[v] And shouldn't I endeavour to permeate my profession with this lovely adorning and to "be imitators of God, as beloved children, and walk in love"?[w] Will not this temper of the gospel secure my earthly enjoyment of godliness?[x] Will it not also seal my title as a child of God?[y]

[u]Gen 13:7–9; Eccl 10:4

[v]Ps 103:8; 2 Peter 3:15

[w]Eph 5:1, 2

[x]Matt 5:5

[y]Matt 5:9

19 *The way of the sluggard is as a hedge of thorns,*
But the path of the upright is a highway
[*AV—raised up*].[14]

Another picture of the slothful man drawn to life! He plants his own *hedge* and then complains of its hindrance. He is always at a standstill. Every effort is like forcing his way through a *hedge of thorns,* where every *thorn bush* tears his flesh. Indecision, delay, and sluggishness, add to his difficulties, and paralyze his exertion; so that after a feeble struggle of conscience, with much to do, but no heart to do anything, he gives up the effort.

This laziness is ruinous in worldly matters. One or two hills vigorously climbed *make the way* plain for future

[12] *A man of wrath, Heb constantly indulging it; unwilling to put it away; a firebrand—SCHULTENS. Comp. 29:22.*

[13] *Verse 1. References.*

[14] *"A highway—a path so formed, as to be easy to the foot of the traveller"—FRENCH and SKINNER. Comp. Isa 35:8. Also 2 Chron 9:11.*

triumph. But to work half-heartedly; to drag to work as an unavoidable task; to avoid present difficulties in order to find a smoother path, makes *a hedge of thorns* harassing to the end of the journey.

But this evil is much more ruinous in the Christian life. The lazy Christian is never at ease. He knows that he needs a change. He makes an effort to pray; or he takes up a good book. But he doesn't go through with anything because he has no purpose of heart. To him, exertion is impossible. He sees no hope of success and sinks again.

And this isn't just at the beginning of his path. It is *his way*—his whole course. The righteous may loiter or decline, but that's not *his way. The sluggard* may have a fit—sometimes an astonishing fit—of exertion; but he relapses to his former state,[z] still surrounded by a *hedge of thorns,* unable to change *his way,* and so, he is disheartened to the end.

[z]Prov 12:27

Observe God's estimate of him. He doesn't contrast him with the diligent, but with *the upright.* He calls him a *"wicked, lazy slave"*—all because of his laziness in spiritual things.[a] The difficulties are far more in the mind than in the path. For while *the sluggard* sits down by the side of his hedge in despair, *the path of the upright,* which in itself is no easier, is made plain, *a highway.* He doesn't expect God to work for him in his lazy ways. But he finds that God helps those that help themselves. Working with diligence, he finds that he can work in comfort. Following God's commands, feeding upon His promises, continuing in prayer, in waiting and watching for an answer to prayer—his *path* is raised up, before him. He believes what is written, and acts upon it without disputing, without delay. The minute the light comes into his mind—it determines the direction of his steps, and the way in which he proceeds, His stumbling blocks are removed.[b] Hard-working wisdom performs what lazy foolishness thought impossible. To be sure, there are *thorns* in the way, but not an impassable *hedge of thorns;* just those that, while they pierce his flesh, are overruled as a blessing to his soul."[c]

[a]Matt 25:26

[b]Num 13:30; 14:6–9; Isa 57:14

[c]2 Cor 12:7, 8

Now, let me apply this to myself—to my great work. It is of greatest importance to me to have *my path a plain* highway. For this—confidence of success is indispensable. Let me then examine the grounds of my confidence. Suppose up to this moment I have been living in enmity with God; yet now He does not will my death;[d] He invites me to come to Him;[e] He guarantees my acceptance.[f] I have His word to depend upon. Why should I stagger in unbelief? His truth claims my confidence and justifies my expectation of certain blessing. I don't begin, hoping to make things right for past neglect, but believing in Him for free pardon and strength. The physician heals my helplessness. Faith expels slavish fear, and "the way of the Lord," instead of a *hedge of thorns,* is "a stronghold to the upright."[g] The prospect brightens, and instead of "the hard man," which *the sluggard* pictures to himself, a reconciled God appears before me.[h]

[d]Ezek 33:11
[e]Matt 11:28
[f]John 6:37
[g]Prov 10:29
[h]Matt 25:24; 2 Cor 5:19

This is no easy way. What fluctuation of faith! What weariness and discouragement! But at last *the path is made a highway.* Difficulties are faced, surmounted, carried by assault, and what cannot be removed is endured. The mountains are leveled before Zerubbabel.[i] The feeble worm threshes them by the energy of faith.[j] Hope, love, and joy are conquering principles. Christianity, with all its crosses, is found to be a practicable thing.[k] The victory over laziness opens a happy and triumphant way to heaven.[l]

[i]Zech 4:7
[j]Isa 41:15
[k]Phil 4:13
[l]Matt 11:12

The sluggard has enjoyed the same advantages. But he has not gone through the *thorn hedge* of his own corruptions. He has never learned that the cross is the discipline to the end of the way. He does not think what is spoken to faith but what is agreeable to feeling. He has never broken through the *thorn* of unbelief. He has compromised and failed in the unreserved trust and surrender of himself to his Savior. Therefore, he comes to God in confidence. All his service is with a festering conscience and with that timidity and delay which ensures defeat. His way at every turn is restless trouble; struggling with a *hedge of thorns* to the very last.

Child of God, beware of a sluggish spirit. Even the morbid, strife about your condition may sometimes be a slothful indulgence in direct opposition to the plainest declarations of God. Don't let unbelief snatch the promise from your hand or paralyze the hand that holds it. If *the pathway* has been made plain, don't sit down in the indulgent comfort of it. But go in this your strength to more important advantage. Prize every particle of success you've gained by exertion. Oh! it's worth everything, if, though we have permitted ourselves to be entangled by spiritual laziness, we rise, even though it's at the close of day, and clear away the clouds, that "at evening time there will be light."[m] Happy indeed will it be to be stirred, though late, to a firmer confidence; to be brought, though only a step nearer to Christ—to have one thorn less to battle with in the struggle of death.

[m]Zech 14:7

20 *A wise son makes a father glad,*
But a foolish man despises his mother.

Do not the brightest joys,[n] and the bitterest sorrows[o] in this world of tears, flow from parents' hearts? Whatever be the delight to see a son prospering in life; the Christian father finds no rest, until *a wise son makes him glad.* And here we don't need any development of talent, or superior attainment, but the true *wisdom*; humble and docile, marked (as the contrast suggests) by filial reverence, specially by the cordial choice of that, which is the beginning of wisdom—the fear of the Lord. Such a son does indeed rejoice his father, as he watches, with equal pleasure and thankfulness, the daily growth and healthiness of his choice vine.

[n]Prov 10:1; 23:24; 1 Kings 1:48
[o]Prov 17:25; 2 Sam 18:33

But what if *folly,* instead *of gladdening, despise a mother*[p]—her, whose tender love,[q] and yearning faithfulness,[r] are a faint picture of the heart of God? The law of God commands honor[s] and reverence,[t] and the transgression of the law will not be forgotten.[u] But isn't this neglect a chastening rebuke for playful indulgence? What grace and wisdom are needed, that the parents may be a valuable blessing to their children for their highest interests! A single eye is the primary concern.

[p]Prov 19:26; 23:22
[q]Isa 66:13
[r]Isa 49:15
[s]Exod 20:12
[t]Lev 19:3
[u]Prov 20:20; 30:17; Ezek 22:7

21 *Folly is joy to him who lacks sense,*
But a man of understanding walks straight.

This Book of instruction probes our Christian reality. What do we think of *folly?* Not only does the ungodly practice it. But *it is joy* to him. He sins without temptation or motive. He cannot sleep without it.[v] It is "the sweet" morsel "under his tongue."[w] He "obeys its lusts."[x] He works it "with greediness."[y] He hates the

[v]Prov 4:16, 17
[w]Verse 14; 9:17; Job 20:12
[x]Rom 6:12
[y]Eph 4:19

[z]Matt 1:21; Acts 3:26

[a]Rom 7:24, 25; 8:1

[b]Isa 33:14; Jon 2:8

[c]Prov 21:15

[d]Prov 4:18

gospel, because it "saves."[z] But hear the humbling confessions of a child of God—"I am carnal, sold under sin. O wretched man that I am! who shall deliver me?" Verily would he sink under his hated burden, but for the confidence—I thank God, there is "no condemnation."[a]

This appetite for sin proves the man to be *without wisdom.* That which has turned this fair world into a graveyard; no!—that which hath kindled "continual burnings," is *his joy.* And so he goes on, intent upon the trifles of the day; and trifling with eternal concerns; preferring shadowy vanities to everlasting glory. Won't he ever open his eyes to the discovery, that "those who regard vain idols forsake their faithfulness"?[b] The Lord save him, before it's too late, from reaping the bitter fruit of his foolish choice!

But the man of understanding gives himself to the Word of God. He has *joy* in *wisdom,*[c] as the sinner in folly. Even his painful discoveries of indwelling corruption establish him deeper in his Christian convictions, than those who know only the surface. He is taught of God and his straight walk is a bright "light of dawn."[d] Give me, O my God, *understanding,* that my *joy* may be in your wisdom, not in my own *folly.*

22 *Without consultation, plans are frustrated,*
But with many counselors they succeed.

[e]Prov 11:14

[f]Prov 20:18; 24:6

[g]Acts 15:6, 31

The value of this Proverb as a political truth is sufficiently obvious. A nation *without counsel* can never *succeed.*[e] *Many counselors* are an indispensable advantage to the ruler for his own purposes.[f] And by the neglect of them many good *plans are frustrated.*[15] In the church, also, combined counsel has greatly tended to Christian *success.*[g] Its influence also in our religious institutions is of the highest importance. Clear and commanding is the duty of godly and able men as *many counselors* to take an active part in their *plans.* In many individual perplexities we are led highly to estimate this advantage. For how weak and ignorant we are! Were our judgment perfect, the first impressions would always be right. But feeble and shaken as it is by the Fall, every dictate needs careful thought. How much evil has been done by acting upon

[15] *Rehoboam—1 Kings 12:13–19. Ahab—22:18–39. Even David—2 Sam 24:1–4, 15.*

impulse in a hasty moment or by a few warm words or lines without consideration![h] Our wisdom lies in self-distrust; at least leaning to the suspicion that we may be wrong. Yet, on the other hand, we must guard against that indecision of judgment, which is carried about by every person's opinion; the expediency, especially in important matters, of experienced *counsel* will be generally felt. But even here the wisest can be wrong and often is. In the use of human means, let us mainly look up to the great "Counselor"[i] of His church for guidance, and in reverential thankfulness say "Thy testimonies also are my delight; *they are* my *counselors*."[j] Blessed be God for this special privilege of *counsel* always at hand! In humility and confidence we shall not seriously wrong.[k]

[h] Prov 19:2
[i] Isa 9:6
[j] Ps 119:24
[k] Prov 3:5, 6

23 *A man has joy in an apt answer,*
And how delightful is a timely word!

This is a true Proverb when the mouth is under God's control. *A word* for our great Master to our fellow-sinners he will condescend to bless. The remembrance—"Who has made man's mouth?"[l]—does away with pride. But don't we have *joy by the answer of our mouth?*[m] The pain that every right-minded Christian feels in giving "open rebuke," is abundantly compensated by *the joy* of the happy outcome.[n] Even an unsuccessful effort brings *the joy* in the testimony of our conscience. It must however be *a word spoken in due season*[o] though it be from feeble lips.[16] For—though "there are some happy seasons, when the most rugged natures are accessible," said Bishop Hopkins (*Works*, 4:485), yet many a good word is lost, by being *spoken* at the wrong *time*. Obviously a moment of spoken irritation is always at the wrong time. We must wait for the return of calmness and reason.[p] Sometimes indeed the matter forces itself out after long and seemingly ineffectual waiting. It has been brooded over within for a long time and must have expression. But this explosion sweeps away every prospect of good and

[l] Exod 4:11
[m] Prov 12:14; 13:2
[n] Prov 27:5; 2 Sam 12:1–13
[o] Prov 25:11
[p] 1 Sam 25:37

[16] *Prov 24:6. Thus Luther, after the pattern of the great apostle, gladly acknowledged his obligation—"The word of a brother, pronounced from Holy Scripture in a time of need, carries an inconceivable weight with it. The Holy Spirit accompanies it, and by it moves and animates the hearts of the people, as their circumstances require. Thus Timothy and Titus, and Epaphroditus, and the brethren who met St. Paul from Rome, cheered his spirit; however much they might be inferior to him in learning and skill in the word of God. The greatest saints have their times of faintness, when others are stronger than they"*—SCOTT'S Contin of Milner, *i. 332. See the ministry of Christ, Isa 7:4.*

leaves a disgusting impression. Instead of a fertilizing shower, it has gathered into a violent and destructive tempest.

It is most important, that our entire behavior should bring conviction, that we yearn over the souls of those whom we are constrained to reprove. The general rule is, to give reproof privately;[q] not exasperating, except when the occasion calls for it,[r] by public exposure. Never commence with an attack; which, because it is an enemy's position, naturally provokes resistance. Seek out a pointed application. A word spoken for every one, like a coat made for every one, has no individual fitness. Since "the wise heart knows the proper time and procedure,"[s] the word is doubly effective. Manoah's wife upheld her husband's faith.[t] Abigail restrained David's murderous intent.[u] Naaman's servants brought their master to sober reason.[v] Paul withheld the jailor's hand from self-destruction and opened salvation to his soul.[w] Sweet indeed also is the minister's *joy from the apt answer* when the gifted tongue of the learned speaks *a word at the proper time* to him that is "weary."[x] And will it not be part of His consummating joy "at His coming," when He shall welcome those instrumentally saved *by the answer of their mouth*, as His "glory and joy"?[y]

[q]Matt 18:15
[r]1 Tim 5:20; Acts 13:6–11
[s]Eccl 8:5
[t]Judg 13:23
[u]1 Sam 25:32, 33
[v]2 Kings 5:13, 14
[w]Acts 16:28–31
[x]Isa 50:4
[y]1 Thess 2:19, 20

24 *The path of life* leads *upward for the wise,*
That he may keep away from Sheol below.

Another beam of light and immortality here shines upon the Old Testament dispensation. For if the *life leading upward* is beyond animal sensation, it must be the life eternal. *The Sheol (hell) below,* opposed to it, must stretch beyond the grave into eternity. But *the path of life*—the way in which alone life is found, the way to God, the way to glory—is but one. That way is Christ.[z] If therefore I come to Him, putting aside all other hope, casting all my hope on Him, and every step of my way "fixing our eyes on Jesus"[a]—am I not in this way? And if I follow Him in the obedience of faith, isn't my course, my daily walk, advancing in that way?[b]

[z]John 14:6
[a]Heb 12:2
[b]John 8:12

This way is above—of heavenly origin—the fruit of the eternal councils—the display of the many-sided wisdom of God. Fools don't rise high enough to see it, much less to plan by it and walk in it. The highest point they reach is a prostrate position on the ground. God doesn't allow them even the name of life.[c] Cleaving to the dust of earth, they sink into *the hell below.* But *the path of the wise leads upward.* They are born from above; taught from above; therefore they walk above, while they are living upon earth. A soaring life indeed! The soul mounts up, looks aloft, enters into the holiest, rises above herself, and finds her resting place in the heart of her God. An incomparable life! to be "partakers of *the* divine nature!"[d] the life of God himself;[e] in humble splendor, rising above things under the sun, above the sun itself. Not only is it out of the reach of carnal men but beyond the understanding of all.[f] It is such *a path* that neither men nor angels could ever have dreamed it up. It can only be thought of with reverential faith. The wise in their most favored moments cannot fully conceive their present privileges; how much less the glorious unfolding when the clouds shall never more be known.

[c] 1 Tim 5:6
[d] 2 Peter 1:4
[e] Eph 4:18
[f] Job 11:7–9

The further we walk in *this upward path,* the further we keep away *from hell below.* Heaven and hell are here before us. Soon our state will be fixed for eternity—What then am I? Where am I? Those "who set their minds on earthly things," their end is the *hell below.* Those who walk in *the path upward*—their "citizenship is in heaven"; their hope is fixed on the Lord's coming from heaven; their everlasting joy will be the complete transformation into His own image.[g] There is no downward tendency. It is still upward. It is all rising ground. No matter how high we go, there is always more to climb; heaven still appears at a great distance, and it will be long before we reach it. Yet the moment we desire this heavenly state, we have begun to know it, and we shall rise higher and higher heavenward, till we take our place before the throne of God. Thus "he that is truly wise, in this holy way of obedience, walketh to eternal life," stated Bishop Hall.

[g] Phil 3:19–21. Comp. Ps 17:14, 15

Children of God, walk like yourselves; with your hearts lifted up "in the ways of the Lord";[h] in holy heights above the debasing pleasure of earth; looking "at the things which are not seen;"[i] looking to the reward;[j] walking *in the upward path,* where all these are; your

[h] 2 Chron 17:6. Comp. Isa 33:16; 40:31; 58:14
[i] 2 Cor 4:18
[j] Heb 11:24–26

[k]2 Cor 5:1–5; Col 1:27
[l]Matt 6:20
[m]2 Cor 5:6–8; Heb 11:19; 13:14
[n]Col 3:1

hope,[k] your treasure,[l] your home,[m] above all—your ascended Savior;[n] and where one golden ray of His favor, one reflected beam of His glory, will outshine all the glare of a shadowy world. Had we more of heaven in our hearts, we should have more of its spirit in our Christian lives. We should think less of the roughness of the way, if we more fully realized the rest beyond. But except we know—in its measure—heaven as our state now, how can we hope to enjoy it as our everlasting home? "Grant, we beseech thee, that, like as we do believe thy only-begotten Son, our Lord Jesus Christ, to have ascended into the heavens; so we may also in heart and mind thither ascend, and with him continually dwell," reads the Collect for Ascension Day.

25 *The LORD will tear down the house of the proud,*
But He will establish the boundary of the widow.

GOD HELPS THE OPPRESSED

[o]Luke 1:51, 52
[p]Esther 7:10; 9:10; Jer 22:13–30
[q]Ps 10:14, 18; 12:5; 58:11

God humbles *the proud* and exalts the humble.[o] The *proud* tyrant steals God's rights, and, as a traitor to God, he *tears down,* not only himself, but *his family,* as well.[p] Can anyone see this as anything but rightful punishment by the Judge of the earth?[q]

[r]Prov 23:10, 11
[s]Jer 49:11. Comp. 1 Tim 5:5
[t]Ps 68:5; 146:9; Deut 10:17, 18
[u]Ruth 1:7–18; 4:14–17
[v]2 Kings 4:1–7
[w]2 Kings 8:1–6
[x]Hos 14:3; Ps 14:2, 3

But the *widow,* with few having any concern for her, and many ready to trample on her—what a friend and protector she has in Christ![r] "Let your widows trust in Me."[s] God condescends to link Himself with them in a special relationship; devoting all His care and tenderness on their sad condition.[t] Didn't He provide for the sorrowing widow, Naomi, a pillar of strength in her faithful daughter-in-law and ultimately *establish her* in Israel?[u] Didn't He supply the pressing need of the minister's widow[v] and take up the cause of the Shunammite widow and *establish* her in her land?[w] And shall we forget how He teaches the returning repentant soul, to prove His gracious promise—"In Thee the orphan finds mercy"?[x]

26 *Evil plans* [AV—*Thoughts*] *are an abomination to the LORD,*
But pleasant words are pure.

Most men take the responsibility of their thoughts so lightly! They regard them as their own, to do with as they please, without restraint. One basic sin terrifies men, who don't think about God for months and years and are totally unaware of guilt. But *thoughts* are the seed principles of sin.[17] And as the cause includes its effects; so do thoughts (like the seed in its little body), contain all the after fruit. They also reveal character. Watch their unending variety; not so much those that are under the control of circumstances, or produced by the occasion, but the natural flow that grows out of our normal associations. "For as he thinks within himself, so he is."[y] Just let the Christian yield himself to the Word, as a discerner of the thoughts and intents of the heart,[z] and what a mass of vanity it will reveal in a day or even an hour as to *the evil.* "Evil plans" are the first bubbling of the corrupt fountain.[a] The tide of evil rolls on unceasingly in "thoughts of iniquity,"[b] giving expression to a malicious disposition; at ease with wickedness and pursuing it with determined purpose. How can such thoughts be other than *an abomination to the Lord?*

But His mind toward His own people is very different! The *words of the pure,* as the expression of *their thoughts*[c] *are pleasant words. How pleasant* is plainly seen by His invitation to fellowship with Him;[d] but even more so by the open reward He has prepared for them to be given before the assembled world. They that "feared the Lord spoke one to another"—and *thought* upon His name—"they shall be Mine, says the Lord of hosts, on the day that I prepare My own possession."[e]

[y] Prov 23:7
[z] Heb 4:13
[a] Matt 15:19
[b] Isa 59:7
[c] Matt 12:34; Ps 37:30, 31
[d] Song of Sol 2:14

27 *He who profits illicitly troubles his own house,*
But he who hates bribes will live.

THE EVILS OF GREED

What awful evils God identifies with greed: idolatry;[f] abomination;[g] an evil eye: the cause of poverty;[h] the "root of all sorts of evil"![i] Not only is it a curse to the sinner, but often a trouble to his house. Lot,[j] Achan,[k] Saul,[l] Ahab,[m] Gehazi,[n] Jehoiakim,[o] and the Jews[p] found it that. And often in our own day, greed for gain has

[17] *Prov 24:9. Gen 6:5. PLUTARCH: "If thou wouldest unlock the door of thine heart, thou wilt find a storehouse and treasury of evils diversified, and full of numberless passions."*

[e] Mal 3:16, 17
[f] Eph 5:5; Col 3:5; Job 31:24
[g] Ps 10:3
[h] Prov 28:22
[i] 1 Tim 6:9, 10
[j] Gen 13:10, 11; 14:12; 19:14, 30
[k] Josh 7:1, 15, 24; Deut 7:26
[l] 1 Sam 15:19–26
[m] 1 Kings 21:1–14, 19–22; 2 Kings 9:24–26
[n] 2 Kings 5:20–27
[o] Jer 22:13, 18–30
[p] Jer 6:12, 13; 8:10

[q]Hab 2:9, 10
[r]Exod 18:21; 23:8; Deut 16:9
[s]Gen 14:22, 23
[t]Acts 8:18–20
[u]Ps 15:5; Isa 33:15, 16; Jer 22:15, 16; Ezek 18:5–9
[v]Heb 11:24–26; Matt 19:29, 30

plunged whole families into misery by ruinous speculations![q] (Where the enriching blessing of God is not desired or asked for, we cannot wonder that it is withheld!)

But the man of God *hates* bribes[r] and would refuse them, or any other gift, that would bring dishonor to his God. Abraham refused the gifts of the king of Sodom[s] and Peter the bribes of Simon.[t] The man who walks in that kind of integrity, *lives* on high in the special favor of his God.[u] He, who *hates* this world's gifts for the affliction of the cross, "shall receive many times as much, and shall inherit eternal life."[v] "Let their money perish with them, that prefer all the world's wealth before one day's communion with Jesus Christ, and his despised people," said the Marquis of Vico, nephew of Paul V.[18]

28 *The heart of the righteous ponders how to answer,*
But the mouth of the wicked pours out evil things.

THINK TWICE BEFORE YOU SPEAK ONCE

[w]Eccl 10:2
[x]Prov 10:31, 32; 16:23
[y]1 Peter 3:15
[z]Verses 16, 23
[a]Ps 31:22; 116:11
[b]Josh 9:14, 15
[c]1 Sam 25:13–21
[d]Matt 16:22

Consideration is an important part of Christian character, and nowhere is it more important than in the discipline of the tongue. Think twice, before we speak once. "A wise man's *heart* directs him toward the right"[w] that he may weigh his words, and *ponder how to answer,*[x] and be "ready to make a defense to every one who asks [him] to give an account for the hope that is in [him]."[y] Though there may be "good treasure" within, yet we must carefully ponder to draw from it "a timely word."[z] Often we may rebuke ourselves for speaking hastily. And indeed when that which is uppermost comes out, nothing but the scum of evil can be looked for. Many have stumbled for having spoken from the impulse of the moment, from hot feelings, rather than from a well-balanced and considerate judgment.[a] In such haste, Joshua was beguiled by the Gibeonites;[b] David indulged a burst of murderous revenge;[c] Peter would gladly have persuaded his Master to turn from the work[d] which He came down from heaven to do and without which we should have been a world eternally lost. Cultivate a pondering mind. If you are ever asked to open an important subject, don't throw it off hastily, nor give an answer, till you have

[18] *See his interesting history in Dr. M'CRIE'S* Reformation in Spain.

obtained it from God. For *the heart's study to answer* necessarily implies prayer, the only way to receive the wisdom "that has the advantage of giving success."[e] Nehemiah darted up his prayer; and how graciously was *the answer* for the moment granted![f] This is especially a ministerial responsibility for the many cases of conscience, that require "the tongue of the wise"—a word of wisdom, conviction, or consolation. How can "the lips of a priest . . . preserve knowledge,"[g] unless *the heart* under his Master's teaching *ponders how to answer?*

The wicked has no such restraint. He cares not what he says. It means little to him whether it's true, or well-timed, or whom it wounds. His poisoned fountain *pours out* poisonous waters.[h] Yet how fearful it is to think of how every light word must be accounted for,[i] and will be found a "hot coal to make the fire of hell burn more fiercely," commented Cartwright. Such a plague often infests the church.[j] From such "constant friction withdraw yourself."[k] Separation is the keeping of the soul. soul.

[e] Prov 2:1–6; Eccl 10:10; James 1:5
[f] Neh 2:1–6
[g] Mal 2:7
[h] Eccl 10:3, 12–14
[i] Matt 12:36
[j] Titus 1:10, 11
[k] 1 Tim 6:5

29 *The LORD is far from the wicked,*
But He hears the prayer of the righteous.

See the difference the Lord makes between these two classes! He is equally near to them both in his essence.[l] But in his favor, *He is far from the wicked*[m] and rejects their prayer.[n] He is near to *the righteous and hears them.*[o] His distance from *the wicked* is to their hearts' desire.[p] Yet, He sometimes makes them groan,[q] as they will sink hereafter, under the everlasting curse[r] of their wickedness. But who can estimate the grace, that calls these "stubborn-minded, who are far from righteousness. I bring near My righteousness, it is not far off; and My salvation"?[s] The guilt of despising such abounding mercy[t] must be inexpressible.

But *to the righteous*—He is most graciously near.[u] *He* hears their breath, when there is no voice;[v] their desire and weeping, when there are no words;[w] their stammering, when there is no gift.[x] Wonderful indeed is it, that He should *hear such prayers,* polluted as they are in their very breath. Yet our compassionate High Priest waits for these vile offerings at the door of the holy of holies, and in His golden censer they appear spotless

[l] Jer 23:24; Acts 17:27, 28
[m] Ps 34:16; Jer 18:17; Amos 9:4
[n] Isa 1:11; Jer 14:12; Ezek 8:18
[o] Ps 34:15; 1 Peter 3:12
[p] Job 21:14
[q] Exod 33:1–7; 1 Sam 28:6; Hos 5:15; Mic 3:4
[r] Ps 73:27; Matt 25:41; 2 Thess 1:9
[s] Isa 46:12, 13
[t] Acts 13:38–46
[u] Ps 34:18; 145:18, 19
[v] Lam 3:56
[w] 1 Sam 1:13; Ps 38:9; 6:8
[x] Isa 38:14

[y]Rev 8:3, 4 before the throne.[y] For His sake we are not only borne with, but accepted. Our sighs are the breathings of faith, [z]Rom 8:26, 27 and His own Spirit has prompted our broken words.[z] So then ... how can He turn away from them?

Yet the enemy will suggest the doubt. Does God hear? How well the enemy knows what a shelter prayer is from his assault; and he does everything he can to keep us from it. "Am I righteous?" We hear the whisper—maybe [a]1 John 2:1 you aren't. But what about your advocate—isn't He?[a] Then put your prayer in His hands. You can't doubt *His* access to God; that His ear, if shut to you, is open to Him. [b]2 Kings 4:13 Do you want to be "spoken for to the king?"[b] Then, stammer out your prayer to your Friend—"O Lord, I am oppressed; undertake for me." Dr. Bates commented, "It would tire the hands of an angel to write down the pardons, that God bestows upon one penitent sinner."

"But I see no answer." Correct the errors of sense by faith in His word, which declares, whatever appearances may be—*He hears*. Don't judge by your feelings or conceptions, but by His own unchangeable Word, by the [c]Ps 65:2 manifestation of His name.[c] You can be sure that He will refuse you nothing that is really good; that you receive, if not what you desire, yet what, upon the whole, is best and most fitting for you. Have patience with God. Dictate nothing. Commit your will to Him. Say not—"I want you [d]Mark 6:25 to give me right away."[d] Leave time and all to Him. If He doesn't answer in your time, He will in His own, which is [e]Isa 30:18 far better.[e] He has clearly shown His sovereign appointment, that those who pray must wait His time and His [f]Luke 18:1–7 will.[f]

Yet, let us look out and see how our prayers speed. The husbandman looks for his harvest. And when we have sown in a fruitful soil—in the very heart of God—shouldn't we look for the return, wait in hope, strengthen our heart in God's promises, and never cease looking up, till the answer comes down? No prayer will be without God's fruit.

Study the character of God, not as the judge on his bench; or the king on his throne of state; but as the Father in the full flowing of His love. In the sharpest trial, not all the world, not all the power of hell, can bar your access to Him. No child runs to his father with such confidence as yours. God will never disappoint the child of His, who fully throws himself upon His love.

Then honor Him in this confidence. Show that you really mean what you say. Don't just bring general petitions but definite requests. Tell Him *what* you want and *all* you want. Show that prayer is no penance, or irksome endurance, but a pleading exercise; a conscious reality, a living soul speaking to a living God. Prize His presence above all else—the pleasures of prayer above all other privileges. No creature, not even an apostle, could compensate for the loss of His presence. *Wrestle* in prayer, but *sit still* in faith. He has bound himself by His own promises. And the fulfillment of them in answer to prayer will quicken confidence and praise.

30 *Bright* [AV—*light of the*] *eyes gladden the heart;*
Good news puts fat on the bones.

The eye is the medium of the greatest enjoyment. Most thrilling is the sight of the wonders of the creation![g] The Psalmist's hymns of praise finely portray his delight.[h] Glowing was the joy, which burst from Solomon's heart in the sight of the morning glory—"The light is pleasant, and *it is* good for the eyes to see the sun."[i] Look also at his gracious and unexpected provision—how bright were the aged Patriarch's eyes and *his heart gladdened,* when he embraced his long-lost son! In the cloud of despondency, it was truly sunshine! And when the eye fastens upon the one subject of attraction, even one look casts a glory on the soul and fills it with life and joy.[j] "They looked to Him and were radiant."[k] And what will it be, when the whole soul, made alive with divine power, shall center in the eye; when *bright eyes* shall see Him with an unclouded view, whom all heaven adores with everlasting praise!

But let's look at the joy of hearing. How the patriarch's heart bounded at *the good news* of his beloved Joseph![l] The absent minister seems to live again in *the good news* of his thriving people.[m] "How delightful it must be to the humbled sinner to hear the *good report* of salvation, and to have *his eyes* enlightened to behold the glory of God in the face of Jesus Christ!" said Scott. The delight, with which the shepherds saw the *good news* realized before

[g] Ps 19:1; 111:2
[h] Ps 108; 104
[i] Eccl 11:7
[j] Gen 46:29, 30; Prov 13:12
[k] Ps 34:5
[l] Gen 45:27, 28; Prov 25:25
[m] 1 Thess 3:8

[n]Luke 2:15–17
[o]Isa 52:7
[p]Ps 89:15

their eyes, can hardly be imagined.[n] It is still so joyful to the humbled sinner that the very "feet of him who brings good news" are lovely in his eyes.[o] "Blessed are the people who know the joyful sound!"[p]

31 *He whose ear listens to the life-giving reproof,*
Will dwell among the wise.
32 *He who neglects discipline despises himself,*
But he who listens to reproof acquires
understanding.

[q]Verse 12
[r]Prov 6:23
[s]Verse 5; 12:18; Ps 141:5
[t]Lev 19:17, 18

What a contrast to the "scoffer" earlier described, who does "not go to the wise"![q] By nature we are unteachable, neither knowing, nor caring to know. But the Lord gives humility and self-knowledge. Our unteachableness yields. Light pours in. We learn the meaning of words once familiar to us only in sound. The purified *ear* now *listens to the* reproof that tends to *life*[r] and welcomes the medicine.[s] This exercise of *reproof* is the law of social life; part of the love of our neighbor;[t] the solemn obligation to be "our brother's keeper" to the utmost of our power.[19] The way we receive reproof is a test of principle. Humility, sincerity, self-knowledge—the exercise or the defect of these graces—is brought out to our honor or dishonor. Beautiful indeed is the sight of "a wise reprover to a listening ear."[u] The man of God *lived with the wise.* He took his meek reprover to be his wife.[v] He honored the faithful messenger of his Father's rod with his highest confidence. The apostle's affectionate testimony to his reproving brother showed that he had *listened to the reproof* of life.[w] This considerate and humble disposition always *acquires understanding.*[x] Nothing teaches like experience; and no experience is more useful, because none is so abasing, as rebuke.[y]

[u]Prov 25:12
[v]1 Sam 25:39–42
[w]2 Sam 12:7–12; 1 Kings 1:32. Comp. Prov 28:23
[x]Gal 2:11, with 2 Peter 3:15
[y]Prov 1:5; 9:9; 12:1

Reproof indeed may be considered one of the wholesome bitter experiences of life.[z] Thoughtless merrymaking may prefer "the song of fools" to "the rebuke of a wise man."[a] But afterthought will show the wisdom of honoring those, who deal faithfully with our faults, even with severity; rather than those, who would soothe us with the poisoned sweets of flattery and wink at or encourage our waywardness.[b] Unhappily, however, many a man lacks sincerity and has no real desire to be corrected.

[z]Prov 29:15; Rev 3:19
[a]Comp. Eccl 7:5
[b]Prov 27:5, 6

[19] *This obligation was repudiated by the first murderer, Gen 4:9.*

He makes a hollow truce with his conscience just because it disturbs him. By throwing a protective cover over all his faults, he shields his most dangerous enemies. In this unfavorable state of mind, *he neglects discipline* because it is contrary to flattery and *despises himself.*[c] Many are the examples of this ruinous folly.[20] The fool will not admit to the charge. But doesn't he underrate its high value and imminent danger when he despises God's warning and provision for its salvation?[d] "Be warned, O Jerusalem, lest I be alienated from you."[e]

[c]Verse 10
[d]Matt 16:26
[e]Jer 6:8; Zeph 3:2

33 *The fear of the* LORD *is the instruction for wisdom,*
And before honor comes *humility.*

The fear of the Lord is elsewhere described as the substance[f] and the beginning or principal part[g] of wisdom. Here it's set forth as *the instruction of wisdom.* The teachers, inspired by divine *wisdom,* made it a grand subject of their instruction.[21] Nor is it less important in this the new dispensation, linked as it is with the full privileges of the gospel.[h] The fear of terror melts away. A reverential fear fills the soul. God rejoices in His mercy; the child of God in His confidence. But as wisdom realizes the presence of a holy God, it must always be connected with *humility.* Indeed, no Christian grace can exist without this preserving principle. Every dispensation of God strikes at the root of self-exaltation and leads to that real absence of self-esteem and self-sufficiency, which most of us long after rather than attain.

[f]Job 28:28
[g]Prov 1:7; 9:10; Ps 111:10
[h]Acts 9:31; Heb 12:28

Most wise, therefore, is our Father's discipline—*humility before honor.* Indeed, without *humility, honor* would be our temptation, rather than our glory. If the apostle had not been kept down by a most humbling trial, his *honor* would have been his ruin.[i] Often, then, the exaltation of the Lord's people in God's providence often leads through the valley of *humiliation.* Joseph was raised from the prison to the throne.[j] Moses and David were taken from the sheepfold to feed the Lord's sheep.[k] Gideon acknowledged himself to be of the least "of the families of Israel.[l] Ruth was humbled by adversity before she was raised to the high honor of a mother in Israel and

[i]2 Cor 12:7–9
[j]Gen 41:14–44
[k]Exod 3:1–12; Ps 78:70–72
[l]Judg 6:15, 16

[20] *The young man—Prov 5:11–13; Korah and his party—Num 16:12–14, 31–33; Zedekiah—Jer 27:17; 38:14–23, with 39:1–7.*
[21] *Moses—Deut 10:12; Josh—24:14; Samuel—1 Sam 12:14, 20, 24; David—Ps 34:9–11; Solomon—Eccl 12:13.*

[m]Ruth 2; 4:13–22; Matt 1:5

[n]1 Sam 25:41, 42

[o]Luke 14:7–11

progenitor of the Savior.[m] Abigail confessed herself unworthy to wash the feet of her lord's servants before she was honored to be his wife.[n] And in the daily walk of life, the humble place is the pathway to *honor*.[o]

[p]Luke 18:14; 1 Peter 5:6

The same principle holds true in the dispensation of grace. "He who humbles himself shall be exalted"—in due time.[p] And that doesn't mean that, in the forgetfulness of our high privileges and confidence, we are to be weighed down by a sense of degradation. The true humility, which realizes our sinfulness, casts us most simply upon the full resources of the gospel, so that the most humble believer is most triumphant. "The lower then any *descend* in humiliation, the higher they shall *ascend* in exaltation. The lower this foundation of humility is laid, the higher shall the roof of honour be overlaid," said Trapp.[22]

[q]Ps 22:6

[r]Phil 2:9

[s]Matt 11:29; 20:28; John 13:14

And wasn't this the track of our beloved Lord—before *honor and humility*—the cross before the crown? How deep was that descent, by which He, who was infinitely more than man, became "a worm, and not a man"![q] And yet, what tongue can tell *the honor* which rewarded this *humility!*[r] "We must not disdain to follow Jesus Christ," said Cope. Is it a light privilege to follow in the pathway consecrated by His steps, brightened by His smile?[s]

[22] *The more humble I am, the more fit I am to come to God, and the more willing He is to come into the soul, and dwell in it. The highest heavens are the dwelling place of God's glory; and the humber heart has the next highest honor, to be the habitation of His grace—paraphrase of LEIGHTON.*

CHAPTER SIXTEEN

1 *The plans of the heart belongs to man* [*AV—the preparations of the heart in man . . . is from the* LORD],
But the answer of the tongue is from the LORD.

The grand question "Who is the first mover in the work of conversion?" is answered here. "Can man prepare his own heart for the grace of God?" *The preparations of the heart in man are from the Lord.*[1] He takes the stone out of the heart, that it may feel;[a] draws it, that it may *follow;* quickens it, that it may *live.* He opens the heart that He may imprint His own law on it and mold it into His image.[b] He works, not merely by moral persuasion, or by the bare proposal of means of uncertain power; but by the invisible almighty agency. The work then begins with God. It is not that we first come and then are taught. But first we learn; then we come.[c] His grace prevents and also cooperates; not working upon a stone and leaving it dead, but, as He did in Paradise, He breathed into the lifeless earth a principle of life and energy.[d]

Shall we then just idly wait until He works? Far from it. We must work, but in dependence upon Him. He doesn't work without us. He works through us, in us, by us; and we work in Him.[e] Ours is the duty; His is the strength. Ours the agency; His the quickening life. His commands do not imply our power to obey, but they do imply our dependence upon Him for the grace of obedience. The work, as a duty, is ours; but as a performance, it is God's. He gives what He requires, and His promises are the foundation of our performances. Our works are not the cause of His grace, but the effect; they could

[a]Ezek 36:26
[b]Acts 16:14; Jer 31:33
[c]John 6:45
[d]Gen 2:7
[e]Phil 2:13; Job 11:13

[1] *Ps 10:17. "From whom all holy desires, all good counsels, and just works do proceed"—Liturgy.*

never have come out of us, until God had first put them in us.

The fruit also, as well as the root—*the answer of the tongue,* no less than *the preparation of the heart—is from the Lord.* The tongue of the ungodly is under God's restraint.[f] And when the Christian's thoughts are marshaled in due order, doesn't he depend upon the Lord for uttermost?[g] Often in prayer, the more we speak, the more we leave unspoken, till *the answer of the tongue* is fully given, "crying, 'Abba! Father!' "[h] But the fluency of the tongue without the preparation of the heart; when prayer is without special business; when we read the precious promises, and don't carry a word from them to plead before the throne—this is man's dead formality. It's not *from the Lord;* it's an abomination in His sight.

[f] Num 22:18
[g] Eph 6:19
[h] Gal 4:6

This habit of dependence must continue to the end. We can no more prepare ourselves *after* grace received, than *before* it.[2] He who is "the author," must be "the perfecter of faith."[i] He is "Alpha and the Omega," the beginning and the end,[j] in this almighty work. Our happiness and prosperity is in the humbling acknowledgment of praise—"By the grace of God I am what I am."[k] Dependence is not the excuse for laziness but the spring of active energy.

[i] Heb 12:2
[j] Rev 1:8
[k] 1 Cor 15:10

And if man's reason disputes, "If God does not give me grace, how can I come?"—we ask, did you ever desire, did you ever ask for, grace? If not, how can you complain that you have never received it? If helplessness is really felt, if it brings conviction, grace is ready to be given. "Ask, and it shall be given to you."[l]

[l] Matt 7:7

2 *All the ways of a man are clean in his own sight,*
But the L*ORD* *weighs the motives.*

If man were his own judge, who would be condemned? But man judges by acts; God by principles. His eye therefore beholds a mass of corruption; while *all the ways of a man are clean in his own eyes.*[m] In fact—man will never believe his real character, until the looking glass is held to his face with convincing light,[n] or some subtle temptation makes the hateful discovery. He confesses himself indeed to be a sinner. But he has no idea

[m] Gen 6:5; Ps 14:3
[n] Rom 7:9

[2] *Isa 26:12; 2 Cor 3:5; "I beg," said Jerome, "that I may receive; and when I have received, I beg again."*

what his sins are! He believes they are probably only minor and abundantly balanced out by his fanciful virtues. "You are those," said our Lord to men of this character, "who justify yourselves in the sight of men, but God knows your hearts; for that which is highly esteemed among men is detestable in the sight of God."[o] [o]Luke 16:15

Sometimes we see this delusion under the most shadowy cover: Pilate washed his hands from the blood of his condemned victim and was *clean in his own eyes*.[p] [p]Matt 27:24 The murderers of Christ were clean, by avoiding the defilement of the judgment hall and by eating the passover.[q] [q]John 18:28

The persecutors of the church blinded their consciences in the sincerity of unbelief.[r] [r]Acts 26:9 Often the self-deceiver has passed into eternity, professing to be saved. But how does he stand before God? He never acted from principle. He had the form and appearance of a Christian, so true-to-life as to pass for a living man. But the eyes that are as a flame of fire, bare witness—"You have a name that you are alive, and you are dead."[s] [s]Rev 3:2

External form without a sanctified heart is baseless. Our real worth is what we are in the sight of God. He weighs, not only the "actions,"[t] [t]1 Sam 2:3; 16:7 but *the motives* also. His eye can spot one missing grain and pronounces the sentence. Saul was thus "weighed on the scales and found deficient."[u] [u]1 Sam 15:11; Dan 5:27 And "if Thou, Lord, shouldst mark iniquities"—the shortcomings of your full and righteous demands—"O Lord, who could stand?"[v] [v]Ps 130:3; 143:2 Must we not fly from Omniscience to satisfied justice, and there find, that "there is forgiveness with Thee"?[w] [w]Gal 3:10, 13, with Ps 130:4 Joyous, indeed, is it to note the even balances of our Judge; in one scale, His own perfect law; in the other, His Son's perfect obedience. Here, O my God, is my peace, my security. "Thou, most upright, dost *weigh* the path of the just."[x] [x]AV—Isa 26:7 But oh! place the blood of your beloved Son even in the scale of your justice; and we will render to you the glory of your wondrous work of grace.

3 *Commit your works to the* L*ORD*,
And your plans [AV—*thoughts*] *will be established.*

An unsettled mind is a serious evil—a canker to Christian peace. Every faculty is thrown into disorder. The memory is confused, the judgment undecided, the will unsteady. No moral rules can bring order out of such chaos. Faith is the only principle of solid *establishment.*[y] That is where our original happiness and security rested. But independence destroyed our well-being.[z] The return to this humble simplicity is the privilege of the gospel: "In all your ways acknowledge Him"[a]—is the rule of peace. Eliezer's *thoughts were established in committing his work to the Lord.*[b] This confidence kept our beloved Lord unmovable in His great work.[c] Prayer was the exercise of His faith. *Establishment* was the issue.[d] Has the fretting spirit ever tried this true remedy? Actively join the two hands of faith and prayer in turning our burdens over to our Father. To have a sanctuary to flee to—a God, on whom to roll our cares;[e] to lean to His wisdom and rest on His faithfulness—here is a chamber of quietness in the most distracting anxieties—"So He gives to His beloved *even in his* sleep."[f]

[y]Ps 112:7; Isa 26:3
[z]Gen 3:5
[a]Prov 3:6
[b]Gen 24
[c]Isa 49:4; 1:7–9
[d]John 17:4
[e]Ps 37:5
[f]Ps 127:2

Commit then all your works to Him. Look to Him for strength and guidance in all. Look to Him for success in all. Roll on Him the great *work* of your soul's salvation. Be satisfied with His management of your concerns. Put your works, as you would put your children, with confidence, into the hands of God. Christian self-possession will be the result. Let your heart habitually turn to the throne of grace; so that in a crisis of trouble instant faith, instant—perhaps speechless[g]—prayer, may bring instant composure and courage. This active energy of faith will enable us to collect *our thoughts, establish them* in the peace of God and keep our souls in fortified security.[h] Indeed a great part of our worship is to *commit our works to Him* "free from concern," not in a general dependence on His goodness or wisdom, but in a particular dependence for our special need. The burden being now cast upon one who is better able to bear it,[i] the mind is easy, the thoughts composed, quietly waiting the outcome of things; knowing that all, that is for our good, and the glory of our God, shall be brought to pass.[j] Thus "we who have believed enter that rest."[k] But "if we will not believe"—so speaks the solemn warning—"surely [we] shall not last."[3]

[g]Neh 2:4
[h]Phil 4:6, 7
[i]1 Cor 7:32; 1 Peter 5:7
[j]Ps 112:7
[k]Heb 4:3

[3] *2 Chron 20:26; Isa 7:7–9. To paraphrase Knox,—Nothing can be more erroneous than for those who fear God, to suppose themselves as liable as ever to the changes and chances of*

4 *The* LORD *has made everything for its own purpose, Even the wicked for the day of evil.*

Every workman has some purpose for his work. God's purposes are the highest. As the apostle Paul reasons concerning the oath of God—because "he could swear by no one greater, He swore by Himself";[l] so here—because he could propose no higher end, he proposed Himself. Indeed, it is His exclusive right, that, since He has been "the beginning,"[m] so He should be the end of all His works.[4] The Lord hath created all things—all the works of the creation—all the events of nations—all the dispensations of Providence—*for Himself;* not to fill up a vacuum (for what vacuum could there be to the fountain of sufficiency?); but for the display of His glory to His intelligent creatures.[n] It cannot be doubted, but that from His tremendous power and wisdom, from His loving and diffusive goodness He displayed, an unlimited weight of glory is reflected upon the great source of all these perfections. "Let the Lord be glad in His works"[o] with inexpressible delight and satisfaction. And so, all things return to that boundless ocean, from which they originally came. Even *the wicked,* whose existence might seem scarcely inconsistent with God's perfections. He *includes* in the grand purpose of exalting His Name. "It is the greatest praise of His wisdom, that He can turn the evil of men to His own glory!" said Bishop Hall.[p] *He has made even the wicked for the day of evil*—but He didn't *make* them wicked[q]—they made themselves *wicked.* He compels them not to be wicked.[r] He abhors their wickedness. But He foresaw their evil. He permitted it; and though God said "I take no pleasure in the death of the wicked,"[s] He will be glorified in them *in the day of evil;*[t]

[l]Heb 6:13
[m]Col 1:18; Rev 3:14
[n]Isa 43:21; 60:21
[o]Ps 104:31
[p]Comp. Exod 14:17
[q]Gen 1:27; Eccl 7:29
[r]John 3:19
[s]Ezek 33:11
[t]Job 21:30; 2 Peter 2:9

this mortal life. They may experience change, yes—if God sees it's for good—but the true Christian, fully trusting His Lord, is forever done with chance. Having once cordially committed himself to God's Fatherly care, he can meet nothing in life, which is not the result of God's adjustment, or His wisdom, which cannot make a mistake; of His love, with which even the tenderness of the tenderest parent cannot compare. With our lives under His incomparable care and management, what can we fear? It's for us, through His grace, to keep ourselves within the circle where these movements are carried on. Then we need not doubt, that, though we see nothing remarkable in our course, an unseen hand is directing every circumstance, in the most effectual manner, to keep from us what might hurt us, to make sure we have what will benefit us, and to direct all our concerns to the best possible outcome—ALEXANDER KNOX'S Remains, *vol. ii. "Divine Providence"—a work full of instructive thought, but deeply tinctured with unsound principles.*

[4] *Isa 43:7; 48:11, 12; Rom 11:36; Rev 4:10, 11. See President Edwards's profound and interesting reasoning—"God's chief end in Creation" Chap. 1. Works i. Could there be a clearer demonstration of the deity of Christ, than the representation of Him as the great end of creation—"All things have been created through Him and for Him"?—Col 1:16.*

and when they sin by their own free will, He ordains them to punishment, as the memorials of His power, justice, and long-suffering.[u]

[u] Rom 9:17, 22

Clearly God is not the author of sin. He can't give away what He doesn't have—what is contrary to His nature. Perfection cannot produce imperfection. Absolute holiness cannot be the cause of sin; though, like the law,[v] it may be the innocent occasion or excitement of it. What he foreknows—as Edwards profoundly observes, "proves the necessity of the event foreknown; yet it may not be the thing, which causes the necessity."[5] He can decree nothing but good. If He permits evil, so far as not to hinder it, He hates it as evil and permits it only for the greater good—the greatest of all good—the more full manifestation of His own glory in it and out of it. He will be glorified in, or on, all His creatures. "All Thy works shall give thanks to Thee, O Lord!"[w] His retributive justice, no less than the riches of his grace, reveals His glory.[x] It would seem as if the redeemed are permitted to see this and to participate with God's satisfaction. The flames of hell excite the reverential praises of heaven—"And a second time they said, 'Hallelujah! Her smoke rises up forever and ever.' "[6]

[v] Rom 7:5, 8, 11–13; 1 Cor 15:56

[w] Ps 145:10

[x] Rom 9:22, 23

5 *Everyone who is proud in heart is an abomination to*
the LORD;
Assuredly, [*AV—though hand join in hand*] *he will*
not be unpunished.

The hatefulness of a proud look has been mentioned.[y] But the searcher of hearts sees *the proud of heart* under a humble look.[z] Men see no *hatred* in this spirit. It brings no disgrace. Instead, it is often thought to be high-minded. But it keeps back the heart from God. It lifts up the heart against Him. It contends for supremacy with Him.[a] So . . . when it strikes at God, what wonder that God strikes at it,[b] as *a hateful abomination to Himself?*

[y] Prov 6:17

[z] Matt 6:16

[a] Ezek 28:2

[b] 1 Peter 5:5

In addition, how unbecoming such sin really is! A creature so utterly dependent, so fearfully guilty, yet *proud*

[5] Treatise on Will, *Part 2: Sect. 12. See also Doddridge's valuable note on Luke 22:22.*

[6] *Rev 19:3. "God made man neither to save nor damn him, but for His own glory. That is secured, whether in man's salvation or damnation (See 2 Cor 2:15). God never did, and does not now, make man wicked. He made man upright. Man* makes himself *wicked; and because man is wicked, God may justly appoint him to damnation for his wickedness; in doing which He glorifies His justice"—GILL.*

in heart! A true child of a fallen parent, who, in dreaming to be as God, made himself like the devil.[c] Many are the forms of this hateful spirit. Some are *proud* of their beauty; some of their talents; some of their rank; some of their goodness—all forgetting, that "what do you have that you did not receive?"[d] all unconscious, that these attitudes of the heart are *an abomination to the Lord.*

[c]Gen 3:5
[d]1 Cor 4:7

Perhaps, however, this declaration applies more distinctly to *proud* combinations against God—*hand joining in hand.*[e] What is all this force, but the worm striving with his Maker?[f] "Who is the Lord?"—was the boast of haughty Pharaoh. Let him and his people go to the Red Sea and learn.[g] *Hand joining in hand* shall *not* be held innocent—shall *not go unpunished.* The Babel combination was blasted with confusion.[h] The associations against the holy child Jesus were "broken" in pieces.[i] The ungodly conspiracies of Voltaire and his school have been overthrown. And thus in our own day, will all banding together for wickedness, only manifest more gloriously—"There is no wisdom and no understanding and no counsel against the Lord."[j]

[e]Prov 11:21; Ps 59:3; 12, 13
[f]Isa 45:9
[g]Exod 5:2; 14:26–30
[h]Gen 11:1–9
[i]Isa 8:9; Ps 2:1–5
[j]Prov 21:30

6 *By lovingkindness* [AV—*mercy*] *and truth iniquity is atoned for,*
And by the fear of the LORD *one keeps away from evil.*

The true exposition of this verse requires much care and consideration. We protest against that false principle of theology which substitutes the grand doctrine of the gospel in the place of its practical statements. The cleansing of sin seems here however to direct us to atonement.[7] Therefore to connect it with man's *lovingkindness and truth* is to overturn the foundation of the gospel. These are duties to be performed;[k] not atonement for sin: and often are they performed by men devoid of the grace of God, whose *sin therefore is not atoned for.* They may indeed, in the government of God, be available for avoiding national judgments.[l] But there's a vast difference between simply keeping things peaceful and the actual cleansing of sin. On the other hand—considering that God's *lovingkindness and truth* are frequently shown in

[k]Prov 3:3
[l]Dan 4:27

[7] *It is the ordinary sacrificial term. Exod 30:10; Lev 4:20; 5:6; 16:6; Dan 9:24. Also Ps 65:3.*

[m]Exod 34:6; Ps 57:3; 86:15; Mic 7:18–20; John 1:17. Comp. Prov 14:22
[n]Ps 85:10
[o]Comp. Ps 89:2, 3, 14; Ps 117:1
[p]Prov 8:9

connection with this invaluable blessing;[m] the analogy of faith appears to link it here with these combined perfections, "which kiss in Christ the Mediator,[n] and with that covenant of grace, in which they shine so brightly," said Henry.[o] This view may seem to some to depart from the general purposes of this book, which deals more with practical points and matters of common life, than with the deeper articles of faith. But it should be noted, that, when some of its pages are so fully illuminated by evangelical sunshine,[p] we might naturally expect—besides this connected splendor—occasional rays of doctrinal light to shine upon this system of Christian morals.

[q]Isa 53:6; 2 Cor 5:21
[r]Rom 8:32
[s]Rom 3:26
[t]1 Kings 7:21
[u]Rom 7:14–25; 8:1

Taking, therefore, in accordance with most of our best critics and soundest expositors, this ground of interpretation—we see the great controversy between God and man. Man tries to get rid of his sin by repentance or external ceremonials. God determines it by *sacrifice;* not by negating the authority of His law through a simple act of *mercy*; but by meeting the requirements of His law on the basis of the *substitutionary atonement* His mercy provided.[q] No show of *mercy* can be conceived in force and emphasis to compare with that awful moment when God "did not spare His own Son,"[r] but permitted blameless love and purity to agonize on the cross. And yet, this wondrous display of *mercy* was a display of *truth* no less wondrous; since it was the means, by which inflexible justice could justify the guilty.[s] So gloriously do these two attributes harmonize! We don't ask to which we owe the deepest obligation. *Mercy* promises, *truth* fulfills the promises. *Mercy* provides, *truth* accepts—the ransom. Both mercy and truth sat together in the eternal councils of God. They came into the world together. Both, like the two pillars of the temple,[t] combine to support the Christian's confidence; that, though there is abundant cause for condemnation even in the holiest saint; actual condemnation there is not—and cannot be.[u]

[v]Ps 130:4. Comp. Jer 32:40
[w]Prov 3:7; 8:13; 14:16, 27

But if in the first clause of the verse we see how the guilt of *sin is totally removed,* the second clause shows, how its *power is broken.* The very exercise of forgiveness is to implant a preserving principle.[v] *By the fear of the Lord, men keep away from evil.*[w] To suppose that a sinner who does not repent of his sins can be pardoned would be to unite the two contrary principles of reconciliation and enmity. We are not cleansed from our sins that we should go back and wallow in them again.[x] The beam of light, which burns away every record of condemnation, is convincing, sanctifying, healing to the soul. Indeed God shows the deepest hatred of sin in the very act of the atonement He made for it through the death of His Son. Yet the implanted principle of obedience is no legal bondage. *The fear of the Lord* is at once a bridle to sin and a spur to holiness. It changes the slave into a child. And the trust of a child for his father is like a sevenfold shield from sin. Sin's very touch is hateful, and all its ways are abhorred and forsaken.

[x]Luke 1:74, 75. Comp. Rom 6:1; 2 Cor 7:1

7 *When a man's ways are pleasing to the* L*ORD*,
He makes even his enemies to be at peace with him.

Often the man of God enjoys the favor of both God and man.[y] Yes, he will always have *his enemies,* if from no other source, they "will be the members of his household."[z] To seek *peace with them* by compromising his principles would be to forfeit his character at a dreadful cost. Let him hold fast his principles in the face of *his enemies*. "Though they mean him no good, they shall do him no harm," said Bishop Sanderson (sermon on text).

How then do we explain the persecution of the saints,[a] of Him especially, whose *ways always pleased the Lord?*[b] Each statement limits the other. The one shows the native enmity of the heart: the other its divine restraint. It shall be let loose, so far as is for the glory of God. Beyond this, it shall be restrained.[c] His church had her season of rest.[d] He has all tongues, all hands, all hearts, under His power. When a man walks with God, why should he fear man?[e]

"The best way for *our enemies* to be reconciled to us, is for us to be reconciled to God," said Bishop Patrick. All our danger lies in His wrath, not in their anger. No creature can touch us without His permission.[f] Laban followed Jacob as *an enemy* but was constrained to be *at peace with him.*[g] Esau when about to execute his long-planned threat was melted down into brotherly endearment.[h] Israel's lands were preserved from invasion, while they were engaged in the service of God.[i] The

[y]Prov 3:3, 4; Rom 14:18
[z]Matt 10:36
[a]2 Tim 3:12
[b]John 8:29, 37
[c]Ps 76:10
[d]Acts 9:31
[e]Rom 8:31
[f]See Job 1:9–12; Ps 105:13–15
[g]Gen 31:24
[h]Gen 27:41; 32:1–4
[i]Exod 34:23, 24

enemies of the godly kings were chained and bowed before them.[j] Often has the majesty of the godly brow commanded the reverence of the wicked and even bound up their hands.[8] And such will be the ultimate victory of the church over all opposition.[k]

[j] 1 Kings 4:21–25; 10:23–29; 2 Chron 17:10

[k] Rev 3:9

But even if *the enemies* are let loose; yet if their harm is overruled to larger good, isn't the promise substantially fulfilled? No wise man will sue with breach of promise, because he promises a hundred dollars and gives a thousand instead." Or who can truly say, that that man is not so good as his word, that is apparently much better than his word?" said Bishop Sanderson. God will take care of His people. Peace or war shall turn to their everlasting good.[l]

[l] Rom 8:28; Phil 1:12–19

8 *Better is a little righteousness*
Than great income with injustice.

We have already had this Proverb in substance;[m] except that the treasures are more distinctly shown to be *income with injustice.* It seems almost too plain to need illustration. Yet so blind is the love of gain, that it looks only at its own selfish end, and the present moment; and fancies, what never can be enjoyment[n] and security.[o] Merited justice is at hand.[p] Far *better is the little with righteousness.* Wasn't the widow of Zarephath richer with her scanty fare than Jezebel in her royal attire;[q] the poor prophet, sharing her pittance, than the king with his *great income with injustice;*[r] Zaccheus, when reduced to his comparative *little with righteousness,* than with his former abundance of the unrighteous?[s] If the sight of a man's possession arouse envy, his scantiness of enjoyment might shortly melt it away in compassion. We learn the valuable lesson—the fewer desires, the more peace. This is what we see now. But soon the day will declare it much more clearly. The *little, righteously* used, will then find a gracious acceptance.[t] The treasures of wickedness will be found treasures of wrath eternal.[u]

[m] Prov 15:16

[n] Ps 127:2; Eccl 5:12
[o] Prov 10:3; 21:6, 7; Jer 17:11
[p] James 5:4

[q] 1 Kings 17:10; 2 Kings 9:32–37

[r] 1 Kings 21:19; with 17:15

[s] Luke 19:2, 8

[t] Matt 25:34–40; Luke 16:9
[u] Hab 2:6, 9, 12; James 5:1–3

Few however possess *great income.* But the most trifling gains *without right* will canker. Beware of the hairbreadth deviation from straight principle. Be dead to immorality which "amounts to idolatry"[v] against God

[v] Col 3:5

[8] *David—1 Sam 24:17; Daniel and his fellow-captives—1 Sam 1:6–21; 3:26–30; 6:24–28; John the Baptist—Mark 6:20; Paul—Acts 27:43.*

and "the root of all sorts of evil" to ourselves.[w] Godliness is great riches in this life; what will it be in eternity![x]

[w] 1 Tim 6:10
[x] 1 Tim 5:6; 4:8

9 *The mind of man plans his way,*
But the LORD *directs his steps.*

A fine description of the sovereign government of God! Inscrutable indeed is the mystery, how He accomplishes his fixed purpose by freewilled agents. Man without his free will is a robot. God without his unchangeable purpose ceases to be God.[y] As rational agents we think, consult, act freely. Upon us, as dependent agents, the Lord exercises His own power in permitting, overruling, or furthering our acts.[z] Thus man proposes; God disposes. *Man plans; the Lord directs.* He orders our will without infringing on our liberty or disturbing our responsibility. For while we act as we please, we must be answerable.

[y] Mal 3:6
[z] Prov 19:21; 21:30; Ps 33:2; Isa 46:10; Lam 3:37

We observe this supremacy, in *directing,* not only an important end, but every step toward it; not only the great events, but every turn;[9] not only in His own people,[a] but in every child of man.[b] How little did Joseph's brethren contemplate the overruling direction to their evil schemes![c] When Saul's *heart was planning* "threats and murder against the disciples of the Lord";[d] when the renegade slave was running in his own path in the Epistle to Philemon, little did they think of that gracious *direction of their steps,* to the salvation of their souls. When David simply went at his father's bidding, little did he know the grand crisis to which *the Lord was directing his steps.*[e] And little did the captive girl guess what weighty results would come from her banishment from her country.[f] Often also the path of the Lord's people has been encouraged by the counteracting of their enemies' *planning,* and the backward *direction of their steps,* at the moment when they were ready to grasp their prey![g] In fact, as Bishop Hall remarks, "Every creature walks blindfold. Only he that dwells in light sees [where he goes]."[h]

[a] Ps 37:23
[b] Prov 20:24; Jer 10:23
[c] Gen 37:26–28; 45:5
[d] Acts 9:1–6
[e] 1 Sam 17:17, 18, 23, 58
[f] 2 Kings 5:2, 3
[g] 1 Sam 23:27; Isa 37:7, 8
[h] 2 Kings 5:2, 3

This doctrine of Providence is not like the doctrine of the Trinity—to be received by faith. Experience gives a demonstrable stamp of evidence—even in all the minutiae of circumstances which form the parts and

[9] *What vast results hung upon the sleepless night of the Eastern autocrat, Esther 6:1.*

pieces of God's plan. A matter of common business;[i] the indulgence of curiosity;[j] the supply of necessary want;[k] a journey from home[l]—all are connected with infinitely important results. And often, when our purpose seemed as clearly fixed, and as sure of accomplishment, as a journey to the city, this *way of our own planning* has been blocked by unexpected difficulties, and unexpected facilities have opened an opposite way, with the ultimate acknowledgment—"He led . . . also by a straight way."[m] God's control of the apostle's movements, apparently thwarting their present usefulness, turned out rather to the furtherance of the gospel. Philip was transferred from an important sphere in Samaria from preaching to thousands into a desert. But the Ethiopian Eunuch was his noble convert, and through him the gospel was doubtless widely circulated.[n] Paul was turned aside from a wide field of labor to a more restricted ministry. A few women and a family were his only church. Yet how did these small beginnings issue in the planting of flourishing churches![o] After all, however, we need much discipline to wean us from our own plans that we may seek the Lord's direction *in the first place*. The fruit of this discipline will be a dread of being left to our own devices; as before we were eager to follow them.[p] So truly do we find our happiness and security in yielding up our will to our heavenly guide! He knows the whole way—every step of the way—the end from the beginning. And never shall we miss either the way or the end, if only we resign ourselves with unreserved confidence to his keeping and *direction of our steps*.

[i] 1 Sam 9:3, 15, 16
[j] Luke 19:4, 6, 9
[k] John 4:7
[l] Acts 16:14
[m] Ps 107:7; Isa 42:16
[n] Acts 8:37–39
[o] Acts 16:6–15, 34, with Phil 1:1; 1 Thess 1:1
[p] Ps 143:10

10 *A divine decision is in the lips of the king;*
His mouth should not err in judgment.

11 *A just balance and scales belong to the* L*ORD;*
All the weights of the bag are His concern.

12 *It is an abomination for kings to commit wickedness,*
For a throne is established on righteousness.

13 *Righteous lips are the delight of kings,*
And he who speaks right is loved.

Here is a manual for kings; showing, not what they are, but what God requires them to be, that they may be a blessing to their people and benefactors to the world.[q] If this standard is neglected, the wisely arranged ordinance fails in its objective. "A man has exercised authority over *another* to his hurt";[r] and ruler and people may each become a curse to the other.[s]

[q] 2 Sam 23:3, 4
[r] Eccl 8:9
[s] Judg 9:20

The king is not indeed wiser by birth than his subjects; but he is under stronger obligations to seek wisdom.[t] And when God's law is his law, *a divine decision is in his lips.* Such was the wisdom of Solomon, when in a delicate and difficult cause *his mouth did not err in judgment.*[u]

[t] Prov 25:2; 1 Kings 3:9; 2 Sam 14:17
[u] 1 Kings 3:26–28

Such a king (and this is the glory of royalty) will have no interest of his own, apart from the public good. The remembrance that the *balances and weights are the Lord's concern*—made by his appointment—dictates an even-handed justice.[10] Not only will he refrain *from wickedness;* but it will be *abomination to him to commit it.* Not only will he be careful to remove all evil from his person;[v] but he will surround himself with faithful counselors.[11] *Righteous lips will be his delight.* Admirable was Eli's regard to Samuel's *lips,* even when they spoke daggers to his heart.[12]

[v] Prov 20:8, 26. Contrast 29:12

Nothing is lacking in such a reign but stability. And thus speaks the word, unnoticed indeed by worldly statesmen, but well-warranted by experience—the throne is *established on righteousness.*[w] Thus Mr. Hooker said the government "acknowledges itself indebted to religion. Godliness, being the chiefest top and well-spring of all true virtues," is the foundation of national prosperity.[x] The *righteous* are the pillars of the earth,[y] the lions around the king's throne, his glory and defense.[z]

[w] 1 Kings 2:3; 2 Chron 32:22, 23; Jer 22:13–20
[x] Prov 14:34
[y] Ps 75:3
[z] 1 Kings 10:19, 20

[10] *Deut 24:15, 16; Ezek 45:10. The Jews used to keep their weights in* bags. *Mic 6:11.*

[11] *Prov 22:11; Ps 101:6, 7; Dan 3:28–30; 6:24–28. Constantius, the father of Constantine, tested the character of his Christian servants by the imperative command to offer sacrifices to his gods. Some sank under the trial. Those, who had* really *"bought the truth," would sell it for no price (Prov 23:23). They were inflexible. He banished the base compliants from his service. The true confessors he entrusted with the care of his own person. "These men," said he, "I can trust. I value them more than all my treasures." This was sound judgment. For who are so likely to be faithful to their king, as those that have proved themselves faithful to their God?*

[12] *1 Sam 3:15–18. Contrast 1 Kings 22:8; 2 Chron 15:7–10; 25:15, 16; Mark 6:17, 18. Clarendon perhaps was the finest example in modern times of unbending uprightness; boldly reproving his shamefully wicked master and beseeching him "not to believe, that he had a prerogative to declare vice to be virtue." Well had it been for Charles had these* righteous lips been his delight.

And shall we not plead for our leaders that they may embody this noble standard in their personal character and high responsibilities?[a] And may we not see here some faint delineation of the glorious King of Zion? What sentences of discriminating *judgment* dropped from His lips![b] How even are *the balances* of His perfect standard![c] How fully is His *throne established on righteousness!*[d]—himself loving righteousness, and hating iniquity! And what and who are *His delight?*—*righteous lips—He that speaketh right.*[e]

[a] 1 Tim 2:1, 2; Ps 72:1
[b] Matt 22:15–46
[c] Ps 45:6, 7; Isa 11:3, 4; 32:1
[d] Isa 9:7; Jer 23:5
[e] Prov 11:1; 12:22; Ps 15:1, 2; 24:3–5

14 *The wrath of a king is* as *messengers of death,*
But a wise man will appease it.
15 *In the light of a king's face is life,*
And his favor is like a cloud with the spring rain.

The vast power of a king is here developed in a graphic picture of Eastern despotism. Life and death are in the king's hands. His will is law.[f] Every sign of *his wrath*—even the frown of his face or the word out of his mouth—*is a messenger of death.*[g] The despot issues his order, and the executioner performs his command without delay or resistance.[h] No common *wisdom* was needed to *appease his wrath.* Jonathan appeased his father's *wrath.*[i] Daniel *appeased* the outrageous autocrat of Babylon.[j] What a blessing, in contrast with this tyranny, is our own constitution! Such an admirable counterpoise between the power of the people and the caprice of the sovereign! The just authority of the crown is preserved, without invading the rightful liberty of the subject.

[f] Eccl 8:4
[g] Esther 7:7–10
[h] 1 Sam 22:16–21; 1 Kings 2:24, 25, 46; 2 Kings 6:31–33; Matt 14:10
[i] 1 Sam 19:4–6
[j] Dan 2:15, 16. Comp. Acts 12:20–22

The king's favor marks the same absolute power. The restoration of Pharaoh's butler to his place was as life from the dead.[k] The captive monarch found renewed *life* in the light of his master's countenance;[l] Nehemiah's depression was cheered by his king's kind manners and still kinder favors.[m] And wasn't the king's golden sceptre, held out to Esther,[n] like a reviving *cloud of the spring rain*—the security of the joy of harvest?[13]

[k] Gen 40:20, 21
[l] 2 Kings 25:27–30
[m] Neh 2:1–8
[n] Esther 5:2, 3, with 4:16

But think of the King of Kings, before whom the mightiest monarch is as dust.[o] How much more is His *wrath to*

[o] Isa 40:22

[13] *Deut 11:14; Job 29:23; Joel 2:23; Zech 10:1; James 5:7. When the Jews began their civil year after the Autumnal Equinox, the latter rain fell in the spring; "and the more wet the spring," says Dr. Russel, "the later the harvest, and the more abundant the crop"—HARMER's Observ. i. 71.*

be dreaded as a messenger of death![p] The kings themselves will fly to the rocks in vain for a shelter from its fury.[q] *Wise* indeed is *the man who appeases it.* What do we owe to that blood (of Christ) that speaks our peace?[r] Sinner—before it's too late—listen to the pleading call—"Be reconciled to God."[s] And then whose *wrath* does he need to fear, who knows that God is favorable to him?

[p] Matt 22:13; Luke 12:5
[q] Rev 6:15
[r] Col 1:20; Heb 12:24
[s] 2 Cor 5:20; 6:2

Certainly, if there is "life" *in the light* of the earthly *King's smile,* how much more so is it in God's favor.[t] One smile scatters the thickest cloud and brings gladness infinitely more than all the treasures of earth;[u] refreshing as the latter rain.[v] "Christ liveth," said the noble Luther, "else I would not desire to live one moment." Yes, Christian!—bitter and deep as your sorrow may be, there is something to dread, above all your troubles—the clouding of your Lord's countenance. Take every opportunity to get a glimpse of it. Seize every leisure moment to exchange a word or a look. Note how difficult every brief period of separation is to you. Above all, look forward to that time when you shall walk up and down in the unclouded *light.* Oh, my Lord, Let the splendor of that day irradiate my soul, even though it may still be far away; and don't allow any place in my life to be without its light and comfort. Yes, Lord, let it eclipse all other joys, and by its glistening beauty cause the small contentment of this world to be just so many glowworms, which shine only in the night. Give me such a sense of your presence and your glory, Lord, that I would sooner forget myself, than you and your appearing.

[t] Ps 30:5
[u] 2 Cor 4:6, 7; 21:6
[v] Hos 6:3

16 *How much better is it to get wisdom than gold!*
And to get understanding is to be chosen above
silver.

Even apart from divine inspiration, this must be considered to be competent judgment. It was formed by one who had both human and divine wisdom in greater measure than any man ever had.[w] In your quiet times before the Lord, think about the overwhelming interest of heaven above earth, of the soul above the body, of eternity above time. And who's going to argue the point? One who made his choice of heavenly things above

[w] 1 Kings 3:12, 13

earthly, counted all things but loss and refuse by comparison.[x] They are more valuable,[y] more abiding,[z] more fruitful,[a] more satisfying. They are inexpressibly *better. Yes, how much better it is to get wisdom than gold, understanding than silver!*[b] Wisdom is the only thing under the sun exempted from the universal verdict—"All is vanity."[c] The spiritual apprehension of it is like the sudden discovery of a rich treasure ready for immediate use.

The security of the possession of it also heightens its value. Multitudes labor night and day for *gold*; yet miss the treasure. But who was ever disappointed in the effort to *get wisdom*?[d] When has earnestness and prayer failed of success?[e] "The beginning of wisdom is: Acquire wisdom; and with all your acquiring, *get understanding.*"[f] Nothing less than salvation is the great end.[g] How rich must be that blessing of which the Son of God is the storehouse! For in Him "are hidden all the treasures of wisdom and knowledge."[h] And nobody can rob us of our portion.

[x]Phil 3:8
[y]Prov 3:13–15; 8:10, 11, 18
[z]Prov 23:5
[a]Eccl 7:12
[b]Eccl 5:10
[c]Eccl 1:2
[d]Matt 11:12
[e]Prov 2:3–5; James 1:5
[f]Prov 4:7
[g]2 Tim 3:5
[h]Col 2:3

17 *The highway of the upright is to depart from evil;*
He who watches his way preserves his life.

The highway is the plain beaten path. *The highway of the upright*—his normal course in life—is "the highway of holiness"[i]—*departing from evil.* Here let him be seen as peculiar in his practice as in his principles. Each of us has our own world of *evil*—an inner circle, where the conflict is far more sharp; where the need of divine discipline is felt far more keenly, than in the grosser form of sin. Show great tolerance with others but none to yourself. Admit no faults or weaknesses. Count nothing small that hinders the completeness or consistency of your Christian profession. The real injury is not from our living in the world but from the world living in us. So delicate is the vital principle that it never can release its glowing influence, except in the atmosphere of heaven.

Therefore, to keep this way is to preserve our life.[j] Indeed, if Christianity really did possess sincerely and sufficiently the minds of all men, there wouldn't be any other restraint from evil needed. It was so with Joseph,[k] but David forsook the path and fell into a grievous sin.[l]

[i]Isa 35:8; Ps 119:1–3
[j]Prov 4:23–27; 19:16
[k]Gen 39:9, 10
[l]2 Sam 11:2

The quick perception of evil—the sensibility of danger from lawful things—at once proves our heavenly birth and protects us from many subtle schemes.[m] "The unclean will not travel on it," but the redeemed shall walk there.[n]

[m] 1 John 5:18

[n] Isa 35:8, 9

18 *Pride* goes *before destruction,*
And a haughty spirit before stumbling
[*AV—the fall*].
19 *It is better to be of a humble spirit with the lowly,*
Than to divide the spoil with the proud.

ADAM, WHAT HAVE YOU DONE?

What more vivid explanation of these Proverbs is needed than our own ruined condition? Our father's *pride*, desiring to be as God, hurried his whole race to *destruction*. "O Adam," was the exclamation of a man of God, Mr. Adam, "what hast thou done!" (*Private Thoughts*). "I think," said another holy man, "so far as any man is proud, he is related to the devil, and a stranger to God and to himself," said Baxter (*Narrative*). It is with most awful eloquence that God shows the true character and ruin of pride.[o] He gives us endless examples throughout His Word,[14] with each sounding this solemn command: "Be not conceited, but fear."[p] Terrible, indeed, is our danger if we ignore that caution; if the need for it is not deeply felt!

[o] Isa 14:4–19; Ezek 28; 29; Job 40:11, 12

[p] Rom 11:20. Comp. 1 Cor 10:12; 1 Tim 3:6

The haughty spirit carries the head high. The man looks upward, instead of watching his step. It's no wonder, then, that he doesn't see where he's going and *stumbles and falls!* He loves to climb, and the enemy is always at hand to help him;[q] and the greater the height, the more dreadful the *fall*. There is often something in the fall that marks the Lord's special judgment. God smites the object of which the man is *proud*. David glorified in the number of his people, and the Lord diminished them by fatal disease. Hezekiah boasted of his treasure, and the Lord marked it to be taken away. At the moment that Nebuchadnezzar was proud of his Babel, he was banished from the enjoyment of it. "The daughters of

[q] Matt 4:5, 6

[14] *Pharaoh—Exod 9:16, 17; Amaziah—2 Chron 25:15–20; Haman—Esther 5:11; 7:10; Pharaoh—Ezek 29:3–5; Nebuchadnezzar—Dan 4:29–33; Herod—Acts 12:21–23;* In the Church, *David—2 Sam 24:1; Uzziah—2 Chron 26:4–16; Hezekiah—2 Chron 32:25; Isa 39; Peter—Matt 26:33, 69–74.*

Zion are proud," priding themselves on their ornaments, and they were covered with disgrace.[r] Yet after all, it's *the state of heart,* that prepares man for *the fall,* that is the worst part of his condition. For whatever it is that is our pride, that is our danger. "Why," a wise man asks, "are earth and ashes proud? Pride was not intended for man."

[r] Isa 3:16, 24

But have we been preserved from open disgrace? Examine secret faults. Trace them to their source—a subtle confidence in gifts, attainments, and privileges. And then praise your God for His painful discipline that preserves us from ruinous self-exaltation. Truly the way down to the valley of humiliation is deep and rugged. *Humility,* therefore, is the grand preserving grace. The truly repentant publican was safe, while the boasting Pharisee was condemned.[s] *Better* then—more happy, more honorable, more acceptable to God and man—is *a humble spirit,* keeping company *with the lowly, than the spoil* of the proud conqueror, bringing on his own *destruction.*[t] Better is a *humble spirit,* than a high condition; better to have our spirit brought down, than our outward condition raised. But who believes this? Most men strive to rise; few desire to lie low! May your example—blessed Savior—keep me low! "When Majesty," said Bernard, "humbled Himself, shall the worm swell with pride?"

[s] Luke 18:14

[t] James 1:9

20 *He* [*AV—that handleth a matter wisely*] *who gives attention to the word shall find good,*
And blessed is he who trusts in the LORD.

TWO GOLDEN KEYS TO SUCCESS

Two things are needed for the success—*wisdom and faith.* One teaches us what to do for ourselves; the other what to expect from God. "Wisdom has the advantage of giving success,"[u] especially in important matters. Joseph's *wise* management in a great emergency *found good.*[15] The apostles *wisely* handled the matter of the care of the widows by relieving themselves from secular work, and, for greater satisfaction, choosing the officers (as seems probable from the original of the names) from among the complainers. And great *good did they find*

[u] Eccl 10:10

[15] *Gen 41:25–44. Hence the removal of wise men is a national judgment, Isa 3:1, 2. Comp. also Prov 13:15; 17:2; 19:8.*

resulting from this arrangement.[16] Let the young Christian eagerly seek this *wisdom*. His first glowing impulse would be to cast away every trace of his former life and stamp his new life in Christ with needless singularity. But he may learn, that true self-denial is more an internal change of heart than an external badge of difference; that we may be marked by a "martyr" spirit but without the genuine love; that the difference between enthusiasm and zeal is not the energy, we apply, but the direction in which we are moving. This *wisdom* will produce Christian humility and consistent living.

After all, the greatest human wisdom may be outsmarted.[v] Man's wisdom, without faith, will surely fail.[17] [v]2 Sam 17:14
True *wisdom doesn't trust in self*.[w] Eliezer's wise and [w]Prov 3:5, 6
careful *handling* of things was in the spirit of faith. In the same spirit, Jacob conducted his wise defense against his brother.[x] Esther *wisely handled her* critical problem with [x]Gen 32:33
the king by using "a *fast* to call upon God, and a *feast* to obtain favor with the king," said Bishop Reynolds.[18] This is in all cases true wisdom—to make man the inspiration to earnest effort; God the object of trust.

RECIPE FOR HAPPINESS

And where, as in this practical *trust*, shall we find so godly, so simple, a recipe for happiness? Never did God intend for us to create our happiness out of our own resources. To feel that we know nothing, that we can do nothing, contrive nothing; then to look up to Him as our supreme good, and to trust Him as our only friend—when did such reliance and expectation ever bring disappointment? We feel that we, and everything we have, are in His hands. This is our peaceful security. "I have had many things," said Luther, "in my hands, and I have lost them all. But whatever I have been able to place in God's, I still possess."[19] In this quiet confidence we have nothing more to do with ourselves. A thousand perplexing thoughts are scattered to the winds. God now takes the place once filled by disturbing agitations. The soul is fixed in God. He reigns over all with an all-seeing eye

[16] *Acts 6:1–7. Similar* good *result was obtained in the* wise handling of *the difficult matter of circumcision, Acts 15.*
[17] *Isa 22:5–11. Comp. 2 Kings 18:13–17. Man is* at his best estate, *vanity, Verses 5, 6.*
[18] *Esther 4:16; 5:5; 7:1–7. Bishop REYNOLDS on Hos 14:3.*
[19] *D'AUBIGNE'S* History of the Reformation, *Book 14, chap. 6.*

and an all-moving hand. The eye of faith pierces through the darkest cloud and reads God's thoughts of peace and love. All the world cannot rob us of one word of God. Sometimes God may seem to oppose His own promises. But there is more reality in the least promise of God, than in the greatest performance of man. Bishop Hall commented, "I will therefore ever trust Him on his bare word; with hope, beside hope, above hope, against hope, for small matters of this life" (Works viii. 8). For how shall I hope to trust Him in impossibilities, if I can't trust Him in probabilities. This simple habit of faith enables us fearlessly to look an extremity in the face and to hold on, knowing that His honor is at stake, and He has obligated Himself to put His own seal to His Word. Whoso "trusts in the Lord" happy is he.[y]

[y]Ps 2:12; Jer 17:7, 8

21 *The wise in heart will be called discerning,*
And sweetness of speech increases persuasiveness.

The heart is the proper seat of wisdom.[z] There it dwells "with prudence."[a] Two two—wisdom and good judgment—working together, are essential to the completeness of a Christian profession. Intellectual *wisdom* without cautions and careful application produces no practical results. The great lack of prudence gives needless offense to the gospel and destroys influential weight of character. Often, also, spiritual affections are wasted for lack of careful direction or discipline. Moral habits from this lack become either unhealthy or hardened. There is either superstitious and overconscientiousness or reckless indifference; sometimes conscience about everything, sometimes about nothing. *Discerning wisdom* gives consistency to the whole system. The eye directs the foot, and we walk safely upon firm ground. Bright and sparkling parts are like diamonds, which may make the wearer look better, but they are not necessary for the good of the world. Whereas common sense (substantially identified with *discerning wisdom*) is like current coin. We have use for it everyday in the ordinary tasks and experiences of life. And if we would just use it, it would enable us to progress much farther than we could ever imagine.

[z]Prov 2:10; 10:8
[a]Prov 8:12; Hos 14:9

These internal qualities gain much from external gifts. "In everything [we] were enriched in Him, in all speech and all knowledge";[b] when we are enabled to clothe our thoughts in a flowing style and clear expression; this doubtless gives a great advantage in communicating knowledge.[c] *The sweetness of speech increases persuasiveness.* Ambrose's smooth eloquence caught Augustine's attention and gradually brought conviction to his mind. Yet much more does this advantage belong to "the *sweet* words of consolation, which come forth of a godly trust," reads *Reformers' Notes. Wisdom is in the heart,* as in a treasury; and "the mouth speaks out of that which fills the heart."[d] When therefore the "heart overflows with a good theme; I address my verses to the King;" the tongue, like the Apostle's[e]—without any external attractiveness, is "the pen of a ready writer."[f] And when without measure "grace is poured upon" the lips[g] of the King Himself, what wonder that He should have commanded the admiration[h] and fixed the attention[i] of His hearers! How rich the privilege of His true disciples to sit at His feet.

[b] 1 Cor 1:5
[c] Eccl 12:10, 11
[d] Matt 12:34. Comp. verse 23
[e] 1 Cor 2:1–4
[f] Ps 45:1
[g] Ps 45:2
[h] Matt 7:28; Luke 4:22; John 7:46
[i] Luke 19:48

22 *Understanding is a fountain of life to him who has it,*
But the discipline of fools is folly.

WELL-SPRING OF LIFE

A religion of notions—what is it? A dreaming theory! All is death. There is no pulse in the affections, no motion in the heart. But when the understanding is enlightened, to grasp and understand spiritual things in their spiritual glory, notions become principles. Feelings flow from light and are filled with *life.* The Book of God shines forth with new glory. Every verse is a sunbeam. Every promise sparkles with divine love. What before was unmeaning sound now becomes "spirit and . . . *life.*"[j] This spiritual *understanding* is indeed *a fountain of life,*[k] not a work on the surface; not merely a forced impulse; not the summer stream, but a deep-flowing fountain.[l] If it be not always bubbling, there is always a supply at the bottom fountain.

[j] John 6:63
[k] John 4:14; 7:38
[l] Prov 18:4

But the contrast leads us to speak of this *fountain,* as not only refreshing *to him who has it,* but a blessing to all around him. Indeed, every Christian will feel the responsibility of enriching his sphere, narrow or wide. The fountain in the apostle's heart, filled with knowledge and spiritual *understanding,* communicated widespread blessing.[m] Let the humblest member of the church pay attention to the valuable advice of an ancient one, Theophilus of Alexandria and "by the daily reading of the Scriptures pour oil into his faculties, and prepare the lamp of his mind; so that, according to the precept [teaching] of the gospel, it may give light to all that are in the house" (quoted by Nicholls).

[m] Acts 14:21, 22

Yet the stream can't rise above its level. It can be only what the fountain makes it. So what can we expect, but *folly,* from the *instruction (discipline) of fools?*[n] Such in the fullest sense was the whole system of heathenism;[o] *the instruction* of its dark philosophy;[p] and the creed of the sensual Epicureans.[q] Justly, our Lord rebuked the senseless instruction of the Scribes and Pharisees.[r] What else could it be, but "if a blind man guides a blind man, both fall into a pit"?[s]

[n] Prov 15:2
[o] Isa 44:9–20; Jer 10:1–8
[p] Rom 1:21–25; 1 Cor 1:19, 20
[q] 1 Cor 15:32
[r] Matt 23:16–26
[s] Matt 15:14

Professing Christian, think about this. Unless your *understanding* is filled with heavenly light, it will be a poisoned fountain, not a *fountain of life.* What if your *understanding* is clear, but your heart is dark; if you are learned in the truth of Christ, *yet not "taught in Him ... as truth is in Jesus";*[t] if like Balaam, you are sound in theology, yet damned in sin![u] "Let us not think much of ourselves," says Bishop Reynolds, in a sermon before the University of Oxford, "though God should have adorned us with the most splendid natural gifts; with quickness of *understanding,* almost like that of angels; unless at the same time he adds to all, the gift of his spiritual grace, by which we may attain to a knowledge and delight in the heavenly mystery."

[t] Eph 4:20, 21
[u] Num 33:19–23; 2 Peter 2:15

23 *The heart of the wise teaches his mouth,*
And adds persuasiveness to his lips.

THE EXCELLENCY OF THE BELIEVER

The *fountain of life,* however silently it may flow, cannot be concealed. The deep instruction, pouring out from a divinely instructed heart, reveals the heavenly source, from whence the *fountain* is supplied. While "mere talk leads only to poverty,"[v] *the teaching of the heart adds persuasiveness.* Who does not know the difference between one, who speaks of what he has read or heard, and one, who speaks of what he has felt and tasted? The one has the knowledge of the gospel—dry and spiritless. The other has "the sweet aroma of the knowledge"[w]—fragrant and invigorating. The theorist may have more knowledge (for Satan—as an angel of light—is fearful proof how much knowledge may be consistent with ungodliness) but the real difference applies, not to the amount, but to the character, of knowledge; not to the matter known, but *how* it is known. "Unbelievers," as Dr. Owen *(On the Mortification of Sin in Believers)* admirably observes, "may know more of God, than many believers; but they know nothing as they ought" to know it; nothing correctly; "nothing with holy and heavenly light." The excellency of a believer is, not that he has a great understanding of things; but that, what he *has* apprehended (which perhaps may be very little) he sees in the light of the Spirit of God, in a saving, soul-transforming light. And this is what gives us communion with God. It is not therefore the intellectual knowledge of divine truth that makes the fruitful Christian. The only truly effective Christian, is he, who knows holy things in a holy manner; because he is gifted with a spiritual appetite and hunger for them. What he has learned, therefore, is truly of God. His object has a real existence. Without any theological aid, he comes to the enjoyment of "all the wealth that comes from the full assurance of understanding";[x] to a clearer certainty of the truth, than by the most demonstrable theory.[y] And this experimental theology gives a rich anointing to his communications. Godliness is not spoken by rote. *The heart teaches the mouth.*

Take as an illustration the doctrine of the Trinity—that mystery, of which every letter is mysterious. The debtor in the schools, in attempting to teach it, only "darkens counsel by words without knowledge."[z] *The heart of the wise*—heaven-taught—realizes the indwelling of the three sacred persons in undivided essence; and every act of prayer is through God—by God—to God.[a] Conscious weakness needs divine breath. Conscious guilt trusts in God's support. *The heart,* thus taught in the school of

[v] Prov 14:23
[w] 2 Cor 2:14
[x] Col 2:2
[y] 1 John 2:27; 5:20
[z] Job 38:2
[a] Eph 2:18

experience, teaches the doctrine in simplicity, and *adds persuasiveness to the lips*. How much better is faith understood by seeing a godly life, than in listening to accurate definitions of it! He who lives most simply a life "by faith in the Son of God"[b] will explain most clearly its office and influence. Contrast also proud reasoning man replying to the sovereignty of God, with the heart humbled, and *teaching the mouth* the adoration of wonder and praise.[c]

[b]Gal 2:20; 1 John 5:10
[c]Rom 9:19, 20; 11:33

This *heart-teaching* gives the minister the tongue of the learned for the refreshment of the weary soul, when he declares, not only what he has seen and heard,[d] but what his "hands handled ... of the Word of life."[e] He then speaks, not only the message of God, but from the mouth of God; and his "gospel did not come in word only, but also in power and in the Holy Spirit and with full conviction."[f]

[d]Isa 1:4, with 2 Cor 1:4
[e]1 John 1:1–3
[f]1 Thess 1:5

Man's religion begins with the head; God's with the heart. Out of the heart "flows the springs of life."[g] Let me be careful which I have—man's or God's. Intellectual religion brings me into the icy zone: cold, and clear and cold.[20] But the experimental application brings forth the glow of evangelical light and warmth. Let me look mainly, not to intellectual or theological attainments but to heavenly teaching. Let me be concerned that my *heart* be first *taught*. Then let *it teach my mouth, and add persuasiveness to my lips* for the praise of my God and the edifying of His church.

[g]Prov 4:23

24 *Pleasant words are a honeycomb,*
Sweet to the soul and healing to the bones.

The sweets of pleasure are not always *healing*.[h] *The honeycomb* combines both. Description may give some idea of what honey is like. But only actual eating can give me understanding of what it really is. So is the mysterious delight and refreshment given to us in *pleasant words*. When they are words of counsel, sympathy, or encouragement, they are medicinal also; not only *sweet to the soul*, but *healing to the body*. Much more are the

[h]Prov 5:3–5

[20] *"Going over the theory of virtue in one's thoughts, talking well, and drawing fine pictures about, this is so far from necessarily or certainly conducting to form the habit of it in him, who thus employs himself, that it may harden the mind in a contrary course, and form a habit of insensibility to all moral considerations."* Such is the weighty and solemn warning of Bishop Butler, Analogy, *part 1. chap. 5.*

pleasant words of God both sweet and wholesome. The professing believer may enjoy a passing sweetness in them.[i] But only by drinking them in will he realize their solid *pleasure*[j]—"*sweeter also than honey* and *the drippings of the honeycomb.*"[k] We go on our way, like Samson, eating our honeycomb;[l] like Jonathan, revived.[m] We take the Lord's words to the throne of grace; and, pleading them humbly and thankfully, we find them most *pleasant* to our taste. Often, their richness is so overwhelming that we can only ask, concerning the manna—"What is it?"[n] And they are as healthful as they are *pleasant;* invigorating to our inner being, the strength—*the bones,* so to speak—of our spiritual system.[o]

[i] Ezek 33:32; Matt 13:20; Heb 6:4, 5
[j] Heb 6:7
[k] Ps 19:10. Comp. 119:103
[l] Judg 14:8, 9
[m] 1 Sam 14:27
[n] Exod 16:15
[o] Prov 3:8; 4:22

Pleasure and healing, alike, flow from the words of man in the things of God.[p] How David and Jonathan in the wood strengthened each other's hands in God![q] How the Eunuch was cheered by Philip's exposition of the precious Scripture![r] What health did Paul's most *pleasant words* pour into the heart of the desponding jailor![s] And how his own spirit was revived by the meeting at Appius Forum;[t] as the disciples had been refreshed by fellowship with their divine Master on the walk to Emmaus![u] When He is the subject and His Spirit the teacher, pleasant indeed will be the words of Christian communion beyond any earthly enjoyment.

[p] Verses 21, 23; 15:23; 27:9
[q] 1 Sam 23:16
[r] Acts 8:35–39
[s] Acts 16:27, 34
[t] Acts 28:15
[u] Luke 24:32

25 *There is a way* which seems *right to a man,*
But its end is the way of death.

ASHES OF DELUSION

Again we have this solemn, searching caution. For so fearful is the danger of self-delusion, that we are only safe by warning upon warning.[v] Not lack of understanding, but love of sin is the cause.[w] The judgment is perverted because the heart is blinded.[x] It is no proof that *a way is right,* just because it *seems right.*[y] "All the ways of a man are clean in his own sight";[z] yet *their end is the way of death. The way of* disobedience seems to be necessary; or it is only a small turning from the way; yet it was punished as divination . . . and idolatry."[a] *The way* of deceit seems *to be right;* an easy way of escaping difficulty;[b] or gaining a present advantage.[c] "But a lying tongue is only for a moment";[d] and the unrepenting liar

[v] Phil 3:1
[w] John 3:19
[x] Isa 5:20; Eph 4:18
[y] Prov 12:26; John 16:2; Acts 26:9
[z] Verse 2; 12:15
[a] 1 Sam 15:20–23
[b] 1 Sam 21:2
[c] 2 Kings 5:22
[d] Prov 12:19

finds his "part *will be* in the lake that burns with fire and brimstone."[e] The Pharisee is dazzled with his own goodness. All his religion is outward; sufficient ground for his own acceptance with God.[f] He has combined it with the internal work to add to the pomp of the heartless ceremonial. He brings to God the formal duty, which he abhors,[g] and he refuses the spiritual service, which God demands.[h] Yet his *way seems to be right.* But his countenance is hated,[i] his prayer is cast out;[j] his goodness is an abomination.[k] The professing believer takes up his opinion and puts on appearances, only to keep the Spirit out of his heart and to quiet his conscience, without coming to grips with the real issue. Yet *his way*—with so much doing in religion—*seems right to him.* Often considerable natural feeling enters in. Joy is mistaken for faith, till the scorching sun has withered it away.[l] Alarm is mistaken for penitence; better, of course, than total indifference; yet proving itself to be only a fit of selfish terror, passing away with the apparent danger.[m] Thus, "he feeds on ashes" of his own delusion, and "cannot deliver hisself."[n] Onward he goes to the grave; yes—even to the presence of his God, when a closed heaven, and an open hell, show him the truth too late.[o] It is madness to dream of heaven, when, actually every step is another step toward hell. *It's the end* of the journey that tests the safety of the path. And Satan is determined to keep that, so that he may make his *way seem to be right. The ways of death are many. The way of life is but One*—"I am the way, and ... no one comes to the Father, but through Me."[p] Oh! What a blessing to have our eyes opened to see the awful danger of our own way, and our ears opened to hear the voice behind us, saying—"This is the way, walk in it"![q]

26 *A worker's appetite works for him,*
For his hunger urges him on.

LABOR ON EARTH, REST IN HEAVEN

When man sinned in the Garden of Eden, God appointed him to earn his living by the sweat of his brow.[r] But, the curse is mingled with mercy. What if there were no necessity for man to work? "Every intent of the thoughts"[s]—unmingled, unceasing "evil"—would, for

[e] Rev 21:8
[f] Prov 30:12, with Rom 9:33; Luke 18:11, 12
[g] Isa 1:10–14
[h] Matt 15:7–9
[i] Verse 5; Prov 6:16, 17
[j] Luke 18:14
[k] Isa 65:5; Luke 16:15
[l] Matt 13:20, 21
[m] Ps 78:33–37
[n] Isa 44:20
[o] Matt 7:22, 23; 22:11–13; 25:10–12
[p] John 14:6
[q] Isa 30:21; Jer 6:16
[r] Gen 3:19
[s] Gen 6:5

lack of other occupation, be left to its own devices. Wise then and gracious is the decree—labor on earth, rest in heaven. Earning a living through hard work is the necessary condition of the great mass of mankind. Hunger drives us on. We labor so that we can eat.[t] This is laboring for ourselves. The harvest is our rich recompence. Only we need to be careful, that we don't labor for vanity,[u] or for "evil gain."[v] This is working our own ruin.[w]

[t]Eccl 6:7

[u]Prov 23:4, 5; Isa 47:12, 13; Heb 2:13
[v]Hab 2:9; Isa 5:8
[w]Prov 28:22; 1 Tim 6:9, 10

But even where we are exempt from physical labor, there's enough going on in the world to fill up our daily life with wearisome mental occupation. Under Christian discipline, that brings its own reward, the *worker's appetite works for him.* But millions live for pleasure alone. The popular notion is that "man is nothing more than his pleasure." But if this is true and man is nothing more than this; then surely he is the most pitiable and wretched creature in the world. For there is far more for man to do than live just for his own pleasure. And the man who doesn't have to work for his living actually has more responsibility than those who do. No man is under greater obligation to work hard than he.

And yet all labor, whether bodily or mental, is evil, if it prevents concentration of interest on the only satisfying object of labor: "Do not work for the food which perishes, but for the food which endures to eternal life."[x] Think about the certain harvest it provides—The Son of Man will give it. Look over the field of labor—the gospel of His grace. Every promise is there to meet you, to wait on you, "God . . . accomplishes *all things* for me"[y] and yet, it's all of no avail, if you don't act upon it and make it your own. How wonderful for us, when a spiritual appetite is created; and drives us on to labor for the things that endure. Everything else finds its place, when life's primary object occupies the central place in our lives. We don't renounce all other interests in this world, which have rightful claim to us, and we care for them. Our hands and our time are given to the world; our hearts to God. Our activity is in our calling; our affections above it. This is in the highest sense laboring for ourselves—for our best, our most enduring good. All is centered in God. Indeed, without Him life is nothing. Whatever its momentary enjoyments, it is all a gloomy world of emptiness and van-

[x]John 6:27

[y]Ps 57:2

ity. Most truly does the Christian's heart respond to Augustine's confession—"All other plenty besides my God is mere beggary to me" (Confess. Lib. 13. c. 8).

27 *A worthless man digs up evil,*
While his words are as a scorching fire.
28 *A perverse man spreads strife,*
And a slanderer separates intimate friends.
29 *A man of violence entices his neighbor,*
And leads him in a way that is not good.
30 *He who winks his eyes* does so *to devise perverse things;*
He who compresses his lips brings evil to pass.

STRIFE IN EVERY FURROW

The man of Belial *(worthless man)* labors hard; but not for himself; certainly not for his own good. Yet his labor presents a vivid picture indeed of the energy of sin. He has broken away every yoke of restraint. Every member of his body, every power of his mind, is a slave "to impurity and lawlessness."[z] May we not learn from him in humiliation the true standard of concentration of mind, singleness of object, hard work, delight, and perseverance? His pleasure is to *dig up evil;* pursuing his *evil* projects with intense activity,[21] as if searching for hid treasure. The tongue is usually the chief instrument of mischief. In what black color God's Word pictures this vile criminal—*a scorching fire*—a world of iniquity, set on fire of hell![22] And as he digs, so he *sows, evil*—seed that comes up only with a disease that kills. He sows strife in every furrow;[a] jealousies among nations,[b] war between ruler and people,[c] divisions among churches,[d] coldness between ministers and their flocks,[e] ill-will among friends[f]—a spirit eminently hateful to God.[g] Where open contentions might not work, whisperings,[23] evil-surmisings, idle and slanderous reports are employed to *separate even intimate friends.*[h]

[z]Rom 6:19
[a]Prov 15:18
[b]2 Sam 10:3
[c]2 Sam 20:1
[d]1 Cor 1:11, 12; 3:3
[e]1 Cor 4:8; 2 Cor 12:15; Gal 4:16
[f]2 Sam 16:3
[g]Prov 6:16, 19
[h]Prov 6:14; 18:8

Truly he is an evil man. If he doesn't tell direct falsehoods, his dark whispers of *slander* are plain enough to

[21] *Ps 7:14, 15; Saul—1 Sam 18:21, 22; Ahab—1 Kings 18:10; Jeremiah's enemies—18:18; the chief priests seeking false witnesses against our Lord—Matt 26:59.*
[22] *James 3:6–8; Ps 52:1–4; 57:4.* "His tongue is a burning firebrand, *to set all the world in combustion"—Bishop HALL.*
[23] *1 Sam 24:9; Ps 35:15; 2 Cor 12:20. This sin is numbered in the black catalog of heathen abominations, Rom 1:29.*

be understood and sure to be exaggerated. The well-meant word or act may be misinterpreted. He has seen or heard probably only a little. He guesses at the rest to make his story complete. And by this report, half true and half false, he plays with his neighbor's name, to his great injury. No wonder, that this evil gossiper should be classed with "a murderer, or thief."[i] For the man, who loosens the closest ties, and breaks up the peace of whole families, sins against those commandments, which charge crime against the thoughts, the word, the principle, as well as the outward act.[j] Again, we find him a tempter, *a man of violence* indeed, combining with loud and overbearing speech *enticements for his neighbor, to lead the* unwary *into a way that is not good.*[k] His whole soul is filled with these Satanic plots. Sometimes we may see him *wink his eyes* to outward distractions; *compressing his lips,* as if engaged in deep thought to *bring evil to pass;*[l] all expressing the intense study, with which he contrives his neighbor's ruin!

[i] 1 Peter 4:15
[j] Matt 5:21, 22
[k] Prov 1:11–14; 4:16, 17; Acts 20:30; 2 Peter 2:1, 2
[l] Prov 6:12–14; 10:10

Such is the heavy service of the most cruel of all masters—Satan. He wears out both the minds and bodies of his slaves and pays them, at the end, only the fearful wages of eternal death.[m] If the way to heaven is "small" is not "the way of the treacherous . . . hard"?[n] Is there not harder work in the way to hell;—without one beaming hope of the cheering home, one bit of encouragement from heavenly promises, that upholds the servants of God in all their weariness and trial? "Do not take my soul away *along* with sinners . . . In whose hands is a wicked scheme," and where "destruction and misery are in their paths."[o]

[m] Rom 6:23
[n] Matt 7:14, with Prov 13:15
[o] Ps 26:9, 10; Rom 3:16

31 *A gray head is a crown of glory;*
It is found in the way of righteousness.

Gray hair is the old man's glory[p] and claim for reverence.[q] God solemnly links the honor of it with his own fear.[24] "The head is the elder" and they are numbered with the "honorable."[r] The sin of despising them is marked,[s] and, when shown toward His own prophet, was fearfully punished.[t] Wisdom and experience may justly

[p] Prov 20:29
[q] Prov 23:22; 2 Sam 19:32, 39
[r] Isa 9:15
[s] Isa 3:5
[t] 2 Kings 2:23, 24

[24] *Lev 19:32. The Roman satirist intimates, that the neglect of "rising up before the hoary head" was punishable with death—JUVEN. Satire, 13, 54–56. The reverence paid by the Lacedaemonians to the hoary head is well known. They probably borrowed this law from the Egyptians, who inculcated this respect to its full extent, HEROD. Lib. ii. c. 26. Comp. also OVID,* Fasti, *v. 57, 58. See a serious and instructive paper in the* Rambler, *No. 50.*

[u]Job 12:12; 32:4–7
[v]1 Kings 12:13–20

be supposed to belong to them;[u] and the contempt of this wisdom was the destruction of a kingdom.[v]

CROWNS OF GLORY

[w]Gen 47:7–10
[x]1 Kings 49:18; Luke 2:28, 29
[y]Luke 1:6
[z]Luke 2:36, 37
[a]Ps 71:18
[b]Philem 9
[c]Ps 92:13–15

But the diamond in *the crown* is, when *it is found in the way of righteousness.* Even a heathen monarch did homage to it;[w] an ungodly nation and king paid the deepest respect to it.[25] The fathers of the Old and New Testament reflected *its glory.* The one died in waiting faith in the Lord's salvation. The other was ready to "depart in peace" in the joyous sight of it.[x] Zacharias and Elizabeth walked in all the ordinances of the Lord "blameless";[y] Anna—"a widow" indeed in the faith and hope of the gospel;[z] Polycarp, with his fourscore and six years in his Master's service—*Crowns of glory were their gray heads* shining with all the splendor of royalty. How earnestly the holy Psalmist pleads this crown for usefulness to the church;[a] the apostle Paul for the cause of his converted slave.[b] And who more honorable than those, who, having been "planted" in youth within the courts of the Lord, grow up to "yield fruit in old age," manifesting the glory of the Lord's faithfulness and love?[c] Truly is an old man's "diadem that, which not the art of man but the kingdom of God, has fashioned and set on his head," said Muffet. And is not the earthly glory brightened by its nearness to the unfading, everlasting crown?

TIME: NO EMPTY DURATION

[d]Rom 2:5

But separate the heavenly virtue from *the gray head* and the crown is fallen. It lies dishonored in the dust. For what is a more lamentable spectacle, than a graceless old man, only gaining by his score of years a greater share of guilt? Time is no empty duration. It is filled up with talents for eternity, a field for their exercise, helps for their improvement, and an accounting for their neglect or abuse. The white hairs of ungodliness speak of ripeness for wrath—"storing up wrath" with every day's uninterrupted increase against "the day of wrath."[d] "The one who does not reach the age of one hundred shall be thought accursed."[26]

[25] *Samuel—1 Sam 25:1; Elisha—2 Kings 13:14; Jehoiada—2 Chron 24:15, 16.*

[26] *Isa 65:20. "There is not on earth a more venerable and delightful spectacle than that of an aged pilgrim walking with God; and a more affecting and deeply melancholy sight can*

32 *He who is slow to anger is better than the mighty,*
And he who rules his spirit, than he who captures a city.

THE HEART: A FIELD OF BATTLE

A great conflict and a glorious victory are here set forth; a conflict not in thought, but in action; hidden from the *mighty* ones of the earth: known only to those, who having enlisted under the baptismal banner are "manfully fighting" reads The Baptismal Service, against their spiritual enemies. The heart is the field of battle. All its evil and powerful passions are deadly foes. They must be defeated in the strength of God. Those who are ignorant of God and of themselves make light of them. They scarcely acknowledge them. Instead of being *slow to anger*, under provocation, they think that they "have good reason to be angry."[e] It is a disgrace to put up with wrong. A hasty temper is an infirmity. They are hardly responsible for it. Instead—the indulgence is a relief, and they hope to cool down in time, utterly unconscious of any sin against God. Thus, instead of *having rule over their spirit,* they are captives, not conquerors.

[e]Jon 4:9

But can a Christian do so—"present yourselves to God as those alive from the dead"?[f] "How shall we who died to sin still live in it?"[g] Must I not vigorously "buffet my body and make it my slave";[h] especially that "small part," which is such a mighty instrument of evil? To bridle the tongue, so as to check the expression of passion, or "speaking unadvisedly with our lips"—is a victory,[i] that can only be achieved by almighty strength. The pains and cost of the conflict are beyond human calculation. But the victory compensates for all.

[f]Rom 6:13
[g]Rom 6:2
[h]1 Cor 9:27; James 3:5
[i]James 3:2

hardly, on the contrary, be imagined, than that of a hoary-headed sinner, who has lived his fourscore years 'without God in the world,'—all that time God calling and he refusing, and the almighty 'angry with him every day:' his body now bowed down beneath the weight of years; all his powers of action and of enjoyment decaying; every hour likely to be his last; time all behind him, and eternity all before him; and his soul still 'dead in trespasses and sin;' the hour of his departure come, and no readiness for the world to which he is bound. Oh! With what opposite emotions do we contemplate old age in this character, and in the saint of God; who in approaching the close of his earthly pilgrimage is drawing near to what has been the goal of his hopes and desires; who, while outwardly decaying, is inwardly maturing for heaven; in whom every symptom of coming death is but a symptom of approaching life; and who, in the final exhaustion of nature, bids adieu to the world in the words of aged Simeon—'Lord, now lettest thou thy servant depart in peace, for mine eyes have seen thy salvation' "—WARDLAW, on Eccl 12:7.

MY WORST ENEMY: MY OWN HAUGHTY HEART

The glory of this victory is indeed far above *the mighty. The capture of a city* is child's play, compared with this struggle which "is not against flesh and blood."[j] That is only the battle of a day. This, the weary, unceasing conflict of a life. There, the enemy might be mastered with a single blow. Here, he is to be chained up and kept down with unremitting perseverance. The magnifying of the conflict exalts the glory of the triumph. Gideon's *rule over his spirit* was *better* than his victory over the Midianites.[k] David's similar conquest was *better* than could have been the spoils of Nabal's house.[l] No less glorious was that decisive and conscious mastery over his spirit, when he refused to drink the water of Bethlehem, obtained at the hazard of his bravest men; thus condemning the excessive appetite, that had desired refreshment at so unreasonable a cost.[m] On the contrary, Alexander, renowned conqueror of the East, lived and died a miserable slave. He lost more honor at home, than he gained by his conquests abroad; famous in war, but shamefully degraded by a brutish foe.[27] Though valor is commendable, as a natural gift of God;[n] yet "to be our own master, is far more glorious for us, than if we were the masters of the world," said Lawson. "Among all my conquests," said the dying emperor Valentinian, "there is but one that now comforts me. I have overcome my worst enemy—my own haughty heart." This then is to subdue an enemy that has vanquished conquerors—this surely is to be "overwhelming" conquerors. Christian! never forget the source of victory—"through Him who loved us."[o]

[j] Eph 6:12
[k] Judg 8:1–3
[l] 1 Sam 25:33
[m] 2 Sam 23:17
[n] Judg 6:12
[o] Rom 8:37

This recollection brings us to the true point. Keep close to the glorious standard of an almighty, most loving Savior. Never can victory be had apart from it. Trials may be appointed, yet only to discipline for triumph; to draw us from our fancied to our real strength.

[27] *"So old and no older," wrote Philip Henry in his Diary. "Alexander was only thirty, when he had conquered the great world: but he said, "I have not yet subdued the* little world—myself." *"Thou art a slave of slaves," said the proud Philosopher (Diogenes) to this mighty conqueror—"for thou art a slave to those appetites, over which I rule." The complaint of the Czar Peter, "I can govern my people, but how can I govern myself?"—was a practical acknowledgment of the difficulty.*

YOUR ARMOR: WEAR IT—DON'T STORE IT!

Often the Christian soldier wins the day, even when he has been wounded in the fight. Yet, think not the war is ended because a battle is won. No quarter can be given, no truce allowed on either side. The enemy may have been stabbed in the heart; yet will he get up and renew the fight. You must walk—yea—sleep—in your armor. It must be *worn*, not stored away. There is no discharge from this war, till your body of sin and death is laid in the grave. Meanwhile victory is declared, before the conflict begins. Let every day then be a day of triumph. The promises are to present victory.[28] With such stirring, stimulating hopes, you shall surely *have rule,* if you will but dare to have it. And if you have not courage enough to be a Christian, you must then be a slave for life to the hardest of taskmasters.

This bloodless victory, so contrary to the turmoil of war,[p] is the crown of Christian grace.[q] No other grace of the gospel can be exercised without its influence. Yet the daily conquest anticipates the final victory, the rewards of which will be reaped through eternity.[29]

[p]Isa 9:5
[q]Rom 12:19

33 *The lot is cast into the lap,*
But its every decision is from the LORD.

The lot cast into the lap, or into the bottom of an urn,[30] often determined important matters. Officers were thus chosen;[r] work determined;[s] dwellings fixed;[t] discoveries made;[u] contentions caused to cease.[v] Yet the *Lord's decision* was manifestly shown. Canaan was divided in that way; so as to accord fully with Jacob's prophecies.[w] The offender was brought to justice.[x] What could be more beyond human direction? Yet what more entirely under divine determination? No one doubted the *decision.* Saul was acknowledged to be King;[y] Matthias was numbered

[r]1 Chron 24:5
[s]Luke 1:9
[t]Neh 11:1
[u]1 Sam 14:41
[v]Prov 18:18
[w]Num 26:55; Josh 18:8
[x]Josh 7:16
[y]1 Sam 10:20–24

[28] *Rev 2:7 and 3. Him that* overcometh.

[29] *Many striking sentiments from heathen ethics might illustrate this maxim. Cato the elder (in Plutarch) declared him to be the best and most praiseworthy general, who had rule over his own passions. Livy brings in Scipio speaking to his friend, "The danger of our age—believe me—is not so much from armed men, as from the pleasures scattered all around us. He that has disciplined them by his own temperance, has obtained to himself much honor and a greater victory, than we had in the conquest of Syphax"—Lib. 30. c. 15. "In all ages fewer men are found, who conquer their own lusts, than that conquer an army of enemies"—CICER. Ep. Lib. xv. Ep. 4. Thus Seneca writes to a friend, "If you wish to subject all things to yourself, subject yourself to reason. You will rule many, if reason ruleth you." Alas! that this should be all fine barren sentiment, not Christian principle!*

[30] *Parkhurst translates the word to mean the bottom or midst of an urn or vessel, into which the lots were cast.*

[z]Acts 1:26

[a]Esther 3:7; 9:1, 2

[b]John 19:24, with Ps 22:18

[c]Jon 1:7

[d]Ezek 21:21, 22

among the apostles[z]—without disputing. Even when *cast* profanely or superstitiously, the same authority overruled. Haman's lot was so disposed, as wholly to overthrow his scheme to destroy the Israelites; giving full time for the deliverance of his intended victims.[a] The soldier's lot was direct fulfillment of a prophecy that could not otherwise have been accomplished.[b] The heathen sailors *cast* it in ignorance; yet it was the divine discovery of the guilty criminal.[c] Heathen lots were controlled by the same absolute power.[d]

WHEEL OF PROVIDENCE

[e]Acts 1:24–26

[f]2 Peter 1:19

[g]Ps 119:105

[h]Prov 3:6

The lot is however a solemn matter, not to be lightly *cast.*[e] It is an acknowledgment of absolute authority and power, giving up our personal responsibility, and virtually appealing to an Omniscient, Omnipresent, Omnipotent God. It teaches us that things that we conceive to be accidental are really under God's control. "What is chance to man is the appointment of God," said Scott. *The lot, cast* "at peradventure, carrying a show of casualty," said Bishop Hall, is under a certain *decision.* Yet admitting it to be a scriptural custom, its expediency under our more complete spiritual light is more than doubtful. "We have" at least "the prophetic word *made* more sure, to which you do well to pay attention, as to a lamp shining in a dark place."[f] The Book of God is given us expressly as "a lamp to my feet, and a light to my path."[g] The rule is more clear in itself and linked with a most encouraging promise—"In all your ways acknowledge Him, and He will make your paths straight."[h] It is far better to exercise faith, than indifferently to tamper with personal responsibility.

[i]1 Kings 13:2
[j]Isa 44:28

[k]Matt 10:29, 30

The practical lesson to learn is that there is no blank in the most minute circumstances. Things, not only apparently dependent on chance, but upon a whole series of uncertain conditions are exactly fulfilled. The name of a king,[i] or of a deliverer,[j] is declared many hundred years before their birth—before, therefore, it could be known to any—save the Omniscient governor of the universe—whether such persons would exist. The falling of a hair or a sparrow is directed, no less than the birth and death of princes or the revolutions of empires.[k] Everything is a wheel of God's care. Who directed the Ishmaelites on their journey to Egypt at the very moment that Joseph was cast into the pit?[31] Who guided Pharaoh's daughter to the stream, just when the ark, with its precious deposit, was committed to the waters?[l] What gave Ahasuerus a sleepless night that he might be amused with the records of his kingdom?[m] Who prepared the great fish at the very time and place that Jonah's lot was cast?[n] Who can fail to see the hand of God, most wonderful in the most apparently casual happenings, overruling all second causes to fulfill His will, while they work their own? "When kingdoms are tossed up and down like a tennis-ball;[o] not one event can fly out of the bounds of His Providence. The smallest are not below it. Not a sparrow falls to the ground without it. Not a hair, but it is numbered by it," said Polhill (*Divine Will,* p. 159).

[l] Exod 2:3–5
[m] Esther 6:1
[n] Jon 1:17
[o] Isa 22:18

[31] *Gen 37:25. "The unparalleled story of Joseph," as Dr. South remarks in his striking sermon on this text, "seems to be made up of nothing else but chances and little contingencies, all tending to mighty ends."*

CHAPTER SEVENTEEN

1 *Better is a dry morsel and quietness with it*
Than a house full of feasting [AV—*sacrifices*] *with strife.*

HOUSE OF PLENTIFUL PROVISION

The reference is to the Jewish custom of feasting at home upon the remains of the *sacrifices.*[a] *A house full of feasting (sacrifices)* was therefore a house of plentiful provision. Yet when the spirit of love does not rule, self rules, over the fruitful source of *strife* and confusion. Well may the Christian be content with his *dry and quiet morsel,* to be delivered from such jarrings. "Holy love, found in a cottage," said Henry, *is better* than the most luxurious feast in the palaces of *strife.*[b] Happiness is not adding to our condition, but limiting our desires, and cutting them down to our condition. The secret dew of the Lord's blessing brings the rich gain of godly *quietness*[c] and contentment, and provides a satisfying meal, and a well-furnished house in the poorest dwelling.

[a]Lev 7:16; 19:6; 1 Sam 9:24

[b]Prov 15:17

[c]1 Tim 6:6

The marriage feast perhaps was comparatively *a dry morsel.* Yet was this a feast of love better than the Pharisee's house, *full of sacrifices with strife.*[d] Would you like to really enjoy your material blessings. Then welcome the Savior to them. Cherish His Spirit. Look to His glory in their enjoyment. Whether we have little or much, it will be blessed with the token of His presence and the seal of His everlasting love.

[d]John 2:1–3, with Luke 7:36–39; 11:37, 38, 45, 53

Think about things that will lead to quiet contentment. Maybe you don't have as many comforts as you had, or as you might have, or as others less deserving enjoy; yet, don't you have far more than you deserve? If you had more, wouldn't you be tempted to forget God and to live for the world? Won't the remembrance that this is the earthly lot your Savior chose, turn every thought of discontent into adoring rapture of thankfulness and love? Such is the great gain of godliness with contentment.

2 *A servant who acts wisely will rule over a son who acts shamefully,*
And will share in the inheritance among brothers.

Foolishness naturally leads to *shame*; wisdom to honor.[e] *The son,* the heir of the family, may degrade himself by misconduct, and, instead of being the glory of the house, *cause shame. A wise servant,* though having only a temporary interest in the house,[f] may be promoted to *rule over him.* The Scripture hath recorded no literal instances of this interchange of place. But a punishing God has determined that "the foolish will be servant to *the wisehearted.*"[g] The prodigal son, in conscious *shame,* was ready to take his place among the "hired men."[h]

[e]Prov 3:35; 12:8
[f]John 8:35
[g]Prov 11:29
[h]Luke 15:19

DANGEROUS PROMOTIONS

The wise servant has however sometimes shared the *inheritance among the brothers* in the family. Jacob, by marrying Laban's daughter, was included in the inheritance.[i] Solomon's own *servant,* in his own experience, probably verified this Proverb.[j] Abraham also would have made his *wise servant* his heir but for the interposing mercy of God.[k]

Yet this promotion is dangerous. No one can bear elevation safely without special grace and painful discipline.[l] Great wisdom, much prayer, and constant watchfulness are needed to promote humility and Christian consistency; as well as to silence the envy and jealousy, which unexpected prosperity naturally excites.[m] Honor from man calls for humility before God and careful holiness in adorning our Christian profession.

[i]Gen 30:27–34; 31:1
[j]1 Kings 4:7, 11
[k]Gen 15:3, 4
[l]2 Cor 12:1–7
[m]Dan 6:3–5

3 *The refining pot is for silver and the furnace for gold,*
But the LORD *tests hearts.*

GOLD IN THE FURNACE

The refining pot and furnace try the refiner's metals. But Jehovah reserves to Himself the right of *testing hearts.*[n] His eyes are as a flame of fire.[o] Nothing deceives

[n]1 Kings 8:39; Jer 17:10
[o]Rev 1:14

Him; nothing escapes His probing search. The gold must be put into *the furnace.* So mixed with dross is it, that the workman's eye can scarcely see it. But for the *furnace,* the dross could not be separated from the gold. The refiner's process burns it out, and the pure metal is left behind. No burnishing is of any avail. Till it has undergone the fire, it is unfit for use. And must there not be a furnace for the child of God?[p] None of us knows himself, until "the fire itself will test the quality of each man's work."[q] We can only exclaim in witnessing the result—Lord! What is man—the heart of man of the holiest saint thus revealed laid open to view?

[p]Isa 31:9; Jer 9:7
[q]1 Cor 3:13

But the Lord will have the metal cleansed. We cannot do the work. It is no common power that can separate the base mixture. No milder remedy will accomplish the purpose. But by this process the hidden evil is brought out for humiliation;[r] the hidden good for honor.[s] Deep personal or relative affliction; "knowing the affliction of his own heart";[t] the discovery of secret sins; circumstances of daily trial in trifles, known perhaps only to the heart that feels them[u]—all or any of these are a searching, piercing *furnace.*

[r]Deut 8:2; 2 Chron 32:31
[s]Gen 22:12; Matt 15:23–28
[t]1 Kings 8:38
[u]Prov 14:10

Painful indeed is the purifying process. The flesh trembles at the fire. Yet shall we not let the refiner do his work though it be by Nebuchadnezzar's furnace?[v] Shall we not commit ourselves with well-grounded confidence in His wisdom, tenderness, and love?—"Correct me, O Lord, but with justice."[w] Isn't any *furnace,* that purges away our worldly dross,[x] that brings us to know ourselves, our God, and His dealings with us—a mighty blessing? The best materials for praise come out of this consecrated *furnace.* But we need to carefully examine these trials before we can see their value. When the action of fire upon the metal brings it into its best state for use, we look for the results: the displacing of all worldly idols, the melting away of the stubbornness of the will, the full surrender of the heart to God. For as gold cast into the *furnace* received new luster, and shines brighter when it comes out than before; so are the saints of God more glorious after their great afflictions, and their graces even more resplendent. The refiner's process may be slow, but its results are sure. Nothing but dross will

[v]Dan 3:19
[w]Jer 10:24
[x]Isa 1:25

perish. The vilest earth will be turned into the finest gold. No refiner ever watched the *furnace* with such exactness and care. Many glittering particles may be swept away. But the pure residue—the solid particles—comparatively scanty in amount, but sterling in quality, will be delivered into the mold. It may seem strange to see the gold left in the fire, but He who put it there is carefully guarding over it. Not one grain will be lost![y] He "will sit" in patient watchfulness[z] moderating the heat, and carefully marking the moment, when it will be brought *"through the fire,"*[a] and set out in all the purity produced by the purifying trial. Every hour of the trial is worth far more than gold—a richer vein of Christian attainment. A suffering Savior is known better and loved more.

[y] 1 Peter 1:7
[z] Mal 3:2, 3
[a] Zech 13:9

Here then in the *furnace*—child of God—see the seal of your election;[b] the ground and establishment of your confidence;[c] your joyous anticipation, that, when your Lord shall appear, your faith here in the furnace shall then be made up into a crown of pure gold, and be found unto His praise and honor, and glory.[d]

[b] Isa 48:10
[c] Zech 13:9
[d] 1 Peter 1:7

4 *An evildoer listens to wicked lips,*
A liar pays attention to a destructive tongue.

Here's a black but true picture of human nature. *The evildoer* isn't satisfied with the stirring impulse of his native lust. But he has such a craving for sin, that he seeks foreign stimulants to give it increasing activity.[e] Amnon thus stimulated his own lust, by *listening to his wicked friend.*[f] Ahab, to secure his desired object, eagerly listened to the advice of his murderous wife.[g] The Jews gladly listened to the false prophets, who flattered them in their wickedness.[h] The malice of the ungodly was active and intense, in digging up false witness for our Lord's condemnation.[i] Yet there wouldn't be so many open mouths, if there weren't so many willing ears to listen to them. But remember that the *listening ears* share responsibility with the *destructive tongue,* since they're every bit as much involved in the treason.

[e] Prov 4:16, 17; Ps 64:5, 6
[f] 2 Sam 13:5, 6
[g] 1 Kings 21:4–7
[h] Isa 30:9–11; Jer 5:30, 31; Mic 2:11; 1 John 4:5
[i] Matt 26:59, 60

The liar gladly talks with anybody who countenances his own wickedness.[j] If he didn't love a lie, he wouldn't listen to it. That's the way he shrinks from the condemning light of truth into his own atmosphere of darkness.[k]

[j] Prov 28:4
[k] John 3:20

How opposite this spirit is to the true charity of the gospel, which "does not rejoice in unrighteousness, but rejoices in the truth"![l] "If then," says Bishop Hall in *Works*, "I cannot stop other men's mouths from speaking ill, I will either open my mouth to reprove it; or else I will stop mine ears from hearing it." And he continued that he would let the person see in his face, that he didn't approve of what the speaker said.[m] Let the guilty talker think how certainly will this "reproach against his friend" bring the frown of heaven upon him! Oh, Lord! Fill my heart and tongue with your own gracious Spirit!

[l] 1 Cor 13:6

[m] Ps 15:3

5 *He who mocks the poor reproaches his Maker;*
He who rejoices at calamity will not go unpunished.
(held innocent, marg.)

The sin against our *Maker* of oppressing "the poor," has been noted before.[n] In this mocking, there probably is no power to oppress. The *poor* aren't poor by fortune but by God. The *reproach* therefore falls, not on the *poor*, but on their *Maker*—on Him who made them, and made them poor, "Woe to the one who quarrels with his Maker"![1] To pour contempt upon the current coin with the king's image on it is treason against the ruler. The sacred majesty exercises no less contempt in despising *the poor,* who—no less than the rich—have the King's image upon them.[o] This view marks contempt of the poor as a sin of the deepest dye.

[n] Prov 14:31

[o] Gen 9:6

Especially, when poverty is brought on by *calamity;* when the hand of God is therefore more evident, then to *rejoice at calamities* is a fearful provocation. This was the sin of Shimei, scorning his fallen ruler.[p] This sin brought the enemies of God's people under His severest punishment.[2] Very different is the spirit of the Bible: teaching us, even where *calamity* is the fruit of misconduct, instead of being glad—to sympathize; instead of crushing, to raise, a fallen brother, or even a fallen enemy.[q]

[p] 2 Sam 16:5–8

[q] Prov 24:17, 18; Job 31:29; Ps 35:13, 14; Rom 12:20, 21

All slight of *the poor* is strongly rebuked here. And who, knowing himself and his own obligations, could

[1] *Isa 45:9. Comp. Job 40:2. See Bishop Sanderson's* Sermon on 1 Peter 2:17, 13.

[2] *Babylon—Lam 1:21, 22; Ammon—Ezek 25:6, 7; Tyre—26:2, 3; Edom—Obad 10–15. Contrast this barbarous delight with the godly tenderness of the Lord's prophets in foretelling calamities. Isa 16:9–11; Jer 9:1; 17:16; Mic 1:8. The* gladness, *elsewhere expressed* in the calamities *of the enemies of God's people was obviously the admiring discovery of the Lord's faithful keeping of His people and of His glory in the deserved punishment of his irreconcilable rebels, Exod 15; Ps 35:8–10, 19–26; Rev 18:20.*

ever disdain the poor, "Why should I," asks Bishop Reynolds (*Works,* p. 905), "for a little difference in this one particular of worldly wealth, despise my poor brother?" He continued to say that when so many great things *unite* us, can we allow wealth to *disunite* us? "One sun shines on both; one blood bought us both; one heaven will receive us both; only he hath not so much of earth as I, and possibly much more of Christ. And why should I disdain him on earth," Reynolds said and added, "whom the Lord might elevate above me in heaven?"

6 *Grandchildren are the crown of old men,*
And the glory of sons is their fathers.

This Proverb has its limit. What a *crown* of thorns to each other are ungodly children and graceless parents! Little *glory* indeed did Rehoboam and his son add to *their fathers.*[r] And the reputation of Israel's godly King Hezekiah was not helped by his sinful father.[s] Gehazi brought shame, not glory, to his children.[t] But in the ordinary course, gracious children and parents reflect honor upon each other. Such parents rejoice in the number and growth of their *children.* Such children regard *their father's* name as *their glory.* Joseph was indeed a *crown* to his aged father;[u] as was Jacob himself *the glory of his son,* even in a heathen nation.[v] "A good root maketh the branches to flourish, by virtue of the lively sap that it sendeth up. And flourishing branches win praise to the root, for the pleasant fruit which they bring forth, said Clever.[w]

The Old Testament promise—"length of days"[x]—was enhanced, when accompanied with the blessing of children; yet more—when crowned with the increase of *children's children.*[y] The true blessing, however, could only be known, when children, were brought up to know and love the Lord, and were trained early in His ways, and declared Him to their children, that they might also set their hope in God.[z] "Blessed is the man whose quiver is full of them [children]."[a] Happy the children crowned with the example of such fathers! Abraham was the honorable, boast of his descendents.[b] David was *the glory* of his children, preserving for them the throne of Judah for seventeen generations.[c] And may not godly parents,

[r] 1 Kings 17
[s] 2 Chron 28, 29
[t] 2 Kings 5:27
[u] Gen 47:11, 12
[v] Gen 47:7–10
[w] Prov 1:1
[x] Prov 3:2, 16
[y] 2 Kings 48:11, 12; 50:23; Job 42:16; Ps 128:6
[z] Ps 78:5–7
[a] Ps 127:5
[b] Matt 3:9; John 8:33
[c] 1 Kings 11:12, 13; 15:4; 2 Chron 21:7

under the broader government of grace, educating their children by example, no less than by precept—may they not look for a godly seed[d] who shall acknowledge infinite, eternal obligations to parental faith and godliness?[e]

[d]Ps 127:3
[e]2 Tim 1:5; 3:15

7 *Excellent speech is not fitting for a fool;*
Much less are lying lips to a prince.

Men naturally speak as they are. The *lip* is the organ of the heart. *The lip of excellency,* that speaks properly of high and lofty things, obviously *doesn't belong to the fool.*[f] A grave discourse on godliness doesn't become an ungodly man.[g] It carries no weight, and, so far from doing good, it often brings contempt.[h] Christ would not accept even a true statement from the lips of Satan, lest it should be a cause for stumbling.[i] So out of place was proper speech from so corrupt a source!

[f]Prov 26:7, 9
[g]Ps 50:16, 17
[h]Matt 7:3–5; Rom 2:21–24
[i]Mark 1:34. Comp. Acts 16:16–18

Much less are lying lips fitting to a prince—the minister and guardian of truth.[j] Yet in a world, where self reigns supreme, such inconsistencies are all too many![3] The pure doctrine of our divine master alone secures Christian consistency in heart, lip, and life. Never let us forget, that if *excellent speech is not fitting for a fool, it does fit the gospel of Christ—the saints of God.*[k] And oh! let it be fully exercised in all earnestness and power, for the nourishing of the church,[l] and for the conviction of those who know not Christ.[m]

[j]Prov 16:10
[k]Phil 1:27
[l]Eph 4:29
[m]Col 4:6

8 *A bribe* [AV—*gift*] *is a charm in the sight of its owner;*
Wherever he turns, he prospers.

"A gift is so tempting, that it can no more be refused than a lovely jewel, by him to whom it is presented; and such is its power, it commonly prevails over all men, dispatches all business, carries all causes, and—in a word—effects whatever a man desires," said Bishop Patrick.[4] Such is the sympathy between a lusting eye and a

[3] *Heathen morality from the lips of one of her wisest teachers did not rule out* the lying lips of princes, *because they governed for the public good. "All others," Plato adds, "must abstain." Far more* becoming a prince *was the saying of Louis IX, of France—"If truth be banished from all the rest of the world, it ought to be found in the breast of princes." Alphonsus of Arragon declared that one "word of a prince should be a greater security than a private man's oath." Undoubtedly the royal character ought to display a grandeur and dignity of principle, that should shine through every dark cloud of trial and perplexity.*

[4] *"What a description," adds Mr. Scott, "of the mercenary selfishness of mankind!" Comp. also verse 23; 18:16. Even the heathen conscience seems to have had a right understanding of this evil. The saying of Philip of Macedon is well known, that "there was no fortress so strong, but it might be taken, if a donkey laden with gold was brought to the gate." The poet finely illustrated this remark, referring also to the current report, that—"not Philip, but Philip's*

glittering *bribe*. The covetous prophet[n]—yes, even an apostle[o]—was willfully deceived by its fascination. The heathen soldiers sold themselves to its slavery.[p] A king's minister was won over by its allurement.[q] Even a king—and such as the man after God's own heart—was sinfully perverted in the snare.[r] Seldom does it fail to *prosper wherever it turns*. But who would envy a *prosperity* for evil? All ministers of law were wisely directed (like fabled justice) to give their decisions blindfolded, not looking at this *charm*, lest they should be dazzled by its sparkling attraction.[s] Unfaithfulness was always visited with the heavy displeasure of the great Judge.[t]

[n]Num 22:7, 8, 21; 2 Peter 2:15
[o]Matt 26:14–16
[p]Matt 28:12–15
[q]Acts 12:20
[r]2 Sam 16:1–4
[s]Exod 23:8; Deut 16:19
[t]Deut 27:25; Isa 5:22, 23; Mic 7:3, 4

And isn't even the child of God often tempted in this way? Doesn't the influence of a *bribe*, the sense of obligation, ever repress the bold consistency of godliness? Doesn't the bias of friendship, or a plausible advantage, entice into a crooked path? Oh! be determined, in a greater strength than your own, to resist sin! The battle isn't with violent temptation, or with open sin, but with subtle and apparently harmless strayings from the straight path. Exercise your "integrity and uprightness" in the spirit of faith; and don't doubt that they will "preserve" you.[u] The man of God, who "will dwell on the eights" with his God, "shakes his hands so that they hold no bribes"; as the apostle Paul "shook" off the viper that had fastened on his hand.[v] From this height he looks down upon this corruption with indignant loathing—"Keep your gifts for yourself . . . may your silver perish with you."[w]

[u]Ps 25:21
[v]Isa 33:15, 16, with Acts 28:5
[w]Dan 5:17; Acts 8:18–20. Comp. 1 Sam 12:3

9 *He who covers a transgression seeks love,*
But he who repeats a matter separates intimate friends.

Seeks love! A beautiful expression that ought to be kept in mind! It shows a delight in the atmosphere of *love*—man's highest elevation in communion with his God.[x] It implies not merely exercising love but searching and making opportunity for it. Yet how seldom do we rise to the high standard of this most-important grace, exalted as

[x]1 John 4:16

gold,—conquered Greece." "Gold and silver pervert many things, especially motives of right. Money hath a great power with those that are in power. A golden key will open any prison door, and cast the watchman into a deep sleep. *Gold will break open gates of iron, as well as silence the orator's voice, and blind the judge's eyes. It will bind the strong man's hands, and blunt the edge of the sword. It makes war, and it makes peace. What almost can it not do with corrupt minds?"—CARYL* on Job 31:21.

[y] 1 Cor 12:31; 13
[z] Eph 5:1, 2

it is far above "the greater gifts";[y] and illustrated and enforced by no less than the divine example![z] Yet too often it sits at the door of our lips, instead of finding a home in our hearts; forgetting that the exhortation is not, that we should talk of love, but that we should walk in it; not stepping over it, crossing it, walking by the side, but in it, as our highway and course. One step of our feet is better than a hundred words of the tongue.

A loving spirit demonstrates this heavenly grace in a wonderful way. Our motives are often misunderstood. We meet in a world of selfishness and cold reserve, instead of glowing confidence. Prejudice builds a wall against Christian communication and fellowship. Wounded pride returns unkindness with contempt. Resentment causes retaliation. Disappointment kindles unhealthy suspicion. Here is a noble field for Christian victory; instead of resenting, to *cover a transgression* with a mantle of love;[a] with that act of pardon, by which we are saved—the most aggravated *transgression,* the most unprovoked injuries, being *covered* in eternal forgetfulness.[b]

[a] Prov 10:12; 1 Cor 13:7
[b] Heb 8:12

Repeating gossip about others often separates close *friends* by uncovering a forgotten quarrel.[c] There may be no harm intended. But to amuse ourselves with the follies or weakness of our brethren is sinful trifling, filled with injury. "Gossips and busybodies" are justly described as "talking about things not proper to mention."[d] A disciplined tongue is a gracious mercy to the church.

[c] Prov 16:28
[d] 1 Tim 5:13

10 *A rebuke goes deeper into one who has understanding*
Than a hundred blows into a fool.

If we should *cover our sins,* we shouldn't hold back *rebuke. Rebuke* distinguishes the wise man from the *fool.*[e] A word is enough for the wise. But fools require stern and forceful discipline. Parents and teachers should especially study the character of children that they may temper *rebuke* wisely. Many a fine spirit has been spoiled by wrong discipline.

[e] Prov 13:1

If this be true of man's *rebuke,* much more of God's. A word was enough for David.[f] A look *went deeper into* Peter's heart,[g] than a *hundred blows into* Pharaoh,[h]

[f] 2 Sam 12:1–7; 24:13, 14
[g] Luke 22:61, 62
[h] Exod 9:34, 35

Ahaz,[i] Israel.[j] Whippings only bruise the fool's back; they never reach his heart. So he remains a fool. Though you should pulverize him with a pounding tool, as wheat is ground, he'll still be as foolish as ever.[k]

[i] 2 Chron 28:22
[j] Isa 1:5; 9:13; Jer 5:3
[k] Prov 27:22

What then makes the difference in the effect of *rebuke*? "I will remove the heart of stone from your flesh and give you a heart of flesh."[l] A needle pierces deeper into flesh than a sword into stone. A wakeful ear, a tender conscience, a softened heart, a teachable spirit—these are the practical exercises, by which our wise and loving Father disciplines His children for His service, for His cross, and for His crown.

[l] Ezek 36:26

11 *A rebellious man seeks only evil,*
So a cruel messenger will be sent against him.
12 *Let a man meet a bear robbed of her cubs,*
Rather than a fool in his folly.
13 *He who returns evil for good,*
Evil will not depart from his house.

THE RAGE OF THE BEAST

Some awful pictures of man are seen here. Look at his waywardness—*seeking only rebellion*—resisting all authority of God and man. This is no light sin.[m] Therefore a *cruel messenger,* one who can't be distracted from his job, shall be turned from his work *and sent against him.* The disobedient son in the family;[n] Korah in the "congregation";[o] Absalom,[p] Sheba,[q] and Pekah,[r] in the kingdom—all stand out as moments of deserved justice. Not that *rebellion* is the only sin, but it *is* the surfacing of the stubborn will. It may be hidden under a peaceful and attractive cover, not dead but sleeping.[5] Let God remove the restraint! Let Satan set up an occasion for temptation; then see what happens! Where everything seemed love and unity before, now it seems to be nothing but hatred for one another.[s]

[m] 1 Sam 15:23
[n] Deut 21:18
[o] Num 16
[p] 2 Sam 18:15, 16
[q] 2 Sam 20:1, 22
[r] 2 Kings 15:27–30
[s] Titus 3:3

Take another look at man in his foolishness. His strength and accuracy can scarcely be surpassed. A savage beast under the strongest excitement—*a bear robbed of her cubs*—is less dangerous to meet. Witness Jacob's sons taking a whole city by surprise because of one man's

[5] *The philosophical remark of Burke—"Those who do not love religion, hate it"—is the spirit of our divine Master's saying, Matt 12:30.*

[t] Gen 34:25
[u] 1 Sam 22:18
[v] Dan 3:13–19
[w] Matt 2:16
[x] Acts 9:1
[y] Gen 1:27
[z] 1 Sam 25:32, 33

foolishness;[t] Saul slaying a large company of innocent priests;[u] Nebuchadnezzar heating the furnace sevenfold;[v] Herod murdering the children in Ramah;[w] "Saul still breathing threats and murder against the disciples of the Lord"[x]—wasn't all this the rage of a beast, not the reason of a man? Surely this is a very humbling picture of man, once created "in the image of God."[y] But it's even more humbling to see this foolishness in a child of God; to see David binding himself with an oath to murder a whole family, some of whom had taken up his cause against the drunken offender. Yet the melting away of his fury under wise remonstrance showed the man of God covered with the shame of his *folly*; not the *fool* living *in it* as his nature, habit, and delight.[z]

But now, getting closer to home, aren't there households where uncontrolled anger takes charge of everybody at will? Doesn't the self-willed victim remember, that nothing is said or done in a passion, that can't be better said or done afterward? Don't we ever see the Christian, whom his Master's discipline and example ought to have transformed to a lamb, still *like the bear robbed of her cubs?* Man—the holiest, "God left him alone only to test him, that He might know all that was in his heart"[a]—"man," so left to himself, "at his best is a mere breath."[b] We ought to hate that all too common, empty excuse—"It is my way." Isn't this why a contrite soul grieves, calling for deep humiliation and increasing watchfulness?

[a] 2 Chron 32:31
[b] Ps 39:5

THE ASTONISHMENT OF HEAVEN AND EARTH

Look again at man in his ingratitude. God forbids returning evil for evil; much more *evil for good.* Even the heathen believed that this sin included every other.[c] Yet was it the aggravation of their own sin. It is so hateful to God, that it not only brings evil upon the sinner *himself,* but on *his family.* Israel was punished for the ill return to Gideon.[d] The traitor's *house* was doomed to a curse.[e] And how fearful *the evil* to the ungrateful nation![f]

Such ingratitude is common, but the conscience is asleep. What else can we expect, when the ungodly resent attempts to prompt their best interests? *David* complained of this unkind and undeserved payment in return

[c] Rom 1:21
[d] Judg 8:35; 9:56, 57. Comp. Jer 18:20–23
[e] Ps 55:12–15; 109:9–13
[f] Matt 27:25, with 23:32–39

for the good he was doing.[g] Such a recompence is marked out for special disapproval.

[g]Ps 38:20

And surely *evil rewarded for good* was the stamp of our father's sin.[h] And ever since, the curse has been fearfully verified. *Evil will not depart from his house.* And this is not unjust severity. What do we say to a child, who has been nourished with the tenderest care, yet casts off all love for his parents and rewards good with evil? Could any other virtue make up for this unnatural hatred, this awful sin—the astonishment of heaven and earth—the mark of every child of fallen Adam? "Sons I have reared and brought up, But they have revolted against Me."[i] Without the transfer of this mighty mass of guilt, how could we stand before God? And who of us, still suffering under this load won't seek to fully experience that no less perfect work, by which the rebel spirit is tamed and humbled into the meekness and love of the gospel?

[h]Gen 3:5, 6, with 2:8–18

[i]Isa 1:2

14 *The beginning of strife is* like *letting out water,*
So abandon the quarrel before it breaks out.

OPEN THE DAM—PREPARE FOR A FLOOD

Both the destructive elements—fire and water—illustrate the danger of the beginning of strife.[j] To neither element can we say—"Thus far you shall come, but no farther"![k] We can no more command our uncontrolled passions—"Hush, be still"[l]—than we can the raging storm. The dam may restrain a large body of water; but open the valves, and the water loosed may be a sweeping flood. So fearfully has *the beginning of strife* issued in the murder of thousands;[m] and even in the destruction of kingdoms.[n]

[j]Prov 26:21; Judg 9:19, 20; James 3

[k]Job 38:11

[l]Mark 4:39

[m]Judg 12:1–6; 2 Sam 2:14–27

[n]2 Chron 10:14–16; 13:17; 25:17–24

And it's no less destructive in ordinary life! One provoking word brings on another. Every angry response widens the breach. Not very often, once we hear the first word, do we hear the last. A flood of evil is poured in, that destroys peace, comfort, and conscience. Doesn't grace teach us the Christian victory—hold back expression of resentment, and, bear the irritation rather than break the bond of unity?

It's a wise rule to stop evil at *the beginning.* It's much easier to preserve the dam than repair it. Once a break is made, even if it just lets out a drop of *water,* it's the *beginning* of an evil, the fruit of which cannot be calculated. How soon was the indignation of the ten apostles turned against the two. If the Lord hadn't stepped in between them so promptly, it might have led to a serious *quarrel*![o] For—as one forcefully said—Man *knows the beginning* of sin; but who *bounds the issues* thereof? Abraham nobly yielded in the *contention* with Lot, and the quarrel ended.[p] But with Paul and Barnabas—because neither would yield—"there arose such a sharp disagreement that"—sad record!—"they separated from one another."[q] Moses restrained himself in the rising quarrel with his wife. Israel wisely refrained from contention with Edom in the angry refusal of water.[r] David answered gently to his brother's irritating suspicion.[s] He was "like a deaf man" to his enemies, who were seeking contention with him.[t] The prompt decision of the apostles in the care of widows, preserved the infant church from serious division.[u] Under similar threatening circumstances, wouldn't it be well to consider, whether we're contending for shadow or for substance? If substance, then we need to determine whether it might not be an exercise of forbearance, rather than a handle of dissension;[v] or, if its importance justified the dissension,[w] whether our judgment and conscience had fully and intelligently determined the real principles involved. "Peace" and holiness are the main points we are commanded to "pursue";[x] and they are so much one, that we look in vain to advance in holiness, unless we "pursue the things which make for peace."[y] In guarding against the deadly issue of *quarrels*: let it be remembered, that the time to leave off is not when we see it at its worst, but at its *beginning*; restraining the first rising in ourselves; controlling our own proud tempers, and cultivating our Master's meek and self-denying spirit.[6]

[o] Matt 20:24
[p] Gen 13:8, 9
[q] Acts 15:39
[r] Num 20:14–21
[s] 1 Sam 17:28, 29
[t] Ps 38:12–14
[u] Acts 6:1–4
[v] Rom 14
[w] Gal 2:5
[x] Heb 12:14
[y] Rom 14:19; Col 3:12–15; James 3:18

15 *He who justifies the wicked, and he who condemns*
the righteous,
Both of them alike are an abomination to the LORD.

[6] *The following remarks from Mr. Burke are well worth consideration—"The arms with which the ill dispositions of the world are to be combated, are moderation, gentleness, a little indulgence of others, and a great distrust of ourselves; which are not qualities of a mean spirit, as some may possibly think them; but virtues of a great and noble kind, and such as dignify our nature, as much as they contribute to our repose and fortune. For nothing can be so unworthy of a well-composed soul, as to pass away life in bickerings and litigations, in snarling and scuffling with every one about us"*—Letter to Barry. *PRIOR's* Life of Burke.

JUDGE RIGHTEOUS JUDGMENT

Judicial iniquity is an awful abuse of God's authority.[z] The judge or magistrate "is a minister of God to you for good."[a] The appeal is to him for justice as the representative of God.[b] If the great Judge "loved righteousness, and hated wickedness,"[c] this unrighteousness justifying *"the wicked"* must *be abomination to him.*[d] This guilt of Samuel's sons, so contrary to his own integrity, was the immediate cause of the abolition of the theocracy.[e] The judges in David's time seem to have been guilty of both these branches of injustice.[f] Ahab's house was ruined by *his condemnation of the righteous.*[g] "Not this Man, but Barabbas"[h]—combined the double sin. It was the perfection of injustice, the most aggravated abomination.

[z]Exod 23:7
[a]Rom 13:4
[b]Deut 25:1
[c]Ps 45:7; Deut 32:4
[d]Isa 5:23
[e]1 Sam 8:3–5, with 12:3
[f]Ps 82:2; 94:20, 21
[g]1 Kings 21:13–19
[h]John 18:40

But we're not to confine the application to official iniquity. All of us need great watchfulness, that we may "judge with righteous judgment";[i] that no corrupt bias may prejudice the exercise of our private judgment, either in favor of *the wicked,* or in the *condemnation of the righteous?*

[i]John 7:24

But let us place ourselves before the Judge of all, accused by Satan, our own conscience, and the righteous law of God; convicted of every charge; yet justified. Does God then in thus justifying "the ungodly"[j] oppose this rule? Far from it. If he *justifies the wicked,* it is because of righteousness.[k] If he *condemns the righteous,* it is on the charge of unrighteousness. Nowhere throughout the universe do the moral perfections of the governor of the world shine so gloriously as at the cross of Calvary.[l] The satisfaction of the holy law, and the demonstration of righteous mercy, harmonize with the justification of the condemned sinner.[m] And this combined glory tunes the song of everlasting praise.[7]

[j]Rom 4:5
[k]Rom 3:25, 26
[l]Isa 53:5–10; 2 Cor 5:21
[m]Ps 85:10; Isa 42:21; 45:21

16 *Why is there a price in the hand of a fool to buy wisdom,*
When he has no sense?

[7] *Bishop Davenant justly quotes this text, as an example of the suitable use of the term justification—"not the infusion of a quality, but the pronouncing a sentence."* (Discourse on Inherent Righteousness, *chap. 22. Allport's Translation). In this true sense it is used in reference to our justification before God—pronounced* just *in God's own court of judgment.*

THE PRICE IN THE HAND OF A FOOL

A question of wonder and indignation! We often find this reckless lack of sound judgment in temporal things. A young man will spend a large sum at the university, professing to buy wisdom, and yet idle away all his time! Isn't *the price* obviously *in the hand of a fool,* who *has no* concern for the advantages? The thoughtless fool might be warned even by his worldly friends. He is losing important opportunities, turning his best friends away, getting into debt, harming himself physically, ruining his reputation. Isn't this throwing away good money by reckless foolishness?

Yet it's far sadder to see foolishness like this in spiritual things. Why is *a fool* so blessed, when he has no desire to improve his blessings? Birth, spiritual privileges, talents, time, influence, opportunity—all are part of the *price for buying wisdom.* If the *fool* throws them away, the account of unprofitableness seals his sentence.[n] The means to buy wisdom is in our hands.[o] Yet how many thousand *fools* have no desire to buy, and would rather lose the opportunity, than to work for it; rather go sleeping to hell, than working to heaven! Those remaining of the ten tribes despised the opportunity put within their reach to come up to the feast of the Lord.[p] The town where Jesus was brought up,[q] the cities where He wrought his miracles,[r] willfully despised the price of wisdom. The Gadarenes threw away the pearl.[s] Herod eyed it with curiosity;[t] Pilate with indifference;[u] the Jews with scorn.[v] The rich youth preferred his own goodly pearls to it.[w] Felix hoped to turn it to his own selfish purpose.[x] Agrippa dared not purchase it.[y] Weren't all these pictures of the *fool* that every day meets our eye? That which is "more precious than jewels"[z] is to him more worthless than a pebble. That which "is more sweet than honey, is tasteless as the white of an egg," said Lawson. He lives for himself, as if there were no God in the world. His heart is given to the world, as if it could be a God to him, or could fill up God's vacant place in his heart! Yet, the realities of eternity—the mighty things of the gospel—are like a tale that is told. Isn't it enough that they should have a place in our creed though never in our hearts? The world is preferred to heaven,

[n] Matt 25:24–30
[o] Prov 8:4, 5; 9:4–6; Isa 55:1–3; Rom 10:8; Rev 3:20
[p] 2 Chron 30:10
[q] Luke 4:28
[r] Matt 11:21
[s] Matt 8:34
[t] Luke 23:8. Comp. Acts 17:21, 32
[u] John 18:38
[v] Acts 13:46
[w] Mark 10:22
[x] Acts 24:25–27
[y] Acts 26:28
[z] Prov 3:15

time to eternity; and the immortal soul, for which such a cost has been paid, and such prospects prepared, perishes in folly. But those who linger will stop short of heaven. And won't it be like a sword in the awakened conscience—"I might have been enriched, if I hadn't wasted the golden opportunities of salvation and fooled away the glorious days of the Son of Man?" Won't this be the sting of the never-dying worm—"Had I come to Christ when I might have come, I wouldn't have been in this place of torment. I *would* not come then.[a] I *cannot* come now."[b] "Lord, save me," cries the pious Howe, "from trifling with the things of eternity."

[a] Matt 23:37; John 5:40
[b] Matt 25:10; Luke 13:25–28; 16:26

But if I have a strong enough desire *to buy wisdom* and am willing to pay the price, I'll get it. I'll find blessing beyond price by putting my talent to work and by diligently improving my privileges. I shall find Him whom my soul needs above all, and desires to love above all; whose lovely names are not empty names but full of truth. Brother—Husband—Savior—if the fool would only think about these, wouldn't the picture attract his heart; as One able to promote him to honor, to give him unmeasurable compensation for his toil or loss; whose very reproofs are pity, whose strivings are tenderness; whose rebukes are love, whose smile is heaven.

17 *A friend loves at all times,*
And a brother is born for adversity.

TRUE FRIENDSHIP

This beautiful picture of friendship has been drawn by moralists, sentimentalists, and poets. But the reality is only found, where God's grace has melted away natural selfishness and turned it into disinterested love. If virtue is the best ground of friendship, then is this most heavenly virtue in the firmest ground of all. What passes under the name is too often, as Bishop Hall (*Works*, 8:38. *Meditations and Vows*) describes it, "brittle stuff." The fickle excitement is cooled by distance or by the coldness of our friend. Degradation of worldly circumstances reduces friendship into indifference[c] or even into hatred.[d] The friend, who has left the right path, is forsaken, instead of being followed, watched over, and every opportunity used for reclaiming him. But the true *friend loves*

[c] Job 6:14, 15
[d] Prov 19:7; Job 19:17–20

at all times, in spite of "evil report and good report." He does not change when circumstances change. He is the same whether we are in wealth or need. He proves himself in *adversity,* by rising in wrath, and exerting every nerve, in proportion as his help is needed.[e] He is not ashamed of poverty or of a prison.[f] In any jarrings of the flesh, *adversity* cements love. *The loving friend* becomes now *a brother born for adversity.*[g] Such was the love of Joseph to his brethren; unshaken by changes, not lessened by ingratitude.[h] Such was the firm cleaving of Ruth to her desolate mother-in-law;[i] the unity of heart between David and Jonathan;[j] the affectionate sympathy of the beloved disciple to the mother of his Lord;[k] the faithful love of the brethren to the great apostle Paul in his troubles.[8]

[e]2 Cor 6:8; 2 Sam 15:19–22; 17:27–29
[f]Phil 2:25; 2 Tim 1:16–18
[g]Comp. Job 2:11–13
[h]Gen 45:5–8
[i]Ruth 1:16, 17
[j]1 Sam 18:3; 19:2; 23:16
[k]John 19:27

We can't expect perfection. Can we doubt the sincerity of the disciples, while we are humbled, instructed, and warned by their frailty?[l] For frailty it was; not willfulness, nor hypocrisy. "You are those who have stood by Me in My trials"—was their Master's kindly acknowledgment in that time of weakness when they all forsook Him and fled.[m]

[l]Matt 26:40, 41
[m]Luke 22:28, with Matt 26:56

LIVING BEYOND THE REACH OF DISAPPOINTMENT

It is to Him that we must look for the perfect example. To see the Son of God in our nature that He might be our *friend and brother;*[n] to hear Him "not ashamed to call them brethren"[o]—this is a mystery of friendship that is unsearchable. Truly, this Friend—He, alone, is worthy of our unlimited confidence. Such is the constancy of *His love—at all times*[p]—even unto death[9]—unchanged by the most undutiful returns—"turned and looked at" the disciple (a look so full of tenderness and power!)[q] whom we would have excommunicated. Such is the sympathy of His love—*born for adversity;* so joined to us—the Friend and the Brother we need; never nearer to us than when He is with us in our lowest depths of trouble; and, even though He is now our glorified Brother in heaven, yet He can still "sympathize with our weaknesses,"[r] still

[n]Heb 2:14
[o]Heb 2:11–13
[p]John 13:1
[q]Luke 22:61
[r]Heb 4:15

[8] *Aquila and Priscilla—Rom 16:3, 4; Epaphroditus—Phil 2:25, 26—when a prisoner; the Philippian church—Phil 4:15.*

[9] *John 15:13.*
"Mine is an unchanging love;
Higher than the heights above;
Deeper than the depths beneath;
Firm and faithful, strong as death."—COWPER

afflicted "in all our affliction";[s] presenting us to his Father, as His own elect, the purchase of His blood, the "members of His body," of His flesh, and of His bones.[t] Here is sympathy in all its fullness, and all its helpfulness. Here is indeed *a Brother born for adversity*. Howell said, " 'Trust him', O ye trembling believers, 'at all times,' and in all places. You will then be possessed of the happy art of living beyond the reach of all disappointment."[10]

[s]Isa 63:9
[t]Eph 5:30

18 *A man lacking in sense*[11] *pledges,*
And becomes surety in the presence of his neighbor.

Though we are to feel ourselves *born for adversity*, ever ready to "bear one another's burdens";[u] yet we must not befriend our *brother* at the risk or expense of injustice to our family. We have therefore another warning against unwise suretyship.[v] Beware of pledging in agreement without determining whether we can fulfill our obligation or whether *our neighbor* is not equally able to fulfill it himself. This shows *a man lacking in sense;* especially if he does this *in the presence of his neighbor*. For why is his word taken, except because of the suspicion of insolvency or dishonesty? A lavish, thoughtless kindness may gain us a popular name. But the principle, closely examined, will be found to be another form of selfishness. There is no true generosity in rash engagements, which may involve our name and family in disgrace or ruin. True indeed—if those hands that were nailed to the cross, had not been wounded in paying our debt, the handwriting that was against us could never have been cancelled.[w] Yet the eternal plan is no pattern for our simple foolishness. Nor is infinite love combined with perfect wisdom a plea for our rash generosity. Religion, though it warns its professors to be cautious, all too often unjustly bears the blame for them. If we would adorn the Christian profession and avoid causing the ungodly to stumble, we must "have regard

[u]Gal 6:2
[v]Prov 6:1–5; 11:15
[w]Col 2:14

[10] *HOWELL'S* Sermons, 2. 252. *"Though solitary and unsupported, and oppressed by sorrows unknown and undivided, I am not without joyful expectations. There is one* Friend who loveth at all times: a Brother born for adversity—*the help of the helpless; the hope of the hopeless; the strength of the weak; the riches of the poor; the peace of the disquieted; the companion of the desolate; the Friend of the friendless. To Him alone will I call, and He will raise me above my fears"*—Memoir of Mrs. Hawkes, *pp. 127, 128. The ancient Jews applied this Proverb to Christ, adducing it as a testimony, that the divine Messiah would by His incarnation become the Brother of man.*

[11] *Prov 7:7; 10:13; 11:12; 15:21; 24:30. "It reveals the want of all the faculties of the soul, through ignorance, carelessness, and the prevalence of evil tendencies of various kinds," SCOTT on 11:12.*

for what is honorable, not only in the sight of the Lord, but also in the sight of men."[x]

[x] 2 Cor 8:20, 21

19 *He who loves transgression loves strife;*
He who raises his door seeks destruction.

BRANCH FROM THE ROOT OF SIN

It's possible, of course, to fall into conflict without *loving* it.[y] But let's always look at it as a branch from the root of sin,[z] and the fruitful source of sin.[a] To *love* strife, then, is to love sin. The man involved in *strife* argues that he loves peace, that it's his neighbor's stubbornness that drives him into *strife.* And yet, if we are in it frequently; if we don't take any pains, or make any sacrifice of self-will or interest,[b] to avoid getting into *strife*—doesn't conscience make the charge against us? The love of *transgression* lies deeper than we usually see it. It shows itself in forms that the world may overlook but which prove it to be carnal.[12]

[y] Gen 13:7, 8
[z] Gal 5:19–21
[a] 2 Cor 12:20; James 3:16
[b] 1 Cor 6:1–7

Usually it proceeds from the root of pride.[c] the man tries to lift his door[13] above his neighbor's, pretending to be higher in rank than he really is. Or, he lets his ambition walk all over his neighbor. Sometimes he rises above his ruler[d] or even stands in defiance of his God.[e] The lazy man sees his ruin before him and idly waits for it, not making any effort to prevent it.[f] But the proud man *seeks destruction.* He puts himself in the way of it, and sooner or later his day comes; and his name, glory, and honor are swept away.[g] Watch over me, O my God, to preserve me from the first rising of my proud heart. Or if my frailty yields to it, O keep me from generally practicing this presumptuous sin that hurries me, as a rival against your throne, into the pit of *destruction.*

[c] Prov 13:10; Mark 9:33, 34
[d] 2 Sam 15:1; 1 Kings 1:5; 16:9–18
[e] Rom 13:1, 2
[f] Prov 6:11
[g] Prov 16:18; Isa 22:15–19; Jer 22:13–19

20 *He who has a crooked mind finds no good,*
And he who is perverted in his language falls into evil.

[12] *1 Cor 3:3, 4. "I never loved those salamanders, that are never well, but when they are in the fire of contention. I will rather suffer a thousand wrongs, than offer one. I will rather suffer a hundred, than inflict one. I will suffer many, ere I will complain of one, and endeavor to right it by contending. I have ever found, that to strive with my superior is furious; with my equal doubtful; with my inferior sordid and base; with any, full of unquietness"—Bishop Hall,* Meditations and Vows, *Works, viii. 18.*

[13] *An illusion to the* gates *of splendid palaces in the East, generally elevated according to the vanity of their owner—MORIER, quoted in BURDER'S* Oriental Customs.

NOT MY OWN WAY, LORD!

The history of God's ancient people is a picture of willfulness with all its empty results. Let their long-suffering God do what He would *to* them and *for* them, they *found no* satisfying good.[h] Self-will even in its fullest exercise, instead of bringing the desired *good,* always ends in disappointment; and, when *the perverted language* breaks out, in frightful evil.[i] The best of us are too often controlled by this waywardness. Even when we seek to walk with God, how the *crooked* mind struggles to walk by its own inclination! May the good Lord give us a self-denying spirit, to restrain us from being guided by our own corrupt fancies! Many an erratic course in the church we trace to some unhappy prejudice not disciplined by the divine Spirit, not molded to reverential faith. Most graciously therefore does our God assert His own right to supremacy; promising us—not freedom from restraint, but a yoke,[j] a binding law, a strict obligation, and—above all—the heart to love and obey.[k] Here is now self-control and stability; not impulse and feeling, but fixed and steady principle. Should we not cry with filial simplicity—"Not my will, O Lord. Let me have anything but my own way. Leave me not to my perverse heart." In proportion as *the crooked mind* is thus subdued, *the perverted language* is bridled; and we have the perfect man in Christian consistency, humility, and love.

[h]Ps 78

[i]Prov 11:20; 18:6, 7; Num 16; Acts 13:8–11

[j]Matt 11:29

[k]Jer 31:33; Ezek 36:26, 27

21 *He who begets a fool* does so *to his sorrow,*
And the father of a fool has no joy.

HARVEST OF RAIN

Among the vanities, to which the creature is made subject, Solomon elsewhere lists one, of which he probably had an emotional experience—leaving the labor of his hand—he knows not to whom—whether he would be a wise man or a fool.[l] As it turned out, it was *a fool.* A weeping parent not only finds *no joy* in the fondly cherished object of his hopes; but a consuming grief embitters all his joys, and often brings him down with sorrow to the grave.[14] And how this sorrow is aggravated,

[l]Eccl 2:18, 19

[14]*Gen 42:38. Hasn't many an afflicted parent fellowship with the impassioned cry of Augustus—"Would that I had lived single, or died childless?"*

when there's an unhappy, humbling awareness, that we have been unduly indulgent, or too severe, or unwise. Or most of all, if we've been neglectful—of real prayer for the child,[15] and diligent improvement of God's appointed means, we have allowed the evil tendencies to grow to produce a terrible harvest of ruin!

Yet let the godly parent expect everything from prayer—provided it isn't paralyzed by despondency.[m] In the deepest distress never lose sight of God's love.[n] Let the determined faith of a praying mother encourage perseverance.[o] God exercises faith; but He never fails to honor it. He delays to answer prayer; but every word, every sigh, is registered for acceptance in His best time. Let Solomon's word be a quickening—not a discouraging—word "profitable" indeed "for reproof, for correction," but also, as much "for training in righteousness."[p]

[m] Gal 6:9; John 11:40
[n] Gen 17:7
[o] Matt 15:22–28
[p] 2 Tim 3:16

22 *A joyful heart is good medicine,*
But a broken spirit dries up the bones.

THE BEST MEDICINE!

This is not true of all *joyfulness.* The wise man rightly describes the loud and noisy mirth of fools to be, no *medicine,* but "madness";[q] a transient flash, not an abiding source of enjoyment. Probably this merriment here means nothing more than cheerfulness, which, in its proper measure, on proper subjects, and at a proper time, is a legitimate pleasure, especially belonging to Christianity.

[q] Eccl 2:2. Comp. 1 Sam 25:36, 37

Our Lord made *a joyful heart* by his message of divine forgiveness;[r] and this doubtless was a more healing *medicine* to the paralytic than the restoration of his limbs. If I am a pardoned sinner, an accepted child of God, what earthly trouble can get me down? "Paul and Silas were praying and singing hymns of praise to God" in the inner prison with "their feet in the stocks."[s] The martyrs glorified God in the "fire." They were "tortured, not ac-

[r] Matt 9:2–7
[s] Acts 16:25

[15] *Bishop* SANDERSON'S Sermon on Rom *15:5. "Think none of you, you have sufficiently discharged your parts towards those that are under your charge, if you have instructed them, corrected them when they have done amiss, and rewarded them when they have done well, so long as your fervent prayers for them have been wanting. In vain shall you wrestle with their stubbornness and other corruptions, (though you put forth all your strength) so long as you wrestle with them only. Then, or not at all, shall you wrestle to purpose, when you enter the lists with the Father of Spirits, as Jacob did: wrestling with him by your importunate prayers; and not giving him over, till you have wrung a blessing from him, either for yourselves, or them, or both."*

cepting their release, in order that they might obtain a better resurrection."[t] All earthly enjoyments are now doubly blest with heavenly sunshine.[u]

[t]Heb 11:34, 35
[u]Eccl 9:7–9

There is also the Christian flow of natural spirits. For when consecrated to the Lord, they become a means of enjoyment, not only to ourselves,[v] but to those around us. Often has the sorrowing saint been encouraged, often also has the worldling been convicted, by a brother's cheerful words or looks.[w] To the former it has been a *medicine;* to the latter a rebuke.

[v]Prov 15:13
[w]Prov 12:25; Eccl 8:1

THE WITHERING INFLUENCE

A *broken spirit* in an evangelical sense is God's precious gift; stamped with His special honor, and always constituting an acceptable service. But here it describes a brooding spirit of despondency; always looking at the dark side; and, if connected with Christianity (which is not always the case), flowing from narrow and misdirected views, a false humility centering in self. The influence *dries up the bones.* The bodily system is noticeably affected. "It contracts and enfeebles the animal spirits; preys on our strength; eats out the vigor of the constitution. The radical moisture is consumed; and the unhappy subject of this passion droops like a flower in the scorching heat of summer," said Bishop Horne.[16]

Not less deadly is its influence upon the spiritual system. Hard thoughts of God develop, as though he had forsaken, neglected, or forgotten us. From doubting, the soul goes to chilling fear; then to gloomy despondency. The power of the telescope fails to bring distant objects near. Hence the present hold of the grand object is feeble. The hope of future enjoyment is dark. Distance too often lessens communication. Prayer is less frequently or powerfully sent up. The answers therefore and the supplies of cheering grace are fewer. We are not only weakened in comfort but cut short in strength. The mind is clothed in sable. The chariot's wheels are taken off, so that we drag heavily. Discontent and a quarrelsome, unbelieving sadness take possession of the soul and totally unfit us for the service of God.

[16] Sermon on a Merry Heart. *The English proverb is "Dry sorrow drinks the blood—sorrow that cannot weep!"*

Therefore, we should be most watchful against this withering influence, not allowing the imagination to dwell needlessly in gloom. Basic temperament will have its effect. External things act upon the body and through the body upon the mind. Some of us are creatures even of weather, not the same on a misty day as on a bright one. There is much in our physical system that is more within the province of the physician than the minister; much perhaps that we may be inclined too hastily to censure in a brother, when a more accurate knowledge would call forth our sympathy. When outward and inward troubles unite, what wonder, if the vessel, like Paul's ship, "where two seas met,"[x] give way?[17] Still, let it be remembered, that every indulgence increases the evil; and that allowed prevalence may end in a fixed melancholy.

[x]Acts 27:41

Turn and see what materials can be gathered for resistance to this ruinous evil and induce a well-regulated cheerfulness. Why am I not, at this moment, utterly overwhelmed with distress? How seldom, if ever, am I in pain all over at the same time! How faithfully do our greatest supports combine with our greatest trials![y] Surely in these recollections some excitement of pleasurable feeling might be directed into the channel of gratitude to God! How many rays of collected mercy shine from the great center of joy!

[y]2 Cor 1:5

But to come more immediately to the gospel—unquestionably there is abundant matter for the deepest humiliation. No words can adequately describe the shame that we ought to feel for our insensibility even on account of one single act of infinite love. Yet the gospel encourages humiliation, not despondency. It deals with realities, not of woe and despair, but of hope, peace and joy. Its life and glory is that "bind up the broken-hearted,"[z] who will not break the "bruised reed,"[a] or "crush under His feet" the prisoners of hope.

[z]Isa 61:1
[a]Isa 42:3; Lam 3:34

A CHEERFUL HEART

If then—Christian—you believe the gospel to be "good news," *show* that you believe it, by lighting up your face with a smile. Don't go around bowed down like you've got the weight of the whole world on your shoul-

[17] *Prov 12:25; 15:13; Job 30:30; Ps 32:3, 4; 102:3–5; 119:83; 38:18. The mixture of bodily and mental anguish formed the completeness of our Lord's sufferings, Ps 22:15; 69:3.*

ders. And don't be spreading gloom everywhere you go.[b] Show that the gospel you received is the daylight of your soul, that you have found true joy and peace.[c] Show that you know the *joys* of the gospel, not just because you read and heard of them, but because you have tasted them. If they truly make you happy, don't belie your happiness by wearing a face that makes you look like you're really suffering. Don't give people any reason to think that Christianity is nothing but incurable gloom. It's true that joy is a forbidden fruit to the ungodly.[d] But let it be the adorning of your Christian testimony.[e] It's a sin against God for the Christian to be without it.[f] The gloom of the servant reflects unfairly upon our Lord and Savior Jesus Christ. It makes people think that you've found Him to be a very "hard man."[g] So then . . . resist all sorrow that suggests such dishonorable thoughts of Him. Don't belittle His heavenly comfort, by too loudly bemoaning His counterbalancing affliction. No cloud can cover you, but the "bow may be seen in the cloud."[h] And in all this world's afflictions, one beam of His love might scatter all your clouds and fill your heart with "joy inexpressible and full of glory." Let the Lord then be magnified, which hath pleasure, not in the misery, but in "the prosperity of His servant."[i] He gives you the right to be cheerful and the reason; and He will give you a cheerful heart that's alive with gladness.

[b]Luke 1:19; Isa 58:5
[c]Prov 3:17
[d]Hos 9:1
[e]Isa 52:1, 2; 60:1
[f]Deut 28:47
[g]Matt 25:24
[h]Ezek 1:28
[i]1 Peter 1:8; Ps 35:27

Still, let each of us be careful to keep a just and even balance. Liveliness needs a guard. Otherwise it might degenerate into flippancy and instability. Be much in secret with God. Cherish a solemn, reverential spirit before the Throne of Grace. Christian joy is a deeply serious thing. The froth and lightness that pass for it don't deserve the name. The carnal element must be destroyed so that the heaven-born principle might be introduced. It comes from God and helps us maintain communion with Him.

Yet on the other hand, a too-serious temperament must be resisted. It could sink into morbid depression. Gloom isn't from God, and it shouldn't stamp the character of God's children. It may often be in conflict with a man's own self, either in body or mind. But it won't be long before, instead of *the broken spirit which dries up the bones,* our spirits will be so full of joy that we'll need another body to contain them. In the meantime, Christian discipline on both sides will be the principle of increased happiness and steady consistency.

23 *A wicked man receives a bribe* [AV—*gift*] *from the bosom*
To pervert the ways of justice.

Again we are warned of the corruption of *bribes.*[j] No sin has a deeper stamp of wickedness; none a more awful mark of divine punishment.[k] The temptation tests principle. Sir M. Hale (as his biographer writes) "had learned from Solomon, that *a gift perverteth the ways of judgment.*" Therefore, he always rejected gifts with courteous sincerity. Not even a good cause will justify evil practices. The apostle Paul, though held in bondage and kept from his great and blessed work, would not gratify his covetous judge by buying his freedom.[l] The rules of the gospel are clear and decisive. Let us not "do evil that good may come . . . Do not let what is for you a good thing be spoken of as evil . . . abstain from every form of evil."[m]

[j] Verse 8
[k] Isa 1:23, 24; Ezra 22:13
[l] Acts 24:26
[m] Rom 3:8; 14:16; 1 Thess 5:22

Even a corrupt world is ashamed of this sin. *The bribe* is in the bosom,[n] hidden from the eye of man. But how fearfully uncovered it is to the eye of God, who will not overlook any attempt *to pervert the ways of justice!* One day He will defend His Omniscience from all the insults heaped upon it in the world by those foolish men, who were not ashamed to do the things in the very face of God Himself, that they would not have wanted the lowest of His creatures to discover!

[n] Prov 21:14

Let every child of Abraham hear the command given to his father—"Walk before Me, and be blameless."[o] "He who walks righteously, and speaks with sincerity . . . And shakes his hands so that they hold no bribes . . . he will dwell on the heights."[p]

[o] Gen 17:1
[p] Isa 33:15, 16; Ps 15

24 *Wisdom is in the presence of the one who has understanding,*
But the eyes of a fool are on the ends of the earth.

WANDERING EYES, SCATTERED THOUGHTS

Let's trace our interest in *wisdom* from the beginning. First it "will enter your heart."[q] There it "rests in the

[q] Prov 2:10

heart of one who has understanding,"[r] as his principle of conduct. Now it is in the presence of *his eyes* in the Book of wisdom, as his rule of faith and life.[s] It is the center toward which all his thoughts, motives, and pursuits move. All is now order. Every faculty, desire, and affection finds its proper place. "*He that hath understanding* fixeth his eyes upon wisdom, and contenteth himself with that object; whereas *the eyes of a fool* are constantly wandering everywhere; and his thoughts settle upon nothing that may avail to his good, states Bishop Hall. *His eyes are on the ends of the earth,* rolling and wandering from one object to another. His thoughts are scattered. He has no definite object, no settled principle, no certain rule. Talent, cultivation of mind, improvement of opportunity—all frittered away. He cares for those things furthest from him and for which he has the least concern. concern.

[r]Prov 14:33

[s]Prov 14:8

RUBBISH FOR GOLD

In the following paraphrase of Rev. Thomas Adams, he vividly portrays this inconstancy: Today he goes to be shipped for Rome. But before the tides come, his tide is turned. One party thinks him theirs; the opposite party thinks he's theirs; he is with both; and he is with neither. He doesn't have an hour with himself. Indifference is his stabilizer and opinion his sail; he resolves not to resolve. He doesn't know what he holds. He opens his mind to receive notions, just as one opens his hand to take water. He has a great deal of it, if he could hold it. He is certain to die, but he doesn't know what religion to die in. He objects, like a posed lawyer, as if delay could remove some obstacles. In a debated point, he sides with the last reasoner he read or heard. The next distracts his attention, and he and his opinion with him perhaps sides with him, so long as its teacher is in his sight. He will rather take rubbish for gold, than test it in the furnace. He receives many judgments, but he keeps none. He loathes manna after two days' feeding. The best place for him to live could be his bedroom, where he wouldn't bother anything but his pillow. He is full of business at church; a stranger at home; a doubter outside his own house; an observer in the street; everywhere a fool (*Works*, Folio, 1630—"The Soul's Sickness").

These diversionary tactics are one of the enemy's most effective weapons. His great objective is to turn the mind aside from what is *immediate* to what is *indefinite,* from what is *plain and important* to what is *unsearchable;*[t] from what is *personal* to what is *irrelevant.*[u] Many trifles take the place of the one thing "necessary." And the time he wastes by allowing himself to be so easily diverted—isn't it often a temptation to him? Where are his eyes, or his thoughts, at prayer? All too often, instead of "fixing our eyes on Jesus"[v] His great object, the life of prayer, the only way to God—aren't they *on the ends of the earth,* as though there were no nearer, or better object of attraction? Don't we want simplicity of spiritual *understanding* to keep Him, the great uncreated *Wisdom,* constantly before our eyes? Lord! Forgive me for my great instability. You alone can help! "Turn away my eyes from looking at vanity."[w] Fix them—O fix them—on Him, on whom all heaven, all the redeemed, delight to gaze forever.

[t] Deut 29:29; Col 2:18
[u] Luke 10:42; 13:23, 24; John 21:21, 22
[v] Heb 12:2
[w] Ps 119:37

25 *A foolish son is a grief to his father,*
And bitterness to her who bore him.

PARENTAL AND FILIAL RESPONSIBILITY

Surely the divine Spirit did not repeat this Proverb[x] for nothing. Wasn't it to deepen our sense of parental responsibility and filial obligation? Can parents be insensible to the prospect of this grief? Can children be so hardened, so unnaturally selfish as to pierce a parent's heart with such bitterness?[y] The mother's anguish is here added to the father's grief.[z] As a sword in her bones is the apprehension of bringing out "children for slaughter."[a] How uncertain are the dearest comforts of earth! Our fallen mother anticipated the joy of "having gotten a manchild"—perhaps the promised seed—"of the Lord."[b] Yet to the *bitterness* of her soul, he "was of the evil one, and slew his brother."[c] Her daughter naturally "remembers the anguish no more, for joy that a child has been born into the world."[d] Already she grasps the delightful vision of his infant training and ripening maturity. And yet, too often he proves in the end *a foolish son, and bitterness to her who bore him.*

[x] Verse 21
[y] Prov 19:13
[z] Gen 26:35
[a] Hos 9:13
[b] Gen 4:1
[c] 1 John 3:12
[d] John 16:21

Absalom was named "His father's peace." And still, he was the cause of his father David's most painful *grief.* This isn't the weeping of a "night," succeeded by a joyous "morning";[e] but "anxiety in the heart of a man weighs it down,"[f] perhaps for years, perhaps to the end of days. Its connection with eternity gives to the trial its keenest edge. To see a *foolish son* rushing with no way to return, into his eternal doom—this to the godly parent is a most terrible and upsetting emotional experience.[g] Strong indeed must be that faith (yet such faith has been promised)[h] which bows reverentially to God and maintains the serenity of peaceful submission.

[e] Ps 30:5
[f] Prov 12:25
[g] 2 Sam 18:33
[h] Lev 10:1–3; 1 Sam 3:18

But parental anxieties and sorrows must raise the question: "How can the parent be spared this piercing thorn, this bitter *grief*—the bitterest that ever a parent's heart can know!" The primary root of this sorrow is self will.[i] The vast power of parental influence must be used wisely, at once, at any cost. We must not instruct, or entreat only, but command.[j] We must allow no appeal to our authority, no reversal of our decision. This discipline in the spirit of love, and enforced by example, is God's honored command.

[i] Prov 29:15
[j] Gen 18:19; 1 Sam 2:23–25

Then to give power to all other means, there must be a living faith in the Word of God. For if I really believe the awful fact, that my child is a child of wrath, that Satan claims a right in him, and that if he should die unconverted, hell must be his everlasting portion. If I truly believed that, wouldn't I work with all the earnestness and energy at my command for his soul's salvation. Wouldn't I work under the clear conviction, that if he is not saved, good were it for him "if he had not been born"?

But this faith brings encouragement fully tailored to the tremendous anxiety. As a Christian parent, I can claim God's salvation for my child.[k] I can plead with him and for him. Here I desire to exercise a sound balance of well-disciplined confidence; encouraging parental hopes and moderating parental anxieties. The law of the kingdom is, that men "ought to pray and not to lose heart."[l] I may not see my most cherished desires realized until the last moment. There may be many stops, many disappointments, many turns in the road. But the bread cast

[k] Matt 26:24; Gen 17:7
[l] Luke 18:1

[m]Eccl 11:1

"on the surface of the waters," shall be found, even though it may not be until "after many days."[m]

The main thing for us is to make sure our faith proves its soundness as a *practical* principle. See how inconsistent we parents sometimes are, praying that God will take our children as His own, and yet, training them, as though they belong to this world? Are we sure, we *don't* desire something more for them than eternal life or unrelated to it.[18] One desire like that stirs up another; and *that one,* another; until finally, the little things seem even more important than the main blessing and replace it.

[n]Gen 5:29

When it comes right down to it, what are we doing—raising them so they can take care of us when we need them?[n] We need to make sure we try to keep them close to the Lord—connect them early with His church—not to ourselves. Turn them to the Lord early in life. Teach them to know Him and serve Him. Then, instead of being a great disappointment to us, they'll be "the restorers of life and a sustainer of your old age."[o]

[o]Ruth 4:15

And instead of their turning out to be rebels against God and making our lives bitter, they will love and serve Him and bring praise to His name.[p]

[p]Ps 22:31; 92:13

26 *It is also not good to fine the righteous,*
Nor *to strike the noble for* their *uprightness.*

[q]Prov 16:29; 18:5; 20:23; Ps 51:17; Ezek 36:31
[r]Verse 15
[s]Phil 1:28; Rom 13:3
[t]1 Kings 21:11–13; Matt 26:3, 4; Acts 4:1–3
[u]Isa 28:17, with Mal 3:2, 5

Often Solomon's meaning is far beyond his words. To punish the *righteous,* not only *is not good,*[q] but it is "the abomination"[r]—an evident "sign of destruction."[s] If rulers are "a cause of fear for good," they are ministers of God in authority, but ministers of Satan in the way they use that authority.[t] And how will such injustice "endure the day of His coming," when He shall "make justice the measuring line, and righteousness the level"![u]

[v]Job 34:18
[w]Acts 23:5. Comp. 1 Sam 24:5, 6; 2 Sam 16:5–7
[x]Prov 20:8

No less wicked is the sin of the people. To rebel against a ruler is high treason against God.[v] The apostle confessed the unwilling sin of his smiting words.[w] And it's even more of a sin *to strike them for uprightness.* A godly king—ruling righteously, "disperses all evil with his eyes"[x]—will cause many and powerful enemies to rise up against him. The evil-minded will undermine his

[18] *Mark the golden rule on which all hangs—Matt 6:33.*

influence[y] or resist his authority.[z] If they don't dare to confront him openly, they will "curse" him in their thoughts.[a] To attack, even by word, is our sin.[b] To pray is our *duty*. And who knows but what a prayer-hearing God would send a righteous administration, a shelter and blessing to the land?[c]

[y] 2 Sam 15:1–6
[z] 2 Sam 20:1
[a] Eccl 10:20
[b] 2 Peter 2:10; Jude 8
[c] 1 Tim 2:1–3; 2 Sam 23:3; Isa 32:1, 2

27 *He who restrains his words has knowledge,*
And he who has a cool spirit is a man of understanding.
28 *Even a fool, when he keeps silent, is considered wise;*
When he closes his lips, he is counted *prudent.*

THE GOOD TREASURE

The wisdom of these Proverbs will be acknowledged by those, who know the sins of the tongue, and the immense difficulty of restraining that unruly member. A *man of knowledge will hold his words,* when the probable prospect is harm rather than good.[d] The good treasure is far too valuable to be unprofitably spent. *Silence* is often the best proof of wisdom.[19] Our Lord in His divine knowledge, careful as He was to improve every opportunity for teaching, sometimes *withheld His words*.[e]

[d] Ps 39:1, 2; Matt 7:6
[e] Matt 16:4

This restraint is most important when we are angry.[f] Passion demands immediate judgment. A *cool,* well-tempered *understanding* asks further time for consideration. Christ judged the fiery, emotional outbursts of the apostles to be a lack of right *understanding*.[g] Nehemiah, by holding back the first expression of his righteous anger, gave a reasonable and convincing answer for the occasion.[20] The prophet wisely refrained even a message from God to a king in the moment of passion.[h] "A little spark blows up one of sulphurous temper; and many coals, greater injuries, and reproaches are quenched, and lose their force, being thrown at another of a cool spirit," commented Leighton. Indeed, *a fool* may purchase[i] to

[f] Num 12:1, 2; Ps 38:12–14; Isa 53:7
[g] Luke 9:54, 55
[h] 2 Chron 25:16
[i] 1 Peter 3:9

[19] *Prov 10:19; Job 13:5. Dr. Good in his note on John 13:5 gives a translation of an Arabic poetical proverb.*
Keep silence then; but when besought;
Who listens long, grows tired of what is told;
With tones of silver though thy tongue be fraught,
Know this—that silence of itself is gold.

[20] *Neh 5:6–11. Cicero advises his brother Quintus (a proconsul in Asia) most diligently to restrain his tongue under anger, which, he adds, is no less a virtue, than freedom from anger itself*—Epist. ad *Q. FRATREM, lib. i. 1.*

himself the reputation of *wisdom,* if he just *keeps his mouth* shut, instead of exposing his foolishness openly for everyone to see.[j] "He cannot be known for a fool, that says nothing. He is a fool, not who hath unwise thoughts, but who utters them. Even concealed folly is wisdom," said Bishop Hall (Works, 8.83).

[j] Contrast Prov 15:2; 19:11

How infinitely momentous is the account which God takes of the tongue! "Death and life are in the power of the tongue."[k] Our eternal acceptance or condemnation will hang on it—in part at least.[l] How could we endure judgment for every idle word we've spoken, let alone every wicked one, if there weren't for the self-abased sinner, a covering from this condemnation, a cleansing from this guilt, a seal of acceptance.[m]

[k] Prov 18:21

[l] Matt 12:36, 37

[m] Isa 6:7

CHAPTER EIGHTEEN

1 *He who separates himself seeks* his own *desire,*
He quarrels against all sound wisdom.
2 *A fool does not delight in understanding,*
But only in revealing his own mind.

THIS ONE THING I DO

Desire is the chariot wheel of the soul, the spring of energy and delight. The man of business or science is filled with his great object; and *through desire he separates himself* from hindrances, so that he may devote all his attention and energy to it. "One thing," saith the man of God, "I do."[a] This one thing is everything with him. He *separates himself* from all outward hindrances, vain company, trifling amusements or studies, needless engagements, that he may *seek all wisdom.* John *separated himself* in the wilderness,[b] Paul in Arabia,[c] our blessed Lord in frequent retirement,[d] in order to have greater concentration in their momentous work. The Christian minister deeply feels the responsibility of this holy *separation,* that he may "be absorbed" to his office.[e] Without it—Christian—your soul can never prosper. How can you experience the great wisdom that comes from knowing yourself, if your whole mind is occupied with this world's chaff and vanity? There must be a withdrawal to commune with your own heart and to ask the questions —"Where am I? What am I doing here?" There's a great deal to look into and to think about. Everything here calls for our deepest, closest thoughts. We must walk with God in secret, or the enemy will walk with us, and our souls will die. "Get up, go out to the plain, and there I will speak to you."[f] "When you were under the fig tree, I saw thee."[g] Deal much in secrecy, if you

[a]Phil 3:13
[b]Luke 1:80
[c]Gal 1:17
[d]Mark 1:35; 6:31; Luke 6:12
[e]1 Tim 4:15; 2 Tim 2:4
[f]Ezek 3:22
[g]John 1:48

would know the secret of the Lord. Like your divine Master, you will never be less alone than when you are alone.[h] There is much to be done, much to be gained, and enjoyed. Your most spiritual knowledge, your richest experience will be found here. Men who live, without drawing apart to be alone with the Lord, may be fluent talkers, and accurate preachers, but nothing they say comes from a broken and contrite heart. The lack of unction paralyzes all spiritual impression. All intelligent, self-observant Christians feel the great need for combining holy solitude with active life in order to nourish his faith, and along with that, every Christian grace. Sir M. Hale left this testimony, "I have endeavoured to husband this short, uncertain, important talent (time) by dedicating and setting apart some portion of it to prayer and reading of thy word; which I have constantly and peremptorily observed, whatever occasions interposed, or importunity persuaded to the contrary" (*the Good Steward.* Contemplations, pp. 238, 239).

[h]John 16:32

And then, when we look around us into the great, broad field of the Revelation of God, what a world of heavenly wisdom there is to converse with! In the hurry of this world's atmosphere, how little can we grasp of it! And yet, so great is the wonder of it, that meditation of just one point overwhelmed the apostle Paul with adoring astonishment.[i] Here are "things into which angels long to look."[j] The redeemed will be occupied throughout eternity in this happy searching; exploring "the breadth and length and height and depth," until they are filled with all the fullness of God."[k] Surely then if we have any *desire,* we will *separate ourselves* from the cloudy atmosphere around us, so that we may have fellowship with these happy investigators of God's mysteries.

[i]Rom 11:33

[j]1 Peter 1:12

[k]Eph 3:18, 19

Yet *the fool does not delight in understanding.* His only desire is to pour out his own trivialities, to get away from public view, in order *that he may reveal in his own mind*—He makes a humiliating discovery, indeed, of both the limits of his knowledge and the emptiness of his mind.

3 *When a wicked man comes, contempt also comes,*
And with dishonor comes *reproach.*

PREPARE FOR THE FURNACE

Selfishness marks *the wicked.* "Wheresoever he cometh, he is apt to cast *contempt and reproach* upon every man's face, stated Bishop Hall.[l] His neighbor's circumstances or infirmities provide him opportunities to hold him up to scorn. The Word of God holds no attractions for him. God's people are the objects of his *reproach.* Their seriousness he calls gloom, their cheerfulness levity.[m] If "no negligence or corruption" can be found,[n] he is great at inventing one. "As the proverb of the ancients says, 'Out of the wicked comes forth wickedness.'"[o] We must prepare for this furnace, even though the fires of martyrdom are extinguished. Our blessed Lord bore all the evils of the world without flinching. But *contempt and reproach* pierced His soul more keenly, than the nails did His hands and His feet. "Reproach," saith he, "has broken my heart."[p] And shouldn't the servant expect to be like his Master?[q] Often, however, retributive justice overwhelms *the wicked* themselves with *dishonor* and disgrace.[r] A scornful spirit against the godly is never forgotten. Every bitter word is registered against the great day.[s] And what a sight it will then be, when the reviled shall stand forth, clothed with all the glory of the King of saints, and the faces of their persecutors shall be covered with "disgrace and everlasting contempt!"[t] The sight of that day will never be blotted out! The rebuke of His people shall be taken away from off all the earth, "for the Lord has spoken."[u]

[l]Comp. Prov 29:16
[m]Matt 11:18, 19
[n]Dan 6:4
[o]1 Sam 24:13
[p]Ps 69:20; Matt 27:39–44
[q]Matt 10:25; John 15:20
[r]2 Sam 6:20–23; Esther 7:9, 10
[s]1 Peter 4:4, 5; Jude 14, 15
[t]Dan 12:2
[u]Isa 25:8

4 *The words of a man's mouth are deep waters;*
The fountain of wisdom is a bubbling brook.

SO DEEP ARE THE WATERS!

"This sentence expresses the depth, the abundance, the clearness, and the force of the counsels of *the wise man,*" stated Calmet. The last clause gives this restriction to *wisdom.* When a man has conversed with all wisdom, his *words* are in themselves *deep waters,* and in their communication fruitful *as a flowing brook.* His wisdom is a *fountain,* "which sends up full brooks, that are ready to overflow their banks. So plentiful is he in good discourse and wholesome counsel!" exclaimed Bishop Hall.[v] So *deep were the waters* from the wise man's fountain that *his words* nearly overwhelmed the capacity of his royal hearer.[w] One greater than Solomon "amazed" the people by the clearness, no less than by the *depth of the waters.*[x] No blessing is more valuable than letting "the word of Christ richly dwell within you," ready to be brought out on all suitable occasions of instruction.[y] If the wise man sometimes spares his words,[z] it is not because he doesn't have anything to talk about but for greater spiritual improvement. The stream is ready to flow, and sometimes can scarcely be held back.[a] The cold-hearted, meditative professing believer has his flow—sometimes a torrent of words, yet without a drop of anything profitable; chilling, even when doctrinally correct; without life, fervor, or love. Lord! deliver us from this barren "talk."[b] May our *waters be deep,* flowing from Thine own inner sanctuary, refreshing, and enriching the church of God!

[v] Prov 10:11; 16:22; 20:5
[w] 1 Kings 10:4–8
[x] Matt 7:28, 29
[y] Col 3:16; 4:6
[z] Prov 27:27
[a] Job 32:19; Jer 20:9; Acts 17:16
[b] Prov 14:23

This *fountain* is specially strengthening, when, as in John Chrysostom it gives a heavenly glow to outward eloquence. Consecrated mind and talent are the gifts of God. Oh! let them be improved in simplicity, not for the creature's honor, but for the glory of the great giver.

5 *To show partiality to the wicked is not good,*
Nor *to thrust aside the righteous in judgment.*

THE STAMP OF GOD

Were not "the foundations of the earth . . . shaken," would we hear of so great a violation of the rule of right?[c] But in a world, of which Satan is "the God and the prince," injustice is a natural principle of administration. The godly king of Judah pointed his judges to the divine example—look, and be like Him.[d] Everything revolting is connected with *wickedness.* There is no one so noble, that it does not degrade; so lovely, that it does not deform; so learned, that it does not deceive. *To show partiality to the wicked is not good.*[e] "Abomination," is its true name—the stamp of God.[f] "Whatever excuses man may make for its course, it is an offense to God, an affront

[c] Ps 82:2–5
[d] 2 Chron 19:7
[e] Prov 17:26; 24:23; 28:21
[f] Prov 17:15. Comp. Lev 19:15; Deut 1:16, 17

to justice, a wrong to mankind, and a real service done to the kingdom of sin and Satan," said Henry. *In judgment,* let the cause be heard, not the person. Let the person be punished for his wickedness, not the wickedness be covered for the person's sake. When, as in the case of Naboth, the wicked person was accepted, *to thrust aside the righteous in judgment,* it overthrows the throne of judgment in the land. The Shechemites were sharply punished for their sin, in accepting Abimelech to the overthrow of the righteous claims of Gideon's house.[g] No wonder. In such wickedness the rights of God are despised; the claims of His justice are cast off. "He who rules over men righteously, Who rules in the fear of God."[h] Such was our divine pattern in the flesh "of quick understanding in the fear of the Lord," and therefore "with righteousness He will judge."[i] Such will be His judgment, when "He will judge the world in righteousness."[j] His decision will be exact; His sentence unchangeable.

[g]Judg 9
[h]2 Sam 23:3
[i]Isa 11:4
[j]Acts 17:31

6 *A fool's lips bring strife,*
And his mouth calls for blows.
7 *A fool's mouth is his ruin,*
And his lips are the snare of his soul.

THE TONGUE— A WORLD OF INIQUITY

It is quite remarkable, that the apostle Paul, when describing man's depravity, dwells mainly on the "small part"—the tongue and all its related parts—the throat—the lips—the mouth.[k] Actually, the tongue is such a world of iniquity, that it defiles the whole body![l] We often see what it does to others; but here's what it does to us, ourselves. *The fool's lips bring strife.* What foolishness! The wise man may be drawn into it by an unruly temper[m] or by the force of circumstances.[n] But "so far as it depends on you, be at peace with all men,"[o] holding down even the first signs of strife.[p] *The fool* enters into it by intruding into other people's business and needlessly[q] and willfully stirring up strife,[r] like "the alarm of war" and drums beating up to the battle. He makes a rod for his own back.[s] He puts a weapon into Satan's hands for him to use against his own head.[t] The willful quarrel-

[k]James 3:5; Rom 3:13
[l]James 3:6
[m]Acts 15:39
[n]Gen 13:8
[o]Rom 12:18; 14:19
[p]Prov 17:14
[q]Prov 20:3; 26:17
[r]Prov 16:27, 28
[s]Jer 4:19; Prov 14:3; 19:19, 29
[t]Prov 26:21

ling of the men of Succoth and Penuel with Gideon called for retaliation.[u] The scoffing mouth of the little children brought about the destruction they deserved.[v] The slanderous *lips* of Daniel's persecutors were *the snare of their soul.*[w] There is no need to dig a pit for the *fool.* He digs it for himself.[x] The mouths of wild beasts devour each other. *The fool's mouth is his own ruin.*[y] The fowler's snare is not needed; for he "is snared by the transgression of his lips."[z] He is not only the cause, but the agent of his own *ruin.*

[u] Judg 8:4–17
[v] 2 Kings 2:23, 24
[w] Dan 6:13
[x] Ps 7:15; 64:8
[y] Prov 10:8, 14; 13:3; Eccl 10:12, 13
[z] Prov 12:13

And shall not the child of God watch in godly fear, lest his folly should call for his Father's discipline? Sharply may they have to be "hewn" by the sword.[a] He may act as though he would kill, in order to make alive. All this is that he may embitter sin and endear returning mercy. It is always wise and gracious love, as one of the fathers says—"threatening, that he may not strike: and striking, that he may not destroy." If just showing the rod will produce the desired effect, gladly will he withhold punishment. But if our folly, as Leighton speaks (*Works,* v. 114), "pulls punishment out of his hands," whom do we have to thank for the pain but ourselves.

[a] Hos 6:5

8 *The words of a whisperer are like dainty morsels,*
And they go down into the innermost parts of the body.

THE WORLD'S MOST DEADLY POISON

Do men deny, question, or minimize the depravity of our nature? See again how the deadly poison of only one member destroys practical godliness, social order, and mutual friendship. *The whisperer* was expressly forbidden by the law,[b] even more, he is opposed to the spirit of the gospel.[c] No character indeed is more despicable; no influence more detestable. It is right indeed, that we should exercise interference with each other, and mutual inspection. It is hard-hearted selfishness, that asks the question—"Am I my brother's keeper?"[d] The rule is clear—"Do not merely look out for your own personal interests, but also for the interests of others."[e] The rule is illustrated and enforced at the same time by an example magnificient and compelling. It is "the attitude . . . which was also in Christ Jesus." Had the Son of God looked at

[b] Lev 19:16
[c] 1 Cor 13:6
[d] Gen 4:9
[e] Phil 2:4

His own things, and not at the things of others, would He have emptied himself of His divine glory? Would He have "humbled Himself" to the accursed cross?[f]

[f]Phil 2:5–8

Again—the uniting force of the interference will be determined by the principle of love for our neighbor. It is right therefore to bring an evil report,[g] for the prevention of sin. That's how Eli was enabled, though without effect, to rebuke his sons.[h] The life of an apostle was by this means preserved.[i] Serious evils in the church were restrained or corrected.[j] But no good results can arise from the spirit of *the whisperer,* because with him it is pure selfishness,[k] without a principle beyond the love of sin for its own sake. He lives upon the scandal of the place, and makes it his hateful business to carry about tales, or slanders of his neighbor's faults.[1] Such reports are eagerly devoured, and the mischief-maker feeds with greedy appetite upon the fruit of his cruel indulgence. To him this may appear harmless play. But if it draws no blood, and no outward hurt is shown, an internal, and often incurable, wound is inflicted.[l] We may seem to make light of the gossip brought to our ears and wholly to despise it. But the subtle poison has worked. We think, "Suppose it should be true. Perhaps, though it may be exaggerated, there may be some ground for it." The thought indulged only for a moment brings suspicion, distrust, coldness; and often it ends in the separation of the best of friends.[m] That's how dangerous the tongue is without stern, determined control!

[g]Prov 24:11, 12; Gen 37:2; Lev 5:1

[h]1 Sam 2:23, 24

[i]Acts 23:13. Contrast Jer 40:13–16; 41:1, 2

[j]1 Cor 1:11; 11:18

[k]Jer 20:10

[l]Prov 26:22

[m]Prov 16:28; 17:9; 1 Sam 24:9; 26:19; 2 Sam 16:1–4

The gossip of an unguarded moment may cause tremendous, irreparable injury. The evil humor may meet with a welcome audience in good society, where (but for the food which scandal supplies) conversation would drag heavy. But no whitewash can change its real character, as an abomination both with God and man. Ah! what but the power of holy love, opening freely the channels of kindness and forbearance, can overcome this mischievous proneness? And what will bring this spirit of love, but a true interest in Christian privileges, and a corresponding sense of Christian obligations?[n]

[n]Col 3:12–14

[1] *The word properly signifies a pedlar, who buys goods (stolen ones it may be) at one place, and sells them at another, taking care to make his own market of them. So a talebearer makes his own visits, to pick up at one place, and utter at another, that which he thinks will lessen his neighbor's reputation, that he may build his own upon it—M. HENRY'S* Sermon on Friendly Visits. *Comp. Prov 11:13; 20:19.*

9 *He also who is slack in his work*
Is brother to him who destroys.

THE LOSERS

Note the similarity between the principles and workings of corruption. The sluggard and the prodigal belong to the same family. The man who hid the Lord's "talent," was just as unfaithful with him as the one "squandering his possessions."[o] The lazy man has no heart for *his work*. He lets important opportunities slip by. Instead of increasing his stock, he allows it to gradually dwindle away. God "dost open Thy hand, and dost satisfy the desire of every living thing."[p] But unless we have hard-working hands, with which to receive it, we may starve. He that by the laziness of his hand deprives himself of the means of getting, is as near to being a waster as can be.[q] *He is the brother of him who destroys*—the lord of a large estate, who, instead of managing, improving, and enjoying it—*destroys* it away in extravagance and folly.

It is the same in spiritual things. Some settle for heartless orthodoxy. They pray secretly and then forget what they asked for. Their family worship is routine formality, not an established, meaningful daily practice. They commune with their own hearts in empty generalities, gaining no accurate, humbling understanding of themselves. How do they differ from the careless *destroyer* of his privileges? What's the difference between those who pray, read, and work formally, and those, who cast these high privileges away? Both take the same course, though by a somewhat different track. The one folds his arms in sluggishness. The other opens his hands in wastefulness. The one gets nothing. The other spends what he gets. The one rushes into poverty. The other sits and waits for it to come to him.[r] The one dies by a rapid and violent disease. The other by a slow, but sure, wasting away. Fearful is the guilt, solemn is the account, certain is the ruin, of both. God gives talents, not only for enrichment, but to be used. And whether they are selfishly neglected, or carelessly thrown away—"You wicked slave" will be the condemnation; "outer darkness" will be the just and eternal doom.[s] Servant of Christ! let your Master's life be your pattern and your standard. He never lost a moment through idle neglect or unprofitable waste. He was as

[o] Matt 25:25; Luke 16:1
[p] Ps 145:16
[q] 1 Cor 7:24
[r] Prov 6:11
[s] Matt 25:26–30

much in earnest in his daily work, as in his nightly prayer. Follow Him in his work, and you'll be honored with His reward.[t]

[t]John 12:26

10 *The name of the LORD is a strong tower;*
The righteous runs into it and is safe.
11 *A rich man's wealth is his strong city,*
And like a high wall in his own imagination.

Consciousness of danger makes even the animal creation look for a refuge.[u] To man, a strong tower offers such a hiding place.[v] But man as a sinner—is he aware of the danger closing in on him, threatening his ruin? Oh, if he could only know how welcome he would be in the *strong tower* ahead of him! Such is *the name of the Lord;* not the bare outward words, operating like a charm, but His character; that by which He is known, as a man by His name. The full calling upon "the *name* of the Lord" sets out most powerfully *the strength of the tower.* Every letter adds confirmation to our faith.[w] Every renewed manifestation brings a fresh sunbeam of light and blessing.[2]

[u]Prov 30:26; Ps 104:18
[v]Judg 9:51; 2 Chron 14:7; 26:9
[w]Exod 34:5–7

AN UNSHAKEABLE FORTRESS

Consider the sinner in his first awakening conviction. He trembles at the thought of eternal condemnation. He looks forward—all is terror; backward—nothing but remorse; inward—all is darkness. Till now, he had no idea of his need of salvation, and his enemy suggests that it is beyond his reach; that he has sinned too long and too much, against too much light and knowledge; how can he be saved? But *the name of the Lord* meets his eye. He spells out every letter and putting it together, cries—"Who is a God like Thee?"[x] He runs to *it, as to a strong tower.* His burden of conscience is relieved. His soul is set free, and he enjoys his *safety.*

[x]Mic 7:18

Consider—again—the child of God—feeble, distressed, assaulted. "What, if I should return to the world, look back, give up my profession, yield to my own deceitful heart, and perish at last with even greater condemnation?" You are walking outside the gates *of your tower;* no wonder that your lack of judgment exposes you to "the flaming missiles of the evil one." Read again *the name of*

[2] *See the New Testament names of God. Rom 15:5, 13; 2 Cor 1:3; 5:19; 1 Peter 5:10.*

the Lord! Go back within the walls—see upon the *tower the name*—"I, the Lord, do not change."[y] Read the direction to trust in it—"Who is among you that fears the Lord, that obeys the voice of His servant, that walks in darkness and has no light? *Let him trust in the name of the Lord,* and rely on his God."[z] Mark the warrant of experience in this trust—"Those who know *Thy name* will put their trust in Thee; for Thou, O Lord, hast not forsaken those who seek Thee."[a]

[y]Eph 6:16; Mal 3:6
[z]Isa 50:10
[a]Ps 9:10

So . . . sense of danger, knowledge of the way, confidence in *the strength of the tower*—all give a spring of life and earnestness to *run into it.*[3] Here the *righteous*—the man justified by grace, and sanctified by the Spirit of God—*runneth* every day, every hour; realizing at once his fearful danger, and his perfect security. Within these walls, who of us needs to fear the sharpest or swiftest dart that may be shot against us? We realize our security from external trouble[b] and in trying exercises of faith! We are *safe* from his avenging justice, from the curse of His law, from sin, from condemnation, from the second death.[c] We joy in our safety[d]—yes—in our exaltation.[e] Our best interests are beyond the reach of harm;[f] and the righteous nation takes up the song of triumph—"We have a strong city; He sets up walls and ramparts for security."[g]

[b]Deut 33:27–29; Ps 61:3; 91:2; Isa 54:14
[c]Job 13:15
[d]Ps 18:1–3; Isa 25:4
[e]Isa 33:16
[f]Col 3:3
[g]Isa 26:1–4

But only the righteous are found here. What do the ungodly know of this refuge? "Our God's mercy is holy mercy. He knows how to pardon sin, not to protect it. He is a sanctuary to the penitent, not to the presumptuous," stated Bishop Reynolds.[h] Yet what joy it is, to know that the gates of this city are always open! No time is unseasonable. No distance, no weakness hinder the entrance. The cripple may *run,* like "swift-footed" Asahel."[i] All that enter are protected unto salvation. To paraphrase Leighton: Satan is raising heavy guns against the fort, using every means to take it, by strength or stratagem, unwearied in his assaults, and very skillful in knowing his advantages.[j] But notwithstanding all his disturbing power, "the peace of God" daily fortifies our hearts against fear of evil.[k] Such is our *strong tower!* What we owe to our gracious Savior, who has made our way to it so

[h]Hos 14:1, 2
[i]2 Sam 2:18
[j]1 Peter 1:5
[k]Phil 4:7; Gr. Comp. Prov 1:33; 14:26

[3] *See the examples of Jacob—Gen 32:11, 28, 29; David—1 Sam 30:6; Ps 56:3; Asa—2 Chron 14:11; Jehoshaphat—20:12; Hezekiah—2 Kings 19:14–19; the apostles—Acts 4:24–33.*

free, so bright.[l] We rest in the heart of God, and are at peace.

[l] Matt 11:27; John 1:18; 14:6

But the rich man's wealth is his strong city—yes—and his *high walls*.[m] Well does Solomon add—*in his own imagination*. Little does he think that in a moment they may crumble to dust, and leave him unsheltered and in fearful ruin. "Trouble will find an entrance into his castle. Death will storm and take it. And judgment will sweep both him and it into perdition," expounded Scott.[4]

[m] Prov 10:15

The histories of David and Saul show most strikingly the contrast between trouble with a refuge and trouble without a refuge.[n] Our Lord draws a vivid contrast between a real and an imaginary refuge![o] Every man is as his trust. A trust in God communicates a divine and lofty spirit. We feel that we are surrounded with God and dwelling on high with Him. Oh, the sweet security of the weakest believer, shut up in an unshakeable fortress! A vain trust brings a vain and proud heart, the immediate forerunner of ruin.

[n] 1 Sam 30:6, with 28:15. Comp. Isa 1:10, 11
[o] Matt 7:24–27

12 *Before destruction the heart of man is haughty,*
But humility goes *before honor.*

IN THE LOW VALLEY

We have had both these Proverbs separately.[p] Surely this repetition, like our Lord's often-repeated parallel,[q] was intended to deepen our sense of their importance. It is hard to persuade a man that he is proud. Every one protests against this sin. Yet who does not cherish the viper in his own bosom? Man so little understands, that dependence upon his God constitutes his happiness, and that the principle of independence is madness, and its end—destruction.[r] The *haughty* walk on the brink of a fearful precipice—only a miracle preserves them from instant ruin. The child of God is most secure when he lies prostrate in the dust. If he soars high, the danger is near though he is on the verge of heaven.[s]

[p] Prov 16:18; 15:33
[q] Matt 23:12; Luke 14:11; 18:14
[r] Gen 3:5, 6
[s] 2 Cor 12:1–7

The danger to a young Christian is a too-forward profession. The glow of his first love, the aroused concern over the condition of his perishing fellow-sinners: ignorance of the subtle working of inbred vanity, the mistaken

[4] *Comp. Ezek 28:1–10; Luke 12:18–20. See also a fine passage in the* Rambler, *in Dr. Johnson's best style of solemn instructiveness, No. 65.*

zeal of unwise friends—all tend to foster self-pleasing. Oh! let him know, that *humility goes before honor.* In the low valley of humiliation special manifestations are given.[t] Enlarged gifts, and apparently extending usefulness without growing more deeply into the humility of Christ, will be the decline, not the advancing of grace. The spirit that is the most humble has most of the spirit of Christ. The first entrance requirement into His school, the first step of admission to His kingdom is—"Learn from Me, for I am gentle and humble in heart."[u]

[t]Job 42:5, 6; Isa 6:5, 7; Dan 9:20–23

[u]Matt 11:29

The spring of this humility is true self-knowledge. Whatever external advantages a man may have, he still needs to keep looking within; and the real sight of himself will lay him low. When he compares his secret follies with his external decency—what appears to his fellow-creatures with what he knows of himself—he can but cry out—"Behold, I am insignificant"![v] The seat of this precious grace is not in words, great emotion, or tears, but in the heart. No longer will he delude himself with a false conceit of what he has not, or with a vain conceit of what he has. The recollection—"Who regards you as superior?"[w] is ever present, to press him down under the weight of infinite obligations. Its fruit is lowliness of mind, meekness of temper, thankfulness in receiving reproof, forgetfulness of injury, readiness to be lightly regarded. There cannot be any true greatness without this deep-toned *humility.* This is he "whom the king desires to honor." "Blessed are the poor in spirit; for theirs is the kingdom of heaven ... He raises the poor from the dust ... to make them sit with princes, with the princes of His people."[x]

[v]Job 40:4

[w]1 Cor 4:7

[x]Esther 6:6; Matt 5:3; Ps 113:7, 8

13 *He who gives an answer before he hears,*
It is folly and shame to him.

LISTEN BEFORE YOU ANSWER

Too often this Proverb is confirmed in everyday life. Men will scarcely listen to what is unacceptable to them. They will break in upon a speaker, before they have fully heard him, and therefore *give an answer,* which they have hardly considered and only imperfectly understood. The eager debater prides himself on his quick judgment. He interrupts his opponent, and disproves arguments, or contradicts statements, *before he has fairly heard them.* Job's friends seem to have erred here.[y] Elihu, on the other hand, considerately restrained himself, till he had thoroughly *heard* the matter.[z] Job himself prudently "investigated the case which I did not know."[a] This impatient spirit doesn't speak well for candor or humility, and only stamps a man's character with *folly and shame.* It is fraught with injustice in the court of law.[b] Here at least the judge must carefully hear and weigh both sides for a satisfactory verdict. The wise man thoroughly heard his difficult case, before he gave judgment.[c] Job was scrupulously exact in contending with his "slaves."[d] The rich man, when his "steward was reported accused to him as squandering his possessions," did not turn away upon the mere report, but he examined his reports.[e] On the other hand, Potiphar, from lack of this upright considerateness, was guilty of the most flagrant wrong.[f] The Eastern autocrats seldom cared to sift accusations. Even the man after God's heart grievously sinned in this matter. But their hasty decisions brought shame upon them, being either covered over, or virtually withdrawn.[g] Our Lord's testimony was answered, *before it was heard.*[h] The apostle Paul met with similar treatment,[i] though at other times he found a more impartial judgment.[j]

This *folly* was directly forbidden by God's law.[k] It was no less contrary to His own procedure. He examined Adam, before He pronounced judgement.[l] He came down to see Babel and Sodom, previous to their destruction, for the more clear demonstration of His justice.[m] While on earth, patient investigation marked His decisions.[n] "All His ways are just; a God of faithfulness and without injustice, Righteous and upright is He."[o]

[y] Job 20:1–3; 21:1–6
[z] Job 32:4, 10, 11
[a] Job 29:16
[b] John 7:45–52
[c] 1 Kings 3:16–28. Comp. Prov 25:2
[d] Job 31:13
[e] Luke 16:1, 2
[f] Gen 39:17–20
[g] Esther 3:8–11; 8:5–13; Dan 6:9, 14, 24; 2 Sam 16:1–4; 19:26–30
[h] Luke 22:66–71
[i] Acts 22:21, 22; 23:2
[j] Acts 23:30–35; 24:1–22; 25:1–5, 24–27; 26:30–32
[k] Deut 13:12–14; John 7:24
[l] Gen 3:9–19
[m] Gen 11:5; 18:20, 21
[n] Matt 22:15–33, with Isa 11:3
[o] Deut 32:4. Comp. 1 Sam 2:3

14 *The spirit of a man can endure his sickness,*
But a broken spirit who can bear?

A BROKEN SPIRIT—WHO CAN BEAR IT?

Man is born in a world of trouble with strong powers of endurance. Natural courage and vivacity of spirits will bear us up even under the pressure of great evils, poverty, pain, sickness, want. Instances of heathen fortitude abound in the records of history. But Christian principle *strengthens* the natural strength. David, in the most fearful extremity, "strengthened himself in the Lord his God."[p] Job could bless God under accumulated external trials.[q] The apostle was "well content with weaknesses."[r] The martyrs were "overwhelmingly" conquerors under the most cruel tortures.[s] Outward troubles are tolerable, yes—more than tolerable, if there is peace within. *The spirit of a man can endure his sickness.* But if *the spirit is broken*—if the prop itself is broken—everything goes under. If the strength that is in me be weakness, how great is that weakness. The wound of the spirit is so much the more piercing, as the spirit itself is more vital than the body. The grief gains the victory and becomes intolerable.

[p] 1 Sam 30:6
[q] Job 1:21
[r] 2 Cor 12:10
[s] Rom 8:37

The most powerful minds are easily vulnerable. Even our great Newton, "endowed with an intellectual strength, which had unbarred the strongholds of the universe," and distinguished also by "unbroken composure," in middle life was a prey to mental depression that, as he informs us, shook his "former consistency" (firmness).[5] Boyle describes his wounded *spirit,* as so overpowering for many months, that, "although his looks did little betray his thoughts, nothing but the forbiddenness of self-dispatch [suicide] hindered his committing it."[6] So long as the evil is without us, it is tolerable. Natural courage can bear us up. *But who can bear a broken spirit?*

In the spiritual realm—the pressure is even more overpowering. When He who made *the spirit broken,* or permits Satan to break it, we might challenge the whole creation. *Who can bear it?* The suffering of the soul is the soul of suffering. Spiritual wounds, like the balm that heals them, can never be known, till they are felt. It is sometimes, as if the arrows of the almighty were dipped in the lake of fire, and shot flaming into the very midst of the soul, more sensitive than the apple of the eye.[t] The best joys of earth can never soothe the poisoned sting. Mirth is madness and vexation.[u]

[t] Job 6:4
[u] Eccl 2:2

There is a hell for the wicked on this side eternity. Man becomes a burden to himself. Cain said, "My punishment is too great to bear!"[v] Saul was given up to the

[v] Gen 4:13

[5] *Sir D. BREWSTER'S* Life, *pp. 224, 232–235.*
[6] *JONES'* Christian Biography—*Article, Boyle.*

blackness of despair.[w] Zimri in rebellious madness threw himself into the flames.[x] Pashur was made a terror to himself.[y] Ahithophel and Judas chose strangling rather than life.[z] So the torments of eternity are preceded by fearful torments on earth. One hell is kindled within, before entering into the other. Such is the foretaste of hell—only a few drops of wrath—for a few moments. What will be the reality—the substance—for eternity!

[w]1 Sam 28:15
[x]1 Kings 16:18
[y]Jer 20:4
[z]2 Sam 17:23; Matt 27:5

Observe the poignancy of the *broken spirit* in the children of God. Job, delivered for a small moment into the enemy's power, "cursed the day of his birth."[a] David "roared for the disquietness of his heart." The "arrows" of the almighty stuck in him, and His hand "pressed down on" him.[b] The martyrs[7] in a moment of temporary apostasy could not endure the anguish of the *broken spirit* and chose the flames as the less bitter alternative. Such is the sharpness of the Lord's sword and the weight of His hand that every stroke is deadly. Conscience is the seat of guilt, and its vivid power turns—so to speak—"the sun will be turned into darkness, and the moon into blood"[c]—the precious promises of free forgiveness into arguments of hopeless despondency. Many a penitent is held back awhile from fully understanding God's acceptance of Him and from the settled enjoyment of the peace of the gospel. And but for the gracious restraint of the Lord's power and love, hardened despair would be the successful "advantage" of Satan's "schemes."[d]

[a]Job 3:1
[b]Ps 38:1–8
[c]Joel 2:31
[d]2 Cor 2:11

But let us gaze at the meek and glorious sufferer in Gethsemane. Look at *the broken spirit* there—the fainting humanity of the Son of God—His was "grieved and distressed," His prostrating sorrow, He was "deeply grieved to the point of death," under the darkness of desertion.[e] Human nature, even when exalted to a personal union with the divine, is human nature still; forced to confess its inborn weakness in the conflict with almighty wrath. If all the support of the indwelling Godhead were demanded for this passion of unknown weight and infinite intensity; with trembling astonishment we cry:—Who can bear a wounded spirit? Irresistible, is the logical conclusion, "If they do these things in the green tree, what will happen in the dry?"[f] The flame,

[e]Matt 26:38
[f]Luke 23:31

[7] *Bainham—Bilney—Cranmer. See FOXE'S* Records.

that could but scorch the one, must consume the other to the uttermost.

Yet is not this *broken spirit* the Christian's first seal of
[g]Acts 2:37 mercy, the preparation for all future and eternal mercy?[g] Bitter indeed is the anguish, when the mass of sin is raised from the grave of oblivion, and set "the case in
[h]Ps 50:21 order before your eyes."[h] But isn't this the sight, that
[i]Acts 16:29–33 makes Jesus and his free salvation so very precious?[i] And doesn't this spirit place us within the sphere of His heal-
[j]Isa 61:1, 2 ing commission?[j] We ask now—not, *who can bear,* but who can heal? Luther said it so well: "It is as easy to make a world, as to ease a troubled conscience." Both are
[k]Gen 1:1; Isa 57:19 creation work, requiring the almightiness of God.[k] To Jesus who was wounded for us, we must return for heal-
[l]Hos 6:1 ing.[l] All we need is the sight of Him, suffering in our
[m]Isa 53:5 place.[m] And that sight—so healing—so reviving—how it quickens the soul to a happy, animated faith, that issues in a song of everlasting praise!

15 *The mind of the prudent acquires knowledge,*
And the ear of the wise seeks knowledge.

KNOW THE ROAD—
WALK MORE PLEASANTLY

Knowledge is gathering its rays on every side. But all that is intrinsically valuable centers in divine *knowledge.* "All arts," as Bishop Hall teaches, "are Maids to Divinity. Therefore they bow to her, and do her service" (*Works,* 8.107). Indeed, it is of first importance that she go before, to inspire and indoctrinate the mass. For while we readily admit the importance of intellectual knowledge; the grand object is the salvation of the soul. And all knowledge that is not grounded upon this primary conviction, or that does not directly or indirectly serve this great end, is worse than valueless. It is power for evil. It is a weapon of mighty influence, that will ultimately turn against the man's own self. Never let us forget, that unsanctified knowledge is still, what it was at the beginning, gathering death, not life, and that, if "the tree was good for food, and that it was a delight to the eyes, and
[n]Gen 3:6 that the tree was desirable to make *one* wise,"[n] it is only the enticement to the unwary, flattering them, that they

"will be like God," that, they "become conceited and fall into the condemnation incurred by the devil."[o]

[o]Gen 3:5; 1 Tim 3:6

And yet, in the sphere of God's Word, the value of knowledge is estimated by its character. When it is speculative, not experimental; general, without practical influence, it is mere listening to a sound. It is not the sight, like that of the brazen serpent, that brings life from the dead, with its blessed accompaniment of transformation into the likeness of Christ. How sad it is to think of the mass of triflers in this heavenly knowledge; hearing without retaining; retaining without intelligence, or without personal application. So often "is there a price in the hand of a fool to buy wisdom, when he has no sense?"[p]

[p]Prov 17:16

But here is *the prudent.* He has pondered, and formed a just estimate of the blessing. *His mind* has taken hold of it,[q] and, as the means are free, and success sure,[r] he has *acquired it.* As the proof of his possession, he *seeks* for more. For who that has a treasure, will be satisfied with what he has; content with a lesser measure, while a larger is within his reach? *His ear* is now wakened to seek the ministry of the Word, and the conversation of experienced Christians.[s] Every avenue of instruction is diligently improved.

[q]Prov 15:14
[r]Prov 2:3–6; Hos 6:3; James 1:5
[s]Prov 1:5; 9:9

A word to the young: think how much important *knowledge* is to be *acquired.* Get up early and go after it. Let it have your first and your best time and more of it than anything else. Begin before your minds are corrupted with false principles; before you have learned too much, that must be unlearned as disciples of Christ. Examine your prayers? What is their tone? Is it the concentration of the soul, filled with one desire, and carrying it, where it will be accepted and satisfied? The only saving *knowledge* comes down from heaven, and we can only receive it upon our knees. Again, let's take the pulse of your efforts? Does it show the heart to be delighting in the object? Or is it only a start for a moment, and then a sinking back to the slumber of the sluggard? *Knowledge* from heaven leads toward heaven. Clearer knowledge sweeps away many clouds. A better sight of your work will make it easier. With a more intelligent knowledge of the road, you will walk more pleasantly. You will not only guide yourselves, but be "able to admonish one another."[t] "Grow in the grace and knowledge."[u] Follow your convictions. Let nothing turn you aside. In particular—be considerate and *wise* in your application of knowledge. Remember its valuable use to regulate judgment. "Walk" wisely before God in a perfect way[v] "that your love may abound still more and more in real knowledge and in all discernment."[w] Hasten onward then. Happiness and usefulness, light and glory, are before you; and while, sitting at your Master's feet, at every step you will enter more fully into the spirit of the confession of Ignatius—"I am now beginning to be a disciple."

[t]Rom 15:14
[u]2 Peter 3:18
[v]Ps 101:2
[w]Phil 1:9

16 *A man's gift makes room for him,*
And brings him before great men.

THE LEGITIMATE USE OF GIFTS

We have before spoken of the corrupting influence of *gifts* (bribes).[x] But we may justly apply this proverb to their legitimate use. Eliezer's *gifts made room for him* in Rebekah's family.[y] Jacob's *gifts made room for him* in his brother's heart.[z] Nor was it inconsistent with his integrity, by sending his present to the governor of Egypt, to bring his sons with acceptance *before the great man.*[a] Ehud's gifts *made room* for his errand;[b] Abigail's for the preservation of her house.[c] Often indeed were they presented simply as a tribute of respect;[d] as now, in some parts of the East, without them an inferior would scarcely have any claim upon his superior for favor or protection. The minister of the gospel recognizes their value, *making room for him,* perhaps also for his message. Sympathy gives weight to his instruction, when, after the example of his divine Master, he combines kindness to the body with love for the soul. However, great wisdom and discrimination are obviously required to prevent the serious evil of a well-intentioned charity. A wise consideration may also *make room* for us with *great men* for the advancement of the Christian cause. But in this most delicate exercise, let our own principles be fully acknowledged; else even in the service of God, we shall be "not fleshly . . . not walking like mere men";[e] not as the dignified servants of a heavenly Master.

[x]Prov 17:8, 23. Comp. 19:6
[y]Gen 24:30–33
[z]Gen 33:1–11
[a]Gen 43:11
[b]Judg 3:17, 18
[c]1 Sam 25:18–27
[d]1 Sam 9:7
[e]1 Cor 3:3

Blessed be God! We need no *gifts to bring us before Him.* Our welcome is free; our door of access ever open; our treasure of grace in His unchanging favor unsearchable.

17 *The first to plead his case* seems *just,*
Until *another comes and examines him.*

FOR A CONSCIENCE
VOID OF OFFENSE . . .

Earlier we had a rule against judging others.[f] Here we are warned against justifying ourselves. Self-flattery is our cherished nature; highly valuing our fancied excellences; very blind to our real imperfections. So ready are we to place our own cause in a strong light; and sometimes, almost unconsciously, to cast a shade over, or even omit, what might seem to balance on the opposite side. It is so difficult to state facts and circumstances with perfect accuracy, where our own name or credit is concerned. Hence, our cause being first with us, *seems just.* But, according to the Proverb, "the first tale is good, till the second is heard." Our neighbor, acquainted with the real case, comes and *examines* us, exposes our fallacy, and puts us to shame. How often has the tale of wrongs from a hard-hearted overseer, landlord, or creditor, roused our indignation, and perhaps provoked our protest. But a close look at the other side of the story has shown us the wrongness of a hasty, one-sided judgment. Saul made himself appear *just in his own cause.* The necessity of the case seemed to warrant the deviation from the command. But Samuel *examined him* and exposed his rebellion.[g] Ziba's cause *seemed just* in David's eyes, until Mephibosheth's explanation *examined him* to his confusion.[8] Job's incautious self-defense was exposed by Elihu's probing application.[h] An eloquent advocate may easily make a bad *cause coming first seem just.* But the plaintiff is always right, till the defendant's case has been opened. Yet the true rule of justice would be, to judge neither one to be right, till both sides have been heard. Let all the evidence be sifted; and often the plausible cover is swept away by a more searching investigation.[i]

[f] Verse 13

[g] 1 Sam 15:17–23

[h] Job 33:8–12

[i] Acts 24:5, 12

[8] *2 Sam 16:1–4; 19:26. Comp. Prov 28:11. See Bishop SANDERSON'S Sermons on Job 29:14–17, Prov 24:10–12*

Judges are bound to "consider it, take counsel and speak up,"[j] carefully guarding against prejudging, they have been able to thoroughly consider the whole case; also he that is last *in the case* comes with disadvantage, though it may be the cause of right. In our *own case,* we should always be alive to conviction. Watch against a self-justifying spirit. Cultivate the spirit of self-distrust. Balance our enemy's statement against our own prejudices. Judge as under the eye of God and with the sincere anxious prayer to lay ourselves open to his searching disclosure of hidden evil. Deceit in any form never answers its end. "A blameless conscience both before God and before men" must be our great exercise.[k]

[j]Judg 19:30
[k]Acts 24:16

18 *The lot puts an end to contentions,*
And decides between the mighty.

DECISIONS BY LOT—
OR BY THE WORD?

The general use of the lot has been explained before.[l] It is here referred to as a means of peaceful settlement. Whether from the evenness of the balance, or from want of confidence in the judgment, a legal appeal might be of doubtful authority. Contending parties therefore agree to abide by the decision of the lot. Important matters of order under the divine theocracy were thus determined.[m] How many contentions would there have been *between the mighty,* in settling the respective boundaries of the tribes, if this means had not been adopted to *put an end to contentions.*[n] When Saul was thus chosen to the Kingdom,[o] and Matthias "numbered with the eleven apostles,"[p] the election was accepted as the voice of God. There seems therefore no scriptural prohibition to the use of this custom provided it is exercised in a reverential dependence upon God[q] and not profaned for common purposes or worldly ends.

At the same time, as we have before observed, the Word of God appears to be, more fully recognized as the arbiter of God's will. All *contentions end* in a simple, childlike, unreserved readiness to be guided by this more sure rule. The extent of forgiveness is here clearly defined,[r] and the principle and motive for its exercise effectively supplied.[s] Perhaps it is easier to abide by the

[l]Prov 16:33
[m]1 Chron 6:63; 24:31; Neh 11:1
[n]Num 33:54
[o]1 Sam 10:20–24
[p]Acts 1:26
[q]Acts 1:24, 25
[r]Matt 18:21, 22
[s]Col 3:13

decision of the lot than of the Word. The latter requires more self-denial, humility, and patience, and therefore is more practically useful.

19 *A brother offended* is harder to be won *than a strong city,*
And contentions are like the bars of a castle.

HOW TO WIN AN OFFENDED BROTHER

Referring to *the end of contentions,* how affecting is this case of special difficulty! A brother—not an enemy—*is harder to be won than a strong city;* as if the nearer the relationship, the wider the breach. The thread, once snapped, is not easily joined. "What a view does it give us of our corruption, that the natural love implanted in us should degenerate into Satanic hatred!" Such was the *contention* of Cain with Abel; of Joseph's brethren with himself;[t] of Absalom and Amnon;[u] the civil wars between Benjamin and his brethren;[v] in later times between Judah and Israel.[w] Cities in old times were strongly fortified with *bars* of iron against a siege.[x] What a long siege did Esau's *strong city* stand, before it was *won* by the power of love, and the bars of his castle opened their avenue for conciliation![9]

[t]Acts 37:3–5, 18–27
[u]2 Sam 13:22
[v]Judg 20
[w]2 Chron 13:16–17
[x]Isa 45:2

Nowhere is harmony so important as in the church. Never can she prosper, except she maintains the form of Jerusalem—"a city that is compact together."[y] Begotten as we are by the word living on the same food, animated by the same life, ought we not, with all our lesser differences, hold "the unity of the Spirit"?[10] If ties so close cannot unite us; at least let our common welfare, and common danger, quench this unholy fire; just as the fear of the enemy without, might alleviate mutual misunderstanding within. But how painfully *the contentions* between Luther and Calvin (not to mention others of more recent date in the church) show the fearful difficulty of *winning an offended brother!*

[y]Ps 122:3

Yet the extreme difficulty doesn't lessen the obliga-

[9] *Gen 27:41–45; 33:5–11. The rooted enmity of the nation seems to render doubtful the cordiality of the reconciliation. See Num 20:14–21; Ezek 35:5; Obad 10–14.*

[10] *Two reasons made a godly and learned man (Strigelius) long to leave the world. "1. That I might enjoy the sweet sight of the Son of God and the Church of God. 2. That I may be delivered from the cruel and implacable hatred of Theologians." Melchior Adam* in vita. *Chrysostom gives this rule—"Have but one enemy—the devil. With him never be reconciled; with thy brother never fall out."*

tion. So don't let it paralyze your effort. Nothing can be more plain and decisive than the gospel rule. Yet so repugnant is it to flesh and blood, to all nature's pride, feelings, and high notions, that we cry with the disciples of old—"Lord, 'Increase our faith!' "[z] Call in this only principle, that can constrain the heart; and Christian victory is assured. Grace reigns triumphant.

[z]Luke 17:5

20 *With the fruit of a man's mouth his stomach will be satisfied;*
He will be satisfied with *the product of his lips.*

21 *Death and life are in the power of the tongue,*
And those who love it will eat its fruit.

WORST OF EVILS, BEST OF BLESSINGS

Who would not be careful of the seed he puts into a fruitful field when he knows that his harvest will be according to his seed?[a] Here is not a field, but a "world,"[b] to be cultivated, so that we may be *satisfied with the fruit, and with the product.* What this *fruit and product* may be, is a fearful alternative. *The fruit of the mouth—the power of our tongue*—will be poisonous or wholesome, *death or life.*[c] Evil words tend to *death,*[d] good words to *life*[e]—to the comfort of the speaker, as well as to the blessing of the hearer. There is no middle ground—nothing but extremes. It is either the worst of evils or the best of blessings.

[a]Gal 6:7, 8
[b]James 3:6
[c]Verse 7; Ps 50:20, 21; Matt 5:22; 12:36; Jude 14, 15
[d]Prov 13:2
[e]Prov 12:14; 13:2; Ps 34:12, 13

This is plainly shown in public responsibilities. The testimony of witnesses, and the legal decision of the judge, fearfully show, that *death or life is in the power of the tongue.* Take even a more important field of illustration—the ministry of the gospel—the doctrine of false and true teachers. Suppose the sinner's conscience is awakened, and he eagerly longs for an answer to that immensely momentous question—"What must I do to be saved?"[f] The answer can blind him to his own state; soothe with false remedies, with the true remedy concealed or obscured. Or . . . he can be directed to the cross as the one object, compared with which all other objects are vanity and delusion. Don't we see, that, according to the use of *the tongue, death and life are in the power of*

[f]Acts 16:30

it? And take another example—perhaps a more solemn, understanding of God's great work, when all is simply and fully exhibited; when man's helplessness and divine sufficiency—sin and the Savior—ruin and the restoration—are clearly shown; according as the message is rejected or welcomed, it becomes "an aroma from death to death . . . " or "life to life."[g] So again, *death or life is in the power of the tongue.* [g]2 Cor 2:16

In the common activities of life also, *the tongue* is "the fountain . . . both [of] fresh and bitter water";[h] as powerful to destroy as to edify; the poison, or antidote, depending on how it is used. A man by using his tongue aright, in talking, exhorting, witnessing, counseling, may save; and, by abusing it in any of these ways, or any other, may destroy. *Either way he will be satisfied with the fruit.* The curse of destroying others will return upon himself. In administering a blessing to his neighbor, his own soul will be fed.[i] They that love it shall eat the fruit of it. It is, however, the habitual, not the occasional, use of this little member, that determines *its fruit.* A saint may speak unadvisedly—a sinner acceptably—with his lips. Neither would thus determine his true character. [h]James 3:11 [i]Prov 11:25

Born as we are for eternity, no utterance of our tongue can be called trifling. A word, though light as air, scarcely marked, and soon forgotten, may rise up as a witness at the throne of judgment for *death or for life* eternal.[j] When I think of this awful power, shall I not—as Chrysostom warns—"guard this little member more than the pupil of the eye"? Are not the sins of *the tongue* an overwhelming manifestation of the long-suffering of God? "Woe is me"—exclaimed a man of God—"for I am ruined! . . . I am a man of unclean lips."[k] Shall I not cry to my God that He would restrain my tongue;[l] yes, cry more earnestly, that He would consecrate it[m] as a sacred gift, stamped with His image, that it might be my glory, not my shame; my organ of praise, my exercise of joy?[n] In the inner man the heart is the main thing to be kept;[o] in the outer man, the tongue.[p] O my God! take them both into Thine own keeping, under Thine own discipline, as instruments for Thy service and glory. [j]Matt 12:37 [k]Isa 6:5 [l]Ps 141:3 [m]Ps 51:15 [n]Ps 57:7, 8 [o]Prov 4:23 [p]Prov 21:23

[q] Prov 15:10; 16:10; 22:1; 29:4; Eccl 7:28

22 *He who finds a wife finds a good thing,*[q]
And obtains favor from the LORD.

"A CROWN FOR MAN'S HEAD"

[r] Judg 13:23
[s] Job 2:9, 10
[t] Prov 12:4
[u] Gen 2:18; Eccl 4:9, 10
[v] 1 Cor 7:39
[w] 2 Cor 6:14

This is obviously to be taken with limitation. Manoah *found a good thing in his wife.*[r] But Job didn't.[s] Some find "the crown of [the] husband"; others, "rottenness to his bones."[t] That which alone deserves the name is indeed *a good thing.* If in a state of innocence it was "not good for the man to be alone"; how much more in a world of care and trouble "two are better than one," for mutual support, helpfulness, and sympathy.[u] *The good thing* implies godliness and fitness. Godliness is found, when the man marries "only in the Lord,"[v] and only one, who is the Lord's. The "do not be bound together with unbelievers"[w]—the union for life of a child of God with a child of Satan, is a most awful abnormality. "I wish," said Bishop Hall, "that Manoah could speak so loud, that all our Israelites might hear him—'Is there never a woman among the daughters of thy brethren, or among all God's people, that thou goest to take a wife of the uncircumcised Philistines?' If religion be any other than a cipher, how dare we not regard it in our most important choice? Is she a fair Philistine? Why isn't the deformity of the soul more powerful to dissuade us, than the beauty of the face to allure us?"[11]

But there may be godliness on both sides, without that mutual fitness which makes the woman "a helper" for the men. *The good thing is,* when he honors her, not as the wisest or the holiest of women, but as the person, whom God saw to be the best and most fit for him in the whole world, a comfort for life, a help for heaven.[12] Thus she becomes the one object of his undivided heart. Mutual faith is pledged in the Lord. Such a communion sanctifies his affections and elevates him from earth to heaven.

[11] *Contemplations, 10:3. Bishop Beveridge's Resolution is well worth recording—"I shall always endeavor to make choice of such a woman for my spouse, who hath first made choice of Christ as a spouse for herself; that none may be made one flesh with me, who is not made one spirit with Christ my Savior. For I look upon the image of Christ as the best mark of beauty I can behold in her, and the grace of God as the best portion I can receive with her. These are excellences, which, though not visible to our carnal eyes, are nevertheless agreeable to a spiritual heart; and such as all wise and good men cannot choose but be enamored with. For my own part, they seem to me such necessary qualifications, that my heart trembles at the thoughts of ever having a wife without them," Resol. 2.*

[12] *Luke 1:6. See the beautiful picture, Prov 31:10–31.*

But how is this *good thing found?* Isaac *found it,* where every Christian looks for his blessing, as an answer to prayer.[x] A man's choice for his own indulgence will bring a curse upon himself and his family.[y] "He chooses our inheritance for us"[z]—is the cry and confidence of the child of God. Then truly will he *obtain* the gift, not as the result of fortune, or as the proof of his own good discernment; but, as Adam received his wife, "from the Lord,"[a] a token of his special *favor.*

[x]Gen 24
[y]2 Chron 18:1, 2; 21:1–6
[z]Ps 47:4
[a]Prov 19:14

23 *The poor man utters supplications,*
But the rich man answers roughly.

POOR AND RICH BEFORE GOD'S THRONE

It is natural to *the poor,* aware of their dependence, to *use supplications.* And this humiliation may be the discipline for that poverty of spirit, which the Lord sealed with his first blessing.[b] Yet it is a shame to *the rich,* that he should often answer these pleas *roughly.* Instead of the kindly feelings flowing out, he seems to be bound against them with iron chains. He closes his ears to the tale of woe; and, never having tasted the bitter bread of poverty, he has no heart of sympathy and helpfulness. The cultured man of the world, all courtesy and refinement in his own circle, is often insufferably rude and unfeeling toward those under his feet. His good breeding is often just the polish of selfishness. The proud "worm" knows so little the proper use of his power, that the exercise of it only transforms him into a tyrant. Instead of scattering his blessings around, he only makes himself feared and hated by his misused responsibility.[c] If he would just study the character of his divine Master, he would see the exercise of power come alive with true greatness. Wasn't our Lord as considerate to blind Bartimeus, as to the nobleman of Capernaum?[d] All ranks alike shared in his tenderest sympathy.

And yet, as the rich in their conscious superiority may be overbearing, *so the poor, in using their supplications,* may show a servile, crouching spirit,[e] lacking that bold integrity of character, which gives dignity alike to the lowest as to the highest of men. To all of us our providential circumstances bring their besetting temptations. Walking close to God is our only safeguard.

[b]Matt 5:3
[c]1 Sam 25:17
[d]Mark 10:49; John 5:48
[e]1 Sam 2:36

But *the rich, in his rough answering* of the poor, ought to consider, how much more dependent he himself, is upon his God, than his poorest brother is upon himself! And when he comes before his God, he must wear the garb of poverty, though he be a king.[f] *He, too, must use supplications.* Yes—all of us alike are *poor* before the throne of grace, all of us, alike, are poor and must make entreaties. Yet, when does our gracious Father ever *answer* his poor pleading child *roughly;* except as He wisely disciplines his faith, while his heart is full of yearning parental love toward him?[g]

[f]Ps 40:17; 86:1

[g]Matt 15:26. Comp. Gen 42:6, 7

24 *A man of* many *friends* comes *to ruin,*
But there is a friend who sticks closer than a brother.

TO HAVE A FRIEND IS TO BE RICH

To be without a friend, marks a state of painful desolation.[h] On the other hand, a true friend is no common acquisition.[i] There are many who profess friendship. But the jewel itself is as rare as it is precious. Yet, what is life without this cheering, enriching blessing? For its enjoyment, kings have even left their thrones for a time.[j] To Alexander, the conquered world without his Hephaestion would have been a wilderness.[13] But if *a man has friends,* and would keep them, he must show himself friendly. To throw friends away by neglect, caprice, unreasonable disgust, or needless offense, is to show himself utterly unworthy of the blessing. Observe Ruth and Naomi—each warmly tender toward one another, each laying herself out for the other.[k] David acknowledged the kindness of his friends in distress.[l] Paul dealt most delicately with his friend's wounded sensibility[m] and showed the most considerate care for his companion's comforts.[n] It is by such kind consideration that the bond is mutually cemented. A man having friends shows himself friendly. Love begets love and is accompanied by love. Not that this will show itself in extravagant professions, or lavish praise, gratifying to the weak, but revolting to an intelligent mind. The true expression will be in

[h]Ps 88:18

[i]Prov 17:17

[j]Ps 55:14

[k]Ruth 1:16; 2:11, 18, with 3:1–14, 16; 4:16

[l]1 Sam 30:26–31

[m]Philem 8–20

[n]Titus 3:13

[13] *Friendship's the wine of life.*
A friend is worth all hazards we can run.
Poor is the friendless master of a world:
A world in purchase for a friend is gain.—YOUNG

that unmistakable integrity, which at once shows the man, and makes the Christian shine.

Therefore, we need to take care to base our friendship upon the true foundation. Otherwise it may be snapped asunder by the merest trifle, or it may become idolatrous love, usurping God's place in the heart. Sanguine and affectionate dispositions are much given to sudden fancies and mistaken impressions. But the charm is broken by empty professions or the cold return of the misplaced love; and the illusion is swept away in humbling disappointment. Wise men will refrain from the choice of *many* close friends, or involving a multiplication of duties, and, too often, entangling difficulties.

The bond of real friendship is often closer than the natural tie. "Your friend ... is as your own soul."[o] Such was Jonathan unto David—*a friend who sticks closer than a brother*[14]—tender and sympathizing, while his *brother* was fraught with unkind suspicion.[15] He dared the deadly displeasure of his father by openly clinging to David, while his wife showed her love at the expense of his name.[p] Hiram's cordial kindness to Solomon, contrasts with *his* brother's unjust attempt to keep him from the throne.[q] Job's friends, despite their harsh misconceptions, stayed close to him in his afflictions, when his wife and family were strange to him.[r] And do we not remember, that when *the brethren* of Jesus avoided a near position to His cross, *"there were standing by the cross"* the disciple whom Jesus loved, gladly receiving from His lips the charge to care for His bereaved mother?[s] Even natural minds of high feeling may exhibit this strength of friendship. But its surest bond is that, which unites the whole family of God. The identity of sanctified taste; sympathy of experience; holy consecration for mutual helpfulness; above all—union as members of one body to one Head—in all these, flows the magnetic attraction of heavenly, divine friendship.

But where shall we find the complete fulfillment of this exquisite picture, except in Christ, who became our Brother, that he might cleave to us *closer than a brother,*

[o] Deut 13:6

[p] 1 Sam 18:20, 28; 19:12–17, with 20:24–33

[q] 1 Kings 5, with 1:5

[r] Job 2:11–13, with 19:13–17

[s] John 19:25–27

[14] *Bishop Coverdale's version is very beautiful—"a friend that delighteth in love, doth a man more friendship, and sticketh faster unto him than a brother."*

[15] *1 Sam 17:28, with 18:3; 19:2–4; 2 Sam 1:26. It is interesting to observe the reciprocity with one exception (2 Sam 16:1–4) on David's part to the end of life, 2 Sam 9:1; 21:7.*

[t]Heb 2:11, 14–18

in tenderness and help?[t] Let His people bear witness, whether He is not the greatest, best, most loving, most faithful of friends. Truly He loves at all times. He is a friend to them that have no other friend; to those who have been His bitterest enemies; a friend who abides, when all others have fallen away. Mark him as a present friend, known and tried, able to enter into all that most deeply affects us; in temptation opening, when needed, "the way of escape";[u] in affliction cheering with the divine Comforter;[v] sustaining "him upon his sickbed";[w] in death sustaining us by "Thy rod and Thy staff";[x] in eternity receiving us to Himself.[y] What *brother sticks* so close as He, esteeming Himself more honored, the more we lean upon him, "put no confidence in the flesh"?

[u]1 Cor 10:13
[v]John 14:17, 18
[w]Ps 41:3
[x]Ps 23:4
[y]John 14:3; 17:24; Phil 3:3

And then, looking on the objects of His love;[z] its freeness;[a] its costliness;[b] its perseverance in spite of all the discouragements of our obstinacy and foolishness;[c] "He loved them to the end,"[d] as parts and members of Himself—how can we duly honor this, our faithful, tender, unchanging, unchangeable Friend? Aren't there any, who boast of their faithfulness to the creature, who yet have no sympathy with this divine friendship, no give-and-take affection to this surpassing Friend? Won't our very sensibilities condemn our indifference? For what stronger proof can there be of their wickedness and confusion, than that they should be flowing to the creature-objects, cold and dead to the divine Friend? Oh! let Him be the first choice of youth, the tried and chosen Friend of maturing age, the Friend for eternity! Cultivate a closer acquaintance with Him. Set the highest possible value upon His friendship. Live a life of joyous confidence in His all-sufficiency and love. Make Him the constant subject of conversation. Avoid whatever is displeasing to Him. Be found in those places where He meets His people.[e] Long to be with Him forever. Thus testify to all around—"This is my beloved and this, my friend."[f] Is it not because men have no eyes to see Him, that they have no heart to love Him? Were but the eyes really opened, they would soon affect the heart; and all would be for Him in entire devotedness of service.

[z]Rom 5:8
[a]John 6:37
[b]John 15:13; 1 John 3:16
[c]Isa 42:4; Hos 11:7, 8; Mal 3:6
[d]John 13:1
[e]Isa 64:5
[f]Song of Sol 5:16

CHAPTER NINETEEN

1 *Better is a poor man who walks in his integrity*
Than he who is perverse in speech and is a fool.

Poverty is never a disgrace, except when it is the fruit of bad conduct. But when adorned with godly uprightness it is most honorable. *Better is the poor man, than* he whom riches lift up in his own eyes, and he is given up to his wickedness and foolishness.[a] Often man puts under his feet those, whom God lays in His bosom. He honors the wicked for their riches and despises *the poor* for their poverty. But what does the rich have, if he doesn't have God? And what is a poor man, if he has God? Better be in a wilderness with God, than in Canaan without Him.[b] Was not Job on the dunghill, *walking in his integrity, better* than ungodly Ahab on the throne?[c] Wasn't Lazarus in his rags better off than Dives with his "fine linen" and "living in spendor"?[d] Calculate wisdom by God's standard, who judges not by rank or station in life but by character. Judge things in the light of eternity. How soon will all accidental distinctions pass away, and only personal distinctions count! Death will strip the poor of his rags, and the rich of his "purple," and bring them both "naked" to the earth, from whence they came.[e] Meanwhile, let us hear our Lord's voice to His despised people, "I know ... *your poverty* (but you are rich)."[f] How glorious the stamp upon the outcast believers *walking in their integrity*—"Of whom the world was not worthy"![g] For them is prepared the honor that comes from God only—His seal, His smiles, and His everlasting crown.

[a] Prov 28:6
[b] 1 Tim 6:17–19
[c] Job 2:7, 8
[d] Luke 16:19–21
[e] Job 1:21; Eccl 12:7
[f] Rev 2:9
[g] Heb 11:37, 38

2 *Also it is not good for a person to be without knowledge,*
And he who makes haste with his feet errs.

THE BLESSINGS OF KNOWLEDGE

"Also"—seems to trace the *fool's sinful ways* to their source. He *is without knowledge*. Ignorance gives continuity to folly. *Knowledge* is valuable even to the mind. It expands and sharpens its reasoning powers, and, when rightly directed, preserves from many besetting temptations. Be assured, to paraphrase Chalmer, it is not because the people know much, that they ever become the willing subjects of any hostile rabble-rouser, who is without principle. It is just because they know too little. It is just because ignorance is the field, on which the pretension of a political impostor ever reaps his most abundant harvest, he added. *Knowledge* also opens much wholesome enjoyment. The intelligent poor are preserved with their comforts of home from the temptations of the bar. The most educated are raised above the trivialities of loose living. So both classes are restrained from the sensualities of ungodliness.

That the person made for God *should be without knowledge, is not good*. The blessing is not merely expansion of mind, or restraint of evil, but light and life eternal.[h] *Without it*, all is thick darkness—the darkness of death. Man has no directory for his ways. He doesn't know how to walk and please God. He knows nothing of spiritual duties, heavenly affections, the life of faith, the entire surrender of heart, or living to the glory of God. As a result, he substitutes services of his own, carnal and unprofitable. He "who walks in the darkness . . . does not know where he goes."[i] He has no remedy for his sins, so he devises penance, or at least repentance or reformation. Not knowing the mystery of the gospel, he cannot come to God by Christ and wash in "a fountain . . . opened," and, therefore, he can't obtain peace with God, or in his own conscience.[j] He has no support in his trouble, nothing better than vain philosophy, or natural hardness. He doesn't know where it comes from, the love of God in it, its true intent, its humbling, quickening, and sanctifying operation. He cannot "exult in . . . tribulations" from a sense of its beneficial effects;[k] and therefore he either despises it, or hardens himselt against it, or faints under it. He has no strength for his duties—none but his own, which is perfect weakness. He knows not

[h] John 17:3

[i] John 12:35

[j] Zech 13:1; Rom 9:31, 32

[k] Rom 5:3–5; Heb 12:11, with 5

how to be strong in the Lord, to be strengthened by the Spirit, to use the Christian armor, to mortify sin, to resist Satan, or to overcome the world. He might be given unconquerable strength and be able to "do all things through Him [Christ] who strengthens" him.[l] But he doesn't know Christ. And, therefore, he has no interest in Him; and, "apart from Me you can do nothing."[m] He has no hope in his end. All is fearful uncertainty. He has no knowledge of the free grace of the gospel, no reliance on its promises, no confidence in the Savior, no title which he can bring to God for acceptance, and no view of God's faithfulness. And thus "fools die for lack of understanding."[n] They "are destroyed for lack of knowledge."[o] "For they are not a people of discernment, therefore their Maker will not have compassion on them. And their Creator will not be gracious to them."[p] The terror of the great day will be, that "the Lord Jesus shall be revealed from heaven with His mighty angels in flaming fire, dealing out retribution to those who do not know God."[q]

[l]Phil 4:13
[m]John 15:5
[n]Prov 10:21
[o]Hos 4:6
[p]Isa 27:11
[q]2 Thess 1:7, 8

What then must we think of the thoughtless trifler, lost in pleasure, playing with trinkets, and despising priceless knowledge? What is he, but a man "without understanding," justly compared to "the beasts that perish"?[r] Is ignorance then the mother of devotion? Is it not the worst of evils, the center of all evil,[s] the parent of irreligion, and the forerunner of ruin?[t] Awful indeed are its aggravations—to be ignorant in a time of knowledge, blind in a land of light, unenlightened in "the valley of vision"!

[r]Ps 49:20
[s]Isa 1:3, 4; Acts 3:17
[t]Luke 19:42; Isa 22:1

"RUSHING WITH THE FEET IS SIN"

But let us mark the evil of the lack of soundly-disciplined knowledge in temporal matters. The uninstructed child or savage acts rashly. The man of impulse is impatient to finish his work before the time, and therefore crowds into the day far more than belongs to it, forgetting that "things are not done by the effort of the moment, but by the preparation of past moments," said Cecil in *Remains*. Our wise moralist has well remarked, "He that is in a hurry proves, that the work in which he is engaged is too much for him," advised Dr. Johnson. Certainly this *making haste with the feet* may be considered to be sin, inasmuch as it proceeds from a want of simple trust in God, and submission to His orderly arrangements and claims of regular duty.

[u] 1 Kings 8:59

The true method is to do "as each day requires."[u] This is all that God requires to be done. The affair of one day at a time is as much as can be quietly committed to God in the daily exercise of faith. This principle should be carried into all important responsibilities. Burnet's account of Sir M. Hale is most valuable in this view. He was often heard to say, that he had seen many witty men run into great errors, because they did not give themselves time to think; but, the heat of imagination making some notions look good to them, they, without staying till that cooled, were violently led by the impulses it made upon them; whereas calm and slow men, who pass for dull in common estimation, could search after truth, and find it, with more deliberation, so with greater certainty.

WHEN THE SOUL IS NOT WELL

[v] Prov 4:26

[w] Ps 119:60; Luke 19:6

[x] Josh 9:14, 15

[y] 1 Sam 13:12

[z] 2 Sam 16:3, 4

[a] 1 Kings 13:18, 19

[b] 2 Chron 18:1–4; 19:2

[c] Prov 28:20, 22

But far more serious is this evil in spiritual matters. "Where no discretion is, there the soul is not well" Bishop Coverdale advised, (*Translation*). The man, therefore, *without knowledge,* instead of watching "the path,"[v] *makes haste with his feet* and errs. Haste, as opposed to sloth, is the energy of divine grace.[w] Here, as opposed to consideration, acting hastily in sin. This impatience is the genuine exercise of self-will, not taking time to inquire; not waiting for the counsel of the Lord. Godly Joshua offended here.[x] Saul's impatience cost him his kingdom.[y] David's haste was the occasion of great injustice.[z] The prophet, not taking time to ponder the evidence contradicting his own message, was *without knowledge. He rushed with his feet and erred.*[a] Jehoshaphat's hurry to ask counsel *after,* instead of *before,* was sharply rebuked.[b] Rash experiments, the result of *haste,* often threaten serious evils in the state. The same spirit rends the church with schism. The heady professing believer wanders from church to church and from sect to sect without thinking. In common life how much *sin* has been the fruit of a few rash words or hasty lines! A sudden impulse has taken the place of considerate principles. Let's always remember, that without self-discipline there can be no Christian consistency or stability. In a thousand cases *haste* may plunge *our feet into sin,*[c] if not into ruin. The best-intentioned purposes, unwarranted by the will and Word of God, are only blind impulses, to be checked, not followed. The real peace of faith, is to stand or sit still, and see how God will appear on our side, to make a way for us through many a deep water of bewilderment.[d] "He who believes in it will not be disturbed."[e]

[d] Exod 14:14; Isa 30:7
[e] Isa 28:16

3 *The foolishness of man subverts his way,*
And his heart rages against the LORD.

ADAM'S FOOLISH CHILDREN

Such was *the foolishness* of Adam! First he *subverted his way;* then he charged God for its bitter fruit. God, making him "upright," made him happy. Had he been ruled by God's will, he would have continued so. But, he "sought out many devices,"[f] he made himself miserable. As the author of his own misery, it was reasonable, that he should fret against himself. But such was his pride and baseness, *that his heart raged against the Lord,* instead, and blamed Him.[g] So his first-born child, when his own sin had brought "punishment" on him, *raged*, as if it were "too great to bear!"[h] This has been the *foolishness* of Adam's children ever since. God has linked together moral and penal evil, sin and sorrow. The fool rushes into the sin, and most unreasonably *rages* for the sorrow; as if he could gather grapes from thorn bushes, or "figs from thistles."[i] He charges his crosses, not to his own wickedness, but to the injustice of God.[j] But God is clear of all blame[k] He had shown the better; man chooses the worse. He had warned by his Word and by conscience. Man, deaf to the warning, plunged into the misery; and, while eating the fruit of his own ways, his heart *rages against the Lord.* He mumbles, "It's wrong that I should have these strong desires and then be punished for indulging them. I could not help it. Why did he not give me grace to keep from yielding to them. I can't help giving in to them. Why doesn't God give me the strength to resist them?"[l] That's the pride and blasphemy of an unhumbled spirit. The criminal blames the judge for his righteous sentence.[m]

[f] Eccl 7:29
[g] Gen 3:6–12
[h] Gen 4:8–13
[i] Matt 7:16
[j] Ezek 18:25
[k] James 1:13, 14
[l] Jer 7:10
[m] Isa 8:21, 22; Rev 16:9–11, 21

THE DISEASE WITHIN

But let's take a closer look at this bold accusation of God's righteousness. "Why didn't He give me power to resist?" Is that God's obligation and responsibility? Actually, do we have any claim upon God? Isn't God's grace his own?[n] Isn't the fool following his own will, and therefore responsible for his doing? Why can't he turn to God? He can, but just refuses to listen and obey. The way is open to him—and he's free to make his own choice. No force of natural impossibility hinders. His stubbornness alone makes him powerless. He *can't,* because he *won't;* and therefore, if he perishes, the problem lies, not in his weakness, but in his stubbornness.[o] The worst part of his wickedness is his wicked will.

[n] Matt 20:15; Rom 9:19–21

[o] Matt 23:37; John 5:40

NEEDED: CHANGE OF HEART, NOT LOCATION

It is not only that his nature is wicked, but that he is willing for it to be wicked. If he just felt and recognized his moral inability, wouldn't he then turn for help to Him who is eyes to the blind, ears to the deaf, feet to the lame. If he did, then overcoming power and victory would surely be his.

This stubbornness shows itself in every new uprising of corruption. The Pharisee mocks God by his hypocritical service, and then *rages,* because no good comes from it.[p] The proud "worm" cherishes an attitude of discontent toward God. Either the desired comfort is withheld, or the will has been crossed. If he doesn't talk about it, still he carries a grudge in his heart against God. If he had been placed differently, he would have succeeded better. God therefore gets the blame for his failure. And yet, it's obvious, that if he is not ready now to serve God, he needs a change of heart, not a change of place. The disease is within, and therefore would follow him through whatever circumstances with the same result; leaving him as far as ever from happiness. The constant struggle of the will is to be anywhere, but where God has placed us for our best welfare.

[p] Isa 58:3; Mal 3:14; Job 25:6

And how humbling it is to see this *foolishness* in the Lord's people! Our carelessness or waywardness provokes and deserves discipline; yet the heart frets under the rebuke.[q] While we shun what is positively sinful, too often we allow occasions of sin. We are found in circumstances or society, which, experience has taught us, hinder prayer, dampen spiritual taste, and wound the conscience. If therefore we allow this willful indulgence, at

[q] 2 Sam 6:8

least let us take the blame for it ourselves and not charge God with it in trying to hold Him responsible for the bitter consequences.

DOUBLE BURDEN

Then, too, we rebel against what we can't change, thereby doubling our burden, by adding guilt to our trouble. If a fool's quarrel with his brother calls for punishment,[r] how much more the "grumblers, finding fault" against God deserve punishment[s]—"Woe to the man who quarrels with his Maker";[t] or rather the child kicking against his Father's discipline, instead of humbling himself "under the mighty hand of God."[u] If he only knew himself, if he would only trust his God, he would look, not at the rod, but at the hand that holds it.[v] Should *the heart rage* to see it in his father's hands? Should he not kiss it, even while it smites him; shouldn't he peacefully, yes, even thankfully accept the punishment of his "iniquity"?[w]

[r]Prov 18:6
[s]Jude 16
[t]Isa 45:9
[u]1 Peter 5:6
[v]1 Sam 3:18; 2 Sam 16:11; Ps 39:9
[w]Lev 26:41

This stormy rebellion against God's rule brings its own torment. It knocks all the powers of the soul out of course. There is no peace or tranquility, except in agreement with the will of God, being fully reconciled to His doings. While Ephraim "was like an untrained calf," unaccustomed to the yoke, it was only the more irksome. Once he was brought "back . . . restored . . . instructed," he found peace and release from the irritation.[x]

[x]Jer 31:18, 19

Let us, therefore, always be ready with the cry—"Let me know why Thou dost contend with me . . . Teach Thou me what I do not see; If I have done iniquity, I will do it no more."[y] Instead of offering "complaint in view of [our] sins . . . Let us examine and probe our ways, And let us return to the Lord." "I will bear the indignation of the Lord because I have sinned against Him."[z] The extent of the evil is little known, till we are brought under the hands of God. It requires no less than His almightiness to break the stubborn will into ready obedience. "Thy will be done"—is easily prayed, but not so easily learned. If things aren't just the way we want them, all too often we struggle to break loose from the affliction; professing indeed to live by faith, yet becoming discouraged over difficult situations.

[y]Job 10:2; 34:32
[z]Lam 3:39, 40; Mic 7:9

WHEN THE MYSTERY IS FINISHED

For our own happiness, our great desire should be, that our own will may be destroyed and replaced by the will of God. The discipline, therefore, that schools the will into subjection, brings with it nothing to cause complaining thought. Actually it reveals the secrets of God's heart toward us, and of our hidden corruptions; that, since it comes from *His* hand, and He controls the handling of it, the discipline can only bring blessing, if we allow it to. We must only believe that all that God does, will appear to be right and best when the mystery is finished; that all His care will be expounded with the full display of His glory. It will then be seen that the cross of disappointed wishes was the gracious means of saving us from ruining ourselves, and of preparing us for endurance, and ultimately for enjoyment. It will bring great joy and delight, indeed, to look back upon every step of the "straight way" which our Father has led us to "go to an inhabited city,"[a] and to see, how needful was the discipline at every point, how suited to every crisis. How we ought to praise God for His unwearied patience, with which He lovingly "put up with them in the wilderness."[b] Meanwhile let us take a closer look at God and His gracious plans. "O Lord, take away our ignorance, that we may know thee; our idleness, that we may see thee; our unbelief, that we may find and enjoy thee," prayed Bishop Hall.

[a]Ps 107:7

[b]Acts 13:18

4 *Wealth adds many friends,*
But a poor man is separated from his friend.

THE DIVINE PRINCIPLE OF LOVE

We have had the substance of this Proverb before.[c] It is quite true, that *wealth adds many friends.* But such friendships don't generally amount to much. Their friendship isn't really with us but with our money. The basis of such friendships is selfishness. Therefore, they don't lead to lasting friendship. Few among them will be found loving "at all times, And a brother ... born for adversity."[d] God has made poverty a graduation of rank; and as such we are bound to regard it. Man makes it a wall of separation. It not only tries our own faith and

[c]Prov 14:20. Comp. verse 6

[d]Prov 17:17

patience, but the love and sincerity of our faith as well.

This lack of sympathy for the poor is a serious evil. It *separates* those, whom God has linked together by a mutual bond of interest, each toward each, the rich being the guardians and protectors of the poor; *the poor* being the strength and support of the rich. But too often *the poor* know their wealthier neighbors, only as living in the most luxurious indulgence, while they themselves are left in the sense of their poverty, unaided and uncared for. This could never be, if the gospel had penetrated the mass with its own divine principle of love. But what if the Lord's *poor be separated from* his selfish *friend.*[e] There is One that knows "the troubles of my soul,"[f] and that has pledged His word—"I will never desert you, nor will I ever forsake you."[g] Yes—this is the joy and the stay of his confidence—"I am afflicted and needy. Let the Lord be mindful of me."[h] Poverty may *separate him from his friend.* But who or what shall separate him from his God?[i] Heirs of God and fellow-heirs with Christ . . . whom He [God] appointed heir of all things," what can he lack?[j] "If it were possible for him to stand absolutely in need of the use and service of the whole creation, all the creatures in the world would surely wait on him, and be appropriated to him," stated Bishop Reynolds (*Works,* p. 11). With such an inheritance as his, why should he fret over a few years of poverty or neglect? Earth's short dream will soon be past; and then comes the eternal reality of unclouded joy.

[e]Verse 7
[f]Ps 31:7
[g]Heb 13:5
[h]Ps 40:17
[i]Rom 8:38, 39
[j]Rom 8:17; Heb 1:2, with 1 Cor 3:21–23

5 *A false witness will not go unpunished,*
And he who tells lies will not escape.

HOW BIG CAN A LIE BECOME?

If "a truthful witness saves lives,"[k] *a false witness* destroys them. What fearful guilt and responsibility, reaching, without the atoning sacrifice, throughout eternity! Can we wonder that the detection should bring him under certain condemnation?[l] It is an offense against both tables of the law. The liar takes God's name "in vain." *False witness* is a direct transgression against the law of our neighbor. This wickedness does not however come to this height at once. But the habit of *telling lies,*

[k]Prov 14:25
[l]Deut 19:16–21; Exod 20:7

[m]Rom 3:8 the allowance of untruth under the pretense of a good end,[m] or only in play, grows to this aggravation.[1]

In this view, strict attention to truth forms a primary point in a Christian education. The boundary line must never be trifled with. Not even a child can pass it without paying a price. It will soon lose its respect, if it isn't reverenced at any cost and under all circumstances. A child must never be allowed to play with a lie. It must constantly be pressed upon him that anything less than truth is a lie. Even if no one is deceived by it, a habit is fostered, and we can't tell how big it will actually become. "He who is faithful in a very little thing is faithful also in much."[n] The fostering of a lie soon banishes all fear of being under oath. The careless liar, if occasion demands, has no conscience against becoming *a false witness*. But neither in the higher or lower indulgence will falsehood be forgotten. It may escape detection from man. But it lies open and unveiled before the eye of God. It shall *not go unpunished; it shall not escape* there. The liar may perhaps have thought or intended no harm. But there is no mercy at the bar of God. "And *all* liars, their part will be in the lake that burns with fire and brimstone."[o]

[n]Luke 16:10

[o]Rev 21:8

6 *Many will entreat the favor of a generous man,*
And every man is a friend to him who gives gifts.
7 *All the brothers of a poor man hate him;*
How much more do his friends go far from him!
He pursues them with *words,* but *they are gone.*

FRIENDS IN THE DAY OF CALAMITY

The fourth verse is here further opened with an accurate description of man's native selfishness. "A prince never wants suitors for his favour," warned Bishop Patrick. Every one loves, or professes to love, those from whom they expect benefit. False friends enjoy flattering people for the sake "of gaining an advantage,"[p] valuing them for their possessions, not for their virtues. Yet if "wealth certainly makes itself wings . . ." and "flies toward the heavens,"[q] will not the false friends take their

[p]Jude 16

[q]Prov 23:5

[1]*Jer 9:3–5. There is much instruction in the wise reply of Solon on first seeing the rude theatricals of Thespis. Asking him how he dared to tell so many lies before the people, and receiving for answer, that he only did it in play—"Yes," said the legislator, striking his staff with force into the ground, "But if we begin with telling lies in play, we shall end with telling them in earnest."*

flight with them? If the same person, now fought over for his gifts, were by God brought to poverty, the same *friends would hate* or neglect him. "Which of them," asks Bishop Hall (*Works,* xiii. p. 77), "would dare acknowledge him, when he is going to prison?" As the winter brooks, filled from the opening springs and the torrents from heaven, are dried up and vanish before the summer heat; so these friends of *the poor go far from him,* cold, distant, and vanishing in the day of his calamity. If *he pursues them with words,* yet they are deaf to his pleas for help and sympathy. Job found these "summer" friends a great aggravation to his affliction.[r] Jerusalem in its days of prosperity was "the joy of the whole earth." After its destruction, "they have called you," said the mournful prophet, "an outcast, saying, 'It is Zion; no one cares for her.' "[s]

[r]Job 6:15–22; 19:13–19; 29:30

[s]Ps 48:2; Jer 30:17

But how ought we to entreat the favor of *our* Prince? What gifts does He give to His beloved people? And shall not those who are enriched with them exhibit His rule of mercy to their poorer brethren,[t] especially to His poor, the princes and heirs of his kingdom?[u] "Lord! in my greatest plenty help me to mind and feel others' poverty; and in my most prosperous condition keep me from forgetting the afflictions of thy Joseph," prayed Swinnock (*Christian Man's Calling,* Part ii. 338).

[t]Gal 6:10; Heb 6:10

[u]James 2:5

8 *He who gets wisdom loves his own soul;*
He who keeps understanding will find good.

WISDOM IS THE THING

It would seem that self-interest might win us to Christ. Careless sinner! little do you know your loss of solid happiness! If anything is worth *getting,* and, when got, worth *keeping,* wisdom is the thing.—"Acquire wisdom! Acquire understanding! . . . with all your acquiring, *get understanding.*"[v] How this blessing is to be obtained, Solomon has before explained. Apply your heart diligently to the search; then bring your heart to God for His light and teaching; and the treasure is your own.[w] Yet it's as hard to *keep* the blessing as to *get* it. It doesn't take long for it to slip away from a negligent hand. "Keep your soul diligently,"[x] and you will keep your treasure; as the man, who, finding hidden treasure in the field, buys the

[v]Prov 4:5–7

[w]Prov 2:1–6

[x]Deut 4:9

[y]Matt 13:44 field to make sure he can keep it.[y] But what he has found here certainly doesn't benefit the flesh. The Christian's present portion requires the sacrifice of all.[z] And yet, as a reward, abundantly overpaying for all that can be endured, it is real, unlimited, heavenly. To *get wisdom* therefore, whatever the cost, is *to love our own soul.* "For he who finds me finds life"[a]—all in me, all with me.

[z]Luke 14:26, 33
[a]Prov 8:35

PEBBLES AND PEARLS

Isn't finding life in Christ better than anything earth can offer?[b] Here is the eternal good, when every earthly good shall have passed away?[c] We should be ashamed to even wonder whether Christ or the world shall have our highest love, our utmost trust, the best of our time and talents. Doesn't just asking the question give us our answer? Isn't it like comparing pebbles with pearls, dust with diamonds, rubbish with gold? To have our own way is to destroy, not *love, our own souls.* "But he who sins against me injures himself; All those who hate me love death."[d]

[b]Ps 4:6, 4
[c]Ps 73:25, 26
[d]Prov 8:36

9 *A false witness will not go unpunished,*
And he who tells lies will perish.

EVIL THINGS IN GOD'S SIGHT

"For all His ways are just.... Righteous and upright is He.... God ... cannot lie."[e] That's the character of Jehovah! We can't wonder at the repeated condemnation of deceit. So openly dishonoring is it to His unchangeable character! Here, one addition is made to the former sentence.[f] Not only will the punishment be certain—he that speaks lies shall not escape—but it will be utter ruin—He shall perish.[g] "Lies and violence" are linked together.[h] " 'I will be a swift witness against ... those who swear falsely ... and do not fear Me,' says the Lord of hosts."[i]

[e]Deut 32:4; Titus 1:2
[f]Verse 5
[g]Jer 28:15–17; 29:31, 32; 2 Peter 2:1–3; Rev 22:15
[h]Hos 12:1
[i]Mal 3:5

10 *Luxury is not fitting for a fool;*
Much less for a slave to rule over princes.

What has *a fool* to do with luxury? This world's prosperity, so far as he knows it, can only be a curse to him.[j] "Praise is becoming to the upright,"[k] suitable to his character. He has a right and title to it.[l] But it *is not fitting for the fool.* To be sure, he has his fun.[m] But he

[j]Prov 1:32
[k]Ps 33:1
[l]Ps 32:11
[m]1 Sam 25:25; Eccl 7:5, 6; Isa 5:11, 12; 22:12–14; Hos 7:3–5; Amos 6:3–6

knows nothing of solid joy. What he really deserves is a chastening rod.[n] And should the Lord graciously make this dispensation holy—as He has so often done!—it will introduce him to *luxury* which will then be fitting for him.[o]

[n]Prov 10:13, 14; 26:3

[o]2 Chron 33:11–13; Luke 15:14–24

Much less fitting is the exhibition of *a slave having rule over princes.* Such a high position is dangerous to the individual. In God's kingdom, it is one of the things at which "the earth quakes . . . it cannot bear."[p] The servant has the same rational power with his ruler. But his limited reasoning powers make him unfit to rule. There are exceptions, as in the case of Joseph.[q] But usually God's order cannot be reversed without anarchy and confusion.[r] Peace and happiness belong to godly contentment.[s] "Let every man remain with God in that condition in which he was called."[t] To those whom He has placed under the authority of others, our Father's voice is full of instruction—"Are you seeking great things for yourself? Do not seek them."[u]

[p]Prov 30:21

[q]Gen 41:39–45

[r]2 Sam 3:24, 25, 39; Isa 3:5

[s]1 Tim 6:6

[t]1 Cor 7:24

[u]Jer 45:5

11 *A man's discretion makes him slow to anger,*
And it is his glory to overlook a transgression.

ANGER: TEMPORARY MADNESS

What is *anger* but temporary madness? When we yield to angry outbursts or act impulsively, there's no telling what we might do. One thing is certain, though, we're more than likely to do something we'll be sorry for.[v] The time between the first stirrings of anger and their outward expression is most important.

[v]Prov 14:17, 29

A MAN'S WISE JUDGMENT DELAYS HIS ANGER

Being mindful of his own infirmities, he will guard against offensive bursts of temper, taking time, instead, to carefully weigh the offense that is causing his anger and to be sure he doesn't attach more importance to it than it deserves.[2] Whatever tends to anger him is the test, whether he has wisdom, or is the slave of his own pas-

[2] *Prov 16:32; Eccl 7:9; James 1:19. Comp. 1 Sam 10:27. Even heathen moralists acknowledge the value of this* discretion—*"I would have beaten you," one said to his offending servant, "if I was not angry." Augustus under the impulse of anger was requested to repeat the alphabet to give him time to cool. "It is easier," as Seneca wisely observed, "not to admit the passion, than, when admitted, to govern it." Justin Martyr, when asked what was Christ's greatest miracle, named His so great patience in such great trials.*

sion. Most people figure we ought to get even—to return one insult for another. God's standard for the Christian is to rise above, "not returning evil for evil, or insult for insult, but giving a blessing instead."[3]

POISON LURKING WITHIN

We are likely to feel that overlooking an offense against us shows lack of courage and bold spirit. But Solomon, a wise man and a king, declares it to be weakness, rather than strength or greatness, not to be able to graciously bear things that offend us. *It is honorable to pass over a transgression against us.* It must be, because it is likeness to God. What a motive! So what, if we let it pass for a kind of sheepishness to be meek. It is a likeness to Him, who was "a sheep that is silent before its shearers, so He did not open His mouth."[w] It is a portion of His spirit.[x]

[w] Isa 53:7
[x] 1 Peter 3:3, 4

And what an example of His long-suffering in the midst of such willful daily, hourly, provocations![y] If He creates us anew, it must be, as before, in His own image. Forbearance and forgiveness will therefore take the place of resentment and malice. Moral strength may, in some men, curb the outward expression. But the poison lurks within. Forbearance from a pure motive, *overlooking transgression* in love, is a noble triumph of grace. It is most honorable to God and fraught with the richest spoils to our own souls.

[y] Eph 4:31, 32; Col 3:13

12 *The king's wrath is like the roaring of a lion,*
But his favor is like dew on the grass.

The king of the forest is very much like the king of the land.[z] "A lion has roared! Who will not fear?"[a] The rocks and hills echo the terrifying cry. And all the animals of the forest run off in every direction or are petrified to the spot. The king's wrath in a land of despotism[b] is just as frightening. He reigns without law, above law. His will is his only law; an awful picture of cruelty;[c] tyranny,[d] and caprice![e] Proud human nature just cannot bear to have unlimited power, except with special grace from above. But *the king's favor* is a reviving blessing, as *dew upon the grass.*[f]

[z] Comp. Jer 4:7; 50:17; 2 Tim 4:17
[a] Amos 3:8; Rev 10:1–3
[b] Prov 16:14; 20:2; 28:15
[c] Matt 2:16–18
[d] Exod 5:4–9; Dan 3:1–19
[e] Dan 2:5–12
[f] Prov 16:15; 2 Sam 23:3, 4

[3] *1 Peter 3:9. The example of Joseph—Gen 45:4–15; 50:21; David—1 Sam 24:7–19; Ps 35:7–14; 38:12–14. The prophet—1 Kings 13:4–6. Mr. Scott justly remarks on the identity of the Old Testament standard with that of Christ and His apostles. Comp. Matt 5:38–42; 18:21, 22; Rom 12:17–21; with Prov 25:21, 22.*

THE KING'S TERRIBLE WRATH

But if *the wrath of a king* is so terrible—oh, my soul, what must the wrath of God be![g] If it's so terrible in this world, where every drop is mixed with mercy; what will it be in eternity, where it is "mixed in full strength and without cessation;[h] where His power is so fearfully manifested, not only in tormenting, but in preserving and establishing "them to correction"?[i] Oh! let this wrath be the grand object of my reverential fear. Let me flee from it by the only way of escape, while escape is open to me; and seek His *favor,* as the enriching "dew" unto Israel, invigorating and nourishing my barren soil.[j]

[g]Luke 12:4, 5
[h]Rev 14:10, 11
[i]Hab 1:12
[j]Hos 14:5–7; Ps 72:6

13 *A foolish son is destruction to his father,*
And the contentions of a wife are a constant dripping.

"Many," observes an old commentator, "are the miseries of a man's life; but none like that, which cometh from him who should be the stay of his life." As "a wise son makes a father glad,"[k] so *a foolish son is the father's destruction*[l]—a multitude of calamities meeting in one, such as no earthly portion, no riches, honor, or station, can outbalance. If this denunciation—"Write this man down childless"[m]—could be written over him, it would be a comparative blessing to him. The throne of grace to the Christian *father* will be the only refuge for his grief. There he will pour out the bitterness of his soul in humiliation for himself and supplication for his child; and find rest.[n] Oh! Is it possible for us to be too earnest for the prevention of this *destruction?* Shouldn't we be greatly concerned for the salvation of our children early in life, and—combined with this—shouldn't we seek special sustaining grace from God for ourselves,[o] to keep us from carelessly and unknowingly sowing the seed in their young hearts, that will afterward spring up with such deadly fruit?

[k]Prov 10:1; 15:20
[l]Prov 17:21, 25
[m]Jer 22:30
[n]2 Sam 23:5
[o]Judg 13:12

RAIN ON THE ROOF

Another domestic calamity is mentioned, no less painful. The *contentions of a wife* are as *a constant dripping*[p] of rain through the roof of an old house. Such a dripping utterly destroys a man's comfort in his home and wears away a heart firm as a stone. This trial is the more dif-

[p]Prov 27:15, also 21:9, 19; 25:24

ficult because there is no lawful escape. The *foolish son* may be ordered out.[q] But the *contentious wife* must be endured.[r]

[q]Deut 21:18
[r]Matt 5:32; 19:9

The question is—would this problem have developed at all, had the plain scriptural rule of subjection been obeyed?[s] Or isn't it the rightful chastening for the neglect of the divine command, so essential to bring about happiness in the marriage yoke?[t] Or, couldn't it be the "thorn in the flesh," the needful restraint from some imminent, subtle, and fearful danger?[u] Self-will and impatience would flee from the cross. Faith will seek strength to bear it meekly to the honor of God, extracting a solid blessing out of a heavy trial.[v] And who knows but what *the contentious wife* may give herself to persevering prayer and patient forbearance, as a helper to her husband, and both shall ultimately dwell as "a fellow-heir of the grace of life"?[w]

[s]Gen 3:16; 1 Cor 14:34; Eph 5:22–24; Col 3:18; Titus 2:5
[t]1 Cor 7:39; 2 Cor 6:14
[u]2 Cor 12:7
[v]2 Cor 12:8, 9
[w]1 Peter 3:7; Gen 2:18; 1 Cor 7:16

But surely our God teaches us a valuable lesson of this world's vanity by fixing disappointment on our greatest comforts. Let His children beware of putting their trust in any earthly portion, or being ensnared by their blessings. If they do, their jealous Father will embitter their sweetest sources of enjoyment and teach them by painful discipline to enter into no rest but His.

14 *House and wealth are an inheritance from fathers,*
But a prudent wife is from the L*ORD.*

FOR MEN ONLY—
A SPECIAL GIFT FROM GOD

"Every perfect gift is *from above*";[x] only, some of them come in the ordinary course of living; others more directly from Him. *Houses and wealth,* though His gifts, come from our fathers—*they are the inheritance of fathers.*[y] The heir is known, and eventually he takes possession of his estate. But *the prudent wife* is wholly unconnected with the man. There has been no previous bond of relation.[z] She is often brought from a distance.[a] "The Lord God . . . brought her to the man"[b] by His special providence, and therefore as His special gift. The history of Ruth beautifully illustrates the train of matrimonial providence. The Moabitess married, contrary to all human probability, a man of Israel, that she might be

[x]James 1:17
[y]Prov 13:22; Num 27:7; Deut 21:16; 1 Kings 21:3, 4; 2 Cor 12:14
[z]1 Sam 25:39–42
[a]Gen 24:4, 5
[b]Gen 2:22

brought into Naomi's family, return with her to her own land, and in the course of filial duty be brought under the eye, and drawn to the heart of Boaz, her appointed husband.[c] Often do the wheels of the Lord's working in this interesting matter constrain the admiration of men who aren't very spiritually observant.[d] And how much more endearing and secure is a special gift of God! The bread coming down from heaven was more valued, than if it had been the fruit of labor. Thus is *the prudent wife* honored, as "a special blessing of God's immediate choosing, and therefore to be obtained by our prayers at the hand of the giver," advises Bishop Hall. The *prudence,* however, here described, implies not only her wise governing of her household,[e] but that godly consideration connected with divine wisdom,[f] by which she becomes the joy and confidence of her husband:[g] as *the contentious wife* is his trouble and disgrace.

[c] Ruth 1:1–4; 4:13
[d] Gen 24:50
[e] Prov 31:27
[f] Prov 8:12
[g] Prov 18:22; 31:11, 23, 28

But isn't the husband, no less than *the wife, from the Lord?* Let each prospective bride seek the blessing of God's ordinance; never trusting to her own judgment and affections, without primary reference to His guidance.[h] Let us realize the responsibility, as well as the indulgent comfort, of the union; ever counting it a talent for God, for His service and glory: and not doubting for ourselves, that all things shall turn to our comfort and usefulness, if we pull together.

[h] Prov 3:6

15 *Laziness casts into a deep sleep,*
And an idle man will suffer hunger.

THE ROAD TO POVERTY

All experience and observation confirm that lazy habits destroy mental energy, and idleness is the road to poverty. What could we expect from someone who lies in bed all day? No more than we can expect from the lazy person who works as though he's in a deep sleep.[i] Even when the sleep is not *deep,* it still partially paralyzes active performance. The lazy person doesn't have thorough use of his faculties even when he's awake. And if he has made any false move, he doesn't even have enough energy to correct it.[4] If there is any reward of

[i] Prov 6:9–11

[4] *Marshall Turenne expressed his warm obligation to a friend, who had given him the following advice, when first setting out in life—"When you have made a false step, spend not a moment in vexing yourself, and moaning over it; but think how it may best be repaired, and instantly set about it."*

perseverance, be sure that laziness will never find it. *The idle man will suffer hunger.*

Thoughtless sinner! Apply this to the work of God. You convince yourself that everything's okay, just because you won't open your eyes to the truth. You're content to let things run their course.

SLEEP OF DEATH

You don't rebel against the gospel. But has not our Lord said, "He who is not with Me is against Me"?[j] You feel that you've done no harm. But *is it* no harm to have wasted every opportunity for eternity to have wandered about in vanity from your cradle, instead of living for the Lord? At any rate, you're determined to sleep. And though your two greatest treasures—God's favor, and your own soul—are in grave danger; yet still you say to your soul, "Soul . . . take your ease."[k] Instead of weeping in love, wrestling in prayer, and working hard—you remain in *a deep sleep.* "Awake, sleeper";[l] else wilt thou sleep the sleep of eternal death.

[j]Matt 12:30

[k]Luke 12:19

[l]Eph 5:14

How often we find people active and working hard—all eyes, ears, and heart in worldly matters, hating laziness, yet devoured by it themselves. They know that something needs to be done. But when it comes to denying self, crucifying the flesh, coming to Christ, loving the Lord, and dedication to His service—then it's *deep sleep.* So then . . . does the grace of God work as a charm, without, or independent of means? This were a deadly delusion that cast people into *the deep sleep* of presumption. *Such an idle man will suffer hunger!*[m] The enduring meat is the gift of God; but, like every other blessing of the gospel, it is given only to labor.[n] *The idle mouth*—full of nothing but heartless complaints, perhaps sending up a dull prayer for the present quiet of conscience—*shall suffer hunger.* The soul can never flourish, unless it's in earnest with God. It may be roused for a while; but only to be *cast into a deeper sleep* than ever. For godliness can never thrive with this deadly illness. Of course, a lazy person can be a sincere Christian, but his laziness causes him the loss of some of his spiritual privileges and detracts from the sincerity of his experience. And undoubtedly a lazy habit is utterly inconsistent with the vitality of true godliness. Soon only a dead form of reli-

[m]Prov 10:4, 5; 20:4

[n]John 6:27, with Heb 6:11, 12; 2 Peter 1:5–11

gion remains—just the bare walls of the house, instead of the temple filled with God's glory.

And now, let's look at the child of God awakened out of *a deep sleep.* He has set out in good earnest for the kingdom; he has begun to fight—yea—to conquer. But sleep has followed; and, instead of improving his advantage in the battle, a sudden assault of the enemy has laid him low. Mind your work and your conflict more than ease and comfort or you will be, not a conqueror, but a captive. In time of ease, how naturally, as Bunyan's pilgrim found it, the air of the plain tends to make us drowsy! And then the soul, instead of being "satisfied as with marrow and fatness,"[o] *suffers hunger,* and becomes faint for want of its proper nourishment. The heartless outward appearance of godliness will be lost. But the spirit that breathed life into them is gone. Nothing but the unceasing prayer and exercise of a self-denying spirit can shake off this evil disease that cleaveth to us. Be thou, Lord, our helper, our strength, our physician!

[o]Ps 63:5; 41:8

16 *He who keeps the commandment keeps his soul,*
But *he who is careless of his ways will die.*

The fearing of *the commandment* is the path of honor.[p] *The keeping* of it is our security. *Keep the Word,* and the Word will keep us securely. Our duties are thus identified with our privileges.[q] This is the first successful effort to wake ourselves from *the deep sleep of laziness;* when we arouse ourselves "to take hold of Thee ... choose what pleases Me, And hold fast My covenant ... to minister to Him, and to love the name of the Lord."[r] Yet the power to keep the commandment is not in a man's self.[s] Is it not God working in us, through, by, with us?[t] Thus "his deeds having been wrought in God;"[u] and nothing is left to us, but the thankful, humbling acknowledgment—"Yet not I, but the grace of God with me."[v] Let the world know, then, that we do not exercise obedience in a covenant of works, nor reject it as a system of bondage and despondency; but that *keeping the commandment* evangelically is *keeping our own souls*[w]—the way of present happiness,[x] the seal of everlasting mercy,[y] the pathway to heaven.[z]

Yet the multitude, instead of *keeping the commandment* to "obey Me,"[a] are careless about their ways and

[p]Prov 13:13
[q]Ps 19:11; 119:165
[r]Isa 64:7; 56:4–6
[s]Jer 10:23
[t]Isa 26:12; Phil 2:12, 13
[u]John 3:21
[v]1 Cor 15:10
[w]Prov 10:17; 16:17; 22:5
[x]Isa 64:5; John 14:21–23
[y]Ps 103:17, 18
[z]Isa 35:8–10; Rev 22:14
[a]Lev 26:21

unconcerned about their final end. With them, it's hardly worth finding out whether God is displeased or not; and whether they are walking in the broad way or the narrow; or what the end of that way may be. It's unbelievable! The greatest issues man can ever face are always before him, not in dreams or visions, but in reality. He has either the favor of God or His curse upon him. In the presence of God, he must choose between salvation and damnation. He sees them in the light of God. He acknowledges the stamp of God upon them; and yet, even with this tremendous insight, this fearful responsibility, he hasn't a serious thought in his head. Instead of being overwhelmed by the great eternal issues he faces and the choice he must make between heaven and hell, he's ready for any trifle or momentary pleasure that crosses his path. He remains indifferent to it and dies.

Even those, coming out of Christian homes, where they have been exposed to spiritual things from childhood, face a constant struggle between their conscience and their wicked desires and ways. For a time, they are controlled by the Word of God or the corrections of the rod. But soon their lack of steadfastness and their inconsistencies drag them into "worse" hardness than before they knew anything about Jesus Christ.[b] They are "led astray to the dumb idols,"[c] and become slaves of their wills, their lusts, their fancies. They don't know, and they don't *care* to know, "that God will bring you to judgment for all these things."[d]

Young people—think about "the path of your feet." Watch every step you take, that your ways "may be" established[e] in God's keeping grace, the only security for Christian steadfastness.[f] Keep your conscience tender, have God's Word always before you and His promises in your heart. Let your spirit always be pliable for God's guidance. How solemn the warning—*He that is careless of his ways shall die!* Sinner! Think about *that!* It's not just something someone dreamed up to scare you into good behavior. It's *death.* It's brought on by our own lusts, which gave birth to sin, which, when it is full-grown, brings death.[g] It is harvest from that seed.[h] It is the death that a *soul* can die; everlasting reality and a condition of infinite misery, that can never be changed. It

[b]2 Peter 2:20–22
[c]1 Cor 12:2
[d]Eccl 11:9, with 2 Kings 10:31; Jer 44:17
[e]Prov 4:26
[f]2 Peter 3:17, 18
[g]James 1:14, 15
[h]Gal 6:7, 8

doesn't end your *existence*—that would be a blessing!—it ends your *happiness*. What must it be like to be so linked to the wrath of God that you can never, under any circumstances, be freed from it! Just think what it would mean to have the wrath of eternal God filling the conscience of your never-dying soul, with all its power eternally enlarging to receive the full and never-ending impression! While you are going on through life, doing everything your wicked heart desires,[i] remember "there is hardly a step"—who knows how short, or how soon taken?—between you and this death.[j] "Why then will you die," when God testifies, that He has "no pleasure" in your death, when His gracious voice tells you to "turn . . . and live."[k] "Consider your ways!"[l] Oh! listen, before you learn the wisdom of fools, and be wise too late.

[i]Isa 57:17
[j]1 Sam 20:3
[k]Ezek 33:11; 18:32
[l]Hag 1:5, 7

17 *He who is gracious to a poor man lends to the* LORD,
And He will repay him for his good deed.

YOUR BEST INVESTMENT: LEND YOUR MONEY TO THE POOR

The promise of God is, that "the poor will never cease to be in the land."[m] Hence the universal obligation is, to *be gracious to the poor*. This is according to the New Testament standard, which requires that the *spirit* of the act must be right, as well as the *act, itself*.[n] We must open our *heart* as much as our *hand*,[o] "give yourself to the hungry, And satisfy the desire of the afflicted;"[p] thereby doubling the alms, by giving a part of ourselves. Did you know it is possible to "give all my possessions to feed the poor," without one bit of love from the heart.[q] But whatever we give, if we show no compassion to our brother, how can it be that the love of God is in us?[r] The good Samaritan showed true, practical *graciousness*. There is a great lesson here for us. Our Lord doesn't want us to miss it. "Treat them in the same way," He said.[s]

The appointment of the deacons in the early church;[t] the concern of the apostles when delegating a commission to their brethren in Christ;[u] the high commendation of the Macedonian churches;[v] the weekly rule of charity, laid down (not enforcing a fixed standard, but "as God hath prospered")[w]—all this shows the acceptableness of this Christian service. Sir Thomas More used to say,

[m]Deut 15:11
[n]Luke 6:30–36; Col 3:12; Comp. Prov 14:21
[o]Deut 15:7, 10
[p]Isa 58:10
[q]1 Cor 13:3
[r]1 John 3:17
[s]Luke 6:28–31
[t]Acts 6:2–6
[u]Gal 2:9, 10
[v]2 Cor 3:9
[w]AV—1 Cor 16:2

"There was more rhetoric in this little sentence, than in a whole library." The worldly philanthropist, however, has no conception of this divine principle. If our brother is the object of our compassion, then the very majesty of heaven is concerned. The Lord considers it as a *loan to Himself.* It is *lending to the Lord.* Selfish individuals would evade the obligation on the grounds of being sensible. Why give something if there won't be anything coming back in return! Oh! but wait a minute! What does the Lord say? He tells us that, *what* we give in His name is *just a loan.* It will be paid back, and He offers security that can never fail. God, Himself, becomes liable for the debt of the poor. He takes it upon Himself and gives us the bond of His Word in promise of payment. Though He has a right to all, and is obligated to no one,[x] He willingly becomes a debtor to His own. Many acts of kindness have been buried and forgotten. The joy of giving is its only fruit. But here is a safe deposit in the very heart of God. It can never be lost or forgotten.[y] If then,—we want to save up for the future, where is there a better place to keep it, than in the Christian's treasure? The poor man's hand is the treasury of Christ. What better place in all the world is there for my investments! There's where they will be safely kept and surely returned to me.[5]

[x]Ps 16:2; Rom 11:35

[y]Matt 10:42; 25:40; Heb 6:10

And yet, how foolish we are! Most of us would rather *lend* to a rich man of known integrity, than *to the Lord.* It's true that giving to the poor is certainly an act of faith, when there seems to be no hope of return.[z] But this is the principle, which "the king desires to honor."[a] If we just fully knew the experience of the Lord's people, we would see many examples of His faithfulness to His Word. The Resurrection Day will bring it all to light.[b] Meanwhile, let us admire this, His wondrous grace. He puts the desire to give into our hearts. He makes our hearts responsive to the need, opens the opportunity, and, beyond all that, He accepts the act, as if it had been His own, without spot or pollution!

[z]Luke 6:38. Comp. Prov 28:27

[a]Esther 6:6

[b]Matt 25:34–40

18 *Discipline your son while there is hope,*
And do not desire his death.

[5] Works, *viii. 32. No man is a better merchant, than he that lays out his time upon God,* and his money upon the Poor—*Bishop TAYLOR'S Holy Living, chap. 1.*

PATTERN FOR PARENTAL DISCIPLINE

Christian parents, carefully study the Word of God. See here our Father's wise and loving discipline with His children. "As a father has compassion on his children." "As one whom his mother comforts, so I will comfort you."[c] Yet when His children need discipline, though his heart cries out—Spare; though every groan of His child causes Him deep pain,[d] He loves us so well, that He spares them not for their crying.[e] He uses the rod; even heavily, if need be.[f] He will deprive of brightest comforts, joys, and possessions, if they do not respond; and He does it, "for our good, that we may share His holiness."[g] What child of God has not thanked Him a thousand times, that He did not withhold His discipline, till it had done its perfect work?

[c]Ps 103:13; Isa 66:13
[d]Exod 2:23, 24; Judg. 10:16
[e]Ps 89:30–32
[f]Ps 39:10; 1 Peter 5:6
[g]Heb 12:10. Comp. Lam 3:33

Shouldn't this be our pattern, then—our standard. Isn't this the sound principle of all Christian education? "Fathers, do not exasperate your children, that they may not lose heart."[h] But don't let the rule—*discipline*—spare not—be a hard saying. Isn't there a false tenderness for the child which is a cover for our indulgence of weak and foolish affections? There is much more mercy in what *seems* to be harshness, than in false tenderness.[i] Let the child see, that we are firmly determined; that we are not to be diverted from our duty by the cry of weakness or passion. Isn't it far better that the child should cry under healthful correction, now, than that parents should afterward cry under the bitter fruit to themselves and their children of neglected discipline. Eli could not have devised a better way to have plagued himself and his house as much, as by his kindness to his children's sin. If parents wanted to make themselves miserable, they could find no better way than to spare the rod. Yet very little of the rod would be needed, if they guided and directed their children as they ought to do, by the decisive word, a frown, or a look.

[h]Col 3:21
[i]Prov 23:13, 14

BEGIN EARLY

But the great force of the rule is its *timely* application—*while there is hope*. For the case becomes truly hopeless, if the remedy is delayed. The cure of the evil must begin in infancy. Not a moment can be lost.[j]

[j]Prov 13:24; 22:15

Now is the time, when the good can be accomplished most easily and with the least physical discipline. The lesson of obedience should be learned at the earliest possible moment. One painful struggle and victory in very early life, may, under God, do much toward settling the point, then and there, and for all the years ahead. On the other hand, even harsh chastening later, may fail to accomplish, what an early slight rebuke might have accomplished.

But don't we often allow ourselves to become blind to the situation, because we'd rather not face up to what we know will be painful to correct? The false notion—"Children will be children"—often causes us to pass over their real faults, and to consider their tempers and waywardness too trifling to require prompt correction. Sin, winked at in its beginnings, will soon harden into strong and deep-rooted corruptions. Not many of us would neglect our child's most trifling bodily ailment, if we knew it could lead to most serious results. If they cannot be reasoned with, then they must be controlled. How often have we found in later life the evil of fixed habits, which early correction might have subdued with far less cost of sufferings![k] Oh! what grace and wisdom is needed to discipline our minds, judgment, and affections to self-government in our own lives, which will enable us to train our children practically for the service of God and for their own happiness!

[k] 1 Kings 1:6; 2:24

19 A man of *great anger shall bear the penalty,*
For if you rescue him, *you will only have to do it again.*

THE CURE FOR UNDISCIPLINED PASSION

How often does the unchastened child become a man with an uncontrollable temper, who brings himself into trouble by his boisterous and ungoverned passions! Adonijah, whom "his father had never crossed . . . at any time," rebelled against his brother, and *bore the penalty.*[l] He had learned nothing by experience. Delivered from one noisy quarrel or brawl, he plunged right into another. Indeed, who knows what will be the final end of undisciplined passion? Cain—*a man of great anger*—the murderer of his brother—*the punishment that he suf-*

[l] 1 Kings 1:6; 2:25

fered was "too great to bear."[m] The friendly efforts to restrain this wrath must be repeated again and again,[n] even though too often ineffectually. Meanwhile the man *shall bear his own penalty*—the miseries of a fierce internal struggle, driven about by the fury of his raging lust. Truly, a man's good judgment tells him he ought to learn to control his anger.[o] If he doesn't, every fresh outburst will leave him more degraded and defenseless.[p] He ought to strive to make his *first* effort to restrain his anger successful.

[m]Gen 4:5–8, 13
[n]1 Sam 19:1–11; 20:32, 33
[o]Prov 19:11
[p]Prov 25:28

After all that a man boasts of his self-control, there is no agitation within which restraint cannot subdue. Wounded pride and unquelled resentment leaves one brooding inwardly and *suffering* an intolerable burden of self-inflicted *punishment.* What then is the ultimate cure? "Learn from Me, for I am gentle and humble in heart."[q] The glory and encouragement of the gospel is, that Christianity, with all its difficulties, is practical.[r] "My grace is sufficient for you"—is the cheering word of Him, who sealed the faithfulness of the promise with His blood. Don't ever doubt then, that "The Lord will accomplish what concerns me,"[s] even to the molding of the *man of great anger* into his image of meekness, gentleness, and love.

[q]Matt 11:29
[r]2 Cor 12:9
[s]Ps 138:8

20 *Listen to counsel and accept discipline*
[AV—instruction],
That you may be wise the rest of your days.

A WORD TO THE WISE—CHILDREN!

We have just had a word for parents on Christian discipline. Now children are exhorted to humility. And they are aroused to hear *counsel and discipline.*[t] And constantly they need the word! "Childhood and youth are vanity."[u] Present gratification is the main object. Oh! remember, seeds sown in youth, will produce either blessed or bitter fruit in later life. Take Timothy, for example. How rich was the harvest from his early attention to *discipline.*[v] But how different and fearful was the judgment—the fruit of despising timely wisdom and instruction—upon scoffers,[w] the awful death of the wicked,[x] the ruin of the holy nation.[y] Couldn't Rehoboam[z] and Amaziah[a] have escaped the ruin of their kingdom, had

[t]Prov 4:1, 2; 5:1, 2; 7:1, 2
[u]AV—Eccl 11:10
[v]2 Tim 3:14, 15
[w]Prov 1:26; 29:1
[x]Prov 5:9–14
[y]Matt 23:37–39; Luke 19:41, 42
[z]1 Kings 12:12–19
[a]2 Chron 25:15–20

they *listened to counsel,* and thereby obtained *wisdom for the rest of their days?* "I am going to die," said a thoughtless king on his deathbed: "and yet I have not begun to live." How greatly the wisdom of mature age depends upon diligence in *hearing counsel and accepting discipline*! So ... we value "the yoke"—specially of affliction—"bear ... in his youth"—a "good" thing indeed, loaded with profit.[b] In this yoke, Joseph received and heard much counsel and *discipline* from God, which highly qualified him with wisdom for his high responsibility.[c] Daniel, also instructed early in youth, found wisdom in later life, which God was pleased to prolong beyond the normal span of years. It enabled him to superintend a hundred and twenty provinces with singular honor to his profession.[d]

[b]Lam 3:27
[c]Gen 37; 39–41
[d]Dan 1:4–9; 6:3, 4

And the wisdom to meet that great crisis won't be found in thoughtless disregard. *Counsel and discipline (instruction)* are liberally given. But sad to say, of most of them, the Lord is constrained to complain—"My people do not understand."[e] And who, when viewing the mass of ungodliness, can refrain from the weeping lamentation of the man of God—"Would that they were wise, that they understood this, That they would discern their future!"[f]

[e]Isa 1:3
[f]Deut 32:29

21 *Many are the plans in a man's heart,*
But the counsel of the LORD, *it will stand.*

MAN'S DEVICES AND GOD'S COUNSEL

Here's the striking contrast between man and God, illustrated in a limited way by the vast disproportion seen between the "worm" and his Maker. Man's most serious, well-digested thoughts are only—imagination—uncertainty—of little importance. But God's mind is *counsel,*[g] firm and full purpose. Man's *plans are many;* God's *counsel* is like Himself—*Unity. Man's plans* are full of anxiety. Many are eventually fruitless.[h] All of them are vain.[i] God's counsel is unchanging, and shall stand forever.[j] "I act and who can reverse it!" and "My purpose will be established. And I will accomplish all My good pleasure."[k]

[g]Eph 1:11
[h]Ps 2:11
[i]Ps 94:11
[j]Ps 89:2; 119:89
[k]Isa 43:13; 46:10

Now when God and man were as one, *man's plans* were identified with *God's counsel.* Then it was as the days of heaven upon earth. But ever since the fall, *man's plans and God's counsel* have been in opposition. Which will triumph, who can doubt? "There is no wisdom and no understanding and no counsel against the Lord."[l]

We mark this conflict in everyday life. Man's own way is a way devised by human weakness and folly; and it is impossible to make a solid road out of such frail materials. Even in the most plausible path—a well-calculated moderation in earthly projects, he is only heading for certain disappointment and increasing the certainty and perplexity of that disappointment by his every movement. He plans his whole life, when not a single step is under his own control; not one step can he take, for one moment, in opposition to the Lord's counsel.[m] *It shall stand,* though, reluctant, God is to give him up to his own *plans;* still—even after God has left him—God seems to send a longing, lingering look after him.[n] The malice of Joseph's brethren was the means of fulfilling the divine *counsel* in the salvation of his people.[o] The plot laid for the destruction of Israel furthered their prosperity.[p] The vain attempts at opposition to Christ were secondary and contributed to the great end of "the predetermined plan and foreknowledge of God."[q] The *plans of man* to prevent Paul's journey to Rome was conspicuously defeated.[r]

[l]Prov 21:30; Heb 6:17

[m]Lam 3:37

[n]Ps 81:11–14

[o]Gen 37:19; 45:5, 6

[p]Exod 1:8–12, 20

[q]Ps 2:1–6, with Acts 4:26–28; 2:23

[r]Acts 23:12, 15, with 11

IN HEAVEN—NO CONFUSION

How vain the impious attempt to fight "against God"![s] "Woe to the *one* who quarrels with his Maker"![t] Our liberty does not interfere with His secret purpose. But let us be careful that it does not resist his declared will. As His wisdom chooses our lot, let His Word discipline our desires as the best means of bringing them to a prosperous end. After all, it is a cheering hope. All is clear above, however cloudy it might be below. All is calm in heaven, no matter how stormy it might be on earth. There is no confusion there. God reigns alone. His very purpose reaches its appointed end. "But He is unique and who can turn Him? And what His soul desires, that He does."[u]

[s]Acts 5:39

[t]Isa 45:9

[u]Job 23:13

22 *What is desirable in a man* [AV—*The desire of a man*] *is his kindness,*
And it is *better to be a poor man than a liar.*

WHEN THE POWER FAILS!

The privilege of doing good is within the reach of all. When the power fails, the desire of a man to do good is accepted as the deed and received as the most expensive proof of love. If there be a willing mind, it is accepted, according to that a man hath, and not according to that he hath not.[v] The dealings of God with His people are grounded on this principle. David's *desire* to build the temple was as fully accepted and honored as the act itself.[w] Such also was our Saviour's estimate of the value of the widow's mite[x]—of the box of ointment poured upon himself,[y]—of the "cup of cold water" given to a disciple.[z] *The desire was the kindness,* more rich and fruitful than the offerings of self-pleasing abundance.[a] "It is the comfort of poverty, that our affections are valued, not our presents," stated Bishop Hall.[6]

[v] 2 Cor 8:12
[w] 2 Chron 6:8; 7:12–17
[x] Mark 12:41–44
[y] Mark 14:8, 9
[z] Matt 10:42
[a] Luke 21:4

Yet *the desire* must be active; not lazy excitement, but the communication of effectual faith according to the power given to us.[b] Such *a desire* is far better in the sight of God, in the heart of one of his *poor* people, than a man with large opportunities and hollow professions, who proves himself to be a *liar.*[c] The *poor* man gives readily. The rich cannot afford. He denies that he has the ability. He promises and does nothing. *The poor man is better than the liar.* The main thing is to take heed to the motive. Men don't know the heart, but "the Lord weighs the motives";[d] and "the fire itself will test the quality of each man's work."[e]

[b] Philem 6; 2 Cor 8:11
[c] Verse 1; Ps 62:9
[d] Prov 16:2
[e] 1 Cor 3:13

23 *The fear of the* LORD leads *to life,*
So that one may sleep satisfied, untouched by evil.

HOW TO FIND TRUE HAPPINESS

It is a privilege to be exempt from *the fear of the Lord* as a legal principle.[f] As a grace of the gospel, cultivate it to the uttermost.[g] Threefold fruit is here set before us—*life—satisfaction—security. It leads to life*—not just natural life, common to the ungodly—(though this blessing, so far as is good, is included),[h] but a heavenly, yes—an eternal, life[i] in the favor and enjoyment of God. So far as we are under its influence, we speak, pray,

[f] Luke 1:74; Rom 8:15; 2 Tim 1:7
[g] Heb 12:28; 1 Peter 1:17
[h] Prov 9:11; 10:27
[i] Ps 33:18, 19; 34:11, 12

[6] *"Rich men's presents," said the Venerable Bede when dying, "are gold and silver, or other costly things. Mine must be recommended by the affectionate pleasure with which I give them."*

think, and deal with man, as if God were standing by. The genial beams of "the sun of righteousness" nourish this holy principle;[j] and soon it will be perfected in the service above.[k]

[j]Mal 4:2
[k]Rev 15:3, 4

Meanwhile the *satisfaction* it imparts is a precious privilege. The service of God is now our delight—our great delight. The law is no taskmaster over our heads but a principle of life and joyous energy within. The worldling's heart is torn with an aching void. He travels from one source of happiness to another, crying, "Who will show us any good?" "Lift up the light of Thy countenance upon us, O Lord!"—is the cry and solid *satisfaction* of a child of God, above the best portion of earth.[l] Instead of being cast from wave to wave, here is quiet rest. Whoever wants, "O fear the Lord . . . they who seek the Lord shall not be in want of any good thing," and "His soul will abide in prosperity."[m] *He that has it shall sleep satisified.* Is not this fixed repose and trust in His love the very soul of happiness?

[l]Ps 4:6, 7
[m]Ps 34:9, 10; 25:12, 13

It is said that an object of fear usually brings dread. Now, identify the person as *"he that fears the Lord,"* and that turns it into gold. He that fears *that way, doesn't fear.*[n] He has his "strong confidence"—high and sure, an unshakable fortress.[o] "God . . . has made Himself known as a stronghold."[p] We go to Him as our God, whom we know, and who is engaged in covenant with us. And now, taking our sanctuary in God, we sit and sing under His shadow. In this hiding place how can we suffer any evil?[q] What is evil in itself He will turn to our good.[r] No kind of testing or suffering can separate us from God. It only binds us closer to Him. We do not *fear* God's uplifted arm. But His frown of rebuke enters into our soul. His mercy sweeps away the fear of terror. His holiness maintains the fear of reverence. Conscious security only causes us to dread more than ever any break in our blessed fellowship with Him.

[n]Ps 112:7
[o]Prov 14:26
[p]Ps 48:3
[q]Prov 12:21
[r]Rom 8:28; Heb 12:11

24 *The sluggard buries his hand in the dish,*
And *will not even bring it back to his mouth.*

HOW LAZY CAN ONE GET?

Another striking illustration of the palsy of laziness![s] It so grows on its victim that he has no heart to do even

[s]Prov 12:27; 26:15; Eccl 4:5

necessary things, such as feed himself, for example. He would rather suffer the cravings of hunger, than exert himself to put food into his mouth. A sad picture of many fair intentions and promises and apparently good beginnings in spiritual matters—all brought to a halt for lack of the effort to overcome the least hindrance. Every spiritual duty is a burden. The struggle necessary for prayer—the only means of receiving our spiritual food—is too hard. The soul, that seemed to have been awakened, sinks into its former lethargy; and each new effort to rouse it is fainter and more hopeless. The hand cannot be stretched out, even to take hold of a crown.

Some seem to feel that little or no exertion is necessary; clear profit, that they have never been really in earnest about this momentous concern. The conflict is not imaginary. "Woe to those who," reposing on the lap of indulgence, "are at ease in Zion."[t] If the work of a day, much more the work of eternity, calls for all diligence; if the Emperor Titus could mourn that he "had lost a day," what will be the stinging remorse of having lost a life! And to think, that by a right beginning, followed up "by perseverance in doing good,"[u] we might have effectively "served the purpose of God in [our] own generation";[v] been missed in the world after we had fallen asleep; and sown seed for eternity, so that our "memory," instead of rotting, would have been "blessed"![w] To remember that all this was wished, yes, even resolved; yet not a bit of it accomplished: won't this be a thorn for a dying pillow, perhaps the tormenting worm for eternity?

The mere waste of time is far from being the worst part of the evil. It is fatal alike to our well-being, and our welldoing, to condemn our energies to rust out in inactivity. Thomson's excuse for reposing in his "Castle of Indolence" was that he had nothing to do. And doubtless the want of an objective is sufficient to make an idler of a man of talent. But can this ever be the condition of any one—even the least occupied, or the least influential among us? Are any of us freed from the responsibility of diligence, if not for ourselves, at least in the service of our fellow-creatures. Much less can the Christian plead as an excuse for "standing here idle," that "no one hired us."[x] Isn't the great object always in sight, always worthy

[t] Amos 6:1
[u] Rom 2:7
[v] Acts 13:36
[w] Prov 10:7
[x] Matt 20:6, 7

of all the concentration of mind, talent, and energy—"To me, to live is Christ"?[y]

[y]Phil 1:21

The special time for the resistance of this deadly disease, is when we are most under its power. When the Bible is uninteresting, then is the time to live in it with patient diligence. When prayer is cold and heartless, instead of giving up, hold on, however feebly, yet with perseverance. When in a state of listless exertion, be employed for God and for His church. Form habits of early energy. Beware of a dreaming sentimentalism. Cultivate bodily activity. Regard the incursions of laziness. They are the effects of poisons, though they merely cause sleep, unless they are counteracted by constant resistance, they will prove fatal. Yet with all these means, never forget the one principle, that makes them effectual—prayer, unceasing, believing, "fixing our eyes on Jesus," who not only gives life, but liveliness.[z]

[z]Heb 12:1, 2; John 10:10

LIFE IS SOLEMN REALITY!

Christian! He who has awakened you from the sleep of death, will keep you awake, till the Lord comes. But still, even with you, much drowsiness remains. You trifle away time in a barren profession, such as your Lord will not tolerate. He will awaken you to the fact that life is a solemn reality, that prayer is not a half-hearted work, but a close dealing with the living God, a warm pulse of the hidden life, a continued conflict with mighty enemies.

Are you struggling in this conflict? Then, look for rest, only in the arms of victory. While the conflict lasts, there is no time for loitering or for slumber. Yet, don't forget to thank God for every victory, yes, for the continued strength that enables you to persevere in the fight; for the wise provision also, that brings such holy conflict unto ourselves, as the means of invigorating our faith, our hope, our earned right to the crown, and our joyful expectation of it. If peace with God is our life, "the joy of the Lord is your strength,"[a] our health, our happiness, but it is not to be found listless, enervated living.

[a]Neh 8:10

25 *Strike a scoffer and the naive may become shrewd,*
But reprove one who has understanding and he will gain knowledge.

DOES PUNISHMENT PAY OFF?

There is a difference of opinion about the profit of punishments. Some believe, that, if the will does not give way to reason, forced obedience is of little use. But God's Word and command are our standard, though great wisdom is required in how they are applied. Two ways are mentioned here; each measured out according to the character of the offender, but both wholesome in their results. The *scoffer* is a bold sinner. *Strike him, that the naive who follow him may beware.*[b] It may be a timely warning to those that are led by him. Taking the ringleader out of a mischievous group may put an end to the group. This is the value of laws. Often it pays to make an example of the sinner, and even though he, himself, remains hardened, it will do the whole body good. Thus "God strikes some, that he may warn all," said Bishop Hall.[c]

[b]Prov 21:11; Acts 13:6–12

[c]Comp. Exod 18:10, 11; Deut 13:11; 19:20; 21:21; Acts 5:1–11; Rev 11:13

But a *man of understanding should be reproved.* He doesn't need to be "struck." "A *rebuke* goes deeper into one who has understanding than a hundred blows into a fool."[d] In the *scoffer's* case, the profit is to others. In the *wise man's,* it is to himself. *He will understand knowledge.*[e] His wisdom enables him to profit and to be thankful for the timely reproof.[f] Never let us forget the mercy of being kept from sin, or being restored from it, even though it comes by our Master's sharp (but gracious) rebuke—"Those whom I love, I reprove and discipline; be zealous, therefore, and repent."[g]

[d]Prov 17:10; 15:5

[e]Prov 9:8, 9

[f]Ps 141:5

[g]Rev 3:19

26 *He who assaults* his *father* and *drives* his *mother away*
Is a shameful and disgraceful son.

MONSTERS IN HUMAN FORM

This is not an ideal picture of recklessness. "Unloving"[h]—is an awful mark of unrestrained depravity. Man is the debased slave of his selfish lust. The spendthrift son may *assault his father's* substance by extravagance, and his spirits and health by his bad conduct. Absalom *assaulted his father* by his undutiful rebellion.[i] Often, a mother's tenderness has been repaid with crushing unkindness. The insolence of an ungrateful son virtually *drives* her from her home. Her idol has become her

[h]Rom 1:30, 31

[i]2 Sam 15:1–14

curse! Such monsters in human form, outraging every principle of humanity, have been found in every generation. Yet seldom do they escape without some mark of retributive justice even in this life.[j] And though they may be callous to public opinion, while *causing shame and disgrace* on their names; yet conscience will speak;[k] and, sooner or later, the stroke will fearfully fall. Children! A parent's sorrows carry a heavy account before the bar of God. If "the first commandment [be] with a promise,"[l] will not the breach of the commandment cut off the promise, with an awful and aggravated weight of condemnation?

[j]Prov 30:11, 17
[k]Isa 57:20
[l]Eph 6:2

27 *Cease listening, my son, to discipline,*
And you will *stray from the words of knowledge.*

MINISTERS OF SATAN AND HOW TO RESIST THEM

Hear the same caution from the lips of our divine Master—"Beware of the false prophets," and "Take care what you listen to."[m] All instruction is not to life. Teachers of evil, ministers of Satan[n] abound. And their instruction, causes many to *stray from the words of knowledge* and is more palatable to the evil of the heart; more alluring to the inexperience of the young, than solid scriptural teaching.[o] The apostle Paul reproved the Galatian church for listening to teachers, *causing them to stray* fatally *from the words of knowledge.*[p] And wouldn't he have warned us against the same teaching, so fearfully prevalent: putting rituals in Christ's place, or attaching them to Him; man's proud work of voluntary humility and external service in place of the pure simplicity of reliance on the Redeemer's work? When a soul has reached such a state,[q] what ground of confidence can he bring before God? To him, what is His service, but the bondage of outward ceremonies, leading to unhappy despair?

This instruction is not generally a bold and direct departure from truth. But, as in the first temptation,[r] it causes us to stray so gradually, that the deviation from the straight line is scarcely noticed, till the mischief has been done. Had Eve at once refused *to listen,* she would not

[m]Matt 7:15; Mark 4:24
[n]2 Cor 11:13–15
[o]Isa 30:10; Jer 5:31
[p]Gal 1:6, 7; 3:1–4; 5:7, 8
[q]Mark 5:4
[r]Gen 3:1–6

have *strayed from the words of knowledge.* But the success of the first attempt has emboldened the seducer to deal out his deadly poison to her enfeebled children. And what faithful pastor does not feel grave concern for his flock, lest by the same beguilement, that "your minds be led astray from the simplicity and purity of devotion to Christ"?[s]

[s]2 Cor 11:3

Insinuating infidels, who endeavor to shake the principles of young people, under the pretense of removing heedless scruples, and expanding their minds, and delivering them from the shackles of bigotry—such persons you should shun as the plague. Let us also sound a caution against false teachers of a more plausible, and therefore more dangerous character. Let their schemes and disguises be fully laid open. It is the "wolves" that are "in sheep's clothing."[t] "Trickery . . . craftiness in deceitful scheming" is the distinctive character of their instruction.[u] All that is pleasing is brought out to cover up the delusion.

[t]Matt 7:15

[u]Eph 4:14

Perhaps never was the poison commended in so attractive a form. All the charms of elegant fiction are employed to give effect to it. A lovely picture of practical religion is exhibited. Or the deliverance from the fowler's open snare is portrayed with glowing, colorful interest. Superficial readers are captivated by the external loveliness. But the wise watchman would raise his warning voice—*Cease, my son, from listening.* To hear—to regard—is to stray. All these beauteous sketches of fancy are the framework that conceal unscriptural principles. Weigh them in the balances of the sanctuary, and they will be found wanting. Trace them to their source, and it will be found to be a corrupt fountain. When anything but Christ is the foundation principle, a human standard, not the Word of God, is the rule. *Cease listening.*[v]

[v]Rom 16:17, 18; 1 Tim 6:3–5; 2 Tim 2:16, 17

Indeed, we would like to give the warning everywhere that needless tampering with error is "entering into temptation." In fact, it is most hazardous to deal with it at all, before our minds are thoroughly grounded in the truth, and we have obtained that "it is good for the heart to be strengthened by grace."[w] Yet we have senses given for discernment. Use increases this discernment.[x] Increasing clearness should be the matter of daily prayer.[y]

[w]Heb 13:9

[x]Heb 5:14

[y]Phil 1:9, 10

We are bound therefore to exercise our sense by the plainest commands.[z] Our divine Master distinctly rebukes laziness.[a] When the words came with the stamp of an apostle, the appeal to the unerring standard was highly commended.[b] Should we give up our judgment to the church? Not when we remember, that "each one shall bear his own load," and "shall give account of himself to God."[c] Maintain your right of private judgment which constitutes your personal responsibility.

[z]1 Thess 5:21; 1 John 4:1
[a]Luke 12:57
[b]Acts 17:11. Comp. Isa 8:20
[c]Gal 6:5; Rom 14:12

This Christian independence, however, must be held with humility and simplicity. The duty of private judgment must be felt as one's own burden to be cast on none but God. Therefore, we must carefully restrain self-will. We must attend the ordinances in the spirit of learners rather than judges; desiring to gather instruction in childlike simplicity, and watching lest the appetite for wholesome food should give place to a spiritual lust.[d] While the right of judgment is our great privilege, let's never forget, that unrestrained it is a cankering evil.

[d]2 Tim 4:3

But what if our lot is plainly cast, and our sphere of Christian obligation opened, where words of knowledge are not found? We would suggest right at the start, that particular cases require particular application. There may be cases, when the call would be very specific: *cease from listening.* If the teaching is heretical, or wholly unevangelical, if the teacher's life is immoral or scandalously worldly; if the children of the family are obviously in danger of being *caused to stray,* the path may be made plain to depart. And yet, in this case, much exercise of mind, much personal sacrifice would be called for to separate from the minister, not from the church. And under no circumstances let the ungodliness of the minister be an excuse for the neglect of Christian responsibilities. At the same time, in many more cases than are ordinarily supposed, the mature Christian will remain in his place, continue in prayer, and abound in a labor of love. As occasion may allow, he will meekly use the weapons of admonition and reproof, maintain a consistent example, and take up his appointed cross. In some cases, when the offense is open and the error obvious, sound discipline may bring the heretical or ungodly teacher to punishment, and thereby open the way for better instruction.

To the majority, who are mainly dependent upon the ministry for instruction, some forbearance must be shown, even should they be constrained by hunger to *cease listening to* those, who would give them a stone for bread. At least the main guilt lies on "the stranger," not on them, that flee from him, for they "do not know the voice of strangers."[e] Fearful indeed will be the witness of many a soul neglected, if not destroyed, for lack of hearing the *words of knowledge.* Assured as we are, that the preaching of Christ is the only preservation from this tremendous evil, if Christ be preached, and sinners are converted to Him by other less accredited teachers, "I rejoice, yea, and I will rejoice."[f] Yet where Christians can abide, let them do so—let them "trust in the Lord, and do good."[g] The deficiency in privilege will be abundantly supplied. Christian activity will be a stimulating means of grace. The constant application of the touchstone will be a preservation for error. The food of the Word will be more precious. And who knows but an enlightened minister may be given to the power of believing prayer and to the living influence of godly meekness, patience, and consistency?

[e] John 10:5
[f] Phil 1:18
[g] Ps 37:3

28 *A rascally witness makes a mockery of justice,*
And the mouth of the wicked spreads iniquity.
29 *Judgments are prepared for scoffers,*
And blows for the back of fools.

LOOK OUT FOR THE BAITED HOOK!

This man is justly called a witness of Belial. Satan himself has taken him for his own malicious purposes.[h] *Mocking* judgment, instead of esteeming it, his testimony is worthless. He has cast Me [God] behind [his] back. He *spreads iniquity* with greediness, feeds upon it as his proper food, and, sinning without remorse, he is always ready to use deceit, either for gain or revenge.

[h] 1 Kings 21:13; 14:9

But in his greediness he has swallowed the hook with the bait. *For such scoffers, judgments are prepared.* For such *fools* that "mock at sin"[i]—*blows* are ready *for their backs,* often inflicted by men who are the instruments of God. Scoffers are warned "lest your fetters be made stronger"[j] for judgment, which, no matter how much they may despise it, they cannot resist it. Can your heart en-

[i] Prov 14:9
[j] Isa 28:22

dure, or your hands be strong, in the day that I shall deal with you? Who shall dwell with the devouring fire? Who shall dwell with everlasting burnings? It is a fearful thing to fall into the hands of the living God.[k] Oh! that thoughtless, light-minded young people would take such words to heart! When they join in the laughter of their more hardened companions, and learn from them to *scoff at judgment,* in spite of the accusings of a conscience not yet silenced; let them tremble, lest from standing "in the path of sinners," they may go on to "sit in the seat of scoffers,"[l] and may even exceed their companions in despising the threatenings of God.

[k]Ezek 22:14; Isa 33:14; Heb 10:31

[l]Ps 1:1

And when under these slighted *judgments,* who is to be blamed for them? "Our sin," says Bishop Hall, "is our own, and the wages of sin is death. He that doth work, earns the wages. So then the righteous God is cleared both of our sin and our death. Only his justice pays us what our evil deeds deserve." What a wretched thing a willful sinner really is, who will be guilty of his own death! Blessed—blessed day! should it ever see him bemoaning himself like this—"Thou hast chastised me, and I was chastised, like an untrained calf; Bring me back that I may be restored, For Thou art the Lord my God."[m]

[m]Jer 31:18

CHAPTER TWENTY

1 *Wine is a mocker, strong drink a brawler,*
And whoever is intoxicated by it is not wise.

TAKE HEED TO YOURSELVES

[a]Gen 9:21

The history of the world from the days of Noah[a] proves, that the love of *wine and strong drink* is a vice, more dangerous than it may seem. The wretched victims are convinced too late that they have been *mocked* and grievously deceived. Not only does it overcome them before they are aware, but it promises pleasures which it can never give. And yet, so mighty is the spell, that the stupefied slave consents to be *mocked* again and again, till "at last it bites like a serpent, and stings like a viper."[b]

[b]Prov 23:29–32

Its power degrades below the level of the beasts. (The government of reason is surrendered to lust, appetite, or passion.[c] Ahasuerus, with his merry heart, showed himself most irrational.[d] The conqueror of the East murdered his friend.) All is tumult and recklessness. The understanding is gradually impaired.[e] The "mind will utter perverse things."[f] Other sins of the same black dye follow in its train,[g] often hurrying a person into the very jaws of destruction.[h] Surely then *whosoever is intoxicated by it is not wise.*

[c]1 Sam 25:36; Isa 56:12; Hos 7:5
[d]Esther 1:10–12
[e]Isa 28:7; Hos 4:11
[f]Prov 23:33
[g]Gen 19:33; Isa 5:11, 12, 22, 23
[h]2 Sam 13:28; 1 Kings 16:8–10; 20:16; Jer 51:39, 57; Dan 5:1–4; Nah 1:10

How humbling it is to human nature, to see, not only the mass of the ignorant, but splendid talents, brutalized by this lust; that which was once created "in the image of God," now sunk into the dregs of shame! Yet more humbling is the sight even of God's own people "wallowing in the mire." The examples of Noah and Lot are recorded,[i] not as a laughingstock to the ungodly, but as a beacon to the saints. "Let him who thinks he stands take heed lest he fall."[j] Even an apostle had practically

[i]Gen 1:27; 2 Peter 2:22; Gen 19:33
[j]1 Cor 10:12

learned that his security lay not in the innate strength of his principles but in the unceasing exercise of Christian watchfulness.[k] "Be on guard, that your hearts be not weighted down with dissipation and drunkenness and the worries of life, and that day come on you like a trap," is the needful warning of our divine Master. The great apostle Paul said, "Do not get drunk with wine, for that is dissipation, but be filled with the Spirit."[l]

[k]1 Cor 9:27

[l]Luke 21:34; Eph 5:18

2 *The terror of a king is like the growling of a lion;*
He who provokes him to anger forfeits his own life.

THE POWER OF THE KING

The wrath of the king has been mentioned before under this figure.[m] Here *his terror* is described, the effect for the cause. Even Joab with all his valor trembled at this *growling of a lion* and fled for refuge to the horns of the altar.[n] Jonathan felt the strong necessity for appeasing it.[o] Such was the power *of a king*, the sole, the uncontrolled arbiter of life and death[p]; *whosoever therefore provoked him to anger, forfeits his own life,* as Adonijah found to his cost.[q] How terrible it must be then to fear the King of Kings! Armies of terrors and doubts are nothing to a look of His angry countenance. "Lord," says the Psalmist (considering the frailty of poor man, and the power of God) "who understands the power of Thine anger, and Thy fury according to the fear that is due Thee?" Even a little stirring up of God's wrath brings ruin beyond comprehension and without remedy.[r] His very long-suffering and patience, with those who deserve only destruction, just kindle the fires of His wrath against them more fiercely.[s] Miserable sinner, plead against His wrath. Seek a Mediator. Beware of continuing to sin.

[m]Prov 19:12

[n]1 Kings 2:28–34

[o]1 Sam 19:4–6; Eccl 10:4

[p]Prov 16:14; Esther 7:8

[q]1 Kings 2:23

[r]Ps 90:11; Ps 2:12

[s]Rom 9:22

3 *Keeping away from strife is an honor for a man,*
But any fool will quarrel.

The fact that this teaching is so opposite to what the world teaches proves it to be from God. A world of sin must always be a world of *strife*, because it is controlled by the wisdom of sinful man that brings only "disorder and every evil thing."[t] And yet, an evil world is an ideal place for the display of the grace of God, in the fruits of "the wisdom from above"—meekness, gentleness.[u]

[t]James 3:14–16

[u]James 3:17, 18

We've already been reminded, that "it is [man's] glory to overlook a transgression";[v] here we are strongly urged to *keep away from strife.* Many, just to keep peace and quiet, if not from a better motive, would overlook an injury. Yet if they were to get into a fight, they would feel honor-bound, not to quit—not to cease from it, as God says we should—but to give it all they have and to strike the last blow. But God knows that it is far more difficult to gather the waters once they are let out of the dam, than to keep them there in the first place. To stop quarreling or fighting, especially when we see that we are in the wrong; or—*if* we are in the right, but find that no good will come from it—this is a high *honor for a man,* a noble triumph over the flesh.[w] Abraham *kept away from strife* by making an impartial concession.[x] Isaac showed himself a man of peace in dealing with the greedy, quarrelsome Philistines.[y] The prophet "went his way," to prevent a further kindling of anger.[z] These all set a good example for us, but how much more common it is to see quarreling and fighting encouraged by man's pride than brought to a halt by a peaceful and loving spirit![a] *The fool* can't wait to get into a fight,[b] because that's his element, but he only torments himself and becomes a pain-in-the-neck to those around him. To return "a gentle answer" to grievous words,[c] and to keep out of the way of an angry person,[d] is the path of wisdom. To "put on a heart of . . . gentleness and patience," and to "let the peace of Christ rule in your hearts"—these are the marks of the called of God, following the example of our wonderful Lord.[e]

[v] Prov 19:11
[w] Prov 16:32; Rom 12:21
[x] Gen 13:8, 9
[y] Gen 26:17–31
[z] Jer 28:11
[a] Judg 8:1; 12:1
[b] Prov 18:6; 2 Sam 10:1–14; 2 Kings 14:8
[c] Prov 15:1
[d] Prov 25:8
[e] Col 3:12–15

4 *The sluggard does not plow after the autumn,*
So he begs during the harvest and has nothing.

LAZY PEOPLE ALWAYS HAVE EXCUSES

Again[f] we are instructed by a vivid picture of a most deadly habit. Lazy people always have excuses to keep them from doing any hard work. They will not plow after cold weather sets in, although autumn really offers no hindrance to plowing, if we have our heart in our work. This is just as true in God's service. When the heart is cold, any little difficulty will hinder. Every Christian might well ask himself if all his praying during his whole

[f] Prov 19:15, 24

lifetime has cost him even as much exertion as one hour's plowing. What have we really given to God? Anything more than the shadow of duties, when the world has had our heart and energy? The flesh wants to avoid suffering at any cost, even when the heart is under temporary conviction.[1] Good-bye heaven forever, if it calls for any suffering along the way. What a contrast between our work for Christ, and His work for us! We so grudgingly work for Him, but He is totally absorbed in His work for us. He just can't wait to get it done![g]

[g]Luke 12:50

But the lazy man must reap the fruit of his sin. If he will *not plow* in *seedtime,* he cannot reap *in harvest.* At that happy season—when the laborer is rewarded for his hard work—*he will beg and have nothing.* Poole warns, "Men's hearts are justly hardened against that man, who by his own sloth and sinfulness hath brought himself to want" (*Annotations*). And what else can the spiritual *sluggard* look for? The cold keeps him from the house of God. His soul is therefore perishing for lack of good. If wishing were all it took to make sure of heaven, who wouldn't have it? But heartless wishes, without the crucifixion of the flesh, will stop short of the promise. Millions have perished in serious religion from want of diligence and self-sacrificing devotedness. And what will it be to *beg during the great harvest,* and beg in vain;[h] when all wicked excuses are silenced, and fearful doom is pronounced upon the unprofitable servant![i]

[h]Matt 25:3–9; Luke 16:24

[i]Matt 25:26–30

Professing Christian, is there time to stand idle, when we stand at the door of eternity?—to be slack, when so near our great salvation?[j] "Blessed are those, who have sown much for God in their lifetime," exclaimed Burroughs. "Oh! the glorious harvest that those shall have! The very angels shall help them to take in their harvest at the great day. And oh! the joy that there shall be in that harvest! The angels will help to sing the harvest-song, that they shall sing, who have been sowers of righteousness."[k]

[j]Rom 13:11

[k]Hos 10:12

5 *A plan* [AV—*counsel*] *in the heart of a man is like*
deep water,
But a man of understanding draws it out.

[1] *Matt 19:21, 22. The shrinking from* the cold—*(as Melancthon observes in his brief comment on this verse)—is the avoiding of the cross.*

What goes on in *the depths of the heart* of man is not easily discovered. Often it is no more than crafty evil.[l] David was deceived by the smooth promises of Saul[m] and afterward by the religious hypocrisy of his ungodly son.[n] The plan of Daniel's enemies was too deep for Darius to see to the bottom of it.[o] The *plan* of Herod probably blinded the wise men to his real intentions.[p] And yet *a man of understanding* will often *draw out* a deceitful *plan* and set it in its true light. David described the *deep plans* of his enemies, as one who had penetrated to the very bottom of them.[q] Job accurately discovered the true, but indirect, counsel of his mistaken friends.[r] Paul *drew out* the secret counsel of selfishness in the devisive preachers of the gospel.[s]

[l]Jer 17:9
[m]1 Sam 18:17–26
[n]2 Sam 15:7–9
[o]Dan 6:4–9
[p]Matt 2:8
[q]Ps 64:5, 6; 119:98
[r]Job 21:27, 28
[s]Phil 1:15

But let us look at the bright side. Observe a man of God, instructed by God. Natural intelligence and keen perception are deepened and enlarged by spiritual light. His mind is enriched with the fruits of scriptural study and meditation. Here are *the deep waters of heavenly counsel.*[t] The talkative, professing believer, in his superficial judgment, sees nothing. But *a person of understanding* will discover and *draw out* valuable instruction. The Queen of Sheba *drew* wholesome water from the depths of Solomon's great well of "wisdom" and understanding.[u] Often, however, men with great minds keep aloof from general society. We may be in contact with them without having any idea of their intellectual stature. The *waters are deep,* but there is no bubbling up. Yet an exciting interchange of thoughts and ideas will draw out flowing water from the wellspring of wisdom. And often such communication with a godly and experienced minister, or a soundly instructed Christian, becomes most precious—"He who walks with wise men will be wise."[v] But to be prized above all is familiarity with the *deep* waters of the counsel of God. Don't say, I "have nothing to draw with and the well is deep."[w] A thinking habit in the exercise of prayer will enable you to "joyously draw water from the springs of salvation."[x] Will it not bring into your own soul "a well of water springing up to eternal life"?[y]

[t]Prov 18:4. Contrast 26:7, 9
[u]1 Kings 10:1–7
[v]Prov 13:20
[w]John 4:11
[x]Isa 12:3
[y]John 4:14

6 *Many a man proclaims his own loyalty*
[*AV—goodness*],

But who can find a trustworthy [AV—*faithful*] *man?*

A TRUSTWORTHY MAN— WHO CAN FIND HIM?

The last Proverb showed *the depth* of the heart—its deceitfulness and pride. So ... when we hear a man's own estimate of himself, we need no further proof of his lack of self-knowledge.[z] Even the ungodly *proclaims his own loyalty*. Jehu took no heed to walk in the way of the Lord. Still—said he, "Come with me and see my zeal for the Lord."[a] Absalom, even while he was planning acts of treason against his king and country, "stole away the hearts" of the people by his loud pretensions to goodness.[b] The whole nation while given up to all manner of sin and wickedness boasted of its integrity.[c] The Pharisee *proclaimed his goodness* at the corner of the streets;[d] yes—even in the presence of his God.[e] Such is the blindness of a self-deceiving heart! Lord! teach me to remember—"that which is highly esteemed among men is detestable in the sight of God."[f]

[z]Prov 16:2
[a]2 Kings 10:16, 19–31
[b]2 Sam 15:1–6
[c]Jer 2:23, 35; 5:1. Comp. Rom 2:17–23
[d]Matt 6:1, 2, 5, 16; 23:5. Comp. Prov 27:2
[e]Luke 18:11, 12
[f]Luke 16:15

After all, however, doesn't this mirror, honestly used, reveal more resemblance to our own features, than we would readily admit? We all condemn the open boasting of the Pharisee. But too often we eagerly reach out for the good opinion of the world. We scheme to gain the shadowy prize! We pretend shyness and reluctance to participate in things, but only, in order that others may bring us forward. Somehow we make certain it be known that *we* were the authors, or at least, that we had a considerable part in some work, that might raise our name among our friends and associates. Sometimes we are all too ready to take credit to ourselves, which we do not honestly deserve;[2] while we shrink from real reproach and abuse for the gospel's sake.

In opposition to this self-complacent goodness, Solomon, an accurate observer of human nature, exclaims almost in despondency—A *trustworthy man*—as a parent—a reprover—an adviser—an "upright person"—*who can find* him?[g] Look close. Look at yourself in the mirror of God's Word.[h] Does your neighbor or

[g]Mic 7:1, 2
[h]Ps 101:6

[2] *Prov 25:14. Thus Lysias, the chief captain, represented the governor, that he had interposed for Paul from his zeal for a Roman citizen, when the simple truth was, that he was ignorant of the fact at the time, and was about to scourge him as a rebel. Acts 23:27, with 21:38; 22:24.*

friend find you *trustworthy*? What does our daily communication tell them? Don't we often say things to be agreeable at the expense of truth? Don't we often profess regard for others that really doesn't express our true feelings at all? In today's society, while glaring sins and violations of the law are restrained, a thousand petty offenses are allowed that break down the wall between sin and duty. Judged by God's standard, they are really guilty steps upon forbidden ground. Never let it be forgotten that the sound influence of social virtues can only be maintained by the graces of the gospel. Never let the professing Christian regard moral integrity as a low attainment. The man of God bursts forth into fervent praise for upholding grace in this path.[i] After all, what can bring greater honor to God, than proof shown by the conduct of His people, that their daily transactions are animated with the soul of integrity, and that they faithfully keep their word? Never does godliness shine more bright, than in "showing all good faith ... in every respect."[j]

[i] Ps 41:11, 12

[j] Titus 2:10

7 *A righteous man who walks in his integrity—*
How blessed are his sons after him.

Here is a full portrait of the faithful man, rich in the blessing of his God.

Take the history of the father of the faithful. Abraham was *the righteous man,* accepted with God, and *walking* before Him *in his integrity.* And the covenant of his God promised an everlasting *blessing for his sons after him.*[k] And so does every child of God, who walks *in the same integrity,* secure "an inheritance [for] his children's children."[l] It is "not however for the merits of the parent, that they deserve it: but such is the mercy of God to the root and the branches; that, because the fathers are loved," said Muffet, "their children also are embraced."[3] But we must show our *integrity*, as did Abraham, in the practical habit of faith on our children's behalf.[m]

[k] Gen 17:1, 2, 7

[l] Prov 13:22. Comp. Ex 20:5, 6; Ps 25:12, 13; 37:26; 112:2

[m] Prov 22:6, with Gen 18:19

SAP IN THE ROOT

Christian parents!—let *integrity*, as before God, be the stamp of our family relations. Don't walk according to the

[3] *"The branches fare better for the sap of grace in the root"—SWINNOCK'S* Christian Man's Calling, *p. 383. When God saith—He will be a God to the godly man and to his children, I believe he intended more in that promise for the comfort of godly parents than most of them think of, Acts 2:39; Gen 17:7.*

teachings of the world yourselves, nor allow your children to do so. Let us make God's Word—His whole Word—our universal rule; His ways, however despised, our daily portion. Let us "seek first," for our children as for ourselves, "His kingdom and His righteousness."[n] Then, *walking in our integrity,* we may look for the honored blessing of being the parents of a godly race. *Our sons are blessed after us*; perhaps after we, having served our own generation by "the purpose of God," we shall fall asleep.[o] But well may we be content to wait the coming of that day, when the "thoughts from many hearts may be revealed." For then surely will the *son's blessing* be found in the secret records of heaven, linked with the prayerful, practical exercises of the parent's faith and love.

[n] Matt 6:33; 1 Sam 2:30

[o] Acts 13:36; Luke 2:35

8 *A king who sits on the throne of justice*
Disperses all evil with his eyes.

IN THE CONGREGATION OF PRINCES

This is the picture of a godly king, such as Solomon's father, David, described and exemplified; just, ruling "in the fear of God";[p] making it his great care and business to execute judgment. In those days he *sat on the throne of justice* and decided the law.[4] And his influence appears to have been so great that the wicked dared not come and sin in his presence. Another sovereign exclaimed indignantly, "Will he even assault the queen with me in the house?"[q] He was concerned that, not only the queen's and his own rights were obscenely outraged, but also royalty itself. David, as a man of God, and a sovereign of his people, could not endure the wicked in his presence.[r]

At present, "God takes His stand in His own congregation . . . of the rulers"[s] watching how they execute the power delegated to them; but hereafter He shall sit as a judge even of them, who, by reason of that delegated power, are styled gods. The concern then of the magistrate, when he goes up to the judgment seat, will be to put on righteousness as a glorious and beautiful robe, and

[p] 2 Sam 23:3, with 2 Sam 8:15; 1 Kings 15:5

[q] Esther 7:8

[r] Ps 101:3–8

[s] Ps 82:1

[4] *1 Kings 3:16–28, with 10:9. A Roman commentator (Corn. a Lapide) mentions the custom of St. Louis of France to sit twice a week in the throne of judgment, and make his dying charge to his successor, not only to appoint the most upright judges, but to overlook them in the discharge of their office. Does not the Court of the Queen's Bench in England suppose God to be sitting there in determination of judgment?*

to render his tribunal a fit emblem of that eternal "throne," of which "righteousness and justice are the foundation."[t] And always to the extent the ruler realizes his solemn responsibility, evil will be made to flee, and scattered away from him.[5]

[t] Ps 89:14

But what is to be ever standing before the King of heaven, who scatters away all evil with his eyes? "Thine eyes are too pure to approve evil, and Thou canst look on wickedness . . . The boastful shall not stand before Thine eyes . . . All things are open and laid bare to the eyes of Him with whom we have to do."[u] May the High Priest ever stand between the sinner and the Holy God, so that, while we walk in reverence, we may not be "frightened by any fear"!

[u] Hab 1:13; Ps 5:5; Heb 4:13; 1 Peter 3:6

9 *Who can say, "I have cleansed my heart,*
I am pure from my sin"?

IN THE PRESENCE OF THE KING

Behold the Great *King sits on the throne of justice,* and challenges every child of Adam—"Now gird up your loins like a man, And I will ask you, and you instruct Me."[v] The question is confusing. The answer humbles us in the dust. *Who can say*—truly say—*I have made my heart clean?* A sinner in his self-delusion may believe that he is a Christian, claiming that he cleaned himself up to become one. But that is impossible, for a true Christian knows he did not become one by his own doing, that it was only Jesus Christ who could and did save him and cleanse his heart from sin. *Who can say I am pure from my sin?* What! no vain thoughts, no sinful imagination lodging within! No ignorance, pride, coldness, worldliness, unbelief indulged! The more we search the heart, the more we'll see its impurity. "Yet you will see still greater abominations,"[w] evils never before suspected. Sure, there are many who boast about their goodness. But their boasting proves, not their goodness, but their blindness; that man is so sinful, that he cannot understand his own depravity.[x] What do those say who have entered into the presence of the King of Kings, whose holiness disperses *away all evil?* "Behold! I am insig-

[v] Job 38:3

[w] Ezek 8:13

[x] 1 John 1:8. Comp. 1 Kings 8:46; Eccl 7:20; Jer 2:35; Hos 12:8

[5] *Verse 26; 25:4, 5. Comp. 2 Chron 15:16. Plutarch tells of Cato, that such was the reverence of his character, that the bad women of Rome could not bear his look.*

nificant!" said Job. "Now my eye sees Thee. Therefore I retract." "Woe is me," said another, "I am ruined! Because I am a man of unclean lips ... For my eyes have seen the King, the Lord of hosts."[y] And what about the one who is considered the foremost of the saints of God; a very flame of love for Christ and His Church; "in far more labors," in tenderness as a mother for her newborn child; in walk "holy and blameless"—does he speak of his *purity from sin*? Not for a moment! In his highest state of Christian attainment, he feels himself to be the chief of sinners—a wondrous "example ... [of] perfect patience."[z] Such was the mighty power of depravity, mingled with such shining grace, that but for a miracle of instant help from God, he might have been thrown from "the third heavens into the snare of the devil."[a] Now, coming closer to our own time. "Once I thought," said a holy man of God, Venn, "some humiliating expressions of the saints of God, too low for me—proud, blind wretch that I was! Now I can say with Edwards—'Infinite upon infinite only reaches to my sinfulness'" (*Life*, p. 183). "And indeed there is not a conscious child of God, that does not share in this self-abased spirit. But for the clear manifestation of gospel grace, every one of us would have cause to tremble, lest our sins—after we lived in them so long, and after such tender long-suffering on God's part—should remain uncancelled in the great day of accounting, and send us into just and everlasting punishment? The *clean heart,* therefore, is not the heart pure from sin, but *the heart cleansed and renewed by grace*. And truly, if none can *say—I have cleansed my heart*, myriads can witness to the blood of Him, who is the Son of God, cleansing it from all guilt,[b] and to the mightiness of the Creator to renew it unto holiness.

[y] Job 40:4; 42:5, 6; Isa 6:5

[z] 2 Cor 11:23; Col 1:22; 1 Tim 1:15, 16

[a] AV—2 Cor 12:2–7, with 1 Tim 3:6, 7

[b] 1 John 1:7

But there are not many, who in the house of God will confess themselves miserable sinners, and at the holy table acknowledge the burden of their sin to be intolerable, who still will go back to the world, and boast or comfort themselves in the confidence of their goodness? Oh yes, they will confess that they are sinners, but still will deny every charge of sin. But they are not the "heavy-laden," to whom Christ hath promised "rest";[c] not "the lost ... the Son of Man has come to seek and to

[c] Matt 11:28

[d]Luke 19:10; 2 Kings 5:12

save."[d] They will come and lie beside the cleansing fountain, but never care to "wash . . . and be clean." But see in this Proverb the fundamentals of the gospel—man's total corruption; his inability to make his heart clean; and his grievous tendency to self-deception. All of which reveals his desperate need. Only when that need is truly felt, does God's cleansing remedy become valid. "If I do not wash you, you have no part in Me." If this is so, then, "Lord, not my feet only, but also my hands and my head."[e] "Wash me thoroughly from my iniquity . . . and I shall be whiter than snow . . . . Create in me a clean heart, O God, and renew a steadfast spirit within me."[f]

[e]John 13:8, 9

[f]Ps 51:2, 7, 10

10 *Differing weights and differing measures,*
Both of them are abominable to the L*ORD*.

WATCH YOUR WEIGHTS

This probably refers to the dishonest practice of having *different weights and measures* for buying and for selling—one stone too heavy—the other too light. Such practices seem to have been among the crying sins of the nations that brought down the judgment of God upon it.[g] So opposite are they to the character of "a God of faithfulness and without injustice,"[h] that the very stone and ephah were abomination to him.[i] The disuse of barter, and the more accurate system of inspection, have in some measure restrained this open form of fraud. But the cheats of trickery and close dealing, the evasion of legal duties, taking advantage of the ignorance of the unwary—all those deviations from the scriptural standard are *alike hateful to the Lord.* A very grievous thing it is to think of the several kinds of frauds and deceits, wherein men are grown wondrously expert, and so shameless, that they think it rather a credit to them, as an argument of their perfect understanding in their many mysteries and particular professions, than any blemish on their Christian profession. What a fearful exposure will be made on that great day, to the "disgrace and everlasting contempt" of the dishonest and ungodly merchant! Every man of moral integrity will scorn the flagrant breach of the golden rule. But let this, as every other temptation, be a matter of prayerful watchfulness. And don't be satisfied with just abstaining from that hateful

[g]Hos 12:7; Amos 8:4, 5; Mic 6:10, 11

[h]Deut 32:4

[i]Verse 23; 11:1; Ps 5:6

vice. Do something positive. Blot out its darkness by the bright, steady shining of an upright profession, full of simplicity, love, self-forgetfulness, and active sympathy with your neighbor's needs. "Let integrity and uprightness preserve me, for I wait for Thee."[j]

[j]Dan 12:2; Ps 25:21

11 *It is by his deeds that a lad distinguishes himself,*
If his conduct is pure and right.

THE BUDDING OF THE YOUNG TREE

Let parents watch their children's early habits, tempers, and *deeds.* Generally, the discerning eye will note something in the budding of the young tree, by which the tree in maturity *may be distinguished.* The child will tell what the man will be. No wise parent will pass over little faults, as though it were only a child doing childish things. Everything should be looked at as the index of the secret principle, and the work or word should be judged by the principle. If a child is deceitful, quarrelsome, obstinate, rebellious, selfish, how can we help but tremble when we think about his growth? A quiet, truth-loving, obedient, generous child—how joyous is the prospect of the blossom and fruit from his hopeful budding! From the childhood of Samuel,[k] Timothy,[l] much more of the Savior,[m] we could not but anticipate what the manhood would be. The early *purity* and *right* principles promised abundant and most blessed fruit.

[k]1 Sam 1:28; 3:19, 20
[l]2 Tim 3:14, 15, with 1:5; Phil 2:20, 21
[m]Luke 2:50–52

But do we mourn over the evil of our child, specially when tracing it to its original source? Oh! Let it send us to our knees in prayer for God to work in his heart and life that entire change which we so intensely desire. Put the finger on the parental promise,[n] and plead—"Remember the word to Thy servant, in which Thou hast made me hope."[o] The answer may be delayed. But "though it tarries, wait for it; For it will certainly come, it will not delay." Meanwhile live by faith;[p] work in faith. Never forget that we serve the God of Hope. Don't despair of His grace. Don't doubt His faithfulness. Hold on in active energy and patient hope. The tears of despondency shall be changed into tears of joy, giving a happy glow of warmth to every tender correction. The prodigal shall yet return. The Lord's plan will finally put unbelief to shame.[q] Hard was the trial of the faith of Augustine's

[n]Gen 17:7
[o]Ps 119:49
[p]Hab 2:3, 4
[q]James 5:11

mother. But most glorious was the crown of her patient wrestling constancy. And the old Christian's remark about Augustine—"It is impossible that the child of so many prayers could ever perish"—has been treasured as a source of great encouragement to Christian parents ever since.

12 *The hearing ear and the seeing eye,*
The LORD has made both of them.

THE SPIRITUAL SENSES—GOD'S SPECIAL GIFTS

Seeing and hearing are the two senses by which instruction is conveyed to the mind. They are component parts of that divine structure, so "fearfully and wonderfully made."[6] The natural senses are gifts common to all. The spiritual senses are the special gifts of sovereign power and grace.[r] It was left for man to make the ear that cannot hear and the eye that cannot see; and then to degrade himself to the senseless level, by worshipping the work of his own hand.[s] But *the hearing ear, and the seeing eye, the Lord has made both of them.*

[r] Matt 13:16, with Deut 29:2–4

[s] Ps 115:4–8

Man is deaf and blind in the things of God—"While seeing they do not see, and while hearing they do not hear."[t] The voice of mercy is disregarded. He is insensible to both his need and his remedy. His ear is open to sound advice, to moral doctrine, to the dictates of external decency. But as to the gospel, he is a mere statue, without life. All his senses are blinded, deadened, chained.[u] His moral disabilities can only be removed by that almighty power, which on earth gave ears to the deaf and sight to the blind.[v] We could just as easily create our natural self as re-create our spiritual self. "The hearing ear," which Solomon speaks of, is that which believes and obeys what it hears. The *seeing eye* is that, which not only sees the good, but follows it as well.[w] But who of us, whose *ears* are wakened, and whose *eyes* are opened, will not rejoice in the adoring acknowledgment—*The Lord has made both of them?* Would Lydia have ascribed the opening of "her heart" with a new power of attention and interest to her own natural effort?[x] O my God—may the ears and eyes which Thou hast made be

[t] Matt 13:13, 14

[u] 2 Cor 4:3, 4

[v] Mark 7:34; 8:22, 25, with Isa 35:5

[w] Job 34:3

[x] Acts 16:14. Comp. Isa 1:4

[6] *Ps 139:14. Comp. Ps 94:9; Exod 4:11. The celebrated Galen is said to have been converted from atheism by an attentive study of the perfect structure of the eye.*

for Thyself alone! to hear Thy voice[y]—to "behold the beauty of the Lord."[z]

[y] 1 Sam 3:9; Ps 85:8
[z] Ps 27:4; 63:2

13 *Do not love sleep, lest you become poor;*
Open your eyes, and *you will be satisfied with food.*

THE MOST PAINFUL CHRISTIAN CONFLICT?

Use sleep, as tired nature's sweet restore. Man requires it. God graciously gives it.[a] Without it "a man" could not go "forth to his work and to his labor."[b] Recruited for the active diligence of the day, he *opens his eyes,* "by the sweat of your face you shall eat bread,"[c] *and is satisfied with it.* But *don't love sleep* for its own sake. Bishop Taylor advised, "Let your sleep be necessary and healthful, not idle and expensive of time beyond the needs and conveniences of nature" (*Holy Living,* Chap. 1). Otherwise it is liable to become a ruinous and deadly habit, that can lead even a competent man—who carries much responsibility, but with no heart to fulfill it—*to become poor.* Valuable opportunities for improvements are allowed to slip by, and "strangers" quickly seize his prey.[d] What strange inconsistency and delusion! Man wants long life, and yet willfully shortens it by sleeping it away,[7] and the time given to prepare for eternity is wasted. The talent entrusted for trading is hid in a napkin. Nothing is done for God, for the soul, for his fellow-creatures, or for heaven. Rightfully, he is cast out as a wicked (because he is lazy) servant.[e]

[a] Ps 3:5; 4:8; 127:2
[b] Ps 104:23
[c] Gen 3:19
[d] Prov 5:9–11
[e] Matt 25:14–30

Without question, the Christian who sleeps beyond his needs, chooses to live on the level of an animal, rather than the God-given level, elevating him to fellowship with angels. Furthermore, he certainly doesn't regard communion with God very highly, if he isn't willing to sacrifice fleshly pleasure for the enjoyment of that privileged fellowship. The evil, however, doesn't end there. For the one given to too much sleeping, his whole day is in trouble. His daily habits are weakened. His mind is—at least partially—asleep, during his routine

[7] *Prov 19:15. Dr. Doddridge's life, though far from reaching the age of man (Ps 90:10) was yet, by the resistance of this besetting temptation, virtually extended to the ordinary bounds. By his successful energy in redeeming time from sleep he accomplished his invaluable work in the midst of multiplied engagements. See* Family Expositor *on Rom 12:13. "I take it for granted, that every Christian, who is in health, is up early in the morning. For it is much more reasonable to suppose a person up early, because he is a Christian, than because he is a laborer, or a tradesman, or a servant, or has business that wants him"—LAW'S* Serious Call.

activities. Whatever permits loafing, or calls for little effort, is all that is acceptable. Every exercise of self-denial is revolting. It is quite obvious that this spirit has little sympathy with the genuine spirit of Christianity—life, joy, energy. It sinks far below the level and obligation of those, who are "a temple of the Holy Spirit,"[f] "sons of light and sons of day,"[g] "virgins" with "their lamps" trimmed[h] for the bridegroom's coming, lively, vigorous candidates for an incorruptible eternal crown.[i]

[f]1 Cor 6:19
[g]1 Thess 5:5, 6
[h]Matt 25:7
[i]1 Cor 9:24, 25

Especially should we, who are of drowsy habits, listen to the call—*love not sleep.* Right here could be our most painful Christian conflict. But may we not hear the gentle rebuke, "So, you men could not watch with Me for one hour? Keep watching and praying, that you may not enter into temptation."[j] When resisted, it is an infirmity; when allowed, or only feebly opposed, it is sin. At all events, in the service of God it is safer to consider it, not as a weariness to be encouraged, but as an indulgence to be vigorously denied and overcome. Otherwise, while the self-denying Christian will *open his eyes, and eat plentifully,* the flesh may gain the victory over the spirit, and lead to a lifeless habit of prayer, hearing, and meditation.

[j]Matt 26:40, 41

14 *"Bad, bad," says the buyer;*
But when he goes his way, then he boasts.

ANALYSIS OF DECEIT

The Bible gives abundant proof, that man has always been the same in every generation since the Fall. In all the centuries that have followed, man's dealings with his fellowmen have never been free from fraud and selfishness. The buying and selling of goods—God's way of binding man to man, is marred by man's corruption. Solomon had before detected the deceitfulness of the seller. Now he exposes *the buyer,* and to bring it home more closely, he gives even the market language—*"It is bad, it is bad."* Then the buyer adds, "The article is of inferior quality. I can get it cheaper elsewhere. It isn't worth that much to me. I don't have any need for it, nor do I have any particular interest in it now." After he has been able to make a shrewd bargain by his convenient lies, he goes his way, boasting about his conquest and laughing at the stupidity of the seller, and is probably highly commended for his cleverness.[k]

[k]James 4:16

The same principle of fraud applies to the seller. If the one says, *"It is bad,"* the other no less eagerly cries, "It is good." So neither one says what he really believes and what he knows is true.[l] The one is determined to buy cheap; the other on selling high. The one decries unjustly; the other praises untruly. He asks one price, when he means to accept another, and takes advantage of the confidence of his customer to impose on him a worthless article.[8] In fact, no one can even begin to know the endless number of clever little, secret lies that are told every day and everywhere under the sun.

[l]1 Sam 12:3

We all are engaged in money transactions; and with many of us, it is our main business in life. Yet, so great are temptations—from our own interest or self-defense; the selfishness of others; and the general example of the world—to be dishonest; that we should be most thankful for this probing analysis of deceit. The man of God stands at the dividing line, between total honesty and subtle deceit. To pass over that line, even by a single step, is to defy God. The gain may be insignificant, but the sin is enormously far-reaching. (Remember, there was enough sin in the dimensions of the single piece of fruit, that Adam and Eve partook of, to bring sin and death into the whole human race.) Here now, by dishonest business dealings, God's law is deliberately broken,[m] conscience is violated, deceit is practiced; evil is called good, "and good evil";[n] our duty to our neighbor transgressed; and all this—perhaps without a moment of remorse—only to satisfy man's greed.

[m]Comp. Lev 19:11; 25:14

[n]Isa 5:20

But do professing Christians prove themselves beyond reproach in such matters? Yet, how can we be worthy to bear Christ's name, if we are not so trustworthy during the week as we are on Sunday, or as honest in our dealings with men, as with God? How can we be true disciples of Christ, unless we yield to His authority? Every one of us ought to ask ourselves, Have I trembled

[8]*Amos 8:6. Contrast the disinterested transaction (Gen 23:3–18). Augustine mentions a somewhat ludicrous, but significant story. A medicine man announced to a capacity crowd gathered around him, that in the next entertainment he would reveal to all present what was in their hearts. An immense crowd attended, and the man redeemed his pledge to the vast assembly by a single sentence—"You all wish to buy cheap, and to sell dear"—a sentence generally applauded; every one, even the most trifling (as Augustine observes) found the confirming witness in his own conscience.*

[o]Col 3:25; I Thess 4:6
[p]Matt 5:37
[q]Matt 7:12
[r]Acts 24:16

before the solemn warnings of God, the great lawgiver?[o] Am I ready to be tried by His rules of guileless simplicity,[p] and his golden rule for the treatment of others?[q] Have we always acted as under the eye of God? Are there any of our money transactions, that we would be ashamed to have proclaimed upon the housetops? Can we honestly say we are ready to face a heart-searching God, with "a blameless conscience both before God and before man"?[r] Let us never forget that the gospel of Jesus Christ—through its active exercise of grateful, devoted love, and its untiring spirit of doing all to the glory of God—is the only principle that can expel selfishness from the heart of man.

15 *There is gold, and an abundance of jewels;*
But the lips of knowledge are a more precious thing.

GOODLY PEARLS

[s]Matt 19:22, with Luke 4:22
[t]Job 31:24, with 1 Tim 6:9, 10
[u]1 Kings 3:9
[v]1 Kings 10:27
[w]Luke 19:42
[x]Matt 13:45, 46; Luke 2:10

This is not the standard of the world; for there, *gold and jewels* are worth far more than *lips of knowledge.* So the young man made his choice, preferring his "much property" to those gracious words of the Lord Jesus that arrested the admiration of the multitude.[s] But when "fine gold" is our hope "and trust," it will surely be our ruin.[t] Solomon's estimate—that knowledge is above riches—was that of one, to whom the Lord had given a wise and "understanding heart."[u] *Gold* and precious *jewels* were abundant in his days.[v] Yet all these earthly treasures were as nothing in Solomon's eyes in comparison to heavenly teaching. *The lips of knowledge were a more precious thing.*[9] But it is *divine* knowledge only, however, that stands out so high. Human wisdom only captivates the imagination and furnishes its measure of useful information. But the words of man, for the most part, die away in the ear. They do not feed the heart. They furnish no comfort to the afflicted, no hope to the desponding, no teaching to the ignorant in "those things which make for" everlasting "peace."[w] If therefore they be "fine pearls," at least they are not the "pearl of great value"—that *more precious thing,* which dims the luster of earth's most splendid vanities.[x]

[9] *Prov 3:15; 8:10, 11, 19; 16:16. Job gave the same verdict, Job 28:12–19.*

How *precious a jewel are the lips of knowledge,* when the messenger of the gospel brings "good news of a great joy" to the burdened conscience—to him that is ready to perish! Truly the very sound of his "feet" is welcome for the sake of his message.[10] *Precious* also will be the communications of Christian fellowship. Though falling infinitely short of the grace that dwelt in our wonderful Lord; to the extent we are taught of Him, will our tongues be "as choice silver,"[y] and our "lips ... spread knowledge"[z] *as a precious thing,* enriching, and adorning with the glory of our heavenly Lord.

[y]Prov 10:20
[z]Prov 15:7

16 *Take his garment when he becomes surety for a stranger;*
And for foreigners, hold him in pledge.[a]

[a]Prov 27:13

Again and again, we are warned against suretyship for a stranger[b]—any new acquaintance, especially one whose character has lost all credit. To lend to him is the sure road to poverty and ruin. He is not fit to be trusted. Lend nothing to him without good security. If necessary, *take his garment* as his pledge. The letter of the law forbade this extremity.[c] But the spirit and intent of the law was concerned with the protection of the poor and unfortunate, who were forced to borrow for their own needs, and therefore claim pity. The command here is aimed at the inconsiderate, who deserve to suffer for their folly, because they have willfully plunged themselves into ruin. Nor does it in any degree suggest the just suspicion of covetousness or close dealing. The love of our neighbor does not involve the forgetfulness of ourselves. The path of godly wisdom is the safest for all parties. It never can be wise to assist someone when our kindness will only hurry him on to ruin. Our refusal may be an exercise of self-denial, as it should be. Let it be clearly understood that this is the sacrifice; not the indulgence, of self-gain. This grace is one of the combined perfections of our Lord.[d] Don't let it be lacking in the lives of His people. Without it, our Christian profession is not complete, and we will frequently bring offense to the gospel.

[b]Prov 6:1–5; 11:15; 17:18
[c]Exod 12:26, 27; Deut 24:12, 13. Comp. Job 22:6; Amos 2:8
[d]Prov 8:12

[10] *Isa 52:7; Rom 10:14, 15. Such was the delight of hanging upon the lips of the golden-mouthed Chrysostom, that the common proverb was—"Rather let the sun not shine than Chrysostom not preach."*

17 *Bread obtained by falsehood is sweet to a man,*
But afterward his mouth will be filled with gravel.

DON'T MIX YOUR FOOD WITH GRAVEL!

"Holiness is sweet in the way *and end* too. Wickedness is sometimes sweet in the way, but always bitter in the end," warned Caryl.[e] It is with deceit, as with every other sin, that Satan always holds out a bait; always promises gain or pleasure as the wages of his service, but most surely disappoints the victims of his delusion.[f] Corn that is thrashed on a *gravelly* floor will spoil the sweetness of any bread made from it. How many this arch-deceiver has allured by the *sweetness of his bread,* whose *mouths have been afterward filled with gravel!* The *bread,* which *a man* hath got by fraud and trickery, seems *sweet* and pleasant at the first taste; but by the time he has chewed it for awhile, he'll find it to be nothing but hard gravel, that grinds between his teeth, galls his jaws, wounds his tongue, and offends his palate.[g] "Everything gotten wrongly is here implied," cautioned Bishop Patrick. Bitter was Achan's "sweet," deceitfully hid in the tent, which brought ruin upon himself and his family.[h] Look at Gehazi. What profit had he from his talents of silver and changes of garments? Bitter indeed was *the bread of falsehood* to him.[i] Even Jacob, a true servant of God, was chastened heavily almost to the end of his days with the bitter fruits of deceit.[j] To the mass of such blinded sinners it is eternal ruin. Whatever advantage the tempter offers, you can be sure his price is your soul, to be paid in your dying hour. What a terrible bargain—an eternal treasure traded for the trifle of a moment! We may be very charmed with the present *sweetness;* but how bitter the after-fruits will be, when the poor deluded sinner shall cry—"I indeed tasted a little honey . . . Here I am, I must die."[k] That's how certain it is that the bitterness that springs out of sin is the bitterness of death.

Not a single step can be taken in the way of godliness, without renouncing every sinful practice. Not the smallest violation of the law can be excused. Even to venture into what we believe to be insignificant sins is most dangerous. The smallest sin breaks down the fence; and once we get through the fence, self-restraint is impossi-

[e] Job 20:14
[f] Prov 9:17, 18; 23:31, 32; Job 20:12–16
[g] Comp. Lam 3:16
[h] Josh 7:21–24
[i] 2 Kings 5:20–27
[j] Gen 27; 42:36–38
[k] 1 Sam 14:43; Eph 4:30

ble. Total uprightness is the mark of the true servant of God. Let the man, who loves and studies God's word, exhibit its holiness in his life. Never should we separate our Christianity from our business. Instead, we should let the image and glory of the Lord dominate our entire lives. Every stepping aside from the straight path grieves "the Holy Spirit of God," darkens the sunshine of our soul, blasts the consistency of our profession, and wounds the church of God.

18 *Prepare plans by consultation,*
And make war by wise guidance.

WE ARE DEPENDENT ON ONE ANOTHER

This is true wisdom—to deliberate before we act and to *prepare plans by* sound and experienced *counsel.* Even the wisest of men valued this strengthening help.[l] God has made us more or less dependent upon each other. And therefore, while it is most important to possess a calm and decided judgment; it is no less important to guard against clinging obstinately and exclusively to our own opinions.[m] Especially is it true in government: "In abundance of counselors there is victory."[n] Wars of ambition for power or riches are *never wise.* The result may be fearful. David took counsel of the Lord;[o] Nehemiah, while supporting his courage by faith,[p] *prepared his plans by counsel,* and called his counsel to deliberate in all emergencies.[q] Ahab, asking counsel of his false prophets;[r] Amaziah, despising the sound counsel given to him[s]—both with bad *guidance, made war* to their own ruin. Even godly Josiah—making every allowance for his circumstances, can probably be charged with impulsive action. Neglecting *to prepare plans by counsel* of the Lord's prophets then living among his people, he was chastened with temporal destruction.[t]

[l] 1 Kings 12:6
[m] Prov 15:22
[n] Prov 11:14; 24:6
[o] 2 Sam 5:17–23
[p] Neb 2:17–20; 3; 4
[q] Neh 4:19, 20
[r] 1 Kings 22:6
[s] 2 Kings 14:8–12
[t] 2 Chron 35:20–24

THE ENEMY AT OUR FACE

Now ponder Bishop Hall's description of the spiritual *war.* "It admits of no intermission. It knows no night, no winter. It abides no peace, no truce. It calls us not into garrison, where we may have ease and respite, but into pitched fields continually. We see our enemies in the face always, and are always seen and assaulted; ever resisting, ever defending, receiving and returning blows. If we're negligent or weary, we die. What other hope is there, while one fights, and the other stands still? We can never have safety and peace, but in victory. Then must our resistance be courageous and constant, when both yielding is death, and all treaties of peace mortal" (*Holy Observations,* 25). Does not this war bring the greatest need of deliberate *counsel,* carefully counting the cost;[u] cleaving to our all-wise Counselor[v] and almighty helper? Under His *counsel,* and the support of His grace, don't be afraid to take up the song of praise—"Blessed be the Lord, my rock, who trains my hands for war, and my fingers for battle fight"![w]

[u]Luke 14:31, 32
[v]Isa 9:6
[w]Ps 144:1

19 *He who goes about as a slanderer reveals secrets,*
Therefore do not associate with a gossip.

DID YOU EVER MEET ANYBODY WHO'S ALL TONGUE?

Don't ever forget that all communication in social life must be based on love. Any breach of this is highly displeasing to God. Look at *the slanderer.* Obviously he has much time on his hands not being used for any good purpose. Therefore, he spends it on other people's business; digging up secrets, snooping into family affairs. It all furnishes material for scandal and for using up his idle time. As he visits in one home, he talks about the affairs of the last family he was with. His present visit will furnish matter for idle talk in the next house. His name—slanderer—describes him well. The joy of his life is to satisfy his impertinent curiosity and make gossip out of everything he sees or hears. He makes it the business of his life, sacrificing all other business for it. It's as if he were nothing but tongue, and his restless babbling, perpetual motion. Don't associate with that kind of person! Why, you wouldn't want to have him looking over your wall, let alone entering your house, to associate with your family circle. You know very well all he would be doing is drawing gossip out or putting it in.

The flagrant blot, however, in this contemptible, and dangerous character, is his unfaithfulness as he goes about revealing secrets.[x] This is extremely offensive to a God of truth. Even when matters are given to him by a

[x]Prov 11:13

friend, in strictest confidence, he can't wait to spread them around. That's sacrilege and desecration of friendship. Don't ever regard this as trivial. Don't ever receive a trust without the strongest determination of Christian faithfulness.

Notice this about the slanderer also that he works his way into the *secrets* of others, gaining his materials for talebearing by flattering the person present at the expense of the one who is absent. Watch and pray earnestly against this deadly evil. Keep your own vineyard carefully.[11] Otherwise, while you're busy with other people's business when you ought to be caring for your own, your vineyard will be like the "vineyard of the man lacking sense ... completely overgrown with thistles"[y] like the "curious people," whom Augustine rebuked, who "pry into another's heart and life; but are slothful to amend their own." Be diligent in your own calling, serving the Lord and His church. Study the obligation of Christian character, according to the standard of Jesus Christ, our supreme example, whose every word was full of love. How many in self-indulgence and forgetfulness of their own obligations, because they don't have anything to keep their hands busy, set their tongue to work instead![z] Such people bring, as it were, a plague of flies with them;[a] buzzing from house to house, from one neighbor to another, to bring a report on all the gossip they've been able to pick up. A sharp rebuke is what they deserve, and it would be an effective means of driving them away.[b]

[y]Prov 24:30, 31

[z]1 Tim 5:13

[a]Exod 8:24

[b]Prov 25:23

20 *He who curses his father or his mother,*
His lamp will go out in time of darkness.

YOUTH'S RESPONSIBILITY TO PARENTS

If *darkness* is the punishment of this atrocious sin, is it not also the cause? For surely even the light of nature should be extinguished, before the child should *curse* those, who under God have taught it to speak—the authors and preservers of its existence; the child's greatest earthly benefactors. Even an undutiful look, much more a word, is an offense against God's commandment. How heavy then must be the weight of guilt involved in the *cursing* of them! The deepest reverence is due to them

[11] *Mark the complaint, Song of Sol 1:6. Comp. our Lord's probing advice, Matt 7:3–5.*

[c] Jer 35:1–10

when they are dead.[c] How great then must be the provocation that causes a child to sin against his parents while they are living for their children, in all the active, self-denying energy of love and service! This *cursing*, according to our Lord's standard, includes taking lightly their responsibilities toward their parents,[12] and willful disobedience—a fearful, palpable mark of the last days.[d] Let God's own curse on Mount Ebal,[e] and His judgment of temporal death,[13] testify to how He regards it. If the temporal sentence of death is repealed, the more awful judgment still remains unchangeably upon the divine statute book—*darkness*—the blackness of darkness—eternal darkness without a ray of light, of which blackness is only the shadow, to show what the reality must be.

[d] 2 Tim 3:2; Rom 1:30, 31
[e] Deut 27:16

21 *An inheritance gained hurriedly at the beginning,*
Will not be blessed in the end.

THE MOST WORTHWHILE INHERITANCE—WHAT IS IT?

Solomon is obviously limiting his observation to an inheritance gotten dishonestly, not the advancement of Joseph in the glory of Egypt,[f] or a Mordecai in the Persian[g] courts, or a Daniel in Babylon.[h] All these were *gained hurriedly* under the special care of God. But the greedy one, overly anxious to get rich[i] or great, may *get an inheritance at the beginning; but in the end it will be accursed*[j] not *blessed.* Absalom[k] and Adonijah[l] strove for a kingdom and met their ruin. One king of Israel after another, trampled on each other as they hurried hastily on to destruction.[m] In his day, Napoleon rose with astonishing rapidity to a magnificent *inheritance.* Yet he ended his days in disgraceful banishment. Even less splendid possessions end in the same disappointment. What a price Ahab paid for his wickedly and *hurriedly gotten inheritance* of Naboth's vineyard![n] Let not the warning be in vain—that "those who want to get rich" shall suffer "many foolish and harmful desires." What is their end?—"ruin and destruction."[o] Place the cross and crown of Jesus before you. The world fades, selfishness dies, at the very sight of them. One object only attracts

[f] Gen 41:14–45
[g] Esther 6:11; 8:15; 10:3
[h] Dan 2:46, 48
[i] Prov 28:20, 22
[j] Prov 10:2, 3; 21:5; 28:8
[k] 2 Sam 15:10; 18:9–17
[l] 1 Kings 1:5–9; 2:25
[m] 1 Kings 16:8–22
[n] 1 Kings 21:1–15, 19. Comp. Job 15:29; 20:18; Amos 6:4–8
[o] 1 Tim 6:9, 10

[12] *Matt 15:3–6. The original words in Deut 27:16 precisely correspond.*
[13] *Exod 21:15, 17; Lev 20:9; Deut 21:18–23. Comp. 30:17. The Roman punishment for one who murders his parents was to be sewed up in a sack and cast into the sea.*

and satisfies. "I said to the Lord, "Thou art my Lord . . . the portion of my inheritance."[p] Here is *blessing* beyond understanding—and without end.

[p]Ps 16:2, 5

22 *Do not say, "I will repay evil";*
Wait for the Lord, *and He will save you."*

BE SATISFIED WITH GOD'S MANAGEMENT!

"Vengeance is Mine"—is the awful proclamation of God.[q] Most reverently do His people adore God's rightful and exclusive privilege.[r] Who else is able to exercise and control all that power? He is omniscient—He knows all things, but we know imperfectly. We are blinded by our selfish desires. He is just, "without hypocrisy"; we are prejudiced in our own behalf. What presumption, let alone impiety, for the crawling "worm" to intrude upon His exclusive rights and privileges! Revenge is indeed a cherished lust of the flesh. Were it not for God's restraining hand, this world would be a "Field of Blood." But never did the Lord allow it in His people.[14] Not even an Edomite, their most bitter enemy; not even the Egyptian, their most cruel oppressor—was to be abhorred.[s] The folly and sin of this passion are alike manifest. He that holds revenge in his heart, keeps his own wounds open. His enemy could not do him a greater injury than to cause him to have a revengeful spirit. The tongue, which "speaks rashly like the thrusts of a sword,"[t] is here the instrument of this passion. Yet often when the outward act prompted by hatred is restrained, still the passion that is prompting it broods more fiercely within.[u] Or at least it is only a reluctant obedience, not the glorious victory exhibited in the history of the men of God—"do not be overcome by evil, but overcome evil with good."[15]

[q]Deut 32:35; Rom 12:19; Heb 10:30
[r]Ps 94:1; Rev 6:10; James 3:17
[s]Job 25:6; Matt 27:8; Deut 23:7
[t]Prov 12:18; 25:18
[u]Gen 27:41; 2 Sam 13:22

What then is the remedy? In humility and faith we must lay these problems before the Lord. Put them in His hands. Wait on Him, and He shall save us. Revenge rises, only because we have no faith. For if we really believed that God would take up our cause, wouldn't we leave ourselves completely in His hands? See how He concerned Himself with the cause of the man who was "very

[14] *Prov 24:29; Lev 19:18. Observe the identity of this standard with that of the New Testament—the teaching of our Lord—Matt 5:38, 39; and His apostles—Rom 12:17, 19–21; 1 Thess 5:15; 1 Peter 3:9.*
[15] *Rom 12:21. Comp. Joseph—Gen 45:5; David—1 Sam 24:18–21.*

[v]Num 12:1–10
[w]2 Sam 16:12; Ps 38:12–15
[x]Ps 37:5, 6
[y]1 Peter 2:23

humble ... more than any man on ... earth"![v] And see also, with what confidence David rested himself in the midst of reproach,[w] thereby living what he preached.[x] And so did David's Lord—even the Son of God, Himself, entrusted "Himself to Him who judges righteously."[y] After His blessed example, therefore, "let those also who suffer according to the will of God entrust their souls to a faithful creator in doing what is right."[z] Isn't it enough for us to know that all shall be made right one day? God will set all straight at last; but that day is not yet. Be satisfied then with His management. It is enough to know, that "the salvation of the righteous is from the Lord."[a] As His praying people, let us keep our hearts and minds fixed on that coming great day, when God shall "bring about justice for His elect, who cry to Him day and night, and will He delay long over them? 'I tell you that He will bring about justice for them speedily.' "[b]

[z]1 Peter 4:19
[a]Ps 37:39, 40
[b]Luke 18:7, 8

23 *Differing weights are an abomination to the* LORD,
And a false scale is not good.

HONESTY IN BUSINESS

[c]Verses 10, 14, 23
[d]Matt 6:7
[e]Isa 28:10
[f]Rom 10:2, 3

Here let us search into the mind of God. Three times He brings home one point of practical detail.[c] Yet this is not a "meaningless repetition."[d] There is a reason for it. Instead of "order on order ... line on line,"[e] the infinite treasures of wisdom and knowledge might have poured forth endless variety of instruction. We aren't surprised when we see the apostles emphasizing, over and over, the argument of a sinner's justification before God.[16] And we understand from this repetition the primary importance and the peculiarly offensive character of the doctrine.[f] Doesn't this repeated emphasis on honesty in business show the great importance God places upon it? And doesn't it show, too, how much resistance there must be to it? If we feel we can't hear too much about the grace of God, why do we shrink from practical application of God's principles in our everyday lives? If we love to be told, what we owe to God on Sunday, but rebel from living as a Christian the rest of the week, in our business activities, we are not accepting the whole revelation of God. Ours is not "the wisdom from

[16] *See Epistles to the Romans and the Galatians.*

above" that "is first pure, then peaceable ... without hypocrisy."[g]

[g]James 3:17

The need for this particular teaching is most understandable because of the evil that prevails throughout our business world; cheating and all dishonesty in business (the differing weights) are declared to be *an abomination*[h] to God, yet how often are they excused, as something that happens all the time, perhaps even of necessity! But the short measure will fill up a full measure of guilt, and the light weights bring upon the soul heavy weight of judgment. If Job, was fearful, lest his "land cries out" against him,[i] let the businessman beware, lest his *weights and scale* bear witness against him. Certainly there is cause for watchfulness! What's the meaning of this massive and costly government with all its checks and counterchecks, its endless numbers of laws, and penalties, if not, that man cannot trust his fellowman? But in all this, let me not forget, that of all this deceit my heart is the native soil; that nothing but the culture of divine principle keeps down these poisonous weeds, and, supplies in their place, "the fruit of righteousness ... to the glory and praise of God."[j] The love of God constrains His servant. God is true to him; and He will not be false to others. God is merciful to him, and He will not be unjust to others. This is the practical influence of the gospel.

[h]Prov 11:1; Mic 6:10, 11

[i]Job 31:38

[j]Phil 1:11

24 *Man's steps are* ordained *by the* L*ORD*,
How then can man understand his way?

HERE IS THE WAY—WALK IN IT

God's great power and sovereignty and man's absolute dependence and helplessness—these are foundation principles. They do not infringe on the free will of man, and they do not excuse man's indolence. Man often acts, as though he were the master of his own life; as if *his steps* were of himself. Or else, he wrongly believes that every event has been predetermined, and therefore, instead of diligently working out the Lord's purposes, he thinks his "strength is to sit still" and do nothing.[k] But the humble, heaven-taught Christian exercises free agency in the spirit of dependence. Though utterly powerless for obedience, he looks to God for the strength to

[k]AV—Isa 30:7

obey. The consciousness that *his steps are of the Lord,* gives energy to his faith. It is written—"a man's way is not in himself."[l] It is written again—"This is the way, walk in it."[m] In this way, Scripture guards against Scripture. Here is dependence without passive inertia (a tendency to remain in a fixed position without change); diligence without presumption or self-confidence. Here, then opposite principles work together harmoniously.

[l]Jer 10:23
[m]Isa 30:21

The true liberty of the will is the power of acting according to choice, without outside restraint. Divine agency, not only does not hinder man's freedom, but it removes the obstacle of a corrupt and tyrannizing prejudice. With this removed, man can act more freely, and more effectually. You see, man is not moved as a machine, which is unconscious of what it is doing and the results of its activity. He is acted upon by intelligent principles. He is not carried along the way, but enabled to walk. He is "led," not driven, "with cords of a man," not of a beast; and those cords are so wisely applied, that they are felt to be "bonds of love."[n] He is enlightened, so that he sees; softened, so that he turns; drawn, so that he runs.[o] He is moved effectually, but willingly; strongly, but without constraint. Divine grace acts, not as in a lifeless machine, but as in a purposing, willing, everworking creature. Nothing is therefore distorted. There is no unnatural violence. It is "the day of Thy [Lord's] power," who "is at work in you both to will and to work for *His* good pleasure."[p] *His steps are ordained by the Lord,* who at once inspires the effort, and secures its success.

[n]Hos 11:4
[o]Song of Sol 1:4; Ps 119:32
[p]Ps 110:3; Phil 2:13

The world of God shows the same overruling agency. Man determines and acts freely in the minute circumstances of the day. Yet the active overall influence, arranging every step at the right time and place, makes it plain, that *his steps are of the Lord.* Rebekah came to the well just at the moment that Abraham's servant was ready to meet her. "The Lord has guided me in the way."[q] Pharaoh's daughter goes out to bathe just at the crisis moment when the infant Moses was committed to the water.[r] Was this the working of chance or some fortunate coincidence? Who can doubt the finger or the leading of God? A curse of destruction was pronounced against Eli's

[q]Gen 24:27
[r]Exod 2:1–5

house. The word was fulfilled by a combination of apparently casual incidents. David fled to Abimelech for relief. That very day Doeg was there; not in the ordinary course, but "*detained* before the Lord." He gives information to his cruel master, and in a moment of anger the curse was accomplished.[s] Who can doubt but *the steps* of Doeg and of David meeting together *were of the Lord*? All parties acted freely. What was false in Doeg was righteous in God, whom we adore as a sin-hating God, even while, as in the crucifixion of Christ,[t] He makes use of sin for the fulfillment of His own purposes.

[s] 1 Sam 2:30–32, with 21:6, 7; 22:9–18

[t] Acts 2:23

Man's steps, therefore, being *of the Lord,* must often be clothed in mystery. *How then can man understand his own way*? Often does it run counter to his plans. The Babel-builders raised their proud tower to prevent their dispersion: but it became the very means of their dispersion.[u] Pharaoh's plan to "deal wisely" for increasing the power of his kingdom brought about its destruction.[v] Haman's project for his own glory was the first step of his ruin.[w] Often when our way is not counter to our plan, it is far beyond our own understanding. Little did Israel *understand* the reason of their roundabout way to Canaan. Yet in the end it proved "a straight way."[x] As little did Ahasuerus *understand* the profound reason, why "during that night the king could not sleep"; so incidental a happening it hardly seemed worthy to record, yet it became a necessary link in the chain of the Lord's everlasting purposes of grace to His people.[y] Little did Philip *understand his own way,* when he was moved from the wide sphere of preaching the gospel in Samaria, to go into the desert, which ultimately proved a wider extension of the gospel.[z] As little did the apostle Paul understand, that his prosperous journey to see his beloved flock at Rome, would be a narrow escape from shipwreck and going to Rome in chains.[a] Little do we know what we pray for. "By awesome deeds Thou dost answer us in righteousness, O God of our salvation."[b] We go out in the morning *not understanding our way*; "not [knowing] what a day may bring forth."[c] Some turn, connected with our happiness or misery for life, meets us before night.[d] Joseph in taking his walk to search for his brethren, never anticipated a separation of more than twenty years' from

[u] Gen 11:4–9

[v] Exod 1:8–10, with 14:30

[w] Esther 6:6–13

[x] Exod 13:17, 18, with Ps 107:7

[y] Esther 6:1

[z] Acts 8:5–12, 26, 27

[a] Acts 27; 28:20, 30, with Rom 1:10

[b] Ps 65:5

[c] Prov 27:1

[d] John 4:7

[e]Gen 37:14

his father.[e] What can we learn from those cross ways or dark ways? Not constant, trembling anxiety but daily dependence. "I will lead the blind by a way they do not know, in paths they do not know I will guide them." But . . . what then? Will they be left in dark perplexity? "I will make darkness into light before them and rugged places into plains. These are the things I will do, and I will not leave them."[f] Often do I look back amazed at the mystery of my course, so different, so contrary to my way. But it is enough for me, that all is in Thy hands, O Lord, that "the steps of a man are established by the Lord."[g] I dare trust Thy wisdom, Thy goodness, Thy tenderness, Thy faithful care. Lead me—uphold me—forsake me not. "With Thy counsel Thou wilt guide me, and afterward receive me to glory."[17]

[f]Isa 42:16

[g]Ps 37:23. Comp. Prov 16:9

25 *It is a snare for a man to say rashly, "It is holy!"*
And after the vows to make inquiry.

In every path the great bird-trapper has laid his snares. Perhaps, however, the most subtle are reserved for the service of God. Offerings made *holy* to the Lord often were devoured by the hypocritical worshipper, sacrilegiously used for himself. Achan, for example, robbing the treasury of the Lord, found it a snare to his ruin.[h] This was the sin of "the whole nation"; and fearful indeed was the judgment—"You are cursed with a curse."[i] Voluntary vows were commonly practiced;[j] and often *inquiry was made afterward,* which ought to have been made before. They were at full liberty not to vow; but having vowed, they were bound to pay.[k]

[h]Josh 6:19; 7:1

[i]Mal 3:8–10

[j]Lev 27:9, 10, 28–33

[k]Deut 23:21, 22; Eccl 5:4–6

RASH PROMISES—BETTER LEFT UNMADE

As the counterpart to this hollow, half-hearted profession—a man in trouble will often make far-reaching promises to God; but once he gets what he wants, he looks for a way to get released from his obligation. Often, too, in a moment of deep emotion—perhaps under the glow of a gospel service, we make pledges to God, but,

[17] *Ps 73:24. Augustine mentions the weeping prayers and pleadings of his godly mother, because of his voyage from Carthage to Italy. Her anxiety was grounded probably on his absence from her control, and her concern, that, once away from her influence, he would plunge deeper into sin. But it proved in the end to be the providential purpose for his conversion—"In thy deep and hidden counsel"—to paraphrase Augustine, "listening to my mother's desire, you didn't grant the particular thing she asked for then, but instead, the overall prayer she constantly made on my behalf for my salvation."*

afterward, when the impulse has subsided, and we think things through, we begin to look for ways to get released from our pledges. What sickening examples of man's deceitfulness! He entangles his soul in the snares of death, who takes back for unholy use what has already been consecrated to God, and who, after he has vowed something to the Lord, finds a way to withdraw his vow and deprive God of what is rightfully His. Withdrawal of the gift proves the prior withdrawal of the heart. Let Ananias and Sapphira testify that God is a jealous God.[l] Fulfill your rash promises and be faithful to those you make thoughtfully and prayerfully. *Before* entering into the service of God, find out everything that is required. Beware of spiritual commitments based solely upon emotion. Commitments on emotion are far different from those on deep, solid, permanent principles. Whatever the cost, be true to the consecration of yourself as "a living and holy sacrifice"[m] on the altar of your God.

[l] Acts 5:1–10, with Deut 4:24
[m] Rom 12:1

26 *A wise king winnows the wicked,*
And drives the threshing *wheel over them.*

THE GREAT SIFTING DAY

Solomon, as *a wise king,* was constantly looking over his own responsibilities. His standard was not to commit wickedness himself,[n] nor to allow it in his people; to *winnow,* not to encourage, *the wicked.* As the farmer's *wheel,* gathered the grain, cut the straw, and separated the chaff;[18] his sifting administration of justice brought the wheel of vengeance on *the wicked,* and *winnowed* them as worthless chaff,[o] or crushed them in ruin.[p] It was the same spirit in which his father David destroyed them when they boldly came to him for his support.[q] Godly Asa cast out wickedness from the high place nearest his own throne and heart.[r] Amaziah justly punished it with death.[s] Nehemiah—that true reformer—rebuked it even in the family of the high priest.[t] But it is the King of Kings alone that can make this separation complete. He often sifts His people by trial, to produce in them, greater purity and full preservation.[u] But what will it be, when He

[n] Verse 8: Prov 16:12. Comp. 1 Kings 14:16
[o] Ps 1:4
[p] 1 Kings 2:25–46
[q] 2 Sam 1:2, 16; 4:5, 12. Comp. Ps 101:7, 8
[r] 2 Chron 15:16
[s] 2 Chron 24:25; 25:3, 4
[t] Neh 13:28, 29
[u] Amos 9:9

[18] *Isa 28:28, 29. This is an obvious allusion to the way of threshing in the East. One mode was by a wagon, having* wheels, *with iron teeth like a saw. The axle was armed with notched* wheels *throughout. It moved upon three rollers armed with iron teeth, or wheels, to cut the straw—See Bishop LOWTH'S* note on Isa 28:27. *Comp. Amos 1:3.*

shall come with "His winnowing fork ... in His hand, and He will thoroughly clean His threshing floor"![v] What a *winnowing* of chaff there will be! Not the least bit will go into the garner. Not a grain of wheat will be cast away. O my soul! how will you fare at this great sifting day! "Who can endure the day of His coming? And who can stand when He appears?"[w]

[v] Matt 3:12
[w] Mal 3:2

27 *The spirit of man is the lamp of the* LORD,
Searching all the innermost parts of his being.

THE CANDLE OF THE LORD

We are placed under a solemn system of divine government. Infallible judgment is constantly exercised, our principles examined, their standard estimated, and sentence pronounced. There ought to be something in the soul that acknowledges the judgment of God. That's why conscience is often called—God in man. God has not left Himself without witness in His own benighted world.[x] He brings the searching light of *His bright lamp* in the darkness. At the first creation, God's lamp was exceedingly bright, as it shone in man's little world.[y] But every faculty of man's being took part in the ruin of the Fall. Still there was enough left in man's inner mind and conscience to reveal God's perfections, the just penalty of sin,[z] and faint glimpses of right and wrong standards,[a] even in the thick darkness of heathenism. Yet dim, indeed, is *this lamp* unless it is lighted at God's *lamp.*[b] But when the Word and Spirit of God give light to it, it will effectually perform its important offices—(as Bishop Reynolds defines them)—"direction, conviction, and consolation";[19] not only showing the outward acts, but also *searching the innermost parts of man's being*—all the hidden acts and conduct of the inner man.[c] This unwelcome intruder follows everywhere, interpreting the administration of the rod, not—as men would have it—as the incidents or phenomena of the day, but as righteous punishment. Certainly, the ungodly man would be glad if he could put out God's lamp. But he is too great a coward to venture into his secret chamber in the dark. He "hates the light,"[d] which, in spite of all his opposition, still drags forth into day many secret, lurking evils; never permit-

[x] Acts 14:16, 17
[y] Gen 1:26
[z] Rom 1:20, 21, 32
[a] Rom 2:14, 15
[b] Prov 6:23; Ps 119:105
[c] 1 Cor 2:11. Comp. Job 32:8
[d] John 3:20

[19] *Treatise on the Passions, chap. 41.*

ting the pleas: Is it not a little one? Whatever his happy, thoughtless pleasures, might have been, the time will come, when he must leave them, and be alone. And then, "What is all that a man can enjoy in this way for a week, a month, a year, compared with what he feels for one hour, when his conscience shall take him aisde, and rate him by himself?" asked South in *Sermon on Prov 3:17*.

Most valuable also is *this lamp,* throwing the light of God upon the narrow path; so that we are not exceedingly careful in small matters, but negligent in the more important ones; and we are still curious in substantial points, and yet not careless in minor things; regarding no duty so small that it should be neglected, and no care so great that it is beyond our best efforts to cope with.

Now let me ask—when God causes *his lamp* to shed a clearer light, can I endure it? Do I welcome the hateful discoveries it brings out? Do I value its light, as opening the secret communion between a sinner and a holy, jealous God? Do I exercise myself to preserve the light from being dimmed in the atmosphere of sin, and to guard its purity, as the means of establishing my confidence with God?[e] Oh! let there be no *innermost part* of my soul, where I am not most willing, most earnest, to bring *the lamp of the Lord,* that all secret indulgences may be searched out and mortified. "He who practices the truth comes to the light, that his deeds may be manifested as having been wrought in God."[f]

[e] Acts 24:16; 1 John 3:20, 21

[f] John 3:21

28 *Loyalty and truth preserve the king,*
And he upholds his throne by righteousness.

Punishment is indeed a necessary security against the infringement of the law.[g] Yet a wise *king* will follow the example of the great sovereign, and make judgment "His extraordinary work," and mercy his delight."[h] And so long as sacred *truth* is his guiding principle, the abuse of *loyalty* need not be greatly feared. No, *loyalty is the upholding* pillar *of His throne.*[i] But who doesn't know, that, though *truth* commands reverence, it is *loyalty* that wins the heart? Solomon himself had a strong bodyguard, for the safety of his person.[j] Yet were the *loyalty and truth* of His government, not only the most spendid jewels of his crown, but "the best guard of His body, and supporters of His throne," said Trapp.

[g] Verse 26

[h] Comp. Isa 28:21; Mic 7:18

[i] Isa 16:5

[j] Song of Sol 3:7

How wonderful is this combination in the administration of the Great *King!* "Righteousness and justice are the foundation of Thy throne; *loving kindness and truth* go before Thee."[k] Much brighter is the manifestation of these glorious perfections in that great work, by which God sacrificed even His Beloved Son, that man might be saved without the tarnish of one spot upon his infinitely adorable name.[l]

[k] Ps 89:14

[l] Ps 85:10

29 *The glory of young men is their strength,*
And the honor of old men is their gray hair.

THE GLORIES OF YOUTH AND OLD AGE

Every stage of life has its peculiar honor and privilege. "Youth is the glory of nature, and *strength is the glory of youth.* Old age is the majestic beauty of nature, and the *gray head* is the majestic *beauty,* which nature hath given to old age," said Jermin. Yet these pictures describe the use, not the abuse. It is their youth usefully exercised, especially consecrated to God, and employed for His glory. Otherwise, as an occasion of cruelty,[m] or vain-glorious boast,[n] *its strength* is its shame, and will end in vanity.[o] The silver crown brings honor, reverence, and authority—but only in the way of righteousness.[p]

[m] 2 Sam 2:14–16

[n] Jer 9:23

[o] Isa 40:30

[p] Prov 16:31

Yet *the honor of the gray head* is most likely to be found, *where the strength and glory of youth* have been dedicated to God. The young plant, stunted, and deformed in its youth, will generally carry its crookedness into advancing growth. But who can calculate what the extent of fruitfulness may be, where the beginning of our strength—"the dew" of our youth—has been given to the Lord?[q] Let youth and age, however, both beware of defacing their glory. Each has advantages over the other in some things and disadvantages in others. Therefore, they shouldn't envy or despise each other. The world—the state—the church needs them both—*the strength of youth for energy* and the maturity of *age* for wisdom.

[q] Ps 110:3; Ps 92:13–15

30 *Stripes that wound scour away evil,*
And strokes reach *the innermost parts.*

BLESSED PUNISHMENT!

Punishment is the Lord's way of bringing pain to a person's flesh to bring the spirit under control; sometimes even "the destruction of his flesh, that his spirit may be saved in the day of the Lord Jesus."[r] It describes not the gentle stroke, but the severity of parental discipline; not by whim or impulse, and certainly not in anger, but for profit.[s] The diseased body needs medicine no less than food, both for healing and enablement to receive nourishment from its food; the diseased soul needs chastening no less than consolation, and as the main preparation for consolation. But if the *stripes that wound*—the mark of severe chastisement—*scours away evil,* is it not a lesser evil, serving as the means of subduing a greater evil? Do not the Lord's *strokes reach the innermost parts*? Miserable beyond measure is the untamed stubbornness of self-will. A gentle stroke is first tried. When this remedy fails, then the *stripes* are needful. Manasseh's Babylonish chains doubtless prevented the "eternal bonds under darkness."[t] Similar discipline was effectual with Israel, the prodigal son,[u] and the immoral Corinthians.[v] Multitudes have borne witness to the love, wisdom, and power of their Father's discipline—"disciplined by the Lord in order that we may not be condemned along with the world."[w] *The evil was scoured away;* and those, who groaned under *the stripes,* to all eternity will tune their harps to the song—"I know, O Lord, that Thy judgments are righteous, and that in faithfulness Thou hast afflicted me."[x]

Child of God! Think of your Father's character. "He Himself knows our frame." And "He does not afflict willingly."[y] No more will be given in weight or measure than is needed.[z] But truly blessed are *the stripes* that humble and break the proud will.[a] Rich indeed are "peaceful fruit of righteousness" from the conflict and suffering of the flesh.[b]

[r] 1 Cor 5:5
[s] Heb 12:10
[t] 2 Chron 33:12, 13, with Jude 6
[u] Luke 15:16–20
[v] 2 Cor 2:6–8
[w] 1 Cor 11:32
[x] Ps 119:75
[y] Ps 103:14; Lam 3:33
[z] Isa 27:8; Jer 10:24
[a] Jer 31:18–20
[b] Job 34:31, 32; 36:9, 10; Isa 27:9; Heb 12:11

CHAPTER TWENTY-ONE

1 *The king's heart is* like *channels of water in the hand of the* LORD;
He turns it wherever He wishes.

GOD AND THE KING'S HEART

Most thinking persons acknowledge God as the door of all things. On inert matter He acts by physical force; in brute animals, by instinct and appetite; in intelligent beings, by motives suited to their faculties, in His redeemed people, by the influence of grace. We are here reminded of one course of His providential acting. The general truth of man's entire dependence is stated earlier and is taught by the strongest possible illustration—God's uncontrollable sway upon the most absolute of all wills—*the king's heart.*

The channels of water are an apt emblem of this agency. Its commencement is a single spring; scarcely capable of turning a handmill to grind a day's corn. But increased by other small or great streams joining with it, it may turn hundreds of mills and provide food for thousands. So the thoughts of *the king's heart* are first a single desire for the good of his subjects; which, strengthened by additional ideas, drawn from his mental resources, becomes, finally full accomplishment. But after all, God who is the great sovereign *turns* the most despotic rule and all political projects, to His own purposes, with the same ease, that *the channels of water are turned* by every curve of the river.[1] While the course of the river is directed, yet *the waters* flow naturally and unforced on their own level. But *the king's heart* is di-

[1] *The allusion evidently is to channels made for the distribution of waters according to will, for irrigation of gardens or fields—See PAXTON'S Illustrations, i. 173., Bishop LOWTH'S note on Isa 1:30.*

rected as a responsible agent, without interfering with the moral liberty of his will.

Nehemiah fully recognized this privilege, when, having a favor to ask of the king, he "prayed to the God of heaven."[a] And indeed Scripture witness is plentiful. Abimelech's *heart was in the hand of the Lord* for good.[b] Pharaoh's heart was turned toward Joseph.[c] The Babylonian monarchs showed kindness to Daniel and his captive brethren.[d] The Persian monarchs supported and assisted in the building of the temple.[e] The hearts of wicked kings are alike in *the hand of the Lord;*[f] yet He has no part in their wickedness.[g] The hatred of Pharaoh, the ambition of Sennacherib and Nebuchadnezzar[h] were His instruments for His own purposes. Ahab's murderous heart was restrained and even made to accomplish the downfall of Baal.[i] The counsels of the kings of the earth against Christ were under God's control.[j] So "the wrath of man shall Thee praise; with a remnant of wrath Thou shalt gird Thyself."[k] So an almighty agency is visible by its effects in the minutest affairs. Ahasuerus's sleepless nights;[l] Nebuchadnezzar's attempts to foretell the future by mystic arts;[m] appointment of the year of general taxation[n]—these seemingly unimportant events were turning points in the dispensations of God, full of immensely momentous results.

[a]Neh 2:4, 5
[b]Gen 20:6; Ps 105:14, 15
[c]Gen 41:37–45
[d]Dan 1:19; 2:48; 3:30; 6:1–3, 28; Ps 106:46
[e]Ezra 1:1; 6:22; 7:27; 9:9; Neh 1; 11:4–9
[f]Rev 17:16, 17
[g]Exod 1:8–22; Ps 105:25
[h]Isa 10:7; Jer 25
[i]1 Kings 18:10, 40
[j]Acts 4:25–28. Comp. John 19:10
[k]Ps 76:10
[l]Esther 6:1, 2
[m]Ezek 21:21
[n]Luke 2:1

Knowing this, we are encouraged to turn all anxious care for the church to her great head; to rejoice that not kings, but the King of Kings reigns.[o] And shall we not be quickened to earnest prayer for our rulers,[p] that their *hearts being in the Lord's hand, as channels of water,* may desire to rule for His glory, as princesses for nurses[q] to His people.

[o]Isa 9:6
[p]1 Tim 2:1–3
[q]Isa 49:23

2 *Every man's way is right in his own eyes,*
But the L*ORD weighs the hearts.*

LORD, SHOW ME TO MYSELF!

Let us be thankful for the repetition[r] of this mighty Proverb; most valuable for the close probing of our hearts, and the testing of the spirituality of our profession. So "the heart is more deceitful than all else"[s] that it deceives, not others only, but—what even Satan never does—itself. Every intelligent Christian bears painful

[r]Prov 16:2
[s]Jer 17:9

witness to this self-deception. How differently do we judge the same action in ourselves and in others. How often do we excuse if not justify, in ourselves the very habits, which we condemn in others. Therefore, the prayer of the Psalmist is never out of season—"Search me, O God, and know my heart; Try me and know my anxious thoughts."[t] There's nobody in the world about whom we make so many mistakes as ourselves. But, oh to be approved of God in heart, and in sincerity—that's no common mercy!

[t] Ps 139:23

Hid as the self-deluding professing believer is from himself, *his way is right in his own eyes.* But is it right in God's eyes? *The Lord judges the heart*—a solemn and rousing reminder! He thoroughly reads every heart. And what defilement He sees in those *ways of a man* that are *most right in his own eyes!* Saul thought that he was serving God acceptably. But the all-searching eye discovered pride, covetousness, disobedient rejection of his God.[u] What is more self-satisfying than the soul's strict fast and humiliation? But Saul's wrong motive marred the sacrifice. Did ye at all fast to me, even to me?[v] Little did the self-complacent king suspect the spiritual pride, false confidence, and worldliness, which, God, in his deep heart-searching, brought to view.[w] And how much vile mixture is hidden even in a sound-hearted profession of faith! The disciples covered their own spirit by pretending great zeal for their Master.[x] *The Lord weighs the heart.* He "weighs the motives";[y] proving exactly what is of Himself, and what is of a baser kind; what, and how much, there is of God, and what there is of man. The principles of the heart lie deep. The work may be good in itself. But what are the ends? The same work, according to its end, may be accepted, or be cast away. Jehonadab and Jehu both were engaged in the same exterminating work. With the one it was right service; with the other, vile hypocrisy.[z] Self-distrust is therefore the wisdom of true godliness;[a] daily, hourly, trembling in ourselves; yet boldly grounding our confidence in God! Except for the covering of the High Priest, how could we stand for one moment under the piercing eyes of our Judge? Did our dearest earthly friend know what was passing in our thoughts at any one hour, could he ever regard us worthy

[u] 1 Sam 15:13–26
[v] Zech 7:6; Isa 58:5; Jer 2:35
[w] Matt 19:21
[x] Luke 9:54
[y] Prov 16:2
[z] 2 Kings 10:15
[a] Prov 28:26

of his confidence? Wouldn't his heart revolt from contact with such vileness? Yet does our gracious Lord—*while weighing our hearts,* and knowing all their hidden corruptions—forgive, accept, yes, and even rejoice in us as His people.

3 *To do righteousness and justice*
Is desired by the LORD *rather than sacrifice.*

SACRIFICE OR SERVICE?

Did Solomon mean to undervalue *sacrifice?* Never! No man ever more highly honored it.[b] Perhaps the splendor of his sacrificial service may have given rise to the frequent national perverted trust in external forms. *Sacrifice* was appointed as a type of Christ who was the great sacrifice for sin.[c] But never was it intended to take the place of that universal moral obedience, which the law of God had from the beginning indispensably required. Yet how soon man mistook the intention of the practice! How easily did he substitute the offering of bulls and goats for the more self-denying service of the heart.[d] Israel abounded in the observance of their outward ceremonials, while indulging the sin of Sodom and Gomorrah.[e] Their offerings to God took the place of their duties as God's people. And so with us! We tithe so carefully, but neglect "the weightier provisions of the law: *justice* and mercy and faithfulness."[f] Justly therefore did our Lord commend the judgment and wisdom of the scribe, who gave due place and proportion to both ceremonial and moral service.[g] Both are His requirements; and a well-instructed conscience will strive to fulfill both. Yet, plainly, God has in some instances, done away with ceremonial service,[h] but never moral service.[i] He has often accepted the moral without the ceremonial observance; but never the ceremonial without the moral. What would the world be without such *righteousness and justice,* which at once establish the "throne,"[j] "exalt a nation,"[k] and make real to their disciples a true interest in the richest of all possessions—the love of God![l]

There certainly is no sacrifice we could put in the place of these invaluable principles. Nevertheless, the same preference, the same exaltation, of external service

[b] 1 Kings 3:4; 8:64
[c] Heb 10:12
[d] 1 Sam 15:22; Ps 1:13, 14
[e] Isa 1:11; Jer 7:22; Hos 6:6; Amos 5:21; Acts 7:42; Mic 6:6–8
[f] Matt 23:23
[g] Mark 12:34
[h] Matt 12:7; Acts 10:34, 35
[i] Matt 22:37–39
[j] Prov 16:12
[k] Prov 14:34
[l] Prov 15:9. Comp. Isa 64:5

prevails among us—something to recommend us to God's favor; something easier and less humbling than the "living and holy sacrifice"[m] for His service. You, who profess Christ, take a good look at the character of your service. Let it be free and cheerful; not painful duty. You may look in weakness but let it always be in willingness with love. What do you see? Are you resting in the shell and surface, or are you worshiping in the spirituality of service? Do you hear the voice calling you away from dead forms, to seek the living power of godliness? Cain brought his sacrifice, not his heart. If you speak more, "what do you do more *than others?*"[n] Remember, those externals that stand in the place of a consecrated heart are the delusion of the great deceiver. Keep your heart with God. Walk with Him in the honest exercise of Christian obligation; honoring God's stamp on every commandment; making conscience of every duty; and though we come short of every one, yet daring not to neglect any.[o]

[m]Rom 12:1
[n]Matt 5:47
[o]Ps 119:5, 6, 128

4 *Haughty eyes and a proud heart,*
The lamp [AV—*plowing*] *of the wicked, is sin.*

SINFUL PLOWING

Another stamp of abomination upon pride![p] We cannot mistake the mind of God so frequently revealed. Yet this sin assumes so many shapes that, until the Spirit of God shows a man to himself, he rejects the idea of having any concern for it. Instead, he will be proud of his very pride, proud of a high spirit. He will regard those Christians, mean and cowardly, who, in the true spirit of the gospel, yield their right to a stronger hand.[q]

But not only the haughtiness, but even the *natural actions—the plowing of the wicked, for example, is sin.* "This is a difficult statement; who can listen to it?"[r] How can *the plowing* of the soil, in itself a duty,[s] become *a sin?* Because it is the motive that determines the act. The most natural actions are intended for Christian ends.[t] Therefore, they become moral actions, good or bad according to their own motives. The man, who *plows* the soil, acknowledging God in his work, and seeking His strength and blessing—does it acceptably to the glory of God. It is essentially a religious action. But *the wicked man,* who does the same work without any regard to

[p]Prov 3:34; 8:13; 16:5
[q]Matt 5:39–41; 1 Cor 6:7
[r]John 6:60
[s]Gen 3:19
[t]1 Cor 10:31; Col 3:17

God—for want of a godly end, *his plowing is sin.*[2] His idleness is sin against a plain command.[u] His work is the sin of ungodliness, putting God out of His own world. The substance of his act is good. But the corrupt principle defiles the very best actions.[v] "Every intent of the thoughts of the heart was only evil continually."[w] If the fountainhead be bitter, how can the waters be pure? Sin indeed defiles every motive in the Christian's heart. But *here* it is the *substance* of sin. In the one case, it is infirmity of walk in the straight path. In the other, it is habitual walk in a crooked path. With *the wicked*—his eating as well as his gluttony; his drinking as well as his drunkenness; his business dealings, and his buying and selling, as well as his greed, and excessive love of the world, are all set down and regarded by God as sins, and such sins as He must take responsibility for with God. What a fearful condition is his! If he could only see it for himself! Whether he prays,[x] or neglects to pray,[y] it is hateful in God's sight. He cannot but sin; and yet he is fully accountable for his sin. To die, is to plunge into ruin.[z] To live unsaved is even worse; it is daily "storing up wrath for yourself in the day of wrath."[a] Wouldn't it be better, then, for him to leave his duties undone? Man's helplessness "must not prejudice God's authority, nor diminish man's duty," said Bishop Reynolds (*Works,* p. 94). What should he do then? Let him learn the absolute necessity, the vital change in his life and heart—"You must be born again."[b] The leper taints everything that he touches. But let him turn to God, the great physician, whose word is sovereign healing,[c] whose divine blood cleanses from every spot.[d] His nature once cleansed, his works will be clean. His thoughts and principles, all will be for the glory of God; all acceptable to God.

[u] 2 Thess 3:10
[v] Titus 1:15
[w] Gen 6:5
[x] Verse 27. Prov 15:8; Isa 1:13
[y] Ps 10:4
[z] Ps 60:17; Matt 25:41–46
[a] Rom 2:5
[b] John 3:7
[c] Matt 8:3
[d] 1 John 1:7

5 *The plans of the diligent* lead *surely to advantage,*
But everyone who is hasty comes *surely to poverty.*

HASTE MAKES POVERTY

The diligent is usually contrasted with the lazy,[e] but here with the *hasty*. *The plans* of each produce their own

[e] Prov 10:4; 12:24, 27; 13:4

[2] *Holy intention is to the actions of a man that, which the soul is to the body, or form to its matter, or the root to the tree, or the sun to the world, or the fountain to the river, or the base to a pillar. Without these, the body is a dead trunk, the matter is sluggish, the tree is a block, the world is darkness, the river is quickly dry, the pillar rushes into flatness and ruin, and the action is sinful, or unprofitable and vain"—Bishop TAYLOR'S Holy Living, chap. 1: Sec. 3.*

fruit, *for advantage or for poverty.* The patient, plodding, hard-working man perseveres in spite of all difficulties; content to increase his material possessions by degrees; never relaxing, never yielding to discouragement. This perseverance is profitable under the blessing of God.[f] "You might just as well expect," says an old writer, "riches to rain down from heaven in silver showers, as to provide for your family without hard work in your calling." *Haste* may have perseverance and hard effort marking it. But just as laziness is its defect, undisciplined impulse is its excess. The hand too often goes before and acts without the judgment. So a wise philosopher counsels us—not to measure our success by the effort applied. The test is the advancement of the business. A wise man had this wise saying for people he saw in a hurry to get things done—Slow down a little, friend, so we can get this job done sooner. Use your time carefully, and you save time, but just going through the motions is simply beating the air.

[f]Prov 10:22

The evils of *haste* under wrong impulses are truly fearful. Haste can drive a man into rash projects; and his high delusive hopes turn out to be the short, sure road to *poverty.*[g] By contrast, how rich the harvest of Christian *diligence,* of patient "perseverance in doing good"—"eternal life"?[h] The heavenly race is not to be run by so many spurts but by a steady course. "Run," not with *haste* or *speed,* but *"with endurance* the race that is set before us." Remember the seed that sprang up *in haste* withered.[i] Excitement is delusion and ends in disappointment. What is more important than to cultivate a deep work of grace, throughout our whole being, and abounding with fruit to the glory of God?

[g]Prov 19:2; 23:5; 28:22

[h]Rom 2:7; Heb 6:12

[i]Heb 12:1; Matt 13:20, 21

6 *The getting of treasures by a lying tongue*
Is a fleeting vapor, the pursuit of death.
7 *The violence of the wicked will drag them away,*
Because they refuse to act with justice.

A graphic picture of *the hasty-spirit*—its own dishonest ways lead to poverty. *Treasures may be won by lying;* but they turn out to have no value. They are "put into a purse with holes"[j] and slip away. They are like a ball tossed to and fro in a storm or dust blown about by the

[j]Hag 1:6

wind.[k] Unrighteous gain is a costly bargain. The wrath of God mingles bitterness with the wages of sin.[l] Judas eagerly desired to get rid of his ill-gotten treasure that had so quickly become an unbearable curse. Yet he could not escape from his torturing conscience. His misery drove him to suicide.[m]

[k] Prov 10:2; 22:8; Jer 17:11
[l] Zech 5:4. Comp. Isa 1:23, 24; Jer 7:9–11, 15; Ezek 22:13, 14; Hab 2:6–8
[m] Matt 27:5

In fact, this seems to be the way of the ungodly. It's as though they seek death as their reward, they are so in love with *eternal death!* Their sin is the seed of their destruction. Their *getting of treasures* virtually destroys them.[n] And there is no one to blame but themselves! They can't lay it to ignorance or inconsideration, because it is really willful sin that destroys them. "Do you not know that the unrighteous shall not inherit the kingdom of God?"[o] That "the wages of sin," invariably, inevitably—"is *death*"?[p] What else did *the getting of treasures* of Achan and Gehazi bring to them?[q] Short was the enjoyment of Ananias and Sapphira in the part of the price kept back for themselves at the expense of *a lying tongue.* Sudden and everlasting *destruction* was their doom—a solemn warning to worldly, half-hearted, self-deceivers, who profess to know God.[3]

[n] Prov 1:11, 18, 19; 22:22, 23; Hab 2:10–13
[o] 1 Cor 6:9
[p] Rom 6:23
[q] Josh 7:21–26; 2 Kings 5:20–27

8 *The way of a guilty man is crooked,*
But as for the pure, his conduct is upright.

Observe the striking contrast between man by nature and man by grace. Who will say that man is today what he was when he first came from his Maker's hands?[r] How is he born? Wild, as a beast of the field.[s] And how soon he develops his nature! "Foolishness is bound up in the heart of a child; childhood and the prime of life are fleeting."[t] Need we add that this is *a crooked way?* How distant from the God, who made and loved him! Turned from God; "turned to his own way";[u] with no law but his lust, no rule but his will;[v] loving his own liberty, but despising true liberty; made by his own self-delusion the "slaves of corruption";[w] ignorant, morally unrestrained, wasting his life in luxurious pleasures; desiring only to

[r] Eccl 7:29
[s] Job 11:12
[t] Prov 22:15; Eccl 11:10
[u] Isa 53:6
[v] Eph 2:3; Titus 3:3
[w] 2 Peter 2:19

[3] *Prov 12:19; Acts 5:1–10. Aggravated destruction, probably with shame seems to be implied. Comp. 2 Sam 12:31; Heb 11:37; Also Luke 12:46. "Search your chests; search your hearts, all ye that hear me this day; and if any of you find any of this adulterated gold among your heaps, away with it. As you love yourselves, away with it. Else know, that (as Chrysostom wittily says) 'You have locked up a thief in your counting-house, which shall carry away all: and—if ye look not to it the sooner—your soul with it!' "—Bishop HALL'S* Sermon on the Righteous Mammon. Works, *v. 109, 110.*

be the fountain of his own happiness, the maker of his own sufficiency.

Take him in his noblest path—the pursuit of wisdom. Here, too, *his way is guilty and crooked.* Forbidden wisdom his delight—wisdom, not as wisdom, but as forbidden; intruding into the counsels, prying into the ark, of God?[x] Such was the first appetite of stubborn willfulness, not desiring to know God, which "is life eternal";[y] but to know as God knows,[z] which was pride in its principle, and death in its issue.

[x]Col 2:18
[y]John 17:3
[z]Gen 3:5

But man, by grace made *pure,* "created in the likeness of God"[a]—mark him well. His will is now conformed to God; his actions are regulated by this perfect standard. Therefore, his rule and aim being right, *his conduct is upright.*[b] He lives now, as does his divine Savior, "to God."[c] Such is the dignity of his great object! Such his fellowship with his glorious head! Such his token of heaven and growing fitness for it! Oh! the mercy of being turned from our own *crooked way* to the *pure service* of our God! Yet so much in him remains uncontrollable. And there is still so much self-deceit; such twisted workings of depravity! "O heart, heart"—cries a deeply-taught, earnest Christian, Rev. John Berridge—"what art thou? The vainest, craftiest, wickedest thing in nature!" And truly, when the stroke goes deep into the soul, when the inner circle, the very center of our being, is reached and probed, what hidden evils come to light! O my God! Show me to myself, so far as I can bear the sight, that I may be kept humbled and self-abased; always near my Savior; always applying His precious blood; always covering myself in His *pure* and perfect work of righteousness!

[a]Eph 4:24
[b]Titus 1:15
[c]Rom 6:10, 11

9 ***It is better to live in a corner of a roof,***
Than in a house shared with a contentious woman.

GOD'S MARRIAGE COUNSELING

In the spacious houses in the East, several families lived together in groups. *A contentious woman* would be a grievous disturbance to such a community; and a peaceable man would prefer the *corner of a roof,*[d] exposed to all the inconvenience of wind and weather, to the ample accommodation of a house in an atmosphere of

[d]Comp. Deut 22:8; Josh 2:6–8; 2 Sam 11:2; Acts 10:9

contention.[e] A solitary life outside the house would be better than a quarrelsome life within. Some times of comfort might be enjoyed outside the home, but none in it. This trial becomes so much greater, when it comes from a man's own flesh; when she, who ought to be a "crown to her husband," becomes "rottenness to his bones";[f] when she, who is supposed to be his choicest treasure, becomes his piercing scourge. It can't be other than miserable for them, who are of necessity compelled to live with one another, but can't live peacefully together. The intent of God's ruling is contradicted here. For it would seem "good for the man to be alone," rather than that his "helper"[g] should turn to be his hindrance and his curse. But how many bring this bitter trouble upon themselves! They plunge into marriage as an adventure; with no thought of the obligations involved, the temptations to be avoided, the crosses to be borne. They never looked to God for guidance in this all-important matter—the choice of a life's mate! And so, not asked for from the Lord, the wife doesn't come from the Lord, and she comes without His blessing.[h] Sinful pleasure, greed, or waywardness, brings only disaster that can't be counterbalanced by high position or riches.

The only safe entrance into this honorable estate is, when each party (as Chrysostom instructs) commits himself to God—"Bestow me as Thou wilt, and on whom Thou wilt." The only security for happiness is, when, with due regard, for mutual fitness, mutual love is reverently founded upon God's command, which makes of them "one flesh."[i] *Contentions* will be restrained by preventive habits of Christian discipline; each considering that anger improves nothing, and patience helps much, and that it is far better to give place to each other than to "the devil."[j] The husband in his claim for submission will remember, that he has found, *not a servant, but a wife.* She, on her side, will not forget the beauty and order of graceful sacrifice and ready agreement; and that her glory is departed from her, should she lose "the quality of a gentle and quiet spirit," precious in the sight of man, and "in the sight of God."[k] When each is faithful in his vows to the other, their marriage becomes firm and stable.

[e] Verse 19; Prov 25:24

[f] Prov 12:4

[g] Gen 2:18

[h] Prov 19:14; 18:22

[i] Gen 2:24, with 24:67

[j] Eph 4:27

[k] 1 Peter 3:4

10 *The soul of the wicked desires evil;*
His neighbor finds no favor in his eyes.

SELF: GOD OF THE WICKED

A lively portrait of Satan himself! not only doing, but *desiring evil! Evil* is the very nature of the *wicked.* Is it any wonder, then, that his very *soul desires it?* His heart "is given fully to do evil."[l] He craves it as his appetite, his main delight.[m] What preparation "for destruction" must there be in "vessels" so full of sin and wrath![n] And here lies the difference between the godly and *the wicked;* not that the one is pure from evil and the other commits it; but that the one does it because he is constrained to do it; the other, from delight. The one testifies—What I hate—the other—What *my soul desireth*—that do I.[o] As the fruit of this native cherished principle, *self,* to *the wicked,* becomes both his god and his object. He is so intent upon his own lust, that, not only his enemy, or a stranger, but even *his neighbor,* who might have a claim upon him, *find no favor in his eyes.* His love does not extend beyond his own door.[p] No one who stands in the way of his own interest, remains a friend for long. In fact, everyone he associates with must give way to his selfish gratification.

[l] Eccl 8:11
[m] Prov 4:16; 12:12; 13:19
[n] Rom 9:22
[o] Rom 7:15–21, with 6:12, 16, 17
[p] 1 Sam 25:11

Such is sin in its hateful character and deadly fruits. "Men will be lovers of self, lovers of money, boastful . . . unholy!"[q] But look at the man of God with his heart enlarged and softened by the life-changing influence of the gospel. Where is *the neighbor* in distress that does not *find favor in his eyes?*[r] "Love . . . does not seek its own"[s] —is his spirit. "Bear one another's burdens"[t]—is his rule. "In the body . . . the members should have the same care for one another."[u] Oh! for a larger measure of this gracious spirit, as "the dew of Hermon, coming down upon the mountains of Zion,"[v] upon the church of God!

[q] 2 Tim 3:2; Titus 3:3
[r] Luke 10:31–35
[s] 1 Cor 13:5
[t] Gal 6:2
[u] 1 Cor 12:25
[v] Ps 133:3

11 *When the scoffer is punished, the naive becomes wise;*
But when the wise is instructed, he receives knowledge.

PROFITABLE AFFLICTION

This Proverb in substance has been given before[w] as an instructive illustration of the Lord's providential dis-

[w] Prov 19:25

cipline. No stroke of his rod is without its effect. The blow that strikes one, reaches two—*the scoffer for punishment; the naive for improvement.* The *scoffer* describes a character far more common than is usually conceived. It includes much more than the evil outbreaking of the revolting heart. Under more decent, external dress, we often see the utter lack of that awful reverence for God, that humility of mind, that submission of our will, that surrender of desire, which is the glory and happiness of those above, who "cast their crowns before the throne." The very idea of the grace of God is an object of scorn and contempt. We don't wonder, therefore, that the daring offender should be marked out for *punishment.* And yet, if (as is too frequently the case) *the punishment* doesn't correct *the scoffer,*[x] at least it becomes a lesson to the *naive* one, who had been in danger of being misled by the scoffer's example.[y] Why even the man of God learns a lesson of love mingled with wholesome trembling, from this fearful demonstration of divine authority and power—"Thou hast removed all the wicked of the earth like dross; therefore I love Thy testimonies. My flesh trembles for fear of Thee; and I am afraid of Thy judgments."[z]

[x]Rev 4:10; Isa 1:5; Jer 5:3

[y]Ps 64:7

[z]Ps 119:119, 120. Comp. Heb 10:26–31

Though already taught of God, *the wise* thankfully receives additional knowledge through the Lord's daily instruction.[a] Among his most fruitful lessons are the *instructions* of the rod—*instructions* (mark the difference of the term)—not *punishment.* Often the teaching rod confirms the teaching law. And the well-disciplined child of God is ready with his acknowledgments—"Blessed is the man whom Thou *chasten,* O Lord, and dost *teach* out of Thy law." And "I will bless the Lord who has counseled me; Indeed, my mind instructs me in the night." And "it is good for me that I was afflicted, that I may learn Thy statutes."[b]

[a]Prov 1:5

[b]Ps 94:12; 16:7; 119:71

12 *The righteous one considers the house of the wicked,*
Turning the wicked to ruin.

WHAT FAITH SEES

The punishment of *the wicked* spells out a lesson, not only of love and trembling, but of *wise consideration.* Yet the perplexing mysteries of God are many. The *righteous*

[c] Ps 73:2–14

[d] Ps 73:16–22

[e] Gen 18:25

[f] Ps 74:22; 82:8; 2 Thess 2:8

[g] Job 20:4, 5; Ps 37:35, 36

[h] Prov 12:7; 13:3–6; 15:25; 2 Peter 2:4–9

[i] Job 21:28–30; Ps 58:10, 11

[j] Job 22:15–20; Ps 73:23–26

man doesn't always see things in their proper perspective. The prosperity of the wicked staggers his faith, excites his envy, and brings on hard thoughts of God.[c] But when he looks at things with the eye of faith, he sees far beyond the dazzling glory of the present moment. He sees, not the outer splendor and adornments, but its final end. Then he justifies God and puts himself to shame.[d] "Shall not the Judge of all the earth deal justly?"[e] Here we rest, until He shall "arise, O God, and plead Thine own cause," and "with the breath of His mouth and bring to an end by . . . His coming"[f] the very essence of evil, wiping it out forever. Meanwhile, where the superficial eye sees nothing but confusion, *the righteous man should learn* deeply-practical lessons; the short duration of the prosperity,[g] and the certainty of *the overthrow of the wicked;*[h] the assurance of a day of recompense;[i] the contrast of the blessings of the godly for time and for eternity[j]—these are what faith sees. Don't all these things marvelously set forth the perfections of God and call to each of His children—My son, give glory to God?

13 *He who shuts his ear to the cry of the poor*
Will also cry himself and not be answered.

A HELPING HAND—AND A FEELING HEART

[k] Deut 15:7–11; Isa 58:6–9

[l] Rom 12:8; 2 Cor 9:7

[m] 2 Cor 8:1–4

[n] Prov 29:7; Neh 5:1–8

[o] Luke 10:30–32

[p] James 5:4

[q] Luke 18:2–4

If there were no poor, much of the Word of God, applying to their comfort, and directing our obligations, would have been written in vain. The obligation implies not only a helping hand, but a feeling heart; *hearing the cry of the poor* with sympathy,[k] cheerfulness,[l] self-sacrifice.[m] *Shutting the ears* implies cruelty or insensibility;[n] turning away from real and known distress;[o] any kind of oppression; cheating the laborer of his pay,[p] depriving him of the power of earning the necessities of life; and failing to do all in our power, to defend him against oppression.[q]

[r] 2 Thess 3:10

[s] Prov 29:7

To be sure, it may sometimes be our duty to *shut our ears.* The law of God does not tolerate the trade of begging with all its pathetic cries and appeals.[r] To support the poor in his idleness, however compassionate or self-pleasing the motive, is to encourage, if not to participate in sin. Good common sense, not feeling, should direct our charity.[s] Genuine hardship and need causes most of us to want to do all we can to help. We take our responsibility to the poor and needy seriously, and we give as we are able, whether it be much or little. When we must withhold our help to others, let it be in order to keep our feelings of sympathy in proper control, not to indulge our selfishness. We ought to count it a privilege, no less than an obligation, to minister to the poor. Think of it as conforming to our Lord's spirit and work.[t] Don't be miserly in giving because you feel you have so little to offer. Instead, think of the needless expenses that limit our power to help others; think of the luxuries we enjoy that keep us from giving as much as we might to our brethren who are starving around us. All this is, in a very real sense, *shutting our ears* to the cries of the poor. Greed and sensuality harden the heart; and when the heart is hard, the ear is deaf.[u] This sin was wrongfully charged to Job.[v] But wherever it actually exists, the stamp of God's displeasure is found upon it;[w] and the sin of failing to help the needy will, in that great and final day, be openly condemned.[x]

[t]Matt 14:14–21
[u]1 Sam 25:10, 11
[v]Job 22:5–7, with 29:16; 31:16, 17, 20
[w]Prov 11:24, 26; 28:27; Jer 34:10–22; Matt 18:30–34
[x]Matt 25:41–45

And now, as selfish hardness shows that the man has no love for God,[y] he will find no love from God. "Whatever measure you deal out to others, it will be dealt to you in return."[z] Did he *shut his ears to the cry of the poor?* Then God will close His ears against his cry.[a] He that would not give a crumb on earth was denied a drop of water in hell.[b] "For judgment will be merciless to one who has shown no mercy."[c] Professing Christian! Study the character of your God—"full of compassion and . . . merciful";[d] and be like Him. Remember—you should be tender-hearted and show love and mercy toward others.[e]

[y]1 John 3:17
[z]Luke 6:38; Judg 1:6, 7; 1 Sam 15:33
[a]Job 34:24–28; Zech 7:9–13
[b]Luke 16:21, 24, 25
[c]James 2:13
[d]James 5:11
[e]Col 3:12

14 *A gift in secret subdues anger,*
And a bribe in the bosom, strong wrath.

KEEP YOUR HEART IN ORDER

We have noted before,[f] cases of resentment, where a legitimate and prudent distribution of *gifts* may quell the storm and restore the calm. But *a gift in secret* implies something abnormal,[g] otherwise, why should the light be dreaded?[h] Both parties are involved in the guilt. The giver acts as a tempter. The receiver willfully breaks the law of God.[i] The passions of men are easily charmed. But rarely will a covetous man be so angry with his friends, as

[f]Prov 18:16
[g]Prov 17:23
[h]John 3:20
[i]Exod 23:8; Deut 16:19

not to be *subdued with his gift,* especially when, *given in secret,* it tells no tales. A *bribe* to such a man is stronger far than *strong wrath;* and when it has shown its errand, the melting process is rapidly accomplished.[j] So it is that the wounded pride is expelled by another ruling passion—greed! Who then can excuse himself by irresponsibly crying out: "I can't control my passion; I just can't overcome it!" If it can be *subdued* by sordid motives, it leaves us inexcusable, if we do not subdue it by Christian motives. But it is too evident that secret covetousness ruins many an exercise in forbearance. How closely we need to watch and keep our own hearts, in order, as a Christian to walk with God!

[j]Eccl 10:19

15 *The execution of justice is joy for the righteous,*
But is terror to the workers of iniquity.

TRUE SERVICE BRINGS ITS OWN SMILE

It is not that the *righteous does justly.* Conscience may dictate this, at least externally, while the prejudice of the heart is on the side of sin. But *it is joy to the righteous to do it.* His rest, purpose, affections—all center in it. He has as much delight in *the execution of justice,* as "the soul of the wicked desires evil,"[k] as his own soul desired it.[l] *It is joy* but only to the righteous.[m] To the mere professing Christian, it is conviction and fear; the service of a slave. He knows God only as a Master and conceives of Him as a taskmaster. He has never known him as a Father and therefore never served him as a child. But his true service—identifies holiness and happiness, and brings its own smile and income of *joy* with it, as naturally as heat accompanies fire, and beams flow from the sun. And so "the way of the Lord is a stronghold to the upright."[n] Wasn't that true of our beloved Lord? He could say—"I delight to do Thy will, O my God . . . I have food to eat that you do not know about . . . My food is to do the will of Him who sent me, and to accomplish His work."[o] Oh! that the servant might be in spirit like his Lord!

[k]Verse 10
[l]Eph 2:2, 3; Titus 3:3
[m]Ps 32:11; 97:11, 12
[n]Prov 10:29
[o]Ps 40:8; John 4:32–34

So then, do we blame Christianity for the gloom and sadness in the world? The truth is the children of this world have never tasted the clusters of Canaan. So how can they know their sweetness? Christian! Look up and be cheerful, for the honor of your God and His gospel.

Don't live as though you are suffering from some affliction. Instead, live as one snatched from destruction; as a child of God, an heir of heaven. You know far more than you can tell. But you can at least tell enough to make the world inexcusable, if they turn away. And you can let them see, that "the work of righteousness will be peace," and "the yoke" of Christ is easy;[p] and you can show them that the greatest sacrifices for Him are sweet; that there is more pleasure in plucking out the "right eye" for Him, than in using it for sin or for Satan. And then for yourself, think further, if this is the kind of happiness you now enjoy among all hindrances of sin, what will it be, when these hindrances are removed, and we shall serve Him without sin forever![q] If this is what the wilderness is like, what will Canaan be!

[p] Isa 32:17; Matt 11:30; 5:29

[q] Rev 7:15; 22:3

But what do the ungodly know about all this? Sin is to them a mockery,[r] a sport,[s] even a joy.[t] But never can it be their *solid joy.* It is their weariness, never their rest.[u] *To the workers of iniquity* belong only vanity and disappointment, that end in *terror.*[v] Hear the testimony of God—"Destruction and misery are in their paths, and the path of peace have they not known." And "there is 'no peace,' says my God, 'for the wicked.'"[w]

[r] Prov 14:9
[s] Prov 10:23; 26:18, 19
[t] Prov 15:21
[u] Isa 47:13; 57:10, 20; Jer 9:5
[v] Prov 5:22; Matt 7:23

[w] Rom 3:16, 17; Isa 59:7, 8; 57:21

16 *A man who wanders from the way of understanding*
Will rest in the assembly of the dead.

THE WANDERERS

This seems to describe the fearful ruin of those who abandon their faith.[x] God has opened *the way of understanding. Wandering out of it* implies that *the man* was once in it—at least that he was instructed and professed to walk in it. The end of willful wandering is eternal death. Such was the character and end of the wicked son of Jehoshaphat;[y] and the rebellious children of godly Josiah;[z] apostates from the religion received by tradition from their fathers.

[x] Ps 125:5

[y] 2 Chron 21:1, 4–6, 18, 19
[z] 2 Chron 36:1–17; Jer 22:17–19, 28–30

But we don't have to go back into the Old Testament to see those guilty of apostasy. It's very common today, to see the children of godly parents—children who despise their birthright—cast away its privileges. Though, from an early age, they have been instructed in the Holy Scriptures, instead of continuing "in the things" which they

[a]2 Tim 3:14, 15
[b]Jer 14:10
[c]Matt 6:23

have learned "and become convinced of,"[a] they have "loved to wander."[b] They have never really gained a real appreciation of its value. They found the way too confining and too humbling. Novelties have been preferred; self-confidence indulged; self-pleasing delusions cherished; the want of godly sincerity has darkened their path;[c] conscientious error, disguised with outward holiness, is readily accepted, and *the man* totally without solid Scriptural standards, *wanders out of the way of understanding.*

[d]1 Sam 16:14–23

This state of *death* is often connected (and stands out more strongly by the connection) with outward observances of religion, the practice of many moral duties, and with a certain measure of moral taste, partially formed according to Scriptural standards. But there is also occasional conviction that the heart is really wanting; and whatever might be the temporary excitement—like Saul under the soothing notes of the harp of the son of Jesse,[d] there is no change from the state of hardened rebellion against God. The true cause of the death is that in the full blaze of religious knowledge, a living faith is absent. Hence, there is no reality of prayer; therefore no genuine desire, no vital effort, no hearty perseverance. With all his light, knowledge, and privileges, the man is still *a wanderer out of the way of understanding.*

CONGREGATION OF THE DEAD

[e]Isa 53:6
[f]1 Sam 28:12, 13; Zeph 1:4–6

Indeed, *wandering* is the character of man's fallen nature.[e] But the light, convictions, and advantages of instruction he has had, greatly intensify his responsibility.[f] Beware of the first *wandering* step, whether in doctrine or in practice. It may be all that's needed to firmly establish you in a state of apostasy, like Bunyan's blinded *wanderers* in *The Pilgrim's Progress* who were out of the straight path and found among the tombs, *resting in the assembly of the dead.* It will be a special mercy, if the wayward *wanderer* does not find his last and final abode among the mighty dead "for whom the black darkness has been reserved forever."[4] "It would be better for them not to have known the way of righteousness, than having known it, to turn away from the holy commandment de-

[4]*Jude 12, 13. Comp. Isa 14:9; See Prov 2:18; 4:18, 19; 8:35, 36; 12:28; 14:32; in evidence of the knowledge of the future state under the old dispensation.*

livered to them."[g] Such need to remember, that, by *resting in the assembly of the dead,* they show their character, their state, and their home. Though they have been born of godly parents, yet, *wandering from the way of understanding,* they are out of the way of life.

[g]2 Peter 2:21

One can only wish to view such sad apostates, as Bunyan's characters Faithful and Hopeful did, with tears gushing from our eyes, thinking very solemnly about their condition. Don't they stand as warnings to us that we should tremble—yes—be in an "uproar"?[h] While we "stand only by . . . faith," we need to remember the needful caution—"Do not be conceited, but fear"?[i] We need to always combine self-distrust with our Christian confidence; "let us fear lest, while a promise remains of entering His rest, any one of you should seem to come short of it";[j] thankful alike for the warnings to make us fear, and for the encouragements to preserve us from despair.

[h]Ps 2:11
[i]Rom 11:20
[j]Heb 4:1

But the great mass of the world's population are also described here. They never profess; they never have professed. They know that "wisdom shouts in the street," yet they refuse to "hear the voice of charmers."[k] Many will occasionally listen, but still they go "away . . . immediately" forgetting "what kind of person he was."[l] This was true of Noah's mighty generation; and they *rest in the assembly of the dead.*[m] And won't all, who refuse—their opportunities to gain wisdom and depart and turn away—won't they be found to be "dead in . . . trespasses and sins" eternally?[n]

[k]Prov 1:20; Ps 58:5
[l]James 1:24
[m]1 Peter 3:19, 20; 2 Peter 2:5; Gen 6:4
[n]Eph 2:1

17 *He who loves pleasure* will become *a poor man;*
He who loves wine and oil will not become rich.

HOW TO KEEP FROM BECOMING RICH

What then? Aren't we supposed to have *any pleasures?* If this were the case, it would turn people away from Christianity. Actually, *pleasure* is the very character of the ways of God[o]—*pleasure* infinitely more satisfying "than when their grain and new wine abound."[p] Aren't we to rejoice in our earthly comforts? "God . . . richly supplies us with all things to enjoy."[q] This great flow of happiness is more than doubled by the rule of "gratitude."[r] Yet, strange as it may seem, the way to enjoy

[o]Prov 3:17
[p]Ps 4:6, 7
[q]1 Tim 6:17. Comp. Eccl 2:26; 3:22; 9:7–9
[r]1 Tim 4:4, 5

pleasure is not to *love it,* but to live above it;[5] to "rejoice, as though they did not rejoice; and those who use the world, as though they did not make full use of it."[s] The man, who gives his whole heart and time to *the love of pleasure,* and sacrifices all his wisdom and foresight to it, is surely on the high road to poverty.[6] On the same road he finds him that loveth wine, under the power of a "mocker."[t] He that loves oil—one of the most precious fruits of Cannaan[u]—may find, that those who could not live without dainties lost the necessities.[v] But the saddest sight in all the universe is the man, in the prison house of selfishness, who sacrifices his immortal soul to the love of pleasure. Salvation is thrown away as a thing of no consequence.[w] Fearful indeed is *the poverty,* the utter, eternal ruin of this willful, unreasoning passion. "Woe to you who are rich, for you are receiving your comfort in full." And "Child, remember that during your life you received your good things, and likewise Lazarus bad things; but now he is being comforted here, and you are in agony."[x]

[s]1 Cor 7:30, 31

[t]Prov 20:1; 23:21

[u]Deut 8:8; 11:14; Judg 9:9; Ps 23:5; Mic 6:15; Hab 3:17

[v]Isa 32:9–12; 47:8, 9; Zeph 2:15; Rev 18:7

[w]Eccl 11:9; 1 Tim 5:6; 2 Tim 3:4; 1 Peter 4:3–5

[x]Luke 6:24; 16:25. Comp. Ps 17:14

Youth indeed dreams of uninterrupted *pleasure* and is unaware of the misleading appearance of the charming prospects. Yes, earthly joys are vain indeed. They *may* leave us; we *must* leave them. To place our happiness in them, is to build upon the wave, which rolls from under us, and plunges us into the depths of despair.

But the double-minded professing Christian asks: "May we not combine both the *pleasures* of the world and the pleasure of Christianity?" But the object of the man of God is: first, to awaken, then, to satisfy, a holy appetite. And, in order to accomplish this, he knows he must separate himself from worldly pleasure, which so far from quickening or nourishing, tends utterly to quench it.

BABES IN THE CRADLE

"Thrice fools are we," exclaims a glowing Christian, "who, like new babes in the cradle, know not that there is a kingdom before them!" reported Rutherford in *Letters.* Small wonder, then, that those, who do not know heaven,

[5] *It is a fine remark of Cyprian's—"The greatest pleasure* is to have conquered pleasure; *nor is there any greater victory than that, which is gained over our own appetites."*

[6] *Verse 20. The instance of the profligate—5:10, 11; of Samson—Judg 16:1–21; of the Prodigal—Luke 15:13–16.*

try to get everything they can out of *this* life. But shouldn't the heirs of heaven live above the love of earth, having no more sympathy with those devoted to sensual pleasures, than with the pleasures of the pig "wallowing in the mire"? Mark well, then, the danger and temptation, the need for unceasing watchfulness, that you keep your heart, loosened from things of earth and fixed on things above.[y] For, if you are growing in the *love of* earthly *pleasure, you shall be a poor man* indeed. You will be growing indifferent to prayer; heartless and dead to God; fancying shadows to be substance; and despising the true substance as a shadow. Heavenly pleasures will lose their sweetness, as earthly *pleasures* are relished. Certainly the more a man drinks from the cup of worldly pleasures, the more he will become intoxicated by them. Our spiritual character is our glory. Personal holiness is indispensable to spiritual enjoyments. So keep always before you, as the witness of your better experience, the emptiness[z] and bitterness[a] of the world's *pleasures,* and the all-sufficiency of your real portion—the Lord Himself.[b] Shall a man's debased appetites and poisoned tastes destroy the credibility of these records in God's Word—and the solemn verdict of experience. God forbid!

[y] 2 Peter 2:22; Luke 21:34
[z] Eccl 2:11
[a] Prov 14:13
[b] Ps 16:5, 6; 17:15; 73:25, 26

18 *The wicked is a ransom for the righteous,*
And the treacherous is in the place of the upright.

GOD'S OWN—SO PRECIOUS IN HIS SIGHT

The *ransom* is here spoken of only in a popular sense, as equivalent to a substitute.[c] God sometimes, for wise reasons, involves *the righteous* in the same judgment with *the wicked.* Sometimes the punishment of *the wicked* is God's ordained means of sparing a *righteous* nation from calamity.[d] Often, in the Lord's retributive justice, *the wicked* are brought into the very trouble, which they designed for *the righteous.*[7] There, since they are suffering in the place of the righteous, they are as it were *a ransom for them.* When God's people are in trouble, it may sometimes seem that God sells His "people" for nothing;[e] yet so precious are they in His

[c] Ps 49:7, 8
[d] Josh 7:24–26
[e] Ps 44:12

[7] *Prov 11:8, and references. See also the first-born son of Egypt given for the deliverance of Israel. Exod 11:4–8; 12:29–36.*

sight, that a whole nation shall, if needful for their preservation, be brought to ruin. Egypt and Ethiopia were such a *ransom* for Jerusalem, when God turned Sennacherib's fury against them and warded off the threatened attack upon the sacred city.[8] It was like tossing bait to a beast of prey, to give the beloved victim a chance to escape. Often, God turns the enemies of Christians to fight among themselves, so that the destined scourge for His people is turned in another direction. It's as though the crushed nation is *a ransom,* taking the innocent victim's place. However, threatening the prospects of the church may be, yet there is no ground for faintness or trembling. His promises to His people are not empty sounds. They are more solid than rocks. "No weapon that is formed against you shall prosper." And "he who touches you, touches the apple of His eye."[f] The night may be dark; but morning will come forth gloriously.

[f]Isa 54:17; Zech 2:8

19 *It is better to live in a desert land,*
Than with a contentious and vexing woman.

POISON IN THE CUP

Look back at verse 9 to see perhaps even a stronger picture of the misery of domestic disagreements! *It is better* to be despised altogether of the communion of social life, if it must be purchased at a price so dear—the companionship of one, whose *contentions* will turn every comfort into bitterness. *It is better to live,* not only "in a corner of a roof," where there might be peace, but even *in the desert;* giving up all social indulgences for desolation, solitude, and even dangers.[9] Oh! it is the poison in the sweetest cup of earth's best joy, where "the two shall become one flesh";[g] yet not joined "to the Lord," and so made "one spirit with Him."[h] Only the woman is mentioned. But the disruption is just as frequent, and at least as guilty, from an arrogant, dominating husband, as from a scolding wife. Surely our gracious God here teaches His children a lesson too often neglected at their own expense—to put their necks into this

[g]Matt 19:5
[h]1 Cor 6:17

[8] *Isa 43:3, 4. Ransom, the same word in the original. Comp. 2 Kings 19:7–9.*

[9] *See Mark 1:13. "I had rather," said the wise son of Sirach, "dwell with a lion and a dragon, than keep house with a wicked woman."*

sacred yoke, reverently, discreetly, advisedly, solemnly, and in the fear of God. Let them carefully consider the fact, that a choice, influenced by the fascination of beauty, manners, or disposition, by intellect or accomplishments, but not godliness, can give no promise of God's blessing, or individual happiness. Instead, it often issues in a state of degradation, too painful to talk about, into which one or both parties are content to plunge, making themselves hateful for the sake of indulging their angry passions. Nor does this apply only to the marriage. All members of the family circle, bound together by natural ties, and living together by providential arrangements, can also do a lot toward killing each other's happiness. The owners of these uncontrolled tempers must, however, reap the natural harvest of the seed they sow, and suffer under the mortifying consciousness, that others steer clear of them and would gladly choose, if necessary, the alternative of living in the desert land, as a welcome change from constant irritation.

The family is sometimes a fierce fire. The child of God is bound to recognize God's effectual and Fatherly discipline in his trials from the tempers of those around him. Yet no less strange is the fact, that even among Canaan's pilgrims, words are often uttered that must produce pain; and so, thorns, which our heavenly Father has not planted, are strewn in our brother's or sister's path. Effects still more regrettable are seen in impressions made upon the young, or on others watching the exhibition of such inconsistencies, where better things might have been expected.

The matrimonial "thorn in the flesh" may be a needful chastening, overruled as a preventive against self-confidence,[1] and for the exercise of adorning Christian graces.[10] Yet much prayer and forbearance are required, to avoid being upset by every trifle; to avoid giving needless occasion and opportunity for irritation; to resist impulsive outbursts of uncontrolled passion; and to draw present support, under this heavy cross, from the assured

[1] 2 Cor 12:7

[10] *Buxtorf quoted a Jewish saying—"How will a man prove his spirit? By enduring a bad wife." Socrates was asked, why he endured his wife. "By this means," he replied, "I have a schoolmaster at home, and an example how I should behave myself abroad. For I shall be the more quiet with others, being thus daily exercised and taught in the forbearance of her"*—Homily on Matrimony.

prospect and intense longing for the home of everlasting peace.[11]

20 *There is precious treasure and oil in the dwelling of the wise,*
But a foolish man swallows it up.

[j]Verse 17
[k]Prov 10:22
[l]Matt 6:19
[m]Luke 12:16–22

To love an earthly *treasure* is the way to poverty.[j] Yet we may thankfully enjoy the wise gathering, as the fruit of the Lord's blessing,[k] like the oil of Canaan,[12] for refreshment. This is not the forbidden laying "up for yourselves treasures upon earth,"[l] a hoarding for selfishness and distrust of God.[m]

THE GRAND TREASURE

[n]Prov 10:5; Gen 41:48
[o]Prov 22:3

This *treasure is in the home of the wise.* For sound judgment is not worldliness;[n] an indifference to coming testing, is not faith, but foolishness.[o]

Even the cottage of the godly poor often contains this desirable *treasure,* the reward of perseverance and hard work. Yet poor indeed is the palace, where the Bible, with its stores of unsearchable riches, is not the grand treasure, and where *the oil* of gladness, while it pours out richly, is not the choicest comfort.[13] Wherever this treasure is prized, above all else, there is *the dwelling of the wise,* whether it's occupied by the prince or the pauper.

[11] *It is not a grave question—whether divorces or conventional separations, such as we hear of even in the church, are not rather the flinching from, than the enduring and honoring the cross. The supposition that* it is better to dwell in the wilderness *implies, that the worst alternative to* the contentious and angry woman *should be chosen. This was Job's lot. "The devil" (as M. Henry observed) "spared his wife to him, not only to be his tempter, but his tormentor." Yet he didn't put away his matrimonial cross. The endurance of it was doubtless a component part of Job's patience, which is commended to our imitation, and which was honored with a double increase of family blessing (James 5:11; Job 43:12, 13). Our Lord, in restoring this command to its original sternness of obligation, admits but one exception, thereby excluding every other (Matt 5:32; 19:1–9). According to this rule, an unfaithful wife must be put away as a sin; but a* contentious *wife restrained, and endured as a cross. Paul in discussing the questions of right and wrong submitted to him (1 Cor 7:2–5), lays down the general law, and admits no revulsion of taste or feeling, much less pretense of religion, to put asunder (save* for a time, *by mutual consent, and for a spiritual purpose, 5) what God hath joined together. If in an extremity the unbeliever was suffered to depart, no analogy can be applied from a heathen marriage, where the light of revelation had never shown the obligation, to that of professing Christians, where its full force was intelligently understood, and voluntarily recognized. Enforced separations brought about or permitted by the Lord, where the hearts are in unity, keep the marriage bond. But willful, settled separation rejects the distinct ground, on which marriage stands. The woman (save where the primary law of nature—self-preservation—dictates) is obviously bound by the same indissoluble tie (1 Cor 7:10). If on the other side it be defended, as avoiding the open scandal of continual contention; let the duty of humiliation and mortification of the sins, which have produced this painful extremity, be first of all instantly and habitually applied. Let the high offense of the direct breaking of God's law be deeply pondered. And let it be considered, whether such action does not shake the foundation of an appointment, expressly framed to "make of twain one flesh." (Gen 2:24; Matt 19:5); ordained as a type of the unchangeable relation of Christ and His church (Eph 5:32); and of which "the Lord, the God of Israel," saith, "that He hateth putting away" (Mark 2:16).*

[12] *See note on verse 17.*

[13] Treasure and oil *are mentioned; first the general term, then one of its valuable items. A similar idiom may be found in Mark 16:7.*

There dwells as much happiness as can be known on earth—how shall we find such joy in the same world with such men!

But whatever *the treasure of the foolish man* is, or however it is obtained, his lack of foresight will cause him to spend it, all too soon. It all goes one way. Drunkenness, wasteful expenditure, idleness, gambling, soon gobble it up. He serves a master, who will leave him nothing at the year's end and make utter destitution the only reward for his drudgery. That's what happened to the prodigal son. Yet, in the gracious mercy of his Father, he came to his senses and became a possessor of *a treasure more precious* than his earthly appetite had craved.[p]

[p] Luke 15:13–24

But there are other *foolish men* besides the drunkard and the spendthrift; and other *treasure* infinitely more desirable. Admission to *the dwelling of the wise*—the opportunity of thereby growing rich in knowledge and holiness[q]—what a "price" would it be "in the hand of a fool," had he but "sense" for it! But the golden moment is lost; *the treasure* is spent. Time is wasted in reckless pursuits. The entire absence of a holy aim in his daily work deadens all sense of responsibility. He lives only as the creature of the present moment, with no object connected with eternity. Oh, Lord! Please don't leave me to my own foolishness, for I would quickly spend my *treasure,* instead of *trading* with it and adding to it for my best welfare.

[q] Prov 13:20; 17:16

21 *He who pursues righteousness and loyalty*
Finds life, righteousness and honor.

THE HIGHEST PRIZE

Here the *precious treasure* is not wasted but handled with a distinctness of purpose that shows an awareness of its value. This is the Christian standard—"Not that I have already obtained it, or have already become perfect, but I press on in order that I may lay hold."[r] Heaven, "the prize of the upward calling," is the bright and completing object. But *righteousness and loyalty*—all our obligations to God and man—are, not only the pathway to heaven, but, also, what fits us for it.[s] Holiness must be our daily habit, as well as our Christian service—"in all your behavior."[t] Whatever we do or say must glorify

[r] Phil 3:12–14

[s] Ps 15; Isa 33:15–17; 35:8

[t] 1 Peter 1:15

God.[u] The true proof of divine grace in the heart is the practical influence it has upon the temper and conduct.[v]

[u]1 Cor 10:31; Col 3:17; Zech 14:20
[v]Titus 3:8

But this *pursuing* is not the toiling at a daily task; not a compulsory law, that chains the conscience against the will. It is joy, and freedom, and enlargement;[w] the rising flow of the heart filled with fearless love.[14]

[w]Ps 63:8

This "*pursuing,*" finds its own reward.[x] And it must be a reward of grace, it is so infinitely above our faint and sinful efforts. He who *pursues after it finds life*[y]—that which is the life of life—the treasure of the best happiness; fellowship with God; the sunshine of His face; the enjoyment of his love.[z] *He finds righteousness*—an earned reward from a God of grace.[a] He *finds honor.* For "if any one serves Me," saith our divine Master, "the Father will honor him." "To those who by perseverance in doing good seek for glory and honor and immortality," He gives "eternal life."[b] Then—to depart in the joy of conscious acceptance—"I have finished the course . . . in the future there is laid up for me the crown of righteousness."[c]

[x]Ps 19:11; Isa 32:17
[y]Prov 8:35; 12:28; 22:4
[z]Prov 15:9; Isa 64:5; John 14:21–23
[a]Matt 10:41, 42; Luke 6:38; Heb 6:10
[b]John 12:26; Rom 2:7
[c]2 Tim 4:7, 8

ON THE "HOME STRETCH"

Such is godliness with its faithful and precious promises for both worlds![d] Are they worth following after—now? Yet, how many play with this grand opportunity, as if it were a trifle and easy to get! How often laziness and sleepiness degrade it into a lifeless task, an exercise that is "only of little profit"! Where do we see this strenuous, sustained effort; this applying to the real work of the daily cross; all of which shows the reality of a man's Christian experience. We look for the picture of runners on the home stretch—all energy; all pursuit; nothing diverting them from the task at hand; pressing all their might with constant urgency in their vital service; up to a point that they had never reached before. But even this high standard of perseverance will only bring us to the goal.[e] The half-hearted, temporary professing Christian, the creature of impulse instead of the child of faith,

[d]1 Tim 4:8
[e]1 Peter 4:18

[14] *"The will is in love with those charms, which draw us to God. . . . No man will complain, that his temples are restrained, and his head is prisoner, when it is encircled with a crown; so when 'the Son of God hath made us free,' and hath only subjected us to the service and dominion of the Spirit, we are free as princes within the circle of their diadem; and our chains are bracelets, and the law is a law of liberty, and 'God's service is perfect freedom,' and the more we are subjects, the more we 'reign as kings;' and the further we run, the easier is our burden . . . and Christ's yoke is like feathers to a bird; not loads, but helps to motion; without them the body falls"*—Bishop Taylor.

though for a while he may run well, will utterly fall short.

22 *A wise man scales the city of the mighty,*
And brings down the stronghold in which they trust.

The art of war has already shown the superiority of wisdom over strength.[f] Wise tactics, or a wise application of courage, triumphs over mere personal skills. Joshua's battle plan for taking Ai was a proof of military *wisdom.*[g] Solomon seems to have known of *a wise man* single-handedly delivering his city from the power of a mighty king; a proof of *wisdom* quite equal to the strength of an aggressor *scaling the walls,* and so *bringing down the stronghold.*[h] Much more, therefore, will spiritual *wisdom,* the immediate gift of God, overcome difficulties as formidable and frightening as *the scaling of the city of the mighty. A wise* estimate of the cost is helpful in achieving most important triumphs.[i] For doesn't conscious weakness lead to a great dependence upon God. What difficulties are too great for an almighty arm? "By Thee," said a valiant soldier in the army of faith, "I can run upon a troop; and by my God I can leap over a wall."[j] "The weapons of our warfare are not of the flesh, but divinely powerful for the destruction of fortresses,"[k] unconquerable to the power of man. All the promises are to him who overcomes.[15] Let the soldier go to the conflict, "strong in the Lord," and putting "on the full armor."[l] The triumph is sure. The heavenly *city will be scaled.* "The kingdom of heaven suffers violence, and violent men take it by force."[m]

[f]Prov 24:5, 6; Eccl 7:19
[g]Josh 8:3–22
[h]Eccl 9:13–18
[i]Luke 14:31, 32
[j]Ps 18:29; Ps 144:1
[k]2 Cor 10:4
[l]Eph 6:10, 11
[m]Matt 11:12

23 *He who guards his mouth and his tongue,*
Guards his soul from troubles.

How frequently the wise man reminds us of the responsibility connected with the use of this "small part."[n] As the test of a sound or unsound conversion, we cannot see it too often![o] Indeed, the soundness of the regenerate heart is never more plainly seen, than when speaking of moral judgment. The corruption of the heart indeed is the main source. But its evil is fearfully increased by the outbursts of the lips. How large a portion of this world's ceaseless *troubles* may be traced to this prolific source! It

[n]James 3:5; Prov 10:14; 12:13; 13:3; 14:3; 17:20; 18:6, 7, 21
[o]James 1:26

[15] *Rev 2:7, and to all the apocalyptic churches.*

is the unbridled horse that brings his rider into fearful jeopardy. *The mouth* has been opened rashly. *The tongue* has flowed unguardedly; and "behold, how great a forest is set aflame by such a small fire!"[16] Our neighbor has been injured; God has been dishonored; and bitter *trouble of soul* has been the fruit.

YOUR TONGUE—KEPT FOR HIS SERVICE!

What then is our preventive from this ever-present temptation? Cultivate watchfulness and sensitivity. Walk closely with God. Cherish the tender touch of His restraining hand. *Guard your tongue* for His service; asking for His grace at once to restrain or use it.[p] When consecrated to God, it becomes the "glory" of man;[q] not only *guarding him from trouble,* but lifting him to happy fellowship in the unceasing praises of Heaven.

[p] Ps 141:3
[q] Ps 57:8

24 *"Proud," "Haughty," "Scoffer," are his names,*
Who acts with insolent pride.

SCORNER IS HIS NAME

And who gave him these names? Even the Lord, who will "cut off all flattering lips, the tongue that speaks great things; who have said, 'With our tongue we will prevail; our lips are our own; who is lord over us?' "[r] See how God covers him with disgrace. Man's rebuke may be "a curse without cause."[s] But God's stamp is indelible. *Proud and haughty scorner!* Such is *his name.* He may pride himself upon his *scorning.* But contrast him with the man, to whom God "will look, to him who is humble and contrite of spirit, and who trembles at My word."[t]

[r] Ps 12:4
[s] Prov 26:2
[t] Isa 66:2

See this vivid picture in Pharaoh—that *haughty scorner* bursting out in his *insolent pride*—"Who is the Lord that I should obey His voice?"[u] in Sennacherib, who reproached and blasphemed the Holy One of Israel.[v] Haman meets with an insult. His *insolent pride* kindles. He cares neither for God, nor man. The ruin of

[u] Exod 5:2
[v] 2 Kings 18:35; 19:21, 22, 28

[16] *James 3:5. See how strongly Job protests against the imputation of the injury of the tongue, Prov 31:30. "The tongue," says Bishop Taylor, in his bold imagery, "is a fountain both of bitter water and of sweet. It sends forth blessing and cursing. It is sometimes 'set on fire,' and then it puts whole cities into combustion. It is unruly, and no more to be restrained than the breath of a tempest. It is volatile and fugitive. Reason should go before it; and when it does not, repentance comes after it. It was intended for an organ of divine praises. But the devil often plays on it, and then it sounds like the screech-owl, or the groans of death. Sorrow and shame, folly and repentance, are the notes and forcible accents of this discord"*—Sermon on the Good and Evil Tongue.

his one enemy will not satisfy him. He must glut Himself with the blood of a whole unoffending nation.[w]

[w] Esther 3:5, 6; 5:9

Scorner is his name. Not an empty *name.* Never let us separate *the name* which God has given, from the doom which He has denounced. "For the Lord of hosts will have a day of reckoning against everyone who is *proud* and lofty, and against everyone who is lifted up, that he may be abased." And "'Behold, the day is coming, burning like a furnace; and all the arrogant and every evildoer will be chaff; and the day that is coming will set them ablaze,' says the Lord of hosts, 'so that it will leave them neither root nor branch.'"[x] "Now we call the arrogant blessed . . . But who can endure the day of His coming?"[y] Oh! With such a revelation of the mind of God, never think lightly of a *proud* thought, or a *scornful* feeling or expression.

[x] Isa 2:12; Mal 4:1
[y] Mal 3:15, with 2

It may be, that God's own children are guilty of this hateful abomination.[z] Yet He will not wink at this sin, nor spare His rod. The glory of their name shall be darkened. His frown shall be made visible. If Asa's "heart" was in the main "wholly devoted to the Lord all his days," yet for the sin of haughtiness and insolent pride, his sun went down in a cloud.[a] "For our God is a consuming fire."[b]

[z] Prov 6:16, 17; 8:13; 16:5
[a] 1 Kings 15:14; 2 Chron 16:10–13
[b] Heb 12:28, 29

25 *The desire of the sluggard puts him to death,*
For his hands refuse to work;
26 *All day long he is craving,*
While the righteous gives and does not hold back.

THE MISERIES OF LAZINESS

We've already seen the shame and miseries of laziness many times. But here is the finishing stroke. *The desire of the lazy man kills him!* It leads to no effort, therefore to no fruit. "Hope deferred makes the heart sick";[c] and perpetual frustration frets him to death. What he longs for, he makes no effort to obtain. He would rather sit still and starve. He thinks he can live by wishing, not by working.[d] Oh, he may have some faint *desire* to work. But the effort to put his hands to work[e] is too great. Therefore, his *hands* as if they were given him only to be folded, *refuse to work.* It isn't that he doesn't have physical power and activity. He could spend his whole time in

[c] Prov 13:12
[d] Prov 12:27; 20:4
[e] Prov 19:24

[f]1 Tim 5:13

busy idleness;[f] but for useful *work* he has no heart. Meanwhile, with all his inactivity, he is a prey *all day long* to *craving*, tormented with insatiable desires. The hope of enjoyment is never out of sight, but, for lack of exertion, it is always out of reach. So ... dreaming of the end without self-denial or godly exercise, he dies with his desires in his mouth; envying those, whose hard work enables them to give and spare not.[g]

[g]Ps 37:26; 112:9; Eph 4:28

THE STAMP OF DEATH

Such is the temporal evil of laziness, one of the many forms of moral selfishness, that paralyze both our energy and comfort. But far more ruinous it is in the higher and deeper concern. The stamp of death is plainly evident upon the disheartened professing Christian.[h] We ask—where does he stand spiritually? He hopes he has it; and he has often heard that the very desire for grace is grace. And this is true, *if the desire* is strong. Yet, faint as it may be in its first dawn, it is "the day of small things" not to be despised.[i] It is the "smoldering wick," which the Savior "will not put out,"[j] but kindles into a flame. But if it's never any more than *a desire*, which is, habitually overcome by an opposing inclination; instead of grace, it's a delusion, just sentimental excitement to lull the conscience to sleep. "How can an object, which standeth in a fixed distance from the nature which it should perfect, be procured by idle and standing affections? Those affections must have life in them, [if they] would bring life after them. Dead desires are deadly desires," writes Dr. Reynolds (*Treatise on the Passions*, chap. 17). Look out for the sluggard's cry. His *desires*, instead of carrying life in them, are cold things, that strike death into the soul. Earnest seeking is the test of godly desire.[k] No opportunity where we might find our God will be left unexplored;[l] no means of grace unimproved, where we might enjoy His presence.[m] Here is a paraphrase of an excellent prayer of Sir Thomas More—"Lord! make me work hard to get those things, instead of asking for them from Thee in prayer."

[h]Rev 3:1

[i]Zech 4:10

[j]Matt 12:20

[k]Ps 27:4; Isa 26:8, 9; Ps 24:6

[l]Job 23:3, 8, 9

[m]Isa 64:5

If some will call this active energy legal, our Lord's command to "work"[n] proves, that it is Scriptural. Whoever does not strive to come near to the standard has never really understood it. Whoever *desires* only, and

[n]John 6:27; Luke 13:24

refuses to work to be a growing Christian daily, gives doubtful evidence whether he is a Christian at all. Some profess to be hindered from duty because they have no heart for it, like the man who would allow cold to keep him from the fire that was intended to warm him. The lazy man talks about grace—His soul "craves and gets nothing."[o] Effort is the death of laziness. It sweeps away most difficulties and endures the remaining ones, confident of ultimate success. [o]Prov 13:4

PRAYER AND HARD WORK

And it isn't that the power is in ourselves. But when did God ever fail to help the sinner's efforts? Thou dost give to them, they gather."[p] The ship is likely to be steered with greatest certainty and success, when the pilot's eye is looking toward heaven and his hand is at the stern. And so, prayer and hard work, dependence and independence, go together in the Bible however opposite they may be in man's thinking. God's help is given, not to excuse the neglect of human effort, but to encourage its improvement.[q] The means are as much the matter of divine foreknowledge and counsel, as the ends with which they are connected.

[p]Ps 104:28

[q]Phil 2:12, 13

What then do we want for active service but the continuing exercise of faith? This gave power at first; and it alone sustains that power. Just don't ever suppose that trying for the prize is too late. If ever you're discouraged—much more—if ever you are inclined to be lazy—make a mental note of it and pray that God would write it there clear as a sunbeam—"it is yours—yours for all time, and the fruit of it shall be yours for all eternity." There is never a time, when the Lord is not giving; when He has not bound Himself to give, by infinite and most loving commitment. Deliberately dedicate yourselves. Put your resolve into practical form, habit, and place. Make all sacrifices for it. Seize all opportunities for making it good. Our work will be our recompense; our labor our wages. And while the lazy man only *craves* for himself, the *righteous*, out of a willing heart, lives for the Lord. He loves to *give, and he does not hold back*. He is "a blessing in the midst of the earth."[17]

[17] *Isa 19:24. The following exhortations are well worth our pondering—"Our heart being naturally at a distance from God, it is not a single step, that will bring us near to Him. Neither will a few minutes of cold prayer suffice to support our souls.—Let us beware of*

27 *The sacrifice of the wicked is an abomination,*
How much more when he brings it with evil intent!

ABOMINABLE WORSHIP UNACCEPTABLE

This is the repetition of a former Proverb[r] with additional intensity. At no time, under no circumstances, can the *sacrifice of the wicked* be acceptable. All the true requisites of holy worship are lacking. There is no heart. The service is therefore only formality or hypocrisy.[s] There is no way of access;[t] no "altar" to sanctify the gift.[u] Therefore it is presumption, self-righteousness, will-worship.[v] There is no faith—"without faith it is impossible to please Him."[w] The actual act, considered in itself, may be good; but the corrupt principle makes *the sacrifice an abomination.*[x]

[r] Prov 15:8
[s] Matt 15:7–9
[t] John 14:6
[u] Heb 13:10; Matt 23:19
[v] Gen 4:3–5
[w] Heb 11:6
[x] Mal 1:7, 8

How much more hateful (the sin is double) *when he brings the sacrifice with evil intent!* The mind under the dominant power of sin produces a disease-filled atmosphere, which infests everything within its sphere of influence. That is the way it was, when Balaam brought his *sacrifice,* in order that he might curse Israel;[y] Saul, in wayward disobedience;[z] Absalom and Jezebel, to cover their treachery;[a] the adulteress, in order to lull her unwary prey;[b] the Pharisees, as a handle to their covetousness.[c] What an *abomination* their service must be before Him, who is of eyes "too pure to approve evil, and Thou canst not look on wickedness"![d]

[y] Num 23:1–3, 13
[z] 1 Sam 13:8–15; 15:21–23
[a] 2 Sam 15:7–13; 1 Kings 21:9–12; Isa 1:13–16
[b] Prov 7:14, 15
[c] Matt 23:14
[d] Hab 1:13

And yet, apparently, *the sacrifice of the wicked,* is sometimes accepted. God, as the moral governor of the world, externally rewards actions externally good.[e] But never does He fail to punish the evil principle in those very actions, which are the subjects of His reward. Our Lord's love of the victim of self-delusion revealed His humanity, not His divine complacency; and was fully consistent with His holy hatred of his proud rejection of the gospel.[f]

[e] 1 Kings 21:27–29; 2 Kings 10:29–31
[f] Mark 10:17–21

indolence. Many are the hours and days we lose on our road to heaven. These days will soon amount to years.... We should willingly exert ourselves to climb a mountain for the sake of a fine view, or pure air. Let us then use all our strength to climb the mountain of Zion, where we shall breathe a truly vivifying atmosphere, and from whose heights we shall behold the true Eden, the valley of peace, through which flow living waters, and where the tree of life flourishes. May the Lord bestow upon us all the necessary will and energy!—Letters and Biography of Felix Neff—*a most interesting supplement to Dr. Gilly's Memorial of a short life filled up with usefulness and crowned with glory.*

ONLY ONE REFUGE

So . . . what are *the wicked* to do, rejected as they are under the most favorable circumstances? Shall they give up in despair or harden their hearts in rebellion?[g] Or shall they wait for better opportunities and prepare themselves for the gospel? The door of prayer is their only refuge.[h] *That* door opens the gospel to them with a free guarantee of faith, abundant encouragement, and sure acceptance.[i]

[g]Jer 2:25; 7:10

[h]Acts 8:22

[i]Isa 1:16–18; 55:6, 7

28 *A false witness will perish,*
But the man who listens to the truth *will speak*
forever.

HOW TO SPEAK AND BE HEARD

The last clause of this Proverb seems to establish and restrict the first. A *false witness* often becomes one by the evil habit of thoughtlessly repeating what he hears, without examination or certain knowledge. In that way, he may very seriously injure his neighbor's character or property. It proves a very loose conscience, and an utter lack of "love" which "covers," instead of exposes faults.[j] It is rejoicing in iniquity, rather than rejoicing in truth.[k] This false witness will certainly be punished by God;[l] and even by man he will be confounded and silenced. No one will ever again receive or trust his testimony. *But the man who listens*—the true witness who speaks only what *he hears,* and is fully acquainted with—*he speaks truth*—to conviction. He holds to his testimony and never contradicts himself. As we hear in court he "speaks the truth, the whole truth, and nothing but the truth." His word, even if it had been slighted at first, gains more and more credit and authority, after *the false witness shall have perished.*[m]

[j]Prov 10:12

[k]Contrast 1 Cor 13

[l]Prov 19:5, 9

[m]Prov 12:19

Thus the faithful and true Witness speaks for himself and his servants—"We speak that which we do know, and bear witness of that we have seen."[n] The apostles, to give solid weight to their testimony, would fill up the vacancy among them, only from among those who had "accompanied us all the time that the Lord Jesus went in and out among us";[o] as if those only, who had heard, would speak consistently. They claimed authority for their commission that they had heard it directly from the

[n]Rev 3:14; John 3:11

[o]Acts 1:21, 22

[p]1 Cor 1:23; 15:3, 4; 2 Peter 1:16–18; 1 John 1:1–3
[q]2 Cor 1:17
[r]2 Cor 4:13

mouth of God. Because of that, we are assured of its divine guarantee.[p] It is *that,* which is the main power of testimony. A feeble and hesitating tone is spiritless and ineffective.[q] But a definite, straight-forward presentation of truth—repeating the same thing consistently—commands conviction. "I believed, therefore I spoke."[r]

29 *A wicked man shows a bold face,*
But as for the upright, he makes his way sure.

THE HARDENED FACE

[s]Gen 4:8, 9
[t]2 Kings 5:25
[u]John 13:21–30
[v]Matt 26:47–49
[w]Prov 7:10–13
[x]Num 13:20–22, 32
[y]1 Kings 22:3–6, 18–29
[z]Jer 36:23, 24
[a]Jer 44:16, 17, with Job 15:25, 26
[b]Isa 3:9
[c]Phil 3:19
[d]Rom 2:5

A bold face, without shame or blushing for sin, is a fearful indication of a hardened heart. Cain standing boldly in the presence of his God with his hands covered with his brother's blood;[s] Gehazi with his fearless lie;[t] the traitor Judas, willing to be singled out by his Master, without visible emotion,[u] then afterward with unblushing boldness kissing His sacred cheeks[v]—how bold their faces must have been in determined *wickedness*! The adulteress, too, clothing her seductive witcheries with shameless face, stands out before us.[w] Sometimes *the wicked man* is determined in his way with a *bold face* against the plainest possible warnings and statement of the will of God. Nothing would hinder Balaam from his own perverse way. He even anticipated the conditional permission of God, lest it should ultimately stand in his way.[x] Ahab, with great determination, made his face *bold* against the clear forbidding will of God.[y] Jehoiakim, before his whole council, defied God.[z] His people ran with the bravery of madmen.[a] Doesn't sin stand out before us with a brazen face?[b] The drunkard staggers drunkenly at noonday. The profane man swears in the open crowd. The sensualist glories in his "shame."[c] Truly, this is the spirit of Satan. How near to hell! How awful is the plain stamp of the seal of wrath![d] Truly we have no stay and command of ourselves. We are so headstrong and our wills so demanding, that, if God were ever to leave us wholly to the control of our unruly nature, and to our own course, we should soon end up in ruin!

THE TENDER SPIRIT

It's so refreshing to contrast with that, the tender spirit of the child of God. This is rest indeed—to put ourselves in the Lord's hands, fearful of taking one step alone; carefully ordering our steps, lest by carelessness, or, much more by willfulness, our actions would bring shame upon His face.[e] Godly simplicity greatly clears the eye of the soul. When the heart is set on the work to be done, there usually won't be any great problem in discovering the path.[f] Secret heavenly guidance is asked for.[g] But an indecisive, unsettled mind gives great advantage to the enemy's assault. Here's the contrast—*The wicked man* makes his face *bold* against God's commands, but the godly obeys them and allows them to direct his *way*. He doesn't sit around doing nothing, waiting for miraculous leading. Instead, he does all he can by ordinary means, allowing them to throw light upon every step. Temporal, as well as spiritual; trifles, as well as important matters, are brought under the eye of our gracious God. Childlike confidence brings sunshine and acceptance, and bright and glorious privileges.

[e]Ps 119:5, 6, 80
[f]Matt 6:22
[g]Prov 3:6

30 *There is no wisdom and no understanding*
And no counsel against the LORD.
31 *The horse is prepared for the day of battle,*
But victory belongs to the LORD.

VICTORY IS THE LORD'S

This Proverb is not true in the strictest sense. All the *wisdom* and policy of earth and hell are really in active operation. But all is in vain *against the Lord*. The history of the church abundantly proves tnis. The decrees and counsels of God are firm as stone; immoveable, notwithstanding all human plotting and scheming. They can no more be altered than the course of the sun. *Wisdom and understanding* and the best-contrived *counsel*, when *against the Lord*, utterly fail.[h] "He captures the wise," not in their ignorance, but in "their own shrewdness";[i] not when their *wisdom* is fading, but when it is at its greatest height. Ahitophel's counsel was discovered for what it was when his every word was received as though it came from the very mouth of God.[j] Pharaoh's *counsel* to keep Israel's population down resulted in its increase.[k] His murderous decree, as a link in the chain of God's care, instead of resulting in the death of Israel's leader and lawgiver, actually prepared him for even greater

[h]Ps 33:10, 11
[i]Job 5:13; 1 Cor 3:19
[j]2 Sam 16:23; 17:7, 14, 23, with 15:31
[k]Exod 1:8–12

[l]Exod 1:15, 22, with 2:1–10
[m]Num 24:10
[n]1 Kings 11:11, 40
[o]1 Kings 22:30–34
[p]1 Kings 21:21; 2 Kings 10:1–7
[q]2 Kings 11:2
[r]Neh 6
[s]Isa 8:10; 14:27; 46:10
[t]Matt 2:8, 16
[u]Matt 22:15–46
[v]Lev 24:16
[w]Isa 53:9
[x]Matt 27:62–66
[y]Gal 3:13
[z]Isa 53:9. Comp. Matt 27:57–60
[a]Matt 28:1–15
[b]Comp. Acts 2:23, 24; 4:27, 28
[c]Ezek 1:18

leadership.[l] Balak's desire to curse Israel was overruled for blessing.[m] The wise, in his darker days, vainly set up his own *wisdom* against the declared purpose of God.[n] Ahab's project to ward off the threatened stroke against his life;[o] his determination to prevent the extinction of his family;[p] Athaliah's deep-laid plot to wipe out the family of David,[q] and so to keep God's promises from being fulfilled; the enmity against the builders of the temple[r]—this varied and diversified mass of *wisdom and counsel,* and understanding against the Lord—all came to nothing.[s] "They all signify nothing, if they oppose the counsels and decrees of heaven," said Bishop Patrick.

Mark the history of our Lord. It would seem as if nothing could have hindered the success of Herod's *wisdom and counsel* against His infancy.[t] What an impressive mass of *wisdom* from all quarters vainly tried to "trap Him in what He said"![u] How near to failure were the prophecies connected with His death, burial, and resurrection! Stoning was the sentence for the charge laid against Him![v] His burial was appointed among the wicked.[w] His resurrection, so far as man could do, was effectually prevented.[x] But God had ordained crucifixion for His death,[y] His burial among the rich,[z] His resurrection as the confusion of all their counsel.[a] The event proved that there *was no wisdom, nor understanding, nor counsel that could stand against the Lord.* "God's desire is fulfilled to those who have the least mind to it. All man's wisdom, while it strives for masteries, is overmatched," said Trapp.[b]

Let us look at that kingdom of God, so finely represented by "the rims of all four of them ... full of eyes round about."[c] To deny an absolute superintending control, is to "place an idle scepter in the hands of Him, who governs the universe."[18] How many movements baffle both previous calculation and inquiry that follows; effects, for which no adequate cause can be found; departures from the general rule that were plainly intended to take our eyes off second causes to the Lord—the first great spring—of agency, moving alone, and in spite of all opposition! The raging Dioclesian inscribed on his medal—"Christianity is extinguished," and this great au-

[18] *Archbishop Magee's interesting Sermon on this text,* Works, 2:354. *Comp. Job 12:21, 22; Isa 44:25.*

thor brings out from the very fire the tangible proof that "the blood of the martyrs is the seed of the church." "Oh! the folly and blindness of men, that think to carry all to their minds, and walk as masters of their own designs, and never have any serious thought of Him, in whose hands both they, and all their business, and all the affairs of states and kingdoms of this world, are as a piece of wax, to frame them to what He pleases!" exclaimed Leighton.[d] And don't some of us remember with shame our "quarrels" with our "Maker"[e]—how long we endeavored to defeat His purposes of love, until at length we were brought to cast our weapons at His feet and to acknowledge, that *there is no wisdom, no understanding, no counsel that can stand against the Lord?*.

[d] Jer 10:23, 24
[e] Isa 45:9

SALVATION IS OF THE LORD

But in putting away rebellion—beware of vain confidence, scarcely less displeasing to the Lord. *The horse* was a forbidden confidence in *the day of battle.*[f] The most glorious days of victory were, when God instructed Israel to disable the horses and then victory would be theirs.[g] Israel's decline commenced from the transgression of the law; defeat from the very quarter of confidence.[h] The after-renunciation of this confidence was a time of gracious acceptance.[i] *The horse* indeed may be legitimately employed as a means of defense. But never let the material of warfare be our confidence. Use the means but don't idolize them. They that trust in them fall. Those that remember that *safety is of the Lord,* are "risen and stood upright."[j] "*The horse* is a false hope for *victory.*"[k] The remembrance of "the name of the Lord" was mightier to the young warrior than the strength of the giant.[l] Much more—in spiritual warfare, let us have the active exercise of dependence. "Salvation of the righteous is from the Lord"[m]—free, complete, triumphant, and everlasting victory over all the powers of hell.

[f] Deut 17:16
[g] Josh 11:6, 9; Judg 4:3–15; 2 Sam 8:4
[h] 1 Kings 10:26–28; 2 Chron 12:8, 9. Comp. Isa 31:1–3
[i] Hos 14:3, 4
[j] Ps 20:7, 8
[k] Ps 33:17
[l] 1 Sam 17:45
[m] Ps 3:8; 37:39, 40; 68:20; Jon 2:9

CHAPTER TWENTY-TWO

[a]Prov 18:22

1 *A good name*[a] *is to be more desired than great riches,*
Favor is better than silver and gold.

HOW PRICELESS IS A GOOD NAME!

[b]Gen 11:4

[c]2 Sam 18:18

[d]Luke 6:26; 16:15

[e]Isa 5:20

[f]1 Sam 2:26; Luke 2:52

[g]Acts 2:47

[h]Neh 1:10, 11; Phil 2:15, 16; 4:8, 9

But what is this *good name,* here commended as a precious jewel? Not the *name,* which the Babel-builders would "make for ourselves."[b] Not as Absalom, who raised a pillar to "preserve his *name*" or rather to commemorate his shame.[c] It is not the popular voice. So different is God's standard from man's that to have "all men speak well of you," would be a bad name![d] So likely are men to substitute darkness for light and light for darkness,"[e] that the reputation too often serves in the place of reality, the false glare for the genuine principle, the shadow for the substance, the tinsel for the gold. The good name is gained by godly consistency.[1] The possessor is either unconscious of the gift, or humbled with the conviction, that it is wholly undeserved. The *favor* connected with it is often seen in early childhood.[f] It was the heavenly seal upon the early Christians.[g] And every servant of God values it as a trust and talent for his Master's service and glory.[h]

[i]1 Sam 25:3, 17, 25

[j]Prov 23:5

[k]Luke 7:4, 5; Acts 9:36–39

[l]Gen 39:4, 21; 41:37; Dan 2:48, 49; 6:1–3

So great is its value, that it is *rather to be desired than great riches, than silver and gold.* A byword may be attached to riches.[i] Add to which they—"Like an eagle that flies toward the heavens."[j] But the good name will be in everlasting remembrance.[k] And even now it brings confidence and respect.[l] It largely adds to usefulness; gives

[1] *Heathen intelligence seemed to have some glimpse of this medium. Agesilaus—being asked how a good name was to be obtained—replied, "By speaking the best, and doing the most upright, things." Socrates to the same question answered, "By studying really to be what you wish to be accounted."*

authority to reproof, counsel, and example; so that, if the world cannot love, neither can they despise. So, we have the Christian obligation to be "blameless and innocent ... appear as lights in the world."[m] And the honor of having a good report of all men, and of the truth itself.[n] And the qualification for efficiency in the sacred office—"above reproach" and of "a good reputation."[o] But how often do the "dead flies" spoil "a perfumer's oil"![p] Satan, when he cannot hinder the instruments, will mar them, to give currency to error, and to cause the ungodly and unstable to stumble.[q]

[m]Phil 2:15
[n]3 John 12; Acts 16:2; 2 Cor 8:18
[o]1 Tim 3:2, 7; 4:16
[p]Eccl 7:1; 10:1
[q]2 Sam 12:14

We must not overvalue man's estimation, much less take it as the standard of our principles, or the motive of our conduct. Yet we must not on the other hand underrate it. "I never thought," said the wise Sir M. Hale, "that reputation was the thing primarily to be looked after in the exercise of virtue (for that were to affect the substance for the sake of the shadow); but I looked at virtue and the worth of it, as that which was the first desirable, and reputation as a handsome and useful accession to it" *(Good Steward).*

Some, however, judge—"So long as my conscience is clear, I don't care what the world thinks or says of me. Other people aren't my judges." Now, in resisting the efforts of the world to turn us aside from the path of duty, we may, from time to time, comfort ourselves in our own innocency, fly for refuge against the injuries of tongues into our own consciences, as into a castle; and there repose ourselves in security, disregarding the reproaches of evil men.[r] But we should be very much concerned with stopping the mouths of those who oppose and criticize us, and while we count it a "very small thing" to be "examined by ... human court," we should most anxiously provide "what is honorable, not only in the sight of the Lord, but also in the sight of men."[s]

[r]Eccl 7:1, 30
[s]1 Cor 4:3, with 2 Cor 8:21. Comp. 1 Cor 9:15; 2 Cor 11:12

Yet precious as this blessing is, be careful that you don't purchase it at the expense of conscience. Far better that others should blot our name, than that we should wound our consciences. "Two things there are," saith St. Augustine, "whereof every man should be specially chary [cautious] and tender—his conscience, and his credit. But that of his *conscience* must be his first care; this of his name and credit must be content to come in the second place. Let him first be sure to guard his conscience well; and then may he have a due regard of his name also. Let it be his first care to secure all within, by making his peace with God and in his own breast. That done—but not before—let him look around if he will, and do the best he can, to strengthen his reputation with and before the world."

But though it is true, that reputation and the affection of others are *more desired than riches;* yet we must not forget, that they may be in themselves vanity and a snare. And as seeking them is the infirmity, or rather (when made an idol) the sin of a noble mind, the most severe discipline is needed to preserve Christian simplicity and singleness. But the honor that comes from God only is always safe. How much more important it is for us to register a *good name* in the church,[t] "a book of remembrance,"[u] and "in the book of life."[v] Oh! Isn't this infinitely above all this world's glory?[w] And how gladly will our Lord acknowledge these jewels as His own at the day of His appearing![x] How sure and glorious is His promise to his faithful servant—"I will not erase his name from the book of life, and I will confess his name before My Father, and before His angels"![y]

[t] Matt 26:13
[u] Mal 3:16
[v] Phil 4:3
[w] Luke 10:20
[x] Mal 3:17
[y] Rev 3:5

2 *The rich and the poor have a common bond,*
The LORD *is the maker of them all.*

RICH AND POOR—HOW MUCH IN COMMON

There is great diversity in the many levels and circumstances of mankind. Yet the difference is mainly superficial, and the equality in all important matters is very obvious. *The rich and the poor* apparently so remote from each other, actually have most everything in common. All have the same birth.[z] All enter the world naked,[a] helpless, unconscious beings; all stand in the same natural relation to their God; dependent on him for their birth;[b] the children of his care;[c] the creatures of his moral government.[d] All are subject to the same sorrow, sickness, infirmities, and temptations.[e] At the gate of the invisible world the distinction of riches and poverty is dropped. "All go to the same place"[f]—alike having kindred with worms and corruption. And when they shall come forth

[z] Job 31:15; Mal 2:10; Acts 17:26
[a] Job 1:21; Eccl 5:15
[b] Job 12:10; Acts 17:25, 28
[c] Ps 145:9, 15, 16
[d] Dan 4:35
[e] Heb 13:3
[f] Job 3:19; Ps 89:48; Eccl 2:16; 3:20; 6:6; 9:11; Heb 9:27

from the long home in the final day, all—"great and the small, standing before the throne."[g]

[g]Rev 20:12

COMMON NEED—COMMON SALVATION

We meet together also on the same level as sinners. All are tainted with the same original corruption.[h] "All of us, like sheep, have" personally "gone astray."[i] All need alike the same birth to give them life, the same precious blood to cleanse them, the same robe of righteousness to cover them.[j] It is in fact a common need,[2] and a common salvation.[k] In all these matters *the rich and the poor* are as one. "God is not one to show partiality."[l] The difference appears only as the outward garment.[m] Yet what a distance it makes! The one scarely hears of or knows the other!

[h]Gen 5:3; Job 25:4; Ps 51:5
[i]Isa 53:6
[j]Rom 3:21, 22
[k]Jude 3
[l]Acts 10:34; Job 34:19
[m]Luke 16:19, 20

And when redeemed into the family of God, isn't every member of the family our brother?[n] Here then rich and poor meet on an equal footing at the same throne of grace, in the same spiritual body,[3] at the same holy table.[o] We communicate to each other the same blessed hopes, feel the same sympathies, and anticipate the same home.

[n]Gal 3:28; Col 3:11
[o]1 Cor 10:17; 12:13

Nor is this accidental or thoughtlessly arranged. *The Lord is the maker of us all.* Not only does He makes us as men; but He *makes us rich and poor.*[p] How wonderful—that divine arrangement has knit *the rich and the poor* together so closely in mutual dependence that neither can live without the other;[q] neither can say to the other, "I have no need of you."[r] The lower rank may be the feet and the hands, working out the purposes of the mind. The higher may be the head, the seat of counsel, absolutely necessary for the direction and preservation of the social system. Truly indeed—in considering the balance, by which perfect order is drawn out from the selfish passions of men, we must acknowledge the moral, no less than the natural, system—"In wisdom Thou hast made them all."[s]

[p]1 Sam 2:7
[q]Eccl 5:9
[r]1 Cor 12:21
[s]Ps 104:24

Yet this Christian equality before God doesn't do away with rank before men. "Let those who have believers as their masters not be disrespectful to them because they are brethren, but let them serve them all the more, because those who partake of the benefit are believers and

[2] *In the ordinance of redemption all were to give alike, as an acknowledgment of equal need, Exod 30:15.*
[3] *See this implied in the rebuke, James 2:2–5.*

[t]1 Tim 6:2

beloved."[t] If all were equal in rank could men continue for a single day? The differences of mind and talents, industry, self-denial, providences, would upset the balance before the morning was gone. God never meant to level the world of men, any more than the surface of the earth. The distinction of *rich and poor* still remains in His appointment, and all attempts to change it will end in confusion. To each of us are committed our several talents, duties, and responsibilities, both to God and man. Let each of us, therefore, be assigned to our own work and be content to "remain with God."[u] "Let the brother of humble circumstances glory in his high position; and let the rich man glory in his humiliation."[v] Soon we shall all be one family in our Father's house—to "go out" no more.[w]

[u]1 Cor 7:24
[v]James 1:9, 10
[w]Rev 3:12

3 *The prudent sees the evil and hides himself,*
But the naive go on, and are punished for it.[x]

[x]Prov 27:12

It is a great part of wisdom to see what God is doing or about to do. When evil comes, most men can see it. But the *prudent foresee it.* Not that God has given us knowledge of the future. This would only have encouraged arrogance. But He has given us *wisdom* to naturally foresee evil and to forecast the most effectual means of deliverance. In that way, David was directed to hide himself from Saul;[y] Elijah from Jezebel.[z] The disciples were taught to *hide* from impending *evil.*[a] Paul repeatedly *hid himself* from threatened destruction.[b] Even our divine Master acted on this rule of prudence[c] till His hour was come.[d]

[y]1 Sam 20:19; 23:19–21; 26:1
[z]1 Kings 17:3; 19:3
[a]Matt 10:23; 24:15–18
[b]Acts 9:23–25; 17:14; 23:17
[c]Mark 3:6, 7; Luke 4:29, 30; John 8:59; 10:39
[d]Matt 26:46

But let's apply it to spiritual *evils foreseen*—"Noah . . . prepared an ark for the salvation of his household."[e] Josiah endeavored to ward off the threatened judgment by humiliation before God.[f] Paul labored for the protection of present acceptance with God, foreseeing the tremendous evil of appearing unsheltered "before the judgment seat of Christ."[g]

[e]Heb 11:7
[f]2 Chron 34:21
[g]2 Cor 5:9, 10

Not that the wise man is gifted with supernatural knowledge. He only uses the discernment God has given him. He notes the signs of the times. He studies the Word of God in connection with coming judgments; and he acts accordingly. To walk carelessly in the midst of evil is reckless and foolish. We stand by "faith" balanced with fear;[h] yet not the fear of bondage and a slavish attention to details, but of care, watchfulness, and diligence.[i] Guilty, wandering, tempted, afflicted, dying as we are, common—at least Christian—*wisdom,* shows us our need of a hiding place. Unless we seek one in time, we are lost for eternity. If we could just realize the huge mass of guilt lying upon us, and the infinite wrath that, for that guilt, hangs over us, could we rest without protecting cover? Shouldn't we just run over anything that gets in our way in our rush to shelter? Judgments there will be. But let us set our face toward our hiding place. God will undertake for our danger. His own most loving voice points us to a shelter within His own perfections.[4]

[h]Rom 11:20
[i]Heb 4:1, 11

Very different is the course of the *naive.*[j] Without any wisdom; foreseeing no evil and fearing none; given up to his own ways, and reckless of all consequences, he passes on, and is punished by his own foolishness.[k] Oh! Many such there are, that "Thy hand is lifted up yet they do not see it";[l] who will not hear the distant thunder, warning of the approaching storm; who in their fancied security laugh at those, who are preparing for an evil day; laugh on the brink of that destruction, which, unless God's grace is interposed, will make them wise too late.

[j]Prov 14:15, 16
[k]Prov 7:7, 22, 23
[l]Isa 26:11

4 *The reward of humility* and *the fear of the* LORD
Are riches, honor and life.

THE TRUEST GLORY

Who will say then—"it is vain to serve God"?[m] *Riches, honor—and life* to enjoy them—all this accumulation and completeness of happiness belong to His service. But note the two marks of His ways, *humility and the fear of the Lord. Humility* is not the mere meekness of modesty.[n] Though it is a lovely quality, it is not a Christian grace. Nor is it the cringing humility of the hypocrite for his own selfish ends;[o] or the temporary conviction of outward humiliation.[p] We may easily, distinguish the genuine principle by its accompaniment—*the fear of the Lord*—that blessed holy reverence, which none but His

[m]Mal 3:14
[n]1 Sam 10:22
[o]2 Sam 15:5
[p]1 Kings 21:27

[4] *Isa 26:20. "It is nature which teaches a wise man in fear to hide himself. But grace and faith doth teach him where. Where should the frighted child hide his head, but in the bosom of his loving Father? Where a Christian, but under the shadow of the wings of Christ his Savior?"–HOOKER'S* Remedy against Fear.

children express, and which, while it represses presumption, establishes *humility.* A just understanding of God will always lay us in the lowest dust before Him. The contrasted sight of His majesty with our meanness, of His holiness with our defilement, caused one to cry out—"Behold! I am insignificant"[q]—from another—"Woe is me, for I am ruined!"[r] Then *humility* is the truest glory. The most humble is the most triumphant Christian. Depressed indeed he may be; yet he is highly exalted. *Riches* are his, both of grace and of glory. None can deprive him of them.[s] *Honor* is his—the true fruit,[t] the gracious reward[u] of *humility*—high and glorious; the title and present privilege of a child of God, as "heir of God and fellow-heirs with Christ."[v] Life is his[w] *lives,* every kind of life, not natural only, but spiritual and eternal; life with the Father and the Son, now "hidden with Christ in God. When Christ, who is our life, is revealed," then to be manifested in all its fullness of everlasting joy.[x] Shall we look then beyond the narrow limit of time and search out the character of the heirs of glory? He "will beautify the afflicted ones with salvation." "Blessed are the poor in spirit, for theirs is the kingdom of heaven."[y] How glorious is the end of this lowly path of *humility and godly fear!*

[q]Job 40:4; 42:5, 6
[r]Isa 6:5
[s]Prov 8:18
[t]Prov 15:33; 18:12
[u]Luke 18:13, 14
[v]Rom 8:17
[w]Prov 19:23; Ps 22:26
[x]Col 3:3, 4
[y]Ps 149:4; Matt 5:3

5 *Thorns* and *snares are in the way of the perverse;*
He who guards himself will be far from them.

ONLY GOD CAN MAKE THORNS A BLESSING

A forcible image to show that nothing stands so much in a man's way as the indulgence of his own unbridled will. The man, who is most perversely bent on his purposes, is most likely to be thwarted in them. He thinks to carry all before him; whereas his stubborn willfulness makes *thorns and snares* for *his way.*[z] He is as a man, encompassed on all sides with *thorns and snares.* His stubbornness brings him into endless perplexities, out of which he can find no escape. Sarah,[a] Jacob,[b] Balaam[c] found *the way of the perverse* contrary and full of hindrance and entanglement. It's only by God's special mercy that *the thorns* make the way better, and causes the willful sinner to come, as a humbled child, asking

[z]Jer 23:12, 13; Judg 2:2, 3
[a]Gen 12:10, 20; 16:1–6; 20:2–14
[b]Gen 27
[c]Num 22:22–32

and seeking the road to his Father's house.[d] If there are difficulties in the ways of God, can it be that there are none in the ways of sin? An honest balance would prove which yoke, which burden, is the more easy and light. The sting of conscience; the rebukes of God; the disappointment of cherished desires; the tyranny of lust—all help to make "the way of the treacherous ... hard."[e] And—not the world only, but even the holy gospel, is made *a snare in the way of the perverse.* Such are "the deep things of Satan"[f] that the perverse "continue in sin that grace might increase," thus giving them an occasion or excuse for sin.[g]

[d]Luke 15:12–20
[e]Prov 13:15
[f]Rev 2:24; 2 Cor 2:11; 11:14
[g]Rom 3:8; 6:1; Jude 4

Our happiness and security, therefore, lie in a humble submission to the Lord; desiring nothing so much as conformity to His will; dreading nothing so much as being left to our own waywardness. So ... by *guarding,* we shall be *far from the thorn and snare of the perverse;* we shall "make straight" and safe, if not smooth, "paths for your feet," and "all your ways will be established."[h] "He who was born of God *keeps him* and the evil one does not touch him."[i]

[h]Heb 12:13; Prov 4:26
[i]1 John 5:18

6 *Train up*[5] *a child in the way he should go,*
Even when he is old he will not depart from it.

THE OBJECT OF GREATEST CONCERN IN ALL THE UNIVERSE,

The hopes of at least two generations hang upon this most important rule. How can we look on a child without thoughtful anxiety? In the child, an existence for eternity is begun. No power of earth or hell can crush it. The whole universe does not afford an object of deeper interest. The child's life is "like arrows in the hand of a warrior"; a most powerful instrument of good or evil, according to the direction that is given to it.[j]

[j]Ps 127:4

Everything hangs on his *training.* Two ways lie before him—the way in which he *would go,* headlong to ruin; and the *way in which he should go,* the pathway to

[5] *All commentators by their different versions admit the significance of the original term.* Imbue—*Schultens, Geier—"Give it the first dip, dye, seasoning."* Initia—*Begin the first instruction—Lay the groundwork—the first stone.* Instrue—*This is substantially like Abraham's servants—instructed alike in the art of war and in the fear of God, Gen 14:14; 18:19. The word elsewhere conveys the idea of dedication to the service of God (Comp. Deut 20:5; 1 Kings 8:63; 2 Chron 7:5; title to Ps 30). In this view a judicious expositor illustrates it—"As a house, altar, or temple, newly built, and not yet profaned, is fitted by certain rites and sacrifices for its future use, so a child, as a newly-formed edifice, is fitted by a certain course for the service and the church, and his heart is made a fit habitation of God, and the temple of the Holy Ghost"—GEIER.*

heaven. The rule for *training* implies a turning aside from immoral conduct. A young and healthy tree shoots straight upward, and, instead of putting forth crooked and deformed branches, gives promise of a fine and fruitful matuurity.

But all *training*, unless it is based on the principles of the Bible, must be injurious. To expand the mind, without soundly enlightening it, is but to increase its power for evil. It would be far better to turn it over to total ignorance, inasmuch as the uninstructed savage is less responsible, less dangerous, than the well-furnished infidel.

Yet the religious *training* must not be the border of the garment, which might easily be cut off. It must be spread throughout. Begin, as Hannah did, with the dedication *of the child* to God.[k] When this is done, train him as God's child, entrusted to your care. Ask guidance from day to day—"What shall be the boy's mode of life and his vocation?"[l] Train him. Pray for him. Teach him to pray. Instruct him—"from childhood you have known," the sacred writings as the sole rule of faith and directory of conduct.[6]

[k]1 Sam 1:28

[l]Judg 13:12

Remember, unless you give a child principles, you leave him utterly helpless. And yet, too often parents have no established principles of education themselves. The children are theirs. Something therefore must be done for their training for future life. But because they are ignorant of their moral state, and of their besetting evils, they are utterly unable to apply any effectual discipline. The child, therefore, becomes the victim of his parent's ignorance. His education in all its important departments is neglected. The impulse of caprice gives the only direction, and, in this atmosphere of confusion, parental authority soon fails to control the far mightier influence of passion.

Certainly, when we admit that the Scriptures are inspired of God, nothing could be more ruinous than to thrust them out of their place, as the sum and substance of educational principles. Never was Scriptural training more momentous. Because of a failure here, many young people are tossed to and fro by every poisonous error;

[6] *Tim 3:15. Comp. the wise man's own training, Prov 4:3, 4.*

and the anxious attempt to set them right we find to be "building where there is no foundation, or rather, where there is not so much as ground to build upon," said South on the text. In fact, the mind, abhorring a vacuum, must have some thoughts. The alternative is not between *sound* principles and *no* principles, but between wholesome truth and those crude or poisonous errors, which the subtle enemy is always ready to inject, and the corrupt heart is equally prepared to receive. Don't let the formation of sound practical habits, diligence, industry, and self-government, be forgotten. Let *the child be trained,* like the soldier under arms, to endurance, order, and subjection.

But we must not forget the distinct track of the educational training—*the way in which the child should* (not that in which he would) go! Heaven and hell, themselves, are not more opposite than these two ways. In fact, they are identified with the narrow and broad way, and every child of Adam is walking in one or the other of these ways. The child's will, revolting from God, is the certain way to ruin. The way back to God, marked out in the Bible, is consecrated by His blessing and is the sure way to heaven. Solomon wisely directs us to begin at the entrance of his way—at the first sign of intelligence. The earlier the *training,* the easier the work, and the more encouraging the results. Our character largely takes the form of that mold into which our early years were cast. Much in afterlife, both good and evil, may be traced back to the seed sown in the days of infancy. It is a matter of experience, that what is learned in early childhood, is most firmly retained. It stands the wear of time with the least damage. It is far better, instead of waiting for the maturity of reason to work upon the pliability of childhood.[7] The gardener begins to graft in the first rising of the sap. If the crooked shoots of self-will and disobedience are not cut off, their rapid growth and rapidly growing strength will greatly increase the future difficulty of bending them. Present neglect leads to later risk and perplexity. We may begin our work too late, but we can hardly begin it too soon.[m] If the child is too young to be

[m] Eccl 11:6; Isa 28:9, 10; Lam 3:27

[7] *Mr. Locke does not hesitate to affirm, "that of all the men we meet with, nine out of ten are what they are, good or bad, useful or not, according to their education"* (Thoughts Concerning Education). *The heathen moralists seem to have understood the subject well. Horace, after alluding to the early discipline of the colt and the hound, applies it.*

taught to read, he cannot be too young to teach to obey. Don't let the watchfulness to check the buddings of evil, and to cherish the first tenderness of right feeling, be relaxed. The ceaseless activity of the great enemy teaches the value of early *training.* Get to the child before Satan does. Sow the ground with good seed. That's the best way to keep his evil tares out.[n] Be at the start *of the way* with wholesome food, before Satan has the opportunity of pouring in his "bread obtained by falsehood"; before the child's nature is hardened by the habits of sin, or brutalized by familiarity with vice.

[n] Matt 13:25-28; Prov 20:17

But this *training* must be practical. Just talking to a *child* about God's Word, without bringing it to bear upon his loose habits, and self-will, is utterly ineffective. None of us lives to himself alone. We are all spreading an influence around us, whether for good or for evil. Here, therefore, in our families lies the responsibility of Christian consistency. When a child *hears* about godliness, but *sees* only wickedness, it is like bringing him bread with one hand, and poison with the other; "beckoning him with the hand to heaven, and at the same time taking him by the hand, and leading him in the way to destruction," said Archbishop Tillotson in his *Sermon on Education.* Who would receive even the choicest food from a leprous hand? Neglect is far better than inconsistency; forgetfulness, than contempt of principle. A child learns more by the eye than by the ear. Imitation is a far more powerful principle than memory. A well-trained child gladly looks to his parent's godliness as his model, to copy. A wayward child eagerly tries to excuse his own sinfulness. The discovery of a wrong parental example will harden him in infidelity and ungodliness.

Actually, this *training* is a work of watchful anxiety, attended with a painful, and often long-prolonged exercise of faith and patience. Who could hold on in it, without God's support of the promise to parents—*When he is old, he will not depart from it?* The man *will be,* as the child *is trained.* Education is totally distinct from grace. But, when it is conducted in the spirit and on the principle of the Word of God, it is a means of imparting it. Sometimes the fruit is immediate, uniform, and permanent to the end.[o] But often the bread cast "on the surface

[o] 1 Sam 1:28; 3:20; 12:2, 3; Ps 92:13–15

of the waters" is found, not till "after many days";[p] perhaps not till the godly parent has been laid in the grave.[8] Yet the fruit, though late, will not be any less sure.[q] *The child may depart* when he is young. But *when he is old*—in after years, convictions long held down, will rise up and bring back the power of early impressions. The seeds of instruction will burst forth into life.[9] He will find it hard in a course of sin to kick against the pricks.[r] Scriptures, learned by heart, will force themselves upon him with many a sharp and painful struggle. Conscience will disturb his pleasures, and embitter the sweetness, which he had found, or fancied that he had found, in his sins. The remembrance of his father's house brings the prodigal "to his senses," and he comes home with shame in his face, tears in his eyes, and godly sorrow in his heart.[s]

[p]Eccl 11:1
[q]Hab 2:3
[r]AV—Acts 9:5
[s]Luke 15:17–20

If the promise has not been fulfilled, it is because the duty has not been performed. God never gives a command, without giving his sincere servant grace to obey it. It's not for us, therefore, to lie down in despair, or even in heartless prayer, but to go forward[t] in painful obedience. With such a plain promise—the promise of Him who cannot "lie," or "repent," and who will be true to every title of His word[u]—there's no reason for us to ever be cast down. "Is anything too difficult for the Lord?"[v] Cultivate, then, the exercise of parental faith; trusting, not in what we *see,* but in what God has pledged; like our father Abraham, "in hope against hope he believed."[w] Expect the fulfillment of the parental promise as confidently as any other free promise of the gospel. Exercise faith in the full energy of Christian diligence and in the patience of Christian hope. Leave God to accomplish His own gracious will. If his sovereignty reserves the time and means to Himself, His faithfulness secures the promise to us, which is, and ever must be—"Yes," and "Amen"—"I will ... be God to you and to your descendants after you." And "I will pour out My Spirit on your offspring, and My blessing on your descendants."[x]

[t]Exod 14:13
[u]Num 23:19
[v]Gen 18:14
[w]Rom 4:18–20
[x]2 Cor 1:20; Gen 17:7; Isa 44:3–5

This is the reward of faith to those who make the salva-

[8] *2 Chron 33:11–13. "It is no small mercy," said Mr. Flavel, alluding to his case, "to have thousands of fervent prayers lying before the Lord, filed up in heaven for us"*—Fountain of Life, *Sermon 20.*

[9] *Timothy was instructed as a child, but not converted till adult age. Comp. 2 Tim 3:15, with 1 Tim 1:2.*

tion of the soul the primary object of education. But most of mankind deal with their children, as if they were born only for the world, with nothing to look to after death. Wholly leaving out the mighty questions—the great end of life—how this or that matter affects their soul—the only thought is—"Don't our children have to be like others to make their way in the world?" Therefore, they fearlessly bring them into contact with the evil around them, set their feet in the broad road of destruction, and bid them go on with the rest. In all important matters they educate them consistently for *time*, not for *eternity*. They concentrate their grand interest on matters, in which the soul has no concern; accomplishments or scholarship, not godliness; refinement of taste and manners, not soundness of faith. Need we say, that this is an education without God, without His promise, without rest? The parents of such children, and the children of such parents, are alike objects of compassion. Eternity will bring a solemn account to both.

7 *The rich rules over the poor,*
And the borrower becomes *the lender's slave.*

ONE TO RULE, ONE TO SUBMIT

[y]Verse 2

"The rich and the poor have a common bond"[y] for mutual sympathy and helpfulness; yet God has appointed one to rule and the other to submit. And this gradation of rank in all its forms involves distinct obligations to be carefully sought out and followed. Subjection, on the one hand, is cheerfully acknowledged as God's own command; while the sense of responsibility is enlarged on the other. *The rule* applies to all the domestic relations between dependents and superiors. Yet, let it be *the rule* of order, not of pride, caprice, or selfishness. And especially, when exercised over young persons of refined minds and education, let dependence be soothed by the law of kindness, elevating them to a rank far above the servants of the house. The golden rule of love will diffuse Christian happiness without disorder or compromise of obligation.

[z]Prov 18:23; Amos 2:6; 4:1; 5:11, 12; 7:4–6; James 2:6; 5:4

Too often, however, it is *a rule* of harshness.[z] And indeed, without a practical submission to God's rule over us, we can scarcely be trusted with power over our fellowmen. Such obligations as that of the *borrower to the lender*, often force the dependent to a servile bondage. Man becomes an alien to his brother; the victim of his gratification, not the object of his sympathy.[10]

It is very important to maintain an independence of mind, quite distinct from pride, which elevates the mind far above evil doing or scheming, for the sake of pleasing a patron. Many have been forced to great entanglement of conscience, perhaps to vote contrary to it, in order to keep favor with the political leader currently in power. Often, too, the influence of capital becomes an iron *rule of the rich over the poor.* Many, who profess to conscientiously resist state interference, have little regard for the consciences of their dependents. Money-masters exercise control over their workmen, which reveals all too plainly their purpose: to make them the creatures of their own will—a powerful tyranny that should be denounced with utmost and vigorous protest.

The true Christian line is to shun that proud independence, which scorns the kindly offer of needed help; but at the same time to avoid all needless obligations. "Sell not your liberty to gratify your luxury," said Henry. If possible, "owe nothing to anyone except to love."[a] "Guard against that poverty, which is the result of carelessness or extravagance. Pray earnestly, labor diligently. Should you come to poverty by the misfortune of the times, submit to your lot humbly; bear it patiently; cast yourself in child-like dependence upon your God," said Geier.

[a] Rom 13:8

8 *He who sows iniquity will reap vanity,*
And the rod of his fury will perish.

SEEDS FOR ETERNITY

Scripture often gives the practical illustration of the seedtime and harvest.[b] They are linked together in the spiritual, as strongly as in the natural, world. The harvest is according to the seed.[c] Such is the dignity and worth of the soul, that eternity is stamped upon all its actions. Every thought, every principle (is not this a solemn recollection?) is a seed for eternity. It will certainly bring a harvest of eternal joy, or "incurable pain." The wise man

[b] Ps 126:5, 6; Hos 10:12; Matt 13:3, 24–30

[c] Gal 6:7, 8

[10] *2 Kings 4:1; Neh 5:3–5; Matt 18:25, 29. Compare the blessing, Deut 15:6; 28:12.*

here seeks to avoid the latter. All experience and observation testify to the fact that the diligence of the ungodly *sower* can only end in *vanity,* in utter and eternal disappointment.[d]

[d]Isa 17:11; Job 4:8; Rom 6:21

The connection, however, of the two clauses of this proverb may intimate that the iron rod of the rich ruling over the poor, following his own selfish dictates, guarantees disappointment. But this is not necessarily so. Their abused power *will perish,* and they *will reap* nothing but the harvest of their injustice. But it is plainly evident, when we look about us, that oppressors often prosper for a time. God may even use them as His chastening rod. But the seedtime of *iniquity* will end in the harvest *of vanity;* and when they have done their work, *the rod of their fury shall perish.* Such was Hitler and also Sennacherib of old,[e] such was Napoleon. Napoleon, in his day, was the rod of anger to the nations of the earth. But how utterly was the rod permitted to fail, when its purpose was accomplished, forcefully depriving him of empire and greatness, and making him an exiled captive. But such is not the harvest from *God's* seed—"A true reward,"[f] not of *vanity,* but of substantial, everlasting joy.[g] Here let us sow "bountifully" that we may "also reap bountifully."[h]

[e]Isa 10:5–12, 24, 25; 30:31; Zech 10:11
[f]Prov 11:18
[g]Ps 126:5, 6
[h]2 Cor 9:6, 9

9 *He who is generous will be blessed* [AV—*hath a bountiful eye*],
For he gives some of his food to the poor.

CARETAKER'S OF GOD'S BOUNTY

The heart often looks out through the eye.[i] *The bountiful or good eye* is contrasted with the envious eye.[j] The man with the selfish eye can look with indifference on distress,[k] satisfy himself with the heartless expression of good will,[l] and find many reasons for withholding his charity. But the man with *the good eye* delights in seeking out ways to show kindness.[m] He not only helps with needs brought to his attention but he searches out other needs and is delighted when he finds them. Nehemiah, instead of using his great power for his own benefit, spent his own material possessions in feeding the poor, *giving of his food to the poor* at his own table.[n] His great work required a large heart. And such a heart God had

[i]Luke 10:33–35
[j]Prov 23:6; Deut 15:9; 28:54–56; Matt 20:15
[k]1 Sam 25:3, 10, 11; Luke 10:31, 32; 16:19–21
[l]James 2:15, 16
[m]Isa 32:8
[n]Neh 5:16–18

given him. Always remember—Christian—that God's standard is sacrifice, not convenience; *giving of our food;* letting *the poor* share with ourselves.[o] Nor should it be wrung from us by begging. "God loves a cheerful giver."[p] His charge is that we "be generous and ready to share."[q] This is His own pattern of bountifulness, "Thou dost open Thy hand, and dost satisfy the desire of every living thing."[r] We are only the caretakers of His bounty. Of our property, whether little or much, we must be ready to acknowledge that, as of our very selves[s]—It is not our own. But, let the motive be higher than the mere gratification of kindly feelings. Cherish carefully godly simplicity. "Let your light shine before men . . . and glorify your Father," not for your own.[11]

[o]Job 31:17
[p]2 Cor 9:7; Deut 15:10
[q]1 Tim 6:17, 18
[r]Ps 145:16
[s]1 Cor 6:19, 20

This *bountifulness* is a privilege which earth possesses above heaven. Many a rich blessing is sealed to it.[t] "Beneficence is the most exquisite luxury; and the *good man* is the genuine epicure," said Bishop Horne.[u] He "has a continual feast," because the objects (the poor people he helps) are always before him. Men will *bless* him according to their ability;[v] and don't fret when "*they* do not have the means to repay you; for you will be repaid at the resurrection of the righteous";[w] when "one good work done for God will be seen," as Luther says, "to show more glory than the whole frame of heaven and earth." It is the working of His grace, the following of His pattern, the reflection of His image, the showing forth of "His marvelous light."[x]

[t]Deut 15:10; Isa 58:10, 11; Matt 5:7
[u]Ps 41:1
[v]Prov 15:15; Job 29:11–13; 31:16–20
[w]Ps 41:1, 2; Luke 14:14; 1 Tim 6:19
[x]1 Peter 2:9

10 *Drive out the scoffer, and contention will go out,*
Even strife and dishonor will cease.

THE SCOFFER— FIREBRAND OF CONTENTION

This is a word to rulers. *The scoffer* is a firebrand of *contention* in the church.[y] He must be restrained.[z] If restraint proves ineffectual, he must, if possible, be *driven out.*[a] If his "seat" be allowed in the family,[b] *strife and dishonor* must be the result. A jeer or biting taunt is more provoking than a blow. If therefore "peace be to this house," and "peace will rest upon him,"[c]—*drive out the*

[y]3 John 10
[z]2 Tim 3:8, 9
[a]1 Tim 1:20; Titus 3:10, 11
[b]Ps 1:1
[c]Luke 10:5, 6

[11] *Matt 5:16, with 6:1–3; 25:34–40. It is stated of a very generous Christian that he strictly forbade the recipients of his bounty to return thanks. Probably the knowledge of his own heart suggested this prohibition.*

[d]Gen 21:9, 10. Comp. Prov 15:18; 16:28
[e]Prov 26:4; 2 Kings 18:36
[f]2 Tim 3:1–7
[g]Prov 3:34
[h]Ps 119:115. Comp. Neh 13:28
[i]1 Cor 6:11

scoffer, and the contention will go.[d] He must not be argued with.[e] We must make no terms with him. We must meet him with bold and open rebuke, lest his influence should overthrow the faith of the simple.[f] If God "scoffs at the scoffers,"[g] what less can we do than banish him from our society?[h] Yet if we *drive him out,* cast him not off. Pray for him. Remember "such were some of you."[i] While we abhor the sin, pity the shame.

[j]Ps 35:21–24; 69:11–13
[k]Ps 120:5–7
[l]Heb 12:3
[m]1 Tim 1:13–16
[n]Gal 1:23, 24

But what if we should not be able to cast him out? He may be a husband or a child. At least give a protest. Show that you stand in strict disagreement. Turn away from his scoffing. This will mortify, if not silence. Turn from him to your God.[j] This will bring peace. Dwell with him sighing, as David in Mesech.[k] One greater than David teaches us by His example. Honor your divine Master by enduring, as He did, year after year, "hostility by sinners."[l] And who knows, but this meek and silent endurance, with a loving, bleeding heart, may have power to *drive out* the scoffing, and to mold *the scoffer* into the lowliness of the cross? Then who would be a more welcome member of the church or of the family? *Strife and dishonor* would cease in both, should the persecutor of the faith become a monument of grace,[m] a shining witness to the truth.[n]

11 *He who loves purity of heart*
And *whose speech is gracious, the king is his friend.*

THE KING'S FRIEND

[o]Phil 3:12–15
[p]Matt 12:33, 34
[q]Prov 31:10, 26

Purity of heart describes not the natural, but the renewed man. It is no external varnish, no put-on holiness; but sincerity, humility, shrinking from sin, conformity to the image of God. He who has fully attained this *purity* is before the throne of God. *He who loves it* is the child of God on earth. His perfection is desire, constant progress, pressing toward the mark.[o] When the fountain is cleansed, it sends forth sweet waters. When the tree is made good, the fruit will be good. "For the mouth speaks out of that which fills the heart."[p]

Purity of heart sheds such refinement over the whole character, and pours such *gracious speech,* it attracts the admiration of those, who do not understand its source, and cannot appreciate its principle.[q] Such was the *gra-*

cious speech of the holy Savior, "for the people were hanging upon His words ... wondering at the gracious words which were falling from His lips."[r] The moral influence also of this *purity* of character is to put impurity to shame.

[r]Ps 14:2, 7; Luke 19:48; 4:22

Solomon doubtless spoke his own determination, that *the king should be the friend* of the gracious servant. This had been his father's resolution.[s] This character smoothed the way to royal favor for Joseph,[t] for Ezra,[u] and Daniel.[v] And we find godly Obadiah in the confidence of wicked Ahab.[w] So powerful is the voice of conscience, even when God and holiness are hated! Yet this choice of the gracious lips is too often rather what ought to be, than what is.[x] It is good for the kingdom when the ruler's choice is according to this rule.[y] Such alone the great King marks as *His* friends. Such he embraces with his fatherly love.[z] Such he welcomes into His heavenly kingdom.[a] "Blessed are the pure in heart, for they shall see God."[b]

[s]Ps 101:6; 119:63
[t]Gen 41:37–45
[u]Ezra 7:6, 21–25
[v]Dan 6:1–3, 28
[w]1 Kings 18:3, 12; 2 Kings 13:14
[x]Prov 16:12, 13
[y]Prov 28:2; 25:5
[z]Prov 15:9
[a]Ps 15:1, 2; 24:3, 4
[b]Matt 5:8

12 *The eyes of the* L*ORD* *preserve knowledge,*
But He overthrows the words of the treacherous man.

THE KEEPING OF GOD'S WORD

"The eyes of the Lord" often means His searching Omniscience;[c] but in this case, it refers to His fatherly care.[d] The human mind and heart have many doors through which false principles can enter and warp the judgment. But for the gracious coverings to *preserve knowledge* in our hearts, the *words of the treacherous* might "overthrow our faith."[e] Oh! Let us seek, in close communion with Him, continued *preservation* from a cloud upon our intellectual faculties and spiritual understanding to help us in our spiritual growth.

[c]Prov 5:21; 15:3; Ps 11:4
[d]2 Chron 16:9; Ps 34:15; Zech 4:10
[e]2 Tim 2:17–19

But the proverb illustrates upon a wider scale His faithful keeping of the truth in the world. In fact, it may be regarded as a prophecy in the course of fulfillment to the very end of time. For how wonderfully has the *knowledge* of God been *preserved* from age to age; and all the plausible or malignant schemes to blot it out been *overthrown*! The Scriptures, as the words of knowledge, have *been preserved* in a far more accurate state than any other book of corresponding antiquity; though man's wisdom has never been lacking in ingenuity to corrupt it. When *knowledge* seemed on the eve of perishing, a single copy of the Scriptures, found as it were accidentally, *preserved* it from utter extinction.[f] For successive generations God's Word was in the custody of faithful librarians, handed down in substantial integrity.[g] In the dark ages, witnesses prophesied, as from the earliest eras of Revelation,[12] some indeed for a long time in sackcloth,[h] until the dawn of a brighter day. Nor was this in peace and quietness. Often has the infidel's *treacherousness* labored with all the might of man for its destruction.[13] Often it has been suppressed, committed to the flames, or circulated in perverted copies and false interpretations. Yet all these *words* and deeds of the *treacherous* have been overthrown. And notwithstanding all heretical corruptions, *the eyes of the Lord have preserved knowledge.* Still His word is among us, with its divine credentials unimpaired, and its unsearchable store undiminished—a standing miracle of the faithfulness of its almighty keeper. Full of joy and confidence is the believer's acknowledgment—"Of old I have known Thy testimonies, that Thou hast *founded them forever.*"[i]

[f] 2 Chron 34:14–18
[g] Rom 3:2
[h] Rev 11:3–11; 12:14–17
[i] Ps 119:152

13 *The sluggard says, "There is a lion outside;*
I shall be slain in the streets!"[j]

[j] Prov 26:13

OVERCOMING DIFFICULTIES IN THE WAY

"This sentence belongs to those who flinch from the cross," said Melancthon. Real difficulties in the way of heaven exercise faith. And such there are, far too great for those, who never did "calculate the cost," or who goes at any time to serve as a soldier in warfare at his own expense?[k] But imaginary difficulties are the indulgence of laziness. *The sluggard* is a coward. He has no love for his work, and therefore he is always ready to cheat his soul, "inventing some vain excuse, so he will not have to do his duty," reads *Reformer's Notes.* He shrinks from every work likely to involve trouble.[l] Fancied dangers frighten him from real and present duties. *There is a lion without; I shall be slain in the streets*—an absurd excuse!—as if

[k] Matt 8:19–20, with 11:12; Luke 14:28–30; 1 Cor 9:7
[l] Prov 15:19; 19:24

[12] *Enoch—Jude 14, 15; Noah—2 Peter 2:5.*
[13] *Jer 36:23. The company of Voltaire and his associates.*

public *streets* except in special cases, were the haunts of wild beasts.[m] He is afraid of being *slain outside* when he willingly gives himself up to be slain within.[n] Thus the unbelieving spies, when holding up to view the luscious fruit of Canaan, added—But we be not able to go up against the people. The cities are walled up to heaven; and the giants are there.[o] As if the promises of God were not a stronger ground of faith than the giants of fear![p] But much sadder is it to see Moses shrinking[q]—and Jonah running away, from the Lord's work.[r] All excuses against doing it reveal this cowardly spirit. And who has not felt the temptation, when called to a plain but self-denying duty; to encounter painful opposition to the gospel, or to a faithful rebuke of sin?—*There is a lion outside.* True. But have you forgotten the promise in the ways of God? "You will tread upon the *lion* and cobra, *the young lion* and the serpent you will trample down?"[s] Doesn't our Master call us to follow Him in a life of self-devoted conflict and energy? Ponder the terms of discipleship. "If anyone wishes to come after Me, let him deny himself, and take up his cross daily, and follow Me."[t] Godly courage, "suffer hardship," "put on the full armor of God"[u]—all this is needed; all this must be daily and hourly looked for, not only by those who stand at the front of the battle, but by the lowliest soldier of the cross; else, though "equipped with bows . . . they turned back" disgracefully "in the day of battle."[v]

[m] Ps 104:20–22
[n] Prov 21:25
[o] Num 13:27–33
[p] Num 14:6–8, with Gen 12:7
[q] Exod 4:10–14
[r] Jon 1:1–3
[s] Ps 91:11–13
[t] Luke 9:23
[u] 2 Tim 2:3; Eph 6:11, 13
[v] Ps 78:9

14 *The mouth of an adulteress is a deep pit;*
He who is cursed of the L*ORD will fall into it.*

AT THE EDGE OF THE PIT

This fearful temptation has already been frequently discussed.[w] But in a book especially for the young, who, knowing the power of "youthful lusts,"[x] and the seductive witcheries of sin, will think a fresh warning unnecessary? Is it not the voice of mercy? For what but unbounded compassion could stand as it were at the edge of *the pit,* and unfold to the incautious its awful dangers? A *deep pit* indeed it is,[y] easy to fall into; hard, next to impossible, to get out of.[z] So stupefying is this sin to the flesh, to the mind, and to the conscience![a] It is *the mouth of a pit far deeper.* "Her feet go down to death,

[w] Prov 2:16–19; 5:3; 6:24–29; 7:5; 9:16–18
[x] 2 Tim 2:22
[y] Prov 23:27
[z] Prov 2:19; Eccl 7:26
[a] Judg 16:19, 20; Neh 13:26; Hos 4:11

[b]Prov 5:5; 2 Peter 2:10–12; Rev 21:8

[c]Rom 1:28; Ps 81:11, 12

[d]Prov 5:37

[e]Ezek 18:32

her steps lay hold of Sheol."[b] What more humbling proof can there be of the total depravity of man's nature, than the fact, that those affections, originally given as the purest enjoyments of life, should become the corrupt spring of such defilement. The sin and snare would seem to be a judicial infliction for those, whose willful rejection of God has made them *cursed of Him.*[c] They have turned away from instruction, hated reproof, resisted conviction, been given up to their abomination; they give therefore all too plain proof that they are abandoned by God,[d]—abhorred of the Lord! Is the embrace of *the adulteress* a companion for such a judgment? Every curse, eternal frown and banishment, the weight of infinite unmingled wrath, is involved in this awful name. Not that God desires the death of the vilest sinner.[e] But shouldn't His justice and His holiness be marshaled against those, who willfully choose evil and reject alike the warnings of His wrath and the invitations of His love?

15 *Foolishness is bound up in the heart of a child;*
The rod of discipline will remove it far from him.

JOHNNY'S FIRST CLASSROOM

What parent, what instructor of children, will not bear sad, but decisive testimony to the *foolishness of the child.* The early development of waywardness and passion,—even before the power of speech;[14] before the child is capable of observing and imitating those around him—is a touching, but, undeniable evidence of inborn sin. Resistance therefore cannot begin too early. Education should commence even in the cradle.

[f]1 Cor 13:11

[g]Luke 2:52

Note—it is *foolishness,* not childishness. No moral guilt attaches to the recollection—"When I was a child, I used to speak as a child; when I became a man, I did away with childish things."[f] "A child is to be punished," as Mr. Scott wisely observed, "not for being a child, but for being a wicked child." Comparative ignorance, the imperfect and gradual opening of the faculties, constitute the nature, not the sinfulness of the child. The holy child increased "in wisdom."[g] But *foolishness* is the mighty

[14] *Augustine mentions a living demonstration of the fall—the sight of an infant, before it could speak, showing an evident look of envy and passion toward another infant about to share its nourishment. He adds—in reference to himself—"When? I beseech thee, O my God, in what places, when or where, was I innocent?"—Confess. lib. i.c.7.*

tendency to evil—imbibing wrong principles, forming bad habits, entering into an ungodly course. It means the very root and essence of sin in a fallen nature—the folly of turning away from a God of love. It includes all the sins of which a child is capable—lying, deceit,[h] willfulness, perverseness, want of submission to authority[i]—a fearful tendency toward evil and revulsion against good. It is not the sheet of pure white paper; not the innocent, or even the easily controlled creature, easily guided by proper means, that we are looking at; but a little heart full of sin, containing all the seeds of future evil, multiplying to a fruitful harvest.

[h]Ps 58:3
[i]Job 11:12

We delight in our children's harmless play. We would make ourselves one with them in their activities and fun. But this foolishness—visible every hour before our eyes—never let it be a subject of sport but of deep and constant concern. Don't ever excuse this *foolishness* by remarks like, "Oh, he's just a child," or "Children will be children, you know!" It's true, of course, that children's sins cannot be chargeable with the guilt of adult responsibility; yet God has awfully shown, that they are sins against Himself. The judgment on the "*young lads*" of Bethel is enough to make both the ears of thoughtless parents to tingle.[j]

[j]2 Kings 2:23, 24

But what's the origin of this sinfulness? "Look to the rock from which you were hewn." Look unto "Abraham" our father, and to "Sarah who gave birth to you."[k] As is the root, so are the branches. As is the fountain, so are the waters. Our nature was poisoned at the spring. Our sinful parent, having lost God's image, could only "become the father of a son in his own likeness"[l]—a sinner begetting a sinner. "That which is born of the flesh is flesh,"[m] and could be nothing else. Now "who can make the clean out of the unclean?"[n] The creature therefore is produced into being with a basic enmity toward God;—"by nature" therefore "children of wrath."[o] The entailed inheritance, held from our first father, can never be cut off. And there is no dividing it. Each child inherits the whole of it. His Maker testifies, that he has been "called a rebel from birth", and "the intent of man's heart is evil from his youth."[p] In shame he acknowledges the testimony—"Behold, I was brought forth in iniquity, and in sin my

[k]Isa 51:1, 2
[l]Gen 5:3
[m]John 3:6
[n]Job 14:4; 25:4
[o]Eph 2:3
[p]Isa 48:8; Gen 8:21

[q] Ps 51:5
[r] John 16:21

mother conceived me."[q] If the joy of a child's birth blots out the remembrance of its pain and sorrow,[r] yet must not this joy be lessened in the humbling recollection of what the child brings into the world—sin? That self-will, that proud independence, that shakes the very foundations of society, is the birth-sin of our fallen nature. And it doesn't lie just on the surface, like some childish habits, easily corrected. *It is bound up in the child's heart,* "held firmly there by chains invincible to human power," said Cartwright. It is incorporated into his very nature. And so many are its forms, so subtle its workings, that the wisest parent is often at a loss to know how to detect and treat the evil.

[s] Prov 19:18; 23:13, 14; 29:17

The prescribed remedy, however, is clear. It is vain to bid the sin depart. And there's very little inclination in the child himself to *remove it from him. The rod of discipline* is distinctly named and repeatedly and insistently urged as God's own means for this important purpose.[s] And surely the thought of having been an instrument of producing nature, poisoned against a God of love, must constrain the parent to use these divinely-appointed means for destroying the deadly poison.

THE RULING PRINCIPLE

[t] Prov 13:24, with 3:11, 12
[u] 2 Chron 33:12, 13
[v] Heb 12:10
[w] Prov 29:15

Only let the child see, that, as with our heavenly Father, love is the ruling principle;[t] that we follow the example of the wisest and best of parents, that we use God's rod for *removing* men *from sin,*[u] that, like him, we "discipline" not for our pleasure, but for our child's profit;[v] not from whim or passion, but from tenderness to his soul. Use the Lord's means, and then we can do, what we cannot otherwise do—wait in faith for the promised blessing. Many a stirring movement of the flesh will be restrained, man's will be put down, and God's will gain the supremacy. Shame, brought about by sin, will cause sin to be detested, and in sorrow and humiliation the path of wisdom will be chosen, loved, and followed.[w]

We have indeed no right to demand to see God's reasons for his commands. Yet we may be permitted, in part at least, to examine their workings. Habits are of immense value, as they are built into the character by the Holy Spirit. But there must be a beginning and the use of means to establish the principle. If a child is punished for falsehood; to avoid future punishment, he abstains, and speaks the truth. As he advances, he finds the blessing and comfort of the right path. He learns gradually to speak truth from a higher motive. Insensibly his conscience acquires tenderness in regard to it; and it becomes a principle in his character. In that way, *the rod of discipline* performs its work with permanent benefit.

16 *He who oppresses the poor to make much for himself*
Or who gives to the rich, will *only* come to *poverty.*

MOUNTAINS OF GOLD

These two cases seem to be opposite. Yet they meet at the same center. Both are equally devoid of the love of God and the love of their brother. Both alike are obsessed with their own gain. The one *oppresses* the poor to increase his riches. The other *gives to the rich,* hoping for something in return. Both courses—paradoxical as it may appear—are the road to poverty. " 'Because of the groaning of the needy, now I will arise,' says the Lord." And "one who loves violence His soul hates."[x] "Sin pays its servants very bad wages; for it gives the very reverse of what is promised. While the sin of oppression promises mountains of gold, it brings them poverty and ruin.[y] Injuries of the poor are sorely resented by the God of mercy, who is the poor man's friend, and will break in pieces his oppressor," said Lawson.[z] But if *oppression* is the road to poverty, is not liberality the way to riches? Doubtless it is, if it is for God.[a] But here the man was putting forth a false show of generosity to ensure gifts in tenfold return; while he could at the same time indulge his selfishness in grinding the poor without penalty. Our Lord, therefore, forbids His friends to make a feast for the rich, looking for "repayment."[15] "If you do good to those," said He to His disciples, "who do good to you . . . if you lend to those from whom you expect to receive, what credit is that to you?"[b] *To give to the rich* is perverting our stewardship for the service of the poor. But merited justice will destroy the ill-gotten gains of selfishness;[c] and hypocrisy will meet its just reward of shame and disappointment.[d] Oh! let the Christian ever hear his

[x]Ps 12:5; 11:5
[y]Jer 12:13–15
[z]Comp. verses 22, 23
[a]Prov 3:9, 10
[b]Luke 6:33
[c]Job 20:19–22; Isa 5:8, 9; Mic 3:2–5; Zech 7:9–14; James 2:6, 13; 5:1–4
[d]Luke 12:1, 2

[15] *Luke 14:12. Martial often alludes to the expectation of a legacy with keen rebuke of selfishness.*

Father's voice—Walk before me, and be thou perfect.

17 *Incline your ear and hear the words of the wise,*
And apply your mind to my knowledge;
18 *For it will be pleasant if you keep them within you,*
That they may be ready on your lips.
19 *So that your trust may be in the* LORD,
I have taught you today, even you.
20 *Have I not written to you excellent things*
Of counsels and knowledge,
21 *To make you know the certainty of the words of truth*
That you may correctly answer to him who sent you?

CHOICE SILVER

Solomon here changes his manner of speaking. From chapter 10 he had chiefly given detached, pointed sentences in opposite forms; contrasting right and wrong principles with their respective results. His observations are now more connected and personal, and, like a wise minister, he preaches *to* his people, not *before* them; preaching to them, not only as a group, but to their individual consciences.

The wise man here "shows the power and use of the Word of God," said Melancthon. He begins with an earnest call to attention, speaking no ordinary matters, but *the words of the wise. Incline your ear—apply your heart to my knowledge*[e] as to a message from God. Lord! Waken "My ear to listen as a disciple."[f]

[e]Prov 2:2; 23:12
[f]Isa 50:4

See the attractiveness of wisdom! It is a *pleasant,* as well as a profitable thing. And who is not alive to the call of pleasure? Yet, the world cannot associate Christianity with pleasure. Rather than adding to their fun, worldlings feel, it spoils it. And how can it compensate for that? In their view, it just sets up a lot of things to do, but nothing to enjoy; something very serious, perhaps important in its place; but sobering and gloomy; a duty, not a privilege. Yet how little our profession has done for us, if it has not found it to be *a pleasant* thing; if it has not adorned it with somewhat of an angel's face! Often indeed, by our own fault, it fails to comfort and invigorate us; a body of truth, indeed but a body without the spirit—cold and lifeless. *It is pleasant* only if *we keep it within us.*[g] Heart-religion conveys vital happiness. The fruit is of "the tree of life";[h] its taste sweeter than "honey" or the honeycomb.[i] "Thy words were found and I ate them, and Thy word became for me a joy and the delight of my heart."[j]

[g]Prov 6:21; 7:1, with 2:10
[h]Prov 3:18
[i]Prov 24:13, 14; Ps 19:10; 119:103
[j]Jer 15:16

Note also the connection between an experience of the *mind and of the lips. Keep it within thee.* "Let my lips utter praise"; and how graceful the lips will be, fitting them to speak with natural simplicity, and suitable application![k] When the "heart overflows a good theme," the tongue is as "the pen of a ready writer."[l] It becomes as choice silver. The words are fitted "like a string of rich and precious pearls," said Diodati. "The lips of the righteous feed many."[m] Yet *the words* will be sparingly *ready on the lips,*[n] where there is no treasure in the heart. Never let the mouth attempt to "speak wisdom," until "the meditation of my heart" has been "understanding."[o]

[k]Ps 119:171; Matt 12:34; Col 3:16
[l]Ps 45:1
[m]Prov 10:21. Comp. 15:23; 16:21; 25:11
[n]Prov 26:7, 9
[o]Ps 49:3

But how powerless even words of wisdom are without personal application! Let each of us isolate himself from his fellowmen for a while and be alone with God, under the clear, searching light of His Word. If our praying is cold; graces are languid, privileges clouded, and profession unfruitful, is it not because "religion" has been taken up as a whole without immediate personal contact with the truth of God? O my soul, the message of God is to thee, even to thee[16]—this day. Today, while it is called today,[p] welcome His voice with reverential joy. "Take hold of instruction, do not let go. Guard her, for she is your life."[q] *That your trust may be in the Lord;* that you may claim your interest in Him; that you might seal His truth upon your heart—*He has made it known to you, even to you.* Believe, love, obey, be happy here, and for eternity. And who can doubt the excellency of the things that are written, so rich in counsel and knowledge—"words fit for a prince to speak, and the best man in the world to hear"? said Scott.[r] So free, so pleading an invitation![s] Such deep manifestations of the divine counsels![t] Such wise, earnest, parental warning against sin![u] Such encouraging exhibitions of the service of God![v]

[p]Heb 3:13; 4:7, with Ps 95:7
[q]Prov 4:13
[r]Prov 8:6
[s]Prov 1:8, 9
[t]Prov 8
[u]Prov 6, 7
[v]Prov 3

[16] *See the same emphatic reduplication, Prov 23:15.*

Such a minute and practical standard for relative life and social obligations.[w]

[w] Prov 10–22

But let us not forget the great end of this Revelation—that we may know the certainty of the things; that we may give an answer concerning our confidence. The gospel itself was written with special reference to this important objective.[x] Yet this confidence is a divine attainment. The gospel came in word and power with the Holy Spirit, in order to come "with full conviction."[y] That cannot be a sound faith which doesn't encompass all our being. And even a general admission of the authority of the whole, without individual application, would, if carefully analyzed, prove to be a lack of cordial reception of any part of the revelation. A lodgment in the heart can alone bring that full conviction—"We believe, for we have heard for ourselves and know that this One is indeed the Savior."[z]

[x] Luke 1:1–4; 2 Peter 1:15, 16

[y] 1 Thess 1:5

[z] John 4:42

Doubts may arise as to the integrity of the foundation. But a candid and intelligent survey of the outward evidence would satisfy all reasonable minds.[17] And a fair trail for ourselves would confirm the mass of proof with all the weight of internal evidences. Far better to make the test at once, than to paralyze the small bit of remaining strength by unreasonable doubtings. The Bible exhibits a divinely-appointed remedy equal to man's infinite distress and accepted of God in its power and widespread influence. Let this at least encourage the effort to apply our case to the remedy and the remedy to our case. There may be shaking in the exercise, but not in the foundation, of our confidence.

No further proof can be expected. None, in fact, could be given, except a voice from heaven. But even that would be seized upon by the busy enemy and readily converted into a vehicle of doubt by working upon our imagination. Actual demonstration would leave no room for faith, which is clearly man's discipline, humbling him in the consciousness of his ignorance and his dependence upon God. We have only therefore thankfully to receive, and diligently to improve, the sufficient evi-

[17] *See Dr. ALEXANDER'S* Canon of the Old and New Testament Scriptures Ascertained—*a valuable volume printed in America—reprinted in London.*

dence entrusted to us. Paley has given us a golden maxim of Christian philosophy when he defines true fortitude of understanding to consist "*in not suffering what we do know to be disturbed and shaken by what we do not know*," (*Natural Theology*, chap. 5). Therefore, to hold off the "obedience of faith,"[a] until we shall have solved all the ten thousand objections of a proud infidelity, is to lose the urgent responsibilities of the present moment in an unwarranted expectation of light, which was never intended to be given. Perhaps time was, when these questions were welcome, nurtured by pride or sensuality; rather insinuated than formally presented. Simplicity was revolting. Imagination took the place of faith, instead of supporting it. But the tossings of the mind in theoretical uncertainty have been arranged to enhance the value of a soundly assured trust.

[a]Rom 16:26

The importance of such a trust cannot be overestimated. It constitutes the major strength of the sacred office. "The lips of a priest should preserve knowledge, and men should seek instruction from his mouth; for he is the messenger of the Lord of hosts."[b] But unless he, himself, is certain of the *truth*, how can he answer them that call upon him, with assurance. And it is hardly less necessary for the Christian to always be "ready to make a defense to every one who asks you to give an account for the hope that is in you."[c] Temporary doubt may be punishment for an argumentative spirit; but prayer, and humility, with all their attendant graces, will ultimately lead to Christian establishment. In that way, we shall be preserved from the fearful, but all too-prevalent danger, of receiving and accepting with authority, the traditions of men instead of the testimony of God. Ours should not be a blind faith in the leaders of the church, or in the church, itself, but *only* in "the law and to the testimony";[d] "your faith should not rest on the wisdom of men, but on the power of God;"[e] stamped by the impress of the Spirit, as "the witness in himself."[f] No power of Satan or his secret agents will drive us permanently from this stronghold. We "know whom" and what we "have believed,"[g] and are "convinced," for the support of our weaker brethren, "that this is the true grace of God. Stand firm in it!"[h]

[b]Mal 2:7
[c]1 Peter 3:15
[d]Isa 8:20; Acts 17:11
[e]1 Cor 2:5
[f]1 John 5:10; 2:20, 27
[g]2 Tim 1:12
[h]1 Peter 5:12

22 *Do not rob the poor because he is poor,*
Or crush the afflicted at the gate;
23 *For the* Lord *will plead their case,*
And take the life of those who rob them.

THE LAW OF LOVE

Perhaps after so solemn an exhortation, we might have expected something more important. Yet what can be more important than the law of love and to rebuke the breaches of that law? *Robbery,* under any circumstances, is a breach of the commandment. But to *rob the poor, because he is poor,* and has no means of protection, is a cowardly aggravation of the sin.[j] And it is even more low-down to *crush the afflicted in the gate*—the place of judgment[k]—to make his only refuge a market for bribery,[l] and to corrupt the sacred authority of God, given for his protection.[m] It is God, who is most resisted when we wrong those who cannot resist or defend themselves. "The threatenings of God against the *robbers of the poor* are sometimes laughed at by the rich and great. But they will find them in due time to be awful realities," said Lawson.[n] "Weak though they be, they have a strong One to take their part," commented Bishop Sanderson (*Sermon on 1 Sam 12:3*). He *will plead their cause.* And woe to the man against whom He pleads. "What do you mean, demands the poor man's pleader, "by crushing My people, and grinding the face of the poor?"[o]

The accumulation of divine vengeance is heaped upon this sin.[p] Ahab's judgment testified to the fearful *robbing of those who rob the poor.*[q] The captivity in Babylon was the scourge for this wickedness.[r] And when the deeds of secrecy shall be brought to light, how black will be the catalog of sins of oppression! How tremendous the judgments of the oppressor![s] Meanwhile let the poor commit himself to His God;[t] yea, take up the song of praise,[u] in the confidence that the divine *pleader* will "maintain the cause,"[v] to the eternal confusion of his *spoilers.*

[i]Exod 20:15
[j]2 Sam 12:1–6
[k]Ruth 4:1; 2 Sam 15:2; 19:8; Job 5:4; Amos 5:15
[l]Exod 23:6; Amos 5:12
[m]Ps 82:4. Comp. Ps 72:1–4
[n]Verse 16
[o]Isa 3:15. Comp. Prov 23:10, 11; Jer 1:33, 34
[p]Ps 109:6, 16
[q]1 Kings 21:18–24. Comp. Isa 33:1; Hab 2:8
[r]Ezek 22:29–31. Comp. Jer 21:12
[s]Mal 3:5
[t]Ps 10:14
[u]Ps 109:30, 31
[v]Ps 140:12

24 *Do not associate with a man* given *to anger;*
Or go with a hot-tempered man,
25 *Lest you learn his ways,*
And find a snare for yourself.

ANGER ISN'T HARD TO LEARN

Sin is contagious. Our corrupt constitution makes us susceptible to it in any form in which it comes to us. The ugly passions of *an angry man* repel rather than attract.[w] But sin never loses its infectious character. Friendship blinds the eye; and where there is no light in the mind, no true tenderness in the conscience, we can see hateful things done by those we love, because of blunted sensibilities. Common dealing *with an angry man* is like living in a house that is on fire. His unreasonable conduct stirs our own tempers. One fire kindles another. Occasional bursts of passion soon form the habit. The habit becomes the nature. Thus *we learn his ways, and find a snare for ourselves.*[x] How soon a young person, living with a proud man, gets the mold of his society, and becomes arrogant and overbearing! Evil ways, especially when they fall in with our natural temperament, are learned much more quickly than good ways, and are much more able to corrupt "good morals,"[y] than are good manners able to correct the evil. We learn anger easier than meekness. We convey disease, not health. Therefore, the rule of self-preservation, no less than the rule of God is—*"do not associate with a man given to anger."*

[w] Prov 21:24; 25:28; 27:4

[x] Ps 106:35, 36

[y] 1 Cor 15:33

26 *Do not be among those who give pledges,*
Among those who become sureties for debts.
27 *If you have nothing with which to pay,*
Why should he take your bed from under you?

DON'T SIGN FOR YOUR OWN EXECUTION

Avoid contention, not only *with angry,* but with unwise, perhaps unprincipled associates. Don't make a pledge[z] as *a surety,* without forethought, and inadvertently without upright principle. Repeated warnings have been given of this danger.[a] Making a pledge, becoming surety for a friend, often wounds our own hearts. Signing someone else's bill, to become responsible for it, if he should fail, may almost be signing a warrant for your own execution. In any event, it is fraudulent to give security for more than you are worth; promising what you are unable to perform. The creditor may fairly in this case proceed to extremities[b]—not with the debtor (whom he

[z] Prov 6:1

[a] Prov 6:1, 2; 11:15; 17:18

[b] Prov 20:16

knows to be worth nothing, and whom indeed the law of God protected)[c]—but with the surety. And why—the wise man asks—should you rashly incur beggary and ruin, *to have the bed taken from under you?*

[c]Exod 22:26, 27; Deut 24:12, 13

There is, however, so much danger of erring in over-caution, and of indulging selfishness under the cover of prudence, that these wholesome cautions must be considerately applied. Yet in devising liberal "plans,"[d] we must combine the most careful regard to justice and truth;[e] otherwise, our very charity will prove the scandal, instead of the glory, of our profession.[f] We may take "*joyfully* the seizure of . . . property," for the testimony of a good conscience. But what is the fruit of our own rashness and folly, we cannot but take it heavily.[g] Oh! let our Lord be honored in our profession; by well-doing "you may silence the ignorance of foolish men."[h]

[d]Isa 32:8
[e]Phil 4:8
[f]Rom 14:16; 1 Tim 5:22; Heb 12:13
[g]Heb 10:34
[h]1 Peter 2:12, 15; 3:16

28 *Do not move the ancient boundary*
Which your fathers have set.

DON'T DESTROY THE BOUNDARIES!

Everyone has an undoubted right to what is his own. He must therefore have the means of knowing and securing his right. Even the heathen admitted the sacredness of *the boundary.* The dividing stone was honored as the god, without whose kindly influence every field would be the subject of contention.[18] The *boundary* line was protected by the wise laws of Israel. God Himself set the bounds to the respective parts of His own world, restricting each part within its proper limits.[i] But He distributed the different nations[j] and appointed the same security for the many allotments of His own people.[k] *The ancient boundary* line stood as the witness and memorial of each man's rights, *which his fathers had set.* Its *removal* therefore was forbidden, as a selfish and unjust invasion of property,[l] included in the curses of Ebal,[m] and noted, in following ages, as the beginning of national provocation.[n]

[i]Gen 1:6–10; Job 38:10, 11
[j]Deut 32:8
[k]Num 34
[l]Deut 19:14. Comp. Prov 23:10; Job 24:2
[m]Deut 27:17
[n]Hos 5:10

All sound Bible teachers warn us, from this Proverb, to reverence long-tried and well-established principles and not to rashly make changes in them. Some scorn *the ancient boundaries* as relics of bygone days of darkness.

[18] *See Ovid,* Trist, *2:630–648.*

And because they are impatient of restraint, they want a wider range of wandering, to indulge either their own lustful appetite for novelties, or the gloomy cravings of others for this unwholesome excitement.[o] Endless divisions and dissensions have been the fruit of this deadly evil. The right of individual judgment oversteps its legitimate bounds; and under its sinful exercise, "everyone" feels justified to do and think "what was right in his own eyes."[p]

[o] 2 Tim 3:7; 4:3, 4
[p] Judg 21:25

The last age witnessed a rude, but, by divine mercy, an unsuccessful effort to root up her landmarks. We have seen an offensive and subtle attempt to *remove* them from the place, where *our* well-instructed *fathers have set* them. This is indeed the rooting up of the foundations of the grace of God, which ought, if need be, to be "resisted to the point of shedding blood."[q] The Lord makes us valiant for the truth and consistent witnesses of its power!

[q] Heb 12:4

29 *Do you see a man skilled* [AV—*diligent*] *in his work?*
He will stand before kings;
He will not stand before obscure men.

WHO STANDS BEFORE KINGS?

Do you see a man? He is marked out for a special notice.[r] And who is he? *A man skilled in his work;* quick, ready, actively improving his time, his talents, his opportunity for his work; like Henry Martyn, who was known in his college "as the man who had not lost an hour" (*Life,* chap. 2). An obscure sphere is too low for such a man. *He will stand,* as Joseph,[s] Nehemiah,[t] Daniel—*all diligent in their work*—did—*before kings.* If the letter of the promise be not fulfilled, "*the diligent* will rule" in his own sphere.[u] Such was the honor put upon Eliezer's care, forethought, and activity for his master's interest.[v] "Nobleness of *condition* is not essential as a school for nobleness of *character.* It is delightful to think that humble life may be just as rich in moral grace and moral grandeur as the loftier places in society; that as true a dignity of principle may be earned by him, who, in homeliest drudgery, conscientiously fulfills his task—as much so as he, who stands entrusted with the fortunes of

[r] Prov 26:12; 29:20
[s] Gen 39:3–6; 41:42
[t] Neh 1:11; 2:1; Dan 6:1–3; 6:28
[u] Prov 12:24
[v] Gen 24

an empire," said Chalmers *(Commercial Discourse,* p. 107).

Diligence, even without godliness, is often the way to worldly advancement. Pharaoh chose Joseph's brethren, as "*capable men,*" to be rulers of his cattle.[w] Jeroboam owed his rise in Solomon's house to his "industrious" habits.[x] But when a man is "serving the Lord" in fervency of spirit,[y] wisely using his own talent for the day of reckoning;[z] not only the poor man, but the mighty man of the world, will be too low for him. *He shall stand before the King* of Kings with unspeakable honor, with unclouded acceptance—"Well done, good and faithful slave . . . enter into the joy of your master."[a]

And if the men of this wise king were "blessed" *which stood "continually" before him,* and heard "his wisdom"; what must be the joy of *standing before* the great King, seeing His face and serving Him forever![b] "This is the honor for all His godly ones."[c] "If any one serves Me," saith our gracious Master, "where I am, there shall My servant also be; if any one serves Me, the Father will honor him."[d]

[w] Gen 47:6
[x] 1 Kings 11:28
[y] Rom 12:11
[z] Luke 19:13
[a] Matt 25:21–23
[b] 1 Kings 10:8, with Rev 7:15; 22:3, 4
[c] Ps 149:9
[d] John 12:26

CHAPTER TWENTY-THREE

1 *When you sit down to dine with a ruler,*
Consider carefully what is before you;
2 *And put a knife to your throat,*
If you are a man of great *appetite.*
3 *Do not desire his delicacies,*
For it is deceptive food.

BEWARE OF THE KING'S DELICACIES

The Word of God is our rule of practice, not less than of faith. It enforces us, not only in our spiritual, but in our natural, actions as well.[a] It directs us in the daily details of common life. Suppose we are invited, in the way of God, to the table of a man of rank—how wise the caution—*consider carefully what is before you!* Think where you are; what is your besetting temptation; what impression is your conduct likely to make? Excessive appetite or a flippant attitude give the ungodly legitimate grounds for prejudice against us, or it can be the cause of "a stumbling block to the weak."[b]

But after all, it's we, ourselves, who are mainly concerned. Isn't it possible that the luxuries on the table may cause us to eat too much? If so, then the rule is plain and urgent. *If you are* conscious of being *given to overeating,* making it your greatest delight, even if you have to force yourself, put a halt to it.[c] Act as if *a knife were at your throat.* Be stern and resolute with yourself.[d] Don't give way to lust. Resist every renewed temptation to indulge. *Remember that the delicacies are deceptive food,* sometimes from the insincerity of the host;[e] always from the disappointment of the anticipated pleasure.[f] To use them may be lawful. To *be desirous of them* is fearfully dangerous.

[a] 1 Cor 10:31
[b] 1 Cor 8:9; Rom 14:21
[c] Matt 18:8, 9
[d] Prov 23:31; Ps 141:4
[e] Prov 23:6–8
[f] Eccl 2:10, 11

[g]Gen 3:6
[h]1 Cor 11:21; Phil 3:18, 19; Jude 12, 13
[i]Gen 25:28; 27:4, with 26–29
[j]Luke 21:34

What man who knows his own weakness will think this caution needless? Alas! Wasn't the lust of the flesh the first inlet to that sin, which has overwhelmed us all?[g] How often it has tarnished a Christian profession[h] and dampened spiritual anticipation and joy.[i] If Christ's disciples, conversant only with mean and homely food, needed a caution to "be on guard";[j] much more must it apply to *a ruler's table,* where everything ministers to the temptation to overindulge.

[k]Gen 1:26, 28; 9:2
[l]Matt 6:11, 25–33
[m]Ps 78:18
[n]Rom 13:14

It is man's high *right* to "rule over ... every living thing."[k] It is *his shame* therefore that the creature in any form should have dominion over him. God gives us our body to feed, not to pamper; to be the servant of the soul—not the master. He gives bread for our necessities,[l] man craves "food according to his desire."[m] We are to make "provision" for the needs of the flesh, not its lusts.[n] And surely a soul that puts "on the Lord Jesus Christ" can never degrade itself to live only to satisfy the lusts of the flesh. If the unsaved Seneca could say, "I am greater and born to greater things, than to be the servant of my body"—is it not a shame for a Christian, born as he is, the heir of an everlasting crown, to be the slave of his carnal appetites?

[o]Ps 19:13
[p]1 Cor 9:27
[q]2 Peter 1:5, 6

To go as near as we can to the bounds of intemperance is to place ourselves in almost certain danger of exceeding them. He that takes his *full* liberty in what he may, shall regret it. A wise person advises, "If I see any dish that tempts me to overeat, I fear a serpent in that apple, and I would make a willful denial." Temptation presses hard. So then ... put the strongest guard at this weak point. Curb your desires, however pressing they may seem, and you will find unbelievable benefit from it.[o] Take this old prayer, for example: "Grant unto us such abstinence, that our flesh being subdued unto the spirit, we may ever obey thy godly motions." Join with it the resolution of the apostle Paul—"I buffet my body and make it my slave"[p]—and the rule of Peter—"applying all diligence, in your faith."[q] This practical warfare will break the power of many a strong temptation and triumph over the flesh gloriously.[1]

[1] *Dan 1:8. Compare Augustine's ingenuous and instructive* Confessions, *book 10.100.31.*

4 *Do not weary yourself to gain wealth,*
Cease from your consideration of it.
5 *When you set your eyes on it, it is gone.*
For wealth *certainly makes itself wings,*
Like an eagle that flies toward *the heavens.*

ETERNITY AT THE DOOR

So here we have a warning against covetousness. If riches come from the blessing of God, receive them thankfully,[r] and consecrate them wisely and freely for Him. But to labor to be rich, is the dictate of our own wisdom, not of that which is from above. Let them be gotten if they can, and how they can, without undue concern and attention.[s] Solomon, however, beautifully describes their true nature—a mere nonentity, an illusion—*it is gone.* Foolish it is, then, to *set the eyes* (to cause them to fly, like a ravenous bird upon his prey[t]) upon this, that is so elusive and fleeting. One moment it seems to be within reach. The next it has eluded our grasp, and *flown away as an eagle* toward heaven.[2]

[r] Prov 10:22; Gen 31:9

[s] Prov 28:20, 22; Ezek 28:4, 5; Luke 16:4–8

[t] Jer 22:17; Hos 9:11

And yet, to practically acknowledge the stamp of vanity upon this idolized treasure, is a lesson we don't learn in a day. It is learned only in the school of discipline. The eagerness for earthly things, and the neglect of heavenly, shows, either that eternity is a delusion, or that the world is mad. For it we *really believed* in the things of eternity, wouldn't our thoughts be fixed on them, and our heart filled with them, leaving very little time or room for the meaningless vanities of life? As to their true worth, Luther truthfully and boldly declared—that "the whole Turkish empire in all its vastness was only a crust, which the great Father of the family cast to the dogs." And then—as to abiding, there is no need to invent *wings. Wealth makes them for themselves.* The man who concentrates all his wisdom, talents, and energy, who sacrifices all his peace; will "rise up early, to retire late,"[u] in *gaining riches,* and he has often been at one stroke deprived of all, just when he supposed himself to have it all in his grasp. Divine chastisement,[v] laziness,[w] extravagance,[x] injustice,[y] robbery,—can quickly reduce one to lowest poverty.[z] The longest wealth stays is but for a

[u] Ps 127:2

[v] Gen 13:5–11; 14:12
[w] Prov 6:9–11
[x] Luke 15:12–16
[y] Prov 20:21; 21:6; James 5:2, 3
[z] Job 1:14–17

[2] *A frequent Scripture illustration of a speedy flight. Comp. Deut 28:49; 2 Sam 1:23; Lam 4:19.*

moment. Eternity is at the door;[a] and naked shall we go out of the world, as we came into it.[b] Yet even all this fails to teach us to cease from our own wisdom, to seek true "wealth" on earth,[c] and in God's wisdom to lay up enduring "treasures in heaven."[d]

[a]Luke 12:20
[b]Job 1:21; Ps 49:17
[c]Prov 8:18–21
[d]Matt 6:20

Here then lies the contrast. The world sees reality only in the objects in front of them; the Christian, only in *invisible things*. Therefore, if our judgment looks upon the one as a shadow, and the other as reality; let us see that we set our affections accordingly; giving little attention to the things of earth, and our heart to the things of eternity. Thank God for the present possession of "a better possession and an abiding one."[e] But are there not moments when we relax and become lazy, and allow "uncertainty of riches" to become our confidence?[f] It is then we need a sharp lesson to remind us, how *certainly they make to themselves wings and fly away*. Oh! Think, Christian, of your heavenly birth, your eternal expectations; what manner of man you will be in a short moment, when the false pageant of earth shall have given way to the real manifestation of the Son of God, and you will be on the throne with Him forever![g] With this glory in prospect, what a degradation it is to *set your eyes* upon that which "is passing away."[3]

[e]Heb 10:34
[f]1 Tim 6:17
[g]Phil 4:5; Col 3:1–4

6 *Do not eat the bread of a selfish man,*
Or desire his delicacies;
7 *For as he thinks within himself, so he is.*
He says to you, "Eat and drink!"
But his heart is not with you.
8 *You will vomit up the morsel you have eaten,*
And waste your compliments.[h]

[h]1 Cor 5:10, 11; 10:27

We ought not to entertain the invitation of a selfish man, who grudges the very food we eat, or of a deceitful man, whose friendship is a cloak for selfish purposes. The evil eye of the *selfish man* will peep through the covers of his delicacies, and betray him, in spite of his

[3] *1 Cor 7:29–31. It is a fine remark of an ancient philosopher—"Nothing can be called great, which to despise is great. Thus riches, honors, dignities, authorities, and whatever beside may have the outward pomp of this world's theatre, cannot be to a wise man pre-eminent blessings, since the contempt of them is a blessing of no mean order. Indeed those who enjoy them are not so much entitled to admiration, as those who can look down upon them with a noble superiority of mind"—Longin,* De Sublim. *sect. 7. The Roman Satirist adverts to Solan's warning to Croesus, when he refused to admire his immense riches (a warning despised at the time, but remembered when he was bound to the stake).*

attempts to conceal them. We judge him not by his words; *for as he thinks within himself, so is he.* And while *he says, Eat and drink,* it is all too plain, that *his heart is not with you.*[i] "Better is a dish of vegetables where love is," than his delicacies. "It is better to be a poor man than a liar."[j] Every *morsel* at his table is loathsome; and we *waste compliments* we gave our hypocritical and unworthy host.

[i] Luke 11:37
[j] Prov 15:17; 19:22

There's no danger like that attached to the invitation of the gospel. There is no selfishness,[k] no grudging—"Ho, Every one who thirsts, come to the waters."[l] The table is set. The herald is sent to spread the word.[m] Hunger is the only requisite. *While he says,* "Eat, friends; Drink and imbibe deeply, O lovers,"[n] his whole *heart is with us.* There are no repentings, no disappointments here. Every taste increases the appetite for more. And the prospect is near at hand, when we shall be abundantly and eternally satisfied with the abundance of "Thy house."[o]

[k] 2 Sam 11:13; 13:26–28
[l] Isa 55:1
[m] Comp. Prov 9:2, 3
[n] Song of Sol 5:1
[o] Ps 36:8; 16:11

9 *Do not speak in the hearing of a fool,*
For he will despise the wisdom of your words.

A TIME TO KEEP SILENCE . . . A TIME TO SPEAK

Our Lord's rule is to the same purpose—"Do not give what is holy to dogs, do not throw your pearls before swine, lest they trample them under their feet, and turn and tear you to pieces."[p] Cast not away your good counsels upon incorrigible sinners. So long as there is any hope of reclaiming *the fool,* make every effort for his precious soul. In the true spirit of our Master, bring the gospel to the worst and the most unwilling; and never find an excuse for being lazy and neglectful in these matters. Yet there is "a time to be silent, and a time to speak."[q] Such a time we shall understand by the trial of our own spirit. We long to speak in compassion. But self-denial, not self-indulgence, restrains.[r] We have before been warned against untimely rebuke.[s] This caution extends further—*Do not speak in the hearing of a fool.* Such was our Master's silence before Herod.[t] If he would hear, there would be hope. But instead of being thankful for instruction, *he will despise the wisdom of your words*[u] and take occasion from them only to scoff and

[p] Matt 7:6
[q] Eccl 3:7; Prov 26:4, 5
[r] Ps 39:1, 2
[s] Prov 9:8
[t] Luke 23:9
[u] Prov 1:7

blaspheme the more. Many doubtful cases, however, require much wisdom. And the safe rule will be, never to speak without prayer for divine guidance, and simplicity, and love.

10 *Do not move the ancient boundary,*
Or go into the fields of the fatherless;
11 *For their Redeemer is strong;*
He will plead their case against you.

GOD GIVES ORPHANS SPECIAL HELP!

The general command not to remove the old boundary has been given before.[v] Now, a special warning and a powerful reason are added here. Many would not dare to touch the rich, yet they oppress the poor at will. But *the fields of the fatherless* are under almighty protection. It isn't that anyone has a right to trespass upon the rich man's field. But the *fatherless* have no might, and God pleads with the invader for the wrong done to them. It's as though it were a wrong done to Himself, because it is done to those, whom He undertook to protect. They may seem to be helpless. But *their Redeemer is strong; He will plead their cause against you.*[w] Was the nearest of kin bound to be the redeemer of his kinsman's wrongs?[x] How marvelous and unsearchable, the pity, grace, and condescension of Emmanuel! When He could not redeem as God, He became our kinsman, that He might be our Redeemer![y] And He now bears the endearing title of the "father of *the fatherless*."[z] His moral government shows, that "in Thee" they find not "mercy"[a] only but justice also.[b] Here is their strong confidence, when human help is gone: "The unfortunate commits himself to Thee; Thou hast been the helper of *the orphan*."[c] "This is pure and undefiled religion in the sight of our God and Father, to visit orphans and widows in their distress."[d] Special provision was made in the apostolic ministration for these friendless objects of Christian help.[e] The gospel reflects the image of Christ when native selfishness is melted away in sympathizing love.

[v] Prov 22:28

[w] Prov 22:22, 23; Jer 1:33, 34. Comp. Exod 22:22–24; Job 22:9, 10; 31:21–23; 34:28; Isa 10:1–3

[x] Lev 25:25; Num 35:12; Ruth 3:12

[y] Heb 2:14–16

[z] Ps 68:5, with 18

[a] Hos 14:3; Ps 146:9

[b] Ps 103:6

[c] Ps 10:14, 17, 18

[d] James 1:27

[e] Acts 6:1; 1 Tim 5:3–5, 9, 10

12 *Apply your heart to discipline* [AV—*instruction*],
And your ears to words of knowledge.

TREASURE HOUSE OF KNOWLEDGE

The frequent repetition of these counsels[f] implies a humbling truth familiar to every day's experience—man's natural turning away from divine *discipline,* and his inattention to *the words of knowledge.* It is well to have these commands renewed from time to time. We all need "order on order, order on order";[g] and that to the very end of our course. The best taught and most advanced Christian will be much in earnest in seeking more *instruction* and will gladly sit at the feet of the Lord's ministers, to hear the *words of knowledge.* Here lies the value of the Bible, as the one source of *instruction,* and the only treasure house of *the words of knowledge.* The simple reference to this standard is the keeping of the soul from errors.

[f]Prov 2; 3; 4; 8; 19:20
[g]Isa 28:13

Note the connection between *the application of the heart and of the ears.*[h] *The heart* is open to sound advice or moral precept, but yet it is closed to Christ and His doctrine. It is closed up in unbelief, prejudice, indifference, and the love of pleasure. A listless heart, therefore, produces a careless ear. But when the heart is graciously opened, softened, and enlightened, the attention of the ear is instantly captured.[i] This indeed is the Lord's Sovereign creation work;[j] yet it is wrought by a God of order in the use of His own means. Awakened desire brings to prayer.[k] Prayer brings the blessing.[l] And then, *every word of knowledge* is precious, more "than thousands of gold and silver pieces"![m]

[h]Prov 2:2
[i]Acts 16:14
[j]Prov 20:12; Rev 3:7
[k]Ps 119:18; 19:10
[l]Prov 2:3–6
[m]Ps 119:14, 72, 127

13 *Do not hold back discipline* [AV—*correction*] *from the child,*
Although you beat him with the rod, he will not die.
14 *You shall beat him with the rod,*
And deliver his soul from Sheol.

SPARE THE ROD, SPOIL THE CHILD

Christian parents do not always recognize the Scriptural standard of discipline. "Foolishness is bound up in the heart" of the parent, no less than "of the child." "The foal of a wild donkey"[n] must always need its measure of discipline. The rule therefore is, notwithstanding all the pleas of pity and love—don't withhold it! Do the work

[n]Prov 22:15; Job 11:12

wisely, firmly, lovingly. Persevere, notwithstanding apparently unsuccessful results. Connect it with prayer, faith, and careful instruction.

We admit that it is revolting to give pain and call forth the tears of those we so tenderly love. But while hearts are what hearts are, it is not to be supposed that we can train without discipline. If it be asked—will not gentle means be more effectual? Had this been God's judgment, as a God of mercy, He would not have provided a different course of treatment. Eli tried them, and the sad issue is written for our instruction.[o] "Must I then be cruel to my child?" No—certainly not! Instead, God charges you with cruelty, if you *withhold correction from your child.* He goes on in his own "foolishness."[p] Unless he is restrained, he will die in his sin. God has ordained the rod to purge his sins, and so *deliver his soul from Sheol.* What parent then, that trembles for his child's eternal destiny, can *withhold correction?* Is it not cruel love, that turns away from painful duty? To suffer sin upon a child, no less than upon a brother, is the same as hating him "in your heart."[q] Is it not better that the flesh should smart, than that *the soul should die?* Is there no danger of stirring up native wickedness, and thereby becoming accessory to the child's eternal destruction? What if he should reproach you throughout eternity, for the neglect of that timely *correction,* which might have *delivered his soul from Sheol?* Or even if he be scarcely saved, can he not charge against you, much of his increasing difficulty in the ways of God?

[o] 1 Sam 2:23–25; 3:13

[p] Prov 22:15; Eccl 11:10

[q] Lev 19:17, with Prov 13:24

Yet, let it not be used continuously. Point to the problem. Our heavenly Father never stirs the rod with His children, if His gentle voice of instruction prevails. Continual faultfinding; applying *correction* to each bit of childish trifling or troublesome thoughtlessness, would soon bring a callous deadness to all sense of shame. Let the correction be reserved, at least in its more serious forms, for willfulness. It is medicine, not food; the remedy for the occasional diseases of the constitution, not a daily, regulated system for life and nourishment. And to convert medicine into daily food, gradually destroys its remedial qualities.

Some parents, indeed, use nothing but *correction.*

They indulge their own passions at the expense of their less guilty children. Unlike our Heavenly Father, they "afflict" and grieve their children "*willingly*";[r] to vent their anger, not to subdue their children's sins. Self-recollection is of great significance. "Am I about to correct my child for his own good?" Uncontrolled use of this Scriptural command discredits it on the basis of its effectiveness and sows the seed of much bitter fruit. Children become hardened under an iron rod. Sternness and severity of manner close up their hearts. It is most dangerous to make them afraid of us. A spirit of bondage and concealment develops, which often leads to a lie; sowing the seed of hypocrisy—sometimes the seed of disgust, and even of hatred, toward their unreasonable parents. "If parents," said a wise and godly father, "would not correct their children, except prayerfully, when they are able to 'lift up their hands without wrath,' it would provoke neither God nor them."

[r]Contrast Lam 3:33; Heb 12:10

Other parents freely threaten *the rod,* yet withhold it. It was meant only to frighten. It soon becomes an empty and powerless sound. This again opposes the Lord—our great example. *His* threatenings are not vain words. If His children will not turn to Him, they will find Him true to His threatenings. This threatening play is solemn trifling with truth; teaching children by example, what they had learned from the womb,[s] to "speak lies." Let our words be considerate, but certain. Let our children know, that they must not trifle, either with our words or with us. The firmness of truthful discipline alone can convey a wholesome influence. Any defect here is a serious injury.

[s]Ps 58:3

We must learn however not to expect more than is reasonable from our children; nor to be unduly depressed by their naughtiness. Yet we must not wink at their sinful actions. We must not love them less, but more. And because we love them, we must *not withhold needed correction from them.* All of this is more painful to us than to them. And most humbling! Since it is the corrupt root that produces the poisoned sap in the bud, what else is it but the *correction* of our own sin? Yet though "discipline for the moment seems not to be joyful, but sorrowful";[t] when given in prayer, in wisdom, and in faith, the saving blessing is assured.[u] Lord, do thou be pleased to have

[t]Heb 12:11

[u]Comp. 1 Cor 5:5; 11:32

part in every stroke, so that the rod of correction may be a rod of instruction. "It is a rare soul," said good Bishop Hall, "that can be kept in constant order without smarting remedies. I confess, mine cannot. How wild had I run, if the rod had not been over me! Every man can say, he thanks God for his ease. For me, I bless God for my *trouble*."[4]

15 *My son, if your heart is wise,*
My own heart also will be glad;
16 *And my inmost being will rejoice,*
When your lips speak what is right.

NONE BUT A PARENT KNOWS

[v] Prov 1:8, 10, 15

Solomon now turns from parents and speaks most tenderly to children,[v] perhaps to his own child. What Christian parent can help but respond? Could we be happy to see our child honored in the world, admired, talented, prosperous, without godliness? *If your heart is wise*—this is the spring of parental joy—*my heart will be glad.* His health, his comfort, his welfare is inexpressibly dear to us. But while we watch over the casket, it is the jewel that we value most. The love of our child's soul is the heart and life of parental love.[5] None but a parent knows the heart of a parent. None but a Christian parent knows the yearning anxiety, the many tears, and prayers, and travailing in birth again for the soul of a beloved child; or the fervor of joy and praise, when the first budding of heavenly *wisdom* bursts to view.[6] The sight brings joy into the innermost depths of the bosom. Parents, who don't experience these sensations, and with whom Solomon's language is unfelt and uninteresting, realize neither their responsibilities nor their privileges.

Greatly is the parent's joy heightened to hear *his son's lips speaking what is right;* to see him, in a day of apostasy and unstable profession, openly standing on the Lord's side. But surely this child, now the father's joy, is one, *from whom correction has not been withheld.* The "foolishness" bound in his heart has been driven from

[4] Silent Thoughts, *21.*

[5] *See Solomon's own education, Prov 4:3, 4.*

[6] *Verses 24, 25; 10:1; 15:20; 29:8. "Lord, let thy blessing so accompany my endeavour" (were the pleadings of a godly parent) "that all my sons may be Benaiahs (the Lord's building); and then they will be all Abners (their Father's light); and that all my daughters may be Bethiahs (the Lord's daughters); and then they will be all Abigails (Their Father's joy)"—SWINNOCK'S* Christian Man's Calling, *2:29, 30.*

him;[w] and its place graciously filled by a *wise heart*—a witness to the subsequent rule and promise—"Correct your son, and he will give you comfort."[x]

[w]Prov 22:15; 29:15

[x]Prov 29:17

And are not ministers also partakers of this parental joy? Paul the aged was filled with prayerful delight in his "beloved son" in the faith.[y] The thriving churches were his "glory and joy."[z] Another apostle "was very glad to find some of your children walking in truth."[a] And may we not rise higher and adore the manifestation of this joy in heaven[b]—yes, in the bosom of God himself over the return of His *corrected child* to a *wise heart*—"This son of mine was dead, and has come to life again; he was lost, and has been found"?[c]

[y]2 Tim 1:2–5

[z]1 Thess 2:19, 20; 3:8, 9

[a]2 John 4; 3 John 4

[b]Luke 15:7, 10

[c]Luke 15:24; Prov 29:13–24

17 *Do not let your heart envy sinners,*
But live *in the fear of the* LORD *always.*
18 *Surely there is a future,*
And your hope will not be cut off.

BE CONTINUALLY WITH YOUR GOD

David's counsel is exactly the same. He shows how little reason we have to *envy sinners,* and what is the true path of duty and quietness.[d] He was, however, himself, for a while shaken by this temptation. And though he did not *envy sinners,* so as to covet their worldly prosperity, yet he compared their condition with his own chastening, "it was troublesome" for the Psalmist until he went "into the sanctuary of God; Then [he] perceived the end,"[7] and learned to rest in the assurance—*Your hope will not be cut off.*

[d]Ps 37:1–9, 35, 36. Comp Prov 24:1, 2, 19, 20

What then is the safeguard proposed? Just what the Psalmist had found so effective—being "continually" with his God[e]—the very spirit of the rule—*live in the fear of the Lord always.* Here he gathered confidence for both worlds—"With Thy counsel Thou wilt guide me, And afterward receive me to glory."[f] With such a portion, both for time and for eternity, could his heart then *envy sinners*? "I have set the Lord continually before me ... Thou wilt make known to me the path of life; in Thy presence is fullness of joy."[g] What more could he desire? *His heart,* instead of *envying sinners,* would be drawn

[e]Ps 73:23

[f]Ps 73:24

[g]Ps 16:8–11

[7] *Ps 73:3, 16, 17. Even a non-believer discovered the power of this temptation. Socrates being asked—What was most troublesome to good men?—he answered, "The prosperity of the wicked."*

[h]Ps 17:14; Luke 16:25
[i]Prov 24:20

out in compassionate pleading for those, who have no portion but a dying world;[h] no expectation, but that which shall quickly be *cut off.*[i]

But this habitual *fear of the Lord* is not separate from everyday life. Actually, it gives to it a holy character. It makes all its minute details not only consistent with, but component parts of, godliness. Acts of kindliness are done "in a manner worthy of God."[j] Instead of one duty thrusting out another, all are done "heartily, as for the Lord rather than for man."[k] Some professing believers confine their spiritual attitudes and actions to extraordinary occasions. But Elijah seems to have been content to await his translation in his ordinary course of work;[l] an example that may teach us to lay the greater stress upon our daily and habitual, not extraordinary, service. Others are satisfied with a periodical religion; as if it were rather a rapture or an occasional impulse, than a habit. But if we are to engage in morning and evening devotions, we are also to "wait" upon the Lord "all the day."[m] If we are to enjoy our service and worship on the Lord's day, we are also to "remain" in our calling with God."[n] Thus the character of a servant of God is maintained—"reverence for Thee."[o]

[j]3 John 5, 6
[k]Eph 6:6; Col 3:23
[l]2 Kings 2:1–12
[m]Ps 25:5
[n]Ps 84, with 1 Cor 7:20, 24
[o]Ps 119:38

In this Christian walk with God, all is safe for eternity. The hope of the ungodly,[p] the hypocrite,[q] the worldling,[r] shall perish. But *your hope will not be cut off.*[s] It is a hope that "does not disappoint."[t] It is grounded upon "the unchangeableness of His purpose," and "enters within the vail."[u] Surely there is an end for this. If your cross is heavy, remember you have but a little time to bear it. If the way is wearisome to the flesh, *the end* drawing nearer will abundantly compensate. If the light is not visible, it "is sown like seed" for Thee.[v] And in waiting for the glorious harvest—"here is the perseverance and the faith of the saints."[w] Meanwhile, don't judge the Lord hastily by sense and feeling. Hold fast by God's word. Give time to His providence to explain itself. Conclude nothing upon an unfinished work. Wait, and see "*the outcome* of the Lord's dealings." " 'I know the plans that I have for you,' declares the Lord, 'plans for welfare and not for calamity to give you a future and a hope.' " Jesus said, "What I do you do not know now; but

[p]Prov 11:7
[q]Job 8:13, 14
[r]Luke 12:19, 20
[s]Prov 24:14; Ps 9:18; Eccl 8:12; Phil 1:20
[t]Rom 5:5
[u]Heb 6:17–19
[v]Ps 97:11
[w]Rev 13:10

you shall understand"—and not only know—but approve "hereafter."[x]

[x] James 5:11; Jer 29:11; John 13:7

19 *Listen, my son, and be wise,*
And direct your heart in the way.
20 *Do not be with heavy drinkers of wine,*
Or *with gluttonous eaters of meat;*
21 *For the heavy drinker and the glutton will come to poverty,*
And drowsiness will clothe a man *with rags.*

LOOK OUT FOR SATAN'S POISONED BAIT!

These repeated exhortations to *listen,* remind us of our Lord's earnest and affectionate call—"He who has ears to hear, let him hear."[y] They show the great importance of *listening,* as the first step to being wise. For wisdom, no less than "faith comes from hearing."[z] *"Direct your heart in the way."* The promise makes this call effectual—"I walk in the way of righteousness, in the midst of the paths of justice."[a]

But the call specially warns against a besetting temptation. God's creature abuses his gifts.[b] *Wine* becomes the occasion of excess. *Gluttons,* as slaves of the body, degrade the soul. Not only, don't be one of them, don't even associate with them.[c] Is it possible to be among diseased people without contracting infection? Can't we easily get a stain that can't be wiped out?

Aren't we unconsciously molded by the company we keep?[d] Didn't Lot probably learn his dreadful wickedness by contact with the ungodly?[e] The truest love is not to sit down with them, but to labor for their conversion; and, if this is ineffectual, to avoid them. Young people! "Remember—tinder is no more apt to take fire, wax the impression of the seal, paper the ink, than youth to receive the impression of wickedness," said Greenhill.[f] Don't think that the enemy of your soul wants you to have even present happiness. His malice holds out a poisoned bait. *Poverty* and shame are the temporal fruits.[g] But the eternal ruin of his deluded victims is his far more deadly design.

Noah as a winebibber[h] and the Corinthian converts, profaning the sacred feast by *drunkenness and gluttony,*[i] warn the man of God—"watching and praying, that you

[y] Matt 11:15; 13:9
[z] Rom 10:17, with Prov 1:5
[a] Prov 8:20
[b] Isa 5:11, 12, 22; 22:13; Hab 2:5, with Ps 104:14, 15; 1 Tim 4:3–5
[c] Prov 28:7
[d] Ps 106:35. Comp. Matt 24:49
[e] Gen 19:30–32, with Ezek 16:49, 50
[f] Ezek 19:4
[g] Prov 6:11; 20:13; 21:17; Isa 28:1–3; Joel 1:5; Luke 15:13–16
[h] Gen 9:20, 21
[i] 1 Cor 11:21

may not enter into temptation."[j] However, be sure that you always evangelize your parental warnings with the gospel. "Behave properly . . . not *in carousing and drunkenness . . . But put on the Lord Jesus Christ*"—the only effectual protection from the wickedness of the flesh. "*Having these promises,* beloved, let us cleanse ourselves from all defilement of flesh and spirit."[k]

[j] Matt 26:41
[k] Rom 13:13, 14; 2 Cor 7:1

22 *Listen to your father who begot you,*
And do not despise your mother when she is old.

"We had earthly fathers to discipline us, and we respected them."[l] Such is the rule of nature. Such is the law of God.[m] The wise man here enforces its special application to an aged parent. Certainly these—love and reverence—are doubly due. "A thing comely and pleasant to see," says Bishop Hall, "and worthy of honour from the beholder, is a child understanding the eye of his parent," reads *Holy Observations,* 5. More lovely still is this filial devotion, when the child is of age, and free of the restraints of parental authority, for then, the respect shown is prompted by principle and gratitude. The child doesn't feel any more free to *despise* his parent's wishes, than if he were subject to their early discipline. The Scripture examples are beautiful patterns for our imitation. Isaac with Abraham;[n] Jacob with both his parents;[o] Joseph's deference to his aged father, and desiring his blessing on his own children;[p] Moses with his father-in-law;[q] Ruth with her mother-in-law;[r] Solomon in the grandeur of royalty paying respect to his mother;[s] the Rechabites hearkening to their deceased father's command;[t] and—above all the rest—the Savior's tender care for His mother in his own dying agonies.[8]

[l] Heb 12:9
[m] Exod 20:12; Lev 19:3; Eph 6:1, 2. Comp. Prov 1:8; 6:20
[n] Gen 22:9
[o] Gen 28:1–5
[p] Gen 48:9–14
[q] Exod 18:13–24
[r] Ruth 2:22, 23
[s] 1 Kings 2:19
[t] Jer 35:6

The contrary conduct comes under God's most awful disapproval.[u] It is typical of heathen depravity[v] and is one of the signs "that in the last days difficult times will come."[w] That kind of behavior will always bring a blot upon the child's name and character.[x]

[u] Prov 20:20; 30:17; Deut 21:18–21; 27:16; Isa 3:5
[v] Rom 1:30
[w] 2 Tim 3:1, 2
[x] Prov 19:26

But isn't neglect by our children, the Lord's chastening of our foolish fondness for our children when young, and

[8] *John 19:26, 27. Dr. Taylor's godly exhortation to his son, as Foxe writes in his exquisite biography, "is worthy of all youth to be marked"—"When thy mother is waxed old, forsake her not; but provide for her to thy power, and see that she lack nothing; for so will God bless thee, give thee long life upon earth, and prosperity, which I pray God to grant thee," Vol. 6:692.*

our unwise treatment, or inconsistent conduct? Sinful indulgence will always make us *despised* in their eyes and lay our authority in the dust for them to trample under foot. Christian dignity and consistency, on the other hand, command respect, even where they fail to produce the full practical results.[y] Oh! what need we have for divine grace and wisdom, in order to honorably maintain parental responsibility!

[y]Prov 31:28

23 *Buy truth, and do not sell* it,
Get *wisdom and instruction and understanding.*
24 *The father of the righteous will greatly rejoice,*
And he who begets a wise son will be glad in him.
25 *Let your father and your mother be glad,*
And let her rejoice who gave birth to you.

KEEP THE BLESSING IN FULL VIEW

This is the "merchant" who to purchase the "one pearl of great value, he went and sold all that he had."[z] The blessing can indeed only be bought "without cost."[a] It is as free as it is precious. But the value of it determines the importance of gaining it at any cost. First, however, let us satisfy ourselves that the seller is no deceiver; that he is perfectly upright in His dealings. "Buy from Me,"[b] saith the Savior. This puts the matter at rest. If we do not really want the article, we won't pay much attention to the invitation to buy. "Buy the things we have need of"[c]—is the rule. Ponder also its inestimable value. It is *the truth,* the only means of salvation,[d] the only deliverance from sin,[e] the only principle of holiness,[f] the "one thing needful."[g] Keep the blessing in full view—"The surpassing value of knowledge [of] Christ Jesus my Lord . . . that I may gain Christ, and may be found in Him . . . that I may attain to the resurrection from the dead."[h] We cannot be defrauded in the purchase. It is inexpensive at any price.[i] The lover of pleasure values the baubles of Vanity Fair most highly. But Bunyan beautifully describes the pilgrims, answering the sneering reproach—"What will you buy?" They lifted up their eyes above—"We will buy the truth."

But, like the well-practiced merchant, we must secure the genuine article. Many a counterfeit article is offered.[j] Measure everything by God's standard.[k] That which

[z]Matt 13:45, 46
[a]Isa 55:1
[b]Rev 3:18
[c]John 13:29
[d]1 Tim 2:4
[e]John 8:32; 2 Tim 2:25, 26
[f]John 17:17
[g]AV—Luke 10:42
[h]Phil 3:8–11
[i]Prov 3:15
[j]2 Cor 11:3, 14; Gal 1:6, 7
[k]1 Thess 5:21; 1 John 4:1; Isa 8:20

brings *wisdom, instruction, and understanding,* is *the truth* of God.

Then having determined its riches and its purity—not only wish for it, gaze at it, commend it; but *buy the truth.* Not only bid, make an offer; but settle the agreement. Make it yours. The man did not wish for the field with the hidden treasure; but he "sold all that he had" and bought it. And let your purchase be the whole truth. Every particle, the very filings of the gold, are invaluable—"Give attention *to all* that I am going to show you."[l] Many are willing to make some little effort, but they stop short of the prize.[m] Shrink not from the full price; as did Herod;[n] the young ruler;[o] Agrippa;[p] and therefore they didn't buy it. Moses gave up "the treasures of Egypt" for it,[q] Paul, his Jewish privileges, and high reputation.[r] The Hebrews "accepted joyfully the seizure of... property."[s] The martyrs "did not love their lives even to death."[t] And who among them regretted paying the price?

[l] Ezek 40:4
[m] 2 Tim 3:7
[n] Mark 6:17–20
[o] Luke 18:23
[p] Acts 26:28
[q] Heb 11:24–26
[r] Phil 3:4–8
[s] Heb 10:34
[t] Rev 12:11; Acts 20:23, 24

Having made the purchase, shall we part with it? Should we not find it all we expected; or should we after all discover that we did not want it. We should be glad to get rid of it. Many an estate has been bought, and sold again, because of disappointed expectations. Though we are usually at liberty to *sell* what we have bought, here is a command to *buy,* but an order not to *sell.* And a merciful prohibition it is! For those who *sell the truth,* sell their own souls with it. And "what will a man be profited, if he gains the whole world, and forfeits his soul?"[u] Can we look at Esau,[v] Judas,[w] Demas,[x] *selling* their treasure for something worthless, experiencing real sorrow? Yet their apostasy clearly proved that "they did not receive the love of the truth so as to be saved":[y] that it was some shining shadow, no more than a notion, theoretical, not practical, never engrafted in their hearts. Having therefore never felt the power, or known its price, they could *sell it* for this world's pleasure, or for the more flattering delusions of their own hearts. Reader: have you ever known that apprehension of divine truth, that has made it in your eyes worth every sacrifice to *buy it?* No one—be assured—who has really *bought* it, will ever be willing to *sell* it.

[u] Matt 16:26
[v] Heb 12:16, 17
[w] Matt 27:3–5
[x] 2 Tim 4:10
[y] 2 Thess 2:10; 1 John 2:19

A joyous sight it is to see children realizing their parents' fondest hopes; proving their "heart is wise"[z] by earnest questioning about this only gainful purchase; not content with receiving it by education, but making the contract for themselves; discovering that Christianity must be a personal concern, an individual transaction between God and their own souls. It is cause for *greatly rejoicing,* to see our righteous children enriched for eternity, in possession of a treasure which they can never spend, and which no troubles, changes, or even hatreds of hell, can touch. If the godly parents have had a seed-time of tears, these precious sheaves of joy are an abundant recompense.[a] The stern exclusive system which recognizes little, apart from God's purpose and sovereignty, cancels out, or at least weakens, the responsibility of means, and thereby loses the privilege, both of trusting the promise, and seeing its accomplishment. Won't the child feel the constraining obligation to fulfill his parent's *rejoicing* so vividly portrayed? That son must be most unnatural, if his heart does not glow with the desire to repay *his father's* anxious love, and the yearning tenderness of *her who gave birth to him.* They ask no other repayment, than *the rejoicing and gladness* of seeing *a righteous and a wise son.* Selfishness itself might supply a motive; since parental *gladness* is the child's own joy for walking in *wisdom's* ways of pleasantness and peace.

[z] Prov 23:15, 16

[a] Ps 126:6. Comp. Prov 10:1; 15:20. Contrast 17:25

26 *Give me your heart, my son,*
And let your eyes delight in my ways.
27 *For a harlot is a deep pit,*
And an adulterous woman is a narrow well.
28 *Surely she lurks as a robber,*
And increases the faithless among men.

Here Solomon rises above himself and speaks in the name and person of divine wisdom.[b] For who else could claim *the gift of the heart*—the work of His own hands, the purchase of His own blood? *My son.* Such is the relationship which God acknowledges; including every blessing which He can give, and all the obedience that He can claim. No obedience can be given without the believing and practical acknowledgment of this relationship—my son; not a stranger; not an enemy; not a

[b] Prov 1:20; 8:1

slave, but *a son!* invited to return. A pardon of the past, and a perpetual jubilee of joy, awaits you at your Father's house.

GOD WANTS THE LOVE OF ALL OUR HEART

Many claim *the heart* of man. Heaven and hell contend for it. The world with its riches, honors, and pleasures; and science with its more plausible charms—cries—*Give me your heart.* Yes, even Satan dares to put in a loud and urgent plea—"if You worship before me, it shall all be Yours."[c] The loving Father calls—*My son, give me your heart.* The answer too often is—"I have no heart for God. It already belongs to the world. I cannot make up my mind to become a Christian, at least not yet." And so, even where there is no wickedness—perhaps even some plausible semblance of piety, the "darling" is given to the lion;[d] *the heart* to the murderer. Not one is naturally ready to offer the gift of his heart to Him who alone deserves it. Only a few are moved in a moment of conviction; and then, not till they have proved, at great cost, the falsehood and disappointment of all others who would lay claim to their hearts.

[c]Luke 4:7

[d]AV—Ps 35:17

It is a great honor He places upon His creatures, in condescending to receive as *a gift,* what is already owed to him in debt, and what He might at any moment that He wishes, command for Himself. But His call wakens His child to recollection and conscious dependence. It is the Father's striving with His child's will. It is the test of His child's obedience. It is a pointed arrow of conviction to his conscience for willful resistance to God's call; the only hindrance to his *giving his heart* is, that he has already given it to others who are infinitely unworthy of it. "My guilt is damnable," exclaimed a humbled saint, "in withholding my heart; because I know and believe His love, and what Christ has done to gain my consent—to what?—my own happiness."[9]

And yet, this call, holds no interest whatsoever. To them it would be like laying up a treasure in the clouds. To others, it is more like the funeral knell than a jubilee sound; as if we are called to surrender all our pleasures, instead of adding to them one of preeminent value and

[9] *ADAMS'* Private Thoughts.

pervading influence. Indeed most truly is our happiness bound up in this gracious command. For what else can fill up the aching void within, but "the love of God [which] has been poured out within our hearts through the Holy Spirit"?[e] Created objects only seem to widen the chasm. If our appetite is satisfied, it is but for a moment; while every irritation increases the general dissatisfaction. The heart, willfully remaining at a distance from God, can find its home only in a land of shadows. It grasps nothing solidly; while its never-ending conflict with conscience is, "the tossing sea . . . [which] cannot be quiet."[f]

[e]Rom 5:5

[f]Isa 57:20; Heb 7:25

Very little thought is given to the One who demands the gift—the ever-blessed God, whose smile is heaven, whose frown is hell. To rise to a higher obligation—it is claimed by Him, whose love brought Him from the throne of glory to the accursed cross; whose grace will cast out no one that comes to Him; who will find a place for His bitterest enemies near to His heart; who will be to each of them all that a lost sinner, with an immortal soul, can need; who "is able to save forever"; who has saved countless myriads; who is ready—Sinner! ponder it well —to save you!

But remember—He will never abandon any of His full requirements. He doesn't ask magnificent temples, costly sacrifices, pompous ceremonials, but the spiritual worship of the heart.[g] He demands, not the hands, the feet, the tongue, the ears; but that which is the moving principle of all the members—*the heart.* Give Him that! —It's all He desires. Withhold it, and He will reject everything else we can offer. What the heart doesn't do, it's as if it were not done at all. The cold formality of a lifeless faith is a dead, not "a living," and therefore, not a "holy sacrifice" or acceptable "spiritual service."[h] "How can you say, 'I love you,' when your heart is not with me?"[i] The man, who gives his heart to the world, rises above all his difficulties, persevering, resolved, successful. Never can we triumph over the hindrances of the gospel without the supports, that come only through the complete surrender of our heart to God.

[g]Isa 66:1, 2; John 4:23, 24

[h]Rom 12:1

[i]Judg 16:15

Never will He dispense with His claim for the love of *all our heart.*[j] We must not deal with Him as Lot's wife

[j]Matt 22:37

[k]Gen 19:26
[l]Ruth 1:14
[m]Matt 6:24
[n]Matt 10:37
[o]Hos 11:4

did, moving slowly forward, while the heart is behind;[k] or like Orpah, stopping at the very moment that the cross is to be borne.[l] Don't even consider dividing your heart with the world.[m] God loves *a broken heart.* He spurns *a divided heart.* Satan will seem to be content with a part; because he knows that, God will accept nothing less than all, so that Satan will get the whole heart anyway. It is far beneath the Majesty of heaven to possess anything less than the throne[n]—a lowly throne at best for the almighty Sovereign of the universe. But his claims are paramount. And never are we truly our own, until we unreservedly acknowledge ourselves to be His. Indeed all false religions in the world are but vain substitutes for this plain and most happy privilege. However plausible our profession, if it does not lead the heart to God, it is a fearful delusion. Whatever principles, practices, or society, turn our hearts from God—it is the highroad of ruin.

And does He ask His child for *his heart*; and will His child refuse to *give* it? Does it open immediately to Satan and the world—even before they knock? and is the beseeching Father to be excluded? Are there no "bonds of love" to draw?[o] Out of what rock was it hewn, that it can withstand the pleadings of divine parental love? Can't you give it to Him? Surely, if you had the will, you would have the power, too. If you have the faintest will, at least show it, even if it is by the feeblest effort. Offer it, even if you do so with a trembling hand. His hand will meet yours and take it from you. The happiest day of your life will then have arrived; a day, you will never in the slightest regret.

If you have not done it, do it now. Don't let it be half-giving. To hesitate—to delay—is to refuse. And why should you delay? Has Satan been so good a master, that you are reluctant to leave him? Can you find a better friend than Jesus, who has cared so long for you, than He who has died for you? Now then, with the help of God's Spirit, without whom this cannot be done—resolve, decide—once for all—forever. But if you have already done it, renew your pledge daily. He is still the same; still as deserving of *your heart* as ever. You cannot give it to Him too soon or rededicate it too often. The command does not compel us to enter the service of God. The citadel is not stormed, but it opens its gates. A principle of immortal energy constrains the heart; yet only by making it "volunteer freely."[p] All reluctance is melted away, and *by the power of love* the heart is compelled to "come."[q] What other gift is so free? And never is the will so free, as when it moves toward God. Weak as the child is, he can testify, that to *give his heart* is his first desire; that he never intends anything less; that he longs for the consuming of every corruption, which hinders his full surrender. O Lord, Your grace alone can enable me. I am ashamed of the gift. Nothing can be more unworthy. But because it has been purchased by Your death, and You call for it, it is Your own, and it *shall* be Yours. Take it then as it is, I pray. Make it what it is not. Keep it with Yourself. Bind it so close to You with the cords of love, that it may never cast a wishful look away from You. If I had a *thousand* hearts, every one would be Yours. You alone can fill it. You alone are worthy of it. Exalt Your own throne in it forever.

[p]Ps 110:3

[q]2 Cor 5:14; Luke 14:23

Think how everything hangs on this point. Give it and all the blessings of the gospel are yours. Refuse to give it, and you trample the blessings under your feet; you live a life of base rebellion to your best Friend, and of cruel madness to your own soul; you live without Christ; you will die without hope; accursed, lost forever. The command of authority is an invitation of love—Think about it. Think how right, how reasonable, how winning, how much it is beyond everything else, how much worth accepting in spite of every hindrance and objection. How much beyond every other joy is the delight of *giving your heart* to the tender compassionate love of your dying Savior! And then, having made Him the object of your desires, and all your wishes for happiness and dependence; be determined to seek, and confident to find all in Him, and firm in rejecting every temptation to seek it elsewhere. Having therefore *given your heart, let your eyes delight in his ways.*[r] "*Our heart* given, gives all the rest. This makes eyes, ears, tongue and hands, and all, to be holy," said Leighton.[s] His Word will be our rule;[t] His Holy Spirit our interpreter.[u] The *heart,* no longer divided, is now at full liberty for His service. *The eyes,* no longer wandering, like "the eyes of a fool are on the ends of the

[r]Prov 4:23–25

[s]1 Peter 2:4, 5
[t]Prov 6:23; Ps 119:9–11, 105
[u]Ps 117:43

earth,"[v] are now fixed upon an object supremely worthy, and abundantly satisfying.

Here also is our power of resistance to the clever seductions of the enemy[w]—"I have given my word to the Lord, and I cannot," I will not, "take it back."[x] He has *my heart,* and He *shall* have it. So long, indeed, as we carry about us a body of sin and death, we need a continual supply of "the Spirit" to put "to death the deeds of the body."[y] But in our new atmosphere of heavenly light, the mask falls off from the allurements of sin. *The harlot* appears frightful as *a deep pitch,* or, what is even more, *a narrow well,* with no room to escape.[z] Mighty and strong men have fallen into it.[10] The tempter hides the danger, while she lays wait for the prey; and thus she successfully *increases the faithless among men.*[a] Blessed be God! if while fleshly lusts have destroyed "numerous,"[b] we have, by *giving our heart* to its gracious Lord, been enabled to resist the temptation, and to ascribe to our faithful-keeping God the glory of our deliverance.

[v]Prov 17:24
[w]Prov 2:10, 11, 16
[x]Judg 11:35. Comp. Gen 39:9
[y]Rom 8:13; Gal 5:16
[z]Prov 22:14; 2:19
[a]Prov 7:6; 9:13–18
[b]Prov 7:26

29 *Who has woe? Who has sorrow?*
Who has contentions? Who has complaining?
Who has wounds without cause?
Who has redness of eyes?
30 *Those who linger long over wine,*
Those who go to taste mixed wine.
31 *Do not look on the wine when it is red,*
When it sparkles in the cup,
When it goes down smoothly;
32 *At the last it bites like a serpent,*
And stings like a viper.
33 *Your eyes will see strange things,*
And your mind will utter perverse things.
34 *And you will be like one who lies down in the middle of the sea,*
Or like one who lies down on the top of a mast.
35 *"They struck me,* but *I did not become ill;*
They beat me, but *I did not know it.*
When shall I awake?
I will seek another drink."

[10] *1 Kings 11:1–8, with Neh 13:26; Judg 16:4–20. "He* [Samson] *broke the bonds of his enemies; but he could not break the bonds of his own lusts. He choked the lion; but he could not choke his own wanton love"—Ambrose quoted by Jermin.*

THE DRUNKARD'S MIRROR

A warning was lately given against keeping company with sensualists—those who live for the pleasure of the senses.[c] Here it is enforced by the most graphic description of the sin in all its misery, shame, and ruin. It is the drunkard's looking glass! Let him see his own face. Let him hang it up in his cottage. Fix it in the wine cellar that he may see himself when he goes there. The picture is drawn with such vivid color! "No translation or paraphrase can do justice to the concise, abrupt, and energetic manner of the original," said Scott. Drunkenness is a time of merriment. But what must be the stupifying insensibility that can find a moment's joy, with such an accumulation of *woe*! Every sin brings its own mischief. But such woe! Such sorrow!—in all its multiform misery! *Who has it*? The brawls and *contentions* over the cup;[d] the *complaining* words of pollution;[e] *the wounds,* often to murder,[f] *without cause*; the *redness of the eyes,* showing the effect of liquor on the countenance; the impure appetites that are kindled; the infatuation almost incredible—this is sensuality in all its wretchedness.

[c] Verses 20, 21
[d] Prov 20:1; 1 Tim 3:3
[e] Dan 5:4
[f] 2 Sam 13:38; 1 Kings 16:9, 10; 20:16–20

Where did this world of *woe* and *sorrow* come from? It is the curse of self-will indulged. Not satisfied with their healthful refreshment, many will "add drunkenness to thirst."[g] *They linger long,* "who rise early in the morning that they may pursue strong drink."[h] *They go to taste the mixed wine,* strongest and most intoxicating of drink.[11]

[g] AV—Deut 29:19
[h] Isa 5:11

Wisdom's voice therefore is—avoid the allurements of sin. Often has a *look,* harmless in itself, proved a fearful temptation.[i] *Do not look on the wine when it is red.* Its very color; its sparkling transparency *in the cup*; the relish with which it *goes down smoothly,* "or goes down pleasant," said Holden[j]—all tend to excite the irregular appetite. Crush it in its beginnings, and prove that you have learned the first lesson in the school of Christ—"Deny himself."[12] Whatever is its present zest, *at the last it bites like a serpent, and stings like a viper.*[k] If it *bit* first, who would touch it? If Satan presented the cup in his own naked form, who would dare to take it? Yet it comes from his hand as truly as if he were visible to the

[i] Gen 3:6; 39:7; Josh 7:21; 2 Sam 11:2
[j] Song of Sol 7:9
[k] Comp. Prov 20:17

[11] *Prov 9:2, note. Homer describes his celebrated Helen, as mixing exhilarating ingredients in the bowl to revive the spirits.*

[12] *Matt 16:24. Augustine gives an instructive example of his mother's nurse,* Confess. 9:8. *See also George Herbert's excellent advice in his well-known poem*—The Temple.

eyes. If poison were seen in the cup, who would take a chance and drink it? Yet, is the poison less dangerous because it is unseen? *The viper's sting* is concealed, yet fatal. The cup of sparkling wine becomes "a cup of trembling" in the hands of the Lord.[l]

[l]AV—Zech 12:2. Comp. Joel 1:5

Sensual indulgences rarely come alone. One lust prepares the way for others. The first step is sure to lead onward. The poor deluded victim cannot stop when he pleases. Drunkenness opens the door for impurity.[m] The inflamed eye soon catches fire with *the harlot*; and who knows what the end may be? Loathsome indeed is *the heart* of the ungodly laid bare. Drink opens it as far as words can do; and by the tongue, it does indeed utter perverse things.[13] "Blasphemy is wit, vulgar language is eloquence to a man that is turned into a brute," said Lawson.

[m]Gen 19:32. Comp. Jer 5:8; Ezek 16:49, 50; Hos 4:18; Rom 13:13; 1 Peter 4:3

But the delirium is the most awful feature of the case. The unhappy victim, having lost all will and power to escape, sleeps quietly amid dangers as real *as lying down in the middle of the sea, or on the top of the mast.*[n] Yes—even his senses seem to be stupified. He may be *struck and beaten.* But "his heart was merry,"[o] and he thanks his drunkenness, that *he didn't know it.* Therefore "like a dog that returns to its vomit is a fool who repeats his folly,"[p] craving fresh indulgence. *When shall I awake? I will seek another drink.* More senseless than the brute who satisfies nature, not lust; so lost to shame; his reasons so tyrannized over by his appetite, that he longs to be bound again, and only seeks relief from his temporary *awakening* to a sense of his misery, by yielding himself up again to his ruinous sin.[q]

[n]Isa 28:7, 8; Hos 4:11. Comp. Prov 31:4, 5

[o]1 Sam 25:36, 37

[p]Prov 26:11; Isa 56:12

[q]Jer 2:25

Oh! how affecting is the thought of the multitude of victims to this deadly vice in every age, around the world, and among all ranks of society! Perhaps there is no sin which has not linked itself with it; which the unconsciousness in the act of sin only serves, not to excuse the guilt, but to increase the responsibility.

While we see the whole nature so depraved in taste, so steeped in pollution—we ask, "Is anything too hard for the Lord?" Praised be His name for a full deliverance from the captivity of sin, and of all and every sin, even

[13] *Ps 69:12; Hos 7:5. The libertine poet praises the inspiring excitement of wine to the genius of posey—HOR. Eph 1:19.*

from the chains of this giant sin.[r] The mighty, though despised instrument is "Christ crucified . . . the power of God and the wisdom of God."[s] It is this, which—when vows, pledges, and resolution—all have failed; works secretly, yet most effectually; imparting new principles, affections, and appetites. The drunkard becomes sober; the unclean holy; the glutton temperate. The love of Christ overpowers the love of sin. Pleasures are now enjoyed without *a sting* (for no *serpent,* nor adder is here) and the newly-implanted principle transforms the whole man into the original likeness to God—"No one who is born of God practices sin, because His seed abides in him; and he cannot sin, because he is born of God . . . He who was born of God keeps him and the evil one does not touch him."[14]

[r]John 8:34–36; 1 Cor 6:10, 11

[s]1 Cor 1:23–25

[14] *1 John 3:9; 5:18. See an affecting evangelical pleading with this case in that valuable manual,* JOWETT'S Christian Visitor.

CHAPTER TWENTY-FOUR

1 *Do not be envious of evil men,*
Nor desire to be with them;
2 *For their minds devise violence,*
And their lips talk of trouble.

[a]Prov 23:17

[b]2 Cor 5:7; Heb 11:1

[c]James 4:5

[d]Ps 73:10–14

[e]Prov 23:18. Comp. verses 19, 20

[f]Prov 1:11–14; 4:16; 6:18; 1 Sam 23:9; Job 15:35; Ps 7:14; 64:2–6; Mic 7:3

[g]Esther 3:8, 9; 5:13

[h]Matt 26:16; 27:3–5; Job 7:15

[i]Ps 26:9; 28:3

This advice was given only a few verses back.[a] But it is very difficult in the false glare of this world's glory to "walk by faith, not by sight... the conviction of things not seen."[b] In the confined atmosphere of impatience and unbelief, "He jealously desires the Spirit which He has made to dwell in us."[c] But the evil spirit, if it does not bring the scandal of open sin, curses our blessings, withers our graces, cankers our peace, clouds our confidence, and stains our Christian profession. The full cup in the house of evil men stirs up *the desire to be with them.*[d] But if their fearful end did not restrain, their awful character is warning enough.[e] It is the great malice of Satan himself, *their minds devise violence; their lips talk of trouble.*[f] Take away then the delusive veil; and who would envy them? When Haman was *devising violence* for the holy nation, the barbed arrow of discontent was eating out his insides.[g] Who would envy Judas, plotting his Master's destruction? In the agony of remorse, his soul chose strangling, rather than life.[h] "Do not take my soul away *along* with sinners"—is the prayer of the child of God—nor "with the wicked and with those who work iniquity."[i] Let me, instead of plotting the destruction, study the salvation, of my fellow-sinners—trying to determine what I can do to win them to Christ? Let me *desire to be with* the man of God, employed in this Godlike work. The Christian is the only enviable person in the world. The seeming blessings of *evil men* are God's heavy curses; and the smart of the stripes is a favor too good for them to enjoy. To judge our condition wisely, it is to be considered, not so much *how* we fare, as *upon what terms*. If we are in a right relationship with heaven, every cross is a blessing; and every blessing a pledge of future happiness. If we are in God's disfavor, every one of His benefits is a judgment; and every judgment makes way for perdition. Instead of *envying evil men* in their successful wickedness, dread their character more than their end, and rejoice that your Father never counted the poor vanities of this world a worthy portion for you.

3 *By wisdom a house is built,*
And by understanding it is established;
4 *And by knowledge the rooms are filled*
With all precious and pleasant riches.
5 *A wise man is strong,*
And a man of knowledge increases power.
6 *For by wise guidance you will wage war,*
And in abundance of counselors there is victory.

TEMPLE OF SOULS

Why should we envy the prosperity of the wicked? Even if their house is built,[j] it cannot be established,[k] by iniquity. "It is only the snow-palace built in the winter, and melting away under the power of the summer's sun," said Geier. "The wise woman builds her house"[l] upon piety and prudence—a far more solid *establishment*. Let every *room* of the mind *be filled with these precious and pleasant* gifts. Without them man is without strength of character; the creature of accident, circumstance, or society, thinking and living upon the opinion of others. A general indecision marks his insignificant course; the soul, when consecrated as God's *house*,[m] is *built on* an enlightened *understanding* of divine truth: and every *room is filled with all precious and pleasant riches* of godliness.[n] Heresy is held down by conceding supreme authority to the Bible. But the crude professing believer acts under feverish impulse, a sickly sentimentalist in religion. Instead of retaining a firm hold of truth, he readily takes on the most monstrous opinions. He is "carried away by varied and strange teachings," instead of exhibiting the good things of a "heart . . . strengthened by grace."[o] Growth in spiritual, as distinct from speculative

[j] Mic 3:10
[k] Prov 12:3; Jer 22:13, 18; Amos 5:11
[l] Prov 14:1
[m] 2 Cor 6:16
[n] 2 Peter 1:2–4
[o] Heb 13:9

"knowledge," will always be accompanied with growth "in grace."[p]

[p] 2 Peter 3:18

And let's also observe, how God has laid the foundations of the spiritual *house,* shaped and framed the materials by His own divine wisdom, and *filled all the rooms with His precious and pleasant riches?* Delightful is the overview of the building, as it is rising, and as it will be, when it is finished. "Oh, the transcendant glory," exclaimed the heavenly Martyn (*Life,* chap. 3), "of this temple of souls; lively stones, perfect in all its parts, the purchase and work of God!"

But let's take another look at the advantages of *wisdom. A wise man is strong.*[q] Every view confirms Lord Bacon's far-famed saying—"Knowledge is power." New discoveries and developments have increased our strength almost immeasurably over physical force. Intellectual *knowledge,* wisely applied, has immense moral dominance. It restrains national leaders from unadvised *wars;*[r] and, if forced into the field, instead of walking their perilous path alone, they ensure the safety of their nations by the *abundance of counselors.*[s] *The man of* spiritual *knowledge* is a giant in strength. He combines the power to draw the bow with a steady hand and eye to guide the arrow to the mark. Conscious ignorance is the first principle of knowledge. "I am but a little child," said the wisest of men, Solomon; and this humility of wisdom was the *establishment* of his kingdom.[t] The Christian, "filled with the knowledge of His will in all *spiritual* wisdom and understanding," is also "*strengthened*" in his warfare "with all power, according to His glorious might."[u] For "the people who know their God will display strength and take action."[v]

[q] Prov 21:22; Eccl 7:19; 9:16
[r] Prov 20:18
[s] Prov 11:14; 15:22
[t] 1 Kings 3:7; 5:12; 10:23–29; 2 Chron 27:6
[u] Col 1:9, 11
[v] Dan 11:32

7 *Wisdom is too high for a fool,*
He does not open his mouth in the gate.

The commendation of wisdom is here continued. The man richly endowed with it comes forth with authority and *speaks at the gate* among the wise. *The fool,* destitute of wisdom is barred from this honor. The simple[w] and diligent[x] prove that the treasure is not really out of reach. But *it is too high for the fool.* His groveling mind can never rise to so lofty a matter. He has no apprehen-

[w] Prov 8:9; 14:6; Matt 11:25
[x] Prov 2:1–6; John 7:17

sion of it;[y] no heart to desire it,[z] no energy to lay hold of it.[a] And therefore, though in the gospel it "is near you, in your mouth and in your heart,"[b] he cannot reach it. Its holy spirituality is *too high* for him. Therefore he commands no respect in his own station of society.[c] No one seeks his counsel. His opinion, if given, is of no account. Though he may have a babbling tongue in the street, yet *he doesn't open his mouth in the gate.* He is utterly unfit to give judgment in the presence of wise and judicious men. And this is not from natural defect but from willful wickedness. His Lord had committed at least one talent to his trust. But he had frittered it away, not trading with it.[d] Oh! Look for *wisdom,* while it is within reach; while it is so freely promised.[e] When found, let it be diligently improved for the great purposes of life. What if we should die without it, having done nothing for our God or fellow-man, having neglected the way of life: and "in the greatness of his folly he will go astray" to everlasting ruin?[f]

[y]Ps 10:5; 92:5, 6; 1 Cor 2:14
[z]Prov 17:16, 24
[a]Prov 13:4; 21:25
[b]Rom 10:6–8
[c]Contrast Job 29:7–10
[d]Matt 25:24–30
[e]James 1:5
[f]Prov 5:23

8 *He who plans to do evil,*
Men will call him a schemer.
9 *The devising* [AV—*thought*] *of folly is sin,*
And the scoffer is an abomination to men.

A PICTURE OF DEPRAVITY

What a picture of human depravity, in its active working, its corrupt beginning, and its fearful end! Talent, imagination, active mind, are so debased, as to be all concentrated upon Satan's own work—*scheming to do evil.*[g] He was the first *schemer,*[h] and he trains his children, till he makes them, like himself, master schemers. He teaches them to contrive new modes of sinning, ways of trickery and deceit; like the degraded heathen, they become "inventors of evil."[i] To do evil is the principle; *planning to do evil* is the energy, or Satan's service. In this craft of evil, Balaam was *a schemer.*[j] Abimelech has earned for himself the same condemnation.[k] Jeroboam's subtle scheming has stamped his name with the black mark of reprobation—"he made Israel sin."[l] Jezebel,[m] and others of less note, equally industrious in evil, will appear in the same ranks at the great day.

[g]Verse 2; Ps 36:3, 4
[h]Gen 3:1
[i]Rom 1:30
[j]Num 31:16; Rev 2:14
[k]Judg 9
[l]1 Kings 12:26–33; 15:30
[m]1 Kings 21:25; Rev 2:20

Even when it is not brought out into action, *the devising* or thought *of folly*—giving it lodgment,[n] instead of casting it out as loathsome—*is sin.* "But what guilt," it is asked, "can there be in a thought? It's just an airy notion—harmless. It doesn't mean anything. It can't make any impression. A malicious thought can't hurt. A covetous thought cannot rob. What guilt or danger can belong to so small a thing as a thought?" Perhaps, in dealing with man, these might be trifling evils. But as the thought is the fountain of the act, God counts it in the act and holds us responsible for it.[o] The smallest sin makes us guilty of the whole law. This is His decision; and who can speak against it? The most spiritual Christians lay their hands upon their mouths and their "mouths in the dust."[p]

The awakened sinner admits that he is totally depraved upon the same demonstration as his own existence—consciousness. One sin gives birth to another. Countless multitudes follow in rapid and continuous succession. "Every intent of *the thoughts of his heart* was only evil continually."[q] If we fully realized the significance of all this, the flitting moments of the day, each bringing with it an increase of guilt, could not slide away so pleasantly from us; not at least without constant application of God's remedy. Job's sensitive conscience caused his sons to continually avail themselves of the atoning sacrifice![r] John Bunyan (unlike many who are only "professing" Christians and never troubled about their thoughts) was deeply afflicted at the memory of just one sinful thought. And let's not condemn this as a morbid temperament! Isn't it rather the tender sensibility of a heart humbled by constantly keeping Jesus Christ as the great sin-offering in view? Our sensibilities rise in proportion to our spiritual understanding. Even just a passing shadow of sin—if we only realized it—might well be a matter of painful bitterness. True sorrow for heart-sins—however involuntary—is a clear mark of divine grace and teaching: issuing in deep humiliation, not with despondency.[s]

But let us follow out this *thought of folly* unrestrained. The brain is never used to its fullest. It is the fruitful principle of sin, which, the more it is committed, the more evil it becomes. The *thought* therefore becomes

[n]Jer 4:14

[o]Comp. Prov 15:26; Ps 94:11; Matt 9:3, 4; 15:19; Acts 8:22; Rom 2:15

[p]James 2:10, 11; Lam 3:29

[q]Gen 6:5

[r]Job 1:5

[s]Rom 7:15–25

stronger with every repeating, till its full influence is developed in the "seat of scoffers"[t]—*an abomination*, not only to God, but to *man*.[u] Regardless of the prominence that misused wit and talent may gain for the fool, he secures no respect, and is generally avoided, or dreaded, and ultimately brought to shame.[v]

[t]Ps 1:1
[u]Prov 21:24; Mal 2:8, 9
[v]Jer 36:23, with 22:19

10 *If you are slack* [AV—*faint*] *in the day of distress,*
Your strength is limited.

HOW TO PREPARE FOR THE STORM

Let this be a word of strengthening encouragement. The marvel is, that those who know not where to look for a refuge when the storm is breaking over their heads, do not always *faint*. But natural courage and buoyancy, or a deeper plunge into the world, as a change from sorrow, raises them above their troubles for a while, but then turns them further from God.

Yet, why should the child of God, contrary to his Father's command,[w] *faint?* Look at your privilege—"The eternal God is a dwelling place, and underneath are the everlasting arms"[x]—your duty—"Call upon Me in the day of trouble; I shall rescue you, and you will honor Me"[y]—*your security*—"I will never desert you, nor will I ever forsake you." And "for a brief moment I forsook you, but with great compassion I will gather you."[z]

[w]Prov 3:11
[x]Deut 33:27
[y]Ps 50:15; 91:15
[z]Heb 13:5; Isa 54:7

Yet we don't speak in parables. Every Christian's heart confesses that he is apt to *faint*. "The strongest and holiest saint on earth is subject to some qualms of fear," stated Bishop Hall in *Contemplations*,[a] not from the greatness of the danger, but from the weakness of his faith.[b] Even those who had "endured a great conflict of sufferings" including accepting "joyfully the seizure of... property," still needed stirring exhortations and encouragements to Christian steadfastness.[c] Having borne the brunt of one battle, they know there are heavier conflicts before them.[d] Let each of us be awake to the besetting danger. Remember—when we seek strength from our resources;[e] when faith gives way to distrust;[f] praise to murmuring,[g] hope to despondency;[h] when forsaken pleasures keep coming vividly to mind,[i] and prolonged labor presses heavily[j]—then we *faint in the day of distress*.

[a]Comp. Prov 15:26; Ps 94:11; Matt 9:3, 4; 15:19; Acts 8:22; Rom 2:15
[b]Matt 14:30
[c]Heb 10:32–36; 11; 12:1–3
[d]Heb 12:4
[e]Isa 49:30
[f]Ps 78:19, 20
[g]Exod 15:1, 24; 17:3
[h]Num 14:3
[i]Exod 16:3; Num 11:4–6
[j]Job 7:1–4

[k]Job 5:7
[l]James 1:4

For this *day* we must prepare. "Man is born for trouble."[k] He inherited that from his first father, Adam. And he may be called to drink deeply of the bitter cup, requiring much *strength*, and "let endurance have its perfect result."[l] *The day* is needful for the trial of our principles. What seemed more promising, than the confidence of the stony-ground hearers, or the longer endurance of the apostle's companions? But the *day of distress* exposed their hollow profession.[m] Often also, even when "the root of the matter is found," a painful exhibition of *faintness*[1] which is unable to weather out a bad day, proves the weakness, not the vigor, of *strength.*

[m]Matt 13:20, 21; 2 Tim 4:16; 1:15; AV—Job 19:28

But why—again we ask—should the child of God faint? If "affliction" came "from the dust," and sprouted "from the ground,"[n] he might be discouraged by his ill-fortune. But where every minute circumstance is the fruit of eternal counsel, where "the very hairs of your head are all numbered,"[o] well may he "lean on the God of Israel." If his soul, like Israel of old, "became impatient because of the journey,"[p] it leads to his Father's house. If he be wearied with his burden, soon he will rest eternally in his Savior's bosom. Never will he be called to a martyr's trial, without a martyr's faith.[2] The chastening rod is the seal of everlasting love.[q] The temporal cross comes from the same hand as his everlasting crown. Never believe, Christian, that your tender-hearted Savior, who knows the weakness of your constitution, will ever mix the cup of affliction with one ounce of poison. *If your strength is limited,* go to Jesus—the strong one—for strength. "He gives strength to the weary, and to him who lacks might He increases power."[r] Commit yourself daily to Him, for His supply of "grace is sufficient for you." So go onward, weak and strong at once; weak in order to be strong; strong in your weakness. His "power is perfected in weakness;" and you will finally "boast" even in your depressing "weaknesses, that the power of Christ may dwell in me";[s] not only sustained, but "strengthened" unto joyfulness.[t]

[n]Job 5:6
[o]Matt 10:30; Isa 48:2
[p]Num 21:4, 5
[q]Prov 3:12; Isa 48:10
[r]Isa 40:29
[s]2 Cor 12:9
[t]Col 1:11

Oh, hasten the time, when the dark and cloudy day

[1] *Abraham—Gen 12:10–13; 20:2. Moses—Exod 4:10–13; Num 11:11. Joshua—7:6–10. David—1 Sam 27:1; Ps 31:1, 22; 116:11. Elijah—1 Kings 19:3, 4. Jeremiah—20:7–18. Jonah—4:8, 9. Peter—Matt 26:35, 69–74. The disciples—Matt 26:35, 56.*

[2] *"Be of good heart," said Ridley to his brother Latimer, with a wondrous cheerful look running to him, and embracing and kissing him—"for God will either assuage the fury of the flame, or else strengthen us to abide it"—FOXE, 7:548.*

shall be changed for unclouded sunshine; the crown of thorns for the crown of glory; "the spirit of fainting" for the garment of everlasting praise.[u]

[u]Isa 61:3

11 *Deliver those who are being taken away to death,*
And those who are staggering to slaughter, O hold
them back.
12 *If you say, "See, we did not know this,"*
Does He not consider it *who weighs the hearts?*
And does He not know it *who keeps your soul?*
And will He not render to man according to his
work?

Suppose a fellow-man is in imminent danger—*delivered to death* and ready to be slain unjustly,[v] or from wickedness.[w] The judge, invested with the power of God[x]—*if he* forbear to deliver, on the false pretense that *he knew it not,* the Lord will require it. This obligation, with all the responsibility of its neglect, is the universal law of the gospel.[y] Whoever knows his brother's danger and *doesn't try to rescue him—doesn't God who knows the heart,* take note? *Will He not provide?* The Hebrew midwives,[z] and Esther in after-ages,[a] delivered their own *people who were facing death.* Reuben *delivered* Joseph from the pit. Job was the *deliverer* of the poor in the extremity;[b] Jonathan saved his friend at great risk to himself.[c] Obadiah hid the Lord's prophets.[d] Ahikam and Ebed-melech saved Jeremiah.[e] Johanan attempted to *deliver* the unsuspecting Gedaliah.[f] Daniel preserved the wise men of Babylon.[g] The Samaritan rescued his neighbor from death. Paul's nephew *delivered* him by informing him of a murderous plot.[h] The rule includes all oppression, which has more or less of the character of murder.

[v]1 Sam 24:11; 26:18–20; 1 Kings 21:8–13
[w]Luke 10:30
[x]Ps 82:3–6
[y]Luke 10:29–36
[z]Exod 1:13–17
[a]Esther 3:6–13; 4:13, 14; 8:4–6
[b]Job 29:12, 13, 16, 17
[c]1 Sam 19:4; 20:26–33
[d]1 Kings 18:4
[e]Jer 26:24; 38:11–13
[f]Jer 40:13–16
[g]Dan 2:12–15
[h]Acts 23:16–22

NO MAN CARED FOR MY SOUL

Excuses are easy to find for passing over their sad condition—*we didn't know*—we had no idea you were in trouble, how you got into it, or how to help you out of it. But the true reason is we don't love others, but we do love ourselves. That is plain to see. You can tell by our hesitancy to help our brethren as we should and our readiness to make all kinds of excuses for ourselves. But doesn't God, who has a balance for every thought, know your brother's wants, the sorrow of his heart, and the grief that presses down his soul? Doesn't he *consider* the excuse of ignorance to be a mere cover for selfishness? There is no use pleading ignorance before the all-seeing God. *He who weighs the heart* will thoroughly sift; His Omniscience will know perfectly; His retributive justice will pay what is due. Indifferent kindness will be considered.[i] But to *hold back deliverance*—whether from cruelty,[j] selfishness,[k] or fear of personal consequence[l]—involves an awful account.

[i] Jer 38:7–13; 39:16–18
[j] 1 Sam 22:9–18
[k] 1 Sam 25:10, 11; Luke 10:30–32
[l] John 19:4–13

But how much more guilty to *withhold the deliverance* of immortal souls!—in ignorance, ungodliness, or unbelief—souls who are drawn *unto death, and ready to be slaughtered!* Shouldn't they be the object of our greatest concern? What can we say then about our cold indifference which makes no effort to help? "We have no right to judge. We didn't know. Am I my brother's keeper?[m] It's no concern of mine," we chant. But wouldn't many a soul have started back from ruin, if only his danger had been discovered before it was too late? Yet the one word, that might have saved, was withheld. Just think—is there some brother, child, or neighbor of yours, whose cries might pierce your soul through eternity with the rebuke—"If only you had been really concerned for my soul, I would never have come to this place of torment."[n] God commits their souls to our care. The Lord save us from being accused in the court of heaven of the murder of our brother's soul, because we were not concerned enough to try to deliver it.

[m] Gen 4:9
[n] James 5:19, 20

And doesn't this sound forth a solemn warning to those, whose special duty it is to *deliver them that are drawn unto* death? "We did not know." But is that a legitimate excuse? Shouldn't we have been watching for souls, "as those who will give an account"?[o] What a terrible accounting will await those who perish by our neglect as their pledged and divinely-appointed guardians! "While your servant was busy here and there"—upon his own pleasure—the soul "was gone"! "But his blood I will require from your hand."[3]

[o] Heb 13:17

[3] *1 Kings 20:39, 40; Ezek 33:8. See Doddridge's striking sermon on this text given from his works in William's* Christian Preacher.

13 *My son, eat honey, for it is good,*
Yes, the honey from the comb is sweet to your taste;
14 *Know* that *wisdom is thus for your soul;*
If you find it, *then there will be a future,*
And your hope will not be cut off.

TASTE AND SEE!

Honey was the choice product of Canaan;[p] the food of its inhabitants,[q] even of children;[r] *good and sweet to the taste.* So, when the spiritual "senses" are "trained,"[s] then you shall find wisdom unspeakably delightful to *your soul;*[t]—that knowledge of Christ, without which we are undone, and in which we are supremely happy.[4] The only way we can learn the sweetness of the honeycomb is to eat it.[u] Experimental knowledge alone gives spiritual discernment and proves the gospel to be, not a golden dream, but a divine reality. And who mistakes *honey* for any other substance? Who would not instantly detect a counterfeit? And what intelligent Christian would mistake something resembling heavenly *wisdom* for the real thing? "Lord! I have long wanted the true manna; all my former food was nothing but empty husks," said Augustine. Truly, the soul, hungering for bread, and feeding upon a practical understanding of Christian doctrine, realizes solidly what no formalist ever knows. He possesses a plausible shadow—emotion, impulse, conviction, external reformation.[v] But the living faith carries its own witness with it. It is all true—"I believed, therefore I spoke"![w] The treasure is *found* with the ecstasy of Archimedes[5]—bringing its own reward.[x]

The expectation of the finder, so far from being *cut off,* shall be infinitely exceeded. "The love" that is manifested passes knowledge.[y] "The peace" that is sealed passes all understanding.[z] The "joy" that is felt is "inexpressible and full of glory."[a] Shall we then timidly exhibit these privileges, as if they would lower the obligations of holiness or paralyze exertion? They don't deaden. They stimulate. They invigorate, while they refresh. Depression unnerves; fear enchains; but "the joy of the

[p] Exod 3:8; Ezek 20:6
[q] Judg 14:9; 1 Sam 14:27; Matt 3:4; Luke 24:41, 42
[r] Isa 7:15
[s] Heb 5:14
[t] Prov 16:24; Ps 19:10; 119:103
[u] Judg 14:18
[v] Heb 6:4, 5
[w] 2 Cor 4:13
[x] Comp. Jer 15:16
[y] Eph 3:19
[z] Phil 4:7
[a] 1 Peter 1:8

[4] *Phil 3:8. "Lo! this," says good Bishop Hall, "is the honey that I desire to* eat. *Give me of this honey, and I shall receive (like Jonathan of old. 1 Sam 14:29) both clearness to mine eyes and vigour of my spirits, to the foiling of my spiritual enemies"*—Soliloquies, *54.*

[5] *Discoverer of the lever and specific gravity.*

[b] Neh 8:10

Lord is your strength."[b] It inspires energy, elevates hope, and makes our service perfect freedom.

15 *Do not lie in wait, O wicked man, against the*
dwelling of the righteous;
Do not destroy his resting place;
16 *For a righteous man falls seven times, and rises*
again,
But the wicked stumble in time of *calamity.*

CAST DOWN BUT NOT DESTROYED

Solomon breaks off his affectionate counsel to the children of God, with a solemn warning to *the wicked man.* Should we exclude him from the circle of instruction? If he is left unconverted, it is his own guilt. But if he has been unwarned and uninstructed, beware lest his blood be upon our hearts.

Hatred against *the righteous* is deeply rooted in the wicked man.[c] He imagines, especially if he is in power,[d] that he can tyrannize them without punishment. But it is venturing upon a dangerous course—"he who touches you, touches the apple of His eye."[e] "I am Jesus whom you are persecuting"—struck down the most relentless persecutor, trembling[f] to the earth. The plots against their *dwelling* of the righteous; *the destroying of their resting place,* may prosper for a while; [g] but if *the righteous man falls even seven times,* overwhelmed by the assault, he rises again.[h] He may fall into trouble, but he will not succumb under it. Instead, he will remain firm. Take courage, then—afflicted soul! Look your foe in the face, and sing triumphantly—"Do not rejoice over me, O my enemy. *Though I fall I will rise.*"[i] He shall deliver you in six troubles; yea in seven shall no evil touch you. Who delivered us from so great a death, and does deliver; in whom we trust, that He will yet deliver. "Struck down, but not destroyed."[j] Here is our conflict and our security. The life is untouched; instead, it is strengthened, and "manifested," by the successive supplies of upholding mercy.[k] Many trials cannot overwhelm the righteous.[l] But all it takes is one to sweep away the wicked. *He stumbles in time of calamity;*[m] and there is no *rising again;*[n] no recovery, no remedy. He lies where he falls, and he perishes where he lies. Sinner! whatever your

[c] Prov 29:27; Gen 3:15; Ps 37:12, 32; 1 John 3:12
[d] 1 Sam 19:11; Acts 12:1–3
[e] Zech 2:8
[f] Acts 9:5, 6
[g] Ps 69; Title; Acts 8:3, 4
[h] Ps 37:24
[i] Mic 7:8
[j] Job 5:19; 2 Cor 1:10; 4:9
[k] 2 Cor 4:11
[l] Ps 34:19; 37:39, 40; 1 Cor 10:13
[m] Ps 7:13–16; 9:16
[n] Job 15:30; Amos 8:14

wickedness; may the Lord save you from the millstone of condemnation—the persecuting of the saints of God![6]

17 *Do not rejoice when your enemy falls,*
And do not let your heart be glad when he stumbles;
18 *Lest the* LORD *see* it *and be displeased,*
And He turn away His anger from him.

But God's chosen people *did* rejoice—with godly rejoicing—over the fall of their enemies.[o] Is not this joy the triumph of the righteous?[p] Is it not the adoration of heaven, as the manifested glory of God?[q] But how different is this sublime sympathy in the triumph of God's people, from the sick joy of private revenge! A secret, if not an avowed pleasure *in the fall of an enemy,* is a natural reaction.[r] But what has grace done for us, if it has not overcome nature by a holier and happier principle? David "bowed down mourning" in his enemy's affliction.[s] David's Lord wept in the prospective ruin of foolish man, full of hatred against Himself. *To rejoice in the fall of an enemy* would be to fall deeper ourselves; to fall not into trouble, but into sin; to break the commandment, which calls us to love our "enemies,"[t] and to repay cursing with blessing and prayers.[u] This selfish cruelty is most hateful to God.[v] It has often *turned away His wrath* from the criminal to the one who mocks at his calamity.[7] Does the mirror of God's Word show our character in the sin that is rebuked or in the contrast of our compassionate Lord?

[o] Exod 15:1
[p] Prov 11:10; Job 22:19; Ps 58:10
[q] Rev 15:3, 4; 18:20; 19:1–6
[r] Ps 35:15, 16: 2 Sam 16:5–7
[s] Ps 35:13, 14; 2 Sam 1:11, 12. Comp. Job 31:29
[t] Luke 19:41–44
[u] Matt 5:44
[v] Prov 17:5; Zech 1:15

19 *Do not fret yourself because of evildoers,*
Or be envious of the wicked;
20 *For there will be no future for the evil man;*
The lamp of the wicked will be put out.

[6] *The just man rising from his fall is, without justification, applied to the* perseverance of the saints. *The word* fall *frequently occurs in this book; but always in reference to trouble, not sin (Prov 11:5, 14; 13:17; 17:20; 27:27; 28:10, 14, 18). The antithesis obviously fixes this meaning. "There are plain texts enough to prove every Scriptural doctrine. But pressing texts into any particular service, contrary to their plain meaning, not only serves to deceive the inconsiderate, but to rivet the prejudices, and confirm the suspicions, of opposers; just as bringing forward a few witnesses of suspicious character would cause all those, however deserving of credit, who should be examined in the same cause, to be suspected also, and create a prejudice against it in the minds of the court and of all present"—SCOTT.*

[7] *"Lest the Lord be angry, and turn his wrath from him to thee"—Bishop COVERDALE. Comp. Judg 16:25–30; Mic 7:10. Edom—Lam 4:21, 22; Ezek 35:15; 36:5–7; Obad 10–14. Tyre—Ezek 26:2. Babylon—Ps 137:7–9; Isa 51:22, 23; Lam 1:21. Moab—Jer 48:26, 27. Ammon—Ezek 25:1–7.*

JUDGE ALL IN THE LIGHT OF ETERNITY

[w]Verse 1; 23:17

This *fretting* must be a deep-rooted disease to need such repeated discipline.[w] One moment's recollection of our mercies might show how little reason there is for it. Mercies infinitely more than we discover might be sufficient to sweep the clouds from our sky and to make us ashamed of our despondency. *The envy of the wicked* is checked by the remembrance that there is an end—surely a happy end for the righteous.[x] Let them wait for it. It will not disappoint them. Here we are further reminded that there is *no future,*[8] *no reward, to the evil man.* Leave him to his Judge. *His lamp,* despite all his efforts to keep it burning,[y] *will be put out.*[z] Sometimes in bold daring he puts out his own lamp. "I give," said the infidel Hobbes, "my body to the dust, and my soul to the Great Perhaps. I am going to take a leap *in the dark.*" And what darkness it was—a leap into "the black darkness . . . forever."[a]

[x]Prov 23:18

[y]1 Kings 21:21
[z]Prov 13:9; 20:20; Job 18:5, 6; 21:17

[a]Jude 13

Let's learn to judge things in the light of eternity. Learn neither to overvalue the fancied sunshine of *the wicked,* nor to undervalue our own *real* happiness. *Envy not* the lot of the wicked. And don't complain about our own. Ours is far beyond his reach. His is far below our *envy.* "His candle burneth; his prosperity flourisheth, until it hath kindled hell-fire; and then it is extinguished; whereas the lamp of the godly is put out here, to shine as a star in heaven," stated Jermin.

21 *My son, fear the* LORD *and the king;*
Do not associate with those who are given to change;
22 *For their calamity will rise suddenly,*
And who knows the ruin that comes *from both of them?*

DESPISERS OF AUTHORITY

[b]Prov 23:17

We have another loving exhortation to *fear the Lord.*[b] And is it any wonder? Isn't it the substance of our holiness and our happiness? Oh! Reverence His majesty. Acknowledge your dependence on Him. Be as careful in walking before Him in your secret thoughts, as in your

[8] *Same word in Heb as Prov 23:18. Previously "end" in AV, and "There shall be none* end *of plagues to the evil man"*—Old version.

outward conduct. Don't tolerate a sinful motive in your heart, any more than you would allow gross outward sin. If there is no outward punishment, won't the thought keenly pierce your heart—how unkindly this defilement responds to such unspeakable love!

The connection between *the fear of the Lord and the king* is not local or accidental. Our Lord and His apostles have, in the same way, linked the throne of supremacy in heaven and the throne of His majesty on earth.[c] One principle is the spring of the other. Disloyalty has often been a libel upon godliness. But the Christian is loyal, because he is godly.[d] "Subjection to the governing authorities" is repeatedly urged,[e] and rebellion is visited with the most heavy condemnation.[9] Yet there is no interference with our first and primary obligation. Solomon "puts God before the king, because God is to be served in the first place, and our obedience is to be given to the king only in subordination to God, and not in those things, which are contrary to the will of God," said Poole.[f]

Man's independence, however, naturally rebels against submission. The popular cry is for the voice and sovereignty of the people; a plain proof, that "there is nothing new under the sun";[g] since the picture of those demagogues (leaders of the common people) who, nearly two thousand years ago—walked after "the flesh in its corrupt desires and despise authority. Daring, self-willed, they do not tremble when they revile angelic majesties."[h] Such men love change for the sake of change. To become leaders of a party, they disturb the public peace by proposing changes without any promise of substantial advantage.[10] They would prefer a storm which would bring them into prominence, to a calm in which they were already quietly secure. They are more eager to fish for a name in troubled waters, than to cultivate those quiet and social virtues, which, if generally cultivated, could restrain the commotion. "Let my soul

[c] Matt 22:21; 1 Peter 2:17

[d] 1 Sam 24:6

[e] Matt 17:24–27; Rom 13:1–7; Titus 3:1; 1 Peter 2:13–17

[f] Comp. 1 Sam 22:17, 18; Dan 3:16–18; Acts 4:18, 19; 5:27–29

[g] Eccl 1:9

[h] 2 Peter 2:10; Jude 8. Comp. 1 Sam 10:27

[9] *Rom 13:2. See two valuable sermons by Bishop Horne and Horsley on this text. Agricola's testimony to the submissive obedience of our uncivilized ancestors is interesting. See TACITUS'* Life of Agricola. *Comp. 1 Sam 22:17, 18; Dan 3:16–18; Acts 4:18, 19; 5:27–29.*

[10] *"He that goeth about," says our judicious Hooker, "to persuade men that they are not so well governed as they ought to be, shall never want attention and favorable hearers." Ibid. Book i. Sallust admirably remarks of these turbulent innovators that "they thought the very disturbance of the established order of things a sufficient bribe to set them at work. That which is wanted in the aptness of their speech is supplied by the aptness of men's minds to accept and believe it." See the whole paragraph opening Hooker's great work,* Eccl. Polit.

[i]Gen 49:6

not enter into their council."[i] It is dangerous to *associate with* them. To oppose all change, indeed, is to set up a plea of perfection. Every improvement (and where is there not room for improvement?) is a change. But public evils are not to be mended by violent complaint. To be *given to change;* to undo all that has been done; to alter for the sake of altering; to be weary of the old and captivated with the new, however untried; to make experiments upon modes of government—is a fearful hazard. It is losing the substance of *real good* in the dream of *imaginary improvements;* as if we must undo everything, rather than be idle. This waywardness we see in Korah's sin;[j] in Absalom's rebellion;[k] in the continual struggle for royalty in the Israelitish kings.[l] How suddenly disaster struck, even when they seemed to be within the grasp of their object![m] *Who knows the ruin, which both* the Lord and the king[11] may inflict on the despisers of their authority;[n] often fearful beyond precedent, without remedy?

[j]Num 16:1–3
[k]2 Sam 15:10–13
[l]1 Kings 16:8–22
[m]2 Sam 15:13; 18:9–16
[n]2 Sam 18:7, 8; 20:1, 2, 22; 2 Kings 17:21, 23; Eccl 8:2–5; Acts 5:36–37

23 *These also are sayings of the wise.*
To show partiality in judgment is not good.
24 *He who says to the wicked, "You are righteous,"*
Peoples will curse him, nations will abhor him;
25 *But to those who rebuke the* wicked *will be delight,*
And a good blessing will come upon them.
26 *He kisses the lips*
Who gives a right answer.

A WORD TO THE WISE

We've had a solemn exhortation directed to the people.[o] Now we have a word *to the wise,* specially to those in authority. God has given many laws against respect of persons in judgment.[p] It is not good.[q] Rather, He rebukes it as a hateful abomination.[r] Let truth be considered, not favor. This is an evil in the church today, as much as in the government. No responsibility is more momentous in our sacred high places, then "doing nothing in a spirit of partiality."[12] Man, corrupt as he is, often

[o]Num 16:29–33
[p]Exod 23:6–8; Lev 19:15; Deut 1:17; 16:19
[q]Prov 18:5; 28:21
[r]Ps 82:2–4

[11] *French and Skinner. The best critics (Geier, Dathe, Lavater) most naturally apply the distinctive term (them both) to the separate persons. The ruin foreboded is thus connected with the persons, who had been described separately as the objects of fear.*
[12] *1 Tim 5:21. Hooker—in "reverence and awe unto the prelates, whom Christ hath placed in seats of higher authority over me"—suggests, that "the ancient canon be specially remembered, which forbiddeth a bishop to be led by human affection in bestowing the things of God"—Eccl. Pol. book 7.c.24.3, 7.*

abhors unrighteous judgment.[s] A bad judge deprives us of the blessing of good laws.

[s] 1 Sam 8:1–5

On the other hand, there is no greater national blessing, than a government *rebuking the wicked.*[t] This was a part of Job's God-fearing character.[u] *The good blessing that came* upon Nehemiah's upright administration is abundantly plain.[v] In fact, generally *everyone will kiss*—pay the homage of love and respect[w]—*to him who gives a right answer* in judgment. He is a public treasure; "a blessing in the midst of the earth." Isn't then, the responsibility of rulers, and the welfare of thousands depending on them, a quickening impulse to prayer? And may not our want of a "quiet life in all godliness" be traced to this neglect?[x]

[t] 2 Sam 25:3, 4
[u] Job 1:1, 8; 29:7, 11–17
[v] Neh 5:7–9; 13:8–11, 25, 28, with 31
[w] Comp. 1 Kings 19:18; Ps 2:12; Hos 13:2
[x] Isa 19:24; 1 Tim 2:1, 2

But we are not rulers. Yet are not many of us in authority—parents—heads of families—teachers and guardians of the young? Uprightness and consistency alone can maintain that influence so essential to usefulness. For a spiritual ruler to *say to the wicked—"You are righteous,"* is indeed treacherous, dealing with his divine Master; cruel deceit to immortal souls; hiding the ruin, which he is bound to reveal; acting the part of a minister of Satan under the cover of a minister of Christ. *His people* will live *to curse and abhor him,* perhaps throughout eternity. Even the very people that hate both his Master and his message, will *kiss his lips who gives a right answer*—a reluctant but honorable witness to his faithfulness.

27 *Prepare your work outside,*
And make it ready for yourself in the field;
Afterwards, then, build your house.

WISE MASTER BUILDERS

This rule of wisdom applies to all worldly matters. Religion, so far from forbidding, insistently urges care and forethought. Much inconvenience and suffering flow from its neglect. Acting upon this useful direction, the wise builder first *prepares his work outside.* He collects his materials, estimates the quantity required; then he makes his work fit together by shaping and bringing the materials into their place; *and afterwards,* having all things in readiness, he builds his house. The work was thus prepared for Solomon's magnificent temple, before *the house was built.*[y] The spiritual house is similarly built of materials prepared and fitted; and so it grows "unto a holy temple in the Lord."[z]

[y]1 Kings 5:18; 6:7

[z]Eph 2:21, 22

But think about the care, with which the great *work should be prepared.* Count the cost carefully. Consider whether the profession will stand the storms.[a] Lay the foundation deep upon the Rock.[b] Be much in prayer for divine strength. Avoid that outward display, which shames the inconsiderate builder, who begins to build his house, without having thoroughly *prepared his work.*

[a]Luke 14:28–30

[b]Luke 6:48

Has not the minister of the gospel special need of *preparing his work?* A minister, unequipped, cannot be a "wise master builder." Even when the foundation is laid, "Let each man be careful how he builds upon it." Let him look well to the day at hand.[c] And let all the Lord's servants weigh deeply their responsibility. Haste, and crude judgment, have ruined many a Christian project. Let us be guided by the well-considered wisdom of experienced men[d] and collect our materials from their wisdom, forethought, and sound-judging energy. *A house will then, in that way, be built* to the honor of our God, and for the service of His church.

[c]1 Cor 3:10–15

[d]Matt 18:17, 18

28 *Do not be a witness against your neighbor without cause,*
And do not deceive with your lips.
29 *Do not say, "Thus I shall do to him as he has done to me;*
I will render to the man according to his work."

For the good of society it may sometimes be necessary to witness against a neighbor. But never let it be *without cause.* Yet, when compelled to this revolting duty, whatever the temptation or consequence, don't lie. Speak plainly, truthfully, the whole truth. Doeg's *witness against his neighbor was without cause;* not from conscience but from malice. The main fact also was that David could have cleared Abimelech from the suspicion of treason and saved his life—but he failed to do so.[e] This garbled *witness* deceived with his lips and bore the black stamp of a "deceitful tongue."[f]

[e]1 Sam 22:9, 10; 21:1, 2

[f]Ps 52:3, 4; 120:2–4

You can bait the thief with profit, the adulterer with lust, the murderer with revenge. But it is difficult to say what advantage it is to this evil *witness* or what allurement belongs to the sin, save that which Satan himself feels—the love of sin for its own sake or for the satisfaction that is vainly hoped for from the commission of sin. Should we, however, be clear from the uglier forms of this sin; yet we resist the unkind *witness against our neighbor,* in magnifying his failings, and measuring them on a far stricter basis than we measure our own; rashly censuring his indifferent or doubtful actions; and censuring even his sins with an unchristian intention?

And then—as to indulging personal resentment—it is natural to say, though only in the heart—*I will do as he has done to me.* But shall we in that way, dare to take the sword out of God's hands and place ourselves upon his bench in court? "Vengeance is mine, I will repay, says the Lord."[g] Let wisdom and grace be set to work to put out the fire from hell before it gets out of control? Far happier will be your recollection of injuries forgotten than revenged. But grace alone can enable us to *"forgive . . . from your heart."*[13] And yet, too often its exercise is so feebly cherished that natural feelings come to the surface; and, if there is no actual recompense of evil, there is merely a negative obedience to the rule, a refraining from a joyful outburst of enthusiasm but just the opposite, instead. Solomon sets forth the true rule in this book,[h] more lovely, more constraining, as enforced by God's own example.[i] Humility and tenderness mark the self-knowing Christian, who forgives himself *little,* his neighbor *much.*

[g]Rom 12:9. Comp. Gen 1:16–19

[h]Prov 20:22; 25:21, 22

[i]Matt 5:44, with Luke 23:34; 1 Peter 2:21–23

30 *I passed by the field of the sluggard,*
And by the vineyard of the man lacking sense;
31 *And behold, it was completely overgrown with thistles,*
Its surface was covered with nettles,
And its stone wall was broken down.
32 *When I saw, I reflected upon it;*
I looked, and *received instruction.*

[13] *Matt 18:35, with Luke 17:3–5. "The excellency of the duty is sufficiently proclaimed by the difficulty of the practice. How hard it is, when the passions are high, and the sense of an injury quick, and the power ready, for a man to deny himself of that luscious morsel of revenge! To do violence to himself, instead of doing it to his enemy!"—SOUTH'S* Sermon on Matt 5:44.

33 *"A little sleep, a little slumber,*
A little folding of the hands to rest,"
34 *Then your poverty will come* as *a robber,*
And your want like an armed man.

THE FALSE SLUMBER

Everything around us holds useful lessons for the observant eye. Every particle of creation may be taxed to add its quota to our store of knowledge. We can extract good, even from evil, and gather "grapes" of "thorn bushes" and "figs from thistles."[j] Solomon describes with his usual vigor of thought and strength of coloring, the affecting sight that had passed before his eyes—*the field and vineyard of the sluggard, grown over with thistles and nettles, and the wall utterly broken down.* Instead of turning away, *he thought about it seriously and learned something.* In the solemn consideration of this picture of desolation, he could not but turn his thoughts to the wretched owner. He fancied himself in the owner's house, looking at the stupid creature stretched out on his bed, and crying out, under the noonday sun—"A little sleep, a little slumber, a little folding of the hands to rest." Stimulated by the outpouring of this sluggish creature, the response almost unconsciously forced itself—*So shall your poverty come as one that robs, and your lack as an armed man.*

[j]Matt 7:16

And yet, by some strange delusion, *the lazy man thinks* himself wise.[k] But how plain it is to see how *lacking in sense* he is and without heart to improve himself! He could enrich himself from *his field and vineyard.* But he has never cultivated or weeded it. *The stone wall,* raised by some more ambitious hand, is *broken down;* and he is too lazy to repair it. *His vineyard* is therefore left prey to every invader; while he lives like an animal, in sensual indulgence, he brings himself gradually, but irresistibly, to *poverty.*[l] Not that he means to become a beggar. He only wants *yet a little sleep, a little slumber* more—and then he will get up and get busy. But his desire to sleep and rest continually increases. Every hour's indulgence strengthens the habit and chains the victim in hopeless bondage. His efforts for exertion are only the struggles of the paralytic, without energy or results. If his dependence is upon his own effort, manual or mental, his lazi-

[k]Prov 26:16

[l]Prov 6:10, 11

ness will soon bring him to ruin. On a higher level, it deprives him of the means of using his influence correctly or of employing his talents to any valuable purpose. There is, indeed, no higher blessing than usefulness; no more moving lamentation than that of the worn-out laborer, who is conscious that his usefulness is over. But *the sluggard* is satisfied, that *his* usefulness will never begin. He is content with a life of utter uselessness. He willfully gives himself up to it; as if laziness were for his greatest good, and every kind of exercise was the object of his shrinking dread. Such a life can never satisfy its own conscience and certainly will never escape the condemnation of God.[m] It brings poverty to himself. He becomes his own enemy. The springs of solid happiness are impoverished, and the true end of life frittered away.

[m]Matt 25:26–36

But let us look at the spiritual sluggard. If a neglected *field* is a melancholy sight, what is a neglected *soul!* A soul which, instead of being cultivated with the seeds of grace, is left to its own barrenness; *overgrown with thistles and nettles.*[n] Time, talents, opportunities have been assured; also, perhaps, the blessing of a godly education, as well as every encouragement for hopeful promise. But if hard work is needed; if the man must "work,"[o] then his field will be left, at least for the present. He must have a *little more sleep* first.[14] And so he sleeps on and shuts eyes and ears against every disturbance of his fatal slumber. Nothing is done or attempted for God, for his own soul, or for his fellow-man. His *vineyard* is left open. All his good purposes are *as a stone wall broken down.* Satan goes out, and returns at "his will."[p] All is devastation and ruin.

[n]Gen 3:18

[o]John 6:27; Luke 13:24

[p]Matt 12:45; 2 Tim 2:26

Christian! Isn't there danger of this evil creeping into our Christian experience? No habit is so ruinous. It weakens, then finally stops the voice of prayer. It hinders the active energy of meditation. It weakens the influence of watchfulness. The way to heaven is steep, rough, hard to climb, immeasurably long, forbidding in its present exercise and doubtful in its end, full of toil and discouragement, without any beaming hope or sunshine. This false apprehension checks every step of progress; so that

[14] *See Augustine's instructive reference to his own case*—Confess. *lib. viii. c.5.*

[q]Jer 31:12

[r]Prov 23:21; 2 Sam 11:2; Ezek 16:49

[s]Matt 21:28

[t]John 17:11

the soul—instead of being "a watered garden,"[q] sending forth refreshing fragrance and grateful fruits—relapses into its former wild state; laid open to every temptation; and too often ultimately a prey to sensual appetites.[r]

Let our Father's voice be instantly heard—"Son, go work *today in the vineyard*."[s] Don't you see, that it is *overgrown with thistles*? Look forward, not backward. Don't complain, but decide. Don't just pray, but do something. Always connect privilege with practice. Prove the principles of *moral character*, as well as *spiritual experience*. Aim at every active exercise, that may strengthen spiritual habits. Surely, if we plan to stand in the faith of the sons of God, we must hourly, and continually, be setting ourselves to work. It was not the meaning of our Lord and Savior in saying—"Father, keep them in Thy name"[t]—that we should be careless to take care of ourselves. Our handwork is required for our own safety.

CHAPTER TWENTY-FIVE

1 *These also are proverbs of Solomon which the men of Hezekiah, king of Judah, transcribed.*

This seems to be a third division of this sacred book.[a] The selection was probably made (with several repetitions from the first part[1]) from the three thousand proverbs which Solomon "spoke";[2] and which, having been carefully preserved *the men of Hezekiah transcribed,* nearly three hundred years after. Thus the Word of God, brought out of obscurity for the instruction of the people, stamped the reformation of this godly king;[b] as it did the reformation of Josiah in aftertimes.[3] The New Testament fully authenticated this section of the book as a part of the inspired canon.[c] We are not reading therefore the maxims of Solomon—the wisest of men, but the voice from heaven proclaims—These are the true sayings of God.

[a]Prov 1 and 10–24

[b]2 Chron 31:21

[c]Verses 6, 7, with Luke 14:7–10; 21, 22, with Rom 12:20; 26:11, with 2 Peter 2:22; 27:1, with James 4:14

The Holy Spirit mentions not only the author, but the copyists, of these Proverbs. And often has good service been done to the church, not only by original writers, but by those who have copied and brought out their writings into wider circulation. The world usually honors only the grand instruments and casts the humbler agency into the shade.[d] But God honors not only the primary, but the subordinate instruments; not only the five—but the one talent—faithfully put to use for Him. The blessing is not promised according to their number, but to their improvement.[e]

[d]Eccl 9:15, 16

[e]Matt 25:21–23

[1] *Verse 24, with 21:9; 26:13, with 22:13; 26:15, with 19:24; 26:22, with 18:8; 27:12, with 22:3; 27:13, with 20:16; 27:15, with 19:13; 28:6, with 19:1; 28:18, with 10:29; 28:19, with 12:11; 28:21, with 18:5; 24:23.*

[2] *1 Kings 4:32. Comp. Eccl 12:9. Does not the divine discrimination, which has withheld the whole of Solomon's writings, reprove the indiscriminate publication of all that eminent men may have left in manuscript? Crudities, and even gross errors, have in that way been accredited by the authority of great names, not less unjustly to their memory, than injuriously to the church.*

[3] *2 Chron 34:14–30. We mark the same divine stamp of mercy upon our own precious, though reviled, Reformation.*

2 *It is the glory of God to conceal a matter,*
But the glory of kings is to search out a matter.
3 As *the heavens for height and the earth for depth,*
So the heart of kings is unsearchable.

GOD'S UNSEARCHABLE MYSTERIES

The great King of heaven and the puny kings of earth are here contrasted. *The glory* of each is opposite—*of God to conceal; of kings to search out.* Whether He "dwells in the thick cloud,"[f] or whether "covering thyself with light as with a cloak"[g]—*it is the glory of God to conceal a matter.*

[f] 1 Kings 8:12; Ps 18:11; 97:2
[g] Ps 104:2; 1 Tim 6:16

What glory indeed could belong to a God, whose name, and ways, and works were open to the view, and could be fully understood by the "worm" as Bildad in Job called men of the earth? Those things He *has* brought to light, only show how much He has *concealed.* We look at His works. These are parts of His ways; but how little "we hear of Him!"[4] We study his providential ordering of events, and we feel that we need to pray over them once more, before we venture to interpret them—"Thy way was in the sea, and Thy paths in the mighty waters, and Thy footprints may not be known!"[h] We adore also that *glorious concealment* of his great work of forgiveness, of which Dr. Owen most truly remarks—that "were it not somewhat beyond what men could imagine, no flesh could be saved."[i] But so far is it removed from our sight that no human wisdom can understand the full extent of this vast work. It is forgetfulness of this unsearchable forgiveness, cutting it down to where we can understand it by our own wisdom, that shuts out a glowing confidence and restrains many a sincere penitent from fully understanding and habitually enjoying the peace of the gospel. In another area of this widely extended field, we think deeply about His great purposes of grace; and our hearts only find release in reverential adoration—"Oh! the depth!"[j]—"rather standing on the shore, and silently admiring it, then entering into it," said Leighton.[k] To wade in those depths is the sure way to be overwhelmed by them.

[h] Ps 77:19; 36:6
[i] Ps 130
[j] Rom 11:33
[k] 1 Peter 2:8

So God educates His children in mystery, that He may

[4] *Job 26:14. "Lo! these are the outlines (marginal or boundary lines) of his ways, and the mere whisper (opposed to the crashing 'thunder' of the next clause) we can hear of him,"—Dr. GOOD.*

exercise them in the life of faith,[l] acting and living upon objects too wonderful to comprehend and coming to His revelation without any mind or will of their own. So . . . in the boundless and bottomless works of His grace—the voice speaks from the inner sanctuary—"Cease striving and know that I am God."[m] And isn't this shade of mystery our highest joy, as the dwelling place of our adorable God and Savior? Are not the clouds of His *concealment* the brightness of His glory,[n] as the most simple, yet the most incomprehensible Being, whom the mightiest intellect can never "by searching find out to perfection"?[o] "As there is," says Bishop Hall, "a foolish wisdom, so there is a wise ignorance. I would fain know all that I need, and all that I may. I leave God's secrets to himself. It is happy for me, that God makes me of his court, though not of his council. O Lord! let me be blessed with the knowledge of what thou hast revealed. Let me content myself to adore thy divine wisdom in what thou hast not revealed."[5]

[l]John 13:7
[m]Ps 46:10
[n]Hab 3:4
[o]AV—Job 11:7

So . . . it is the glory of God to conceal a thing—to do many things, of which the full development of their great end is far beyond our sight. The highest glory of earth is at infinite distance—*God conceals*. For who could bear His full brightness?[p] *But the glory of kings is to search out a matter.*[q] They must not pretend to be like God. By themselves they know nothing beyond their people. Yet as everything depends upon them, they must take advantage of all stores of wisdom, to *search out* the mysteries of true policy, in order to govern by them; the mysteries of iniquity, in order to correct; and the minute details of individual cases, in order to give suitable judgment. This is the reason for God's command that they should write out a copy of the law for their daily study and direction.[r] This wise king had himself attained singular discernment in *searching out a matter*, even without external evidence, and with all the perplexity of conflicting testimony.[s]

[p]Exod 33:20; Dan 10:5–8, 17; Rev 1:12–17
[q]Ezra 4:15, 19; 5:17; 6:1, Comp. Job 29:16
[r]Deut 17:18, 19
[s]1 Kings 3:16–28

[5] *Bishop Hall, 8:5; 11:84. This* glorious concealment *is however no precedent for the Tractarian principle of Reserve, which at once eclipses the freeness and fullness of the gospel, and paralyzes the energy of Christian life and hope. Blessed be God! "The things that belong to our peace are brought to light by the Gospel." The doctrine of the atoning cross is* "delivered first of all" *(1 Cor 15:3)—the primary truth in the forefront of the gospel. With self-abasing humility we acknowledge, that "secret things belong to the Lord our God." But guilty, indeed, is the presumption of casting a cloud of* concealment *on "the things that are revealed, and which belong to us, and to our children forever"—not only as the foundation of our hope, but as the principle of our obedience. Deut 29:20. Yet don't some of us need to be drawn further from the "secret things," and nearer to the things that are revealed?*

And yet, the sovereign must often frame His counsels with much caution and reserve. Many of His purposes are far beyond the comprehension of the great mass of His people; so that to their minds *the heart of kings is unsearchable;* and they might just as soon think of measuring *the heaven for height* or fathoming *the earth for depth.* Shouldn't this teach forbearance in pronouncing judgment? Are not the "daring, self-willed [who] do not tremble when they revile angelic majesties," convicted of the guilt of "reviling where they have no knowledge"?[t] Are not "prayers . . . for kings and all who are in authority," far more fruitful and acceptable?[u]

[t]2 Peter 2:10, 12; Jude 8, 10
[u]1 Tim 2:1–3

4 *Take away the dross from the silver,*
And there comes out a vessel for the smith;
5 *Take away the wicked* from *before the king,*
And his throne will be established in righteousness.

AN OFFERING IN RIGHTEOUSNESS

The *smith* produces "the vessel for honorable use," by *taking away the dross from the silver,*[v] which mars its beauty and purity. Such is the destructive influence of *the wicked* in the royal counsels.[w] *Take them then away from before the king.* Let him purify his court and government from this *dross.* Let him keep it from high places. Let him reject it in authority at any cost.[x] That's how David *established his throne in righteousness*[y] and commended this resolution by his dying counsel to his wise son.[z] This is political wisdom on scriptural principles. If "righteousness exalts a nation,"[a] the open acknowledgement of it is the sure path to national prosperity.[b] And won't *the throne* of our great King *be established* by the entire and eternal removal of the wicked?[c] In the great day of trial and decision shall I be found disapproved or purified silver? Lord! Let me, under the refiner's hand, be purified, and purged as "gold and silver, so that [I] may present to the Lord offerings in righteousness" in that day.[d]

[v]Rom 9:21; Mal 3:2
[w]1 Kings 12:10–16; 2 Chron 24:17–24
[x]Prov 20:8, 26
[y]Ps 101:4–8
[z]1 Kings 2:5, 6, 32, 33, 44, 45
[a]Prov 14:34
[b]1 Kings 15:13; 2 Chron 14:1–7
[c]Mal 3:17, 18; Matt 13:41–43; 25:31–46
[d]Mal 3:3

6 *Do not claim honor in the presence of the king,*
And do not stand in the place of great men;

7 *For it is better that it be said to you, "Come up here,"*
Than that you should be put lower in the presence of the prince,
Whom your eyes have seen.

Our Lord applies this Proverb more generally.[e] Who doesn't need this caution against ambition? But even to godly Baruch the Lord said, "You, are you seeking great things for yourself?"[f] Not even the fellowship of the Savior, His heavenly instruction or His divine pattern of holiness[g] could restrain the strife among the disciples as to who should be the "greatest";[h] it was repeated even after the most wondrous exhibition of humility;[i] after they had just partaken with Him of the holy feast.[j] Loving "to be first among them," is the bane of godliness in the church.[k]

[e]Luke 14:8–11
[f]Jer 45:5
[g]Matt 11:29
[h]Matt 18:1–4
[i]John 13:1–15
[j]Luke 22:19–27
[k]3 John 9, 10

Wolsey's fall is an instructive beacon to ambitious men, not to *push themselves forward to set forth their glory in the presence of the king.*[6] The seizure of *the place of great men* usually subjects man to be put lower, to his own embarrassment. Not that we would disapprove of fit and able men putting themselves forward in public responsibilities. But the eagerness for a big name, with an obvious incapacity for handling the work, should be strongly condemned. "Humility goes before honor";[l] shown in a reluctance to force either our presence or our opinion upon those in higher positions; shrinking from external respect, rather than courting the "vain show." Thus were Gideon,[m] Saul in his early and better days,[n] and David advanced to honor.[o]

[l]Prov 18:12; AV—Ps 39:6
[m]Judg 6:15
[n]1 Sam 9:21, 22; 15:17
[o]1 Sam 18:18. Comp. Ps 131:1

Let each of us give himself to the work of casting down our high tower of conceit; cultivating a deep sense of our utter worthlessness, and carefully pondering that example, which is at once our pattern and our principle. Oh! Think of Him, who was "fairer than the sons of men," being the most humble of men—of Him, who was infinitely more than man, making himself "a worm, and not a man."[p] Think of that day, which will set us all on our own true base; when each of us shall stand before "the ruler of the kings,"[q] and will be taken for just what we are, for that which He counts us to be. What will it be to be put

[p]Ps 45:2, with 22:6
[q]Rev 1:5

[6] *The poet elegantly contrasts Daedalus and Icarus—father and son, both provided with wings. The father, contenting himself with skimming the ground, was safe. The son, soaring aloft, perished. A vivid lesson in humility.*

lower; to be utterly cast out in *His presence,* whom our eyes shall then see to our eternal confusion![r]

[r]Rev 1:7

8 *Do not go out hastily to argue* your case;
Otherwise, what will you do in the end,
When your neighbor puts you to shame?
9 *Argue your case with your neighbor,*
And do not reveal the secret of another,
10 *Lest he who hears* it *reproach you,*
And the evil report about you not pass away.

IS IT REALLY WORTH QUARRELING OVER?

Quarreling under any circumstances is a serious evil. The considerate Christian will rather yield rights than insist upon them to the hazard of his own soul and to the injury of the church.[s] *Hasty arguing* is always wrong. Think well beforehand, whether the case is right, or, even if it is worth quarreling over. Carefully consider the uncertainty or the consequence of *the end.* See the fruits in Gaal's quarrel with Abimelech,[t] Amaziah's *strife* with his brother king of Israel,[u] godly Josiah's unadvised contention with Pharaoh.[v] So little do *we know what to do in the end!* Often has a man brought himself to ruin by a *hasty argument* at law. Instead of triumphing, *he has been put to shame by his neighbor.* Let's never forget, that not "outbursts of anger" only, but "disputes" and "dissensions" are "deeds of the flesh," excluding from heaven.[w] Hence the constraining obligation to "seek peace, and pursue it";[x] after the noble example of our father Abraham, who quenched the beginning of the "strife," by yielding to his nephew his natural superiority, and his just rights.[y]

[s]1 Cor 6:1–7
[t]Judg 9:26–40
[u]2 Kings 14:8–12
[v]2 Chron 35:21, 22
[w]Gal 5:19–21
[x]Ps 34:14
[y]Gen 13:8. Comp. Prov 17:14

Yet if, after all, strife is inevitable, then let us ponder how much wisdom and rule over our own spirit is needful to conduct it honorably in line with our Christian profession. *Argue your case with your neighbor himself.* Show him that the great object is not to justify *your case,* but to put a speedy end to the strife. Abraham, instead of complaining to others, carried his wrongs straight to the king, who was answerable for them.[z] Jephthah *argued his case* with the king of Ammon himself, as the best means of bringing it to a peaceful, friendly settlement.[7] But to

[z]Gen 21:25–32

[7]*Judg 11:12–27. Comp. the rule of the great lawgiver, Matt 18:15.*

tell secrets to others, even though we urge them to secrecy, is a breach of integrity.[8] And if, as often is the case, confidence is betrayed, the just consequence must be dishonor to ourselves that may *not pass away*. Backbiter will be our name. And many privacies hitherto unknown may be published in retaliation to our shame.

How many unholy and heated quarrels would be restrained by the practice of these rules of wisdom and love! Obviously the one most at fault should be the one to yield. But if, as usually happens, he is too unreasonable to do so; let a generous, self-forgetting kindness deny ourselves the pleasure of a triumph, instead of standing upon very exact forms, or waiting for an apology from the offender. And if we find it easier to talk of our neighbor's faults to others, than it is to wisely and prayerfully tell him of them alone, ask for self-discipline and the mind of Christ. "Let the peace of Christ rule in your hearts, to which indeed you were called in one body."[a] [a]Col 3:15

11 Like *apples of gold in settings of silver*
Is a word spoken in right circumstances.
12 Like *an earring of gold and an ornament of fine gold*
Is a wise reprover to a listening ear.

WORDS UPON WHEELS

The allusion is to the curiously wrought baskets of *silver* network in which delicious fruits were served. The beauty of the texture sets off the fruit with additional charms. So does a lovely setting enhance the attractiveness of truth.[9] "The Preacher sought to find delightful words"[b]—*words spoken in right circumstances*—giving to each their proper meat—and that "at the proper time,"[c] suited to their ages and difference of temperament. "Honest words are not painful."[d] Our Lord witnessed of Himself, as with "the tongue of disciples, that [He] may know how to sustain the weary one with a word"[e]—a word upon the wheels—not forced or dragged, but rolling smoothly along, like the chariot wheels. His messages on the living water and the bread of life[f] arose naturally out of the conversation,[g] and therefore the mes-

[b]Eccl 12:10; Prov 15:23
[c]Luke 12:42. Comp. 2 Tim 2:15
[d]Job 6:25
[e]Isa 50:4
[f]John 4:6
[g]Comp. Luke 14:15, 16

[8] *"To tell our own secrets," says our great moralist, "is generally folly"—but, without guilt. To tell about others the things with "which we are entrusted is always treachery, and treachery for the most part combined with folly"*—Rambler, No. 13.
[9] *See Bishop Lowth's beautiful exposition. Praelect. 24.*

sages were full of powerful application. Paul powerfully charged the Athenians with superstition by an inscription on their own altar; and strengthened. His reasoning by quoting from one of their own poets.[h] To a dishonest and corrupt judge he preached "righteousness, self-control and judgment to come."[i]

In general conversation much depends, not only upon the *word spoken* but upon the occasion and spirit of speaking. We must not only put ourselves out to do good, but we must watch for the most fitting time for doing it. Under affliction, or tender impressions of conviction, *a word spoken in right circumstances* might be as the descent of our gracious Lord to the soul, "like rain upon the mown grass."[j] The plough enters most easily into earth when it is softened. Under all circumstances our lips should know "what is acceptable."[k] Unseemly language makes wholesome truth more unacceptable. As far as possible, let reproof be introduced naturally, without formality or constrained effort. Many, who strongly feel the impulse of being "ready ... out of season," neglect the not-less Christian obligation of being instant "*in* season"?[l] We may hope to relieve our conscience by speaking our mind. But to do it rudely and harshly, may put a stumbling block in our brother's way. The *apples of gold* in their beautiful cover, evidently imply good sense and good taste with good things. A well-meaning absurdity rather brings contempt than conviction.[m]

All of us are bound to rebuke broad and easily-recognized sins;[n] yet, on more doubtful individual cases the duty is far more restricted. Who will give direction? There must be intimate connection, full knowledge of the case, some right from age or station to warrant it. From its extreme difficulty, no duty calls for more delicate feeling, and more meekness of wisdom. Yet where reproof is well-timed and well-taken, *a wise reprover to a listening ear is an earring of gold, and an ornament of fine gold* set out to the best advantage. Such was Eli's word to Samuel;[o] Abigail's and Nathan's to David;[p] Isaiah's to Hezekiah.[q] We see the good fruit in Jehoshaphat, who, instead of being revolted by reproof, was stimulated to higher service for God.[r] The apostle Paul's

[h] Acts 17:22–28
[i] Acts 24:25
[j] Ps 72:6
[k] Prov 10:32
[l] 2 Tim 4:2
[m] Prov 31:26
[n] Lev 19:17
[o] 1 Sam 3:11–18
[p] 1 Sam 25:31–34; 2 Sam 12:1–13
[q] 2 Kings 20:14–19
[r] 2 Chron 19:2–4

heart-searching reproof was so well received by the Corinthian church and worked so efficiently that "in everything you demonstrated yourselves to be innocent in the matter."[s] What a triumph of grace is it when the kindness of *reproof* is acknowledged[t] and the motive of love appreciated![u] Faithful indeed is the blessing, when the gift of *a listening ear* prepares the Lord's children for a profitable hearing of His *reproof.*[v]

[s]1 Cor 5:1; 2 Cor 2:1–3; 7:11
[t]Ps 141:5. Comp. Prov 9:8
[u]Prov 27:5, 6
[v]Hab 2:1–3; Prov 20:12; 15:31

13 *Like the cold of snow in the time of harvest*
Is a faithful messenger to those who send him,
For he refreshes the soul of his masters.

GOD'S FAITHFUL MESSENGERS

Snow itself would be out of season *in the time of harvest.* But *the cold* of snow would be most refreshing to the parched and fainting reapers. *So is a faithful messenger to those who send him.*[w] How Eliezer *refreshed the soul of his masters,* when "he returned with a true account and speedy dispatch of the important affair committed to him!" stated Poole. Think of Judge Isaac's feelings in the evening walk of meditation—his heart full of the great matter under suspense, when "he lifted up his eyes and looked, and behold, the camels were coming," fraught with the desired blessing.[x] How Cornelius was *refreshed,* when his *messenger* returned with the joy of his heart and the answer to his prayers.[y] Often does the apostle Paul acknowledge this *refreshment* to his anxious "spirit," when burdened with the care of all the churches.[z] And may we not ascend to the highest, and with reverence mark even God himself condescending to receive *refreshment* through his *faithful messengers?* *"We are a fragrance,"* says Paul, *"of Christ to God."* He appears to be overwhelmed with contemplation, and in utter amazement, he cries out, "Who is adequate for these things?"[a] Wondrous condescension! Our great Master acknowledges *the messengers* of His churches as "a glory of Christ."[b] And He will honor them, as His crown, at the great consummating day. They that turn many "to righteousness" shall shine "like the stars forever and ever."[c]

[w]Prov 13:17
[x]Gen 24:63, 64
[y]Acts 10:4–6, 25
[z]1 Cor 16:17, 18; Phil 2:25–30; 1 Thess 3:1–7
[a]2 Cor 2:15, 16
[b]2 Cor 8:23
[c]Dan 12:3

14 Like *clouds and wind without rain*
Is a man who boasts of his gifts falsely.[10]

WIND WITHOUT RAIN

The preceding Proverb described an invaluable blessing. This one marks a destructive curse. Imagine a drought, as in the day of Elijah, threatening desolation to the land,[d] and a thick *cloud,* seemingly big with fruitful blessing, yet passing over—*wind without rain.* This is a true picture of *the boaster;* rich in promises, but performing nothing; arousing great expectations, then sinking them in disappointment. Whether it is a vain conceit of his own understanding, or a hypocritical desire to maintain a profession, it is a *boasting falsely.* If it is bad to promise and deceive, it is far worse to promise with an intention to deceive. This was the very character of Satan, the great deceiver. Did he not offer a false gift to our unhappy parents (Adam and Eve)—a promise, which could never be realized—"You will be like God, knowing good and evil"?[e] And—didn't he, with a presumption, that hell itself might almost be ashamed of, *boast himself of his false gift;* when he offered the world to his own Maker—Jesus—as a temptation to the vilest blasphemy?[f]

How sad to find this character in those who stand in the place of God! The church has ever been chastened with *false* teachers; ministering delusion, instead of instruction.[g] And are there none among ourselves, feeding the flock with *false gifts,* seeking to maintain their hollow profession even in the sight of Him, whose frown at the great day will banish them forever from His presence?[h] Oh! let those that bear the Lord's message, take heed, that, if they be counted "as deceivers," they may be "yet true";[i] not as those, which corrupt the Word of God; but as of sincerity, as of God, in the "sight of God," let them "speak in Christ."[j]

[d] 1 Kings 18:5
[e] Gen 3:3–5
[f] Matt 4:8–10
[g] 1 Kings 22:11; Jer 5:31; 2 Cor 11:13–15; Gal 1:7; 2 Peter 2:17–19; Jude 12–16
[h] Matt 7:22, 23
[i] 2 Cor 6:8
[j] 2 Cor 2:17; 4:2

15 *By forbearance a ruler may be persuaded,*
And a soft tongue breaks the bone.

THE MOST BRILLIANT JEWEL OF ALL

Solomon has before given a general rule for gentle-

[10] *"Whoso maketh greate boasts, and giveth nothing"—Bishop COVERDALE.*

ness.[k] Here he takes an extreme case, and shows its power with the ruler, whose unrestrained anger may rise to immediate revenge.[l] Yet submission and *forbearance* has mighty power to *persuade*. This was David's response to Saul's enraged temper.[m] Often by putting a case before an angry *ruler* at an opportune time, he may be persuaded by "the gentleness of wisdom" against his present mind.

[k]Prov 15:1

[l]Eccl 8:3; 10:4; 1 Sam 22:17, 18

[m]1 Sam 24:8–20; 26:13–25; James 3:13

But the general principle is most instructive. The *soft* member *breaking the hard bone* may seem to be a paradox. But it is a fine illustration of the power of gentleness above hardness and irritation. Apply it to those who are set against the truth. Many a stout heart has been won by a *forbearing*, yet uncompromising, accommodation to prejudice.[n] In reproof Jehovah showed what He could do in "the strong wind" and the "earthquake." But His effective rebuke was in the "still small voice"; without upbraiding; sharp, yet tender.[o] So powerful is the energy of gentleness! Indeed among all the graces that adorn the Christian soul, like so many jewels of various colors and lusters, against the day of her marriage to the Lamb of God, there is not one more brilliant than that of patience. Its enduring spirit is a manifest fruit of regeneration;[p] a clear exhibition of the mind of Christ,[q] and the practical resemblance of His own *forbearance* amidst our continued and most aggravated provocations. For, when we have been indulged with the privilege of the beloved disciple—"reclining on Jesus' breast,"[r] we have felt nothing being there but gentleness, tenderness, and love.

[n]2 Tim 2:24–26; 1 Cor 9:20–22

[o]AV—1 Kings 19:11–13

[p]James 1:18, 19
[q]Matt 11:29

[r]John 13:23; 21:20

16 *Have you found honey? Eat* only *what you need,*
Lest you have it in excess and vomit it.

TOO MUCH OF A GOOD THING

Solomon lately had invited us warmly to eat honey.[s] Here, however, he imposes a restraint. The old saying applies: "Too much of a good thing." *Eat only what you need.* It is enjoyable only to that point. Beyond this it is nauseating. Cultivate in all things the wisdom of sobriety. Enjoy earthly blessings but do so thankfully and temperately. "Everything created by God is good, and nothing is to be rejected, if it is received with gratitude."[t]

[s]Prov 24:13

[t]1 Tim 4:4

But as a needful balance to this universal privilege—"Let your forbearing spirit be known to all men."[u] Satisfy the wants, but mortify the lusts, of the flesh.[v] Then the gifts of God become blessings to us, and we glorify Him *in* them and *by* them. But the greatest pleasures of earth become, in the excess, distasteful and injurious; full of disappointment, when separated from the great end.[w] Our affections can never safely flow out to any object, unless they are primarily fixed on God. Then we may be sure not to offend, either in the object or measure. No Christian can love whom he should not; nor immediately love whom he would. This holy respect both directs and limits him, shutting up his delights in the conscience of a lawful fruition. In earthly pleasure, however, we can never forget, how slight the boundary line is between the lawful and the forbidden path. Sin and danger begin on the extremity of virtue. For doesn't the legitimate indulgence of appetite to its utmost point bring us to the brink, and often hurry us to the allowance, of gluttony? Doesn't the undisciplined flow of earthly affections endanger idolatry? Why, even spiritual luxury may need self-control; lest it be excitement without deep principle, which must eventually prove unsubstantial and delusive.

[u] Phil 4:5; 1 Cor 7:29–31
[v] Rom 13:14; Col 3:5; Luke 21:34
[w] Eccl 2:10, 11

CELESTIAL HONEY

But in *eating* the real *honey* of the gospel there is no danger of excess. We will never be overfilled in feeding on God's Word. The increasing desire will be fully satisfied only in eternity. "O God, let me but taste and see how sweet the Lord Jesus is in all his gracious promises; in all his merciful and real performances. I shall want no more to make me happy," said Bishop Hall (*Works—Soliloquies*, 54). This is not the *honey*, whereof I am bidden not to eat too much. No, Lord, I can never eat enough of this celestial *honey*. Here I cannot overeat, or if I could, it would improve my health.

17 *Let your foot rarely be in your neighbor's house,*
Lest he become weary of you and hate you.

THE CHRISTIAN AND THE COURTESIES OF LIFE

No code of laws enters, as the Bible does, into minute regulations for the courtesies of life. Yet surely we do not mar the sanctity of religion by spreading it over the face of human society. Daily life is evangelized by the pervading influence of its wholesome principles. This rule illustrates one of our own sayings, which has lost nothing of its significance by constant repetition—"Familiarity breeds contempt." This saying was however never intended to give a chill to the flow of neighborly love or to restrain its practical exercise. It only suggests that happy fellowship cannot be maintained without consideration on the part of all involved. An ordinary acquaintance would give offense in claiming the free and unrestrained communication of intimate friendship. And the intruder would probably receive a plain hint that he was an unwelcome guest. To avoid such embarrassment, the intruder should simply withdraw his foot from the premises. *"Make your foot precious"*[11] *to your neighbor* by not giving it too often. It is far safer to err on the side of reserve than to incur contempt by the opposite mistake.

Even the closer band of friendship requires its measure of wise restraint. It is worth all the effort to preserve the invaluable blessing of fellowship with our friends and neighbors. It is the "sweet" of life. And yet in this *honey*[x] there may be the temptation to indulge to excess. Without mutual respect it may nauseate. Unseasonable intrusion into our friend's time; frequent visits without call or object;[12] interference with his necessary engagements, or family comforts; inconvenient expense—perseverance in this course might produce *weariness,* if not disgust, or even *hatred.*

[x]Verse 16

Blessed be God! There is no need of this caution and reserve in our approach unto Him. Once acquainted with the way of access, there is no wall of separation. Our earthly friend may be pressed too far, and kindness, may be worn out by frequent use. But we can never come to our heavenly Friend at the wrong time. He never gets tired of our repeated requests.[y] His gates are always open; "blessed is the man . . . watching . . . waiting."[z] The more frequent our visits, the more welcome, and the more fruitful. What with man would be intrusion, God welcomes. He earnestly invites us into His closest and most endearing fellowship.[a] And does His child take un-

[y]Luke 11:5–9; 18:1
[z]Prov 8:34
[a]Song of Sol 5:1

[11] *Hebrew. See Holden. Comp. 1 Sam 3:1—precious in both cases, because rare.*
[12] *See a valuable paper,* On the Robbery of Time, *in "The Idler." Vol. I. No. 14.*

fair advantage of this most gracious privilege? Far from it. Though He has the "boldness and confident access";[b] he seeks for "gratitude, by which we may offer to God an acceptable service with reverence and awe."[c]

[b]Eph 3:12; Heb 4:16; 10:19, 20

[c]Heb 12:28

18 Like *a club and a sword and a sharp arrow*
Is a man who bears false witness against his
neighbor.

MURDER WEAPONS IN THE CHURCH

False witness is universally condemned. But where, except in the Word of God, are its true character and deep burden of guilt adequately set forth? What a picture we have here of cruelty and malice—even intentional murder! Three murderous instruments are before us, bringing together the sixth and ninth commandments: (false witness and murder). The tongue, intended as "a tree of life," becomes a weapon of death.[d] Who can bear the sin involved in this fearful corruption? Often the open lie as *a sword and sharp arrow* pierces the fountain of life.[e] And little better are those slanders and unkind insinuations—all violations of love—uttered so freely in everyday conversation. Consider, you that deal in such conversation, whether you could think of treating the objects of your slanderous talk, as Jael did Sisera,[f] or as Joab did Abner.[g] Would you shrink with horror at the thought of beating out your neighbor's brains with a *club* or of piercing his heart with *a sword, or a sharp arrow*? Then why do you indulge in similar savagery; destroying as far as you can his reputation, which is as dear to him as his life, and wounding all his best interests, by tearing down his reputation?[13] A man can outlive and overcome other injuries. But slander, regardless of all efforts to heal the wound, too often leaves a scar to his dying day.

[d]Prov 15:4, with 12:18; Jer 9:3, 8

[e]Gen 39:14–20; 1 Kings 21:10–13; Matt 26:60–66; Acts 6:13, 14

[f]Judg 4:21

[g]2 Sam 3:27

It's truly appalling to think of how many of these *clubs, swords, and sharp arrows* there are, even in the church of God. And they are not being used against the enemy (army against army),[h] but brother against brother. The test word of a party, not the standard of the cross, is the watchword for the destructive conflict.[i] How long! Lord! how long?

[h]1 Sam 17:21

[i]Judg 12:6

[13] *See God's estimate and threatening. Ps 1:19–21; Ezek 22:5.*

19 Like *a bad tooth and an unsteady foot*
Is confidence in a faithless man in time of trouble.

WHEN YOU NEED HIM WHERE IS HE?

The bad tooth and unsteady foot are not only useless for their respective purposes, but a source of pain and uneasiness. So is a *faithless man in time of trouble.* "A friend loves at all times, and a brother is born for adversity."[j] But many have the name only. They are very friendly, when they are not needed; when we are giving, not receiving, our gifts; when there is no price to pay. But *in the time of* trouble, "who can find a trustworthy man?"[k] Job experienced this so keenly *in his time of trouble.*[l] David was sorely tried in this way, too,[m] even at the very last stage of life.[n] The brethren came out to meet the apostle Paul at Appius Forum. Yet there was a time when their support would have been especially cheering, but he had to record: "At my first defense no one supported me, but all deserted me."[o] But why should we wonder that Paul had to bear such a cross? Didn't his Master have to endure it before him, and God's Word reminds us, "it is enough for the disciple that he become as his teacher."[p]

[j]Prov 17:17
[k]Prov 20:6
[l]Job 6:14–17
[m]Ps 55:12–14
[n]1 Kings 1:19, 25
[o]Acts 28:15, with 2 Tim 4:16
[p]Matt 26:56, with 10:24, 25

This world is full of instances of this disappointment. Micah's Levite ungratefully repaid the trust placed in him.[q] Mephibosheth's trust in Ziba;[r]—and Israel's dependence upon an arm of flesh; revealed a broken reed, not a staff of support.[14] Actually, when did the world ever fulfill its bright promises *in time of trouble*? A merciful correction to the child of God, when he turns aside from his true trust (in God) to vain dependence.

[q]Judg 17:7–12; 18:20–24
[r]2 Sam 16:1–4; 19:24–28

GOD IS FAITHFUL

But no matter who else is *unfaithful,* God is true. Who ever trusted in Him and was disappointed? Who has ever built upon God's sure foundation and not experienced its unshaken security?[s] Though he has pledged himself never to forsake His servants,[t] yet, He has especially promised: "I will be with him *in trouble* . . . a very present help in trouble."[u]

[s]Isa 28:16
[t]Heb 13:5
[u]Ps 91:15; 46:1; Jer 17:5–8

[14] *See also Assyria—2 Chron 28:20, 21; Hos 5:13. Egypt—Isa 30:1–3; 31:1–3; Jer 36:5–7; Ezek 29:6, 7.*

20 Like *one who takes off a garment on a cold day, or*
like *vinegar on soda,*
Is he who sings songs to a troubled heart.

YOUR PAIN IN MY HEART

What could be more inhuman than *taking away* a poor man's *garment,* or the blanket on his bed, *in cold weather*? Such an act of cruelty was forbidden by the God of the poor.[v] Again—what could be more inappropriate than pouring *vinegar upon soda or* gunpowder; which, instead of being serviceable, would only quickly dissolve it into bubbles?[15] And it would be just as inappropriate to sing merry songs to a heavy heart.[w] "Give . . . wine"—is the inspired rule—"unto those that be of *heavy* hearts."[x] But however great are the charms of music,[y] loud, boisterous songs are ill-suited to soothing the pangs of sorrow.[z] A forced, unnatural song did not ease the pain of the Israelites in captivity.[a] And even where no unkindness is intended, inconsiderate frivolity, or even excessive cheerfulness, is as a sword in the bones. The tenderness, that shows a brother's tears; that knows how to "weep with those who weep,"[b] as members of the same body;[c] and directs the mourner to the mourner's friend and God—this is Christian sympathy—a precious balm for the broken heart. The outward expression of this sympathy may not always be necessary. But oh! let its spirit be deeply cherished, especially by Christians of either a cheerful or cold temperament; most of all by the minister of Christ, that he may sit at the mourner's side, and comfort him with the same comfort, wherewith he himself is "comforted of God."[d] Much may be done to improve a person's health, but excessive emotion, no less than coldness, needs self-control. However, never let us forget, that it was for these reasons, that our divine Savior "took our infirmities, and carried away our diseases," that he might be touched with the feeling of them.[e] Yes—"He Himself knows our frame;"[f] and His work is not to *take away the garment* from His child *on the cold day,* but to cherish him with all the tenderness of His own bosom.[g] Instead

[v] Deut 24:12, 17; Job 24:7–10; Isa 58:7
[w] Eccl 3:4
[x] AV—Prov 31:6; Ps 104:15
[y] 1 Sam 16:23; 2 Kings 3:15
[z] Job 30:31; Dan 6:18. Comp. Eccl 22:6
[a] Ps 137:1–4
[b] Rom 12:15. Comp. Job 2:11–13
[c] 1 Cor 12:26; Heb 13:3
[d] 2 Cor 1:4–6
[e] Matt 8:17; Heb 4:15
[f] Ps 103:14
[g] Isa 49:11

[15] *The nitre (soda) of Scripture is not that salt that commonly goes by the name, but a soda or mineral alkali (the Roman natrum) which strongly ferments with all acids. Dr. Blayney remarks on Jer 2:22 (the only other example of the word), "In many parts of Asia it is called soap-earth, because it is dissolved in water, and used like soap in washing."*

of unsuitably *pouring vinegar on soda;* which would only increase the suffering, like the good Samaritan, he pours in His "oil and wine" for the healing of the wound.[h]

[h]Isa 61:2, 3, with Luke 10:34

21 *If your enemy is hungry, give him food to eat;*
And if he is thirsty, give him water to drink;
22 *For you will heap burning coals on his head,*
And the LORD *will reward you.*

PERFECT LOVE

In what heathen code of morals shall we find this perfect love? Every system yields largely to selfishness. None reaches beyond loving "those who love you," of which the true lawgiver—God—justly asks, What reward have ye?[i] Certainly the corrupt Jewish teachers could not rise to this sublime standard. "They did not, it seems, perceive anything to be disapproved in hatred, more than in good will. And according to their system of morals, "our enemy" was the proper and natural object of one of these passions, as "our neighbor" was of the other. They could not come up to the law: and therefore, twisting the rule of *judicial* vengeance, to authorize private vengeance,[j] they brought the law down to their own level.

[i]Matt 5:46, 47

[j]Matt 5:43; Deut 7:1, 2; 23:6; 25:17–19

The agreement between the Old and New Testament codes[k] is most complete. Both were dictated by the same Spirit. Each stamps the other with divine authority. "The law of love is not expounded more spiritually in any single precept, either of Christ or his apostles, than in this exhortation," said Scott. Therefore, we don't need to discredit one system, in order to exalt the other. The "new commandment" is that "which you have had from the beginning;" old in its authority; "new" only, as enforced by a new principle and example.[l] To suppose that the gospel stretches beyond the measure of the law, would imply, either that the law demanded too little, or the gospel too much. Neither supposition honors the law, as the unchangeable reproduction of the divine perfections.

[k]Comp. Rom 12:20, 21, with text. Exod 23:4, 5, with Matt 5:44

[l]John 13:34; 1 John 2:7, 8; 2 John 5

There may be no open infraction of the law, even though the heart rebels against its high standard. Circumstances may hinder open retaliation. Our enemy may be out of our reach, or may be too great to offend without punishment. But the grudge remains.[m] There would be

[m]Lev 19:18; James 5:9

[n]Prov 24:17, 18

[o]2 Sam 13:23, 28

[p]Col 3:12, 13

[q]Matt 5:44

[r]1 Sam 24:16–20; 26:25

delight in his misfortune.[n] We think of him only in connection with our injuries. The spark may be controlled for years, but someday when conditions are right, it may burst out into a murderous flame.[o] How many stops and starts there are at best before we fully avail ourselves of the opportunity! How guilty we are of a retaliating spirit; how much we measure our conduct toward our enemy by his conduct toward us! And if on any point we have persuaded our selfish hearts to return good for evil, how we minister to self-complacency, or self-righteousness!

We are not bound to trust our enemies; but we are bound to forgive them. And yet too often our love to them is only ceasing to quarrel with them. If we put off revenge, as inconsistent with our Christian name; do we go further and put on, as the elect of God, hearts of mercy—"forgiving each other, whoever has a complaint against anyone"?[p] Love is of too substantial a nature to be made up of mere negatives; and thereby too effective to end up as no more than bare desires.[q] We may speak of our good will toward *our enemy* and that we forgive and pray for him from our heart. But unless we are ready to exercise practical sympathy—*feeding him when he is hungry and giving him to drink,* when thirsty—we are simply the victims of our own self-delusion. "O noble revenge of Elisha," exclaims Bishop Hall, "to feast his persecutors! To provide a table for those, who had provided a grave for him! No revenge but this, is heroical, and fit for Christian imitation."[16] To *feed our hungry enemy* with the tenderness of a nurse, who breaks the portion into morsels for her infant's nourishment—what a splendor does nature's opposition give to this victory of grace!

No man ever conquered his enemy's heart by revenge; but many have by love. Wasn't that how our almighty Savior overcame the hardness of our unyielding hearts? Try it yourself! Cover the unruly metal beneath and above. Don't just put it over the fire, but *heap burning coals upon it.* Few hearts are so hardened they won't melt under the mighty power of patient, self-denying, burning love.[r] Or, if it should be dross, that resists the intense flame, everything won't be lost. If your enemy will not repay you for all the good done to him, don't be

[16] Contemplations, *Book 19: Cont. 2, on 2 Kings 6:22, 23. See another equally noble example in the most degenerate times of Judah. 2 Chron 28:12–15.*

concerned. The Lord will reward you. The God of love will honor His own image on His own children.[s] David in this assurance held back the rising vengeance in his zealous servants,[t] and in similar forbearance found that his "prayer" for his enemy's good was filling his own heart once again.[u] We are directed to return blessing for insult, knowing that hereunto are we called, that we should "inherit a blessing."[v] Our chief aim therefore must be to gain the victory of meekness and love. The wickedness of our enemies will then work to our advantage. We shall be indebted to them for some measure of conformity to our divine Master that we may have gained.

[s]Matt 5:44, 45

[t]2 Sam 16:9–12; Ps 7:4

[u]Ps 35:13. Comp. Matt 10:13

[v]1 Peter 3:9

To dispute the reasonableness of the rule is to say, that "man is the proper object of good will, whatever his faults are, when they respect others; but not when they respect myself. I am sure," adds Bishop Butler (*Sermons at the Rolls*), "there is nothing in it unreasonable." Actually, it means no more than that we should not indulge a passion, which, if generally indulged, would reproduce itself so abundantly that it could almost lay the whole world waste.

But as reasonable as this rule is, it is far removed from man's inborn power. The rules, no less than the doctrines, of God, are "foolishness to Him."[w] Let those who expect to enter into eternal life by keeping the commandments begin with this. In no time at all, they would see that they might as easily turn the sun backward; that they could as readily cut off a right hand as reach it out *to feed an enemy* in distress. Such an exhibition of love would be ideal perfection in their eyes; or at least, like a beautiful piece of workmanship, which every one admires, but no one attempts to imitate.

[w]1 Cor 2:14

Yet, isn't it really capable of being used? That's how the world feels about it, and that is how my corrupt heart finds it. But "I can do all things"—this then among the rest—"through Him who strengthens me."[x] It shall then be done willingly and joyfully. My enemy has no claim upon my life; yet He that bids me love Him, claims and deserves my full obedience.[y] "We are the disciples of Him, who died for His enemies."[17] If we only drank more

[x]Phil 4:13

[y]John 14:15

[17] *Bishop Wilson* (Sodor and Man) *Rom 5:10; Comp. Luke 23:34. Was not this His own obedience to His own law? Matt 5:44.*

fully into His spirit, this useless rule would not be our task, or our cross, but our delight and the satisfaction of our own desires.

23 *The north wind brings forth rain,*
And a backbiting tongue, an angry countenance.

[z]Prov 26:20
[a]Prov 16:28
[b]2 Cor 12:20

Who can tolerate *the backbiter*? He is a pest in society;[z] in the circle of friendship;[a] in the church of God.[b] Even though he may not look the part, and even travel in good company, he cannot hide his real character. Let the very sight of him bring a rebuke of holy indignation. This is to "be angry, and yet do not sin."[18] Indeed, *not* to be angry here, would be to sin. *Holy* anger is a property in God.[c] It was plainly displayed in the humanity of Jesus.[d] When God's name was dishonored, the "humblest" man upon earth waxed hot[e] in anger, even while His heart was melting in love for the rebels.[f] And shouldn't *we* feel this, when *the backbiting tongue* breaks His law of love, as dear to God as His own Godhead? And yet very rare is the exception—even with Christians—when the faults of others, real or imagined, do not occupy the conversation: or at least, when some discrediting of the absent ones or some ridicule of their weaknesses, is not discussed!

[c]Deut 9:8; Ps 7:11; Nah 1:2
[d]Mark 3:5; 8:33
[e]Exod 32:19, with Num 12:3
[f]Exod 32:30–32

This tongue wounds four at one stroke—*the backbiter* himself, the object of his attack, the hearer, and the name of God. All involves the professing Christian in the fearful guilt of offending the "little ones."[g] For how can the weak and inexperienced help but stumble at such an inconsistent exhibition of the gospel of love?

[g]Matt 18:6

But if he is drawn into the group rather than repelled by it, and becomes a willing listener, isn't he a partaker of the gossiper's sin? Don't allow yourself to become a part of it. Keep your ears and your mouth away from the terrible poison, and let an angry look drive the slander away from the gossiper, or *him* away from you. Where you are not in a position to rebuke the offender, a marked show of displeasure will often get your point across to the shameless offender.

24 *It is better to live in a corner of the roof*
Than in a house shared with a contentious woman.

[18] *Eph 4:26. To paraphrase Philip Henry—You know, what an angry countenance does; and we may sometimes reprove by our looks, when we don't have opportunity of giving it otherwise. (See his* Life.)

HOUSE OF CONTENTION

This Proverb has been given before.[h] God's Word doesn't repeat because it lacks subject matter. It repeats because of the importance of the subject being discussed. So great is the trouble caused by contention that the most uncomfortable part of the house (into which the soul might withdraw for communion with God) would be a grateful alternative.

This Book presents a graphic picture of marital happiness, where the wife is as the "loving hind and a graceful doe"—her husband's most satisfying delight.[i] But here is a vivid contrast of misery from which even a big house provides no refuge or rest.

God has wisely appointed the relative positions of husband and wife. Equality would have provoked contention for superiority. But the divine appointment preserves peace without degradation.[j] If man is "to rule over" the woman, "the woman is the glory of man"[k]—the diadem in his domestic circle,[l] and, upon her level, still his support, solace, and "helper."[m] *The contentious* wife, revolting against her Maker's rule of submission to her husband, torments herself as well as her husband.

Let the professing Christian beware of trifling with God's command, that he marry—"only in the Lord."[n] If he goes into the world, instead of coming out; if he unites himself in the closest possible bond with the world, instead of being "separate"; if, when forbidden to "touch what is unclean," he makes himself "one flesh" with it,[o] then he need not wonder, if his God "curse your blessings,"[p] and leave him to choose for himself a house of contention, without one ray of heavenly sunshine. Young man! Think of the deep responsibility of the marriage choice! Let it plainly be the Lord's choice for you, not your choice for yourself. Best of all, let *Him* be your first choice and He will put all the rest in order.[q] Watch and distrust your own will. Turn for guidance to God's Word, the "lamp . . . light to my path."[r] Mark the care of your God;[s] and "It is the blessing of the Lord that makes rich, and He adds no sorrow to it." He will surely sanctify his own gift.[t]

Christian woman! Don't feel that these Proverbs are unworthy of your attention, too. You may not be the con-

[h] Prov 21:9
[i] Prov 5:18, 19
[j] Gen 3:16; 1 Tim 2:11–14
[k] 1 Cor 11:3–7
[l] Prov 31:28
[m] Gen 2:18
[n] 1 Cor 7:39
[o] 2 Cor 6:14–17, with Eph 5:31
[p] Mal 2:2
[q] Matt 6:33
[r] Ps 119:105
[s] Gen 24:12–60; Ruth 3:18
[t] Prov 19:14; 10:22

tentious wife spoken of. But certainly the repeated reference to that kind of woman implies the need for the wife to cultivate the opposite graces, without which she will fail to measure up to her greatest potential.[u]

[u]1 Tim 2:9, 10; 1 Peter 3:1–6

25 Like *cold water to a weary soul,*
So is good news from a distant land.

GOOD NEWS FROM A DISTANT LAND

What were the *cold waters* to Hagar and her child in the wilderness;[v] to Israel at Rephidim;[w] to Samson at Lehi![x] Such is the *good news from a distant land.* Solomon had before spoken of the refreshment of *"the messenger";*[y] he speaks here of *the message.* This Proverb, like many others, was probably written out of personal experience. Solomon's fleets, returning from *a distant land* with precious merchandise were doubtless (like our own merchant ships) welcomed with great delight.[z] One who is exiled from his homeland or has special interests in a foreign land—perhaps near and dear relatives, from whom he has been separated for a long time—well understands Solomon's living illustration. Had Joseph's brethren brought their sorrowing father as many pieces of gold as grains of corn, all that would have been nothing to the *good news from a distant land*—"Joseph is still alive."[a] Information from afar is naturally more cheering than tidings in themselves equally interesting, but nearer home. The long interval of these tidings; the lengthened separation from loved ones; the anxiety necessarily excited by lack of communication; the uncertainty of the loved ones welfare and prospects—all combine to make these *cold waters* specially refreshing *to the weary soul.* "Hope deferred makes the heart sick, but desire fulfilled is a tree of life."[b]

[v]Gen 21:16–19
[w]Exod 17:1–6. Comp. Num 20:11
[x]Judg 15:18, 19
[y]Verse 13
[z]1 Kings 9:26–28
[a]Gen 45:25–28. Comp. 43:27–30
[b]Prov 13:12. Comp. 15:30. Contrast Neh 1:2–4

Reader! if your light, vain heart has ever leaped within you at the news of some earthly advantage, have you heard and welcomed the *good news from a distant land*? Do you know your need, your danger of perishing? Then what refreshment can compare with the "good news of great joy" brought to you from heaven—"There has been born for you a Savior"?[c] Yet, these joyous tidings would be in vain, unless faith could hear their repeated proclamation as from the angel's lips or from the Savior's cross.

[c]Luke 2:10, 11

But the influence they have on the receptive heart, melts away the mass of sin in the glowing splendor of this grand work of God. Yes, sinner—mountains of gold could never have purchased the blessing now brought to your ears, even to the very door of your heart, without "money."[d] Doesn't your heart almost burst with praise—"how lovely on the mountains are the feet of him who brings good news, who announces peace"![e] Most welcome also are the messengers' tidings from *a distant land,* telling of the welcome reception of their message.[f] The angelic harps strike up the song.[g] Even the heart of God is filled with adorable joy![h]

[d]Isa 55:1
[e]Isa 52:7
[f]Acts 15:3. Comp. 11:18, 23
[g]Luke 15:7, 10
[h]Luke 15:20–24

26 Like *a trampled spring and a polluted well*
Is a righteous man who gives way before the wicked.

Eastern *wells and springs* (where the rains are only periodic, and separated by long intervals) are of great value.[i] The results of corrupting them are proportionate.[j] The well is therefore a blessing or a curse, according to the purity or impurity of the waters. A righteous man in his proper character is "a fountain of life," a blessing on the "earth."[k] But if *he gives way before the wicked* by his inconsistent life,[19] the blessing becomes a curse, the *well is polluted, and the spring trampled.* How degrading it was to Abraham to *give way* under the rebuke of a heathen king;[l] to Peter, to yield to a servant-maid in denying his Lord![m] How terribly David's sin *polluted the well,* both to his family[n] and his people![o] And how the idolatry of his wise son *trampled the spring* through successive generations![p]

When a minister of Christ turns from the faith[q] (and such spectacles have been quite frequent) or compromises his principles from the fear of man,[r] *the springs and wells* of truth are fearfully corrupted. When a servant of God, with standing and influence, crouches and *gives way before the wicked,*[20] the transparency of his profession is grievously tarnished. Actually, Satan makes more effective use of God's people than of his own. The great wickedness of the ungodly passes in silence. But he

[i]Gen 26:18–22; Deut 8:7; Josh 15:18, 19
[j]See Ezek 32:2; 34:18
[k]Prov 10:11; Gen 12:3
[l]Gen 12:18–20. Comp. 20:10; 26:10
[m]Matt 26:69–72
[n]2 Sam 11:2, with 13:11–14; 16:22
[o]2 Sam 12:14
[p]1 Kings 11:1–8; 2 Kings 33:13
[q]Philem 24, with 2 Tim 4:10
[r]Gal 2:11–14

[19] *Giving way is to be taken in a moral sense (making a slip), Parkhurst.*
[20] *2 Kings 18:5, 6, with 13–16. Contrast with these humbling instances of infirmity the great confessor, who would not fall* down before *false apostles—not even before a true apostle—Gal 2:4, 5, 11.*

makes the neighborhood ring with his talk of the failings of professing Christians. When Christians live consistently for Christ, sinners are convicted. But when Christians stumble by the wayside, sinners clap their hands with joy to see the Lord "wounded in the house of . . . friends."[s] The consciences of the ungodly are lulled. The "lame," instead of being "healed," are "put out of joint."[t] The scandalous falls of good men are like bags of poison cast by Satan into the *well* that supplies the whole town with water.

[s] Zech 13:6
[t] Heb 12:13

And let's not get the idea that only prominent Christians are responsible to live consistently. Every Christian, by his very profession, should be "the salt of the earth," and "the light of the world." So it's up to each one of us to see that the salt does not "become tasteless," and that we let our light shine, as our Savior says we should.[u] None of us stands or acts alone. "Not one of us"—think of it carefully—"lives for himself."[v] The conduct of each one of us has its measure of influence on the whole body of Christ. Each is the center of a circle more or less extended. Each is either a pure *spring*, or a *polluted well*. Lord! cast the salt into "the spring of water," that they may be "purified."[w]

[u] Matt 5:13–16
[v] Rom 14:7
[w] 2 Kings 2:21, 22

27 *It is not good to eat much honey,*
Nor is it glory to search out one's own glory.

BEWARE OF THE DEAD FLY THAT SPOILS THE HONEY!

Sweets are good; but only in moderation.[x] A man's own name and reputation is *honey* to him.[y] Let him carefully preserve it from the "dead flies" that spoil it.[z] God's honor is closely linked with the consistent testimony of His people. But even those Christians who live as consistently as possible are themselves only a step away from the sin of pride, for to be "puffed up" over our holy living, to take to ourselves whatever praise may come, to force ourselves into public attention,[a] in order to build up our own reputation,[b] is not glorifying to God. Why, it is as out of place for us to seek *our own glory*, as it is to take credit for our existence.

[x] Prov 24:13
[y] Verse 16
[z] Phil 4:8, with Eccl 10:1
[a] AV—1 Cor 4:6; Prov 20:6; 27:2
[b] Gen 11:4; 2 Kings 10:16; Dan 4:30

Isn't there a danger of seeking the reputation for godliness rather than godliness, itself—a well-known name in the church, rather than an unknown name in the Book of Life? Most all ministers are severely tested here. The temptation for them is to identify their usefulness with their honor; cherishing the desire for public praise, rather than for unnoticed fruitfulness; dreading to be thought of on an ordinary level, as "vessels of wood and of earthenware," rather than of "gold and silver."[c] Oh! It's a mighty victory over self, to trample man's judgment under foot, and seek only God's approval. Nothing is right unless it is done in the true spirit of the gospel; "do nothing from selfishness or empty conceit, but with humility of mind let each of you regard one another as more important than himself."[d] The great apostle spoke of matters of glorying only by compulsion.[21] A boastful spirit ruins many a good testimony.[e] If we should turn away from the flattering glass of self-love to the pure and faithful mirror of the law, the normally unseen deformities would open to view and constrain us to take the lowest place among the most unworthy. It's good to remember—"That which is highly esteemed among men is detestable in the sight of God."[f]

[c] 2 Tim 2:20
[d] Phil 2:3; Gal 5:26
[e] John 5:44; 12:43
[f] Luke 16:15

28 Like *a city that is broken into* and *without walls*
Is a man who has no control over his spirit.

OUR NOBLEST BATTLES

One of the Proverbs we had earlier declared "he who is slow to anger is better than the mighty" and a mighty conqueror.[g] And certainly the noblest conquests are gained or lost over ourselves. *Anyone who has no control over his own spirit* is an easy prey to the invader. Anyone can irritate and torment him.[h] He yields himself to the first assault of his uncontrolled passions, offering no resistance; *like a city that is broken into and without walls*, he becomes the object of contempt.[i] Unable to discipline himself, any temptation leads to sin and causes him to do things he never dreamed of. The first outbreak of anger leads to murder.[j] Unwatchfulness over lust plunges him into adultery.[k] His natural strength, no matter how great it might be becomes utterly feeble in his battle with temptation and sin.[l] How should such a pitiful individual arouse our concern and compassion!

[g] Prov 16:32
[h] Esther 3:5, 6; 5:13
[i] Neh 1:3; 2:17
[j] Gen 4:5–8. Comp. 1 Sam 20:30–33; 25:33; Dan 3:13, 19
[k] 2 Sam 11:2–4
[l] Judg 16:1–19

[21] *2 Cor 12:1–11. See Lyttleton on* Conversion of St. Paul.

But there are many types of this moral weakness, less shameful, but hardly any less injurious to the soul. Every outbreaking of irritation, every spark of pride kindling in the heart, before it ever shows itself in the face or on the tongue, must be attacked, and determinately resisted. It is the beginning of a breakdown *in the walls of the city.* Without instant attention, it will widen to ruin the whole *city.*[m] Man may talk of self-control, as if the reins were in his own hand. But he who has been born of the Spirit, and taught to know "the affliction of his own heart,"[n] is made to feel, that effective self-control is really in God's hands, not his own. So then . . . what can be done? At Satan's first assault, we must fortify the walls with prayer. We must not trust the fortress. Haven't repeated defeats taught us the need for turning to greater strength than our own? How can we even *enter* into the conflict, much less win the battle, but for the promise—"Sin shall not be master over you"?[o] Oh! for simple, cleaving faith, to draw out from God's bountiful supply—energy, continual watchfulness, perseverance, triumphant victory!

[m]Comp. Prov 27:14

[n]1 Kings 8:38

[o]Rom 6:14

CHAPTER TWENTY-SIX

1 *Like snow in summer and like rain in harvest,*
So honor is not fitting for a fool.

The richest blessings lose their value when unsuitably bestowed. *Snow* is the beauteous wintry covering of the earth;[a] preserving the seed from the killing cold.[b] But *in summer,* it is out of season. *Rain* in its season is a fruitful blessing.[c] But in *harvest* it is an unsuitable interruption to the reaper's work, and often a public calamity.[d] Just so, honor, unsuitably bestowed on *a fool, is not fitting for him.* "He neither deserves it, nor knows how to use it," said Poole.[e] *Honor* bestowed on Joseph and Daniel, suitably to their wisdom, was seemly to themselves and a blessing to the land.[f] But when *a fool,* sometimes a scoffer at religion, is promoted to public office, how ungracefully his *honor* sits upon him! In Haman it was only the display of his pride and vainglory, the cause of his more public disgrace.

[a]Job 37:6
[b]Isa 55:10
[c]Job 38:26, 27; Ps 65:9–13; 104:13, 14; James 5:7
[d]1 Sam 12:17, 18
[e]Prov 19:10; 30:21, 22; Eccl 10:5–7. Comp. Ps 12:8
[f]Gen 41:38–40; Dan 6:1–3

We need to learn, then, to adorn our profession with consistency. Seek that heavenly wisdom, which will make us worthy of any honor that may be appointed for us. "He who is faithful in a very little thing is faithful also in much."[g]

[g]Luke 16:10

2 *Like a sparrow in* its *flitting, like a swallow in* its *flying,*
So a curse without cause does not alight.

HARMLESS SHOWERS OF STONES

Groundless fears are real evils and often press heavily upon enfeebled minds. An unprovoked and undeserved curse flies out of an angry mouth, "What if it should come to pass?" But we have no more reason to fear *a curse without cause,* than we do the *birds wandering* over our heads. *The swallow flying* up and down never lights upon us; *so the curse without cause shall not come* to hurt us. Moab's curse was powerless though he attempted to strengthen it with the divination of the wicked prophet.[h] Goliath's curse against David was scattered to the winds.[i] And in what way was David any the worse because of Shimei's curse;[j] or Jeremiah for the curse of his persecutors?[k] Under this harmless shower of stones, we turn from men to God and are at peace. "Let them curse, but do Thou bless; when they arise, they shall be ashamed, but Thy servant shall be glad."[l]

[h]Num 22:4–6; 23:8; Deut 23:4, 5
[i]1 Sam 17:43
[j]2 Sam 16:12
[k]Jer 15:10
[l]Ps 109:28

But if the *curse* is not *without cause,* it *will come* to pass. Jotham's righteous curse came upon Abimelech and the men of Schechem.[m] Elisha's curse fearfully came to the young mockers of Bethel.[n] The curse rests on Jericho from generation to generation.[o] And, reader, if you are an unsaved, unbelieving sinner, without love for the Savior, there is a curse for you, not without *cause,* but justly deserved; and *come* it will.[p] In fact, hasn't it already come from your Maker and your God;[q] not a harmless threat of evil, but the solemn foreboding of everlasting wrath centering in your heart? Oh! flee from it while there is time; while the refuge is still open to you![r] If you are covered it shall not come.[s] You shall rejoice in your redemption "from the curse,"[t] in your complete security.[u]

[m]Judg 9:56, 57
[n]2 Kings 2:24
[o]Josh 6:26; 1 Kings 16:34
[p]Deut 28:15; 29:19, 20; 1 Cor 16:22
[q]Prov 3:33; Zech 5:3, 4
[r]Gen 19:17
[s]Rom 8:1
[t]Gal 3:10, 13
[u]Prov 1:33

3 *A whip is for the horse, a bridle for the donkey,*
And a rod for the back of fools.

This Proverb turns our ideas inside out. We would give the bridle for the horse and whip for the donkey. But Eastern donkeys are very superior, both in beauty and spirit, very valuable to their owners.[v] The *bridle* is necessary to curb and to guide them; while *the horse,* perhaps badly broken in, may need *a whip;* if dull, to speed him up; if fiery, to correct his temper.[1] Every creature subdued for the service of man needs the right of discipline. The Lord "will counsel you with [His] eye." But let them cultivate a pliable spirit; not "as the horse or the mule" whose mouth must be held in with "bit and *bridle.*"[w] *The fool* neither hears the voice, nor sees the directing eye. He will be ruled neither by reason nor persuasion. *A rod* therefore is for the fool's back.[x] Pharaoh provoked this severe chastisement at the hands of God;[y] the men of Succoth and Penuel at Gideon's

[v]Judg 10:3, 4; 12:13, 14; 2 Sam 17:23; 19:26
[w]Ps 32:8, 9
[x]Prov 10:13; 19:29
[y]Exod 10:3

[1] *PAXTON'S* Natural History of Scripture, *p. 221, and Parkhurst.*

hands.[z] Many such *fools* are in the church, self-willed, full of conceit. They need *the rod,* and they have it.[a] Discipline is the most probing test. What is its fruit? In the child submission and tenderness;[b] in *the fool* (except it beat out his folly,[c] which is too often a desperate case[d]) hardness and rebellion.[e] How sad it is that the child sometimes needs the *rod* intended *for the fool's back.* Yet never does his loving Father use it, till gentle means have been tried in vain. Oh, Lord, use your own wise means to save me from my own waywardness and ruin.

[z]Judg 8:5–7, 16
[a]2 Cor 10:6–11; 13:2
[b]Jer 31:18–20
[c]2 Chron 33:11–13
[d]Prov 17:10; 27:22
[e]2 Chron 28:22; Isa 1:5; Jer 5:3

4 *Do not answer a fool according to his folly,*
Lest you also be like him.
5 *Answer a fool as his folly* deserves,
Lest he be wise in his own eyes.

HOW TO TREAT A FOOL

We are forbidden, and yet commanded, to *answer a fool.* One rule says: "*Don't* answer him." The other says "*Do* answer him." But the reason, given with each of these rules, clears up the apparent contradiction. Both together are a wise directory for the treatment *of the fool,* according to the difference of character, time, or circumstances. Suppose a freethinker or scoffer at religion shows the desperate *folly* of his heart by making a "mock at sin,"[f] by witty mocking, or seemingly plausible arguments against the Word or ways of God. Generally speaking, it would be better to follow Hezekiah's command concerning Rabshakeh's blasphemy—"Do not answer him."[g] Jeremiah thus turned away in silence from the folly of the false prophets.[h] If however we are constrained to reply—*don't answer him according to his folly;* not in his own foolish manner; "not returning . . . insult for insult."[i] Moses offended here. He *answered* the rebels *according to their folly*—passion for passion, and thus *he became like them.*[j] David's answer to Nabal was in the same humiliating spirit.[k] The answerer in this case *is like the fool.* He appears at the time to be cast in the same mold.

[f]Prov 14:9
[g]2 Kings 18:36; Jude 9
[h]Jer 28:11
[i]1 Peter 3:9
[j]Num 20:2–10; Ps 106:33
[k]1 Sam 25:21, 22

But that which may be, at one time, our duty to refrain from doing, at another time, and under different circumstances, it may be no less our duty to do. Silence may sometimes be mistaken for defeat. Unanswered words

may be deemed unanswerable, and *the fool* become ar-
[l]Verse 12; Job 11:2
rogant, more and more *wise in his own eyes.*[l] An *answer* therefore may be called for; yet not in folly, but to folly; "not in his foolish manner, but in the manner which his foolishness required," said Fuller (*Harmony of Scripture*); not according to his folly, but *according to your own* wisdom. Yet here our words would be sharp as rods. The fool's back needs them. Such was Job's answer to his wife; grave, convincing, silencing—"You speak as one of *the foolish* women speaks. Shall we indeed accept good from God and not accept adversity?"[m]

[m]Job 2:9, 10

Oh! for wisdom to govern the tongue; to discover "a time to be silent, and a time to speak";[n] most of all to suggest "a timely word"[o] for effective reproof! How instructive is the example of our great Master! His silence and His answers were equally worthy of Himself. The former always conveyed a dignified rebuke.[p] The latter issued in the confusion of his faultfinding enemies.[q] Won't a prayerful meditative study communicate to us a large measure of His divine wisdom?

[n]Eccl 3:7
[o]Prov 15:23; 25:11
[p]Matt 16:1–4; 21:23–27
[q]Matt 22:46; Luke 13:17

6 *He cuts off* his own *feet,* and *drinks violence*
Who sends a message by the hand of a fool.
7 Like *the legs* which *hang down from the lame,*
So is a proverb in the mouth of fools.
8 *Like one who binds a stone in a sling,*
So is he who gives honor to a fool.
9 Like *a thorn* which *falls into the hand of a drunkard,*
So is a proverb in the mouth of fools.

LOADED PISTOL IN A MADMAN'S HAND

Surely this varied exhibition of foolishness is an incentive to the study of heavenly wisdom. The fool is utterly unfit for service. When you send him out with a message, he makes so many mistakes, careless or willful, that it is like ordering him to go, when we have cut off his legs. Indeed we can only *drink violence* from his commission.[r] The unbelieving spies spread discontent and rebellion throughout the whole congregation.[s] How careful we should be to entrust important business to trustworthy people! *Fools* are either unqualified for their mission, or they have their own interests to serve, at whatever cost to

[r]Prov 10:26. Contrast 13:17; 25:13
[s]Num 13:32; 14:1–4

their masters. Solomon himself *drank violence,* by employing an "industrious" servant, but a *fool* in wickedness, who lifted up his hand against the king, and robbed his son of ten parts of his kingdom.[t] Benhadad *drank violence by sending a message by the hands of* Hazael, who murdered his master, when the way was opened for his own selfish purposes.[u]

[t]1 Kings 11:26–40

[u]2 Kings 8:8–15

See—again—how the fool exposes his shame. Never would a lame man show his infirmity so much as he would if he were to pretend to do feats of agility or strength. Never does a fool appear so ridiculous as when making a show of wisdom. It only creates disgust,[v] "A wise saying doth as ill become a fool, as dancing does a cripple," said Bishop Patrick. A *parable*—"an authoritative weighty saying," stated Parkhurst—*in his mouth* becomes a jest. "Is Saul also among the prophets?" and "Why do you look at the speck in your brother's eye, but do not notice the log that is in your own eye?" And the advice: "Physician, heal yourself . . . you, therefore, who teach another, do you not teach yourself?"[w]

[v]Prov 17:7

[w]1 Sam 19:24; Matt 7:3–5; Luke 4:23; Rom 2:21

Place the fool in honor. The sling makes *the stone bound in it* an instrument of death. *The honor given to the fool* makes him a curse to his fellow-man.[x] The prime favorite of a king, had not God restrained him, would have been the murderer of the chosen nation.[y] How dangerous it is to place unqualified persons in authority. "It is like putting a sword or a loaded pistol into a madman's hand," said Scott.[2]

[x]Judg 9:6; 1 Sam 8:1–3

[y]Esther 3:1–5

But the fool also does mischief unconsciously to himself. "It is no more fit for a fool to meddle with a wise speech, than for a drunken man to handle a thorn bush," said Bishop Hall. When the *thorn goes up into his hand,* his insensibility only makes the wound more deadly. *So the fool's proverb*—his wise sayings, gathered he scarcely knows where, *go up into him like a thorn,* sharply pricking his conscience. Yet he feels no pain, no alarm. Sad indeed is the sight (should it not make us tremble for ourselves?) of the ungodly prophet, dealing out from the

[2] *Parkhurst and other critics prefer the reading that* honor *is lost upon a fool, like a precious stone covered up in a mixed-up heap. "He that sets a fool in high dignity—that's as though a man casts a precious stone upon the gallows." Bishop Coverdale—alluding to the custom of throwing a stone to the heap, under which the criminal was buried.*

[z]1 Sam 3:11

mouth of God, yet with hardened indifference, words enough to make "both ears ... tingle."[z]

Such is *the fool*—a pest to his fellowman; awfully responsible to his God! But in the ministry how fearfully are this evil and responsibility increased! The great *message, sent by the hands* of ungodly servants, brings most serious damage to the church.[3] *The parable*—our Lord's wise and holy instruction—*in the mouth of a fool* is misdirected and contradicted by his unholy life. "But to the wicked God says—'What right have you to tell of My statutes, and to take My covenant in your mouth? For you hate discipline, and you cast My words behind you.' "[a] "Almighty God, who alone worketh great marvels, send down upon all Bishops and Curates the healthful spirit of thy grace" (Liturgy); that "stewards" faithful to their trust,[b] workmen that need not "be ashamed,"[c] true and authorized "ambassadors" for Christ, may be multiplied in the church; and that fools—unfaithful ministers—may be rebuked and restrained.

[a]Ps 50:16, 17

[b]1 Cor 4:1, 2
[c]2 Tim 2:15; Eph 6:20

10 Like *an archer who wounds everyone,*
So is he who hires a fool or who hires those who pass by. (AV—*the great God that formed all things both rewardeth the fool, And rewardeth transgressors.*[4])

THE REWARD OF THE FOOL AND THE TRANSGRESSOR

It is difficult to fix with certainty the interpretation of this Proverb. All who expound it, however, believe that it speaks of God's government, direct or permissive. The *God that formed all things* proportions exactly the *reward* of the wicked.[d] *The fool* is responsible for sins of ignorance; not only for the little he knows, but for the much, which, had he not neglected the means, he might have known. The *transgressor* is much more responsible for his sins against knowledge, warning, and conviction. And "because of your stubbornness and unrepentant heart you are storing up wrath for yourself in the day of wrath and revelation of the righteous judgment of God, who will render to every man according to his deeds,"

[d]Ps 31:23; Isa 3:11

[3] *1 Sam 2:17; Jer 23:15. Hence the solemn responsibility of the Ordination Rule. 1 Tim 5:22.*
[4] *The Standard American Edition, 1901, margin reads: "A master worker formeth all things; But he that hireth the fool is as one that hireth them that pass by. The Hebrew text is obscure."*

and the "slave who knew his master's will and did not get ready or act in accord with his will, shall receive many lashes, but the one who did not know it, and committed deeds worthy of a flogging, will receive but few."[e]

[e] Rom 2:5, 6; Luke 12:47, 48

Or suppose the "great" one to be a mighty prince; powerful in *forming* the minds, character, and principles of *all* around him. If he rule "in the fear of God,"[f] will he not *reward the fool and the transgressor,* the ignorant and the arrogant? For how can his kingdom prosper upon the encouragement of the wicked?[g]

[f] 2 Sam 23:3

[g] Prov 25:5; 2 Chron 28:1–8; 33:1–11

Or if he is a wicked prince, he grieves all by his tolerance of sin: *hiring transgressors* as instruments of his will.[h] But still it is the government of God. The scepter is in the hands of unlimited power, wisdom, and goodness. But God uses His sword against the wicked and also the staff of His indignation."[i] Shall we then reply against God? Reverence, faith, humility, patience, expectations are graces of the Lord's children. "Clouds and thick darkness surround Him; Righteousness and justice are the foundation of His throne."[j] His providence never sleeps; and there is no interruption of his government. We are living only in a preparatory state. The veil will soon be lifted up, and the grand revealing will explain all. *Fools and transgressors* will receive their just reward; and one universal chorus will burst from heaven—"Who will not fear, O Lord, and glorify Thy name? For thou alone art holy; for all the nations will come and worship before Thee."[k]

[h] Judg 9:4; 1 Kings 21:10

[i] Ps 17:13, 14; Isa 10:5

[j] Ps 97:2

[k] Rev 15:4

11 *Like a dog that returns to its vomit*
Is a fool who repeats his folly.

POISONED PLEASURES

Is this the picture of man—"made a little lower than God"[l]—made in the "likeness" of God?[m] Who that saw Adam in his universal dominion, sitting as the monarch of creation; summoning all before him; giving to each his name, and receiving in turn his homage[n]—who would have conceived of his children sunk into such brutish degradation? The tempter's promise was—"You will be like Gods."[o] The result of this promise was—You shall be as beasts. The vilest comparisons are used to show man's loathsomeness in the sight of God. Do any feel disgusted

[l] Ps 8:5

[m] Gen 1:26

[n] Gen 2:20

[o] Gen 3:5

at the comparison? Let them remember, that the emblem is far less filthy than the thing it represents; and that the whole race of animals does not afford anything so debasing that it can't be far outdone by the excesses of the morally unrestrained drunkards and gluttons. We naturally turn away in disgust from this sight. If only we had the same disgust for the sin, which it so graphically portrays! If only we would abhor ourselves for those things God infinitely abhors in us!

The apostle Paul uses this "true proverb" to describe the awful condition of apostates[p]—temporary conviction, without real conversion of heart, and falling away into desperate hardness. Many reasons may produce disgust in the sinner's mind for his *folly*. He may loathe and for a while relinquish it. It has proved so full of misery;[q] its very pleasure so filled with poison; that no wonder he makes an occasional, or even a strong effort to get rid of it. But when the sickness has passed away, the sweetness of the forbidden fruit again comes to mind; the heart and affections are again clasped around the world, *and, as a dog returns to its vomit*—to the food, which had caused his sickness; so a *fool repeats his folly*—to that, which had been his hurt and shame.

[p]Peter 2:22
[q]Prov 13:15

Thus greedily did Pharaoh *return* from his momentary conviction;[r] Ahab from his make-believe repentance;[s] Herod from his partial amendment;[t] the drunkard from his brutish insensibility[u]—all to take a more determined course in sin; to take their final plunge into ruin. Even a superficial knowledge of Christ will not preserve an unrenewed heart. The house may be "swept" of outward sin, "and put in order" with external holiness; but if it is empty, if the divine inhabitant is not heartily welcomed, the former tenant will quickly return, and occupy it as his permanent home with sevenfold destruction.[v]

[r]Exod 8:8, 15; 9:27, 34, 35
[s]1 Kings 21:27–29; 22:8, 37
[t]Mark 6:20–27
[u]Prov 23:35
[v]Matt 12:43–45

Isn't sin then justly called *folly*? Doesn't the God of truth call it that now? Won't every *fool* confess it to be so at the end, when its wages shall be fully paid in "disgrace and everlasting contempt"?[w] Child of God! Listen to your Father's voice of "peace." But think also of His solemn warning "to His people, to His godly ones . . . let them not turn back to folly."[x]

[w]Dan 12:2
[x]Ps 85:8. Comp. John 5:14

12 *Do you see a man wise in his own eyes?*
There is more hope for a fool than for him.

THE CONCEITED FOOL

Do you see the man? God is pointing at him.[y] There is something to be learned from him. He retreats in his own conceit—*wise in his own eyes.* He sets himself up as a standard: The false idea he has that he has gained wisdom, totally keeps him from gaining it. He thinks himself wise, because he doesn't know what it is to be wise.[z] His wisdom is "falsely called 'knowledge.' "[a] For he has yet to learn the first lesson in school—his own lack of wisdom—a lesson not to be learned without hard practice. The knowledge of the most intelligent is as nothing compared with his ignorance; and yet how strangely the smallest bit of knowledge "puffeth" him up,[b] and fills him full of himself! "Let no man deceive himself. If any man among you thinks that he is wise in this age, let him become foolish that he may become wise."[c] *There is more hope for the fool,* who knows that he is one. The natural fool has only one hindrance—his own ignorance. The conceited fool has two—ignorance and self-delusion. He has everything to unlearn (which is the hardest lesson in the school) before he can learn anything right. He shows some improvement when he becomes less positive.

It was our Lord's cutting reproof to the conceited Pharisees—"The tax-gatherers and harlots will get into the kingdom of God before you."[d] It was His charge against the Laodicean church—"Because you say, 'I am rich, and have become wealthy, and have need of nothing,' and you do not know that you are wretched and miserable and poor and blind and naked."[e] The prodigal fool, running into all "loose living," is more open to conviction, than the man who prides himself upon his proper religion.[f] To the profane and ungodly we must go. But to warn him, he imagines he is knocking at the wrong door. "God, I thank Thee that I am not like other people,"[5]—is his heart's language before God. "Do not come near me, for I am holier than you!"[g]—is his proud comparison with his fellow-sinners. Offer him light—He walks "in the light" of his own fire.[h] Offer him life—He "is living" in his own eyes.[i] Offer him food—His full soul "loathes honey"![j]

[y] Comp. Prov 22:29
[z] 1 Cor 8:2; Gal 6:3
[a] 1 Tim 6:20
[b] AV—1 Cor 8:1
[c] 1 Cor 3:18. Comp. Prov 3:7; Rom 12:3–16
[d] Matt 21:31
[e] Rev 3:17. Comp. Prov 30:12
[f] Luke 15:11–18, with John 9:40, 41
[g] Isa 65:5
[h] Isa 50:11
[i] Rom 7
[j] Prov 27:7

[5] *Luke 18:11. See Bunyan's Picture of Ignorance.*

Professing Christian! Dread an ill-founded opinion of yourself. The more firmly grounded a man is in error, the more dangerous is his state. Oh! Beware of holding tight to a delusion, which the Word of God, closely studied, would quickly dispel. Suspect your spiritual state, at least till you have given it a most probing search. Is it not possible that you may be deceived; that there may be a lie in your right hand; that you may have been building upon the sand; and mistaken the shadow for the substance? Consider—it is a matter of infinite and everlasting importance—in which multitudes have been mistaken—in which it is easy to be mistaken—in which our hearts are very deceitful—in which a mistake, not corrected in time, will bring ruin for eternity.

Lord! preserve me from this hopeless delusion. Pull down all my pride and fancied wisdom. Take the blindness from my eyes, that I may know what I am in your sight. Clothe me with humility from the sole of my foot to my head.

13 *The sluggard says, "There is a lion in the road!*
A lion is in the open square!"[k]
14 As *the door turns on its hinges,*
So does *the sluggard on his bed.*
15 *The sluggard buries his hand in the dish;*
He is weary of bringing it to his mouth again.[l]
16 *The sluggard is wiser in his own eyes*
Than seven men who can give a discreet answer.[6]

[k]Prov 22:13

[l]Prov 19:24

LION IN THE WAY

The counterpart to these illustrations may be seen in the man dozing away his life in guilty idleness; without an object and therefore without motivation for activity. But let's look at the pictures, as they meet our eye in the church. The gradation shows the almost incredible increase of evil—unresisted.

The sluggard is utterly reluctant to work. When therefore his laziness is disturbed, he is ingenious in inventing excuses, and fancying dangers, which have no real existence. For he, who has no desire to labor, never lacks pretenses for staying idle. His insincerity lulls his conscience to sleep in his false excuses. Were it as easy *to be*

[6] *"Than seven men that [sit] and teach"—Bishop COVERDALE.*

a Christian as it is to *wish* to be one, who wouldn't *be* a Christian? If it took only one great effort, taking only a little while, it would be worth the struggle. But to see no end to the toil, and to see duty upon duty, trouble following trouble, no breathing time of rest—is an appalling hindrance. And therefore *a fierce lion in the road—a lion in the square*[m] excuses him from a decided profession. [m]Heb 12:3

We don't wonder that he shrinks from his work. He loves his *bed* of ease. Here *he turns himself, as you would turn the door on its hinges,* moving indeed, but making no progress. He works from one excuse to another but never moves from his place. Difficulties hinder him from going forward. Conscience keeps him from going backward. And therefore, *as the door on its hinges,* where he was one day, one year, there he is found the next. He moves within a scanty round of duties, always beginning, never finishing, his work; determining nothing; not *quite* at ease; yet with no heart for exertion. Stretched upon his bed of sloth, he cries—"O that this were working! O that I could raise my heart to heaven!" But is heaven to be gained by complaining and wishing?

No—*even the most needful exertion is grievous to him.* Even if he does get out of bed, his situation isn't improved one bit. Ease is still his cry. How to preserve it, his only care. *He buries his hand in the dish;* and never makes an effort *to bring it to his mouth* with his necessary food.[n] So . . . for the lack of the most trifling exercise he starves his soul, even though the Bread of Life (Christ) is placed before him. No marvel, if his life, instead of a continual feast, is a constant problem. [n]Eccl 4:5

Yet—such is the strange union of self-complacency with folly—this worthless being—a mere user of resources, just using "up the ground"—pronounces himself a genius, prides himself upon his wisdom, and looks down with contempt upon his more industrious companions—generally superior in attainment.[o] This foolish dream of his own shrewdness fixes his standard. He has found the road to learning without any inconvenient exertion. Not bothering to think, he sees none of the difficulties that are obvious to an active mind, and he speedily arrives at most unreasonable conclusions. He will not be beaten out of his sloth. Any *seven men could render a* [o]Luke 13:7

reason for his conviction, but he *is wiser in his own eyes than them all.*[7]

In how many striking lights is laziness presented in this book? Don't I think too slightly of it. Let me look closely—in what respect am I influenced by it—bodily, mentally, or spiritually? Doesn't laziness ever follow me in my work, to my knees, to my Bible reading? Don't I excuse myself from work requiring painful effort? Or when conscience forces me to it, how is it done? May God enable me to resist this paralysis in every form! If just about to resolve, let me propose my work to myself, as to be done with full purpose of heart; not opposing difficulties to necessity; not allowing heartless despondency. What if, after all, my faith should turn out to be a fancy and my hope a delusion? Self-suspicion is the first awakening of the soul—"Search me, O God."[p]

[p]Ps 139:23

It is well if sleep is only a little disturbed; far better, if the eyes are fully opened. Active, simple faith carries us onward, in the face of *the lions in the road,* who seem to stand with open mouths to devour us. It is a special mercy to realize the holy violence of the battle. Bunyan put his pilgrims under the direction of Great-heart for their encouragement. Heaven never will be won by folded arms. "Violent men take it by force."[q]

[q]Matt 11:12

17 Like *one who takes a dog by the ears*
Is he who passes by and *meddles with strife not belonging to him.*

THE MEDDLER

If we would honor our God in our Christian walk, we must take time at every step, for prayer, and for the exercise of sound judgment. Otherwise, we shall often rush on, apart from His direction, and to our loss. *If we take a dog by the ears,* we will have good reason to regret it. To *meddle in strife that's none of our business* will surely bring us trouble[r]—our own cross, not our Master's. There's a wide difference between suffering as a busybody, and suffering as a Christian. It's alarming to those, who don't regard being a busybody as being a criminal, to find the apostle Paul classifying it with murder, theft,

[r]1 Kings 22:4, 32

[7] Seven men—*the number of perfection. Comp. Amos 1:3, 6, 9, 13; 2:4, 6.*

evil-doing. In striking contrast, he gives the dignified exhortation—"Let him glorify God."[s] If we shouldn't "go out hastily to argue"[t] in our own cause, we have even less reason to do so in our neighbor's cause. This is entering into "strife"—the waywardness of the fool.[u]

[s]1 Peter 4:16
[t]Prov 25:8
[u]Prov 18:6; 20:3

Even with Christian intentions, many of us are too fond of *meddling with strife not belonging to us.* We're too quick to make ourselves judges of our neighbor's conduct. Remaining neutral is often the better part of wisdom. Uncalled-for interference seldom avails with the quarreling parties; while the well-meaning mediator involves himself in the strife to his own hurt. Our blessed Master reads us a lesson of godly wisdom. He healed the contentions in his own family, but when called to meddle with strife that didn't belong to Him, He answered—"Who appointed Me a judge or arbiter over you?"[v]

Must we then condone sin in our brother?[w] Certainly not. But we should ponder carefully the most effectual way of restraining his sin. Think of the special blessing to the "peacemakers."[x] But the true peacemaker, while he deplores *the strife,* knows very well that interference in the moment of irritation will kindle rather than extinguish the fire. Yet his self-control is not indifference. He commits the matter to Him, whose wisdom he so greatly needs. He will seize the first moment for favorable reproof and "a timely word," how good is it![y] Indeed, the common communication greatly requires that wisdom which "dwells with prudence." "Who among you is wise and understanding? Let him show by his good behavior his deeds in the gentleness of wisdom."[z]

[v]Matt 18:1–6; 20:24–28, with Luke 12:13, 14
[w]Lev 19:17
[x]Matt 5:9
[y]Prov 15:23
[z]Prov 8:12; James 3:13

18 *Like a madman who throws*
Firebrands, arrows and death,
19 *So is the man who deceives his neighbor,*
And says, "Was I not joking?"

How little does the thoughtless man consider the misery which his wantonness causes others! He bears no malice. He just loves a lot of fun. His companions compliment him as clever, and join in laughing at the victim of his cruel jokes. But *"reveling in their deceptions"*[a] is a black mark of ungodliness. What the man calls sport,[b] is the *madman,* scattering murderous—*"firebrands, ar-*

[a]2 Peter 2:13
[b]Prov 10:23

rows and death." What are so slickly called practical jokes—such as are practiced at school, or even at college—come under this awful charge. In this case, there's little difference betwixt fraud and fury. He that purposely deceives his neighbor, "all in fun," harms him just as much as a lunatic, who does wrong out of frenzy and distemper. Yet this solemn line of distinction is drawn. The *madman* is irresponsible for his actions; *the deceiver* is accountable to God and his fellow-man. "He that sins in jest, must repent in earnest; or his sin will be his ruin," warned Henry.

"What hath a Christian," saith Bernard, "to do with jesting?" Let him practically observe the wholesome caution against it, as "not fitting."[c] Let him cultivate the valuable graces of seriousness, consideration, and self-discipline. Let him study his Master's image, embodying both the spirit and the rules of his gospel.

[c] Eph 5:4

20 *For lack of wood the fire goes out,*
And where there is no whisperer, contention quiets down.
21 Like *charcoal to hot embers and wood to fire,*
So is a contentious man to kindle strife.
22 *The words of a whisperer are like dainty morsels,*
And they go down into the innermost parts of the body.[d]

[d] Prov 18:8

The busy tongue makes work, where it does not find it. Such is the despicable trade of *the whisperer* (AV—talebearer)—employing his time in prying into other people's business, ferreting out secrets, diving into family histories, intermeddling with their concerns: all this with the view of putting himself forward, as a keen, intelligent, and active man. In every way where he can please himself "man is naturally his own grand idol. He would be esteemed and honoured by any means; and to magnify that idol self, he kills the name and esteem of others in sacrifice to it," stated Leighton.[e] Real virtue results from this base selfishness.

[e] 1 Peter 2:17. Comp. Jer 9:4

The fire of holy zeal seizes on things nearest home. This is a wildfire scattering its destruction abroad. The *whisperer* (talebearer) should be looked on as an incendiary. For his "tongue is a fire . . . set on fire by hell."[f] His

[f] James 3:6. Comp. Prov 16:27

raking up old and forgotten tales supplies the fuel, without which *the fire of strife, lacking wood, goes out.* To quench the flame, we must take away the fuel. We must remove *the whisperer*; stop him in his words; compel him to produce his authority; face him, if possible, with the subject of his tales. This decisive course will prevent a mass of slander and put him to shame.[g]

[g]Prov 25:23. Comp. 22:10

Closely related is *the contentious man.* The trouble he causes is more out in the open. His determination to have the last word is as coals to burning coals and wood to the fire.[h] It keeps up to the flame, kindled perhaps by a mere angry word or a contemptuous look; and which, for the constant adding of fuel, might quickly have been extinguished. Do we never aim at the wit of a sharp answer, that "stirs up anger," rather than at the wisdom and grace of "a gentle answer" that "turns away wrath?"[i]

[h]Prov 15:18; 16:28; 29:22; 2 Cor 12:20

[i]Prov 15:1

THE STAB OF DEATH

The whisperer's wounds are however the most dangerous. They *go down into the innermost part of the body*—the vitals of the heart. One noiseless word may be the stab of death. But, if he escapes for a while, his secret sins shall be set before God's eyes, and his evil trifling with his brother's character will be justly recompensed.[j]

[j]Ps 50:20; 52:1–5

Are we closely watching against these sins? Do we carefully damp the rising flame of contention?[k] Do we resist the temptation to speak needlessly of the faults of others? Do we dread the character of a polished, well-educated, amusing slanderer? Are we ready to give up the notoriety that comes from telling a good story, for fear of wounding a good name? We may feel indignant at the charge of *whisperer.* Yet it requires no ordinary exercise of Christian discipline to maintain the silence of charity and to regulate both the tongue and the ear within its well-advised limits.

[k]Prov 17:14; Gen 13:8, 9

23 Like *an earthen vessel overlaid with silver dross*
Are burning lips and a wicked heart.
24 *He who hates disguises* it *with his lips,*
But he lays up deceit in his heart.
25 *When he speaks graciously, do not believe him,*
For there are seven abominations in his heart.

26 Though his *hatred covers itself with guile,*
His wickedness will be revealed before the assembly.
27 *He who digs a pit will fall into it,*
And he who rolls a stone, it will come back on him.

BROKEN POTTERY

The sin here described is a disgrace to society! Yet is it often *covered* with flattering dress, as a worthless piece of broken pottery with a thin coat of *silver.* "The tongue of the righteous is as choice silver." Here is only *silver dross*—"the heart of the wicked is worth little";[l] *lips* burning with warm affection, yet covering a *heart* filled with malice and wickedness.[8] Such were *the lips* of Joseph's brethren to their father when they "arose to comfort him" under the bereavement which they had brought upon him.[m] Such was Absalom's smooth hypocrisy.[n] Such were the traitor's *lips* and *heart,* uniting with the rest in protestations of faithfulness; yet betraying the Son of man with a "kiss."[o] An open enemy could be endured much easier.[p] The pious talk of hypocrites, the charitable activities of infidels, the smooth enticement of the false angel of light—all answer to this wrong figure. Hypocrisy is often spun of a very fine thread; and the heart of man, abounding with as much hypocrisy as it does, is the most deceitful thing, yes, and the most *deceivable* too, actively and passively both, of anything in the world.

Often, too, when *the lips* do not *burn,* there is *concealed* hatred. Cain talked with his brother "in the field," while murder was in his heart.[q] Saul pretended to honor David, while he was plotting his ruin.[r] Absalom *deceived* his brother, by seeming to let him alone, for two years *building up deceit within him.*[s] Joab covered his murderous intentions with peaceable pretenses.[t]

Christian wisdom will guard against accepting too readily things *as they seem.*[u] That is in fact the harmlessness of "doves," without the wisdom of "serpents."[v] This weakness cost Gedaliah his life.[w] A sounder spirit saved Nehemiah from the snare of his hateful enemies.[x] The source of this wickedness gives good reason for distrust. *There are seven abominations*—a great variety[y] *of*

[l]Prov 10:20
[m]Gen 37:35
[n]2 Sam 15:1–9
[o]Matt 26:35; Luke 22:47, 48
[p]Ps 55:12
[q]Gen 4:8
[r]1 Sam 18:17, 21
[s]2 Sam 13:22–28
[t]Luke 3:27; 20:9, 10. Comp. Gen 34:15–25; Ps 28:3; 55:20
[u]Jer 9:8; 12:6; Mic 7:5
[v]Matt 10:16
[w]Jer 40:14; 41:6, 7
[x]Neh 6:1–4
[y]Verses 16; 24:16

[8] *Prov 10:17; Ps 55:21. See Bunyan's description of the town of "Fair-Speech."*

abominations—closely folded up *in his heart,* only within discovery by that heart-searching eye, "all things are open and laid bare."[z] And here lies the root of the disease. A deceitful heart makes a deceitful tongue and lips. The heart is the workhouse, where the forge of deceit and slander is found; and the tongue is only the outer shop, where they are mended; and the lips the door of the shop; so then, only the goods made in the workshop (the heart) can be sent out of the outer shop (the tongue) through the door (the lips). From evil thoughts comes evil speech; from a deceitful heart, deceitful words, well-varnished, but lined with rottenness.[a] Oh! Let this contemptible character be a beacon to us to steer clear of all approaches to false dealings. Better to risk giving offense by being truthful (though let this, so far as conscience allows, be avoided) rather than *cover our hatred* by flattering words.

[z]Jer 17:10; Heb 4:13

[a]1 Peter 3:16

Pretense is never the answer. The providence of God brings dark deeds to light. "The voice" of Abel's blood cried "from the ground."[b] "The sins of some men are quite evident, going before them to judgment; for others, their sins follow after."[c] The hand strips off the mask and exposes the flatterer to shame. *His seven abominations* shall be proclaimed, if not more privately, at last before the whole congregation, when all shall appear before men and angels as they really are, and when the hypocrite shall receive his just recompense of everlasting contempt.[d]

[b]Gen 4:10

[c]1 Tim 5:24

[d]Luke 12:2

However, retribution often reaches the offender in this world. "He will fall into the pits, which he has bestowed pains to dig for his neighbour, and be crushed by the stone, which he meant to roll upon him," said Scott. Even the last place of sinning is sometimes made the place of punishment.[e] Those who plot evil against others, will be overwhelmed by it themselves.[f] Moab, in attempting to curse Israel, himself fell under the curse of God.[g] Haman's gallows for Mordecai was his own promotion of shame.[h] The enemies of Daniel were devoured in the ruin, which they plotted against him.[i] So does God "take the wise by their own shrewdness,"[j] the wicked in his "greed."[k] The death of Christ, which was to be the means of warding off national judgment, was the just cause of the dreaded punishment for all nations.[l] The

[e]1 Kings 21:19, with 2 Kings 9:26; Jer 7:31, 32

[f]Ps 7:15

[g]Num 22:6; 24:17

[h]Prov 3:35; Esther 7:10

[i]Dan 6:24

[j]Job 5:13

[k]Prov 11:6

[l]John 11:50; Matt 23:32, 38

hatred that plans the evil, often brings about its own overthrow. What a place of bloodshed this world would be, apart from the restraining grace of God! Oh! May my heart, my soul, every member, every principle, not only be restrained from hateful passions; but be filled with the spirit of the gospel and consecrated to the service of God!

28 *A lying tongue hates those it crushes,*
And a flattering mouth works ruin.

Rarely do we see a solitary sin. One sin begets another. *Lying* and malice are here linked together. The *lying tongue* against our Lord was the fruit of hateful malice.[m] The slander against Stephen came from the same source. The silent reproach of his holy life was intolerable.[n] If men *crush* because they hate; much more do they hate them whom they have crushed, and thus made their enemies. Ammon, having *crushed* his sister Tamar, hated her with greater hatred than his former love, because she was a witness against his own shame.[o]

[m] John 8:44, with 40
[n] Acts 6:9, 14
[o] 2 Sam 13:5–15

But again and again—beware of the flatterer. It's sad but where *isn't* he welcomed as a friend? From some angles he presents an attractive face. But a nearer view shows him as a subtle, murderous enemy, *working ruin.*[p] But he has a great advantage—a bosom friend: the sweet song of our own praises that lulls us to sleep, and the moment we feel secure and comfortable, the net is thrown over us.[q] *The flattering tongue works the ruin* of the world. The temptation—"You will be like God"—proved irresistible.[r] And still in the path of sin,[s] in the determined satisfying of the wayward will,[t] flattery is the snare; *ruin* is the end.

[p] Ps 5:9; 10:7–10
[q] Prov 29:5
[r] Gen 3:5
[s] Prov 2:16; 5:3; 7:5, 21–23
[t] 1 Kings 22:6, 11, 12; Jer 5:31; 14:14–16

How then should we treat the *flatterer*? Homer puts it into his hero's heart to regard him as a friend of hell.[9] Our safety then is in flight,[u] or at least in frowning resistance.[v] "Be as much troubled," said godly Philip Henry (*Life*, chap. 10), "by unjust praises, as by unjust slander." Show plainly that they please us least, who praise us most. Give timely warning, that the repetition of the offense threatens to disrupt your friendship. Hold tightly to the deepest views of inborn corruption. They will quickly prove false any flattering comments made to us or about

[u] Prov 20:19
[v] Prov 25:23

[9] Iliad *1:312, 313.*

us. Pray for wisdom to see the snare; for gracious principles to raise us above vain praises; for self-denial to be content, and even thankful without them. This will be our security.

All these Scriptures strongly teach, how hateful our attempts to deceive are to a God of truth. All warn us against the common habit of slight departures from the truth, and of any lack of sincerity of expression, as totally inconsistent with a Christian profession, a breach of the law of love, and often leading to habitual deceit.

CHAPTER TWENTY-SEVEN

1 *Do not boast about tomorrow,*
For you do not know what a day may bring forth.

BOAST NOT OF TOMORROW

Let the apostle James expound the wise man—"Come now, you who say, 'Today or tomorrow, we shall go to such and such a city, and spend a year there and engage in business and make a profit.' " Both apply the same rebuke to the boast;—*you do not know what a day may bring forth*—whereas "you do not know what your life will be like tomorrow."[a] To provide for the morrow is a scriptural duty.[b] The farmer, when he has reaped his harvest, sows his seed for the next harvest. The Christian in his calling, depending on God's providence, walks with God. But to *boast about tomorrow*—"All such boasting is evil."[c] Actually, it is absurd to boast of what is not our own. *Tomorrow* is finely described as an unknown birth. It may be in eternity. And yet the person who lives after the flesh, and the worlding [d] *boast*, as if it were their own; and thereby virtually put God out of His own world. The ungodly count on being saved *tomorrow*, and therefore put off coming to Christ, forsaking the world, and living for eternity, to some infinitely future day.[e] Would they do this if they did not count on *tomorrow* being given to them? No. And we're all alike in that respect. We all naturally cherish looking forward. But we need to be careful. The great enemy uses it to bring about practical forgetfulness of God. Yet we must not live, as if tomorrow would not come. If we did, the world would stagnate. The present duties of the day would be put aside so we could make immediate preparation for the coming eternity. But we flee from death, when he enters our houses,

[a] James 4:13, 14

[b] Prov 6:6–8; 10:5; 24:27. Comp. Gen 41:35; Acts 11:28, 29

[c] James 4:16

[d] Isa 56:12; Luke 12:16–19

[e] Acts 24:25

as if we did not expect him. How little do we die daily![f] We can even coolly calculate upon the death of others for our own benefit. Our intense anxiety about earthly, and indifference to heavenly things speak all too plainly. The very young look forward to being a teen-ager; the more advanced teen-ager to becoming twenty-one; the worker to retirement. All, contrary to their Christian profession, do what God's Word warns us against: *boast ourselves of tomorrow.*

[f]1 Cor 15:31

How awfully has this *boasting* been put to shame! In the days of Noah, "they married wives, they were being given in marriage, until the day that Noah entered the ark, and the flood came and destroyed all."[g] Abner promised a kingdom but could not be certain of life for an hour.[h] Haman dressed his best in anticipation of the queen's banquet but was hanged like a dog before night.[i] The fool's soul was required of him on the "very night" of his worldly projects for many years to come.[j] "Serious affairs to-morrow"—was the laughing reply of Archias, warned of a conspiracy, which hurried him into eternity the next hours. The infidel Gibbon planned on fifteen years of life and died within a few months at a day's warning. *We do not know what a day may bring forth.*

[g]Luke 17:26–29

[h]2 Sam 3:9, 10, 27

[i]Esther 5:12; 7:1–10

[j]Luke 12:19, 20

How natural is it for the young to be looking for *tomorrow's* prospect! But haven't you ever seen a lovely flower cropped or faded in the blossom? Aren't the robust, as well as the feeble, cut down in their prime?[k] Who is there with a lease on life? It's time that there is a promise of forgiveness to the repenting, but where is the promise of *tomorrow* for repentance? Will concern naturally come with years? Or will rather long-protracted habits of ungodliness harden into a second nature? What if, in the midst of your boasting, flattering yourself that you will see another and another day—you should be taken by surprise, totally unprepared, and be left to lament your presumption in the lake of everlasting fire[l] forever? Stop and consider; weep and pray—believe—now—while conscience speaks; while you are halting between God and the world. Now in this "acceptable time" devote yourself to God. Enthrone the Savior in your heart.

[k]Job 21:33

[l]Matt 24:48–51; 25:10–12; Luke 13:25; 2 Cor 6:2

The universe doesn't present a more moving sight than an aged sinner, with one foot in the grave, losing all in the world, and infinitely more in eternity. A moment, and he is gone. Heaven and hell are no trifles. *Tomorrow* counted upon, today neglected, ruins all. Standing on the brink of the precipice—how precious the moment for prayer—ere the door of mercy is closed forever!

Has the child of God reason to *boast about tomorrow?* What a change tomorrow can make in your worldly circumstances,[m] or Christian experience?[n] You can never be more sure of anything than that you can never be sure of anything. We have no security for a single hour. Share your cares with God. Place them all in His hands.[o] Let disappointment prepare you for your heavenly rest and bind all your wishes and pleasures by His gracious will.[p] If you actually believed that "the time has been shortened" and "the form of this world is passing away," wouldn't you "rejoice, as though they did not rejoice"?[q] Would pleasures of earth be so highly prized, if we didn't secretly depend on *tomorrow?* Surely this thought would more than sustain one in the loss of those pleasures: The shadow only is gone—the body of my happiness remains immovable. To see temporal things without really seeing them is the life of Christianity.[r] To remember "this world as the grand laboratory for the perfecting of souls for the next" is Sir M. Hale's caution and to have our "loins" girded about for our Lord's coming; to live, as not to be surprised by the call, and in readiness to open to Him "*immediately*"—this is our secret and our happiness. "Blessed are those slaves whom the master shall find on the alert when he comes."[s]

[m]Job 1:21
[n]Ps 30:7
[o]Ps 37:4
[p]James 4:15
[q]1 Cor 7:29–32
[r]2 Cor 4:18
[s]Eph 6:14; Acts 16:26; Luke 12:37

2 *Let another praise you, and not your own mouth;*
A stranger, and not your own lips.

"Praise," says Jermin, "is a comely garment." But though you, yourself, wear it, *another* must put it on, or else it will never fit well. Praise is sweet music, but it is never tuneable in *your own mouth.* If it comes from the mouth of *another,* it sounds in tune to all ears that hear it. Praise is a rich treasure, but it will never make you rich, unless another tell the same. Indeed—except as the vindication of our character,[t] or our Master's honor[1] may

[t]1 Sam 12:3; Ps 7:3–5; 2 Cor 1:17–19

[1] *2 Cor 11:5–12; 12:11. To paraphrase Whichcote—St. Paul was pressed into speaking of himself more than he chose to do; and when he speaks of things concerning himself, he always puts in, "I speak as a fool"—intimating, that unless there be very great cause, whoever talks much of himself, talks like a fool—WHICHCOTE'S* Sermons.

require—nothing lowers a man so much in the eyes of his fellowmen as singing his own praises. For though every man is his own flatterer,[u] yet men usually despise pride in others, while they cherish it in themselves. "Whatever is of good repute ... let your mind dwell on these things."[v] But "let [our] works," not our tongues "praise [us] in the gates."[w] And while our works shine, see to it, that we ourselves are hid. "Confess your sins to one another."[x] But let someone else speak our *praise.* "Scarce any shew themselves to advantage, who are overly-solicitous to do so," said Bishop Butler.

[u]Prov 20:6
[v]Phil 4:8
[w]Prov 31:31; Ruth 3:11
[x]Prov 25:27; Matt 5:16; James 5:16

Our name will lose nothing by this self-renouncing spirit. If *our own mouth* is silent, *another's* will be opened on our behalf. John was "not even fit" in his own eyes to "remove His sandals." Yet his Lord's mouth proclaimed him as the greatest of all that had been "born of women."[y] The centurion spoke of himself, as "not qualified that [Christ] come under [his] roof." Yet did the elders testify, that "he is worthy for You to grant this to him." Yea—the Savior's own mouth confirmed the testimony—"I say to you, not even in Israel have I found such great faith."[z] Luke mentions nothing in his records to his own credit. Yet *another praises him* warmly as "the beloved physician" and his sole faithful companion in his trials.[2]

[y]Matt 3:11; John 3:30, with Matt 11:11; John 5:35
[z]Matt 8:8, with Luke 7:3, 4, 9

Self-seeking is a shameful blot upon a Christian testimony. What! Shall one that has said before God—"Behold, I am insignificant"—be ready to say before his fellowmen—"Come with me and see my zeal for the Lord."[a] Come, see how humble I am! Oh! for the self-abased spirit of our glorious Master—ever ready to endure reproach; but never receiving "glory from men"; never seeking His own "glory."[b] Contrast what God shows us of ourselves in the closet with our "good showing in the flesh." And doesn't this put self-complacency to shame? Surely that we are so little *really* humble is reason enough for the deepest humiliation.

[a]Job 40:4; 2 Kings 10:16
[b]John 5:41; 8:50; Gal 6:12

3 *A stone is heavy and the sand weighty,*
But the provocation of a fool is heavier than both of them.

[2] *Col 4:14; 2 Tim 4:11. It was a fine touch in Sallust's portrait of Cato—"He would rather* be, *than* seem *to be, a good man; so that the less he sought glory, the more he obtained it."*

4 *Wrath is fierce and anger is a flood,*
But who can stand before jealousy?

THE DEADLY PASSION

The *wrath* even of a wise man in the moment of folly is *fierce.*[c] What then must *a fool's wrath* be, "where there is not a drop of heavenly water to quench the fire?" said Cartwright. It is indeed *the weight of a stone or sand*[d]—intolerable, "being without cause, measure, or end," said Poole.[e] An angry fool stays sullen for a long time. That's what distinguishes his anger from the temporary impulse that the child of God may too hastily yield to. Absalom kept his anger for two years.[f] David's anger melted away under the first conviction of reproof, and "the sun" went not down upon his "anger."[g]

And yet *fierce* as wrath may be,[h] overflowing as the springtide, it can be appeased. Esau's wrath was soothed into brotherly love.[i] The outrageous despot was subdued in witnessing the pretense and power of God.[j] But *jealousy* is a passion that can't be appeased, the native principle[k] with a fearful train of evils.[l] *Anger* is stirred up by offense; envy by godliness,[m] prosperity,[n] or favor.[o] Reason operates rather as the oil to fan the flame, than the water to quench it. Proud men want to be admired by all, and preferred above all; and if they aren't, a secret hostility takes over their lives. Men cannot endure the real or reputed excellency of others. The proud creature would shine alone.[p]

Solomon has before described the curse of this deadly passion to the man who indulges it.[q] Here he shows its subtle, and almost irresistible power, upon its victims. For indeed, in contrast to the excellent description of mercy, it is twice cursed. It curses both its subjects and its object. Like the star called "Wormwood," that embittered all the rivers and fountains of waters on which it fell,[r] it poisons and robs of their sweetness all the sources and streams of human enjoyment.[s]

So it might well be asked: "Who is able to stand before envy?" Even the perfect innocence of Paradise fell before it. Satan lost his own happiness. Then he envied man and ceased not to work his destruction. It shed the first human blood that ever stained the ground.[t] It quenched the yearnings of natural affection and brought

[c] 1 Sam 25:13, 21
[d] Exod 15:5
[e] Comp. Prov 17:12
[f] 2 Sam 13:22, 23
[g] 1 Sam 25:32, 33; Eph 4:26
[h] Gen 49:7; Matt 2:16
[i] Gen 27:41; 33:4
[j] Dan 3:13–30
[k] Mark 7:22; Gal 5:20, 21; Titus 3:3; James 4:5
[l] Rom 1:29, 30; 2 Cor 12:20; James 3:14, 16
[m] Eccl 4:4; Dan 6:3–5
[n] Gen 26:14; Ps 73:3
[o] Gen 4:5–8; 1 Sam 18:6–9, 16, 17
[p] Ps 119:77
[q] Prov 14:30
[r] Rev 8:11
[s] Eccl 4:4
[t] 1 John 3:12

bitter sorrow to the patriarch's heart.[u] Even the premier of the greatest empire in the world was its temporary victim.[v] More than that—the Savior in His most benevolent acts was sorely harassed[w] and ultimately sank under its power.[x] His servants therefore must not expect to be "above [their] master."[y]

[u]Gen 37:3, 4, 23–35; Acts 7:9
[v]Dan 6:6–17
[w]John 12:10, 11
[x]Matt 27:18–20
[y]Acts 5:17; 13:44, 45; 17:4, 5, with Matt 10:24

But Christian, remember—though the promise is sure, that "sin shall not be master";[z] yet the struggle is sharp to the end. Let us probe deeply into this corruption. Men will look at grace, as we have seen, with an envious eye. They will darken the lives, that outshine their own, and defame the holiness, which they have no desire to follow. But "those who have true worth in themselves, can never envy it in others," said Sir Philip Sidney *(Aphorisms).* Do we then love to see a brother's superior position and his larger gifts or graces?[a] Do we take pleasure in his prosperity, in honor paid to him, though to our own slight?[b] Is our tone of praise as definite toward him as we wish that of others to be toward us? Can we bear to be passed by in favor of those who may seem to be doing our work in opposition to us?[c] Oh! How hateful the hidden depths of our deceitful hearts would appear if they were exposed! "Who can discern his errors? Acquit me of hidden faults."[d]

[z]Rom 6:14
[a]Num 11:28, 29
[b]John 3:30
[c]Phil 1:15–18
[d]Ps 19:12

5 *Better is open rebuke*
Than love that is concealed.
6 *Faithful are the wounds of a friend,*
But deceitful are the kisses of an enemy.

FRIENDSHIP'S SUPREME OBLIGATION

Which is the friend who will be a real blessing to my soul? Is it one that will humor my fancies and flatter my pride? Is it enough that he loves my person and would spend his time and energies in my service? This comes far short of my requirement. I am a poor, straying sinner with a wayward will and a blinded heart; going wrong at every step. The friend for my case is one who will watch over me with *open rebuke;* a reprover, when needful; not a flatterer. The genuineness of friendship without this mark is more than doubtful; its usefulness utterly paralyzed. That *concealed love,* that dares not risk a *faithful wound* and spares *rebuke* rather than inflict pain,

[e]Lev 19:17

[f]Prov 9:8; 28:23; Matt 18:15

[g]Gal 4:12–16

[h]Rom 15:2

[i]Matt 18:15; 1 Tim 5:20

[j]Gal 2:11–14

judged by God's standard is hatred.[e] Far better the wound should be probed than convered. *Rebuke*, kindly, considerately, and prayerfully administered, cements friendship, rather than loosens it.[f] The contrary instances only prove that the union had never been based upon substantial principle.

Many indeed profess their value for a true friend; and yet in the most valuable discharge of friendship, they count him their "enemy." The apostle had some well-founded apprehension because of this, though so wise and affectionate, and speaking from the mouth of God.[g] As if the rule of friendship was that we should absolutely "please," without reference to the divine restriction—"for his good, to edification."[h] Christian faithfulness is the only way of measuring up to our profession. And much guilt lies upon the conscience in the neglect.

But this *open rebuke* must not contravene the express rule of love—telling the fault between you and "him in private." Too often, instead of pouring it secretly into our brother's ear, it is proclaimed through the wide medium of the world's ear; and thus it passes through a multitude of channels, before it reaches its one proper destination. The *openness of the rebuke* describes the free and unreserved sincerity of the heart, not necessarily the public exposure of the offender; save when the character of the offense; or the interests of others, may appear to demand it.[i]

But don't ever allow a false tenderness to weaken a supreme obligation. Could Paul have answered to God for his *concealed love* to a brother apostle, when the compromise of a fundamental principle called for open rebuke?[j] Obviously, the sin should be brought to view, ere we *rebuke*. Nor should we vehemently reprove involuntary slips; much less forget the exercise of a loving spirit. Leighton's gentleness gave such a power to his reproof, that the offense was rarely repeated; but from shame, not from a new principle. The mark of true godliness is readiness to have our faults pointed out; and a thankfulness to those who undertake the self-denying office.[3] "A faithful reprover is a very great help in our Christian course. He is to be valued above the greatest

[3] *Neh 5:7–13. Even when given most rashly and unkindly, one of the meekest of men could say, "I was thankful to God for admonishing me, and my gratitude to the man, was I think, unfeigned." In his journal, the reprover's name was found specially remembered in prayer—MARTYN'S life, chap. 3.*

treasure . . . He that would be safe," says Bishop Kidder, "must have a faithful friend, or a bitter enemy, that he may fly from vice by the warnings of the one, or the strong denunciations of the other." Much more valuable is this *faithfulness*, than the smooth politeness of people of the world in their dealings with one another.

The truest friend of man—*His wounds are faithful*. He will not pass by a single fault in His people. He acts upon His own rule from the most considerate regard to their best welfare. And who would not choose this *faithful wound*, however painful at the moment of infliction, rather than the *deceitful kisses of the enemy*?[k] *The kiss* of the apostate was a bitter ingredient in the Savior's cup of suffering.[l] His foreknowledge of the treachery,[m] in no degree weakened His intense feelings, which, from their close union with the Godhead, made Him capable of suffering beyond all comprehension.[4]

[k] Prov 26:23–26; Neh 6:2
[l] Matt 26:48, 49, with Ps 41:9; 55:12, 13
[m] John 6:70; 13:18–26

7 *A sated man loathes honey,*
But to a famished man any bitter thing is sweet.

HOW'S YOUR APPETITE?

This is true of the enjoyments of this life. The more we have, instead of increasing our happiness, deprives us of the peace and joy that come with smaller portions.[n] The man, whose appetite is turned off by overeating, can't stand to look at even the most appealing food, but even *bitter* and distasteful things are greatly enjoyed by a starving soul.[o] Such a healthful appetite is one of the many counterbalancing advantages of poverty. The epicure, with his highly-developed taste for fine foods, might well envy the luxury of a plain home-cooked meal. Israel, after eating "the bread of angels" *loathed* and trod it under foot "as miserable food."[p]

[n] Eccl 5:11
[o] Job 6:7; Luke 15:16, 17
[p] Ps 78:25; Num 11:4–20; 21:5

And isn't this just as true in spiritual things? The Laodicean professor—"I am rich, and have become wealthy, and have need of nothing"—*loathes the honey* of the gospel.[q] Christ in His bitter sorrow is "nothing" to him, while he passes by.[r] His love excites no tenderness; the hope He offers arouses no interest. "The consolations

[q] Rev 3:17, 18; Matt 9:12; Rom 9:30, 31
[r] Lam 1:12

[4] *Philip Henry beautifully describes the proper offices and uses of Christian reproof. "To reprove a brother is like, when he is fallen, to help him up again; when he is wounded, to help to cure him; when he hath broken a bone, to help to set it; when he is out of the way, to put him in it; when he is fallen into the fire, to pluck him out; when he hath contracted defilement, to help to cleanse"*—Life, *chap. 10.*

[s]Job 15:11

of God" are "small," of little account with him.[s] He can spare them without feeling any loss. He reads the Bible only to quarrel with it and find fault with its most precious truths. He finds it offensive, because to him, it speaks of a ruin, of which he has no apprehension, and which he has no desire to look into. And so, he is nauseated by the most nourishing of all food—God's Word—having no relish for it, because he feels no need. And there is another case to be considered. Fullness of bread—richness of spiritual customs—doesn't always bring a corresponding appetite. Can't overfilling be as great a curse as famine? Is it not fearfully written upon many a professing Christian—"A sated [full] man *loathes honey*"?

Actually, *the famished soul* is far more to be envied, feeding upon unpleasant truths, yes—and welcoming even *bitter* experiences, as medicine for the soul's health.[t] Don't we learn *the sweet* of the gospel by this *bitterness*? Doesn't this *bitterness* make Christ *sweet* to the soul? A sinner in all his guilt; and a Savior, who, in His perfect merit and love, answers fully to the sinner's needs. Every view of Christ makes sin more *bitter*. Every view of sin makes Christ more dear. And there is no terror in the conviction that makes the Savior more dear. Instead, it prepares the way for a solid confidence in the glad tidings of the gospel.

[t]Ps 119:67, 71

What then is the true pulse of my Christian experience? Am I willing to receive the Word in its completeness—the *bitter* as well as the *sweet*? Do I love its humbling spirituality, its self-denying requirements? Do I subordinate every desire to an unreserved obedience to my God? Am I ready to walk in His narrowest path, to have my most secret corruption exposed; to have my conscience laid open to the sharp piercing of the "two-edged sword"?[u] Oh! May my soul be preserved in this all-out devotedness to my blessed Lord!

[u]Heb 4:12

8 *Like a bird that wanders from her nest,*
So is a man who wanders from his home [AV—*place*].

ROLLING STONES

Instinct teaches *the bird,* that *the nest* is the only place of safety or repose. Here God has provided her special cover.[v] Nothing therefore but danger awaits her in her *wanderings*. And seldom does she return without some injury to herself or her nestlings. Perhaps *her nest* is cold and inconvenient. But her *wanderings* make her more restless and dissatisfied. She is safe and happy only while she stays in and near her nest. [v]Deut 22:6, 7

No less senseless and dangerous is it for a man to leave the place, society, or calling, which God has marked out. Here, he is in God's neighborhood, and so under God's protection; and if he will be content to remain in *his home,* God will bless him with the rich gain of godly "contentment."[w] But *the man wandering from his place* is the rolling stone that gathers no moss. He is always restless, as if he had a windmill in his head. Every new idea sends him off in a new direction. His want of fixed principles and employment exposes him to never-ending temptation.[x] Always wanting to be something or somewhere different from what and where he is, he only changes imaginary for real troubles. The better part of wisdom is to know and keep our place. The soul, the body, the family, society—all have a claim upon us. This feverish excitement of idleness is the symptom of disease, wholly exposed to Christianity, the ruin of both our comfort and our usefulness. [w]1 Tim 6:6 [x]Prov 21:16

The basic rule cannot ordinarily be broken without sin—"Let each man remain with God in the condition in which he was called."[y] Do we really want to abide in fellowship with God? Then, we must "remain" in our calling. Every step out of the path He has chosen for us, without a clear scriptural warrant, is departure from God. We are only safe in following His leading. But by going ahead of His leading, and much more, by breaking away from His guidance[z]—*a man wanders from his place* and must pay a price for his disobedience. Never can we step out of God's ways, but we shall take the path back with a cross. [y]1 Cor 7:24 [z]Jon 1:1–4

It is often the wayward impulse of idle pleasure; but it always yields the same fruit. Dinah was safe in the circle of her family, *as the bird in her nest.* But when the unsuspecting wanderer "went out to visit the daughters of the land,"[a] the fowler's snare soon entangled her. [a]Gen 34:1, 2

Let's take a look at this spirit in the church. *The idler*

[b] 1 Tim 5:13

[c] Prov 26:17

[d] Matt 12:43; Luke 16:2

[e] Prov 14:8

[f] 1 Thess 4:11

[g] Prov 22:28; Num 21:5

[h] 2 Tim 3:7

wanders "around from house to house,"[b] neglecting his own duties, and therefore he has plenty of time on his hands to meddle with what does "not [belong] to him."[c] (So busy is the enemy in finding his own work for those who have no heart to work for God!) The discontented professing Christian is unhappily so shut up in so obscure a corner, that he will die, before the world knows his worth. He wants a larger sphere. The world is scarcely wide enough for him. Thus he *wanders from his place,* "seeking rest, and does not find it." The gifted pretender is full of zeal for God and His church. His talents were not intended to go to waste. What he can do, he thinks he should do. He sees the minister of God neglecting his flock. Why shouldn't he, since, in his own opinion, he is well able to take over? But wouldn't he then be *wandering from his place*? Our Master's charge is—"Give an account of your," not of your *neighbor's,* "stewardship."[d]

If grace gives the desire for usefulness, God must open the path. We need the "wisdom ... to understand *his way,*"[e] our duty, is to "attend to *your own business.*"[f] Not a single talent need be wasted. Every Christian has his own field, large enough for the exercise of his measure of gifts, without moving "the ancient boundary," that separates the sacred office, as the Lord's consecrated service. Many might be found to manage the ambassador's office competently. But who would venture into it without God's call and leading? The unsteady professing Christian has no spiritual home. No church is sound enough for him; none will even fully satisfy his taste. Like the *wandering bird,* he is always on the wing. Any one place is too limiting for him. The accustomed food, even though coming down from heaven, is loathed "as miserable food."[g] His spoiled appetite leaves him on a Lord's day morning undecided whom to hear, his own will being his only guide. He is anxious to hear from all; and, as the sure result, he learns from none.[h] In this self-willed delusion the basic concept, the true form and substance of the church is destroyed. God did not intend for it to be made up of a few wandering sheep. He meant it to be a fold with a shepherd; not a heap of loose, scattered stones, but stones cemented, fitted into their several places; and "the whole building being fitted together growing into a holy temple in the Lord."[i] The church is terrifying to the enemy, not in her single members, but "as an army with banners";[j] close in rank, where each soldier keeps his own place. The individual profession, in the stead of collective unity, is a purely divisive spirit, the essence of pride and selfishness.

[i]Eph 2:21, 22

[j]Song of Sol 6:10

And is not this spiritual wandering the history of many, who under the pretense of conscience have separated from the church, which had "reared and brought" them up as children? *After their own lusts* they "accumulate" to themselves teachers, "wanting to have their ears tickled." The end of this *wandering from their place,* like that of the bird from her nest, is the loss of everything valuable—*They "will turn away their ears from the truth, and will turn aside to myths."*[k]

[k]Isa 1:2; 2 Tim 4:3, 4

Professing Christian! Beware of this tampering with simplicity and godly steadfastness. This *wandering* spirit proves, not expanding love, but ever-broadening indifference; freedom, not from prejudices, but from settled principles. Our Lord restrained His disciples saying "do not hinder him"—the man, who was doing a good work. But He did not direct them to *wander from their own place* and follow him.[l] The rule to "examine everything" is coupled with—"Hold fast to that which is good."[m] Christian establishment is the result of a scriptural balance. "Discipline and ... stability"—"favor, and ... union"—are the two staves of the Good Shepherd; the strength of the church, the joy of her ministers.[n] If the order is broken, the "stability" soon fails. Confusion reigns, instead of peace and unity. The enemy's watchwords prevail—Divide and conquer. Let every man therefore be in *his own place* in the church; not weakening his minister's hands to please his own fancy; but marking carefully the footsteps of the "flock"; and seeking to find him whom his "soul loves," by feeding beside the "tents of the shepherds."[o]

[l]Mark 9:38–40

[m]1 Thess 5:21

[n]Col 2:5; Zech 11:7

[o]Song of Sol 1:7, 8

9 *Oil and perfume make the heart glad,*
So a man's counsel is sweet to his friend.

FRIENDSHIP TO THE SOUL

Most refreshing are *oil and perfume* to the senses.[p] Not

[p]Comp. Ps 133:2; Song of Sol 1:3; 3:6; 4:10; John 12:3; Dan 2:46

[q]Prov 17:17
[r]Prov 27:5, 6
[s]Deut 13:6; Philem 12
[t]Rom 12:15; Job 2:11, 12; 42:11

less so is friendship to the soul.[q] Who does not feel the need of a brother's or sister's love, their hands, their heart? Cold indeed is social fellowship without individual sympathy. "Faithful are the wounds of a friend."[r] But his very faithfulness alone would crush. *His sweetness* and tenderness soundly heal the wound. Sympathy is the balm of friendship. My "friend . . . is as [my] own soul,"[s] the sharer of my joys and my sorrows.[t] How, without him, could I more than half enjoy my pleasures? How could I bear my sorrows alone? What *ointment and perfume must have gladdened the heart* of the two bosom friends in the wood when their hearty counsel "encouraged" each other's hand "in God"![5]

[u]Exod 18:17–24
[v]Gen 21:17
[w]Ps 34:2; 66:16
[x]2 Cor 1:4
[y]Isa 50:4
[z]Job 34:31, 32

The loving warmth of a *friend's counsel* constitutes its excellence. It is not official, or merely intelligent. It is the counsel of his soul. He puts himself in our place, and counsels, as he would wish to be counseled himself. In that way, Moses' *heart was gladdened* by Jethro's *counsel,* relieving him from a heavy and needless burden.[u] And in that way, many cases of spiritual perplexity have been solved. When unable to see the needful consolation, *a friend's counsel,* like the angel of old, has pointed to the well of water near at hand for our support.[v] Often the sympathy of a brother's experience has cleared our path,[w] and turned the stumbling block into a waymark set up for our direction and encouragement. Shouldn't we then "comfort" our fellow-sufferers "with the comfort with which we ourselves are comforted of God"?[x] "The Lord God has given" us, as He did our divine Master, the gift of "the tongue of disciples"![y] Matchless Teacher! He teaches more in one hour than man can do in a whole age! That we may be learned in real Christian living we sit down at your feet! What I know not teach Thou me.[z]

[a]Eph 1:21; Song of Sol 1:3; John 12:3

But the real comfort and blessing of this *counsel,* will be to the degree in which we are living in communion with our Lord. Then, indeed, will there be *oil and perfume to gladden* the heart. That beloved "name" which is "far above" every name will be as "oils" poured forth, and "the house" will be "filled with the fragrance of the ointment."[a]

[5] *1 Sam 18:1–3; 20:17; 2 Sam 1:26, with 1 Sam 23:16. Similar must have been the joy of Peter from his brother Andrew's counsel. John 1:40–42.*

10 *Do not forsake your own friend or your father's friend,*
And do not go to your brother's house in the day of your calamity;
Better is a neighbor who is near than a brother far away.

FRIENDS—CLOSER THAN BROTHERS

Man without principle is the creature of whim. His friendships have no quaranteed stability. *The oil* soon loses its fragrance. *The sweetness of counsel*[b] is forgotten. New friends gain influence; and even *the father's friend*—the long-tried family friend—*is forsaken*. Solomon exemplified his own rule by cultivating kindly communion with Hiram, *his father's friend*.[c] The unprincipled contempt of this rule cost his foolish son his kingdom.[d] If other things are better when new, a friend is better that is old and tried. (For how can you trust an untried friend?) Never forget his rare price. Never be tempted by the lure of advantage to incur the risk of losing him. *His* house, *not your brother's*, may be your shelter *in the day of your great need*.[e] For though blood relationship ought to be the closest bond; yet, without a higher principle, selfishness will too often predominate. Joseph found far greater kindness among foreigners than from his own kindred.[f] Jonathan's affection afforded to David, what his brothers' jealousy would never have given him.[g] The Savior found His most soothing sympathy *in the day of His calamity*, not in his brother's house, but in the persevering attachment of his devoted friends.[h] *One friend and neighbor* closely knit in unity, near at hand, and in readiness to assit, is *better than a brother as far off* in affection, as in distance.

[b]Prov 27:9
[c]1 Kings 5:1–10
[d]1 Kings 12:6–19
[e]Prov 18:24
[f]Gen 39:4, 21; 41:39–45, with 37:4–18
[g]1 Sam 20, with 17:28
[h]Luke 22:28, with John 7:3–5

"But if it be an indecency, and uncomeliness, and a very unfit thing—that is—contrary to the precept of studying 'whatsoever is lovely, and thinking of these things'—to forsake *my friend and my father's friend;* how much more horrid must it be to forsake my God, and my father's God. 'My father's God shall not be my God,' " said Howe (*Works*, 7, 529). But was I not solemnly given up to this God at my first coming into the world? And was this transaction a trifle at the time and to be regarded as a trifle at the end of life? How could Solomon ever forget the injunction of his aged parent—"as for you, my son . . . know the God of your father"?[i] Exquisitely beautiful is the picture of the venerable patriarch, commending *his friend and his father's friend* to his children for His heavenly blessing—"God before whom my fathers Abraham and Isaac walked, *the God who has been my shepherd* all my life to this day, the angel who has redeemed me from all evil, bless the lads."[j] Here is *a wise Friend,* who knows our need;[k] *a sympathizing Friend* who feels our distress;[l] *a mighty Friend* able to cover and provide;[m] a *faithful Friend,* true to his word;[n] *a fast Friend,* who will never leave.[o] Young people, do you know Him as your *father's Friend*? Make Him *your own* in the hearty receiving of His gospel. Cleave to Him. He will never disappoint you.

[i] 1 Chron 28:9
[j] Gen 48:15, 16
[k] Col 2:3
[l] Ps 31:7
[m] Isa 63:1; Matt 28:18
[n] Num 23:19; Rev 19:11
[o] Heb 13:5

11 *Be wise, my son, and make my heart glad,*
That I may reply to him who reproaches me.

FAITHFUL CHILDREN

The Christian parent takes his full share of the minister's greatest "joy" to see his "children" walk "in truth."[p] Then indeed are "your children like olive plants around your table"[q]—the ornament of his family—yes, "a plant of renown"—the glory of the church and of the land. All else for them we rest with the Lord, for "still I know that it will be well for those who fear God, who fear Him openly."[r] *Our heart is gladdened* by their godly *wisdom*; and strengthened are we by what flows from this wisdom—their holy prayers. And truly will we put our seal to the choice this parent expressed: "I had rather have my house filled with my children's prayers, than filled with gold."

But an *ungodly* child is indeed the parent's *reproach.* He can only cause his father weeping. "Alas! my daughter! You have brought me very low, and you are among those who trouble me."[s] On this account the offending damsel was stoned at the "doorway of her father's house."[t] The graceless children of gracious parents are a special *reproach,* even upon the name of God.[u] The world will charge it (however in many cases most wrongfully) to their parents' example or neglect. Here, therefore, *a wise son makes the heart glad.*[v] He is his father's

[p] 2 John 4; 3 John 4
[q] Ps 128:3; AV—Ezek 34:29
[r] Eccl 8:12
[s] Judg 11:35
[t] Deut 22:21
[u] Gen 34:30; 1 Sam 2:17
[v] Prov 10:1; 29:3

weapon of defense, "when they speak with their enemies in the gate."[w] Should not the children of the church ponder the deep responsibility of bearing the kind of testimony that may answer *him that reproaches* and stop the mouths of those who are always ready to speak against the gospel? Especially children of ministers should feel this responsibility; "to adorn, not only their Christian testimony, but their parents' principles; showing that the principles of their father's house and ministry are the rules of their conduct, and their real delight."[6]

[w]Ps 127:5

12 *A prudent man sees evil* and *hides himself,*
The naive proceed and *pay the penalty.*[x]

[x]Prov 22:3

A FORTRESS OF ROCKS

Even animal instinct demonstrates wisdom.[y] Every intelligent man acts upon it. It is natural to see the evil when it has come or is close to our door. But *the prudent man foresees evil* coming long before it is near. God is the same unchangeable God of holiness and justice. He hates sin as much as He always has. There must therefore be *evil* to the sinner. *The prudent man* sees the effect in the cause. Therefore, he provides himself a shelter. We often see the Christian's patience, security, and hope. This is his *wisdom*—obtaining a refuge. The *evil* is near. But God in Christ is to him, a fortress of "rocks"; not a cold and barren refuge, safe from enemies, but still exposed to hunger; but instead He is a storehouse of food, as well as—"my refuge"—a citadel of defense. "Bread will be given him; his water will be sure."[z] The man, who has never been aware of the coming evil, is without a hiding place. The man outside the gate perishes, as if there were no refuge. Only he, who runneth into the "strong tower . . . is safe."[a] A mighty blessing is anything that awakens from slumber, and brings concern, *wise* action, and confidence!

[y]Jer 8:7
[z]Isa 33:16. Comp. Ps 142:5
[a]Prov 18:10

The Israelites, warned of the destruction of the firstborn,[b] and many ages after, of the ruin of their city, *hid* themselves.[c] This *wisdom* combined with faith, rouses us (as the man-slayer) to flee from impending danger, and to

[b]Exod 12:12, 13, 21–23
[c]Matt 24:15–21

[6] Life, *pp. 294-295. The Mosaic law severely punished the sins of the priest's daughter for the disgrace brought upon the holy office, Lev 21:9. "Faithful children" is a ministerial qualification. 1 Tim 3:4, 5; Titus 1:6. It was a frequent petition in Philip Henry's family worship, that "ministers' " children might have grace to carry it, that the ministry might in nothing be blamed"—See the Author's* Christian Ministry, *Part 3, Chap. 9.*

[d]Heb 6:18
[e]Num 35:11–13
[f]Acts 4:12

lay "hold of the hope set before us."[d] For him, there were six cities.[e] For us there is but one.[f] Nothing short of vital faith brings us into it.

But the naive—the willfully foolish—let things take their course. They mutter, "God is so merciful. Everything's going to turn out okay eventually, so why worry?" They will not be warned. The foolish things of the world occupy their hearts. Everything else is forgotten; they pass on, and are punished. The *wise hide* themselves in God. *The naive* rush blindfolded into hell. Oh! sinner, does not your ruin lie at your own door? What good will it do you to try to enjoy the world's mad pleasures here, if you have to "lie down in torment"?[g] The tears of those who repent are but for a moment and end in everlasting joy.[h] But for those who will not turn to God in repentance, there is nothing but the "weeping" of utter despondency.[i] Will you scorn this warning? The ox is driven to destruction. The sinner plunges into it, in spite of every effort to restrain him.

[g]Isa 50:11
[h]Ps 126:5, 6
[i]Matt 8:12

13 *Take his garment when he becomes surety for a stranger;*
And for an adulterous woman hold him in pledge.

[j]Prov 20:16

This Proverb also we have had before.[j] In order to fix it firmly in mind, it is necessary to remind ourselves again and again, what contributes to a happy life. This may be an illustration of the wisdom just described; *foreseeing evil,* and, instead of rushing into it, avoiding it. For what can be more unwise, than to trust a man, *that is surety for a stranger or for a strange woman*? Such lack of wisdom is utterly unworthy of confidence. And therefore *take his garment,* as full security for a debt. Be willing to be charged with selfishness, rather than, by lack of wisdom, hinder yourself from helping more worthy projects. The perfection of Christian graces is that they do not encroach on one another. Kindness loses the name of virtue, when shown at the expense of wisdom. Yet caution is needed, lest in repressing an impulse, we crush or hazard a valuable principle. We would not too quickly frown upon a generous act; because it may have overstepped the bounds of wisdom. Time, growing consideration, and experience, will correct the error. Meanwhile, don't let the discipline of wisdom chill the glow of active, self-denying love. Let every grace be in the right order, proportion, and combination, "that the man of God may be adequate, equipped for every good work."[k]

[k]2 Tim 3:17

14 *He who blesses his friend with a loud voice early in the morning,*
It will be reckoned a curse to him.

Is it a sin, then, to *bless our friend?* Our Lord openly acknowledged the love of His friends.[l] And yet *a loud voice,* and extravagant praises, bring insincerity into question. When a man exceeds all bounds of truth and decency, affecting pretentious words and exaggerated expressions, we cannot but suspect some sinister end.[m] Real friendship needs no such assurance. One act of love is more than many *loud blessings*. There is no wise man, but had rather have one promise than a thousand fair words, and one performance than ten thousand promises. For what does it cost a man to spend a little breath, to give one his word, if that's all he intends to give? He may be *getting up early in the morning,* so no one else can get ahead of him, in case there might not be enough time to finish this great business; and yet, while harping on the same string, he may be secretly condemning me all the day. Contrast David's *early rising* for the service of God, with his son's *early rising* for the hypocritical *blessing of his friends*.[n] The apostle could not endure this exaggerated praise.[o] Indeed every intelligent man must look upon it rather as *a curse to him*. For—to accept such excessive flattery as encouragement—would stamp him as a fool. And the deceitful *blessing* would end in a fearful *curse*.[p]

[l]Luke 22:28
[m]Prov 26:23–25
[n]Ps 5:3; 119:147, with 2 Sam 15:2–7
[o]2 Cor 12:6. Comp. Rom 12:3
[p]2 Sam 16:16–19; 17:7–13; Acts 12:22, 23

Toward our friends, this should be our rule: "Let us not love with word or with tongue, but in deed and truth."[q] The rule for ourselves is—"Walk before Me [God]," not before men.[r] Let worldly things and worldly men be of small consequence in our eyes. Man's day will soon have passed away.[s] Eternity in all its substance and glory is at hand.

[q]1 John 3:18
[r]Gen 17:1
[s]1 Cor 4:3

15 *A constant dripping on a day of steady rain*
And a contentious woman are alike;

16 *He who would restrain her restrains the wind,*
And grasps oil with his right hand.

CLOUDS AFTER RAIN

The figure of *the dripping* has been given before.[t] The time is here added—*a day of steady rain,* shutting us up at home.[u] There is rain without and within, both alike troublesome; the one preventing us from going out with comfort; the other from staying at home in peace. The storm within is however much more pitiless. Shelter may be found from the other, but none from this. The other wets only to the skin; this even to the bones. *Contention* with a neighbor is a sharp shower, over and gone. But this is a constant dripping, the curse of a house, even though it has every luxury.

[t] Prov 19:13
[u] Rom 15:24

Whether *the woman* lusts for rule, or frets under the obligation to submit; either principle breaks the rank in which God has placed her. Occasions always present themselves for the display of this unhappy temper. After the attempts to soothe and pacify her, the return of clouds "after the rain" betokens more showers and dispels the hope which a passing sunbeam may have raised. Unrestrained by divine grace, she becomes her husband's torment and her own shame. It would be as easy to *restrain the wind,* or *grasp the oil with our right hand,* as to restrain her tongue, or *hide* her stormy attitude. No—as the wind when it is held in check, howls more frightfully; so the attempt to quiet her only makes her more noisy.

Such repeated warnings seem to be needful. "Fleshly lusts" too often rule conscience and judgment in the important choice. "Such will have trouble in this life."[v] Wisdom and prayer, not blind love, give the only security of happiness and peace.

[v] Eccl 12:2; 1 Peter 2:11; 1 Cor 7:28

17 *Iron sharpens iron,*
So one man sharpens another.

Man was made, not for solitude, but for companionship.[w] It is only as a social being that his powers and affections are expanded. *Iron sharpens iron.*[x] Steel, whetted against a knife, sharpens the edge. So the collision of different minds whets each the edge of the other. We owe some of the most valuable discoveries of science

[w] Gen 2:18
[x] 1 Sam 13:20, 21

to this mutual reaction. Useful hints were offered, which have resulted in the opening of large fields of unexplored knowledge. In the sympathies of friendship, when the mind is dull, and the countenance overcast, a word from a friend puts an edge upon the blunted energy, and exhilarates the countenance.[y] The commanding word in the field of battle puts a keen edge upon *the iron.*[z] The mutual eagerness for evil is a solemn warning against evil communications.[a] But how refreshing it is, when, as in the dark ages of the church, "those who feared the Lord spoke to one another."[b] *Sharpening* indeed must have been the fellowship at Emmaus, when the "hearts" of the disciples "burned within" them.[c] The apostle was often so invigorated by *the countenance of his friends,*[d] that he longed to enjoy "your company for awhile."[e] Upon this principle—"two" are better than one—our Lord sent His first preachers to their work.[f] And the first divine ordination in the Christian church followed this precedent.[g]

"The communion of saints" is an Article in our Creed. But do we practically acknowledge it in its high responsibility and Christian privilege? We should gladly take up the bond of brotherhood. If a brother seems to walk alone, *sharpen his iron* by fellowshipping with him in Christian love. Walk together, considering one another's infirmities, trials, and temptations; and mutual "stimulation"[h] of each other's gifts and graces. "If the axe is dull" the edge will thus be sharpened.[i] If this high obligation and privilege were more fully realized; if we walked more closely with God in this holy atmosphere,[j] we wouldn't so often complain of social fellowship, where much might have been communicated, and yet all ended in barrenness and disappointment.

18 *He who tends the fig tree will eat its fruit;*
And he who cares for his master will be honored.

What an encouragement to earnestness in our calling! The fig tree was a valuable product of Judea.[k] Its cultivation was probably a profitable labor, and therefore illustrated the general reward of faithfulness. The gardener's hard work was recompensed by *eating its fruit.*[l] The faithfulness of his servant will be similarly honored.[m] Eliezer's uprightness[n] and Deborah's long and faithful

[y] Job 4:3, 4
[z] 2 Sam 10:11–13
[a] Prov 10–13; 1 Kings 21:25; Isa 41:6, with 1 Cor 15:33
[b] Mal 3:16
[c] Luke 24:32
[d] Acts 18:5; 28:15; 2 Cor 7:6
[e] Rom 15:24
[f] Luke 10:1–3, with Eccl 4:9–12
[g] Acts 13:2–4
[h] Heb 10:24, 25; also 3:13
[i] Eccl 10:10
[j] 1 John 1:7
[k] Mic 4:4; Hab 3:17; Luke 13:6
[l] 1 Cor 9:7; 2 Tim 2:6
[m] Prov 22:29
[n] Gen 24

[o]Gen 35:8

[p]2 Kings 2:3–5

[q]Luke 7:2
[r]Gen 31:7

services[o] were suitably *honored.* Elisha's affectionate devotedness to *his master was honored* with a double portion of his spirit.[p] The centurion's care for his servant was probably an acknowledgment of earnest *care for his master.*[q] The excepted cases of ingratitude[r] do not invalidate the rule.

There are no exceptions, however, in the service of the divine *master.* Our happiness is in receiving His Word and studying His will. Our *honor* is secured by His promises—"If any one serves Me, the Father will *honor* him." "Blessed are those slaves whom the master shall find on the alert when he comes; truly I say to you, that he will"—adorable condescension!—"gird himself to serve, and have them recline at table, and will come up and wait on them."[s] Their *honor* will be told to each before the assembled world, "Well done, good and faithful slave . . . enter into the joy of your master."[t] It will seal their portion in eternal happiness—"His bond-servants shall serve Him; and they shall see His face, and His name shall be on their foreheads."[u]

[s]John 12:26; Luke 12:37

[t]Matt 25:21, 23

[u]Rev 22:3, 4

19 *As in water face* reflects *face,*
So the heart of man reflects *man.*

SCRIPTURE PORTRAITS

This Proverb does not cram everyone together in one confused mass; as if all were alike under a never-ending variety of conditions. We cannot identify infancy with age or all the proper and distinct features of physical make-up and education. But under the same circumstances, and on the same level, the coincidence is most remarkable and instructive. As *in* the reflection of *the water, face reflects face; so in another heart we see the reflection of our own.*[v] Human nature has experienced no change since the fall. The picture of man's corruption, drawn more than four thousand years after the fall, is man, as we see and know him now.[w] The apostle's graphic description of the Christian conflict is as if we had been sitting before him having our own picture taken.[x] This identity of Christian experience is most valuable. "No one," exclaims a tried child of God, "has ever felt as I do." But let him open his case to a brother or a sister, compare notes with their testings, and who will

[v]Ps 33:15

[w]Gen 6:5; Ps 14:2, 3; Rom 3:10, 11

[x]Rom 7:14–25

not add his own name to his complaints? Thus, instead of being "surprised at the fiery ordeal among you," he learns that "the same experiences of suffering are being accomplished by your brethren who are in the world."[y] The same features and "measure of the stature ... of Christ," mark the whole family; "one and the same spirit works inasmuch as all these things, distributing to each one individually just as He wills."[z]

[y]1 Peter 4:12; 5:9

[z]Eph 4:13; 1 Cor 12:11

Scripture history also illustrates this unity. Ishmael's mocking shows the enmity of the heart in all ages.[a] Who of us does not find something answering to Jonah's evil temper in our own fretfulness, waywardness, or ingratitude? Job shows us our impatience, our mistaken judgments of God's dealings with us, and the special trial of Satan's temptations. David's *heart* in all its varied exercises *answers to our heart.* How else could we speak *his* confession, praises, conflicts, and triumphs, and feel that the words are our own? It is these Scripture portraits that make the Word of God so "profitable for teaching, for reproof, for correction, for training in righteousness."[b]

[a]Gal 4:29

[b]2 Tim 3:16

Through them we learn sympathy with the members of Christ. We share their joys and sorrows, their confidence and temptations. Self-knowledge also teaches us concerning human nature,[c] and how to deal wisely and profitably with our fellow-sinners. The practical lesson of humility and forbearance is also deeply taught. A man sees *a face* reflected *in the water.* It disgusts him, but he has no idea that it's *his own face* he sees. He exclaims with vain self-preference against the ungodliness of the sinner, or the infirmities of the saint. Actually, he is reviling himself! For you, who are guilty of this, your only hope is to change your language from scorn to self-abhorrence and shame!

[c]Ps 36:1

20 *Sheol* [AV—*hell*] *and Abaddon* [AV—*destruction*]
are never satisfied,
Nor are the eyes of man ever satisfied.

A striking picture of the two great devourers—*Sheol and Abaddon*[d]—*never satisfied! Hell*—ever since Adam's sin has been insatiable. It has opened its mouth to receive countless millions; and still it yawns, craving for more.[e] Generations have sunk into *destruction,* doing the work, and earning "the wages of sin." Still the pit is not full. The broad mouth is always open for more.

[d]Prov 15:11

[e]Prov 30:15, 16; Isa 5:14; Rom 6:23

[f]1 John 2:16

And so it is with *the eyes*—the desires[f]—*of man*, always requiring new gratification. "He enlarges his appetite like *Sheol*, and he is like death, *never satisfied*." His "eye is not satisfied with seeing, nor is the ear filled with hearing."[g] Curiosity, love of novelty, coveteousness, ambition—all these desires, like thirst in sickness, are aggravated as we try to satisfy them.[h] Man is always seeking for what he can never find—satisfaction in earthly things. He toils after his object, and when he has grasped it, he toils still more; the possessor of abundance, not of happiness.[i] His best efforts only bring him meager enjoyment, not deserving the name. The summit of ambition, when reached, is not his resting place; only the point, where he stretches after something higher. All the affections of fallen man are filled with unquenched thirst. He may think his desires moderate. He may set bounds for them and flatter himself that he will never overpass them. But give him a world, and, he will weep for another, and sink at last into a wretched eternity of unsatisfied desires.

[g]Hab 2:5; Eccl 1:8. Comp. 2:1–11

[h]Eccl 6:7

[i]Eccl 5:10–12

And this isn't the full effect of his depravity! Corruption also leads us to seek rest in something less than God. But it is our nature not to find it. How can an immortal being quench his thirst except from an infinite source? The soul was originally created to find a suitable and infinite gratification in the love of its Creator. And now that it is turned aside by the fall, it has never-ending depth that craves to be filled. Nor do we speak here of refined and educated minds. The most unlettered individual, awakened to a sense of his consciousness, might breathe out Augustine's confession—"Thou hast made us for thyself; and our heart can have no rest, til it rests in thee" (*Confess.* book I. chap. 1). And here the gospel offers the answer: "Come to Me, all who are weary and heavy laden, and I will give you rest."[j]

[j]Matt 11:28

THE KING IN HIS BEAUTY

So often as the eager question is asked, "Who will show us any good?"[k]—the answer comes back—"Ho! Every one who thirsts, come to the waters;" for "if any man is thirsty, let him come to Me and drink." Because he who comes to Me shall never thirst."[l] Here our desires are increased and *satisfied* at the same time. A fountain

[k]Ps 4:6

[l]Isa 55:1, 2; John 7:37; 6:35

of infinite fullness is at our door. We are welcomed to a haven of rest, to a heart of peace and love. And when new-created in the image of God, and made capable of communion with Him in grace, and of enjoying Him in glory, can our desires be *satisfied* with anything less, with anything else? Is He not now our supreme delight, our satisfying object, never leaving us without complete satisfaction for a single moment?[m]

[m]Ps 16:5; Lam 3:24

Now let me ask: Have I seen God, as that, which alone is sufficient for my soul? Have I made the important discovery that all my uneasy cravings from morning to night arise from not seeking Him as my only satisfaction? Let me sit down to the richest banquet of life, and every dish will be tasteless, and without nourishment, if He is not above all, and in all. To delight in anything independent of Him[n] is as if we cast Him down from His throne. All is misery and delusion. But delighting in Him, everything ministers to our comfort, flowing from this great center. In that great final day, how complete the *satisfaction of the eyes* and heart will be! The eternity of being will be an eternity of joy—"Your eyes shall see the King in His beauty; and "as for me, I shall behold Thy face in righteousness; *I will be satisfied* with Thy likeness when I awake."[o]

[n]Ps 73:25

[o]Isa 33:17; Ps 17:15

21 *The crucible is for silver and the furance for gold,*
And a man is tested *by the praise accorded him.*[7]

TRIAL OF THE HEART

The crucible and furnace have been mentioned before, as the Lord's trial of "hearts."[p] The most searching *furnace* is seen here. He that is praised is not only much approved, but much proved. The courting of the *praise* of our fellowman is the world within. *Praise* is a sharper trial of the strength of principle than reproach. "If a man be vain and light, he will be puffed up with it. If he be wise and solid, he will be no whit moved therewith," stated Bishop Hall. A haughty, proud spirit: loving "to be first";[q] forwardness to give our opinion, and offense, if it is not taken—this is the dross brought out of the furnace. Count the discovery a special mercy. Know your need of

[p]Prov 17:3

[q]3 John 9

[7] *Gesenius (Gibbs) translates this verse—"What a crucible is to gold, that let a man be to the mouth that praiseth him"—i.e., let him examine the praise carefully.*

purifying, and let the great refiner—God—do His perfect work.[r]

[r]Mal 3:2, 3

But see *a man* humbled by praise, aware of how little he deserves it, and "who regards you as superior?"[s] See him made more careful and diligent, bearing his honor meekly, and the same man as before; here *the furnace* proves the real metal, and brings out "a vessel for honor, sanctified, useful to the Master."[t]

[s]1 Cor 4:7
[t]2 Tim 2:21

Absalom was tried in *this crucible* and found to be "rejected silver."[u] Herod, under the shouting praise of his flatterers, "did not give God the glory," and was destroyed in shame.[v] Joseph[w] and David[x]—maintained their humility; Daniel his consistency;[y] the apostles their singleness for their Master's glory. Here was the bright *gold* in the heated *furnace.*

[u]2 Sam 14:25; 15:6, with Jer 6:30; Ezek 22:18
[v]Acts 12:21–23
[w]Gen 41:41–43; 45:5–8
[x]1 Sam 18:7, 8, 15–18
[y]Dan 6:3–5

How fearful the trials of a minister of Jesus Christ so often are. When He becomes popular, the idol of his people;[z] when men of strong impulse and weak judgment put the servant in the Master's place[8]—then he is in *the crucible.* He that is but dross is consumed. Even if there is true metal, the man of God "shall be saved, yet so as through fire." Without painful discipline his usefulness would be withered and his spirituality deadened.[a]

[z]Acts 3:11–16; 10:25, 26; 14:11–15
[a]1 Cor 3:15; 2 Cor 12:7

HOW TO GIVE AND RECEIVE PRAISE

Two rules strongy present themselves—Be careful in giving praise. Even the children of the world can discover the deadly persistence of pride in our nature. "Do you know," remarked M. de Stael on her deathbed, "what is the last thing to die in man? It is self-love." We cannot therefore do our brother a greater injury than by supplying fuel for pride by uncontrolled praise. God doesn't always see him as the church does. It may be that the best-known servant of God is one, of whom the church has taken little notice. And at best we are far too short-sighted to know accurately where our brother stands spiritually. We can't know his true worth without the balances of the sanctuary, which are *fully* in the

[8] *"We should feel," said the venerable Mr. Simeon in his own way, "as if our ears were stung with blasphemy, when we discover any attempt to transfer the crown of glory from the head of the Redeemer to that of any of His servants." Henry Martyn continually expresses his sensitive conscience upon this besetting temptation—*Life, *chaps. 2, 3. Dr. Payson—a careful self-observer—mentions among his trials—"well-meant, but injudicious commendations!" When I am praised,—"God! humble me,"—was the prayer of one marvelously preserved in the fearful furnace—*Life of Mrs. Godolphin, *p. 22. See also Author's* Christian Ministry, *part 3, chap. 7.*

hands of Him, who searches the heart. Therefore, till the day appointed when all things will be open to view, it is well to judge each other, whether for good or evil, with appropriate moderation. Is it merciful to expose a weak fellow-sinner to the frown of a jealous God, by stirring up the inborn corruption of his heart?[9] For put even the finest *gold into the furnace,* how humbling is the spectacle of the dross that still clings to it![b] Don't be any less careful in receiving praise. While our taste revolts from extravagant flattery, yet we are apt to think that it is meant kindly, and it is very rare not to take unconsciously a drop of the poison. But the praise of the church is by far the most dangerous poison,—so refined, so luscious! Especially when we feel it to be lawfully earned, how hard to receive it with self-renouncing consecration to God! Christian! you know you carry gunpowder with you. So be sure to keep those who carry fire at a distance. "It is a dangerous crisis, when a proud heart meets with flattering lips," said Flavel. And isn't it possible that even the habit of speaking humbly of ourselves is a snare of the devil? Wouldn't it be safer not to speak of ourselves at all? At least—to confine our conversation in strict sincerity to what we are, not what we appear to be, and it would be wise "to restrain our lips."[c] Guard against dwelling even in thought upon anything that brings man's approving eye upon us. Delight mainly in those works that are only under the eye of God. Value His approval only. Think always of the love of human praise as the most deadly enemy of a Christian profession to be resisted with intense energy and perseverance.[d]

[b] Isa 39:2; 2 Chron 32:31

[c] Prov 10:19

[d] John 5:44; 12:43, 44

22 *Though you pound a fool in a mortar with a pestle*
along with crushed grain,
Yet his folly will not depart from him.

WHO CAN CHANGE THE LEOPARD'S SPOTS!

The allusion is to the Eastern way of beating off the

[9] *"I do not know," said Neff, "that I ought to thank you so very warmly for what I have too much reason to fear the old man will be ready to take advantage of; his life being, you know, principally supported by praise"*—Biography, p. 369. *"Every one here," writes Dr. Payson to his mother, "whether friends or enemies, are conspiring to ruin me. Satan, and my own heart, of course will lend a hand; and if you join too, I fear all the cold water, which Christ can throw upon my pride, will not prevent it from breaking out into a destructive flame. As certainly as anybody flatters and caresses me, my Father has to scourge me for it, and an unspeakable mercy it is, that he condescends to do it."*

husk from the corn by pounding it in a hard bowl.[10] Yet the husk doesn't stick as tightly to the grain, as *folly to the fool.* The beating of *the mortar* may separate the husk from the grain, but foolishness cannot be beaten out of a fool. Much is said of the effectiveness of correction.[e] But by itself it accomplishes nothing. What can it do for *the fool,* who despises it?[f] "The rod" as an ordinary means, "will remove" *folly* out of the "heart *of a child.*"[g] But when the child is become a man in strength of habit and stubbornness of will, foolishness can no longer be beaten out of him. The Ethiopian can no more "change his skin or the leopard his spots," than those can do good, "who are accustomed to do evil."[h]

[e]Prov 23:13, 14; 29:15, 17
[f]Prov 12:1; 15:10
[g]Prov 22:15
[h]Jer 13:23

Examples of this incurable hardness are everywhere. The flood, for example—that cleansing broom of divine vengeance destroyed the race, but not the folly, of man. Even God, Himself, declared He would never use a flood again for that purpose,[i] Pharaoh was once and again *pounded in the mortar; yet his folly did not depart from him.*[j] Ahaz under the same infliction "became yet more unfaithful to the Lord," and stands out as a beacon to all ages— *This is that king Ahaz!*[k] "Where will you be stricken again?"—was the sorrowful complaint of God concerning His Israel.[l] The deepest infliction of chastisement produces only the fruit of blasphemy and hardened impenitence.[m] If Manasseh's *folly, when pounded in the mortar, departed from him;*[n] this was not the natural power of affliction, but the super-added power of sovereign grace, which can turn any evil, even sin itself, to eternal good. The belief in the necessary working of affliction for our saving good is a fatal delusion. Never did it of itself bring one soul to God. In all cases, it is only what God is pleased to make it. It may even be tenfold more severe. The blows may be so mighty, as to make the most stupefied soul quiver with intense feeling. Still if the rock be broken, the broken pieces will retain all their native hardness. The man may be crushed, yet not humbled. Still will he cling to his *folly;* and turn away from Christ and heaven, rather than part with that which is interwoven into every part of his nature. Wasn't it so

[i]Gen 8:21
[j]Exod 9:27; 10:16; 12:29–32; 14:5
[k]2 Chron 28:22
[l]Isa 1:5. Comp. 9:13; Jer 5:3; 44:9, 10, 15, 16. Ezek 24:13; Amos 4:11, 12
[m]Rev 16:10, 11
[n]2 Chron 33:12, 13

[10] *Many commentators conceive a reference to this mode of punishment still practiced in the East. See Calmet-Parkhurst. HORNE's* Introduction, *3:157. BURDER'S* Oriental Customs. *But perhaps the figurative allusion is more simple.*

with you, too, Christian until God's all-powerful love awakened (what chastisement alone could never have stirred) the cry of unreserved submission?—"Lord, Don't spare me. Bruise me; humble me; do anything with me, but don't leave me under my sins. Who can deliver me, if you do not?" How welcome is the "grieving" of the penitent child to his yearning father. The Lord said, "I have surely heard . . . 'Thou hast chastised me, and I was chastised, like an untrained calf; Bring me back that I may be restored, for Thou art the Lord my God. For after I turned back, I repented; And after I was instructed, I smote on my thigh; I was ashamed, and also humiliated, Because I bore the reproach of my youth.' Is Ephraim My dear son? Is he a delightful child? Indeed, as often as I have spoken against him, I certainly still remember him; therefore My heart yearns for him: I will surely have mercy on him."[o]

[o] Jer 31:18–20. Comp. Hos 14:1–4; Luke 15:18–24

23 *Know well the condition of your flocks,*
And *pay attention to your herds;*
24 *For riches are not forever,*
Nor does a crown endure *to all generations.*
25 When *the grass disappears, the new growth is seen,*
And the herbs of the mountains are gathered in,
26 *The lambs* will be *for your clothing,*
and the goats will bring *the price of a field,*
27 *And* there will be *goats' milk enough for your food,*
For the food of your household,
And sustenance for your maidens.

THE BIBLE:
DIRECTORY FOR ALL EMPLOYMENTS OF LIFE

"This declareth the great goodness of God toward men, and the diligence that He requireth of him for the preservation of His gifts," said *Reformers' Notes.* It is a living picture of the occupations, advantages, and responsibilities of rural life in olden days. It is specially appropriate to a nation, whose chief riches were, in its early origin, in *pastures and flocks.* Their father Jacob admirably exemplified this rule. He *knew well the condition of his flocks and herds.*[p] Even King David, mindful of his ancient occupation, kept his *flocks and herds* under constant inspection.[q] Uzziah also deemed a pastoral charge

[p] Gen 30:32–42; 31:38–40; 33:13
[q] 1 Chron 27:29–31, with 1 Sam 16:11; Ps 78:70, 71

[r] 2 Chron 26:10
[s] Ruth 2:4, 5; 3:7
[t] Prov 23:5

no degradation to his royal dignity.[r] The rule requires personal attention. Everything should not be left to servants. The master's eye, like Boaz,[s] should, as far as possible, overlook the work. *Riches* are a fickle possession. *They would not be forever.*[t] Even *the crown might not endure to every generation.* Native produce is more permanent wealth. Honest, hard work secures a more certain maintenance, springing up out of the earth, a more immediate gift of God.

[u] Col 3:22–24
[v] Rom 12:11
[w] Acts 13:36
[x] Matt 5:14–16
[y] 1 Cor 7:20, 24
[z] Ps 147:4; Matt 10:30

The Bible is a directory for all the diversified employments of life. It teaches that every man ought to have a business and rebukes the neglect of practical everyday duties. God may be glorified by a single eye and purpose in every station; by the laborer, the farmer, the servant, no less than by the master.[u] We must "serve" the Lord being "fervent in spirit," but a part of this service is that we be "not lagging behind in diligence."[v] Laziness would make the cares of life an excuse for a low standard of Christianity. But to withdraw from the burden would be to neglect serving "the purpose of God" in our generation;[w] to put our light "under the peck-measure, but on the lampstand"; to cover it, instead of letting "your light shine."[x] Our own calling is the way of God for us; and in this way, let us commit ourselves to God and be at peace.[y] His providence extends to little things, as well as to things of greater importance. The least is under His care, as if there were nothing else. There is no weariness, perplexity, or labor. A single glance is sufficient. Nothing escapes His all-seeing eye. He that "counts the number of the stars," numbers also "the very hairs of your head."[z] Sweet balm for that cankering care which is the ruin of all godliness!

[a] Job 31:20

This picture also exhibits the fruits of hard work, as far more preferable than those of ambition. The comparison with those, whose position places them above the need for labor, affords no reason for envy, but much for thankfulness. The various produce of the field—*grass* in the pastures; *the herbs of the mountains;* the suitable *clothing from the lambs;*[a] *the goats paying the price of the field;* the sufficiency of wholesome food *for the household and maidens*—all is the overflowing bounty of our gracious God. "How precious is Thy lovingkindness, Oh

God!"[b] Thus "man goes forth to his work and to his labor until evening," singing his song of praise—"O Lord, how many are Thy works! In wisdom Thou hast made them all; The earth is full of Thy possessions."[c]

[b]Ps 36:7

[c]Ps 104:23, 24

CHAPTER TWENTY-EIGHT

1 *The wicked flee when no one is pursuing,*
But the righteous are bold as a lion.

THE INVISIBLE PURSUER

The wicked may appear *bold* in facing danger, so long as they avoid serious thought, and stupefy conscience. But when conscience is roused, guilt is the parent of fear. Adam knew no fear, until be came a guilty creature. Then, to the searching question—"Where are you?" he replied, "I heard the sound of Thee in the garden, and I hid myself."[a] But *the wicked flee,* not only when their enemies pursue,[b] but also *when no one pursues.*[c] Yet, isn't conscience an invisible *pursuer,* following close, the herald of the wrath of God? And there are times, when "the sound of a driven leaf will chase them;[d] when "the shadow of the mountains" shall make their hearts melt away.[e] Cain was terrified with the apprehension of murder, when there was no man, save his own father, living on the earth.[f] Many a daring infidel has shown himself a coward in a moment of sudden danger. In unwelcome thoughts of judgment to come, conscience has turned pale at the question—"What will become of the godless man and the sinner?"[g]

[a]Gen 3:9, 10
[b]Deut 28:25
[c]Lev 26:17; Ps 53:5
[d]Lev 26:36; Job 15:21
[e]Judg 9:36
[f]Gen 4:13, 14
[g]1 Peter 4:18

THE BELIEVER'S LION—LIKE BOLDNESS

But if guilt brings fear, the removal of guilt gives confidence.[h] *The wicked flee; the righteous are bold as a lion.* Fearless as the king of the forest,[1] they dare to do anything but offend their God. The fear of Him has drowned

[h]Heb 10:22; 1 John 3:21

[1] *Comp. Prov 30:30; 2 Sam 17:10. "This noble animal is the most perfect model of boldness and courage. He never flies from the hunters, nor is frightened by their onset. If their number forces him to yield, he retires slowly, step by step, frequently turning upon his pursuers. He has been known to attack a whole caravan, and when obliged to retire, he always retires fighting, and with his face to his enemy"—PAXTON'S* Illustration of Natural History of Scripture, *pp. 295, 296. Pindar refers to the lion as the figure of courage, Isth. 4.* Antistr.

every other fear. "Though a host encamp against me," saith the man of God, "my heart will not fear."[i] Moses feared not "the wrath of the king."[j] Caleb and Joshua stood firm against the current of rebellion.[k] Elijah dared Ahab's anger to his face.[l] Nehemiah in a time of peril exclaimed, "Should a man like me flee?"[m] The three believers stood undaunted before the furious autocrat of Babylon.[n] The apostles' boldness astonished their enemies.[o] Paul before the Roman governor,[p] and even before Nero himself, "witnessed a good confession."[q] Athanasius before the Imperial Counsel of Heresy; Luther at the Diet of Worms, finely exemplified the *lion-like boldness*. Nor is this the character of individuals only. The faithful and constant Christians will be *bold* to walk contrary to the course of this world; withstanding the scorn of man; valiant for despised truth; glorying in a persecuted name—Jesus. Fearless is he of men. "If God is for us, who is against us?"[r] And he's no less fearless of Satan. Though Satan is a "roaring lion,"[s] he is also a chained lion. "Resist the devil," and—coward like, "he will flee from you."[t] If there is a want of *boldness*, is there not a wound of conscience, neglect of prayer, or want of faith? The boldness itself is the sense of weakness, and divine "power is perfected in weakness."[u] When God intends us to do great things, He makes us feel, that "apart from Me you can do nothing."[v] Thus pride receives its death-blow, and He receives all the glory to Himself.[2]

[i] Ps 27:3; 3:6; 46:2; 112:7
[j] Heb 11:27; Exod 10:28, 29
[k] Num 14:6–10
[l] 1 Kings 18:10, 17, 18; 21:20; 2 Kings 1:15
[m] Neh 6:11
[n] Dan 3:16
[o] Acts 4:13
[p] Acts 24, 26; Rom 1:15, 16
[q] 2 Tim 4:16, 17
[r] Rom 8:31
[s] 1 Peter 5:8
[t] James 4:7
[u] 2 Cor 12:9
[v] John 15:5

2 *By the transgression of a land many are its princes,*
But by a man of understanding and *knowledge, so it endures.*

"THIS THING IS FROM ME"

Is God concerned in the falling of a sparrow?[w] Surely then much more in the control of kingdoms.[x] If we realized more deeply our national dependence, we should see the clouds of lawlessness and confusion work-

[w] Matt 10:29
[x] Dan 4:25

[2] *Bishop Hall has finely worked out this contrast*—"The wicked *is a very coward, and is afraid of everything; of* God, *because he is his enemy; of* Satan, *because he is his tormentor; of* God's creatures, *because they, joining with their Maker, fight against him; of* himself, *because he bears about with him his own accuser and executioner. The godly man ... is afraid of nothing; not of God, because he knows Him to be his best friend, and will not hurt him; not of Satan, because he* cannot *hurt him; not of afflictions, because he knows they come from a loving God, and end in his good; not of the creatures, since 'the very stones in the field are in league with him'; not of himself, since his conscience is at peace"*—Medit. and Vows, *Cent.* 2. 74.

ing His wise, mysterious, or gracious purposes. Rival *princes* desolate the land with the horrors of civil war.[y] A quick succession of *princes* rises by treason, violent seizure of power, or by natural course.[z] Therefore, there follow a change of laws, loss of privileges, adding of new burdens, or wasteful expenditure of treasure or blood. Man traces these evils to political causes. But God's voice speaks from the cloud—"This thing has come from Me."[a] *By the transgression of a land many are its princes.* The bloody battles and wars in Britain's early history, which swept away the flower of her nobility; and those of a later date, which overturned for a time her long-established institutions—did they not betoken the same awful scourge of national *transgression?* Would that the nation had learned from her own records of bygone days, the sound and practical lessons of repentance with all its blessed fruits![3]

[y] 1 Kings 12:16–21
[z] Zech 11:8
[a] 1 Kings 12:24

But no less must we acknowledge God's hand in the preservation *of the state by men of understanding and knowledge.* By a man of this high character *the state* of Egypt was prolonged by preservation from famine.[b] The long and prosperous reigns of the godly kings of Judah strongly contrast with the records of Israel after the revolt.[c] And perhaps this may be a mark of the Lord's quarrel with us; that the detached political parties present few—if any—masterminds—*men of understanding and knowledge*—raised up at a grand national crisis for the *endurance of the state.* Such men guided by Christian principle, we would pray might be the counselors of our leaders, that *our country may endure* "in all godly quietness."[d]

[b] Gen 41:38, 39
[c] 1 Kings 15:25–34; 16:8–29; 2 Kings 15:8–31, with 1 Kings 15:10; 2 Chron 17:1–5; 32:20–26
[d] 1 Tim 2:1, 2

[3] *Thus wrote Jeremy Taylor of his sorrowful times, in his fervid coloring, and deep-toned instructiveness; and with some solemn application to later times. "It is a sad calamity to see a kingdom spoiled, and a Church afflicted; priests slain with the sword, and the blood of nobles mingled with the . . . sand; religion made the cause of trouble, and the best of men most cruelly persecuted; government turned, and laws ashamed; judges decreeing in fear and covetousness, and the ministers of holy things setting themselves against all that is sacred. And what shall make recompense for this heap of sorrows, when God shall send such swords of fire? Even the mercies of God, that shall then be made public when the people shall have suffered for their sins. For I have known a luxuriant vine swell into irregular twigs and bold* [outgrowths], *and spend itself in leaves and little rings, and afford but little clusters to the wine press. But when the Lord of the vine has caused the dressers to cut the wilder plant, and make it bleed; it grew temperate in its vain expanse of useless leaves, and knotted into fair and juicy branches, and made account of that loss of blood by the return of fruit. It is thus of an afflicted kingdom, cured long of its* [excesses], *and punished for its sins. It bleeds for its riot, and is left ungoverned for its disobedience, and chastised for its wantonness. And when the sword hath let forth the corrupted blood, and the fire hath purged the rest, then it enters into the double joys of restitution, and gives God thanks for His rod, and confesses the mercies of God in making the smoke to be changed into fire, and His anger into mercy"—Works, 6:182.*

3 *A poor man who oppresses the lowly*
Is like *a driving rain which leaves no food.*

RAIN UPON THE MOWN GRASS

Unrestrained power is often an engine of *oppression;*[e] but never more so, than when it is in the grasp of the *poor.* Place an unprincipled spendthrift in power, and he is a destructive flood in his sphere; greedily serving every advantage by *oppression* to redeem his substance. *A poor man* suddenly raised to power, instead of sympathizing with grievances familiar to his former condition[f] is usually preeminently characterized by selfishness. Only a fool will admire the splendor of his power, reckless of the evil, that it is spreading all around. Esther, when raised to a throne from an obscure station, was well reminded to use her power for God; for that, some great work was surely intended by the remarkable providence.[g] But a base mind becomes more corrupt from hasty promotion. A man's necessities inflame his desires; and being without a spark of generous humanity, he is only interested in improving his uncertain opportunities for selfish gain.[4] Some of the rulers in the French Revolution came up from the lowest ranks. And their *oppression* was indeed a *driving rain, leaving no food* in fertile districts.

How cheering is the contrast of Him, once *poor* himself by His voluntary abasement, now raised to honor and glory; yet pitying, not ashamed of, his poor "brethren."[h] Truly, His administration is not the *driving rain* of desolation, but the "rain upon the mown grass," rich in mercy. "He will deliver the needy when he cries for help, the afflicted also, and him who has no helper . . . He will rescue their life from oppression and violence; and their blood will be precious in his sight."[i]

[e] Gen 31:29; Eccl 4:1
[f] Matt 18:28–30
[g] Esther 4:14
[h] 2 Cor 8:9; Phil 2:7–11, with Heb 2:11, 12
[i] Ps 72:6, 12–14

4 *Those who forsake the law praise the wicked,*
But those who keep the law strive with them.

[4] *It is in matter of power—to paraphrase Bishop Sanderson—as it is in matter of learning. They that have but a smattering of learning, you shall ever observe to be the most forward in the show of the little they have; because they fear there would be little notice taken of their learning, if they didn't show it when they can. It is even so in this case. Men of base spirit and condition, when they have gotten the advantage of a little power, conceive, that the world would not know what goodly men they are, if they did not do something or other, to show forth their power to the world. And then, their minds being too narrow to comprehend any generous way whereby to do it, they cannot devise any other way to do it, than by trampling upon those that are below them;* and that *they do beyond all reason, and without all mercy*—Sermon on Prov 24:11, 12. *Comp. also on 1 Sam 12:3.*

PREACHING WITH OUR LIVES

How responsible we are for the influence of our testimony, influencing all around us for evil or for good! Similarity of taste directs the choice of our companions. Those who love sins, naturally "give hearty approval to those who practice them."[j] *They praise the wicked,* because, like themselves, *they forsake the law,* and cast it to "hiding places."[k] "The world would love its own."[l] Each sees his brother in sin.[m] Each makes *the other's conduct,* not *the forsaken law,* the standard of action. *The wicked* may possess some praiseworthy qualities.[n] But to *praise them* for their wickedness, identifies us with them. "It is fearful to sin; more fearful to delight in sin; yet more to defend it," said Bishop Hall (*Works,* 8:36).

[j]Rom 1:32
[k]1 Sam 23:23; Neh 4:17–19
[l]John 15:19
[m]Isa 12:6
[n]Luke 16:8

The servants of God maintain the same unity of spirit. They cannot call sin by smooth names and gloss over an ungodly character. If *they keep the law,* they *strive with those who forsake it.* Noah thus contended with the ungodly in his day, condemning them not merely in word, but in life; and though "a preacher of righteousness," he preached more powerfully by his life, than by his doctrine.[o] But this contention must be aggressive. We must "expose," as well as separate from, "the unfruitful deeds of darkness."[5] Our divine Master's open testimony was the grand offense.[p] So let us plainly show that His enemies are ours;[6] that we hold neutrality in His cause to be treason. For "he who is not with Me is against Me."[q]

[o]2 Peter 2:5; Heb 11:7
[p]Matt 15:10–12; Luke 20:19; John 7:7
[q]Matt 12:30

Oh! the appalling recollection of our former influence for evil! The deadly, perhaps the eternal, injury, which all our subsequent labors have never undone! The encouragement, which our *praise of the wicked* gave to sin, hardening our companions in their wickedness! What wouldn't Manasseh have given to have undone his sin in all its evil consequences upon his son and his kingdom![r] How intolerable would be our thought of the past, but for the blood which covers our guilt, while it deepens shame and self-abhorrence.[s] But let it ever be present before us, as our constraining obligation to redeem what has been lost, as far as possible, by a holy contention against sin, and by the convincing protest of consistent godliness.[t]

[r]2 Chron 33:15–17, with 22; 2 Kings 23:26
[s]Ezek 16:63
[t]Phil 2:15, 16; 1 Peter 2:12; 3:16

[5] *Eph 5:11; Elijah—1 Kings 18:18. Elisha—2 Kings 3:13. John—Matt 3:7; 14:3, 4.*
[6] *Ps 139:21, 22. See the rebuke given to a godly king, 2 Chron 19:2.*

5 *Evil men do not understand justice,*
But those who seek the LORD understand all things.

DARKENED UNDERSTANDING

Ignorance and knowledge are here contrasted and each traced to its proper source. The apostle draws the same contrast. "A natural man does not accept the things of the Spirit of God ... But he who is spiritual appraises all things."[u] This unity of statement is beautiful and instructive. "The two Testaments, like our two eyes, mutually enlighten us, and assist each other," said Serle (*Horoe Solitarioe*, vol. 1, 585).

[u] 1 Cor 2:14, 15

Evil men do not understand justice.[v] They do not know the true standard of right and wrong, the true way to God, or the end of God's dealings with them. Their ignorance is willful.[w] "Being darkened in their understanding ... *because of the hardness of their heart* ... Men loved the darkness rather than light; for their deeds were evil." They "substitute darkness for light and light for darkness."[x] The most distinguished scholar is a fool in *understanding justice;* and, unless he is humbled by the consciousness of his ignorance, and seeks light from above, he will perish in gross darkness. What a curse are learning and intellect without a humble heart!

[v] Ps 82:5; Jer 4:22

[w] Job 21:4

[x] Eph 4:18; John 3:19; Isa 5:20

Sometimes knowledge, no less than ignorance, hinders a right *understanding.* Where the knowledge of the truth goes before or beyond the power of it, the mind is often perplexed with difficulties, which the less intelligent, but more simple, escapes. When knowledge stands in the place of faith; when man reasons, instead of submitting to divine teaching; knowledge abused becomes a positive hindrance to a correct understanding. Nothing is more revolting to our evil nature, than the study of Scripture, with an earnest and sincere desire to follow its light and teaching.

An undisciplined imagination is a great hindrance to spiritual judgment. But turn it in the right direction and it will give vivid understanding of divine things, clothing the picture with brilliant but truthful coloring. Within its own province, a consecrated imagination can be a valuable handmaid to the gospel. But a ray of faith is better than a rainbow of fancy. The picture, if it is not closely connected to reality, fades away without permanent influence. But even the feeblest faith, grounded on the fundamentals of the gospel, proves steadfast and enduring, even when overcome by natural and intellectual power, and "the whole head is sick, and the whole heart faint."

THE MYSTERIES OF LOVE

But pride fastens upon every faculty of man. And this is the general cause: the source of light is despised.[y] So "there is none who *understands,*" because "there is none who seeks for God."[7] *They that seek the Lord,* babes though they may be in intellect, and ignorant in worldly things—shall have an accurate *understanding of all things* profitable, such as no natural man can attain.[z] The words "are straightforward to him who *understands,* and right to those who find knowledge."[a] Many things, dark to human reason, are simplified to humility.[b] The harmony of the divine attributes staggers reason and can only be apprehended by humble faith. "In thinking of the justice of the Deity" (as a reclaimed infidel, De La Barpe—the French poet and philosopher—describes his own conflict) man "is at first ready to doubt his [God's] compassion. But the gospel answers him by the voice of an Apostle—'God so loved the world' that 'He spared not His own Son, but delivered Him up for us all'—It is then that the penitent sinner apprehends this awesome mystery. His proud and blind reason had rejected it. His humble and contrite heart profoundly feels it. He believes because he loves; because he is grateful; because he sees all the goodness of the Creator proportioned to the miseries of the creature. Oh my God! all thy mysteries are mysteries of love, and therefore are they indeed divine."[8]

[y] AV—Isa 1:5; Ps 10:4

[z] Ps 25:9, 12; 119:98–100, 130; Matt 11:25

[a] Prov 8:9

[b] Ps 25:14, with Prov 24:7

Again—God is working in the spring of hard work, not of inactivity. Man works, but under the Master-worker. He is free, but under the free-making Spirit, giving him a will for the service. Thus, while active, he is kept depen-

[7] *Ps 14:2; Rom 3:11. "Wickedness," Bishop Taylor justly observes, "corrupts a man's reasoning, gives him false principles, and evil measuring of things"*—Sermon before University of Dublin. *"I regard it as a fundamental error in the study of Divinity," remarks Professor Franke, "for any one to persuade himself, that he can study divinity properly without the Holy Spirit. As long as he remains in this error all labor is lost on him"*—Lect. Paron. *p, 184. "A grain of true faith is more estimable than a mass of mere historical knowledge"*—Ib. Idea Studiosi Theologioe. *"A man may as soon read the letter of Scripture without eyes, as properly understand their mysteries without grace"—Bishop* BEVERIDGE.

[8] *Quoted in* SHEPPARD'S Thoughts on Devotion, *pp. 308–310.*

dent.[c] He works with deeper humility and more assured confidence.[d] This is a mystery to reason. But they that seek the Lord understand it. Practical experience shows it to them. Again—*how dark are the Lord's ways to man's proud reason!* Hard arrangement of events! A world of sorrow! But the child of God, seeking to know the end, *understands* them all to be "loving kindness and truth."[e] Isn't it the sharp trial, to probe the wound; the bitterness, to wean from the creature comfort; the burden, to prove "the perseverance and the faith of the saints"; the sifting, to separate the chaff from the wheat; the furnace, to purify the gold? In these ways, seeking *the Lord* expounds the mysteries of providence and grace! We are neither tripped by the stones, perplexed by the course of events, nor discouraged because of the length and weariness of the way. Those who desire the light shall have it.[f] To those who improve it, more shall be given.[g]

[c]Ps 119:4, 5, 8, 10, 32, 173
[d]Phil 2:12, 13
[e]James 5:11, with Ps 25:10; Rev 13:10
[f]John 7:17
[g]Matt 13:12; 25:29

THE HEART'S REAL PRAYER

But—I cannot seek—that is—I cannot pray." Nor can you do anything right of yourself. But does this discharge you from the obligation? Does it not often mean—if we would be honest—"I don't care for the blessing." But suppose the confession to be sincere—"I cannot pray." Then do as you are taught. Carry this confession to the Lord. Repeat it again and again upon your knees. Don't let inability be laziness, but faith. There is not one of the Lord's people, who doesn't understand the complaint. The confession of your utter helplessness is most profitable, as confirming the divine testimony.[h] Yet remember the help provided for weakness and ignorance.[i] If you cannot pray *as you would, pray as you can. Desire—sincere and supreme*—is the heart's real prayer, God's own work upon the soul.[9] Is this plain? Wait in the constant use of the means. Be found in the way.[j] "Light is sown," and the seed in God's best time will bring the harvest.[k] No one fails to make progress who is really in earnest. It is a grand mistake to suppose that some impression must be felt as the authorization to seek. The only true authorization you need is the free invitation

[h]2 Cor 3:5
[i]Rom 8:26
[j]Isa 64:5
[k]Ps 97:11

[9] *Ps 38:9; Isa 26:8, 9. See Homer's fine description, "Prayers, the daughters of Jove"—perhaps the most remarkable view of prayer to be found in heathen literature—as Cowper in his Notes writes—"well worthy of observation, considering where it is found"—Il. I. 502–514.*

and promise of the gospel. You must come, if at all, as a sinner, not as a saint; as you are, not as you would be; now, not waiting for some better time or preparation; seeking your fitness in Christ, not in yourself. And then plead His promise—"the one who comes to Me I will certainly not cast out."[l] Tell Him that you are come on the ground of this promise, and to claim the fulfillment of it—"Remember the word to Thy servant, in which Thou hast made me hope."[m] This must prevail. "He cannot deny Himself."[n]

[l]John 6:37
[m]Ps 119:49
[n]2 Tim 2:13

But if *as yet* you cannot come that boldly, don't brood over your state. Ask for divine teaching to understand, and divine grace to follow, the light given. You don't need any depth of learning, or any extraordinary inspiration. Simplicity, humility, diligence, will bring the unction "from the Holy One, and you all know."[o] In God's best time, the heart is given, as well as the mind. The senses are "trained to discern good and evil."[p] All is light, because the creative word has been given anew—" 'Let there be light'; and there was light."[q] Are Christians then to be despised as fools? They are the most intelligent people in this world. Established at Wisdom's gate, their religion is divine wisdom; and "Wisdom is vindicated of all her children."[r]

[o]1 John 2:20
[p]Heb 5:14
[q]Gen 1:3; 2 Cor 4:6
[r]Luke 7:35; Prov 8:34

6 *Better is the poor who walks in his integrity,*
Than he who is crooked though he be rich.

THE BLESSINGS OF THE POOR

This Proverb is repeated[10] for its valuable instruction. One part of the comparison, implied before, is here expressed—*though he be rich.* Before, he was described as *perverse in speech.* Now, a deeper trait of character is here given—*perverse* in his ways, or his principles. This is one of those paradoxes that sometimes cause even God's children to stumble.[s] *A man may walk in his integrity,* and yet be *poor.* He may be *crooked in his ways,* and be *rich.* And yet the poor man, with all his external disadvantages, *is better;* more honorable, happier, more useful *than the rich,* with all his earthly splendor.[11]

[s]Ps 73:2–16

[10] *Prov 19:1. the Septuagint translation of this verse, 28:6, is—"A poor man is better than a rich lie"—the abstract for the concrete. Comp. Prov 19:22; Ps 62:9.*

[11] *There is a fine passage from Cicero, which it is difficult to translate without losing much of its spirit—"A contented mind is as good as an estate. Frugality is itself a revenue. To be*

To come to a solid scriptural decision on this point is of great practical importance. For if we are dazzled with the glitter of this world's glory, we shall reverse the golden rule;[t] and "seek" *first* the world as our grand object: and the "kingdom" of God, the interests of the soul, the stake of eternity, will occupy only the second place; that is—virtually they will be crowded out.

[t]Matt 6:33

This is a just balance, however opposite it may be to common opinion. Dishonesty is the besetting temptation of *the poor.*[u] Yet in spite of this temptation, *he walks in his integrity.* Is there not a glory around his poverty, infinitely beyond the vain show of this world? *The rich man is crooked in his ways;* "a double-minded man," endeavoring to walk in two ways:[12] outwardly following godliness, inwardly deceit; pretending to go one way, walking in another. Who can trust him?

[u]Prov 30:9

So far then as concerns character, the comparison is in favor of *the poor.* As regards condition—Who would not prefer the lot of Elijah, subsisting upon his barrel of meal, to Ahab in all the glory of his throne?[v] Who does not see a dignity in Paul standing at man's judgment bar that throws the worldly rank of his judges into utter insignificance?[w]

[v]1 Kings 17:13–15, with 21:1–4, 19

[w]Acts 24:24–26; 26:27–29; 2 Tim 4:16, 17

But the truth is of general application. Outward superiority only affects our state before God, increasing proportionately our responsibilities.[x] How many will wish that they had lived and died in obscure poverty with "a blameless conscience both before God and before men"[y] rather than have been entrusted with riches.

[x]Luke 12:48

[y]Acts 24:16

7 *He who keeps the law is a discerning* [AV—*wise*] *son,*
But he who is a companion of gluttons humiliates his father.

satisfied with one's lot is to be really and infallibly rich. If landed possessions are most highly valued by shrewd judges of human affairs, as a property, which is least liable to injury; how inestimably precious must true virtue be. It cannot be snatched from us by force or by fraud; cannot be damaged by shipwreck or by fire; [*it cannot be changed by*] *tempests or political disturbances! They alone, who are endowed with this treasure, can be said to be truly rich. They alone possess what is fruitable and durable. What is allotted to them they deem sufficient. They covet nothing. They really want nothing. They require nothing. The wicked and the avaricious, on the contrary, so far from being rich, are in reality miserably poor; inasmuch as they have no certain treasure, and are always impatient, for some addition to their stores, never satisfied with their present possessions"*—Paradox 6:3.

[12] *Hebrew perverse in two ways, James 1:8.*

WHO IS A WISE SON?

Keeping the law is national wisdom and honor.[z] How valuable is that training which leads young people, under the Lord's blessing, to make this happy personal choice.[a] Such are obviously taught of God and guided by His spirit into true wisdom. For suppose a son of polished manners and intellectual gifts, yet without right principle; or another son of moderate ability, in a humble walk of life, who is yet deeply and practically godly—would it be hard to determine which is the *wise son,* bringing honor to his father's name?[b] Yet how often is *humiliation* instead of honor, the father's bitter experience. For how is his name blotted, when the depraved son, seeking his own gratification, chooses the *companionship of* the ungodly, and soon becomes one of them![c] Young man! in your noisy fun-making have you found solid, enduring peace?[d] Let the man of God direct you in "keeping [your] way pure—by keeping it according to Thy word."[e] Let his choice be thine—"I am a *companion,*" not of gluttons, but "of all those who fear Thee, and of those who keep Thy precepts."[f] Meet the temptations of your former *companions* with a firm protest—"Depart from me, evildoers, that I may observe the commandments of my God."[g] Here is honor to your father, happiness to yourself, usefulness to the church, fitness for heaven.

[z]Deut 4:6
[a]Isa 56:6, 7
[b]Prov 23:24
[c]Prov 19:26; 23:19–22; 29:3, 15; Luke 25:13
[d]Prov 14:13; Eccl 2:2; 7:6
[e]Ps 119:9, 11
[f]Ps 119:63
[g]Ps 119:115

Parents! Do we shrink from this overwhelming *shame?* Let us more earnestly, more prayerfully cultivate that wise and holy training of our children, which is God's appointed plan; and which, however long or severely He may try our faith, He will not fail to honor in His own chosen time.[h]

[h]Prov 22:6

8 *He who increases his wealth by interest and usury,*
Gathers it for him who is gracious to the poor.

GOD'S SECRET PROVIDENCE

What a deadly curse it is to be under the spell of covetousness! Everything that is "true . . . honorable . . . right . . . pure . . . lovely . . . of good report," is sacrificed to this idolatrous principle. No laws can bind it. God had fenced in the rights of his poor people with solemn and plain obligations.[i] And He will not suffer their rights to be

[i]Phil 4:8; Exod 22:24; Lev 25:36; Deut 23:19, 20; Ezek 18:13

regarded lightly. "I know," says the man of God, "that the Lord will maintain the cause of the afflicted, and justice for the poor."[j] As a God of fairness, how often does He make selfishness punish itself, and even to turn to the advantage of the oppressed.[k] Ill-gotten gains are a dangerous and uncertain possession.[l] A man labors for himself, and his harvest falls into better hands; not that he planned it that way; but "it is brought about that way through God's secret Providence," said Diodati.[m] In this, as in every view, godliness "holds promise for the present life."[n] It brings "great gain when accompanied by contentment,"[o] and restrains those excessive desires for wealth, which ruin all right principles, and "plunge men into ruin and destruction."[p] A man's life consisteth not in the "abundance . . . of his possessions."[q] Why should we seek to *increase our wealth* by unjust gain, when we have our Father's promise—"All these things shall be added to you"[r]—when His divine power has given unto us all things pertaining unto life and godliness?[s]

[j]Ps 140:12
[k]Prov 13:22; Job 27:13, 16, 17
[l]Prov 10:2; 21:6
[m]Eccl 2:26
[n]1 Tim 4:8
[o]1 Tim 6:6
[p]1 Tim 6:9
[q]Luke 12:15
[r]Matt 6:33
[s]2 Peter 1:3

9 *He who turns away his ear from listening to the law,*
Even his prayer is an abomination.

REJECTION OF GOD AND ITS CONSEQUENCES

This does not mark the frailty, infirmity, or temptation that too often interrupts *the listening to the law* and dampens attentive interest; or even the occasional rebellion against God's commands. The case described is that habitual and obstinate rejection of God, that despises his commands, and refuses the instruction of his ministers. It's an awful thing that there should be such a rebel. Yet, this is how the ungodly, while they take God's "covenant" into their mouth, "hate discipline," and cast His "words behind" them.[t] Why, even in His church "they come to you as people come, and they sit before you as My people, but they do the lustful desires expressed by their mouth."[u] If such a *one turns his ear away from God's law* every *prayer* that he may offer in time of distress, the Lord will regard as an *abomination*.[v] It's a fearful thought, that, however showy and smoothly fashioned his prayer may be to impress men, in the sight of God it is wisely cursed. The door of audience is justly closed against the presumptuous hypocrite. "Great reason that

[t]Ps 50:16, 17
[u]Ezek 33:31, 32
[v]Prov 1:28, 29; Zech 7:11–13

God shall refuse to hear him, who refused to hear God," said Bishop Reynolds.[w] And what if his language now—"Depart from us!"—should be taken out of his mouth at the great day, as the seal of his everlasting doom![x]

[w] Hos 14:8

[x] Job 21:14; 22:17, with Matt 25:41

What a strange contradiction that this open rejection of God should be connected with any form or semblance of religion! And yet how often does the self-deceiver try to make up for disobeying God's plain command by performing some outward duty. Israel presented "the multitude of sacrifices" as a price for the neglect of practical obligations. "Worthless offerings ... incense" that was "an abomination."[y] Often now *praying* at home is an excuse for *turning away from hearing the law* in God's own house. Such *prayer* is solemnly declared to be *abomination.* Often also is the law of love and even of solemn duty evaded, to maintain a profession of godliness, hateful in God's eyes, who will bring to open shame every hypocritical service.[z] God doesn't trifle with man and, most certainly, He will not allow man to trifle with Him.

[y] Isa 1:11–15; Ps 66:18

[z] Matt 15:8

Always remember, that godliness is God's whole service; that "the wisdom from above is first pure ... without hypocrisy";[a] that to praise one holy practice at the expense of another; to decry preaching for the sake of commending prayer; is proof alike of false judgment and an unsound heart. To reject any divine command is proud will-worship; a plain proof, that the privilege has never been enjoyed. For no beggar would slight the door, where he had been used to receive his blessing. O my God! let me lie close to Thine own heart, or at Thy feet that my will may be lost in Thine, and my happiness found in a whole-hearted devotedness to Thee!

[a] James 3:17

10 *He who leads the upright astray in an evil way*
Will himself fall into his own pit,
But the blameless will inherit good.

IN THE PRESENCE OF OUR ENEMIES—GOD!

To delight in the enticing of sinners *in an evil way* is the very appearance and image of the tempter. But his chief delight, his main effort, is to *cause the upright to go astray.* No rejoicing is so great, as when a standard-bearer faints by the wayside. Because, while it shows the seducer's enmity to the truth, it supports him in his sin. Yet how fleeting is his joy! Success is his ruin. By the punishing justice of God, he often *falls into his own pit.*[b] The snare of Balaam for the people of God ended in his own ruin.[c]

[b]Prov 26:27

[c]Rev 2:14; Num 31:15, 16, with 8

The malice of Satan and his agents sets out the faithfulness of our almighty keeper. "Thou dost prepare a table before me in the presence of my enemies," who gnash their teeth at the sight.[d] Even if they succeed for a while *in leading the upright astray,* recovering mercy is in store for them;[e] and brought out of the snare in deep humiliation, *the upright,* instead of the evil meditated against them, *have good things to inherit.* What *good things* they are, can never be fully written or thought of. For "eye has not seen and ear has not heard, and which have not entered the heart of man."[f] But whatever they are—Christian—take them to yourself, claim your right, and don't be robbed of your portion. And if we *have good things to inherit,* much more we have in the future "an inheritance which is imperishable and undefiled," that no one can take from us.[g] Who shall separate us from our Father's love? "Neither death, nor life, nor angels, nor principalities . . . nor any other created thing."[h]

[d]Ps 23:5

[e]Num 31:3; Luke 22:31, 32

[f]1 Cor 2:9

[g]1 Peter 1:4

[h]Rom 8:39

11 *The rich man is wise in his own eyes,*
But the poor who has understanding sees through him.

THE MOST DIGNIFIED MAN—WHO IS HE?

To be truly wise, and *wise in our own eyes* are two things often confused, but essentially opposite. But though riches do not always bring *wisdom,*[i] *the rich man* often pretends they do, and attributes his success to his own intelligence, though he may really be simple and foolish. The apostle therefore, with a reference to this besetting temptation, directed a charge to the "rich in this present world not to be conceited."[j] The prophet brings the wealthy prince of Tyrus on the stage and shows him to us in *all* the folly of his conceit.[k] Obviously, *the rich man* has many advantages over *the poor,* in leisure and opportunities of instruction. Yet on the other hand, worldly elevation operates against him. He is shut out from many opportunities of Christian instruction.

[i]Job 32:9

[j]1 Tim 6:17

[k]Ezek 28:2

The atmosphere of flattery clouds the faculty of self-knowledge, which is the basis of true wisdom. And how natural for him to think himself as wise as his flatterers represent him; as high above his neighbors in *understanding* as in station! Hence he becomes dogmatic in his conceit, loving to display his fancied superiority in every way. Yet, as in the case of Naaman's servants,[l] the intelligent, good *understanding of a poor man may see through him,* and his superficial show. Especially when he is endued with a measure of spiritual *understanding, the poor man* may expose his superior to deserved embarrassment.[m] Indeed, there is no more dignified character in all the universe than the poor wise man. Did not the incarnate Lord honor this station supremely by taking it on himself?[n] To walk in His footsteps, in His spirit, is wisdom, honor, and happiness, infinitely beyond what this poor world of vanity can offer.

[l] 2 Kings 5:13
[m] John 9:30–34
[n] Phil 2:7

12 *When the righteous triumph, there is great glory,*
But when the wicked rise, men hide themselves.

WHAT GLORY SO GREAT!

"We are made," said *a righteous man,* "as 'the scum of the world and the dregs of all things, even until now.' "[o] Yet these are the men, who bear up the "pillars" of the state.[p] *When therefore they triumph*—when they are raised to honor—*there is great glory.*[q] The whole kingdom feels more or less the influence of this national blessing. Godliness is accepted. Men are protected in the free exercise of their religion. When "Mordecai went out from the presence of the king in royal robes of blue and white ... the city of Susa shouted and rejoiced. For the Jews there was light and gladness and joy and honor. And in ... every province ... a feast and a holiday."[r] The same result is seen in the experience of the church. When the churches "enjoyed peace" from the fiery trial, they were "built up; and, going on in the fear of the Lord and in the comfort of the Holy Spirit."[s] And what *glory is so great* as the sunshine of the enjoyment of their God!

But when the wicked rise to honor, how is this *glory* eclipsed! The people of God are removed into corners, silenced, *hidden.*[t] The light of some hundred prophets, and even of Elijah himself, was *hidden* for a while under

[o] 1 Cor 4:13
[p] Ps 75:3
[q] Prov 11:10; 29:2
[r] Esther 8:15–17
[s] Acts 9:31
[t] Acts 9:28

the tyranny of Ahab.[u] And in every age the power of *the wicked,* especially under a despotic rule, *hides* much valuable influence. Yet it *is hidden* only to the eye of sense. For of those, who "went about in sheepskins, in goatskins, being destitute . . . in deserts . . . and caves and holes in the ground," what greater *glory* could we give, than the divine inscription stamped upon them "of whom the world was not worthy"?[v]

[u] 1 Kings 17:2, 3; 18:4; 19:1–4

[v] Heb 11:37, 38; Rev 12:6

13 *He who conceals his transgressions will not prosper,*
But he who confesses and forsakes them *will find*
compassion.

VAIN COVERINGS FOR SIN

God and man each *conceal sin*; God, in free unbounded grace;[w] man, in shame and hypocrisy. The sinners here contrasted are chargeable with the same guilt. But how opposite are the remedies adopted and their many results! The contrast is not between great sins and small, but between *sins concealed, and sins confessed and forsaken. Whoso conceals* even the smallest *sin, shall not prosper. Whoso confesseth and forsaketh* even the greatest, *shall find compassion. "Love covers"* our neighbor's sins;[x] pride our own. The proud sinner naturally wishes to be thought better than he is. His sin must have some cover.[13] He must at least give it a good name.[y] He would *conceal* it, if possible, from himself; putting it out of mind; banishing all serious thoughts; stifling conviction; and then trying to persuade himself that he is happy. To escape evil consequences, a lie is resorted to.[14] Or if the facts are too plain to be denied; he says, "the worst part is unfounded. We were not in it so much as our neighbor." Ignorance, good, or at least not bad, intentions, custom, necessity, strong temptation, sudden surprise, the first offense; bodily infirmity; even the decrees of God[z]—one or more are pleaded in excuse. Or to save our honor—rather our pride—the blame must be shifted on another.[15] Even God himself is made account-

[w] Ps 85:2

[x] Prov 10:12

[y] Isa 5:20

[z] Jer 7:10

[13] *Cicero stamps* confession *of wickedness as disgraceful and dangerous. Thus does heathen morality develop the pride of depraved nature.*

[14] *Cain—Gen 4:9; Rachel—31:34, 35; Joseph's brethren—37:31–35; David—2 Sam 11:15, 25; the adulteress—Prov 30:20. Comp. Jer 2:23; Peter—Matt 26:70; Ananias and Sapphira—Acts 5:1–8. Is not this a sad tendency in children? The first offense may be trifling. But the fear of punishment induces a lie. Another lie is necessary to* conceal *the first. Every step adds to sin.*

[15] *Adam and Eve—Gen 3:12, 13. Comp. Job 31:33; Aaron—Exod 32:21–24; Saul—1 Sam 15:20, 21; Pilate—Matt 27:24–26.*

able—a secret but daring charge, carrying with it its own self-contradiction. Indignantly he challenges the proof and lays the sin at the right door.[a] More commonly, but most wrongfully, it is laid upon Satan. The most of his power is that he is a tempter. And no claim could he have ever established, had not we willingly sold ourselves to his service. Our father Adam—again—must bear the burden. Must our "teeth [be] set on edge" for the "sour grapes" which he ate?[b] Must the unborn children be held responsible for the inheritance which their father lost? But it was the nature that sinned, of which we are a component part. We were in his "loins"[c] at the time, and therefore we share his responsibility. Our own personal sin has approved the deed by our own free and repeated consent. All these attempted transfers are vain coverings. Conscience bears witness to the truth that no man takes harm but from himself.

But even this admitted—man with ceaseless originality still attempts a frame *to conceal his sin.* Some supposed good deeds are put forth as a compensation.[d] And by balancing good and evil respectively against each other, he hopes to establish some weight in his favor. Yet all these fig leaf coverings[e] for his nakedness only show his determination to hold his sin; and his pride of heart, which would rather hide it from God himself, than submit to receive free mercy as a self-condemned sinner.

These attempts however to *conceal sin will not prosper.* The voice of an offended God summoned Adam from his hiding place to receive his sentence.[f] "The voice" of Abel's blood cried "from the ground," and the murderer became "a vagrant and a wanderer on the earth."[g] Conscience lashed Joseph's brethren with the sin of bygone days.[h] Saul's *concealing his sin* cost him his kingdom.[i] "The leprosy of Naaman shall cleave to [Gehazi and his] descendants forever."[j] The proud accusers of their fellow-sinner were convicted by their own conscience.[k] "There is no darkness or deep shadow where the workers of iniquity may hide themselves."[l] Their darkest deed is open to the scrutiny of an all-seeing God, and set "in the light of Thy presence,"[m] to "be proclaimed upon the housetops" before the assembled world.[n]

This unsuccessful attempt to cover sin, while it adds to the guilt,[o] is full of misery.[p] The love of sin struggles with

[a] Isa 50:1; James 1:13
[b] Ezek 18:2
[c] Heb 7:10
[d] Mic 6:6, 7
[e] Gen 3:7
[f] Gen 3:9
[g] Gen 4:10–12
[h] Gen 42:21
[i] 1 Sam 15:21, 23
[j] 2 Kings 5:27
[k] John 8:9
[l] Job 34:22
[m] Job 34:21; Ps 90:8
[n] Luke 12:2, 3; Eccl 12:14; 1 Cor 4:5
[o] Isa 30:1
[p] Isa 28:20

the power of conscience. The door of access to God is barred.[q] Christian confidence is clouded;[r] and, unless God in His mercy intervenes, it must end in the sting of the never-dying "worm." The *concealing* of the disease rules out the possibility of a cure. Only the penitent confessor can be the pardoned sinner.

[q]Ps 66:18
[r]Ps 32:3, 4; Isa 66:24

THE ONE TRUE COVERING FOR SIN

Long indeed is the struggle, before every false cover is cut off; before the heartless general confession—"We are all sinners"—is exchanged for the deep-fat personal acknowledgment, "give glory to the Lord . . . Truly, have I sinned against the Lord . . . and this is what I did . . . Behold I am insignificant; What can I reply to Thee? I lay my hand on my mouth."[s] But glorious is the divine victory over pride and sullenness, when this first act of repentance, this first step of return,[t] is heartily accomplished. God doesn't need confession for His own information. But He demands it for our good. It brings no claim on His mercy. But it opens the way for the reception of it. Christ has fully satisfied the claims of justice. But the claims must be acknowledged in the humble acceptance of the benefit. The mercy is ready; but the sinner must draw it out—"Only acknowledge your iniquity."[u] Our yearning Father is waiting for this moment, that He may have "compassion."[v] There is no further keeping of anger. *He shall have compassion,* instant reconciliation.[16] Words may be few, while the heart is full. With David it was but a single sentence; but the closest workings of his heart witnessed to the enlargement and straightforwardness of his sorrow.[17] So *man confesses* his debt; God crosses it out from His book; and sweet is the penitent's song—"Blessed is he whose transgression is forgiven."[w] The dying thief confesses, and the condemned criminal is crowned with life eternal.[x]

[s]Jos 7:19, 20; Job 40:4
[t]Luke 15:17, 18
[u]Jer 3:13
[v]Luke 15:20; Hos 5:15
[w]Ps 32:1
[x]Luke 23:43

But we must not overlook the distinctive feature of this *confession.* It is not that of Pharaoh, extorted on the rack;[y] or of Saul, and Judas,[z] the stinging of remorse; or of the Pharisees and Sadducees,[a] mere formal profession; or of the harlot,[b] a cover for sin. Penitent faith *confesses* in the

[y]Exod 9:27, 34
[z]1 Sam 24:16, 17; 26:3, 4; Matt 27:4, 5
[a]Matt 3:7
[b]Prov 7:14

[16] *Ps 32:5. Comp. similar examples, 2 Chron 33:12, 13; Jer 31:18–20; Jon 3:5–10; Luke 15:21–24, 23:40–43. See also the promises, Lev 26:40–42; 2 Chron 7:14; Job 33:27, 28: Isa 1:16–18, 55:7; Ezek 18:21, 22, 1 John 1:9.*
[17] *2 Sam 12:13, with Ps 51. See also his tender dread of* covering sins. *Ps 139:1, 23, 24.*

[c]Lev 16:21

act of laying the hand upon the great sacrifice,[c] and hence draws strength of purpose to *forsake* all that has been here *confessed.* For awhile the hypocrite confesses with forsaking (remember Pharaoh and Saul), the hearty *forsaking* is here the best proof of the sincere *confessing.*

[d]Job 40:4; 42:6; Ezek 16:63

[e]Ps 25:11, with Luke 18:11. Comp. Isa 43:24–26

[f]Jer 1:20

And this first act of the penitent is matured into the daily habit of the saint. The further we advance, the deeper will be the tone of *confession.*[d] The moment sin is seen to be sin, let it be laid on Christ. Every moment of unconfessed sin adds to its burden and guilt. The thought of a nature estranged from God: a heart full of corruption; sins of youth and age; before and after conversion; against light and conviction, knowledge and love; the sins of our very confessions, their defilement, coldness, and too often self-righteous tendency; all supply abundant material for abasing acknowledgment. Plead the greatness, not the smallness of our sin.[e] Never regard any sin so trifling, as not to need the *immediate* application of the blood of atonement. Genuine conviction gives no rest, until, by the believing application of this remedy, the peace of God is firmly fixed in the conscience. As Bunyan so accurately pictured, it was not at the wicket gate, but at the sign of the cross, that Christian found the grave of sin. Here it is lost, forgotten, never found.[f]

SORROW FULL OF JOY

[g]Josh 7:1

[h]1 Sam 15:20

[i]Mark 6:17–20; 9:43–48

[j]Matt 12:43–45

[k]Job 34:32

[l]Isa 55:7

This evangelical humiliation lays the only solid ground for practical godliness. It is a sorrow full of joy, and not less full of holiness. No Achan will be reserved;[g] no Agag spared;[h] no right hand or right eye favored.[i] It will not be "the unclean spirit [going] out" and returning to his house with sevenfold influence;[j] or the man, who leaves his home, but *forsakes* it not, all his heart and joy being still there. Here the *forsaking* will be without the thought of returning, with the fixed determination never to return.[k] It will not be the exchange of one path in the broad road for another more attractive; but the giving up of the whole road with all its bypaths. The inner principles as well as the outer walk; "the unrighteous ... thoughts," no less than "the wicked ... ways" will be *forsaken* heartily and forever.[l]

14 *How blessed is the man who fears always,*
But he who hardens his heart will fall into calamity.

This Proverb fitly follows the last. Confession precedes, godly *fear* follows, the reception of mercy, as the end for which it is given, and the proof of its reception.[m] It implies no uncertainty of our safety; but, by guarding us against fresh wounds of conscience, it more firmly maintains our confidence. If we believe and rejoice in the Lord as our "sun," we would always *fear Him* as "a consuming fire."[n] This fear is our security.[o]

We may here profitably glance at some Christian paradoxes. *How is happiness to be found in constant fear?* Is fear to be the atmosphere or the spirit of a child of God? Where love makes "perfect," there can be no unquiet tremblings or doubtings of heart.[p] But godly fear preserves the sunshine and seals our special acceptance.[q] We walk with our Father in holy watchfulness and peace. Again—we readily conceive the happiness of trust.[r] How do we link with it the happiness of fear? So far from fear being contrary to faith, it is a component part of it, or at least its inseparable addition;[s] the discipline, that preserves it from presumption. Faith without fear is self-confidence and self-delusion. No—the assurance of our "stand only by ... faith" is balanced by an instant and most needful exercise of *fear.*[t] Who grasped a more triumphant confidence than Paul? Yet without presuming upon a long and consistent profession, self-distrust, watchfulness, and diligence established his confidence. "If there be truth in the Christian's assurance, not sin itself can disappoint him, it is true. But it is no less true, that if he does not fear sin, there is no truth in his assurance," said Leighton.[18] Instead of being afraid to mix faith and fear, we should be afraid that they will be separated. Again—the righteous is bold as a lion;[u] yet *he fears always.* But Christian courage, though opposed to slavish fear, forms the very essence of godly *fear.* The three confessors were bold before the Babylonish ruler; yet they so *feared* to offend God, that "the furnace of blazing fire" was the better alternative in their eyes.[v]

[m] Ps 130:4
[n] Ps 84:11, with Heb 12:28, 29
[o] Hab 3:16
[p] 1 John 4:18
[q] Isa 66:2
[r] Prov 16:20
[s] Heb 11:7
[t] Rom 11:20
[u] Verse 1
[v] Dan 3:16–18; Gen 39:9; Neh 5:15

[18] *On 1 Peter 1:17. How many have no other idea of fear, than as excluding the certainty of acceptance; whereas its true influence is not fluctuation in doubt, but carefulness in preservation.*

So is holy *fear* every way identified with happiness. It is a fear of reverence, not of bondage; of caution, not of distrust; of diligence, not of despondency. In proportion as we are raised above tormenting fear, we cherish a deep reverence of the majesty and holiness of God, a childlike fear of displeasure, a jealousy over our motives, desires, and the risings of our evil tendencies, and an abhorrence and shrinking, not only from sin, but from the temptations and occasions of sin. Well does the Christian know the value of this conservative principle; as far removed from legality as from presumption. One, whose mournful experience gives additional weight to His words, warns us, as "sojourners" in a world of evil, and with hearts so often betraying our steps, to pass our time "*in fear*."[w] Though we are surely saved we are also "with difficulty . . . *saved*."[x] Though there be no uncertainty in the end, there is appalling difficulty along the way—"Let him who thinks he stands take heed lest he fall."[y] The man who stands in his own security requires the caution more than any. Guard against an unheeding confidence. Keep the sentinel at the door. Watch for the enemy at every turn. Suspect a snake in every path, a snare in every creature. Feed with fear.[z] "Rejoice with trembling." Yes—"work out your own salvation with fear and trembling."[a] None are so established in grace, but in unwatchfulness they may fall into the greatest sin. Live then in constant fear of yourself. This godly *fear* proves self-knowledge, preserves from self-confidence, produces self-distrust. In wariness against a fall we are most likely to stand. If weakness is our frailty, the consciousness of it is our strength. "When I am weak, then I am strong."[b] The importance of this principle will be seen by the contrast with its opposite. *Fear* keeps the heart tender, and the soul safe. Security and presumption *harden* the sinner, and he *falls into calamity*. Pharaoh's *hardness of heart*, and its consequences, were but the bravery and ruin of the devil.[c] When David's self-indulgence and carelessness had swept away his tenderness, he fearfully *fell into sin*.[d] The latter history of his wise son. It sounds the same awful warning.[e] Peter's fearlessness, though the fruit of ignorance rather than willfulness, almost destroyed him.[f]

[w] 1 Peter 1:17
[x] 1 Peter 4:18
[y] 1 Cor 10:12
[z] Contrast Judg 12
[a] Ps 2:11; Phil 2:12
[b] 2 Cor 12:10
[c] Exod 14:5–8, 23
[d] 2 Sam 11:2
[e] 1 Kings 11:1–11
[f] Matt 26:33–35, 41, 74

A deep sensitivity to sin is a special mercy. To think what it is; what it may be; that, indulged only in thought, without the Lord's restraint, it will end in apostasy. Dare we trifle with it? The man, who takes liberties with it, thinking it too harmless for eternal punishment, and promises himself peace by way of his own heart—why, the terrible horrors of his case could hardly be described even by a voice from heaven. Every word of God is a thunderbolt leveled at him.[g] Scarcely less pitiable is the man, who makes light of his eternal state; living without prayer; so much better in his own eyes than his more ungodly neighbor; and fully satisfied with a mere external preparation for eternity. Don't forget—professing Christian—we may be strong in confidence, only because we are sleeping in delusion, or *hardened* in insensibility. From all the mischief of self-ignorance and "hardness of heart,"[h] O Lord, deliver us!

[g]Prov 29:1; Deut 29:19, 20

[h]Matt 19:8

15 Like *a roaring lion and a rushing bear*
Is a wicked ruler over a poor people.
16 *A leader who is a great oppressor lacks understanding,*
But *he who hates unjust gain will prolong* his *days.*

A godly ruler is to a land the clear sunshine of an unclouded morning; the fruitfulness of the springing grass after the rain.[i] But what a curse is *a wicked ruler,* where arbitrary tyranny takes the place of right! We might as well live among the savage wild beasts of the forest. *The lion roaring* for the prey, and *the bear rushing* in hunger are appropriate emblems of this tyrant *over a poor people.*[j] "No sentiment of pity softens his [heart]. No principle of justice regulates his conduct," said Paxton.[19] "Complaint only provokes further demands. Resistance kindles his unfeeling heart into savage fury. *Poor* and miserable indeed are the people . . . under his misrule."

[i]2 Sam 23:3, 4

[j]Prov 29:2; Zeph 3:3; 2 Tim 4:17

And so, indeed, injustice is allowed to reign upon a wide scale. A whole nation is afflicted by the ruthless tyranny of one man. Perhaps the scourge extends from the *wicked ruler* downward, through all its various levels, to the petty fawning favorites, delegated with the sword of power. The wise man, in thinking about all the

[19] Nat. Hist. of Script. *p. 333. Comp. 1 Kings 21:1–7; Neh 5:15.*

material that makes up a world of vanity, couldn't help but take this desolating curse into account. And so bitter was the view to his own mind, that he would have preferred even death itself or non-existence, to the alternative of having to look at the world's sorrows without being able to help.[k]

[k]Eccl 4:1–3

The leader who oppresses may justly be charged with *lacking understanding.*[l] Even if he had established a previous reputation for wisdom, yet abused power, with all its alluring corruptions, is enough to cause him to lose sound judgment. The struggle of the love of rule with the better principle often shakes the sound balance, till step by step his conduct loses all traits of wisdom, and exhibits a man—if not wholly deprived of understanding, yet without what is closely related to it because he is swayed by the tumult of passion. As one proof of his *lack of understanding,* his foolish choice of wicked officers often alienates the affections of his people from his person, probably to the shortening of his rule.[m] And so . . . his perverted power fearfully backfires upon himself.

[l]Isa 3:12

[m]1 Kings 12:12–19

Widely opposite is the character of a considerate ruler, *hating unjust gain,* and living only for the good of his people.[n] He may usually be expected to *prolong his days.* "He may hope to reign long and happily, having his throne erected in the hearts of his subjects," said Scott.

[n]Exod 18:21

What need for rulers to seek for understanding that they may rule as the fathers of their people![o] And what cause have we to bless God for our mild and happy government; preserved as we are from wicked despots,[p] who would not stop at any tyranny that might serve their selfish purposes![20]

[o]1 Kings 3:6–9

[p]1 Sam 22:17–19; Dan 3:6, 19

17 *A man who is laden with the guilt of human blood*
Will be a fugitive until death; let no one support him.

CAPITAL PUNISHMENT: THE MURDERER MURDERS HIMSELF

The first law against the murderer must not be broken

[20] *Of Tyndal's celebrated work—"The obedience of a Christian Man"—Henry VIII declared—"This book is for me, and for all kings to read." He probably only referred to those parts that he might use to accredit his own selfish greed. Well would it have been, had he pondered such important instruction as—"The king is but a servant to execute the law of God, and not to rule after his own imagination! He is brought to the throne—'to minister unto, and to serve his brethren, and must not think, that his subjects were made to minister unto his lusts.' "*

down. It was in force from the beginning. "It was enacted and published before him, out of whose loins the whole world after the flood was to be repeopled; to show that it was not meant for a national or temporary [practice], but for a universal and perpetual law," said Bishop Sanderson *(Sermon on Prov 24:10–12)*. The reason given for the command confirms its universal obligation. To commit murder is to destroy "the image of God" and that is high treason against God Himself.[q] Again did God declare his mind in the Levitical law. No satisfaction must be taken for the murderer. Another reason is given—"Blood pollutes the land," and only the murderer's blood can cleanse it.[r] Yes—even the heathen judged this awful transgressor to be under divine vengeance.[s] The death therefore of the murderer is an imperative obligation. The love for mankind, that protests against all capital punishment, is not honest love. (Can a man pretend to be more merciful than God?) Pity is misplaced here. The murderer therefore of his brother is his own murderer. He shall flee, hurried by his own horror of conscience,[t] by the sword of justice,[u] or by the certain judgment of God.[v] *Let no one support him.* Let God's *law* take its course.

[q] Gen 9:6
[r] Num 35:33
[s] Acts 28:4
[t] Deut 19:13
[u] 1 Kings 2:32; Exod 21:14; 2 Kings 11:15
[v] 1 Kings 21:19; 22:38; 2 Kings 9:33–37

Yet we must not cast off concern for his soul. Visiting the cell of the condemned is a special exercise of mercy. While we bow to the stern justice of the great law giver, joyous indeed it is to bring to the sinner, who is under the sentence of the law, the free forgiveness of the gospel; not canceling his sin, but showing the overabounding of grace above the abounding of sin.[w]

[w] Rom 5:20

18 *He who walks blamelessly will be delivered,*
But he who is crooked will fall all at once.

THE SALVATION OF THE UPRIGHT

This contrast was already considered.[x] The Proverb itself has been given. The security of the upright, "he walks securely," noted before, is here included in his salvation. The hypocrite's known[y] ruin is here set out as complete—*at once.*[z]

[x] Verse 6
[y] Prov 10:9
[z] Prov 24:16; 29:1

This *blameless walk* will show itself in extreme carefulness; in all doubtful points keeping on the safer side; not venturing upon a precipice, when we can walk upon

[a]Gen 17:1
[b]Gen 28:17
[c]Heb 11:1, 27

level ground. This is most certainly Christian perfection—Walking before God.[a] There is no need for Jacob's vision[b] to realize God's presence. "Faith" sees that which is invisible.[c] This life may seem to miss much temporal advantage. But what if the *upright* is not rich, honorable, esteemed? "If God shall not cease to be; if He will not let go the reins; if his word cannot deceive—*he that walketh uprightly* doth proceed upon sure grounds," said Barrow (*Sermons*. Ps 140:13). He is saved. This one blessing includes all. It is the substance of time and of eternity. Everything else is shadow and vanity. To dwell in the presence of God; in the sunshine of His countenance;[d] in the light and gladness of His joy,[e] and at length in His unclouded glory[f]—that is the salvation *of the upright*.[g] Christian! would you part with all this even for kingdoms? What earthly comforts could be substituted for it? This is everything!

[d]Ps 11:7
[e]Ps 97:11
[f]Ps 15:1, 2; Rev 14:5
[g]Ps 125:4

Any lack of uprightness will bring the child of God under the rod. *But he that is crooked in his way will fall at once.*[h] His double-mindedness, his vain attempt to "serve two masters," only bring him to shame.[i] Even when we walk in the highest conscious integrity, what need we have to still cry out, "Redeem me, and be gracious to me!"[j]

[h]Ps 125:5
[i]Matt 6:24
[j]Ps 26:11

19 *He who tills his land will have plenty of food,*
But he who follows empty pursuits *will have*
poverty in plenty.

LABOR—SOURCE OF HAPPINESS

This Proverb also has been given before.[k] Such memories and hearts as ours need "line on line" in the enforcement of practical obligation.[l] Though labor became our lot as punishment for sin,[m] still there is such blessing in it, that, should we be deprived of it, our greatest source of happiness would quickly diminish. Man was not born to be a stone without energy; or a machine to be moved by mere passive force. Our true happiness is active dependence. Constant, persevering effort is the means of working it out fruitfully. The earth "both thorns and thistles it shall grow for you." But *he who tills his land will have plenty of food.*[n] The blessing

[k]Prov 12:11
[l]Isa 28:13
[m]Gen 3:19
[n]Gen 3:18, with Prov 14:4; 27:23–27

comes, not by miracle, to encourage laziness; but in use of means, to stimulate effort.

The contrast to this *plenty of food* is *great poverty*. The experiences of the prodigal are a warning beacon. In his father's house, doubtlessly taking part in meaningful activity, he had "more than enough bread." But when, in his waywardness, he left his *plenty,* and followed after vain persons, soon he found himself in *great poverty,* "I am dying here with hunger!"[o] Idleness is a sin against God, against our neighbor, against ourselves. "Not lagging behind in diligence, fervent in spirit, serving the Lord"—is the rule of prosperity in this world's concerns; much more in the momentous concerns of eternity.[p]

[o] Luke 15:17
[p] Rom 12:11; Eccl 9:10

20 *A faithful man will abound with blessings,*
But he who makes haste to be rich will not go unpunished.

The study of the contrast shows the definite meaning of the terms. *A faithful man* is opposed, not to the rich, but—mark the careful accuracy—to him *who makes haste to be rich.* A man may be rich by the blessing of God.[q] But he hurries to be *rich* by his own covetousness.[r] He may be rich and yet *faithful. He makes haste to be rich* at the expense of *faithfulness.*[21] *The faithful man* makes no big claims. But we can learn a lot from him, even in the slightest trifles.[s] He is true to his word. He fulfills his engagements. He has only one principle—"for the Lord"; under His eye; in His presence; "to the glory of God."[t] Measure his principle by a worldly standard. He will prefer his conscience to his interest. He would rather be poor by God's design than rich by sin. This is the man of faithfulness. "Who shall find a trustworthy man?"[u] But when you have found him, note his *abounding blessings;* blessings covering his head;[v] blessings for both worlds.[w] Is there not infinitely more promise in the ways of God, than in the ways of sin? Let the path be ever so tried and perplexing, just let it be a straight path,[x] and the Lord's sunshine will brighten it, "in the hand of God"—said a wise man—"is the prosperity of man."[y]

[q] Prov 10:22; Gen 24:35; 1 Kings 3:13
[r] 1 Tim 6:10
[s] Luke 16:10
[t] Col 3:23; 1 Cor 10:31
[u] Prov 20:6; Matt 24:45
[v] Prov 10:6
[w] Ps 37:37; 112: Isa 33:15, 16
[x] Prov 4:26, 27; Heb 12:13
[y] Job 20:10

But the man who has no faith can only walk in a crooked path. He leaps over every bound of principle. *He*

[21] *Verse 22. Prov 19:2; 20:14. Even the heathen moralists could see this.*

makes haste to be rich. He cannot wait for God in the path of Christian service. The promise isn't fulfilled fast enough for him. And he becomes rich too soon, scarcely knowing or caring how. He is only concerned that he doesn't lose his hold on what he has gained. Yet all this *haste* only leads to his own ruin. Instead of *abounding with blessings,* he shall not be innocent. Jacob, as *a faithful man,* was paid with full wages for his work. Though his master treated him harshly, God dealt bountifully with him. He *abounded with blessings;* while Laban, *hurrying to be rich,* became poor.[z] "I will study more," said Bishop Hall, "how to give account of my little, than how to make it more."

[z]Gen 31:7–9

It's extremely hard, if not impossible, to remain innocent in this path of temptation.[a] Yet, how does the Scripture combat the vice of covetousness? Not by claiming that gold is only earth, in a different form, and therefore not worth seeking; but by telling us, that "covetousness ... is idolatry," that "the love of money is a root of all sorts of evil"; that it has resulted for some, even in the "shipwreck in regard to their faith,"[b] and is always, in whomsoever it gains a foothold, an abomination? Even if no criminal means is resorted to, yet the overpowering desire, the perseverance in every path leading to riches, the laboring night and day for the grand object, the delight and confidence in getting it[c]—all prove the idolatrous heart,[d] and will not go unpunished. "Those who want to get rich fall into temptation and a snare and many foolish and harmful desires which plunge men into ruin and destruction. But flee from these things, you man of God."[e]

[a]2 Kings 5:25, 27. Comp. Prov 13:11; 20:21; 21:6

[b]AV—Col 3:5; 1 Tim 6:10, 1:19

[c]Job 31:25

[d]Job 31:24, 28

[e]1 Tim 6:9–11

21 *To show partiality is not good,*
Because for a piece of bread a man will transgress.

This Proverb has been more than once repeated.[22] The act itself *is not good.* It is positive *transgression.* The principle is worse—ugly selfishness. Here is perhaps a man, not of slavish or naturally degraded mind, but—such is the debasing influence of lust!—*a man* of weight and influence; and yet abusing his power for his own ends. It is a rich man, or a relative, or he is under some

[22] *Prov 18:5; 24:23, and references.*

obligation, and therefore he *shows partiality*. Now what is right for the rich is right for the poor. So the trampling of the poor under foot, the great Judge regards as rebellion against His own just law.[23] Principle once overpowered seldom regains its high position. Each successive trial proves its weakness; until he, who once thought himself able to resist a large bribe, for the smallest trifle will break with God and his conscience. *Even for a piece of bread, that man will transgress.*[24]

Isn't this often a pulpit sin? Isn't the minister sometimes drawn away from godly simplicity by some selfish motive?—*to transgress* his God-given obligation *for a piece of bread*? In old times this was a besetting temptation of the sacred office.[f] Let the beacon be solemnly regarded.

[f]Ezek 13:19; Mic 3:5; 2 Peter 2:3

In ordinary life, a man's bread hanging upon favor is a strong temptation to *transgress* upright principles. Cowardice and unbelief shelter themselves under the cover of wisdom. Christian reproof is neglected from fear of losing custom or advantage. Our interest is preferred to God's. And a plain Bible obligation is put aside *for a piece of bread*.[g] Are Christians wholly guiltless in this matter? Isn't conduct sometimes ruled by the fear of man, rather than by trust in the Lord?[h] Let the temptation be resisted at the first step, manfully, prayerfully, in the Lord's strength; and the victory is gained.

[g]Lev 19:17

[h]Prov 29:25

22 *A man with an evil eye hastens after wealth,*
And does not know that want will come upon him.

HASTE TO BE RICH—HIGHROAD TO POVERTY

Another warning word! "Beware, and be on your guard against every form of greed." "The lust of the eye"[i] brings deadly damage to the soul. Abraham was rich without *haste*, with God's blessing.[j] Little did Lot consider that his *haste to be wealthy* was the highroad to poverty. But step by step he entered into temptation.[k] Every worldly prospect withered and died; and he ended his days, a poor, forlorn, degraded tenant of the desolate cave of Zoar.[l] Thus he who sought the world, lost it; he

[i]Luke 12:15; 1 John 2:16

[j]Gen 13:2

[k]Gen 13:10–13; 14:12

[l]Gen 19:30

[23] Transgression *in this place is the same word as rebellion. Isa 1:2. See also 1 Kings 12:19; 2 Kings 1:1; 3:5.*
[24] *Amos 2:6. Cato used to say of M. Coelius the Tribune, that "he might be hired* for a piece of bread *to speak, or to hold his peace"!*

who was ready to lose it, found it. When Ahab's *evil eye* envied Naboth's enjoyment of his vineyard; when Jehoiakim was grasping by unjust means all that came into his reach, little did they consider, how this *haste to be wealthy* would end in disgrace.[m] But many and loud are the warnings against covetousness, which will surely end in shame, filled with the curse of an avenging God.[n]

[m] 1 Kings 21:2, 18, 19; Jer 22:13–19

[n] Prov 23:5, with Job 20:18–22; 27:16, 17; Jer 17:11; Luke 12:19, 20

Man of God! "I have made a covenant with my eyes;"[o] or else you can never keep your covenant with your God. Remember—it isn't he who knows most the things of heaven, but he who loves the most, who will be most fully deadened to the riches of earth. The *evil eye* fixed on earth can never look above. To the extent you love earth, by that much you lose heaven. If heaven is your possession, and you have so much waiting for you there, isn't your shame that you think about it so little and have so little love for it? Hold back your eagerness to rise in the world. For in its highest glory, the world holds nothing worthy of your heart. Keep the things of earth as your outer garment, which you can "lay aside," when it hinders you in the heavenly race.[p] But keep heaven next to your heart—your treasure—your love—your rest—your crown. Happy are you if you have the mind of the godly Christian Paulinus (the Bishop of Nola), who in the fifth century when he heard of the loss of all his property—looked up—and said, "Lord, you know where my treasure has long been!"

[o] Job 31:1; Ps 119:36, 37

[p] Heb 12:1

23 *He who rebukes a man will afterward find* more *favor*
Than he who flatters with the tongue.

YOUR FRIEND—THE REPROVER

Too often the flatterer finds more favor than the reprover.[q] "Few people have the wisdom to like reproofs that would do them good, better than praises that do them hurt," said Dr. South *(Life)*. And yet, a frank, honest man, notwithstanding the momentary struggle of wounded pride, will *afterward* appreciate the purity of the motive, and the value of the discovery. He who cries out against his doctor for hurting him, when he is examining his wound, will still pay him well, and thank him too, when he has cured it.

[q] 1 Kings 22:6–8, 27; Jer 26:7, 8

Unbelief, however, makes Christian *rebuke* powerless. Actual displeasure, or the chilling of friendship, is intolerable. But Paul's public *rebuke* of his brother apostle produced no disruption between them. Many years *afterward* Peter acknowledged his "beloved brother Paul" with most affectionate regard.[r] The apostle's painful *rebuke* of his Corinthian converts eventually increased his *favor* with them, as the friend of their best interests.[s] *The flatterer* is viewed with disgust;[t] the reprover—*afterward* at least—with acceptance.[u] A less favorable result may often be traced to an unseasonable time,[v] a harsh manner, a neglect of prayer for needful wisdom, or a want of due consideration of our own liability to "be tempted" and to fall.[w] Let us study the spirit of our gracious Master, whose gentleness ever poured balm into the wound, which His faithful love had opened. A rebuke in this spirit is more like the support of a friend, than the chastening of a rod.

[r] Gal 2:11–14, with 2 Peter 3:15
[s] 1 Cor 5, with 2 Cor 2:1–10
[t] Prov 27:14
[u] Prov 9:8; 27:5, 6; Ps 141:5. Comp. Eccl 7:5
[v] Prov 15:23
[w] Gal 6:1

24 *He who robs his father or his mother,*
And says, "It is not a transgression,"
Is the companion of a man who destroys.

OBLIGATION TO PARENTS

The damage caused by sin is measured by our obligation to the one sinned against. A murderer is an extremely wicked sinner, but how much worse is the murderer of his parents. *To rob* a stranger, a neighbor, a friend, is evil; how much more sinful it is to rob a father or mother. It breaks the son's or daughter's obligation to love and care for them. Ingratitude is added to injustice. Where will such a hardened sinner stop? But often the sin of robbery against parents is committed without the awareness that it is wrong,[x] as if the children might dispose of their parents' property at their own will. These *robbers* would be insulted if they were called thieves. But God, who sees men as they are, and judges them in sure balances, ranks them among "the wicked," and will deal with them accordingly.[y]

[x] Gen 31:19, 34, 35; Judg 17:2
[y] Prov 21:7

Nor is this guilt limited to the more glaring sins. Surely it is no better, when the young spendthrift wastes *his father's* property, and counts it *no transgression* to incur debts on his father's account without his knowledge or

[z]Prov 19:26
[a]Matt 15:5, 6
[b]Matt 15:9
[c]Ps 119:5, 6, 80, 128

consent.[z] Our Lord calls attention to another kind of *robbery*—the denial of the absolute duty of providing for parents; and this under the pretense of devotedness to God![a] But the gospel allows no substituting of one duty for another.[b] The upright Christian will place *all* duties upon the same ground of Christian obedience.[c]

[d]1 Sam 2:25

Young people! As you value your soul, your conscience, your happiness—consider how great your obligation to your parents really is. Think of the honor, respect, and consideration involved; the clear stamp of God's authority upon it; the mark of his disapproval when duty to parents is despised;[d] the certain seal of His blessing upon its practical and self-denying acknowledgement.

25 *An arrogant man stirs up strife,*
But he who trusts in the L**ORD** *will prosper.*

STRIFE—CANCER OF GODLINESS

[e]1 Kings 4:29
[f]Esther 3:1, 2
[g]3 John 9
[h]Prov 13:10
[i]Esther 5:11–13
[j]Eccl 5:10, 11
[k]James 1:11
[l]Prov 16:20; Ps 84:12; Jer 17:7, 8

The contrast between *the arrogant, and him who trusts in the Lord,* is very remarkable. It shows that pride is the root of unbelief. The man, having cast off God, expects nothing, fear nothing, from him. He lives as if there were no God. His proud heart is large; not, like the wise man's, in fullness of capacity,[e] but in ambitious grasp, and insatiable appetite. Never is he content within his own bounds. In the world he would be a Haman[f] in the church, a Diotrephes—"one who loves to be first among them."[g] It is his nature *to stir up strife.* Every one that does not agree with his own opinion of himself, is supposed to be disrespectful. Thus "through presumption comes nothing but strife."[h] And always will there be some thorn of mortified ambition,[i] or some fresh craving of unsatisfied desire,[j] eating at him, so that he will "fade away" in his ways.[k] What an empty shadow of fleeting happiness! So contrary to the blessings *of him who puts his trust in the Lord.*[l] "He shall be filled with good and solid things," said Diodati.

[m]Mark 9:33, 34

Christian! Avoid *stirring up strife.* It is the cancer of godliness. Keep near to your Lord. It was when the disciples were talking together by the way, instead of walking in close communion with their Master, that strife was stirred up.[m] Doesn't this point to the one thing most needful of all—faith! Truly—as Luther says—"Faith is a precious thing."[n] It rolls away all disquieting care.[o] It enables us to entrust to our blessed Lord whatever is troubling us and be at rest.[p] How much more, when the great burden is removed! Smite, Lord, smite; for thou hast pardoned. "My name, the sun of righteousness, will rise with healing in its wings; and you will go forth and skip about like calves from the stall.[q]

[n]Comp. 2 Peter 1:1
[o]1 Peter 5:7
[p]Ps 37:5–7
[q]Mal 4:2; Isa 58:11

26 *He who trusts in his own heart is a fool,*
But he who walks wisely will be delivered.

THE HEART—THE GREAT IMPOSTER

Contrast the sound and fruitful confidence just mentioned with man's natural *trust*. Our confidence determines our state.[r] To *trust* an imposter, who has deceived us a hundred times, or a traitor, who has proved himself false to our best interests, is surely to deserve the name of *fool*. This name therefore the Scriptures—"using great plainness of speech"—gives to him *who trusts in his own heart*. Well does Bishop Hall call it, "The great Imposter."[25] For has it not been practicing deceit upon us from our first moment of consciousness? Yes, the traitor makes his home within us, plotting, in partnership with our deadly enemy, the most elaborate efforts for self-destruction.

[r]Matt 7:24–27

The wise man illustrates his own proverb. It must have been some bitter root of self-confidence that brought his wondrous wisdom to the lowest degradation.[s] Peter also—how he fooled himself in his *trust!* Presuming upon the willingness of the spirit, and forgetting his Lord's most needful caution against the weakness of the flesh; though he was named a Rock, he fell as a reed before the first breath of temptation. If the everlasting arms had not been underneath, it would have been like the fall of Judas into the depths of hell. An instructive lesson to show us that all dependence upon feelings, impulse, our own strength, sincere purpose or conviction—is vain confidence. Sad experience has convinced us of this. Yet in the blindness of our folly, we are always ready to *trust* again, to our ruin, if the Lord doesn't intervene.

[s]1 Kings 11:1–8

[25] *Title of Sermon on Jer 17:9. See Bunyan's Discourse between Christian and Ignorance.*

Truly, there is no sin, which a man ought not to fear, or to think himself incapable of committing, since we have in our corrupt will the seeds of every sin. None of us can safely presume, that our heart might not hurry us into grievous sin, that we cannot now regard without horror.[t] If Eve in a state of innocence could believe a serpent before her Maker;[u] if "the holy one of the Lord" could worship the golden calf;[v] if the man after God's own heart could wallow in adultery, murder, and deceit;[w] if the wisest of men, and the warm-hearted Peter just referred to, could sink so low—what might we not do? Surely "all men are liars." The best of men, when left to themselves, are sad spectacles of weakness and instability.

Blessed be our God! Our standing is not on the uncertainty of man's best purpose; but upon the faithful promise, the unchangeable will, the free grace, and almighty power of God; not therefore on ourselves, but on the Rock—Jesus—on which the church is immovably built. We appreciate, then, a deep understanding of our indwelling weakness and corruption. Painful and humbling as it is, it helps strengthen our faith; and grounds us in the gospel far better than walking over the mere surface. This study of the heart strengthens the principle of that holy fear, which enables us to *walk wisely,* and thereby *delivers* us from the evils of a self-confident state. Surely in a path, where every step is strewn with snares, and beset with enemies, we have great need to heed these cautions—"Be careful how you walk"—looking on all sides—"not as unwise, but as wise."[x] A sound confidence is a proof of wisdom. We ought to be willing for the Lord if He chooses, to deprive us of the inviting and seemingly good pleasures into which we may have been drawn by the dictates of *our own heart.* Let it be a standing rule of conduct in our Christian walk to cultivate self-distrust, never to suppose security where God warns us of danger, never to trust ourselves with our own keeping. We are weak and should not needlessly expose ourselves to harm. We cannot pray—"Do not lead us into temptation"—when we are rushing headlong into it—or—"Deliver us from evil"—when we seem to invite its approach.[y]

[t] 2 Kings 8:13–15
[u] Gen 3:1–6
[v] Exod 32:2–5, with Ps 106:16
[w] 2 Sam 11:4, 17; Ps 116:11
[x] Eph 5:15. Comp. Prov 3:5, 6
[y] Matt 6:13, with 26:41

27 *He who gives to the poor will never want,*
But he who shuts his eyes will have many curses.

HOW TO AVOID POVERTY

Nobody wants to be poor. And therefore the carnally minded to avoid poverty, carefully gathers together, and latches onto, as much wealth as he can by any means possible; and he thinks that by such means he will avoid being poor. According to man's judgment, it is the best way that a man can take. But the Holy Spirit teaches us another way, totally contrary to natural reason. *He who gives to the poor will never want.* This is against reason, which says, that we must gather and hold tightly, to avoid poverty. Reason doesn't see what God can and will do. She is blind to the works of the Lord, especially those that he works according to his free promise.

However carefully we may guard our possessions, who can guarantee that we won't fall into proverty? But this promise gives a security, that no earthly abundance can give. Covetousness combines with reason to contradict the Word of God. Yet the promise is given by Him, who has full power to make it good; who has a thousand ways of repaying what is done or sacrificed at His command.[z] The fruit of our God-directed labors is the best preventive against poverty. What it is—is putting money into the bank of heaven, which can never fail us when we need credit. The best securities on earth will not prevent the fact that "wealth certainly makes itself wings, like an eagle that flies toward the heavens."[a] But when have the promises of heaven ever failed?[b] Nevertheless, with the carnal mind, covetousness prevails above faith, and a trust in uncertain riches makes the living God "a liar."[c]

[z] Ps 24:1
[a] Prov 23:5
[b] Num 23:19; 2 Cor 1:20
[c] 1 Tim 6:17; 1 John 5:10

Do we, the professed followers of Christ, really take these truths to heart, testing our own principles and practice by them? Do we honestly intend to make them, instead of self-judgment and self-interest, our rule and measure of conduct? Our Christian testimony is strengthened, and a sure seal of blessing is placed upon our family, when we refuse to plead family needs, as an

[28] *Prov 3:9, 10; 11:24, 25; 13:7; 14:22; 19:17; 22:9; Deut 15:7–10; Ps 41:1–3; 112:5–9, with 2 Cor 9:6–11; Eccl 11:1; Isa 32:8; 58:7–11; Matt 5:7; Luke 6:38. Observe the glowing exuberance of this last promise—Not only "shall it be given you"—but* good measure—*justly*

excuse for cutting back on our giving to the Lord. Again and again, God confirms this committment.[26] Yet many, who are "earnest in contending for the faith" of the gospel, and who would resist at any cost the invasion of heresy—we fear—would be ashamed to reveal how little they actually give to the Lord and His work.

If we really believed the promise linked to this duty, we wouldn't nearly so often *shut our eyes* to a case of distress. Yet, not only do we fail to look for others needing our help, but we actually turn away from them, as the servant of God would turn away from sin;[d] and then justify ourselves on the grounds that there are too many demands for our giving—too many needs, however worthy they may be. *Many a curse* falls upon this kind of grudging spirit, both from God and man.[e] And isn't there danger here of the everlasting curse?[f] Ponder it well—lest self-wisdom and careful examination check the glow of charity, prove a cloak for selfishness, and obscure the light of Christian benevolence and love, which ought to shine forth in the testimony of God's true children.

[d] Job 31:1, with Gen 39:10
[e] Prov 11:26; 1 Sam 25:17, 25, 26, 38
[f] Matt 25:41–45; James 2:13; 5:1–4

28 *When the wicked rise, men hide themselves;*
But when they perish, the righteous increase.

This Proverb has, in essence, been given before.[g] *The rise of the wicked* to power is indeed a national judgment, greatly to be protested against as the means of exercising cruel hatred against the church of God, the way it has been in all her persecutions, and the way it will be, so long as she is in the wilderness.[h] But what a tremendous weight of guilt and punishment is involved in fighting against God![i] Little do *the wicked* know the preciousness of the saints in His sight,[j] their perfect security under His cover,[k] the sovereign restraint which He has placed upon her enemies,[l] and the triumphant outcome of all opposition against her.[m]

[g] Prov 28:12
[h] Prov 29:27; Gen 3:15; Rev 12:6, 17
[i] Acts 9:4
[j] Zech 2:8
[k] Isa 26:20
[l] Ps 76:10
[m] Exod 15:1; Isa 51:9–11; Rev 18:20

The power of the wicked even here, however, is but for a moment; and *when they perish*—as perish they will—*the righteous will increase.* A great increase was there among the people of God in the days of godly Hezekiah, when the doors of the temple, which his wicked father

proportioned to the exercise of love—pressed down—*to secure it as full measure*—shaken together—*as with corn, that it may lie closer in its place—and as if this were not enough*—running over—*without bounds*—given into your bosom—*so that you shall enjoy the resulting blessing to the fullest.*

had shut up, were opened because of a national profession and consecration to God.[n] The immediate result of Haman's overthrow, was not only tolerance and encouragement of the true religion, but a large increase in the number of those professing it.[o] In the early ages of the Christian church, after the death of the persecuting Herod, "the word of the Lord continued to grow and to be multiplied."[p] Thus "out of the eater came something to eat, and out of the strong came something sweet."[q] The cross is the enriching blessing to the church and to every individual member of it.

[n] 2 Chron 28:24; 29; 30:13–25

[o] Esther 8:17

[p] Acts 12:23, 24

[q] Judg 14:14

CHAPTER TWENTY-NINE

1 *A man who hardens* his *neck after much reproof*
Will suddenly be broken beyond remedy.

THE HIGH PRICE OF INTENSIFIED SIN

This is indeed an awful word. The unruly ox, *hardening his neck* against the yoke,[a] is all too perfect a picture of the stubborn sinner, casting off the restraints of God. This was the standard complaint against Israel,[b] a true picture of the mass of the ungodly before our eyes. Conviction follows upon conviction, chastening upon chastening. Still the rebel *hardens his neck,* stops his ears against the voice of God, and invites his threatened judgments.

Very frequent are these instances among the children of godly parents or hearers of a faithful minister.[c] Every means of grace is a solemn, but despised, *reproof.* Intensified sin makes the judgment of a righteous God more evident. The more enlightened the conscience the more *hardened the neck.* Every beating pulse is rebellion against a God of love.

Sometimes it is more the immediate voice of God. An alarming illness, a dangerous accident, or the death of a companion in wickedness, is "the rod and reproof" intended to "give wisdom."[d] But if the "fool" continues to despise all God's reproof, his destruction will be *sudden,*[e] and *without remedy.*[f]

Such was the destruction of the old world, and of the cities of the plain, long *hardened* against the patience and forbearance of God.[g] Pharaoh grew more stubborn under the rod and rushed madly to his *sudden* ruin.[h] Eli's sons "would not listen to the voice of their father," and in one day both died.[i] Ahab, *much reproved* by the godly

[a]Jer 31:18

[b]Exod 32:9; 2 Chron 36:13–16; Neh 9:29; Isa 48:8; Jer 17:23; Zech 7:11, 12; Acts 7:51

[c]Prov 5:12, 13; 1 Sam 2:12

[d]Verse 15

[e]1 Thess 5:3

[f]Prov 1:22–30; 6:15; 28:14, 18; Isa 30:12–14

[g]Luke 17:27–29

[h]Exod 9:27, 34; 10:27, 28; 14:28

[i]1 Sam 2:25, 34; 4:11

prophet, *hardened his neck,* and the bow drawn "at random," received its commission.[j] How must Judas have steeled his heart against his Master's reproof![k] Onward he rushed, that he might turn "aside to go to his own place."[l] Truly God's patience has its end. And this fearful moment, once it arrives, the "vessels of wrath ... endured with much patience," are now revealed more plainly as "prepared for destruction."[m] There is no help—not even the gospel—for their circumstances. As they lived, so they die, so they stand before God—*beyond remedy.* No blood and no lawyer pleads for them. As they sink into the burning lake, every billow of fire, as it rolls over them, seems to cry out—*beyond remedy.*

[j]1 Kings 18:18; 21:20; 22:28, 34
[k]John 6:70; 13:10, 11, 18–27
[l]Matt 26:14–16; John 13:30; Acts 1:25
[m]Rom 9:22

Sinner—Oh! that you would be wise to consider your guilt, your state, your prospect, while your "judgment" and "destruction" linger! Is not the Spirit of grace pleading with your heart? Wouldn't He save you now, if you would just obey His call? You are standing upon mercy's ground between heaven and hell. O thou God of almighty sovereign grace, show "an example" of your "perfect patience."[n] Let the sinner sing your everlasting praise, as "a brand plucked from the fire" a monument of your over-abounding grace.[o]

[n]1 Tim 1:16
[o]Zech 3:2

2 *When the righteous increase, the people rejoice,*
But when a wicked man rules, people groan.

"The robes of honor to the righteous are the garments of gladness to *the people.* The sceptre of *authority* to the godly is the staff of comfort to *the people.* On the other hand, [the official robes of authority are the garments] to *the wicked ...* of *mourning to the people.* The throne of command to the one is the dungeon of misery to the other. The titles of honor given to the one are sighs of sorrow wrung from the other," said Jermin.[p] The contrast of the government of Mordecai and Haman illustrates *this rejoicing and groaning.*[q] The special rejoicings at the crowning of Solomon probably showed the people's confidence, that he would walk "in the statutes of his father David."[r] The reigns of *the righteous* kings of Judah were marked by great national happiness.[s] The world's most glorious era, yet to come, is when "the Lord" shall "bless" His own kingdom, as "the city of righteousness, a

[p]Prov 28:12, 28
[q]Esther 8:15, 16; 10:3, with 3:15; 4:1–3
[r]1 Kings 1:39, 40, with 3:3. Comp. 4:20
[s]2 Chron 15:12–15; 20:27–30; 29:36; 30:21

[t]Jer 31:23; Isa 1:26
[u]Ps 72:1–7; Isa 32:1

faithful city."[t] For what but righteousness can truly bless an individual, a family, or a nation.[u]

[v]Eccl 10:5, 6; Isa 3:4, 5; Mic 3:9–12

When therefore *the wicked rule—the people*—not the godly—only *groan*. The depth of the *groaning* surely turns to joy at the removal of the scourge. Meanwhile it is borne by the faithful in the land as a national scourge.[v] And if tears are their drink, patience will be their bread, till God have mercy on them. How we need to thank God, that our guilty country, with so much to humble us in shame, should have been spared so long from the curse of *wicked rulers!* The tyrant rules for his own sinful ends. The Christian sovereign for the good of the people.

3 *A man who loves wisdom makes his father glad,*
But he who keeps company with harlots wastes his
wealth.

THE LOVE OF WISDOM

[w]Prov 10:1; 15:20; 23:15, 24, 25; 27:11; 28:7
[x]Prov 4:7

These Proverbs in substance have been given before.[w] Yet there are variations that are instructive. For instance, the wisdom is here more distinctly described as *loving wisdom*. For he is wise not only who has arrived at a complete habit of wisdom, but who, as yet, *loves it*, or desires it, and listens to it. Don't we hang too loosely from its heavenly influence? Let it plainly be our main concern, not as a good thing, but the best—"the beginning" thing.[x] The awakened sinner *loves it* from the sense of need; the Christian from its satisfying delight. The taste gives a keen edge to the appetite. What we have already grasped of the blessing is nothing compared with what is yet to come. This world of vanity no longer captures our love.

[y]Prov 3:17
[z]Prov 8:20; 4:11, 12
[a]Prov 3:14, 15; 8:18, 19
[b]Prov 3:35
[c]Jer 3:4
[d]Prov 23:23–25

Let the young man consider wisdom's "pleasant ways, and ... peace,"[y] her light and security,[z] her "enduring wealth,"[a] and glorious inheritance;[b] and "now" won't you call to the God of wisdom—"My Father, Thou art the friend of my youth?"[c] Let Him have the best years of your life. Isn't the best sacrifice due to Him, who is above the songs of heaven, who has obtained a kingdom for those that love Him? No worldly honor, no success of talent, will make a godly *father* as happy as will this choice for eternity.[d]

Folly brings its own shame and sorrow. "The *compan-*

ion of gluttons" is readily found in fellowship *with harlots* saddening his father, by *wasting his wealth*.[e] One course of vanity leads to another. All end alike in ruin.[f] He may possess the external talents. But *the love of wisdom* is the only protection from "an adulteress" and "foreigner."[g]

[e]Prov 28:7, 19
[f]Prov 5:9; 6:26; Luke 15:30
[g]Prov 4:6; 7:4, 5

Deep indeed is the anxiety—the joy or the sorrow—connected with children.[h] May it give a deeper tone of simplicity and pleading in dedicating them to God[i] and training them up for His service! Let us present them early, as the "children" are "a gift of the Lord"; but as His, more than our own—His property—His inheritance.[j] Here are our springs of perseverance, of hope, and of ultimate reward.

[h]Prov 17:21, 25
[i]1 Sam 1:26–28
[j]Ps 127:3

4 *The king gives stability to the land by justice,*
But a man who takes bribes overthrows it.

GOD'S JUSTICE ESTABLISHES THE LAND

What good are the best laws if they are badly administered? Partiality and injustice make them null and void. And yet it requires great integrity and moral courage to withstand the temptations of worldly policy and self-interest. God's own throne is built and established *by justice*.[k] This then can be the only *stability* of the land.[l] To compromise it to some private ends provokes the anger of God to chastise, if not *overthrow* the land. The article in England's Magna Carta—"We will sell justice to none"—is plain evidence of how corrupt social principles were before that great standard was raised up.

[k]Ps 89:14; 97:2; Isa 9:7
[l]Verse 14; 16:10–12; 20:8, 26; 25:5; 2 Chron 9:8

Under the godly government of Samuel the land *was made stable by justice*.[m] But "his sons, however, did not walk in his ways." They were priests. They received gifts: and the theocracy—the security of the land—*was overthrown*.[n] The righteous administration of David bore up the "pillars" of the land at a time of great national weakness.[o] The same principles in the godly successors were the source of strength and prosperity.[p] The want of uprightness in Saul shook the kingdom from his grasp;[q] and the covetousness of Jehoiakim[r] destroyed its foundations and buried him in its ruins. Let the same consistency pervade every grade of official responsibility. No respect will be paid to dignity, temporal or spiritual, ex-

[m]1 Sam 7:3–12, 15–17
[n]1 Sam 8:2–7
[o]Ps 75:2–6, 10; 2 Sam 8:15
[p]2 Chron 1:1; 14:2–7; 19:6, 7, with 20:27–30; 31:20, 21; Isa 32:1, 2
[q]1 Sam 13:12
[r]Jer 22:13–19

cept it be *stabilized with justice.* Let men of God be in our high places; and "righteousness exalts a nation," and the church will be the joy and praise of the whole earth.[s]

[s]Prov 14:34

5 *A man who flatters his neighbor*
Is spreading a net for his steps.

LOOK OUT FOR THE SINFUL MAN CLOTHED IN WHITE!

Bunyan's pilgrims were warned most wisely: "Beware of *the flatterer.*" Yet "forgetting to read the note of directions about the way," they fell into *his net,* and, even though delivered, were justly punished for their folly. The doctrine of man's goodness, strength, or freedom; innocent infirmities; pardonable offenses; softening down the statements of man's total corruption; a general gospel, without close application; its promises and privileges, without the counterbalance of its trials and obligations—all this is frightful flattery—the sinful man clothed in white—"Satan disguises himself as an angel of light," and "his servants also disguise themselves as servants of righteousness."[t] Unwary souls are misled. Even watchful Christians fall into *the net.* And while they have to thank their faithful God for deliverance, they cannot forget His sharp and needful chastening of their foolishness. Where heresy, or apostasy, are not the root of the matter, then it is the bad fruit of the flatterer.[u]

[t]2 Cor 11:13–15

[u]Rom 16:17, 18; 2 Peter 2:1–3

But let us guard against this net in our daily path. Too readily we are deceived by the *flatterer's* words. Even when we know we do not possess the loveliness attributed to us; when we know the *flatterer* doesn't mean what he says; instead of being justly upset by his smooth hypocrisy, is there not sometimes a secret self-satisfaction because he thought us sufficiently important to make us the object of his deceit? Even when it is so ridiculous as to create disgust, is that disgust always without pleasure? Besides—what else is much of the language of smooth courtesy or lively interest and affection? Who would venture to act with confidence on this deceitful talk? The *net is always spread* to allure into some evil path; often into the greatest wickedness. *The flattering* woman beguiled her prey.[v] The parasites of Darius defied him for a month, to make him the tool of their mali-

[v]Prov 2:16; 7:21; 26:28

cious plot.[w] The enemies of Christ *spread the flatterer's net for His steps.* But here the wisdom of God was infinitely above them and God "is the one who catches the wise in their craftiness."[x]

[w]Dan 6:6–9

[x]Matt 22:15–23, with 1 Cor 3:19

BEWARE OF THE FLATTERER'S NET

The feet of many strong men have been entangled in this *net.* Indeed seldom has the frailty of the man of God been more painfully exposed. David honored his God in the endurance of Shimei's curse. But Ziba's smooth words drew him to an act of great injustice.[y] Usually some lack of integrity has predisposed the mind for this poison. David was struggling to discover a plea for leniency to his murderous son, when the woman of Tekoah spoke to him with her *flattering* lips. The bribery of passion was far more powerful than her arguments.[z] But bitterly the misguided parent reaped the fruit of entering into *the net spread for his steps.*[a] Ahab was fully prepared for his own ruin by listening to *the flattery* of his lying prophets.[b]

[y]2 Sam 16:1–12

[z]2 Sam 14:4–24

[a]2 Sam 15:1–14

[b]1 Kings 22:11, 12

Remember, when a man loads us with commendation, it is *the flatterer's net.* "Watch the path of your feet."[c] Exchange confidence for suspicion.[d] Fearful is the snare to those, whose rank or influence causes them to walk before men, rather than God. Indeed, religious *flattery* is a common snare to a Christian profession. It may be natural, perhaps well-intentioned, to be willing to profit by more advanced experience, and to inquire of a brother, by what means he has been able to rise above the ordinary level; or—even to express our envy at his higher knowledge, faith, or love. But all this tends to encourage self-complacency, "confidence in the flesh" —the ruin of that self-renouncing confidence in his Savior, which is the clear stamp of the faithful follower of his Lord.[e] Too often is the same *net spread for the steps* of the minister of Christ, whether to gain his good opinion, or from the genuine but indiscreet, warmth of affection. But Oh!—think—He is a man as you are—beset with temptation—perhaps even besides those that are "common to men." His heart, like yours is fully responsive to self-exalting fancies. And to know that he has a reputation for holiness; that he is a man of influence; that

[c]Prov 4:26

[d]Prov 26:24, 25; 27:14

[e]Phil 3:3; 1 Cor 10:13

his character is looked up to; that his opinion is valued—this is indeed a fiery trial in "the crucible" that brings out to view much of the rubbish of vanity.[f] Far better would it be, that our Christian communication with each other should be molded by the wise resolution to refrain from flattering titles, "be partial to no one," as this is hurtful to the creature and displeasing to God.[1]

[f] Prov 27:21

6 *By transgression an evil man is ensnared,*
But the righteous sings and rejoices.

SNARES FOR THE SOUL, SONGS FOR THE HEART

There is always a snare in the ways of sin; always a song in the ways of God. Which then are the "ways" of pleasantness and "peace"?[g] The light-hearted sinner goes on in his flowery path. Soon he is taken captive "in *the snare* of the devil";[h] often in a snare of his own making.[i] *Transgression* is in fact *the snare* of the soul. Now, doesn't it make sense to avoid a snare? Sinner—think for a moment. What are the pleasures of sin to the pleasures of heaven? Remember—sin and ruin are bound together; and who is there that can separate them?

[g] Prov 3:17, with 13:5
[h] 2 Tim 2:26; Job 18:9–11
[i] Prov 5:22; 11:5, 6; 12:13; Job 17:8

Outwardly, the righteous man's lot may seem the same as *the evil man's*. But how wide is the gulf between them.[j] Joseph's brethren in prison, under the sting of conscience, sink in despondency. Paul and Silas in prison *sang and rejoiced.*[k] But only very little can be judged by their outward state. The ungodly are in prosperity, and the children of God "chastened every morning,"[l] yet rise triumphant in the most difficult experiences—"Do not rejoice over me, O my enemy. Though I fall I will rise; though I dwell in darkness"—my cause apparently forgotten, my light obscured, my character defamed—"the Lord is a light for me."[m] What does it really mean to possess all the promises of God? The wealth of this golden mine can never be described in human language. Even an angel can't comprehend it! And how solid is the basis for this *rejoicing!* The com-

[j] Isa 65:13, 14
[k] Gen 42:21, with Acts 16:25
[l] Ps 73:14
[m] Mic 7:8

[1] *Job 32:21, 22. "Surely it is enough for us to have foes within and without to contend with, without having snares for our feet laid by our fellow pilgrims. Oh! it is a cruel thing to* flatter. *The soul is often more exhausted and injured by disentangling itself from these nets, than by the hottest contest with principalities and powers. Those who have once known the torture the believer undergoes, while this poison is pervading his soul, the bitter ... medicines he must take as antidotes, the frightful oblivion of lessons of humility which he has been studying for years, will, I think (unless much under the influence of the enemy of souls), not administer the* [poisonous *drink*] *a second time"—HELEN PLUMPTRE'S letters, pp. 43, 44—a most profitable volume.*

pleteness of the Savior's work; His constant love; the fullness of His Spirit; the sufficiency of His grace; His faithful promise; watchful eye; ready help; perpetual intercession. All this joy is not like that of the world, flowing and ebbing; but heightening and overflowing through all eternity.

But the righteous also *sing*—they and only they. Yet often they don't sing. Why? Because their harp is on the willows, as if they could not "sing the Lord's song in a foreign land."[n] Or ... unbelief remains unchecked in their lives. They apply God's promises so timidly in their lives that distrust outweighs all encouragement. Their brighter seasons are enjoyed again and again, without moving on to greater things. They lay nothing up for the future, and, therefore, "in a day of clouds" and "doom" they spend their time complaining, instead of improving and enjoying their situation.

[n] Ps 137:4; Ezek 30:3

Isn't it worth tracing the reasons for this dishonorable evil to its sources? Are we unable to sing or just disinclined? It is time we seek a stronger exercise of faith, rouse ourselves out of lethargy, and get rid of mistaken fears. And in faith, repent, return, watch, and pray, and mortify besetting sins. Let's think about it seriously. Do we not sing because we no longer have any cause for rejoicing? Certainly this can't be! We have countless blessings, far greater than any disappointments we may be passing through just now. We ought to put faith to work counting them, and then, surely, even under the deepest gloom that ever could rest upon the soul, the harp would be taken down from the willows, and *the righteous would sing and rejoice.*[2]

But not only do we *have* all these mercies remaining with us, though others may be taken away, but, with the eye of faith, we see them more clearly and enjoy them more deeply, in the darkness when it seems so much harder to *sing and rejoice.* But never is God's grace so cheering, so triumphant, as when it raises us above our trials; and enables us to take up the song of victory on the

[2] *To some Christians of a morbid temperament, Bernard's advice may be important—"Let us mingle honey with wormwood, that the wholesome bitter may give health, when it is drunk tempered with a mixture of sweetness. While you think humbly of yourselves, think also of the goodness of the Lord."—"Always are there evil days in the world; always good days in the Lord"—AUGUSTINE on Ps 33.*

[o]Rom 7:24, 25; 1 Cor 15:55–57

field of battle;[o] rebuking unbelief, and strengthening our confidence for renewed conflict.

Indeed, it is when we are most bowed down, when we are wounded and disheartened by the sense of our own guilt and waywardness, that, we need to grasp the glorious word—"Where sin increased, grace abounded all the more."[p] Can we then be without cause for singing? Won't our harps reach an even higher pitch? Yes, praise God! We are moving rapidly toward a world where our harps will never be unstrung, the heart never out of tune, and the song ever new. We will *rejoice and sing* without one faltering note in our song and without one jarring note in the song of our brethren.[q]

[p]Rom 5:20

[q]Isa 35:10; Rev 5:8–10

7 *The righteous is concerned for the rights of the poor,*
The wicked does not understand such *concern.*

EVIL DAYS IN THE WORLD; GOOD DAYS IN THE LORD

The original language gives this Proverb a judicial aspect, according to Holden, Geier, and Bishop Patrick. To respect the person of the poor is no less unjust, than to "defer to the great."[r] But *the righteous* judge will consider *his rights,* judge it as for God, investigate it thoroughly, and make sure it will not be lost by any inability of His to defend it.[s] This was the considerate administration of the great King of righteousness.[t] The man of God will follow his godly example.[u] Let him have the desire first, and then, certainly he will have the patience to search into the truth of things. He'll not be stingy with his efforts, though matters may be complicated and require long and irksome labor.

[r]Lev 19:15; Exod 23:3

[s]Ps 82:3, 4

[t]Ps 72:2–4, 12–14

[u]Job 29:11–16; 31:13, 20; Jer 22:16

Selfishness however, not truth, justice, or mercy, is the standard of *the wicked.* He considers, first *the poor* man's person, then *his rights.* The unjust "judge" would not have avenged the "widow" of her adversary, except to save himself trouble.[v] Felix professed not to know the apostle's cause, only that he might satisfy his own greed.[w] But how fearful a thing it is to sit in the place of God[x] as His representative, only to pervert his judgment for selfish gain.[y] For he, who rejects the complaints of the poor and brushes them aside with hard words and threatening looks, out of the hardness of his heart, or

[v]Luke 18:2–5

[w]Acts 24:26, 27

[x]Ps 82:6; Rom 13:1, 2

[y]Prov 24:11, 12; Jer 5:28, 29; Ezek 22;7, 29–31; Mic 3:1–4

because he doesn't want to be disturbed, cannot justly excuse himself by pleading—"See, we did not know this."[z]

[z]Prov 24:10–12

These truths, however, obviously apply more generally to the considerate attitude of the righteous toward the poor, and the cruel disregard that *the wicked* has toward them. The declaration that "the poor will never cease to be in the land"; and the inequality of rank, prevailing throughout God's management of affairs, were doubtless intended to arouse Christian sympathy and response.[a] Consideration of *the poor* is the true spirit of Christian sympathy; putting ourselves as much as possible in their place.[3] Oh! how different this is from the impatient, ungracious manner in which the suit of a poor client is sometimes dispatched, as if we grudged our time and effort. Our beloved Lord not only "went about doing good,"[b] but He did it so tenderly, so considerately. He was always ready to yield His own convenience and even necessary comfort to the call of need.[c] The same *concern for the poor* marked the apostolic administration.[d] Sympathy with the poor is the practical acknowledgment of our own undeserved mercies: especially remembering the Lord's poor, as His representatives,[e] who is first and last, and all to us; and who, "though he was rich, yet for your sake He became poor, that you through His poverty might become rich."[f]

[a]Deut 15:7–11; 2 Cor 8:14, 15
[b]Acts 10:38
[c]Mark 6:31–34
[d]Acts 4:34, 35; 6:1–6; 1 Cor 16:2; 2 Cor 9:12, 13; Gal 2:10
[e]Matt 10:42; 25:40
[f]2 Cor 8:9

Well do those who choose not to know about other's needs, deserve their name—*the wicked.* Like Cain, they acknowledge no interest in their brother.[g] Like Nabal—It is no concern of mine.[h] If the "poor man" must be fed rather than starve—it is casting food to a dog, rather than holding out a helping hand to a fellow-sinner.[i] This total absence of the image of a God of love[j]—this utter casting off His royal law[k]—surely He will treat him accordingly.[l]

[g]Gen 4:9
[h]1 Sam 25:10, 11
[i]Luke 16:20, 21
[j]1 John 3:17
[k]James 2:8; Lev 19:18, with Luke 10:31, 32
[l]Prov 24:12

8 *Scorners set a city aflame,*
But wise men turn away anger.

[3] *Ps 41:1. Most striking was the* concern of the poor *in Bishop Ridley. In his last moments at the stake, he implored the queen in behalf of certain poor men's leases likely to become void by his death. FOXE, 7:545, 546. In the same noble spirit was the remembrance of the dying Scott to his son, of the arrival of the season, when he had been used to plant a root for the supply of the poor.*

THE SCORNER: PUBLIC NUISANCE NUMBER ONE

The comparison is here between a "Proud . . . Haughty . . . Scoffer,"[4] and *a wise man*. The one causes public trouble; the other brings public blessing. The one raises a tumult; the other quells it. The man, who *scorns* to be bound by common restraint, will *set the city aflame* by his presumption,[m] or *set it on fire* by blowing the fire of divine wrath upon it. Happily *wise men* are scattered through the land: and their energy and prudence *turn away anger*.[n] "Proud and foolish men kindle the fire, which wise and good men must extinguish, said Henry.

[m] 1 Sam 11:2, 11; 2 Sam 10:4; 12:31

[n] 2 Sam 20:1, 15–22; Acts 19:23–41

Another instructive illustration of this Proverb suggests itself. Not the tyrant over his fellowman, but the *scorner* against his God, is the public nuisance. Many of the kings of Judah and Israel *set the city aflame with problems*. By provoking God's anger, they did more to bring about its ruin, than the most powerful foreign enemies. Their influence led the people into deeper sin and ripened them for judgment.[o]

[o] 2 Kings 21:9–15; 23:26, 27; Isa 28:14–22; 2 Chron 36:16, 17; Jer 36:23–34; Matt 21:33–43; 23:34–39; 1 Thess 2:15, 16

But wise men stand in the gap and turn away anger.[5] Surely it was wisdom in the king and people of Nineveh, instead of bringing their *city* into a snare by *scornful* rebellion, to turn away threatening destruction by timely humiliation, humbling themselves before God, just in time.[p] Let the people be gathered; let the ministers of the Lord prepare themselves to their work of weeping and as accepted pleaders for the land.[q] Surely "unless the Lord of hosts had left us a few survivors" of these powerful intercessors, "we would be like Sodom," and "we would be like Gomorrah."[r] Praise be to God! The voice is yet heard—"Do not destroy it, for there is benefit in it."[s] The salt of the earth preserves it from corruption.[t] Shall we not then honor these *wise men* with deep respect and gratitude—"My father, my father, the chariots of Israel and its horsemen!"[6]

[p] Jon 3:5–10

[q] Joel 2:17

[r] Isa 1:9

[s] Isa 65:8

[t] Matt 5:13

[4] *Hebrew Men of scorn. Prov 21:24.*

[5] *Moses—Exod 32:1–14; Deut 9:8–20; Ps 106:23. Aaron—Num 16:48. Phinehas—25:11; Ps 106:30. Elijah—1 Kings 18:42–45; James 5:16–18; Jer 18:20; Dan 9:3–20; Amos 7:1–6. The righteous remnant—Isa 1:9, 6:13. Comp. Gen 18:32; Job 22:30; Jer 5:1; Ezek 22:30, 31. Contrast 13:5. "Nothing therefore can make a man so good a patriot as religion"—Bishop HALL.*

[6] *2 Kings 2:12. This acknowledgement is sometimes forced from the consciences of the ungodly. Prov 13:10–16.*

9 *When a wise man has a controversy with a foolish man,*
The foolish man either rages or laughs, and there is no rest.

It would generally be far better not to meddle with such *a fool* as is here described. We can only deal with him at a great disadvantage and with little prospect of accomplishing anything.[u] If *a wise man has a controversy* with the wise, he can make himself understood, and there is some hope of bringing the debate to a good conclusion. But in *controversy with a fool there is no rest,* no peace or quiet. It will go on without end. He will neither listen to reason, nor yield to argument. He is so stubborn that he will either *rage or laugh;* either release against us the fury of an ungoverned temper, or *laugh* us to scorn. This kind of *controversy* was a point of painful trial to our Lord. What could be more revolting than sometimes their murderous rage,[v] sometimes their scornful laugh,[w] both rejecting His counsel against themselves?[x] And what if *a controversy with such fools* should be appointed for me? Let me remember the days when I, too, was stubborn and foolish. And while this vivid impression reminds me that I was once the same as they are now, can I return their unreasonable treatment of me with anything but tenderness and compassion?[y] Yes—when, as the most effectual means for their benefit, I would commend them to the almighty and sovereign grace of God—the most helpful thing I can do for them, is to remember that it was this grace that healed *my* deep-rooted stubborness, and that it is just as free, and no less sufficient for them.

[u] Prov 17:12; 26:4; Eccl 10:13; Matt 7:6
[v] Luke 4:29; John 7:1; 8:59; 11:53
[w] Luke 16:14
[x] Matt 11:16, 17
[y] Titus 3:2, 3

10 *Men of bloodshed hate the blameless,*
But the upright are concerned for his life.

"CHRISTIANS TO THE LIONS!"

This bloody hatred is the fulfillment of the first prophecy from the mouth of God.[z] The first history of the fallen world puts the seal to the prophecy—"Cain rose up against Abel his brother and killed him."[a] Ever since, this same testimony has been given.[b] "Which one of the prophets did your fathers not persecute?" was the indignant remonstrance of Stephen to his countrymen. They

[z] Gen 3:15
[a] Gen 4:5–8
[b] Verse 27; Ps 37:12–14, 32; Gal 4:29; 2 Tim 3:12

"fill up then the measure of the guilt of your fathers;" by being the betrayers and murderers of the Son of God.[c] The noble army of martyrs stands before us. What intense hatred they were subjected to by their persecutors and what unbelievable tortures they suffered. *The men of bloodshed hate the blameless.*[d] Why? Because of their innocency. That was the only ground of their hatred; and when any outbreak of evil threatened, the swelling cry of the multitude was—The Christians to the lions! The next picture in the annals of the church is just as vivid—"I saw the woman"—awful sight!—"drunk with the blood of the saints, and with the blood of the witnesses of Jesus."[e] Such fierce cruelty against Jesus Christ and His followers still exists, and nothing but the gospel can overcome it. Everything less than this only holds down the violence. But it still retains all its substance and power, and waits only for the removal of present restraints to develop the same hatred as ever *of the men of bloodshed.*

[c] Acts 7:52; Matt 5:12; 23:32
[d] Heb 11:36, 37
[e] Rev 17:6

God's Word explains this murderous and revengeful spirit. Why did Cain kill his brother? "Because his deeds were evil, and his brother's were righteous."[f] Darkness cannot endure the light.[g] The condemning light[h] of godliness arouses the enmity of the ungodly. That's why Ahab hated his upright prophets,[i] and the Jews and Romans the holy Savior.[j] Conformity to His will is still the great offense. Such precise fools, contrary to everybody else—turning the world upside down!—how can they be endured? Getting rid of them is something to rejoice over.[k] That is the world's attitude toward those who love and serve Jesus Christ.

[f] 1 John 3:12, 13
[g] John 3:19, 20
[h] Heb 11:7
[i] 1 Kings 21:20; 22:8
[j] John 7:7
[k] Rev 11:9, 10

And yet, God is not unmindful of the persecution and troubles they bear. *The men of bloodshed hate the blameless; but the upright are concerned for his life.* Saul wanted to murder David: but his son Jonathan protected him.[l] Jezebel was thirsting to destroy the prophets of the Lord; Obadiah "hid them ... in a cave, and provided them with bread and water."[m] The enemies of Jeremiah plotted against him; Ededmelech saved his life.[n] Herod was trying to take Peter's life; the church shielded him with their prayers.[o] The men bound themselves to murder Paul; "Priscilla and Aquila" were ready

[l] 1 Sam 18:11, 25, with 18:1–4
[m] 1 Kings 18:1–4
[n] Jer 38:1–13
[o] Acts 12:5

to "risk their own necks" for his life.[p]

[p] Acts 23:12; Rom 16:3, 4

What a life of conflict is this world of sin! What are we to do about it—quit loving it? Shouldn't we instead ask the Lord for patience to endure it? But most important for us is that, we should be found definitely on the Lord's side,[q] "join with me," if need be, "in suffering for the gospel."[r] We should never stand aloof from our brethren's cause.[s] When we help them, we are workers with God Himself. If union is so effective against the church, it ought to be just as effective *for* the church; strengthening her stakes, establishing her foundations, and enlarging her usefulness.

[q] Matt 12:30
[r] 2 Tim 1:8
[s] 2 Tim 16, 17

11 *A fool always loses his temper* [AV—*uttereth all his mind*],
But a wise man holds it back.

A TEST OF CHARACTER—CONTROL OF THE TONGUE

"There is an appointed time for everything"—the wise man writes elsewhere—"a time to be silent, and a time to speak."[t] It is a mark of true wisdom to be able to discern the times.[u] Indeed the discipline of the tongue, or lack of it, is a sound test of character. The man, who speaks hastily and with conceit, will be put to shame in his foolishness.[v] He might have been "considered wise" in his silence.[w] But silence is beyond his power—he has to speak all his mind—tell all he knows, thinks, or intends, and runs on, until he "spouts folly."[x] It is sometimes thought a proof of honesty to speak our mind. But actually, it simply proves our lack of wisdom and good sense. For there is so much it would be far better never to speak about; yes, to hold down even in our thoughts![y] How much "silly talk" and "jesting";[z] how many angry, detracting, unkind words do we utter, because we have neglected to watch, or rather to entreat "set a guard, O Lord over my mouth," as the door of our hearts![a] And what wrong judgments we often pass upon men's actions because we utter all our mind, as it were, in one breath, without stopping to think, or perhaps without the information we need to form a correct judgment!

[t] Eccl 3:1–7
[u] Eccl 8:5; Amos 5:13
[v] Prov 18:13
[w] Prov 17:28
[x] Prov 15:2
[y] Prov 30:32; Mic 7:5
[z] Eph 5:4
[a] Ps 141:3

Indeed the words of the fool, as the Bible scholar Cartwright remarks, "are at the very door—so to speak—of his mind, which being always open, they readily fly abroad. But the words of the wise are buried in the inner recess of his mind, [so] the coming out is more difficult."[b] This is wisdom to be valued and cultivated. Many things we may *hold back,* which will then be far better spoken than at the present moment.[c] By then, we may find reason to doubt what, at the time, we were fully convinced of. There is often a lightness of faith—the fruit of sudden impulse, breaking out in sudden profession. Beware of a loose foundation. Men under the present excitement run through all the sects and parties of the church, everywhere uttering their whole mind; "tossed here and there by waves, and carried about by every wind of doctrine"—seeking rest, and finding none.[d] How much better to take time for second thoughts, to wait, and weigh again! We should then, instead of exhibiting a changing and doubtful face, gain that "it is good for the heart to be strengthened by grace."[e]

[b]Comp. Prov 10:14; 12:16, 23; 13:16; 14:33
[c]1 Sam 25:36
[d]Eph 4:14
[e]Heb 13:9

This godly wisdom holds in common life. Samson fell a victim to the folly of uttering all his mind.[f] Samuel was restrained by God from such rash behavior. He regarded his own safety. We should never speak against our mind. But we don't always have to speak our whole mind. Be careful to speak nothing but the truth. But the whole truth (as in the instance of Samuel) may sometimes be legitimately restrained.[g] The apostle was two years at Ephesus without uttering all his mind against the worship of Diana. Was that cowardice, shrinking from the truth? His weeping ministry, and unceasing efforts, proved his faithfulness.[h] His open protest *held back* was self-discipline, consistent with Christian courage and decisiveness.

[f]Judg 16:17
[g]1 Sam 16:1, 2
[h]Acts 19:10, 23; 20:31

12 *If a ruler pays attention to falsehood,*
All his ministers become *wicked.*

WICKED PRINCE—WICKED PEOPLE

The influence of the *ruler's* personal character upon his people involves a fearful responsibility. A wicked prince makes a wicked people.[i] In his more immediate sphere, *if he pays attention to falsehood,* contrary to the laws of God and love;[j] he will never want those about him ready to minister to his foolishness. "Lies will be

[i]1 Kings 15:30; 16:2
[j]Exod 23:1. Comp. Prov 13:5

told to those that are ready to hearken *to them,*" said Henry. Envy, ambition, malice, self-interest will always be at hand for prejudice and scandal. The *ruler,* who is too easily convinced, becomes the tool of all manner of wickedness. His corruption pushes the godly out of his presence; and *all his ministers become wicked.* There are exceptions to this rule (as Obadiah in the court of Ahab,[k] Ebedmelech in the service of Zedekiah,[l] Daniel in Nebuchadnezzar's court[m]). But this is the natural tendency, the general result, to his own disgrace and ruin. If he would, therefore, rule in uprightness and in the fear of God; instead of lending himself to belittling or flattery, he must carefully close his ears against doubtful characters, lest he should approve *wicked ministers,* and discourage those that will boldly speak the truth.

[k] 1 Kings 18:3
[l] Jer 38:7–13
[m] Dan 2:48, 49

How wise was David's determination—both as the sovereign of his people and the *ruler* of his house—to frown on lies, and uphold the cause of faithful men![n] Contrast Ahab surrounded with his wicked prophets; all combining in one lie to please their weak and ungodly master. We see how ready he was to listen to falsehood, and how well the flattery worked; when he punished the only man who was "valiant for the truth," and who persisted in declaring it—not fearing the wrath of the king.[7]

[n] Ps 101:2–7

But all in authority may learn a lesson of responsibility. Let ministers, especially, not only hold the truth in its full integrity, and take heed that their character will bear the strictest scrutiny; but let them turn away from the fawning flattery of those, of whose uprightness there is at best but doubtful proof.

13 *The poor man and the oppressor have this in common:*
The LORD gives light to the eyes of both.

GOD IS NO RESPECTER OF PERSONS

The doctrine of this Proverb, as of one like it,[o] seems to be the real equality of the divine exemptions under apparent inequalities. The rich seem to be used by *the oppressor;* so called, from the deceitfulness of riches,[p] and

[o] Prov 22:2
[p] Prov 23:5; Matt 13:22

[7] *1 Kings 22:6, 26, 27. Comp. Hos 7:3. AV—Jer 9:3. "Many kings have been destroyed by poison; but [no poison has been so] efficaciously mortal, as that [taken] in by the ear"—SOUTH. Massillon well taught his young prince, that the flattery of the attendant in court was little less dangerous than the rebellion of the traitor.*

[q]1 Tim 6:9
[r]Comp Prov 22:7

of the means, by which they are too often obtained.[q] The moneylender[r] appears to point to the same purpose; implying the oppression too often connected with riches.[8] Both these classes, so distinct in their relative condition, meet together on the same level before God. However *men* may differ; however one may oppress and despise, and the other envy or hate; however *the poor* may be tempted to murmur because of the oppressions of his richer neighbor; however the rich by charging too high a rate of interest, or unjust gain, may take advantage of the necessities of the poor—*the Lord gives light to the eyes of both*—"God is not one to show partiality."[s] Both are partakers of His providential blessings.[t] Both are the subjects of His Sovereign grace; "members of the same body, animated by the same spirit, appointed for the same inheritance; partakers of the same 'great and precious promises.' There [is] not one prize for the soul of the poor, and another for the rich. There [is] not one table for the [poorer] guests, and another for the greater," said Bishop Reynolds (*Vanity of The Creature,* Sect. 8). *The poor* Lazarus and the usurer Zaccheus have long met together in one *common* home; both alike, are the undeserved monuments of wondrous, everlasting mercy;—*the eyes of both enlightened,* spiritually, eternally.[u]

[s]Acts 10:34
[t]Matt 5:45
[u]Luke 16:22; 19:9

Isn't it presumption to judge hastily the way of God; or to judge them at all by the plummet of our own reason?[v] Let's wait the appointed time, and all will be clear, as all is right. How far beyond our limited understanding is every exercise and display of this manifold wisdom, grace, and love!

[v]Ezek 18:25

14 *If a king judges the poor with truth,*
His throne will be established forever.

[w]Prov 29:4, 7; 20:28

This rule has often been repeated in substance.[w] The writer of this book was a king. He was naturally led to write for his own benefit, while the divine Spirit guided his pen for the use of other rulers to the end of time. May every ruler and national leader keep the picture of a godly ruler constantly before our eyes! It is natural for *the king* to desire *the establishment of his throne;* but not natural for him to seek it in God's own way. Jeroboam

[8] *Ps 57:9, 10; James 5:1. For the same reason our Lord denominates riches generally the distinctive term of "the mammon of unrighteousness" AV—Luke 16:9.*

sought it by wickedness;[x] Rehoboam by worldly policy;[y] Ahaz by worldly alliances.[z] The far more sure way is the faithful administration of justice, not neglecting the rich, but specially protecting the poor, who from their weakness were in the greater need of a covering.[a] David appears to have been a poor man's king, giving the lowest of his people familiar access to him for judgment.[b] Solomon, and many of his godly successors, ruled their kingdom in the same principles of justice, and were abundantly honored by their God.[9] Bad administration by the rulers never failed to bring a curse upon the government.[c] "For those who honor Me I will honor, and those who despise Me will be lightly esteemed."[d]

[x] 1 Kings 11:26
[y] 2 Chron 11:22, 23; 12:1
[z] 2 Chron 28:16–20
[a] Prov 31:9; Ps 82:3, 4
[b] 2 Sam 19:8
[c] Isa 3:13, 14; 10:1; Jer 22:13–19; Zeph 3:3
[d] 1 Sam 2:30

When our great Savior King walked on earth, His enemies bore testimony, whether in flattery or conviction, to his righteous character.[e] No less beautiful than accurate is this description, as applied to the principles of His government, in the connection with the promise of the *establishment of his throne.*[f]

[e] Matt 22:16
[f] Ps 72:7, 11, 15; Isa 9:7; 11:4, 9

15 *The rod and reproof give wisdom,*
But a child who gets his own way brings shame to his mother.

Discipline is the order of God's government. Parents are His dispensers of it to their children. The child must be broken in to "bear the yoke in his youth."[g] Let *reproof* be tried first; and if it succeeds, let *the rod* be spared.[h] If not, let it do its work. Eli gave the *reproof,* but spared *the rod.*[i] *The rod* is evidently to be taken literally, not metaphorically; corporal, not spiritual punishment.[j]

Some give *the rod* without *reproof,* without trying to get the conscience to respond. This is either tyrannical or whimsical and no matter which, nothing can be expected from it. But the two together not only drive "foolishness" far away, but, as a positive blessing, *give wisdom.*[k] God's own children grow wiser under correction. They see their folly, and in genuine shame turn from it, blessing Him for His rod for faithfulness and love.[l] It teaches us how foolish it is to reject medicine because it is bitter.

But look at the child *who gets his own way*—without restraint. A more perfect picture of misery and ruin can-

[g] Lam 3:27
[h] Prov 17:10
[i] 1 Sam 2:22–25; 3:13
[j] Prov 23:13, 14. Comp. 19:29; 20:30
[k] Prov 22:15
[l] 2 Chron 33:12; Ps 119:67, 71, 75; Luke 15:13–17; Mic 6:9

[9] *1 Kings 3:16–28. Jehoshaphat—2 Chron 19:5–11; 20:30. Josiah—Jer 22:14–19. Comp. Daniel's advice to Nebuchadnezzar, 4:27.*

not be conceived. His terrible temper is thought to be due to his tender years."It will pass away as his reason improves. Time alone can correct it," says the misinformed mother. But, actually, time of itself mends nothing. It only strengthens and matures the growth of the native principle. This, being a decided tendency to evil, will lead to deadly injury. The mother cannot guess the future stature, health, talents, or prospects of her newborn infant. But of one thing she may be absolutely certain—her child does have and will have a corrupt and wayward will. It is just that the poison doesn't appear at first. But no one gets upset about it. Why worry? The child isn't being raised in a wicked environment or under the influence of bad example. He just *gets his own way.* See what happens to the restive horse, left in the same condition with his rein loosened, full of his own spirit. What happens to him? He plunges headlong down the precipice. The child, without parental control, rushes on under the impetuous impulse of his own will; and what but almighty sovereign grace can save him from destruction? Many a hardened villain on the gallows was once perhaps the pleasing, susceptible *child*; allowed *his own way,* to his own appetite, pride and self-willed obstinacy.[10]

The sound discipline of heavenly guidance is our Father's best blessing. His most fearful curse is for us to be given up to our own ways, "to walk in [our] own devices."[m] A *child* left like that is at the furthest point from salvation, in the very jaws of the devouring lion.

[m]Ps 81:12

Now let's turn from the ruined child to the disgraced, broken-hearted parent. *The mother* only is mentioned, as the chief superintendent of the early discipline; perhaps

[10] *Comp. 1 Kings 1:6–9; 2:23–25. Rousseau inculcated this system to its fullest extent—"That no kind of habits ought to be impressed on children; that you should leave them to the natural consequences of their own actions; and that, when reason comes to exert itself in a maturer state, all will be right." Upon which the following beautiful quotation has been given—"Emilius! how I tremble for thee, while I see thee, while I see thee exposed to the care of thy too ingenious tutor. I see thee wilful to thy parents; domineering in the nursery; surfeiting on meats; inflaming thy body with noxious humors, thy mind with unquiet passions; running headlong into dangers, which thou canst not foresee, and habits which thou canst not eradicate; mischievous to others, but fatal to thyself"—See Bishop HORNE'S* Sermon on Self-Denial. *"We pity orphans," remarked a wise Christian parent, "who have neither father nor mother to care for them. [But a] child indulged is [even] more to be pitied. It has no parent. It is its own master, peevish, forward, headstrong, blind; born to a double portion of trouble and sorrow above what fallen man is heir to; not only miserable itself, but worthless, and a plague to all who in the future will be connected with it. What bad sons, husbands, masters, fathers, daughters, wives and mothers are the offspring of fond indulgence, shown to little masters and misses almost from the cradle! Wise discipline gives thought and firmness to the mind; and makes us useful here, and fit for the world of perfect subordination above"—VENN'S* Life, *p. 257.*

also as the most susceptible of the grievous error. For if the father's stronger character induces him to "exasperate your children";[n] to rule rather by command than by persuasion; does not *the mother's* softer mold tend to the opposite evil? And so far as she yields to mistaken indulgence, she bears the greater share of the punishment. It is not, that she is *brought* to trouble, or even to poverty; but to that, which is the most keenly felt of all distress—to *shame.* Nowhere is God's retributive justice more strongly marked. The *mother's* sin is visited in the proportioned punishment. What greater neglect of obligation, than a *child who gets his own way?* What greater affliction, than the *shame to which he brings her?* Parental influence is lost. The reverence of authority is forgotten, as a bygone name.[o] The child rules; instead of being as a corrected child, in subjection.[p] The parent fears, instead of the child; and thus virtually admits to her own degradation. Instead of "a wise son makes a father glad"; it is "a foolish son" is "bitterness" to *his mother.*[q] The sunshine of bright prospects is clouded. The cup of joy is filled with wormwood. The father's mouth is dumb with the confusion of grief. The dearest object of *the mother's* tenderness, instead of being the staff and comfort of her age, *brings her to shame.* Truly *children,* thus left to themselves, will mingle the bitterest cup that man can ever have to drink, and stir up the saddest tears that ever eyes can have to weep.

[n] Col 3:21
[o] Prov 19:26
[p] Heb 41:9
[q] Prov 10:1; 17:21, 25

This is not a trial, which, like many others, she might keep to herself. *The shame* is too public to be concealed. What must have been the open dishonor upon Eli's name, when the sins of his children made men abhor the offering of the Lord! When the treason of David's sons *brought him to shame* in the sight of all Israel; surely his own conscience must have brought his own sin to mind, as the cause of their ruin; both left to themselves—one condoned in the most serious sin;[r] the other having not even been corrected by a word.[s] And if the shame before men is so bitter, what will be the overwhelming confusion at the great consummation, when the evil tendencies, cherished with such cruel fondness by the parent, shall produce their harvest "in a day of sickliness and incurable pain."[t]

[r] 2 Sam 14:21, 23; 15:6; 18:33
[s] 1 Kings 1:5–9
[t] Isa 17:11

Oh! as our children's happiness or misery, both for time and eternity, is linked with our own responsibilities; shouldn't we watch and pray, and resist the weakness of the flesh, in self-denying firmness? "Take this for certain," says Bishop Hopkins (*Works*, 1:450), *"that as many deserved stripes as you spare from your children, you do but lay upon your own back.* And [the children] you refuse to chastise, God will make [of them] severer scourges to chastise you." At whatever cost, establish your authority. Let there be but one will in the house. And let it be felt, that this will is to be the law. The child will readily discover, whether the parent is disposed to yield, or resolved to rule. But however trifling the requirement, let obedience be, in small matters as well as great, the indispensable point. The awe of parental authority is perfectly consistent with the utmost freedom of childlike confidence. Actually, it is the very foundation of it (for the child can hardly appreciate the kindness of a parent, whom he thinks afraid to strike), while it operates as a valuable safeguard against a thousand acts of uncontrolled waywardness. But let us always keep the awful alternative vividly before us. Either the child's will, or the parent's heart, must be broken. Without a wise and firm control, the parent is miserable; the child is ruined.[11]

16 *When the wicked increase, transgression increases;*
But the righteous will see their fall.

The increase of transgression obviously equals the increase of transgressors.[u] And it is not merely a numerical increase, but also an increase in the power and daring of sin. "Men began to multiply on the face of the land" and were giants in sickness, as in strength, until the striving of the "Spirit" of God could endure it no longer.[v] This is the way it was with the Babel-builders[w] and the cities of the plain.[x] Combination emboldens in sin.[y] Each particle

[u] Hos 4:7
[v] Gen 6:3
[w] Gen 11:8
[x] Gen 18:20
[y] Isa 41:7

[11] *"I earnestly entreat you," writes the wise and experienced Josiah Pratt to his children, "to subdue the wills of your children most tenderly* if you can? *But if not, your duty and your love require measures, which shall enforce obedience. Commit yourselves as little as may be into a contest with your children. But having once done this, you must maintain the contest till the child yields. Every such victory will make the next easier, and in all likelihood deter the child from entering on another contest. And you must make thorough work of it, if you would bless the child. The guile of the heart is seen in combination with its self-will, in trying to evade your authority. A very young child puts forth perhaps his first approaches to sin in acts of cunning and rebellion. Rely with unshaken confidence on that divine maxim—'Train up a child in the way he should go, and when he is old, he will not depart from it'*—MEMOIR, *chap. 19.*

of the mass is corrupt. The mass therefore of itself ferments with evil. Thus the prevalence of infidelity in our densely crowded districts above the more thinly populated villages. There is the same evil in individual hearts; but not the same fermentation of evil.

If it weren't for the prospects of faith, the Christian eye could not bear the sight. *But the righteous will see their fall.*[z] Noah saw the destruction of the old world,[a] Abraham the ruin of the devoted cities;[b] "Israel saw the Egyptians dead upon the seashore."[c] "Let not the righteous," said Bishop Patrick, "be discouraged; for the wickeder men are, the shorter is their reign." The faithful minister, conscious of his inability to stem the everflowing torrents of sin, would sink in despair, but for the assured confidence that he is on the conquering side; that his cause, as the cause of his Lord, must eventually prevail. Yes—though now sin *seems* to triumph, and Satan boasts of his victories; yet "the kingdom of the world," with all their vast population, shall become the kingdom of our Lord, and of His Christ; and He will reign forever and ever."[d] This is indeed the supporting joy of faith; to realize the glory of this day, when *the righteous will see the fall* of the now triumphing *wicked;* and one universal shout shall swell throughout the earth—"Hallelujah! Salvation and glory, and power belong to our God; because His judgments are true and righteous ... For the Lord our God, the Almighty, reigns."[e]

[z]F

[a]G

[b]G

[c]Ex

[h]Isa 2 1 C

[d]Rev 11:15

[e]Rev 19:1–6, with 15:4; 18:20. Comp. Isa 66:24

17 *Correct your son, and he will give you comfort;*
He will also delight your soul.

DISCIPLINE IS A MUST!

Once more Solomon returns to the subject of discipline. These repeated reminders[f] strongly show its importance. The command is positive—*Correct your son.* How can an upright judgment evade or explain away a plain, literal order? This Book of Proverbs is not out of date. Like every other part of the Sacred Volume, it is the Book for every age; "All Scripture is inspired by God and profitable for teaching, for reproof ... for training."[g] To try more self-pleasing rules, therefore, is to set up our will in opposition to God's; reason or feeling in place of

[f]Verse 15; Prov 13:24; 19:18; 22:15; 23:13, 14

[g]2 Tim 3:16; Rom 15:4

faith. It is making ourselves wise above that which is written.

The measure and kind of correction must depend, of course, upon the age, sex, and temper of the child, and the character, seriousness, and circumstances of the fault. But let it be, like our gracious Father's discipline, never more than can be borne.[h] Make due allowance for any marks of frank and honest confession. Yet, with a wise application of the principle, there must be no exception to the rule. Different tempers, like different soils, require corresponding difference of treatment. But discipline there must be; not relaxed in fondness, not pushed on in harshness; but authority tempered with love. If a gentle hand cannot control, a stronger hand must be applied.

We may take *comfort* without *correction;* but such comfort will bring trouble in the end. The true *comfort* is that, which our *child will give;* and that he may *give* it, the rule is—*Correct.* We may be assured, that God would not have so insisted upon it, if a blessing were not with it. If Eli was rejected, it was because in this matter he honored "his sons above" God.[i] Those then "who honor Me" above their sons "I will honor." Pain is the present exercise both to parent and child,[j] but the after blessing is secured.[k] Ground well tilled and trees carefully pruned bring forth more "fruit."

Observe how the objection of parental weakness is anticipated. "If I put my son to pain, will he not hate me?" No—when "a child gets his own way," he is a deep and anxious trouble. Now *he will give you comfort.* Before—he "brings shame."[l] Now he shall give delight to your soul.[m] The momentary feelings of the child under *correction* will give way to the conviction of the parent's wisdom and regard for his profit.[n]

Yet, the rule against discouragement would not have been repeated had there not been some parental evil to be corrected. Provocation revolts, transfers confidence to most unworthy associates, and brings into ruinous temptations. Children claim considerate treatment. They must not be driven by brute force. Authority must be tempered with love. The grounds of extraordinary commands should be explained to them. What is good should be liberally commended. The best construction should be

[h] 7:8; 57:16; r 10:13

[i] 1 Sam 2:29, 30. Contrast Gen 22:12

[j] Prov 15:10

[k] Heb 12:11

[l] Prov 29:15

[m] Prov 23:13–16, 24, 25

[n] Heb 12:9

put upon defective efforts. The distinction should be carefully drawn between weakness and willfulness, between heedlessness and obstinancy. Home should be gladdened with the invigorating joy of spring and replete with every wholesome pleasure. Every attempt should be made to gain confidence, so that the child, instead of a cold trembling reserve, should run into our arms. But in this glowing atmosphere, forget not God's rule. The completeness of discipline is the father's firmness combined with the mother's tenderness; each infusing into the other the quality of each. A wise parent will put his seal to the testimony that this well-disciplined education is the surest means of securing the children's affection, gratitude, and reverence.

On this important subject so often enforced—we are not taught to believe without promises, or to obey without understanding why. The Book of Proverbs exhibits cause and effect—the certain consequences of a given course of action, whether good or evil. It sets our promise and obligation—promise fulfilled in the way of obligation. The promised blessing to godly parental discipline is written in beams of living light. If the grace of the promise is lost, it is only by unbelief in the promise, or by a presumptuous confidence in it (separating the end from the means) such as brings shame in the issue. It is not that God is untrue, but that we are unfaithful. God has given the promise. Man either slights, rejects, or abuses it. He attempts to put aside the Scripture by an appeal to experience, instead of proving the faithfulness of God by "obedience of faith."[o] The commands—the directions—the promises—the blessing—all are the Lord's. Put His word to the test. The simplicity and perseverance of faith will be richly honored in His own best time and way.

[o] 1 Cor 16:26

18 *Where there is no vision, the people are*
unrestrained [AV—*perish*],[p]
But happy is he who keeps the law.

The vision—as appears from the contrast—is divine instruction. The ministry is God's appointed means to communicate this blessing,[q] and therefore the main instrumentality of conversion,[r] and subsequent Christian perfection.[12] There can be no greater calamity, therefore,

[p] Comp. Exod 32:25; 2 Chron 28:12; Matt 9:36

[q] 1 Sam 3:1; 1 Sam 9:9; Mal 2:7; Eph 4:11

[r] 1 Cor 1:21; James 1:18; 1 Peter 1:23

than the removal of the *vision* (instruction). The temporal famine, affecting only the body, is a light judgment, scarcely to be mentioned, compared with that, by which *the people are unrestrained*—"a famine . . . for hearing the words of the Lord."[s] For "when there is none that can edify, and exhort, and comfort the people by the word of God, they [will] *perish*. They become [enslaved] captives unto Satan. Their heart is bound up. Their eyes are shut up; they can see nothing. Their ears are stopped up; they can hear nothing. They are carried away as a prey into hell, because they have not the knowledge of God," said Bishop Jewell.

[s] Amos 8:11, 12; Isa 8:16

Israel often brought on this most fearful judgment—the removal of the open vision.[t] The "lampstands" of the apocalyptic churches has from the same cause been long since removed out of its place; and for the most part little more remains than the ceremonial of bygone days.[u] From the apostate church, *the vision* is well-nigh withdrawn, and *the people perish* in ignorance and delusion. For as Cranmer nobly testified, "I know how Anti-Christ both obscured the glory of God, and the true knowledge of His Word: overcasting the same with mists and clouds of error and ignorance through their false glosses and interpretations. It [moves me]," he adds, "to see the [simple] and hungry flock of Christ led into corrupt pastures, to be carried blindfold they know not whither."

[t] 1 Kings 12:28–32; 2 Chron 15:3–5; Ps 74:9; Lam 1:4; 2:9; Ezek 7:26; Hos 3:4

[u] Rev 2:1–5; 3:1–3, 15, 16

In many bodies the complaint is as real as in days of old—"My people are destroyed for lack of knowledge."[v] The sun doesn't shine on more wretched objects, than on the awful masses of our fellow-sinners, growing up in habitual estrangement from God.

[v] Hos 4:6

It has been calculated that millions of our countrymen are living in habitual separation from the worship of God. Whether from the guilty neglect of leaders, the willful

[12] *1 Cor 14:3; Eph 4:11–14; 1 Thess 3:10. And yet, this most fruitful divine agency (preaching), which our blessed Lord honored as the grand medium of His own teaching (Ps 40:9, 10; Isa 61:1, 2) is now depreciated as the mark of "a Church only in a weak and a languishing state, and an instrument, which Scripture*—to say the least—*has never much recommended"* (Tracts for the Times, *87, p. 75). Far more orthodox is the sentiment of one of our venerable reformers. "Thus we may learn the necessity of preaching and what inconvenience follows when it is not used. 'Where preaching fails'—saith Solomon—'there people perish.' Therefore, let every one keep himself in God's school-house, and learn his lesson diligently. For as the body is nourished with meat; so is the soul with the word of God"—Bishop PILKINGTON'S* Works, *p. 112, Parker Society's edition. "The meanest village," Luther would say, "with a Christian pastor and flock, is a palace of ebony."*

neglect of individuals, or from the population having grown far beyond the extent of the instruction provided, it is certain, that even in the most enlightened countries in the world, to vast masses of the poor *there is no vision, and the people are unrestrained* in ignorance—"the things which make for peace . . . have been hidden from your eyes"![w]

[w]Luke 19:42

Take the most awful illustration of this Proverb that can be imagined. If to be without *vision* is the mark of a *perishing* state, what ray of scriptural hope is there for the heathen world? Being "separate from Christ," they are described by infallible testimony as "having no hope."[x] Salvation is indeed free to all, "whoever will call upon the name of the Lord." But how shall they call without faith; believe without hearing; "hear without a preacher?"[y] If, therefore, there is *no vision,* how can they but perish? They "perish without the Law"[z] (not condemned under the law of revelation, which they have never known); but still *they perish* "without excuse,"[a] alienated from the life of God through the ignorance that is in them, because of the "hardness of their heart."[b] Proud reasoning man revolts and presumes to be more merciful than God. But this false love is only the cover for selfishness. Men deny the danger, because they are too indolent, too self-indulgent, to stretch out the helping hand, or to make one sacrifice for the rescue. True charity is the fruit of reverential faith. And, while it realizes the tremendous peril, it concentrates all the energy of compassionate tenderness, believing prayer, and self-denying effort upon their salvation.

[x]Eph 2:12
[y]Rom 10:13–17
[z]Rom 2:12
[a]Rom 1:20
[b]Eph 4:18

But the contrast is not between those who have not *the vision* and those who have it; but between the destitution and the improvement of the blessing. The mere profession of the gospel may nullify it. Of what use is light, if we don't open our eyes to see it? So far from becoming a blessing, it will only issue in deeper condemnation.[c] If some are enlightened, multitudes are struck blind.[d] But this true *vision*—the object really seen as life and light to the soul—is the spring of that happy *keeping of the law,*[e] which knows no less a privilege than communion with our God and Savior here and for eternity.[f] Yes, truly—to be interested in the promises of God; to be an inheritor of

[c]Matt 11:20–24; Luke 12:47, 48
[d]John 12:40
[e]Prov 3:21–24; 4:5–9; 8:32–35; 19:16; Luke 11:28; John 13:17
[f]John 14:21–23; Rev 22:12, 14

everlasting glory; to be the present possessor of divine favor; to be secured from the peril of everything against him, and assured of the supply of all things that will work for his good—this is the *happy* portion of the practical disciple. And indeed in the ordinary course of life, as Hooker observes in his godly instruction—"what event soever ensue, it breedeth, if not joy and gladness always, yet always patience, satisfaction, and reasonable contentment of mind. Whereupon it hath been set down as an axiom of good experience, that all things religiously taken in hand are prosperously ended; because, whether men in the end have that, which religion did allow them to desire, or that, which it teacheth them contentedly to suffer, they are in neither case unfortunate."

Who then can justly cast a cloud of gloom over the ways of God? Let the Pentecostal Christians witness to their gladness.[g] Let every servant of the Lord invite his fellow-sinners to enjoy the privileges he enjoys and manifests through his holiness and joy.

[g]Acts 2:46, 47

19 *A slave will not be instructed by words* alone;
For though he understands, there will be no response.

AUTHORITY MUST BE MAINTAINED AT ANY COST!

Discipline must be carried, not only into the family,[h] but throughout the whole household, in order to preserve God's authority and order. An important hint is here given relative to the management of servants. Though it does not apply to all, it shows a very common temptation to self-will. There is a proud as well as humble silence; which is as plain a proof of an unsubdued spirit, as a flippant answer. The patience of Job was sorely exercised by this trial; and that under circumstances, that made the treatment more aggravated.[i] We must guard against harshness in our spirit.[j] But with servants, as with children, authority must be maintained at any cost. And therefore, if *a servant understands* the command, but *will not answer;* if *he will not be instructed by words,* it is better to dismiss him, than to lower our authority, and tolerate evil by yielding to his waywardness.

[h]Prov 29:15, 17

[i]Job 19:16

[j]Lev 25:43

The Scripture fully sets out the duties of servants—

"Not argumentative . . . With good will render service, as to the Lord, and not to men."[k] Sullen resistance to reproof is most inconsistent with the profession of a Christian; and, if the offender escapes the correction of an earthly master, he will be visited with the rod of his angry Lord, as a self-deceiver or backslider from his high obligation.[l]

[k] Titus 2:9; Eph 6:7

[l] Prov 19:29; 26:3

20 *Do you see a man who is hasty in his words?*
There is more hope for a fool than for him.

ONLY A FOOL UTTERS ALL HIS MIND

We have just been warned against sullen silence. The next warning is directed against *hasty words.* When a man flows on in his words, evidently without time for consideration;[m] when he gives his opinion as if it were a loss of time to take counsel or regard the judgment of others; when you find him foward in pronouncing judgment before men of acknowledged wisdom and experience; this is the "fool [who] uttereth all his mind";[n] the man lately marked out for our warning,[o] as *a hopeless fool,* "wise in his own eyes."

[m] Prov 18:13

[n] AV—Prov 29:11

[o] Prov 26:12

It is very difficult to deal effectively with him. Until the stronghold of his own conceit is shaken, argument and instruction are lost upon him. The man who is conscious of his weakness, distrusts himself, and is ready to ask and receive counsel; is more likely to be led right, than he, who thinks himself to be right already.

It is a special mercy to be preserved from hasty judgments or expression of judgments. The first stamp upon a perfect mind is infallibly correct. On an imperfect mind it must be subjected to a careful scrutiny. It is sound wisdom to admit that our judgment may be mistaken. Self-control and hesitancy to assert oneself give solid consistency. This character of mind is most important in religious arguments. Be careful to defend or oppose nothing, till you have tested it by the true standard. Moses deferred judgment on the sin before his eyes, till he had brought the matter to God.[p] "Let every one be quick to hear, slow to speak."[q]

[p] Lev 24:12

[q] James 1:19

21 *He who pampers his slave from childhood*
Will in the end find him to be a son.

We have another valuable rule for domestic discipline; directing masters to a wise treatment of their servants. It is a grievous error for us to step out of the path which a God of order has marked out for us. And it is just as sad a thing for us to induce others to do so. God, in His wisdom, has framed the constitution of society, assigning to each their station and their duties. If a servant aspires to be in the house anything but a servant, his character loses its value. A master acts—to say the least—most unseemly, when he forgets his own place and authority, and *pampers his servant* by the allowance of undue freedom. It is difficult to preserve the true medium between distance and familiarity. A haughty, menacing demeanor toward our servants forgets the respect justly due to them.[r] An inconsiderate fondness takes them out of their place, greatly to their own injury. Our Lord's distinction shows, that friends—*not servants*—should be admitted to our familiar fellowship and entrusted with our confidence.[s] But to promote a servant therefore to the rank of a confident, unfits him for his own condition, and defeats our own end by the natural results of this unnatural treatment. True kindness keeps him in his place. "Good usage does by no means imply [the kind of pampering] that would ruin a child," said Scott. *A servant pampered*—often from *a child*—if he is not made to know his place in time—soon relaxes in respect and attention. Instead of this false kindness stimulating to diligence, and inducing gratitude; he becomes idle, insolent, and ungovernable; assumes the place of the young master, and in effect, *becomes a son*. This unseemly taking over is an evil, and "the earth ... cannot bear ... a slave when he becomes king."[13] Ishbosheth must have allowed Abner undue liberty, when he so far forgot the respect due to his sovereign that he insulted him before his face.[t] David also must have loosened the reins of proper authority, when Joab murdered the commander-in-chief at the head of his army, without being instantly subjected to the penalty of the law.[u] Even the wise man Solomon appears to have forgotten his own prudent caution, when *he pampered* Jeroboam in authority; and promoted him too sud-

[r] Eph 6:9

[s] John 15:15

[t] 2 Sam 3:8

[u] 2 Sam 20:10

[13] *Prov 30:21, 22. Lord Bacon suggests for the good ordering of servants—1. That we promote them by steps, not by leaps. 2. That we occasionally deny their wishes. "Sudden elevation," he adds, induces insolence. The constant granting of their wishes makes them only more imperative in their demand"*—Advancement of Learning, *Book 12.*

denly. He lived to regret his error, when with the pretension *of a son* he combined the pride of a rebel.[v] The confusion and anarchy of after years in the kingdom originated in the same false step.[w] The greatest kindness to servants is to "grant to your slaves justice and fairness"[x]—*but no more.* Any defect in this rule will be sure to bring trouble. What need we have of the daily supply of divine grace to rule our house well in due subjection! The resolution to "behave ourselves wisely in a perfect way" can only be accomplished in the habitual prayer—"When wilt Thou come to me?" Then indeed "I will walk within my house in the integrity of my heart."[y]

[v] 1 Kings 11:26–28
[w] 1 Kings 16:9–12
[x] Col 4:1
[y] Ps 101:2

22 *An angry man stirs up strife,*
And a hot-tempered man abounds in transgression.

"LET NOT THE SUN GO DOWN ON YOUR WRATH"

Anger is not necessarily a sinful passion. Even a *hot temper*—the overflowing of the torrent—is a property in God.[z] We can readily conceive of its energy in the unfallen nature of man. Had Satan appeared to Eve in his own open hatefulness, her anger against him would have been a holy principle. But in a fallen nature, to preserve its purity is a rare and most difficult matter. It must be confined to points, where God's honor is concerned;[a] and even on these points the rule must be observed—"Do not let the sun go down on your anger."[b] The short period of the day is abundantly sufficient to express right motives and to accomplish holy purposes.

However, the general tendency of anger is here most truly described. Its active energy *stirs up strife.*[c] It quarrels even about trifles[d]—or matters, which forbearance might have satisfactorily explained.[e] And when suppressed, but not laboriously controlled, how often does it become more intense, and break out more furiously—being loaded with sun! Indeed, it is difficult to take a full view of the mighty power of this mass of sin. It gives a shove to every besetting sinful tendency. It may be blasphemy![f] It stops at nothing. How many murders do we owe to this outburst of the moment![g] But for divine restraints the very foundations of society would be torn up!

Parents! Do we feel the responsibility of checking

[z] Nah 1:2
[a] John 2:15–17
[b] Eph 4:26
[c] Prov 15:18; 26:21; 30:33; James 3:16
[d] 1 Tim 6:4; 2 Tim 2:23, 24
[e] Acts 15:39
[f] Lev 24:10, 11
[g] 1 Sam 18:9, 10; 22:6–19; Matt 2:16; Acts 7:54–59; 12:19

these sudden outbursts early in the life of our children? And do we earnestly watch against these outbursts in ourselves, praying continually that they may be brought and kept under control? How beautiful are the instances of almighty grace—such as Henry Martyn—transforming *the angry man* into the likeness of his meek and holy Master!

But we must not be satisfied with just outward constraint upon passion. God condemns the deep-rooted principle that gives it birth. O my wretched heart—filled with soul-destroying corruption! Every time I give way to my own desires even the least bit, how fearfully my sinful heart takes over. So much time spent in excitement! So much more in the restless waiting for the desired opportunity! And all given to the great murderer! Oh! for the mystery and doctrine of the cross to mold our character into its genuine spirit and influence!

23 *A man's pride will bring him low,*
But a humble spirit will obtain honor.

HUMILITY—CROWN OF FINITE BEINGS

This Proverb—Bishop Hall (sermon on text, *Works*, 5.270) says, "is like unto Shushan: in the streets whereof honour is proclaimed to the humble Mordecai; in the palace whereof is erected an engine of death to a proud Haman." It exhibits the spirit of our Lord's oft-repeated declaration made plain by His daily providences—"Whoever exalts himself shall be humbled; and whoever humbles himself shall be exalted."[14] The real value of man in himself is so small that the Psalmist is at loss where to find it.[h] His undue value of himself is utter delusion; having lost all; stripped of all; yet proud, as if he were the possessor of all. He raises himself to heaven in his airy visions; but soon he meets with his own punishment—*A man's pride will bring him low.*[i] We see this in the world. The proud conceit of rank, talent, or any superiority must be under continual control;[j] while on

[h] Ps 8:3, 4; 144:3; 39:5

[i] Job 40:12; Ps 18:27. Comp. Zeph 2:15; Rev 18:7, 8; ref. on Prov 16:18, 19

[j] 1 Kings 21:1–4; Esther 5:13

[14] *Matt 23:12; Luke 14:11; 18:14. The speech of Artabanus to Xerxes before his invasion of Greece is a striking testimony from a heathen. "God delights to depress whatever is too highly exalted. Thus a large army is often defeated by a small one. When God in His jealousy throws them into a panic, or thunders against them, they miserably perish. For God suffers no mortal to think magnificently"—HERODOTUS Book 7, c. 10.*

the other hand, humility, at first considered to be worth little, eventually comes to be recognized for its true value.

The world counts nothing great without display. But mark the substantial "honor that cometh from God only." "Heaven is my throne, and the earth is My footstool ... But to this one I will look, to him who is humble and contrite of spirit."[k] Yes—"I dwell," said the high and lofty One that inhabits eternity, "with the contrite and lowly of spirit."[l] Humility is indeed true greatness—"the crown"—as Mr. Howels in *Sermons* (i. pp. 335, 336) finely remarks—"of finite beings, made and jewelled by the hand of God Himself. Supremacy is the glory of God; humility is the ornament of His child." "I am but dust and ashes ... I am not worthy of the least of all the mercies ... I abhor myself ... Sinners—among whom I am foremost of all"[m]—such are the self-abasing confessions of men great in Jehovah's eyes. They shine with the reflection of His glory; but they turn away with genuine humility from their own shining.

[k]Isa 66:1, 2

[l]Isa 57:15

[m]Gen 18:27; AV—32:10; AV—Job 42:6; 1 Tim 1:15

Men of this stamp the king delights to honor. Their dignity begins on earth and is crowned in heaven. "Blessed are the poor in spirit for theirs is the kingdom of heaven."[n] They may be poor in rank. But they shine forth as mightier conquerors than Alexander. Their real glory eclipses the glare of the pomp and pride of life.

[n]Matt 5:3; 18:4

The elevation of *the proud* is often the step to their downfall. But God's *honor*, put upon his own people, upholds them, as Joseph and Daniel, in their high eminence, as witnesses for His name. Fitness for heaven is that adorning clothing of humility, which leads us to ascribe all our grace to God, and all our sin to ourselves. This is the prostrate adoration of heaven.[o] The Lord fill us richly with this spirit.

[o]Rev 5:9–12

Indeed all chastening discipline is for the great purpose, to "keep man from pride,"[p] and *to bring us low* in our own eyes, that His *honor* may "exalt you at the proper time."[q] It is with us as with our Lord—*honor* comes out of humiliation.[r] Thou meanest to be not our Savior only, but our pattern too. If we can go down the steps of Thine humiliation, we shall rise up the stairs of Thy glory.

[p]Job 33:17

[q]1 Peter 5:6; Job 22:29

[r]Prov 15:33; 18:12

24 *He who is a partner with a thief hates his own life;*
He hears the oath but tells nothing.

This is a warning under the eighth commandment. Do we realize the same solemnity of obligation as under the first? Many professing believers attach a degree of secularity to a detailed application of the duties of the second table of law. But both stand on the same authority. The transgressions of both are registered in the same book. The position in the Ten Commandments cannot be of great importance if it is there with nothing more than the approval—I am the Lord thy God. The law acknowledges no difference between *the thief and his partner.* Consenting to sin—receiving the stolen goods—involves us in the guilt and punishment.[s] The accomplice may be less practiced in sin. He may be just starting in it. But the first step is the way of death—acting as if *he hated his own life.*[t] One step naturally leads on to another. Suppose he is called to give evidence, under oath, concerning his secret knowledge of the deed. Wouldn't this be a temptation to lie; rather than to betray his fellow? Under the perverted obligation of his bond of secrecy *he hears the oath*—the solemn order to tell the truth on pain of the curse of God[u]—and he refuses to betray his partner in crime!

[s]Prov 1:10–15; Ps 50:18–21; Isa 1:23, 24

[t]Comp. Prov 6:32; 8:36; 15:32

[u]Comp. Lev 5:1; Num 5:21; 1 Kings 22:16; Matt 26:63.

Oh! how frightful is the history of thousands, whose fellowship with sinners has drawn them into fellowship with sin, and ultimately to take the lead in sin!—whose entrance into the path has led them step by step into the very depths of depravity! And of these thousands, how few I fear—retrace their steps, and become, like Onesimus as we read in Philemon, true followers of Christ, and faithful servants to man!

25 *The fear of man brings a snare,*
But he who trusts in the LORD *will be exalted.*

A snare brings a man into difficulties. He is not master of himself. Here Satan *spreads the snare,* and *the fear of man* drives into it. And a fearful *snare* it is and always has been to thousands. Many, once entangled, have never escaped. It besets every step of the pathway to heaven, every sphere of obligation. The king turns aside from strict trustworthiness.[v] The judge willfully pronounces

[v]1 Sam 15:24; Matt 14:9

an unrighteous sentence.[w] The minister faints under the cross;[x] and to avoid it, compromises the simplicity of the gospel.[y] They are too timid and afraid to carry out an unpopular teaching. The people cannot bear the *full* light. The sun of righteousness—Christ—is therefore exhibited under a mist; but dimly visible; shorn of His glowing beams. The strictness of the rule is distasteful. It must therefore be softened down, modified, or explained away.[z] Or inconstancy of profession must be quietly dealt with, lest the good opinion of some influential man must be forfeited. Such is the power of evil shame! Such low thoughts, not only concerning God, but of immortal souls as well! This timeserving shows a man-pleaser, not a true "bond-servant of God,"[a] and brings damage alike to his work and soul.[15]

[w] John 19:8, 13, 16
[x] 1 Kings 19:3; Jon 1:1–3
[y] Gal 2:12; 6:12
[z] Isa 30:9, 10; Jer 5:31
[a] Gal 1:10

The same deadly influence operates in families. Sometimes even parents shrink from openly protecting their child.[b] They dare not promise a supreme concern for his primary interests, or declare in opposition to many around them, the patriarch's godly determination—"As for me and my house"—however evil it may seem to others—"we will serve the Lord."[c]

[b] John 9:22
[c] Josh 24:15

Every class of society exhibits this corrupt principle. Perhaps the highest are bound in the most abject and hopeless chains; and to their tyrant they seem to acknowledge a sort of conscience or religious obedience. They will put aside all religious profession without fear: except that they are slaves to the attitudes and demands of this world's fashion, that they "trembled violently"[16] at the thought that people around them may think them religious; thereby giving honor to a vain idol but ashamed to honor the Lord of heaven and earth. Many would bravely face danger, who would shrink from being regarded as religious. They would fearlessly face the cannon's mouth, and yet they panic at the ridicule of a puny worm. Or even if some public excitement roused an impulse of boldness for religion, yet in a small grasp,

[15] *Zech 11:17. "Remember Dr. Dodd," writes Mr. Venn to his son, "I myself heard him tell his own flock, whom he was lecturing in his house that he was obliged to give up that method of helping their souls, because it exposed him to so much reproach. He gave it up, and fell from one compliance to another, with his corrupt nature; and under what reproach did he die!" Let the concluding advice of this excellent minister be well pondered—"Be afraid of nothing more than the detestable cowardice of a selfish and unbelieving heart"*—Life, *pp.* 255, 256.

[16] *Gen 27:33. The same word in the original.*

there is a cold timidity of silence. They shrink from the bold consistency of being a living witness. They are afraid to be thought peculiar. They are satisfied with just a little outward appearance of godliness, with no spiritual character or privilege. All is heartless delusion.

What—again, makes so many, especially among the young, ashamed to be found upon their knees; to be known as readers of their Bibles; or to take a definite stand with the saints of God? They know the Christian to be on the right side; and often they hear a whisper of conscience—"How I wish that my soul were in his place!"[d] But they are only half-hearted about religion. *The fear of man brings a snare.* And therefore they ask—not "What is the right thing for me to do?"—but, "What will my friends think of me?" They cannot brave the finger of scorn. And if they seem for a while to be in earnest, "their slavish fears" (as Bunyan well describes the case) "overmaster them. They have second thoughts—namely—that it is good to be wise, and not to run, for they don't know the hazard of losing all, or at least falling into unavoidable and unnecessary troubles."[17] They would rather wrestle with their convictions, till they have worn themselves out, than welcome what Moses esteemed "greater riches than the treasures of Egypt . . . *the reproach of Christ.*"[e]

[d] John 7:13; 12:42, 43; Acts 26:11; 2 Tim 1:15; 4:16

[e] Heb 11:26

But how painful to see the children of God entangled in the *snare!* The father of the faithful twice denied his wife.[f] His son follows his weak example.[g] Aaron fashions the golden calf.[h] The man after God's own heart sinks himself into the lowest degradation.[i] Hezekiah, distinguished for his *trust,* gives way to his *fear.*[j] The zealous disciple, even after the most solemn pledges to his Savior, and after an act of great boldness in His defense, yields up his courage to a servant girl and solemnly renounces His Lord.[k] Oh! Do we not hear the warning voice against entrance "into temptation"—against the weakness of the "flesh"?[l] Let us run into our hiding place, and cry—"Uphold me that I may be safe."[m] Humbling, indeed, is the contrast between the boldness of the servants of Satan and the timidity of the soldiers of Christ! Who of us has not cause of painful self-condemnation?

[f] Gen 12:11–13; 20:2, 11
[g] Gen 26:7
[h] Exod 32:22–24
[i] 1 Sam 21:10–13
[j] 2 Kings 18:13–16; 2 Chron 16:1–7
[k] Matt 26:69–74
[l] Matt 26:41
[m] Ps 119:117

[17] *Conversation between Hopeful and Christian.*

How different this cringing attitude is from the godly *fear* of sin, which the wise man says is the true meaning of happiness![n] *That* is a holy principle, *this* an opening to sin.[o] *That* is our keeping grace;[p] *this* wounds our conscience, and draws us from our allegiance. "By the fear of the Lord men depart from evil;[q] by *the fear of man* they run themselves into evil," said Flavel *(treatise on fear,* chap. 2). The one is that pathway to heaven.[r] The other, involving the denial of the Savior, plunges its wretched slave into the lake of fire.[s]

[n]Prov 28:14
[o]Gen 39:9, with Isa 57:11
[p]1 Cor 10:12; Heb 4:1
[q]Prov 16:6
[r]Prov 19:23
[s]Mark 8:38; Rev 21:8

But even apart from this tremendous end, see what a great hindrance it is to Christian integrity. Indeed as Mr. Scott most truly observes "It is," often at least, "the last victory the Christian gains." He will master, by that grace which is given of God, his own lusts and passions, and all manner of inward and outward temptations. He will be dead to the pleasures of the world, long before he has mastered his fear of man. This kind of spirit does not go out but grows by very spiritual and devout living. The hindrance meets us at every turn and slows us down. Oh! for a free deliverance from this kind of bondage; scarcely to be expected, however, till we have been made to feel its power!

Thank God—there is a way of deliverance. Faith frees the soul from fear. If fear makes the giant tremble before the worm, *trust in the Lord* makes the worm stronger than the giant. Neither the fury of the king,[t] nor of the people;[u] neither the fire,[v] nor the den of lions,[w] daunts and hurts him that believes in his God. "He that fears to flinch, shall never flinch from fear," said Hildersham. Faith gives power to prayer. The strength from prayer makes us cheerful in obedience, and unwavering in trial. Here is safety, strength, courage, peace. Nothing but faith gives the victory; but the victory of faith is complete.[18] He only, *who puts his trust in the Lord,* is prepared, when God and man are at odds, to "give heed to" God rather than man.[x] A secret union with God is implanted in the soul by this faith; a union as mighty, as it is secret; a sacred spring of life—the energy of God him-

[t]2 Kings 6:31, 32
[u]Num 14:6–10
[v]Dan 3:17
[w]Dan 6:10
[x]Acts 4:19

[18] *1 John 5:4, 5. Comp. Heb 11:27. "I cannot wield the sword of the Spirit," said the weak and timid Haller to his friends, "If you do not stretch your hands to me, all is over." He then threw himself trembling at the feet of the Lord, and soon rose enlightened, and exclaiming—*"Faith in the Savior *gives me courage, and scatters all my fears"—DAubigne's* Hist. Refor. *Book 15. Chap. 2.*

[y]Gal 2:20

[z]Ps 69:29; 91:14; Isa 33:16
[a]Prov 18:10
[b]1 Peter 1:5

[c]Gal 6:14

self[y]; triumphant therefore in the mightiest conflict with the flesh. The man, dependent on the world for happiness, is in bondage. The servant of God is at liberty. It doesn't matter to him, whether the world smiles or frowns. He is safe, beyond its reach—set on high.[z] Faith brings him to his strong tower.[a] There he is "protected by the power of God through faith for ... salvation."[b] *Fear brings us into the snare.* Faith brings liberty, safety, *exaltation.* Oh! Thou God of power and grace, may my soul praise Thee for this mighty deliverance, this joyous freedom! May I never be ashamed of my Master! May I be bound to His people and glory in His cross![c]

26 *Many seek the ruler's favor,*
But justice for man comes *from the* LORD.

THE LIBERTY THAT FAITH BRINGS

[d]Ps 30:5
[e]Ps 146:3; Isa 2:22; Jer 17:5, 6
[f]Isa 30:1–3; 31:1–3
[g]Prov 19:6

[h]Gen 40:1, 2

[i]Ps 47:4; Prov 16:33

[j]AV—James 1:17; Isa 49:4; Job 34:29

Therefore, seek God to be your friend. "His favor is for a lifetime."[d] Confidence in man is no less sinful[e] and dangerous[f] than *the fear of man.* Yet, with what earnestness will men seek earthly advantage! *Many seek the ruler's favor*[g] more than God's, and sacrifice their consciences, and hazard their souls, to get it. But when they have bought it at such a price, what is it?—as easy to lose, as it was hard to gain. The whim of the moment may destroy the hard-earned object.[h] And then, what have they to live upon? All this is forgetting, that *every man's justice comes from the Lord.* Here then is the solid ground of faith. First, begin with God; all judgment is in His hands. "Commit your way to the Lord, trust also in Him, and He will do it."[19] Let Him choose and dispose our lot.[i] Consider everything that passes as coming from Him. In everything, great and small, deal with Him. Reason with Him. His favor, unlike the changing *favor of the ruler,* is without "variableness, neither shadow of turning." And when, through the fickleness of man, earthly prospects are fading, then rest in quiet—"Surely the justice due to Me is with the Lord."[j] "As thou wilt, what thou wilt, when thou wilt," said Thomas à Kempis. This is the shortest, the surest, way of peace—Only believe.

[19] *Ps 37:5, 6. "He needeth not to flatter the ruler; for what God hath appointed, that shall come to him"*—Reformer's Notes. *"The determination concerning a man is from Jehovah"—Bishop LOWTH'S* Prelim. *Dissertation to Isaiah.*

27 *An unjust man is abominable to the righteous,*
And he who is upright in the way is abominable to the wicked.

POISON IN THE SERPENT'S SEED

Here is the oldest, the most rooted, the most universal quarrel in the world. It was the first fruit of the fall.[k] It has continued ever since and will last to the end of the world. It is always kept up at the highest point. Each party is *abominable* to the other. It is not only that they are as opposite in character, as light is to darkness; but there is a mutual dislike that can never be softened down.

[k]Gen 3:15

Let us look at each of the parties in this open opposition to each other. *An unjust man is an abomination to the righteous.* Is it then his sin to be at such odds with his fellow-sinner? No, rather—it is the very holiness of his character and profession. If he has any fear of the holiness of God; if through grace he is delivered from the love and dominion of sin, is not the sight of sin hateful to him? And while he abhors it most of all in himself, yet does not the watching of the evil in his own heart deepen his abhorrence and hatred of it in those around him? He would not overlook it in those most dear to him. He appeals to his God in a burst of holy indignation: "Do I not hate those who hate Thee, O Lord? And do I not loathe those who rise up against Thee? I hate them with the utmost hatred; they have become my enemies."[l]

[l]Ps 139:21, 22. Comp. Prov 28:4

Looking at the other party—*the wicked* holds *the righteous* in similar *abomination.*[m] "The mind set on the flesh is hostile toward God," and cannot therefore bear His image in His children.[n] Gladly would the wicked, were not their enmity restrained, "uproot" them "from the land"; just as they never rested, till they had nailed the Son of God to the tree. Here however is the main difference. The enmity of *the just* is against the sins, not the persons, of the wicked. How they, with all this principle, love their souls and pray for them![o] How gladly would they win them to Christ and salvation! The enmity of the wicked is against *the persons*—the ways of *the righteous*—all that belongs to them. "This is that strong poison in the serpent's seed," said Leighton,[p] the murderous spirit of their father the devil!

[m]Verse 10

[n]Rom 8:7; John 15:17–19; 1 John 3:12, 13; Ps 52:5

[o]Rom 9:1; 10:1

[p]1 Peter 3:14

[q]Ps 55:6

[r]Ps 45:3, 4; Rev 19:11–16; Gen 3:15

The soul is wearied with the unceasing struggle with the enemies of truth. How can one resist the wish for the "wings like a dove! I would fly away and be at rest."[q] And how could we continue on in the battle except for the blessed hope—O Lord! hasten it in Thy time—when the woman's conquering "seed . . . shall bruise "the Serpent's head, and the head of all[r] his seed, finally and forever; and then He shall reign King and Savior over His redeemed people.

CHAPTER THIRTY

1 *The words of Agur the son of Jakeh, the oracle.*
The man declares to Ithiel, to Ithiel and Ucal:
2 *Surely I am more stupid than any man,*
And I do not have the understanding of a man.
3 *And I have not learned wisdom,*
But I have knowledge of the Holy One.

"CARNAL—SOLD UNDER SIN"

The two concluding chapters of this book are an appendix to the Proverbs of Solomon. Nothing certain is known of the writers; and it is vain to speculate when God is silent. It is far better to give the full interest of our mind and heart to instruction, than to indulging unprofitable curiosity about the writers. Our ignorance of the writers of many of the Psalms doesn't hinder their profit to us. We know God—their Author, when the penmen are hid. It is enough for us to be assured that they were "men" who wrote as they were *"moved by the Holy Spirit."*[a]

[a] 2 Peter 1:21

Agur was doubtless one of the wise men found in many ages of the Old Testament. *His words* were *the oracle*—that is—divine instruction[1] given to *Ithiel and Ucal* (*Ithiel* especially) probably two of his scholars, whose names are equally unknown to us. Perhaps they came to him for instruction, and he was led to express himself in the most humbling sense of his own ignorance—You come to me for instruction. But *surely I am more stupid than any man;* not having the advantages of *learned wisdom,*[b] *but I have knowledge of the Holy One.*[c]

[b] Amos 7:14, 15
[c] Dan 4:18

His language is certainly strong. He could scarcely have used any stronger. He confesses himself to be, not

[1] *This was a frequent Scripture name for ordinary instruction. Prov 31; 1 Cor 14:1, 3, 4; 1 Thess 5:20.*

only stupid as man is by nature;[d] but, even though enlightened by heavenly teaching, *more stupid than any man.*[e] Were these the words of truth? Or were they the affectation of modesty? Or was it false humility, dishonorably denying the work of God? He was now speaking from the mouth of God. And how could he pretend ignorance in His name? He spoke the truth, as it really is, as consciousness could only speak; as self-knowledge under divine teaching dictated. For let a man take "the lamp of the Lord"; given him to search "all the innermost parts of his being,"[f] and what a mass of vanity will he find there! Such folly mixed with his wisdom! Such ignorance with his knowledge! that, instead of priding himself upon his elevation above his fellowmen, he can but cry out in shame—*Surely I am more stupid than any man!* Whoever knows his own heart, knows that of himself, that he can hardly conceive of any one else being so degraded as himself.[2]

[d]Job 11:12; Ps 49:20
[e]Jer 10:14
[f]Prov 20:27

IF YOU WON'T STOOP, YOU CAN'T ENTER THE DOOR

And what is more—it is the child of God comparing himself with his perfect standard. And in the perception of his own shortcomings, the most discerning clear-sighted penitent feels that he can never abase himself as he ought before his God—He would lie low, lower still, infinitely lower, in the dust. Holy Paul, comparing himself with the spirituality of the perfect law, exclaims—"I am of flesh, sold into bondage of sin."[g] Isaiah, in the presence of a holy God—cries out—"Woe is me, for I am ruined! Because I am a man of unclean lips."[h] Job in the manifestation of the power of God sinks into absolute nothingness and unworthiness.[i] David in the full view of the wisdom of God is made to see the wickedness of his own irrational conduct and take up the very confession of Agur—"I was senseless and ignorant; I was like a beast before Thee"![3] The nearer our contemplation of God, the

[g]Rom 7:14
[h]Isa 6:5
[i]Job 40:4; 42:6

[2] *Comp. Prov 14:10. The following remarks of Edwards* (Religious Affections, *Part 3, Sec t. 6) will illustrate this subject—"He that has much grace, apprehends much more than others that great height to which his love ought to ascend; and he sees better than others, how little he has risen towards that height. And therefore estimating his love by the whole height of his duty, hence it appears astonishingly low and little in his eyes—True grace is of that nature, that the more a person has of it, with remaining corruption, the less does his goodness and holiness appear in proportion, not only to his past, but his present deformity, in the sin that now appears in his heart, and in the abominable defects of his highest and best affections."*

[3] *Ps 73:1–22, "a bear." Bishop Horsley gives it, "I was as a brute before thee."*

closer our communion with Him, the deeper will be our self-abasement before Him; like the winged seraphs before the throne, who with their wings "covered his face, and with two [wings] . . . covered his feet."[j] Well, therefore, may the wisest and holiest of men, though "renewed to a true knowledge according to the image of the One who created him,[k] take up the humiliating confession, "*Surely I am more stupid than any man.*" Genuine humility is the only path of wisdom. Unless a man stoops, he can never enter the door. He must become "foolish that he may become wise."[4] And when he is humbled in his shame, then let him see the house of his God in its breadth and length;[l] enjoying clearer, and longing still for clearer manifestations of the incomprehensible God.

[j]Isa 6:2

[k]Col 3:10

[l]Ezek 44:5

But how reverently should we approach His divine presence! With what holy hands should we open His revelation, dreading a careless, light and presumptuous spirit; yet cherishing those nobly ambitious desires for deeper and higher knowledge; yes, reciting them before our God with that repetition which to a carnal mind would be nauseating repetition; but which He, who knows our hearts, loves to hear, and will beyond our desires abundantly fulfill.

4 *Who has ascended into heaven and descended?*
Who has gathered the wind in His fists?
Who has wrapped the waters in His garment?
Who has established all the ends of the earth?
What is His name of His son's name?
Surely you know!

"BE STILL AND KNOW THAT HE IS GOD!"

Can we wonder that Agur should have confessed his ignorance, now that he was contemplating the majesty of God, so wondrous in His works, so incomprehensible in His nature? The eye was blinded by the dazzling blaze of the sun. To behold Jehovah *ascending and descending* in His own glorious person:[m] afterward in the person of His dear Son[n] (for in His great work was not His Father's name in Him[o]); to see Him holding the loose *winds* as

[m]Gen 11:7; 17:22; 18:21; Exod 3:8
[n]John 1:51; 3:13; 6:62; Eph 4:9, 10
[o]John 10:30, 38; 14:10. Comp. Exod 23:21

[4] *1 Cor 3:18. There is a fine ray of wisdom in that consciousness of ignorance, that led Socrates to confess—"I only know one thing—that I know nothing." Comp. 1 Cor 8:2.*

firmly as a man might hold in his *fists,*[5] to see His almighty control of the *waters,*[p] and His establishment of the *ends of the earth*[q]—this is a sight that might make the highest and wisest of men sink into nothingness before Him? Who has done this, none can doubt. The challenge is a demonstration that it was God alone. "Shew me the man, that can or dare [to take] this power to himself," said Bishop Hall.

[p] Job 26:8; 38:8–11; Isa 40:12; Jer 5:22
[q] Job 26:7; 38:5; Ps 93:1; 119:90

But when we pass from the works to their great Maker, truly we are overwhelmed. *What is His name or His son's name?* "Can you discover the depths of God? Can you discover the limits of the Almighty?" He "dwells in unapproachable light; whom no man has seen or can see."[r] How can we express Him in words or conceive of Him in thought? Child of God! "Cease striving and know that I am God."[s] Restrain your reason. Humble your faith. "Put your hand over your mouth." Lie in the dust before Him. "Oh, the depth!"[t]—open only to Him whose "understanding is infinite."[u]

[r] Job 11:7–9; 1 Tim 6:16. Comp. Job 38:3, 4
[s] Ps 46:10
[t] Job 21:5; Rom 11:33
[u] Ps 147:5; Isa 40:28

But how the mystery increases! *What is His name . . . Surely you know!* And who can tell? "No one knows the Son, except the Father."[v] Yet there is a Son in the eternal Godhead; a Son, not begotten in time, but from eternity;[w] His name, therefore, not, as some would have it, a component part of His humiliation, but the manifestation of His Godhead: co-existent with His Father in the same indescribable nature, yet personally distinct.[6] *What is His name or His son's name?* Sovereignty—omnipresence—omnipotence is His. He, too, controls the winds and waters,[x] and establishes the earth,[y] as one who is in the visible "form of God, [and] did not regard equality with God a thing to be grasped."[z]

[v] Matt 11:27
[w] Prov 8:22–30
[x] Matt 8:26; 14:32
[y] Heb 1:3
[z] Phil 2:6

What is His name? The secret name is easily spelled.[a] But the mystery is hid. We must not inquire too curiously.[b] Be careful that we stop where Revelation stops. Beyond this bound every step is a trespass on forbidden ground, intruding into those things which we have not seen, "inflated without cause by his fleshly mind."[c] Many, however, are so bewitched by their own fancy that

[a] Rev 19:12, 13
[b] Gen 32:29; Judg 13:18
[c] Col 2:18

[5] *Job 28:25. Comp. Ps 104:3; 135:7. The heathen dreamed of a lower deity, whom Jupiter appointed as storekeeper, to still or raise the winds at his pleasure. HOMER. Odyss. K. 21, 22. VIRGIL. Aen. i. 69, 70.*
[6] *"We have a full and clear testimony of the distinction of persons, and that the Son is equal to the Father, and of the same substance with Him"—LAVATER.*

they conceive themselves to understand this name. They think far higher of their wisdom than Agur did of his and are at no loss at all to explain what they conceive in their proud ignorance to be the full meaning of the incomprehensible subject. But the genuine disciple acknowledges the nature of the Son to be alike unfathomable with that of the Father. He humbly lies at His feet and thankfully adores the mystery, which he cannot by searching "discover."[d]

[d]Job 11:7

Yet, what Revelation has brought up to us from these untraceable depths are pearls of great price. Let us reverently gather them for the enriching of our souls. So far as our divine Teacher leads us by the hand, let us faithfully follow Him. Within His bounds let us wander freely through the length and breadth of the land. The wholesome dread of being wise above that which is written, must not dampen the holy ardor to be wise and wiser continually in that which is written. To inquire just out of curiosity is rashness; to believe is piety; to know indeed is life eternal. Unsearchable as He is in His greatness; yet so near is He to us that we can rest in His bosom. Yours, Christian, is the unspeakable privilege to be one with Him, who is One with God. And therefore, if you tell *His name,* as you are bound to tell what is revealed, is it not all that is infinitely great, combined with the endearing relationships: husband, brother, Savior, King?

5 *Every word of God is tested;*
He is a shield to those who take refuge [AV—*put their trust*] *in Him.*
6 *Do not add to His words*
Lest He reprove you, and you be proved a liar.

Nothing is learned solidly by abstract speculation. Go to the Bible. Here all is light and purity. Though "secret things belong to the Lord our God, but the things revealed" are our holy directory. Everything is intended to influence the heart and conduct.[e] How unlike the sacred books of the heathen or the sensual religion of Mahomet! Here there is no license, or encouragement to sin, no passive cooperation with it. All lurking sins, cherished in the dark cavern of pollution, are brought to light and reproved. *Every word of God is tested.* Of what other

[e]Deut 29:29

book in the world can this be said? Where else is the gold found without mixture with a cheaper metal. The Word is tried. It has stood the trial, and no dross has been found in it. "Having God for its Author, it has truth without any mixture of error for its matter," stated Locke. "*The words of the Lord are pure words,* as silver tried in a furnace of earth, purified seven times."[f]

[f]Ps 12:6. Comp. Ps 119:140; Prov 8:8, 9

But if *every word of God is tested,* take care that no word is slighted. How few range over the whole revelation of God! To take a whole view of the universe, we should embrace not only the fruitful gardens but its barren deserts, coming equally from the hand of God, and none of them made without purpose. To take a similarly comprehensive view of the sacred field, we must study the apparently barren, as well as the more manifestly fruitful, portions of the Bible. Meat will be gathered from the detailed code of laws, from the historical annals of the kings, and from the "quarrels and conflicts,"—the prolific results of "your pleasures."[g] The whole Scripture is Scripture, and "all Scripture is . . . profitable."[h]

[g]James 4:1

[h]2 Tim 3:16

But usually we read and reread our favorite passages. We take a small part all too often, instead of the whole, or as if it were the whole. One is absorbed in the doctrinal, a second in the practical, a third in the prophetical, a fourth in the experimental, Scriptures; each seeming to forget, that *every word of God is tested.* That this is not the right way to study God's Word becomes clear in our character and conduct. The doctrinist becomes loose in practice; the Christian, most interested in studying the practical teaching of the Word, becomes self-righteous in principle. The prophetic disciple, absorbed in his imaginative atmosphere, neglects present obligations. The experimental religionist mistakes a religion of feeling, excitement, or fancy, for the sobriety and substantial fruitfulness of the gospel. All remind us of our Lord's rebuke—"You are mistaken, not understanding the Scriptures."[i]

[i]Matt 22:29

The great exercise therefore is—to bring out the whole mass of solid truth in all its parts and glory. So wisely has God linked together the many parts of His system that we can receive no portion soundly, except in connection with the whole. The accuracy of any view is more than suspicious, that serves to put a forced construction upon

Scripture, to dislocate its connection, or to throw important truths into the shade. Apparently contradictory statements are in fact only balancing truths; each correcting its opposite, and, like the opposite muscles, contributing to the strength and completeness of the frame. Every heresy probably stands upon some insulated text or some exaggerated truth, pressed beyond "the proportion of . . . faith."[j] But none can stand upon the combined view and testimony of Scripture. Nor let it be sufficient, that our system includes no positive error, if some great truths are lacking. Let it be carefully grounded upon the acknowledgment—*Every word of God is tested.* Some of us may err in presumptuous familiarity with Scripture; others in unworthy reserve. But if the heart is right, self-knowledge will expose the error, and self-discipline will correct it.

[j]Rom 12:6

Christian simplicity will teach us to receive every divine truth upon the ground—that *it is the Word of God.* Though it is not all of equal importance, it will be regarded with equal reverence. With complete confidence, we acknowledge God as the author of all Scripture, and that *every Word of God is tested.* To reject therefore one "jot or tittle is a sufficient demonstration," as Dr. Owen admirably observes, "that *no one jot or tittle of it* is received as it ought [to be]. Upon whatsoever this tittle and inscription is—'The Word of Jehovah'—there must we stoop, and bow down our souls before it, and captivate our understandings unto the obedience of faith."[7]

This holy reverence is combined with God as our *refuge.* Blessed trust, which brings *a shield* of special favor over His trembling child![k] Sometimes Satan is permitted to cover him in darkness, and to picture, as it were, frightful images upon his prison wall. What would he do in this time of terror, if he could not find *a shield* and a *refuge* in the bosom of His God? Yes—if *the Word of God is tested,* it must be a sure ground of trust. We may take its statement with undoubting confidence, *that He is a shield,* as to Abraham of old,[l] so to Abraham's children, that put their trust in Him.[8] In all circumstances from within and from without—when I quake under the ter-

[k]Ps 2:11, 12; Isa 66:2

[l]Gen 15:1

[7] *OWEN on the* Perseverance of the Saints, *chap. 10. See* Life of Mary Jane Graham, *chap. 5.*
[8] *Ps 5:12. Comp. the same connection, 18:30.*

rors of the law, in the hour of death, in the day of judgment—"Thou art ... my *shield*."[m] Nothing honors God like this turning to Him in every time of need. If there is rest, peaceful confidence, safekeeping, anywhere, it is here. Where is it found otherwise? Despondency meets the poor deluded sinner, who looks for some other prop. And even the child of God traces his frequent want of protection to his feeble and uncertain use of his divine *shield*.

[m]Ps 119:114

But *the Word of God is* not only *tested,* and cannot deceive. It is also sufficient; and therefore, like tried gold, it needs no addition for its perfection. Hence to *add to His words,* stamped as they are with his divine authority, will expose us to His tremendous reproof and cover us with shame.[n] Israel virtually *added* their oral law and written traditions.[o]

[n]Deut 4:2; 12:32; Rev 22:18, 19
[o]Mark 7:7–13

The needlessness of this addition is obvious. For if "the sacred writings ... are able to give you the wisdom that leads to salvation,"[p] what more do we need? And if this were spoken of the Old Testament Scriptures, the sufficiency of a part confirms the larger sufficiency of the whole, while it excludes all reference to any othe sufficiency; just as the sufficiency of the early light for all practical purposes, while it does away with the necessity of the light of a candle, it establishes the fuller advantage of the light of perfect day. If "Scripture is ... profitable for teaching, for reproof, for correction, for training in righteousness;" if the "man of God ... be adequate, equipped for every good work,"[q] what clearer demonstration can be given of its absolute completeness? To reflect, therefore, upon the integrity of this divine rule of faith and to shake confidence in its sole authority, is to bring in a false principle, the source of every evil and corruption of the faith.

[p]2 Tim 3:15
[q]2 Tim 3:16, 17

Never was it so important to clear from all question the momentous controversy as to what is, and what is not, the Word of God. The Lord has most carefully guarded His *tested Word* from all human mixture. May He preserve His ministers from "teaching as their doctrines the precepts of men"; saying, "the Lord declares," when He hath not spoken![r] What reverential awe, what godly jealousy, should they exercise, to *keep from adding to*

[r]Ezek 13:7–9, with Matt 15:9

His Word by words of false interpretation; inserted between the lines; not to expound their own minds, instead of the mind of God!

7 *Two things I asked of Thee,*
Do not refuse me before I die:
8 *Keep deception and lies far from me,*
Give me neither poverty nor riches;
Feed me with the food that is my portion,
9 *Lest I be full and deny* Thee *and say, "Who is the Lord?"*
Or lest I be in want and steal,
And profane the name of my God.

BORDERS OF TEMPTATION: RICHES, POVERTY

Though Agur had confessed his brutishness before his God; yet his prayers (the most accurate test of a man of God) prove him to have been possessed of deep spiritual understanding. "You ask and do not receive, because you ask with wrong motives, so that you may spend it on your pleasure."[s] How wisely gracious, therefore, is the teaching of the divine Comforter, helping "our weakness" in prayer, and by molding our petitions, "according to the will of God," ensuring their acceptance.[t] Agur's heart must have been under this heavenly teaching; dictating his prayers by a primary regard for his best interests, and by a spiritual discernment of what would probably be beneficial, and what injurious to them.

[s]James 4:3

[t]Rom 8:26, 27

Two things he especially *asked*—not as though he had nothing to ask, but as being the pressing burden of the present moment. And these he asks—as if he would take no *refusal*[u]—with all the intense earnestness of a dying sinner, *"Do not refuse me before I die."*

[u]Gen 32:26

His prayers are short but comprehensive. Though little is said, yet that little is full of many things, all arranged in their proper order. Spiritual blessings are first; temporal blessings, second, on a lower level.

Keep deception and lies far from me. Isn't this the atmosphere of the world?—characterized by vanity, deluded by lies: promising happiness, only to disappoint its weary and restless victims? How can the heaven-born soul breathe in such a world? Everything deadens the heart and eclipses the glory of the Savior. "My soul cleaves to the dust." "All that is in the world, the lust of the flesh and the lust of the eyes and the boastful pride of life, is not from the Father, but is from the world."[v] And, therefore, "those who regard vain idols forsake their faithfulness."[w] A soul that knows its dangers and its besetting temptations will live in the spirit of this prayer of the godly Agur—*keep from me—far from me*—as far as possible, *deception and lies*. "Turn away my eyes," prayed a saint of God in the same watchful jealousy—"from looking at *vanity. Remove the false way from me*."[x]

[v]Ps 119:25; 1 John 2:16
[w]Jon 2:8
[x]Ps 119:37, 29

But how singular, yet how filled with instruction, is Agur's second prayer! All are ready to pray against poverty. But to disapprove *riches*—this is not nature's desire, but an impulse of godly fear and trembling, that comes from above. "Give me not riches"—is the prayer of hardly one in ten thousand. Agur, as a wise man, desired the safest and happiest lot; not, as Israel of old, "food according to their desire,"[y] but *food* convenient for him, measured out in daily allowance,[z] suitable to his need. This is obviously not a predetermined measure. It implies, not a bare sufficiency for natural life, but a provision varying according to the calling, in which God has placed us. "If Agur [is] the master of a family, then that [provision] is sufficient to maintain his wife, children, and household. If Agur [is] a public person, a prince or a ruler of the people; then that is Agur's sufficiency, which will conveniently maintain him in that condition," said Mede *(Sermon on Agur's Choice)*. Jacob when he had "become two companies," evidently required more than when, in his earlier life, "with my staff only I crossed this Jordan."[a] What was sufficient for him alone, would not have been sufficient for the many that were then dependent upon him. The immense provisions for Solmon's table, considering the vast multitude of his dependents, might be only enough for the demand.[b] The distribution of the manna was food convenient—nothing too much, but no deficiency—"He who had gathered much had no excess, and he who had gathered little had no lack."[c] And thus, in the daily dispensation of God's care, a little may be plenty for one, while an overflowing

[y]Ps 78:18
[z]Comp. 1 Kings 4:27; 2 Kings 25:30
[a]Gen 32:10
[b]1 Kings 4:22
[c]Exod 16:18

plenty is not adequate for another. Only let Christian self-denial, not depraved appetite, be the standard of competency. Proud nature never stoops so low.[d] The apostle distinctly traces to the influence of divine teaching his Christian moderation in his different conditions of abundance and of want.[9] Philosophy may have introduced the lesson; but almighty grace alone can command the practice of it.

[d]Eccl 5:10; Hab 2:5; 1 Tim 6:9, 10

"It is a question," says Dr. South, "whether the piety or the [wisdom] of this prayer [is] greater."[e] Agur was well persuaded of the temptations that accompany these two opposite conditions—*the deception and lies* belonging to *riches,*[f] and the discontent and occasion of sin, which are the snares of *poverty*. Yet he does not pray against these states, absolutely only submissively. It is the prayer of his choice, the desire of his heart, that God would graciously exempt him from both, and bless him with a middle condition. Nor does he ask this to satisfy the flesh. He disapproves, not the trouble, anxieties, and responsibilities of *riches,* which might seem to indicate a lazy, self-pleasing spirit; nor the miseries and sufferings of *poverty*; but he cries for deliverance from the snares of each condition—"Let me not be *rich, lest I be full, and deny Thee.* Let me not be poor, *lest I steal, and profane the name of my God.*"

[e]James 3:16

[f]Ps 62:9

Sadly enough, the danger of these results is all too evident. Both extremes are the borders of fearful temptation. Strange and irrational as it may appear, such is the depravity of our nature, that mercies lead to neglect, and often, casting off, of God.[g] Lust is too strong for conscience. Rarely does "the daughter of Tyre . . . come with a gift"; or "the rich among the people will entreat . . . favor" of their God.[h] Too often, the more we receive from God, the less He receives from us.[10] The intertwining thorns choke the heavenly plant.[i] And as we prosper in the flesh, we are impoverished in the spirit. But not less threatening are the dangers of extreme poverty; nor is it every Christian, that can honorably grapple with them. Dishonesty is a besetting temptation,[j] followed up by

[g]Job 21:13, 14; 22:17, 18

[h]Ps 45:12

[i]Matt 13:22

[j]Prov 6:30

[9] I have learned—I have been instructed—*expressions taken from the instructions in the* Heathen Mysteries. *Phil 4:11, 12.*

[10] *Deut 6:11, 12; 8:10–13; 32:15; Hos 13:6. What a deep knowledge of the heart is implied in that petition of the Litany for deliverance* in all time of wealth! *How hard to realize the* time of wealth *as the time of* special need!

[k]Prov 29:24. Comp. Lev 6:2, 3; 19:11, 12; Zech 5:3, 4
[l]2 Tim 2:26

lying to escape punishment.[k] Thus two commandments are broken, and the sinner is in "the snare of the devil, having been taken captive by him to do his will."[l]

[m]Gen 28:20
[n]Jer 45:5
[o]Phil 4:11, 12; 1 Tim 6:6–10

The "golden mean" (for even a heathen could describe it) that way, is recommended by patriarchs,[m] prophets,[n] and apostles.[o] No, our Lord teaches us to pray for it in terms identical with this petition. For what else is our daily bread but *food that is my portion*?

We must however be careful that we use Agur's prayer in his spirit. Perhaps the gospel teaches us to leave the matter entirely with God. Both *riches and poverty* are His appointment.[11] It may please Him to place us in a high condition; to entrust us with much *riches*, or to exercise us with the trials of *poverty*. Many of His children are in both these conditions.[12] And shall they wish it otherwise? No, let them, instead, seek for grace to glorify Him in either state. Of, if it seem lawful to pray for a change of condition, let us not forget to pray for a single eye to His glory, that His will, not ours, may be done in us. "Whatsoever God gives," said the pious Bishop Hall, "I am both thankful and indifferent; so as, while I am rich in estate, I may be poor in spirit; and while I am poor in estate, I may be rich in grace."[13]

10 *Do not slander a slave to his master,*
Lest he curse you and you be found guilty.

Let not this Proverb be an excuse for unfaithfulness. How much evil goes on in a family, because those that are aware of it, and ought to inform, shrink from accusing a servant *to his master*! They think that they must not make mischief in the house, or bring themselves into trouble. But we owe it alike to master and to servant[p] not to wink at sin. We may owe it to ourselves to accuse the servant *to his master* for injury to ourselves.[q] Yet, let a fellow-servant first observe our Lord's rule of privacy.[r] Let every exercise of faithfulness be in the spirit of love.

[p]Matt 7:12; Lev 19:17
[q]Gen 21:25, 26
[r]Matt 18:15

[11] *Riches are His gift, 1 Kings 3:13. Poverty is His will, Deut 15:11. Comp. Job 1:21.*
[12] *Abraham—David—Solomon—with Lazarus and the heirs of his kingdom, James 2:5.*
[13] Works, *8:195. "Our Saviour, in the prayer he taught, directs us to pray in general, that God would give us daily bread, and deliver us from evil; without specifying the external comfort we might desire, or the particular disagreeable occurences we might wish to be secured against: but leaving it to the goodness of our heavenly Father to determine what is* convenient for us, *and what would prove upon the whole really evil. Let us therefore from hence learn to pray, that God would always put us into that condition, which He sees to be fittest for us, and that He would fit us more and more for that condition, in which He places us, whatever it might be: granting us wisdom and grace to behave in it after a right manner, and both to discern and improve the advantages annexed to it. By this means, when there is no appearance but of a barren desert, we shall discover mines of gold"*—Grove's Sermons.

Beware of the busy maliciousness of the talebearer.[s] Never make trouble for trifles; or *slander the servant,* when he may not have the full liberty and power to defend himself. When conscience does not constrain us to speak, the law of love always supplies a reason for silence. The Jewish servants were ordinarily slaves, for the most part crushed by their masters' oppression. It would be most cruel, therefore, to be without strong cause to heap degradation upon a sinking fellowman, for whom the Mosaic law prescribed kindness and protection.[t]

The rule, however, may be more generally applied. David suffered severely from unkind accusations to his royal master.[u] Those who take the most eager pleasure in finding fault are usually those, who can least bear the retort upon themselves. Take heed, lest, while thou art exposing "the speck in your brother's eye, you be reminded to your deeper disgrace of the "log that is in your own eye."[v] A curse from your injured brother may not come "without cause" to you.[w] The motive, which plainly actuated the accusation of the adulteress, only brought shame upon the accusers, The conviction of their own consciences brought their own guilt to mind.[x] Should not this remembrance constrain us to "malign" *needlessly* "no one"?[y] Should not the covering of our infinitely provoking offenses, cause us to gladly throw a covering over our offending brother, where the honor of God does not forbid concealment?[z]

[s] Lev 19:16
[t] Deut 23:15
[u] 1 Sam 22:9, 10; 26:19
[v] Matt 7:3–5
[w] Comp. Prov 26:2; Deut 15:9; 1 Sam 26:19. Comp. James 2:13
[x] John 8:3–9
[y] Titus 3:2
[z] Eph 4:31, 32; Col 3:12, 13

11 *There is a kind of* man *who curses his father,*
And does not bless his mother.
12 *There is a kind who is pure in his own eyes,*
Yet is not washed from his filthiness.
13 *There is a kind—Oh how lofty are his eyes!*
And his eyelids are raised in arrogance.
14 *There is a kind of* man *whose teeth are* like *swords,*
And his jaw teeth like *knives,*
To devour the afflicted from the earth,
And the needy from among men.

FOUR KINDS OF SINNERS

Agur here gives in artificial order (as in some of the Psalms) his observations, probably in answer to his disciples' inquiries. He describes four different classes of people that came under his eyes—not a few individuals, but *a kind of man*; a race of men, like a large stock, descending from father to son. Truly "that which has been is that which will be, and that which has been done is that which will be done. So, there is nothing new under the sun."[a] For these four *kinds* belong to every age. They always have been, and always will be, to the end of time.

[a]Eccl 1:9

Take the first class. What a disgrace to human nature! Those who curse their parents! Solon, when asked why he had made no law against parricides (murderers of parents), replied, that he could not conceive of any one so impious and cruel. The divine lawgiver knew his creature better, that his heart was capable of wickedness beyond conception;[b] and this wickedness was beyond the imagination of the heathen sage. He has marked it with his most tremendous judgment.[c] The cursing of a parent was visited with the same punishment as the blaspheming of God;[14] so near does the one sin approach to the other. The rebel against his parent is ready to stretch "out his hand against God" Himself, and "rushes headlong at Him with his massive shield."[d] Many are the forms, in which this proud abomination shows itself; resistance of a parent's authority,[e] contempt of his reproof,[f] shamelessly defiling his name,[g] needlessly exposing his sin,[h] coveting his substance,[i] denying his obligation.[15] Most fearful is the increase of this *kind*. Every city bears sad testimony to this crying sin that brings down many a parent with sorrow to the grave, and it spreads lawlessness throughout the whole land. No excuse can be allowed to justify the sin. The authority of parents, even in the lowest degradation, must be respected, but we dare not, must not, follow their examples. But what can be done to hold back the threatened invasion of this devastating flood? Once and again let us remember; before it is too late, *discipline*—wise, tender, early discipline; *prayer*—pleading, patient, believing prayer; *diligence*—active, direct, wisely applied. Will not our God bless His own means and give us yet to praise Him? Trust, and doubt not.

[b]Jer 17:9
[c]Prov 30:17; 20:20; Deut 21:18–21; 27:16
[d]Job 15:25, 26
[e]2 Sam 15:1–10
[f]1 Sam 2:25
[g]2 Sam 16:22
[h]Gen 9:22
[i]Prov 19:26; Judg 17:2

In what church do we not find this second *kind*—*pure in his own eyes, yet not washed from his filthiness*?[j] The

[j]Isa 65:5

[14] *Lev 20:9, with 24:11–16. See the same close connection, Isa 45:9, 10; 2 Tim 3:2.*
[15] *Matt 15:4–6—showing that* cursing and not blessing, *the parent, are one and the same.*

Pharisees of the gospel[k] were the living picture, devoted to the externals of religion, and to them exclusively; they were washing the outside of the cup and platter, while the inward part was wholly *unwashed from its filthiness*. We see them *in this third kind,* in the Laodicean church.[l] The family at this distance of time is far from being extinct. Many lineal representatives abound among us. Their religion, as of old, is mere ceremony; rigid in forms, but with a deeply rooted hatred of vital godliness. In the service of the church, they will go through the exercise of confession of sin, and supplication for mercy, as miserable offenders; still *pure in their own eyes,* with no conscious *filthiness,* from which they need to be washed. They will, even at the Lord's table, engage in a service, as full of contrition and self-renunciation as language could express; yet they do all this, not to humble their soul in sorrow and confidence, but to feed self-righteousness and delusion. All is formality, and confidence in the flesh.

[k] Matt 23:25–27. Comp. Luke 16:15; 18:10; John 9:40, 41

[l] Rev 3:17, 18

Indeed a thin cloak of profession suffices to maintain this self-gratifying judgment, because everywhere it is the great work of Satan to delude the sinner into a good opinion of himself. His open profession is according to the course of this world, plunging without scruple into all its follies and pleasures. His baptismal engagement is thrown to the wind. He does not pretend to renounce the devil, the world, or the flesh. Creeds are a matter of indifference. For the hearty service of his God he has no care or concern. And still, he is *pure in his own eyes*. He estimates himself by some plausible qualities, or some course of external decorum,[m] but he is a blind infidel as to the depravity of his nature, which—not the gross acts of sin—gives the stamp to his whole character. Sometimes partial obedience maintains this delusion; while he hides from himself the genuine hypocrisy of secret reserves, which mars everything.[n] He was once impure; but he has gone through a course of purifying observances, has *washed* himself *from his filthiness,* little knowing the infinite distinction between being *pure in his own eyes* and being pure in the sight of God.

[m] Matt 19:20; Rom 7:9; Phil 3:6

[n] 1 Sam 15:13, 14

We often see this self-deceiver in the spiritual church, exhibiting a full and clean profession to his fellowmen; while he—awful thought!—lives at an infinite distance

[o]1 Cor 13:1; Jude 3

from God.[o] He has notions of the grand doctrines of the gospel, and he finds it convenient to profess them. Salvation by free grace is his creed, and he will "contend earnestly for" its purest simplicity. He conceives himself to distinguish accurately between sound and unscriptural doctrine. He regards it as legal to search for inward evidences, lest they should obscure the glorious freeness of the gospel. All this is a cover for his slumbering delusion. His conscience is sleeping in "a form of godliness," while his heart is wholly untouched by "its power."[p] Or perhaps there may be alarming conviction of some powerful corruption in his life, which, if he could master, he would be at peace. But while fixing his eye upon this single sin, he has no idea of the great fountain of evil within. He tries to substitute penance, (voluntary suffering or punishment) for true repentance; some external work of sacrifice for the deep worked-in principle of sin; and periodical routine of humiliation, instead of a habit of daily or momentary confession of sin. But with all this, there is no mourning for his innate guilt and pollution; no awareness of sin in his thoughts, acts, motives, or prayers; no apparent change from a proud, self-willed, or worldly spirit. Everything he does serves only to soothe his conscience. He is *pure in his own eyes*—in his own imaginary view and perverted judgment! Yet, until he becomes disturbed in his complacency, how hopeless his condition![q]

[p]2 Tim 3:5

[q]Prov 3:7; 12:15; 16:2

Whatever allowance we may make in other cases for the pressure of our basic temperament, here, at least, the lack of any redeeming influence is a plain proof of self-delusion. Vital Christianity is the sugar in the liquid which permeates the whole contents of the cup. The path may be thorny and our light darkness. But sweetness will be mingled in our sorrow, even till the last drop in the cup of life shall be spent. The formalist's religion is a piece of polished marble in the cup, externally beautiful, but cold and dead; permeating nothing with an atom of sweetness.

The power of this self-delusion is that man has no natural conception of the deep stain of sin, so deep that nothing but the blood can erase it. The man of God, bathed in the tears of remorse, cries out for this blood alone to "purify me."[r] The tears of the purest repentance in themselves are impure and hateful.[s] We can't begin to really know the full extent of our corruption in a day. As the Lord leads us into the light of our own hearts, we behold greater and "still greater abominations."[t] The conscience purged from sin becomes more clear for the discovery of remaining pollution. Those who are the most purified will have the deepest sensibility of impurity,[u] and will most deeply value the "fountain . . . opened for . . . sin and for impurity," with its free invitation—"Wash, and be clean."[v]

[r] Ps 51:7
[s] Job 9:30, 31; Jer 2:22
[t] Ezek 8:6
[u] Comp. Rom 7:9; Phil 3:6, with Rom 7:14–24; 1 Tim 1:15
[v] Zech 13:1; 2 Kings 5:13.

Sinner! if you are found *unwashed from your filthiness,* must it not be certain exclusion from that place, into which shall enter "nothing unclean"?[w] Awful indeed will be the final sentence—"Let the one who is filthy, still be filthy."[x]

[w] Rev 21:27
[x] Rev 22:11

The next *kind* truly amazes us. *Oh, how lofty are his eyes! And his eyelids are raised in arrogance.* Such intolerable arrogance! What greater irregularity does the conscience furnish than that of a proud sinner, his *eyelids raised,* instead of being cast down to the ground. Such is his self-confidence, even in the presence of his God![y] And before men—all must keep their distance from these swelling worms! We may see this pride embodied in a system—the Man of sin "takes his seat in the temple of God, displaying himself as being God"![z] We may see it in worldly greatness—in the pride of Moab;[a] the prince of Tyre;[b] the boasting Anticohus;[c] Haman in all his glory;[d] Herod arrayed "in his royal apparel";[e] Nebuchadnezzar in his self-pleasing contemplations, before the severe chastening of his God had taught him the wholesome lesson—Those that walk in pride He is able to abase.[f] On a lower level, it is the pride of birth, rank, wisdom, riches, or accomplishment. But in every circumstance this high look is especially hateful to God;[g] and the day is appointed in His own purpose for its utmost humiliation.[h] Meanwhile, it is hardly conceived, how really contemptible such pride makes these deluded creatures appear before their fellowmen.[i] One beam of the divine glory[j] and one sight of the cross of Calvary[k] would at once dispel their vain, splendid illustration.

[y] Luke 18:11
[z] 2 Thess 2:4
[a] Isa 16:6; Jer 48:29
[b] Ezek 28:2
[c] Dan 11:36
[d] Esther 5:11
[e] Acts 12:21
[f] Dan 4:30, 31
[g] Prov 6:17; 21:4. Comp. Ps 131:1
[h] Isa 2:12
[i] Ps 101:5
[j] Comp. Job 42:5, 6; Isa 6:5
[k] Phil 2:5

The last *kind* appears before us as a monster of iniquity. We can scarecely draw the picture in its full colors. Conceive of brutes with iron teeth—a wild beast opening his mouth and displaying, instead of teeth, *swords and knives*, sharpened ready for their murderous work.[l] Yet, these cruel oppressors are marked by pitiful cowardice. They vent their wickedness, only where there is little or no power of resistance. It is not the wolf with the wolf, but with the defenseless lamb; *devouring the afflicted and needy from among men,*[m]—eating "up my people"—not like an occasional indulgence, but "as they eat bread" their daily meal, without intermission.[n] Such cruel oppressors appear from time to time as a chastening curse to the land; but not only that, they were also found among the rulers of God's own people,[o] even among the teachers of religion,[p] cloaking their covetousness under robes of special holiness. That is God's picture of man left to himself. When the reins are loosened or given up is there any length of wickedness to which he will not go? Yet so depraved is man that he does not understand his own depravity. Nothing is so much hidden from him as himself.[q] He keeps a good opinion of himself by keeping the light out of his heart and conscience. His imagination fancies good, where there is nothing but hateful deformity. Under this self-delusion, we deal so gently and tenderly with sin, that no conflict is maintained with it, no sorrow or burden felt concerning it. How deeply do we need the searching light and convincing power of the Spirit of God, to show us our abominations; to make us tremble at the sight of them; and to let us see, that our remedy must come from God every moment; that no partial change, no external polish, nothing less than the creating power of God, can reach the case for a cure![r]

Adored, indeed, is the grace of God, if we are not in one or other of these *kinds of men!* But let us remember—"Such were some of you"—either disobedient to our parents, or self-righteous in the church, or proud and contemptuous, or cruel and oppressive. But *we are washed from our filthiness.*[s] Therefore—"who regards you as superior?"[t] is the profitable recollection, when we are disposed to forget from whence we were raised, and to whom we owe all that we have and are for His service.

[l] Ps 57:4
[m] Eccl 4:1; Isa 3:15; Amos 2:6, 7; 8:4; Mic 2:1, 2; Hab 3; 14
[n] Ps 14:4
[o] Amos 4:1; Mic 3:1–3
[p] Matt 23:4
[q] 2 Kings 8:13
[r] Ps 51:10
[s] 1 Cor 6:11
[t] 1 Cor 4:7

15 *The leech has two daughters,*
"Give," "Give."
There are three things that will not be satisfied,
Four that will not say, "Enough":
16 *Sheol* [AV—*the grave*], *and the barren womb,*
Earth that is never satisfied with water,
And fire that never says, "Enough."

Agur describes in an artificial way[u] but with forcible imagery, the cravings of human lust. If viewed in reference to the last *kind of man,* they form a perfect picture of the merciless and greedy tyrant. They are like the *leech which has two daughters, crying, "Give, give."* They are like these *four things: the grave, the womb, the earth, and fire.*[v] But with a more general reference, the figures are graphically instructive. The *leech* with its two-forked tongue, like *two daughters,* sucks the blood with an insatiable appetite. *The grave* opens the mouth for fresh victims.[w] *The barren womb* eagerly covets the blessing.[x] *The parched earth,* after large supplies of water, still thirsts for more. *The fire,* when the spark first kindles a coal, or lights upon combustible matter, never ceases to burn as long as fuel is supplied, and in many a disastrous fire, leaves us to cry out in fearful wonder, "Behold, how great a forest is set aflame by such a small fire!"[y] And yet these are scarcely adequate representations of that insatiable thirst within, that *never* says, "Enough." The greater the portion, the greater the lust. Every indulgence provokes the appetite. *"The horse leech hath but two daughters.* But we have," says Bishop Sanderson, "I know not how many craving lusts, no less [insistently] clamorous than they; till they be served, incessantly *crying, Give, give;* but much more unsatisfied than they. For they will be filled in time, and when they are filled, they tumble off, and there is an end. But our lusts will never be satisfied. Like Pharaoh's [cattle], when they have eaten up all the fat ones, they are still as hungry and as whining as they were before."[16]

[u] Prov 30:21, 24, 29; 6:16; Amos 1:3, 6, 9; 2:1, 4

[v] Ps 59:12, 14, 15

[w] Prov 27:20; Hab 2:5

[x] Gen 30:1; 1 Sam 1:6, 11

[y] James 3:5

How blessed then is the state, to which the gospel brings us—having "food and covering, with these we shall be content." What a merciful deliverance from that

[16] *Sermon on Phil 4:11.* "By the daughters of the horseleech [*bloodsucker*] *may be understood* covetousness and *prodigality. Both then cry,* Give, give. *The former cries,* Give *to keep; the latter cries* —Give, *to spend. Neither of them saith it is enough"—CARYL* on Job *20:20.*

[z] 1 Tim 6:6–10 "ruin and destruction," the certain end of lawless lust.[z] Happy child of God!—weaned from his old indulgence! disciplined under his father's yoke! satisfied abundantly with his father's love. Whether he have "abundance" or "suffering need," he can say, "I have received everything in full, I am amply supplied."[a] Has he not found that, which answers every demand, supplies every need, and satisfies every desire? What but God can fill the soul, which God hath made, and made for Himself?

[a] Phil 4:12, 18

17 *The eye that mocks a father,*
And scorns a mother,
The ravens of the valley will pick it out,
And the young eagles will eat it.

Agur here returns to the first *kind of man*—the unnatural despisers of their parents.[b] He had before described their character. Now he links it with the punishment. Observe the guilt only of a scornful look, or the *mocking eye,* when perhaps not a word is spoken. Certainly if the fifth commandment is "the first commandment, with a promise,"[c] it is also the first with judgment. No commandment in the breach of it is visited with more tremendous threatenings. What a picture is here given of infamy! Perhaps the case of Absalom furnishes the most striking illustration—a self-willed youth or rebel against his father and his sovereign, made a spectacle of shame before his people! the vengeance of God inflicting the punishment, which was due at the bar of human justice![d] But we may observe a more general illustration of the frightful picture. How many confessions on the scaffold or beside the electric chair have borne testimony that the first step toward the untimely end was contempt of parental authority and restraint! The bodies of such criminals were deprived of the rites of burial; exposed either on the gallows, or cast out into the valley, as meat for the fowls of the air.[e] Thus *the eye,* that has scornfully *mocked his father,* became the choice morsel of the *eagle or the raven of the valley.*[17]

[b] Prov 30:11
[c] Eph 6:2
[d] 2 Sam 18:17
[e] Gen 40:19; 1 Sam 17:46; 2 Sam 21:10

But even where there is no such literal fulfillment, the curse is not the less sure. Seldom do we see the disobedient rebels prospering and blessed in their own chil-

[17] *Bochart conceives the allusion to be to the valley—Jer 31:40—where probably the dead bodies of the criminals were sent. At all events the denial of the rites of burial was one of the*

dren. Deserved punishment may come to them late, but it is certain to come; and the painful anguish of many a disappointed hope, and many an arrow shot from their own bow, may bear to them the message of their chastening Father—"Your own wickedness will correct you, and your apostasies will reprove you."[f] [f]Jer 2:19

18 *There are three things which are too wonderful for me,*
Four which I do not understand:
19 *The way of an eagle in the sky,*
The way of a serpent on a rock,
The way of a ship in the middle of the sea,
And the way of a man with a maid.
20 *This is the way of an adulterous woman:*
She eats and wipes her mouth,
And says, "I have done no wrong."

FOUR UNSEARCHABLE THINGS

The kingdom of nature is full of wonder and these wonders full of instruction. Where the philosopher cannot give a reason, the humble disciple may learn a lesson. The depths of nature represent the depths of sin—of the unsearchable deceitful heart.[g] *The eagle* soars *in the air* [g]Jer 17:9
with so lofty and rapid a flight, that the eye cannot follow *her way*. She leaves no scent nor footsteps, by which we might trace her, as the beast on the ground.[h] *The serpent* [h]Job 39:27
on the sand would leave its mark. But *the serpent* on the rock leaves no slime like the worm, no feathers like the birds; who then can discover *its way*? *The ship,* like the great monster of the deep, "makes a wake to shine."[i] But [i]Job 41:32. Comp. Ps 104:26; 107:23, 24; Rev 2:24
while she ploughs *in the middle of the sea,* her furrows are quickly closed up, and her way is untraceable. No less mysterious is *the way of a man with a maid.* The seducer is well-practiced in "the deep things of Satan," and he uses a thousand arts to allure the affections of his unwatchful victim. And it is often as difficult to see through his designs and to escape his snares, as to trace *the way of the eagle, the serpent, or the ship.* Let this be

severest marks of divine chastisement. Comp. Jer 7:33; 22:18, 19. The heathen felt this deprivation to be a special affliction. Homer represents the dying Hector, as entreating Achilles not to give his body to be torn by his Grecian dogs, but restore it to his parents for burial. Lib. 11. 337–343. Virgil also represents Palinurus as begging Aeneas either to throw the earth himself upon his body, or to carry it with him through the water, rather than expose it to the birds of prey—6. 363–371.

a warning to young and inexperienced girls, not to trust to their own purity, or to the strength of their own resolutions, or to place themselves in unprotected situations.

Equally unfathomable are the devices of *the adulterous woman* to entangle her prey and to deceive her unsuspecting husband. Solomon has described the picture with striking and minute accuracy.[j] Such a course of abomination, wickedness, and hypocrisy, as hers, can scarcely be conceived; enjoying her sin as a sweet morsel under her tongue; feasting greedily upon her "stolen waters" and secret bread;[k] yet keeping up the semblance of innocence and purity;[l] *wiping her mouth,* to prevent all suspicion, suffering no sign of the action to remain. A woman must be advanced very far in the way of sin before she can present so unblushing a front. Yet every fresh yielding to lust gives rise to new artful devices, "hardening" her heart more fully in the "deceitfulness of sin."[m] Its fascinations blind it to its real character. Let then the first step be avoided, the most distant path that may lead to temptation. Where shame ceases to accompany it, the ruin of the victim is accomplished. Abundant warning is given; solemn instruction—many beacons in the path—to show the certain end of this flowery road.[n]

[j] Prov 7:5, 6
[k] Prov 9:17
[l] Gen 39:13–19
[m] Heb 3:13
[n] Prov 5:3–5; 7:24–27; 9:18

21 *Under three things the earth quakes,*
And under four, it cannot bear up:
22 *Under a slave when he becomes king,*
And a fool when he is satisfied with food,
23 *Under an unloved woman when she gets a husband,*
And a maidservant when she supplants her mistress.

FOUR INTOLERABLE THINGS

Next to things which were unsearchable, Agur now mentions some things that were intolerable—*things, for which the earth quakes,* bringing confusion wherever they are found. Who does not naturally condemn things out of place, as unsuitable and unseemly? Order is the law of the works of God in the world, no less than in the church;[o] and any breach of order is to be disapproved. *Four* such evils are here mentioned—two connected with men, two with women; the one class in the community, the other in the family.

[o] Eccl 3:11; 1 Cor 14:40

The first evil mentioned is—*a servant,* when he reigns. This is a serious evil in the family, whether it arises from the mismanagement of the family head; or from his own intrigue.[p] He is obviously out of place; and ruling, where he ought to serve, he must bring disorder.[q] The evil is far greater in a kingdom. Men of low birth may indeed rise honorably by their own merit to a high station. God may call them, as he did Joseph,[r] to reign. The evil is the advancement to power of ignorant, fawning, and unprincipled followers.[s] Men of mean spirit cannot bear to be raised. Intoxicated by sudden elevation, these upstarts show themselves not only fools, but tyrants; swelling with all the insolence of their unseemly honor. Such was the enmity of Tobiah the Ammonite[t] and the misrule of Haman.[u] What national evil resulted from the elevation of Jeroboam![v] What anarchy from the Zimri's successful but unlawful seizure of the throne![w] Well might the reign *of servants* be deplored, as a component part of the calamity of dejected Zion![x] In the ordinary course it can only be viewed as chastening.[y] Let us acknowledge with thankfulness our deliverance from it.

[p] Prov 30:23
[q] Gen 16:4
[r] Gen 41:41
[s] Prov 19:10; Eccl 10:5–7
[t] Neh 2:10
[u] Esther 3:1
[v] 1 Kings 11:26–28; 12:30
[w] 1 Kings 16:9–20. Comp. 2 Kings 8:12
[x] Lam 5:8
[y] Isa 3:4, 5

Then look at *the fool* (not an idiot, but a willful sinner) *when he is satisfied with food.* Can we wonder that he should be a trouble and a curse; giving the reins to his appetite and becoming yet more devoid of understanding than before? The history of Nabal, sunk into brutishness by his own sensual lust;[z] Elah murdered by his servant, while "drinking himself drunk" in his steward's house;[a] Belshazzar giving himself over to the lust of ungodliness[b]—all these were evils, *for which the earth quakes and which it could not bear. Satisfied with food*—with overeating and drunkenness they dig, as it were, their own graves with their teeth and are set forth as an example in the just punishment of their wicked folly.

[z] 1 Sam 25:36
[a] 1 Kings 16:9, 10; Hos 7:5
[b] Dan 5:1–4, 30; 1 Sam 30:16; 1 Kings 20:16

Look again into the inner room of the family. What is the origin of discord and recognizable misery? *An unloved woman* is in rule. She quarrels with all around her. Her ungoverned tongue and temper are an unceasing source of agitation. Had she known herself, much better for her never to have entered into the marriage bond, than to become the inseparable tormentor of her husband and family.[c] Woman is to man either his greatest curse or

[c] Prov 21:9, 19; 27:15

blessing. If love is not the basis of this sacred union, it will surely be a bond of misery from which only the special mercy of God can deliver. Let the worldly portion of the wife be the last consideration. Take heed, lest worldly glitter open a door for misery without remedy.

The unloved woman, when she gets a husband, if she is in authority, becomes a national evil. Jezebel was a scourge to Israel, the spring of all Ahab's wickedness that brought the heavy judgment of God upon the land.[d] *The earth quaked* for her, and at the last cast her out.[e] Herodias brought upon her husband and his nation the guilt of the blood of the murdered prophet crying from the ground.[f] If marriage is the ordinance of lust, not of godliness, what wonder if the *unloved woman* should be the result, a canker to every domestic comfort?

[d] 1 Kings 16:31; 21:25
[e] 2 Kings 9:30–37
[f] Matt 14:8

The last evil noticed is a frequent source of family trouble—*a maidservant when she supplants her mistress.* Lack of discipline, simplicity, or integrity, leads to waywardness and self-indulgence; and the house, instead of being under wholesome rule, becomes a prey to envy and strife. The ill-regulated connection between Abraham and Hagar, when *the servant supplanted her mistress*—occupying her mistress's place with her husband—became the source of most baneful contention.[g] History presents sad illustration of this intolerable evil. Anne Boleyn and Jane Seymour were *maidservants,* and unhappily heirs, to their respective mistresses while living, in the affections of the king of England. The royal example of selfishness and lust was a national grievance, in which *the maidservants* were not wholly guiltless.

[g] Gen 16:4

And thus, in modern society, a woman servant, treated with that familiarity, which breaks down the divine divisions between the ranks, has sometimes become heir to her mistress; either succeeding to her property—perhaps to the exclusion of more rightful claimants;[h] or rising into her place by a poorly matched union, like those just mentioned, usually productive of much family trouble. Or again, in the higher ranks, she is the heir to her mistress' dresses. This encourages in her the love of dress and vanity, habits unsuitable to her station in life, and too often hurtful to her solid respectability and eternal interests.

[h] Prov 29:21

How needful is it to preserve consistency in every part of our profession! Oh! Let us be careful that no lack of wisdom, godly contentment, or self-denial, brings reproach upon that worthy name for which we are called; that there are no spots, to mar that adorning beauty, which might attract those around us to the ways of God.

24 *Four things are small on the earth,*
But they are exceedingly wise:
25 *The ants are not a strong folk,*
But they prepare their food in the summer;
26 *The badgers are not mighty folk,*
Yet they make their houses in the rocks;
27 *The locusts have no king,*
Yet all of them go out in ranks;
28 *The lizard* [AV—*spider*] *you may grasp with the hands,*
Yet it is in king's palaces.

FOUR SMALL BUT WISE CREATURES

The mind of man spreads over the length and breadth of creation and draws instruction from every part of the universe presented to his senses. Everywhere God teaches us by His works as well as by His Word;[18] by His works, small as well as great. He instructed Job by Behemoth and Leviathan.[i] Here He instructs us by *the ants and the badgers*. And indeed in the minute creation his splendor shines as gloriously as in the more majestic. "At one end," of the scale, as Dr. Paley finely draws the contrast in the conclusion of *Natural Theology*, "we see an intelligent power arraying planetary systems; fixing, for instance, the trajectory of Saturn, or constructing a ring of two hundred thousand miles diameter, to surround the boy, and be suspended like a magnificent arch over the head of the inhabitants; and at the other, bending a hooked tooth, planning and providing an appropriate mechanism for the clasping and re-clasping of the filaments of the feathers of the hummingbird."

[i] Job 40:41

Agur had before mentioned four things that seemed great but were really despicable. Here he produces *four*

[18] *The stupid beasts reprove our ingratitude (Isa 1:3). The fowls of the air, our inattention (Jer 8:7); our unbelieving carefulness (Matt 6:26); and anxious fears (Matt 10:29–31).*

things, little upon the earth, but exceedingly wise. Therefore, don't despise them for their *littleness:* but admire the wonderworking hand, which furnished these little creatures with such sufficient means of provision, defense, and safety. As has been beautifully remarked—"God reigns in a community of ants and [mongooses] as visibly, as among living men or mighty [angels]," said McCheyne (*Life,* p. 34). Truly, everything was made for some purpose. The world of instinct shows that which will put to shame our higher world of reason. Yes—these four remarkable instances of almighty skill, the natures and habits of these four little animals, teach many useful and important lessons, to which the greatest philosopher might pay attention with profit, and he that has ears to hear may hear words of suitable wisdom, rebuke, direction, and encouragement for himself.

"Industry is commended to us by all sorts of examples, deserving our regard and imitation. All nature is a copy thereof, and the whole world a glass, wherein we may behold this duty represented to us," said Barrow in *Sermon on Industry.* "Every creature about us is incessantly working toward the ends for which it was designed; [tirelessly] exercising the powers with which it is endured: diligently observing the laws of its creation." *The ants* have already brought the lesson before us[j]—a people not strong:[19] indeed so weak, that thousands are crushed by one tread of the foot; yet *wise in preparing their food in the summer.* A wise sermon do these little insects preach to us! They make preparation for the coming winter. How thoughtless people are who make no provision for eternity, whiling away life in inactivity, as if there were no work for God, for the soul, or for eternity! Should we learn to be wise, before it's too late, to improve the present moment of salvation; not to wait for the winter—the transition of life, when that grace, offered now, shall be offered no more? Sinner! If you lose everything by your indifference how great a loser you will be! What else do you have to do, but to prepare for eternity? What hope can you have of heaven at the last, if you have never seriously thought of heaven before? Oh!—before it

[j] Prov 6:6–8

[19] *The term—nation or people—is applied to the animal creation. Joel 1:6; 2:2. This is a frequent classical allusion. Homer spoke of a nation of bees; of hogs; Virgil, of fishes,* Geor. *4. 430.*

is too late throw yourself at His feet, whose heart overflows with love. If you are ready, "everything is ready." If you are left out, it is your own doing, not the Savior's.[k] [k]Luke 14:16–24; John 6:37

The ants are not strong. Yet—apart from their wisdom—what people are more diligent, more persevering, or more effective? Indeed, the union of so many noble qualities in so small a creature is one of the most remarkable phenomena in the works of nature. Weakness, then, is no excuse for laziness, no occasion for despair. Instead, isn't it uplifting to our faith?[l] The worm "will thresh the mountains."[m] To the diligent laborer shall be given the food "which endures to eternal life."[n] Working "out your salvation" in helpless dependence, his "toil is not in vain in the Lord."[20] [l]2 Cor 12:9, 10 [m]Isa 41:15 [n]John 6:27

As the ants prepare their food, so do *the badgers* their refuge. *Not mighty folk,* they secure themselves from impending danger by *making their houses* in the holes of inaccessible *rocks.*[21] Thus what they want in strength they make up in wisdom. Not less feeble are we; not less exposed to assault, and is not our refuge, like theirs, "the impregnable *rock*"?[o] Are we then, like them, *making our house,* our home, there; in the foresight of evil hiding ourselves; abiding in our shelter in conscious security?[p] [o]Isa 33:16 [p]Prov 22:3

Observe again the instinct of *the locusts.* Some *insects,* like the bee, are under monarchical government. But *the locusts have no king.* Yet how wonderful is their order, *going out in ranks;* like an army with unbroken ranks, and under the strictest discipline![q] Jerome mentions what he had lately seen—"When the swarms of locusts came, and filled the lower region of the air, they flew in such order, by the divine appointment, and kept their places as exactly, as when several titles or party-colored [q]Joel 2:7, 8, 25

[20] *Phil 2:12, 13; 1 Cor 15:58. Chrysostom ingeniously remakes upon the wonders of divine wisdom, in inspiring so minute a body with such a perpetual desire for labor; teaching us so strongly the lesson, not to affect softness and delicacy or to fly from toil and labor. He adds—that the wise man, sending us to learn of these little creatures, is just as we should in our families put to shame the disobedience of the elder children, by pointing to the little ones—Behold one much younger and smaller than yourself; yet how pliable and ready he is to do as he is bid!—Hom. 12, ad Pop. Antioch.*

[21] *Ps 104:18. There is much difficulty in determining this animal which was reckoned among the unclean (Lev 11:55; Deut 14:7). Dr. Shaw (with whom Parkhurst agrees) considers it to be "the Daman of Mount Libanus, though common in other parts of Syria and Palestine, of the rabbit size and form. As its usual residence and refuge is in the holes and clefts of the rocks, we have so far a presumptive evidence, that this creature may be the coney of the Scriptures."* Travels, *vol.* 2, 160, 161. *Mr. Bruce strongly confirms this account from his own observation—adding— "He is above all other animals so much attached to the rock, that I never once saw him on the ground, and from among large stones in the mouth of caves, where is his constant residence. He is in Judea, Palestine, Arabia and consequently must have been known to Solomon."* Travels, *vol.* 5, 139–147.

stones are skillfully placed in a pavement, so as not to be a hair-breadth out of their several ranks."[22] Do not these little insects read to us a lesson on the importance of unity and unanimous movement? Here is not an ungoverned, disorderly multitude flying in different directions. But *all go out by ranks.* All keep their ranks. Many professing Christians, instead of *going by ranks,* prefer an individual course. They belong to no cohort. They are under no discipline. This unsettled principle can never issue in a Christian steadfastness. Unity, not diversity, brings "good for the heart to be strengthened by grace."[r] The church is strong—not when she goes into battle as an army of irregular soldiers, a regiment in loose disorder, with individual troops, separated from each other; but when she *goes out* in united, well-disciplined groups, every officer at his post, every soldier in his ranks, each under rule, helpful to each other and to their great cause![s] When shall it ever be, Lord? Heal our unhappy divisions. Unite our energies in "the unity of the Spirit in the bond of peace," and "faith, patience, love, perseverance."

[r] Heb 13:9

[s] Num 2; Eph 4:3; 2 Tim 3:10

And what lessons does *the spider* teach, of ingenuity, patience, and untiring labor and perseverance! Its claws or spinning-organs serve both as hands and eyes. She forms her web against the walls, as if she took hold of them with her hands. She frames her fine-spun house with such exactness of proportion, you would think her conversant with a slide rule. She steals her way, into the cottage of the poor and *king's palaces;* as if God wants to instruct even the great ones of the earth by her pattern of diligence. Such perseverance; such diligence in the work of our high calling, if it shall not bring us into the king's palaces,[t] it will ensure the full reward of the man, whom the great king "desires to honor."[u]

[t] Prov 22:29

[u] Esther 6:6

The general lesson to learn from these diminutive teachers is the importance of acting wisely according to the principles of our nature, as the best means to secure the greatest amount of happiness of which we are capable. God has provided happiness for every nature and for each *its* own happiness. How many of us stand condemned by the sermons of these little insects! Let us not

[22] *Quoted by Lowth on Joel. The mystical locusts have a king. Comp. Rev 9:3–11.*

be too proud to learn, or too careless to attend to, the humbling but most valuable lessons taught in this school of instruction: "A wise man will hear and increase in learning."[v] [v]Prov 1:5

29 *There are three things which are stately in* their
march,
Even four which are stately when they walk:
30 *The lion* which *is mighty among beasts*
And does not retreat before any,
31 *The strutting cock* [AV—*greyhound*], *the male goat*
also,
And a king when his *army is with him* [AV—*against*
whom there is no rising up].

Agur lingers upon this vast field of natural wonders; such a splendid exhibition of divine perfections, the source of so much light to the world, before the Book of Revelation (the Bible) was fully opened![w] After having mentioned some striking instances of wisdom, he now singles out a few objects, which appeared to him remarkable for *their stately* movements—the lion, firm and stately in its walk, fearless and proud, *not retreating* from any creature in the way, no matter how powerful; *the strutting cock; the male goat* at the head of the flock, as their guide and protector; and the majesty of *the king,* inspiring all who approach him with reverence for his authority, and not suffering any rising up against the exercise of his power.[x] From all of them, many practical lessons may be learned by the man, "Who is wise? Let him give heed to these things." [w]Job 12:7–10 [x]Eccl 8:2–4

Let us have regard, not only to the various duties of the Christian life, but also to the manner and spirit of their performance. Cultivate not only the integrity, but a *stately* Christian character—the beauty and uniformity of holiness; that there be nothing misshapen or distorted; that there be proper proportion in all the parts and features. Christians should be attractive and engaging in their general demeanor. It is not enough to observe "whatever is true, whatever is honorable, whatever is right, whatever is pure." But "whatever is *lovely, whatever is of good repute* ... let your mind dwell on these things."[y] Any obvious lack of a *stately manner* repels the [y]Phil 4:8

world from the gospel of Christ. "If we desire to reign in heaven, we must present ourselves there with this beautiful crown, from whence radiate all kinds of virtue and praise," said Daille.

And let us not forget to imitate the features of the *stately* ones here portrayed; to be fearless as *the lion*, when pursuing the path of duty, *not retreating from anything*,[z] to be useful as *the male goat*, as we lead a band of God's people; and to maintain our proper authority, as the *king* does, in any place of trust, as parents or guardians of families; and not to allow any rising up against us.

[z]Neh 6:3, 11

32 *If you have been foolish in exalting yourself*
Or if you have plotted [AV—*thought*] evil, put your
hand on your mouth.
33 *For the churning of milk produces butter,*
And pressing the nose brings forth blood;
So the churning of anger produces strife.

This evidently applies to the preceding illustration—a *king, against whom there is no rising.* But *if you have risen up* to despise his authority;[a] or even *if you have but thought evil; lay your hand on your mouth,* restraining your emotion in silent and humble submission.[b] As a general rule, however, we may be thankful for the caution. If we have *done foolishly* by provoking irritation, *in rising up* even in some *evil thought,* against a brother; quench the rising spark, before it kindles into a flame. "*The devising of folly is sin.*"[c] Yet is is more sinful, when it forces its way to the mouth. Words increase the sin, show more of its power, and are more hurtful to others. Obviously it is wise to *put our hand on our mouth,* and to restrain the expression, when we cannot prevent the thought. Better to keep in the infirmity, than to give it vent. But when, instead of *the hand put on the mouth,* there is no discipline, guard, or restraint; "the mouth of fools spouts folly,"[d] overflowing at the lips, and bringing a flood of trouble upon the soul.[e]

[a]Rom 13:1, 2
[b]Prov 27:28; Job 21:5
[c]Prov 24:9; Jer 4:14
[d]Prov 15:2
[e]Prov 15:18; 16:28, 29; 17:14; 18:7

How much more, when the lying, heartless, proud worm *lifts up itself against* the great King! *The foolishness* even of an *evil thought* against Him is such, that no tongue can express it. The Lord humble us in a tender sensibility of this sin! "Behold, I am insignificant; what can I reply to Thee? *I lay my hand on my mouth.*"[f] [f]Job 40:4, 5

Toward man, however, it is often *anger produces strife,* not natural irritation. A peaceable man may be driven to anger;[g] as the violent shaking of the milk in the *churn produces butter; or the pressing of the nose brings blood.* The action of force produces results that would not otherwise have been accomplished. But fearful is *the strife* of this *anger.* In this way, Sihon provoked his own ruin;[h] the Ephraimites stirred up a murderous strife;[i] Asahel sharpened Abner's spear by his willful waywardness;[j] Amaziah plunged into destruction by *the anger-produced strife* of Josah, who wanted only peace and quietness.[k] How multiplied are the sources of misery—the fruit of ungovernable temper and self-will! "Through presumption comes nothing but strife";[l] and where that contention may end, who can say? "I am, and profess to be," said Bishop Hall, "as the terms stand, on neither, and yet on both, parts; for the peace of both; but to satisfy the whims of neither."

[g]Prov 15:1; 26:21; 29:22
[h]Num 21:23, 24
[i]Judg 12:1–6
[j]2 Sam 2:22, 23
[k]2 Chron 25:17–23
[l]Prov 13:10

A humble heart will repress the sparks of this unholy fire. A sorrowful spirit for the evil of our thoughts is a vital part of the cure.[m] We should not readily yield to the sin, for which we had been truly humbled before our God. Whereas, in the absence of this genuine spirit, how reluctant we are to acknowledge our offense toward each other! We can always find some good reason for *rising up against someone or for thinking evil.* And how hard it goes with our proud tempers to be the first to *put our hands on our mouths!* How much more ready we are to open our mouths in self-justification, than in self-abasement. Thus, instead of quenching, we *produce strife.* Instead of the "gentleness of wisdom," there is "jealousy and selfish ambition . . . disorder and every evil thing";[n] enmity between professing believers of the gospel, and distance even between those, who believe themselves to be members of the same body, heirs of the same inheritance,[o] and bound by the same obligation to love one another.[p] Oh! Hasten the blessed time when the church shall be fully transformed into the image of her divine Lord; when it shall be a church of perfect love in a world of love!

[m]Eccl 7:4
[n]James 3:13, 16
[o]Eph 4:4–6
[p]John 13:34, 35

CHAPTER THIRTY-ONE

1 *The words of King Lemuel, the oracle which his mother taught him.*
2 *What, O my son?*
And what, O son of my womb?
And what, O son of my vows?

Of King Lemuel we know no more than of the prophet Agur in the last chapter.[1] All that we know is that he was endowed, like many of God's people,[a] with the invaluable blessing of a godly mother; who, like Deborah of old,[b] was honored of God to be the author of a chapter of the sacred volume.

[a]Ps 116:16; 2 Tim 1:5; 3:15

[b]Judg 5:1

What an animating burst from the yearning of a mother's heart! *What, O my son? . . . O son of my womb . . . of my vows?* Happy mother—when *the son* of her *womb* is the son of her *vows,* like Samuel, a dedicated child, a child of many prayers; asked of the Lord, led into His service.[c] If there were more Hannahs, would there not be more Samuels? If you would have, Christian mother, your child a Samuel or an Augustine, be yourself a Hannah or a Monica. The child of your prayers, of your *vows,* and of your tears, will be, in the Lord's best time, the child of your praises, your rejoicings, your richest consolation. Yet, your faith will not end with the dedication of your child. *Lemuel—the son of her vows*—his

[c]1 Sam 1:11

[1] *Both have been identified with Solomon, though without any historical evidence. It seems unlikely, that Solomon, having given his own name more than once in this book (Prov 1:1; 10:1), should give two mystical names at the close, without any distinct personal application. Nor is there any Scriptural testimony in favor of Bathsheba that would lead us to stamp her with this peculiar honor as one of the writers of God's word. "The admonitory verses composed for King Lemuel by his mother, when in the flower of youth and high expectation, are an inimitable production, as well in respect to their actual materials, as the delicacy with which they are selected. Instead of attempting to lay down rules concerning matters of state and political government; the illustrious writer confines herself, with the nicest and most becoming art, to a recommendation of the gentler virtues of temperance, benevolence, and mercy, and a minute and unparalleled delineation of the female character, which might bid fairest to promote the happiness of her son in connubial life"—Dr. GOOD.*

mother taught him. And such is the practical habit of godliness, that faith in vowing quickens diligence in teaching. The child, truly consecrated, will be brought "up in the discipline and instruction of the Lord."[d]

[d]Eph 6:4

3 *Do not give your strength to women,*
Or your ways to that which destroys kings.
4 *It is not for kings, O Lemuel,*
It is not for kings to drink wine,
Or for rulers to desire strong drink.
5 *Lest they drink and forget what is decreed,*
And pervert the rights of all the afflicted.
6 *Give strong drink to him who is perishing,*
And wine to him whose life is bitter.
7 *Let him drink and forget his poverty,*
And remember his trouble no more.

Solomon has given us his father's wise counsels.[e] Lemuel gives us his mother's. Both have an equal claim to reverence.[f] Filled with deep anxiety, the impassioned tenderness bursts out in this godly mother, as if some besetting enticements were near at hand, perhaps already working poison in her beloved son. *What, O my son? . . . O son of my womb . . . of my vows*? My heart is full. I must give vent. Have I endured all this travail in vain? Beware! *Do not give your strength to women.* What a beacon Solomon had set up![g] What a beacon had he himself become![h] These forbidden gratifications were ways *that destroy kings*. Such was the judgment upon David. His kingly authority was shaken.[i] Solomon's sin *destroyed* his kingdom.[j] The fruit of this sin is shame. The end of it, without repentance, is death.

The anxious mother next warns against another related sin—intemperance.[k] The vice that degrades a man into a beast is shameful to all, but especially unseemly *for kings*. They are "a city set on a hill." Men look, or ought to look, to them for guidance and example. What a sight for *kings to drink wine and strong drink*—to be given to it! Witness Elah[l]—Benhadad[m]—Belshazzar—"the princes" of Israel "became sick with the heat of wine"![n] How their high office and glory were covered with shame! Sometimes it is used as an excuse for sin. But if the drunken king *forgets the decree, and perverts the*

[e]Prov 4:4
[f]Prov 1:8
[g]Prov 2; 5; 7
[h]Neh 13:26
[i]2 Sam 12:9, 10
[j]1 Kings 11:11
[k]Hos 4:11
[l]Matt 5:14; 1 Kings 16:8, 9
[m]1 Kings 20:16
[n]Hos 7:5

[o]Esther 1:10, 11
[p]Mark 6:21–28
[q]Isa 28:7; 56:12
[r]1 Tim 3:3; Titus 1:7

judgment,[2] won't he be held responsible? Ahasuerus was doubtless responsible for his unseemly conduct to Vashti.[o] Herod murdered John the Baptist at an ungodly feast.[p] Priest and prophet "are confused by ... *strong drink.*"[q] A wise veto therefore is set for the rulers of the church—"not addicted to wine."[r]

[s]Ps 104:14, 15
[t]Judg 9:13
[u]Luke 10:34
[v]1 Tim 5:23

And yet the abuse of God's blessing does not destroy their use. Wine is the gift of God. "Wine ... makes man's heart glad."[s] Yes, by a bold figure of its refreshment—it is said that it "cheers God" also.[t] Yet it is *not for kings*—for their indulgences and sinful excitement but for those that need it. As restoratives and refreshments, cordials are seasonable in the hour of need. *Give strong drink to him that is ready to perish*; as the Samaritan gave it to the wounded traveler;[u] as Paul prescribed it for the "ailments" of his beloved son in the faith.[v] Many a man with sinking spirit may be revived and forget his misery under a well-trained restorative. The rule therefore of love and self-denial is, instead of wasting them upon yourself in the indulgence of appetite, which will only debase your nature; see that you dispense your luxuries among those who really require them. Seek out cases of poverty and misery. Let it be an honor to you to bring into your house the poor that is cast out, and then *he may forget his poverty and remember his trouble no more.* May not this remind us of Christ—the messenger of love, dealing with those that are ready to perish?[w] Their conscience is loaded with guilt. Their hearts are heavy with a burden, which they can neither bear nor get rid of. He tells them of God's love to sinners; the ransom found for them; the welcome assured to them. This is a medicine of *strong drink* and wine, such as they need. The heavy heart is "no longer sad."[x] The former *poverty is forgotten,* and its *trouble remembered no more,* and "the blessing of the one ready to perish came upon me ... who brings good news." Happy minister, gifted like his divine Master, with the "tongue of disciples, that I may know how to sustain the weary one with a word."[y]

[w]Isa 61:1, 2; Matt 11:28
[x]1 Sam 1:18; Acts 16:34, Job 29:13; Nah 1:15
[y]Isa 50:4

[2] *A woman wrongly condemned by Philip of Macedon, when he was drunk, boldly exclaimed, "I appeal to Philip, but it shall be when he is sober." Roused by the appeal, the monarch examined the cause and gave a righteous judgment.*

8 *Open your mouth for the dumb,*
For the rights of all the unfortunate [AV—*appointed to destruction*].
9 *Open your mouth, judge righteously,*
And defend the rights of the afflicted and needy.

Very soundly the wise mother pleads mercy for her royal son. This is one of the pillars of the king's throne.[z] He must be the father of his people, employing all his authority to protect those, who cannot protect themselves.[a] No case of distress, when coming to his knowledge, should be below his attention. So our law makes the judge the counsel for the prisoner, who is unable to plead for himself—*opening his mouth for those who cannot speak.* Therefore, magistrates should be extremely careful, so that no one should lose his just right from want of ability to defend it.[b] The *unfortunate* who are, or appear to be, *appointed to destruction,* should have their fair and open course to plead and save their lives.[c]

That is what made the difference between the prosperity of godly Josiah and the ruin of his wicked son.[d] How repeatedly did Jonathan *open his mouth* for his friend *appointed for destruction*![e] How effectively did Esther plead the cause of her helpless and devoted people![f] To descend into lower ranks (for why should we restrict these wise injunctions to the narrow limits of royalty?) what a complete pattern of this mercy Job exhibits! He "was eyes to the blind, and feet to the lame," and doubtless he perfected his character as "a father to the needy.[g] How was Ebedmelech honored for this merciful advocacy of the condemned![h] How awful is the threatened vengeance for the neglect of this mercy![i] Jesus, though He had found an advocate in earlier times, yet stood as a sheep before His shearers—*dumb, appointed for destruction.* No one was found to *open his mouth* for Jesus Christ, the divine afflicted victim.[j] And yet, how He reverses this picture of pitiless neglect, in His powerful, effectual pleading on behalf *of those,* whom the voice of justice so loudly, so justly *appoints for destruction*! Let his representatives on earth study the character of their king in heaven and be conformed more fully to his image of forgiveness and love.

[z] Prov 20:28
[a] Ps 72:12–14
[b] Deut 16:18–20; Ps 82:3, 4
[c] Contrast 1 Kings 21:9–13, with John 7:51
[d] Jer 22:15–19
[e] 1 Sam 19:4–7; 20:32; 22:14, 15
[f] Esther 7:3, 4
[g] Job 29:15, 16
[h] Jer 38:8, 9; 39:15–18
[i] Prov 24:11, 12; Jer 5:28, 29
[j] Isa 53:7; Matt 26:59, 63

10 *An excellent* [AV—*virtuous woman*] *wife, who can find?*
For her worth is far above jewels.

PORTRAIT OF A VIRTUOUS WOMAN

We now come to the principal part of the chapter. The wise mother of Lemuel had warned her royal son against the seduction of evil women, and attendant temptations, and had given him wholesome rules for government. She now sets before him the full-length portrait *of an excellent wife*—that choicest gift, which is emphatically said to be "from the Lord."[k] It is an elegant poem of twenty-two verses—like Psalm 119, artificially constructed—each verse beginning with one of the successive letters of the Hebrew alphabet.[3] It describes a wife, a mistress, and a mother. It is something that every young girl should be taught to read and learn by heart.[4] The more deeply it is practically studied—the more its beauty will be understood and felt. Genuine simple fact without coloring or pretensions commends the virtuous woman's character to our warmest interest.

[k]Prov 19:14

So rare is this treasure that the challenge is given—"*Who can find an excellent wife*?"[l] Abraham sent to a distant land for this inestimable blessing for his beloved son.[m] Perhaps one reason for the rarity of the "virtuous woman" is that she is so seldom desired or searched for. Too often the requirements for a wife are accomplishments, rather than internal, godly worth. Even Adam's portion in innocence was not complete till his bountiful Father made "a helper suitable for him."[n] Truly *her worth is far above jewels.* No treasure is comparable to her.

[l]Comp. Prov 20:6

[m]Gen 24:3, 4

[n]Gen 2:18

11 *The heart of her husband trusts in her,*
And he will have no lack of gain.
12 *She does him good and not evil*
All the days of her life.

The price of the virtuous woman has been told. Her different features will now be given. The first lines of the portrait describe her character as *a wife.* Her faithfulness and oneness of heart, and affectionate dutifulness, cause

[3] *Comp. also Ps 145. The Lamentations of Jeremiah.*
[4] *See the counterpart of* "The virtuous man" *in the exquisite picture, which the sorrowful patriarch drew of the simple habit and feelings of his own life. Job 29; 31.*

the *heart of her husband to trust in her.*[5] He feels his comfort to be regarded, his burdens relieved, and his mind freed from many vexations. He is at ease in constrained absence from home, having left his interests safe in her keeping; while he is sure that his return will be welcomed with a gladdening smile. A faithful wife and a confiding husband thus mutually bless each other. With such a jewel for his wife, the husband has no misgivings. His home is the home of his heart. He needs not to look into what he entrusts to her with a suspicious eye. He has no reserves or jealousies. Ruling in sphere without, he encourages her to rule in her sphere within. Everything is so carefully and economically managed, he is never tempted to dishonesty to fulfill his desires; no need to leave his happy home. The love and loyalty of such a wife will endure throughout their marriage—constant and consistent. Instead of abusing confidence, she seeks constantly to make herself more worthy of it; not fretful and uncertain, but caring "how she may please her husband,"[o] *doing him good, and not evil, all the days of her life.* Would that it were always so! But look at Eve—the helper[p] becoming a tempter; Solomon's wives drawing away his heart;[q] Jezebel stirring up her husband to abominable wickedness;[r] Job's wife calling upon her husband to "curse God and die";[s] the painful cross of "a contentious woman"[t]—this is a fearful contrast—*evil, not good.* Often again it is a mixture of *evil with the good.* Rebekah caring for her husband in the act of opposition to God, yet wickedly deceiving him;[u] Rachel loving Jacob, yet bringing idolatry into his family;[v] Michael *doing good* to David at first in preserving his life, *evil* afterward in despising him as a servant of God.[w] Often we hear of careful management, but not in the fear of God, connected with an annoying disposition. But in this picture it is *good, and not evil.*

[o] 1 Cor 7:34
[p] Gen 2:18, with 3:6
[q] 1 Kings 11:1–5
[r] 1 Kings 21:25
[s] Job 2:9
[t] Prov 21:9; 25:24
[u] Gen 27
[v] Gen 31:19; 35:1–4
[w] 1 Sam 19:12; 2 Sam 20–22

Her husband's comfort is her interest and her rest. To live for him is her highest happiness. Even if her minute attentions to this object are not always noticed, yet she will never harbor the suspicion of indifference or unkindness; nor will she return fancied neglect with sul-

[5] *Such was Luther's description of his wife—"The greatest gift of God is a pious amiable spouse, who fears God, loves his house, and with* whom one can live in perfect confidence."

lenness, or start arguments over trifles.

This course of disinterested regard and devoted affection, when conducted on Christian principles, commends most graciously the holy and honorable estate of matrimony. If it implies subjection, it involves no degradation. Indeed no greater glory could be desired, than that which is given to it, that it should illustrate the great "mystery"—"Christ and the church"[x]—the identity of interest between them; her trials, His;[y] His cause, hers.[z]

[x] Eph 5:32
[y] Acts 9:4
[z] Ps 139:22

13 *She looks for wool and flax,*
And works with her hands in delight.
14 *She is like merchant ships;*
She brings her food from afar.
15 *She rises also while it is still night,*
And gives food to her household,
And portions to her maidens.
16 *She considers a field and buys it;*
From her earnings she plants a vineyard.
17 *She girds herself with strength,*
And makes her arms strong.
18 *She senses that her gain is good;*
Her lamp does not go out at night.
19 *She stretches out her hands to the distaff,*
And her hands grasp the spindle.
20 *She extends her hand to the poor;*
And she stretches out her hands to the needy.
21 *She is not afraid of the snow for her household,*
For all her household are clothed with scarlet.
22 *She makes coverings for herself;*
Her clothing is fine linen and purple.
23 *Her husband is known in the gates,*
When he sits among the elders of the land.
24 *She makes linen garments and sells* them,
And supplies belts to the tradesmen.
25 *Strength and dignity are her clothing,*
And she smiles at the future.
26 *She opens her mouth in wisdom,*
And the teaching of kindness is on her tongue.
27 *She looks well to the ways of her household,*
And does not eat the bread of idleness.

This beautiful portrait may be considered old-fashioned, but the general principles are universal and timeless. It describes not only the wife of a man of rank, but a wise, useful, and godly matron in her domestic responsibilities. It is a woman "making a claim to godliness," adorned with "good works";[a] a Mary no less than a Martha. "It may be necessary to retouch the lines of the picture that have been obscured by length of years; in plain terms—to explain some parts of the description which relate to ancient manners and customs, and to show how they may be usefully applied to those of our own age and country," explained Bishop Horne.

[a]1 Tim 2:10

One thing, however, is most remarkable. The standard of godliness exhibited here is not that of a religious recluse, shut up from active obligations, under the pretense of greater spirituality and consecration to God. There aren't any habits of monastic self-denial set forth here that have often been extolled as the highest point of Christian perfection. One half, at least, of the picture of *the virtuous woman* is occupied with her personal and domestic work. What a rebuke this also conveys to self-pleasing inactivity! Her many tasks show her praiseworthy and genuine simplicity of manners, and practical, yet liberal, thrift. This is indeed a difficult and rare attainment; economy without a miserly spirit; seen and felt as little as possible, and conducted with all care and consideration for the comfort of her family.

But let us look in greater detail at the features of the portrait before us. Her personal habits are full of energy. Manual labor, even menial service, in the old days, was the occupation of women of all ranks.[6] Self-denial was a main principle, with *the excellent wife* leading her servants in hard work, no less than in dignity; expecting nothing from them, that she wouldn't do herself; ruling her household most efficiently through self-discipline. And so, she rounds up her tools and materials and puts them to work for her family. Instead of murmuring at some inconvenient demand, she sets a worthy example *and delights in the work of her hands.* She works early and late. The fruit of her work she turns to good account. In the days of Proverbs she sold the work to merchants. She puts her whole being into her work, ready to do any work befitting her sex and station.

[6] *Sarah—Gen 18:6–8; Rebekah—24:18–20, with 12–14; Rachel—29:9, 10; the daughters of the Prince of Midian—Exod 2:16; the daughter of a king—2 Sam 13:5–9.*

One more particular, connected with her character as a wife, is mentioned—*her dress*. Her clothing is according to the New Testament rule of sobriety.[b] In general, her dress should be suitable without paying too much or too little attention to it. While it is true that her main concern should be the inward "quality,"[c] that, in no way, excuses her from keeping up a respectable outward appearance. In fact, a good wife should strive always to appear as attractive to her husband as she did when he was first attracted to her.

[b] 1 Tim 2:9; 1 Peter 3:3
[c] 1 Peter 3:4; 1 Tim 2:10

Now, we again observe her conduct. Here she is not praised for spending all her time reading the Bible and praying (though she prizes these devotional exercises as "a woman who fears the Lord"[d] should). According to the Scriptures, she keeps her "house,"[e] carefully fulfilling her various responsibilities. If "man goes forth to his work and to his labor until evening,"[f] the women find work as "workers at home."[g] And beautiful indeed is it to see, how by her hard work, self-denial, and heartiness she "builds her house."[h] *She rises while it is still night, to give food to her household.* The delicacy also with which she stays within her own sphere is remarkable. While she provides food for the whole *household*, she assigns work responsibilities—not to the manservants (these with great propriety she leaves to her husband), but *to her maidens.*[7] Their clothing is also provided with every regard to their comfort. *She is not afraid of snow for them.* They are clothed with double garments, well clad for a severe winter. *So well does she look to the ways of her household*, such untiring energy does she show in every department, that none can accuse her of *eating the bread of idleness.* In her household, order is the principle of her rule. Timely orders are given, and they must be obeyed. Nothing is neglected, that belongs to order, level-headedness, frugality, or general management. She understands well the exact responsibilities of each one under her care and their different abilities; when they need to be directed, and when they may be left to their own responsibility; what belongs to her own province of superintendence, and what is beyond it.

[d] Verse 30
[e] 1 Tim 5:14
[f] Ps 104:23
[g] Titus 2:5
[h] Prov 14:1

But never let the wife and mother limit her oversight to

[7] *See Foxe's beautiful picture of Anne Boleyn as the mistress of her household, 5:63.*

her role as a mere housekeeper, with her whole time and mind devoted to the outward routine of her household. While she exercises sound discipline and maternal anxiety, her primary concern is to give special attention to their moral habits and their Christian instruction, encouraging them in private prayer, reading of the Word of God,[8] and involving them in daily family worship; impressing upon them the need for careful observance of the Lord's Day; and watching with concern over their manners, habits, and circle of friends. We would be careful not to overwork our children, yet we should never permit them to *eat the bread of idleness.* We should guide them in their work for us and their work for God. We must regard them as a solemn and responsible trust for God and for eternity. Who can claim to be an *excellent wife* who does not feel this weight of family responsibility?

And her care shouldn't be limited to her own dependents. She should be working, not only for herself, or *for her household,* but for *the poor and needy,* as well. And, having first satisfied her soul,[i] she stretches out her hands[j] to embrace those at a distance from her with the flow of her love; and so, "the blessing of the one ready to perish came upon" her.[k] Her spirit and manner also are of the same character; all in full agreement with the testimony of her lips. Clever, brisk, and managing minds are often deficient in the softer graces. Their tongues are unrestrained and lawless under provocation. Children, servants, and neighbors suffer from this revolting hardness, and find "it is better to live in a corner of a roof, than in a house shared with a contentious woman."[l] But the godly wife and mother has not only the law of love in her heart, but *wisdom in her mouth, and the teaching of kindness* in her tongue. The same love that binds her heart, governs her tongue, not impulsively but kindly and wisely, molding her whole spirit, so that "she says nothing that is foolish, nothing that is ill-natured," said Bishop Horne.[9] Richly endued with "the wisdom from

[i] Isa 58:10

[j] Deut 15:7, 8

[k] Job 29:13; Acts 9:39

[l] Prov 21:9

[8] *Esther must surely have been in the habit of instructing her maidens; else they could not have been prepared for the extraordinary services of the fast, Esther 4:16. Thus it is recorded of one, who shone as a sparkling jewel in the licentious court of Charles II, that "she provided her servants books to read, prayers to use by themselves, and constantly instructed them herself in the principles of religion"*—Life of Mrs. Godolphin, p. 195.

[9] *Mr. Hooker probably had the portrait before his eyes, when in his exquisite funeral sermon for his* "virtuous gentlewoman" *he enumerates "among so many virtues hearty devotion*

above," she is "gentle, reasonable, full of mercy and good fruits."[m]

[m]James 3:17; 1 Peter 3:8

Thus indeed *"an excellent wife* is the crown of her husband."[n] *He is known in the council chambers* [*gates*], *when he sits with the civic leaders* [*elders*], as one who is blessed with no common treasures of happiness; "as one who is indebted perhaps for his promotion to the wealth acquired by her management at home, and, it may be, for the preservation and establishment of his virtue, to the encouragement furnished by her example and conversation.

[n]Prov 12:4

For herself—evident and many are the blessings that rest upon her. *Strength and dignity are the clothing* of her inner self. Christian courage and resolution lift her up above appalling difficulties. *The clothing of dignity* stamps her with the Lord's acceptance, as His faithful servant, the child of His grace, and the heir of His glory. *She smiles,* not only in her present happiness, but the greater happiness of *the future.* Having so wisely provided for the morrow, she is not overburdened with its cares. Having lived in the fear of God and honored Him with the fruits of righteousness, there is sunshine in her hour of trial, in "the valley of the shadow of death," in the unclouded day of eternity. She shall rejoice in *the future,* when the ministering angels, and with those blessed by her goodness and generosity, recipients of her bounty,[o] shall welcome this daughter of Jerusalem into the joy of the Lord.

[o]Ps 23:4; Luke 16:9

28 *Her children rise up and bless her;*
Her husband also, *and he praises her,* saying:
29 *"Many daughters have done nobly,*
But you excel them all."
30 *Charm is deceitful and beauty is vain,*
But *a woman who fears the* LORD*, she shall be praised.*

towards God, towards poverty tender compassion; motherly affection towards servants; towards friends even serviceable kindness; mild behavior and harmless meaning towards all"—Remedy against Sorrow and Fear. *Bishop Taylor's finely-drawn portrait of Lady Carbery is after the same pattern of completeness. "If we look on her as a wife, she was chaste and loving, discreet and humble. If we remember her as a mother, she was kind and severe, careful and prudent, very tender . . . a great lover of her children's souls than of their bodies, and one that would value them more by the strict rules of honour and proper worth, than by their relation to herself. Her servants found her prudent and fit to govern, and yet open-handed and apt to reward; a just exalter of their duty, and a great rewarder of their diligence"*—Funeral Sermon.

31 *Give her the product of her hands,*
And let her works praise her in the gates.

THE REWARDS OF A GODLY WOMAN

An excellent wife is obviously serving her own interest. What greater earthly happiness could she know than *her children's* reverence and her husband's *blessing*? We may picture to ourselves her condition—crowned with years, *her children* grown up; perhaps themselves surrounded with families, and endeavoring to train them, as they had been trained. Their mother is constantly before their eyes. Her tender guidance, her wise counsels, her loving discipline, her holy example, are vividly kept in remembrance. They continue *to call her blessed,* and to bless the Lord for her, as His invaluable gift. No less warmly does *her husband praise* her. His attachment to her was grounded, not on the *deceitful and vain* charms of *beauty,* but on *the fear of the Lord.* She is therefore in his eyes to the end, the stay of his declining years, the soother of his cares, the counselor in his perplexities, the comforter of his sorrows, the sunshine of his earthly joys. Both *children and husband* combine in the grateful acknowledgment that *many daughters have done nobly, but you excel them all.*

But why—it may be asked—do external recommendations form no part of this portrait? All that is described is a true appraisal of her excellence. A graceful form and manner often end in disappointment, more bitter than words can tell, because they are often just a cover-up for the vilest corruptions. And then outward *beauty*—what a fading *vanity* it is![p] One siege of sickness sweeps it away.[q] Sorrow and care wither its charms.[r] And even while it remains, it contributes little to our happiness.[s] It proves a frequent occasion of trouble and the source of many harmful temptations and snares;[t] and, without honor and uprightness, it becomes to a well-judging mind, an object of disgust rather than attraction.[u]

The portrait, here drawn for us by divine inspiration, begins with the touch of *an excellent wife,* and fills up the sketch with the features of *a woman who fears the Lord.*[v] For the lovely features described—her faithfulness to her husband, her active personal habits, her good management and hard work for her family, her considera-

[p] Gen 12:14, with 23:4; 1 Peter 1:24
[q] Ps 39:11
[r] Ps 6:7
[s] Gen 29:17; 30:1, 2
[t] Prov 6:25, 26; Gen 12:11–19; 20:1–2, 11; 26:7; 2 Sam 11:2; 13:1
[u] Prov 11:22
[v] Prov 31:10, 30

tion for the necessities and comforts of others, her watchfulness of conduct, her tender concern for the poor and afflicted, her kind and courteous behavior to all—this completeness of character and grace could only flow from vital godliness. They are the "good fruit," that prove the "good tree."[w] They are the fruit that grows out of right belief.

[w] Matt 7:17

A good wife doesn't seek the praise of others. She is content to be known and loved within her own circle, never pressing herself into the limelight. But as a public blessing, she cannot be hid.[x] And if she has no herald to sound her praise, all will say—*Give her the product of her hands, and let her works praise her in the gates.* "Let every one," says Bishop Patrick, "extol her virtue." Let her not be without the just commendation of her dedicated labors. But while some are honored for the nobleness of the ancestry from which they come; others for their fortune; others for their beauty; and some for other things; let the good deeds, which she herself has done, be publicly praised in the greatest assemblies; where, if all men should be silent, her own works would declare her great worth. Add to this—*as her works praise her in the gates,* so will they "follow" her. "The memory of the righteous is blessed."[y] All will see in her the light and luster of a sound and practical profession; that the promises of godliness are the richest gain, the grace of God the best portion, and his favor the highest honor.

[x] Acts 9:39

[y] Rev 14:13; Prov 10:7

If this picture is viewed as an exhibition of godliness, we observe that Christianity does not lessen attention to temporal duties. Instead, it causes a woman to become more scrupulously exact in all her household obligations, in everything within her province; careful not by her negligence to bring reproach upon her Christian testimony. Why should she be careless or slovenly, putting her important duties out of time and out of place? Of all people, it is more rightfully expected of her that she should have diligently followed "every good work."[z]

[z] 1 Tim 5:10

HOW TO CHOOSE A WIFE

How valuable this picture also is, as a directory for the marriage choice! Let *virtue,* not *beauty,* be the primary object. Set against the *vanity of beauty,* the true happiness of having *a wife who loves the Lord.* Here is the solid basis of happiness. "If," says Bishop Beveridge in *Resolution,* 2, "I choose her for her *beauty,* I shall love her no longer than while that continues; and then farewell at once both duty and delight. But if I love her for her virtues; then, though all other sandy foundations fail, yet will my happiness remain entire." The external choice was the cause of the destruction of the world.[a] A flood of iniquity came into a godly man's family from the self-pleasing delusion.[b] The godly choice uniformly has God's approval and blessing.

[a]Gen 6:2–7

[b]2 Chron 18:1; 21:5, 6

Finally, "if women," says Bishop Pilkington in *Works* (Parker Society Edit. p. 387) "would learn what God will plague them for, and how; let them read the third chapter of the prophet [Isaiah[c]]. And if they will learn what God wants them to do, and be occupied withal, though they be of the best sort, let them read the last chapter of the Proverbs. It is enough to note it, and point it out to them that *will* learn." "That which is last to be done," concludes an old expositor, "is to read it and heed it, and let it become a part of herself, as much as she is able. Let every man be ashamed, if any woman shall excel him in virtue and godliness."

[c]Isa 3:16–24

"Thus—and once more," says Matthew Henry, in his quaint style, "is shut up this looking-glass[d] for ladies, which they desired to open and dress themselves by; and if they do so, their adorning will be found to praise, and honour, and glory, at the appearing of Jesus Christ."

[d]Prov 31

SUMMARY

We should conclude with a brief summary of a few prominent points from our study of this most instructive Book of Proverbs.

Let us note the connection between inward principle and outward conduct. Let us never forget that the truths taught here presuppose an internal source. It is the light within that shines out. The hidden life is brought into plain view. The fountain sends forth its wholesome waters. The "good tree" brings forth good fruit. A good man out of the "good treasure" of the heart brings forth good things.[a] These therefore are the evidences, not the inborn principles. They result from the nourishing of the source within. *Nothing permanent is produced by change of opinion, excitement of feeling, conviction of conscience, but by a change of heart.* The "gentle answer"[b] is the outward expression of the softened and humble heart. The religion of sincere purposes, however promising, withers away, having "no firm root" in itself.[c] The ways and fashions of the world, therefore, rule with a far mightier power, than the dictates of God's Word or the voice of conscience. An outward grasp of Christian teachings also is powerless without the internal principle. They exhibit a body of truth indeed, but a body without life, without any spring of influence or reward. Only Christ in the heart will change the outward conduct and put everything in its proper place and proportion.

[a]Matt 12:33, 35
[b]Prov 15:1
[c]Matt 13:21

Let us note, too, the flow of true happiness throughout the whole sphere of godliness. Solomon has described this connection with the most glowing interest.[d] Most important is it to leave the impression upon the minds of all, especially of our young readers, that Christianity is joyous. Only as the world sees it, is it something to be

[d]Prov 3:13–18; 4:4–13; 8:17–21, 32–38

endured, not *enjoyed.* The Pharisaic professing believer just sees a lot of things that have to be done but nothing to be enjoyed. With many it is a matter of serious and honest concern. But often they see no joy in it whatsoever. The man, who lives only for pleasure, sees Christianity only in an atmosphere of gloom. But despite all these misconceptions there is no greater or surer reality in life than this—to know *Jesus Christ is happiness.* It isn't the merrymaking of the fool or the silly gaiety of the thoughtless. It is Christ, alone, who is the source of true happiness; the only solid, permanent source.

"Happy the believer," as an eloquent preacher forcibly puts it in this paraphrase of his words, "who in his warfare with his spiritual enemies, is able to oppose pleasure with pleasure, delight with delight; the pleasures of prayer and meditation with the pleasures of the world; the delights of silence and retirement with public entertainment or sinful pleasures. Such a man is steady and unmoved in the performance of his duties; and because he is man, and man cannot help loving what opens to him sources of joy; such a man is turned to Christianity by motives like those, that lead men of the world to attach themselves to the objects of their passions, because they bring him unspeakable pleasure."[1] In fact, the world's limited vision hardly qualifies them to pass judgment on what they have never received. They see our infirmities, not our graces; our cross, not our crown; our affliction, not our joy in the Holy Spirit, which compensates and infinitely overpays for all we can endure.

We don't wonder, therefore, that the uninstructed mind naturally associates Christianity with restraint, never with freedom or confidence. But in fact actions, that are valued according to their agreement with the will of God, though they are secular in character, are a part of the Christian's service and assure his acceptance. Adopting this right standard, we shall be able to resist our ruling passion. We won't waver. We shall adopt no questionable course. We will not lend our influence to the spirit of this world. We shall feel, that we have only one object in life—only one true obligation—to maintain the honor of our God. And yet this yoke of strict discipline is

[1] *Saurin's* Sermons, *quoted by Alexander Knox,* Remains, *3. 365.*

our happiness, not our burden. It is linked with a foretaste of heavenly happiness, of which none of us has an adequate conception. Speculative religion is indeed dry and barren. But true and practical godliness is rich in its delights.[e] And while the shortcoming of earthly joy is, that it comes to an end; the perfection of godly happiness is, that it will endure throughout eternity. Truly, it is not just a temporary privilege. It doesn't just dry our eyes and divert our sorrow for a time. It is "eternal comfort."[f] Present joy arises from the belief that it will be everlasting and from looking forward and foretasting that which will be eternal. Surely, then, in our most sorrowful hours, we have far more reason for joy than for mourning; and we are moving rapidly onward to the home, where "the days of your mourning will be finished,"[g] forever.

[e]Ps 19:11; 119:14, 127; Isa 32:17; James 1:25
[f]2 Thess 2:16
[g]Isa 60:20

It is very important that we note Solomon's estimate of real good. Every particle of the chief good he centers in God. To find Him is life.[h] To fear Him is wisdom.[i] To trust Him is happiness.[j] To love Him is substantial treasure.[k] To neglect Him is certain ruin.[l] Now man is naturally an idolator. He is, himself, his center, his object, his end. Instead of submitting to guidance, he guides himself. He disputes the rightful lordship of God. He would change the laws of the Great Lawgiver to suit himself. Need we add that his "way" is "foolish"?[m] What then is the true good? "Yield now and be at peace with Him."[n] Known excellence quickens the desire. Our known God will be our portion.[o] He will claim our entire service.[p] He will show Himself to us as our chief good—a privilege worth ten thousand worlds to know—a satisfying portion for eternity. For indeed so intense is his divine love toward us, that He cannot be satisfied without accomplishing for us the whole eternal duration of enjoyment, that He has laid up for us in Himself. All that we could look for here in the most full and conscious enjoyment of our portion, we should "consider that the suffering of this present time are not worthy to be compared" with a single moment in heaven, when we shall see "face to face," and "know fully just as I also have been fully known."[q]

[h]Prov 8:35
[i]Prov 1:7
[j]Prov 16:20
[k]Prov 8:18–21
[l]Prov 8:36
[m]Ps 49:13
[n]Job 22:21
[o]Ps 16:5; Lam 3:24
[p]Ps 45:11; Matt 22:37
[q]Rom 8:18; 1 Cor 13:12

Let us study Christian completeness and consistency. The elements of this character will be brought out by a diligent and prayerful study of this important Book of Proverbs. Let them be put together in their due connection and proportion; and "the man of God may be adequate, equipped for every good work."[r] We want Christ to be to the soul, what the soul is to the body—the animating principle. The soul operates in every member. It sees in the eye, hears in the ear, speaks in the tongue, animates the whole body, with ease and uniformity, without show or effort. So Christ should be allowed to control every thought, word, and act in our lives. In this day of light and knowledge, ignorance of our duty all too often implies neglect of our educational opportunities. The grand objective is that our lives should be under God's complete control. Then our daily walk will be carefully directed by Him. Never turn aside a single step from His guidance. We must never allow the teachings or habits of this world to take over in our lives. We must guard against everything that dampens vital spirituality, lowers high scriptural standards, or slackens our Christian watchfulness. Let our path be steadily balanced between compromising concession and needless individuality. Let the Christian walk only with God in the way of the gospel. He will never be satisfied with appearing to just hold his ground. But he will acknowledge the wisdom of the discipline which allows him no enjoyment of the present moment except in reaching out and "to press on" for something beyond him.[s] We don't want a profession that will just give us a name in the church, nor a stamp of reproach in the world; but one which keeps Christ always before our eyes, and brings us into a growing conformity to His standard for us.[t] When our heart readily follows His leading, we will resist even the sins that seem less reproachful to the world than those which are more revolting. We will no more tolerate an uncharitable spirit than disgraceful corruption. An angry tone, threatening look, sharp retort, or disparaging word, will cause grief to the conscience, and will be visited by its rebuke, as severely as those stormy outbursts, which disgrace our character before men. Walking "before God," not before men, as a Christian who is "blameless."[u] His eye is our restraint—His judgment our rule—His will our delight.

[r] 2 Tim 3:17

[s] Phil 3:12–14

[t] Matt 5:48

[u] Gen 17:1

But who is sufficient? Child of God! Let the trembling of insufficiency in yourself be overcome by the recollection of all-sufficiency in your God.[v] What He demands of you, that He works in you, His redemptive work on your behalf secures your holiness, no less than your acceptance—*your holiness, not, as some would have it, as the ground, but as the fruit, of your acceptance.* Let the one then be primarily sought; and the other will assuredly follow.

[v] Comp. 2 Cor 2:16, with 3:5; also 12:9

"*I* WILL PUT MY LAW WITHIN THEM, AND ON THEIR HEARTS ... FOR *I* WILL FORGIVE THEIR INIQUITY, AND THEIR SIN *I* WILL REMEMBER NO MORE."[w]

[w] Jer 31:33, 34

TOPICAL INDEX